INVENTING AMERICA

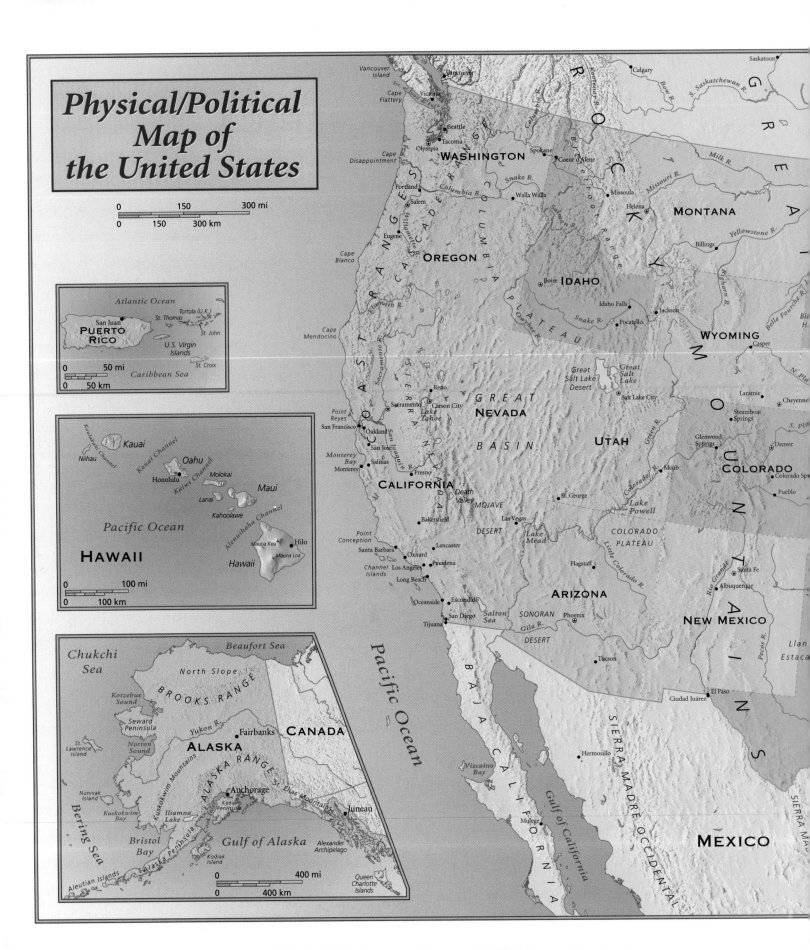

Physical/Political Map of the United States

0   150   300 mi

0   150   300 km

PUERTO RICO

Atlantic Ocean

San Juan
St. Thomas   Tortola (U.K.)
St. John
U.S. Virgin Islands
St. Croix

Caribbean Sea

0   50 mi

0   50 km

HAWAII

Kauai
Niihau   Kauai Channel
Honolulu   Oahu   Molokai
Lanai   Kaiwi Channel   Maui
Kahoolawe
Alenuihaha Channel
Mauna Kea   Hilo
Hawaii   Mauna Loa

Pacific Ocean

0   100 mi

0   100 km

ALASKA

Chukchi Sea
Beaufort Sea
North Slope
BROOKS RANGE
Kotzebue Sound
Seward Peninsula
Yukon R.   Fairbanks   CANADA
St. Lawrence Island
Norton Sound
Nunivak Island
Kuskokwim Mountains
Kuskokwim Bay   ALASKA RANGE   St. Elias Mountains
Iliamna Lake   Anchorage
Kenai Peninsula
Bering Sea   Alaska Peninsula
Bristol Bay   Gulf of Alaska   Juneau
Aleutian Islands   Kodiak Island   Alexander Archipelago
Queen Charlotte Islands

0   400 mi

0   400 km

CANADA

Saskatoon
Calgary
Vancouver Island   Vancouver
Cape Flattery   Victoria
Str. of Juan de Fuca
Seattle   Spokane
Cape Disappointment   Tacoma   Coeur d'Alene
Olympia   WASHINGTON   Kootenay R.   Bow R.   S. Saskatchewan R.
Portland   Snake R.   Milk R.
Columbia R.   Walla Walla   Missoula
Salem   Helena   MONTANA
Eugene   OREGON   Boise   IDAHO   Billings   Yellowstone R.
Cape Blanco   Idaho Falls   Jackson   Bighorn R.   Belle Fourche R.
Klamath R.   Snake R.   Pocatello   WYOMING
Cape Mendocino   Great Salt Lake Desert   Great Salt Lake   Casper   N. Pl
Reno   Salt Lake City   Laramie   Cheyenne
Sacramento   Carson City   GREAT   Steamboat Springs   S. Pl
San Francisco   Lake Tahoe   NEVADA   UTAH   Green R.   Glenwood Springs   Denver
Oakland   BASIN   Moab   COLORADO
San Jose   Colorado R.   Colorado Sp
Monterey Bay   Salinas   Pueblo
Monterey   Fresno
CALIFORNIA   Death Valley   St. George   Lake Powell
MOJAVE   COLORADO PLATEAU
Bakersfield   DESERT   Lake Mead   Little Colorado R.
Point Conception   Las Vegas   Flagstaff
Santa Barbara   Lancaster   ARIZONA   Santa Fe
Oxnard   Pasadena   Albuquerque
Channel Islands   Los Angeles   NEW MEXICO   Pecos R.
Long Beach   Gila R.   Phoenix   Llan
Oceanside   Escondido   Salton Sea   SONORAN   Estaca
San Diego   DESERT   Tucson
Tijuana   SIERRA
El Paso
Ciudad Juárez

Pacific Ocean

BAJA CALIFORNIA

Hermosillo

SIERRA MADRE OCCIDENTAL

Vizcaino Bay

Gulf of California

Mulege   MEXICO

SIERRA MA

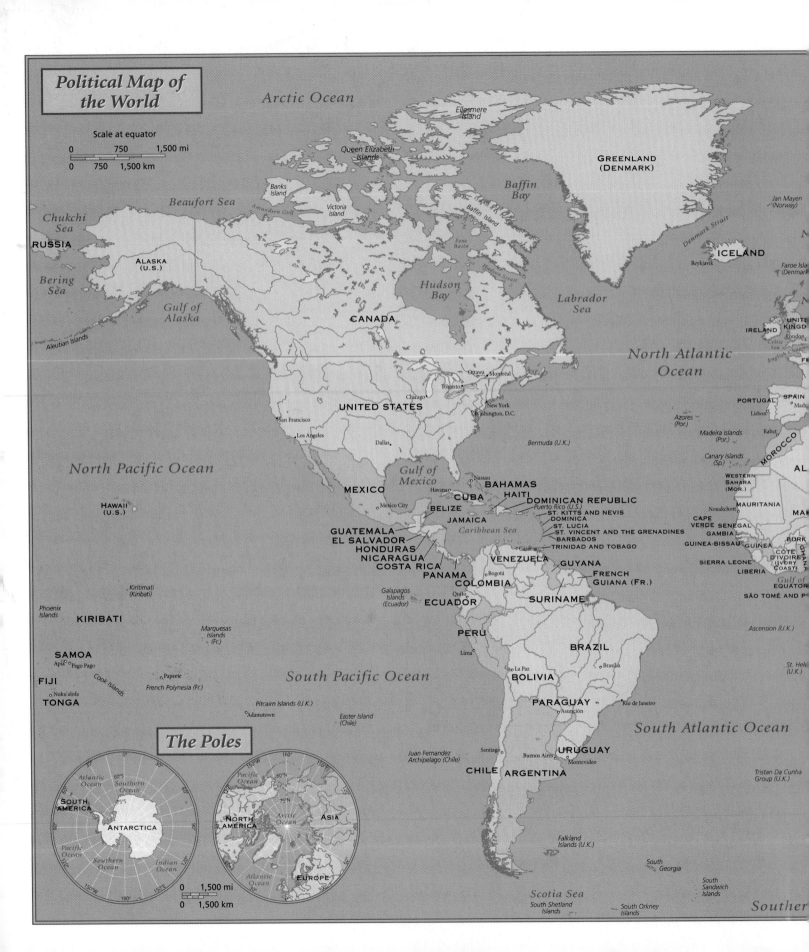

Scale at equator

0   750   1,500 mi
0   750   1,500 km

Arctic Ocean

Chukchi
Sea

RUSSIA

Bering
Sea

Beaufort Sea

Banks
Island

Amundsen Gulf

Victoria
Island

Queen Elizabeth
Islands

Ellesmere
Island

Baffin
Bay

GREENLAND
(DENMARK)

Jan Mayen
(Norway)

ICELAND

Reykjavik

Faroe Islands
(Denmark)

Denmark Strait

ALASKA
(U.S.)

Gulf of
Alaska

Aleutian Islands

Foxe
Basin

Hudson Strait

Hudson
Bay

Baffin Island

Labrador
Sea

North Atlantic
Ocean

IRELAND

UNITED
KINGDOM

London

Celtic
Sea

English Channel

North Pacific Ocean

CANADA

Ottawa   Montréal

Toronto

Chicago

New York
Washington, D.C.

UNITED STATES

San Francisco

Los Angeles

Dallas

Bermuda (U.K.)

PORTUGAL

SPAIN

Madrid

Lisbon

Azores
(Por.)

Madeira Islands
(Por.)

Rabat

MOROCCO

AL

Canary Islands
(Sp.)

WESTERN
SAHARA
(MOR.)

MAURITANIA

Nouakchott

MA

MEXICO

Gulf of
Mexico

Mexico City

Havana

Nassau

BAHAMAS

CUBA   HAITI

DOMINICAN REPUBLIC

Puerto Rico (U.S.)

ST. KITTS AND NEVIS

DOMINICA

ST. LUCIA

ST. VINCENT AND THE GRENADINES

BARBADOS

TRINIDAD AND TOBAGO

BELIZE

JAMAICA

Caribbean Sea

CAPE
VERDE   SENEGAL

GAMBIA

GUINEA-BISSAU   GUINEA

SIERRA LEONE

LIBERIA

CÔTE
D'IVOIRE
(IVORY
COAST)

BURK

GHA

Z

HAWAII
(U.S.)

GUATEMALA

EL SALVADOR

HONDURAS

NICARAGUA

COSTA RICA

PANAMA

Caracas

VENEZUELA

Bogotá

COLOMBIA

GUYANA

FRENCH
GUIANA (FR.)

SURINAME

Gulf of
EQUATOR

SÃO TOMÉ AND P

Kiritimati
(Kiribati)

Galapagos
Islands
(Ecuador)

Quito

ECUADOR

Phoenix
Islands

KIRIBATI

PERU

Lima

BRAZIL

Brasília

Ascension (U.K.)

Marquesas
Islands
(Fr.)

SAMOA

Apia   Pago Pago

FIJI

Nuku'alofa

TONGA

Papeete

French Polynesia (Fr.)

Cook Islands

South Pacific Ocean

La Paz

BOLIVIA

Rio de Janeiro

St. Helena
(U.K.)

Pitcairn Islands (U.K.)

Adamstown

Easter Island
(Chile)

PARAGUAY

Asunción

South Atlantic Ocean

Tristan Da Cunha
Group (U.K.)

Juan Fernandez
Archipelago (Chile)

Santiago

Buenos Aires

URUGUAY

Montevideo

CHILE   ARGENTINA

0   1,500 mi
0   1,500 km

Atlantic
Ocean

Southern
Ocean

SOUTH
AMERICA

60°S

75°S

ANTARCTICA

Pacific
Ocean

Southern
Ocean

Indian
Ocean

Pacific
Ocean

NORTH
AMERICA

Arctic
Ocean

60°N

75°N

ASIA

Atlantic
Ocean

EUROPE

Falkland
Islands (U.K.)

South
Georgia

South
Sandwich
Islands

Scotia Sea

South Shetland
Islands

South Orkney
Islands

Souther

Inventing America

A HISTORY OF THE UNITED STATES

VOLUME 2: FROM 1865

PAULINE MAIER

MERRITT ROE SMITH

ALEXANDER KEYSSAR

DANIEL J. KEVLES

W. W. NORTON & COMPANY
NEW YORK   LONDON

Copyright © 2003 by Pauline Maier, Merritt Roe Smith, Alexander Keyssar, and
    Daniel J. Kevles

The text of this book is composed in Minion, with the display set in Frutiger,
    Copperplate 31, and Texas Hero.
Composition by UG / GGS Information Services, Inc.
Cartography by maps.com
Manufacturing by the Courier Companies, Inc.
Book design by Joan Greenfield
Cover designer: Brenda McManus/Skouras Design
Page layout: Alice Bennett Dates
Editor: Steve Forman
Manuscript editor: Susan Gaustad
Production manager/project editor: JoAnn Simony
Photo researchers: Ede Rothaus, Neil Hoos, Nathan Odell
Editorial assistants: Lory Frenkel, Julia Paolitto

The Library of Congress has cataloged the one-volume edition as follows:

Inventing America: a history of the United States/Pauline Maier . . . [et al.].
        p. cm.
    Includes bibliographical references and index.
    ISBN 0-393-97434-0
    1. United States—History. I. Maier, Pauline, 1938–

E178.1.I58 2002
973—dc21
                                                                                2001044648

ISBN 0-393-97762-5 (pbk.)
W. W. Norton & Company, Inc., 500 Fifth Avenue, New York, NY 10110
                                www.wwnorton.com

W. W. Norton & Company Ltd., Castle House, 75/76 Wells Street, London,
    W1T 3QT
1 2 3 4 5 6 7 8 9 0

For Eleanor Smith Fox (1908–2001), mother, guiding light, friend. —Merritt Roe Smith

For Anne Kevles, who so much wanted to cast her vote in the next election;
Eric F. Goldman, who shepherded a young physicist into American history;
Bettyann, partner in all things; and Jonathan, Beth, David, and their children
here and to come, shapers of the new century. —Daniel J. Kevles

To the memory of my parents, Alexander and Grace Atkinson Keyssar, who
made many things possible. —Alexander Keyssar

For my parents, Irvin L. and Charlotte Rose Rubbelke; my children, Andrea,
Nicholas, and Jessica, and also Corinne Maier (b. 2000), who will help make
American history in the twenty-first century. —Pauline Maier

Contents

CONTENTS

Maps

Inventing America is a new history of the United States whose unifying theme is innovation. It aims to integrate into a compelling narrative the persistent inventiveness of Americans in devising new political institutions and practices, economic arrangements, social relations and cultural motifs, adaptations to the natural environment, and exploitations of science and technology.

Americans have repeatedly resorted to experiment in the face of changing circumstances, drawing on ideas and practices from abroad or from native soil. They have long considered this penchant for innovation a distinguishing feature of their culture and history. The willingness of Americans to remake their world has run from the adaptations the colonists made to survive in an unfamiliar environment to the New Deal's try-anything response to the Depression; from the adoption of a radically redesigned corporation as a distinctive and powerful economic institution to the establishment of regulations intended to bind industry to the public interest; from the forging of an African American culture by slaves to the resourceful efforts of women to find ways of combining family and career. And since the late nineteenth century, Americans have sought to remake their position in the world, mixing pragmatism with evangelism, drawing from the experience of failure as well as success.

Our text is concerned throughout with the bold experiment in popular self-government that characterized the birth of the United States and continues in our politics and society. While writing a national narrative, we weave together numerous stories on the ground, tales of regions, institutions, businesses, social groups, and individual men and women. We place renewed emphasis on national and state governments; both have often acted as powerful agents of social and economic change, and the states have provided laboratories of political innovation. We also recount the transforming dynamism of business enterprise and its effects throughout society.

We are acutely aware that a good deal of the American story does not merit celebration. It has entailed retreat as well as advance, conflict as well as consensus, and the use of government to block change as well as to advance it. We probe the gap—originally wide and, in many respects, ongoing—between the promise of the United States and the reality of its practices, including slavery, the brutal treatment of Native Americans, the discrimination against women, immigrants and minorities, political and economic inequities, and the degradation of the environment. Yet we are also concerned with how Americans have narrowed that gap by enlarging the scope and meaning of the nation's founding ideas and ideals.

The most original aim of this text is the treatment of science and technology as integral elements of American history. Technical innovation has been important from earliest times, when, in a remarkable feat of plant breeding, pre-Columbian peoples cultivated primitive grains into maize. With the arrival of Europeans, Americans began importing knowledge, technology, plants, and animals from abroad, a process that mirrored the import of capital, people, and culture, and they established themselves as members of a global exchange. They adapted the imports to their own needs while developing an indigenous capacity for innovation that produced its own, increasingly transforming effects. The activities of naturalists and scientific societies in eighteenth-century America contributed to the creation of an American identity. The technological and organizational innovations of the nineteenth century changed the ways Americans worked, lived, and spent their leisure. And at least since the nation's centennial, in 1876, science and technology have been crucial to its security, economy, health, and quality of life.

Despite the enormous importance of technology and science in American history, most texts do not come to grips with it. Our book seeks to remedy that neglect, while refraining from giving technological change undue weight in the overall narrative. We have introduced science and technology as parts of mainstream history, recounting their broad social and economic consequences—how electricity lit up the urban night, for example, or how domestic innovations changed the daily lives of women. At the opening of the twenty-first century, the enormous impact of science and technology on the world is beyond dispute. Our text seeks to explain to students how they came to exercise so much influence and power in the United States, emphasizing that both are the products of human agency rather than of forces beyond human control. We have found that such a focus provides students in survey courses with a recognizable bridge to periods in the past when science and technology were also transforming the world. Students respond to accounts of these changes and readily acknowledge their importance.

Readers will find that the integration of science and technology into the story enriches and, in certain respects, reconfigures our understanding of familiar events. For example, antebellum reform movements take on new meaning when seen as intersecting with the technological changes that were helping to spread their messages. In the late nineteenth century, inventors, entrepreneurs, and then corporations began drawing on the boundless frontier of scientific laboratory knowledge to supplement the resources of the closing physical frontier. In the nineteenth and twentieth centuries, technologies such as moving conveyor belts and electrically driven cutting tools made industrial production more efficient but also fostered unrest among workers. And advances in communications such as radio contributed to the emergence of the United States as a world power, as did the new understanding of yellow fever, which protected the crews building the Panama Canal.

Our attention to science and technology sheds new light on the impact of war on U.S. history. War and preparedness have incubated or accelerated social, economic, and technological change. The War of 1812, for example, emerges as a watershed in American economic history. It created the conditions in which entrepreneurs were able to establish the first successful integrated textile factory—at Waltham, Massachusetts. Moreover, as a direct result of the war, the U.S. Army collaborated with arms manufacturers to pioneer the development of interchangeable parts. Both developments were critical to the nation's early industrialization.

Before World War I, the armed services encouraged the new technologies of radio and aircraft, and their development was whirled ahead by mobilization for the conflict. World War I also opened new opportunities for women and blacks and other minorities, and so even more dramatically did World War II, which also stimulated vast migrations across regions and fueled economic recovery and expansion around the country. Further, World War II established the federal government as the dominant patron of scientific research and produced the atomic bomb, microwave radar, electronic computers, jet aircraft, and antibiotics. Under the goad of the Cold War, federal patronage stimulated compara-

ble innovations and provided industry with the knowledge that, in the last quarter of the twentieth century, made possible the creation of biotechnology, personal computers, and the information economy.

Each of the coauthors took responsibility for drafting different sections of the text: Maier, Chapters 1–8; Smith, Chapters 9–16; Keyssar, Chapters 17–22 and 24; Kevles, Chapters 25–33; and Kevles, Maier, and Smith, Chapter 23. However, all of us fully collaborated from the beginning of the project, jointly developing its themes and an outline of the book, and then reading and critiquing each other's chapters with the aim of achieving consistency in approach throughout.

We have made every effort to produce a history that is fully accessible to students, including those who are new to American history. We consider it essential to guide students through the discussions, taking care to facilitate their understanding of the material. We use anecdote and vignette to bring the narrative to life. We also include boxed inserts of primary source materials throughout. Called "American Journal," this feature is intended to illustrate commonplace life as it was shaped by science and technology. Under titles such as "What's for Dinner?" and "What if You Get Sick?," the Journal entries speak directly to the broader themes of the text, and, perhaps more important, are fun to read.

The design and pedagogy of the text are also meant to support student readers throughout. Each chapter opens with a Chapter Outline and a set of Focus Questions on the key subjects that students need to address. The Focus Questions then reappear in the running heads of the chapter to help students keep sight of the main issues in play. The chapters end with Chronologies and brief lists of further readings. (More extensive lists of the sources on which the book rests are provided in the Bibliography on the Norton website for the text.)

With innovation as our main theme, we saw an opportunity to introduce a new dimension to the traditional survey book. Even the most vital prose falls short of conveying, say, the din of the weave room at the Lowell mills when the machinery was operating at full speed, but a palpable, sensory experience of history can be gained from archival audio and visual materials. Digital technology has for some time promised the integration of audio and video materials with print text, and with the support of the Alfred P. Sloan Foundation, *Inventing America* attempts to achieve that goal. Packaged with each new copy of the print text is a CD-ROM (two with the hardcover edition) that contains archival and original multimedia materials designed to enhance the discussion in the text itself. (Icons in the print text signal the corresponding multimedia materials on the CD.) Students reading about the Lewis and Clark expedition, for instance, will be able to listen to audio readings from their journals recorded by studio professionals. The CD includes a wealth of materials ranging from readings from the court records of the Salem witch trials through recordings of slave spirituals to a video of Franklin Roosevelt's "Day of Infamy" speech. It also contains multimedia teaching/research units on the following subjects: slavery and Washington's Mount Vernon, the Lowell mills, Ellis Island, and the Hanford Nuclear Reservation on the Columbia River. The CD was researched and composed by Robert Martello, of Olin College. We hope that the combination of CD and print text makes *Inventing America* a valuable innovation in the survey course.

DJK
AK
PM
MRS
April 2002

Acknowledgments

The authors of this text have accrued many debts in writing it, and they take pleasure in thanking those who helped. Daniel J. Kevles is grateful to John L. Heilbron for helping to point the way to this book; to Ellen Chesler and James Hershberg for early advice; to William Deverell and Peter Westwick for comments on chapters; to Michelle Brattain and Richard Kim for research reports on particular subjects; and to Frederick M. Hodges for aid with the proofs. He is greatly indebted to Wendy Wall for her research during the project's start-up phase and for her insights in a jointly taught course on recent America. His debt is immeasurable to Karen Dunn-Haley, who lived with this project almost as long as he did, unflaggingly providing material and analyses, historiographical assessments, critical commentary, and encouragement. He is also grateful for the assistance of the Division of the Humanities and Social Sciences at the California Institute of Technology, especially John Ledyard, Susan Davis, Marion Lawrence, and Michelle Reinschmidt; and of the Department of History of Yale University, particularly Jon Butler, Jean Cherniavsky, Carolyn Fitzgerald, and Michael Margonis. And he wishes to thank the Andrew W. Mellon Foundation, whose support enabled him to spend more time on the writing.

Alexander Keyssar would like to thank D'arcy Brissman, Elisa Slattery, Eve Sterne, Nicole Perrygo, Andrew Neather, Noeleen McIlvenna, Daniel Levison Wilk, and especially Paul Husbands for their labors in gathering materials for this book. He is also grateful to the many undergraduates in his introductory U.S. history courses on whom he first tried out much of the material in his chapters. He would like to acknowledge the valuable and cheerful support of the History Department staff at Duke University, especially Vivian Jackson, Andrea Long, and Caroline Keeton.

Merritt Roe Smith is grateful for help with research from Karin Ellison, Greg Galer, Rebecca Herzig, Hannah Landecker, David Mindell, Jennifer Mnookin, Russell Olwell, and Tim Wolters. He also thanks Charles Dew, who undertook some of the revisions of Chapters 14–16 at a crucial stage. Pauline Maier is indebted to Meg Jacobs, Karen Ordahl Kupperman, Mary Beth Norton, and Harriet Ritvo for their generous, expert help on parts of her chapters. Both Maier and Smith are happy to express their gratitude to Greg Clancey and Rob Martello for the research assistance they provided; Victor McElheny for the excellent substantive and stylistic comments that arose from his reading of their chapters; and the students in their team-taught course on American history to 1865, whose responses to their draft chapters led to several improvements. Both greatly appreciate the support of the staff in the MIT Department of Science, Technology, and Society, especially Judy Spitzer, Debbie Meinbresse, and Christine Bates.

The coauthors collectively are grateful for the critical comments provided by the readers of their manuscript:

Robert Angevine, George Mason University
James Axtell, College of William and Mary
Michael Barnhart, State University of New York at Stony Brook
Mark V. Barrow Jr., Virginia Tech
Amy Bix, Iowa State University
Angela Boswell, Henderson State University
Albert S. Broussard, Texas A & M University
Anthony Carey, Auburn University
Paul G. E. Clemens, Rutgers University
Charles B. Dew, Williams College
Glen Gendzel, Tulane University
A. W. Giebelhaus, Georgia Institute of Technology
Larry Gragg, University of Missouri at Rolla
Michael G. Hall, University of Texas at Austin
Dwight Henderson, University of Texas at San Antonio
Richard R. John, University of Illinois at Chicago
Frank Lambert, Purdue University
Daniel Lewis, California Polytechnic State University, Pomona
Eric T. L. Love, University of Colorado, Boulder
David S. Lux, Bryant College
William M. McBride, United States Naval Academy
Robert M. S. McDonald, United States Military Academy
James Mohr, University of Oregon
Jerald E. Podair, Lawrence University
Chris Rasmussen, University of Nevada at Las Vegas
Jan Reiff, University of California at Los Angeles
Susan Rugh, Brigham Young University
Andrew Schocket, Bowling Green State University

Ron Schultz, University of Wyoming
Bryant Simon, University of Georgia
Robert Stoddard, University of British Columbia
David Tanenhaus, University of Nevada at Las Vegas
Stanley J. Underdal, San Jose State University
Helen M. Wall, Pomona College
Wendy Wall, Colgate University
Jessica Wang, University of California at Los Angeles
Kenneth Winkle, University of Nebraska

The authors are deeply indebted for generous support of the project to the Alfred P. Sloan Foundation, especially to Arthur Singer for his decisive early interest, and Doron Weber for his ongoing enthusiasm. They are very grateful to W. W. Norton for the care it has taken in producing the book—in particular, to Steve Forman, their editor, for his patience, advice, and critical readings; and to Susan Gaustad for her skilled copyediting of the manuscript. At Norton they owe many thanks also to JoAnn Simony, Lory Frenkel, Julia Paolitto, Sarah Hadley, Neil Hoos, Nathan Odell, Ede Rothaus, and Alice Bennett Dates for keeping this big project on the rails. Rob Martello conceived, researched, and drew together the digital materials on the CD. The efforts of Steve Hoge at Norton were critical in bringing the digital history component to fruition. Finally, the authors wish to thank Karen Dunn-Haley for digging up the materials for the "American Journal" entries and parts of the CD.

About the Authors

PAULINE MAIER is William R. Kenan Jr. Professor of American History at the Massachusetts Institute of Technology. Her specialty is the period of the American Revolution, on which she has published extensively, including *From Resistance to Revolution: Colonial Radicals and the Development of American Opposition to Britain, 1765–1776* and *The Old Revolutionaries: Political Lives in the Age of Samuel Adams*. Her most recent book is *American Scripture: Making the Declaration of Independence*.

MERRITT ROE SMITH is Leverett and William Cutten Professor of the History of Technology at the Massachusetts Institute of Technology. Roe's research focuses on the history of technological innovation and social change. His publications include *Harpers Ferry Armory and the New Technology* and *Military Enterprise and Technological Change*. He is a fellow of the American Academy of Arts and Sciences.

ALEXANDER KEYSSAR is Matthew W. Stirling Jr. Professor of History and Social Policy, John F. Kennedy School of Government, Harvard University. His specialty is the social and political history of the late nineteenth and early twentieth centuries. Alex's first book was *Out of Work: The First Century of Unemployment in Massachusetts*. His most recent book is *The Right to Vote: The Contested History of Democracy in the United States*.

DANIEL J. KEVLES is Stanley Woodward Professor of History at Yale University. Dan has published extensively on the history of science and the intersections of politics, science, and technology in the twentieth century. His works include *The Physicists: The History of a Scientific Community in Modern America* and *In the Name of Eugenics: Genetics and the Uses of Human Heredity*. His most recent book is *The Baltimore Case: A Trial of Politics, Science, and Character*.

INVENTING AMERICA

Chapter 17

RECONSTRUCTION:
1865-1877

This contemporary engraving shows freedmen electioneering in the South in 1868.

FOCUS QUESTIONS

■ **What were the major issues at stake in the political Reconstruction of the United States?**

■ **How did blacks and whites piece together their lives in the postwar South?**

■ **Why did Reconstruction come to an end in the South?**

■ **What national issues were resolved during Reconstruction, and what issues remained unresolved?**

"The trail of war," noted an English traveler to the Tennessee Valley in the late 1860s, "is visible throughout the valley in burnt up gin-houses, ruined bridges, mills, and factories ... and in large tracts of once cultivated land stripped of every vestige of fencing." The city of Charleston, South Carolina, was "ruined"; "many fine mansions, long deserted, were fast mouldering into decay." Carl Schurz, a leading Republican and a general in the Union army, wrote that it was "difficult to imagine circumstances more unfavorable for the development of a calm and unprejudiced public opinion than those under which the southern people are at present laboring.... When the rebellion was put down they found themselves not only conquered in a political and military sense, but economically ruined."

The North's military victory had settled two critical issues: the **states of the Confederacy** would remain part of the Union, and slavery would be abolished everywhere in the United States. But the end of military hostilities did not mean that the problems that had spawned the war had all been solved, and the conquest of one region by another brought new issues to the fore. When would the rebellious states again participate in the national government? On what terms would these states be readmitted to the Union? How severely would the rebel leaders be punished? Most important, what would become of the South's black population, the ex-slaves—and, with them, of southern society as a whole? What should southern society look like after the war and after slavery?

The nation wrestled with these questions for more than a decade after the Civil War. Most white southerners hoped to restore as much of the antebellum order as they could; the 4 million freed slaves, not surprisingly, had very different visions of the future. Northerners were divided over how harsh or magnanimous a peace to impose on the conquered South; they also disagreed about the degree to which southern society would have to be transformed for the states of the Confederacy to regain power in the national government. The era of Reconstruction was tumultuous, filled with sharp partisan and regional conflict, bitter contests between Congress and the president, and recurrent outbreaks of violence in the South.

The changes wrought during this period, moreover, were not confined to the South. Reconstruction was national in scope, characterized everywhere by the growing economic prominence of industry and the political ascendancy of industrialists and financiers. Between 1865 and 1873, the nation's industrial output rose by nearly 75 percent, while more new miles of railroad track were laid than had existed before the Civil War. Manufacturing towns boomed throughout the Northeast. Chicago tripled its 1860 population and became a center of iron and steel production, meat packing, and the manufacture of agricultural machinery. Even more striking was the opening of the trans-Mississippi West through formal and informal—and sometimes downright shady—partnerships of government with railroad corporations and mining, lumber, and agricultural interests. Largely unsettled by Europeans in 1860, the West became the scene of rapid, helter-skelter development encouraged by the pro-business Republican Party.

The Fate of the Union

RECONSTRUCTION IN WARTIME

Even before the war ended, officials in Washington were taking steps to shape the contours of the postwar South and chart a course for its reintegration into the Union. The most fundamental issue on the agenda was slavery. Lincoln's 1863 Emancipation Proclamation clearly signaled the North's intention to bring an end to the peculiar institution. That intention was translated into law by the **Thirteenth Amendment to the Constitution,** approved by the Senate in 1864 and the House of Representatives in 1865: once ratified by the states, later in 1865, it permanently abolished slavery throughout the nation.

Lincoln, in 1863, also issued a Proclamation of Amnesty and Reconstruction, which spelled out the terms on which rebellious states could rejoin the Union. His action was based on the belief that Reconstruction was primarily an executive, rather than congressional, responsibility. The proclamation, commonly called the Ten-Percent Plan, reflected both his personal impulse to be magnanimous in victory and the hope that a generous Reconstruction policy might speed the end of the war. The plan offered a full pardon and the restoration of all property, except slaves, to all "persons" who took a loyalty

oath and vowed to accept the abolition of slavery. Only a small number of high-ranking Confederate officials were deemed ineligible. When, in any state, such pledges numbered 10 percent of the number of votes cast in 1860, those who had vowed their loyalty could form a new state government. Once that government had determined to abolish slavery and provide for the education of black children, the state could be represented in Congress.

The Ten-Percent Plan was sketchy in its details and lenient in thrust: it did not address the political or civil rights of freedmen, and it put few obstacles in the way of ex-rebels who might seek to regain control of their state governments. The plan, consequently, drew criticism from congressional Republicans who believed that Reconstruction ought to include active support for the freedmen as well as a transformation of social and political life in the South.

The Republican alternative, sponsored by Senator Benjamin Wade of Ohio and Representative Henry Davis of Maryland, offered a more punitive approach. The Wade-Davis Bill, which Congress approved in July 1864, permitted

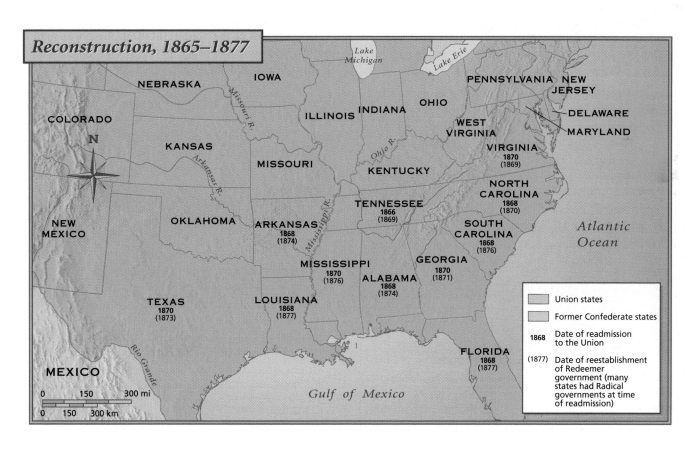

Reconstruction, 1865–1877

the states of the Confederacy to hold constitutional conventions and form new governments only after a majority of their voters had taken an "ironclad" loyalty oath. Officials of the Confederacy and those who had borne arms "voluntarily" would not be permitted to vote for, or participate in, these conventions. The state constitutions themselves had to ban slavery and repudiate all Confederate debts. Lincoln pocket-vetoed the Wade-Davis Bill (by not signing it), which angered his congressional critics and left the Ten-Percent Plan as the official, if vague, blueprint for Reconstruction.

Federal officials also found themselves confronted with another issue: once freed, how would ex-slaves support themselves? Should the government help them to become economically independent of their former masters? Lincoln, intent on restoring the southern states to the Union with maximum speed, believed that federal intervention in the affairs of the South ought to be held to a minimum. (His deepest hope, in fact, was that the "problem" of the ex-slaves would be solved by their emigration—a notion that was neither practical nor statesmanlike.) But many Radical Republicans, including Congressmen George Julian and Thaddeus Stevens, were convinced that the liberty of the freedmen would be illusory unless they owned property, landed property in particular. Four million landless, impoverished black laborers would, according to Julian, quickly be reduced to "a system of wages slavery . . . more galling than slavery itself."

Julian and other Radicals proposed to address the problem by confiscating Confederate lands and redistributing them to the freedmen. This idea came to the fore as early as 1862, when Congress passed the second Confiscation Act, which made all rebel property liable to confiscation. (A previous act applied only to property used in support of the rebellion.) At Lincoln's insistence, however, the second Confiscation Act limited any seizure of land to the lifetime of the owner, which effectively prohibited its permanent redistribution to freedmen. Moreover, the Ten-Percent Plan, by guaranteeing to return all property to rebels who took a loyalty oath, seemed to preclude the mass redistribution of land. Nonetheless, in 1864 and 1865, proconfiscation sentiment mounted in Congress, and both houses repealed the limiting clauses of the 1862 resolution: there was significant sentiment in favor of a program that would substantially alter the distribution of land, and economic power, in the South.

> *"Nearly everywhere, the freedmen displayed a preference for becoming self-supporting, for dividing the land into plots on which they could grow foodstuffs rather than cotton."*

Meanwhile, in parts of the South that had been captured by northern armies, military commanders found themselves dealing concretely, and urgently, with the same issues. On the South Carolina Sea Islands, in southern Louisiana, and eventually throughout the Mississippi Valley south of Vicksburg, victorious northern armies ended up in possession of fertile lands temporarily abandoned by their owners; at the same time, they became responsible for the welfare of tens of thousands of impoverished freedmen, many of them refugees. What ensued was a series of experiments in land and labor policy. Nearly everywhere, the freedmen displayed a preference for becoming self-supporting, for dividing the land into plots on which they could grow foodstuffs rather than cotton. In Davis Bend, Mississippi, a large group of slaves demonstrated they could also organize cotton production by themselves, as they took over and profitably ran plantations owned by Jefferson Davis and his brother. In most locales, however, northern officials adopted more traditional arrangements: they leased the lands to white owners and mobilized the freedmen to work as agricultural laborers, for low wages and on year-long contracts enforced by the army. By the war's

A depiction from *Harper's Weekly* of a freedmen's village, established under the auspices of the Freedmen's Bureau at Trent River, North Carolina, 1866.

end, hundreds of thousands of ex-slaves were working on plantations that were directly or indirectly superintended by the government.

It was against this backdrop that Congress, just before adjourning in March 1865, created the Bureau of Refugees, Freedmen, and Abandoned Lands, commonly called the Freedmen's Bureau. The bureau was charged with monitoring the condition of ex-slaves and delivering fuel, food, and clothing to the destitute, white and black alike. It also had the power to divide confiscated and abandoned lands into forty-acre parcels that could be rented, and eventually sold, to the freedmen. Although the bureau's powers were extraordinary—and set a precedent for public activism and intervention—Congress did not appropriate any funds for the bureau and anticipated that it would exist for only a year.

ANDREW JOHNSON AND PRESIDENTIAL RECONSTRUCTION

Six weeks after the Freedmen's Bureau was created, Abraham Lincoln was dead, and Andrew Johnson had become the fifteenth president of the United States. Johnson, a pro-Union Democrat from Tennessee, had been nominated for the vice-presidency by the Republicans in 1864 to broaden their appeal in the border states. He seemed eminently qualified for the job. Born in humble circumstances in North Carolina, Johnson had served an apprenticeship as a tailor and then moved to the mountains of eastern Tennessee, where he married, learned to read and write, acquired a farm, and began a long career in politics. Elected first to the state legislature, he then served as governor, U.S. congressman, and U.S. senator. Johnson courageously stuck by his Unionist principles when Tennessee seceded, presenting himself as a champion of the yeoman farmer and antagonist of the southern plantation elite. "I will show the stuck-up aristocrats who is running the country, " he once declared. "A cheap, purse-proud set they are, not half as good as the man who earns his bread by the sweat of his brow."

Experienced as he was, Johnson possessed personal traits that were not well suited to politics and that served him ill in the presidency. He was stubborn, intolerant of those who disagreed with him, reluctant to negotiate or compromise. "A slave to his passions and prejudices," as one contemporary noted, he was given to "unreasoning pugnacity." Indecisive and tactless, he lacked both close confidants and the suppleness of mind and vision so characteristic of his predecessor. A

Andrew Johnson, seventeenth president of the United States (1865–69), shortly before his inauguration.

deeply insecure man, he also seemed to crave approval from the very aristocrats he claimed to despise.

Johnson's political beliefs, moreover, differed in key respects from those of Lincoln and other Republicans. A Democrat and not a Whig, as Lincoln had been, Johnson's vision of the good society was Jacksonian and agrarian, rather than industrial or urban; he was wary of northern commercial interests and hostile to government intervention in the name of economic progress. Of equal importance, his racial views were conservative even by mid-nineteenth-century standards. Although Johnson fought the political dominance of aristocratic planters, he was not, until late in his career, an opponent of slavery. Indeed, he had bought some slaves himself, and he once voiced the peculiar wish "that every head of a family in the United States had one slave to take the drudgery and menial service off his family." In 1866, after a meeting with Frederick Douglass, Johnson commented that Douglass was "just like any nigger . . . he would sooner cut a white man's throat than not."

Nonetheless, Johnson's accession to the presidency was initially welcomed by the Radical Republicans, who believed that the Tennesseean's vision of Reconstruction was closer to their own than Lincoln's had been. Senator Zechariah Chan-

539

dler of Michigan even proclaimed that "the Almighty continued Mr. Lincoln in office as long as he was useful, and then substituted a better man to finish the work." In the wake of Lincoln's assassination, a punitive mood swept the North, and Johnson's public utterances lent support to the notion that he would not be lenient in his treatment of the rebels. "Treason is a crime and must be made odious," he declared. "Traitors must be impoverished. . . . They must not only be punished, but their social power must be destroyed."

Johnson's first acts as president suggested that he would depart little from the course charted by his predecessor. Although Congress had adjourned in March 1865 and was not scheduled to meet again until December, Johnson declined to call a special session because he, like Lincoln, believed that Reconstruction was primarily an executive responsibility. In May and June, he issued a series of proclamations that replaced the Ten-Percent Plan. The first was a proclamation of amnesty and restitution that granted pardons and the restoration of all property rights (except slave ownership) to everyone who took an oath avowing loyalty to the Union and support for emancipation. Confederate officials, as well as owners of taxable property valued at more than $20,000, were ineligible, although they could apply for amnesty individually to the

Under the Black Code of Florida, any man fined for vagrancy and unable to pay the fine could have his services sold to the highest bidder. This engraving depicts a freedman's services sold at auction, 1867.

president. (Johnson, true to his rhetoric, was taking aim at the rich as well as at political and military leaders.) Johnson then issued orders appointing provisional governors and instructing them to call state constitutional conventions; only white men who had received amnesty would be eligible to vote for delegates to the conventions. In order to rejoin the Union, these conventions were expected to abolish slavery, nullify their acts of secession, and repudiate all Confederate debts.

Although most Radical Republicans were critical of Johnson's willingness to exclude blacks, including ex-soldiers, from the suffrage, his plan seemed, for a time, to be working. The provisional governors were generally pro-Union Democrats, and most delegates to the constitutional conventions were either Unionists or reluctant Confederates. Ex-rebels took the loyalty oath en masse, while 15,000 members of the elite applied to Johnson personally for pardons.

But the white South—perhaps sensing the president's personal sympathies as a southerner as well as his hopes of rebuilding a national Democratic Party that could carry him to reelection—grew defiant of its northern conquerors. The elected governor of Louisiana began to fire Unionist officeholders, replacing them with ex-Confederates. Mississippi and South Carolina refused to repudiate their Confederate debt; Texas and Mississippi chose not to ratify the Thirteenth Amendment; several states repealed without repudiating their secession ordinances. In the fall elections of 1865, large numbers of ex-Confederates were elected to office, particularly in the lower South: among them were twenty-five ex-Confederate leaders (including Alexander Stephens, the former vice-president of the Confederacy) who were elected to the U.S. Congress. Meanwhile, rebels whose lands had been seized were demanding their return, a demand that Johnson often bent over backward to satisfy.

Led by Mississippi and South Carolina, the new state governments also passed elaborate laws to govern the civil, social, and economic behavior of the freedmen. Some of this legislation, such as prohibitions on intermarriage or black jury service, also existed in the North. But the Black Codes, as these laws came to be called, went a great deal further, severely restricting the economic rights of the freedmen. In Mississippi, freedmen were required to sign year-long labor contracts that they could not break without forfeiting their wages and being subject to arrest; prospective employers could not offer a higher wage to a laborer already under contract; freedmen were prohibited from renting land in urban areas and could be arrested for vagrancy if they could not provide evidence of being employed. In South Carolina, African Americans had to obtain a license and pay a tax to perform any work other than farm work or domestic service, while Louisiana and Texas tried to force black women to work by specifying that labor contracts had to include "all the members of the family able to work." Young blacks deemed to lack "adequate" parental support could be forcibly bound out as apprentices to their former masters. The Black Codes made clear that ex-slaves would be second-class economic citizens, at best.

By the time the Thirty-ninth Congress finally convened in December 1865, all of the Confederate states had formed new governments and elected representatives to Congress. President Johnson, acknowledging that Congress had the constitutional right to judge the qualifications of its own members, urged that these representatives be seated—which would, in effect, have brought an end to Reconstruction. Congress, however, declined to do so. Instead, expressing deep concern about reports emanating from the South, it formed a Joint Committee on Reconstruction to investigate the impact of Johnson's policies.

> *"The Radicals were moralists whose political views were forged by the struggle against slavery and by the successes of small-scale, competitive capitalism in the North. They sought to remake the South in the image of the North."*

Despite this rebuff, the president was well positioned to carry out his Reconstruction policy or something close to it. Although Republicans dominated Congress by three to one, there were serious divisions within the party. Roughly half of all congressional Republicans (and more in the Senate) belonged to a loose coalition of moderates and conservatives. They sought more ample guarantees of black rights as well as legislation to protect freedmen and Unionists from violence, but they were not altogether dissatisfied with Johnson's approach, and they shared his desire to readmit the rebel states as expeditiously as possible. Standing in opposition to this coalition was the strong and ideologically coherent Radical wing of the party. Drawn primarily from New England and the northern states west of New England, the Radicals were moralists whose political views were forged by the struggle against slavery and by the successes of small-scale, competitive capitalism in the North. They sought to remake the South in the image of the North, a goal that demanded an active federal government, black suffrage, and land distribution. Committed and passionate as they were, most Radicals were nonetheless aware that they were out ahead of northern public opinion (three northern states had rejected black suffrage in 1865), and that they themselves were outnumbered in Congress.

Soon after Congress convened, the Joint Committee on Reconstruction, chaired by "moderate" senator William Fessenden of Maine, began extensive hearings, at which witnesses testified to the upsurge of violence, discrimination, and Confederate sentiment in the South. "It is of weekly, if not of daily, occurrence that freedmen are murdered" in Texas, reported General George Custer. In rural Alabama, "gangs of ruffians, mostly operating at night, hold individuals under a reign of terror," another general observed. A Confederate colonel was quoted as saying, "You have not subdued us; we will try you again." In response to such testimony, Republican moderates, led by the influential senator Lyman Trumbull of Illinois, drafted two pieces of legislation to protect the freedmen. The first extended the powers and life of the Freedmen's Bureau: the bill called for direct funding of the bureau, empowered it to build and support schools, and authorized bureau agents to assume legal jurisdiction over crimes involving blacks and over state officials who denied blacks their civil rights. The second measure, the Civil Rights Bill, defined blacks (indeed all native-born persons except Indians) as U.S. citizens; it also specified the rights inherent in citizenship, including the right to make contracts, own or rent property, and have access to the courts. No state could deprive any citizen of those rights; cases involving such violations would be heard in federal rather than state courts; and individuals who deprived a citizen of his rights would be subject to fine or imprisonment. Sweeping as the Civil Rights Bill was, it did not enfranchise blacks, permit them to sit on juries, or desegregate public accommodations.

To the shock of many, especially in moderate Republican circles, President Johnson vetoed both the Freedmen's Bureau and Civil Rights Bills in February and March of 1866. In his veto messages, he insisted that the bills were illegal because they had been passed while the states of the South were unrepresented in Congress, a claim that completely denied Congress the right to formulate Reconstruction policy, or any policy, for that matter. Johnson attacked the Freedmen's Bureau as a fiscally unsound and constitutionally dubious agency, while maintaining that the Civil Rights Bill was an unconstitutional intrusion of the federal government into the affairs of states. His quarrel was not with the details of the bills but with the principles that lay behind them.

The president's vetoes were grounded in both conviction and political strategy. As a lifelong Democrat, Johnson believed in strong state governments and limited national power; he was also convinced that blacks were not the equals of whites and that government policies designed to promote equality could only have undesirable consequences. (He raised the specter of interracial marriage in one of his veto messages.) Yet Johnson's actions were also aimed at dividing the Republican Party and isolating the Radicals. Doing so would leave a coalition of Democrats and moderate-to-conservative Republicans in control of Congress and boost his chances of being elected president in 1868.

Here, Johnson miscalculated badly. Instead of dividing the Republican Party, his vetoes pushed the moderates toward more radical positions. While Democrats, North and South, celebrated Johnson's actions, moderate and even conservative Republicans found themselves with a choice between allying with the Radicals or abandoning goals for which the war had been fought in the first place. In fact, they had no real choice, unless they were prepared to leave the freedmen at the mercy of the same southerners who had enslaved them. Moderate and conservative Republicans broke with the president and sharply attacked his policies. "Those who formerly defended [Johnson] are now readiest in his condemnation," observed one Republican leader.

THE FOURTEENTH AMENDMENT

The Republicans seized the initiative in the spring of 1866. In April, Congress overrode Johnson's veto of the Civil Rights Bill (marking the first time that a significant piece of legislation was passed over a presidential veto), and it then revised the Freedmen's Bureau Bill so that it, too, could be passed over a veto. In addition, the Joint Committee on Reconstruction worked throughout the spring to draft a constitutional amendment that would secure key objectives in a form that could not easily be reversed by presidential action or shifting legislative majorities. By the middle of June, the **Fourteenth Amendment** had received the necessary two-thirds majority from both houses of Congress and was sent to the states for ratification.

The Fourteenth Amendment contained three clauses that dealt with specific post–Civil War issues. One clause upheld the validity of the national (Union) debt while declaring that neither the United States nor any individual state would repay any debts incurred by the Confederacy during the rebellion. A second barred from public office anyone who, as an office-holder, had taken an oath to support the Constitution and then violated that oath by engaging in insurrection. A third mandated that a state that kept any adult male citizens from voting would have its representation in Congress reduced proportionately. This last section was designed to prevent southern states from increasing their representation as a result of the demise of slavery (a slave, in the original Constitution, had counted as only three-fifths of a person for the purpose of representation) while still denying freedmen the right to vote. It implicitly recognized that states had the right to deny men the franchise because of their race, but it reduced their power in the national government if they did so. To the chagrin of women's suffrage advocates, the amendment, by using the word "male," also implicitly recognized the right of states to deny women the vote without incurring any penalty.

Section 1 of the Fourteenth Amendment also addressed immediate issues but in language that was deliberately general and that would long reverberate across the constitutional landscape. This section nullified the *Dred Scott* decision (which had denied the citizenship of blacks) by declaring all native-born and naturalized persons to be citizens; at the same time, it prohibited the states from abridging the "privileges or immunities" of citizens. Section 1 also declared that no state could "deprive any person of life, liberty, or property, without due process of law"; nor could a state deny to any person "the equal protection of the laws." Although the precise meaning of these phrases would be debated by lawyers and judges for more than a century, their core intent was clear. The Fourteenth Amendment enshrined the principle of "equality before the law" in the Constitution; it also authorized the federal government to actively defend equal rights when they were threatened by state governments. Written to protect African Americans in the post–Civil War South, the amendment articulated principles so significant and far-reaching that they would, over time, be applied to people and circumstances well removed from Reconstruction.

The Fourteenth Amendment became the platform of the Republican Party in the congressional elections of 1866, which were widely regarded as a referendum on Reconstruction. Opposing the Republicans was a new political grouping, the National Union Movement, organized by President Johnson as a coalition of conservatives from both parties. Johnson hoped that the movement could mobilize support for ending

Reconstruction and readmitting the southern states while avoiding the taint of treason that still clung to the Democrats.

Yet the National Union was destined to defeat: the northern electorate remained suspicious of Democrats, whatever they called themselves, and incidents of mob violence against blacks in Memphis and New Orleans graphically underscored the need for the continued protection of black rights. Johnson himself antagonized voters with an ill-tempered campaign tour around the nation. "Why not hang Thad Stevens and Wendell Phillips?" he shouted to an audience in Cleveland. The Republicans won a far more lopsided victory than anyone had predicted, gaining ground in every northern state and retaining large majorities in both houses of Congress.

RADICAL RECONSTRUCTION AND THE IMPEACHMENT OF ANDREW JOHNSON

Despite the election results, neither Johnson nor the political leaders of the South seemed ready to capitulate, or even conciliate. Johnson defiantly predicted that his allies would win the next round of elections, while the southern legislatures, with Johnson's backing, emphatically rejected the Fourteenth Amendment. This intransigence tipped the balance for many moderate Republicans, leading them to embrace black suffrage as a central element in reordering the South. Without the franchise, blacks would be powerless to protect themselves against whites who would not accept them as equal citizens.

Working together, the moderates and the Radicals devised a Reconstruction Act that was passed in March 1867 over Johnson's veto. The act declared existing state governments to be merely provisional and reinstituted military authority everywhere in the ex-Confederacy except Tennessee, which had ratified the Fourteenth Amendment and been readmitted to the Union. The bill also outlined the steps that states would have to follow to regain full membership in the national government: holding new constitutional conventions (elected by adult males), ratifying the Fourteenth Amendment, and adopting constitutions that permitted blacks to vote. In the first months of 1867, Congress passed measures to limit the president's ability to obstruct Reconstruction. Among them was the Tenure of Office Act, which required the president to obtain the consent of the Senate before dismissing any official whose appointment required senatorial confirmation.

The Republicans were right to anticipate that Johnson would attempt to obstruct their program. Throughout 1867

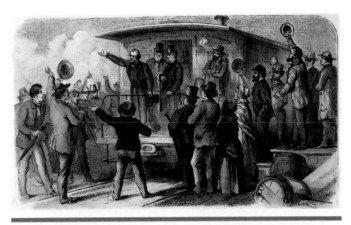

A contemporary engraving showing Andrew Johnson's attempt to undermine Radical Republican candidates during his midwestern "swing around the circle" in late 1866.

and early 1868, he interfered in every way he could, appointing military commanders unsympathetic to the Republicans' goals, removing officials who seemed too sympathetic, insisting on interpretations of the Reconstruction Act that weakened its thrust, and encouraging the South to defy federal law. The skirmishing came to a head early in 1868 when Johnson removed Secretary of War Edwin Stanton, a Lincoln appointee and the one member of Johnson's cabinet who favored Radical Reconstruction. As secretary of war, Stanton occupied a critical place in the chain of command between Washington and the Union armies occupying the South. His removal, according to the Republicans, constituted a violation of the Tenure of Office Act.

Johnson's attempt to remove Stanton (who refused to turn in the keys to his office) prompted the House of Representatives to take the unprecedented step of impeaching the president. According to the Constitution, federal officials could be impeached for "treason, bribery, or other high crimes and misdemeanors," and many Radicals had talked of impeachment for more than a year, but it was the removal of Stanton that prompted some moderates to join their ranks. After two-thirds of the House had voted to impeach, the process moved to the Senate, where a two-thirds vote was necessary to convict the president and remove him from office.

The trial of Andrew Johnson in the Senate lasted from March 13 to May 26, 1868. Johnson's defenders maintained that what he had done was not an impeachable offense, that the president was merely testing the constitutionality of the Tenure of Office Act, and that the act didn't actually apply to

543

A cartoon implying that President Johnson lacked the capacity to grasp the U.S. Constitution and was subsequently flattened by it.

Stanton anyway (because he had been appointed by Lincoln). Yet the legal arguments never did more than cloak the real issue: did Johnson's unceasing opposition to congressional Reconstruction, coupled with his apparent intention of restoring ex-Confederates to power and to the Union, constitute sufficient grounds to remove him from office? Most senators thought that they did. But a sizable minority did not—in part for legal reasons, in part because they feared setting a destabilizing precedent, and in part because they did not want Benjamin Wade, the Radical leader of the Senate, to ascend to the presidency. Johnson, who behaved with uncharacteristic decorum during the Senate proceedings, was acquitted by a margin of 1 vote. The final tally was 35 to 19 in favor of conviction, with 7 Republicans voting for acquittal.

Johnson's acquittal was not the only defeat suffered by the Radical Republicans in 1867 and 1868. In the state elections of 1867, black suffrage was rejected in Ohio, Minnesota, and Kansas, while the Democrats, who openly paraded their hostility to black rights, registered electoral gains in many northern states.

THE DEFEAT OF LAND REFORM

The Radical idea of confiscating Confederate lands and distributing them to the freedmen was never widely embraced in the Republican Party, but it had powerful supporters. Among them were Thaddeus Stevens of Pennsylvania, the leader of the Radicals in the House, and his counterpart in the Senate, Charles Sumner of Massachusetts. Stevens, the Republican floor leader of the House and the senior member of the Joint Committee on Reconstruction, was widely respected for his honesty and idealism while feared for his sharp tongue and mastery of parliamentary tactics. Although frequently outvoted, Stevens saw himself as the leader of a righteous vanguard that would press forward the cause of social and racial justice against all opposition; even in death, he made a statement for racial equality by asking to be buried in a black cemetery. Sumner similarly was a man of principle, devoted to the notion that all individuals had to be equal before the law. An eloquent, charismatic figure, he had little patience for day-to-day politics, but he wielded enormous popular influence and was regarded by many African Americans as their most devoted champion in government.

The obstinacy of the white South lent support to the land-reform arguments of Stevens, Sumner, and others. Confiscation and redistribution, as Stevens pointed out, would simultaneously destroy the power of the plantation aristocracy and provide an economic foundation for black political and civil rights. "Strip a proud nobility of their bloated states; reduce them to a level with plain republicans; send them forth to labor and teach their children to enter the workshops or handle the plow, and you will thus humble the proud traitors." Appealing as this vision may have been, however, the confiscation of land conflicted with basic Republican values: private property was to be protected, not seized, and free labor was to be rewarded with wages, not with gifts of land from the government. *The Nation*, a respected Republican magazine, voiced the fear that the government giving freedmen land would imply "that there are other ways of securing comfort or riches than honest work." The *New York Tribune* proclaimed that "people who want farms work for them. The only class we know that takes other people's property because they want it is largely represented in Sing Sing." The Radical argument that blacks had already worked hard for this land, for two centuries, fell on few receptive ears.

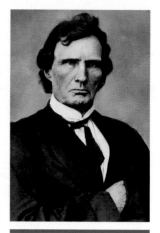

Thaddeus Stevens.

This ideological resistance thwarted efforts at land redistribution in the mid-1860s. The issue came to a head in the spring and summer of 1867 when Stevens—gravely ill but fiercely committed to the cause—introduced a bill to give forty acres of confiscated land to each freedman. Stevens hoped that continued southern defiance would finally prod exasperated moderates to accept confiscation, just as they had come to endorse civil rights and black suffrage. But his hopes were not fulfilled. Although the possibility of land reform captured the imagination of both the freedmen and poor whites in the South, northern Republicans were simply not prepared to go that far. Investment in the southern economy was rumored to be frozen because of fears of confiscation, and moderate Republicans began to worry that confiscation would both hinder the growth of the party in the South and harm relations between labor and capital in the North. By the end of the summer of 1867, a congressional committee of Republicans issued a declaration that Reconstruction would not infringe property rights in the South. Land redistribution—the most radical approach to reconstructing the South—was a dead letter.

While these momentous events, and nonevents, were transpiring in Washington, the program of congressional Reconstruction was proceeding in the South. Under the supervision of the army, whites and blacks were registered to vote, and in the fall of 1867 elections were held for new constitutional conventions. Many whites boycotted the elections, so a large majority of the elected delegates were Republicans, roughly a third of whom were black, with another quarter consisting of recent migrants from the North.

These delegates, derided by southern conservatives as "ignorant Negroes cooperating with a gang of white adventurers," drew up impressively progressive constitutions. Not only did they institute male suffrage (often expressly repudiating financial and literacy requirements for voting), they also created statewide public school systems for both whites and blacks and set up

progressive tax systems that lightened the tax burden of small landowners. The constitutions were ratified, beginning in the spring of 1868, and Republican state governments began to be elected soon thereafter, thanks in good part to black voters. The Republican governments quickly approved the Fourteenth Amendment, which made their states eligible to be readmitted to full membership in the Union. In the summer of 1868, the representatives of seven states were seated in Congress (joining Tennessee); by 1870, Virginia, Mississippi, and Texas were also readmitted. In formal terms, at least, the Union was restored.

THE ELECTION OF 1868

Although the Republicans had failed to remove Andrew Johnson from office, they had high hopes of electing a new president in 1868. To carry the party's banner, they nominated sixty-six-year-old Ulysses Grant, a West Point gradu-

Lithograph showing a parade held in Baltimore in May 1870 to celebrate ratification of the Fifteenth Amendment, which prohibited states from denying men the vote because of their race, color, or previous condition of servitude. President Grant is at the upper left, Vice-President Colfax at the upper right; also pictured are Abraham Lincoln (lower left), John Brown (lower right), and, in the threesome at top, Frederick Douglass (middle) and Hiram Revels (right).

ate, career military officer, and the successful leader of the Union army. Grant was a political moderate who had long opposed slavery and had endorsed congressional Reconstruction, thereby becoming a public adversary of Johnson's. Grant was opposed by Democrat Horatio Seymour, a former governor of New York, and his overtly racist running mate, Frank Blair of Missouri. (Blair referred to the freedmen as "a semi-barbarous race of blacks who are worshippers of fetishes and poligamists.") In a heated campaign marred by outbreaks of violence in some southern states, the Democrats threatened to roll back Reconstruction, while Grant presented himself as a peacemaker, promising to bring an end to the turmoil that had lasted for nearly a decade. Grant was elected by a large electoral college majority (214–80), although the popular vote was much closer. In all likelihood—and as a harbinger of things to come—a majority of white voters cast their ballots for Seymour and the Democrats.

Even before Grant took office, Congress was drafting what would become the **Fifteenth Amendment,** which declared that the right to vote "shall not be denied or abridged . . . on account of race, color, or previous condition of servitude." Support for such an amendment—which was outside the range of mainstream debate only a few years earlier—reflected the rapidly growing Republican conviction that the rights of freedmen would never be secure without the franchise: the amendment was designed to permanently guarantee the political rights of blacks by placing suffrage beyond the reach of state legislatures or state constitutional conventions. It would affect the North as well as the South: in 1868, blacks were unable to vote in eleven northern and all of the border states, a circumstance that undercut the moral authority of northern advocates of black suffrage for the South. As the 1868 elections made clear, moreover, the Republicans had a partisan interest in the amendment: almost all blacks would vote Republican. The Fifteenth Amendment thus promised to enhance the fortunes of both the freedmen and the Republican Party.

Although pathbreaking, the amendment did not go as far as many members of Congress had hoped. Led by Massachusetts senator (and later vice-president) Henry Wilson, some Republicans advocated an alternative version that would have prevented the states from denying any male citizen the franchise "on account of race, color, nativity, property, education, or creed." Far broader in scope, the Wilson amendment would have brought universal male suffrage to the entire nation: in Wilson's words, it would carry out "logically the ideas

"The First Vote," a depiction of freedmen casting their ballots in the South. Note the presence of an African American in a Union army uniform (third in line).

that lie at the foundation of our institutions." The Wilson amendment, in addition, would have prevented the southern states from disfranchising blacks through literacy tests or poll taxes. Many members of Congress, however, opposed this more inclusive language because they did not want to broaden the franchise in their own states, where literacy, tax, and nativity requirements were still in force.

After prolonged debate and considerable parliamentary maneuvering (during which each house of Congress actually passed the Wilson amendment), Congress approved a version that referred only to race, color, and "previous condition of servitude." Charles Sumner, among others, was so angry at this outcome that he refused to vote in favor of the amendment. But even without Sumner's support, the Fifteenth Amendment was sent to the states in the spring of 1869 and ratified a year later.

The Recovering South

The drama of Reconstruction was enacted on several stages. While grand matters of policy were being decided in Washington, the people of the South were trying to rebuild their lives in a world shattered by four years of war and by Yankee victory.

Thousands of blacks left the South and migrated west after the end of Reconstruction. In this 1879 engraving, a group of "Exodusters," as they were called, leave Mississippi.

Much of this world was physically scarred. Railroad lines were torn up nearly everywhere, roadbeds were destroyed, station houses burned, rolling stock gone. Bridges had been blown up, levees had collapsed from neglect, and roads were in poor repair. Through broad stretches of the countryside, the routines of rural life were stilled: livestock was dead or scattered; fences were nowhere to be seen; fields were overgrown; houses, barns, and sheds stood empty. Some villages had simply vanished: a traveler noted that the site of a "once bustling town" was marked by a "single standing chimney." The cities—except, perhaps, for New Orleans—had suffered just as badly. Half of Atlanta had burned to the ground; the warehouses of Mobile had been destroyed by "the great explosion"; eighty blocks of Columbia, South Carolina, lay in ruins.

The South's economy had also collapsed. Agricultural output had plummeted; mines, mills, and factories were shuttered; and banks had virtually ceased to exist. The billions of dollars in capital that had been tied up in slaves had vanished, Confederate paper had become worthless, and nearly all insurance companies were bankrupt. In many areas, the transportation of goods had become impossible by rail, difficult and slow by river. Moreover, the war had claimed the lives of

one-fifth of the region's adult white males and thousands of blacks. Poverty was widespread, destitution common. "In Alabama alone, two hundred thousand persons are in danger of extreme suffering, if not of actual starvation," reported *Harper's Weekly* in December 1865. "Women and children . . . begging for bread from door to door," noted a Freedmen's Bureau official, were an "everyday sight" in Randolph County. As late as 1870, per capita output was 39 percent lower than it had been in 1860; the total value of all property (excluding slaves) had fallen by 30 percent.

THE EXPERIENCE OF FREEDOM

For African Americans, Reconstruction was, above all, the experience of freedom. For some, this experience began before the end of war, with the arrival of Union troops and, often, the flight of their masters. For most, the first moments of freedom came in the spring of 1865.

First reactions to emancipation varied widely. One ex-slave in South Carolina recalled that "some were sorry, some hurt, but a few were silent and glad" when the master of their plantation called them together to announce that they were free. At another plantation, more than half the slaves were "gone" before the master had even finished speaking. Immediate displays of celebration were rare, but rapid changes in demeanor—from the deferential, compliant, cheerful slave to a more reserved, assertive, sometimes angry freedman—were not uncommon. Many plantation owners, particularly those who had abandoned their properties and returned after emancipation, were shocked by the lack of warmth displayed by their former slaves.

Perhaps the most common early response to emancipation was to move. Some men and women left their slave residences the instant their freedom was proclaimed; others waited a few days, weeks, or months before packing their meager possessions and departing. For most **ex-slaves,** feeling free meant leaving the place where they had lived in bondage, moving as

An engraving of the First African Church at Richmond, Virginia, 1874. Churches were among the most important institutions in the lives of freedmen in the years after the war.

they had not been permitted to move as slaves. As Richard Edwards, a black preacher in Florida, observed in 1865: "So long ez de shadder ob de gret house falls acrost you, you ain't gwine ter feel lake no free man, an' you ain't gwiner ter feel lak no free 'oman. You mus' all move—you mus' move clar away from de ole places what you knows, ter de new places what you don't know, whey you kin raise yore head douten no fear Marse Dis ur Marse Tudder."

Yet moving did not mean going far. Although there was a visible migration from the countryside to the city and, over time, a significant postwar migration southward (to the belt of states stretching from Florida to Texas), most freedmen chose to remain in nearby rural areas. Their first postemancipation homes were different spots in a familiar world.

They also began rebuilding that world, starting with their families. One of the most compelling goals of the freedmen was to reunite families that had been torn apart by slave sales: "in their eyes, the work of emancipation was incomplete until the families dispersed by slavery were reunited," observed a Freedmen's Bureau agent in South Carolina. "They had a passion for getting together. Every mother's son among them seemed to be in search of his mother; every mother in search of her children." Freedmen and women placed ads in newspapers in search of their loved ones and walked hundreds of miles to find them. Men and women also formalized relationships they had not been permitted to solemnize under slavery: mass weddings, with dozens of couples at a time, were

frequent occurrences in the early months of emancipation. Family identities were further reinforced as the freedmen began to take last names, often selecting the name of someone known to them. "Precious few of 'em ever took that of their old masters," noted an overseer in Louisiana.

In addition to their families, the freedmen sought to build or rebuild two other institutions: churches and schools. Denied equal footing in the biracial, yet white-dominated, churches that the South inherited from the antebellum era, African Americans withdrew from those congregations and created their own religious communities. In Charleston, the first new building erected after the war was a black church, and ten more had been constructed by 1866. Churches—sometimes makeshift, sometimes not—sprouted up across the countryside, serving both as places of worship and as centers for community social life.

Schools were built with even greater ardor. Since schooling had been denied to most slaves (90 percent of whom were illiterate in 1860), the freedmen greeted their emancipation as an opportunity to learn to read and write and to obtain education for their children. Helped by funding from the Freedmen's Bureau, northern benevolent societies, and, later, the Republican state governments, the freedmen began operating schools everywhere—sometimes committing large portions of their own meager funds to keep schools running. Schools held sessions in churches, warehouses, storerooms, and stables; the Bryant Slave Mart was transformed into a school in Savannah, and in New Orleans a former slave pen was reborn

A congregation of African Americans in Washington, D.C., 1876.

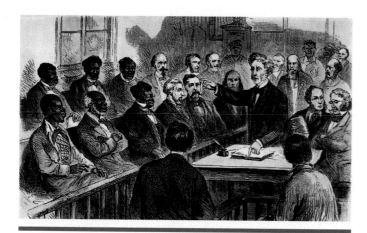

A racially integrated jury in a southern courtroom, 1867.

as the Frederick Douglass School. In rural areas, freedmen negotiated labor contracts that included educational provisions for children; field hands in Selma, Alabama, demanded that their employer provide the materials to build a school, which they would construct and operate by themselves. Education was a source of independence and autonomy, second in importance only to the ownership of land.

Although ex-slaves tacitly accepted racially separate churches and schools, they pressed for changes in the rules and conventions governing social interactions between blacks and whites. Particularly in urban areas, freedmen did not always stand when spoken to by whites or touch their hats or cede sidewalks to their "betters." They also began to question rules that either banned blacks or gave them inferior accommodations on railroads, streetcars, steamboats, or other public facilities. Grounded as much in custom as in law, these rules were sometimes challenged by freedmen through civil disobedience, litigation, and appeals to Union army commanders; occasionally the freedmen even won. A newspaper article in 1867 reported that in Charleston, "another streetcar difficulty occurred today. Two negroes got inside a streetcar, and, refusing to leave, were ejected by the police." In some states, the Republican governments of the late 1860s and early 1870s passed legislation outlawing discrimination in public facilities. Although rarely enforced, these civil rights laws did, at least briefly, help to diminish the strength of the color line.

To most whites, in contrast, the end of slavery only heightened the need for racial separation: "if we have social equality, we shall have intermarriage, and if we have intermarriage we shall degenerate," warned one anxious survivor of the war. Indeed, whites, too, were rebuilding their world during Reconstruction, socially as well as physically. In the sugar- and rice-growing regions of the coastal Carolinas, Georgia, and Louisiana, patterns of land ownership, wealth, and power changed substantially in the wake of the war—although that was not true where the economy was based on tobacco or cotton. Yet even where the social structure changed little, whites had to adjust to a postemancipation social order that was unsettling. Ex-slaves could not be counted on to be deferential, to remain apart, to take orders, to stay in their "place." Whites often described the freedmen as "insolent" or "saucy."

White southerners also found that they could not count on the coercive powers of the state to compel the freedmen to act "properly." In contrast to the antebellum world, state power, particularly after 1866, was wielded by Union army commanders and elected officials who were no longer committed to maintaining white control over blacks. In part for this reason, whites frequently began to take the law into their own hands, making this one of the most violent—if not *the* most violent—periods in the nation's history. Acts of violence against blacks, provoked by black "impudence" or "disrespect," were commonplace. In Greenville, South Carolina, a group of young white men stabbed a black man who had refused to step off a sidewalk when their paths crossed. Race riots, in which blacks were attacked and beaten by whites, erupted in Memphis, Charleston, New Orleans, Atlanta, Richmond, and Norfolk (Virginia): during the Memphis riot in 1866, white mobs killed forty-six African Americans.

This engraving depicts an incident that occurred in early May 1866, when whites assaulted blacks in Memphis, killing forty-six.

"Worse Than Slavery," an 1874 cartoon by Thomas Nast, depicts the plight of African Americans in the post–Civil War South.

Antiblack violence was also expressed in a more organized fashion, through groups such as the Ku Klux Klan. The Klan was founded in Tennessee in 1866 as a social club, but it rapidly became a terrorist organization, dedicated to restoring full-blown white supremacy throughout the South. Klansmen—who came from all walks of life, including the landed elite—roamed the countryside dressed in white sheets and assaulting, beating, and sometimes murdering freedmen, northerners, Republicans, and wartime Unionists. They attacked black churches and schools as well as interracial couples, individuals who had been "impudent" or had financial disputes with whites, and freedmen who were outspoken politically or successful economically. Intent on destroying the Republican Party and preventing blacks from wielding political power, the Klan particularly targeted political leaders: at least 10 percent of the black members of the constitutional conventions of the late 1860s became victims of violence. And over time, the Klan's violence succeeded in silencing opposition.

LAND AND LABOR

Agriculture remained the heart of the southern economy, but just how it would be organized was sharply contested. Most freedmen wanted to own their own land, but within a year after the end of the war, almost all the land that had been dis-

tributed to blacks had been returned to its white owners, and the possibility of any significant governmental distribution of land soon became remote. It was, moreover, exceedingly difficult for ex-slaves to buy land even if they had the means to do so: most whites would not, or were afraid to, sell land to freedmen. Consequently, the great majority of ex-slaves remained landless tillers of the soil; as late as 1880, only 20 percent of all black farm operatives owned land.

Whites, on the other hand, owned land, but needed labor to make their property productive. In pursuit of inexpensive, hardworking labor, southern whites tried to attract immigrants or to import gangs of Chinese workers, but had limited success. The agricultural labor force would have to be black, and in the eyes of many whites, it would therefore have to be coerced and closely supervised. "The nigger," commented one Alabama farmer, "*never* works except when he is compelled to." Becoming a cheap, disciplined plantation labor force was not, however, what the freedmen envisioned as their postemancipation future, even if they failed to own land. They preferred to farm small plots of land as families rather than to work in closely overseen gangs, reminiscent of slavery; they also wanted the freedom to move, change employers, and bargain over terms.

This clash of interests was played out in annual, sometimes daily, skirmishes between employers and employees: over the payment of wages, the terms of credit, the timing of pay-

This 1886 engraving shows a field hand in the South harvesting cotton with an early mechanical harvesting machine.

ments, the rental of land, the selection of crops, the payment of debts. It was also expressed legally and politically. Landowners, often with the support of the Freedmen's Bureau and the Union army, tried to impose annual contracts on the freedmen, which were particularly stifling when the freedmen were paid only at year's end and were penalized for leaving early. The Black Codes passed by the Johnson governments sought to limit the physical mobility of blacks (as did vagrancy laws aimed at discouraging urban migration) and restrict their job options. Landowners also sought to pass laws that would prevent employers from hiring someone else's employees—laws that would, in effect, prohibit the labor market from functioning as a market. When the Republican governments were in power, the tables were turned: laws restricting labor's rights were repealed, new measures helped to guarantee that workers would be paid when employers sold their property (including crops), and taxes on land were increased to encourage large landholders to sell portions of their property.

From this skirmishing and experimentation emerged the system of sharecropping that would dominate southern agriculture for decades. Sharecropping was a fairly simple mode of organizing agriculture: the landowner provided land and tools, the sharecropper performed all the labor, and they split the crop (often fifty-fifty, but the terms varied widely). Or, stated differently, land was rented to tenants, with the rental payment being a share of the crop. This system appeared to have advantages for both blacks and whites. Blacks were able to work in individual household units, with some autonomy and independence; whites were assured that blacks had an incentive to work hard and produce a good crop. By 1880, more than half of all rural blacks worked on shares.

Alongside sharecropping, there developed another institution that proved to be just as durable but far more pernicious in its consequences: the crop-lien system. Farmers always needed credit—to purchase seed, supplies, fertilizer—and before the war, they had borrowed annually from "factors," or banks, pledging their land as collateral for loans that would be repaid once their crops were sold. After the war, however, the banking system was shattered, and the breakup of plantations into small farms operated by tenants (whether sharecroppers or cash tenants) meant that there were many more farmers who needed to borrow, most of whom did not own land that could serve as collateral.

Into this vacuum in the credit system stepped country merchants, many of whom were also landowners. These mer-

chants advanced supplies to farmers, who secured the loans by giving the merchants a "lien" on their crops, which meant, in effect, that the merchant owned, or had the right to sell, the crop. The merchant, in addition, charged the farmer interest on the supplies advanced (often at exorbitant rates) and sometimes was able to set the price at which the crop would be sold. In theory, this was a mutually beneficial set of transactions: a farmer who worked hard, had good weather, and sold his crop at a good price would pay off his debt to the merchant at the end of the year and pocket the difference.

But things rarely worked that simply. Most merchants had monopolies in their local areas and thus had the power to dictate the terms of the transaction, limiting the chances of a farmer actually profiting from his labors. Moreover, bad weather or declining prices would often leave the farmer in debt to the merchant at the end of the year; this generally obliged him to borrow from the merchant (and perhaps rent the merchant's land) again the following year. Most important, perhaps, merchants decided what crops the farmers

Upland Cotton, a painting by Winslow Homer of sharecroppers at work, 1879.

551

The Way They Live, a painting by Thomas Anshuntz depicting sharecroppers, 1879.

would grow, and they commonly demanded that farmers grow *the* cash crop: cotton. Consequently, farmers grew more cotton and less food, which obliged them to buy foodstuffs from the merchants and increase their indebtedness. Even worse, this practice led to a sharp increase in cotton production, which lowered cotton prices (and thus incomes) through much of the 1870s. In this way, small farmers became trapped in a system of "debt peonage," while the South's economy became excessively dependent on cotton.

Thanks in part to declining cotton prices, southern agriculture had difficulty recovering from the war. The region's per capita agricultural output remained below prewar levels for the remainder of the nineteenth century, while the per capita income of whites in the cotton states declined by one-third between the late 1850s and 1879. The income of blacks, of course, increased sharply in the first years after emancipation, but that trend was not sustained, and blacks continued to earn only half as much as whites.

Of equal importance, the stagnation of southern agriculture was accompanied by the region's failure to generate much industrial growth. In the eyes of many Republicans, North and South, such growth was essential: railroad construction and industrial development, they believed, would stimulate urban growth and immigration, thereby enriching the region and reducing the power of landowning planters. State and local governments, particularly those dominated by the Republicans in the late 1860s, sought to encourage railroad construction and industrial growth. They offered railroad corporations financial inducements, including outright monetary grants, to get them to rebuild old lines and build new ones. To lure private enterprise, state legislatures passed laws to protect the property rights of corporations, to provide cheap labor in the form of leased convicts, and to exempt many enterprises (including railroads, banks, and factories) from taxation.

These efforts failed. Although the railroad system was rebuilt and even extended to many interior towns, the overall growth was modest: 7,000 miles of new track were laid in the South between 1865 and 1879, compared with 45,000 miles in the North. The state governments had difficulty paying for the ambitious railroad projects they had launched, and they ended up both raising taxes and, later, cutting back on their commitments. The flow of funds between the public and private sectors, moreover, created fertile soil for corruption: bribery became commonplace in some states, and the Republican Party was tainted by publicly visible corruption. Despite the incentives offered to private enterprise, the politically unstable southern states had difficulty attracting northern and European investment, a problem that was compounded after 1873 by the economic depression that gripped the nation. The fruits of the Republican dedication to the "gospel of prosperity" were limited, and the planting of new industries proceeded far too slowly to alter the overwhelmingly agricultural character of the region.

The Road to Redemption

While the South was rebuilding, the North was booming. The economy grew rapidly, if unevenly, during the war, and, after a brief pause, the growth resumed after Appomattox. Between 1865 and 1873, industrial output soared, while 3 million immigrants poured into the country, most of them headed for the cities of the North and West. The North's victory was, in a sense, a victory of industrial capitalism over a more agrarian, paternalist social order, and the postwar years were a celebration of that triumph. Not only was the Republican Party (which was closely linked to the interests and personnel of industrial capitalism) in power in Washington, but the first transcontinental railroad was completed, George Westinghouse invented air brakes for trains, and the Bessemer process for making steel (by blowing air through molten iron) was introduced into the United States. With fitting symbolism, the stock ticker was invented in 1872 by Thomas Alva Edison.

This unleashing of productive, and speculative, energies was felt throughout the North and in the West, which, with the issue of slavery resolved, was thrown wide open to new settlement. Businesses were built, fortunes were made, and new territories were inhabited. Yet the very ebullience of the economy, followed later by the shock of economic depression, had the effect of drawing attention away from Reconstruction, the South, and the issues that had led to war. By the mid 1870s, the eyes of the nation were more focused on the stock ticker than on the still-incomplete process of reconstructing the South.

> *"Throughout the South, ex-slaves became active participants not only in politics but in governance."*

THE REPUBLICAN PARTY IN THE SOUTH

By the late 1860s, the fate of Reconstruction was closely tied to the fate of the Republican Party in the South. Yet despite their electoral victories in 1868, the Republicans' hold on power was tenuous. Support for the party came from up-country whites (small farmers, many of whom had been Unionists), from low-country entrepreneurs who sympathized with the economic policies of the Republicans, and from northern immigrants. The great majority of Republican voters, however, were black, and the Republican leadership was convinced that the party's fortunes, North and South, would be imperiled if it failed to attract more white support and became identified as the "black" party.

Despite these concerns, the Republican Party made it possible for sizable numbers of African Americans to participate in electoral politics for the first time. Not only did freedmen vote, they were also elected to office. Fourteen blacks, including some who were self-educated and others who were lawyers, were elected to Congress. Two went to the Senate from Missis-

sippi; one of these, Hiram Revels, was a Methodist minister who had organized black regiments at the outset of the war. Several held statewide office, many were elected to state legislatures, and hundreds of black men held local positions. Only in South Carolina did the freedmen hold office in numbers proportionate to their share of the electorate, but throughout the South ex-slaves became active participants not only in politics but in governance.

The policies implemented by the Republican state governments were aimed at protecting the freedmen, modernizing Southern society, and constructing a more active state. They created public schools for both whites and blacks, revamped the judicial system, and built hospitals, penitentiaries, and asylums. In addition to rebuilding the infrastructure that had been destroyed during the war (roads, bridges, public buildings), the governments actively sought private investment in railroads and industry. Yet these projects cost money—which meant raising taxes and increasing the public debt by issuing bonds. Although not high by northern standards, tax rates by 1870 were often triple or quadruple the rates that had prevailed in 1860. Not surprisingly, such sharp increases in an era of economic stress spawned vehement opposition: in nearly every state, white landowners, who resented not only paying taxes but paying taxes that benefited both freedmen and allegedly corrupt Republican officials, formed taxpayers' associations to demand reductions in state budgets.

LEFT: Joseph Rainey, U.S. representative from South Carolina, First District (1870–79).

RIGHT: Hiram Revels, U.S. senator from Mississippi (1870–71).

High taxes and charges of corruption certainly fueled opposition to the Reconstruction governments, but the heart of that opposition remained what it always had been: the desire to restore white supremacy and to restrict the civil and economic rights of blacks. Although there briefly emerged a group of "New Departure" Democrats who spoke of accepting Reconstruction, putting the Civil War behind them, and coexisting with Republicans, most southern Democrats remained devoted to the goal of "Redemption": driving the Republicans out of power and restoring the South's traditional leadership. Democratic Redeemers began to win elections as early as 1869, and their electoral strength mounted in the early 1870s; so, too, did antiblack and anti-Republican violence, led by the Klan.

THE GRANT ADMINISTRATION

Reconstruction was only occasionally on Washington's front burner after Ulysses Grant assumed the presidency in 1869. With Republican governments elected in the South and southern congressional representation restored, both Congress and the new president—who tended to follow the lead of Congress—turned their attention to other matters.

One such matter was civil service reform. The 1860s witnessed an eruption of criticism of the spoils system so prevalent in American politics: victorious politicians gave government jobs to the party faithful, who, in turn, contributed a percentage of their salaries to the party treasuries. Reformers, most of whom were well-educated Republicans from the Northeast, regarded such patronage practices as corrupt and inefficient, and they demanded that appointments be based on merit, certified by competitive examinations. President Grant endorsed these views but did not act on them very energetically. After a presidential commission recommended both competitive exams and the prohibition of salary assessments, Grant did attempt to implement reforms through an executive order. But Congress, which was even more reluctant than Grant to abandon patronage, refused to appropriate sufficient funds to enforce the regulations, and the spoils system lived on.

Much of the passion generated by this issue stemmed from a widespread concern about corruption in public life, an apprehension that public positions and institutions were being used to serve private ends. That the state, at all levels, was becoming larger only heightened these apprehensions. The Grant administration itself was subject to charges of nepotism and cronyism thanks to the large number of appointees who were either former army officers or relatives of the president's wife. Early in his administration, the president had to intervene to quash a scheme in which speculators were using inside government information to corner the gold market, a scheme from which Grant's sister and perhaps his wife stood to profit. In addition, several high officials in the administration, including the secretary of war, ended up leaving office in disgrace after being charged with accepting bribes. Although personally honest, Grant was both politically naive and altogether too trusting of his friends.

The most celebrated scandal of the era, however, the Credit Mobilier affair, involved congressmen. Credit Mobilier, a company created by the directors of the Union Pacific Railroad (who were also the directors of Credit Mobilier), was constructing major new rail lines with financial assistance from the federal government. To keep Congress from taking any steps that might limit the profitability of the venture or peering too closely at the use of federal loans, shares in Credit Mobilier were given to a number of prominent congressmen in 1867 and 1868. Remarkably, when these transactions were finally exposed in 1872, only one member of Congress was formally censured, although the taint of involvement followed others.

Reconstruction moved back to center stage during the Grant administration only in 1870–71. In an attempt to un-

Ulysses S. Grant, eighteenth president of the United States (1869–77).

dermine the Republican state governments, the Ku Klux Klan and other organizations ratcheted up the level of violence in 1870, killing hundreds of freedmen and causing local Republicans to plead for federal assistance. Congress responded with a series of Enforcement Acts making it a federal crime for state officials to discriminate against voters because of their race or to deprive any individual of his civil and political rights. The third such act, the Ku Klux Klan Act of April 1871, made it a federal crime for individuals to conspire to deprive others of their rights and authorized the president to use the army to enforce these laws and to suspend the writ of habeas corpus, if necessary.

The Enforcement Acts were significant in two respects. First, they enlarged federal power: they gave the national government jurisdiction not only over state actions but also over certain categories of crimes committed by individuals. (The Democrats were so incensed over this expansion of the central government that twenty years later they repealed most provisions of these acts.) Second, the Enforcement Acts worked. The Justice Department, led by Attorney General Amos Akerman, born in New Hampshire but a longtime resident of Georgia, vigorously used its new powers to prosecute the Klan, while president Grant sent troops to, and suspended habeas corpus in, parts of South Carolina. Although the president, sensitive to charges of "military despotism," used his powers sparingly, the government's actions were energetic enough to cripple the Klan and dramatically lower the incidence of violence, thereby bolstering the morale of both the freedmen and southern Republicans.

THE ELECTION OF 1872

Despite the success of some of Grant's policies, many Republicans lost faith in the president personally and in the party that he nominally headed but which seemed to hold him captive; in 1872, these disaffected Republicans joined some Democrats to form the Liberal Republican Party. Most Liberal Republicans were middle-class reformers who supported civil service reform, opposed high tariffs, and favored amnesty for ex-Confederates as well as the end of "bayonet rule" in the South. They were also convinced that the Republican Party, which some of them had helped to found, had lost its moral bearings and been taken over by unsavory professional politicians.

The Liberal Republicans met in convention in the spring of 1872 and, to the surprise of many, nominated journalist

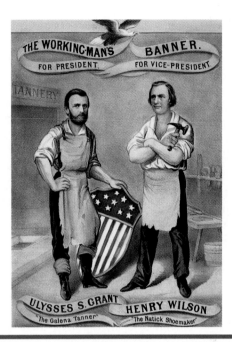

A campaign poster for the Republican ticket in the 1872 election, emphasizing both Grant's and Wilson's backgrounds as workingmen.

Horace Greeley as their presidential candidate. Greeley was a well-known figure with a track record of embracing quixotic, and sometimes contradictory, views; he was also not particularly interested either in civil service reform or lower tariffs. The centerpiece of his campaign quickly became sectional reconciliation and "home rule" by "the best people" of the South. Sensing the chance to beat Grant and to get a president sympathetic to their views, the Democrats also nominated Greeley, despite his having spent much of his career attacking the Democratic Party. But this fusion strategy backfired. Many Democrats could not bring themselves to support an old antagonist, and most Republicans feared that Greeley would deliver the South back to the Klan and ex-Confederates. Grant, despite a lackluster public image, was reelected with 56 percent of the popular vote, winning every state north of the Mason-Dixon line.

RECONSTRUCTION IN RETREAT

Although Grant's reelection seemed to affirm the nation's commitment to Reconstruction, that commitment eroded rapidly, for several reasons. The most important was the absence of any sign that things in the South were improving, that a stable political order was being established. In closely watched Louisiana, for example, disputes about the results of the 1872 elections led to the convening of two legislatures, the inauguration of two governors, and the arrival of federal troops. These episodes were followed, in 1873, by a clash between armed whites and black militiamen known as the Colfax massacre, which left roughly seventy blacks and two whites dead. Violence also enveloped the 1874 elections in Louisiana, setting off a train of events that culminated in federal troops entering the state capitol building and evicting five Democrats before the Democrats could deny key legislative seats to Republicans.

> *"The North's weariness with Reconstruction was also shaped by the severe economic depression that began in 1873."*

Similar conflicts raged throughout the South, as splits emerged within the Republican Party and the Democrats grew emboldened by success. Redeemers, committed to white supremacy, low taxes, and home rule (which meant the removal of federal troops), captured the state governments in Arkansas, Alabama, and Texas, while making inroads in most other states. In 1875, Redeemers in Mississippi—a state with a black majority—put into action what became known as the "Mississippi Plan": a coordinated effort to force whites to abandon the Republican Party and then, through violence and intimidation, to prevent blacks from voting. "Carry the election peacefully if we can, forcibly if we must," declared Democratic newspapers. The plan worked, in part because the Grant administration declined to send troops to protect blacks and Republicans. Democrats in Mississippi gained power in an election in which extraordinarily tiny Republican tallies (for example, 0, 2, and 4) were somehow recorded in counties with large black majorities.

Once in office, the Redeemers were not bashful about dismantling Reconstruction. They cut taxes, education spending (especially for blacks), and state funds for internal improvements. They altered the structure of local government by making key offices appointive rather than elected, and they excluded blacks altogether from law enforcement. The Redeemers also passed new vagrancy laws (designed to inhibit the movement of rural blacks and compel them to work) and lien laws that gave landlords the first claim on crops.

The successes of Redemption made clear that Reconstruction could be continued only with the prolonged, active, and military involvement of the federal government, a prospect that grew increasingly unpalatable in the North. As one northern Republican acknowledged, "The truth is our people are tired out with this worn out cry of 'Southern outrages.'" Republican disillusion with Reconstruction was only deepened by the 1874 elections, in which Democrats scored major gains in all regions and won control of the House of Representatives for the first time in eighteen years.

The North's weariness with Reconstruction was also shaped by the severe economic depression that began in 1873. Precipitated by the collapse of the financial and railroad empire of Jay Cooke, the Panic of 1873 marked the end of the post–Civil War economic boom and the beginning of the longest uninterrupted business-cycle downturn of the nineteenth century. (See Chapter 18.) In the short run, the stock market closed, banks failed, and commercial houses and railroads went under; as the panic dragged on, farm prices declined, wages were sharply cut, and unemployment reached unprecedented levels. The Grant administration did little in response to the crisis, but this was not a failing peculiar to the

An 1868 cartoon by Thomas Nast criticizing the Democratic Party's opposition to Reconstruction. The three men standing represent the urban Irish of the North, unreconstructed southern Confederates, and northern capitalists.

president: the common wisdom throughout the late nineteenth century was that there was nothing much the federal government could do to alleviate a panic.

One critical upshot of the economic downturn was that the buoyant optimism of the late 1860s vanished. People worried about how to pay their rent, feed their families, pay their debts, and find work. In the South, the economic condition of the freedmen worsened because of falling cotton prices; in the Northeast, Midwest, and West, people were preoccupied with their own problems rather than those of African American freedmen in faraway states. Under the best of circumstances, distant political and social upheavals can hold the attention of a people only so long before being overridden by private concerns; and the mid-1870s were not the best of circumstances.

While the North's resolve was weakened by both politics and economics, the ability of the federal government to promote civil and political equality was diminished by the Supreme Court. In what are known as the *Slaughterhouse Cases*, decided in 1873, the Court delivered a highly restrictive interpretation of the Fourteenth Amendment. The cases emerged in 1869 when the state of Louisiana granted one company a monopoly on slaughtering livestock in New Orleans. Other butchers in the city sued, asserting that the state had violated the clause of the Fourteenth Amendment mandating that "no state shall make or enforce any law which shall abridge the privileges or immunities of citizens of the United States." The Court disagreed, arguing that the Fourteenth Amendment protected only the "privileges and immunities" of "national citizenship" (rather than "state citizenship"), and that these privileges and immunities were of a very narrow sort—such as the right to use the nation's navigable waters. This narrow definition clearly limited the reach of the Fourteenth Amendment as a weapon against discriminatory state laws; so, too, did the Court's insistence that the Fourteenth Amendment did not significantly alter the relationship between the states and the federal government and that the Court itself ought not to act as a "permanent censor" of state legislation.

Three years later, in *U.S. v. Cruikshank*, a case that arose out of the Louisiana Colfax massacre, the Court undercut the enforcement clause of the Fourteenth Amendment. Overturning the conviction of three men who had been charged with violating the civil rights of their victims, the Court argued that the postwar amendments only gave the federal government power to prohibit rights violations by states, *not by individuals*. In the same year, in *U.S. v. Reese*, the Court ruled

This Thomas Nast cartoon, published at the beginning of the Panic of 1873, suggests that the "bust up" on Wall Street was well deserved.

that the Fifteenth Amendment did not guarantee anyone the right to vote; it simply specified that certain reasons for denying someone the vote were unacceptable. In practice, *Cruikshank* meant that the enforcement of black rights depended almost entirely on local officials, while the *Reese* decision set the stage for legally disfranchising blacks for ostensibly nonracial reasons.

THE ELECTION OF 1876 AND THE COMPROMISE OF 1877

With the country in depression, Reconstruction faltering, and the Republican Party stained by corruption scandals, the Democrats were well positioned for the 1876 elections. They chose for their standard-bearer the prominent reform governor of New York, Samuel J. Tilden, who was nationally known for having overthrown the Tweed ring (see Chapter 20). Tilden and the Democrats ran in opposition to the "corrupt centralism" of a Republican government, "which, after inflicting upon ten States the rapacities of carpet-bag tyrannies, has honeycombed . . . the Federal Government . . . with incapacity, waste, and fraud." To run against Tilden, the Republicans nominated Rutherford B. Hayes, an ex–Civil War general and

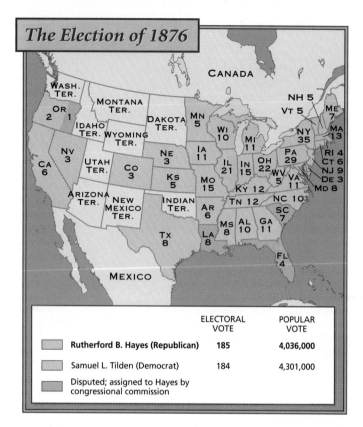

The Election of 1876

	ELECTORAL VOTE	POPULAR VOTE
Rutherford B. Hayes (Republican)	185	4,036,000
Samuel L. Tilden (Democrat)	184	4,301,000
Disputed; assigned to Hayes by congressional commission		

governor of Ohio who also had a reputation as a reformer. Although Hayes had been a moderate on Reconstruction and was noncommittal about the South during the campaign, the Republicans—outraged by new waves of violence aimed at intimidating southern voters—waved the "bloody shirt" of the Civil War for months before the election.

Voters appear to have been more concerned about the economy than about party history. The Democrats ran well, North and South, and Tilden garnered 250,000 more votes than Hayes, although this was partly because many intimidated southern Republicans did not vote. In the electoral college, Tilden was 1 vote short of the 185 needed for victory, with the returns in three states (South Carolina, Louisiana, and Florida) in dispute. In all three, the accuracy of the final tally was challenged by charges of fraud and coercive violence. And in all three, Republican voting boards ended up certifying vote totals that made Hayes victorious, despite the ferocious protest of Democrats.

The result was an unprecedented political and constitutional crisis. The Republican voting boards were, without doubt, certifying returns in a partisan fashion, throwing out Democratic votes in order to guarantee a Republican victory. On the other hand, genuinely free elections, conducted without intimidation, would likely have produced Republican victories in Louisiana and South Carolina, and probably in Mississippi and North Carolina as well. It was thus not clear where the line ought to be drawn between legitimate and fraudulent voting results. It was also not clear who should decide, or how: the Constitution offered no guidelines.

After several months of confusion, investigation, and charges of corruption and dishonesty, Congress and President Grant created a commission to adjudicate the challenged returns. The commission consisted of five senators, five congressmen, and five Supreme Court justices, carefully selected to yield partisan balance. After that delicate balance was tilted slightly by the last-minute resignation and replacement of one member, the commission, by a series of 8–7 votes, certified all the returns in the Republicans' favor.

Meanwhile, some Hayes Republicans and southern Democrats engaged in negotiations that helped pave the way toward a resolution of the crisis. Although no firm evidence exists that a formal "deal" was struck, informal understandings between key players were certainly reached. By the end of February 1877—just in time to permit the inauguration to proceed on schedule—most Democrats agreed not to mount a filibuster in the House of Representatives. Hayes was inaugurated on March 4. His cabinet appointments included men well known for their conciliatory stance toward the ex-Confederacy, and his administration gave enthusiastic support to the federal funding of internal improvements in the South.

More important, in April 1877, Hayes withdrew federal troops from the capitals of South Carolina and Louisiana. This act led immediately to the collapse of Republican governments in those states and to the installation of Redeemer regimes in the only two states where the Republicans remained in power. The withdrawal of troops sent an unmistakable signal. A Republican may still have been in the White House, but Reconstruction was over.

Legacies

The challenge faced by the men and women engaged in Reconstruction was daunting. As many Republicans understood, the task was not simply to restore the Confederate states to the Union but to transform southern society in order to make life in the region more consistent with the professed values of the Republic. To be successful, Reconstruction policies would have had to rebuild the southern economy while simultaneously reshaping both the social structure and the polity: the victors in the war would have had to satisfy the aspirations of 4 million newly freed, propertyless African Americans without provoking the deadly antagonism of white southerners who owned all the region's property yet were utterly dependent upon African American labor. The hatreds and mistrust bred by two centuries of slavery would have to be held in check long enough for more egalitarian patterns of interracial life to form and become commonplace. The task may not have been impossible, but it surely was Herculean and diplomatically delicate.

"For the most part, Reconstruction failed, and its failure had long-lasting consequences for the freedmen, for the South, for race relations, for the nation as a whole."

In retrospect, it is clear that there were positive achievements. The Union was restored, and once-rebellious states became full participants in the national government. Slavery was definitively abolished. Throughout the South, churches were built, as were schools for black children; families were reunited; hospitals, asylums, roads, and bridges were constructed. Thousands of freedmen even acquired their own farms. Perhaps most important, Congress and the states passed constitutional amendments that would ultimately protect a wide array of civil and political rights in the twentieth century. The Fourteenth and Fifteenth Amendments, although sometimes dormant, provided the legal framework for the equal-rights revolution of the mid–twentieth century. It is unlikely that these amendments would have been passed during any other period in the nation's history.

Yet the roster of successes was limited. For the most part, Reconstruction failed, and its failure had long-lasting consequences for the freedmen, for the South, for race relations, for the nation as a whole. The freedmen were granted formal political and civil rights but not the property or state support necessary to protect the exercise of those rights. The collapse of Reconstruction in the 1870s left a large majority of the 4 million ex-slaves as propertyless, agricultural workers in a society in which nearly all economic and political power was wielded by landowning whites. In such circumstances, it is hardly surprising that blacks were exploited, discriminated against, and eventually stripped of rights, such as voting, that they had formally obtained. Southern society became increasingly segregated in the wake of Reconstruction, and racial antagonisms became more pronounced.

Southern blacks and whites, moreover, inhabited a region economically damaged by war and hamstrung by the social and economic order that emerged after the war. It was in the 1860s that there opened up a large income and wealth gap between the North and the South, a gap that did not start to narrow until after World War II. Postbellum southern society was short of capital, ambivalent about industrialization, and reluctant to invest in institutions (such as schools) that might have accelerated development. The organization of agriculture spawned an overreliance on cotton, and cotton culture, with its high rates of farm tenancy, stimulated few agricultural innovations. Relatively unattractive and inhospitable to immigrants, the postwar South settled into decades of quasi-stagnation and high rates of poverty.

1865	Thirteenth Amendment ratified.
March 1865	Freedmen's Bureau created.
1866	Congress passes Civil Rights Bill and Freedmen's Bureau Bill over President Johnson's veto.
	Ku Klux Klan founded in Tennessee.
March 1867	Reconstruction Act passed.
1868	Fourteenth Amendment ratified.
May 26, 1868	Johnson acquitted in impeachment trial.
1870	Last of the Confederate states readmitted to the Union.
	Fifteenth Amendment ratified.
1872	Thomas Edison invents the stock ticker.
1873	Panic sets off longest depression of the nineteenth century.
1875	Mississippi Plan prevents blacks from voting, allowing Democrats to gain power in that state.

Chronology

Reconstruction had political effects as well, some local, some national. The rout of the Republican Party in the South opened the way for the one-party system that came to dominate southern political life for nearly a century, stifling dissent and depressing political participation. The existence of a conservative, one-party region in which most working people were excluded from politics pushed the national political spectrum rightward, complicating or preventing reforms. The wording of the Fourteenth and Fifteenth Amendments, moreover, formalized the exclusion of women from electoral politics.

The era of Reconstruction came to an end without having set the nation on a course that could heal the wounds of slavery and promote greater racial harmony and social justice. Whether any other outcome was possible is difficult to judge; but the shortcomings of Reconstruction set the stage for the troubling history of race in modern America.

Suggested Reading

R. H. Abbott, *The Republican Party and the South, 1855–1877: The First Southern Strategy* (1986)

Michael Les Benedict, *A Compromise of Principle: Congressional Republicans and Reconstruction, 1863–1869* (1974)

Walter L. Fleming, *Documentary History of Reconstruction* (1906)

Eric Foner, *Reconstruction: America's Unfinished Revolution* (1989)

Leon Litwack, *Been in the Storm So Long: The Aftermath of Slavery* (1980)

Geoffrey Perret, *Ulysses S. Grant, Soldier and President* (1999)

Michael Perman, *Reunion Without Compromise* (1973)

Chapter 18

THE RISE OF BIG BUSINESS AND THE TRIUMPH OF INDUSTRY:
1870–1900

An Industrial Economy
  Agriculture and Industry
  Railroads
  Big Business
  Industry and Technology

The Center and the Periphery
  The South
  The West

Classes
  Jobs and Incomes
  Immigrants and Migrants
  Social Mobility

The Wason Manufacturing Company, Railway Car Builders, Springfield, Massachusetts, 1872.

QUESTIONS

- How did the United States become an industrial power between 1865 and 1900?

- What were the regional divisions in the nation's economy in the late nineteenth century?

- How did industrial development affect the class relations of this period?

On May 10, 1876, President Ulysses Grant formally opened the Centennial Exhibition in Philadelphia. Long planned, the exhibition, which filled scores of buildings on a several-hundred-acre site in Fairmount Park, was the centerpiece of the nation's official celebration of its first 100 years of independence. Congress, in authorizing funds for the exhibition, had declared it to be "fitting that the completion of the first century of our national existence shall be commemorated by an exhibition of the natural resources of the country and their development, and of its progress in those arts which benefit mankind."

The opening ceremonies were filled with pomp, music, and dignitaries. The president was escorted by 4,000 troops, and he and Mrs. Grant were joined on the grandstand by the Supreme Court justices, the cabinet members, governors, senators, congressmen, high-ranking military officers, and a host of local officials. Once the president took his seat, an orchestra struck up the *Centennial Inauguration March,* composed for the occasion by German composer Richard Wagner; then a chorus sang the *Centennial Hymn,* with words by poet John Greenleaf Whittier. After a brief speech by Grant declaring the exhibition officially open, 800 singers burst into the "Hallelujah Chorus" from Handel's *Messiah,* artillery on a nearby hillside fired a 100-gun salute, thirteen bells chimed, and the assembled notables, led by the president, marched to the main building, where they were joined by foreign guests and delegates.

The entire cortege then proceeded into Machinery Hall, where acres of motionless machinery surrounded a towering steam engine that rose more than forty feet above the ground. President Grant and Emperor Dom Pedro II of Brazil (the first reigning monarch ever to visit the United States) ap-proached the engine and its builder, George H. Corliss, who showed them how to turn cranks that would start it. Once the cranks were turned, the cylinders and flywheel of the engine began to move, and as they did, all the machinery in the hall, connected to the engine by thousands of feet of underground shafts and pulleys, sprang into motion. The spectators broke into a prolonged cheer. The largest steam engine in the world was providing power to machines that spun cotton, combed wool, printed newspapers, made shoes, pumped water, and performed hundreds of other tasks.

Machinery Hall became the main attraction of the enormously successful Centennial, and the Corliss engine became its celebrated symbol. Fittingly so. The nation's growth since independence had been closely linked to the rise of industry and the success of the steam engine. And the United States in 1876 stood near the beginning of an extraordinary period of economic growth and technological inventiveness. Twenty years later, a writer in *Scientific American* would describe the years since the Civil War as "an epoch of invention and progress unique in the history of the world," and he was exaggerating only slightly. The number of patents issued more than doubled each year, and the list of prominent inventions included Alexander Graham Bell's telephone, Thomas Alva Edison's incandescent lamp and phonograph, the machine gun, the cable car, the electric streetlight, the Linotype machine, and a slew of significant advances in the use of electricity and electric motors.

> *"The United States in 1876 stood near the beginning of an extraordinary period of economic growth and technological inventiveness."*

Technological progress also seemed to be something for which Americans had particular gifts. As novelist William Dean Howells observed after a visit to the exhibition, "it is still in these things of iron and steel that the national genius most freely speaks; by and by the inspired marbles, the breathing canvases, the great literature; for the present America is voluble in the strong metals and their infinite uses." Howells marveled at the "thousand creations of American inventive genius" on display, yet he, like most visitors, was particularly awed by "the majesty of the great Corliss engine" with "its vast and almost silent grandeur." (The engine was "almost silent" because the boilers had been placed outside of Machinery Hall.) Frédéric-Auguste Bartholdi, the creator of the not-yet-completed Statue of Liberty—the arm and torch of which were part of a Centennial sculpture exhibit—went a step further, finding beauty as well as power in the engine. "The lines are so grand and beautiful," he wrote, "the play of movement so skillfully arranged, and the whole machine was so harmoniously constructed, that it had the beauty and almost the grace of the human form."

The nation's centennial thus celebrated not just independence but also progress, not just liberty but technology: its past, its promise, its power, its capacity to generate wealth and improve people's lives. Nearly 10 million people visited the Centennial Exhibition and drank in the happy results of nineteenth-century mechanical, scientific, agricultural, and scientific advances: not only a 700-ton steam engine but harvesters, threshers, printing presses, sewing machines, and locomotives. They also viewed thousands of agricultural and manufactured products, ranging from sugar-coated pills to netted underwear to whiskey and dried cider. The spectacle was exhilarating, a source of optimism, satisfaction, and challenge.

So much so that one would hardly have known that the United States in 1876 was a nation deeply troubled and riddled with conflict. Outside the gates of the Centennial Exhibition, the country was in the midst of a severe economic depression; unemployed workers were demonstrating behind "blood-red banners," and strikes protesting falling wages were breaking out in one industry after another. (Relatively few workers attended the exhibition, both because it charged admission and because it was

closed on Sundays, the only day off most workers had.) At the same time, antiblack violence was mounting in the South, Reconstruction was collapsing, and ex-Confederates were regaining control of southern state governments. Most southern states, in fact, refused to participate in the Centennial—which was hardly surprising, since their membership in the Union was involuntary.

The nation was also encountering some difficulties in the West, where Native Americans were resisting both modern technology and the encroachment of white civilization: in August 1876, the celebrated defeat of Colonel George Custer (who had gone to see the Centennial buildings before making what would be his final trip to the West; see Chapter 19) was a dramatic reminder that the Indian wars were not going well. Back in Washington, political scandals were erupting left and right, only to be overshadowed, late in the year, by a presidential election in which the candidate with the most votes lost.

LEFT: The Corliss engine, the largest steam engine in the world, dominated Machinery Hall at the Centennial Exhibition in Philadelphia, 1876.

RIGHT: The arm and torch of the Statue of Liberty on display at the Centennial Exhibition.

The Centennial Exhibition, in sum, told only half the story. Both the price and the fruits of progress had been shared unequally, creating new conflicts, new social divisions, new challenges. Some of the allure of the Corliss engine, perhaps, sprang from the hope that technology—writ large, towering above the ground—could offer solutions to the many problems, new and old, the nation needed to confront.

An Industrial Economy

AGRICULTURE AND INDUSTRY

Between the end of the Civil War and the turn of the century, almost everything connected with the American economy grew. The population rose from less than 40 million to more than 75 million; the total output of the economy, or gross national product (GNP), more than tripled; and GNP per capita (the quantity of goods and services produced per person) doubled.

Some of this growth was in agriculture, the traditional core of the American economy. The number of farms rose from 2 million in 1860 to 5.75 million in 1900; the number of improved acres of farmland rose similarly from 164 million to 416 million acres. Much of this expansion took place in the Midwest and West, with particularly rapid growth occurring in Missouri, Iowa, Kansas, Nebraska, Minnesota, the Dakotas, and the central valley of California. The 32 million people living on farms in 1900 were producing far more wheat, oats, rice, cotton, sugarcane, potatoes, pork, and beef than their predecessors had in the 1860s. This was so for three reasons: more land was under cultivation; some of the newly settled lands, particularly in the Midwest, were more fertile and easier to farm than land in the Northeast had been; and farmers were increasingly using new and improved technology.

This technology came in many different forms. The seed drill, or drill planter, conserved seed and made it far easier to grow grains in easily tended, regular rows. The chilled iron plow greatly facilitated plowing in the heavy, wet soil of the prairies. Hay balers, mowers, loaders, and forks reduced the labor cost of haymaking. The mechanical reaper, which had come into wide use in the 1850s, became sturdier and more efficient after the war, permitting more farmers to harvest more grain. (Since grains such as wheat had a harvest season of roughly two weeks, the quantity of grain a farmer could grow was always limited by the amount he could harvest in a brief, two-week interval.) Some of the innovative implements put to use after 1865 had been invented earlier, but their adoption was delayed until farms grew larger and machinery prices fell: between 1860 and 1900, the value of farm implements on the average midwestern farm more than doubled. Notably, no such change occurred in the South, where the enormous growth in the cotton crop was achieved almost entirely through increasing acreage rather than productivity.

New technology also came in the form of knowledge. Late nineteenth-century farmers learned about seed selection, soil conservation, the selective breeding of livestock, matching crop varieties to local conditions, and better methods of caring for livestock—all of which made their farms more productive. They acquired this knowledge from diverse sources, including agricultural colleges funded in part through the Morrill Land Grant College Act (1862) and agricultural experiment stations created by the Hatch Act (1887). The federal government thus was a key source of agricultural innovation.

Vastly increased agricultural output led, not surprisingly, to declining prices, a trend re-

A steam-powered wheat thresher on a farm near Fargo in the Dakota Territory, 1878.

inforced by the internationalization of markets resulting from improved transportation. Corn that had sold for seventy cents a bushel in the early 1870s sold for half that fifteen years later; wheat prices fell nearly as much; cotton prices fell from sixteen cents a pound in 1869 to less than six cents a pound in 1898. Since this was, in general, a period of deflation (something difficult for us to imagine in the early twenty-first century), these price drops were less calamitous for farmers than we might think. Still, falling prices were better news for consumers than for farmers, especially those farmers who had not increased their own productivity.

"It was between 1865 and 1900 that the United States became an industrial power."

Significant as the growth of agriculture was, it paled in comparison with the growth of industry. Although the industrial revolution began long before the Civil War, it was between 1865 and 1900 that the United States became an industrial power. According to one index, manufacturing production increased nearly sixfold during these years. Manufacturing output began to exceed agricultural output in the 1880s, and by the turn of the century manufacturing, construction, and mining accounted for two-thirds of the economy. Similarly, by 1880, the number of nonfarm workers topped the number of men and women working in agriculture, and by 1900 6 million people were employed in manufactures, while another 4.5 million worked in mining, construction, and transportation. The United States—which had lagged behind Britain, Germany, and France as recently as 1860—was the world's leading manufacturing nation in 1900, producing 30 percent of its manufactured goods.

Two relatively new industries led this expansion. In 1860, the nation's largest industries had been cotton textiles and lumber milling; both remained important, but they were surpassed by the machinery and foundry industry and by **iron and steel.** The total quantity of raw steel produced—to cite one particularly vivid set of numbers—rose from 30,000 tons in 1868 to more than 11 million tons in 1900. During the same period, the production of bituminous coal (used to make steel) increased by 2,000 percent.

Clearly, the nation's economic center of gravity shifted both to industry and to what William Dean Howells had called the "strong metals." It also moved geographically. During the Civil War, most manufacturing had been concentrated in New York, Philadelphia, and New England. But by 1880, the Midwest, too, had acquired an important industrial sector: Chicago had nearly 80,000 manufacturing workers, while Cincinatti had 59,000 and St. Louis more than 40,000. Industrialization, like the frontier, was moving west.

There were multiple reasons for the enormous expansion of the economy. Population growth, accelerated by immigration, enlarged the market for both foodstuffs and manufactured goods. At the same time, the railroads opened up distant markets for many businesses and farmers, while improvements in shipping brought foreign trading partners closer. These enlarged markets created competition as well as opportunities; both helped to spawn technological advances that made industries more productive.

Growth was also fostered by the tariff policies of the federal government. The Republican Congress had increased

The manufacture of steel through a Bessemer converter at the Thomson Iron and Steel Works in Pittsburgh, 1886.

tariffs (taxes on goods imported into the United States) during the Civil War, both to pay the expenses of the government and to satisfy northern industry's long-standing demand for protection against international competition. In the war's aftermath, high tariffs—often above 40 percent—remained the norm, although they occasionally declined during prosperous periods. How much impact these tariffs had is impossible to measure, but there is no doubt that they stimulated some manufacturing industries and branches of agriculture, while having a negative impact both on consumers (who had to pay higher prices) and on exporters (who wanted free trade).

Dramatic as the growth of the economy may have been, it was hardly continuous or smooth. Panics (as they were called in the nineteenth and early twentieth centuries) occurred each decade, bringing plunging stock prices, business and bank failures, and a temporary halt to economic growth. The Panic of 1873 precipitated a long depression that lasted until 1878; a more moderate downturn occurred in the mid-1880s; and a severe depression gripped the nation from 1893 through 1897. During each of these downturns, production, prices, and wages fell, while unemployment rose.

These widely felt depressions were themselves testimony to the increasing dominance of industrial capitalism. While agricultural economies are subject to the whims of nature, industrial capitalist economies have business cycles: periods of investment and expansion that are followed by periods of stagnation or decline, which, in turn, are followed by new periods of investment and expansion. It was between the Civil War and the turn of the century that the business cycle became a prominent feature of the economic landscape, broadly affecting the rhythms of economic life, transforming the language with the addition of words such as "boom" and "unemployment." This was because the expansion of industry rendered an increasingly large proportion of the population directly vulnerable to business-cycle fluctuations. The men and women who lived through these episodes, moreover, did not have the comfort of believing they were riding the crests and troughs of a cycle: it was only in the second decade of the twentieth century that the concept of a business cycle was embraced by economists (who were themselves something of a late nineteenth- and early twentieth-century invention). To citizens of the late nineteenth century, what happened in 1893 was not a cyclical downturn, but a panic that had no guaranteed ending.

RAILROADS

I see over my own continent the Pacific railroad surmounting every
   barrier,
I see continual trains of cars winding along the Platte carrying freight
   and passengers,
I hear the locomotives rushing and roaring, and the shrill steamwhistle,
I hear the echoes reverberate through the grandest scenery in the
   world. . . .
I see the clear waters of lake Tahoe, I see forests of majestic pines,
Or crossing the great desert, the alkaline plains, I behold enchanting
   mirages of waters and meadows,
Marking through these and after all, in duplicate slender lines,
Bridging the three or four thousand miles of land travel,
Tying the Eastern to the Western sea,
The road between Europe and Asia.

(Ah Genoese thy dream! thy dream!
Centuries after thou art laid in thy grave,
The shore thou foundest verifies thy dream.)

—Walt Whitman, from "Passage to India," 1871

Railroads were at the heart of the economy. The enterprises that built and operated the railroads were the century's largest. They consumed immense amounts of capital, transported most of the nation's freight, and hired an enormous number of workers. The railroads also created a national economy out of what had been a loosely linked network of local and regional economies.

The most celebrated moment in the era's railway history occurred on March 10, 1869, at Promontory Point, Utah, when two teams of laborers, one Chinese and the other Irish, put down rails that linked the Central Pacific and Union Pacific Railroads. Once the rails were aligned, a golden spike was hammered into place by Leland Stanford, the governor of California and president of the Central Pacific, and by T. C. Durant, the vice-president of the Union Pacific. With every blow of the sledgehammer transmitted by telegraph to a waiting nation, the first transcontinental railroad was completed.

This symbolic "tying" of "the Eastern to the Western sea" inaugurated a frantic wave of railroad construction. In 1865, the United States had 35,000 miles of railroad track; by 1900, it had nearly 200,000. By the 1890s, there were five transcontinental railroads, more than a dozen trans-Mississippi lines, and an immense web of track in the East providing multiple connections between all major (and even medium-sized) cities. At the end of the century, the railroads employed more than a million workers tending a system that had 1.4 million freight cars and 35,000 passenger cars in service. The capital to create this system (roughly $10 billion) came from private American sources, overseas investors, and the public sector: the federal government, as well as state and local governments, subsidized the roads through loans, land grants (totaling more than 150 million acres), and tax exemptions.

The rush to build railroads created its own instability. They were overbuilt in many areas, competition was fierce, and business downturns cut revenues and savaged stock prices. In 1876, 40 percent of all railroad bonds were in default; after the Panic of 1893, nearly 200 railroads were unable to pay their debts and were being operated under court supervision. Mark Twain reflected the views of many small investors when he noted that "this is the very road whose stock always goes down after you buy it, and always goes up again as soon as you sell it."

Nonetheless, great fortunes were made in railroading, from stock speculation, mergers, and construction-finance schemes as well as from the actual operation of the roads. Indeed, the men who made these fortunes—including Jay Gould, Cornelius Vanderbilt, Collis P. Huntington, Thomas A. Scott, Leland Stanford, and James J. Hill—acquired a nationally visible wealth that was without precedent. In so doing, they became celebrated (occasionally reviled) figures who seemed to symbolize both the achievements and the excesses of the era.

New technology helped to spur the railroad boom. Steel rails lasted longer than iron, and once the price of Bessemer-produced steel dropped in the 1870s, railroads everywhere began to use the harder, more durable metal. Major gains in efficiency were also realized from the "compound" (or two-cylindered) locomotive, which was more fuel efficient and powerful than its traditional predecessor.

At the same time, two inventions made trains safer: air brakes and the automatic coupler. Braking was a problem for trains in the mid-nineteenth century: mechanical brakes had to be applied individually and separately (by brakemen) to each car, which made for something less than smooth and reliable stops. Several inventors had developed devices (including the air brake) to solve this problem, but the railroads themselves were relatively uninterested until after the Civil War. Then, with both train speeds and the volume of traffic increasing, the railroads turned their attention to braking, just as the young George Westinghouse was receiving a patent on a brake system that used pressurized air to stop all cars simultaneously. Within a year after he had obtained his patent, Westinghouse's air brakes were being used on eight railroads. Once he had invented and perfected the triple valve (1873), a pressure-sensitive gauge that made the brakes virtually fail-safe, Westinghouse brakes, manufactured in Pittsburgh, became the industry standard.

Almost simultaneously, Eli Janney invented a coupling device that permitted cars to be coupled to or uncoupled from one another without brakemen having to step between them while they were moving, a process that had produced extraordinary carnage over the years (65,000 railroad men died on the job between 1870 and 1900). In 1893, one of the first pieces of safety legislation enacted by the federal government,

A ceremony marking the completion of the first transcontinental railroad at Promontory Point, Utah, on May 10, 1869.

The railroad kings: Collis P. Huntington is at top left, Leland Stanford at bottom left.

the Railroad Safety Appliance Act, mandated the use of air brakes and Janney couplers on all interstate rail lines.

Other innovations also served the railroads and their customers. Bridge-building techniques improved substantially—particularly in the wake of several horrific accidents, including the well-known plunge of the Pacific Express into the Ashtabula (Ohio) River when a bridge came apart during a storm. (Train wrecks captured the public imagination in the late nineteenth century much as plane crashes do today.) Passenger comfort was significantly enhanced by the well-appointed, and sometimes luxurious, sleeping cars built by the Pullman Palace Car Company. An entire industry, meatpacking, was given an enormous boost by the development in the late 1870s of refrigerated freight cars that could transport meat without spoilage. The key innovation was to place ice in overhead bins that allowed cool air to drop while keeping the ice from touching the meat (which discolored it and made it spoil more rapidly).

Of equal importance were innovative managerial methods developed first by railroad corporations and later imitated by much of American industry. Railroads were the nation's first big businesses, and because of their size, the physical distance they spanned, and the imperatives of coordination, they faced managerial challenges that were unprecedented. In response, the rail corporations replaced informal lines of authority with a formal, vertical chain of command that governed all divisions of the enterprise; to a considerable degree, management was separated from ownership, and managers themselves became quasi-professional. In addition, the railroads institutionalized long-run planning and developed modern accounting techniques. When the first graduate programs in business management appeared, just before World War I, their programs relied heavily on lessons learned from the railroads.

The impact of railroads on the nation's economy was immense. They provided a great stimulus to the iron and steel industry (and consequently to coal production): in the 1870s and 1880s, about three-quarters of all Bessemer-produced steel ended up as railroad tracks. They spurred the growth of the telegraph industry by encouraging the erection of telegraph lines alongside the rails. The cattle and meatpacking industries were entirely dependent on the railroads, and farmers sold an increasing proportion of their crops in distant markets that could only be reached by rail. Indeed, in 1890 (roughly the peak year), two-thirds of all freight in the United States was carried by the railroads.

Yet the railroads did not just stimulate the economy; they changed it. The 150,000 miles of track laid after the Civil War linked all the cities and most towns of the United States, making it possible for goods to be shipped easily and relatively cheaply from any one place to any other place. This network effectively nationalized the economy, opening markets and breaking down local and regional monopolies. Small entrepreneurs, skilled craftsmen, local factories: all were faced with new competition from outside, even as they simultaneously were able to broaden their own entrepreneurial horizons. Thanks to the railroads, the number of traveling salesmen quadrupled between 1870 and 1880, while mail-order houses like Montgomery Ward and Sears, Roebuck exploded into the forefront of retailing.

The **impact of the railroads** spilled over into countless other dimensions of American life. As both costs and travel times fell, hundreds of thousands of Easterners were able to see the West firsthand. Even a transcontinental trip could be made in less than ten days by

1880. Towns with good rail connections swelled into cities, while well-connected cities boomed: Chicago owed its status as a metropolis to its emergence as *the* railway hub linking the East to the West. Trains carried mail and newspapers everywhere; they brought the circus to small towns; long before radio or television, they encouraged the development of a national culture. They also encouraged people to wear watches—since even farmers whose daily rhythms were dictated by the sun had to abide by train schedules. The first sizable profits earned by Richard Warren Sears, the founder of Sears, Roebuck, came from selling watches in rural Minnesota.

Indeed, standard time zones in the United States were created by the railroads in 1883. Before then, every major city had its own local time, generally based on the position of the sun. This variability created havoc with rail schedules (among other things), but some cities steadfastly resisted any change: the proposition that Cincinnati should alter its clocks by twenty-two minutes "so as to harmonize with an imaginary line drawn through Pittsburgh," concluded a local newspaper, "is simply preposterous. . . . let the people of Cincinnati stick to the truth as it is written by the sun, moon, and stars." But the railroads and their commercial allies prevailed, and on Sunday, November 18, 1883, the "Day of Two Noons," most American cities and towns adjusted their clocks to conform with four standard time zones.

The railways also loomed large in politics, spawning new government agencies and newly configured relationships between private enterprise and the state. Although private corporations, the railroads performed a public function and commonly received governmental subsidies and charters. Consequently, states believed they had a right to oversee the behavior of the railroads. Even before the Civil War, four state railway commissions had been created; by 1897, the number had risen to twenty-eight. The earliest commissions served primarily to investigate and publicize concerns about railroad practices.

Public scrutiny of the railways intensified after the Civil War both because they were wielding increasing power over shippers and consumers and because competition was dri-

> *"Long before radio or television, railroads encouraged the development of a national culture."*

ving the railroads into pricing policies that seemed discriminatory. As more and more track was laid, railroads found themselves having to lower freight rates on lines where competition existed, while holding prices steady or even raising them on routes they monopolized. The result was a disparity between "short haul" and "long haul" freight rates: it was, for example, far more expensive to ship grain from Chicago to Pittsburgh than from Chicago to New York. Residents of small towns with only one rail line often found themselves paying much higher freight rates than shippers in nearby cities. At the same time, railroads began to give rebates or special contracts to preferred shippers—which meant that not everybody was paying the same price for the same service.

In response to these practices, a number of midwestern states passed in the 1870s what came to be called the "Granger" laws because they were supported by farmers who belonged to an organization called the Grange. These laws created railway commissions, empowered them to set maximum or "reasonable" rates, and prohibited discrimination, long haul/short haul disparities, rebates, and other abuses. They constituted a pioneering effort on the part of public authorities to regulate the behavior of powerful pri-

The railroad suspension bridge at Niagara Falls, New York, on the Grand Central route to Chicago and San Francisco, 1876.

Transcontinental Railroad Lines, 1880s

vate corporations. They also reflected a growing preoccupation with what novelist Frank Norris called "the railroad, that great monster, iron-hearted, relentless, infinitely powerful." In late nineteenth-century newspapers, magazines, novels, and paintings, the railroads loomed large, the locomotive often symbolizing both the genius of invention and frightening, inhuman power. Moving trains were common images in the very first motion pictures; and the desire to domesticate and tame

the power of railroads may have played a role in the turn-of-the-century success of the Lionel model train company.

In 1877, the Supreme Court, in *Munn v. Illinois*, upheld the constitutionality of the Granger laws, concluding that private property, when "affected with a public interest . . . must submit to be controlled by the public for the common good." Eight years later, however, the Court partially reversed itself, in *Wabash v. Illinois*, by striking down some state laws on the grounds that the federal government alone had the right to regulate commerce between the states. Since a great deal of freight traffic was interstate, the decision effectively gutted the Granger laws. Congress responded by passing the Interstate Commerce Act (ICA) in 1887, which prohibited discriminatory pricing policies, required published rate schedules, and insisted that all railroad rates should be "reasonable and just." Enforcement of the law was entrusted to an Interstate Commerce Commission (ICC) whose members were appointed by the president. Although much of the law was imprecisely worded and there was little agreement about what constituted "reasonable and just" rates, the ICA was a pathbreaking piece of legislation that established the right of the federal government to actively regulate some private enterprise.

Notably, federal regulation was not unwelcome to many railroad owners and managers. The rate wars of the 1870s and 1880s had threatened their profits, and private efforts to end "cutthroat competition" had repeatedly foundered. The most common such efforts involved establishing "pools," or "cartels," that would fix prices and divide up markets, but these anticompetitive agreements could not be enforced at law, and consequently they tended to collapse whenever a cartel member decided it was in his interest to break the agreement. Regulation therefore seemed to be necessary, and railroad owners agreed that one set of federal regulations was far preferable to a bewildering array of state laws. Federal regulation also promised to standardize rules governing equipment, safety, and rights of way.

The passage of the ICA may also have facilitated the mergers that took place in the 1890s. In their efforts to stabilize the industry, which meant ending price wars, guaranteeing access to key trunk lines, and preventing new lines from sparking competitive chaos, the largest railroads began to reorganize themselves, merge with, or simply acquire their smaller rivals. With the help of investment bankers like J. P. Morgan, five huge rail systems were created that were large enough to stabilize prices and control a hefty proportion of the nation's freight. The mergers that created these systems took place after, not before, the ICC was established.

BIG BUSINESS

Railroads were not the only big businesses in 1900. In most industries, firms and plants became substantially larger between the Civil War and the turn of the century: the number of wage earners per establishment more than doubled, and the amount of capital invested rose even more rapidly. The degree of corporate concentration (the percentage of an industry controlled by its largest firms) also rose, sometimes dramatically: by the end of the century, Standard Oil refined 80 percent of the nation's oil, the Carnegie Company produced 30 percent of all finished steel, and two companies (General Electric and Westinghouse) had complete control of the electrical equipment industry. These were, of course, extraordinary enterprises, yet they aptly symbolized the transformation of industry that occurred between Reconstruction and the beginning of the twentieth century. This was the era in which large corporations, with multiple plants, began to do business *nationally;* it was, indeed, the era that spawned the phrase "big business," an Americanism that made its first appearance in print in 1905 in *McClure's Magazine.*

Yet there was more to this transformation—and more to big business—than just size. Firms did not simply acquire more workers and more capital; they also adopted a new insti-

A cartoon attacking the railroad business headed by William H. Vanderbilt, son and successor to Cornelius Vanderbilt.

tutional structure. This structure—which became the signature of the "modern business enterprise"—had two key, deceptively simple characteristics. The first was the presence of many distinct operating units, each of which had its own administration and kept its own accounts; in theory, each unit could function as an independent business. The second characteristic was that the modern enterprise was managed by a hierarchy of salaried executives.

All firms that became "big" businesses in the late nineteenth century developed or acquired these two structural characteristics, neither of which had appeared in any company before 1840. These features permitted firms by themselves to carry out steps that had once constituted market transactions between individuals or firms. Where grain, for example, had been sold from farmers to wholesale buyers to processors to a series of middlemen who shipped and distributed the processed product, the new multi-unit firms handled all the steps between the farmer and the local retailer. The "invisible hand" of the market, to use economist Adam Smith's famous phrase, was replaced by the visible hands of managers who coordinated the flow of materials, goods, and personnel among the different units of the enterprise.

> *"The modern business enterprise appeared first among the railroads; its spread was linked to revolutionary changes in the ways that goods were distributed and produced."*

The modern business enterprise appeared first among the railroads; its spread was linked to revolutionary changes in the ways that goods were distributed and produced. The changes in distribution came first, as wholesalers (who bought goods from producers and sold them to retailers) took advantage of the new speed of commerce to build regional firms that could move and sell goods quickly. They were joined by mass retailers who were capable of selling large quantities of diverse goods to consumers. Among the first mass retailers to appear in the 1870s were department stores, such as Marshall Field's, Macy's, Lord and Taylor, and Bloomingdale's, as well as Montgomery Ward, the first national mail-order house. Chain stores with branches in different cities (including the forerunners of A and P, Kroger, Grand Union, and Woolworth's) became prominent later in the century. The innovations wrought by these firms spawned institutions that have endured for more than a century.

The transformation of manufacturing came a bit later and depended significantly on new technology. Innovations in technique led to new and better products and more rapid production processes. This was particularly true in industries that depended on the application of heat to raw materials, such as oil-refining and steel-making. The average annual output of a blast furnace, for example, rose from 5,000 tons of steel to 65,000 tons between 1869 and 1899. Equally dramatic shifts occurred in some mechanical industries. In 1881, when a highly skilled cigarette maker could turn out 3,000 cigarettes a day, James Bonsack patented a machine that could produce more than 70,000 in ten hours. Similar advances in speed were obtained by the first automatic canning factories, which led to the successes of Campbell's Soup, Heinz, and Borden's Milk.

Indeed, lured by the enormous markets opened up by the railroads, manufacturers in many industries strove to attain what would later be called "mass production." (The phrase itself became common only in the 1920s in the wake of a widely read, although ghost-written, article by Henry Ford.) Manufacturers introduced technological and organizational innovations to increase the efficiency of each department. Owners and engineers redesigned workplaces to accelerate the movement of materials from one place to another; they

The steam elevator at Lord and Taylor crowded with fashionable customers, New York City, 1872.

also introduced new statistical and accounting methods to measure the effects of their labors. They deployed electric motors (themselves new) to eliminate many of the cumbersome belts and shafts that conveyed steam power to operating machinery. And they designed goods—including farm machinery, sewing machines, and bicycles—with interchangeable parts that would make them easier to manufacture, market, use, and repair. Some manufacturers came closer to this mass-production goal than did others, but the goal was omnipresent.

John D. Rockefeller.

The full-blown modern business enterprise appeared when mass production was integrated with mass distribution within a single firm. One route to this integration was taken in the 1880s by James B. Duke, a North Carolina tobacco manufacturer who recognized the potential of both the market for cigarettes (which were new and exotic) and the Bonsack rolling machine. After signing a contract with Bonsack and installing two of his machines, Duke proceeded to create an extensive sales organization, based in New York, with offices in other American cities and abroad. At the same time, he constructed a purchasing network in the Southeast to buy, dry, cure, and store tobacco—which gave him a secure supply of cured tobacco for his factories. Thanks to the competitive advantages of this "vertical integration" (his firm controlled the entire production process from raw materials to the consumer), Duke became the largest manufacturer in the industry and by 1890 was selling more than 800 million cigarettes a year.

An alternative path to bigness was through merger, or "horizontal integration," a path that became popular in the 1890s. John D. Rockefeller, for example, began his celebrated career as the owner of the Standard Oil Company, an oil refinery in Cleveland. He then bought a number of competitive refineries and formed an alliance with others to control output, keep prices up, negotiate shipping rates with the railroad, and (later) construct their own pipelines. This alliance had several different legal forms in the 1870s and 1880s, including a formal "trust" in which the shareholders of all of the member companies exchanged their stock for certificates

in the Standard Oil Trust. In the mid-1880s, when the trust controlled more than three-quarters of the nation's refining capacity, Rockefeller and his allies moved into marketing, creating their own sales organization; later in the decade, Standard Oil began to buy oil fields and produce crude oil, controlling a third of the nation's supply by 1898.

The drive for bigness was only partially grounded in the imperatives of economic efficiency. In some cases, the impulse to construct large corporations was motivated primarily by the desire to increase profits by suppressing competition and maintaining prices. In the 1870s and 1880s, that impulse led many businessmen to form "pools," in which they agreed on prices and voluntarily divided up markets. When those voluntary pools failed (as they usually did because one member or other would decide that it was in his interest to break the agreement), businesses turned to trusts and holding companies: these were more effective because they held the stock of operating companies and could therefore coerce them into sticking to agreements. When trusts came under legal attack,

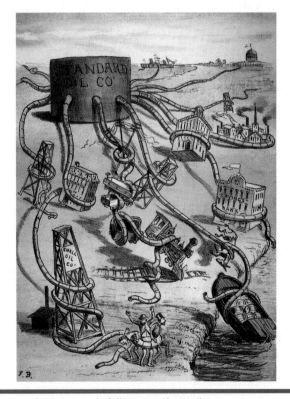

A cartoon depicting Rockefeller's Standard Oil Company as an octopus, a common metaphor of the period.

mergers became the strategy of choice for businessmen intent on dominating markets and avoiding competition.

The formation of large enterprises was facilitated by changes in the laws governing corporations. Most business firms in the first two-thirds of the nineteenth century were sole proprietorships or partnerships, but the expansion of commerce was making corporate organization increasingly desirable: corporations could more easily attract investment because they could limit the liability of investors, and they were permanent legal entities that survived changes in leadership or personnel. Corporations, however, were still encumbered by restrictions put in place in earlier eras, when they were regarded as special franchises chartered by the state to serve public purposes. They were, for example, not permitted to own stock in other companies; nor could they dispose of their assets without the unanimous consent of shareholders. This collision of traditional law with growing economic imperatives was resolved by the emergence of a new legal conception of the corporation as a "natural entity" that required no special regulation by the state. New Jersey led the way, passing laws in 1889 and 1896 that legalized holding companies by permitting corporations to own stock in each other and also authorized corporations to dispose of their assets without a unanimous vote of shareholders. Not surprisingly, there was a vast migration of corporate headquarters to New Jersey after 1889.

The proliferation of large firms, mergers, and trusts was greeted with considerable alarm both within the business community and in the public at large. Owners of small enterprises complained that their larger rivals were monopolists who used illegitimate methods to gain competitive advantages; similar laments came from those who had to buy from or sell to powerful national corporations. Throughout the country, citizens expressed fear of the economic and political power of big business. "The outcry against the concentration of capital was furious," observed a character in Edward Bellamy's best-selling novel *Looking Backward* (1888). "Men believed that it threatened society with a form of tyranny more abhorrent than it had ever endured." Firms like Standard Oil seemed to be destroying the competitive economic order from which they had sprung; distant and faceless corporations seemed capable of callously damaging the livelihoods of millions of people; and big business seemed increasingly able

> *"In key respects, the United States of 1900 more closely resembled the late twentieth-century nation than it did the antebellum world of 1860."*

to control state legislatures. The phrase "to railroad" sprang from popular perceptions of the ability of railroad corporations to ram laws through state legislatures.

Such sentiments spurred state governments to pass new laws to regulate competition and prevent corporate abuse. It also led a half dozen states in the 1880s to take legal action against holding companies. Big business fought such intervention, arguing that large enterprises were natural, inevitable, and beneficial. S. T. C. Dodd, Rockefeller's legal counsel, insisted that "you might as well endeavor to stay the formation of the clouds, the falling of the rains, or the flowing of the streams, as to attempt by any means or in any manner to prevent organization of industry, association of persons, and the aggregation of capital."

In 1890, the federal government responded to the mounting public concern about corporate power by passing the Sherman Anti-Trust Act, which declared that "every contract, combination in the form of trust or otherwise, or conspiracy, in restraint of trade or commerce" was illegal. Similarly, it was unlawful for anyone to "monopolize or attempt to monopolize, or combine or conspire . . . to monopolize any part of the trade or commerce among the several states." The Sherman Act elevated long-standing common-law principles into federal law and offered significant rhetorical support for the virtues of a competitive economy.

Yet it had little impact on the conduct of business at the end of the century. Drafted almost entirely by conservative Republican lawyers, the language of the Sherman Act did not clearly distinguish between legal and illegal activities. What constituted "restraint of trade"? Just what was a monopoly? Such issues were left to the courts, and the courts in the 1890s were sympathetic to big business. In 1895, for example, the Supreme Court ruled that the Sugar Trust, which controlled 98 percent of the nation's sugar-refining capacity, did not violate the Sherman Act, and even if it had, it would have been guilty only of a misdemeanor. In addition, the act was not vigorously enforced and, in its early years, was deployed more often against labor unions than against corporations.

One ironic consequence of the Sherman Act may have been to accelerate corporate mergers. The wording of the act, as well as court decisions, suggested that holding companies and trusts were more vulnerable to legal attack than were outright consolidations. As a result, the years after 1895 witnessed the largest wave of mergers and consolidations in the nation's history. More than 1,800 independent firms disappeared into mergers between 1895 and 1904; and more than 70 of the resulting consolidations ended up controlling at least 40 percent of their industries. In many branches of manufacturing and commerce, oligopoly—the control of markets by a few companies—had come to stay. So had many of the giant firms that would dominate the economy for much of the twentieth century.

INDUSTRY AND TECHNOLOGY

The triumph of industry was accompanied by the arrival of a technologically modern world, a world we could recognize today. In key respects, including the prominence of science-based industries, the United States of 1900 more closely resembled the late twentieth-century nation than it did the antebellum world of 1860. The steel industry, for example, was in its infancy in the 1860s; by 1900, it was a giant. The same was true of the petroleum industry, which produced not only kerosene (and later gasoline) but by-products such as paraffin, petroleum jelly (Vaseline), and naphtha gas (used for lighting). Advances in chemical knowledge also gave birth to the photographic industry and to celluloid, a precursor of plastic, used in diverse products ranging from dental plates to billiard balls to brushes. Even more prominent was the electrical industry. In 1882, there was only one electrical-power-generating plant in the United States; by 1902, there were 2,250, and two of the nation's largest firms, General Electric and Westinghouse, specialized in the design and manufacture of electrical goods.

Indeed, what transpired during these years was not just the growth of new industries but the emergence of new *technological systems,* networks of interrelated products and devices that structured economic, social, and even political activity. People came to depend on these systems, to perceive them as indispensable to their own lives. The railroad network, for example, made long-distance transportation much faster and cheaper than it ever had been, and it shaped expectations accordingly. Not only were goods shipped distances that had been unimaginable a few decades earlier, but mail that had taken months to deliver now took weeks or even days. There were few towns in the late nineteenth century that did not see themselves as utterly dependent on their rail links to the rest of the world. Similarly, nearly a million miles of telegraph wires made rapid communication possible throughout the

United States, as well as across the Atlantic. Newspapers relied on the telegraph to obtain information, as did participants in the booming financial and stock markets. By 1900, more than 80 million telegraph messages were being transmitted annually.

The invention of the telephone launched another communications system. Alexander Graham Bell filed his patent for electromagnetic voice communication in 1876 and founded the Bell Telephone Company a year later. By the time Bell's patent expired (1893), "long-distance" conversations were taking place (between New York and either Boston or Chicago), and more than 250,000 phones were in operation, most of them in businesses. Although some regarded the telephone as a "scientific toy" that could "never be a practical necessity," telephone use surged after 1894, when independent companies flocked into the industry and promoted residential telephones, first in urban and then in rural areas. By 1920, there were 13 million telephones in the United States, and the ability of geographically separated individuals to hold conversations—something startling to nearly everyone in the

Alexander Graham Bell at the New York end of the first long-distance call to Chicago, 1893.

1870s—had become commonplace. "A fellow can now court his girl in China as well as in East Boston," reported one Massachusetts newspaper.

Both the telephone and the telegraph depended on electricity and thus were linked to the electrical system that transformed economic and social life. Many different in-ventors contributed to the electrical revolution of the late nineteenth century, but certainly **Thomas Alva Edison** stood in the forefront. A superb inventor and savvy entrepreneur, Edison was well aware that his inventions—such as the incandescent lightbulb, developed in the late 1870s—were not isolated creations but parts of a larger technological network.

> *It was not only necessary that the lamps should give light and the dynamos generate current, but the lamps must be adapted to the current of the dynamos, and the dynamos must be constructed to give the character of current required by the lamps, and likewise all parts of the system must be constructed with reference to all other parts. . . . The problem then that I undertook to solve was . . . the production of the multifarious apparatus, methods, and devices, each adapted for use with every other, and all forming a comprehensive system.*

The electrical system thus included not only appliances but power generators, transmission lines, relay stations, and electromagnetic devices such as thermostats. In addition, electric motors provided power to streetcars and trolleys, made underground transportation (subways) feasible, and led to the redesign of workplaces and machinery in industries new and old. Particularly after direct current (which had a limited ability to travel distances) was replaced by alternating current in the late 1880s and 1890s, electricity became the preferred source of power for many industries, since it was relatively safe, cheap, and adaptable. In Muncie, Indiana, in the 1890s, for example, electricity transformed production methods in machine shops, ironworks, cutlery manufacturers, and the Ball Brothers Glass Manufacturing Company, the city's largest employer.

The technological advances of the late nineteenth century were based more in science than those of earlier periods, particularly in chemistry and physics. Much of that scientific learning originated in Europe. The Bessemer process in steel manufacture was British (although it was almost simultaneously developed in the United States); and open-hearth furnaces, which displaced Bessemer converters late in the century, were first created in Germany and France. German

Thomas Alva Edison with one of his inventions, the phonograph, 1878.

chemists came up with such innovations as new dyes, fertilizers, synthetics, and brewing methods, which were imported to the United States. Mathematician Charles Steinmetz, trained in Europe, became General Electric's chief engineering consultant and worked out the mathematics for analyzing alternating current. The wireless telegraph was developed primarily by Guglielmo Marconi, based on discoveries in physics by Heinrich Hertz and James Maxwell.

Yet many technological advances were homegrown, made by independent inventors who were not affiliated with major corporations and who were choosing, by themselves, the problems on which they were working. Alexander Graham Bell was one such inventor; another was Nikola Tesla, who held a patent for an alternating current motor and made important discoveries in electricity. Orville and Wilbur Wright, who initiated the era of manned airflight in 1903, were also independent inventors, as were Hiram Maxim (the machine gun) and Lee De Forest, Reginald Fessenden, and Edwin Armstrong (all of whom helped to develop the wireless telephone, or voice transmission).

But the most celebrated independent inventor remained Edison. By the end of his life, Edison had acquired more than a thousand patents for an astonishingly diverse range of inventions and innovations: he made important contributions to the development of the telegraph, the telephone, the phonograph, electric light, electric power, magnetic ore separation, concrete construction, and motion pictures. He was also an extremely successful businessman equally adept at finding investors for his projects and at creating companies to develop and market his innovations. In 1882, for example, backed by financier J. P. Morgan, Edison and the Edison Electric Illuminating Company installed an entire network of power generation and incandescent lighting in lower Manhattan. Less than a decade later, Morgan helped to merge the various Edison companies and several others into the General Electric Corporation.

Edison, moreover, invented a method of invention that symbolized the era's marriage of creativity to economic incentive. Possessing little formal education, he began his career as a Western Union operator, resigning in 1869 to devote himself full-time to invention. Backed by investors who hoped to profit from his improvements to telegraphic devices, Edison rented a building in Newark, New Jersey, equipped it with fine tools and machinery, and hired several talented machinist collaborators. After a half dozen years of success, he amassed enough capital to create what became known as his "invention factory" in rural Menlo Park, New Jersey. Situated between New York and Philadelphia, Menlo Park offered Edison and his collaborators a refuge from urban life, a self-contained country village where the task of invention could be pursued without interruption—in a locale that was still accessible to major centers of finance and industry. At Menlo Park (and later at a larger installation in West Orange, New Jersey), he assembled a team of mechanics and craftsmen, as well as scientists and mathematicians who possessed learning that he himself lacked: "learned men, cranks, enthusiasts, plain 'muckers,' and absolutely insane men," one member of the group later recalled. Edison also purchased the finest equipment that money could buy, as well as a large library. Although he cultivated the image of an eccentric genius, wearing stained shirts and sleeping on a cot in his laboratory, Edison was, in fact, creating a model of collaborative research, a way of institutionalizing the process of technological advance.

Edison's methods were widely emulated, although few inventors could match the creative or financial success of the "Wizard of Menlo Park." But the era of independent invention, though glorious, turned out to be brief. Increasingly, technological research and innovation were carried out not

> *"Edison was also an extremely successful businessman equally adept at finding investors for his projects and at creating companies to develop and market his innovations."*

by the independents but by industrial corporations. Firms had always tried to innovate, but by the end of the nineteenth century they were beginning to undertake systematic research. In 1900, the first formal research laboratory in American industry was founded, appropriately enough at General Electric. The GE Laboratory (which Charles Steinmetz played a key role in creating) had 8 staff members in 1901 and 102 by 1906. The Bell Telephone laboratories followed suit, with Westinghouse not far behind. Science-based industrial research was now being conducted by industry, which meant that industry was selecting the problems to be explored.

The consolidation of large corporations facilitated this trend and was reinforced by it. By the end of the century, firms like General Electric and Westinghouse had become sizable enough to afford full-blown research programs that would both develop new products and protect patents against the next wave of innovation. Moreover, by sponsoring research and controlling the patents and innovations that emerged from that research, they helped to perpetuate their own market supremacy: few small firms could compete with the research operations of giants like General Electric or AT&T.

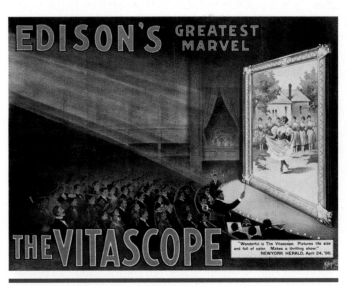

An 1896 poster celebrating another Edison invention, the motion picture. A vitascope, also developed by Edison, was a kind of projector.

These large corporations also acquired the talents of an increasing number of college-trained engineers. Thanks in part to the Morrill Act (1862), which offered federal land to states to establish colleges of "agriculture and mechanic arts," the nation had eighty-five engineering colleges by 1880, and thousands of students each year were earning engineering degrees. In contrast, there had been a mere 2,000 engineers recorded by the 1850 census and still only 7,000 in 1880. As a profession, engineering was a late nineteenth-century creation: professional societies like the American Society of Mechanical Engineers and the American Institute of Electrical Engineers were founded between 1870 and 1910. Most engineers ended up as employees of big business, a vantage point from which they tended to identify the nation's progress with that of their firms.

The Center and the Periphery

However integrated the emerging national economy may have been, significant regional differences persisted. Manufacturing had become predominant in the Northeast and Midwest, but elsewhere that was far less true. The South remained overwhelmingly agricultural, producing cash crops for shipment north and overseas. Meanwhile, the increasingly settled West became primarily an extractive economy, a place where natural resources such as copper and lumber were identified, removed from nature, and shipped away. The southern and western economies, moreover, were not simply different: they were dependent on economic interests in the more metropolitan centers of the Northeast and the Midwest. In the language often applied to colonial relationships, the nation's northern manufacturing and financial belt constituted the economy's center, while the South and West were the periphery.

THE SOUTH

Long after the end of Reconstruction, agriculture, particularly cotton, continued to dominate the economic life of the South. As late as 1900, more than half of the region's labor force was engaged in farming, and the figure was above 60 percent in eight southern states. (In contrast, only 13 percent of the labor force worked in agriculture in the North Atlantic region, and there were only three states outside the South

where the figure was above 50 percent.) The predominance of cotton was equally marked: in 1900, the cash value of cotton was roughly seven times as great as that of tobacco, the second most important cash crop.

There was, to be sure, some industrial development. Advocates of a "New South" promoted not only railroads but manufacturing to lift the region out of its postbellum torpor and reduce its dependence on plantation agriculture. They had some success. Railroad mileage more than doubled in the 1880s alone, and in 1886 the South changed the gauge, or width, of its tracks to match the gauge that was standard in the rest of the nation. In the 1880s and 1890s, textile mills sprang up through the Piedmont region of the Carolinas and Georgia, while tobacco-processing plants revamped their methods and greatly expanded their output. At the same time, an iron and steel industry centered in Birmingham, Alabama, grew rapidly, and the lumber industry flour-

This symbol of the New South arising from the ruin of the Civil War, from the Atlanta Exposition of **1895**, shows her horn of plenty stuffed with steel, pig iron, and other products of the region.

ished, providing one-third of the nation's construction lumber. Still, in industry, the South continued to lag far behind the North, producing only one-tenth of the nation's manufactures (measured in dollars) in 1900. In most southern states, less than 15 percent of the labor force was engaged in manufacturing

The South also remained poor. In 1880, the contrast between the South and the Northeast was similar to that between Russia (one of the poorest nations in Europe) and Germany (one of the wealthiest). In 1900, per capita wealth in the South was less than half the national average, and the disparity in incomes was comparable. Cotton prices remained low, and the new industries, such as textiles, typically generated low-wage jobs. On and off the farm, southern workers earned far less than their counterparts in the North.

Several factors contributed to this persistent poverty. In agriculture, the South had ensnared itself in a cycle that greatly restricted incomes: cotton prices were relatively low, the global demand for cotton was fairly steady, and the more cotton farmers grew, the lower the prices they were paid—which meant that individual incomes increased hardly at all. The combination of sharecropping and the lien system, moreover, hindered the diversification of crops, while average farm size, contrary to the national pattern, was shrinking. In addition, the abundance of cheap labor (as well as the small size of farms) stood in the way of technological innovation. Although patents for cotton-harvesting machinery were issued in the late nineteenth century, landowners had little incentive to develop or purchase new machinery.

The abundance of labor and the isolation of the labor force restrained development in other ways as well. Southern workers did not migrate to higher-wage areas (in part because of the fetters of the lien system), which helped to keep a lid on wages and to encourage the proliferation of low-wage industries. Moreover, in manufacturing, as in agriculture, the availability of inexpensive labor discouraged technological advance. "Instead of installing machinery to do the work, we always undertook to do it putting in another cheap negro," commented one employer in the lumber business. At the same time, conditions in the South discouraged immigration and thereby kept the region from acquiring both skilled workers and the innovative ideas that often traveled with them.

> *"In 1880, the contrast between the South and the Northeast was similar to that between Russia (one of the poorest nations in Europe) and Germany (one of the wealthiest)."*

The inability of southern industry to catch up with the North was further hampered by the region's late start, by the weakness of its infrastructure, by the northern ownership of many railroads and manufacturing plants, and by the absence of a local technological community, including a machine tools industry. These last two factors often reinforced one another: productive machinery tended to be imported to, rather than developed in, the South, and imported technology was not always effective in southern conditions. In the steel industry in Birmingham, for example, the use of imported Bessemer converters was hampered by the high phosphorous content of local ores.

The South's economy between Reconstruction and World War I had something of a colonial cast. Most workers were involved in growing or processing staple agricultural exports. Most industries were labor-intensive (with a high ratio of labor to capital) and paid low wages. To the extent that the region participated in more advanced industries, it did so with northern capital, on terms dictated by executives and investors in faraway cities. Not surprisingly, as late as 1919,

This late nineteenth-century plantation scene illustrates the ongoing dominance of the cotton culture as well as the use of child labor.

the eleven states with the lowest per-capita income were all southern.

THE WEST

According to the superintendent of the eleventh census, the American frontier disappeared sometime between 1880 and 1890. "Up to and including 1880, the country had a frontier of settlement," he wrote, "but at present the unsettled area has been so broken into by isolated bodies of settlement that there can hardly be said to be a frontier line."

The end of the Civil War and the completion of transcontinental railway lines had, in fact, greatly accelerated the development of the trans-Mississippi West. The population of the Pacific and mountain states almost doubled in the 1870s and again in the 1880s; growth in the "west central" states (stretching from Minnesota and North Dakota down to Texas and Louisiana) was even more rapid. By 1910, there were more than 25 million people living west of the Mississippi, 7 million in the Pacific and mountain states alone. At the turn of the century, all of the western territories except

An image of prosperous development in the West, featuring scenes of farming, mining, and, of course, the railroad, 1881.

Oklahoma, New Mexico, and Arizona had been admitted to the Union as states.

Migrants to the West came from nearly everywhere. Large numbers of Scandinavians, Germans, Irish, and Canadians flocked to the farm states just west of the Mississippi. Mexican immigrants were numerous in the Southwest; California became home to tens of thousands of Chinese immigrants; and thousands of African Americans fled northwest, particularly to Kansas, to escape the repression of the post-Reconstruction South. A majority of the westbound, however, were native-born whites drawn from the middling reaches of American society. Farmers, merchants, and professionals, they traveled in family units, moving from east to west along the same latitude. The railroads made their journeys far briefer and less arduous than they had been before the Civil War, although, like most westerners, they tended to move more than once.

Why were these people pouring into the West? For most, the answer was straightforward: they wanted land, to settle and to farm. Between 1862 and 1890, nearly 2 million people claimed free land under provisions of the Homestead Act. The typical westward migrant, however, *bought* land from a public land office, a speculator, or the railroads. To subsidize the construction of the railroads, the federal and state governments had given railroad corporations land equivalent in size to the state of Texas, adjacent to the railroad lines themselves. As a result, some of the most desirable land in the West (desirable precisely because of its location) was removed from federal control and had to be purchased from the railroads. In part for this reason—but primarily because most urban workers lacked the capital and the knowledge to get started in farming, whether or not they had to buy land—the Homestead Act never did offer a realistic escape to impoverished, industrial workers.

Farming in the region offered new challenges to migrants from the East and Europe. As explorer, scientist, and surveyor John Wesley Powell warned in a report written in 1878, the most important natural fact about the West was its aridity: much of the nation west of the 100th meridian did not receive nearly enough rainfall to sustain conventional methods of farming. As one moved across the prairies of the west central states, annual rainfall totals steadily declined; precipitation in the Great Plains averaged only fifteen to twenty inches a year, less than half the norm in the Mississippi Valley. Farmers on the plains and beyond could not expect to grow wheat, corn, or other crops common in the more humid East.

Yet Powell's warnings were ignored. Encouraged by promoters, farmers flooded into the plains in the 1870s and 1880s. The flat, open grasslands were easy to clear and seemed well suited to new farm implements. Besides, most farmers believed that "rain follows the plow," that cultivating the land and planting trees would stimulate rainfall. In the 1880s, that belief seemed well founded: the arrival of the farmers coincided with one of the periodic wet cycles on the plains, and crops, including wheat, were plentiful. But when the rains subsided, beginning in 1889, the results were devastating. Crops failed year after year; the earth turned dusty and hard. Some of the region's settlers stayed in place, awaiting the next wet cycle and eventually learning to "dry farm" with new methods and new crops. But many left: some counties lost half of their population between 1890 and 1900. One Texas family explained its departure on a sign nailed to their cabin: "Two hundred miles to nearest post office, one hundred miles to wood, twenty miles to water, one mile to hell. God bless our home. Gone to live with the wife's folks."

Elsewhere in the West, especially in California, Oregon, and Washington, climatic conditions were more favorable, although water was rarely plentiful and control of the water supply was always a critical economic and political issue. The vastness of the territory, moreover, encouraged farming on a grand scale. In the Red River Valley of North Dakota and Minnesota, as well as in California's Central Valley, "bonanza farms" appeared in the 1870s and 1880s, corporate enterprises with absentee owners, fleets of machinery, hierarchical management, and hundreds of hired hands. Just west of Fargo, Oliver Dalrymple managed farms that employed 1,000 men for harvesting. Hugh Glenn of California, with 66,000 acres of land along the Sacramento River, may have been the single largest wheat grower in the world.

Bonanza farms, however, did not displace family farming. In fact, something close to the reverse happened in the 1890s: many of the enormous "factories in the fields" were subdivided and sold to family farmers. Why did the trend toward consolidation and big business not catch on in agriculture, as it certainly appeared it would in the 1880s? Two factors were important. One was that the new technology that became widely available after the Civil War made it feasible for individual households to run reasonably large farms; there were, in effect, no "economies of scale" that made bonanza farming

"Much of the nation west of the 100th meridian did not receive nearly enough rainfall to sustain conventional methods of farming."

more efficient than family farming. The second reason was that family farmers were better able and more willing to weather bad years. When wheat prices fell in the late 1880s, farm households preserved their property and their way of life by working harder, cutting their expenses, and increasing their acreage. The absentee investors in bonanza farms, however, preferred to put their money elsewhere—which meant that many such farms simply went out of business.

Something similar happened in cattle ranching. The final slaughter of the already beleaguered buffalo in the 1870s (when the railroads and the market for buffalo hides led to the extermination of 5 million animals) created an ecological vacuum on the plains, which was quickly filled by cattle. With the railroads in place and a growing population in the East hungry for beef, cattle ranching became a booming industry: cattle could be fed on the open ranges and free grasslands of the plains and delivered to railroad depots like Abilene, Kansas.

A scene from John Wesley Powell's account of his expedition on the Colorado River, here running a rapid in the Grand Canyon in August 1869.

Herding longhorn cattle aboard a freight train at Halleck, Nevada, to be shipped east, 1877.

Eastern and European investors leapt into the industry, creating cattle companies and large corporate ranches: the Chicago-owned XIT Ranch in Texas had 3 million acres of land. By the mid-1880s, there were 7.5 million head of cattle on the plains north of Texas and New Mexico. Then disaster struck. A combination of overgrazing, dry summers, and severe winters led to huge losses of livestock and the virtual disappearance of investors. What remained in the wake of this econo-ecological crisis were smaller ranches, often family owned (but still employing cowboys), different breeds of cattle, and heightened rancher responsibility for feeding cattle through the winter.

Despite the vicissitudes of business and weather, western agriculture grew rapidly: by 1910, the region grew 65 percent of the American wheat crop, contributing substantially to the nation's agricultural exports. Both in the plains and in parts of the Southwest, agriculture dominated the economy, occupying more than 40 percent of the labor force. Elsewhere in the region, mining, lumbering, and fishing were preeminent. Gold, silver, and copper mines could be found throughout the mountain states and California, while the forests of the Pacific Northwest provided lumber for the West and for export. Outside of California, there was relatively little manufacturing before 1900, particularly of finished goods.

Thanks to the railroads, the West, distant as it may have been, was integrated into a world economy even while remaining thinly populated. Much of what westerners produced was consumed elsewhere; most of what they consumed was produced elsewhere. The inhabitants of the West after the Civil War were not self-sufficient (if they ever had been), but rather participants in an expansive capitalism. Extractive industries such as lumber, copper mining, and even ranching, moreover, required far more capital than the West itself could provide, and consequently promoters of the region frequently sought investment from the East and Europe. For better or worse, they were successful. Investment poured into the West, and outside of California—where San Francisco became a major center of capital, financing development throughout the state—lumber companies, copper mines, and ranches all came to be owned by nonwesterners or by large corporations with financial centers elsewhere. Early in the twentieth century, most of the privately held land in Nevada was owned by nonresident individuals or corporations; two-thirds of the state's industries had absentee owners. Nevada was an extreme case of a pattern that prevailed throughout the region.

Classes

The triumph of industrial capitalism meant much more than the replacement of farms by smokestacks, of small shops by large factories. It also deepened and solidified changes in the class structure that had been underway since the beginning of the industrial revolution early in the nineteenth century. One such change was the emergence of a national elite, an upper class that wielded economic (and sometimes political) power over large terrains and in multiple locales; these were men, and families, whose wealth gave them unprecedented nationwide prominence. Cornelius Vanderbilt, Andrew Carnegie, Henry Frick, John D. Rockefeller, Leland Stanford, James B. Duke, J. P. Morgan: the captains of late nineteenth-century industry and finance, memorialized in institutions that still carry their names, had a visibility and influence far

Cornelius Vanderbilt (left) and J. P. Morgan, captains of industry and finance.

more substantial than regional business leaders had possessed before the Civil War.

More important was a widespread shift in the nature of the middle class, a term that first came into use in the 1850s. The growth of industry and big business made it more difficult for people to be proprietors of one sort or another: farm owners, shopkeepers, artisans, manufacturers. Local manufacturers were bought out by national firms; retailers were driven out of business by Sears, Roebuck or Montgomery Ward. Since the population was rapidly growing, the *number* of persons who owned property on which they could earn a living did not actually decline, but the *percentage* did, as it had for much of the nineteenth century. By 1900, only one out of every four members of the labor force owned productive property; and three-quarters of these were farmers.

At the same time, however, another segment of the middle class grew larger: salaried, white-collar employees. Big businesses created large numbers of managerial positions, clerical jobs, and openings for professionals, such as engineers. The men and women who held these jobs did not possess the kind of independence or control over their working conditions that came with ownership, but they were educated, compensated decently, and reasonably secure in their positions. In the decades after the Civil War, this stratum more than quadrupled in size, increasing from roughly 5 percent of the labor force in 1870 to 11 percent (of a much larger labor force) in 1900.

Both the upper and middle classes flourished in the late nineteenth century. The economy was generating more and more wealth, and most of that wealth went to families in the higher echelons of the occupational structure. In 1870, the richest 1 percent of the population owned more than one-quarter of the nation's assets; the top 10 percent owned 70 percent. This highly skewed **distribution of wealth** did not become any more egalitarian between the 1870s and the beginning of World War I. If things changed at all, they moved in the opposite direction: according to some estimates, the richest 10 percent of the population held nearly 90 percent of the nation's wealth on the eve of World War I.

Incomes were also highly unequal. In 1880, for example, the general manager of the Chicago, Burlington and Quincy Railroad earned $15,000; the railroad's senior executives earned more than $4,000, while middle managers were paid between $1,500 and $4,000. At the same time, clerical workers in the railroad's Chicago office averaged about $800; carpenters, blacksmiths, and other skilled workers were lucky if they made $500–600; and unskilled laborers in Chicago were paid $1.32 a day (and they probably worked fewer than 250 days a year). These differences of income, like those of wealth, did not narrow discernibly before World War I.

An ad for a sewing machine as a desirable feature of middle-class life in New York, 1880.

These inequalities underscore a critical feature of the late nineteenth-century class structure: the presence of an enormous industrial and agricultural working class. By 1870, more than two-thirds of all working Americans were *employees,* a figure that continued to rise in later decades. And most employees performed manual labor. Between 1870 and 1900, 60–70 percent of the nation's workforce consisted of wage earners who labored with their hands. By the turn of the century, the United States had more than 600,000 carpenters, 229,000 tailors and tailoresses, 563,000 miners, 246,000 cotton mill workers, 2.2 million day laborers, and 4.4 million agricultural laborers. The working class was nearly 18 million strong, and its particular circumstances—which had been diverging from those of the middle class throughout the nineteenth century—merit detailed inspection.

> *"By 1870, more than two-thirds of all working Americans were employees."*

JOBS AND INCOMES

The working class itself was a house of many mansions. It included skilled workers, such as machinists, carpenters, and iron puddlers (men who stirred molten iron until it reached the right temperature and consistency), who possessed knowledge that took years to acquire and who often worked at a pace they set themselves, with little supervision. It also included semiskilled factory workers, men and women who tended machines and carried out one stage in a production process. At the bottom of the ladder were the unskilled, who held jobs that anyone could learn quickly: digging, lifting, hauling. One day laborer identified his trade by his tools, calling himself a "pick and shovel man."

The most skilled could support their families in respectable circumstances, even owning a home and providing education for their children. The semiskilled were paid much better in some industries, such as furniture making and stone cutting, than in others, such as textiles; daily wage rates for the unskilled were less than half those of skilled workers, and they also tended to work fewer days. Most semiskilled and unskilled men had difficulty supporting a family on their own incomes. Real wages (adjusted for changes in prices) rose more than 50 percent between 1870 and 1900, but a majority of the working class continued to live in, or not far from, poverty.

Most industrial workers were male. Although the number of women in the labor force reached 18 percent by 1900, women rarely worked outside their homes after they married and had children. (They did, however, often provide critical supplements to household incomes by taking in boarders.) The jobs that single women held were concentrated in certain occupations (such as teaching, domestic service, and—later—clerical work); even within large workplaces, they were restricted to particular, usually poorly paid, tasks. Male and female cotton mill operatives generally did not work the same machines in the same factories.

The contrast between working-class and middle-class lives, moreover, was not just a matter of income. Employees who labored with their hands, for example, usually worked six days a week, ten hours per day. In some industries, conditions were even more arduous: steelworkers routinely worked twelve-hour days, six days a week, and every Sunday half of all employees worked a "long turn" of twenty-four hours so that the blast furnaces could keep running and the day and night shifts could alternate.

Dangers abounded. Between 1880 and 1900, 35,000 workers were killed on the job every year, while another half million were injured. Hundreds, often thousands, of miners died in accidents annually. In 1901, 1 out of every 137 trainmen was killed, 1 out of every 11 injured. The menace of accidents was accompanied by the threat of illness. Black lung disease among miners, brown lung among textile operatives, tuberculosis in many trades: being a worker was hazardous to one's health.

Workers operating lathes in a New York City factory with no protection against accidents, 1900.

In addition, workers suffered from chronic job insecurity. The word "unemployment" first appeared in print in Massachusetts in 1887, announcing—a bit after the fact—the arrival of a new economic and social phenomenon: widespread, involuntary joblessness. The triumph of industrial capitalism had transformed the United States into a nation of employees whose ability to work was dependent on decisions made by employers—when the demand for goods slackened, employers commonly responded by laying workers off. This occurred not only during depressions but year after year, sometimes seasonally and sometimes more episodically. In an average year, between one-fifth and one-quarter of all workers experienced some unemployment, remaining jobless for an average of three months. During depressions, the figure soared: 35–40 percent of all workers were jobless during the worst years of the 1880s and 1890s, and they remained idle, on average, for nearly five months. While employers sought to maintain a "reserve army" of labor so that workers would always be available when they were needed, a distinctive characteristic of working-class life was the unsteadiness of jobs and the unpredictability of incomes.

This chronic uncertainty of employment made workers wary of technological changes that threatened to make jobs even more scarce. New machinery in woodworking, printing, metalworking, and cigar making (to cite just a few examples) permitted individuals to produce far more than they had been able to do, and the machinery consequently seemed to jeopardize people's jobs and livelihoods. In fact, the economy was growing so rapidly that relatively few people were suddenly driven out of their occupations because of new technology. The number of carpenters did not drop precipitously because turn-of-the-century woodworking machinery permitted bathtubs to be built in twenty minutes rather than several hours. Nor did typographers vanish overnight because of the Linotype machine. But skilled workers did often encounter an eroding demand for their knowledge and talents; their incomes slowly declined, and they were joined in their trades by men and women who had fewer skills and understood less about the entire process of production.

In some instances, this technologically induced "skill dilution" was a straightforward consequence of improvements in machinery and production techniques. In others, the process

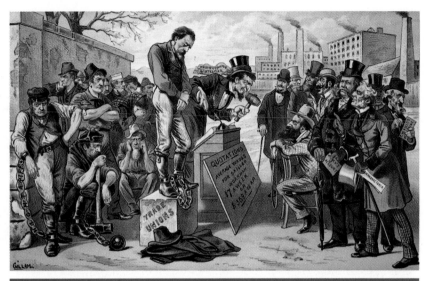

This 1880s drawing, from the humor magazine *Puck*, depicts the condition of workers as akin to those of slaves a few decades earlier.

was more complex and grounded in conflict between workers and managers. The knowledge possessed by skilled workers often gave them substantial power, on the shop floor and in the labor market, and employers could undermine that power by introducing new machinery. In Fall River, Massachusetts, for example, textile mill owners decided to deploy new technology to rid themselves of skilled spinners who had a reputation for insisting on their autonomy. One Saturday, after the spinners had left, "we started right in and smashed a room full of" spinning machines "with sledge hammers," boasted one owner. When the spinners returned to work the following Monday, they found their machines destroyed, new technology in place, and semiskilled "girls" hired to do the spinning.

Similarly, in the iron and steel industry, production in many plants was actually organized by skilled workers, who were paid by the ton, hired their own helpers, and negotiated tonnage rates with their employers. These knowledgeable, experienced workers controlled much of the production process and possessed considerable power when bargaining with owners. The "manager's brains," as early twentieth-century labor leader Big Bill Haywood claimed, "were under the workman's cap." That fact, however, did not sit well with ambitious entrepreneurs like Andrew Carnegie and Henry Frick. In 1892, they responded to a dispute with their skilled workmen by locking the doors to the plant and protecting it with barbed-

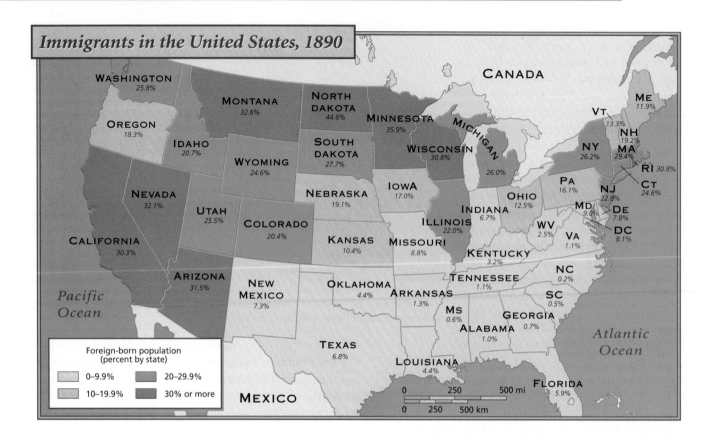

Immigrants in the United States, 1890

Foreign-born population (percent by state)

- 0–9.9%
- 10–19.9%
- 20–29.9%
- 30% or more

WASHINGTON 25.8%
OREGON 18.3%
IDAHO 20.7%
MONTANA 32.6%
NORTH DAKOTA 44.6%
MINNESOTA 35.9%
WISCONSIN 30.8%
MICHIGAN 26.0%
ME 11.9%
VT 13.3%
NH 19.2%
NY 26.2%
MA 29.4%
RI 30.8%
CT 24.6%
WYOMING 24.6%
SOUTH DAKOTA 27.7%
IOWA 17.0%
PA 16.1%
NJ 22.8%
NEVADA 32.1%
UTAH 25.5%
COLORADO 20.4%
NEBRASKA 19.1%
OHIO 12.5%
INDIANA 6.7%
ILLINOIS 22.0%
MD 9.0%
DE 7.8%
DC 8.1%
CALIFORNIA 30.3%
KANSAS 10.4%
MISSOURI 8.8%
KENTUCKY 3.2%
WV 2.5%
VA 1.1%
ARIZONA 31.5%
NEW MEXICO 7.3%
OKLAHOMA 4.4%
ARKANSAS 1.3%
TENNESSEE 1.1%
NC 0.2%
SC 0.5%
MS 0.6%
GEORGIA 0.7%
ALABAMA 1.0%
TEXAS 6.8%
LOUISIANA 4.4%
FLORIDA 5.9%

CANADA

MEXICO

Pacific Ocean

Atlantic Ocean

0   250   500 mi
0   250   500 km

wire fences and armed guards. Frick and Carnegie then installed new technology that transformed most steel mill positions into semiskilled jobs.

Changes in workplace technology tended to alter the structure of the labor force in ways that had mixed results for workers. The proportion of skilled workers declined, but so, too, did the proportion of unskilled workers who often performed backbreaking work for low wages. The major growth was in the percentage of men and women who held semiskilled jobs as machine tenders. New machinery permitted these operatives to produce more and earn more, but it also required them to work harder and faster. As the United States Industrial Commission reported in 1902, "In nearly all occupations an increasing strain and intensity of labor is required by modern methods of production. . . . The introduction of machinery and the division of labor have made it possible to increase greatly the speed of the individual workman." A cotton weaver confirmed that "anybody who works in the mills now knows it is not like what it was twenty-five or thirty years ago, because the speed of the ma-

chinery has been increased to such an extent." A superintendent at a Swift Meat packing plant offered the managerial view: "If you need to turn out a little more, you speed up the conveyors a little and the men speed up to keep pace."

IMMIGRANTS AND MIGRANTS

In much of the country, the rapid growth of the working class—and thus the rapid growth of the economy—was made possible by immigration. More than 1 million immigrants entered the United States during every five-year period between the end of the Civil War and World War I. More than 9 million arrived between 1865 and 1890; another 16 million came between 1890 and 1915.

Until the mid-1880s, the great majority of immigrants came, as they long had, from northern and western Europe: between 1876 and 1880, for example, Great Britain, Ireland, Scandinavia, Germany, and Canada accounted for more than 75 percent of all immigrants. During the final decades of the nineteenth century, however, immigration from these coun-

Immigrants leaving the Ellis Island ferry and landing in New York City, 1900.

England, Canada, and the United States, from southern Italy to Milan, Buenos Aires, and New York, from Portugal to Brazil and Massachusetts, from China to the Philippines, Peru, and California.

There was, then, nothing uniquely American about immigration. The 25 million men and women who came to the United States between 1865 and World War I were a large part, but only a part, of a mass movement of labor that was a significant feature of modern world history. Freed from their moorings, migrants often journeyed to several cities or countries before settling down—a process facilitated both by the railroads and by steamships that made ocean travel relatively fast and cheap. A large proportion of the migrants who came to the United States, moreover, intended to return to their country of origin, and sooner or later many did. Only among the Irish and the Jews was the intention of permanent emigration almost universal.

The immigrants and migrants who came to the United States thus constituted a significant proportion of the nation's working class. In the North and West, factories, mines, and construction sites were peopled largely by immigrants. In

tries began to slow down, while new migratory streams flowed from southern and eastern Europe. Between 1906 and 1910, more than a million migrants came from Italy alone, while another 2 million came from Russia, central Europe, and the Baltic states. To old-stock Americans, these "new" immigrants seemed more alien and less desirable than the "old" immigrants from western and northern Europe.

The story of immigration to the United States has often been told in romantic, even patriotic, terms: the "huddled masses" fled the Old World to seek the New; ambitious, if poor, Europeans escaping political, religious, and economic oppression set sail for the "Land of Freedom" to find liberty and prosperity. Such images contain a kernel of truth, yet they overemphasize the lure of America and pay too little attention to what was transpiring elsewhere. The millions of men and women who migrated to the United States were part of a broader global phenomenon. Throughout Europe and in many parts of Asia, the combination of population growth and economic change (often a restructuring of agriculture by landowners) pressured millions of people to leave their homes and try to make a living elsewhere. Some of these emigrants had property to sell and capital to bring; they became "settlers," intent on farming or establishing a business in a new province or country. But most were not so lucky: they traveled with only their skills or their brawn, from Ireland to

This scene from Horatio Alger's popular "Luck and Pluck Series" shows a lad leaving his rural home to make his way in the world.

Digital History

ELLIS ISLAND AND THE IMMIGRANT EXPERIENCE

Above: An Italian family waiting on their ship for a ferry to take them to Ellis Island. ***Center:*** *A mother and her children about to be examined by the doctor at far left, who is checking a child's eyes for trachoma.* ***Right:*** *In the Registry Room, immigrants who have passed the medical exam wait to be called for the legal inspection.*

"How could it be, I wondered, that after having been so impatient to get there, I suddenly seemed almost frightened by America now that we had arrived. Was it because our uncertain future was only now becoming concrete and unescapable . . . ? We had left home behind; we were not approaching a new home, only an indefinite spot in an unknown vacuum."

—*David Cornel De Jong, a Dutch arrival at Ellis Island in 1917*

In our national memory, we have come to celebrate Ellis Island and the immigrant experience as core components of the American story. There is an important element of truth in this view, but it must be balanced against the vivid testimony of the immigrants themselves to the harsh conditions they encountered at Ellis Island and afterward in America's cities, towns, and countryside. America's immigration history is a story of fresh opportunity but also of inequity and thwarted hope.

Explore both sides of this question through the experiences and reflections of the immigrants who poured through the Ellis Island portal in New York Harbor. Read about the conditions in their home countries that spurred their migrations not only to the United States but to other countries as well. Hear their voices as they recall their experiences on ship and on arrival at Ellis Island. Follow them as they encounter the emotional, material, legal, and medical hurdles to admission.

As you explore the Ellis Island feature on *Inventing America*'s Digital History CD-ROM, consider the following:

■ How would you describe the conditions the immigrants encountered during their stay on Ellis Island?

■ How did the immigrants themselves respond to the obstacles they faced?

■ Based on the materials here and the discussions in the text, how would you assess the significance of the immigrant experience in American history?

1900, 28 percent of the nation's day laborers, 44 percent of all miners, 36 percent of all steelworkers, and 38 percent of all cotton mill operatives were foreign-born. (Excluding the South, which had few immigrants, these percentages were even higher.) As early as 1880, in fact, most American workers were either immigrants, the children of immigrants, or African American. In forty of the fifty largest cities, at least 75 percent of all wage earners belonged to one of these three groups. Conversely, relatively few native whites, whose parents were also native-born, belonged to working-class occupations. Even in small midwestern cities like Dubuque, Iowa, and Joliet, Illinois, less than 20 percent of the working class (but more than 70 percent of the population) came from native white stock.

What this meant was that even before the turn of the century, class boundaries were coinciding with ethnic and racial boundaries. The middle class consisted overwhelmingly of white, native-born Protestants whose parents had also been born in the United States. The working class was predominantly African American in the South, and either foreign-born or of foreign parentage in the North. Workers were also more likely to be Catholic or Jewish. Within the working class, there was additional ethnic and racial stratification. In the South, some jobs and industries came to be viewed as "black," while others, such as textiles, were reserved for whites. In the West, the Chinese and other nonwhites were restricted to arduous, low-paying jobs, including railroad construction and domestic service. In the Northeast, the Italians, Irish, and Jews were similarly concentrated in particular occupations. The nation's labor markets were segmented not only by skill, but by gender, ethnicity, and race.

SOCIAL MOBILITY

From the onset of industrialization, some Americans had worried that the nation's egalitarian promise would be undercut by the formation of a permanent working class. Such apprehensions were often eased by faith in the idea that the nation's bounty was great enough to give all Americans the opportunity to get ahead, to prosper. Inequality certainly ex-

American Journal

What if You Get Sick?

Young immigrant women hoping for a better life in America often ended up performing hard work for long hours—sometimes to the breaking point.

"How many [*immigrant women*] give way under the strain of long hours, bad living conditions, and the confused excitement which comes with their new environment, few people realize. The tragedy of this physical breakdown was illustrated one summer when the services of the Immigrants' Protective League were asked on behalf of a young Polish girl. Although she seemed entirely well when she came and had been passed by the examining doctors at Ellis Island, she had developed tuberculosis after a few months of factory work in Chicago. She was taken to the County Hospital and soon learned that she had no chance of recovery. She was most wretchedly homesick when the visitor for the League saw her at the hospital. She had only a cousin in this country, who could not come to see her because it was the season of overtime work in his trade and the County Hospital was many miles away. She was unable to talk to those around her and found it impossible to eat the strange American food given her, and, worst of all, she realized that all her girlish plans to earn money, send for her mother, and marry well were to come to nothing. Polish food which we were able to procure for her did not comfort her, however, for she wanted only one thing—to be sent back home so that she might die with her mother. In this, too, she was disappointed, for although she improved somewhat when she learned that she was to be deported, she died alone at sea."

Grace Abbott, *The Immigrant and the Community*

isted in the United States, and the growth of manufactures may have made poverty more visible, but there was no cause for alarm; a poor boy who worked hard, studied hard, and saved his money could leave poverty behind.

This ideology received its most well-known nineteenth-century expression in the popular novels of Horatio Alger: the plot of these tales, published between the 1860s and 1890s, usually ended with the rise of a virtuous poor lad to a position of wealth and social respectability (and sometimes, through marriage, into the family of his employer). "In this free country poverty in early life is no bar to a man's advancement," declared one of Alger's characters. Some hard-nosed contemporaries, not surprisingly scoffed at such romantic visions. "If you tell a single concrete workingman on the B and O Railroad that he may yet be the president of the company," observed economist Richard Ely, "it is not demonstrable that you have told him what is not true, although it is within bounds to say that he is far more likely to be killed by a stroke of lightning." Despite the skepticism of men like Ely, there was widespread middle-class faith in the notion that men and women could exit the working class if they were willing to work hard and well.

In fact, both Ely and Alger captured elements of the truth. Ely was certainly correct that a railroad worker had as good a chance of being hit by lightning as he did of becoming a company president. Most men who began their working lives as manual wage earners ended their careers in the same type of position. In Boston and other well-studied cities, for example, three-quarters of all skilled and unskilled workers remained in the blue-collar ranks for their entire careers. Of equal importance, between 60 and 80 percent of the children of blue-collar workers were confined to the working class for their entire careers as well.

Yet there was social mobility in late nineteenth- and early twentieth-century America. Although Horatio Alger–type successes were rare, perhaps as many as one-quarter of all manual wage earners advanced into middle-class jobs; and between 20 and 40 percent of their children may also have experienced some upward mobility. To be sure, these figures did not apply to African Americans, who—North and South—encountered uniquely powerful obstacles to advancement. Nor were they similar for all immigrant and ethnic groups at all historical moments: in many cities, for example, Irish and Italian immigrants did not fare as well as

March 10, 1869	The Central Pacific and Union Pacific Railroads are linked at Promontory Point, Utah.
1873	Panic of 1873 precipitates a five-year depression.
May 19, 1876	President Grant opens the Centennial Exhibition in Philadelphia.
1877	Alexander Graham Bell founds the Bell Telephone Company.
1882	Thomas Edison and the Edison Electric Illuminating Company install electric lighting in lower Manhattan.
November 18, 1883	Four standard time zones adopted across the United States.
1887	The Interstate Commerce Act.
1890	The Sherman Anti-Trust Act.
1893	The Railroad Safety Appliance Act.

Chronology

English and Jewish migrants. Nonetheless, the possibility of advancement existed. Although it was highly unlikely that a day laborer would become rich, it was not unrealistic for a member of the working class to imagine advancing from rags to respectability. Class mattered; it shaped a person's life chances. But it was not a prison with unscalable walls.

Suggested Reading

Alfred D. Chandler, *The Visible Hand: The Managerial Revolution in American Business* (1977)

William Cronon, *Nature's Metropolis: Chicago and the Great West* (1991)

David A. Hounshell, *From the American System to Mass Production, 1800–1932: The Development of Manufacturing Technology in the United States* (1984)

Thomas Hughes, *American Genesis: A Century of Invention and Technological Enthusiasm, 1870–1970* (1989)

Thomas J. Misa, *A Nation of Steel: The Making of Modern America, 1865–1925* (1995)

Stephan Thernstrom, *The Other Bostonians: Poverty and Progress in the American Metropolis, 1880–1970* (1973)

593

AN INDUSTRIAL SOCIETY:

1870–1910

Mulberry Street on New York City's Lower East Side, 1900.

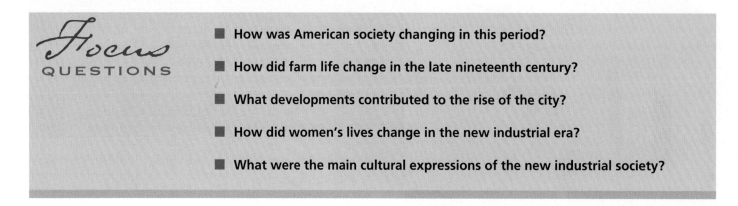

Focus
QUESTIONS

■ How was American society changing in this period?

■ How did farm life change in the late nineteenth century?

■ What developments contributed to the rise of the city?

■ How did women's lives change in the new industrial era?

■ What were the main cultural expressions of the new industrial society?

The triumph of industrialization reverberated through nearly all dimensions of American life. Not only were work and workplaces transformed, but the very fabric of society was rewoven with a more industrial thread. People, things, and words moved faster, over unprecedented distances. Daily life on millions of farms was reconfigured by new technologies and new types of production. Millions of people poured into the nation's cities, living in more densely populated worlds than they had known; their presence transformed the physical environment, as well as the rhythms and contours of urban life. Gender roles, too, were affected, as workplaces became increasingly separated from homes, and as more and more women entered the labor force. Educational institutions revamped their curricula to match the needs of an industrial world; religions were challenged to respond to new moral and social problems; writers, artists, and scientists focused their attention on a social order that was challenging and unfamiliar.

These changes were experienced by a diverse people. The population of the United States included more than 4 million African Americans, as well as several hundred thousand Native Americans from different tribes. It included "old stock" white men and women of northern and western European descent, as well as more than a million Irish immigrants. In the North and West, the diversity was enhanced by the presence of "new" immigrants who seemed even more foreign to native eyes. Italians and eastern European Jews came in large numbers to the Eastern Seaboard; Czechs, Slovaks, Poles, and Hungarians arrived in many cities of the Midwest; Chinese and Japanese immigrants became a visible presence in the West.

Multiple languages were heard on the streets of cities from the Atlantic to the Pacific. Catholics and Jews practiced their religion in locales that had been almost entirely Protestant. Ethnic neighborhoods, governed by different customs and celebrating different holidays, sprouted up in New York, Chicago, Pittsburgh, San Francisco, Portland, and scores of other cities. The society that encountered the new industrialism was far more heterogenous than America had ever been before.

Integration and Segmentation

Between Reconstruction and 1900, the ties that linked different regions and communities became stronger and more numerous. Men and women in New Jersey communicated rapidly with relatives in Illinois or even California. In 1887, free mail delivery started up in communities of more than 10,000 people, and in rural areas in 1896. Trains carried millions of passengers each day, some of them hundreds of miles from home. Thanks to the telegraph, events in Washington were known hours, even minutes, later in Denver and San Francisco. The impact of decisions made by firms in the major cities rippled through the countryside.

At the same time, living patterns, as well as many artifacts of everyday life—furniture, clothing, food, tools, machinery—became similar in communities far removed from one another. Standard time zones meant that men and women living hundreds of miles apart reported to work at the same time and attended church at the same hour on Sundays. Shoes manufactured in Lynn, Massachusetts, were worn from coast to coast; people everywhere bought identical watches from Sears, Roebuck; meat packed in Chicago found its way to dinner tables throughout the nation.

The integration of society was furthered by the extraordinary mobility of the population. In urban areas and rural counties both, men and women were on the move. In Boston, only 60 percent of the city's residents in 1880 were still living there a decade later, and Boston's population was relatively stable compared with some locales. Even more startling, the total number of people who lived in Boston at some point in the 1880s was three times as great as the largest number that ever lived there at one time: men and women were moving in and out of the city at a dizzying rate. This mobility was disproportionately concentrated in the working class, as blue-collar workers repeatedly relocated in response to unemployment and in the hope of finding better opportunities. But Americans of all classes were in motion—which meant that cities and towns were always filled with newcomers, many of whom would not remain long.

The flip side of national integration was the erosion of local communities as the center of people's lives. In 1870, most Americans lived in small communities that were the focal point of their social lives and identities. By 1900, those communities had grown larger, more internally divided, less distinctive, and less self-contained. People looked outward: for jobs, investments, consumer goods, even entertainment. The growth of national corporations made clear that power had shifted, that people's fates were no longer shaped primarily by local events. For many individuals, the community in which they lived ceased to be central to their aspirations or their identities.

"In 1887, free mail delivery started up in communities of more than 10,000 people, and in rural areas in 1896."

While the significance of community declined, the importance of people's occupations rose. Men increasingly identified themselves by the work they performed, forging ties with those in similar pursuits in distant cities and states. Almost all professions formed national associations in the late nineteenth century, to distribute information, maintain standards, and defend professional interests. Workers, too, attached their local labor organizations to national unions of men who belonged to the same trade. The nationalization of social life even extended to recreation. The United States Lawn Tennis Association, which held a national championship, was founded in 1881; the U.S. Golf Association followed suit the following decade; and 1889 witnessed the selection of the first All-American football team.

This integration of American society was, however, accompanied by fragmentation along racial and ethnic lines.

Not only were class cleavages sharpened, but tensions deepened between dominant social groups—always white and generally Protestant—and "minorities" (who in some places constituted a numerical majority). African Americans, Native Americans, Asian immigrants, eastern and southern European immigrants all found themselves excluded from pursuits that were open to those of a different heritage. Although this was the era in which the Statue of Liberty was erected in New York Harbor, American society was not always eager to incorporate "others" into the mainstream of American life.

THE JIM CROW SOUTH

The end of Reconstruction left the social standing of African Americans in limbo. Formally, their rights were protected by constitutional amendments and by the Civil Rights Act of 1875, which made it illegal for blacks to be denied access to streetcars, trains, restaurants, hotels, and other public facilities. In addition, white southern leaders, hoping to reassure northern Republicans, proclaimed their intention of safeguarding the rights of freedmen. South Carolina governor Wade Hampton promised in 1877 to "secure to every citizen, the lowest as well as the highest, black as well as white, full and equal protection in the enjoyment of all his rights." Still, after the withdrawal of federal troops, blacks were at the mercy of those who had "redeemed" the South, men and women who believed that blacks were an inferior race and that close contact between blacks and whites would only "pollute" white civilization. The vast majority of blacks, moreover, were enmeshed in a system of sharecropping and liens that left them economically dependent on white landowners and employers.

In the late 1870s and 1880s, southern society became increasingly divided along racial lines, especially in the cities. Although partially a carryover from antebellum practices, the movement toward segregation also reflected white apprehensions about controlling the behavior of free blacks, particularly in urban settings where social interactions were more common. Children went to racially separate schools almost everywhere, separate churches for blacks and whites were the rule, and blacks were compelled to find work in unskilled, poorly paid "black jobs." Although the extent of racial exclusion varied in different parts of the South (and in some locales race relations remained quite open and fluid), separation of the races became widespread in poorhouses, courthouses, trains, hotels, theaters, and restaurants. Such segregation generally was accomplished not by law but by custom and by the policies of individual enterprises (such as railroad corporations, restaurants, and saloons).

Legally mandated segregation, however, began not long after the end of Reconstruction. Antimiscegenation laws were passed everywhere by the early 1880s, reflecting a powerful white fear of sexual comingling. Indeed, the foremost targets of segregation were places where men and women, particularly black men and white women, might come into close contact with one another. Between 1881 and 1891, nine states passed railway segregation laws that required separate cars for blacks and whites; and after 1890, "Jim Crow" legislation became universal and extensive. (Jim Crow was a stock character in minstrel shows, a happy, childlike rural black man.) Prompted in part by black resistance to informal, customary discrimination, municipal and state governments passed laws systematically separating the races. Not just trains, but railroad stations and ticket windows were segregated. So, too, were parks, playgrounds, swimming pools, streetcars, schoolbooks, and the Bibles on which people swore in court. The law, in effect, formalized the status of African Americans as inferior, dependent, second-class citizens.

At the same time, lawlessness and violence against blacks were on the increase: more than a thousand black men were lynched in the 1890s, often by mobs that publicly tortured their victims before killing them. Lynchings, particularly in rural areas, served as instruments of social control and intimidation, commonly supported by white southerners of all classes. Although the incidence of lynching declined after 1900, more than a hundred blacks were lynched every decade through the 1930s.

The reaction of blacks to this ever-more widespread segregation was mixed. Frequently, there was resistance, both individual and collective. A Richmond minister declared that "the negroes must claim the right to sit with the whites in theaters, churches, and other public buildings, to ride with them on cars and to stay at the same hotels with them." African Americans challenged the rules by sitting in train cars and theaters that had become segregated. Streetcars were boycotted in nearly every city. Some blacks even went to court to try to enforce their rights—and occasionally won. Nonetheless, there was no mass opposition to Jim Crow. African Americans believed that segregated facilities were better than none (which often was the alternative). Others feared economic reprisals—or worse—if they protested, particularly after the outbreak of white race riots that occurred in Wilmington, North Carolina, in 1898, in which blacks were beaten and killed and their homes destroyed. Many acquiesced and tried to make the best of a segregated world, because there simply seemed to be no choice.

Perhaps the most well-known advocate of acquiescence was Booker T. Washington, the most celebrated black leader of the era. Born a slave in Virginia in 1856, Washington worked his way through school and in 1881 founded the Tuskegee Institute in Alabama, a vocational school for blacks. There, he developed the view that for African Americans to progress, they ought to forgo battles for political and social rights and instead concentrate on learning skills, working hard, and acquiring property. In a famous speech to a mixed audience in Atlanta in 1895, he urged blacks to "glorify common labor," and insisted that economic advancement ought to be the primary item on the African American agenda. "Agitation of questions of racial equality," he declared, "is the extremest folly." Social segregation was not necessarily degrading to blacks and ought to be accepted. "In all things that are purely social we can be as separate as the fingers, yet one as the hand in all matters essential to mutual progress."

The Atlanta Compromise, as the speech was called, was well received by whites, who were asked only to act fairly as employers and to lend a helping hand to their poorer fellow citizens. Indeed, whites in both North and South lionized

Booker T. Washington in his office at the Tuskegee Institute, 1900.

W. E. B. Du Bois, leading spokesman for the Niagara movement and a founder of the NAACP.

Washington, who became a prominent national figure and adviser to presidents. Many African Americans, however, regarded Washington as too accommodating, too willing to surrender equal rights. Not surprisingly, perhaps, the most strenuous challenge to Washington came from well-educated northern blacks, such as William M. Trotter, the editor of the *Boston Guardian,* and W. E. B. Du Bois, an elegant writer and rigorous scholar who was the first black man to earn a Ph.D. from Harvard. Du Bois became the primary spokesman for the Niagara movement, a group of northern blacks committed to the militant pursuit of legal, economic, and political equality. "We claim for ourselves every single right that belongs to a freeborn American, political, civil, and social; and until we get these rights we will never cease to protest and assail the ears of America," declared the Niagara Address in 1906. Du Bois and his colleagues envisioned progress spearheaded by the "Talented Tenth," the most cultivated and well-trained blacks, who could both set an example to whites and agitate to improve the conditions of less advantaged African Americans. In 1909, Du Bois and other members of the Niagara movement founded the National Association for the Advancement of Colored People (NAACP), which emphasized the use of legal strategies to end discrimination.

"Du Bois became the primary spokesman for the Niagara movement, a group of northern blacks committed to the militant pursuit of legal, economic, and political equality."

The implementation of segregation was achieved with the support of the Supreme Court, which, in a series of cases, stripped away the protection blacks seemed to have acquired through constitutional amendments and federal legislation. In 1883, the Court ruled that the Fourteenth Amendment outlawed discriminatory action by states but not by private citizens; at the same time, it declared that the Civil Rights Act had exceeded the authority granted to Congress and was not enforceable. Most important, the Court, in *Plessy v. Ferguson* (1896), embraced the doctrine of "separate but equal," legally sanctioning segregation. In 1892, Homer Plessy had boarded an East Louisiana Railway train and taken a seat in a white car in order to test an 1890 Louisiana law mandating separate cars for blacks and whites. The Court's decision maintained that "the underlying fallacy" of Plessy's argument consisted "in the assumption that the enforced separation of the two races stamps the colored race with a badge of inferiority. If this be so, it is . . . solely because the colored race chooses to put that construction upon it." For the following half century, segregation had the imprimatur of the American judiciary.

REFORMING NATIVE AMERICANS

The late 1860s and early 1870s witnessed the launching of a new federal policy toward Native Americans. Often called the "peace policy" (to distinguish it from the largely military approach taken in earlier decades), this initiative was the handiwork of northeastern reformers who prevailed on the government to emphasize honesty and fairness in dealing with the nation's 300,000 Indians. These reformers did not believe that Native Americans were an inferior race, but they did view Indian civilization as inferior, and they were convinced that in order to become the equal of whites, Indians needed to be civilized into the ways of Christian society. To achieve this end, reformers advocated the placement of all Indians on reservations where they could be instructed in agriculture and other skills; they also convinced the government to transfer responsibility for Indian affairs from political appointees and the army to Protestant church groups.

Ironically, the first decade of the "peace policy" was marked by an upsurge of war, particularly on the Great Plains where Indians resisted the encroachments of white civilization as well as the government's efforts to confine them to reservations. Particularly fierce fighting broke out after an army expedition led by Colonel George Custer declared that it had discovered gold in the Black Hills of South Dakota, the heart of Sioux country. The government insisted that the Black Hills be either ceded or leased to whites; when the Indians refused, troops were sent in to protect the gold miners who were already pouring into the region. The war began with several Sioux victories, including one at the Little Big Horn River in 1876 where Custer and all of his troops were killed. Yet the Sioux could not win a war against a large army that pursued them relentlessly, pre-

599

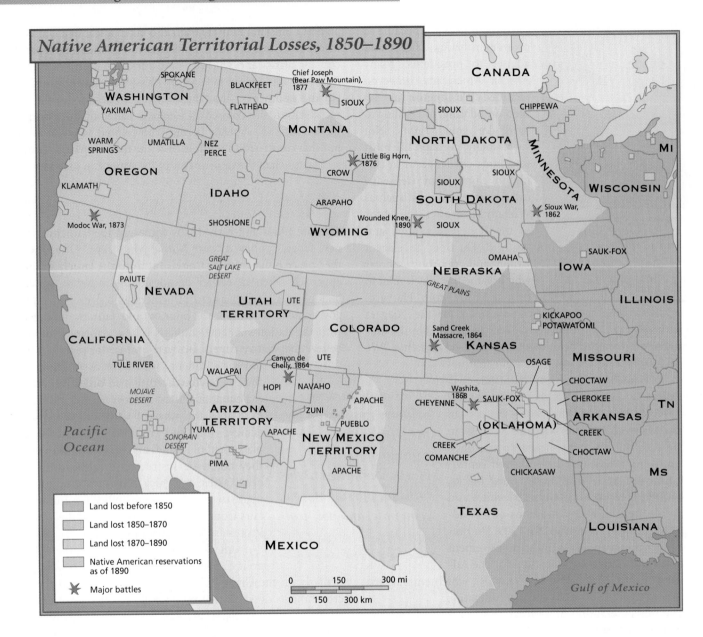

Native American Territorial Losses, 1850–1890

Land lost before 1850

Land lost 1850–1870

Land lost 1870–1890

Native American reservations as of 1890

★ Major battles

venting them from acquiring food, supplies, and shelter. By 1877, most of the exhausted Sioux had surrendered. Similar strategies—of winter campaigns and incessant pursuit—led to the defeat of the Cheyennes, Comanches, Kiowas, and Apaches.

While these campaigns were being waged, the Plains Indians were also being threatened by the destruction of the buffalo. A new tanning process made it possible for buffalo hides to be turned into cheap leather for straps and belts, while the railroads made it much easier to get the hides to market. Responding to this new market, white hunters slaughtered millions of buffalo in the 1870s and 1880s; by the middle of the latter decade, the huge herds that had once roamed the plains had vanished. With them vanished the traditional economy of the Plains Indians and a way of life grounded in communal ownership or use of lands, seasonal buffalo hunts, and tribal sharing of food and other resources. After fifteen years of the "peace policy," the conquest of the plains was complete.

Sitting Bull (left), Sioux leader, and General George Custer.

As the wars drew to a close, the federal government, reflecting the desire of reformers to transform Indians into mainstream Americans, began actively to promote the assimilation of Native Americans. It did so in several different ways. The first was to alter Indian landholding patterns, eradicating communal ownership of lands and redistributing the land to individual families. The Severalty Act of 1887, sponsored by Massachusetts senator Henry L. Dawes, who had close ties to reformers, permitted Indians to acquire title to 160-acre reservation allotments after they had lived on them for twenty-five years; by so doing, they could also become U.S. citizens. The Dawes Act in addition permitted the federal government to sell to whites any reservation lands that were not allotted to individual families. The second element in the assimilation program was the education of Indian children—sometimes at boarding schools, away from their families—in order to imbue them with Christian values and with skills they would need in white civilization. The third was the suppression of Indian culture and religion, which included cutting men's hair, forcibly breaking up religious ceremonies, and banning traditional rituals and marital practices.

The effort to assimilate Indians into mainstream Protestant society was inseparable from the goal of promoting settlement and economic development in the West. Railroads were crisscrossing the region with track, while the population of the West was skyrocketing, particularly in areas with large Indian reservations. Settlers, promoters, and the railroads all wanted access to Indian lands (which in 1880 still covered an area one and half times the size of California), and they supported assimilation because it seemed likely to serve their interests. As a senator from Kansas observed, "The time for bartering with the Indian for his land is passed. We have come to a time when under the operation of natural laws, we need all the land in this country for homes." His impatience was echoed by Senator Henry Teller of Colorado, who advocated opening all reservation lands to settlement and compelling the Indian "to enter our civilization whether he will or whether he wills it not."

In fact, settlers and railroad corporations benefited more from the assimilation policy than did Indians. Between 1880 and 1895, nearly half of all Indian lands were opened up to

Shooting buffalo on the line of the Kansas-Pacific Railroad, 1870s.

601

A classroom at the Carlisle Indian Industrial School in Carlisle, Pennsylvania, part of the effort to assimilate Indian youth to the ways of whites.

instruction, the schools were training Indian children not to become the equals of whites but to hold jobs at the periphery of the white economy.

The promise of citizenship for Indians, moreover, led not to equality, but to a new form of second-class citizenship. Thanks in part to a 1901 act of Congress, more than half of all Indians were U.S. citizens by 1905, and in 1924 citizenship was conferred on all Native Americans. Yet whether citizens or not, Native Americans remained under the guardianship of federal agencies that could control their property and their personal affairs. In addition, states with significant Indian populations restricted their right to vote, disfranchising those who were "not taxed" or "not civilized." By the end of the first decades of the twentieth century, the hundreds of thousands of Indians who, a half century earlier, had possessed their own cultures, governments, and patterns of social organization, had been transformed into a minority group of unequal citizens, living at the margins of American society.

STRANGERS IN THE LAND

The great waves of immigration that carried 20 million people to the United States in the late nineteenth and early twentieth centuries put strains on the social fabric and challenged the nation's receptivity to the foreign-born. A large majority of these immigrants settled in urban, industrial areas, transforming the social landscape of the nation's cities. By 1910, more than half the population of most major cities consisted of immigrants and their children, which meant that the flavor of life in those cities was very different than it had been forty years earlier. The reaction of native-born Americans to this influx was mixed. On the one hand, many industrialists believed that economic growth depended on immigrant labor, and most Americans took pride in their country's role as a refuge for those whom Emma Lazarus, in the poem inscribed on the Statute of Liberty, had called the "tired," the "poor," the "huddled masses yearning to breathe free." At the same time, however, workers increasingly feared immigrants as a threat to their jobs, while members of the middle and upper classes worried about the ways in which "foreigners" were transforming and even taking over "their" society.

The immigrants who faced the most virulent hostility were those who came to the United States from East Asia. Chinese immigrants, overwhelmingly male, began arriving on the West Coast in the 1850s, and by the 1880s the Chinese population peaked at more than 100,000. Most remained in the

settlement or simply seized and given to the railroads. Meanwhile, the Indians—some of whom resisted the policy and some of whom did not—were caught between two worlds. Relatively few were able to convert themselves into the family farmers that the Dawes Act had envisioned; at the same time, communal economic life had become impossible. The education programs, energetic and idealistic as they may have been, tended to disrupt Indian society rather than smooth the way for Indians to enter the white, Protestant world. **Traditional cultures** were severely strained without leading to assimilation. Not surprisingly, the Native American population declined during these years from roughly 330,000 in 1860 to a low of 237,000 in 1900.

After 1900, the situation deteriorated further, partly because the idealistic conviction of reformers that Indians could become the equal of whites was replaced by the more pessimistic view, buttressed by anthropologists, that Indians were biologically inferior to Europeans. Federal policy retained the goal of incorporating Indians into white society, but the vision of Indians as potential equals receded. As a result, Congress, backed by the Supreme Court, began both to abrogate existing treaty provisions and to control the affairs and lands (even allotted lands) of Indians. The extensive network of schools remained in place, but their goals shifted: increasingly limited to providing only the most basic manual

West, working on the railroads or in mining; later they fanned out into agriculture and light manufacturing and began to operate restaurants and laundries. From the outset, the Chinese encountered fierce antagonism and were periodically the objects of mob violence. They were accused of undercutting white labor by working for starvation wages and were routinely described in language depicting them as subhuman—for example, as "groveling worms" or "more slavish and brutish than the beasts that roam the fields."

This hostility mounted in the 1870s, particularly in California, where incidents of violence were frequent and where the Workingmen's Party, led by Dennis Kearny, mounted an all-out campaign to expel the Chinese and to end further immigration. This campaign bore fruit in 1882 when the federal government enacted legislation that halted Chinese immigration for ten years and declared that the Chinese were "aliens ineligible for citizenship." The suspension of immigration was later extended, leaving the Chinese unable to settle legally in the United States until 1943, when Congress passed a new law admitting roughly 100 Chinese immigrants per year. Numerous western states passed discriminatory laws that banned intermarriage, barred the Chinese from certain occupations, and prevented them from owning or leasing land. Several cities and towns, including Tacoma, Washington, and Truckee, California, expelled their Chinese residents; in San Francisco, popular prejudices

A broadside depicting the anti-Chinese sentiment of the Workingmen's Party in California.

made it impossible for the Chinese to find housing outside of Chinatown.

After the 1880s, anti-Chinese fervor began to subside, but it was succeeded by a similar pattern of hostility aimed at Japanese immigrants who began arriving around the turn of the century. Fears of this new "Yellow Peril" mounted rapidly in the West, leading once again to violence and to the passage of overtly discriminatory laws. At the same time, in the Southwest, similar treatment was meted out to Mexican migrants, particularly those who were poor and had darker skins. Although never denied the right to become citizens, they were commonly confined to menial jobs, refused entry to public facilities, and compelled to attend segregated schools.

Discrimination against immigrants was not limited to the West or to men and women from Asia and Mexico. European immigrants—especially those from southern and eastern Europe and from Ireland—also inspired antagonism in many old-stock Americans. This nativism had several strands, all of which grew stronger under the pressure of rapid economic and social change. One, with roots stretching back to the antebellum era, was a middle-class anxiety that the immigrant population was rife with union organizers and dangerous radicals who would destroy the American way of life. In the wake of the Haymarket affair in Chicago in 1886, a notorious incident in which several policemen were killed by a bomb thrown at a meeting called by anarchists, one newspaper declared that the anarchists were "not Americans, but the very scum and offal of Europe." A second long-standing strain of nativism was aimed at Catholics, who were portrayed as adherents of superstition and despotism, breeders of corruption in municipal politics, and foot soldiers in a popish plot to undermine Protestant society. Secret anti-Catholic societies flourished in the 1880s and 1890s, particularly in the Midwest: the most prominent of them, the American Protective Association, founded in Iowa in 1887, attracted hundreds of thousands of members and succeeded in electing its adherents to public office. Everyone who joined the APA was required to take an oath promising never to vote for a Catholic, never to hire a Catholic if a Protestant was available, and never to go on strike with Catholics.

Many old-stock Americans also came to believe that their own (superior) Anglo-Saxon "race" risked being debased or overwhelmed by the arrival of large numbers of non–Anglo Saxon immigrants. Such ideas were articulated, and given respectability, by prominent Protestant clergymen as well as by upper-class Bostonians such as Senator Henry Cabot Lodge. Pressing the distinction between "old" immigrants (from northern and western Europe) and "new" immigrants (from southern and eastern Europe), men like Lodge argued that the latter were inferior human specimens who could not be assimilated into American society. Apprehensions about the "new" immigrants were heightened by social scientists who suggested that old-stock Americans were committing a kind of "race suicide" because their birthrates were far lower than those of eastern and southern Europeans. This racial strain of nativism was given further impetus after the turn of the century by "scientific" ideas linked to eugenics, the theory that the human race could be uplifted by encouraging the breeding of the "best" while restricting the reproduction of the "worst." From the viewpoint of eugenics, the immigration of "degenerate breeding stock" was a threat to the well-being of the nation. Not only would genetic inferiors multiply, but interbreeding would debase the superior genetic stock. "The cross between any of the three European races and a Jew," wrote Madison Grant, one of the foremost advocates of racial purity, "is a Jew."

Many nativists sought federal legislation to restrict immigration. They were joined, particularly after the depression of the 1890s, by a growing number of trade unionists who feared that unrestricted immigration was creating unemployment and depressing wages. "We sympathize with the oppressed of the Old World," noted one union leader, but we are "an asylum whose dormitories are full." Despite such concerns, there were few modifications of the laws regulating non-Asian immigration before World War I. Some states, however, did pass laws that overtly discriminated against immigrants: in New York and Pennsylvania, for example, aliens (noncitizens) were barred from all employment on public works. Idaho even passed a law prohibiting private corporations from hiring aliens who had not yet declared their intention to become citizens.

But legal discrimination was the least of it. Throughout the nation, "new" immigrants were exposed to condescension, hostility, and sometimes violence. Anti-Semitic demonstrations and riots broke out periodically in the North and the South. Italians, stereotyped as violent and lawless, were occasionally assaulted and even lynched: in New Orleans in 1891, eleven Italian men, after being acquitted of murder,

were lynched by a mob, to the approval of local newspapers. More routinely, "undesirable" immigrants were kept out of desirable occupations, denied entry to social events, compelled to live in their own neighborhoods, blamed for urban social problems. The "melting pot" was barely simmering.

Life on the Farm

For the tens of millions of Americans who lived on farms, life changed, though not drastically, in the late nineteenth century. Railroads, refrigerator cars, and urban growth opened up new markets for almost all agricultural products. Nearly everywhere outside the South, technological innovations reduced the drudgery of farm work while increasing the productivity of farm labor. In the grain-growing regions of the Midwest, California, and the Great Plains, new plows, seed drills, threshing machines, harvesters, and combines permitted farmers to grow more with less backbreaking, repetitive toil (see Chapter 18). On dairy farms from New England to Minnesota, the centrifugal cream separator and cream tester made it easier for small farmers to sell their wares profitably to local creameries and butter factories. Progressive farmers were able to avoid waste and increase production by applying new scientific knowledge about breeding, care of the soil, and conservation.

"The catalog offered farm families virtually every kind of product made in the United States: from gasoline stoves, bicycles, and batteries to dresses, underwear, and carriages, to toys, carpets, artworks, and pianos."

Equally important, men and women who lived on farms began to have more contact with the urban world. Faster trains, running all night, brought mail to the hinterland in a matter of days; they also brought big-city newspapers crammed with photographs, tales of urban life, and pages of advertisements. By the 1890s, Chicago newspapers were available in small Illinois towns at seven A.M., not much later than when they hit the streets in the metropolis itself.

The most vivid, and perhaps influential, tissue connecting urban and rural societies consisted of the **mail-order catalogs** of retailers Montgomery Ward and Sears, Roebuck. "The Montgomery Ward catalog," declared a farm woman in Nebraska, "was a real link between us and civilization." Ward's catalog, only eight pages long when the business was launched, mush-

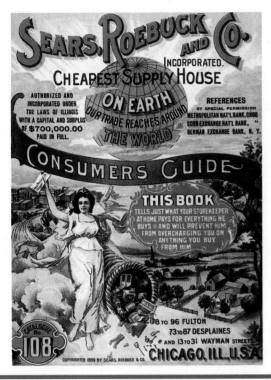

A vision of plenty on the cover of the Sears, Roebuck catalog, 1899.

roomed to 540 pages, offering 24,000 items, by the 1880s; at the turn of the century, it was 1,200 pages, with 17,000 illustrations. The catalog offered farm families virtually every kind of product made in the United States: from gasoline stoves, bicycles, and batteries to dresses, underwear, and carriages, to toys, carpets, artworks, and pianos. Farm families, after placing their orders, sent their payments in advance or paid at a local freight desk once their orders were received: by 1900, Ward was receiving between 15,000 and 35,000 letters a day, some from towns as remote as Bywy, Mississippi.

Thanks to the catalogs, farmers were able to acquire goods that had been rare or unknown in rural America: ready-made clothing, Aunt Jemima's Pancake Flour, hams, foodstuffs made by Heinz and Pillsbury, furniture, musical instruments, tools, and barbed wire so that they no longer had to build fences from hand-wrought rails. And by giving farm families a glimpse of an urban style of living, the catalogs altered the tastes and reshaped the desires of many rural Americans.

Yet despite the growing ties between the countryside and the city and despite the significance of new technology and science, many aspects of farm life changed little. The rhythms of work and leisure continued to be molded by the seasons, by local climates, by the demands of individual crops. And the division of labor within farm households, which had a significant impact on social life, was shaped, as it long had been, by gender.

Margaret Dow Gebby and her husband, Jeremiah, for example, were relatively prosperous farmers in Bellefontaine, Ohio. They owned a 286-acre farm, raising corn and wheat and selling cattle to stockyards in Chicago and Buffalo. Each April, the Gebbys, with their sons and often a hired hand, worked feverishly to get corn planted, sometimes having to repeat their labors if the weather turned cold or wet. In September came the backbreaking work of harvesting corn: men walked the rows, slashing the stalks with one hand and gathering them up in the other, then shucking the corn and hauling it off in wagons to the barn. The Gebbys rushed to complete the harvesting so that they could then plant their winter wheat crop as early in the fall as possible; harvesting the wheat was an even more frenetic period, since the entire crop had to be harvested within a two-week period.

In the 1880s and 1890s, the Gebbys purchased new farm machinery, but the seasonal pace of their efforts did not change. Within the farmhouse, too, seasonal rhythms predominated. The wood-burning stove was moved to the washhouse (where clothes were washed) each May and back into the house in early November. Handwoven rag carpets were put down each winter, cleaned and beaten each spring, and replaced by summer matting. Produce from the garden and the orchards was preserved late each summer and in the fall; windows were cleaned and washed every spring and fall, when the screens were put on and taken off.

Almost all the commercial operations of the farm were the domain of men. Jeremiah, his sons, and a hired hand plowed, planted, and harvested; they were also responsible for daily chores such as caring for the cattle and hogs and maintaining fences, tools, and machines. In addition, Jeremiah controlled the farm's finances: he decided when to sell the wheat crop and what livestock to buy; each year he also journeyed to Chicago, Cleveland, or Buffalo to sell cattle. Margaret had full responsibility for maintaining the household: she did all the cooking and cleaning, baked bread, and preserved produce for the family's consumption. (When her children were young, she also had full responsibility for child rearing.) She produced butter and eggs, some of which she sold at a local store (using the proceeds to buy spices, coffee, and tea), and she made most of her own clothes. (The men wore ready-

A pioneer family alongside their sod house near Coburg, Nebraska, 1887.

made clothing.) Since the family was prosperous, she paid a neighbor to help with laundry, and by the 1890s some of her labors were lightened by the installation of indoor plumbing.

The Gebbys were settled and secure enough to enjoy a rich social life. They attended the Bellefontaine United Church each week; they belonged to a threshing ring, through which families took turns helping one another and socializing; Margaret could also draw on a kin network of sisters, cousins, aunts, nieces, and daughters-in-law for assistance with dressmaking and sewing. Except in the busiest of seasons, the Gebbys visited frequently with family, friends, and neighbors. Margaret also belonged to the local literary society, as well as the Women's Missionary Service, and their entire extended family usually gathered for a week in October to attend the county fair.

Key contours of farm life were similar throughout the nation. Planting and harvesting were hectic periods on all farms; animals had to be tended daily; work was hard, days were long. Men worked in the fields and controlled the cash crops, while women raised children, maintained the house, and endlessly prepared goods for the family's consumption. Networks of friends and neighbors helped and supported one another, while family and church remained the central pillars of social life.

Yet these patterns were often bent by local conditions. The harsh environment of the Great Plains, for example—the

cold, the wind, the capricious rainfall, the lack of wood for fuel or construction—made life far less comfortable than it was for the Gebbys in Ohio. Houses made of sod were easily penetrated by dirt, insects, and snakes, and harvest seasons were extremely short, compelling women and young children to work in the fields. At the same time, the transience of the plains population—as waves of settlers poured in, stayed a few years, and then fled—made it difficult to replicate the social networks and institutions of the rural world farther east. Women, whose work did not require them to go to town, complained of the isolation, the long distances between farms, the lack of contact with friends. Luna Kellie, later an activist in the Populist Party, did not get to town at all in the first eighteen months she lived in Nebraska.

Similarly, in the South, the poverty of the rural population, as well as its overdependence on a single cash crop, forced many women to work in the fields in addition to performing their regular tasks. "The women down this way," observed one sharecropper's wife, "got to the field 'bout as reg'lar as the men. Cotton will be openin' now in four weeks, and that'll be the last of the house except for cookin' and washin' and ironin' till its all picked." Kinship networks were highly developed in the rural South: even in the 1970s, Nate Shaw, who had been a sharecropper in Alabama, could recall the names and precise relationships of scores of family members from the turn of the century. But the combination of poverty (Shaw, for example, did not own a horse), illiteracy, and poor roads limited the geographic and social horizons of most farmers.

Careful estimates suggest that between 1870 and 1900, more than 7 million people moved from rural to urban America, a migration comparable in scale to the movement west in the 1870s and 1880s. This migration had several sources: farm families tended to have high fertility rates, which made it difficult for farmers to leave land to all their children; technological innovations lessened the demand for farm labor, while the cost of technology made it expensive for young people to start farms; and in the Northeast, farmers found it difficult to make a living in the face of competition from more fertile, larger farms farther west. Everywhere, moreover, men and women simply grew tired of the isolation and drudgery of life on a farm.

In addition to these "push" factors, there was also a "pull" from the cities. Wages were higher in urban areas, jobs seemed more abundant, and there were opportunities for advancement into white-collar, managerial, or professional positions. In addition, the cities seemed more glamorous and exciting. There were amusements, stores overflowing with merchandise, thousands of strangers walking through the streets. As a character in a popular play declared: "Who wants to smell new-mown hay, if he can breathe gasoline on Fifth Avenue?"

"Even in the 1970s, Nate Shaw, who had been a sharecropper in Alabama, could recall the names and precise relationships of scores of family members from the turn of the century."

During the 1880s, 40 percent of the nation's rural townships registered population declines; in parts of New England, the figure was as high as 60 percent. In Ohio and Illinois, more than half of all townships lost population. In the Northeast, thousands of farms were simply abandoned. For the first time in the nation's history, there was a mass movement away from farming.

The Rise of the City

AN URBAN SOCIETY

No aspect of late nineteenth-century life was more important, or more dramatic, than the explosive growth of cities. In 1870, only New York and Philadelphia had populations greater than 500,000; by 1910, eight cities did, and three of these contained more than a million people. In 1870, fourteen cities (only three west of the Mississippi) had more than 100,000 people; by 1910, there were fifty, thirteen in the West. Smaller cities, too, multiplied in number. By 1910, 35 million people, or 39 percent of the population, lived in communities with more than 8,000 persons; in 1870, the figure had been 8 million. The growth of cities was fueled both by migrants from the countryside and by immigrants from Europe, Latin America, and Asia: in 1910, in all major cities north of Baltimore, most of the population consisted of immigrants and their children.

The cities were of two types: metropolises and "specialist" cities. Most metropolises had sizable populations as early as 1870, and they were first and foremost commercial centers. Often situated where long-distance water transportation routes met railroad junctures, these were places where a region's products were brought for processing and shipping and where goods from outside the region arrived to be broken down and redistributed within the region. They were also banking and financial hubs and, between 1870 and 1900, became great manufacturing centers: New York, Chicago, and Philadelphia constituted the largest manufacturing clusters in the nation.

The smaller, specialist cities were themselves of two kinds. One provided financial and commercial services to the surrounding rural areas, while also processing and shipping local specialty goods that originated in the countryside. Richmond, for example, handled cigarettes, while Sacramento dealt in canned fruits and vegetables. In the Northeast and the Midwest, a second type of specialty city flourished: the mill city or manufacturing city. Fall River and New Bedford, Massachusetts, made textiles; Lynn and Brockton, Massachusetts, made shoes; Dayton, Ohio, produced machine tools and cash registers; Columbus, Ohio, produced railroad cars. Taken together, these specialized cities made up the two major manufacturing belts: one stretching along the Atlantic coast from Maine to Virginia, and the other extending from Buffalo west to St. Louis and Milwaukee. When linked to the larger, metropolitan centers by the railroads and the telegraph, these cities formed a national urban market as well as a national urban society.

CITIES AND TECHNOLOGY

The dramatic growth of urban populations gave rise to both an expansion and a reconfiguration of urban space. The mid–nineteenth-century city was compact, a walking city whose boundaries were set by the need of almost everyone to walk to work. The doubling or tripling of cities' populations placed irresistible pressures on those boundaries.

Expanding the physical space of cities demanded new modes of transportation. Omnibuses (horse-drawn streetcars on wheels) had appeared in many places by mid-century, opening new areas to settlement, but they were slow, uncomfortable, and too expensive for anyone outside of the middle and upper classes. Similarly, commuter railroads permitted the wealthy to live in suburbs miles out of town, but they did

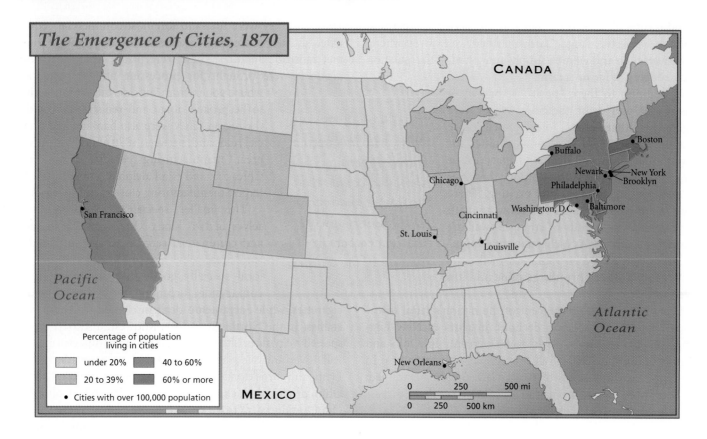

The Emergence of Cities, 1870

Percentage of population living in cities
- under 20%
- 20 to 39%
- 40 to 60%
- 60% or more
- Cities with over 100,000 population

CANADA

Pacific Ocean

Atlantic Ocean

MEXICO

Boston · Buffalo · Newark · New York · Brooklyn · Philadelphia · Chicago · Washington, D.C. · Baltimore · Cincinnati · St. Louis · Louisville · San Francisco · New Orleans

0   250   500 mi
0   250   500 km

not serve the majority of the population. Between 1850 and 1890, the most common form of public transportation became the horse-drawn streetcar on rails, an innovation made possible through a new technique of laying tracks flush on the pavement. These streetcars were larger, faster, and cheaper than omnibuses, and running on rails permitted them to have more predictable schedules. By 1887, 400 streetcar companies, in 300 communities, were conveying 175 million passengers a year.

Yet horse-drawn streetcars were dirty, crowded, and uncomfortable. "You can ride in a horse-car," wrote Mark Twain, "and stand-up for three-quarters of an hour, in the midst of a file of men that extends from front to rear . . . or you can take one of the platforms, if you please, but they are so crowded you will have to hang on by your eye-lashes and your toenails." Many riders were appalled at the spectacle of overworked horses straining to pull overcrowded cars, while the horses themselves contributed to urban pollution and disease. In the 1880s, 15,000 horses died each year on the streets of New York alone, with their carcasses often left to

rot. The average droppings of a dray horse amounted to ten pounds a day.

Entrepreneurs and inventors tried to come up with alternatives to the horse-drawn streetcar. One was the elevated train, driven by steam power and run on tracks mounted on pillars. Elevated lines were constructed in several cities, including New York and Chicago, but they proved extremely expensive to build, they were noisy and caused vibrations for blocks around, and they often dumped oil and hot ashes on unlucky pedestrians walking below. Another experiment was the cable car, pulled by a steam-driven underground cable. The first cable car line was built in San Francisco in 1873, and other cities gave them a try, but they also proved to be expensive to construct, as well as prone to mechanical breakdowns; in addition, since all cars had to move at the same speed, there was no way for a cable car to ever "make up" any lost time.

The decisive breakthrough in transportation technology came with the successful application of electricity to street railways. This became possible through a series of inventions,

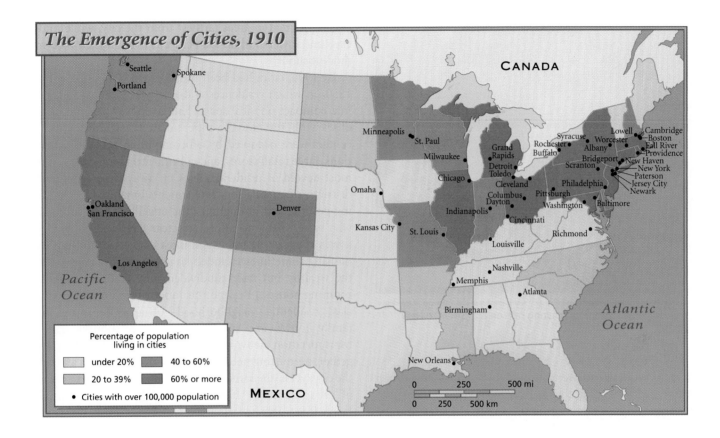

The Emergence of Cities, 1910

Percentage of population living in cities
- under 20%
- 20 to 39%
- 40 to 60%
- 60% or more
- Cities with over 100,000 population

including the dynamo in the 1870s. In 1887, Frank Julian Sprague, who had once worked for Thomas Edison, accepted a contract from the city of Richmond to build an electrified streetcar system. Completed in 1888, after much on-the-spot innovation, Sprague's system used a central power source, with electric current carried to the streetcars through overhead cables. The cables were linked to the cars through wires and a small carriage called a "troller"—all such electric cars thus came to be called "trolleys." Sprague's trolleys were an instant success. Pollution-free, they traveled on tracks at variable speeds, reaching up to twenty miles per hour; they were faster, cheaper, and more comfortable than horse-drawn cars. By 1895, more than 800 trolley systems were in operation in the country, and horse-drawn cars were rapidly phased out.

Other technological innovations facilitated the expansion of cities. Sprague, among others, helped design an electrical system that permitted trains to run underground. (Steam-powered trains could not run any distance underground because of the accumulation of gas, smoke, and dirt.) As a result, Boston opened a subway line in 1897, and New York

followed a few years later. Other engineers improved techniques of bridge building, an essential task in the many cities that were near rivers or harbors. In the 1870s, construction engineers learned to sink stable piers in deep, swift-flowing water, and 1883 witnessed the completion of the Brooklyn Bridge (linking Manhattan to Brooklyn), a strikingly beautiful, mile-long creation that became a symbol of American engineering prowess: the Brooklyn Bridge was not only the longest suspension bridge in the world, but it was sturdy enough to carry two railroad lines, two double carriage lanes, and a footpath.

The enlargement of city space was also made possible by the widespread adoption of a new method of home construction: the "balloon frame" house, so called because it used a light, external frame to replace the heavy timber supporting walls that had dominated residential building for centuries. With its thin pieces of lumber set so that the stresses were spread throughout the structure, and machine-produced nails rather than complex joints, the balloon-frame house could be built inexpensively and rapidly. Complex carpentry

A horse-drawn streetcar moves along rails on 23rd Street in New York City.

and large work crews were unnecessary, and many urban workmen with basic mechanical skills could easily construct their own homes. The result, in the 1870s and later, was the transformation of home building from a specialized craft into a large industry. The balloon-frame house also permitted hundreds of thousands of middle-class and even working-class families to live in private residences in new neighborhoods opened by the streetcars.

The combination of streetcar systems and new modes of construction spawned the development of residential suburbs. Streetcars made outlying towns and villages more accessible to urban centers, and real estate developers constructed new suburbs along the streetcar lines. On the outskirts of Boston, for example, the three suburbs of Roxbury, West Roxbury, and Dorchester swelled in population from 60,000 to 227,000 between 1870 and 1900. Outside Milwaukee, the village of Hart's Mill was transformed into the thriving suburb of Wauwatosa; near Norfolk, Virginia, a real estate company, relying on the streetcars, purchased a large tract of farmland and turned it into the exclusive suburb of Ghent. Nearly all residents of these suburbs were drawn from the middle and upper classes, who were seeking more living space, more community homogeneity, and an escape from the noise, pollution, and "foreignness" of the cities. Yet the suburbs themselves were also class differentiated: the wealthy

usually resided in areas farthest from the city, while middle-class and lower-middle-class citizens lived in their own more modest suburbs.

By 1900, cities had been transformed. The walking city of 1850, in which residences and workplaces were interspersed in a compact physical space, had given way to large metropolises with functionally differentiated neighborhoods. City centers were occupied by office buildings, financial institutions, large retail stores, and cultural attractions; they were almost devoid of residences. Not far away were grimy factory districts, often adjacent to tenements inhabited by the working poor: recent immigrants, the unskilled, men and women who were unable to afford streetcar fares and compelled to live in the least desirable and most congested housing. (This housing sometimes included large homes originally built for the wealthy but later subdivided into small apartments or rooming houses.) Beyond this inner ring were more middle-class residential neighborhoods of apartments or single-family houses, and still farther out were suburbs. The new transportation networks tied different parts of the city together, permitting people to engage in activities in all parts of the city; yet at the same time, they encouraged the segregation of urban space by function and class. In 1890, journalist Jacob Riis published *How the Other Half Lives,* a classic description of life in New York's poor neighborhoods. What was notable about Riis's book was not only its content but

An electric streetcar in Washington, D.C., 1895.

LEFT: The Brooklyn Bridge featured two roads for horse-drawn vehicles, two for trains, and one for pedestrians.

RIGHT: Lower Manhattan had become a business district by the 1890s, with electricity, telephone, and telegraph wires crisscrossing overhead.

that it had to be written at all, that affluent New Yorkers had to turn to a book to find out how their fellow residents were living.

THE IMMIGRANT CITY

The vast majority of immigrants lived in cities, and immigrants from the same country tended to cluster in particular residential areas. These immigrant neighborhoods had population densities two or three times the city average, with families and boarders crowded into tiny, dimly lit apartments. In Chicago's Packingtown district, near the stockyards, an average of twenty-eight people lived in the four small apartments that were typically carved out of a dilapidated two-story frame house. In New York, miserable and unsanitary conditions gave rise to an 1879 law requiring that all new tenements (the word originally referred to any multistory rental building housing more than three families) had to have a window in each room. The result was the "dumbbell" tenement, a design that spread rapidly throughout the country. The walls of dumbbell tenements had indentations on each side to permit the requisite number of windows; unfortu-

nately, since the tenements were tightly packed against one another, the view from most windows was onto noisy, dank air shafts that provided little light or ventilation.

Typically, immigrant apartments housed two or three people per room: a married couple and their children, and often one or more boarders. Men commonly held blue-collar jobs, working unsteadily at low wages. Women contributed to the household economy by performing industrial piecework (such as finishing pants) in the home or, more often, by caring for boarders, usually single men. According to one national study conducted at the turn of the century, 24 percent of all such households contained boarders, and in some locales, such as Packingtown, the figure exceeded 50 percent. Taking in boarders entailed considerable labor on the part of women, but their earnings were essential to make ends meet, to put aside some savings, or to cope with recurrent spells of unemployment. Children, too, were expected to contribute to the family income, either by working at home at jobs such as linking chains or stringing rosary beads or by doing odd jobs in the streets.

Although life in these immigrant neighborhoods has sometimes been depicted with a romantic cast—stores filled with ethnic foods, colorful streets packed with pedestrians speaking a host of different languages, close-knit families struggling to get ahead, preserving parts of the Old World while learning the ropes in the New—hardships were commonplace. Living conditions offered few comforts and little privacy, and immigrants from southern Europe often found the cold intolerable. Diseases such as tuberculosis, bronchitis, and diphtheria were endemic, with death rates generally two or three times higher than they were in middle-class sections of the city. Work was unsteady, and food sometimes scarce. Children, with no alternative places to play, risked accidents in the streets or on roofs.

Nonetheless, immigrants, most from peasant backgrounds, did their utmost to create communities in these unfamiliar urban settings, to build networks of self-help, reciprocity, and recreation. They founded fraternal organizations, burial societies, cemeteries, ethnic clubs, and mutual aid societies; they also organized festivals, sporting events, and outings to parks and the beach. More important, they built churches and syn-

Saloons were neighborhood centers for men of the immigrant city: Steve Brodie's bar in New York City, 1895.

Street life in an immigrant neighborhood, 1888–89, as seen in a photograph by Jacob Riis.

agogues that became centers of community life. Catholics also built their own parochial schools.

Even more numerous than churches were saloons, which were centers of economic and social life for working-class men. Offering men free hot meals when they bought a beer or two, saloons were where immigrant men ate their lunches and relaxed in the evenings. The saloon keeper cashed checks, received mail, kept track of job opportunities, and gave people credit during hard times. The saloons hosted weddings and dances and served as meeting places for fraternal groups and labor unions. One survey of ten residential blocks in Chicago found an average of three saloons per block. Along "Whiskey Row," the streets that stretched from Packingtown to the factories, there were on average twenty-six saloons per block.

For women, patterns of sociability were markedly different. Traditional customs, as well as language barriers and the demands of running households, tended to confine women to their neighborhoods and often to their buildings. Yet in those buildings and neighborhoods, women developed important social ties. As one contemporary observed, "one of the most noticeable traits of the life of the average tenement house dweller . . . is the more or less intimate and friendly intercourse of the families of the house. Washtubs and cooking dishes are borrowed from one another at any hour of the day: a mother leaves her child with a friend across the hall when she goes shopping; a child runs in to learn the time of day from a neighbor whose clock is standard." Women taught newcomers where to shop, how to wash clothes, what kinds of kitchen utensils to buy. A resident of the Lower East Side in New York recalled that "if someone got sick, the neighbor took care of them. My mother went for an operation and the neighbor took the younger children. They would shop and cook. Neighbors gathered in the halls, brought out their chairs, and chatted."

With their parents occupied for long hours, children who were not working roamed the streets by themselves, sometimes getting into trouble. Others attended public schools where they learned English and were inculcated with the values of urban America; their numbers rose substantially by the end of the century thanks to state laws requiring school attendance. Whether they attended school or not, the children of immigrants commonly found themselves torn between the traditions of their families and a new alluring society. Children quickly learned to speak English better than their parents, and they sought an independence that conflicted with parental expectations of obedience and family service. The tension between native-born children and foreign-born parents was an almost universal, if private, dimension of the experience of immigration.

American Journal

What's for Dinner?

When he was twenty-four, Jacob Riis, who had emigrated to the United States from Denmark three years earlier, became a police reporter in New York City. He was assigned to the Lower East Side, where he observed the hardships of tenement life. His book documenting these hardships, How the Other Half Lives *(published in 1890), complete with photographs Riis had taken, outraged enough influential New Yorkers that legislation curbing tenement-house evils was soon passed. Following is a glimpse into the daily life of a Czech immigrant cigar maker and his large family. He was suffering from consumption (as a result of breathing in tobacco fumes) and no longer able to work.*

"In a house around the corner that is not a factory-tenement, lives now the cigarmaker I spoke of as suffering from consumption which the doctor said was due to the tobacco-fumes. Perhaps the lack of healthy exercise had as much to do with it. . . . Six children sit at his table. By trade a shoemaker, for thirteen years he helped his wife make cigars in the manufacturer's tenement. She was a very good hand, and until his health gave out two years ago they were able to make from $17 to $25 a week, by lengthening the day at both ends. Now that he can work no more, and the family under the doctor's orders has moved away from the smell of tobacco, the burden of its support has fallen upon her alone, for none of the children is old enough to help. She has work in the shop at eight dollars a week, and this must go round; it is all there is. Happily, this being a tenement for revenue only, unmixed with cigars, the rent is cheaper: seven dollars for two bright rooms on the top floor. No housekeeping is attempted. A woman in Seventy-second Street supplies their meals, which the wife and mother fetches in a basket, her husband being too weak. Breakfast of coffee and hard-tack, or black bread, at twenty cents for the whole eight; a good many, the little woman says with a brave, patient smile, and there is seldom anything to spare, but——. The invalid is listening, and the sentence remains unfinished. What of dinner? One of the children brings it from the cook. Oh! it is a good dinner, meat, soup, greens and bread, all for thirty cents. It is the principal family meal. Does she come home for dinner? No; she cannot leave the shop, but gets a bite at her bench. The question: A bite of what? seems as merciless as the surgeon's knife, and she winces under it as one shrinks from physical pain. Bread, then. But at night they all have supper together—sausage and bread. For ten cents they can eat all they want."

Jacob Riis, *How the Other Half Lives: Studies Among the Tenements of New York*

THE CITY OF LIGHTS

Not far from the congested immigrant quarters were altogether different urban environments—dazzling, new, vital, prosperous. Almost all major cities acquired new or rebuilt downtowns that served as centers of commerce, both local and national. One distinctive feature of these downtowns was tall buildings, in some cities tall enough to be called skyscrapers. Such buildings were made possible by Elisha Graves Otis's invention of the elevator in the 1850s; by the 1880s, with the application of electric power, elevators became commonplace. At about the same time, a group of architects in Chicago developed a technique of using steel skeletons rather than huge, space-consuming supporting walls as building frames, permit-ting the construction of taller buildings. The perfection of plate glass allowed the new skyscrapers to have large windows, leading some buildings in **New York** and Chicago to be described as "towers of glass."

These skyscrapers were inhabited by large corporations, including the new corporate headquarters of manufacturing firms that, thanks to the telephone, were able to separate their commercial and manufacturing operations. The internal organization of these buildings was itself innovative and hierarchical: different tasks were performed on different floors, with higher levels of management generally segregated from clerks, secretaries, and other white-collar employees. Hundreds, sometimes thousands, of people entered these buildings daily.

The other defining institution of the new downtown was the department store. First appearing in the 1870s, department stores could be found in hundreds of American cities by 1900, and some of them blossomed into urban palaces of consumption. Marshall Field's in Chicago was a small city in itself, selling enormously varied goods, employing as many as 90,000 workers, and equipped with fifty-three elevators, a medical dispensary, a post office, and the largest private telephone switchboard in the world. As distinctive as their size was the emphasis on luxury and the celebration of the latest fruits of American capitalism. This was achieved, in part, through the use of new technologies of glass, light, and color. Glass doors, shelves, and counters filled the interior spaces, while mirrors enhanced the illusion of endless space and abundance. Electric lights and prismatic

Crowds enjoy the Christmas windows of Macy's department store in New York City, 1884.

light, which focused daylight into the stores, created the appearance of "refined Coney Islands," while new colors, manufactured from chemical dyes, dazzled the eyes of shoppers. Some stores enhanced the theatricality by hosting plays and concerts, and almost all built large, flood-lit display windows to give pedestrians an enticing glimpse of their wares. Department stores like Marshall Field's, Macy's and Bloomingdale's in New York and Filene's in Boston were the vibrant nodes of a newly emerging culture of consumption that would endure throughout the twentieth century.

The prosperous, bustling metropolitan centers were undergirded and made more attractive by improvements in their physical infrastructure. Electric street lighting, which provided much brighter light than gas and kerosene lamps, was installed in cities by the 1890s. Electric lighting also permitted businesses to work longer hours and entertainments, such as amusement parks, to remain open at night. In the 1890s, entrepreneur Samuel Insull developed two technologies that made possible the electrification of entire cities. One converted alternating current into direct current (and vice versa), which allowed electricity to be conveyed throughout a city at a reasonable cost. The second was a demand meter that could measure not only a customer's energy con-

> *"Electric street lighting was installed in cities by the 1890s, permitting businesses to work longer hours and entertainments, such as amusement parks, to remain open at night."*

sumption but also the timing and size of the customer's peak demand. Insull was thus able to apportion costs equitably while offering lower rates to those who used more kilowatts or who used them at off-peak hours. The result, early in the twentieth century, was the electrification of nearly all commercial buildings and a growing number of residences.

Between 1870 and 1900, most American cities also paved their streets. (Downtown streets were generally paved first, while politicians often jockeyed to get streets paved in their own neighborhoods.) Asphalt became the pavement of choice because it was inexpensive as well as quiet, durable, and clean; smooth asphalt streets made vehicular traffic more comfortable, while improving conditions for pedestrians, particularly in the rain. Underneath the streets, and on the outskirts of large cities, even more prodigious engineering feats were underway: the construction of thousands of miles of water and sewer lines. To provide water to the skyrocketing population of New York, for example, a new thirty-mile long aqueduct was built: when completed in 1893, it carried 300 million addition gallons of water to the city daily. Water was distributed over 660 miles of water lines, and removed

Electric streetlights and a trolley on State Street, Chicago, 1905.

through 464 miles of sewers. Water systems such as these made the flush toilet and the bathtub standard equipment in the middle-class home; even many poor city residents could enjoy bathroom facilities familiar only to the elite in the nations of Europe.

PUBLIC HEALTH AND THE CITY OF DISEASE

The new water and sewer systems were prompted in part by health concerns. Death rates rose from the early nineteenth century through the end of the Civil War, and they were particularly high for infants and young children. Many deaths resulted from infectious diseases that attacked densely populated cities: in addition to periodic epidemics of cholera, smallpox, and yellow fever, nineteenth-century Americans were vulnerable to pneumonia, influenza, whooping cough, scarlet fever, typhoid fever, dysentery, and—the biggest killer of all—tuberculosis. The medical profession at mid-century could do little to cure any of these diseases and accordingly was not held in very high repute; one prominent Boston physician even claimed that "more die of the practitioner than of the natural course of the disease."

In the first few decades after the Civil War, some progress was made by physicians, engineers, and others who constituted an emerging public health movement. Almost all of these men and women were "anticontagionists," or environmentalists, who were convinced that filth was the primary cause of disease and that the best way to improve health was to clean up the cities. With municipal officials, they worked to remove garbage, clear horse droppings from the streets, empty privies, inspect foods, and install water systems that would keep urban residents from having to drink water from contaminated wells and polluted rivers. They also promoted the construction of sewers and, somewhat later, tried to prevent sewage from being dumped in the rivers and lakes that also supplied drinking water.

Perhaps the most influential anticontagionist was Colonel George E. Waring Jr., a Civil War veteran, agricultural and drainage engineer, and well-known scientific farmer. In the late 1860s and 1870s, Waring became interested in sanitary engineering and embraced the theory that most communicable diseases were caused by "sewer gas," which could originate in "the exhalations of decomposing matters in dung-heaps, pig-sties, privy vaults, cellars, cesspools, drains and sewers" and was often noticeable in the odors that arose from defective water closets. A prolific and ardent popularizer, Waring wrote articles and books urging the universal adoption of the water closet, installed with proper plumbing to prevent sewer gas from leaking into homes. At the same time, he promoted the construction of new sewer systems, a cause that was given a dramatic boost in 1878 by a yellow fever epidemic in Memphis that killed 5,000 and infected thousands more. Appointed by President Hayes to a special commission, Waring argued that the epidemic could be traced to the city's filth, and he convinced the National Board of Health to build a new sewage system for Memphis, a development that gave a strong impetus to sewer construction everywhere. In the 1890s, he was appointed commissioner of street cleaning for New York City, where he launched an aggressive campaign that transformed New York's streets from among the dirtiest to among the cleanest in the world.

Meanwhile, scientific discoveries in Europe were giving rise to new theories of disease, grounded in the notion that specific diseases were caused and transmitted by specific germs or bacteria. The research of Louis Pasteur in France, as well as German discoveries of the bacteria that caused diphtheria and tuberculosis (the cause of roughly one out of every eight American deaths), in the 1880s constituted a serious challenge to the anticontagionists and launched a new era of scientific medicine, introduced to the United States in part by

A Board of Health official inspecting the fruit at a street-side stand, 1873.

physicians who had studied in Europe. The bacteriological revolution did not immediately gain acceptance, but it spawned new laboratories and research facilities designed to test the European theories and, if possible, to discover disease-causing organisms. By the early twentieth century, anticontagionist ideas were largely discredited: some forms of filth did contribute to the spread of disease, but the diseases themselves came not from vapors or sewer gas but from bacteria that could be identified, used to make exact diagnoses, and studied to develop cures and ways of preventing diseases from spreading.

This new, more scientific medicine did not immediately generate effective therapies, but it did have a significant impact on the practice of medicine and on popular conceptions of disease. Research scientists and physicians, few in number in the 1870s, became the elite of the profession. At the same time, cities created diagnostic laboratories to help physicians identify diseases and limit contagion. Armed with new tools, the medical profession grew and gained credibility; and thanks to new, strict sterilization procedures, hospitals became safer places for sick people. The number of hospitals in the nation grew from 178 in 1873 to more than 4,000 by 1909. In addition, the acceptance of bacteriological theories led to a middle-class embrace of public health measures: if diseases were caused by germs that could be carried by air, water, or insects, then the middle and upper classes, however good their plumbing, were vulnerable to the same maladies that afflicted the slums.

George Waring did not live to see his views discredited. In 1898, in the wake of the Spanish-American War, American army commanders in Cuba were alarmed by the prevalence of yellow fever and other diseases in Havana. Waring was appointed chairman of a commission that was sent to Havana to develop a plan for protecting the soldiers. Not surprisingly, Waring concluded that the elimination of yellow fever depended on the construction of a sewage system and paved roads as well as the introduction of water closets. Ironically, four days after Waring returned to the United States, he died of yellow fever. After his death, Havana was cleaned up, much as Waring had advocated, but yellow fever remained rampant. This led to the appointment of a new commission led by the more scientific- and laboratory-oriented Major Walter Reed. Reed's team discovered that yellow fever did not spring from filth but was transmitted by a particular kind of mosquito. When the breeding places of these mosquitos were destroyed, yellow fever was eradicated.

Women in Industrial Society

The economic and social changes that marked late nineteenth-century life opened up new opportunities for women, setting in motion trends that would become more visible in the twentieth century. The percentage of white women who graduated from high school, for example, rose from 15 percent in 1870 to 30 percent in 1900 to 60 percent in 1920; by the latter year, 25 percent of black women (compared with 5 percent in 1870) also graduated from high school. Throughout this period, a majority of all high school graduates were female. Post-secondary opportunities also expanded, thanks both to the founding of women's colleges such as Vassar, Smith, Wellesley, and Radcliffe, and to the creation of state universities (subsidized by the federal government's Morrill Act), many of which were coed; the number of post-secondary institutions open to women quintupled between 1867 and 1900. Although the percentage of women who attended college remained small, their numbers rose from 11,000 in 1870 to 85,000 in 1900.

A female teacher leads a science class at a Washington, D.C., public school, 1899.

Several factors contributed to this advance. Compulsory attendance laws in most states meant that more children went to school in the first place; boys were withdrawn from secondary school more often than girls so that they could help support their families; and an increasing number of white-collar jobs, particularly in teaching and clerical work, that require some education became open to women. There was, in addition, a growing belief that women would benefit from education, either to make them better wives and mothers or because education was intrinsically valuable and would open to women a new range of opportunities. Smith College's original motto was "Add to your virtue, knowledge." M. Cary Thomas, the president of Bryn Mawr, maintained that "the higher education of women" was "preparing the way for the coming economic independence of women."

The expansion of education was accompanied by a steady rise in female participation in the paid labor force. While relatively few married women worked outside their homes, the number of young, single women who did so increased significantly, particularly among immigrants and African Americans. Women also began to enter, and even dominate, new occupations. In 1870, 70 percent of all working women were domestic servants, but the changing economy created abundant opportunities for women in semiskilled factory labor and in lower-echelon white-collar positions. Indeed, by World War I, there were more female clerical workers than domestics, and women predominated in teaching and nursing, while also being widely employed in retail stores. Even black women, although generally relegated to menial jobs, made some gains, particularly in teaching.

What propelled women into the labor force? Households often needed multiple wage earners; employers welcomed women as low-cost employees; a declining marriage rate meant that there were more single women in the population; the educational backgrounds of middle-class women suited them well for jobs in rapidly expanding sectors; and college-educated women, in particular, sought work that was satisfying and fulfilling. Nonetheless, there was resistance to the idea of women working, particularly in middle-class families that upheld an ideal of domesticity and were not in dire need of the earnings that women could generate. Theodore Roosevelt gave voice to this view at the turn of the century, writing that "if the women do not recognize that the greatest thing for any woman is to be a good wife and mother, why, that nation has cause to be alarmed about its future." His widely shared vision helped to keep a lid on the employment of women, particularly married women. One remarkable sign of the tension between work and traditional gender roles was the fact that only a bare majority of female college graduates ever married.

The lives of most adult women, indeed, centered around their families. At the turn of the century, 90 percent of all women did marry, and child rearing, as well as household maintenance, remained a female domain. The number of children in each household, however, declined steadily, a trend that had begun in 1800; by 1900, the fertility rate among white women was about half what it had been a century earlier. Among urban white native-born families, the drop was even sharper, with many couples limiting themselves to two children.

Notably, this drop in fertility took place despite legal changes that limited access to abortion and birth-control devices. Until the mid–nineteenth century, first-trimester abortions were legal virtually everywhere and common among women of all classes. (Most women having abortions were married.) Then, pressed by a medical establishment seeking to professionalize itself and an upsurge of public prudishness, forty states passed anti-abortion laws between 1860 and 1890; by 1900, every state had banned abortion except in cases where the life of the mother was endangered. During this same period, an "anti-obscenity" campaign led by Anthony Comstock, a Connecticut dry-goods salesman devoted to combating sex in art, print, and private correspondence, succeeded in getting federal and state laws passed that drove birth-control information underground. The federal Comstock Law (1873), officially entitled "An Act for the Suppression of Trade in, and Circulation of Obscene Literature and Articles of Immoral Use," banned the importation, mailing, and interstate shipment of birth-control information and devices. The continuing drop in the fertility rate in the face of this legal onslaught suggests both that the laws were ineffective and that women were asserting their right to "voluntary motherhood" by limiting conjugal sex. In an interesting parallel, divorce rates also rose, albeit slowly, despite a tightening of divorce laws in most states.

Smaller families gave a different cast to the lives of women. Not only did they spend less time pregnant, but the diverse burdens of raising children were lightened. Housewives' workload, however, was not lessened by new household technologies. Improved cooking equipment and washing machines, as well as the small electrical appliances that appeared between 1900 and 1920, had the effect not of giving homemakers free time but of raising the standards of house-

"One remarkable sign of the tension between work and traditional gender roles was the fact that only a bare majority of female college graduates ever married."

keeping. Encouraged, in part, by a middle-class movement to ennoble homemaking by professionalizing it, women were expected to cook more diverse and nutritious meals, wash and iron clothes more frequently, keep houses tidier and cleaner, and even study child psychology.

Still, the industrial era offered new social freedoms and a new range of activities to women. Young women who worked outside the home escaped parental supervision each day, and all working women enjoyed opportunities to socialize and enjoy commercial amusements, at lunch or after work. Roughly a fifth of all working women, moreover, were economically independent, living in apartments and forming their own social networks and communities.

By the 1890s, many women were also embracing a new ideal, that of the "New Woman." Generally from middle- or upper-class origins, better educated than most, and often single, the New Woman fused the ideals of Victorian womanhood with social activism and civic participation. These women constituted an important constituency for the women's clubs that began to appear after the Civil War and proliferated rapidly after 1890. The clubs included literary societies, mothers' clubs, alumnae associations, and reform groups; they reflected a desire for self-improvement, camaraderie, and social change. Although the club movement was dominated by middle-class white women, black women also formed clubs, often aiming not only to improve their own lives but to help uplift their race as well.

Perhaps the most important, and certainly the largest, women's association of the era was the Women's Christian Temperance Union, founded in Chicago in 1873. Emerging from an Ohio-based movement that attempted to shut down saloons and control the alcoholic behavior of men, the WCTU, under the leadership of Frances Willard (president from 1879 to 1898), broadened its focus to attack the many evils for which men seemed to be responsible, including domestic violence, prostitution, the exploitation of labor, the abuse of prisoners, and political corruption. By 1890, the WCTU had 160,000 members nationwide and in Chicago alone was running two day nurseries, two Sunday schools, an industrial school, a free medical facility, and a shelter for 4,000 homeless or poor women. The WCTU played a key role in generating the public pressure that ultimately led to Prohi-

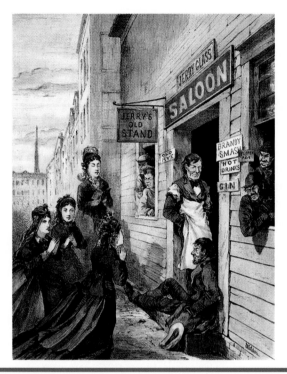

"The Temperance Crusade—Who Will Win?," a cartoon depicting women temperance advocates, 1874.

bition; as important, perhaps, it drew thousands of women into the association movement, often leading them into active support of campaigns for women's suffrage and other social reforms.

The World Viewed

The second half of the nineteenth century was a period of almost unparalleled ferment in intellectual and cultural life. The triumph of industrial capitalism challenged prevailing ideas about the social and economic order, about fairnesss and justice, about the direction of history. At the same time, modern science offered provocative new understandings of the natural world. Most centrally, perhaps, the evolutionary theories of Charles Darwin, as well as their application by others to social issues, instigated wide-ranging debates that resounded through the domains of religion, social thought, law, and culture. The ways in which many, if not most, peo-

ple understood the world in 1900 differed significantly from the understandings that had prevailed in 1860.

EDUCATION

The growth of industrial society generated an enormous expansion of educational institutions. Free, public primary education was already well established in most states by the end of the Civil War, but it was only after 1870 that most states adopted laws making school attendance mandatory for children between the ages of eight and fourteen. It was also during these years that the public high school became a central institution in American life. The number of public high schools rose from 500 in 1870 to more than 10,000 in 1910. In 1870, 57 percent of all children aged five to seventeen attended public day schools; fifty years later, the figure was 80 percent. This national trend was not matched in the still-rural South, where schooling was not compulsory until the twentieth century and where educational opportunities remained limited, especially for African Americans. Well into the twentieth century, most black children did not even attend public elementary schools.

The same years witnessed the proliferation of kindergartens, which were often privately or philanthropically funded. The goal of kindergartens, as articulated by Elizabeth Palmer Peabody, their foremost advocate, was to allow the young child "to take his place in the company of equals, to learn his place in their companionship, and still later to learn wider social relations and their involved duties." Implicitly, the kindergarten movement, as well as the movement for broadened public schooling in general, sought to have public institutions perform tasks that had once been entrusted to families. Schools were also envisioned, in the words of John Dewey, the great educational philosopher of the period, as a "means for bringing people and their ideas and beliefs together, in such ways as will lessen friction and instability."

Both public schools and kindergartens were an expression of diverse, and sometimes contradictory, values. On the one hand, they stemmed from a democratic impulse to provide universal education and enhance the opportunities of all children. Yet they also reflected industry's need for a disciplined labor force with appropriate skills, socialized into American and capitalist norms. This latter impulse became visible in the late nineteenth and early twentieth centuries as public schools developed vocational programs, offering different curricula to students from different class and ethnic back-

Beginning the day with exercises set to music in a New York City public school, 1881.

grounds. In practice, as urban public schools opened their doors to more children, especially immigrant and working-class children, the schools served multiple functions and became contested terrains. Students were disciplined, taught to respect the norms of industry, educated to meet the needs of an industrial economy, and channeled into different types of occupations; at the same time, they were empowered by their literacy, given skills with which they could criticize prevailing values, and offered a chance to compete for the better opportunities the economy had to offer.

This was also the period when the American university acquired its modern form. Although the percentage of young adults acquiring college educations did not increase dramatically, the *number* did: undergraduate enrollment jumped from 50,000 in 1870 to 350,000 in 1910. Despite the skeptical views of some business leaders, a college degree became an important credential. In addition, a new, more secular generation of leaders in higher education was determined to build universities that would be on a par with the great institutions of Europe. Financed both by private benefactors, such as Ezra Cornell, Johns Hopkins, John D. Rockefeller, and Leland Stanford, and by federal and state funds (which turned the Universities of Michigan and Wisconsin, among others, into major academic institutions), universities rapidly became centers not only of higher education but of research. They developed specialized graduate

> *"Despite the skeptical views of some business leaders, a college degree became an important credential."*

programs in the professions and Ph.D. programs modeled on those in German universities, while placing new emphasis on the study of science and social science. In so doing, they transformed the professoriate into a profession, mandated both to teach and to conduct research within specialized disciplines.

One upshot of these changes was the growth of an educated and literate population that could comprehend, and participate in, the shifting intellectual currents of the day. The distinction between "highbrow" and "lowbrow" culture was never very marked in the nineteenth century, and the post–Civil War expansion of education meant that debates carried on among intellectuals were increasingly accessible to millions of citizens. It was no accident that serious works of social thought, such as Edward Bellamy's novel *Looking Backward* (1888) and Henry George's *Progress and Poverty* (1879), a lengthy treatise on the sources of economic inequality, sold hundreds of thousands of copies and were devoured by a large reading public.

SCIENCE AND SOCIETY

No single event had a more profound impact on intellectual life in this period than the publication of Charles Darwin's *Origin of Species* in 1859. Darwin's pathbreaking work, based on decades of research, offered a new, secular explanation of the diversity and character of life on earth. Casting aside the notion that a supreme being had simultaneously created the thousands of species of plants and animals on the planet, Darwin maintained that all living organisms were engaged in a competitive struggle for survival within their particular environments. Those that were most "fit"—the hardiest, most adaptable, or cleverest—triumphed and lived to reproduce; over the long run, this process of "natural selection" led to the evolution of hardier and more fit species.

Darwin's theory of evolution posed an obvious challenge to religious accounts of the creation and to long-standing conceptions of the natural order as static and eternal. As important, it became a model, for scientists and other intellectuals, of an empirical approach to human knowledge, of painstaking, detailed research that could reveal the inner workings of nature and society. Indeed, as evidence accumulated to support Darwin's theory, and as advances in physics, chemistry, and bacteriology became increasingly well known, the undertaking of science itself acquired enhanced importance and prestige.

Darwinism, as developed and applied by Darwin's English contemporary Herbert Spencer, also offered a means of understanding, and justifying, the social changes wrought by industrial capitalism. Applying the principles of biological evolution to the study of society suggested that men, too, were engaged in a competitive struggle, in which the fittest prospered. One implication of this "social Darwinist," or Spencerian, idea was that nations and societies would become stronger only if unfettered competition were allowed to continue: governments, for example, should not interfere with the workings of a laissez-faire, capitalist economy. A second implication was that progress was necessarily slow, that society could improve only through a lengthy evolutionary process.

The foremost American advocate of social Darwinism was William Graham Sumner. Born into a working-class family of English immigrants, Sumner attended public schools in Hartford, Connecticut, graduated with distinction from Yale, and studied to enter the ministry in Geneva, Göttingen (Germany), and Oxford. After serving as an Episcopal priest for several years, but increasingly drawn to secular, social issues, he accepted a newly created chair in political and social science at Yale in 1872. A prolific writer, Sumner spent the next three decades developing and promoting the Spencerian and social Darwinist ideas that first captured his attention in the 1870s. Denouncing government intervention, socialism, protectionism, and social reform, Sumner defended economic inequality by arguing that "millionaires are a product of natural selection," and that the poor, being less fit, deserved their fate. "Let every man be sober, industrious, prudent and wise," he wrote, "and poverty will be abolished in a few generations." Staunchly opposed to any state efforts to regulate the economy, he insisted that the only appropriate role of government was to defend "the property of men and the honor of women." Any other interference with the competitive struggle, including efforts to aid the poor, would only derail the process of natural selection and impede progress. "The law of the survival of the fittest was not made by man and cannot be abrogated by man. We can only, by interfering with it, produce the survival of the unfittest." Not surprisingly, Sumner's views were widely applauded by business leaders and political conservatives.

This conservative strain of social Darwinism set the terms of debate in political and social thought, but it did not go unchallenged. Among the most important dissenters was Frank Lester Ward, the son of an Illinois mechanic and a Civil War veteran. In 1865, Ward obtained a position with the Treasury Department in Washington and acquired a college education and several advanced degrees while working. Strongly interested in science and an ardent supporter of evolutionary theory, he was appointed assistant geologist in the U.S. Geological Survey in 1881, becoming geologist in 1882 and chief paleontologist in 1892.

Yet Ward's interests transcended natural science, and he was most influential as a critic of social Darwinists and as a

This 1882 cartoon, entitled "A Sun of the Nineteenth Century," celebrates Darwin and the significance of his theory of evolution.

621

leader in the new field of sociology. In *Dynamic Sociology* (1883), Ward disputed the notion that the evolution of human societies followed or ought to follow the patterns of the natural world. Humans, unlike other organisms, had minds capable of transforming and controlling the world they inhabited. Informed with reason and guided by scientific investigation, mankind could best progress through invention and planning rather than unfettered and wasteful competition. Laissez-faire economics, he argued, was not mandated by nature, and in fact stifled competition by permitting monopolies to arise. The regulation of economic affairs by democratic governments would serve the interests of society, while widespread educational opportunities would permit even the least talented citizens to improve themselves. "If nature progresses through the destruction of the weak, man progresses through the protection of the weak." Ward, in effect, accepted an evolutionary framework but argued that industrial society would best evolve through the application of human intelligence to economic and social problems.

Both Sumner and Ward were attempting to study society scientifically (an endeavor that gave rise to the field of sociology) in order to address issues raised by industrialization and the political unrest that accompanied it. They were not alone in this quest: many prominent intellectuals were attempting to address the same issues, and some of them attracted a considerable following. Edward Bellamy, writing in the 1880s and 1890s, believed that the abolition of private property was the key to restoring harmony and equality to the United States, and his ideas were so popular that hundreds of Bellamy, or Nationalist, Clubs were founded throughout the nation. Henry George struck an equally resonant note by advocating a "single tax" on land, which, he believed, would reduce inequality and prevent the formation of deep social cleavages. George's views were popular enough that he ran well in the New York mayoral election of 1886, besting Theodore Roosevelt. At the same time, economists such as Richard T. Ely, John R. Commons, and Thorstein Veblen broke with the classical notion that there were immutable laws governing economic behavior and promoted the detailed study of economic institutions.

Scientists also became involved in debates regarding gender and racial inequality. Darwin's argument that the abilities of men and women had diverged in evolutionary history (and that women had smaller brains) was deployed to oppose the

> *"According to Frank Lester Ward, 'If nature progresses through the destruction of the weak, man progresses through the protection of the weak.'"*

advanced education of women, as were also ideas drawn from thermodynamics suggesting that if women spent their energies acquiring education, they would have less energy to carry out their reproductive functions. Somewhat similarly, it was argued that African Americans were less evolved than northern European whites, that they had lesser brain capacities, and that their social condition was the result of their biological inferiority. Given the growing prestige of scientific discourse, it became necessary for opponents of such views to conduct their own research and to present scientific arguments favoring equality.

RELIGION

Although the era was an increasingly secular one, religion remained a potent force in intellectual and social life. The number of churchgoing Protestants, particularly Baptists and Methodists, increased significantly, while immigration brought millions of Catholics and hundreds of thousands of Jews to American cities. By 1900, there were nearly 150,000 Protestant churches in the nation, as well as more than 10,000 Catholic churches. The United States remained a religious and overwhelmingly Protestant nation, and clergymen continued to be among the most influential of Americans.

Organized religion had to confront two distinctive challenges in the late nineteenth century. The first came from science in general and Darwinism in particular: natural, or scientific, explanations of phenomena that had traditionally been understood in biblical terms. Among Protestants, the initial reaction to Darwin and to the growing eminence of science was hostile. Within a few decades, however, there emerged a liberal wing of Protestantism that tried to accommodate these new ideas. These "modernists" sought to bridge the gap between old faith and new science, between static and evolutionary views, even to reinterpret traditional biblical accounts in light of modern knowledge. New York's Henry Ward Beecher, the most influential Protestant cleric of the era, described himself as a "cordial, Christian evolutionist." Although Protestant conservatives continued to resist Darwinism as well as any tinkering with literal interpretations of the Bible, the more liberal, optimistic modernists captured the mainstream by the early twentieth century.

American Jews also felt a need to reconcile traditional beliefs with modern knowledge. Squarely facing this challenge, a convention of Reform Judaism (a tendency that had emerged among German Jews in the United States) declared in 1885 that "the modern discoveries of scientific researches in the domains of nature and history are not antagonistic to the doctrines of Judaism, the Bible reflecting the primitive ideas of its own age." The impact of science was also visible in the most important new sect to emerge during this period: the Church of Christ, Scientist, founded by Mary Baker Eddy in 1879. The Christian Scientists were devoted to the power of prayer, particularly for the sick. Eschewing modern medicine as well as tobacco, alcohol, and caffeine, they believed that illness could be cured through prayer and meditation, which brought one closer to God. Notably, however, they invoked the prestige of "science" in the very name of their denomination and regarded their methods of treating illness as scientific experiments that could be duplicated as proof of the existence of God's laws.

> *"The United States remained a religious and overwhelmingly Protestant nation, and clergymen continued to be among the most influential of Americans."*

The second challenge to religion came from the vast inequalities spawned by industrial capitalism. While the middle and upper classes were thriving, the poor were growing more numerous, powerless, and desperate, and they were expressing their discontent in periodic strikes and riots. How should churches, which had long viewed themselves as the protectors of the weak, respond to these conditions? Among Protestants, two different reactions took shape. One, referred to as the Gospel of Wealth, embraced laissez-faire capitalism and reassured the well-to-do that their prosperity was not only earned but a sign of divine approval. In a famous sermon, delivered an astonishing 6,000 times, Russell Conwell, a Baptist minister in Philadelphia, declared that everyone had "within their reach 'acres of diamonds,' opportunities to get largely wealthy." "I say that you ought to get rich, and it is your duty to get rich," he declared. "Because to make money honestly is to preach the gospel." Henry

Mary Baker Eddy, founder of the Church of Christ, Scientist, in 1879.

Ward Beecher, demonstrating that intellectual modernists could also be social conservatives, expressed little sympathy for striking workers in 1877. He declared that if a man did not smoke or drink, he could easily support a wife and six children on a dollar a day. "Is not a dollar a day enough to buy bread with? Water costs nothing; and a man who cannot live on bread alone is not fit to live." The notion that no one in America suffered from poverty "unless it be his sin" was welcomed by the prosperous.

In opposition to such views, other ministers organized what became known as the Social Gospel movement: they believed that the true task of Christianity was to rescue the poor, renew the social and economic order, and help bring about the Kingdom of God on earth. The two most well-known advocates of the Social Gospel were Washington Gladden and Walter Rauschenbusch, both of whom endorsed workers' rights and pressed Christians to rectify social injustices. Christianity, they argued, ought to be concerned not only with the behavior of individuals but with institutions that harmed men and women: salvation was not merely an individual matter but also a question of constituting a just society.

Catholics and Jews had to confront these issues as well. The 1885 "Pittsburgh Platform" of Reform Judaism thus declared that it was in the spirit of Mosaic law to "regulate the relation between rich and poor," and that "we deem it our duty to participate in the great task of modern times, to solve on the basis of justice and righteousness the problems presented by the contrasts and evils of the present organization of society." Within the relatively small Jewish community, there were few dissenters to such views. Among Catholics, however, a division emerged not unlike the split among Protestants. Although the Catholic Church devoted considerable resources to charity, most church leaders remained convinced that sin and vice, including intemperance, were personal deficiencies rather than social problems, that poverty was the will of God, and that the working poor would be saved by the church, not by legislation or political action. Such attitudes began to shift after Pope Leo XIII issued a famous encyclical, *Rerum novarum* (1891), in which he criticized the greed of capitalists, endorsed workers' right to unionize, and urged governments to care for the poor. But, except in scattered parishes led by progressive priests, change was slow in coming.

LAW, PHILOSOPHY, ART

The triumph of industry and the paradigm of evolutionary theory also had an impact on other realms of thought and culture. One was jurisprudence, where jurist Oliver Wendell Holmes spearheaded an attack on the long-standing notion that the fundamentals of law were unchanging and constituted immutable principles that were to be logically and mechanically interpreted by judges. One of the great legal minds of the era, Holmes in 1881 published *The Common Law,* in which he argued that all laws, in fact, developed in response to the "felt necessities of the time," including the needs of particular interest groups and changing historical conditions. "The life of the law has not been logic," he argued, "it has been experience." The decisions of judges, moreover, should be understood not as the results of impartial logic but rather as reflections of the values and beliefs of judges themselves. Holmes, who joined the Supreme Court in 1902 after twenty years as a justice in Massachusetts, maintained that law did and should evolve, just as economies and societies did. If the law were static and lagged behind social change, it would impede the course of evolutionary progress. Holmes's views did not spark an immediate change in judicial practices, but they became increasingly influential in the course of the twentieth century.

Meanwhile, philosophers William James and John Dewey, among others, challenged the long-accepted philosophical conviction that truth was fixed, abstract, and eternal, that the validity of ideas could be judged by their consistency with fundamental principles. The pragmatists, as Dewey, James, and their followers came to be called, argued that truth resided not in the abstract logic of ideas but in their practical consequences. Influenced both by the natural sciences and by evolutionary theory, they maintained that as the world changed, truths changed, that something was true not eternally but in particular circumstances; the value of an idea thus could be gauged through its application. For Dewey in particular, the appropriate method of truth-seeking was experimental, and the task of philosophers and other intellectuals was to help find positive solutions to real-world, contemporary problems.

Both painting and literature also felt the impact of social change, veering toward realistic depictions of contemporary themes. One of the foremost painters of the era was Thomas Eakins, who studied in Europe in the 1860s and returned to Philadelphia to paint and teach. His paintings fused a meticulous attention to detail with a selection of contemporary subjects. Some of his most well-known, including *The Gross Clinic* (1875), depicted surgical operations, and *The Swimming Hole* (1883) displayed his mastery of the human form while also offering a raw depiction of male nakedness. As a portraitist, he was also unsparing in his attention to realistic detail. Similarly, Winslow Homer, who began his career as a magazine illustrator during the Civil War, traveled through much of the United States and the Caribbean, painting lifelike scenes of farm life, of sailors and fishermen at work, and, with more romantic elements, seascapes.

Novelists in the 1880s and 1890s focused their attention on such social issues as corruption in business and politics, the miseries of life in the slums, and the mounting conflicts between labor and capital. The most influential realist was William Dean Howells, a fiction writer as well as editor of the *Atlantic Monthly* and then of *Harper's*. Both as a critic and as a novelist, Howells encouraged the realistic depiction of urban, industrial society. A realist, wrote Howells, "cannot look upon human life and declare this thing and that thing unworthy of notice, any more than a scientist can declare a fact of the material world beneath the dignity of his inquiry."

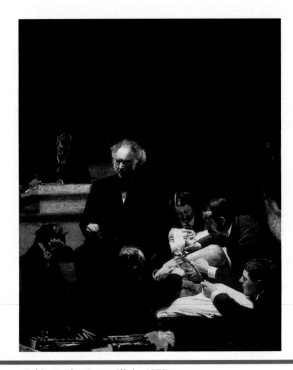

Thomas Eakins's *The Gross Clinic,* 1875.

In *The Rise of Silas Lapham* (1885) and *A Hazard of New Fortunes* (1890), Howells created finely grained descriptions of material life among different classes and the interior dynamics of families, as well as characterizations of contemporary politics.

Ironically, however, the movement toward realism in literature and art was accompanied by a trend that historian Lawrence Levine has called "the emergence of cultural hierarchy in America." During the first half or two-thirds of the nineteenth century, there were no sharp boundaries separating "high culture" from works of mass popular appeal. The plays of Shakespeare were performed in cities and towns throughout the nation, by actors both professional and amateur, to mixed and sometimes rowdy audiences of social elites, middle-class families, and workers. Performances of opera and symphonic music were attended by men and women from all walks of life, seated—in different sections depending on the cost of tickets—in the same concert halls. Museums, containing eclectic collections of paintings and sculpture arrayed alongside mastodons and stuffed animals, attracted men, women, and children seeking diverse types of amusement and edification.

All of this changed during the late nineteenth century. Prompted by the desire of the upper classes to claim "culture" as their own, by the professionalization of actors and musicians, and by a middle-class impulse to weed out audiences whose behavior seemed distracting, the traditionally great works of theater, music, and art became reserved to the middle and upper classes. Music and drama were performed by professionals (thereby increasing the cost of tickets); programs did not mix the classics with popular works; audiences were expected to be silent and reverential; aesthetic elevation was distinguished from mere entertainment. At the same time, museums converted themselves into temples of high culture, repositories of "great works" that were to be appreciated by the educated in silence and solemnity. In 1897, the Metropolitan Museum of Art in New York denied admission, on a weekday afternoon, to a plumber wearing overalls. The museum's director defended its action, saying that "we do

Chronology	
1873	Women's Christian Temperance Union founded in Chicago.
1875	Civil Rights Bill passed.
1881	Booker T. Washington founds the Tuskegee Institute in Alabama.
1883	Brooklyn Bridge built.
1887	Free mail delivery starts in communities of more than 10,000 people.
	First electric trolley cars built.
1896	Supreme Court legally sanctions segregation in *Plessy v. Ferguson*.
1897	Boston opens subway line.
1909	W. E. B. Du Bois founds the National Association for the Advancement of Colored People.

not want, nor will we permit a person who has been digging in a filthy sewer or working among grease and oil to come in here, and by offensive odors . . . make the surroundings uncomfortable for others." The segmentation of industrial society made its mark even in the halls of culture.

Suggested Reading

John Bodnar, *The Transplanted: A History of Immigrants in Urban America* (1985)

John Higham, *Strangers in the Land: Patterns of American Nativism, 1860–1925* (1955)

Lawrence Levine, *Highbrow/Lowbrow: The Emergence of Cultural Hierarchy in America* (1988)

Roy Rosenzweig and Elizabeth Blackmar, *The Park and the People: A History of Central Park* (1992)

Ronald Takaki, *Strangers from a Different Shore: A History of Asian Americans* (1989)

Richard White, *"It's Your Misfortune and None of My Own": A New History of the American West* (1991)

C. Vann Woodward, *The Strange Career of Jim Crow* (1955)

POLITICS AND THE STATE:

1876-1900

A parade in Chicago for the Democratic ticket of Cleveland and Stevenson, 1893.

Focus
QUESTIONS

■ What were the characteristics of city politics in this period?

■ In what ways were state governments the "laboratories of democracy"?

■ What were the major insurgent political movements of the time?

■ What were the major political issues at the national level?

■ How did the courts respond to the tensions of the new industrial society?

■ How did the political landscape change after the 1896 elections?

Reflecting on the years between 1870 and the mid-1890s, historian and writer Henry Adams, the son and grandson of American presidents, wrote that "no period so thoroughly ordinary had been known in American politics since Christopher Columbus first disturbed the balance of American society." In many respects, Adams's judgment was correct. Particularly when viewed against the dramatic backdrop of the Civil War and the first years of Reconstruction, national politics had something of a humdrum flavor during the period that Mark Twain and Charles Dudley Warner dubbed "the Gilded Age." As students of American history have discovered year in and year out, few people remember exactly who the presidents were, or when exactly they served, between 1876 and 1900.

Yet far more was going on beneath the surface—and outside of Washington—than Adams suggested. Political life during these years was riddled with problems, contradictions, and conflict. The economic and social changes of the era posed grave challenges to public authorities: how should governments, at all levels, respond to the nationalization of the economy, the emergence of powerful private corporations, the rapid growth of an urban working class, the plight of farmers newly dependent on international markets and monopolized railways? Should authorities intervene to soften the impact of industrialization and urbanization? If so, should such intervention come from municipalities, from the states, or from the federal government? Answers were not easy to come by. The terrain was uncharted, and many competing interests were at stake.

Popular engagement in these problems, and in politics itself, was immense. Turnout at elections was high, elections were closely contested, new political parties sprouted up, and issues-based movements flourished. In cities, towns, and rural counties, men and women joined together to create new organizations, to learn from one another, and sometimes to take to the streets with their demands. Rallies and mass protests were commonplace, strikes periodically paralyzed parts of the country, and the depression of the 1890s spawned the first national march on the nation's capital, by unemployed workers seeking relief.

Still, as Henry Adams suggested, this was not an era of great political reform or statesmanship. Mainstream political life was characterized more by the evasion than the solution of problems, by corruption rather than idealism, by electoral battles contested more for patronage than for principles. The national political leadership, including the six men who occupied the presidency between 1877 and 1900, often seemed uninspired. The capacities of the state, inherited from a less industrial era and a less national economy, were limited, and the two major political parties, hampered by the courts, lacked the will or ability to transform those capacities. As a result, politics did seem rather ordinary, and the national government seemed oddly distant from the turbulence bubbling in the cities and countryside.

Rule and Misrule in the Cities

In 1890, Andrew White, the president of Cornell University, declared that "the city governments of the United States are the worst in Christendom—the most expensive, the most inefficient, and the most corrupt." White's view was widely shared by his educated contemporaries, many of whom denounced urban governments as corrupt and wasteful models of misrule run by unprincipled political machines and milked by greedy private interests, such as utility companies. Yet the record of urban governments was more complex than these critics suggested. Cities were confronted with immense challenges: as their populations skyrocketed, the demand for municipal services mounted, and the need to invest in expensive **infrastructure**—such as water and transportation systems—became irresistible. City governments met at least some of these challenges successfully; the often-infamous political machines, moreover, responded to the real needs of a significant portion of the urban population.

Between 1850 and 1900, almost all major cities, and many medium-sized ones, did develop political machines, yet they were rarely as monolithic or powerful as the label implied. ("Machine" was a term used by critics; participants referred simply to "the organization.") The pivotal figure in machine politics was the local ward leader in working-class, particularly immigrant, neighborhoods. The ward leader sometimes served as an alderman or a city council member and was often the proprietor of a local business, such as a saloon. He helped to procure city services for his neighborhood, jobs for faithful organization members, permits for street vendors, and access to the city government. In return, he expected his constituents to actively support the organization's candidates on election day. Citywide machines were generally unstable coalitions of ward leaders only periodically "ruled" by a single boss. The machines obtained funds for their operations by legally and illegally cutting deals with private businesses that stood to profit from contracts and franchises granted by the city. Most of these organizations were Democratic, although Republican machines flourished in Philadelphia, Pittsburgh, and Cincinnati.

BOSS TWEED

Surely the most notorious machine boss of the era was William Marcy Tweed, who controlled the **Tammany Hall organization** in New York in the 1860s and early 1870s. Tweed, unlike many bosses, did not come from an impoverished background and had been a successful, skilled carpenter early in his career. He then turned his attention to politics, joining the Tammany organization, which had for decades been the executive arm of the Democratic Party in New York City. Tweed was elected first to the city council and then to Congress; by the late 1860s, he had gained control of Tammany, as well as much of the city government and portions of the state legislature. The Tweed ring was extraordinarily successful at winning elections, in part through fraudulent practices such as hiring "repeaters" to vote in multiple polling places and bribing election officials to alter tally sheets. Tweed also paid $600,000 in bribes to get the legislature to change New York's charter so that his ring could control appointments and the city's finances.

Tweed and his colleagues looted the public treasury, not just for the organization but for their own personal gain. Those who sought contracts from the city were obliged to kick funds back to the ring and were encouraged to pad their bills so that they could kick back even more. The epitome of these practices was reached in the construction of a new county courthouse that eventually cost the city more than $12 million, including $41,190 for brooms and other "articles," $400,000 for safes, and $7,500 for thermometers. Tweed became a wealthy man, owning a Fifth Avenue mansion, an estate in Connecticut, a yacht, and a well-stocked stable of horses; he also distributed large sums of money to the poor and to the Catholic Church.

"The Tammany Tiger Loose: What Are You Going to Do About It?" On the eve of New York city and state elections in 1871, Thomas Nast published this anti-Tammany cartoon, showing Boss Tweed looking on as the Tammany tiger claws the Republic and the rule of law.

Tweed's downfall came in the 1870s when bankers and the city's more respectable leaders, alarmed at the overt corruption and the rapidly growing indebtedness of the city, mounted an investigation of the ring. This resulted in the indictment of numerous officials, including the mayor and eventually Tweed himself. Aided by the testimony of a disaffected sheriff, Tweed was convicted of 104 counts of bribery and fraud. The victim of his own excess and hubris, he died in prison in 1878.

Yet corrupt as Tweed and his cronies were, they did accomplish important things for the city. Circumventing the traditional slow mechanisms of urban administration, the Tweed regime succeeded in getting streets built and extended, in granting franchises to transit and utility companies, in promoting the physical expansion of New York, and in furthering the development of Central Park, one of the most impressive aesthetic achievements of urban America. The Tammany organization was also revered by poor and immigrant New Yorkers who knew that it was Tammany that delivered street cleaning, parks, and bathhouses to their neighborhoods and who turned to the organization for meals, cash, and fuel when they were in dire straits. The organization's popularity permitted Tammany to return to power after Tweed's fall, although his mildly chastened successors reduced the flagrancy of their graft.

DIVIDED RULE

Tweed's ostentatious lining of his own pockets, as well as the centralization of the New York machine under Tammany's control, was exceptional, but the basic dynamics of machine politics were played out in cities across the country. Responding both to the increasing size and complexity of cities and to the needs of working-class immigrants and their children, machine politicians—who were among the nation's first full-time professional politicians—acted as brokers among different constituencies and as representatives of the city's poorer residents. That they felt entitled to profit from their services was an expression of the harsher side of machine politics. "I see my opportunity, and I take it," acknowledged Tammany's George Washington Plunkitt, as he carefully distinguished between "honest graft" (making money from contract letting or from insider knowledge of public construction plans) and "dishonest graft" (such as payoffs from vice establishments). Yet there was always a more positive side to the machines. As Martin Lomasney of Boston's

South End put it, "There's got to be in every ward somebody that any bloke can come to—no matter what he's done—and get help. Help, you understand, none of your law and justice, but help." In Lomasney's own domain, in the early twentieth century, he and his machine were the only significant source of aid for the unemployed.

Rarely did machines govern by themselves: they generally shared power with other political factions, constituencies, and officials. City councils, mayors, and independent commissions often contended with one another for power while possessing legal authority over different domains. Although the machines commonly wielded great influence in city councils, the councils themselves were generally losing power, thanks to legal changes promoted by state governments. Meanwhile, mayors were gaining legal authority, including the ability to appoint department heads and veto city council measures. Big-city mayors, moreover, tended not to emerge from the world of ethnic, ward politics: they were usually successful businessmen, bankers, or lawyers, from old-stock, respectable Protestant families, wealthy enough to pay for their own electoral campaigns. Mayors held most of the reins of city government, furthering the interests of the downtown business community while negotiating deals and compromises with the ward-based machines.

There were also other centers of power, some elected, some appointed. Auditors and controllers were chosen to keep a close eye on financial matters; school officials, who controlled jobs and construction projects, were often elected on their own; independent commissions governed parks, water authorities, and health. Running a city increasingly demanded the employment of professionals and bureaucrats who, particularly after the passage of municipal civil-service laws, remained in office for long periods and wielded substantial influence. Thanks to new technologies—in construction, transit, lighting, water, sewage, and health—experts, such as civil engineers, also became important figures in city administrations.

These governments, moreover, were not autonomous: by the second half of the nineteenth century, it was clearly established in law that cities were subservient to the states. State governments could revise city charters, and they frequently passed legislation dictating the policies of cities. Most often, these state laws were passed in cooperation with the cities, but that was not always the case: sometimes for partisan reasons and sometimes because of conflicts between urban and rural interests, state governments enacted legislation opposed by the city itself. Such legislative meddling ended up spawning a movement for the

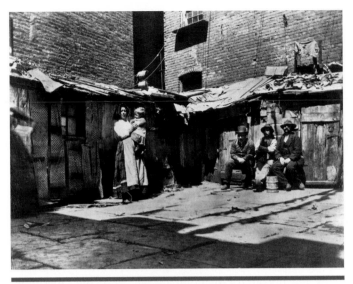

With housing conditions largely unregulated, the urban poor often lived in deplorable conditions. This photo shows Italian immigrant families and their shacks in New York.

"home rule" of cities that was successful in a number of states, including Missouri and California, where cities acquired the right to draft their own charters. This enhanced autonomy was, however, accompanied by a trend that cut in the opposite direction: the creation of statewide commissions—dealing with water, sewage, health, and education—that imposed their own standards on city policies.

In the end, the record of late nineteenth-century city governments was mixed. They succeeded in enlarging municipal services and in creating physical infrastructures that endured for decades: by international standards, American cities had impressively efficient transport, water, sewage, educational, utility, and public health systems. City governments also succeeded, by the end of the century, in streamlining their finances and reducing their debts—which were enormous in the 1870s and 1880s. At the same time, cities were less successful in regulating private property and meeting the material needs of the poor. Housing conditions remained largely unregulated and were deplorable for many urban residents, while public welfare agencies, such as the overseers of the poor, lacked the resources to help the most needy urban residents. In fact, for reasons both fiscal and ideological, the task of caring for the poor was increasingly transferred to underfunded private charities that were less than sympathetic to the plight of men and women unable to support themselves.

Statehouses and Legislatures

State governments in the late nineteenth century were sometimes called the "laboratories of democracy." Decades before the federal government was pressed into action, governors and state legislators were faced with the economic and social problems of the industrial era. The nerve center of each state government was its legislature, comprised largely of part-time, amateur politicians who met for abbreviated sessions once or twice each year; legislators commonly had to broker conflicts between rural and urban constituents while also coping, for the first time in the nation's history, with professional lobbyists hired by corporations. In addition to making state laws, legislators possessed the critical power of electing U.S. senators who shaped national policies and controlled federal patronage.

One core issue faced by state governments was the regulation of large corporations in the financial and transportation sectors of the economy. Responding to popular pressure from farmers, small businessmen, and consumers who felt they were being gouged by "monopolies," states passed laws and created agencies to regulate railroads, banks, utilities, insurance companies, and grain-storage facilities; although such laws were often watered down through corporate influence, they were nonetheless controversial, pathbreaking interventions in economic affairs. State governments in the Midwest and the West also aided farmers by sponsoring irrigation projects and founding agricultural experiment stations, which began to be subsidized by the federal government in 1887. In addition, they passed laws to make public education compulsory, to promote public health regulations, and even to offer a modicum of protection to industrial workers by limiting the hours of women and children and compelling employers to pay wages in cash. Some state governments also dealt with the issue of alcohol consumption by adopting prohibition, while others enacted "local option" legislation.

Both the newness and the limits of state responses to industrialization were visible in the experience of Massachusetts with the problem of unemployment. Massachusetts, an innovator in social and economic policy, founded the nation's first Bureau of Labor Statistics in 1869; its second chief was Carroll D. Wright, who in the 1880s went on to become the first director of the U.S. Bureau of Labor Statistics. Under Wright's supervision, the Massachusetts bureau, in 1878, attempted a systematic count of the unemployed for the first time in the nation's history. This initial effort was followed in

631

1885 by an exhaustive census survey of unemployment, the publication of which marked the first appearance in print of the word "unemployment." That survey was repeated in the 1890s and accompanied by a massive investigation of the "problem of the unemployed."

These studies of what was perhaps the most fundamental problem of an industrial, capitalist society were pioneering: in addition to recognizing the role of the state in addressing social ills, the surveys established that unemployment was a chronic, pervasive problem for workers. Wright and his successors discovered that in any year, 20 percent of all industrial workers experienced some joblessness; during depressions, the figure soared to 35 or 40 percent. Yet despite these startling statistics, the state government did nothing to help. Although jobless workers demonstrated for months during the depression of the 1890s, the governor and the legislature—reluctant to expend state funds and suspecting that many of the unemployed were "idlers" who refused to work—took no action. The unemployed were left to fend for themselves or, if they arrived in the most dire straits, to obtain minuscule amounts of aid from municipal overseers of the poor and private charities. To make matters worse, the state toughened its vagrancy, or "tramp," laws, exposing jobless workers to the prospect of being arrested if they traveled from place to place searching for work.

State governments were also political battlegrounds, and many states, particularly in the Northeast, witnessed the emergence of strong party organizations led by a single powerful figure—who sometimes was also the speaker of the state assembly or the senior U.S. senator. The Republicans dominated state politics in New England and part of the Midwest, while the Democrats, despite remarkably durable opposition, controlled most of the South. Elsewhere—and even, at times, in these regional strongholds—elections were closely contested, with shifting majorities and victory margins so thin that considerable influence was wielded by third parties. High voter turnout was common, and for many citizens party allegiances were strongly felt, shaped by class and regional interests as well as by culture and religion. Those belonging to pietistic religions (such as Methodism, which emphasized a personal faith in God and personal behavior that would bring salvation) often voted Republican, while members of more liturgical faiths (such as Catholicism, with its emphasis on doctrine and avoidance of emotionalism) were more likely to support the Democrats.

The new departures in state activism were less substantial in the South than elsewhere. Although southern states did create public health boards and education commissions, they were underfunded and unable to enforce statewide standards; similarly, state regulation of railroads tended to be weak. The thrust of state government in the region was largely in the direction of fiscal restraint: chastened by the indebtedness incurred during Reconstruction, states adopted low and regressive tax rates while sharply restricting public expenditures.

Political life in the southern states was also distinctive, thanks to the legacy of Reconstruction and to the persistence of race as a preeminent issue. Although the Democratic Redeemers who had captured the state governments in the 1870s remained in power, their reign was troubled. In most states, a majority of blacks continued to vote, and to vote Republican, through the 1880s, and they were often joined by independents and upcountry or mountain whites; at the same time, the Democratic Party itself split into factions, competing as much for office and patronage as for principle. Consequently, elections were fiercely contested, and Republicans, independents, and African Americans won local offices and seats in state legislatures. Elections also tended to be corrupt: all parties purchased votes outright, while blacks were sometimes paid not to vote at all.

In some states, most notably Mississippi, Democrats resorted to violence and intimidation to keep blacks from the polls. Beginning in the 1880s, they shifted their attention to legal techniques of circumventing the Fifteenth Amendment and disfranchising blacks. The first such effort was the written, secret ballot, which kept many illiterate men from voting. After 1890, the techniques became more varied: under the leadership of wealthy Democrats from black-belt counties (those fertile plantation regions that held large black populations), every state government in the South adopted laws and constitutional amendments designed to prevent blacks, and sometimes poor whites, from voting. Among the techniques of disfranchisement were literacy tests, poll taxes, cumulative poll taxes (requiring voters to pay a tax for each year since they had last voted), and primary elections restricted to whites. Such measures, made easier by the federal government's decision in 1893 to abandon all remaining supervision of southern elections, successfully disfranchised the vast majority of the black population: in Louisiana, for example, the number of registered black voters dropped from 130,334 in 1896 to 1,342 in 1904. By removing African Americans from the polity, the Democrats secured their control and placed the region under single-party rule.

The Politics of Insurgency

One of the distinctive features of political life during this period was the breadth and strength of insurgent, grassroots movements. Both in the cities and in the countryside, men and women responded to the stresses of economic and social change by forming new organizations to remedy problems collectively and to promote a more just and democratic society. Millions of people held rallies and marches, went on strike, built alternative economic institutions, ran candidates for political office, pursued far-reaching reforms, and developed ideas that were disturbing, even threatening, to those who had traditionally wielded power. The politics of insurgency reached its peak during the 1890s, shifting the terms of mainstream politics while achieving a mixed record of successes and failures that set the stage for political life in the twentieth century.

LABOR UNITING

Industrial workers first began organizing themselves before the Civil War. They created reform organizations, unions, and workingmen's political parties, all of which tended to be locally based and short-lived. In the decades that followed the war, activist workers sought to build durable movements that would defend the interests of working people in an increasingly national economy. The organizations they built were both economic and political: **unions** to give workers more strength in bargaining with employers; political parties to pressure the state and promote far-reaching changes; and hybrids that operated on both economic and political fronts. These organizations, as well as periodic outbursts of forceful protests, reflected workers' growing sense of exploitation and injustice. Indeed, so deep was their discontent that one of the central issues debated by working-class groups was whether their goal should be the abolition of the "wage system" or the pursuit of concrete gains within the structures of capitalism—or both.

National Unions. After the Civil War, it was clear to activists that local unions had little leverage in a national economy. By

1870, there were thirty-two national trade unions, the strongest of which were the iron molders, typographers, and shoemakers. In 1866, delegates from many of these unions, led by William Sylvis, the president of the Iron Molders' Union, met in Baltimore to found the National Labor Union. The NLU, which included reformers as well as unionists, sought to establish the eight-hour workday (and forty-eight-hour workweek), to reserve public lands for settlers rather than speculators, to create a federal Department of Labor, and to revamp the currency. The NLU also advocated the development of consumers' and producers' cooperatives, so that workers could control their own means of production and avoid being exploited by "middlemen." Shoe workers, for example, banded together to sell the shoes they made directly to retailers (rather than wholesalers) and to buy clothing and food directly from producers. Although the NLU succeeded in getting eight-hour laws passed in seven states, most were ineffective, and the cooperatives floundered because of their inability to obtain adequate credit. The NLU collapsed in the mid-1870s, as did the young national trade unions: jobless members were unable to pay dues, union treasuries shriveled,

Terence Powderly (center), introduced at the Knights of Labor's annual convention in 1886 by machinist Frank J. Farrell (left).

the competition for jobs was fierce, and employers went on the offensive, driving wages down and compelling workers to choose between union membership and their jobs.

The return of prosperity revived the labor movement between 1878 and 1886. The organization leading the revival was the Noble and Holy Order of the Knights of Labor. Founded as a small secret organization in Philadelphia in 1869, the Knights went public in the late 1870s and welcomed as members not only skilled workers but "all producers," including unskilled workers, women, blacks (usually in segregated locals), and some members of the middle class. Only bankers, lawyers, liquor dealers, speculators, and stockbrokers were excluded. Headed by Terence V. Powderly, a former machinist, popular orator, and mayor of Scranton, Pennsylvania, the Knights advocated "a radical change in the existing industrial system." "The recent alarming development and aggression of aggregated wealth," declared its 1878 preamble, "which . . . will invariably lead to the pauperization and hopeless degradation of the toiling masses, render it imperative, if we desire to enjoy the blessings of life, that a check should be placed upon its power and upon unjust accumulation, and a system adopted which will secure to the laborer the fruits of his toil." Echoing some ideas of the NLU, the Knights sought an eight-hour day, the abolition of child and convict labor, equal pay for men and women who performed the same work, the development of cooperatives, and the establishment of bureaus of labor statistics; later, they demanded public ownership of the communication, transportation, and banking industries.

To achieve their goals, the Knights undertook massive educational campaigns and political action. They lobbied at statehouses and in Washington and eventually ran their own candidates for public (usually local) office. At the same time, many "assemblies" of the Knights also acted as unions, bargaining with employers over issues such as wages and hours as well as conducting strikes—despite the organization's official position that striking was to be used only as a last resort. The message of the Knights, as well as the diversity of their activities, struck a resonant chord: workers flocked to join the organization, especially after the Knights won a major strike against robber baron Jay Gould's southwestern rail empire. By 1886, there were local assemblies in nearly every city and midsized town: with 750,000 members, the Knights were the largest labor organization of the nineteenth century. "Never in our history," declared one editorialist, "has there been such a spectacle as the march of the Order of the Knights of Labor . . . it is an organization in whose hands now rest the destinies of the Republic."

The Knights then stalled and fizzled. Absorbing vast numbers of new recruits stretched the organizational capacities of the union, and internal disputes emerged, particularly between those eager to pursue immediate economic gains and others, such as Powderly, who stressed a long-run vision of reform. Meanwhile, employers, including Jay Gould, counterattacked, defeating the Knights in one conflict after another. Most decisively, the Knights were undercut by competition from the resurgent national craft unions, whose leaders concluded that the economic interests of their members would best be served by national organizations consisting only of skilled workers belonging to the same trade. Long-term political goals—which even to many craft union leaders meant replacing capitalism with socialism—

This 1883 cartoon from the humor magazine *Puck* depicts the unequal contest between labor and monopoly, with Jay Gould and others cheering in the stands.

could then be pursued separately, through political parties. Immediate issues affecting labor as a whole, including those that required lobbying, could be addressed through an umbrella organization of trade unions, such as the one created in 1886, the American Federation of Labor.

As workers drifted away from the Knights, many moved toward the craft unions affiliated with the A.F. of L. Comprised almost entirely of skilled white male workers, the national trade unions were designed to maximize the bargaining power of their members and to weather business depressions: it was no accident that nearly all the leaders were men who had personally experienced the collapse of organized labor in the 1870s. Members had to pay substantial dues; they received sickness, funeral, and sometimes jobless benefits; semiskilled and unskilled workers with little market power were excluded; and union officers fought vigorously to maximize and protect the jobs available to their members. These unions generally did not include black workers or women. By 1892, forty trade unions, with roughly half a million members, had joined the A.F. of L.; the strongest were those in the building trades and the "brotherhoods" of skilled railway workers.

Although the national trade unions and the A.F. of L. were less inclusive and visionary than the Knights, neither their members nor their leaders abandoned politics or the desire for significant economic and social change. Many, if not most, adhered to a working-class political culture that resisted the dominant capitalist ethos. A hefty proportion of union members, including key leaders such as P. J. McGuire, president of the carpenters' union, were socialists. The eight-hour movement, which became something of a crusade in the 1880s and 1890s, was fueled by the conviction that a shorter workday would eliminate unemployment and thus enhance the power of workers and yield deep social change. Even the A.F. of L. itself, which later became more conservative, debated proposals for government ownership of all major industries.

The national trade unions, and the A.F. of L., headed by former cigar maker Samuel Gompers, proved their organizational mettle during the depression of the 1890s, by surviving: almost all unions made it through the depression, leaving the A.F. of L. with more than 400,000 affiliated members at the end of the business downturn in 1897. If the depression had deepened the conviction of many workers that the wage system had to be abolished, it had also underscored the need for durable organizations that could protect workers against employers and economic adversity. The trade unions of the A.F. of L. grew rapidly with the return of prosperity: union

Samuel Gompers, head of the A.F. of L.

membership nearly quintupled between 1897 and 1904, transforming craft unions of skilled workers into a durable feature of the institutional landscape.

Politics and Strikes. The insurgency of the working class was also expressed in electoral politics, particularly in the formation and growth of new parties. In the late 1870s, workers played an important role in the Greenback Labor Party, which stressed expansion of the currency and the credit supply to restore power to workers and farmers. In 1878, the party (then calling itself the National Party) polled nearly a million votes nationwide, electing fifteen congressmen and scores of city and state officials. In the mid-1880s, candidates representing the Knights of Labor, as well as local workingmen's parties, ran for office (and sometimes won) on platforms advocating a graduated income tax, government ownership of railroads and the telegraph, currency reform, and an end to child labor. In New York in 1886, the United Labor Party was created to support the mayoral candidacy of author Henry George, who called for public ownership of all means of transportation and communication and for taxing any increases in the value of land—which George believed would discourage land speculation, limit monopolies, make it possible for workers to buy farms, and create a labor shortage that would raise wages and reduce inequality. George finished an impressive second in the mayoral election, well ahead of the third-place candidate, future president Theodore Roosevelt. Radical workers also created the Marxist Workingmen's Party of the United States, the Socialist Labor Party, and an anarchist movement that embraced "equal rights for all without distinction of sex or race" as well as direct workplace action to overthrow capitalism.

Working-class discontents further bubbled to the surface in militant strikes and demonstrations. Nearly every town with a population greater than 20,000 in the Northeast and Midwest witnessed a strike in the late 1880s or 1890s. Some were "sympathy" strikes in which workers walked off their jobs to express solidarity with other striking workers. Others erupted into major national events. In 1877, the announcement by the Baltimore and Ohio Railroad that it was, for the third time, cutting wages by 10 percent sparked a walkout in Martinsburg, West Virginia, that quickly spread to cities and towns throughout the North. Over the course of a month, tens of thousands of railway workers went on strike, dozens were killed by state

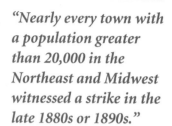

> *"Nearly every town with a population greater than 20,000 in the Northeast and Midwest witnessed a strike in the late 1880s or 1890s."*

militias and federal troops, and railroad property worth millions of dollars was destroyed by enraged strikers and mobs who had long felt oppressed by the powerful rail corporations. The Great Railroad Strike of 1877 raised the specter of insurrection in the minds of many middle-class Americans, prompting state governments to create national guard units to contain labor conflict.

In May 1886, these fears were fanned again when workers across the nation launched a general strike for the eight-hour day, marching in huge parades in Milwaukee, New York, San Francisco, and Chicago, among other cities. The protests were peaceful everywhere but in Chicago. There, on May 3, when eight-hour strikers joined an ongoing strike of iron molders, police fired into the crowd, killing and wounding several workers. The following day, a local anarchist group called for a protest meeting in Haymarket Square. The meeting was thinly attended and quiet until the police, anticipating violence, attempted to break up the crowd. As they charged forward, a bomb was thrown that killed policemen as well as protesters.

Convinced that a violent insurrection was in the offing, Chicago authorities arrested eight radicals for murder; after a blatantly rigged trial that offered little or no evidence, four were convicted and hanged, while another committed suicide in jail. In 1894, the courageous governor of Illinois, John Peter Altgeld, acknowledged that the trial had been a travesty of justice and pardoned the three surviving defendants. To this day, no one is sure whether the bomb was thrown by an anarchist, a police provocateur, or someone else.

No single event captured more ingredients of the conflict between labor and capital than the Pullman Strike of 1894. The strike began among workers who manufactured Pullman cars, the comfortable sitting and sleeping quarters used by middle-class travelers on long rail trips. The company's employees all lived in the much celebrated, model company town of Pullman, just

The walkout at Martinsburg, West Virginia, that sparked the Great Railroad Strike of 1877.

The Haymarket riot in Chicago, May 4, 1886.

At that point, the federal government stepped in on the side of the railroads. Attorney General Richard Olney, a former railway lawyer, hired 3,200 special deputies (paid for by the railroads) to keep the trains running, ostensibly to guarantee the flow of mail. At the same time, federal judges began to issue injunctions to prohibit the ARU and its members from continuing their boycott of trains carrying Pullman cars. One judge, William Howard Taft, later U.S. president and chief justice of the Supreme Court, wrote that things would not improve "until they have had much bloodletting. . . . They have killed only six of the mob as yet. This is hardly enough to make an impression." Over the objection of Governor Altgeld, President Cleveland authorized the use of federal troops to suppress the strike: their arrival in Chicago sparked violence that left dozens of strikers dead. When Debs and other leaders of the ARU refused to obey an injunction targeted at them, they were arrested, convicted of contempt of court, and jailed. This governmental onslaught, coupled with the fierce resistance of the railroads themselves, led to the defeat of the strike and the destruction of the ARU.

south of Chicago. The strike, fueled by resentment of the Pullman company's paternalistic efforts to control workers' lives, was precipitated by a wage reduction unaccompanied by any reduction of the rent that workers had to pay in company-owned housing. After the strike was launched, the Pullman employees asked for support from the fledgling American Railway Union, a bold new organization founded and led by Eugene V. Debs. Debs, who had been secretary-treasurer of the Brotherhood of Locomotive Firemen, had concluded that it would be in the interest of all railway employees to replace the "brotherhoods" of skilled workers with a single industrial union that would include everyone who worked for the railroads, skilled and unskilled. Workers by the thousands had signed up with the ARU, but in 1894 it was still a young and fragile organization.

Fearful that the ARU could not survive a major confrontation with the railroads, Debs opposed active support for the Pullman strikers, but the union nonetheless voted to instruct its members to refuse to work on all trains carrying Pullman cars until the company had agreed to bargain with its employees. Debs, bowing to a majority vote, declared that this act of sympathy and solidarity was "the hope of civilization and the supreme glory of mankind." The railroad corporations then began firing employees who refused to handle Pullman cars, which quickly led to strikes and boycotts that paralyzed train traffic throughout the Midwest.

The Pullman strike had a far-reaching legacy. Debs's legal challenge to his arrest, spearheaded by attorney Clarence

National Guardsmen firing into the crowds in Chicago during the Pullman Strike, July 1894.

Eugene V. Debs, founder and leader of the American Railway Union. He was also a founder and leader of the Socialist Party and the Industrial Workers of the World.

Darrow, produced the Supreme Court ruling (*In re Debs*) upholding the use of blanket injunctions to prevent workers and unions from engaging in "conspiracies in restraint of trade" that might harm the interests of employers. At the same time, Debs was turned into a popular hero: when he left prison after a six-month term, he was met in Chicago by an admiring crowd of 100,000. Debs's own thinking about labor was also changed by the Pullman strike: he concluded that advancing working-class interests required broad-gauged political action rather than simply union organizing. As a result, he first joined the People's Party and several years later helped to organize the Socialist Party of America, which he led for decades.

WOMEN'S SUFFRAGE

The movement for **women's suffrage**, begun before the Civil War, traveled a halting path during and after Reconstruction. Many suffragists, who had been abolitionists before the war, believed that the notion that voting was a "right" belonging to all citizens—an idea that gained increasing acceptance in the mid–nineteenth century—would not only end racial discrimination but would also open the polls to women. Elizabeth Cady Stanton, one of the pioneering leaders of the movement, declared that black suffrage would open the "constitutional door" and that women intended to "avail ourselves of the strong arm and blue uniform of the black soldier to walk in by his side."

But Reconstruction turned out to be a bitter disappointment for Stanton and her colleagues: rather than walking in the constitutional door, women found themselves more formally barred than they ever had been. The Fourteenth Amendment penalized states that deprived any adult males of the right to vote, specifying a link between gender and suffrage for the first time. The Fifteenth Amendment, offering federal protection of the right to vote, made no reference to women: despite the efforts of suffragists to include a gender provision, it declared that people could not be denied the right to vote only "on account of race, color, or previous condition of servitude." The campaign to ratify the Fifteenth Amendment consequently split the suffrage movement and severed the close ties between suffragists and advocates of black voting rights. In addition, the Supreme Court ruled in *Minor v. Happersett* (1875) that the right to vote was not inherent in citizenship; the case had originated in Virginia Minor's attempt to vote on the grounds that she, as a citizen, was already enfranchised.

Disagreements over the Fifteenth Amendment led to the creation of two rival suffrage organizations. The more conservative was the American Woman Suffrage Association, founded by Lucy Stone and her husband, Henry Blackwell. The AWSA supported the Fifteenth Amendment, accepted male members, and focused exclusively on suffrage, which it attempted to obtain state by state. In contrast, the New York–based National Woman Suffrage Association, led by Stanton and Susan B. Anthony, was an entirely female organization that sought to obtain suffrage at the federal level, through a constitutional amendment; it also pursued such goals as equal pay for women and divorce law reform. Neither association had much success between 1870 and 1890,

A meeting of the National Woman Suffrage Association in Chicago in 1880, with Elizabeth Cady Stanton speaking in the center of the platform.

An 1869 Currier and Ives lithograph suggesting that women's suffrage would disrupt family life.

when the two reunited to form the National American Woman Suffrage Association. A constitutional amendment was introduced in Congress on several occasions, but it never received the approval of both houses, and most state referenda were rejected. By the turn of the century, only four thinly populated western states (Wyoming, Colorado, Utah, and Idaho) had granted full suffrage to women. In some others, women did obtain more limited suffrage, such as the right to vote in school board elections.

Resistance to women's suffrage came from two sources. One was the belief that suffrage would be disruptive to family life and harmful to women themselves. Antisuffragists argued that enfranchisement would turn spouses against one another, corrupt women by bringing them into an impure world of politics, force them into contact with saloons and barbershops (which were common polling places), and even lead pregnant women to lose their babies and nursing mothers to lose their milk. The other source was a declining faith in democracy. After the Civil War, in both the North and South, sizable segments of the middle and upper classes were backing away from the notion that voting was a "right": distrusting the ability of masses of people to make sound decisions, they resisted any expansion of the franchise. As a late nineteenth-century chronicler of woman suffrage wrote, "the opposition today seems not so much against women as against any more voters at all."

Partly in response to such ideas and partly because of the growing prominence of a new generation of more socially conservative suffragists, the arguments for enfranchising women tended to shift late in the century. Less emphasis was placed on the equality of men and women and on voting as a right, while more was given to the propositions that women had special qualities that would help clean up politics, and that politically engaged women would become better wives and mothers. More problematically, leaders of the movement argued that enfranchising women would help offset the menace represented by poor, immigrant, and black male voters. In the 1890s, for example, Stanton endorsed a literacy test as a qualification for voting, declaring that "the best interests of the nation demand that we outweigh this incoming pauperism, ignorance, and degradation, with the wealth, education, and refinement of the women of the republic." Belle Kearney, a prominent southern suffragist, claimed that "the enfranchisement of women would insure immediate and durable white supremacy, honestly attained."

The suffrage movement won few electoral victories and lacked a mass following during the late nineteenth century, but it did have an impact. In some states, pressure from the movement led to legal reforms, permitting married women to own property, keep their earnings, make contracts, and enjoy equal custody of their children. Nearly everywhere it

Women voting in Cheyenne, Wyoming, 1888.

639

compelled state legislators and constitutional conventions to think hard about the meaning and limits of democracy. The movement also energized large numbers of women who became active in public affairs and acquired the political skills that would eventually contribute to their enfranchisement.

FARMERS AND THEIR DISCONTENTS

In the South and West, men and women who worked on farms were also drawn down the path of political insurgency. They were angry about the high, and often discriminatory, rates railroads charged to transport their goods; they felt exploited by the middlemen who controlled grain elevators at key points in the transport system; they felt powerless in the face of fluctuating, and generally declining, agricultural prices in the world market; and they felt victimized by high credit costs and deflation, which increased the burden of their chronic and seasonal indebtedness. In the South, the lien system gave its own special twist to the dilemma of farmers.

In "The Grange Awakening the Sleepers," a Granger alerts the public to the menace of the railroad monopoly, 1873.

Among the first collective responses to these conditions was the National Grange of the Patrons of Husbandry. Founded in 1867, the Grange became a large network of local associations, devoted to social and educational activities as well as to the development of cooperatives, owned collectively by groups of farmers, that could demand higher prices for farm products and buy supplies at volume discounts. In the 1870s, Grangers elected sympathetic legislators across the South and West, and they came to wield substantial political influence in Illinois, Iowa, Minnesota, and Wisconsin. In response, several midwestern states passed "Granger laws" regulating railroads and grain-storage elevators, as well as creating agricultural colleges and departments of agriculture. At its peak, the Grange had roughly 1.5 million members, almost all of whom were white. Black farmers created their own organizations, most notably the Agricultural Wheel in the lower Mississippi Valley. The Grange's influence began to wane in the late 1870s, particularly as cooperatives failed in one state after another.

The Grange was succeeded by the more overtly political Farmers' Alliances. The Southern Farmers' Alliance was founded in Texas in 1877 and acquired a significant membership in the 1880s when it started sending "traveling lecturers" out through the countryside to talk about the problems afflicting farmers. Soon a Midwestern Alliance also formed, as did a Colored Alliance of black farmers. By 1889, the three groups claimed a membership of more than 4 million.

The Alliances maintained that railroads, bankers, and the entire credit system bore responsibility for the economic straits of farmers, and, like the Grange, they advocated cooperatives, both as a solution to their problems and as a democratic form of economic organization. But the Alliances also found it difficult to build durable cooperatives in a world already dominated by large corporations that controlled transportation and marketing networks and that were hostile to the cooperative ideal. As a result, they turned quickly to politics, forming a coalition of "producers" with the Knights of Labor, and calling for the free and unlimited coinage of silver (see p. 644), the direct election of U.S. senators, government loans to farmers, and government control of communication and transportation. They also put forward the novel idea, originally proposed by Texas leader Charles W. Macune, of creating government-sponsored "subtreasuries," or warehouses where farmers could store their nonperishable produce. The government would lend money (in effect, issuing new money) to farmers for up to 80 percent of the value of their stored products. The subtreasuries would thus provide farmers with easy, low-interest credit and permit them to keep their crops off the market until they chose to sell them; in so doing, the subtreasury system would create a flexible currency responsive to the actual output of the agricultural economy.

In 1890, the Alliances launched a remarkably successful political campaign, backing major-party candidates who agreed to support their platform. Their candidates won control of nearly a dozen state legislatures, captured numerous congressional seats, and became governors of several states. Most of their victories were in the South. Their electoral success was accompanied by the flourishing of a culture in which masses of people collectively sought significant social change and embraced a vision of society as less hierarchical, less dominated by large corporations, more democratic, more experimental, and more humane. Hopeful as Alliance members were in the wake of the elections, they were nonetheless disappointed by the failure of candidates they supported to translate their platform into law. Consequently, they decided to abandon the strategy of supporting sympathetic major-party candidates and to create their own national party, the People's Party.

"The Democratic Party represented more of the nation's economic periphery, standing for states' rights, limited federal powers, and lower taxes."

The Nation State

While insurgent political movements were gathering steam, national electoral politics proceeded according to its own quadrennial rhythms, with both the major parties and the government in Washington seeming oddly distant from the discontents percolating around the nation. Although four of the five men to occupy the White House between 1876 and the mid-1890s were Republicans, electoral majorities were thin, and the Democratic candidates actually won more votes in four of the five elections. Control of Congress changed hands several times, and there were often Democratic majorities in the House while the Republicans controlled the Senate. Between 1875 and 1897, each party held both the presidency and a congressional majority for only a single two-year interval. Not surprisingly, the number of laws the federal government enacted was relatively modest.

PARTIES AND ISSUES

The two major parties had different regional bases, somewhat different class constituencies, and offered different visions to voters. Republican strength lay in the core of the industrial economy, the Northeast and the Midwest. The Republicans not only embraced industrial capitalism, they advocated an active national state that could foster economic development. "One of the highest duties of Government," noted one Republican senator, "is the adoption of such economic policy as may encourage and develop every industry to which the soil and climate of the country are adapted." In the eyes of the Democrats, the Republican Party was the agent of "special interests," of business, particularly big business. Although that characterization tended to gloss over the close ties between many Democrats and powerful business interests, the most stable pillars of Democratic strength were white farmers in the South and parts of the West, as well as immigrant, particularly Catholic, workers in northern cities. The Democratic Party represented more of the nation's economic periphery, standing for states' rights, limited federal powers, and lower taxes.

The Tariff. The issue that most clearly distinguished the two parties, particularly in the 1880s and early 1890s, was the tariff—a tax on goods imported into the country. Republicans supported protective tariffs, and Democrats opposed them or, at least, favored keeping them at modest levels. Tariffs were not particularly high in the1870s, but the following decade Republicans sponsored a series of bills raising tariffs. By limiting competition from foreign producers, they believed, tariffs would allow domestic industries to prosper, leading to increased profits, more jobs, and higher wages. The Democrats regarded such arguments as fallacious, masking the greed of corporate interests. Tariffs increased the prices of protected goods such as sugar, iron, and textiles by as much as 50–100 percent. In addition, higher prices for manufactured goods increased the cost of agricultural production—which then made it harder for farmers to compete successfully in world markets. The Democrats also maintained, with some evidence, that workers gained little from tariff protection, that the main beneficiaries were businessmen who were pocketing large profits because of the government's interference with free trade.

Tariff policy was hotly debated because it pitted the interests of some individuals and regions against those of others. The tariff was also a powerfully resonant issue because in the late nineteenth century, unlike the late twentieth, it was one of three key instruments of government intervention in the economy. (The other two were the money supply and, later, the regulation of business practices.) Tariffs had a broad impact on both producers and consumers, and they provided a high proportion (often more than 50 percent) of the federal government's total revenues.

Indeed, in the 1880s, increased tariffs swelled the government's coffers, generating a budget surplus that Republicans had to devise some way of spending. One way was expanding pension benefits for Civil War veterans and their families. This pension system, which had begun as a modest program to aid disabled soldiers, soon became a vast federal program, an odd hybrid of patronage and social welfare: some years, more than one-quarter of the federal budget went to the pension system, and by 1893 nearly a million former soldiers and their dependents were receiving pensions, consuming 42 percent of all federal revenues. Not surprisingly, the Civil War pension program provoked regional and partisan discontent. The Democrats opposed its enlargement both because of their opposition to the tariff and because the program aided relatively few of their constituents: until the end of the century, when Spanish-American War veterans were included, the pensions were paid entirely to northerners, and, among northerners, few immigrants could qualify.

Civil Service Reform. A far less partisan issue was civil service reform, which stood at the front of the national agenda in the late 1870s and early 1880s. It was put there by northeastern, liberal Republicans, many of them professionals and intellectuals, who were (at first derisively) called "Mugwumps" (after the Algonquian word for "chief"). Appalled by corruption and by the use of the expanding federal payroll as a source of party patronage, the Mugwumps led a vigorous campaign to make merit, rather than party affiliation, the basis of all federal employment. In so doing, they were implicitly advocating a shift in the financing of political parties, since it was customary for all holders of patronage jobs to give 2 percent of their salaries to the party that had appointed them. Among the reasons for embracing civil service reform was the extraordinary amount of time and energy that politicians had to expend on the distribution of patronage: President Benjamin Harrison estimated that during his first eighteen months in office, he spent four to six hours a day responding to requests for jobs.

By the early 1880s, both Democrats and Republicans were endorsing reform, and in 1883 Congress passed the Pendleton Act, creating a Civil Service Commission to supervise competitive examinations for about 10 percent of all federal jobs. The legislation also allowed the president to add positions to the civil service list and made it illegal for parties to require contributions from federal officeholders. One consequence of this last provision was to make both parties more dependent on contributions from corporations.

The goal of civil service reform, beyond cleansing corruption and patronage from the federal government, was also to build a more efficient, modern administrative state, as required by a complex industrial society. The United States, unlike European nations, lacked a well-organized, central bureaucracy that could carry out the affairs of government and meet the needs of citizens and business for government services. In the industrial world of the late nineteenth century, there was a pressing need for efficient postal and customs services, for national standards, for agencies that could help private interests. A bureaucracy based on merit, in which offices did not change hands with each election, seemed more likely to provide such services than a chaotically shifting patronage network.

The Money Question. One of the dominant issues of nineteenth-century politics was "the money question": deciding what was legal currency in the United States. The issue sounds perplexing to those of us living in the early twenty-first century, but to contemporaries it loomed as one of the most urgent matters of public policy. Between the Civil War and the end of the nineteenth century, the money question was always at or near the center of the political stage.

The issue had deep roots, stretching back to a decision made by the nation's first secretary of the treasury, Alexander Hamilton, who declared both gold and silver to be "legal tender" and thus payable for all public and private debts: their relative values were fixed at a ratio of 15:1, meaning that fifteen ounces of silver could be exchanged for one ounce of gold. However, the relative price of gold on the international market was slightly higher than 15:1, with the result that gold was hoarded and only silver circulated. In 1834, the ratio was changed to 16:1, which had the opposite effect, later intensified by the California gold rush: silver was hoarded, and only gold remained in circulation. The only other currency in use before the Civil War was bank notes, issued by individual banks (not by the government) and backed by gold or silver specie. Since there were thousands of different notes in circulation, many of them counterfeit, bank notes tended to be accepted only at a discount, particularly outside the city in which they originated.

The federal government's need to finance the Civil War further complicated the situation. In 1862 and 1863, the government issued $450 million in paper money, roughly doubling the amount of currency in circulation. Although these "greenbacks" were declared to be legal tender, doubts about their long-term value led them to depreciate in comparison with gold: in 1864, for example, one could buy nearly three times as many goods with one gold dollar as with a greenback dollar. Of equal importance, issuing such a large quantity of money led to a sharp inflation of prices.

All this set the stage for the postbellum conflicts over the currency, grounded in economic self-interest, political beliefs, and passionately held, if often mistaken, ideas about money. The first matter to be addressed was what the government should do about the greenbacks. There were two opposing camps. On one side were those who favored removing the greenbacks from circulation and the "resumption" of an entirely bimetallic or gold currency. Such a step, they believed, would replace inflation with deflation and benefit creditors, who found themselves being repaid in inflated, or depreciated, dollars. Resumption was advocated by creditors, including bankers, and by intellectuals, businessmen, Protestant clergymen, and political leaders who were convinced that a sound currency had to be based on bullion, or specie. Many adherents of "hard money" were Republicans, as well as financial conservatives who opposed any governmental action that might undermine the natural laws of the free market, which was efficiently concentrating power in the hands of large, private financial institutions.

Arrayed in the opposing camp were "soft money" advocates who opposed resumption and wanted to keep the greenbacks in circulation. Among them were debtor businessmen as well as many chronically indebted farmers who did not want to repay debts in deflated, or more valuable, dollars. Soft money (not only greenbacks but any system that

"The federal government in the nineteenth century had few tools with which it could influence economic affairs, and its constitutional capacity to control the money supply was probably the most potent weapon in its small arsenal."

freed the money supply from the need to be backed by gold) was also advocated by entrepreneurs who wanted easier access to credit and by workers who believed that it would raise their incomes and stimulate the economy. Those who favored soft money—many of whom were Democrats—rejected the notion that currency had to be bullion-based and argued that it was the proper role of government to regulate the money supply. Many also believed that a gold standard would concentrate economic power in the hands of the rich, breeding corruption, inequality, and exploitation, and that it was the duty of government to ensure equal opportunities for all citizens by preventing the formation of monopolies.

Arcane as these debates may sound, there was a great deal at stake. The federal government in the nineteenth century had few tools with which it could influence economic affairs, and its constitutional capacity to control the money supply was probably the most potent weapon in its small arsenal. How the government resolved the money question could affect the distribution of wealth, power, and incomes throughout the nation. To contemporaries, it loomed as a critical litmus test: would the state be responsive to the needs and beliefs of the "people" or to the demands and convictions of northeastern and midwestern bankers and capitalists?

In the aftermath of the Civil War, the federal government tried in a rather zigzaggy fashion to find compromises between the hard- and soft-money positions. Between 1866 and 1868, the government withdrew more than $40 million in greenbacks from circulation, but then stopped because of political opposition and fear of an economic contraction. After the panic of 1873, the government briefly reversed course and reissued $26 million worth of greenbacks. Then in 1875, Congress passed the Resumption Act, which declared that the government would begin redeeming greenbacks for gold in January 1879: the act was an attempt to return to a bullion-backed currency without causing a sharp drop in the money supply and prices. Its backers hoped that the knowledge that greenbacks could be redeemed would raise their value to par (the same value as gold) and thus eliminate any incentive for people to actually trade in their greenbacks; this was a critical gamble because, in fact, the treasury had less gold in reserve than the total outstanding issue of greenbacks. But the strat-

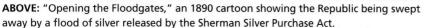

ABOVE: "Opening the Floodgates," an 1890 cartoon showing the Republic being swept away by a flood of silver released by the Sherman Silver Purchase Act.

RIGHT: "The Silver Sun of Prosperity," an 1890 cartoon hailing the Sherman Act as the key to prosperity.

egy worked, thanks in part to favorable economic conditions. Few greenbacks were ever redeemed, and the nation returned to a gold standard without seriously deflating the dollar.

Meanwhile, silver was inching toward center stage. Since silver had dropped out of circulation after 1834, Congress, on the recommendation of the comptroller of the currency, passed the Coinage Act of 1873, which ended the minting of silver dollars. The act was little noticed when it was passed, but that changed quickly with the discovery of major new sources of silver in the western states. The growing supply of silver, coupled with diminishing worldwide demand (because many nations had turned to a gold rather than bimetallic currency), drove the market price of silver down: by 1874, the world price had dropped enough that the government would have been buying and minting silver under the rules that had applied before the Coinage Act. Silver mining interests, as well as advocates of an enlarged currency, were enraged, denouncing the Coinage Act as the "Crime of '73," engineered by banks to limit the currency, maintain a gold standard, and increase their own power. Although many soft-money advocates had been skeptical of silver, they now came to see it as a means of generating a large and flexible currency supply—the need for which seemed pressing as prices continued to drop from the 1870s until the late 1890s.

Thanks to pressure from the silver states, as well as soft-money interests, Congress in 1878 passed the Bland-Allison Act, which required the secretary of the treasury to purchase between $2 million and $4 million in silver each month: since the silver did not have to be put into circulation, the Bland-Allison Act was in some respects simply a subsidy for western silver producers. In 1890, Congress passed the Sherman Silver Purchase Act, which instructed the treasury to buy a larger quantity of silver each month and then to expand the currency by issuing treasury notes backed by the silver. The Sherman Act, too, was a compromise: it did not come close to meeting the demands of silver backers, and it also permitted the treasury to redeem notes in gold alone and thus to continue acting as though the nation were on a gold standard. The stage was set for the eruption of the silver issue into national politics in the 1890s.

Regulating Business. While the tariff and the money supply were two long-standing means through which the federal government intervened in the economy, the regulation of business practices was new to the late nineteenth century. As discussed in Chapter 18, this issue arose first with the railroads at the state level, as public officials attempted to deal with the concentration of economic power acquired by large corporations. After the courts had nullified state laws because of their impact on "interstate commerce" (which the Constitution considered the domain of the federal government), Congress passed the Interstate Commerce Act to regulate railroads in 1887; three years later, it passed the Sherman Anti-Trust Act, which outlawed monopolies that were in "restraint of trade." Although more Democrats than Republicans supported these laws, both parties were split, and the congressional votes tended to be more sectional than partisan, with opposition centered in the Northeast.

The South and the Nation. One issue that sharply divided the two parties was whether or not the federal government should continue to oversee elections in the post-Reconstruction South. The Democrats opposed any continued federal involvement. The Republicans, however, were split on the issue. One faction, the Stalwarts, supported by strong Republican organizations in New York, Pennsylvania, and Illinois, believed that the party should stick to its Reconstruction-era strategy of securing a political base in the South by protecting the voting rights of African Americans. Their opponents (labeled "Half-breeds") thought it better to sacrifice the South to the Democrats than to risk weakening the party in the North with unpopular southern entanglements. In the late 1880s, this issue came to a head as the Democrats consolidated their hold on the South by preventing blacks from voting, which led to a series of contested congressional elections that had to be adjudicated by Congress.

In 1890, Representative Henry Cabot Lodge of Massachusetts, taking advantage of a brief moment when the Republicans controlled the presidency and both houses of Congress, introduced what came to be called the Lodge Force Bill. This measure provided for federally appointed election supervisors in any congressional district or city where 100 citizens requested their appointment; it also authorized the president to use military force, if necessary, to implement the law. Supporters believed that it would both protect black rights and generate enough Republican support in the South to help ensure the party's national dominance; as a happy by-product, it might also undermine the power of urban Democratic machines. The Democrats denounced the bill as an outrageous violation of states' rights; and some Republicans were unenthusiastic be-

cause they feared destabilizing a region in which northern firms had acquired financial interests. Consequently, the Lodge Bill was never passed, and in 1893 Congress repealed all laws authorizing federal supervision of elections.

PRESIDENTIAL POLITICS, 1877–1892

National electoral campaigns were boisterous affairs. Both parties sought to energize the faithful with parades, picnics, rallies, and bonfires, to treat politics as recreation and entertainment. They also resorted heavily to sloganeering and emotional appeals: the Republicans "waved the bloody shirt" to remind voters of the Democrats' ambivalence about the Civil War, while the Democrats charged the Republicans with being the corrupt handmaidens of big business. Both parties sent stump speakers crisscrossing the country to debate issues, and for the first time the mass distribution of pamphlets and tracts became commonplace. Yet the party positions on some key issues—such as business regulation and the money supply—were not very sharply differentiated, in part because both parties were internally split. Closely contested elections, moreover, led both the Democrats and Republicans to avoid controversial issues, such as the prohibition of the sale of alcohol, and to gravitate toward centrist positions on others. Nonetheless, the two parties generally succeeded in bringing 80–90 percent of all eligible voters to the polls.

Office seekers milling in the lobby of the White House as they await an interview with newly inaugurated President Rutherford B. Hayes, 1877.

Hayes, Garfield, and Arthur. The first post-Reconstruction president was Rutherford B. Hayes, who faced an unusual number of handicaps when he assumed office in the spring of 1877. His legitimacy, after the disputed election of 1876, was so clouded that opponents called him "His Fraudulency." Hostile Democrats dominated Congress during most of his term; a long business depression, as well as the ordeal of Reconstruction, had soured the mood of the country; and a deeply entrenched patronage system hindered his ability to wield executive power. He had also announced in 1876 that he would serve only one term.

By all accounts, Hayes, a former congressman, governor of Ohio, and Union general, was an honest, intelligent man, a conciliator by temperament, a mainstream, pro-business Republican. Yet his achievements in office were few. He did strike several blows for civil service reform and against the patronage system, even antagonizing powerful New York senator Roscoe Conkling by removing Conkling's protégé, Chester A. Arthur, from his remunerative position as collector of customs in New York. Hayes also encouraged more humane policies toward Native Americans. Several policy decisions, however, damaged his reputation. In 1877, he sent troops to suppress the uprisings of workers flaring in many cities, leaving him open to the charge of being unsympathetic to working people. Moreover, throughout his presidency, he placed a higher value on promoting national unity than on the rights of African Americans, declining to send troops back to the South and doing little to protect southern blacks against the onslaught of "Redemption." After retiring from politics, Hayes became openly sympathetic to the needs of industrial workers and devoted a great deal of time to helping former slaves.

With Hayes out of the running, several prominent Republicans competed for the presidential nomination in 1880. One was John Sherman, secretary of the treasury and, before that, a congressman and senator from Ohio for more than twenty years. A second was James G. Blaine, Speaker of the House and a congressman since 1863, a charismatic figure depicted by his supporters as the "plumed knight" who threw "his shining lance full and fair against the brazen forehead of every traitor to his country." The third was Ulysses Grant, who, despite two uninspiring terms as president, was popular among professional politicians, including Conkling, who had little use for either Blaine or Sherman.

When the Republican convention remained deadlocked after thirty-three ballots, delegates turned to a lesser-known Ohioan, Senator James A. Garfield, a self-made man, nine-term congressman, and Civil War hero. After Garfield's nomination, the convention, to placate Conkling and help the party win in New York, selected former customs collector Chester A. Arthur as his running mate. Meanwhile, the Democrats nominated General Winfield Scott Hancock, also a Civil War hero and lifetime army officer, and William H. English, a wealthy businessman and former congressman from Indiana. The campaign was hard-fought, with the Republicans abandoning the South to the Democrats and staking their hopes on Garfield's greater experience in government, his stand in favor of protective tariffs (which Hancock, incomprehensibly, labeled a "local issue"), and the taint of treason that still attached to the Democrats in the North. Garfield and Arthur gained a small plurality of the popular vote and were elected thanks to a slim majority of 20,000 votes in New York.

In his first months in office, Garfield voiced a desire to reduce tariffs, institute civil service reform, and strengthen the country's economic ties to Latin America. He spent most of his time, however, trying to satisfy Republican leaders' demands for patronage positions. Day after day, he found himself dealing with what he called "disciplined office hunters" who drew papers "as highway men draw pistols." Exasperated with this ritual of presidential politics, Garfield earned popular support by squaring off against Conkling and refusing to bow to his demands for patronage. But Garfield's efforts were cut short when he was gunned down in early July by Charles

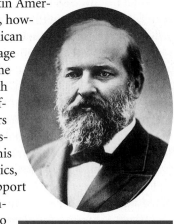

James A. Garfield, twentieth president of the United States (1881).

Guiteau, an unsatisfied office seeker who had a messianic belief that he could save the Republican Party and the nation from destructive conflict by removing Garfield from office.

Garfield lived for nearly three months after he was shot. In September, when he died, Arthur, the very symbol of the spoilsman, became president. Despite the fears of reformers, Arthur served creditably in the presidency and even lent his support to the Pendleton Act, the passage of which seemed even more urgent after Garfield's assassination. Arthur also vetoed bills designed to benefit special corporate interests, and supported federal regulation of the railroads.

Cleveland and Harrison. Despite Arthur's unexpectedly sound performance, the Republicans selected Blaine as their presidential candidate in 1884. A longtime power in the Republican Party, Blaine tried to make protective tariffs the centerpiece of the campaign, while also advocating continued civil service reform, a more energetic foreign policy, and an active federal government that would, among other things, develop the nation's waterways. Blaine's opponent was Grover Cleveland, the governor of New York, who was well-known for running honest administrations: Cleveland ran on that reputation, while defending states' rights and saying as little as possible about the tariff.

The parties' differences on issues were small enough to permit the 1884 campaign to degenerate into a carnival of mudslinging. The Democrats charged Blaine with corruption since he had several times used the power of his office to facilitate business deals from which he had secretly profited. As the details of these episodes became public, he was abandoned by the Mugwumps, as well as by traditionally Republican newspapers; he also found himself the target of cartoons that depicted him as a fawning ally of large corporations. Cleveland, too, turned out to have a personal vulnerability: it was reported, and he acknowledged, that he had fathered an illegitimate child. Republicans sought to undermine Cleveland's candidacy by relaying stories of him as a frequenter of brothels and by holding parades in which men pushed baby carriages, complete with dolls, chanting "Ma, ma, where's my Pa?" After all the mud had been slung, Cleveland won the election by the tiniest of margins, 48.5 percent of the popular vote, compared with Blaine's 48.3 percent. A switch of 550 votes in New York would have given the election to Blaine.

Although the first Democrat to gain the presidency since before the Civil War, Cleveland signaled his allegiance to the conservative, pro-business wing of his party through his cabinet appointments and by announcing his faith in "business principles" in his inaugural address. His administration, marked by a renewal of executive authority (he vetoed more than half the bills Congress passed) and a restoration of respectability for the Democratic Party, did not significantly depart from the policies of his predecessors. Among the more notable pieces of legislation passed between 1885 and 1888 were the Hatch Act, creating agricultural experiment stations, bills furthering Indian policy and civil service reform, and the Interstate Commerce Act—which was a congressional rather than presidential initiative. Cleveland's most serious setback was his failure to push tariff-cutting

LEFT: Grover Cleveland, twenty-second and twenty-fourth president of the United States (1885–89, 1893–97).

RIGHT: Benjamin Harrison, twenty-third president of the United States (1889–93).

legislation through a Congress that was always partially under Republican control.

Cleveland was renominated in 1888, running against Senator Benjamin Harrison of Indiana, the grandson of President William Henry Harrison. Once more, the key issue in the campaign was the tariff: Cleveland maintained his stance in favor of lower tariffs, while Harrison depicted the Democrats as free-traders whose policies would cost American workers their jobs. Thanks to the Republicans' superior organization and the absence of intraparty discord, Harrison was elected in yet another extremely close election. Cleveland, who received overwhelming support in the South, actually won a majority of the popular vote, but Harrison eked out narrow victories in the crucial states of New York and Indiana, which gave him a decisive victory in the electoral college. The Republicans also won majorities in both houses of Congress, allowing them control of the executive and legislative branches for the first time in decades.

Harrison was a capable figure who appointed competent men to his administration while displaying a growing interest in foreign affairs. Yet he gave little active leadership to the nation and left a shallow imprint on its history. The two most important pieces of legislation enacted during his term were the Sherman Anti-Trust Act and the McKinley Tariff, which increased duties on many goods to unprecedented levels. In part because of popular resentment of these tariff increases, the Democrats gained control of the House of Representatives in the congressional elections of 1890, stymying any further presidential efforts to shape legislation with a free hand.

THE PEOPLE'S PARTY AND THE ELECTION OF 1892

In 1892, Harrison and Cleveland squared off against each other again, the first time that two men with presidential experience had faced each other in an election. The campaign was dull, but relatively dignified. The leading issue was again the tariff, with Harrison defending protection while backing away from the McKinley Tariff, and Cleveland favoring tariff reduction while eschewing the more extreme "tariff for revenue only" position of many fellow Democrats. The candidates also disagreed about the coinage of silver and, more sharply, about using the power of the federal government to support black voting rights in the South. Harrison was a supporter of the Lodge Force Bill, while Cleveland, anxious to retain the support of white southerners, opposed it.

A satirical view of the People's Party as "A Party of Patches," including the Farmers' Alliance, the Free Silver Party, and the Old Greenback Party, June 1891.

Cleveland and the Democrats won a decisive victory. He led Harrison by nearly 400,000 votes and nearly doubled the Republican's tally in the electoral college. The Democrats also won sizable victories in the congressional elections and appeared to have become the nation's majority party.

The 1892 election also witnessed the appearance of the People's Party (or Populists), which brought the politics of insurgency into the national electoral arena. The party was formally launched on July 4, 1892, when 1,300 delegates from the Farmers' Alliances, the Knights of Labor, the American Federation of Labor, and a host of smaller organizations gathered in Omaha and nominated candidates for that year's elections. They adopted a platform whose preamble announced the urgency of their mission.

> We meet in the midst of a nation brought to the verge of moral, political and material ruin. Corruption dominates the ballot box, the Legislatures, the Congress, and touches even the ermine of the Bench. The people are demoralized . . . the newspapers are largely subsidized or muzzled; public opinion silenced; business prostrated, our homes covered with mortgages, labor impoverished, and the land concentrating in the hands of the capitalists. . . . The fruits of the toil of millions are boldly stolen to build up colossal fortunes for a few . . . and the possessors of these in turn despise the Republic and endanger liberty. From the same prolific womb of governmental injustice we breed the two great classes—tramps and millionaires.

The Omaha platform, steeped in the notion that "wealth belongs to him who creates it," called for reforms that farmer and labor groups had been demanding: government ownership of the railroads and telegraph; a graduated income tax; the reclamation of lands held by railroads and other corporate speculators; a flexible and inflated currency based on a subtreasury system as well as the free coinage of silver; postal savings banks (to provide a secure place for working people to place their savings); the direct election of senators; immigration restriction; an eight-hour day for government jobs; and outlawing the use of the Pinkerton police (a private, rentable police force) against labor.

The central challenge facing the People's Party was to build a truly national organization that could bridge the divisions among its supporters. Doing so meant unifying farmers from the South and North, despite the legacy of the Civil War and differences in their ideas about currency reform: southern farmers tended to embrace the subtreasury plan developed by the farmers' alliances, while midwestern and western farmers favored the free coinage of silver. To succeed, the party also had to convince a heterogeneous working class to join with a farmer-dominated party and persuade voters everywhere to abandon previous party allegiances. Finally, the Populists had to resolve key conflicts about race: although there were prominent exceptions, such as Georgia's Tom Watson, most southern populists embraced white supremacy, which placed them at odds with black farmers and with many northern populists who rejected racial discrimination and even favored the Lodge Force Bill.

The Populists fared well in the 1892 elections. Their presidential candidate, General James B. Weaver, polled 8.5 percent of the vote, running strongly in the West and Southwest. They also elected three governors, five U.S. senators, ten congressmen, and nearly 1,500 local and state officials, despite substantial electoral fraud in the South that deprived them of hard-earned victories. But the party made few inroads among urban workers and had difficulty prying white southerners loose from the Democratic Party, which insisted that it alone could preserve white supremacy. Nonetheless, adherents of the People's Party were optimistic about its future and looked forward to the elections of 1894 and 1896.

A pro-Cleveland cartoon showing the president defying the hydra-headed free-silver movement.

THE CRISIS OF THE 1890s

Soon after Grover Cleveland took office in 1893, the country plunged into the most severe depression it had ever experienced. Banks and businesses failed, millions of workers were unemployed, and farmers found themselves even more hard-pressed than they had been in the 1880s. The pessimistic vision of the Populists and labor radicals seemed to be vindicated. An economy controlled by large corporate monopolies could not meet the needs of the people; workers and farmers were suffering and angry.

Cleveland's response was far from adequate. He attempted to fulfill his campaign promise of lowering tariffs to stimulate trade, but the new law that was passed, the Wilson-Gorman Tariff, contained so many amendments catering to special interests that it bore little resemblance to reform. In 1894, he authorized the use of federal troops to break the Pullman strike, which made him seem unsympathetic to labor. Most

important, he joined Republicans in repealing the Sherman Silver Purchase Act: the nation's gold reserves were shrinking rapidly, and Cleveland believed, as did most bankers and big businessmen, that maintaining a gold standard was both a moral imperative and the key to economic recovery. Repealing the Sherman Act, however, had no impact on either the depression or the run on gold, which led Cleveland to shore up gold reserves by trading federal bonds for gold from a banking syndicate headed by financier J. P. Morgan. The transaction was immensely profitable to the bankers.

Cleveland's actions ignited a political storm. To many Americans, the depression seemed to call not for a return to the gold standard but rather for inflating the money supply in order to raise prices, stimulate production, and relieve the burden of debt. Cleveland's policies appeared to serve the interests of bankers and other creditors rather than farmers, workers, and small-business owners. The western, prosilver wing of his own party was enraged, and the Populists were heartened. The depression, moreover, bolstered support for the free coinage of silver among Democrats and previously skeptical Populists. One of the most popular publications of the 1890s was William H. "Coin" Harvey's *Coin's Financial School,* an illustrated pamphlet that pressed the cause of silver. A Mississippi congressman wrote to a member of Cleveland's cabinet that the book "is being sold on every railroad train by the newsboys and at every cigar store. It is being read by almost everybody."

The political damage to Cleveland and the Democrats was quickly apparent. In the 1894 congressional elections, many Democrats lost their seats. The Populist vote, centered in the West and South, was more than 40 percent greater than it had been in 1892, while the Republicans gained in the North. By the final year of his presidency, Cleveland was viewed as a conservative, pro-business politician who had failed to end a severe depression and whose monetary policies had shattered the Democratic Party.

THE ELECTION OF 1896

As the 1896 election approached, insurgent political movements and the silver issue were both in the national spotlight. The nation was still sunk in depression, and the route out of economic crisis was far from clear. Proposals for radical political and social change were gaining audiences. Large con-

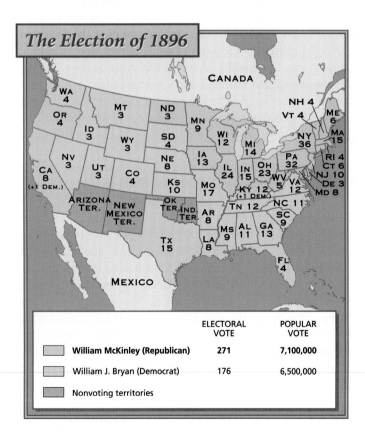

The Election of 1896

	ELECTORAL VOTE	POPULAR VOTE
William McKinley (Republican)	271	7,100,000
William J. Bryan (Democrat)	176	6,500,000
Nonvoting territories		

stituencies believed that the free coinage of silver was essential to restoring prosperity, while others were equally convinced that only a full embrace of the gold standard would turn the trick. (Both groups, in fact, were mistaken, but, as is often true, beliefs were more important than realities in shaping economic policy.) Neither of the major parties, moreover, could ignore the threat of the Populists. Although the People's Party seemed unlikely to win the presidency, it seemed capable of drawing enough votes away from both parties to affect the outcome of the election and to become an important voice in Congress and in state governments.

The Republicans held their convention first, meeting in June to nominate William McKinley, a skillful, nationally prominent former congressman and governor from Ohio. McKinley, best known as a supporter of high tariffs, was the undisputed front-runner because of his popularity with business and labor groups and because of the assiduous preconvention campaigning orchestrated by his wealthy friend, retired businessman Marcus (Mark) Alonza Hanna. The Republican platform embraced protectionism, opposed the free coinage of silver, and insisted that "the gold standard must be maintained." When the platform was passed, a group of western silver Republicans, led by Senator Henry M. Teller of Colorado, walked out of the convention and left the Republican Party.

The Democratic convention, a month later, was less orderly, reflecting the splintering of the party that had occurred under Cleveland. The eastern, pro-gold Cleveland wing fought hard for its positions but was outnumbered by passionate delegates from the South and West. The convention adopted a platform that repudiated much of what Cleveland had stood for, including the gold standard: it endorsed the unlimited coinage of silver as well as a federal income tax. One Missouri delegate labeled Cleveland one of the three greatest traitors in the nation's history, along with Benedict Arnold and Aaron Burr.

The dramatic highpoint of the platform debates occurred when former congressman William Jennings Bryan, a thirty-six-year-old Nebraskan well known for his oratorical skills, delivered a **powerful speech** on behalf of silver, farmers, and westerners. "I come to speak to you in defense of a cause as holy as the cause of liberty—the cause of humanity," he began. Drawing a divide between country and city, East and West, silver and gold, producers and capitalists, Bryan declared, "Burn down your cities and leave our farms, and your cities will spring

William Jennings Bryan in his study at Lincoln, Nebraska, at the time of his first presidential campaign.

up again as if by magic; but destroy our farms and the grass will grow in the streets of every city in the country." The stirring conclusion to his speech, both rebellious and religious, came to symbolize the tenor of the coming election campaign: "Having behind us the producing masses of the nation and the world, supported by the commercial interests, the laboring interests, and the toilers everywhere, we will answer their demand for a gold standard by saying to them: You shall not press down upon the brow of labor this crown of thorns. You shall not crucify mankind upon a cross of gold!" The speech so galvanized the convention that it nominated the young Nebraskan for the presidency on the fifth ballot, balancing the ticket with Arthur Sewall of Maine, a banker who also rejected the gold standard.

The Democratic nomination of Bryan created a quandary for the Populists and exposed divisions within their ranks. Prosilver Populists, most from the West and the Midwest, advocated "fusion" with the Democrats and the nomination of Bryan by the People's Party. Others believed that the coinage of silver was a poor substitute for the subtreasury plan, that more broad-gauged reforms were needed in any case, and that nominating Bryan would destroy the party. Many southerners found fusion to be particularly distasteful because Populism in the South was, in critical respects, a rebellion against the Democratic Party, and they had already burned their bridges with the party of white supremacy. The Populist delegates meeting in St. Louis were faced with a hard choice: they could either risk losing their political identity through fusion or virtually guarantee the election of McKinley by nominating their own candidate. After sharp debate, they chose to nominate Bryan and assert their independence by replacing vice-presidential candidate Arthur Sewall with Georgia's fiery antifusionist Tom Watson. In reaching this decision, they were influenced by assurances—which turned out to be false—that Bryan would ask Sewall to step aside and place Watson in the second spot on a fusion ticket. Bryan,

however, refused to do so, leaving the Populists in the awkward position of supporting a presidential candidate who had repudiated their choice for vice-president.

The presidential campaign was a study in contrasting ideologies and political styles. Bryan took to the hustings, traveling 18,000 miles by train and giving more than 600 speeches. With eloquence and power, the young, energetic "Great Commoner" pressed the cause of silver at every stop, and spoke as well of railroad regulation and the need to halt the "operations of trusts, syndicates, and combines." Raised in a farm family, a man of character and sincerity, Bryan conveyed a faith in the wisdom of the people, an evangelical vision of politics as inseparable from morality, and an optimistic conviction that his cause would eventually triumph. His charisma and message electrified the million or more people who heard him speak and brought an excitement to the election that had not been seen in decades. For farmers, journalist William Allen White noted, "it was a fanaticism like the Crusades."

All of which struck fear in the hearts of many Republicans and eastern Democrats, a fear that the McKinley camp exploited. Mark Hanna realized early on that Bryan would be a

A Republican Party placard shows the party candidate, McKinley, the symbol of "sound government, sound money, and prosperity," and labels his opponent, Bryan, a symbol of "bankruptcy and dishonor."

forceful candidate. He was also among a small group of Republican leaders who had recognized the important role that corporate money could play in elections. Hanna solicited funds from banks, insurance companies, railroads, and other large corporations, raising an official total of $3.5 million, more than ten times the amount that Bryan had available. Standard Oil alone gave Hanna $250,000. Most reports suggest that the Republicans actually spent more than $7 million on the campaign, distributing millions of pieces of literature and funding more than a thousand speakers who were sent out to raise fears about Bryan and to sing McKinley's praises as "the advance agent of prosperity." With the help of special discounts from the railroads, Hanna also paid the expenses of 750,000 people who traveled, in carefully identified groups, to meet with McKinley at his home in Canton, Ohio. There, each delegation attended a reception with the candidate and listened to a short speech delivered from McKinley's front porch: this campaign technique permitted the Republican to meet with voters and repeatedly stress that his party was the vehicle of economic growth and the "full dinner pail" while not seeming to compete with Bryan's superior energy and oratorical skills. The press, overwhelmingly pro-McKinley, carried enthusiastic reports of these events while denouncing Bryan and caricaturing his ideas.

"He's Back Again," an 1897 cartoon suggesting that with McKinley elected, the interests supporting protective tariffs once again hold sway in Congress.

On election day, Bryan won more votes than any previous presidential candidate—nearly 800,000 more than Cleveland had garnered in 1892 and more than any Democrat would win for twenty years. Nonetheless, McKinley received a half million more votes than Bryan and won in the electoral college, 271 to 176. Bryan captured the South, the plains states, and the silver-producing Rocky Mountain states, but McKinley was victorious throughout the Northeast and the Midwest, as well as on the West Coast. The Republicans won every major city, increased their vote in rural areas of the Midwest, and retained control of both houses of Congress.

Bryan's defeat had several sources. One was that he was outspent and placed on the defensive by an unusually united Republican Party backed by nearly all major organs of public opinion. A second was that he failed to win majorities among urban, particularly ethnic workers, which left him with little chance of making any inroads in the Northeast and, more critically, in closely contested midwestern states such as Illinois and Ohio. Workers were intimidated by employers who stated that if Bryan won, "the whistle will not blow on Wednesday." Many workers also had some sympathy for McKinley's high tariff positions and found Bryan's evangelical style alien. Indeed, in 1896, there was a shift in the parties' ethnocultural appeals: it was the Democrats, not the Republicans, who were making a pietistic, cultural bid for votes. This attracted support among some previously Republican voters (Methodists, for example), but it repelled segments of the traditionally Democratic Catholic working class.

The election of 1896 marked the end of the post-Reconstruction era of closely contested national elections and divided government: the Republicans were solidly in power, and they would remain in control of the national government for most of the next thirty-five years. McKinley's victory also signaled the end of the agrarian revolt against industrialism, the final chapter in the rebellion of small producers against corporate capitalism. After a century of uncertainty, wrote Henry Adams, "the majority at last declared itself . . . in favor of a capitalistic system with all its necessary machinery." The dynamics of the election left the People's Party mortally wounded: having lost both the election and its political identity, it did poorly in the 1898 elections and then virtually disappeared from the political stage. Despite the demise of the Populists, however, farmers did well economically after 1896: a year later, a sharp drop in European grain production increased the demand for American exports, and agricultural prices continued to rise well into the twentieth century. But never again would farmers be the powerful political force that they were in the years leading up to the 1896 election.

President McKinley and his fellow Republicans interpreted the election as a mandate to govern in the interest of the business community that had supported them. McKinley appointed bankers to head the Treasury and Interior Departments and a lumber baron as secretary of war. Congress, with the support of the president, passed the Dingley Tariff, which increased already high duties on imported goods to an average rate of 52 percent. And in 1900, the Republicans pushed through the Gold Standard Act, which formally made gold the sole specie backing the money supply. Ironically, the discovery of gold in Alaska and South Africa, coupled with the development of new techniques of extracting gold from low-grade ore, led to an expansion of the currency and inflation—despite the defeat of the silver movement. Thanks in part to these developments and in part to the return of prosperity at the end of the century, the formal adoption of a gold standard had no discernible impact on the economy.

The Conservative Courts

Public policy in the United States has always been shaped by courts, as well as by legislators, governors, and presidents. In the late nineteenth century, the courts expanded their role, taking a more activist and ideological stance toward the "judicial review" of legislation. The federal judiciary was overwhelmingly Republican and consisted almost entirely of men drawn from well-to-do backgrounds. (State judges, many of whom were elected, were less uniform in their party affiliations and social origins, but they, too, tended to come from the upper reaches of society.) These men, responding to the transformations and tensions of the industrial world, came to see themselves as a critical bulwark in the defense of property rights. By the 1890s, they had come to fear the challenges to political and social order posed by working-class protest and

An **1888** cartoon criticizing the courts for crushing anarchy but sparing monopoly.

insurgent political movements, and they saw the courts as defenders of property against the "excesses" of democracy.

This judicial posture spawned a new legal doctrine, often labeled "laissez-faire constitutionalism." It was expressed most consequentially in two arenas. The first was labor law, in which the courts were increasingly hostile to any legislative efforts to intervene in the relationship between employers and employees. In 1885, for example, the New York Court of Appeals, in *In re Jacobs,* struck down an antisweatshop law that prohibited the manufacture of cigars in tenement houses, ruling that the law infringed on the "personal liberty" and freedom of contract of individual workers. For similar reasons, the courts voided an 1893 Illinois law that sought to protect women by limiting them to an eight-hour working day (six days per week). As important, federal judges, after the railroad strikes of 1877, began to issue injunctions to end strikes and compel workers to return to their jobs: originally they were following common law notions that strikes, led by unions, were conspiracies to violate the law and destroy the property of owners. Continuing in the same vein, federal judges after 1890 frequently invoked the Sherman Anti-Trust Act to issue injunctions against striking unions because they constituted "conspiracies in restraint of trade." By the 1890s, injunctions to halt strikes were issued by the hundreds, if not thousands, and new laws sought by labor were likely to be struck down by the courts.

Laissez-faire constitutionalism also had an impact on the ability of state and federal governments to regulate business practices. In the 1870s (see Chapter 18), the Supreme Court had been tolerant of such regulation, ruling in *Munn v. Illinois* that the state of Illinois could regulate prices in grain-storage facilities in Chicago because such facilities were "clothed with a public interest" and because their regulation did not deprive their owners of property without due process of law. In the 1880s, however, business lawyers began to argue that the Fourteenth Amendment justified the judicial narrowing of regulatory laws: the amendment prohibited the states from abridging the "privileges and immunities" of citizens, from denying anyone "the equal protection of the laws," and from depriving "any person of life, liberty, or property without due process of law." Corporations, they argued, were "persons" under the amendment, and "due process of law" was a substantive as well as procedural guarantee—which meant that the ability of government to regulate private enterprise was limited and would be defined not by legislatures, but by the courts.

The federal judiciary, and then the Supreme Court itself, came to embrace these arguments by the 1890s. In a series of cases, the courts overturned or narrowed state regulatory laws and imposed significant limits on the Interstate Commerce Commission. In 1895, the Supreme Court handed down three decisions that became pillars of the new constitutional order. In *U.S. v. E.C. Knight,* the Court ruled that the sugar trust, which refined 98 percent of the sugar in the United States, could not be declared a monopoly under the Sherman Anti-Trust Act because the act referred only to "commerce" and not to "manufacturing." The Court also decided in *In re Debs* that the Sherman Act was a legitimate basis for issuing an injunction against the American Railway Union for engaging in a sympathy strike against the railroads. Unions, it seemed, were more vulnerable to being declared "conspiracies in restraint of trade" than were manufacturers. Then, in *Pollock v. Farmers' Loan and Trust Co.,* the Court declared unconstitutional an 1894 federal law that would have imposed a 2 percent tax on all incomes over $4,000.

These decisions were opposed by labor organizations, reformers, progressive political figures, and even some lawyers and judges. Nonetheless, by the end of the decade, the federal courts had made clear that they would actively intervene to protect the rights of property and freedom of contract against legislative infringement and, more generally, to restrict the scope of government intervention in economic affairs. Many of the decisions handed down by the courts undermined popular legislation while establishing legal precedents that would endure for decades.

The New Political Universe

After 1896, Americans found themselves participating in—or not participating in—what one political scientist has called a "new political universe." Not only did the Republicans gain control of the national government, but outside the thinly populated West the nation was divided into two large, single-party regions. The South and some of the border states were dominated by the Democratic Party, while much of the North was controlled by the Republicans. This shift, underway before the election of 1896, reflected not simply the rebuff of agrarian radicalism but the Republicans' success in presenting themselves as the party of prosperity. By doing so, they were able to divide the politically rambunctious working class and win the support of skilled and unionized urban workers.

One characteristic of this new universe was a decline in the extent to which Americans participated in elections. In the South, the disfranchisement of African Americans had lowered participation levels even before 1896, but the trend became more pronounced thereafter: by 1908, turnout rates in the region had plummeted to 30 percent. In most northern states, turnout was between 80 and 95 percent in 1896, but it then began a gradual decline that would continue, with a few interruptions, through the twentieth century. Single-party dominance meant that parties no longer had to mobilize voters as they had done from the 1870s through the 1890s. Moreover, many citizens, particularly those near the bottom of the economic ladder, stopped going to the polls because they believed that electoral politics had little to offer them. Complex registration systems, literacy tests, and poll taxes in northern states also kept people, especially immigrant workers, from voting.

Linked to the drop in participation was the declining visibility of third parties. The politics of insurgency did not disappear after 1896, but the scale of activity was more limited. In most states, the chaotic, optimistic, rapidly changing multiparty world of the 1870s, '80s, and '90s gave way to a more solidly entrenched two-party or one-party system. The possibilities of insurgent victory, particularly given the complexities of the nation's federal structure of governance, seemed increasingly remote; the enthusiasm and energy so prominent in the late nineteenth century were dampened. The Democratic and Republican Parties, sustained by large organizations and nourished by corporate contributions, had a firm grip on both the institutions of governance and the apparatus of elections. Modern American politics had arrived.

1877	The Great Railroad Strike.
	The Southern Farmers' Alliance founded in Texas.
1886	The American Federation of Labor founded.
May 4, 1886	The Haymarket affair.
1892	The People's Party founded.
1893	Panic and depression.
	Congress repeals all laws authorizing federal supervision of elections.
1894	The Pullman Strike.
1900	The Gold Standard Act passed.

Chronology

Suggested Reading

Henry Adams, *The Education of Henry Adams* (1907)

Lawrence Goodwyn, *Democratic Promise: The Populist Movement in America* (1976)

Richard Oestreicher, *Solidarity and Fragmentation: Working People and Class Consciousness in Detroit, 1875–1900* (1986)

Gretchen Ritter, *Goldbugs and Greenbacks: The Antimonopoly Tradition and the Politics of Finance in America* (1997)

Nick Salvatore, *Eugene V. Debs: Citizen and Socialist* (1982)

Stephen Skowronek, *Building a New American State: The Expansion of National Administrative Capacities* (1982)

C. Vann Woodward, *A History of the South*, vol. 9: *The Origins of the New South, 1877–1913* (1972)

Chapter 21

A NEW PLACE IN THE WORLD:

1865-1914

A contemporary engraving that shows workers excavating the Panama Canal near Emperador.

Focus
QUESTIONS

- What were the main currents of foreign policy in the postbellum years?

- What was the significance of the Spanish-American War?

- How did America extend its power overseas after the war?

- How did the United States become a world power in this period?

In the immediate aftermath of the Civil War, the United States displayed little interest in events transpiring outside its own continental boundaries. Still preoccupied with sectional conflict, possessing a vast, thinly settled West that could absorb its expansive energies for decades, the nation, unlike Britain and other European powers, seemed to have few imperial ambitions. In 1870, the only territory outside of North America that the United States officially controlled was a tiny, uninhabited Pacific atoll, and most Americans were content to keep it that way. "Our country," wrote *New York Tribune* editor Horace Greeley, "has already an ample area for the next century at least."

The country, moreover, had few of the tools necessary to influence affairs beyond its borders. The Department of State in Washington included about fifty employees. The army was shrinking in size daily, on its way to becoming a small force of 25,000 men, 15 percent of whom deserted each year. By 1890, the American army was half the size of Belgium's and slightly smaller than that of Bulgaria. Similarly, the post–Civil War navy consisted largely of small, aging wooden ships with little or no armor, powered by boilers so in need of repair that they could not travel at half their intended speed.

By the eve of World War I, all that had changed. American firms were trading and investing around the globe. American missionaries were spreading the gospel of Christianity and technological progress in Asia, the Middle East, and Latin America. The United States had taken formal possession of territory in the Caribbean and the Pacific, stretching from Puerto Rico and part of Cuba through Hawaii to the Philippines. It had fought its first overseas war, defeating a European empire and seizing some of its colonies. In diverse arenas, the nation had also signaled to all the imperial powers that it intended to be a major player of the international stage.

Meanwhile, the State Department had grown to include nearly 300 employees in Washington, with consular offices in more than 100 cities in 43 countries, while the Commerce Department had acquired a bureau devoted to promoting international trade. The army had 100,000 soldiers under its command, while the navy possessed more than 300 seaworthy ships, including 30 submarines and 35 armored battleships. Furthermore, the United States had exercised its might not only in an overseas war but by dispatching ships and soldiers to secure American interests, collect customs receipts, and police conflicts in locales that it did not legally control. By 1910, the United States stood poised to become one of the foremost powers in the world.

Postbellum Stirrings, 1865–1890

For twenty-five years after Appomattox, American foreign policy was shaped by two traditional yet contradictory impulses. One was expansive: throughout its history, the nation **had grown in population and territory**. Through purchases and conquest, the thirteen states hugging the Atlantic seaboard had become a huge continental nation, and some Americans— particularly among the elite who molded foreign policy— believed that further expansion, in North America and overseas, was both inevitable and desirable. Yet coexisting with this expansive urge was an inclination to steer clear of foreign entanglements, to enjoy the nation's geographic isolation from other powers. The United States could not easily be invaded; through the Monroe Doctrine, it had warned European nations to tread softly in the Western Hemisphere; and any involvement in European affairs seemed unnecessary. Moreover, as citizens of a republic that had once been a colony, many Americans (elite and otherwise) were opposed to the colonial domination of one people by another.

The most influential and prescient advocate of expansion was William Henry Seward, secretary of state under Presidents Lincoln and Johnson. Although once a supporter of the wholesale acquisition of new territories, including Canada and Mexico, Seward by the mid-1860s had begun to pursue a vision of commercial, rather than territorial, empire: the rapidly industrializing United States ought to establish naval bases in the Caribbean and the Pacific and erect a "highway" to Asia in order to gain access to foreign markets and expand its international trade. Eventually, Seward believed, the European colonial regimes would be supplanted by Americans who "value dollars more and dominion less."

In keeping with this vision, Seward signed a treaty purchasing Alaska from Russia in 1867. The secretary was convinced that the acquisition of Alaska, rich in natural resources, would enhance American power in the Pacific, check that of Britain, and nurture America's burgeoning friendship with Russia, which was eager to dispose of Alaska. Although many derided the idea as "Seward's folly" or "Seward's icebox," he eventually convinced the Senate to ratify the treaty and the House to appropriate $7.2 million for the purchase. Seward simultaneously persuaded Congress to annex the tiny, uninhabited Midway Islands to provide the United States with a base halfway between California and the Asian mainland. In May 1867, Seward penned an optimistic poem:

> *Abroad our empire shall no limits know,*
> *But like the sea in boundless circles flow.*

Seward's expansive ambitions were held in check by a Congress riven by internal political conflicts, preoccupied with Reconstruction and largely uninterested in acquiring overseas territories or bases. The secretary signed a treaty with Denmark to purchase the Virgin Islands for $7.5 million, but the Senate refused to ratify it. The Senate also rejected a treaty that would have given the United States exclusive rights to build a canal through the Colombian province of Panama and another establishing tariff reciprocity with Hawaii. In 1870, despite arm-twisting by President Grant, the Senate voted down a treaty that would have annexed the Dominican Republic, because senators were dubious about expansion and wary of adding to the nation's nonwhite population. As Seward himself acknowledged, there was little popular support in the United States for his "empire" with "no limits."

The industrial transformation of the United States, however, led more and more Americans to turn their gaze outward. The spectacular growth and rising productivity of industry made it possible for American firms to compete overseas with the European powers; that growth, coupled with the shock of periodic depressions, also spawned a widespread belief that foreign markets were becoming essential to American prosperity, that the nation's productive capacity had outgrown its ability to consume. Foreign trade increased dramatically after the Civil War: between 1860 and 1897, imports doubled while exports more than tripled, giving the United States a positive balance of trade that would last until the early 1970s. A rising proportion of U.S. exports, moreover, came from industry rather than agriculture: steel, cotton goods, motors, kerosene, and even cigarettes were routinely exported to distant corners of the globe. The well-being of Standard Oil, American Tobacco, and the Singer Sewing Machine Company, as well as farmers in the South and the West, was increasingly yoked to exports. Ties to the international economy were further multiplied by investment abroad (often by opening branches of American corporations) as well as by foreign investment in the United States, and the arrival of millions of foreign workers.

Technological and ideological factors heightened American interest in developments abroad. Faster ships and railroads made foreign lands more accessible, and telegraph cables laid along the ocean floors (the first trans-Atlantic cable was completed in 1866) greatly speeded communication. Tropical territories also seemed more inviting once quinine, an extract from cinchona bark, was recognized as an effective prophylaxis against malaria, the mosquito-borne disease that had killed large numbers of European imperialists. Meanwhile, the "closing" of the frontier in the American West seemed to signal the end of a long era of continental expansion, and social Darwinist notions of the "survival of the fittest" seemed readily applicable to the international arena. Although many social Darwinists were anti-expansionists, in part because they feared adding "inferior" races to American society, others argued that international conflict was inescapable and would surely lead to American economic, political, and cultural triumphs. In the widely read *Our Country* (1885), for example, Protestant minister Josiah

Charles Darwin, 1871.

Strong declared that Anglo-Saxons had a "genius for colonization" and that "God, with infinite wisdom and skill is training the Anglo-Saxon race for . . . the final competition of races."

Pressure for increased government involvement abroad sometimes came directly from Americans who lived and invested in foreign nations. In Costa Rica, for example, American Minor Keith gained control of both the railroads and banana production, becoming the dominant figure in the Costa Rican economy and forming the core of what would become the United Fruit Company (which Central Americans eventually would label "the octopus"). To protect his investments in a region troubled by political strife, Keith encouraged the U.S. government to signal its interest in stability with a show of force by the navy. Similarly, the lush and strategically located islands of Hawaii hosted American planters and missionaries (the two were often indistinguishable) who came to own most of its sugar plantations. To gain access to the American market and tighten Hawaiian ties to the United States, these planters pressed Congress and the State Department for a treaty eliminating tariffs on Hawaiian sugar. Their success in 1875 spawned a dramatic increase in sugar production. When the treaty was renewed in 1887, it included an added provision granting the United States the right to use Pearl Harbor as a naval base. The place of the planters in Hawaiian society, however, remained precarious, thanks to deepening anti-American sentiment in the islands, as well as opposition to the tariff reductions by sugar producers in the United States. To solve these problems, one key group of planters began lobbying the United States to annex Hawaii outright.

Still, the political leadership that controlled foreign policy remained divided, and the government made few territorial acquisitions before the 1890s. Although several Republican secretaries of state, most notably James G. Blaine, who served under Presidents Garfield and Harrison, shared Seward's expansive vision, they were able to take only small steps toward transforming that vision into reality. In 1872, for example, the Senate agreed to lease the Samoan port of Pago Pago but rebuffed State Department efforts to turn Samoa into a protectorate. (Protectorates were diplomatic devices, generally governed by treaties, through which strong states agreed to protect vulnerable territories against third parties in return for specific favors and some control over the weaker territory's policies.) In 1889, Blaine also tried to interest Hawaii in becoming a U.S. protectorate, but the Hawaiians were resistant. Several years later,

pro-annexation whites, with some American support, seized power in a military coup and quickly signed an annexation treaty with Blaine and Harrison. But the treaty was repudiated by Harrison's successor, Grover Cleveland, who was less enthused about overseas acquisitions and wary of implementing an agreement that lacked the support of most Hawaiians. Even in Latin America, where the United States had long-standing interests, efforts to enlarge American influence and capture trade from the Europeans were more rhetorical than concrete.

THE OLD ARMY AND THE NEW NAVY

A similarly halting pattern characterized efforts to build and modernize the armed forces. The army was small and possessed an oversized officer corps, dominated by Civil War veterans, that gave young men few chances to advance through the ranks. It was also slow to embrace new technology. Smokeless gunpowder (which kept guns cleaner and permitted soldiers to fire and remain hidden) was commonly used in Europe, but the army did not adopt a rifle that could use the new powder until 1892—although the widely used, smokeless "Krag" rifle was actually manufactured in the United States. Similarly, the army took years to recognize the potential of the first fully automatic machine gun, which was invented in 1885 by an American, Hiram Maxim.

The navy made more progress, perhaps because it seemed likely to play a larger role in future conflicts. By the early 1880s, the navy was antiquated and in disrepair: fewer than

Hiram Maxim with the machine gun that he invented, c. 1883.

One of the new generation of U.S. Navy cruisers, c. 1890.

hem Steel and Carnegie Steel. By the 1890s, when the decline in new railroad construction reduced the demand for steel rails, steel manufacturers found themselves increasingly dependent on orders from the navy; not surprisingly, these firms often supported an aggressive foreign policy that would require a large navy. The United States also found itself drawn into an arms race with European powers, since larger guns demanded stronger, nickel-plated armor, which in turn created a demand for even more potent guns.

Turning Point: The 1890s

During the final decade of the nineteenth century, the forces and actors favoring a more expansive foreign policy gained the upper hand. The United States asserted itself strongly against the European powers, particularly Britain. It conducted what Secretary of State John Hay called a "splendid little war" against Spain, as well as a less splendid, larger war against nationalist rebels in the Philippines. By 1900, the United States controlled bases, territories, and millions of people from the Caribbean to the western Pacific.

This surge in activity was spawned by a convergence of domestic and international developments. Abroad, the competition for empire was becoming more heated: the Spanish empire was losing strength; British hegemony was being challenged by other European powers, particularly Germany; colonies, bases, and foreign markets were being grabbed or consolidated throughout Africa, Asia, and the Pacific; and an arms race was heightening the military, particularly naval, power of the contenders for empire. At the same time, the subjects of imperial conquest, although unable to match European military technology, were becoming more rebellious, threatening to create either instability or independent local governments, both of which were unwelcome to Western powers. For American policymakers, these movements on the international chessboard seemed both to create opportunities and to generate pressure for a rapid entry onto the global stage.

Foremost among domestic developments was an economy that seemed to require new markets in order to run smoothly. The depression of the 1890s, coming after two decades of sharp swings in the business cycle, appeared to validate the idea that the economy suffered from excess capacity, or overproduction, and that the best cure was to sell more

fifty ships were seaworthy, and none could contend with the more technologically advanced fleets of the European powers or even countries such as Chile and China. Prompted in part by a budget surplus that the Republicans were eager to spend, Congress authorized the construction of a series of steel-armored ships, including three heavily armed, armored battleships in 1890. Even that decision, however, was shaped by ambivalence about overseas involvement: Congress specified that these would be "sea-going, coast-line battleships," with a relatively short cruising range, designed primarily to defend the North American mainland.

Rebuilding the navy had important repercussions for industry and its ties to the government. Building armored ships demanded expertise in the manufacture of high-quality structural steel, as well as specialized facilities for turning out armor and powerful guns. Since the United States lacked such expertise and facilities, the least expensive path was to buy key components abroad. Congress, however, led by Republicans, insisted that domestic sources of armaments be developed. The navy consequently built its own gun factory and subsidized the construction of armor plants by Bethle-

American goods abroad. As Secretary of State William R. Day wrote in 1898, "the output of the United States manufacturers, developed by the remarkable inventive genius and industrial skill of our people . . . has reached the point of large excess above the demands of home consumption. Under these circumstances it is not surprising that greater interest should be exhibited among our manufacturers, exporters, and economists in the enlargement of foreign markets for American goods." Some labor groups, on the other hand, argued that the problem was not overproduction but underconsumption, which could be cured by increasing workers' wages. Yet in the formation of foreign policy, what mattered was not necessarily economic reality but what people believed to be true about economy. And in the 1890s, many businessmen, intellectuals, and political leaders were convinced that the United States needed foreign markets and that it was incumbent on the government to help secure them.

The importance of the government's role was highlighted in one of the most influential books of the era, Alfred Thayer Mahan's *The Influence of Sea Power Upon History, 1660–1783,* published in 1890. Mahan, a Democrat and anti-imperialist until the mid-1880s, was a career naval officer and teacher at the Naval War College. His extensive reading of history, first about Rome and then about Britain, convinced him that the key to any nation's power was its dominance of the seas: "sea power is the centre around which other events move, not it around them." The growth and rising productivity of American industry, he believed, made it imperative for the nation to enlarge its foreign markets, yet this would heighten the possibility of international conflict and war. It was therefore essential that the United States develop a powerful naval fleet that could protect its commerce, destroy an adversary's, and defeat other navies in battle. The only alternative, Mahan claimed, was to stimulate the domestic market through unacceptable "socialistic" measures.

Alfred Thayer Mahan, author of *The Influence of Sea Power Upon History, 1660–1783,* in 1897.

Becoming a great naval power, however, required more than ships. The United States would also need coaling stations, communications centers, repair facilities (especially as ships became more technologically complex), and rest stops for the crews. For this reason, Mahan strenuously advocated the acquisition of permanent bases in the Caribbean and the Pacific; he even abandoned the Democratic Party in 1893 when President Cleveland refused to annex Hawaii. Mahan's arguments lent support not only to officials who sought to enlarge the navy, but to all those who wanted to pursue a more expansionist foreign policy.

Other factors, less closely linked to the economy, also contributed to the actions undertaken in the 1890s. In addition to social Darwinism, deeply embedded convictions about American "specialness" lent support to efforts to implant the American way of life, and Protestant religion, in distant corners of the globe. In 1891 alone, 6,000 American students joined the ranks of Protestant missionaries fanning out to China, India, Japan, Egypt, and other countries. In addition to spreading the gospel, these missionaries were expressing the same sense of racial and cultural superiority that informed the spread of Jim Crow in the South and discrimination against immigrants throughout the nation. Political leaders, moreover, were determined to make the United States one of the world's great powers, and in their vision of "greatness," economic, military, and political power were inseparable.

This did not mean that the entire country embraced expansionism in the 1890s. Independent Mugwumps such as Carl Schurz, *Nation* editor E. L. Godkin, and philosopher William James vigorously opposed expansion, as did numerous Republicans and Democrats, including William Jennings Bryan. The decade witnessed pointed public debates about foreign policy, and no political party or social group, including the business community, was close to unanimous on the subject. Nor did the events of the 1890s constitute a sudden new departure in American foreign relations; the impulse toward expansionism had been gathering strength for decades. But what did happen in the 1890s was a decisive tilt in the balance of forces, the triumph of one tradition over another, the active embrace of a new international role that would endure for a century or more.

BRITAIN, THE MONROE DOCTRINE, AND THE VENEZUELA CRISIS

Early in the 1890s, the Untied States began to flex its muscles in Latin America and to warn European powers, particularly Britain, that American interests would reign supreme in the Western Hemisphere. In 1891, the country squared off

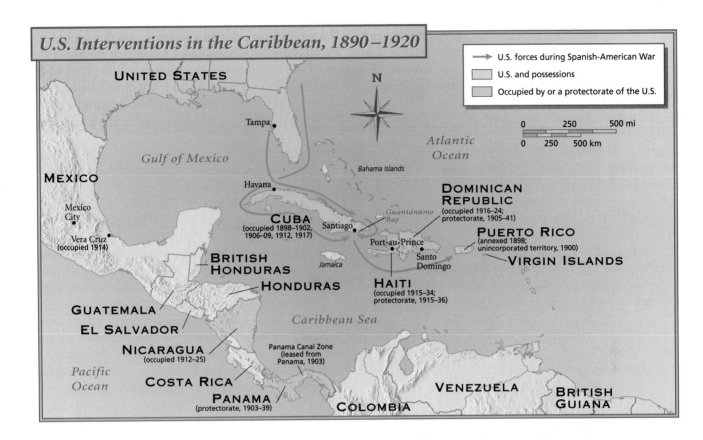

U.S. Interventions in the Caribbean, 1890–1920

→ U.S. forces during Spanish-American War

☐ U.S. and possessions

☐ Occupied by or a protectorate of the U.S.

UNITED STATES

N

Tampa

Gulf of Mexico

*Atlantic
Ocean*

Bahama Islands

MEXICO

Mexico
City

Havana

Vera Cruz
(occupied 1914)

CUBA
(occupied 1898–1902,
1906–09, 1912, 1917)

Santiago

*Guantánamo
Bay*

DOMINICAN
REPUBLIC
(occupied 1916–24;
protectorate, 1905–41)

PUERTO RICO
(annexed 1898;
unincorporated territory, 1900)

VIRGIN ISLANDS

BRITISH
HONDURAS

HONDURAS

Jamaica

Port-au-Prince

Santo
Domingo

HAITI
(occupied 1915–34;
protectorate, 1915–36)

GUATEMALA

EL SALVADOR

Caribbean Sea

NICARAGUA
(occupied 1912–25)

Panama Canal Zone
(leased from
Panama, 1903)

*Pacific
Ocean*

COSTA RICA

PANAMA
(protectorate, 1903–39)

COLOMBIA

VENEZUELA

BRITISH
GUIANA

0 250 500 mi
0 250 500 km

against Chile after two American sailors, on shore leave in Valparaiso, were killed by an anti-American mob. President Harrison demanded an apology and reparations; when the Chilean government responded hesitantly, Harrison sent a message to Congress that virtually invited a declaration of war. Although Chile quickly backed down, the incident only heightened anti-Yankee sentiments. Two years later, after the United States had signed a tariff reciprocity treaty with Brazil, parts of the Brazilian navy, backed by the British, rebelled against their new republican government and formed a blockade of Rio de Janeiro's harbor. Under orders from the secretary of state, American warships broke the blockade, effectively ending the rebellion. At roughly the same time, the United States intervened to terminate a British protectorate in a strategically located region of eastern Nicaragua: Washington encouraged the Nicaraguan government to take formal control of the region, while declaring that the United States would protect the interests of both American and British investors.

These incidents paved the way for the Venezuela crisis of 1895, which marked a major turning point in hemispheric politics. The crisis had its origins in a fifty-year-old boundary dis-

pute between Venezuela and the colony of British Guiana; at stake was an area rich in minerals (including newly discovered gold) and encompassing the mouth of the commercially important Orinoco River. By the 1890s, Britain was acting as though it controlled the region, and it spurned Venezuelan efforts to negotiate the boundary. Venezuela then turned to the United States for help, even hiring an American lobbyist, former diplomat William L. Scruggs, to make its case in Washington.

Scruggs did an excellent job of presenting the Venezuelan viewpoint and tapping American fears of the British. Some Americans believed that Britain, having taken what it could in Africa and Asia, was turning its attention to Latin America, and Britain's refusal to submit the boundary dispute to arbitration was seen as evidence of its imperial designs. To expansionist senator Henry Cabot Lodge of Massachusetts, the implications of such a development were momentous: "If Great Britain can extend her territory in South America without remonstrances from us, every other European power can do the same, and in a short time you will see South America parceled out as Africa has been. We should then find ourselves with great powers to the south of us, and we should be forced to become at once a nation with a powerful army and navy, with difficulties and dangers surrounding us."

In February 1895, Congress unanimously passed a resolution calling on Britain to submit the dispute to arbitration; shortly thereafter, President Cleveland wrote to British prime minister Lord Salisbury reiterating the demand. The British, preoccupied with other matters and believing that their dispute with Venezuela was not the business of the United States, ignored the demands. In the summer of 1895, the president asked his new secretary of state, Richard Olney—who, as attorney general, had broken the Pullman strike and sent Eugene Debs to jail in 1894—to inform the British again how seriously the United States regarded the matter. Olney's extraordinary letter asserted American hegemony over the hemisphere more aggressively than had ever been done before. Beyond invoking the Monroe Doctrine and other traditional arguments, Olney informed the British that "today the

An 1895 cartoon critical of the Cleveland administration's inattention to British encroachments on the Monroe Doctrine.

United States is practically sovereign on this continent, and its fiat is law upon the subjects to which it confines its interposition." Lest Britain fail to understand the sources of that sovereignty, Olney pointed out the "infinite resources" of the United States, "combined with its isolated position render it master of the situation and practically invulnerable as against any and all powers." Accepting arbitration, Olney maintained, was the only way Britain could establish that they were not engaged in an act of imperial aggression against Venezuela and the United States.

Four months later, Lord Salisbury replied to Olney and Cleveland, refusing arbitration and pointedly reemphasizing that Monroe Doctrine or no Monroe Doctrine, the United States had no jurisdiction in the matter. Cleveland responded by sending a message to Congress calling for a U.S. commission to determine the proper boundaries and warning Britain that the United States would "resist by any means within its power" Britain's seizure of territory that it did not rightfully possess. This veiled threat of war caught Britain's attention: recognizing that it had misunderstood the importance of the Monroe Doctrine to the Americans, and still preoccupied with more serious threats to its empire from France and Germany, Britain agreed to arbitration. The crisis ended immediately, and eventually an international commission recognized most of the British claims. In the end, the most significant consequence of the crisis had little to do with the Orinoco or even with Venezuela, whose government was never consulted by the United States. By agreeing to arbitration, Britain had tacitly recognized American hegemony in the Western Hemisphere: the United States had faced off against the greatest power in the world, and it was Britain that had blinked.

CUBA AND WAR WITH SPAIN

The United States had long kept a close eye on Cuba, ninety miles south of Florida. Before the Civil War, southerners had talked of annexing the island as another plantation-dominated slave state; and in 1868, when Cuban nationalists began a decade-long war for independence against Spain, most Americans regarded the rebel cause with sympathy. After the rebellion was defeated, with Spain having promised to undertake significant reforms, the United States became home to Cuban dissidents, including rebel leader Jose Marti, who would become the most revered figure in Cuban history.

Cuban discontent with Spanish rule continued through the 1870s and 1880s, while the island's economy became in-

Cuban rebel leader Jose Marti.

creasingly tied to that of the United States. Americans not only invested close to $50 million in Cuba's profitable sugar industry, but the United States was also the primary export market for Cuban sugar and cigars. Then, in the 1890s, the Cuban economy was rocked, first by a worldwide decline in sugar prices and in 1894 by the Wilson-Gorman Tariff, which, by dramatically raising duties on sugar, cut Cuban exports to the United States by 50 percent. The precipitous decline in the Cuban economy led to strikes, attacks on foreign-owned property, including cane fields, and a renewal of the rebellion against Spain. Marti, probably the one leader who could bridge the class and racial divisions that permeated Cuban society, returned to Cuba in 1895 and was promptly killed by Spanish soldiers.

In 1896, with the rebellion gathering steam, Spain sent 150,000 troops, led by General Valeriano Weyler, to the island. There, Weyler developed a strategy that would become a familiar means of suppressing guerrilla warfare in the twentieth century: he attempted to sever the contacts between rebel forces and agricultural workers by forcibly relocating the workers into prison-like camps. Weyler's *reconcentrado* policy led to the deaths of more than 200,000 Cubans in overcrowded, filthy, and disease-ridden camps, earning him the nickname of "Butcher" in the American press.

The Cubans themselves were divided into several political factions, including a small group who did not oppose continued Spanish rule. Some Creoles (born in Cuba but of Spanish ancestry), as well as American planters and businessmen, originally sought autonomy, or "home rule," within the Spanish empire; as that option seemed less feasible, they considered arranging for the annexation of the island to the United States. Most Cubans, however, wanted complete independence: although they welcomed American support, they feared that the United States might seek to replace Spanish with American rule. As Marti famously asked, "Once the United States is in Cuba, who will get her out?"

The conflict in Cuba was closely watched in the United States. Many Americans, among them members of Congress, believed that the United States should intervene in Cuba, on humanitarian grounds or to protect American investments. Advocates of overseas expansion also saw Cuba as a strategically located island that could help Americans protect a canal in Central America. Led by Democrats and Populists, Congress debated a series of resolutions urging the government to take military action against the Spanish, or at least to formally recognize the rebels. But President Cleveland resisted such calls, preferring to exert diplomatic pressure on Spain to end the warfare and grant Cuba autonomy within the Spanish empire, a solution that would make Spain responsible for protecting American investments there. Cleveland opposed any plan that would join the multiracial, class-torn island to the United States. He also feared that an independent, yet still unstable, Cuba might invite other European forays into the Caribbean.

When William McKinley became president in 1897, he shared Cleveland's reluctance to get too entangled in Cuba. McKinley was, in key respects, the first modern president, centralizing power, particularly over foreign policy, in the White House. As a Republican taking office just as a severe depression seemed to be lifting, his overriding concern was promoting economic growth, and he feared that war would undermine the economy's recovery. A Civil War hero, McKinley had a personal distaste for war: "I have been through one war; I have seen the dead piled up; and I do not want to see another," he told a friend. He also worried that the Constitution would not extend to any overseas territories that the United States acquired. Consequently, he, too, focused on diplomacy, urging Spain to grant Cuba autonomy and bring an end to Weyler's brutal *reconcentrado*.

McKinley's efforts seemed for a time to be working. In October 1897, Spain recalled General Weyler, promising to end the *reconcentrado* and to initiate reforms leading to autonomy within the empire. The Cubans, having heard such promises before, were skeptical, but American cries for war subsided, and McKinley urged Congress to give Spain "a reasonable chance" to fulfill its commitments. Early in 1898, however, the situation began to deteriorate. In January, Spanish soldiers destroyed the offices of a newspaper that had criticized Weyler, provoking anti-Spanish riots in Havana and a widening perception, in the United States and in Cuba, that Spain could no longer keep order.

Then, on February 9, *The New York Journal* published a purloined personal letter written by Enrique Dupuy de Lome, Spain's minister to Washington, in which de Lome suggested that Spain's promise of reform was largely cosmetic and de-

The wreckage of the battleship *Maine*, February 1898.

rided McKinley as a "weak" man, "a bidder for the admiration of the crowd." De Lome resigned immediately, but his letter convinced many that Spain could not be trusted. A week later, the chances of a diplomatic resolution receded further when the American battleship *Maine* exploded in Havana Harbor, killing 266 Americans. Although a modern study of the ship's remains concluded that the explosion was likely caused by the accidental igniting of the ship's coal and powder bins (a common occurrence during the period), contemporaries immediately fixed blame on the Spanish—although the Spanish had much to lose by such an action. "Remember the *Maine*" became the battle cry of those demanding that the United States go to war.

By the end of February, the public clamor for war had grown intense. Sensationalist newspapers such as Joseph Pulitzer's *New York World* and William Randolph Hearst's *Journal* beat the drums loudly, and even some opponents of American intervention began to change their tune. In his own careful way, President McKinley set about preparing for war—which increasingly seemed to be the only way to achieve his objectives of ending the bloodshed in Cuba, protecting American business interests, terminating the uncertainty in the American economy, and

making clear that the United States was able to maintain stability in the Caribbean. He sent a message to Congress asking for $50 million to ready the army and navy for action while reassuring business leaders that a war would not be too costly or damage the economic recovery. At the same time, he continued his diplomatic efforts, sending a series of demands to the government in Madrid. By April, Spain had agreed to almost all of McKinley's demands, including the granting of an armistice, the permanent end to the *reconcentrado,* and the payment of reparations for the *Maine.* The Spanish government, however, refused to agree to the centerpiece of McKinley's proposal: that the United States mediate negotiations for Cuban independence, which would begin without further delay. To have accepted this condition would almost certainly have toppled Spain's government.

On April 11, McKinley sent a war message to Congress. Although approval was never in doubt, Congress spent days debating whether or not to recognize the Cuban revolutionary government. McKinley did not advocate recognition: he pressed instead for intervention that would impose "hostile constraint" on both warring parties in order to guarantee peace and stability in Cuba. McKinley wanted to have as much freedom of action as possible, and he feared that the Cuban rebels might follow a path that would threaten American economic interests. After a week of political infighting, Congress agreed to McKinley's demand: the United States would not recognize the Cuban rebels and thus would not be intervening

A column of Cuban soldiers near the beginning of the Spanish-American War.

on their behalf. In turn, McKinley agreed to an amendment drafted by Senator Henry Teller of Colorado stating that "the United States hereby disclaims any disposition or intention to exercise sovereignty, jurisdiction, or control over said island except for the pacification thereof, and asserts its determination when that is accomplished to leave the government and control of the island to its people," On April 29, 1898, McKinley signed a congressionally approved declaration of war.

THE UNITED STATES AT WAR

The **war in Cuba** was swift and decisive. The American strategy at the outset was to impose a naval blockade, cutting the Spanish forces off from supplies and reinforcements, while simultaneously delivering supplies to the Cuban rebels. In so doing, the United States could buy time to raise and train ground troops. In late May, American warships, far superior to those of Spain, blockaded the Spanish fleet in the harbor of Santiago de Cuba. The navy quickly asked for ground troops to begin an attack on Santiago, and McKinley, shifting his strategy, chose to accelerate the ground war. Thanks to modern telegraph and telephone equipment and the creation of a command center at the White House, McKinley was the first president able to play an active role in military strategy.

Initiating a land war in Cuba meant rushing ill-equipped and barely trained soldiers into combat. Since the army was still a tiny force of 28,000 early in 1898, the United States had to rely on volunteers who, it turned out, were fast in coming: more than 200,000 men enlisted, including a "Silver Battalion" from Nebraska, organized by William Jennings Bryan, and the "Rough Riders" led by the combat-eager Theodore Roosevelt, who had resigned as assistant secretary of the navy in order to enlist. (Roosevelt had his uniforms custom-made by Brooks Brothers.) Supplying, equipping, and training these volunteers, however, was a task that overwhelmed the weak administrative capacities of the army. Chaos and incompetence reigned at the overpopulated training camp and staging area in Tampa. There were not enough guns to go around, and the outdated rifles that were available still used black powder cartridges. Since no American factory produced tropical-weight khaki suitable for uniforms, many soldiers had to wear their own clothes into battle; others were given heavy woolen army shirts designed to be worn in Alaska rather

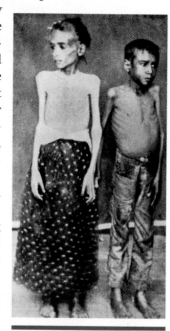

Cubans suffering from starvation during the Spanish-American War.

than the suffocating heat of mid-summer Cuba. Sanitation facilities were grossly inadequate; rations sometimes included "knots of gristle, hunks of rope, and mummified maggots"; and diseases were rampant both in Tampa and Cuba.

The Americans nonetheless quickly defeated the Spanish, with the help of Cuban rebels who secured the beaches for the Americans to land, served as guides, and continued to harass and wear down the Spanish troops. On June 22, American soldiers arrived on the beaches east of Santiago, and, a week later, in the only major land battle of the war, army units broke through Spanish defenses and seized control of San Juan Hill. From the hilltops surrounding Santiago Harbor, they were able to train their artillery on the blockaded Spanish fleet. The Spaniards had little choice but to run the blockade; when they did, the faster and better-armed American warships opened fire, sinking or disabling every Spanish vessel

Members of the U.S. Tenth Cavalry, an African American unit, on San Juan Hill in Cuba.

667

Celebratory cover of an American magazine, 1898.

within four hours, with the loss of only one American life. Demoralized and without any prospect of reinforcements or new supplies, the Spanish army capitulated on July 17. American troops, shunting aside the Cuban rebels, claimed the city. A few days later, American forces, firing few shots and losing only three men, also completed the occupation of the Spanish island of Puerto Rico.

CONQUERING THE PHILIPPINES

The Caribbean was not the only theater of war. Beginning early in 1898, McKinley and his advisers had made plans to seize some or all of the Philippine islands in the event of a conflict with Spain. In the Philippines, consisting of thousands of islands 7,000 miles west of California, Spain was also battling a rebel insurgency, and the islands appeared to be an easy target for a foreign takeover. With the European powers, Russia, and Japan jockeying for power in China, the Philippines held considerable strategic importance for the United States. Commercial interests wished to strengthen American access to Asian markets, and the administration considered

the Philippine port of Manila perfectly located to serve as a base for the navy and commercial shipping. In February 1898, Assistant Naval Secretary Roosevelt sent a message to Admiral George Dewey of the Pacific fleet, instructing him to attack Manila if the United States declared war with Spain. Thus, from the outset, the war to "save" Cuba was also a war for commercial and imperial advantage in the Pacific.

Hostilities actually began in the Philippines before a shot had been fired in Cuba. On April 30, Dewey's small squadron arrived undetected at the mouth of Manila Bay; the next day, it shelled the unprepared Spanish fleet for four hours, completely destroying it without losing an American life. Within a few days, the first American ground troops were dispatched to the Philippines, and by mid-August the American army, acting alongside—if not always with—the nationalist rebels, had defeated the Spanish and occupied Manila. Even before the last ground battles were fought (and unbeknown to troops in the field because of severed telegraph lines), Spain and the United States had signed an armistice.

President McKinley, meanwhile, had taken advantage of wartime conditions to accomplish a goal that he had long sought: the annexation of Hawaii. Convinced that the islands were critical to trade with Asia and concerned that European powers might be tempted to meddle, McKinley in 1897 signed an annexation treaty with the white-dominated, pro-annexation Hawaiian government. "We need Hawaii just as much and a good deal more than we did California," McKinley declared. "It is manifest destiny." Congressional opponents stalled the treaty, arguing that protecting Hawaii would require an expensive navy, that annexation would lead the nation toward an unconstitutional colonialism, and that it would generate an unwelcome migration of cheap Asian labor to the West Coast. A year later, however, circumstances had changed: Dewey had already scored his victory in Manila Harbor, and Hawaii was viewed as a vital coaling station and staging area for American troops. Since opposition still remained strong, McKinley sent Congress a simple annexation resolution that would require only a majority vote of both houses, rather than the two-thirds vote of the Senate needed to ratify a treaty. The president also broke a House filibuster by threatening to use his war powers to seize the islands. Congress approved the resolution in July, and on August 12, 1898, Hawaii became a U.S. territory.

The acquisition of overseas lands continued in October, when delegates from Spain and the United States met in Paris to hammer out a peace treaty. (Notably, neither the Cuban nor Filipino rebels were invited to attend.) Since the United States held all the cards, the negotiations were one-sided: the Spanish government surrendered its sovereignty over Cuba and ceded Puerto Rico, Guam, and several small islands to the Americans. Spain also gave in to President McKinley's demand that it turn over control not just of Manila but of the entire Philippines; to soften the blow, the Americans agreed to make a face-saving indemnity payment of $20 million to Spain. The treaty was signed in December, and McKinley submitted it to the Senate in January 1899.

Ratification, however, was not a sure thing, and the Senate's consideration of the treaty became the occasion for an impassioned national debate over the annexation of the Philippines and, more generally, the desirability of acquiring an overseas empire. Expansionists such as Senator Henry Cabot Lodge argued that the treaty served the nation's economic and diplomatic interest and that there was no feasible alternative to annexation, since an independent Philippines would soon be taken over by another European power. They also maintained that annexation would bring order to the islands, as well as Christianity and civilization to its people.

But some anti-imperialists, such as steel magnate Andrew Carnegie, disputed the claim that "trade followed the flag," arguing that the way to sell goods abroad was simply to make them better and cheaper. Carnegie, in fact, was so enraged that the United States seemed to be following in the imperial footsteps of England that he offered to buy the Philippines for $20 million in order to grant the islands independence. Other anti-imperialists put forward constitutional and political arguments: the United States lacked the constitutional right to acquire colonies; the Constitution could not be applied to distant territories; and American democracy itself would be subverted by the undemocratic subjugation of other peoples. Senator George F. Hoar of Massachusetts voiced the fear that "we are to be transformed from a republic, founded on the Declaration of Independence . . . into a vulgar, commonplace empire, founded upon physical force." Anti-imperialists, who often shared the expansionists' view of Anglo-Saxon racial superiority, also believed that the possession of colonies would compound the nation's already difficult racial problems. As a senator from Missouri put it, "the idea of conferring American citizenship upon the half-civilized, piratical, muck-running inhabitants of two thousand islands seven thousand miles distant . . . is absurd and indefensible."

Above all, perhaps, the anti-imperialists believed that it was simply *wrong,* as well as a violation of key American values, to impose the will of the United States by force on other people. As Senator Hoar argued, invoking the language of abolitionism, "No man was ever created good enough to own another. No nation was ever created good enough to own another." Between 1898 and 1900, the newly formed Anti-Imperialist League attracted thousands of members; centered in urban areas, especially in the Northeast, the ranks of the anti-imperialists included women who identified their own voteless condition with the oppression of colonized people, as well as public figures such as Mark Twain, Samuel Gompers, William Jennings Bryan, William Graham Sumner,

Liliuokalani, queen of the Hawaiian Islands (1891–93), in 1898.

Newspaper illustration of crowds on the docks of San Francisco cheering the departure for the Philippines of the Twentieth Pennsylvania volunteers, June 1898.

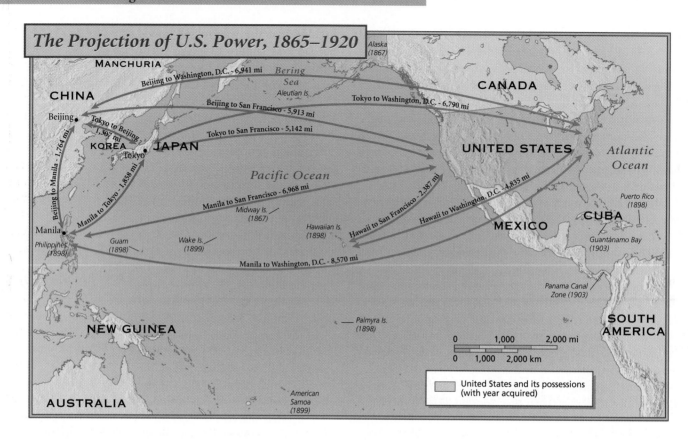

The Projection of U.S. Power, 1865–1920

and Grover Cleveland. Notably, the leadership of the movement consisted primarily of men in their sixties and seventies whose politics were shaped by the moral crusades of antislavery, equal rights, and civil service reform.

For a time, it appeared that the anti-imperialists might be able to block ratification of the treaty with Spain. Early in February 1899, however, word reached Washington that gunfire had been exchanged between the Filipino nationalists and America soldiers who were entering cities run by the Filipinos' provisional government. In circumstances in which a negative vote could be construed as lack of support for soldiers in the field, the treaty was ratified on February 6 by a 57–27 majority, only one vote more than the two-thirds required by law.

SUPPRESSING REVOLUTION
IN THE PHILIPPINES

That shots were fired between American troops and Filipino rebels was hardly surprising. The Filipinos were led by Emilio Aguinaldo, a well-educated former mayor and leader of a revolutionary organization that had fought bitterly against the Spanish. Aguinaldo initially welcomed American intervention, believing that the United States would act according to its own celebrated values and help the Filipinos realize the independence that they declared in June 1898. From the outset, however, the United States was reluctant to link itself too closely to the nationalist cause. Although Aguinaldo's army already controlled much of the Philippines outside of Manila, Admiral Dewey, following instructions from Washington, kept his distance, and when American ground troops finally arrived in the islands, they planned their strategy without consulting the Filipinos. The final battle for Manila was, in fact, a bizarre three-pronged event, as the Spanish fought hard to keep the feared rebels out of the city, while eventually encouraging American troops to enter and accept their surrender.

Even before the defeat of the Spanish, Aguinaldo and his followers had begun organizing a government; by the fall of 1898, they controlled numerous islands, including much of Luzon, the large island that contained the key city of Manila. The

American consul general in Hong Kong described Aguinaldo as "dignified and just as the head of his government," and the revolutionary government as "apparently acceptable to the Filipinos." The nationalist rebels drew up a constitution for their nation and in January 1899 announced the creation of a republic of the Philippines, with Aguinaldo as president. But the United States, pursuing its own goals and convinced that the Filipinos were incapable of self-government, refused to recognize Aguinaldo's republic and began sending troops into areas he controlled. These incursions inevitably led to hostilities. By February, Aguinaldo, recognizing that the Americans had no intention of granting independence, declared war on the United States.

What followed was a war far longer and more costly than the conflict with Spain. During its initial phase, Aguinaldo's large, poorly equipped army fought set battles against American troops. When that strategy proved unsuccessful, his troops reverted to guerrilla war tactics, trying to make American rule costly through small-scale hit-and-run attacks on different islands; they effectively forced the United States to fight a war of counterinsurgency, the first of many in the twentieth century. Subduing the nationalists required more than 120,000 American soldiers over a three-year period, and the nature of the warfare, which was tinged with racial and cultural antagonism, led to brutality on both sides. U.S. newspapers reported that American troops frequently used a water torture to compel captives to talk and

> *" 'And so it has come to pass,' reflected President McKinley privately in September 1899, 'that in a few short months we have become a world power.' "*

that there were incidents of mass killing of unarmed civilians. One American officer justified the brutality to a reporter, claiming that "we must . . . have no scruples about exterminating this other race standing in the way of progress and enlightenment." Ironically, the United States even resorted to a policy of forcing civilians into camps, reminiscent of General Weyler's *reconcentrado* in Cuba.

Thanks to superior weaponry, as well as a strategy of dogged pursuit designed by officers experienced in fighting Native Americans, the American forces did eventually prevail. Aguinaldo was captured in 1901, and most of his troops laid down their arms by the beginning of 1902. "Pacification" of the Philippines was facilitated by a shrewd American policy of granting amnesty to rebels who surrendered and of building close ties with the Filipino elite, many of whom feared the nationalist rebels. The cost of victory, however, was high. More than 4,000 American soldiers died in the war, while thousands more were permanently disabled or weakened by tropical diseases and malnutrition. The carnage was far greater for the Filipinos: 15,000 rebels were killed in battle, and roughly 200,000 civilians lost their lives. "Pacification," moreover, was never really completed: insurgents continued to fight on some islands until 1913, and periodic rebellions against American power and influence would recur until late in the twentieth century.

LEGACIES

"And so it has come to pass," reflected President McKinley privately in September 1899, "that in a few short months we have become a world power." His assessment was correct. The United States in a very short time had enlarged its influence in the Western Hemisphere, while acquiring strategic assets in the Pacific that permitted it to play an entirely new role in Asia. Yet the events of the 1890s also left the United States confronting a new set of questions: what exactly would it do with the territories it possessed and the people it controlled? In the past, territorial acquisitions had always been accomplished through formal annexation, with an eye toward eventual statehood; but to most policymakers, these historical precedents did not seem applicable to the overseas lands the United States now possessed.

Despite the Teller amendment, the fate of Cuba was undecided when the United States took formal possession of

General Emilio Aguinaldo with some of his troops during the insurrection of the Philippines against the United States, 1900.

the island in January 1899. Although many Americans continued to support Cuban independence, others, including Leonard Wood, the military commander of Cuba, believed that annexation alone would yield stability because the Cubans were incapable of self-government. After months of debate, McKinley and his closest adviser, Secretary of War Elihu Root, opted for a compromise. Because of its strategic importance and the scale of American investments, they sought to control Cuba, but they were sensitive to domestic opposition to annexation, reluctant to incorporate a nearby nonwhite nation into the United States, and concerned about provoking the Cubans into a new war for independence. As a result, they decided to grant Cuba formal independence, but with significant strings attached: Cuba could not become deeply indebted to any foreign power; it could not enter into any treaties that would "impair" its independence; it was required to sell or lease lands to the United States to be used as naval bases; and the United States retained the right to intervene in Cuba "for the preservation of Cuban independence" and "the maintenance of a government adequate for the protection of life, property, and individual liberty."

These sweeping provisions, introduced in Congress in 1901 by Senator Orville Platt of Connecticut and later known as the Platt amendment, were attached to a formal treaty between the United States and Cuba. Secretary Root also insisted that they be incorporated into the new Cuban constitution. When the constitutional convention balked in November 1900, its members were informed by Root that they had no choice if they wanted independence and access to American markets: by a narrow majority, the Cubans then accepted the provisions. The Platt amendment remained the cornerstone of American policy toward Cuba for decades, leading to periodic intervention by the United States and becoming a touchstone of rebellion in Cuba. As Leonard Wood commented, "There is, of course, little or no independence left Cuba under the Platt amendment."

The United States imposed a different policy on Puerto Rico, where it did not have to contend with any rebellious forces. In 1900, prodded by McKinley and Root, Congress passed the Foraker act, which established Puerto Rico as an "unincorporated territory" of the United States, ruled by Congress and with a governor appointed in Washington. Puerto Ricans were not made citizens until 1917, and no promise of statehood was ever offered. As a local newspaper noted in 1901, "We are and we are not a foreign country. We are and we are not citizens of the United States. The Constitution applies to us and does not apply to us." This ambiguity received legal sanction from the Supreme Court in 1901 in a series of landmark decisions that came to be known as the "Insular Cases." The Court ruled that the people of unincorporated territories such as Puerto Rico possessed certain "fundamental rights" but not all the rights of Americans. The Constitution, in effect, did not "follow the flag." Or, as Elihu Root slyly noted in response to one of the Court's decisions, "As near as I can make out the Constitution follows the flag—but doesn't quite catch up with it."

The Constitution certainly did not follow the flag to the Philippines. After full-blown hostilities had ended, the Philippines were run by a governor-general appointed by the United States and supported by American troops and then by a U.S.–trained Filipino constabulary. Only Filipinos from the upper classes were allowed to participate in the government.

One other legacy of the Spanish-American War was a permanent shift in the size and mission of the **American armed forces.** In key respects, the war seemed to validate Alfred T. Mahan's theories about the significance of sea power. Accordingly, the United States continued to strengthen its navy, building a large fleet that included new, well-armed battleships. Since its

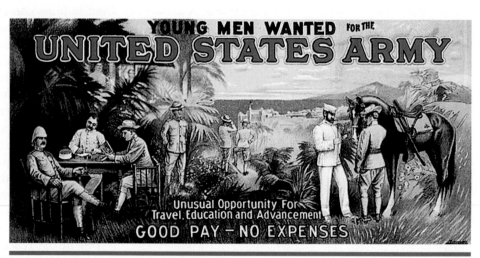

Recruiting poster for the U.S. Army, c. 1900.

The Army Signal Corps extending telegraph lines into the ocean near Manila, 1898.

overseas possessions had to be defended and because these technologically advanced ships demanded sophisticated repair and servicing centers, the country embarked on an ambitious program of naval-base construction, at Pearl Harbor and Cuba's Guantánamo Bay, among other places.

Changes in the army were even more dramatic. In the wake of the war, the United States was obligated to jettison its long-standing ideological opposition to a large standing army: defending far-flung territories required a sizable, more professional force, ready to spring into action at short notice. Under the guidance of Secretary Root, the permanent size of the army increased fourfold, and its command structure was transformed. In addition, Congress passed the Dick Act, which created a new national militia, the National Guard, paid for and controlled by the federal government rather than individual states. One lesson of the war was that the armed forces needed to be nationalized and disciplined: local units of state militias had melded uneasily with career army officers. Money was poured into weapons development, leading to more powerful and accurate artillery, the adoption of the Model 1903 Springfield rifle (which remained in use for decades), and experiments with military aviation.

During the first decade of the twentieth century, the army also began to use motorized vehicles, while telephone, telegraph, and wireless networks were constructed in the Philippines, Alaska, and the Caribbean. (The Spanish-American War was the first in which telephones played a major role.)

The Army Signal Corp, its most scientific and technological branch, was charged with developing the communications needed for overseas operations; the corp exploded in size from 8 officers, 52 soldiers, and an equipment budget of $800 to a dynamic unit of 1,300 a few years later. The United States, in effect, had joined an international arms and communication race: in the three years after the war, the overall military budget increased by more than 300 percent over the prewar level, while nonmilitary federal expenditures rose by less than 25 percent.

The New Century

By the beginning of the twentieth century, the United States controlled what historians have called both "formal" and "informal" empires. In contrast to Britain, France, Germany, and Portugal, its formal possessions—the Philippines, Hawaii, Puerto Rico, Guam, and Samoa—were few, but they were critically located. Less formally, the United States wielded significant economic power and political influence in much of Central and Latin America. As the largest manufacturing nation in the world, with overt global ambitions and a growing military, the United States was the dominant force in the Western Hemisphere and a growing power in East Asia. Between 1900 and the beginning of World War I, the country took further steps to strengthen its position and extend its influence, with little domestic opposition: the anti-imperialist movement so visible at the end of the nineteenth century faded, and most Americans seem to accept the nation's growing role in world affairs.

THE OPEN DOOR TO CHINA

Even before the new century began, the United States adopted a more active posture toward China. In the late 1890s, responding to China's military defeat by Japan and the weakening of its government, the European powers, led by Germany, began to carve out commercial spheres of influence in China acquiring control over ports and railway connections. The United States feared that the Europeans and Japanese would gain enough dominance in China that they could block American exports, particularly of textiles, and close the potentially huge Chinese market to future American trade. Whether the United States could forestall such devel-

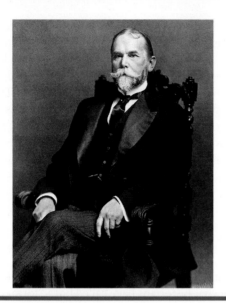

Secretary of State John Hay.

opments was unclear. President McKinley had no intention of using force to pursue American interests, and he feared that aggressive steps in Asia would further arouse the ire of anti-imperialists, jeopardizing his reelection in 1900. As Secretary of State John Hay wrote to McKinley, "We do not want to rob China ourselves, and our public opinion will not permit us to interfere, with an army, to prevent others from robbing her. Besides, we have no army." Hay consequently adopted a purely diplomatic strategy of stating American goals and trying to play the imperial powers off one another.

In September 1899, he sent what became known as the first "Open Door Note" to each of the powers involved in China (although notably not to the Chinese themselves). The note expressed a desire to encourage free trade and preserve Chinese territorial integrity. It asked each power to keep ports open to ships of all nations, to establish nondiscriminatory railroad rates within its sphere of influence, and to let the general Chinese tariff apply to all ports, with the tariffs to be collected by the Chinese. Although none of the imperial powers publicly agreed to Hay's terms, they tacitly assented, permitting Hay to declare in March 1900 that the "Open Door" had been accepted by all parties. The Open Door was a potential boon to American manufacturers, despite their government's relatively weak position in East Asia.

The first Open Door Note was rapidly overtaken by events in China. In 1900, a militant, antiforeign group (who became known in the West as the Boxers, a loose translation of their Chinese name, referring to rituals carried out to protect them against the West's modern weapons) launched a rebellion against the imperialist presence in China. Supported by the empress of the crumbling Manchu dynasty, the Boxer rebels swept through northern China, destroying foreign property, killing foreigners, including Christian missionaries, and eventually placing the foreign legations in Beijing under siege. The imperial powers responded by sealing off their areas of control and sending troops to lift the siege of Beijing in the summer of 1900. Among the expeditionary forces were 5,000 Americans whom President McKinley, in an unprecedented executive action, dispatched without consulting Congress or declaring war.

In the midst of the Boxer Rebellion, Secretary Hay, fearing an imperial splintering of China, issued his second Open Door Note, declaring that the United States respected Chinese "territorial and administrative integrity" and urging the other imperial powers to do the same. For reasons that had less to do with Hay's note than with their own preoccupations and fears, the secretary's wish was granted. In 1901, after the Boxers were suppressed, the imperialist powers withdrew all troops from Beijing, made no attempt to carve

This 1900 cartoon shows Uncle Sam opening China to free trade while England (left) and Russia (right) look on.

up China, and paid lip service to the principle of the Open Door. Behind the scenes, however, several European nations cut secret deals to retain their spheres of influence, leaving the door to China less than fully open.

The Open Door Notes did not achieve very much for the United States, beyond the symbolic assertion of its right to pursue trade opportunities in Asia. They did, however, help President McKinley win reelection against Democrat William Jennings Bryan in 1900. The apparent restraint of McKinley's China policy served to disarm the Democrats' anti-imperialist criticism. McKinley appeared as a careful, sober-minded leader, promoting American economic interests abroad while challenging Bryan's own positions, such as his advocacy of rights for Filipinos that his own party denied to African Americans in the South. At the same time, McKinley's new running mate, the pro-imperialist governor of New York, Theodore Roosevelt, barnstormed the country celebrating the use of force to subdue and eventually uplift "the barbarians." With foreign policy issues politically neutralized, the economy booming, and the coinage of silver losing its appeal as an issue, McKinley won a decisive victory. Less than a year later, however, McKinley was dead, killed by an assassin, and the most ardently expansionist of American public figures was president.

THE PANAMA CANAL

 The most important foreign-policy goal of Theodore Roosevelt's presidency (see Chapter 22) was the construction of a canal through Central America connecting the Atlantic and Pacific. The desirability of such a canal had long been evident: it would reduce shipping costs between the East and West Coasts, and, as southerners hoped, reinvigorate north-south trade routes through the nation's interior. The Spanish-American War and the acquisition of overseas territories added a military dimension to the case for a canal, because the capabilities of the navy would be substantially increased by shortening the transit time from the Atlantic to the Pacific. Roosevelt also viewed a canal, built and controlled by the United States, as a fitting symbol of America's new influence in world affairs.

In the year before his death, President McKinley had set the diplomatic wheels in motion for the building of a canal. Seizing an opportune moment when Britain was preoccupied with conflicts in South Africa, the Far East, and Europe, McKinley dispatched Secretary Hay to negotiate a termination of the 1850 Clayton-Bulwer Treaty, which had committed Britain and the United States to joint construction and control of a canal. After several rounds of negotiations, the two nations signed the Hay-Pauncefote Treaty in 1901, giving the United States the right to build a canal by itself, as long as British ships were charged the same tolls as American ships.

Attention then turned to the site of a canal. Nicaragua had long appeared to be the most promising location: although the route was relatively long, the presence of sea-level interior waterways promised to make construction easier than seemed likely in the Colombian province of Panama, where the French had failed in their effort to hack a canal through dense, unhealthy terrain in the 1870s and 1880s. A newly appointed commission, however, concluded that the Panamanian route was preferable, especially if the United States could, at a reasonable price, buy the charter, some machinery, and property from the French company that had begun construction and still retained the exclusive right to build a canal in Panama. After much debate, Congress in 1902 authorized President Roosevelt to explore the Panama option, but to turn his attention to the Nicaraguan alternative if he could not quickly finalize an arrangement with Colombia.

Secretary Hay then negotiated a treaty with the foreign minister of Colombia, which was signed in January 1903, but the Colombian Senate rejected the treaty as too favorable to the United States and impinging on Colombian sovereignty. Roosevelt, who favored the Panama route, was enraged: denouncing the Colombians as "jackrabbits" and "foolish corruptionists," he refused to return to the negotiating table. Instead, he and his administration lent tacit support to a revolt organized by Philippe Bunau-Varilla, an engineer representing the French canal company and Panamanian investors who stood to lose $40 million if the canal project was abandoned or stalled. On November 1, 1903, Bunau-Varilla and his colleagues, in collaboration with Panamanian nationalists who had long sought freedom from Colombian rule, declared Panama to be an independent state. An American warship cruised offshore as the declaration was made, and a fleet arrived to show American support within days.

Bunau-Varilla, a French citizen who had never lived in Panama, then appointed himself foreign minister and immediately entered into negotiations with Secretary Hay. Before any Panamanians could arrive in Washington to join the negotiations, the Hay–Bunau-Varilla Treaty had been signed, on terms extremely favorable to the United States, including

Cartoon showing death awaiting the builders of the Panama Canal, 1904.

afflicted many of the Americans who went to Panama; others, fearing disease, fled; and the digging was impeded by breakdowns in transportation and machinery. Things got on track only when President Roosevelt, on the recommendation of a railroad tycoon, appointed John Stevens as chief engineer. Stevens was a construction engineer, with long experience in frontier settings, who had spent his career working for the railways, eventually becoming chief engineer and then general manager of the Great Northern Railway. His first step on arriving in Panama in 1905 was to halt construction and to focus instead on creating an environment and an infrastructure that could support the largest construction operation in history.

Stevens had two main concerns. The first was minimizing the threat of disease so that manual workers and professionals would come to Panama. He hired Dr. William Gorgas, who had sanitized Havana to protect American troops, and asked him to clean up Panama City and Colón, the two major cities in the Canal Zone. Given top priority in obtaining workers and ordering supplies, Gorgas pursued his task relentlessly, fumigating the cities house by house. Mobilizing new scientific knowledge about the sources of infectious diseases, particularly water- and mosquito-borne diseases, Gorgas's Sanitation Department remained in action for a decade, disposing of garbage, digging drainage ditches, spraying oil on streams and swamps, and chasing down all possible sources of infection. Stevens meanwhile supplemented Gorgas's work

the granting of virtual sovereignty over the Canal Zone to the United States in perpetuity. Although the Panamanian nationalists denounced the agreement as "the treaty no Panamanian signed," they accepted its terms, thanks to a mixture of American bribes and threats. (The Panamanians were told that if they resisted, the Americans would abandon them, leaving them at the mercy of Colombian authorities.) The episode provoked a storm in the United States, with congressmen and newspapers attacking Roosevelt's dealings with Colombia as an "assault upon another republic over the shattered wreckage of international law." Even Roosevelt's inner circle expressed dismay. After the president had explained his actions at a cabinet meeting, he demanded to know if he had satisfactorily defended himself. "You certainly have," replied Secretary of War Elihu Root. "You have shown that you were accused of seduction and you have conclusively proved that you were guilty of rape." Despite such sentiments, the Senate ratified the Hay–Bunau-Varilla Treaty in February 1904.

The construction of the Panama Canal was an extraordinary feat of organization and engineering, made possible by late nineteenth-century innovations in management, technology, and science. For more than a year after the treaty was signed, the problems that had doomed the French stymied the Americans as well. Yellow fever, malaria, and pneumonia

Dirt and rocks being loaded onto flatbed train cars in Panama by a 25-ton steam shovel.

by building housing for workers and by erecting a supply depot that included a cold storage plant capable of holding 94,000 cubic feet of food, a bakery, an ice cream factory, and a laundry.

Stevens's second concern was transportation—of people, supplies, equipment, and, most important, dirt. Stevens recognized that the central engineering challenge of the project was figuring out where to put and how to move the 232 million cubic yards (338 million tons) of soil and rock that had to be dug from the canal site. To accomplish this task, he transformed the antiquated Panama Railroad, building nearly 300 miles of new track and ordering thousands of pieces of rolling stock, including 300 locomotives and 3,915 flatcars designed for earth removal. He also brought in new types of machinery, such as dirt spreaders, unloaders (to speed the task of getting dirt off the flatcars), and recently developed track shifters that permitted railway lines to be moved quickly so that dirt could be dumped in different spots. By 1907, the Panama Railroad, running 570 trains a day, was said to be the busiest railway in the world.

Stevens also played a critical role in the design of the canal itself. When he was appointed, no design had yet been approved in Washington, although it was presumed that a sea-level canal would be dug through the hilly terrain. Stevens, however, became convinced that a narrow sea-level canal, flanked by high walls, ran too high a risk of being obstructed by landslides, and that a "lock" canal could be built more cheaply and rapidly. By June 1906, he convinced the Canal Commission, the president, and Congress to follow his advice and adopt an engineering plan calling for the creation of an above-sea-level passageway, including a man-made inland lake, connected to a network of locks that would raise and lower ships at each end of the canal. When Stevens resigned as chief engineer in 1907, he left behind a coherent engineering plan, an efficient railroad, and an infrastructure that could support a labor force of thousands.

Stevens's successor was George W. Goethals, a career officer from the Army Corps of Engineers with abundant construction experience. Goethals, who remained on the job for seven years, created an effective managerial hierarchy and oversaw an international labor force that numbered as many as 50,000. A minority (called the "gold roll" because they were paid in gold-backed currency) consisted of skilled white

"The central engineering challenge of the canal was figuring out where to put and how to move the 388 million tons of soil and rock that had to be dug from the canal site."

males, mostly American, lured to Panama by high wages and free transportation and medical care. Their housing was comfortable, recreation and entertainment were provided, and the commissary did its best to provide these men and their families fresh meat, groceries, and at least some of the comforts of home. Most of the men who performed the physical labor of building the canal, however, were unskilled blacks from the Caribbean, joined by thousands of southern Europeans and roughly 1,000 Asians. These "silver" workers (paid in less valuable silver Panamanian currency) lived in cramped barracks, huts, or urban slums; they were poorly paid; they were compelled to use segregated hospitals, dining halls, and post offices; and they were denied rights (including the eight-hour day) that were legally mandated for government employees in the United States. The vast majority of workers who died in accidents or from disease were black.

Workers, digging by hand, during the construction of the Panama Canal.

677

Excavated by De Lesseps Co.
Excavated by New Panama Co.
Excavation for Completion by U.S.

Colon

Bohio Locks Normal Lift 85'

High Water 90 above mean sea level
Low water 85

Obispo Gates
Emperador
Culebra
Pedro Miguel Locks
Miraflores Lock
Panama

High water
Low water

mean Sea Level d.9²

Atlantic Section 14.42 miles   Bohio Lake 13.61 miles   Culebra Cut 7.91 miles 1.55 Pacific Section 8.53

Miles from Colon harbour   15   30   46.70

Colon
Gatun
Bohio Soldado
Obispo
Emperador
Culebra
Panama
Naos Islands

Panoramic view of Panama, showing the route of the canal.

For more than seven years, these workers, "gold" and "silver," dug their way across the Isthmus of Panama. More than 61 million pounds of dynamite were exploded; 300 rock drills were continuously in operation; scores of steam shovels lifted dirt and rock from the site; hundreds of trains shuttled back and forth each day; millions of yards of concrete were poured to form the locks at the two ends of the canal. An ear-splitting cacophony of sound, day and night, the dramatic construction scene became a tourist attraction, with passenger trains ferrying the well-to-do to watch the canal being cut from the earth. Despite major landslides and the periodic buckling of the canal floor, the project was completed in 1913, almost a year ahead of schedule. Its final cost was around $350 million, with disease and accidents claiming the lives of 5,609 workers. The canal saw little traffic during its first years because of World War I, but by the 1920s more than 5,000 ships were passing through its locks each year. The time required for ships to pass from the Atlantic to the Pacific had been cut from weeks to twelve hours. An extraordinary and long-imagined feat of practical engineering had been completed; and the United States owned one of the most important waterways in the world.

THE ROOSEVELT COROLLARY

In addition to superintending the construction of the Panama Canal, Theodore Roosevelt gave a new definition to American policy in the Western Hemisphere. This redefinition was precipitated by Venezuela's default on its debts to Great Britain and Germany. Tiring of unfulfilled promises of repayment, the two European nations, after notifying the United States, set up a naval blockade of the Venezuelan coast. Roosevelt, fearing the blockade might lead to war and German seizure of Venezuelan land or its treasury, pressured Britain and Germany to accept arbitration of their Venezuelan claims. Faced with the threat of American naval intervention, the two countries agreed to arbitration, and their claims were eventually settled by an international tribunal at The Hague in 1904.

The significance of the episode resided in the Europeans' recognition of American primacy in Latin America. It also brought to the fore broader issues: many Latin American and Caribbean regimes were economically and politically unstable, in part because of imperialist interventions, and that instability—characterized by revolutionary movements, violent changes of regime, and unreliable debt repayments—seemed likely to invite outside intervention. As Roosevelt saw the situation, this meant that the United States had to either tolerate European interference in Latin America or police the hemisphere itself. Encouraged by Britain and Germany, Roosevelt adopted the latter course. "In the Western hemisphere," he declared in an address to Congress in 1904, "the adherence of the United States to the Monroe Doctrine may force the United States, however reluctantly . . . to the exercise of an international police power." Although couched as a mere amendment to the Monroe Doctrine, Roosevelt's corollary in fact announced a major shift in America's role. Monroe had warned European nations not to meddle in hemispheric affairs and to respect Latin American revolutions, as well as the independence of Latin American countries; Roosevelt, in contrast, was committing the United States to intervention to suppress revolutions and guarantee a "stability" that the United States alone would define.

Roosevelt soon had the opportunity to put his corollary into action. Between the late 1890s and 1903, social conflict spawned a series of military revolts in the Dominican Republic,

> *"Although couched as a mere amendment to the Monroe Doctrine, Roosevelt's corollary in fact announced a major shift in America's role."*

leading to defaults on foreign loans. In 1903, the turmoil was so great that the United States and several European nations sent warships to Santo Domingo. To stabilize the situation, Roosevelt, in collaboration with Dominican president Carlos Morales, formulated a plan for the United States to take charge of Dominican customs collections and to oversee the repayment of the island nation's foreign debts. The rationale for taking control of customs was strategic and precise: doing so would not only guarantee debt repayment, it would also give the United States *de facto* control of the national budget, since customs revenues were the government's primary source of income. Washington also believed that it would reduce smuggling, graft, and the incentive for rebellion, permit a fractious army to be shrunk, and thus free up funds to stimulate economic development. Although Roosevelt denied any interest in annexing the Dominican Republic ("I have about the same desire to annex it as a gorged boa constrictor might have to swallow a porcupine wrong-end-to"), his plan provoked a storm of opposition among Dominicans and in Congress. The arrangement was implemented nonetheless, and the United States remained in charge of Dominican finances until 1911.

Roosevelt's policy toward the Dominican Republic and other less developed nations was also shaped by ideological and cultural considerations. The president and the men around him saw the world as divided between "civilized" and "barbarian" peoples, and they believed that it was the responsibility of civilized white nations like the United States to train and uplift their less fortunate, usually nonwhite, brethren. "It is a good thing for India," wrote Roosevelt to a friend, "that England should control it." Such cultural and racial condescension was widespread in American society. In 1898, a newspaper, after noting that Admiral Dewey had requisitioned 60,000 pounds of soap for the Philippines, observed that "soap and the Bible go hand in hand . . . in the development of the backward races." In 1904, the Louisiana Purchase Exposition in St. Louis included a display in which 1,200 Filipinos of various "types"—including "savages," "fierce followers of Mohammed," and the "more intelligent class"—lived in mock villages where they could be observed by American fair-goers.

Such views prevented Roosevelt and others from recognizing the real sources of conflict in foreign nations and formu-

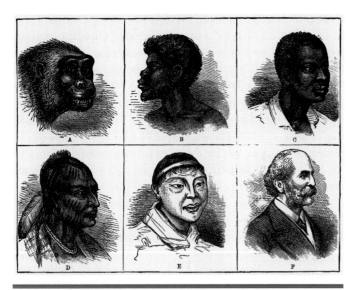

Racist assumptions of the time can be seen in this late nineteenth-century chart depicting the evolution of man from ape to a "civilized," tie-wearing European.

lating appropriate policies. The desire of the Filipinos for independence could be dismissed because most Filipinos were "savages," incapable of self-government—at least until they were schooled by Americans. Similarly, a few years of controlling the finances of a small country wracked by political divisions and economic inequalities were unlikely to bring genuine stability. Five years after the United States turned the customs houses back to the Dominicans, Washington found itself sending troops to Santo Domingo to quell rebellions and restore order. The troops would remain there for eight years.

While Roosevelt was staking out a new role for the United States as the policeman of the Western Hemisphere, he was simultaneously trying to enhance American influence in Asia by acting as a mediator. In 1904, tensions between Russia and Japan over control of northern China and Korea erupted into war, with Japan destroying much of Russia's Pacific fleet. Roosevelt shared a widespread American antipathy to tsarist Russia and quietly supported the Japanese, who had recently made positive overtures to the West. By mid-1905, the war had bogged down, with Japan lacking the resources for a lengthy conflict and the Russian government preoccupied with revolutionary upheaval in its own cities. Roosevelt embraced Japan's suggestion that he mediate the conflict. After rancorous negotiations in Portsmouth, New Hampshire, the

two warring parties agreed to a settlement. Roosevelt won the Nobel Peace Prize for his efforts, but his diplomatic goals were soon thwarted by an agreement between Russia and Japan to carve up northern China and Manchuria. That agreement, coupled with a rising tide of antiforeign (including anti-American) sentiment in China, knocked the final props from under the Open Door policy.

The treaty Roosevelt had brokered between Japan and Russia also spawned anti-American anger among the Japanese, who blamed Roosevelt for robbing Japan of the fruits of military success. Tensions between the two nations were heightened by a domestic event. In response to a sharp increase in Japanese immigration that had begun in 1900, the San Francisco school board decided in 1906 to assign Japanese children to segregated classrooms—displaying once again the West Coast's antagonism to Asian immigrants. The Japanese government demanded that this insulting practice be halted. Roosevelt, who believed that the Japanese (unlike the Chinese) were "highly civilized people," resolved the conflict by negotiating a "Gentlemen's Agreement" in 1907 that called for an end to Japanese emigration to the United States in return for a commitment from San Francisco to stop segregating schoolchildren.

DOLLAR DIPLOMACY AND WILSONIAN IDEALISM

The foreign policy course set by Presidents McKinley and Roosevelt was, in key respects, maintained by their successors, William Howard Taft (1909–13) and Woodrow Wilson (1913–21). Taft, a lawyer by training, was more of a legalist than the rambunctiously nationalist Roosevelt, yet he, too, believed that foreign trade was essential to American well-being and that the government should play an active role in promoting international commerce. Having been the governor-general of the Philippines, Taft was also convinced that international peace was a prerequisite to prosperity and democracy.

Taft's conduct of foreign policy gave birth to the label "dollar diplomacy," a double-edged phrase suggesting both that the government was doing the bidding of Wall Street and that the administration wisely preferred using "dollars" rather than "bullets" to exert influence abroad. Both connotations were apt, and Taft was notably cautious in using force, particularly in response to chaotic conditions on the Mexican border. But his government's preference for dollars did not mean that it avoided the use of bullets. The war in the

Philippines dragged on, soldiers were dispatched once again to Cuba, and Taft several times sent warships and troops to Nicaragua to install or preserve regimes friendly to American business interests.

Taft's successor, Woodrow Wilson, was a moralist in foreign affairs, as in other matters. He personally abhorred the imperialist exploitation of less developed nations, recognized that poverty and oppression bred revolutions, and believed deeply in democracy. Although Wilson, like his contemporaries, was convinced that international trade was vital to the nation's welfare, he was also a scholar and a religious man who believed that Christian values and American political institutions should serve as a model for all nations. Wilson's was a missionary vision in which the role of the United States was to assume leadership in world affairs, uplift other nations, discourage violent revolutions, and sponsor stable, gradual reform.

Wilson, however, became president just as Europe was hurtling into war and during a period when revolutionary movements in many parts of the globe were gathering steam. In those circumstances, despite—or perhaps because of—his idealist democratic convictions, he became one of the most interventionist presidents in American history. Not only did he lead the United States into World War I (see Chapter 23), he also sent troops into half a dozen Latin American nations as well as Russia.

Several of Wilson's interventions in the Caribbean and Central America followed precedents established during the first decade of the century. In Nicaragua, where Taft had already sent troops, marines remained in place under Wilson, eventually controlling the nation's ports, railroads, and financial affairs. In 1916, Wilson insisted that elections be held to replace the American-friendly but unpopular President Adolfo Diaz, and, to no one's surprise, the candidate backed by the United States, Emiliano Chamorro, was elected president. Marines remained in Nicaragua until 1925.

The United States also sent soldiers to take charge of Haiti in 1915, after seven changes of regime in four years, most by assassination. Wilson, troubled by the tumult and by the growing influence of French and German economic interests, proposed an American takeover of Haitian customs offices. When the Haitians refused, the United States sent marines to seize funds from the Haitian treasury, precipitating a collapse of the government and an American military occupation that lasted until 1934. Although the United States did contribute to Haiti's development by sanitizing its cities and building roads and bridges, it also imposed a constitution that contained provisions favorable to itself, including permitting foreigners, for the first time, to own land. Many Haitians resisted the American occupation, and more than 3,000 died fighting the marines. Similar resistance surfaced in the Dominican Republic, where marines were once again sent in 1916. For eight years, the United States occupied the Dominican Republic, combating armed nationalists while establishing an impressive system of public education, controlling the nation's finances, and creating a national guard to maintain the American-enforced peace.

The United States also intervened in Mexico. In the late nineteenth and early twentieth centuries, during the long dictatorship of Porfirio Díaz, Americans had invested heavily in their southern neighbor. By 1910, the United States was the largest foreign investor in the country, and Americans controlled critical industries, including mining and railroads. Foreign investment helped transform Mexico's economic and social structure, which in turn led to a multipronged revolution that began to erupt in 1910. After Díaz was overthrown, the long border between the United States and Mexico became a hotbed of activity, as rebel groups and bandits move back and forth across the border, seeking supplies, arms, and shelter. Despite the threat to American lives and property, President Taft was cautious about intervention, although he did form a 20,000-man Maneuver Division to police the border.

Wilson, faced with different conditions, was less cautious. In 1913, conservative general Victoriano Huerta seized power in a coup, assassinating his predecessor, Francisco Madero. Wilson opposed Huerta's regime, because of the violent way in which it had come to power and because of its ties to British oil interests. Although Huerta's rule was subsequently legitimized by a reasonably free election, Wilson remained eager to seek his ouster. In 1914, the president took advantage of a minor incident in which American sailors were briefly arrested in Tampico to send the American fleet and occupation forces to the important Mexican city of Vera Cruz. A score of Americans and hundreds of Mexicans were killed in the battle for Vera Cruz, which led to an occupation of the city for seven months and eventually to Huerta's resignation. Yet Huerta's successor, Venustiano Carranza, was also resistant to American influence. He advocated a more left-wing program, including agrarian reform, national ownership of all mineral rights, and restrictions on property holding by foreigners. When Carranza's regime was challenged by the forces of an-

Francisco "Pancho" Villa (center) and his fellow revolutionary Emiliano Zapata (with sombrero on knee) in the Presidential Palace in Mexico City, 1914.

new military technology. In Mexico, as in the Dominican Republic, the army introduced aircraft into military operations, which provided vital courier service to far-flung troops, taught important lessons to pilots and the army, and produced pioneering aerial photography. The army also used ten motorized truck companies to chase Pancho Villa, becoming less dependent on railways and more flexible in delivering supplies to combat units. In these respects at least, the Punitive Expedition proved to be America's first experiment with twentieth-century war.

American policies in the Caribbean and Latin America between 1900 and 1917 clearly established the dominance of the United States in the Western Hemisphere. Whatever interest European powers might have had in acquiring bases or colonies in the region was checked, and Presidents Roosevelt, Taft, and Wilson made clear through their actions and words that the United States would police the political and economic behavior of other states, intervening if necessary to protect American interests and keep order. Although these policies protected American property and commerce and limited European involvement, they had profound shortcomings. As often as not, American intervention spawned rebellion and disorder rather than stability. It also created deep reservoirs of anti-American sentiment that would be tapped again and again in the course of the twentieth century.

A New Empire

America's position in the world was transformed between the late 1860s and the beginning of World War I. Americans today often take as a given the global power and reach of the United States, as well as the significance of events abroad to American politics and business. But for much of the nineteenth century, America's relationship to international affairs was far different: rich in resources, devoted primarily to agriculture, geographically protected from external threats, the United States played a small role in international politics and, aside from shifts in the global market for labor and agricultural goods, was little affected by happenings outside its borders. All of this changed in the late nineteenth and early

other revolutionary, Francisco "Pancho" Villa, Wilson briefly threw his support to Villa.

The battles between Carranza's and Villa's forces spilled across the American border. At the same time, small groups of Mexicans launched raids into the United States to reclaim lands that Mexico had lost in the Mexican-American War of the 1840s. In 1915, increasingly absorbed by events in Europe, Wilson finally recognized Carranza's government. Villa, feeling betrayed, then launched a series of attacks across the Arizona and New Mexico borders, trying to demonstrate Carranza's lack of control of the country and to bait the United States into chasing Villa back into Mexico. The United States took the bait, sending a Punitive Expedition of 10,000 troops deep into Mexico in 1916 to capture Villa. The expedition ended up skirmishing not only with the "Villistas" but also with Carranza's troops before it was finally withdrawn in 1917. Although Villa was never captured and made occasional forays across the border for two years, Carranza remained in power.

Despite its failure to eliminate the Villistas, the Punitive Expedition did succeed in lessening conflict along the border. It also provided the United States with an opportunity to deploy

twentieth centuries, setting the United States on a course to becoming a world power and, later, a superpower.

These changes in the nation's global role were inextricably linked to the social and economic transformation of postbellum America. It was during this period that the West was populated by white settlers and that the second industrial revolution permanently altered the nation's economy. Manufacturers as well as farmers, facing competition and becoming more productive, looked increasingly to distant markets for their goods. Workers and managers depended on employment for their livelihoods and equated the availability of jobs with the growth of trade. The widening impact of depressions only heightened the felt need for economic stability. At the same time, the bitterness of racial conflict, as well as the ethnic tensions generated by immigration, made many Americans reluctant to annex new territories and add to the nation's nonwhite population.

The country's impulse and capacity to reach outward were also shaped by science and technology. The productivity gains that led Americans to believe they were overproducing were grounded in the technological advances that transformed workplaces. The desirability of investment in some regions, as well as the feasibility of canal construction in Panama, was enhanced by medical knowledge that reduced the threat of infectious diseases. Advances in military technology strengthened the hand of all industrial nations in their relationships with

1866	First trans-Atlantic cable completed.
1867	United States purchases Alaska from Russia.
1895	Crisis in Venezuela strengthens American power in the Western Hemisphere.
February 1898	American battleship *Maine* explodes in Havana Harbor.
April–August 1898	Spanish-American War.
August 12, 1898	Hawaii becomes a U.S. territory.
December 1898	Spain surrenders sovereignty over Cuba and the Philippines and cedes Puerto Rico and Guam to the United States.
September 1899	John Hay sends Open Door Note to powers involved in China.
1900	Puerto Rico becomes unincorporated territory of the United States.
1904	Roosevelt's corollary to the Monroe Doctrine commits United States to policing the Western Hemisphere.
1913	Panama Canal completed.

Chronology

less developed societies, while the telegraph, the telephone, faster ships, and then airplanes made it easier for men in Washington to monitor and influence events abroad.

What emerged during this period was not simply the American acquisition of "power," but a new structuring of American relationships with overseas nations. In its dealings with the European powers, as well as Russia and Japan, the United States established itself as an economic competitor, insisting on the right to trade and invest around the globe, capable of using military force to achieve its ends. That this outward thrust was accompanied by the maintenance of high tariffs and a special sphere of influence in the Western Hemisphere testified to the malleability of principles when they conflicted with self-interest. In its relations with Latin America, as well as in the Pacific and parts of Asia, the United States acquired colonies and, more commonly, forged relationships that historian William Appleman Williams has aptly labeled "non-colonial imperialism." With the important exceptions of the Philippines, Hawaii, Puerto Rico, and a few other locales, the United States did not assert formal po-

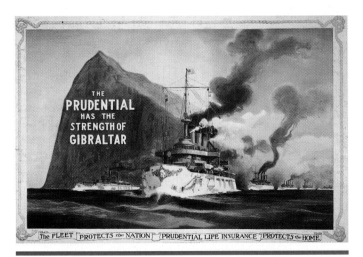

An ad from the Prudential Insurance Company comparing its protection of the home to the Great White Fleet's protection of the nation, c. 1909.

litical or military control over overseas territories; nor did it dispatch colonists to live abroad, as Europeans did in Africa, India, and parts of South America.

What the United States did instead was to establish its dominance over other countries, such as Haiti and Nicaragua, while leaving them nominally independent. The rules governing financial and political affairs were made in Washington. The people who inhabited these countries were regarded as inferiors who were best controlled and tutored by Americans. Military power could be deployed to protect American interests and ensure that the rules were followed. It was fitting that the most prominent exhibit at the 1893 World's Fair in Chicago was the "Great White Fleet," built by the United States Navy, a thirty-acre display that included full-sized replicas of the latest generation of American battleships.

Suggested Reading

Akira Iriye, *The Cambridge History of American Foreign Relations,* vol. 3: *The Globalizing of America, 1913–45* (1993)

Walter LaFeber, *The New Empire: An Interpretation of American Expansion, 1860–1898* (1963)

David McCullough, *The Path Between the Seas: The Creation of the Panama Canal, 1870–1914* (1977)

Emily Rosenberg, *Spreading the American Dream: American Economic and Cultural Expansion, 1890–1945* (1982)

Robert D. Schulzinger, *American Diplomacy in the Twentieth Century,* 3d ed. (1994)

David Trask, *The War with Spain in 1898* (1981)

Russell F. Weigley, *History of the United States Army,* enlarged ed. (1984)

THE PROGRESSIVE ERA:

1900–1916

A women's suffrage parade in New York, 1912.

QUESTIONS

- What were the economic underpinnings of Progressive reform?

- How did developments in technology and science influence Progressivism?

- What were the key elements of Progressive reform?

- How did Progressivism address tensions of class, ethnicity, and race?

- What were the experiences of women in Progressive reform?

- How did Progressive reform influence national politics?

"The Century is dead; long live the Century! Yesterday was the Nineteenth, today the Twentieth." So declared the *New York Times* on January 1, 1901. The citizens of New York marked the dawn of the twentieth century the night before, at a gala outdoor celebration in front of City Hall: the building was bedecked with 2,000 American flags, 2,000 red, white, and blue lightbulbs, and the words "WELCOME, 20TH CENTURY" in gigantic electrically lit letters. An hour before midnight, city council president Randolph Guggenheimer addressed the crowd. "Tonight when the clock strikes 12, the present century will have come to an end. We look back upon it as a cycle of time within which the achievements in science and in civilization are not less than marvelous. The advance of the human race during the past 100 years has not been equaled by the progress of man within any of the preceding ages." Guggenheimer also expressed the "earnest wish" that "the crowning glory of the coming century shall be the lifting up of the burdens of the poor, the annihilation of all misery and wrong, and that the peace and goodwill which the angels proclaimed should rest on contending nations as the snow-flakes upon the land."

A few moments before the clock struck twelve, the lights around City Hall were turned off, returning the crowd to the semidarkness that, until the 1890s, had been the norm of urban night. Then, at the stroke of midnight, lights were turned back on, new floodlights were illumined, and explosions of fireworks rained down from nearby skyscrapers. The whole city was filled with light, with "electric fountains and forests of fire," many of them red, white, or blue. "It was distinctly," as the *Times* observed, "an electric celebration."

Throughout the nation, Americans celebrated the arrival of a new century. Speakers marveled at the changes wrought during the nineteenth century, lauding the material, scientific, and technological advances that had transformed American society and made possible nocturnal festivities such as those in New York. Equally common was the sense of an unfinished agenda, the conviction that the social and political order had not kept pace with the material and the technological. The persistence of poverty and inequality seemed glaring in light of the nation's economic progress, and the absence of any true "brotherhood of man," as one newspaper put it, was all too evident.

The problems confronting American society early in the twentieth century were much the same as they had been late in the nineteenth; so, too, were the economic and social forces shaping Americans' lives. Great wealth and economic power coexisted with broad swaths of poverty. New technologies transformed workplaces and the rhythms of daily life. Immigrants continued to pour into the rapidly growing cities, testing the limits of tolerance in the host society. Racial discrimination remained at the heart of southern social life and politics.

Yet the dawn of the new century marked the beginning of a more optimistic era. The seemingly uncontrollable roller-coaster ride of the late nineteenth century slowed a bit, and many Americans became more confident of their ability to meet the challenges they faced. The effort to grasp the "natural laws" governing economic and social life gave way to empirical investigations of specific issues; the Populist and often working-class cry for sweeping change devolved into a search for concrete, pragmatic reforms. In the words of the young Walter Lippmann, who would become one of the twentieth century's most influential political commentators, "drift" was replaced by "mastery." "We put intention where custom has reigned," he wrote in 1914. Reflecting a shift in middle-class attitudes, government became more active and forward-looking, while politicians from different parties scrambled to identify themselves as "progressive."

Indeed, the first two decades of the twentieth century have long been referred to by historians as "the Progressive Era." They could as well be called the "era of electricity" or the "era of the automobile." There surely was a shift in temper in American public life, a surge of interest in social and political reform, but equally dramatic were the spread of electricity and the beginning of the nation's romance with the automobile. What distinguished these decades from their predecessors was not just the pace of reform but also the material and technological basis of daily life. These different domains were not unrelated to one another: the men and women who wrestled with social, economic, and political issues were influenced by the problem-solving mentality of the scientists and engineers who had wrought technological progress. If knowledge, ingenuity, and persistence could wipe out yellow fever and permit people to talk on the telephone, then surely they could also alleviate poverty, reduce inequality, and rein in the power of large corporations.

A Growing Economy

Undergirding the optimistic temper of the era was a rapidly growing economy. Although the nation did experience two short panics, or recessions, in 1907–8 and 1913–14, growth was steadier than it had been in the late nineteenth century. While the nation's population rose from 76 million in 1900 to 106 million in 1920, gross national product nearly doubled, with the value of manufactured goods increasing sixfold. Although many Americans were troubled by the unusual problem of inflation—rising prices were a new experience for anyone born after the Civil War—middle-class incomes rose substantially, and real wages (adjusted for inflation) increased for most workers.

As was always true, the growth was uneven. Older industries, such as flour milling and textiles, grew modestly, while the steel industry spurted forward between 1900 and 1910 and then slowed considerably because of a dramatic decline in railroad growth. But new industries picked up the slack: the two stars of the era were automobiles and electrical machinery, joined during World War I by a booming shipbuilding industry. Manufacturing remained concentrated in the Northeast and the Midwest, although textiles migrated from New England to the Carolinas and Georgia, while petroleum gravitated toward Texas and Oklahoma.

Farmers did well, although agriculture was becoming a less common pursuit. Between 1900 and 1920, the farm population and the number of acres under cultivation rose only slightly, which meant that the percentage of Americans who were farmers declined. Farm incomes, however, increased substantially, thanks in part to a sustained rise in the prices of farm products. Although the collapse of the Populist movement after the election of 1896 marked a political defeat for the nation's farmers, many of their economic goals were achieved by the prosperity of the Progressive Era.

Farmers' fortunes were also enhanced by technological improvements, most notably stream-traction engines and then gasoline-powered tractors. (The word "tractor" was coined in

New York City's Times Square at night, c. 1900.

689

1905 to identify this new vehicle.) Powerful steam-traction engines were far more productive than horses or mules, but they were expensive, heavy (weighing ten to twenty-five tons), and consumed enormous amounts of fuel and water. Even at the peak of their popularity, between 1908 and 1915, only 5 percent of all farmers owned steam-traction vehicles. Recognizing the shortcomings of steam, inventors competed to develop sturdy, light, relatively inexpensive vehicles driven by gasoline-powered internal-combustion engines. Spurred on by labor shortages during World War I, manufacturers of these new tractors achieved some success: although the great majority of farmers continued to rely on animal power, more than 200,000 tractors—each capable of doing the work of three or more horses—were in use by 1920. Tractors reduced the number of hours of labor needed to produce crops, compensated for a growing scarcity of workers, and freed millions of acres for food production that had been used to support horses and mules.

The gains achieved by science had an equal impact on farm productivity. Advances in plant genetics led to experiments in crossbreeding that yielded improved variants of corn, wheat, and other crops. The new field of bacteriology generated methods of preventing devastating diseases, such as hog cholera. Chemists helped to produce fertilizers in addition to promoting the liming of farmland. These scientific advances were encouraged by the U.S. Department of Agriculture; from 1897 to 1913, under the leadership of James (Tama Jim) Wilson, a former Iowa congressman and professor of agriculture, the department became an important center of scientific research, particularly in genetics and chemistry. It taught farmers about the latest advances in science at experiment stations and on demonstration farms; it also applied scientific knowledge to farm practices and the inspection of livestock. The efforts of the USDA were reinforced by the Smith-Lever Act of 1914 and the Smith-Hughes Act of 1917, which provided federal funds to support agricultural extension programs at land-grant colleges as well as the teaching of new agricultural methods.

Science, Technology, and Industry

Science-based industries, grounded primarily in advances in chemistry and physics, flourished during the first two decades of the twentieth century. New scientific knowledge (much of

which came from Europe) about atoms, molecules, gases, light, magnetism, and electricity lay at the heart of several industries while fostering innovation in others. In physics, for example, X-rays were discovered in 1895, radioactivity in 1896, and the electron in 1897. In 1900, German physicist Max Planck advanced the theory that radiation was emitted in quanta, discrete lumps of energy, rather than in a continuous wave. In 1905, Albert Einstein, then an employee in a Swiss patent office, published his theory of special relativity, with its remarkable implications that mass and

The young Albert Einstein.

energy were equivalent and that physical characteristics such as mass and time can vary depending on the relative movement of the observer.

Such discoveries launched new waves of scientific research in the United States; they were also ripe with possibilities for practical application. The ability to manipulate electrons, for example, made it possible to amplify electrical signals, facilitating long-distance telephone calls and the transmission of radio signals. X-ray technology transformed the practice of orthopedics as well as some surgical specialties. Scientific investigation, in turn, was stimulated by the demands of industry and the search for profits. The industrial research facilities pioneered by General Electric and Bell Telephone (see Chapter 18) were joined by several hundred other industrial laboratories, including those of chemical firms such as Dow, Eastman Kodak, and Du Pont, which employed more than 1,200 chemists by the 1920s. Firms also began to team up with universities such as MIT and the Drexel Institute, to promote scientific research: in Pittsburgh, the Mellon Institute funded graduate students and postdoctoral fellows to solve research problems submitted by industry.

These laboratories produced a wide array of new products for consumers and industry. Researchers at General Electric developed more precise X-ray machines and dramatically improved the quality of electric lighting by developing a tungsten filament and by filling bulbs with inert gas to prevent the blackening that occurred when filaments burned. Leo H. Baekeland, a Belgian-born chemist, invented a photographic paper that could be printed in artificial light (which he sold to Kodak), as well as "Bakelite," the first of a series of synthetic substances that had widespread use (in appliances and jewelry, and as handles and knobs) because they were heat- and chemical-resistant, as well as poor conductors of electricity. Chemists developed improved acids and alkalis (such as caustic and bleaching powders), while scientific advances also spawned the first aluminum products, rayons, and high-speed carbon steel that remained hard at high temperatures and thus led to great improvements in machine-tool technology. Engineers and scientists trained in these laboratories fanned out into older industries, encouraging research and innovation.

In 1901, Congress created the National Bureau of Standards, authorizing the agency not only to establish and maintain standards of measure, such as units of electricity or light, but also to engage in any research necessary to do so. In support of the bureau's creation, the secretary of the treasury, Lyman Gage, testified that the physical sciences were of great importance to the nation's well-being, that "as with all the great things of life," the United States was now competing with the nations of Europe. Foreshadowing developments that would occur later in the twentieth century, the govern-

> *"Electricity was the hallmark technology of the era, capable of transforming every facet of American life."*

ment also established, during World War I, laboratories designed to conduct research with military implications.

TECHNOLOGICAL SYSTEMS

Electricity. As had been true in the late nineteenth century, the fusion of scientific knowledge with entrepreneurial skill inspired not only individual products, such as photographic paper, but the development of large-scale, interconnected technological systems. The electrical system, created in the late nineteenth century but greatly enlarged during the first decades of the twentieth, had the most fundamental impact on society, particularly in cities. Electricity was the hallmark technology of the era, widely regarded as mysterious and all-powerful, capable of transforming every facet of American life. "God is the great electrician," proclaimed one celebrant, while the Sears, Roebuck catalogue in 1901 offered an electric belt that would allegedly restore men's sexual powers. The electrical system included several thousand utility companies by 1907, as well as firms that manufactured goods that ran on electric currents. By 1910, nearly all utilities were generating a standard alternating current, permitting power grids to be interconnected and electrical goods to be produced to uniform specifications. By 1920, one-third of all homes were wired, almost all of which were in urban and suburban areas. Electricity had replaced gas, kerosene, and oils for lighting, and appliances such as electric fans, irons, and vacuum cleaners were becoming commonplace. Electricity also provided the power for urban and suburban rail systems. By 1920, there were more than 200,000 men who fit into the new census occupational category of "electrician."

The spread of electricity to workplaces was even more significant. A rarity in 1890, electricity became first the predominant source of light and then the predominant source of power in factories. The incandescent bulb was a great improvement over the gas lamp: it was brighter, steadier, did not raise temperatures, did not give off fumes, and was less likely to spark fires. It made precise, detailed work much easier: newspaper printers, who generally worked at night, were among the first to embrace electric lighting. Electric motors also had great advantages over those driven by steam or fossil fuels: they provided a steady source of power and light without raising temperatures or consuming oxygen, and they could be regulated by electrically driven sensors and controls.

A cartoon from around 1900 depicting X-ray photography, as discovered by Wilhelm C. Roentgen.

Henry Ford with the first Ford automobile, 1896.

Electricity made it easier to locate machinery in more efficient sequences on the factory floor, and machine tools powered by electricity were faster, lighter, and more portable than their predecessors.

Electricity led to round-the-clock factory schedules, the use of cranes and lifts that carried materials, and ventilation systems that made the air easier to breathe while keeping machinery cleaner. The spread of electricity also meant that manufacturing operations could be located anywhere, since they no longer depended on a nearby source of waterpower or even coal. This critical fact shaped the social geography of the West, where industry, developing in the twentieth century, was concentrated in urban areas rather than in the mill towns that dotted the riverbanks of the East.

The contours of the electrical system were shaped not only by the requirements of science and technology but also by social choices. In a broad-gauged public debate between 1890 and 1920, the vision of electricity as a public service contended with the notion that it ought to be treated as a private commodity. Should generating companies be publicly or privately owned? (Both were in existence in the 1890s.) Should there be many utility companies or just a few? Who should decide what locales or firms would get electrical service and at what cost? Gradually, the view of electricity as a private commodity appropriately controlled by private corporations won out. Although some public utilities endured and some rate

regulations were put in place, the electrical supply became dominated by private enterprises, many of which were partially owned by the two giant manufacturers of electrical goods, Westinghouse and General Electric. One result was that electric power was used extensively for urban, commercial spectacles, such as advertising and store window displays, while most of rural America remained without electricity at all—because it was not as profitable to extend service to sparsely populated areas. Even at the end of the 1920s, most farmers did not have electric lines running to their homes.

The Automobile. The other hallmark technological system of the era revolved around the automobile. Although the first autos were produced only in the 1890s, it was widely believed by the turn of the century that gasoline-powered vehicles would replace the horse-drawn carriage. Hundreds of entrepreneurs and inventors, many of them bicycle makers, machine-shop owners, or wagon manufacturers, rushed into this new industry, with impressive results. In 1899, 2,500 motor vehicles were produced in the United States; by 1907, the figure was 44,000; by 1916, it exceeded 1 million. The basic design was straightforward and durable: a four- or six-cylinder gasoline engine was mounted in the front of the vehicle, connecting through a gear box and propeller shaft to the rear axle. The first car buyers were wealthy sportsmen, businessmen, and professionals; in many towns and small cities, they included doctors who typically traveled to treat their patients.

As early as 1910, a shakeout was occurring in the industry, as successful large firms captured more of the market and

A standard black Ford Model T in 1915.

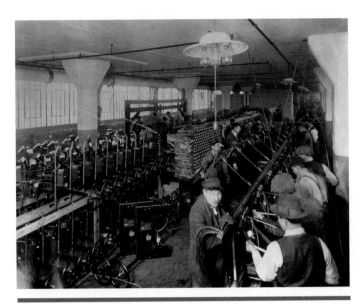

An early assembly line in auto manufacturing, c. 1910.

drove their competitors out of business. The key survivors, including Ford and General Motors, were located in the Midwest, particularly in and around Detroit. Thanks to its plentiful hardwood forests, the region contained a large group of carriage and wagon manufacturers, as well as producers of gasoline engines and an abundant supply of skilled, nonunion labor.

The central challenge confronting the automobile industry was economic as well as technological: how to build an automobile inexpensive enough so that people other than the wealthy could buy it. The man who most successfully tackled this problem was Henry Ford, a former machinist and me-
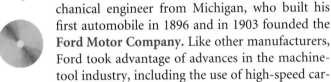
chanical engineer from Michigan, who built his first automobile in 1896 and in 1903 founded the **Ford Motor Company.** Like other manufacturers, Ford took advantage of advances in the machine-tool industry, including the use of high-speed carbon steel and other alloys that allowed parts to be made with greater speed, precision, and interchangeability. Ford, however, went a critical step further, building a single car model that he improved from year to year, a strategy that greatly facilitated the use of standard parts and efficient production processes. The Model T was first introduced in 1908. Eight years later, Ford produced more than half a million lighter, stronger, and less expensive units. By 1927, when production stopped, over 15 million Model Ts had been sold.

Ford achieved this success by improving the techniques of mass production, putting into practice what he called "the principles of power, accuracy, economy, system, continuity, and speed." Particularly in the pioneering plant he opened in Highland Park, Michigan, in 1910, he invested heavily in highly specialized machinery while simultaneously subdividing labor on the shop floor. To further the goals of continuity and speed, Ford in 1913 adopted the moving assembly line, a network of conveyor belts and overhead chains that carried all pieces of the automobile from one worker to the next. "Every piece of work in the shop moves," Ford observed a few years later. "There is no lifting or trucking of anything other than materials." The moving assembly line produced substantial savings, in part because employees were compelled to work more intensively, at a pre-set rhythm. Within a decade, the moving assembly line was adopted throughout the industry, hastening the disappearance of small manufacturers who could not afford to retool their plants.

Ford's assembly line and his production techniques in general were exemplars of "scientific management," a phrase and approach made popular by Philadelphia engineer and businessman Frederick Winslow Taylor. Taylor was one of the nation's first specialists in shop-floor management, and his short book *The Principles of Scientific Management* was the best-selling business book of the first half of the twentieth century. Taylor believed that workplaces could be made more efficient by training, inducing, and compelling workers to labor more steadily and intensively. He conducted time and motion studies to analyze the tasks workers were expected to perform and then encouraged employers to reorganize the work process to minimize wasted motion and time. He also favored piece-rate payment schemes to compel employees, many of whom he described as "stupid," to work more quickly. "Faster work can be assured," wrote Taylor, "only through enforced standardization of methods, enforced adoption of the best implements . . . and enforced cooperation."

Not surprisingly, most industrial workers resisted such schemes. One worker at the Ford Motor Company complained that "when the whistle blows he starts to jerk and when the whistle blows again he stops jerking." At Ford and elsewhere, a common response to the brutal intensification of work was absenteeism and high quit rates: in 1913, Ford's daily absentee rate was 10 percent, while annual turnover exceeded 350 percent. To reduce turnover, which was costly to the company, Ford doubled the daily wages of his most valued employees, to five dollars a day. This strategy was suc-

Table 22.1

MILES OF RAILROAD VS. SALES OF PASSENGER CARS, 1900–20		
	Miles of Railroad Built	Factory Sales of Passenger Cars
1900	4,894	4,100
1905	4,388	24,200
1910	4,122	18,100
1915	933	895,900
1920	314	1,905,500

Source: Historical Statistics of the United States: Colonial Times to 1970, Part 1, Series Q 148, 152, 153, p. 716, and Series Q 239, p. 732.

cessful in stabilizing the labor force and reducing operating costs.

The production of automobiles was only one component of an extensive technological system that would gradually replace the railroad network as the prime mover of the nation's economy (see Table 22.1). The system included manufacturers of rubber tires, car dealers, repair shops, thousands of miles of newly paved roads, the financiers of car purchases, and networks of signals to regulate this new form of traffic. It also embraced the petroleum industry, greatly stimulating the demand for gasoline and spawning that indelible feature of the American landscape, the filling station.

By 1920, the major technological systems of the industrial era had entered the lives of almost all urban Americans and many who lived on farms as well. Homes and workplaces were lit by electricity. Food was processed by electrical machinery, transported by railroads or the first generation of trucks. Men and women communicated with one another through the telegraph or over the phone: by 1920, more than a third of all households had a telephone (see Table 22.2). Americans traveled to work in vehicles powered by gasoline or electricity. Technologies and products that were exotic in 1900 were commonplace by 1920, transforming everyday life.

These technologies, grounded in science-based industry, brought a new profession to the foreground of American life: engineering. As early as 1900, there were 45,000 engineers in the nation, making this profession second only to teaching. That number quintupled over the next thirty years, with the gains most pronounced in electrical and chemical engineering. Almost all engineers were male, and most, like Frederick W. Taylor, came from middle-class, Anglo-Saxon, Protestant families. Engineers in general, and electrical engineers in particular, were the point men of the new economy. They represented the fusion of scientific knowledge with industrial capitalism: most engineers were employed by large corporations, and it was their task to translate the principles of scientific knowledge into practical and profitable applications. As expert problem solvers and symbols of rationality, they were highly esteemed, while their successes stood as testimony to the value of applied science. "Science," wrote Walter Lippmann, "is the culture under which people can live forward in the midst of complexity, and treat life not as something given but as something to be shaped."

Table 22.2

TELEPHONE OWNERSHIP AND CALLS, 1900–20				
	Number of Telephones[a]	Number per 1,000 Population	Average Daily Local Calls[a]	Average Daily Toll Calls[a]
1900	1,356	17.6	7,689	193
1905	4,127	48.8		
1910	7,635	82	35,299	862
1915	10,524	103.9		
1920	13,273	123.4	50,207	1,607

[a]These figures are in the thousands.
Source: Historical Statistics of the United States: Colonial Times to 1970, Part 1, Series R 1–2, p. 783, and Series R 9–12, p. 783.

Progressive Reform

"Reform" was the watchword of political life. Politicians of both major and dissident parties called themselves reformers; and for some citizens reform became a vocation, even a profession. The impulse to reform had multiple sources. These included an upper- and middle-class sense of responsibility for the welfare of society; religious beliefs that linked personal virtue to humanitarian action; the desire of some businessmen to make the economic environment more predictable; and pressure from labor and working-class groups eager to better their own lot. Reformers operated both within and outside the political arena, although all believed that the role of city and state governments, as well as Washington, ought to be expanded. At the heart of progressivism was the conviction that public authorities should help solve the problems of an industrial society.

The desire for reform, however, did not yield a single Progressive "movement" or agenda. Some reformers focused on social issues, such as poverty, the assimilation of immigrants, public education, and child welfare. Others were more interested in what might be called the "political economy" of the era: they attempted to check the power of large corporations, revamp the banking system, and provide compensation for workers injured on the job. Still others devoted their energies to political reform, striving to eliminate corruption and make government officials more answerable to the public. In the West, in particular, reformers were deeply concerned about the natural environment, and throughout the nation reformers tackled such moral issues as banning the sale of alcohol. The goals of Progressive reform were diverse, and they were backed by a varied and fluid set of political actors and coalitions.

> "'Progress' would come not by allowing natural laws to unfold but by seizing the reins of history."

What these reform efforts had in common was the conviction that, in Lippmann's words, life was "something to be shaped": American society could be improved through informed public policies. Progressives had less confidence than their predecessors that laissez-faire economics and Darwinian evolution would inevitably erode the knotty problems of an urban, industrial nation. Progressive reformers believed that human intelligence could devise strategies for ameliorating poverty, lessening the power of big business, and sheltering workers against industrial accidents. "Progress" would come not by allowing natural laws to unfold but by seizing the reins of history. The "promise of American life," wrote Herbert Croly in 1909 in an influential reexamination of American politics, could no longer be fulfilled "automatically" as it had been in the nineteenth century. It would require "official national action."

Whether the reforms of the era were genuinely "progressive" has been a matter of debate among historians. Some of the policies adopted were designed to help those in the lower reaches of the economic and social hierarchy. Others, however, shored up the power of large corporations, emphasizing efficiency at the expense of democracy, expertise rather than popular consent. It was this technocratic face of reform that was bolstered by the problem-solving models of science and engineering, leading at times to an uneasy coexistence of technological and democratic approaches to complex social issues.

URBAN PROBLEMS

The impulse to reform appeared first in the cities, surfacing during the economic crisis of the 1890s and persisting until after World War I. Three related issues were of paramount importance to urban reformers. The first was improving the delivery of basic services, such as transportation, water, and electricity. The second was elevating the living conditions of the working class and the poor, many of whom were immigrants. The third was transforming municipal governance to make cities run more efficiently and to reduce the power of political machines.

Several different types of reformers pursued these goals. One group consisted of left-leaning progressive politicians, such as Mayors Tom Johnson of Cleveland, Samuel "Golden Rule" Jones in Toledo, and Hazen Pingree of Detroit, who tried to eliminate political corruption and enhance the quality of urban life, particularly for working people and the poor. They built public parks, playgrounds, hospitals, and schools and even offered relief to the unemployed during depressions. They also fought against powerful private interests, such as utility and streetcar companies, to keep costs down and services widely distributed. Johnson, who was mayor of Cleveland from 1901 to 1909, led a prolonged fight to lower trolley fares while simultaneously increasing the tax burden on utilities, railroads, and trolley companies. More than 100 cities ended up establishing municipally owned gas, water, electric, or transit companies.

Other political figures, representing more middle-class and elite interests, focused on reforming the structure of city governments. Convinced that machine politicians, partisan rivalries, and ward-based elections produced corrupt and inefficient regimes, these men sought to revamp city governance through several different mechanisms: replacing boards of aldermen and mayors with a small group of commissioners who combined legislative and executive functions; holding at-large, rather than ward-based, elections for city councils; making elections nonpartisan; and vesting executive authority in the hands of appointed city managers. These proposals were based on corporate models: in Dayton, Ohio, the president of the National Cash Register Company claimed that a city ought to be "a great business enterprise, whose stockholders are the people."

One of the first cities to change its structure was Galveston, Texas. In 1900, the city suffered the greatest natural disaster in American history, a hurricane and tidal wave that killed 8,000 of the city's 38,000 residents and left another 10,000 homeless. When the elected city council, already under fire because of sloppy financial practices, was unable to respond effectively to the emergency, it was dislodged by a coalition of bankers, businessmen, and large-property owners. That coalition drafted a new city charter, approved by the state legislature, which provided for the governor to appoint a five-man board to run the city. By 1920, hundreds of cities, particularly in the Midwest and the South, had similarly reconfigured their char-

Scene of the destruction in Galveston, Texas, after the hurricane of 1900.

ters to adopt some version of commission or city-manager government. These reforms weakened the political influence of ethnic, working-class wards, although in most large cities political machines proved to be adaptable enough to weather the change in structure. Parallel measures were adopted for school boards, which were increasingly centralized and de-politicized, with executive power vested in appointed professional superintendents. These reforms were commonly sponsored by local elites, but in some locales they were backed also by labor and working-class groups.

Outside of electoral politics were reformers who worked directly with immigrants and the poor. The most well-known were the women and men who lived in settlement houses, such as Jane Addams, the revered and influential founder of Chicago's Hull House in 1889. A college-educated woman from a well-to-do family, Addams and her colleagues spent decades building Hull House into a diverse community center where middle-class women developed a variety of services for working-class immigrant families. These included kindergartens, English lessons, instruction in domestic skills and disease prevention, as well as employment information and training. Settlement-house res-

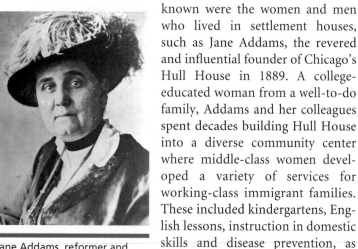

Jane Addams, reformer and founder of Hull House, in a photograph from the 1880s.

idents like Addams learned firsthand about the lives of the poor, often served as unofficial political lobbyists in their behalf, and came to believe that the key to social progress was to empower rather than "uplift" less advantaged citizens. Their efforts were complemented by other activists who focused on specific issues, such as improving public health and housing. Reformers also sought to improve public education by making schooling compulsory and creating vocational training programs for working-class children.

STATE POLITICS

The impulse to reform spread quickly from the cities to state governments, in part because many key issues could be addressed only by state legislatures and governors. A full-blown reform program appeared first in Wisconsin, thanks to the pioneering efforts of Robert La Follette, governor from 1901 to 1909 and one of the first politicians to label himself a "progressive." La Follette beefed up the regulation of railroads, imposed a graduated income tax as well as a tax on corporations, improved the civil service, banned direct corporate contributions to political parties, and instituted primary elections to reduce the power of party bosses. The Wisconsin program became a blueprint for other states, particularly after 1905, when a series of scandals across the country revealed what many had long suspected: that corrupt relationships between business interests and state government officials were epidemic. In one state after another, progressive politicians, often from dissident factions of the Republican Party, swept into office, promising to tame corporations and clean up political life.

These progressive leaders spent much energy on regulating vital industries. More than a dozen new railroad commissions were established, and the regulatory powers of others were strengthened to permit closer oversight of freight rates, illegal rebates to shippers, and safety. State laws were also passed to promote mine safety, as well as the purity of food products. In addition, progressive politicians promoted political reforms, such as recall elections, the direct election of U.S. senators, and initiatives and referenda (which permitted voters to put policy questions on the ballot and make policy decisions).

Such democratizing efforts, however, were often accompanied by measures designed to reduce the size of the electorate. Elaborate registration systems, for example, winnowed the electorate in many states, while in the Midwest noncitizen aliens lost the right to vote. Although commonly touted as anticorruption efforts, such laws served to limit the political power of urban workers; coupled with new regulations governing electoral procedures, they also reinforced the two-

A cartoon favoring the prohibition of the sale of alcohol, 1915.

A cartoon depicting the success of Governor Robert La Follette's reforms in freeing Wisconsin from the grip of the railroad "octopus."

party system, making it more difficult for third parties to compete with the Democrats and Republicans.

Social reforms on the agenda of progressive state officials ranged from mandatory smallpox vaccinations for children to improved hospital and mental health facilities to small "pensions" for mothers with young children. In addition, state governments became enmeshed in the widespread drives to prohibit the sale of alcohol. **Prohibition** and temperance were largely cultural issues, pressed onto the political agenda by evangelical Protestants, mostly from rural areas, who found the drinking habits of urban-dwelling immigrants alien and immoral. Prohibition advocates maintained that drinking ruined families, lowered productivity, drove men and women into poorhouses and prisons, and corrupted politics. Support was particularly strong among women's groups who regarded alcohol as a source of marital abuse. Progressive politicians were not of one mind about prohibition, with eastern progressives joining ranks with their immigrant and Catholic constituencies to combat this intrusion of state power into a new domain of private life. Nonetheless, the prohibitionist forces mustered enough strength to prohibit the sale of alcohol in twenty-one states, many in the South and the West, between 1906 and 1917. Their national triumph came in 1919 with the ratification of the Eighteenth

697

Amendment, which banned the manufacture, sale, and transportation of intoxicating liquors everywhere in the nation.

Class, Ethnicity, and Race

Underlying many of the issues that came to the fore during the Progressive Era was the harsh reality of class differences. While the nation's elites were thriving and the middle class—the buyers of the Model T—was growing rapidly, most adults remained in the industrial and agricultural working class. The nation's 200,000 engineers were vastly outnumbered by the millions of men who were classified simply as "laborers" and millions more who were semiskilled factory operatives, migrant agricultural workers, or sharecroppers in the fields of the South. These men and women typically toiled for sixty hours or more per week, for low wages, in unhealthy or hazardous settings. Their incomes were gradually rising, but relatively few could support a family by themselves. Most workers, moreover, were either immigrants, the children of immigrants, or black. Class boundaries, as was often true in American history, coincided substantially with ethnic and racial divides.

Whether these boundaries would harden or soften was one of the most critical questions facing Progressive Era society. The nineteenth-century answer to the problem of inequality was the view that opportunities were so abundant that anyone could get ahead by dint of hard work. Yet many social critics at the turn of the century believed that the growth of industrial capitalism could only widen the cleavages between social classes. Racial and ethnic divisions seemed to compound the problem, increasing the social distance between the haves and the have-nots, adding to the obstacles to mobility or assimilation.

The significance of this issue—of the class, racial, and ethnic lines that crisscrossed the social order—was apparent to most Americans, but it was not clear what, if anything, could be done about it. Workers, immigrants, and African Americans sought to better their conditions, both as individuals and through collective activities such as the formation of unions, immigrant self-help organizations, and political organizing. They also turned to state governments and to Washington for aid, often with the support of progressive politicians. In the public arena, however, responses to class, ethnic, and racial problems were decidedly mixed. Most business interests opposed state intervention into the "labor question," and social prejudices shaped public responses to African Americans and foreigners. This was a cluster of issues that did not readily succumb to the problem-solving mentality of engineers.

UNIONS AND THE STATE

Trade unions flourished during the Progressive Era. Membership in the craft unions linked to the American Federation of Labor grew steadily after the turn of the century and dramatically during World War I. The unions succeeded in increasing wages and improving working conditions, and by the end of World War I they had made the eight-hour day the norm in industry. Yet the protective umbrella of unions covered primarily skilled workers like machinists, carpenters, railway engineers, and plumbers. Semiskilled factory employees, as well as unskilled day laborers, were left out.

This was so partly because semiskilled and unskilled workers were easy to replace and consequently more difficult to organize—but also because the unions of the AFL (headed by Samuel Gompers until his death in 1924), buffeted by tech-

Textile strikers in Lawrence, Massachusetts, facing off against troops with their bayonets drawn, 1912.

Children working in a vegetable cannery, in a 1912 photograph by Lewis Hine.

nological change and chronic unemployment, were determined to protect the jobs of their members, even at the expense of other workers. They negotiated contracts that guaranteed employment only to union members and, at the same time, restricted access to the unions. The labor movement thus ignored the semiskilled and unskilled and resisted the efforts of blacks, immigrants, and women to enter skilled occupations.

The vacuum left by the exclusive policies of the AFL was colorfully filled by a more radical organization, the Industrial Workers of the World. Founded in 1905 at what was dubbed the "Continental Congress of the Working Class," the IWW sought to organize all workers—and especially the less skilled—in the hope of destroying capitalism and putting in its place a system of industry run and owned by workers. "The working class and the employing class have nothing in common," declared the preamble to the IWW's founding document. Led by "Big" Bill Haywood, the charismatic former head of the western miners' union, the IWW first won support in the West from miners, lumbermen, and agricultural workers. Between 1908 and 1912, the union led free-speech protests in western cities against ordinances that banned street meetings: in Spokane, Frank Little, an IWW organizer, was sentenced to thirty days in jail for reading the Declaration of Independence from a public platform. Within a few years, the IWW's militant determination to organize the unskilled also led thousands of immigrant factory workers in the East to join its ranks. In the textile capital of Lawrence, Massachusetts, in 1912, the IWW led a strike that gripped the attention of the nation: more than 10,000 immigrants from a dozen nations, both male and female, had joined together to protest a pay cut. It was "the first strike I ever saw which sang," noted one journalist.

While the IWW believed that capitalism would be overthrown through the "direct action" of workers who would lay down their tools and refuse to participate in private enterprise, other radicals adopted a different strategy: electing socialists to public office. The Socialist Party, led by Eugene V. Debs, was a respected alternative party in cities and towns throughout the North and West. Socialists believed that the exploitation of workers would not end as long as industry was privately controlled and driven by the profit motive. They were also committed to using the machinery of electoral democracy to peaceably transform the nation's economy. This strategy had its successes. More than 300 cities and towns had socialist officials in 1911; Milwaukee and Schenectady, New York, among others, had socialist mayors. Victor Berger was elected to Congress from Wisconsin, and Eugene Debs himself polled 900,000 votes for president (6 percent of the total) in 1912. Although the Socialist Party never came close to wielding national power, its share of the vote was similar to that achieved in some European countries that in later decades developed strong socialist traditions.

Group portrait of "breaker boys," young miners who sorted coal and picked slate; photo by Lewis Hine, 1910.

LEFT: Boy standing on the floor of a glass factory in Virginia, 1911.

RIGHT: Young girl spinner in a Carolina cotton mill, 1909. Both photos by Lewis Hine.

Pressure from socialists and from progressive Republicans and Democrats put working-class issues on the agenda of state governments. There, they encountered resistance from conservatives who believed that public authorities should not intervene in the labor markets or in relations between employers and employees. In 1908, for example, a Massachusetts proposal to create a system of insurance payments for the unemployed was denounced by the governor as "not only a constitutional impossibility, but a logical absurdity." And Massachusetts was one of the most strongly progressive states in the nation.

One of the few areas of legislative success involved workplace accidents, which killed and maimed hundreds of thousands of workers each year. Under existing law, a worker who was injured on the job (or his heirs in the case of his death) could receive compensation only by suing the company and proving that it was negligent, a difficult, expensive task that few accident victims could accomplish. In response to workers' complaints (as well as employers' fears of unpredictable jury awards), numerous states passed workmen's compensation laws that guaranteed accident victims modest payments, while limiting their right to sue. Although initially most workers were not covered by the compensation laws, the laws nonetheless constituted a pioneering step in state supervision of workplace relationships. The same was true of factory and mine safety laws passed during the period.

Progressives also had some success regulating child labor. In 1900, one out of every six children between the ages of ten and fifteen worked full time, and the figure was much higher in some southern states. Reformers regarded such figures as a scandalous indication that children were being exploited rather than educated. Northern industrialists and workers also considered the prevalence of child labor in the South to be a threat to wage rates in the North. Northern state legislatures consequently passed laws restricting the employment of children, but enforcement was lax, and state courts sometimes gutted the laws—although they gradually became more sympathetic to state intervention on behalf of those too young to protect themselves. In 1916, Congress passed the Keating-Owen Child Labor Act, which prohibited the interstate shipment of goods manufactured or mined by children under the age of sixteen who worked under dangerous conditions or for excessively long hours. The Supreme Court, however, declared the law unconstitutional in *Hammer v. Dagenhart* (1918), on the grounds that the federal government's power to regulate interstate commerce did not extend to the production of goods.

The Supreme Court also killed state efforts to regulate the hours of employment for male workers. Although state courts were growing more tolerant of laws mandating a maximum number of hours in the workday, the Supreme Court in 1905 invalidated a New York law that would have limited bakers to an eight-hour day and a forty-eight-hour week (*Lochner v. New York*). The justices concluded that the law interfered with the freedom of contract of bakers, which the states had no "compelling" interest in doing: baking, they observed, was not a "specially hurtful and unhealthy labor."

IMMIGRATION RECONSIDERED

Everywhere outside the South, the "labor problem" was also an immigration problem. Between 1900 and World War I, the flows of immigration were larger than they ever had been: during the peak year of 1907 alone, more than 1.2 million immigrants arrived in the United States. Although this extraordinary migration spurred economic growth, it heightened the competition for jobs and put downward pressure on wages. Most immigrants of this period came from eastern and southern Europe, and many viewed themselves as temporary workers rather than permanent settlers: their goal was to earn enough money in the New World to buy land or start a business in their own country. Although that goal was sometimes abandoned, more than a third of all migrants from parts of Europe and Asia eventually left the United States. Jewish immigrants, who had little desire to return to the oppression they faced in eastern Europe, were the most prominent exceptions, as the Irish had been in the nineteenth century.

The great majority of Progressive Era immigrants settled in cities, and, in so doing, transformed the urban landscape. Ethnic neighborhoods of Italians, Slovaks, Poles, Jews, Greeks, and Asians turned urban America into a checkerboard of cultural, religious, and linguistic diversity; workplaces, too, were often dominated by immigrants. The immigrant presence was felt also in politics, although many foreign-born residents did not vote either because they lacked citizenship or because they could not meet state suffrage requirements, such as literacy tests.

The ambivalence about immigration that native-born Americans had displayed for much of the nineteenth century was intensified during the Progressive Era, largely because the "new" immigrants appeared more alien and more numerous (see Chapter 19). While manufacturers continued to value immigrants as a source of labor, a growing number of Americans feared that their cities were being "taken over" by for-

> *"Between 1900 and World War I, the flows of immigration were larger than they ever had been: during the peak year of 1907 alone, more than 1.2 million immigrants arrived in the United States."*

eigners. One response to this apprehension, favored by many reformers, was to "Americanize" immigrants, to teach them to speak English, to send their children to school, and adopt the mores of the host culture. A blend of humanitarian concern and condescension, these efforts were grounded in the hope of transforming southern and eastern Europeans into acceptable American citizens.

The period also witnessed a steady strengthening of the movement to restrict immigration. Acts of violence, particularly against Italians and Jews, were not uncommon; nor was social discrimination that kept new immigrants out of particular neighborhoods, schools, or occupations. The Immigration Restriction League, founded by elite New Englanders in 1894, lobbied Congress, with some success, to make it more difficult for immigrants to be naturalized and easier for them to be deported. Laws requiring prospective immigrants to be literate in their own language were passed by Congress in 1896, 1913, and 1915, but they succumbed to presidential vetoes.

The hostility to new immigrants was fed by scientific, or pseudoscientific, theories. Eugenicists, such as biologist Charles Davenport, head of the Carnegie Station for Experimental Evolution, believed that not only physical traits but some personality characteristics—such as "shiftlessness" or a predisposition to crime—were determined by genetics. People with these traits posed a threat to the hardy, virtuous Nordic race that had made the United States great. The most popular statement of these views came in Madison Grant's widely read *The Passing of the Great Race* (1916), which maintained that Americans were committing "race suicide" by allowing millions of inferior men and women to immigrate, procreate, and intermingle with native-born Americans.

Such ideas, together with the stresses that immigration placed on urban living conditions, politics, and the labor market, led to growing support for restriction. In 1906, the American Federation of Labor, after a decade of ambivalence, called for a general restriction law, and many business groups soon did likewise. The issue was shelved during World War I, when immigration from Europe was slowed to a trickle, but after the war fears of a new influx of "undesirable" immigrants strengthened the restrictionist camp.

Congress responded by passing restrictive laws in 1921 and 1924, both of which imposed annual quotas on the num-

Cartoon opposed to unrestricted immigration, 1890.

ber of immigrants to be admitted from each foreign nation. The 1924 measure, which structured immigration policy for decades, was a remarkably overt expression of ethnic and cultural bias. Overall immigration was limited to 170,000 persons, with the quotas for each country based on the number of immigrants from that country residing in the United States in 1890. The formula was designed to restrict immigration from southern and eastern Europe, most of which had taken place after 1890. Asian immigrants were prohibited altogether. In supporting the law, Harvard president A. Lawrence Lowell argued that "homogeneity" was the "basis for popular government" and that democracies, to protect themselves, had to resist "the influx in great numbers of a widely different race."

RACE AND THE NATION

In the South, race remained the critical line of social cleavage. The region received few immigrants, but blacks accounted for a third or more of the total population in eight states. African Americans, moreover, were not simply a separate race but a working class critical to the region's agricultural and service sectors. Much of the white South, while depen-dent on black labor, was committed to minimizing social in-teractions between blacks and whites.

The impulse to reform had little impact on race relations in the South. Jim Crow laws proliferated, particularly in the cities: by 1915, segregation (a term that became current only after the turn of the century) was the norm not only in public conveyances and institutions but also in workplaces and resi-dential neighborhoods (see Chapter 19). Meanwhile, a dense web of legal restrictions made it difficult for rural blacks to search for new jobs or escape the restraints of the lien system. Despite the emergence of a small black middle class, consist-ing largely of shopkeepers, tailors, undertakers, and others who provided services to the black community, most African Americans remained trapped in poverty and rural isolation. Electricity, automobiles, and the telephone were not part of the black experience. The oppression of African Americans was reinforced by a legal system that tolerated lynching while excluding blacks from juries and imprisoning them for petty offenses. With the North turning a blind eye, southern states also completed the process of disfranchisement that had begun in the 1890s. By 1915, there were few black voters any-where in the South or in the border states.

While some African Americans continued to struggle for equal rights, most were pessimistic about the possibility of re-forming the institutionalized racism of the new South. An ever-growing number voted with their feet, migrating to the cities of the North. Between the 1890s and World War I, when the rate of migration accelerated dramatically, thou-sands of southern blacks traveled by boat to Philadelphia and New York or by rail to Chicago or western cities. Some were intellectuals, educated professionals, and business owners, but most were uneducated and had few skills; nearly all were young, the children and grandchildren of ex-slaves.

In the North, they found "no crystal stair," as writer Langston Hughes put it. With manufacturing and white-collar jobs restricted to whites, black migrants generally worked as janitors, day laborers, barbers, and domestic servants. They were also obliged to live in predominantly black neighbor-hoods, a practice reinforced in some places by laws mandating racial segregation. In the largest cities of the North, including Chicago, New York, and Philadelphia, the swelling of the black population, coupled with the refusal of landlords to rent to blacks in most neighborhoods, led to the formation of black ghettoes. By 1920, for example, two-thirds of New York's rapidly growing black population (70,000 people) had migrated to Harlem. Located just north of New York's Central Park,

Harlem had been a popular white, middle-class district until racial discrimination, real estate speculation, and the subdivision of large apartments transformed it into the overcrowded capital of black New York and the national capital of black culture. In many areas newly settled by blacks, outbreaks of racial violence, including lynching, reared their ugly head: in Abraham Lincoln's hometown of Springfield, Illinois, a race riot in 1908 drove 6,000 African Americans from their homes.

Women and Reform

JOBS AND RIGHTS

At the beginning of the twentieth century, Theodore Roosevelt declared that "the greatest thing for any woman is to be a good wife and mother." Most of his fellow citizens seemed to agree. Although women were having fewer children and were increasingly likely to enter the paid labor force, the ideal of domesticity remained pervasive. Ninety percent of American women did marry, and nearly all stopped working outside the home when they had children.

The lives of women were shaped also by their class, race, and ethnicity. Working-class women, whose fathers and husbands held low-paying, unsteady jobs, were more likely than their middle-class counterparts to work outside the home. Irish and black women commonly worked as domestic servants, while Italian women labored in seasonal manufacturing industries, and more educated native-born women took jobs in the mushrooming clerical sector. (Clerical work replaced domestic service during this period as the largest occupation for women.) The daily lives of farm women, white and black, were little different than they had been in the late nineteenth century, although for some the burdens of rural isolation were lightened by advances in communication and transportation as well as by the increase in farm incomes.

The growth of the urban middle class led to a rise in educational opportunities for women: by 1920, 60 percent of white women were graduating from high school, and nearly 10 percent were enrolled in college. Most of these educated women, as long as they remained single, took jobs in traditional, sex-typed, white-collar occupations such as nursing, teaching, and library and secretarial work, all of which were

"Led by those with college educations, women became more visible in public life than they ever had been before."

rapidly growing. But a handful broke into male professions, including medicine, college teaching, and engineering, while others forged independent paths as intellectuals and social activists. One sign of the social strains on these pioneering women was that the marriage rate among college graduates was barely above 50 percent.

Led by those with college educations, women became more visible in public life than they ever had been before. Barred from electoral politics in most states, women became particularly prominent as social reformers, focusing attention on the problems of poverty, alcoholism, child labor, prostitution, public health, and birth control. Women's clubs advocated protective legislation for women and children, reforms of the juvenile justice system, new housing codes, and separate facilities for female prisoners. The well-known founders of settlement houses, such as Jane Addams, were part of a broader movement of women who engaged in hands-on social reform while injecting social issues into political life. Ida B. Wells-Barnett, who had called international attention to the lynching of African Americans in the South in the 1890s, remained a highly audible voice against racial discrimination in Chicago, as well as the South. Late in the Progressive Era, Margaret Sanger pioneered efforts to make birth-control information available, in part to rescue working-class women from the burdens of having large numbers of children.

S. Josephine Baker was emblematic of these pioneers. Born to a wealthy Quaker family in 1873, Baker—whose mother had been in the first graduating class at Vassar—became a physician, graduating from the New York Infirmary for Women and Children in 1898. She began a private medical practice in New York but quickly discovered that distrust of women was so strong that she could not earn a living as a private physician. Accepting a position as an inspector with the New York City Health Department, Baker was appalled by the living conditions and ill health of the city's impoverished immigrants. Anguished by high rates of infant mortality, particularly in the heat of summer, Baker in 1908 sought out the family of every newborn in her district and offered help and instruction in the care of infants—which yielded a dramatic lowering of the infant mortality rate. This stunning success led to her appointment to the newly created post of chief of child hygiene in New York: there, she developed pathbreaking programs in health education while providing vaccinations and uncontaminated milk to

ABOVE: Charlotte Perkins Gilman, a leading theorist of feminism.

RIGHT: S. Josephine Baker.

children throughout the city. In 1916, she began to lecture on child hygiene at the New York University Medical School and received a doctoral degree in public health the following year.

A suffragist and the author of five books, Baker was a self-conscious pioneer, never marrying and always aware that she was breeching the walls of all-male bastions. "I was young and active during the years when women began to be emancipated," she wrote years later in her autobiography. "Women were then making an effort to get out of the shadow-land where they had dwelt for so long." Doing so had demanded personal accommodations. "If I was to be the only woman executive in the . . . department of health, I badly needed protective coloring. . . . My man-tailored suits and shirtwaists, and stiff collars and four-in-hand ties were a trifle expensive, but they more than paid their way as buffers . . . the last thing I wanted was to be conspicuously feminine when working with men."

The experiences of such women helped to generate a new wave of explicitly feminist thought. Indeed, the word "feminist" was coined in the 1910s to refer to someone favoring the full political, civil, and social equality of women. The foremost feminist thinker and writer of the era was Charlotte Perkins Gilman, author of *Women and Economics* (1898) and a member (as was Josephine Baker) of the first feminist organization, Heterodoxy, founded in 1912. Gilman argued that men and women were fundamentally similar, that apparent

> *"The word 'feminist' was coined in the 1910s to refer to someone favoring the full political, civil, and social equality of women."*

differences between them derived from disparate experiences and socialization. She believed that the core of gender inequality resided in the economic dependence of women on men, which over centuries had stunted the capacities of women by limiting their opportunities and confining them to the home. "Only as we live, think, feel and work outside the home," Gilman claimed, "do we become humanly developed, civilized, and socialized." She advocated child care and communal housekeeping to permit even married women with children to work outside the home and realize themselves more fully.

Gilman's vision of a more egalitarian society was not realized, but the women reformers of the era did win their share of victories. They were instrumental in securing passage of the Pure Food and Drug Act (1906), the Mann Act (prohibiting the transportation of prostitutes across state lines, 1910), and the Eighteenth Amendment (prohibiting the sale of alcohol, 1919), as well as the creation of a federal Children's Bureau (1912) that was instructed to "investigate and report . . . on all matters pertaining to the welfare of children and child life among all classes of our people." Female reformers also succeeded in persuading nineteen states to award "pensions" to needy divorced or widowed women with children. Although these "mothers' pensions" were rarely enough to support a household, they were an important step in the state's assumption of responsibility for meeting the needs of the poor.

The rationale for "mothers' pensions" was not a feminist one: it was rather that women, being more vulnerable and less self-sufficient than men, were entitled to greater protection from the state. A similar rationale was offered by the Supreme Court in the landmark case of *Muller v. Oregon* (1908), which upheld the constitutionality of an Oregon law that restricted the hours for female workers; notably, the Court just three years earlier had struck down a similar New York law that applied to men. In explaining its unanimous decision in *Muller*, the Court maintained that it was legitimate for the state to intervene in the labor market to protect women because they were weaker than men and because their health and well-being would affect the vitality of their children. The Court's decision was based in part on a legal brief submitted by attorney Louis Brandeis (but largely written by his sister-in-law, Josephine Goldmark) that offered a detailed description of the lives of women workers.

WINNING THE RIGHT TO VOTE

At the opening of the twentieth century, the movement for women's suffrage was in the midst of a dispiriting period that came to be called "the doldrums." After winning the franchise in several western states in the 1880s and 1890s, the movement had lost momentum. Although women in numerous states were granted the right to vote in school board and other municipal elections, no states fully enfranchised women between 1896 and 1910.

Carrie Chapman Catt, head of the National American Woman Suffrage Association.

Yet leaders of the suffrage cause showed no signs of giving up the campaign for equal political rights, and the movement was energized by steady infusions of educated middle-class women. Under the leadership of Carrie Chapman Catt and Harriet Stanton Blatch (the daughter of Elizabeth Cady Stanton), the National American Woman Suffrage Association (NAWSA) reorganized, raised funds, lobbied politicians, and launched door-to-door publicity drives. In 1906, the movement also abandoned the position that the franchise should be limited to the educated (which had an anti-immigrant and anti-working-class tinge) and linked suffrage to broader issues of social reform. NAWSA sought the support of working-class women and tied the economic exploitation of women to their lack of political power. "Behind suffrage," labor organizer Leonora O'Reilly declared, "is the demand for equal pay for equal work."

NAWSA's organizational efforts were rewarded by victories in Washington, California, Arizona, Kansas, and Oregon between 1910 and 1912. Yet opposition remained strong, and suffrage referenda were defeated in midwestern and northeastern states between 1912 and 1914. Among the opponents were political machines, elite opponents of any further democratization, liquor interests, and some immigrant groups, particularly the Germans and Irish, who viewed the suffrage movement as protemperance. The movement was weakest in the South, where traditional gender views were reinforced by white fears of any expansion of the franchise. Black women in the South formed their own suffrage organizations, arguing correctly that they, perhaps more than anyone, needed political power, but NAWSA, fearing a negative reaction, lent them little support.

In 1915, culminating a debate that had gone on for years, NAWSA joined other organizations in a significant shift of strategy: instead of seeking changes in state laws, they would pursue an amendment to the federal Constitution. The text of the proposed Nineteenth Amendment was modeled on the Fifteenth:

> *Section 1. The rights of citizens of the United States to vote shall not be denied or abridged by the United States or any State on account of sex.*

> *Section 2. Congress shall have power, by appropriate legislation, to enforce the provisions of this article.*

The reasons for the shift were pragmatic. State campaigns were not only costly but nearly unwinnable in the South and in several northern states with particularly byzantine procedures for amending their constitutions. A federal amendment, in contrast, would demand only congressional approval by a

The head of a parade for women's suffrage in Washington, D.C., 1913.

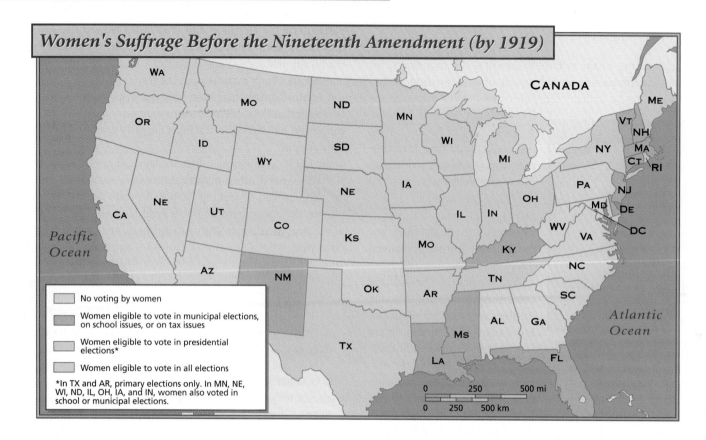

Women's Suffrage Before the Nineteenth Amendment (by 1919)

Legend:
- No voting by women
- Women eligible to vote in municipal elections, on school issues, or on tax issues
- Women eligible to vote in presidential elections*
- Women eligible to vote in all elections

*In TX and AR, primary elections only. In MN, NE, WI, ND, IL, OH, IA, and IN, women also voted in school or municipal elections.

two-thirds vote, followed by majority votes in the legislatures of three-quarters of the states. The major objection to a federal strategy came from advocates of states' rights, particularly in the South, but these objections were overridden, and Catt, the president of NAWSA, devised a "Winning Plan" to build support in the thirty-six states considered most likely to ratify a constitutional amendment.

What followed were several years of intensive grassroots organizing, protests (including daily pickets in front of the White House), and making women's suffrage an issue in national and state elections. Women could already vote in some states and could vote in some elections in many (see map): they could thus threaten to reward their allies and punish their opponents at the polls. By 1917, seven states had passed laws allowing women to vote in presidential elections; that same year, full suffrage was approved in New York, thanks in part to an endorsement from the Tammany Hall machine.

The decisive turn came during World War I. To counter the traditional argument that women should not vote be-cause they did not bear arms, suffrage groups mobilized in support of the war, selling bonds, knitting clothes, holding Americanization classes, and distributing gifts to soldiers and sailors. Such activities, coupled with unrelenting political pressure, finally led President Woodrow Wilson in January 1918 to announce his support of the Nineteenth Amendment. Wilson, who in 1916 had opposed the amendment be-cause he, like most Democrats, regarded it as a state rather than federal matter, delivered an address to Congress in which he urged passage of the amendment "as a war measure." The House of Representatives voted in favor of the amendment the next day. The Senate, where antisuffrage southern Democrats constituted a larger bloc, took an additional year and a half to come aboard.

On August 18, 1920, after NAWSA had carefully executed its Winning Plan, Tennessee became the thirty-sixth state to ratify the Nineteenth Amendment. One of the longest political crusades in American history had come to an end, nearly doubling the size of the electorate.

National Politics

The presidential election of 1900 was a rerun of the election of 1896. President McKinley was renominated by the Republicans, while the Democrats again selected William Jennings Bryan. Bryan, with former vice-president Adlai Stevenson as his running mate, put his oratorical talent and evangelical style on display across the nation. McKinley meanwhile remained in the White House, receiving carefully selected audiences.

Bryan sought to place foreign affairs at the center of the contest, criticizing American imperialism and urging the withdrawal of American forces from the Philippines. Yet whatever misgivings Americans may have had about the Spanish-American War, the campaign was dominated by domestic concerns. The central issues once again were the currency and the tariff. Democrats continued to demand the coinage of silver to inflate the currency, a still-popular cause among debt-ridden farmers in the South and West. They also pressed hard for lower tariffs, which would benefit the consumers of manufactured goods, denounced the influence of big business, called for tougher antitrust regulation, and advocated inheritance and federal income taxes. In response, the Republicans presented themselves as defenders of the nation's business interests in an era of renewed prosperity: they insisted on the legitimacy of the gold standard (which would protect creditors and property owners) and promoted high tariffs to protect industry and the jobs of workers.

The Republicans had the winning formula, improving on their victory of 1896: they were victorious in all states in the Northeast and Midwest, as well as five western states that had supported Bryan four years earlier. The Democrats tightened their grip on the South, thanks in part to the disfranchisement of blacks, and they picked up some support from urban ethnic workers in the North. But the Republicans, aided by campaign coffers five to ten times larger than those of the Democrats, solidified their position as the nationally dominant party, a position they would retain until the 1930s. The regional dominance of each party also contributed to a decline in electoral turnout, a phenomenon that would continue through much of the twentieth century.

The 1900 election ushered a new political figure onto the national stage: the Republicans' vice-presidential candidate, Theodore Roosevelt. A flamboyant hero of the Spanish-American War, Roosevelt was the governor of New York and already a controversial figure. Immensely energetic and ambitious, Roosevelt drew large crowds wherever he campaigned, while creating some unease among party regulars: his nomination to the vice-presidency came about in part because New York's Republican leaders wanted to rid themselves of an unpredictable governor.

THE ROOSEVELT ERA

Less than six months after President McKinley's second inauguration, he was assassinated in Buffalo, New York, by anarchist Leon Czolgosz. At forty-two, **Theodore Roosevelt** became the youngest man ever to occupy the White House. He was also the first president whose personality dominated national public life and whose family received constant attention in the national press. An eastern aristocrat by birth, a western outdoorsman by temperament, Roosevelt was a restless man of action as well as an intellectual who had written ten books, including five serious works of history. Well read in literature, economics, and the natural sciences, he moved easily in the world of ideas and saw himself as the steward of the nation's destiny.

Roosevelt identified himself as an activist conservative who believed that the state had a positive role to play in a society stressed by rapid economic change. He had relatively little sympathy for the working class, fearing that class divisions could spark social revolution. Yet he had equally little patience for corporate greed and worried that the bourgeois life was undercutting the masculine virtues that had made the nation strong. A moralist at heart, he declared the presidency to be a "bully pulpit" from which he could exhort his fellow citizens to act virtuously. Roosevelt was also committed to strengthening the army and navy and to firming up the status of the United States as a great power.

During his first term in office, Roosevelt, lacking any personal mandate, acted cautiously and strove to fulfill promises made by his assassinated predecessor. Even his most celebrated action, which earned him the reputation of a "trust buster," had been set in motion by McKinley: this was the Justice Department's antitrust prosecution of the Northern Securities Company. Northern Securities, put together by financier J. P. Morgan with railroad barons James J. Hill and E. H. Harriman, was a holding company (it held the stock of companies that actually operated enterprises) that controlled virtually all long-distance rail traffic between Chicago and the

West Coast. Since the company was involved in interstate commerce, the Sherman Anti-Trust Act seemed applicable, although lawyers for Northern Securities argued that the act covered only carriers themselves rather than holding companies. The Supreme Court agreed with the government and in 1904, in *Northern Securities Company v. U.S.*, ruled that Northern Securities was in violation of the Sherman Act.

That same year, Roosevelt supported passage of the Elkins Act, which prohibited railroads from giving rebates to large shippers. He also promoted the creation of a new Department of Commerce that would include a Bureau of Corporations empowered to investigate the activities of companies engaged in interstate commerce. Both of these actions strengthened Roosevelt's trust-busting public image, not altogether deservedly. The Bureau of Corporations had relatively little power, and the Elkins Act was supported by the railroads themselves, which were happy to be rid of the pressure to kick back funds to their largest customers.

Roosevelt also seized the spotlight in 1902 when he successfully mediated a strike of anthracite coal miners. The president was shrewd in his choice of an occasion to display sympathy for workers: coal miners were known to work long days for low pay in extremely hazardous conditions, and their union was reasonably flexible in its demands. The mine owners, on the other hand, were stubborn and unpopular, none more so than George F. Baer, who had publicly observed that "God in His Infinite Wisdom has given control of the property interests of the country" to himself and his colleagues. Roosevelt's intervention—which resulted in better wages and working conditions but not recognition of the miners' union—suggested that the federal government, at long last, might be tilting toward an even-handed, rather than promanagement, stance on labor disputes.

Only in one area did Roosevelt break any new ground in his first term: conservation. An outdoorsman and amateur naturalist himself, Roosevelt was repelled by the misuse of wilderness areas, particularly in the West. In 1902, despite opposition from within his own party, he fought hard for the Newlands Reclamation Act, which favored agricultural development while setting aside funds from the sale of public lands to be used to promote irrigation and reclamation projects. The president also promoted the activities of his friend Gifford Pinchot, who headed the nation's small Forest Bureau. With Roosevelt's support, Pinchot won congressional approval to transfer control of the nation's forest reserves to his bureau and to enlarge it into a new agency, the U.S. Forest Service. Pinchot also created the Forest Rangers to manage and protect the nation's undeveloped forests.

Roosevelt's initiatives were designed in part to help him gain control of the Republican Party, which included both traditional probusiness conservatives and progressive insurgents like La Follette of Wisconsin and Congressman George W. Norris of Nebraska. In this endeavor, he was eminently successful, brushing aside concerns about his personality and thirst for power to gain by acclamation the Republican presidential nomination in 1904. With conservative senator Charles W. Fairbanks of Indiana as his running mate, Roosevelt proclaimed that he stood for a "Square Deal" for the American people, but said little on specific issues. He was opposed by an almost equally conservative Democrat, Alton B. Parker of New York, who repudiated the silver issue and represented the northeastern, probusiness wing of the Democratic Party. The most hotly debated issue of the campaign was the tariff.

Roosevelt was elected in a landslide, winning thirty-two states and 57 percent of the popular vote. Parker won no state outside the South. The Democrats' shift to the right did not yield any gains in the business community, but it cost them support on their left flank: with Eugene V. Debs as its standard-bearer, the Socialist Party garnered 3 percent of the national vote (400,000 votes), while the Populists revived to win 100,000 votes in the South and West. Half a million fewer people voted in 1904 than in 1900.

Roosevelt's second term was more contentious and less productive. The economic and political power of big business became the center of policy debate in Washington, in part because key reformers such as Wisconsin's La Follette took seats in the Senate. The reformers, many of them Republicans from the Midwest, raised their voices against the trusts, demanded regulation, particularly of the railroads, and even began to question the virtues of a high tariff, which seemed to be protecting monopolies.

Roosevelt was of two minds on the monopoly question: he thought that big business was inevitable, even desirable, but that the power wielded by large corporations had to be restrained. As Mr. Dooley, the fictional bartender created by humorist Finley Peter Dunne, commented, "Th' trusts are heejoous monsthers built up be th'inlightened intherprise iv th' men that have done so much to advance progress in our beloved counthry. On wan hand I wud stamp thim underher fut; on th' other hand not so fast." Roosevelt accordingly opposed any broad, new antitrust measures while permitting his

Justice Department to prosecute some of the worst abusers of corporate power under the Sherman Act.

The president, moreover, preferred administrative to legislative regulation, which led him to support the Hepburn Act, passed by Congress in 1906. This bill, directed at the railroads, authorized the Interstate Commerce Commission to set maximum freight rates after investigating complaints from shippers: it also required the rail corporations to adopt uniform bookkeeping practices. Although reformers such as La Follette regarded the bill as a watered-down measure that fell short of the rate regulation they sought, the Hepburn Act was one of the most significant bills of Roosevelt's presidency.

A similar achievement was the simultaneous passage of the Pure Food and Drug Act and the Meat Inspection Act in 1906. Reformers had repeatedly expressed concern about the purity of the nation's food supply and the misrepresentation of alleged "medicines," but efforts at regulation had been thwarted by conservatives and industry lobbyists. By 1906, however, several European countries, citing safety concerns, were threatening to stop importing American food and agricultural products. Roosevelt then intervened by mobilizing public opinion to overwhelm the conservative opposition. He received help from an unusual source—a novel, *The Jungle,* by Upton Sinclair, published in 1906. Sinclair's story, a moving portrait of the exploitation of Chicago's immigrant workers, included vivid descriptions of the horrific sanitary conditions in that city's meatpacking industry. The novel sparked "muckraking" magazine articles (as the investigative journalism of the era was called) as well as a government investigation. The resulting Pure Food and Drug Act created the Food and Drug Administration (FDA), which was empowered to test and certify drugs before they went on sale; the Meat Inspection Act authorized the Department of Agriculture to inspect and label meat. Ignored by Congress were the workers in the stockyards who were Sinclair's primary concern. "I aimed at the public's heart, and by accident I hit it in the stomach," the author reflected.

> "The Jungle *sparked 'muckraking' magazine articles (as the investigative journalism of the era was called) as well as a government investigation.*"

Despite this legislative achievement, 1907 marked the onset of political gridlock in Washington. Republican reformers, with some Democratic backing and often with the support of the president, pressed for laws that would further regulate business, restrict child labor, protect injured workers, lower the tariff, and tax the wealthy; but all these measures were beaten back by the conservative Republicans who dominated Congress. The conservatives also clipped the wings of the increasingly controversial Gifford Pinchot and his Forest Service, although Roosevelt did manage to protect more than 15 million acres of western land from further development. To the president's chagrin, moreover, the Supreme Court continued to protect business interests threatened by regulatory reform. In his final address to Congress, Roosevelt observed that the justices, by interpreting laws, inescapably "enact into law parts of a system of social philosophy," and he criticized those justices who continued to adhere "to an outgrown philosophy which was itself the product of primitive economic conditions."

THE SUCCESSOR: WILLIAM H. TAFT

When elected in 1904, Roosevelt had pledged not to run again in 1908: he had already served one almost-full term and respected the "wise custom" that limited presidents to eight years in office. The still-young and energetic president may have regretted that pledge, but in 1908 he prepared to leave the White House, announcing that he planned a lengthy safari to Africa. "Health to the lions," toasted his congressional adversaries.

Roosevelt retained enough clout to handpick his successor as the Republican candidate: his good friend and secretary of war, William Howard Taft. A distinguished lawyer from Ohio, Taft had served both as solicitor general of the United States and as administrator of the Philippines. A centrist within the Republican Party, Taft had strong antilabor credentials but was known to be leery of big business. Although supported by progressive Republicans, he ran on a platform written largely by the party's probusiness, conservative wing.

His Democratic opponent was the durable William Jennings Bryan, whose reform-minded supporters had regained control of the Democratic Party after the election debacle of 1904. Bryan again crisscrossed the country by train, giving eloquent speeches, attacking the Republicans as the handmaidens of large corporations, and promoting his campaign slogan, "Shall the People Rule?" The platform he ran on demanded reduced tariffs, tougher regulation of business, an eight-hour day for government workers, and limitations on the use of injunctions against organized labor. The lines between the parties were drawn with such clarity that the American Federation of Labor abandoned its traditional nonpartisanship and endorsed Bryan's candidacy.

Yet the balance of power in national politics remained unchanged: the Democrats did better than they had done in 1904, but Taft was victorious throughout the Northeast and Midwest and he gained a few western states as well. Bryan won only seventeen states, most of them in the South; his defeat consigned him to the distinguished ranks of dominant political figures who never reached the White House. The election revealed clear ideological schisms within the electorate: taken together, Bryan (running on a very progressive platform) and Socialist Eugene Debs garnered 46 percent of the vote. But the Republicans remained the majority party.

Taft took office just as the crosscurrents of politics began to swirl with great force. Popular movements for women's suffrage, prohibition, immigration restriction, and labor reform were gaining strength, forcing new issues onto the national agenda. Insurgents in both parties, energized by these popular movements, sought new social legislation as well as more effective regulation of business. They also favored democratizing political life through the popular election of senators and changing congressional rules to diminish the power of the conservative old guard.

Taft, attempting to maintain Roosevelt's balancing act between reformers and conservatives, was able to oversee the passage of modest pieces of legislation. With his support, Congress strengthened the Interstate Commerce Commission, established the Federal Children's Bureau, created a system of postal savings banks, and gave the president the authority to lower tariffs as part of reciprocal trade agreements. With less support from Taft, Congress also passed a constitutional amendment, ratified in 1913, giving the federal government power to levy an income tax. On the antitrust front, Taft's administration was far more vigorous than Roosevelt's had been: it even secured the breakup of John D. Rockefeller's Standard Oil Company and the Duke family's American Tobacco Company.

But Taft could not hold the warring factions of his party together. Bitter fights broke out in Congress over the tariff and over the regulation of railroads, telephones, and the telegraph. Taft in the end sided with Republican conservatives, earning him the enmity of the reformers, whom he disliked and distrusted. To make matters worse, a scandal erupted within the administration when Gifford Pinchot leaked to the press the news that his superior, Interior Secretary Richard Ballinger, was being investigated for corruption. After several rounds of investigation and repeated accusations, Taft fired Pinchot, risking a break with Pinchot's patron, the absent yet ever-popular Theodore Roosevelt. Taft sought to shore up his position by campaigning for Republican conservatives in their primary contests against reformers in the 1910 elections. But he was swimming against the tide: in key states, including California and Wisconsin, the insurgents won sweeping victories. Even more worrisome, the Democrats made unprecedented gains in that year's congressional elections, winning control of one house of Congress for the first time in sixteen years.

A few months later, a group of reform-minded Republican senators and congressmen announced the formation of the Progressive Republican League. The group, acting within the Republican Party, criticized the corrupt ties between conservatives and business, demanded greater regulation of the railroads and all large corporations, and declared its opposition to Taft's renomination. Within Congress, the progressives formed alliances with like-minded Democrats, while their leader, Wisconsin's Senator La Follette, became their standard-bearer and candidate for the presidency.

La Follette had little chance of unseating Taft, but he paved the way for Roosevelt's reentry into politics. Roosevelt had returned to the United States in the middle of 1910 and had kept some distance from the internecine warfare: he did, however, speak out often in favor of positions that progressives had endorsed. In the winter of 1912, he announced that he, too, would seek the Republican nomination for president. Aware from the outset that the party's old guard would likely nominate Taft, Roosevelt was propelled both by a desire to join the fray and by the conviction that the historical moment called for a blend of "radical" reforms and conservative leadership, which only he could provide. Frustrated by the thought that he had been president at an inconclusive time, Roosevelt hoped to replicate the role of Lincoln, to lead a new political grouping—and, if necessary, a new party—that would save the Republic.

THE ELECTION OF 1912

Roosevelt's prediction that his party would renominate Taft proved to be correct. When the Republicans met in convention in June 1912, the old guard rebuffed the insurgents, precipitating a walkout by pro-Roosevelt delegates. Two months

Theodore Roosevelt in 1912, shortly after his nomination for president by the Progressive Party.

later, Roosevelt and his followers formed the Progressive Party and launched a crusade to recapture the White House and revitalize American politics. As was fitting, the delegates to the Progressive convention sang "Onward, Christian Soldiers" and the Civil War–era "Battle Hymn of the Republic."

The Democratic Party, meanwhile, was enjoying a revival in national politics. Democrats had gained seats in the Senate, partly as a result of state laws mandating the popular election of senators. (The selection of senators by state legislatures had favored the Republicans in the Northeast and Midwest, because cities were underrepresented in the legislatures.) They had won control of the House of Representatives, and the popular Champ Clark of Missouri had become Speaker of the House. Democrats had also emerged victorious in several key gubernatorial elections. Moreover, the positions they had been embracing for more than a decade—such as lower tariffs and tighter regulation of business—were becoming mainstream. With the Republicans torn apart by conflict, the Democrats believed that they had an excellent chance of winning the White House in 1912.

One of the new Democratic governors was New Jersey's Woodrow Wilson. Born in the South, the son and grandson of Presbyterian ministers, Wilson had earned a doctorate in political science from Johns Hopkins University and taught at several universities. In 1902, he became the president of Princeton University, where he established a reputation as an educational reformer and an opponent of social privilege. A lifelong Democrat with long-standing interests in politics, Wilson drew the attention of the northeastern, anti-Bryan wing of the party, which supported him for governor in 1910. Once nominated, however, he made clear that his sympathies were more progressive than those of his political patrons. An articulate intellectual with an air of rectitude, Wilson was elected by a large majority and proceeded to implement a reform agenda that included the regulation of businesses, workplace safety, and limits on campaign spending.

Wilson emerged immediately as a leading candidate for the Democratic nomination for the presidency in 1912. He was a new face as well as a potential bridge between the southern and northeastern wings of the party. Yet he faced formidable opposition, from House Speaker Clark and southerner Oscar Underwood, the House majority leader, and was regarded with suspicion by Bryan supporters. When the Democrats met in convention in June 1912, they promptly deadlocked. Clark led in the early balloting but was unable to muster the necessary two-thirds majority. After forty-five inconclusive ballots, Bryan threw his support to Wilson, making the governor the Democratic nominee.

The campaign of 1912 was one of the most colorful and substantive of the twentieth century, combining charismatic personalities with an eloquent and sometimes profound debate about the role of the state in an industrial society. It also included the drama of Roosevelt being shot, but not badly wounded, in mid-campaign. President Taft remained largely on the sidelines: knowing he had little chance to win, he loomed as the pessimistic standard-bearer of high tariffs and conservative confidence in the business community. His former mentor, Roosevelt, barnstormed the country, articulating a vision of a conservative yet powerful central government that would lift the nation's moral tone while providing a counterweight to large business enterprises. Wilson was similarly energetic, positioning himself as the champion of opportunity in a more democratized society and economy.

The policy differences between Roosevelt and Wilson were not great. Both advocated political reforms such as direct primary elections, as well as social reforms including maximum hours and a minimum wage for workers and the abolition of child labor. Both opposed restrictions on immigration. Neither had much to say about the oppression of blacks in the South or about suffrage for women—which Roosevelt tepidly supported and Wilson dismissed as an issue for the states rather than for the national government. Foreign affairs were barely mentioned.

Even on the issue of the "trusts"—the centerpiece of the campaign—their differences were more of tone and rhetoric than substance. Roosevelt articulated a vision he called the "New Nationalism," accepting the permanence and value of many big businesses but insisting that the federal government should regulate large corporations to prevent them from unfairly wielding their economic power. Wilson's "New Freedom," in contrast, emphasized the desirability of preserving and restoring competition, by breaking up large businesses and preventing mergers. Both men claimed that they did not oppose large corporations that had triumphed in fair economic competition; they criticized only those that had taken advantage of their size to stifle competition. Wilson thus was for "big business," but against the "trusts"; Roosevelt embraced "good trusts" while opposing "bad trusts." Both believed that "bad trusts" ought to be broken up and that even legitimate big businesses had to be subject to some government regulation. Although neither said so, both candidates were, in effect, agreeing with the Supreme Court's ruling in the Standard Oil case that only "unreasonable" restraints of trade—not restraints of trade per se—were illegal. The line between reasonable and unreasonable restraints of trade was always difficult to draw.

The outcome of the election surprised no one: Taft and Roosevelt split the Republican vote, handing Wilson an easy victory. Fewer people (6.3 million) voted for Wilson than had voted for Bryan in 1908, but he carried forty states to gain an overwhelming advantage in the electoral college. Roosevelt came in second, with 4.1 million votes, while Taft polled 3.5 million. In part because of the continued disfranchisement of blacks in the South, turnout dropped once again. Eugene V. Debs, the Socialist candidate, won twice as many votes (900,000) as he had in 1908, and he ran particularly strongly in the West. Although Roosevelt and Wilson had both claimed to be "radicals," 6 percent of the electorate clearly believed that neither was radical enough.

WILSON: THE SCHOLAR AS PRESIDENT

Wilson's first eighteen months in office were a stunning success. Reflecting his long-standing admiration for British parliamentary politics, Wilson worked closely with Democratic congressional leaders, including Champ Clark and Oscar Underwood, and shrewdly appointed William Jennings Bryan as his secretary of state. Breaking with tradition, he laid out a legislative program in his first inaugural address, held press conferences every week, and became the first president in more than a century personally to address Congress. He also gave speeches designed to educate the public about key issues.

Under Wilson's leadership, Congress passed three clusters of legislation that modernized the political economy of the United States. The first was tariff revision. By effectively painting the protectionist Republican old guard as the tool of corporate lobbyists, the Democrats, led by Underwood, overwhelmed the opposition and lowered most tariffs by about 25 percent. At the same time, they implemented a graduated income tax that applied primarily to the wealthy. This legisla-

President-elect Woodrow Wilson (left) with outgoing president William Howard Taft on inauguration day, March 4, 1913.

tion lessened the government's protection of mature industries, potentially stimulating competition and moving the nation closer to free international trade. It also signaled a shift in the source of the federal government's revenues away from tariffs and toward a tax system grounded in the principle that those with greater resources should shoulder a larger share of the burden.

The second cluster of legislation involved banking reform. At stake were issues that had been prominent in politics for more than a century: the availability of credit outside of the major financial centers of the Northeast, control of the money supply (since issuing credit was a way of creating money), and the desirability of a national banking system that would impose some restrictions on individual banks and enhance financial stability. Pressures for reform were heightened by the Panic of 1907, yet there were major disagreements about the types of change that were necessary.

What emerged after months of debate was the Federal Reserve Act, passed in December 1913. A compromise among competing business interests, the act created a national banking system that blended limited regional autonomy with a network of centralized controls. The regional autonomy was designed to promote the availability of credit outside the Northeast, while the controls were meant to promote stability by preventing banks from engaging in risky practices. The new banking system would be run largely by appointees of the federal government, although the banks themselves were able to select some key officials. In practice, the system was soon dominated by the powerful reserve bank of the nation's financial capital, New York, but the structure proved to be durable and flexible. A technocratic answer to questions that had long been politically prominent—who would control credit, the money supply, and the banking system and whose interests would be served by any such system—the Federal Reserve System effectively removed from the political arena issues that Americans had debated for decades.

After bank reform had been enacted, Wilson turned his attention to the problem of the trusts. His approach was two-pronged. The first was passage of the Clayton Act (1914), which fleshed out the skeleton that the 1890 Sherman Act had created, specifying business activities that constituted illegal restraints on trade as well as penalties for violations of the law. In keeping with Wilson's emphasis on preserving competition, it provided for the breakup of large corporations under some circumstances. To the delight of the American Federation of Labor, the Clayton Act further declared that trade unions were not "illegal combinations in restraint of trade" and thus were exempt from prosecution under the antitrust laws; the ability of federal courts to issue injunctions against unions was also limited. Long overdue in the eyes of workers, the Clayton Act provided a legal guarantee of the right to form labor unions.

The second prong of Wilson's antitrust policy was the creation of the Federal Trade Commission (1914), a new regulatory agency, modeled on the Interstate Commerce Commission, that was vested with the power to investigate complaints regarding violations of the antitrust laws by any corporation engaged in interstate commerce. The FTC also had the authority to order companies to stop anticompetitive practices. As observers pointed out, the FTC seemed to be less in tune with Wilson's rhetoric than with Roosevelt's emphasis on the administrative regulation of big business. But to Wilson, as to Roosevelt, the problem of monopoly seemed complex enough to require ongoing supervision by a permanent agency staffed by antitrust experts. Critics of the FTC, including Roosevelt, charged Wilson with creating the form

> *"The Federal Reserve System effectively removed from the political arena issues that Americans had debated for decades."*

but not the substance of regulation, a criticism that was heightened when Wilson appointed industry representatives to the commission itself.

Although portrayed as efforts to rein in the excesses of corporate power, the Clayton Act and the Federal Trade Commission were welcomed by some business leaders. The new laws served to dampen widespread anticorporate sentiment by interposing an agency, and panels of experts, between the public and large corporations. They also clarified the rules of legal economic competition and thus made the economic environment more predictable. Many businessmen further believed that one set of federal regulations was preferable to a bewildering array of (sometimes more stringent) state regulations. Both the Clayton Act and the act creating the FTC were written in close consultation with representatives of the business community.

Despite the successful passage of major legislation, the congressional coalition of liberal Democrats, Progressives, and progressive Republicans began to unravel. In 1914, conservative Republicans, aided by yet another business downturn, regained many of the governorships and congressional seats they had lost. Nonetheless, Wilson and his allies pressed forward with their reform program. They passed a law banning child labor (later overturned by the Supreme Court), and a federal loan program that would free farmers from dependence on banks and permit them to sell their crops when market conditions were favorable. In 1916, Congress substantially increased the income tax and established an inheritance tax. To the delight of organized labor, it also passed the Adamson Act, which mandated an eight-hour workday on the railroads. Strongly supported by Wilson, who wanted to avoid a threatened national railroad strike, the Adamson Act helped to establish the eight-hour day as the norm in industry and transportation.

Wilson had one other key victory in 1916: his nomination of Louis Brandeis to the Supreme Court. Brandeis was a prominent attorney

Louis D. Brandeis, lawyer, reformer, and later justice of the Supreme Court.

who had championed social reforms and antitrust litigation consistent with the ideals of the New Freedom. Brandeis was also the first Jew ever to be proposed for a seat on the High Court. Many well-known spokesmen for the legal community fiercely opposed the nomination on ideological grounds that were more than a little tinged with anti-Semitism. But congressional Democrats stood firm, and with the help of La Follette and other insurgents, the Senate approved Brandeis's appointment.

Wilson's achievements in office gave him a solid, progressive platform on which to run for reelection in 1916. With the Great War (renamed World War I only in the 1940s) raging in Europe, he also campaigned as the chief executive who had "kept us out of war." He faced a Republican Party that had regrouped with remarkable speed after the schism of 1912. Roosevelt had abandoned the Progressive Party and returned to the Republican fold, leaving the dismayed Progressives without a presidential candidate. The conservative Republican establishment, encouraged by its showing in the 1914 elections, nominated Charles Evans Hughes for president. A moderate former governor of New York, Hughes had the virtue of never having taken sides in the internecine warfare of 1912 because he was a justice of the Supreme Court, a position he resigned after being nominated for president. Although both parties debated foreign policy in general and avoidance of the European war in particular, the central issues of the campaign involved class and regional conflict. While Wilson cheerfully donned the mantle of reform, the Republicans denounced the Adamson Act as "class legislation" and criticized the graduated income tax as an appropriation of northeastern and midwestern wealth by the South and West.

Wilson won the closest election since the 1880s. He led Hughes in the popular vote by a margin of only 3 percent and won the electoral college because of an extremely narrow victory in California. Wilson was victorious throughout the South and, with the backing of many former Progressives, in the West as well. Another key to his victory was the labor vote. Foreshadowing political changes that would be solidified in the 1930s, Wilson lured many urban, industrial workers away from the Republican Party—thanks in good part to the Adamson Act. As a result, the Democratic vote rose throughout the Northeast and Midwest, and Wilson carried the traditionally Republican state of Ohio. Had Ohio followed the sectional pattern that had prevailed for decades, Charles Evans Hughes would have been president.

THE LEGACY OF REFORM

Wilson, the reformer, had won a second term, but the "Progressive" Era was over. By the time of his second inaugural, in March 1917, the war in Europe had seized Wilson's attention, as well as the hopes and fears of the nation he led. With one key exception—the amendment granting suffrage to women—the wave of reform that had marked the first decade and a half of the twentieth century was spent.

The achievements of the Progressive Era at the national level seem relatively slender when matched against the political rhetoric of the period. The most prominent issue, the problem of the trusts, had been addressed, but large corporations continued to dominate the economic landscape. A new banking system had been created, but the centers of finance were unshaken. Workers gained some protection against workplace injuries, but they nonetheless remained vulnerable to most of the risks and uncertainties of industrial capitalism. Democratic rights had been extended in certain domains, such as the popular election of senators (finally made national by a constitutional amendment ratified in 1913), the initiative and referendum, and the enfranchisement of women. Yet African Americans throughout the South faced nearly insurmountable barriers to political participation, while immigrant workers in the North also faced discrimination. Moreover, administrative agencies, ranging from municipal utility agencies to the Federal Trade Commission, were removing key issues from direct popular control.

> *"Reformers of different types erected much of the scaffolding of the modern American state."*

Yet what transpired during this era was not mere noise and bluster: in a piecemeal and halting fashion, reformers of different types erected much of the scaffolding of the modern American state. The national government became far more active than it ever had been in the past, and it assumed responsibility for regulating the rules of conduct and competition in the private sector. To carry out this multifaceted task, it created permanent agencies that could administer policies more flexibly and efficiently than could legislatures and courts alone. Reflecting widespread confidence in the models that emerged from science and technology, these agencies had a technocratic bent, emphasizing the role of experts and expertise in the solution of problems. Alongside these changes was a shift in the financial underpinnings of the federal government, away from tariffs and toward graduated income taxes. This shift altered the regional and class distribution of the tax burden, while tying the federal government's budget more directly to the growth of the economy.

This scaffolding was incomplete, particularly with respect to issues of poverty and inequality that were less amenable to technocratic approaches. But it marked a major advance from the final decades of the nineteenth century and provided institutions and models upon which later generations could build. The achievements of the Progressive Era also reflected a profound shift in the language of politics and public discourse. Roosevelt, Wilson, and others had identified themselves as progressives, even as radicals. They embraced change as well as a vision of an activist state; in so doing, they legitimized the project of reform and carried into the social and political arena the belief in humanly controlled progress that had appeared to be the province of science and technology in the late nineteenth century.

Suggested Reading

Richard Hofstadter, *The Age of Reform: From Bryan to F.D.R.* (1955)

David L. Lewis, *W. E. B. Du Bois: Biography of a Race, 1868–1919* (1993)

Arthur Link, *Woodrow Wilson and the Progressive Era, 1910–1917* (1954)

Richard L. McCormick, *The Party Period and Public Policy: American Politics from the Age of Jackson to the Progressive Era* (1986)

David Montgomery, *The Fall of the House of Labor: The Workplace, the State, and American Labor Activism, 1865–1925* (1987)

Theodore Rosengarten, *All God's Dangers: The Life of Nate Shaw* (1974)

1901	Congress creates the National Bureau of Standards.
1906	The Pure Food and Drug Act.
1908	Ford Motor Company introduces the Model T.
	Supreme Court, in *Muller v. Oregon*, upholds state law restricting hours for female workers.
1913	Ford adopts the moving assembly line.
December 1913	The Federal Reserve Act creates a national banking system.
1914	Federal Trade Commission established.
1919	Eighteenth Amendment ratified.
August 1920	Nineteenth Amendment ratified.

Chronology

Night Life, by Archibald Motley Jr. Motley's earlier paintings of African American life provided a foundation for works that became identified with the Harlem Renaissance in the 1920s.

Focus
QUESTIONS

■ How did the United States get involved in World War I?

■ What were the most important aspects of American involvement in the war?

■ What were the political and social trends in America in the postwar years?

■ What spurred the national economy in the 1920s?

■ How did American culture and society change in the 1920s?

■ What was Hoover's approach to government when he took office as president?

In June 1914, a militant advocate of uniting the Slavic peoples in eastern Europe assassinated Archduke Franz Ferdinand of Austria-Hungary, precipitating a chain reaction of military commitments that resulted two months later in the outbreak of what came to be called World War I. The conflict pitted two large alliances against each other: the Central Powers (led by Germany and Austria-Hungary) and the Allied Powers (Great Britain, Russia, and France). Strategists on both sides expected a short war, but by late 1914 the conflict had turned into a prolonged seesaw, with armies on both sides dug into trenches and attacking each other across the bloodied ground between.

Few Americans, including their president, were impartial toward the combatants. Those of German descent, not surprisingly, favored the Central Powers, and they were joined by many Irish, their sympathies shaped by hostility to Britain. Most Americans, however, felt much greater kinship with England and its allies: President Wilson was well known for his admiration of British institutions, and he privately observed that a German victory would be destructive of "American ideals." Wilson nevertheless asked the American people to be "impartial in thought" as well as in deeds. He adopted a policy of formal neutrality toward the belligerents, and most Americans agreed that the United States should remain detached from the conflict.

In his approach to foreign affairs, Wilson was more reserved than either Theodore Roosevelt or William Howard Taft. He appeared to be more principled, too, at times to the point of righteousness. But he was committed to protecting American interests. When Germany threatened American shipping, his insistence on maintaining freedom of the seas, long a vital American concern, brought the United States into the war on the side of the Allies.

The resulting mobilization accelerated many of the social, industrial, and technological developments under way since the turn of the century. It also crippled reform and ushered in the economically dynamic but politically conservative 1920s, a decade that transformed the way many Americans lived but that was fraught with social, cultural, and economic fissures.

The Road to War

THE STRAINS OF NEUTRALITY

Neutrality toward the war in Europe was practically difficult, if not impossible, to sustain given the extent of British trade with the Allies and British naval control of the North Atlantic. From the beginning of the war, Britain used its power to prevent the shipment of American goods to the Central Powers; at the same time, the Allies relied increasingly on American goods to maintain themselves. In 1914, Wilson's government protested Britain's blockade and in 1916 protested its move to confiscate American cargoes headed to Germany. But the complaints yielded only minor concessions, with the result that overall, despite its declarations of neutrality, the United States' Atlantic trade aided the Allies.

In response, Germany declared in 1915 that all waters surrounding Britain constituted a war zone in which it would attempt to sink, without warning, any Allied merchant vessels.

Germany also warned that neutral vessels, too, were at risk since the Allies frequently flew the flags of neutral countries on their own ships. This new policy, reflecting Germany's awareness of Allied dependence on American supplies, was grounded in the use of a new instrument of warfare: the submarine (also known as the **U-boat**). The Germans relied on U-boats to patrol the Atlantic because at the time they were undetectable when running submerged, and they thus offset the British navy's heavy superiority in surface ships. In violation of conventions governing wartime interference with merchant vessels, German submarines typically attacked without warning, torpedoing ships and inducing heavy casualties.

Americans were made dramatically aware of the impact of Germany's Atlantic strategy when, on May 7, 1915, a German submarine sank a British ocean liner, the *Lusitania*, causing the deaths of almost 1,200 people, including 128 Americans. Although the Germans had, in fact, published warnings in American newspapers that the *Lusitania* was a potential target because they believed it to be carrying munitions as well as passengers—a belief whose truth was confirmed many years later—the attack outraged the American public. Wilson, however, reacted cautiously, demanding an apology and reparations from the German government, as well as a commitment to stop attacking passenger vessels. He insisted on trying to uphold the principle of neutral rights, declaring, "There is such a thing as a man being too proud to fight."

PEACE AND PREPAREDNESS

By the time the *Lusitania* sank, the American public was deeply divided about the war. Many progressives were morally opposed to war in general and feared that entry into the European conflagration would end domestic reform. Since August 1914, they had been organizing, marching, and otherwise lobbying against intervention. Wilson's protest note to the Germans about the *Lusitania* prompted Secretary of State William Jennings Bryan, a resolute anti-interventionist who considered the note too sharp, to resign from the cabinet.

Other Americans, however, took the sinking of the *Lusitania* as reason enough for the United States either to enter the war against Germany or at least to prepare for such a war. According to news reports, many of them originating in British propaganda, the Germans were committing atrocities such as killing babies with bayonets. Just a few weeks before a U-boat sank the *Lusitania*, German troops sent thick clouds of chlorine gas rolling toward the French line on the Belgian front at Ypres, an introduction of chemical warfare that left hundreds of Allied soldiers choking, vomiting, and dying and that further inflamed anti-German opinion. Bankers, industrialists, and other Allied sympathizers mounted preparedness parades and formed a National Security League to lobby for universal military training and increases in arms.

Wilson, his eyes at once on American interests and the election of 1916, threaded his way along the divide between pacifism and preparedness, trying to keep the United States

The *New York Times* reporting the sinking of the British ocean liner *Lusitania* by a German submarine on May 7, 1915.

A cartoon from early 1917 that questions the American position of neutrality while extending loans and selling arms to Great Britain and its Allies.

out of the war while acknowledging that such efforts might be in vain. Hitherto, the government had rejected requests by major bankers such as J. P. Morgan to lend the Allies money, holding that such loans would violate the spirit of neutrality. However, war orders from the belligerents had helped bring the United States out of a recession in 1913–14 and put many Americans back to work. In August 1915, members of Wilson's cabinet advised him that unless credit was extended to France and Britain, those countries would be unable to purchase food and war goods in the United States, and the American economy as well as the Allied war effort would be weakened. In response, Wilson authorized loans to the Allies. American banks would advance up to $2.3 billion in credit to the Allies by April 1917, only $27 million to Germany.

Late in 1915, Wilson asked Congress to increase military expenditures while simultaneously sending a private emissary to Europe to try to negotiate an end to the bloodshed. In August of that year, Germany had pledged that its U-boats would no longer attack passenger ships, but in March 1916 it torpedoed the *Sussex,* a French channel steamer, provoking a storm of protest. Wilson threatened to break diplomatic relations, and through the rest of the year the Germans generally refrained from submarine attacks on passenger vessels.

Wilson owed his victory in the election of 1916 substantially to his success in having kept the United States out of war. In a speech in January 1917, he eloquently envisioned a future based on "peace without victory" and called for the launch of an international organization that would promote "not a balance of power but a community of power."

ENTRY INTO THE WAR

Wilson's efforts were thwarted by a sharp change in German strategy. Early in 1917, concluding that it could win the war by revoking the policy it had pursued since the *Sussex* incident, the German command announced that its submarines would attack without warning all shipping headed for Allied ports. By taking this step, Germany believed that it could cut off food and supplies to Britain and France and gain a military victory before the United States (which Germany fully expected to enter the war) could mobilize an effective army. In February and March 1917, German submarines sank more than a million tons of the Allies' shipping, jeopardizing their lifelines to the United States.

The sinking of merchant vessels galvanized public opinion against Germany, as did the British interception of a telegram from the German foreign minister to his envoy in Mexico suggesting an alliance with Mexico, in return for which Mexico would regain the states of Texas, New Mexico, and Arizona. In early March, Wilson issued an executive order arming the merchant marine; two weeks later, he called up the national guard. Finally, on April 2, the president asked Congress to declare war, asserting, "The world must be made safe for democracy." By April 6, both houses of Congress had overwhelmingly approved the declaration, and the United States was at war.

Prosecuting the War

The United States entered the war woefully unprepared. The army included 120,000 regulars and 80,000 newly federalized national guardsmen—altogether a tiny fraction of the Allied troops fighting in Europe. Most of what the military needed—including guns, munitions, uniforms, and airplanes—was in short supply. The army had no gas masks or industrial suppliers of poison gas. Its meager air service was unequipped with the machine guns or the flight instruments essential to combat operations. And the navy's best submarine detection apparatus could not even sense the presence, let alone determine the location, of a submerged U-boat cruising more than 200 yards away. To prosecute the war, the nation had to finance the mobilization, organize its economy for war production, raise an army, and equip its military services to fight in a conflict that, as a leading business executive remarked, combined the dreams of science fiction "with the horrors of Armageddon."

FINANCING THE WAR

The Wilson administration paid one-third of the costs of the war with revenues from excise taxes, higher estate taxes, and, sanctioned by the recently ratified Sixteenth Amendment, taxes on incomes, some as high as 63 percent. It financed the other two-thirds by borrowing, mainly through a series of bonds called "Liberty Loans." Every one of the bond campaigns was oversubscribed. The direct cost of the war to the U.S. government came to $24 billion, more than twice the total it had spent for all purposes in the fifteen years before the war. The government spent another $11 billion in the form of war loans to other nations.

WAR PRODUCTION

The Wilson administration's prewar emphasis on restoring competition among small producers gave way under the demands of war production to a reliance on big business. Businessmen from major corporations flooded into Washington, taking only a dollar a year in pay while contributing their executive experience to the war effort. In July 1917, the Wilson administration established a War Industries Board (WIB) to oversee producers of key raw materials and manufactures. It also established additional agencies to control trade, shipping, and railroad traffic; and, after passage in August of the Lever Food and Fuel Control Act, it created the Fuel Administration and the Food Administration. In all, nearly 5,000 agencies were established to manage the domestic wartime economy.

Mindful of the business community's long-standing opposition to government control, Wilson tried to mobilize the

economy by relying on voluntarism. For example, the WIB was to act as a clearing agency for the nation's defense industries and encourage production increases as well as the elimination of waste. But by late 1917, it was evident that this cooperative strategy was not working. As a result, while the federal government continued to rely on voluntary cooperation from private enterprise, it came to an unprecedented degree to manage key sectors of the economy.

Faced with an extensive railroad tie-up at the end of the year, Wilson seized control of the railroads, and within months the government had forged thousands of miles of track owned by several thousand companies into an integrated national transportation system. Early in 1918, to conserve fuel for heating and lighting, his fuel administrator introduced daylight saving time. In March, in the hope of inducing greater coordination and productivity in the industrial

A Liberty Loan poster urging ethnic Americans to support the war effort.

war effort, Wilson put teeth into the WIB, appointing Bernard Baruch to head it and giving him the authority to do his job. Grown rich from speculating on Wall Street, Baruch possessed fingertip knowledge of the American economy. Using power and persuasion, he managed to shift a quarter of the economy from consumer to war production. The WIB reached into numerous niches in American economic life, with its conservation division, for example, altering bicycle designs to save 2,000 tons of steel and capturing enough metal for two warships by removing stays from corsets.

The agency that touched the lives of most Americans was the Food Administration, headed by Herbert Hoover, a wealthy mining engineer who had begun devoting himself to public service, most recently as the leader of humanitarian food relief in Belgium. Hoover sought to increase the food supply by emphasizing both conservation and production—for example in

"The WIB altered bicycle designs to save 2,000 tons of steel and captured enough metal for two warships by removing stays from corsets."

wheat, which was in short supply because part of the American harvest was going to U.S. soldiers and the Allies. Hoover urged consumers to practice wheatless Mondays and bake wheat-free breads, cakes, and cookies. Using the powers granted the food administrator in the Lever Act, he got farmers to plant more wheat by guaranteeing them a minimum price and establishing a grain corporation to buy up their harvest. Hoover's policies increased wheat yields from 637 million to 921 million bushels in one year.

To further conserve grain, Congress passed a law limiting the production of alcoholic beverages. The measure boosted the long-standing efforts of moral reformers to outlaw alcohol consumption. In 1919, the states ratified the Eighteenth Amendment (banning the importation or manufacture of intoxicating beverages), and the following year, to enforce these strictures, Congress passed the Volstead Act, which prohibited any beverage containing more than 1 in 200 parts alcohol.

The federal intervention in the wartime economy was unprecedented in scale and scope. While accelerating the efficient organization of mass production, it also ratified progressive beliefs in the value of centralization, federal regulation, reliance on exports, and collaboration among business, government, and labor. Much of the machinery of the intervention was dismantled after the war, but its effectiveness would be recalled when the nation faced the crisis of the Depression in the 1930s and then the need to mobilize for war again.

SCIENCE TO THE FRONT

Early in 1917, a leading scientist declared, "War must mean research." The government had taken steps to reduce the military's technological weakness in 1915 by creating the National Advisory Committee for Aeronautics, intended to foster aeronautical research, and the following year by encouraging the National Academy of Sciences to establish an agency to help mobilize academic science for defense.

After the country entered the war, the National Academy's agency spurred investigations into myriad techniques, devices, and substances for war. Psychologists helped sort out draftees, adapting tests that purported to measure "I.Q." (intelligence quotient) to determine which recruits were competent. Chemists working on chemical weapons were incorporated into the army's new Chemical Warfare Service.

U.S. FOOD ADMINISTRATION

EAT MORE
CORN, OATS AND RYE PRODUCTS — FISH AND POULTRY — FRUITS, VEGETABLES AND POTATOES BAKED, BOILED AND BROILED FOODS

EAT LESS
WHEAT, MEAT, SUGAR AND FATS

TO SAVE FOR THE ARMY AND OUR ALLIES

A Food Administration poster urging Americans to spare wheat and other foods for U. S. soldiers and the Allies.

Physicists developed submarine detectors that in 1918 allowed Allied ships and subchasers to find and sink submarines. The technical mobilization produced new poison gases and defenses against the enemy's, aeronautical instruments, signaling lamps, and new developments in the wireless transmission of voice. It also yielded a heightened appreciation of science by industrialists and military officers.

INTO COMBAT

The Allies cheered the American entry into the war. At the time, their prospects seemed dim. The shipping losses to German submarines in March and April were cutting heavily into their supplies. In the spring of 1917, an American admiral devised an effective means—the convoy—to protect merchant shipping against U-boat attacks. The ships would travel in groups screened on all sides by destroyers. If a submarine torpedoed one of them, it would place itself in dire jeopardy. During May, shipping losses dropped one-third below the April high.

With the **declaration of war,** most opposition to conscription dissolved, and in May 1917 Congress enacted a Selective Service measure. Draft boards peacefully registered more than 24 million men—only 1–2 percent of eligible males failed to register—and inducted about 2.8 million of them. Another 2 million volunteered, bringing the total serving in the war to about 4.8 million.

While the United States built its army, the war on the ground went poorly for the Allies. In November, in a battle in Belgium, the British gained four miles at a cost of 400,000 casualties; and in another near the Austrian border, the Italians suffered a catastrophic defeat. The Allies were further weakened that month by events in Russia. The previous March, a revolution had overthrown the brutal regime of Czar Nicholas II, replacing it with a provisional democratic government under Alexander Kerensky. But on November 6, the Kerensky government succumbed to a Communist revolution spearheaded by the Bolsheviks under the leadership of Vladimir Lenin and Leon Trotsky. The new Bolshevik government, propelled into power partly by the war-weariness of the Russian people, promptly signed an armistice with Germany at Brest Litovsk. Russia's withdrawal from the war allowed Germany to move its thousands of soldiers from the eastern front to fight against the Allies.

Most of the U.S. troops arrived in France after the beginning of 1918, serving as members of the American Expedi-

James Montgomery Flagg's classic recruiting poster for the U.S. Army, 1918.

tionary Force (AEF) under General John J. Pershing, a tough, capable commander hardened by his leadership of the expedition against Pancho Villa. By orders from Wilson, the AEF was to fight in parallel with the Allies while remaining "distinct and separate" from them. Pershing, impatient with the trench-warfare mentality of the Allies, itched to engage in more aggressive combat. But in March 1918, when the Germans launched a massive spring offensive, the AEF was subordinated to a unified Allied command under the French general Ferdinand Foch. The AEF helped beat back the initial German assault. Then, in early June, when the Germans threatened Paris, the Americans helped significantly to halt the German advance in heavy fighting around the town of Château-Thierry and neighboring Belleau Wood. And in the area of the cathedral city of Reims, they assisted in blocking a final German attempt to break through the Allied lines.

In mid-July, the Allies and the AEF, now 1 million soldiers strong, mounted a major offensive against the Germans. In September, given his first independent command, Pershing

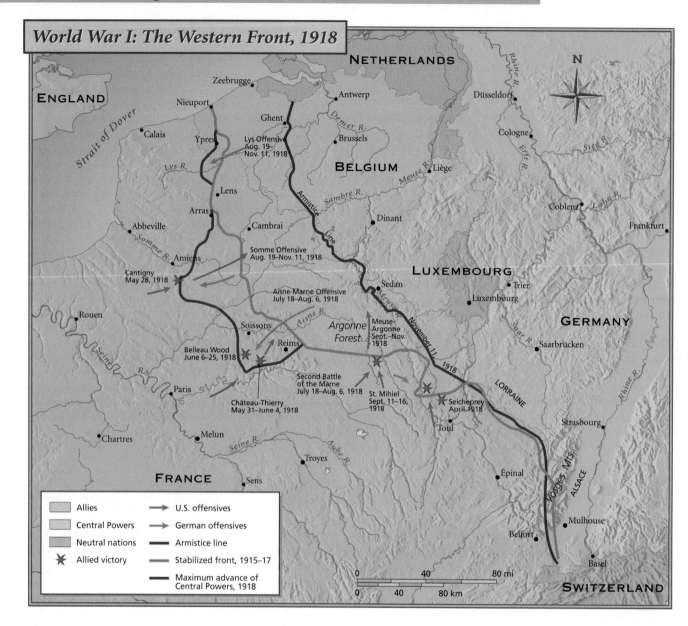

World War I: The Western Front, 1918

Legend:
- Allies
- Central Powers
- Neutral nations
- ★ Allied victory
- → U.S. offensives
- → German offensives
- Armistice line
- Stabilized front, 1915–17
- Maximum advance of Central Powers, 1918

led AEF troops against a German troop concentration around the town of St. Mihiel, about 150 miles east of Paris on the Meuse River. The attack began at 1 A.M. on September 11, when, as one soldier wrote in his diary, in "one instant the entire front . . . was a sheet of flame, while the heavy artillery made the earth quake." Breaking from the seesaw of trench tactics, Pershing organized 500,000 American and 100,000 French troops into a war of movement that, aided by air cover from French and British squadrons, reduced the Ger-

man concentration in four days. On September 26, 1.2 million American soldiers fought alongside the Allies to oust the Germans from the area of the Meuse River and the Argonne Forest. They clawed northward through the seemingly ubiquitous mud and against heavy German opposition, eventually gaining the city of Sedan and severing the major German rail supply route. It was the last major battle of the war.

Unlike the belligerents on the European continent, the United States suffered no physical damage from the war, and its casualty rate was far smaller—8 percent—than the 70 percent rate suffered by the Allies. But adding to the gruesome toll of the war, Spanish influenza struck the United States in mid-September 1918, part of a worldwide epidemic that took 20 million lives. Among them were almost 500,000 Americans, including more U.S. troops (63,000) than had fallen in battle (49,000).

Many of the men who participated in the AEF—all told, a total of 2 million—were marked by the brutality of the war and by the ways that technology had exacerbated the savagery of combat. For ground troops, for example, the ordeal of battle was made worse than in the past by their vulnerability to machine-gunning aircraft and long-range artillery fire. (Among the valued new technical groups in the army was a service led by physicists and engineers that located distant enemy guns by spotting the flash and the sound erupting from their muzzles.) Some soldiers also succumbed to "shell shock," a syndrome that would have earned them condemnation in earlier wars as cowards but that psychologists now treated as type of mental and emotional breakdown.

> *"An increasingly rigid emphasis on national unity led to the suppression of dissent, an intolerant stress on 'Americanism,' and a war against radicalism."*

WARTIME SOCIETY

The war, stimulating most sectors of the economy, changed the lot of industrial labor and created good times for agriculture. It also drew more women into the workforce and accelerated the migration of blacks from the South to northern industrial cities. But an increasingly rigid emphasis on national unity led to the suppression of dissent, an intolerant stress on "Americanism," and a war against radicalism.

A Booming Economy. The demand for war goods added to the prosperity that the war orders from Europe had begun generating. Between 1914 and 1918, factory output mushroomed by more than a third, with automobile production, for example, quadrupling to 1.8 million cars in 1917. Labor shortages drove unemployment down and wages up. Average annual income leaped from $830 in 1917 to $1,407 in 1920. Farm products more than doubled in price during the war, raising farm income significantly but also helping to inflate the cost of living 77 percent, a jump that outpaced the increase in family income.

Samuel Gompers, the head of the American Federation of Labor (AFL), urged workers to refrain from striking during the war, expecting that labor would gain benefits by cooperating with government and business. But a good many workers ignored his call, perhaps remembering that a railroad strike in 1916 had led to passage of the Adamson Act, which established the eight-hour day for the railroads and as a standard for other industries. In the six months following the U.S. entry into the war, a wave of strikes hit American industry.

The National War Labor Board, established in January 1918 to recommend resolutions of labor disputes, issued rulings in 500 cases, many of them guaranteeing labor's right to organize and bargain with management. As a result of pressure from the board, the eight-hour day became more of an industrial norm. Federal agencies pushed employers to honor the federal ban on child labor, allow safety and sanitation inspectors into their plants, raise wages, and offer worker-compensation benefits. In the interest of promoting efficiency and social stability, several states enacted protections and benefits for industrial labor. The tight labor market and the government's encouragement combined to increase union membership from 3 million in 1917 to 5 million in 1920.

Allied troops await the enemy in one of the dirty, damp, vermin-infested trenches of World War I.

But while the government increased its regulation of business, business often unduly influenced the regulatory process. After the Department of Justice granted immunity against antitrust prosecutions to business combinations certified to be serving the public interest, corporate mergers climbed sharply. So did business profits, even though the government tried to curtail them with an excess-profits tax that brought in $2.2 billion, more than three times as much as did the personal income tax. In 1917, for example, the net income of U.S. Steel reached $224 million, a level the company would not achieve again until 1954.

African Americans. Between 1916 and 1918, some 450,000 blacks moved north, substantially increasing the African American population of New York and other cities, especially Chicago, where it jumped by 145 percent to 109,000. They were impelled out of the South by the ravages of floods, boll weevils, and low cotton prices, all of which reduced farm work, and by the region's racially repressive social system. They were pulled to the North by the high demand for labor and the opportunity to earn more in a day than many in the South earned in a week. An African American recently ar-

> *"An African American recently arrived in Chicago from the South wrote, 'Nothing here but money, and it is not hard to get.'"*

rived in Chicago from the South wrote, "Nothing here but money, and it is not hard to get."

But the mass arrival of African Americans sparked conflicts, often with European immigrants, over housing, jobs, and political power. In 1917, rioting broke out in Houston and Philadelphia; and in East St. Louis, Illinois, after whites brutally burned, beat, and stoned residents of a black neighborhood, thousands of people went on a rampage, burning, looting, and killing. After the riots in East St. Louis, blacks marched down New York's Fifth Avenue in silent protest, carrying banners that read: "Mr. President, Why Not Make America Safe for Democracy?"

During the war, some 260,000 blacks enlisted or were drafted. They were assigned to segregated units that were, for the most part, commanded by whites. Sent mainly to training camps in the South, they suffered blatant racial abuse. In late August 1917, provoked by racial incidents, including the beating of a black woman by a white policeman, hundreds of black soldiers of the Twenty-fourth Infantry Regiment stormed out of their Texas camp into the neighboring city of Houston and killed fifteen whites and Hispanics, among them five policemen. Of the sixty-four men tried in courts-martial, five were acquitted, nineteen were hanged, and the rest were sentenced to prison, a number of them for life.

About 50,000 black soldiers went to France. Most were given menial tasks, though some jobs, like unloading cargo from ships, were crucial to the war effort. The AEF allowed only one black regiment, the Ninety-second, which had some of the few black officers trained during the war, into combat in Europe. However, four other black regiments fought under French command, and one was awarded the Croix de Guerre, the French honor for bravery under fire.

Women. In 1917, Florence Thorne of the AFL observed, "Out of . . . repression into opportunity is the meaning of the war to thousands of women." Secretary of the Navy Josephus Daniels brought women into his service, with the result that 11,000 of them worked in the navy as secretaries, nurses, and telephone operators. Women also found employment in new jobs such as running elevators, producing munitions, and delivering messages. Some were appointed to defense advisory boards. During the war, industry employed about 1 million women.

Soldiers of the African American 369th Infantry Regiment, wearing the Croix de Guerre they earned in combat under French command.

Inflation helped bring more married women into the paid workforce: "I used to go to work when my man was sick or couldn't get a job," said one wife, after prices had been rising for four years. "But this is the first time I ever had to go to work to get enough money to feed the kids, when he was working regular." Most working women were not new entrants to the labor force, but the war enabled many to move to better-paying jobs. Even so, they earned less than the men they replaced despite complaints from women and rulings to the contrary from the War Labor Board. And when the soldiers returned after the war, many women were edged out of the industrial labor force.

Women activists did smell victory almost certainly coming for the suffrage movement. President Wilson himself told a leading suffragist that women had earned the right to vote by reason of their contributions to the war effort. In 1919, responding to a torrent of petitions from the states, the Senate and House passed the Nineteenth Amendment, which said that the right of American citizens to vote "shall not be denied or abridged by the United States or by any State on account of sex." It was ratified in August 1920 (see Chapter 22).

Women machinists at work in a refrigerator plant during the war, 1917.

Assaults on Civil Liberties. The enlargement of federal power combined with the emphasis on national unity led to campaigns against dissent from the war. Both the government, using the law, and private citizens, resorting to intimidation and sometimes violence, insisted that everyone adhere to a prowar patriotism and rigid "Americanism" that undermined civil liberties.

In April 1917, the Wilson administration, concerned with mobilizing public opinion behind the war, created a Committee on Public Information (CPI) to publicize the merits of the cause. The CPI soon expanded its role to propagandizing and attempting to control opinions, telling magazine readers to report to the Justice Department "the man who spreads pessimistic stories . . . cries for peace, or belittles our efforts to win the war."

States and local school districts banned the teaching of the German language. Americans boycotted performances of German opera, called sauerkraut "liberty cabbage," and renamed towns with German-sounding names. People publicly flogged German Americans who voiced allegedly seditious thoughts, and they forced many to kiss the American flag. The anti-Germanism soon turned into an animus against all foreign-looking and foreign-sounding people who had recently come to the United States. (About one-third of the population were either immigrants or had at least one immigrant parent; about one-sixth derived from the Central Powers.)

Wilson invoked the Alien Act of 1798, still on the books, to detain or deport enemy aliens. In the Espionage Act of June 1917, Congress provided stiff fines and prison terms for anyone convicted of obstructing the war effort by use of the mails or otherwise. In May 1918, it passed a new Sedition Act, which threatened with a twenty-year prison term anyone who expressed a disloyal opinion or defamed the flag, the government, or the Constitution. Acting under these measures, the federal government prosecuted some 2,000 people and convicted 1,500, including the Socialist leader Eugene Debs, who was sentenced to ten years in prison for having given an antiwar speech. The administration banned Socialist publications from the mails and harassed the Industrial Workers of the World (IWW), arresting and imprisoning its leaders. During the summer of 1917 in Bisbee, Arizona, the town's copper mines disrupted constantly by IWW strikes, 1,186 miners

"In the Land of Freedom," a German comment on the crackdown in the United States on anyone suspected of being a German sympathizer, November 1917.

Empire and the Turkish-led Ottoman Empire, which controlled large areas of the Middle East. Most of the other points urged a new order on the world—absolute freedom of the seas, greater freedom of trade, open rather than secret agreements between countries, and the peaceful resolution of disputes by a "general association of nations," what came to be called the League of Nations.

In October, their last offensive having failed, the Germans conveyed to Wilson that they would accept an armistice based on the Fourteen Points. The French and the British, at first reluctant, agreed to the terms after Wilson threatened to conclude a separate peace. Precisely at 11 A.M. on November 11, 1918, the guns in Europe fell silent. Crowds all over the United States cheered the end of the killing, and soon the troops were sailing home and preparations made for negotiating the peace. In the congressional elections earlier that month, voters weary of the federal government's wartime interventions in the nation's life had given control of both the House and the Senate to the Republican Party. But Wilson unwisely appointed only a single Republican—and at that, one who was on the periphery of power within the party—to the delegation he led to the peace conference. The delegation sailed to a *bon voyage* of ship's horns and whistles aboard the *George Washington* on December 4, 1918, making Wilson the first sitting president to cross the Atlantic.

THE VERSAILLES PEACE CONFERENCE

Arriving in France, Wilson was greeted with exuberant enthusiasm. But the popular accolades masked the difficulty of the task before the American delegation when it met with the Allied heads of state to negotiate the peace at the palace of Versailles, just south of Paris. The chief difficulty was to persuade the Allies, with their colonial interests and bitter experience of the war, to subordinate their hunger for territory and retribution to Wilsonian idealism. The French leader, Georges Clemenceau, commented, "God gave us the Ten Commandments and we broke them. Mr. Wilson has given us the Fourteen Points. We shall see."

What the world saw was the Treaty of Versailles, formally signed on June 28, 1919. The previous October, Kaiser Wilhelm II had abdicated, and a German republic was established. But the treaty was less concerned with stabilizing democracy in Germany and integrating the new republic into Europe than with making it pay for the war and keeping it weak. The treaty stripped Germany of its colonies, granting

were run out of town by the sheriff and 2,000 citizens armed and paid by the mine owners. Arrest, prosecution, and vigilante harassment all combined to chill dissent and protest.

Retreat from Internationalism

Wilson long hoped that the war would produce a more democratic world, and he felt it imperative to articulate his vision of that goal after the Bolsheviks established a Communist regime in Russia and revealed that the treaties signed by the European powers before 1914 included secret arrangements for parceling out territories among the victors. In a speech to Congress in January 1918, the president advanced a framework for the peace spelled out in what were quickly dubbed the Fourteen Points. A majority of the points called for self-determination and autonomy for the ethnic and national minorities under the domination of the Austro-Hungarian

them to the victors as trusteeships that were to lead to eventual independence. It gave parts of Germany to Belgium, Denmark, and Poland. It strictly limited the size of the German armed forces, and it established a thirty-mile-wide demilitarized zone between France's eastern border and the Rhine River. The treaty returned to France the provinces of Alsace-Lorraine, which Germany had taken in 1871, and it awarded France control of the Saar Basin, Germany's rich source of coal, for fifteen years. Finally, it imposed on Germany the obligation to pay huge reparations, later fixed by an international commission at $33 billion.

In the separate Treaty of Sèvres, concluded with Turkey in 1920, the Allies liquidated the Ottoman Empire, awarding the British a mandate to supervise Palestine and Iraq and the French similar responsibility in Syria and Lebanon. In the Balfour Declaration (1917), the British had pledged to help establish a Jewish "national home" in Palestine that would give due regard to the rights of the Palestinians. They also promised to support the creation of independent Arab states—including, so the Arabs thought, one for the Palestinians, a commitment the British later denied they had made. The unresolved fate of the Palestinians would later lead to explosive tensions in the region.

The disposition of Germany's colonies into trusteeships slated for independence expressed Wilsonian principles, and so did the recognition of an independent Poland and the creation of two new nations—Czechoslovakia and Yugoslavia—from the Austro-Hungarian and Ottoman Empires. However, the Versailles Treaty's treatment of Germany was economically unworkable, as the British economist John Maynard Keynes argued in his powerful *Economic Consequences of the Peace* (1919), a best-seller on both sides of the Atlantic. While Germany was required to pay huge reparations, it was denied much of the economic means—for example, the resources of the Saar Basin—to do so. The vindictive features of the treaty provoked a simmering resentment among many Germans.

From mid-1918 until 1920, the United States participated with the Allies in sending troops to the new Communist Russia, declaring that the purpose was to safeguard Allied war stores and protect Russian ports against German attack. But the Allied forces also supported anti-Bolshevik factions in their fight to overthrow the new government. Even after the counterrevolutionary movement failed, the United States refused to recognize the Soviet regime.

BATTLE OVER THE LEAGUE OF NATIONS

Wilson came away from Versailles with the prize of a "covenant," written into the peace treaty itself, to establish a League of Nations. But Senator Henry Cabot Lodge, the Republican head of the Senate Foreign Relations Committee, and other Republican senators refused to accept the League without reservations. They were particularly concerned to ensure that the United States would maintain its autonomy in matters of immigration and tariffs, and that any measures taken by the League to police the peace would not undermine Congress's constitutional right to declare war. Wilson would not agree to any reservations, contending that trying to modify the covenant of the League would destroy the "whole vital structure" of the treaty. When in July 1919 the treaty reached the Senate for ratification, Lodge bottled it up in his committee.

Woodrow Wilson (second from left) and, to his left, Georges Clemenceau of France and Arthur Balfour of Great Britain.

A 1919 cartoon conveying Wilson's strong commitment to the League of Nations.

The United States may have retreated into isolationism, but it was actually less isolated from other nations than at any time in its history. The country was already tied to them in relationships of trade and culture; radio and aircraft promised to link them more closely. Wilson may have been rigid in insisting that the Senate abide by the letter of the League covenant, but his vision of a new world order shaped by a blend of idealism with enforcement would continue to appeal to a number of Americans concerned with maintaining the security of the United States in an increasingly interdependent world.

UNREST AND REACTION

Promptly after the end of the war, the federal government began to demobilize by canceling or curtailing all military contracts for munitions, food, and equipment. These cuts reduced manufacturing jobs at the same time that the veterans, most of them hungry for work, were returning to civilian life.

Early in September, Wilson, furious at Lodge, mounted an arduous speaking campaign in the West to rally public opinion behind the League. Three weeks, 9,000 miles, and thirty-seven speeches later, he collapsed and returned to Washington. On October 2, he suffered a severe stroke that left him an invalid, his mental and physical powers impaired. He was kept isolated by his wife, Edith Galt, who limited the information he received and the people he met.

On September 10, Lodge released the treaty to the Senate with amendments designed to satisfy the Republicans' reservations. Had Wilson been willing to compromise, the Senate might have ratified the treaty and put the United States into the League. But Wilson refused to accede to Lodge's terms. Lacking the necessary two-thirds Senate majority with or without reservations, the treaty died in November, and an attempt to revive it the following March failed utterly. To a significant extent, the Senate's action reflected attitudes toward the treaty in the country at large. Despite Wilson's desperate speech-making tour, U.S. membership in the League enjoyed only limited popular support. In October 1921, the United States ratified the Treaty of Berlin, which normalized its relations with Germany on the basis of the Versailles settlement without the League. Similar agreements soon followed with Austria and Hungary.

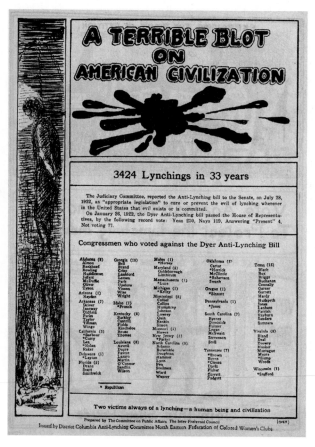

The shocking wave of lynchings after World War I—some against veterans still in uniform—provoked an antilynching campaign in which black organizations like the NAACP played a leading role. This broadside, which lists the names of congressmen who voted against an antilynching bill, was issued by the North Eastern Federation of Colored Women's Clubs in 1922.

By February 1919, about 3 million people were unemployed, and that year labor mounted more than 3,500 strikes, including a general strike in Seattle, a bitter police strike in Boston, and a walkout of some 365,000 workers in the steel industry. Meanwhile, prices continued to soar until, by mid-1920, the cost of living was over twice what it had been in 1914.

Racial and ethnic tensions escalated as white men, many of them veterans, competed for jobs with black migrants and foreign immigrants. Lynch mobs rampaged through parts of the South, and between April and early October 1919 race riots broke out in some twenty-five towns and cities, among them Charleston, Washington, D.C., and Chicago, where the violence left 38 people dead, more than 500 injured, and more than 1,000 homeless. Amid the unrest, fears that Bolshevism might be spreading from Russia to the United States rose to the level of hysteria.

The Red Scare. In late 1918 in Philadelphia, anarchists bombed the homes of a prominent businessman, a police official, and a state judge. The following June, bombs exploded within the same hour in eight cities, one of them damaging the Washington home of Attorney General A. Mitchell Palmer. These and other bombings helped ignite a "Red Scare" that swept through the country in 1919, fueled by fear and anxiety, a readiness to blame strikes and violence on Socialists, anarchists, and Bolsheviks, and alarm over the Soviet government's establishment that year of the Communist International, or Comintern, to spread Communism abroad.

To stem the spread of radicalism, states passed severe sedition laws under which hundreds of accused subversives were imprisoned; others lost their jobs in universities or industry, or fell victim to vigilantes (often war veterans) who stormed radicals' headquarters and seized their literature or disrupted political demonstrations. Attorney General Palmer told Congress that Communists planned "to rise up and destroy the Government at one fell swoop." In late 1919 and early 1920, he mounted a series of raids (the "Palmer raids") on radical groups with neither search warrants nor arrest warrants. His forces found three pistols and no explosives but arrested over 6,000 people. Most were later exonerated, although the government deported some 556 persons of foreign birth. In this atmosphere, the Supreme Court upheld the Espionage and Sedition Acts in *Schenck v. United States* and two other decisions.

The Red Scare intensified the xenophobia (fear of foreigners) that had originated during the war. In 1920, when immigration revived after the wartime lull, a mob burned

This cartoon, published during the Red Scare, shows a Bolshevik lurking under the American flag.

immigrants' homes in the mining town of West Frankfort in southern Illinois; California passed a law forbidding Japanese ownership of land; and Henry Ford launched a newspaper campaign against Jews. The president-general of the Daughters of the American Revolution proclaimed that "nothing will save the life of this free Republic if these foreign leeches are not cut and cast out." The scare abated later that year as spokesmen for industries dependent on immigrant labor began attacking efforts to associate all immigrants with radicalism, and defenders of free speech rallied against Palmer's effort to secure a new federal sedition act to facilitate his campaign against "Reds." There was no panic about a conspiracy of radicals when, in September 1920, a powerful bomb went off outside J. P. Morgan's Wall Street office, killing thirty-eight people and injuring at least fifty-seven.

REPUBLICAN REIGN

The revival of isolationism and the defeat of the Versailles Treaty, the renewed power of business and the attacks on organized labor, the Red Scare and the hounding of radicals—

all signaled that the country was racing to the right. In 1920, the Republican Party looked forward optimistically to retaining the control of Congress it had won in 1918 and retaking the White House.

The Democratic convention nominated Governor James M. Cox of Ohio and Wilson's secretary of the navy, Franklin Delano Roosevelt of New York (a cousin of Theodore Roosevelt). They defended the League of Nations and Wilsonian idealism to an electorate predominantly sick of both. The Republicans, badly split by warring factions, decided on a compromise candidate, Warren G. Harding, an undistinguished senator from Ohio. Harding promised the country "normalcy," by which he meant ending the Wilson administration's foreign and domestic activism. Eugene Debs, defiantly nominated for the presidency by the Socialist Party even though he was in jail, received 1 million votes. Still, amid the postwar swing to conservatism, Harding won the election by a landslide, gaining 60 percent of the popular vote and 404 of the 531 electoral votes. For the first time in memory, the number of qualified voters who cast ballots fell below 50 percent, a signal that many Americans were tired of politics and turmoil.

Harding and his vice-president, Calvin Coolidge, replaced the progressivism and internationalism of the Wilson years with a probusiness conservatism. But while they pursued a formal isolationism, the government was attentive to national security in a high-technology world and helped foster a variety of private engagements abroad.

Harding, Then Coolidge. Harding possessed limited talents and liked amiable relaxation, sometimes with his mistress, Nan Britton, who later described a series of tawdry, adulterous trysts, one in a White House coat closet. He was an enormously popular president, and when he suddenly died of a heart attack on August 2, 1923, the country mourned him like a lost hero. But while Harding had appointed a number of able and accomplished men to his cabinet, he also gave high offices to political cronies from Ohio who took advantage of their positions to line their pockets. The exposure of their crimes (including the illegal sale of leases on federal oil reserves at Teapot Dome, Wyoming) in congressional investigations in 1924 sent many of them to prison.

Calvin Coolidge, Harding's successor, seemed the perfect antidote. Stern, reserved, taciturn, the governor of Massachusetts at the time of the 1919 Boston police strike, he had won admiration then for telegraphing Samuel Gompers of the AFL: "There is no right to strike against the public safety by anybody, anytime, anywhere." Coolidge retained the notable and honest members of Harding's cabinet, including Herbert Hoover, the wartime food administrator and Harding's secretary of commerce; and Andrew W. Mellon, his secretary of the treasury and a financier bent on reducing the tax rates paid by wealthy Americans. In 1924, Coolidge ran for election in his own right in a three-way race that pitted him against Senator Robert M. La Follette of Wisconsin, the candidate of the Progressive Party, and the Democratic nominee, John W. Davis, a little-known corporate lawyer from New York. Coolidge won 54 percent of the popular vote, a decisive ratification of his conservative Republicanism.

The combined legislative records of the Harding and Coolidge administrations emphasized efficiency, limited government, and encouragement of business. In 1921, at Harding's urging, Congress approved a Budget and Accounting Act that required the president to prepare an annual budget with the help of a new Bureau of the Budget and submit it for consideration to the House and Senate. Congress also boosted research in aeronautics and took other steps to assist the fledgling aircraft industry. In 1926 and 1928, Congress gave Andrew Mellon his way, reducing income taxes and inheritance taxes. But Coolidge endorsed only minimal help to farmers and rejected a request for federal assistance from victims, many of them black, of a catastrophic flood on the Mis-

Warren Harding (left), twenty-ninth president of the United States (1921–23), and Calvin Coolidge, thirtieth president (1923–29).

sissippi River, saying that the government was not obligated to protect people "against the hazards of the elements."

FOREIGN AFFAIRS

Despite the retreat into isolationism, policymakers strengthened the military's capacity to deal with the increasingly high-technology character of defense, making the Chemical Warfare Service a permanent part of the army while the armed services installed aeronautics facilities and a new naval laboratory on the banks of the Potomac. Simultaneously, the government sought international agreements for arms control and against war.

In 1921, responding to pressure from progressives in the Senate, the Harding administration convened delegates from nine countries for the Washington Arms Limitation Conference. Secretary of State Charles Evans Hughes, a former governor of New York and an able lawyer, surprised the gathering by calling for each nation to scrap a number of ships; and the delegates surprised the world by agreeing to the proposal in principle. By 1922, when it adjourned, the conference had agreed to nine treaties, including one that allowed the United States and Britain a fixed warship tonnage superior to that of Japan, France, and Italy and imposed a naval holiday by stopping all battleship construction for ten years. Britain, France, Japan, and the United States also agreed to respect each other's possessions in the Pacific. And all nine nations pledged that they would honor Chinese sovereignty and the principle of the Open Door.

In 1928, Frank B. Kellogg, Hughes's successor as secretary of state, and the French foreign minister negotiated the Kellogg-Briand Pact, a treaty outlawing war. The pact was ultimately signed by sixty-two nations, and the Senate ratified it early in 1929 by a vote of 85 to 1. As a practical matter, the pact, which lacked any means of enforcement and allowed military actions for self-defense, was worthless. But the strong support it gained revealed that Americans across a wide spectrum wanted no more of war.

The United States approached Latin America in a similarly benign spirit, for the most part replacing gunboat diplomacy with nonintervention, negotiation, and mutual respect. The country withdrew the marines Wilson had sent to the Dominican Republic, ended military surveillance of Cuba's internal affairs, and ratified a treaty that compensated Colombia for its loss of Panama. The United States also recognized Mexico's revolutionary government in return for an agreement to settle American claims and respect the oil rights granted to foreign companies before 1917. In 1923, Hughes signed a Pan-American treaty providing mechanisms for the peaceful resolution of disputes among the American nations.

Four years later, however, when a liberal insurrection was mounted against the government of Nicaragua, Coolidge dispatched troops and supported a conservative as president there. Instability persisted in Nicaragua, and the troops remained until 1933. In response to criticism of the action by officials at a Pan-American conference, a member of the State Department wrote a memorandum that in effect repudiated the Roosevelt corollary to the Monroe Doctrine, which had claimed the right of the United States to intervene in the internal affairs of Latin American countries. Although the document did not constitute official policy, it was a landmark in the retreat from interventionism.

A Private Internationalism. The government's isolationist policies in the twenties masked a private internationalism—engagements abroad by private citizens, philanthropic organizations, and businesses. Scientists took advanced training in the great European centers of research and brought home the revolutionary new physics of the atom called quantum mechanics. Civic leaders toured European cities, returning with ideas about urban planning and ways that private corporations might serve the greater public interest.

The U.S. government, which often encouraged and protected this private internationalism, was itself involved with agencies of the League of Nations through unofficial observers and connections. From 1921 to 1923, Secretary of Commerce Herbert Hoover revived his wartime program of private famine relief to help feed approximately 10 million starving Russians—a humanitarian gesture he hoped would also thwart Bolshevist ends. American business kept expanding its interests abroad, exporting more and more manufactured goods, agricultural products, and capital. After World War I, for the first time in its history, the United States became a creditor nation, which is to say that it was owed more in loans by foreigners than it owed them.

Business was divided about the kind of encouragement it asked of the government. With their expanding overseas interests, the larger corporations wanted a reduction in tariff

> *"After World War I, for the first time in its history, the United States became a creditor nation."*

rates to promote international trade, but small businesses, with their largely domestic markets, insisted on high rates for protection against foreign competition. Small business won out with the passage of the Fordney-McCumber Tariff Act in 1922. The law raised rates to their highest level in the country's history, but in a concession to big business, the act also provided for granting most-favored-nation status, which meant tariff reductions, to countries that treated American exports favorably. In 1930, the Smoot-Hawley Tariff raised rates to yet new historic highs.

In 1924, the United States intervened in Europe when Germany, its economy reeling from runaway inflation, began defaulting on its reparations payments to the Allies. Faced with a French and Belgian attempt to collect reparations by force, Hoover and Hughes suggested that a committee of private bankers headed by Charles G. Dawes negotiate the dispute. The resulting Dawes Plan adjusted reparations payments to levels consistent with German economic conditions and arranged for an injection of capital into the German economy. The capital, which came largely from American investors, helped restabilize the German currency and create a boom in the German economy. The United States, however, refused to restructure the $10 billion debt the Allies owed the U.S. Treasury.

A Prosperous Nation

The decade of the twenties opened with the American economy in a severe recession brought about by excess inventories, a tightening of credit by the Federal Reserve, and a decline in exports. But in 1922, the economy began to rebound, responding to pent-up demand for housing and consumer goods, especially automobiles, electric appliances, and radios.

CONSTRUCTION

Between 1919 and 1926, construction income doubled to $4.2 billion. The building boom produced thousands of new houses at a rate of almost 900,000 a year, more than twice that of previous decades. The expansion, much of which occurred around cities, made home-owning a real prospect for former renters. People without substantial incomes could now purchase homes with "balloon mortgages," which required only regular interest payments during the life of the loan, deferring repayment of the amount owed until the end of the loan. The houses, fitted with indoor plumbing, included the modern bathroom with a sink and tub, taps for hot and cold water, a toilet, and ceramic tile. Families replaced the old coal or wood-fired stoves with gas or electric ranges, which left no ash residue to be cleaned away.

A modern bathtub in a 1915 advertisement by the Kohler Company, which manufactured sinks, bathtubs, and other bathroom fixtures.

THE AUTO INDUSTRY

Technological improvements helped inflame the American romance with the car. By the 1920s, automobiles could be started with an electric switch rather than by laborious hand-cranking. Their closed steel bodies and roll-down windows protected passengers against wind and road dust. And they were cheap, thanks to Henry Ford, who focused his assembly-line methods of manufacturing—the system that became known around the world as "Fordism"—on the production of the Model T, his "car for the great multitude." The price of the

Model T dropped to $294 in 1924, down by half from what it had been in 1912.

The Ford Motor Company's dominant position in the industry began to erode in the face of competition from the new Chrysler Corporation and General Motors Corporation (GM). Ford, restrained in his approach to marketing, once quipped that Americans could have a Ford in any color they wanted so long as it was black. GM and Chrysler cut into Ford's market by introducing competitively priced cars in a variety of colors, add-on equipment, model and styling changes, and, in the case of GM, the opportunity to buy its cars on credit. Between 1921 and 1929, passenger car production more than tripled, reaching 4.8 million vehicles a year; and the number of cars registered in the United States nearly tripled from 9 million to 26.5 million.

ABOVE: Alfred P. Sloan Jr., the president of General Motors, who made G.M. Ford's leading competitor, 1924.

LEFT: An ad for the 1928 Buick, a General Motors car available in vivid colors.

In 1916, pushed by constituents from both cities and farms, Congress passed a Federal Road Bill that provided funds for states with highway departments, and another in 1921 that designated 200,000 miles of roadway as eligible for a 50 percent federal subsidy. The 1921 act also set up a Bureau of Public Roads to plan a national highway system that, like the canals and railroads of earlier times, would stitch the country's cities and isolated rural communities into a more tight-knit nation.

Car production boosted the economy by its requirements from the steel, paint, textile, electric, and tire industries. Car ownership added to the dynamism by stimulating the oil industry, road construction, and the creation of new businesses—including car dealerships, gas stations, repair shops, parts-supply houses, roadside diners, motor hotels (soon contracted to "motels"), and the fast-food chains pioneered in 1926 by White Castle.

APPLIANCES AND THE RADIO

The economic boom was further fueled by the ongoing electrification of the country. Ever more power lines crisscrossed the cities, lighting factories, homes, and streets, moving streetcars and assembly lines, driving drill presses and lathes. By the end of the decade, about 70 percent of American homes, including most of those in urban areas, were wired for electricity. A new industry sprang up to meet a burgeoning demand for electric appliances—irons, fans, vacuum cleaners, toasters, stoves, washing machines, sewing machines, and refrigerators. Most such purchases were made on the new installment plan, putting consumers at any given moment $2 billion to $3 billion in debt.

The appliance industry at first comprised mainly small firms, but then large companies such as General Electric and Westinghouse entered the market, often buying up the small producers and improving their products in research laboratories. The war had driven home to many businessmen the value of research in the competition for both foreign and domestic markets. By the twenties, organized research had become the standard in American industry, especially its high-technology branches. By the minimum estimate, the number of industrial laboratories doubled over the decade, to more than a thousand. American industry was reported to be spending $133 million a year on research, twice as much as the federal government. "Science is not a thing apart," the *Saturday Evening Post* observed; "it is the bedrock of business."

The star product of the industrial laboratories was the radio. Taking advantage of the new availability of vacuum-tube-based voice transmission, ham (amateur) radio operators around the country began to broadcast recorded music and local news. In 1920, Frank Conrad, a Westinghouse engineer and ham operator in Pittsburgh, began airing regularly scheduled music programs from his garage; he soon moved his transmitter to the top of the Westinghouse factory, obtained a federal license under the call letters KDKA, and proceeded to broadcast the results of the 1920 presidential election—thus transforming radio from two-way conversations into a medium of mass communication.

Radio stations soon proliferated across the country—500 began operating in 1922 alone—often interfering with each other by transmitting programs on the same or closely neighboring wavelengths. In 1927, Congress passed the Radio Act, which set up a Federal Radio Commission to work with the secretary of commerce in issuing broadcasting licenses to radio stations and regulating stations' wavelengths and geographical range. Station transmitters grew far more powerful, able to cover at least 30,000 square miles. Meanwhile, the price of radios dropped, and dealers began to allow purchases on the installment plan. By 1930, almost half of American households owned radios—more than in any European country—and the fraction continued to rise.

The broadcast studio for station WDY in New Jersey, with drapes and towels used for acoustical control, 1921.

Between 1923 and 1929, largely as a result of the explosive growth of the construction, auto, and radio industries, corporate income increased from $8.3 billion to $10.6 billion, while savings jumped from $19.7 billion to $28.4 billion. Even working families could afford some of the products that technological innovation and mass production were making available.

FLAWS IN THE ECONOMY

During the postwar downturn of the early twenties, some industries such as coal and textiles sickened, and the boom years failed to restore them to health. The twenties also produced a redistribution of wealth upward. For example, as a result of Andrew Mellon's tax initatives, people with annual incomes of $1 million paid less than one-third the taxes they had paid at the beginning of the decade. Weak anti-

A gas station designed to blend with the surrounding residential neighborhood in Macomb, Illinois, 1920s.

trust enforcement helped foster corporate concentration in numerous industries, including automobiles, films, coal mining, clothing, and groceries. In 1929, the 200 largest corporations controlled 20 percent of national wealth and 50 percent of corporate wealth. About one-third of families earned less than $2,000 a year, the minimum income estimated for a decent standard of living; about one-fifth earned less than $1,000. This inequitable distribution of the era's prosperity was especially felt by labor and agriculture.

Labor. Organized labor, largely defeated in the 1919 strikes, was further weakened by the economic downturn of 1920–21. Union membership fell from more than 5 million at the end of the war to 3.6 million in 1923 and stayed there. Small- and medium-sized firms still comprised a sizable fraction of American manufacturing, and they employed skilled workers, the kind who formed the backbone of the AFL. But manufacturing was increasingly dominated by industries that relied on mass production, scientific management, and semiskilled and unskilled labor.

The managers of these large industrial firms despised unions. Rather than deal with them, they devised a kind of company paternalism called "welfare capitalism," intended to encourage worker loyalty and promote efficiency with employee programs ranging from life insurance and profit sharing to company-sponsored athletic teams. Such firms often had company unions and formalized systems through which workers could register grievances—except with regard to wages and working hours.

Despite Henry Ford's attempt to make life in his mass-production plants more palatable, the conditions of assembly-line work continued to exact heavy mental and physical tolls. A foreign journalist reported what he saw of a riveter on the line at Ford's huge River Rouge complex near Detroit: "At 8 A.M. the worker takes his place at the side of a narrow platform down the centre of which runs a great chain moving at the rate of a foot a minute.... The chain never stops. The pace never varies. The man is part of the chain, the feeder and the slave of it." Between 1923 and 1929, real wages climbed 8 per-

cent. But while Henry Ford had reduced the work week to forty hours spread over five days, most industrial workers spent six eight-hour days on the job.

Agriculture. During the war, farmers had borrowed money to buy land and machinery with the expectation of producing more crops at the high prices then current. But after the war, agricultural prices spiraled downward, reducing income to where some farmers were unable to pay their debts and were forced into bankruptcy. Many more, beset by rising costs and dwindling prices, sold out.

The small farms were acquired by bigger ones, with the result that agriculture turned increasingly into an agglomera-

The auto assembly line at the Ford Highland Park factory in 1914. Note the rails and chain by which the chassis was moved from worker to worker.

tion of large-scale enterprises (later called "agribusiness"). In the 1920s, "farm factories" sprang up in the wheat-growing regions of Montana, North Dakota, and Kansas, the fruit-growing areas of California, the cotton belt of the deep South, and on livestock and poultry farms from Texas to Delaware. They sought to increase profits by adopting industrial methods of production and exploiting research carried out at land-grant universities, the Department of Agriculture, and privately owned seed companies. These efforts yielded area-specific crop varieties, improved animal-breeding practices, and hybrid corn. Hybrid seed corn had to be purchased each year, but it boosted crop yields by up to 25 percent. Such innovations increased the amount of capital needed to farm efficiently and generally led to further consolidation.

Throughout the twenties, American farms, with all their consolidation, efficiencies, and capital-intensive practices, produced more than the national market could absorb. President Coolidge signed into law several measures to assist farmers, including one to facilitate the cooperative buying and selling of their products. But he twice vetoed the McNary-Haugen Bill, which proposed that the government stabilize agricultural prices by buying up surplus production and selling it abroad. Coolidge argued that the bill sanctioned price fixing and would antagonize foreign producers.

Life on even many of the larger farms remained, for the most part, without access to electricity and thus to most electric appliances. Men might ride a tractor, but women still did their washing with a scrub board, drew their water from a

---

American Journal

What's for Dinner?

In 1930, the Illinois Farmers' Institute gathered a group of farm women together for what they called a Household Science Meeting. One woman described how the new inventions of the radio and refrigerator had become as much a part of farm life as canning and shelling.

"We hear a great deal these days about the non-advisability of canning peas. I gather the peas in late afternoon—which perhaps is not scientific either, then I sit on the back porch in a comfortable chair and watch the birds around the lily pool, look at the snapdragons or the rose arbor, watch the little pigs in the alfalfa pasture, or listen to the radio, and it is really a time of relaxation.

"There may be some farm women who have a problem in regard to their leisure hours, but with most of us I think our greatest problem is trying to find any time when we can have a little leisure, and that time of shelling peas or getting the string beans ready is really a time of relaxation. Then the peas are put in a jar in the refrigerator and are canned in the pressure cooker while I am getting breakfast the next morning, and it really is not a job at all. In addition, I can pork, beef and fried chicken.

"When we moved to our new home we had a house, a barn and one tree, so that everything that is there we have put out. We had to set all of our fruit out. We have strawberries, rhubarb, gooseberries, currants, blackberries, plums, cherries, peaches and apples. We set out two gooseberry bushes. They were little sticks about that long, and I thought, 'Well, I guess my grandchildren will be able to reap some reward from those two sticks.' But this last spring I canned thirty-one pints of gooseberry jam from one bush. We had fourteen apples this last year, so we have had to buy our apples. We hope some day our apple crop will be a little larger. But our apples are bought in the fall, and they keep perfectly in the root cellar until the new crop is ready the next spring, the early summer apples. I think you will agree that we do have a few things to eat at our house anyway.

"The dairy account shows that we sell sweet cream the year round. When we bought our electric refrigerator we had a tinsmith make a rectangular box that fits into a portion of the bottom shelf of the refrigerator. It holds five gallons, and we can keep cream for a week without marketing it, if necessary, because it will keep sweet. The skimmed milk then is fed to the chickens and to the pigs."

From *Thrift for Women*, pamphlet of the Illinois Farmers' Institute

At least one farm family avoided doing the wash by hand despite having no electricity. Nebraska farmer Bill Ott used his car to power a washing machine for his daughter Lizzie.

hand-worked pump, and then heated it on an old-fashioned stove. Family members trudged outside to use a privy even in the depths of winter. Overall during the twenties, some 6 million people left the land for the cities.

METROPOLITAN LIFE

In 1920, for the first time in American history, more people lived in towns and cities than in rural areas. And during the next ten years, the United States grew still more into an urban nation, the result of the continuing migration from farms to factories. Yet the trend was coupled with the movement of a growing number of Americans into the suburbs, satellite towns within commuting distance of cities. Together, cities and suburbs formed a swiftly expanding technological metropolis—an agglomeration of electric lights and streetcars, the clangor and jams of traffic, a locus of communications, consumerism, and creativity.

The Growth of Suburbia. The expansion of suburbs, a process that had begun during the late nineteenth century with the building of electrified streetcar and commuter rail systems, was now accelerated by the mass ownership of automobiles. The suburban population of the nation's ninety-six largest cities grew twice as fast as the cities themselves, in some places

faster. Los Angelenos poured into the San Fernando Valley, which the city had annexed in 1915 but which now became a suburb in all but name. Many suburban residents worked downtown, whisking to and from their homes on "expressways" with no cross streets or stop signs, like New York's handsome Bronx River Parkway, completed in 1923.

While most city dwellers did not own cars, the growing influx of suburban commuters during the 1920s caused severe urban congestion and parking problems. City officials responded by widening roads and building parkways, bridges, and tunnels to ease traffic flows; but the more they built, the more the problem grew. To make matters worse, motorized buses began to replace streetcars during the 1920s, something that General Motors (a leading bus manufacturer) encouraged by acquiring streetcar companies, tearing up their tracks, and closing them down. As a result, New York, a city that operated over 1,340 miles of trolley tracks in 1919, had only 337 miles remaining in 1939.

Businesses began to join people in moving to the periphery, creating a new kind of multicentered metropolis that undermined the old centers, eroded tax bases, and contributed to weaker school systems, higher crime rates, and a reduced commitment to maintaining old neighborhoods and their cultural institutions.

Mass Media. Radio and movies added a national element to American culture. They brought listeners political conventions and prize fights, baseball and football games, comedies, and musical programs—including the crooning of Rudy Vallee and the twanging of "Grand Ole Opry," broadcast from WSM in Nashville, on its way to becoming the mecca of country music. In 1926, AT&T, General Electric, Westinghouse, and the new Radio Corporation of America (RCA) jointly established the National Broadcasting Company (NBC), the country's first radio network, with sixteen member stations. NBC allowed local stations like Westinghouse's KDKA to air programs tailored to their particular markets and share programming with other affiliated stations. But the

LEFT: Yankees slugger Babe Ruth. **RIGHT:** Film star Charlie Chaplin.

network, centered in New York, could reach 54 percent of the American population.

In 1930, movie theaters drew an average of 100 million Americans each week, an increase of 250 percent during the decade. Among the first places to install the new air-conditioning systems—pioneered by the Carrier Engineering Corporation, among others—movie houses were especially popular in the summer. The advent of the "talkies" (motion pictures with sound) with *The Jazz Singer* in 1927 added to the appeal. So did slapstick comedies with performers such as Charlie Chaplin and Harold Lloyd, Walt Disney's animated cartoons (Mickey Mouse was introduced in 1928), religious extravaganzas like *The Ten Commandments* (1923) and *The King of Kings* (1927), and sexually suggestive films that featured stars like Clara Bow, the "it" girl, or the matinee idol Rudolph Valentino.

The number of newspapers declined, with the result that by 1930 people in some cities had only one large-circulation daily to read. National and regional chains owned more than 200 papers, which tended to be conduits for standardized news and opinions for the 13 million people they served. National syndicates, many of them based in New York City, provided the editors of member papers with news reports, editorials, advice columns, and material about science. Magazines such as the new weekly *Time* (1923) appeared on racks across the country, as did *The New Yorker,* a national weekly that linked sophisticated readers in the urban Northeast with fellow spirits as far away as California. *Reader's Digest,* founded in 1921, permitted people to keep up with the proliferation of publications by providing condensed versions of their articles.

Print media covered the spectrum from sex, crime, and romance to moralizing fiction and nostalgic treatments of small-town life. They also helped advance the increasing vogue of celebrity, devoting considerable attention to sports stars like George Herman "Babe" Ruth of the New York Yankees, who in 1927 set a towering record of sixty home runs; boxers Jack Dempsey and Gene Tunney, who in mid-decade twice slugged it out for the heavyweight title; and Gertrude Ederle, who in 1926 became the first woman to swim the English Channel. The media also drew the great German physicist Albert Einstein into the celebrity orbit, applauding him for his theory of relativity and its implication that huge stores of energy were locked in an atom, awaiting release.

Such individuals were appealing because of their glamour or wealth, the sheer human interest of their (sometimes scandalous) lives, or, in Einstein's case, his dreamy humility; but also because they left their mark as individuals in an increasingly organized and corporate world. When in 1927 the young pilot Charles A. Lindbergh flew solo across the Atlantic in his single-engine *Spirit of St. Louis,* he was given a ticker-tape parade back in New York and lionized in print, on the air, and in films. Prominent among the themes in the outpouring of bravos were his courage, character, and tenacity—proof that the individual could prevail against both the scoffers and the odds.

Consumerism. During the twenties, the media reflected the nation's paramount devotion to business and the purchase of its products. The opulent settings of many films aroused consumer desires. Newspapers and magazines had long advertised commercial goods. Whether radio might be publicly funded was an open question in its early days, but it came to be paid for by advertising, a trend that the *New York Times* found "disquieting" but that was too powerful to buck.

Annual advertising budgets doubled during the decade, reaching more than $1.5 billion. Drawing on art, psychology, and sociology, **advertisers** presented products in ways that would stimulate consumer demand. They presented "a dream world," an observer noted, promising that what was displayed would bring idealized benefits, including "shining teeth, school girl complexions, cornless feet . . . odorless breath, [and] regularized bowels." Department stores commercialized the Christmas holiday season by inaugurating Thanksgiving Day parades and in-house Santas. They hired special designers to create artistically staged show windows. The entrepreneurial genius Edward L. Bernays pioneered the field of public relations to develop a favorable climate for the sale of goods to a broad range of customers.

Advertisers sold brand names by invoking the authority of science and even religion, both talismans of the twenties. One social observer remarked, "A sentence which begins with 'Science says' will generally be found to settle any argument in a social gathering or sell any article from tooth-paste to refrigerators." In *The Man Nobody Knows,* a portrait of Jesus Christ, the advertising executive Bruce Barton depicted Christ as a managerial genius for having "picked up twelve men from the bottom ranks of business and forged them into an organization that conquered the world."

No advertising was necessary to encourage the consumption of alcoholic beverages. Americans everywhere mocked the "dry" regime of Prohibition, making moonshine in rural stills and imbibing liquor in city speakeasies; twice as many speakeasies were operating in New York City as the number of pre-Prohibition drinking establishments there. By making illegal what people wanted to drink, Prohibition fostered a variety of criminal entrepreneurs, including bootleggers who smuggled alcohol into the country, gangs (like Al Capone's in Chicago) who had their fingers in virtually every part of the trade, and police who ignored the illegal commerce in exchange for bribes.

Health, Public and Private. Metropolitan life in the twenties brought dramatic health advantages, including better sanitary facilities at home, regular trash collection on the streets, the purification of water supplies, and the inspection of milk. So did vaccines and treatments that allowed doctors to cure, control, or prevent measles, diphtheria, diarrhea, tuberculosis, and syphilis. Nationwide, people could expect to live 20 percent longer, to age fifty-nine. In the cities, infant mortality fell to 69 per 1,000 live births, compared with almost twice as

> *"Eugenicists claimed that 'unfit human traits such as feeblemindedness, epilepsy, criminality, insanity, alcoholism, pauperism, and many others run in families and are inherited in exactly the same way as color in guinea pigs.' "*

many in 1900. Urban mothers, now also concerned with the psychological development of their children, paid attention to the leading behaviorist, John B. Watson, who taught that with proper training, which included forcing children to eat on a rigid schedule, any child could be made into a successful doctor, lawyer, or artist.

Many educated Americans also supported the popular doctrines of eugenics, which sought to exploit the new science of genetics for human biological improvement. Eugenicists claimed, to quote one of their exhibits, that "unfit human traits such as feeblemindedness, epilepsy, criminality, insanity, alcoholism, pauperism, and many others run in families and are inherited in exactly the same way as color in guinea pigs." Biologists, doctors, and psychologists warned that people with the genes for such traits were proliferating so rapidly as to threaten the United States with degeneration, and they urged that these people be prevented from having children. During the 1920s, in pursuit of that goal, twenty-four states enacted eugenic sterilization laws. By the mid-1930s, 20,000 men and women had been sterilized under them; many of these people were "feebleminded" or had been incarcerated for sexual delinquencies— women who bore children out of wedlock, for example. In 1927, in *Buck v. Bell,* the Supreme Court upheld the laws, with Justice Oliver Wendell Holmes Jr. explaining for the eight-to-one majority: "It is better for all the world, if instead of waiting to execute degenerate offspring for crime, or to let them starve for their imbecility, society can prevent those who are manifestly unfit from continuing their kind."

The Jazz Age

The famed novelist F. Scott Fitzgerald called the twenties the "Jazz Age" after its signature music. Jazz had recently been brought to white northern audiences by black musicians up from the South, and metropolitan America was marked by features that echoed the music's character: fast-paced creativity, cultural improvisation, breakaways from convention, and unabashed sexuality. The jazzy elements of the age bypassed many Americans, but those who embraced them—especially

The novelist F. Scott Fitzgerald, who called the twenties "the Jazz Age."

writers and artists, blacks and women, and college students of every stripe—produced innovations in art, self-expression, and identity with impacts that reached beyond their own circles and period.

CULTURAL FERMENT

Many talented writers and artists found themselves out of sorts with the moralizing, self-satisfied America of business, Harding, and Coolidge. A number expatriated to Europe, and some turned alienation into compelling and often salable art. Outlets for their work were provided by the mass-circulation magazines, adventurous new book-publishing houses, and innovative literary marketing methods such as the Book of the Month Club and the Literary Guild, both founded in 1926. New writers were championed by the Baltimore journalist H. L. Mencken in *The American Mercury,* a magazine read avidly in metropolitan America equally for its discerning literary appreciations and its cutting disparagements of pompous politicians, religious fundamentalists, and cultural know-nothings, especially in the South. And the reading audience was expanding as the fraction of Americans attending college grew exponentially—toward the end of the decade, one out of eight high school graduates went on to college.

Sinclair Lewis, a native of Sauk Centre, Minnesota, helped inaugurate the literary decade with the novels *Main Street* (1920) and *Babbitt* (1922), both biting critiques of commercialism, hypocrisy, and conformity in small-town America. Scott Fitzgerald, a recent dropout from Princeton University, debuted simultaneously with *This Side of Paradise* (1920), a novel of lost and gilded youth drawn from the experience of his college years. Himself a paragon of the Jazz Age, Fitzgerald grew rich on royalties and partied on both sides of the Atlantic; but he cast a sharply critical, subtly moral eye on the corruptions of money and social climbing in his fiction, especially *The Great Gatsby* (1925). The next year, Ernest Hemingway, who had been living in Paris, published *The Sun Also Rises,* an exploration of how a loosely connected coterie of young Americans and their British counterparts wandering in Europe coped with the shattering personal impact of the war. A Red Cross volunteer who had been seriously wounded on the Italian front, Hemingway in 1929 published *A Farewell to Arms,* an influential antiwar novel that in direct, stiletto-sharp prose flayed the notions of "sacred, glorious, and sacrifice."

The anonymity and separateness of urban life were hauntingly captured in the paintings of Edward Hopper. In 1921, another artist, Stefan Hirsch, painted *New York, Lower Manhattan* to express, as he put it, his "recoil from the monstrosity that industrial life had become in megapolitania." Some artists commented obliquely on the straitlaced materialism of American society by embracing the sensual images and forms of African and Native American painting and sculpture.

Professors, writers, and poets calling themselves "humanists" indicted science and technology for throwing civilization into a dangerous imbalance. The distortion, they said, threatened to lead to catastrophe if another war occurred, and it was already damaging the United States. The historian Charles Beard summarized how such critics saw urban technological civilization:

> *New York City from the elevated railway, huge sections of Pittsburgh and Chicago, shabby and dilapidated waterfronts, glorious spots of nature made hideous by factories, endless rows of monotonous dwellings, the shameful disregard of beauty along the highways from Boston to San Francisco, magnificent avenues through forest and valley ruined by billboards and gas-filling shacks, fretful masses rushing from one mechanical show to another, the horrible outpourings of radio nonsense, natural and canned, the unceasing roar and grind of urban life.*

THE VITALITY OF SCIENCE

Science and technology nevertheless fascinated some painters, writers, and philosophers. The surrealist painter and photographer Man Ray drew inspiration from innovations such as X-rays. Georgia O'Keeffe refracted the dynamism and congestion of urban life in paintings that endowed steel and concrete with seemingly organic qualities, while Joseph Lozowick, a Ukrainian immigrant, depicted in his prints and oils the underlying order "in the verticals of [the American city's] smoke stacks, in the parallels of its car tracks, the squares of its streets, the cubes of its factories, the arc of its bridges, the cylinders of its gas tanks." Others, like Elsie Driggs, Charles Demuth, and Charles Sheeler, found beauty in the engineering exactitude of American technology, a theme that exemplified their "precisionist" artistic interests.

The humanist critique was heatedly rebutted by the most famous and respected American scientist of the era, Robert A. Millikan, who won the Nobel Prize early in the decade and made the cover of *Time* near the end of it. He insisted that the greatest threats to civilization were not science and its works but the "emotional, destructive, over-sexed" contents of modern literature and art. Scientists like Millikan advanced a conservative syllogism: science was good for business, business was good for America, and in consequence, science was good for the nation's economic and spiritual well-being.

The probusiness climate was also good for university science, which, in recognition of its being the source of technological marvels, was richly aided by gifts from philanthropic foundations, individual businessmen, and state legislatures. American science gained increasing stature in key fields such as chemistry and physics, and it led the world in genetics. During the twenties, Americans won three Nobel Prizes in science, and distinguished European scientists came to visit and often to stay. When in 1932 Einstein announced that he would move to a research institute in Princeton, New Jersey, a French physicist observed that since "the Pope of physics" had moved, the United States would become "the center of the natural sciences."

BLACKS IN THE CITIES

During the twenties, 1 million African Americans migrated northward, with the result that in 1930 cities housed more than 40 percent of the nation's 12 million blacks. The concentration, not to mention the racism they encountered, stimulated increasing activism on behalf of African American rights and cultural identity.

In 1918–19, membership in the NAACP doubled, and the Universal Negro Improvement Association (UNIA) attracted growing attention. Founded by Marcus Garvey, a black Jamaican, the UNIA moved to New York in 1916 and soon had branches in most northern cities. Garvey taught that African Americans needed to be proud of their race and urged them to establish a nation of their own in Africa. Although he made little headway with his back-to-Africa movement—black intellectuals and labor leaders criticized his intense separatism—his emphasis on black pride touched a responsive chord. The UNIA acquired a membership estimated at 80,000 and a much larger sympathetic following. It declined after Garvey was sentenced to prison for mail fraud in 1923 and deported four years later, but he had helped awaken the idea that, as an African American newspaper remarked, "black is beautiful."

That outlook tacitly permeated the work and thinking of the African Americans who gathered in Harlem in the twenties to renew black culture. The novelist Zora Neale Hurston, the poet Langston Hughes, the intellectual and activist W. E. B. Du Bois, and others formed what became known as the

Marcus Garvey, an early advocate of black pride and leader of the Universal Negro Improvement Association.

Harlem Renaissance. They sought an identity for blacks that was somehow authentic, independent of white culture. A number of them contributed essays, stories, and poetry to *The New Negro,* a volume published by the philosopher Alain Locke in 1925 that served as a kind of manifesto for the movement.

What African Americans had to say about themselves, however, caught the attention of whites far less than the jazz they played in Harlem nightclubs. Whites flocked to popular spots such as the Cotton Club to hear and dance to the music. Black jazz and blues artists such as Louis Armstrong and Duke Ellington reached a national audience through "race records" and radio broadcasts of their Harlem performances. Blacks not only gave the age its jazz but also American music one of its native and enduring forms.

> *"What African Americans had to say about themselves caught the attention of whites far less than the jazz they played in Harlem nightclubs."*

WOMEN

After the passage of the Nineteenth Amendment, Congress scrambled to please this mass of new voters, establishing a Women's Bureau in the Department of Labor (1920), granting women equal citizenship rights with men (the Cable Act, 1922), and sending to the states a constitutional amendment outlawing child labor (1924). In the same period, several states started allowing women to serve on juries, and passed equal pay acts and a series of protective acts that set minimum standards for women's pay, limited women's working hours, or prohibited night work.

Women's groups convinced Congress to enter the field of health care. Under the Sheppard-Towner Act (1921), the federal government gave states matching funds for clinics in which nurses instructed mothers on infant care and doctors provided preventive health checkups. Critics condemned the act as a step toward state socialism. It soon became clear, moreover, that women did not vote as a block and often did not vote at all, which weakened legislators' desire to approve laws promoting their interests. The states failed to ratify the child-labor amendment; opposition stalled efforts to get more women on juries; the Supreme Court struck down minimum-wage laws as unreasonable infringments of freedom of contract; and, urged on by the American Medical Association (AMA), which saw the women's clinics as a threat to physicians' control of medical practice, Congress in 1929 repealed the Sheppard-Towner Act.

Women themselves were divided over the legislation designed specifically to protect women. Soon after achieving suffrage, Alice Paul and the National Women's Party (NWP) began arguing for an Equal Rights Amendment (ERA) to the Constitution that said "men and women shall have equal rights throughout the United States and every place subject to its jurisdiction." In one step, the amendment would have rendered unconstitutional all laws, state or federal, that restricted women's right to make contracts and control their personal property, have equal guardianship rights over their children, and serve on juries, or that limited their access to certain jobs—including that "protective" legislation women's groups had won after hard effort. Those laws, Paul argued, in fact restricted women's opportunities: women could, for example, be denied employment by the state legis-

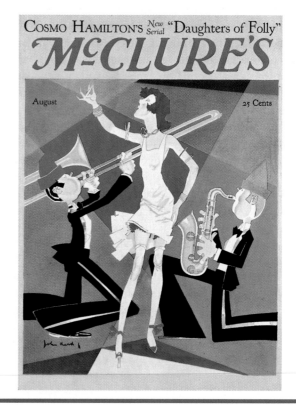

The cover of *McClure's* magazine depicting a "flapper" of the Jazz Age.

lature because, as the Wisconsin attorney general ruled, legislative work "necessitates work during very long and often unseasonable hours." Almost every other women's organization opposed the ERA, which they considered "elitist" since it neglected the real problems faced by working women and catered instead to the ambitions of more educated and prosperous women.

Flappers, Birth Control, and Marriage. To the young women of the twenties, a knowledgeable journalist remarked, "feminism" was a "term of opprobrium," unappetizing to "flappers," as the chic young women of the era were dubbed. Flappers worked hard to look different from their Victorian predecessors: long curls gave way to short "bobs," skirts moved above the knee, and curves became outmoded. Women bound their breasts and dieted to reduce their hips—the bathroom scale made its appearance in the 1920s—and achieve a fashionable boyish shape. They wore makeup, which was once confined to prostitutes, took up smoking and drinking as signs of emancipation, and experimented sexually in the new privacy of automobiles.

Flappers found common cause with more conventional women in the birth-control movement that was championed by Margaret Sanger. Sanger, whose mother had died at forty-nine after bearing eleven children, insisted that women would never be free or equal unless they could control their fecundity. Her attempts to disseminate birth-control information and devices at first aroused strong opposition and led to her arrest. But in 1916, in a Brooklyn storefront, she opened the nation's first birth-control clinic, advertising the facility in handbills written in English, Yiddish, and Italian. By then, the courts were beginning to allow the distribution of contraceptives for the purpose of maintaining health, and five years later Sanger founded the American Birth Control League, a lobbying organization that became Planned Parenthood in 1942. Sanger sought to make birth control respectable by targeting primarily married women and by insisting that diaphragms, the contraceptive she recommended, be fitted by doctors instead of obtained over the counter. She also appealed to eugenicists, arguing that the distribution of contraceptives to lower-income and immigrant groups would improve the quality of the nation's population by helping to reduce their birthrates.

"In 1916, in a Brooklyn storefront, Sanger opened the nation's first birth-control clinic, advertising the facility in handbills written in English, Yiddish, and Italian."

Despite the bravado of the flappers, the prevailing standard for women remained chastity until marriage. The availability of contraception and the liberation of women from notions of sexual and bodily shame put a new premium on the traditional commitment to wedlock, permitting the modern married woman to make a fashion of sexual fulfillment, and even romanticize the bearing of children. The movies added to the romanticism of marriage, dramatizing the single working woman's quest for escape from a boring life as a salesclerk or secretary through marriage to the right man, who was ideally rich and so could buy her the "modern conveniences" that advertising hawked. But modern marriage did not always measure up to what the movies suggested. In 1920, 1 marriage in 7.5 ended in divorce; by 1929, the rate was 1 in 6 and in some cities had risen as high as 1 in 3.5.

Newly married middle-class women of the 1920s could buy rather than make clothing, could purchase items like bread or butter that were once produced at home, had the use of modern appliances to facilitate housework, and could enjoy increased mobility thanks to the automobile. They became less managers of household labor and producers of goods than consumers. In the past, however, in all but the poorest homes servants had done the hardest housework, such as laundry and heavy cleaning. Now, with immigration restriction (see p. 746) and an expansion of new opportunities for unskilled women in factories and shops, the supply of servants declined sharply. Mexicans and African American women from the South could never fill the gap. By the late 1920s, the vast majority of middle-class families had learned to make due without outside help.

In practice, that meant "more work for Mother." To be sure, middle-class women had washing machines and vacuum cleaners, but those devices were not automatic—washing machines, for example, required putting clothes through ringers several times between and after washing and rinsing cycles, then hanging them outdoors to dry—and, in any case, wives were using machines to do work their mothers often did not do. Since the birthrate continued to decline among middle-class urban families (though it remained as high as ever in the country), most urban women had fewer diapers to change and wash. But new sanitary standards meant children and adults in middle-class families changed their underwear daily and sheets every week, so there was, overall, more laundry to do. And the gradual disappearance of peddlers, delivery services, and even home visits by doctors meant that middle-class women spent time driving to stores, clinics, and schools, which again was impossible before the widespread ownership of cars.

Women in the Workforce. The truly modern woman of the day was said to hope for both marriage and a career. The media celebrated events that seemed to herald an explosion of new opportunities for women, such as the famed aviator Amelia Earhart's participation in a flight across the Atlantic in 1927, and the 1921 visit of Marie Curie, the French scientist and twice a Nobel laureate, to the White House to receive from President Harding himself a gram of radium for cancer research.

The number of women college graduates doubled during the twenties, as did the number in the professions. Those with doctorates, including 1,000 with Ph.D.s in science, quadrupled. During this decade, women modestly increased their share in the paid workforce, accounting for about a quarter of it by 1930. By then, some 12 percent of married women had jobs, but most came from lower-income families. More than a quarter of married African American women worked for wages in Detroit, and more than 45 percent did in New York City.

Women who ventured into the professions faced limited opportunities. Most professional women were confined to "nurturing" fields as teachers, librarians, or social workers. About half of American school systems forced teachers to resign once they married; and women academics had trouble getting jobs except at women's colleges. An authoritative survey of the academic world reached conclusions about female academics that could have been generalized to most working women: they were generally paid less, promoted more slowly, and treated with "a considerable degree of discrimination."

For married middle-class women isolated in their suburban homes, exhausted by the amount of hard work a "consumerist" woman had to do and wondering why they didn't feel like smiling while pushing their vacuum cleaner like the women in the ads, or for those aspiring college-educated women whose career ambitions proved to be, like the illusions spun by the movies and advertising, an unrealistic fantasy, discontent took a new form. Without a women's movement to show how their problems were rooted in a system that encouraged women's dreams but made their fulfillment impossible, locked into a set of assumptions that stressed the power of individuals to triumph over all obstacles, they could only blame themselves.

BACKLASH

White, Anglo-Saxon Protestants (WASPs) resented the urban concentrations of Catholics and Jews, of speakeasies and flappers, of science and its intellectually corrosive works. Although WASPs were centered in the dusty towns of rural America, their resentments were shared by numerous city dwellers, many recent migrants from the farms. Together, these people lashed back at what they disliked about metropolitan America, insisting that the country remain alcohol-free ("dry") and warring against minority groups, unlimited immigration, and the teaching of evolution.

Revival of the Klan. The resentments fueled the revival of the Ku Klux Klan (KKK). Reorganized in Georgia in 1915, the Klan soon expanded its traditional zeal for upholding white supremacy against blacks to include the defense of "pure Americanism" against Jews, Catholics, and foreign influences. The KKK spread far beyond the South, gaining strongholds in the Midwest and adherents across the country, largely in small towns but also in major cities. The Klan's white robes, elaborate rituals, and cross-burnings probably gave a psychological boost to ordinary Americans who were on the whole less educated and feeling marginalized by the dynamism of metropolitan society. In 1924, the Klan reached an estimated membership of 4.5 million.

Klansmen often resorted to threats, boycotts, and at times violence to intimidate deviants from traditional morals, punish violators of Prohibition, and keep blacks, Jews, and Catholics in their place. The Klan abruptly faded after 1925, when one of its Grand Dragons was sent to prison for raping his young secretary and then refusing to call a doctor after she swallowed a lethal dose of poison. Nevertheless, bigotry against Catholics, Jews, and blacks remained pervasive: for example, Jews were excluded from home ownership in various neighborhoods as well as residence in resort hotels, and their access to private colleges, universities, and professional schools was severely restricted.

Immigration Restriction. White Protestant resentment of ethnic minorities fueled the long-standing drive for restrictions on immigration. The groups opposed to immigration included parts of organized labor, worried that the influx would adversely affect wages; staunch nativists, convinced that foreign influences adulterated the American character; and businessmen who feared immigrants as infectious carriers of radicalism. Economic factors tended to dominate the restriction debate through 1921, when Congress—in the wake of the Red Scare and postwar unemployment—passed an emergency restriction act.

The more zealous restrictionists lobbied for a permanent law that would discriminate sharply against the most recent wave of immigrants, from eastern and southern Europe. Adding "scientific authority" to the drive, eugenicists claimed that socially desirable traits were associated with the "races" of northern Europe, especially the Nordics, and that the eastern and southern European races carried undesirable ones. Analysis of I.Q. tests given army draftees during World War I concluded that immigrants from eastern and southern Europe were intellectually inferior to native whites from northern Europe. In April 1924, the House and Senate passed with large majorities the National Origins Act, which permanently established restrictions on immigration. Biological and racial arguments figured prominently in the floor debates, with one congressman declaring, "The primary reason for the restriction of the alien stream . . . is the necessity for purifying and keeping pure the blood of America." The act reduced the quota for admission from any one country to 2 percent of the Americans of that national origin in 1890, when the population included far fewer persons from eastern and southern Europe. The new law imposed no restrictions, though, on immigrants from Latin America or Canada. Perhaps half a million Mexicans migrated to the United States in the 1920s, settling mainly in the Southwest and bringing the total Mexican-born population to at least 2 million by 1930.

A Ku Klux Klan meeting in a Washington, D.C., park in the 1920s.

The Sacco and Vanzetti Case. Hostility to immigrants appeared to figure in the most socially charged criminal case of the decade—the trial and conviction (in 1920) of Nicola Sacco and Bartolomeo Vanzetti, both Italian immigrants and political anarchists, for murdering the paymaster of a shoe factory in Braintree, Massachusetts. Both asserted their innocence, and their defenders contended that they had been found guilty on the basis of little evidence and a mass of prejudice. In response to public criticism of the court, the Massachusetts governor appointed a blue-ribbon panel to interview jurors and carefully reexamine the evidence and the trial transcript. The panel concluded that Sacco and Vanzetti had been justly convicted (a finding that divides historians). On August 22, 1927, each died in the electric chair.

The Scopes Trial. In the twenties, many American Protestants felt acutely the challenges to religious faith raised by urban-associated science. Religious modernists, most of them centered in the cities, had found ways to reconcile Darwin's theory of evolution with their biblical beliefs, and in 1923 a dozen of the nation's leading scientists attested to their support of a higher being. But by now a number of Protestants had embraced the doctrines of the recently emergent Fundamentalist movement, which insisted on the literal truth of every word in the Bible.

Under Fundamentalist influence, in the early 1920s several southern states passed laws making it illegal to teach Darwin's theory of evolution in the public schools. Among them was Tennessee, which prohibited any of its public school teachers from teaching any theory that denied the biblical creation story, such as the notion "that man has descended from a lower order of animals." Encouraged by the American Civil Liberties Union, John Thomas Scopes, a twenty-two-year-old biology teacher in Dayton, tested the law and was arrested. In 1925, he was convicted in a trial that drew nationwide attention, but not before his defense counsel, Clarence Darrow, cross-examined William Jennings Bryan, a staunch anti-evolutionist who had traveled to Dayton to join the prosecution. Darrow forced Bryan to affirm that he believed in the literal Bible, including its stories that

Clarence Darrow (left) and William Jennings Bryan at Dayton, Tennessee, where they took opposite sides at the Scopes trial.

Joshua had made the sun stand still and that Jonah had been swallowed by a whale. The ridicule of Bryan convinced many people that anti-evolutionism had been defeated at Dayton. But the Tennessee law was upheld by the state supreme court, and anti-evolutionism, though remaining strong only in the South, worked a chilling, nationwide effect on high school biology texts. In 1930, an estimated 70 percent of public high schools did not teach evolution, a tacit censorship of the curriculum that continued into the 1950s.

The Hoover Peak

The Protestant backlash had largely dissipated by election time 1928. Coolidge probably would have won reelection, but as the contest approached, he distributed to the press a terse pronouncement: "I do not choose to run for president in 1928." In his stead, the Republicans nominated Herbert Hoover, the much-admired secretary of commerce. The Democratic Party was deeply divided between rural American Protestants and urban voters, many of whom were Jews or Catholics. The signature issue of difference between them was Prohibition, which some immigrant groups considered a personal insult. At the Democratic convention, the urban

wing prevailed, nominating Governor Alfred E. Smith of New York, a Catholic and a "wet."

In November, Hoover won in a landslide, receiving 58 percent of the popular vote and 444 electoral votes to Smith's 87. He cut heavily into the normally Democratic South, taking the upper tier of the Old Confederacy as well as Florida. Although anti-Catholicism, which cropped up virulently during the campaign, may have hurt Smith, he carried the country's twelve largest cities, rich in immigrants, all of which had voted Republican in 1924, and he ran well in the distressed agricultural regions of the Midwest. But Smith's support was overpowered by Hoover's strongest card—the nation's prosperity—which the Republican Party had promised to expand, declaring in its campaign slogan, "A chicken for every pot and a car in every garage."

THE "GREAT ENGINEER"

Herbert Hoover commanded enormous public confidence as a can-do figure devoted to the public interest. Orphaned at ten, he had equipped himself with a degree in geology from Stanford University, then earned a fortune as a mining engineer and international businessman, ably applying scientific knowledge to the tasks of finding and processing raw materials for industrial use. Raised a Quaker, he retired at age forty in 1914 to devote himself to public service. People called Hoover a great humanitarian for his work as food administrator during World War I and in food relief afterward. He represented the moderate, internationalist wing within the Republican Party and in the administrations of Harding and Coolidge, speaking out for the League of Nations and against a rigid adherence to laissez-faire.

Hoover approached the affairs of government in the way of the well-intentioned engineer he was. He believed that social and political problems could be solved by the government's encouragement of fact-finding and expertise coupled with voluntarism and hard work. As secretary of commerce, he encouraged the formation of trade

Herbert Hoover, the "Great Engineer," at his inauguration in March 1929.

associations to help industry reduce costs and stabilize employment, strengthened the National Bureau of Standards as a major scientific research laboratory, and mobilized local private relief agencies to create jobs. After his inauguration on March 4, 1929, a journalist remarked that Americans felt they "had summoned a great engineer to solve our problems for us."

BRIGHT CALM

On receiving the Republican presidential nomination, Hoover predicted that the day was in sight "when poverty will be banished from this nation." As president, sensitive to the plight of agriculture, he prevailed on Congress in June 1929 to approve a new Agricultural Marketing Act; the act established a Federal Farm Bureau to promote the creation of farm cooperatives, with the aim of stabilizing markets for agricultural products. If the cooperatives failed, the government would stand ready to purchase surplus crops as means of regulating prices. The mechanism exemplified Hoover's approach: federal action would encourage voluntary efforts, and the government would step in only if voluntarism failed. His administration began collecting data on recent social trends and called a series of conferences on subjects such as child welfare, education, and public health. It also took steps to raise efficiency in oil production, reform and improve the services offered under the Indian Bureau, conserve national resources, and, in general, improve the federal government's efficiency and effectiveness.

But behind the flurry of Hooverian activity, the flaws in the economy were widening. After 1925, the prodigious economic growth rates of the early boom years began to drop in key sectors, notably residential construction and automobiles. Business inventories began to pile up in 1928, nearly quadrupling in value by midsummer 1929. Investors in the stock market indulged in what Hoover called "an orgy of mad speculation," driving glamour stocks like RCA through wild daily changes. A little over six months after Hoover took office, a huge economic calamity began to strike the United States as well as the rest of the world.

During the twenties, the private economy had yielded unprecedented prosperity, turned the United States into a world financial power, and accelerated its transformation into a resourceful metropolitan civilization, diverse in its peoples, disputed in its character, and creative in its culture and science. Government had played little role in the changes beyond providing a hands-off, laissez-faire environment. But as the economic calamity spread, Americans turned for hope and

August 1914	World War I begins.
May 7, 1915	German submarine sinks the *Lusitania*.
1916	Margaret Sanger opens first birth-control clinic, in Brooklyn.
April 6, 1917	United States declares war against Germany.
November 6, 1917	Bolshevik revolution succeeds in Russia.
January 1918	President Wilson presents his Fourteen Points.
September 1918	Spanish influenza strikes the United States.
1919–20	The Red Scare.
June 28, 1919	Treaty of Versailles.
1920	Treaty of Sèvres liquidates the Ottoman Empire.
	Radios broadcast to wide audience for the first time.
1925	Scopes trial in Tennessee.

assistance to their government and the accomplished engineer and humanitarian who headed it.

Suggested Reading

Lizabeth Cohen, *Making a New Deal: Industrial Workers in Chicago, 1919–1939* (1990)

Nancy F. Cott, *The Grounding of Modern Feminism* (1987)

Ruth Schwartz Cowan, *More Work for Mother: The Ironies of Household Technology from the Open Hearth to the Microwave* (1983)

Lynn Dumenil, *Modern Temper: American Culture and Society in the 1920s* (1995)

Robert Ferrell, *Woodrow Wilson and World War I* (1985)

James Grossman, *Land of Hope: Chicago, Black Southerners, and the Great Migration* (1989)

Ellis Hawley, *The Great War and the Search for Modern Order: A History of the American People and Their Institutions, 1917–1933* (1979)

John Higham, *Strangers in the Land: Patterns of American Nativism, 1860–1925* (1988)

Kenneth T. Jackson, *Crabgrass Frontier: The Suburbanization of the United States* (1985)

David Kennedy, *Over Here: The First World War and American Society* (1980)

THE GREAT DEPRESSION AND THE NEW DEAL:

1929–1940

Construction of the Dam, a mural commissioned by the Department of the Interior, by William Gropper, c. 1937.

QUESTIONS

■ **What were the causes and consequences of the Great Depression?**

■ **What was Hoover's approach to the economic crisis?**

■ **What were the major successes and failures of FDR's first term?**

■ **What directions did the New Deal take in Roosevelt's second term?**

■ **What were the major social and cultural trends of the 1930s?**

■ **How successful was the New Deal overall?**

In 1929, the United States was the richest nation on earth, the richest nation the earth had ever seen. Although more than half of all households lived below contemporary standards of acceptable comfort, the first three decades of the twentieth century had witnessed remarkable economic growth. Salaries and wages in most occupations were well above late nineteenth-century levels, and the urban middle class was larger than it ever had been. Renters had become home owners, adding new appliances to their domestic castles each year. Educational opportunities were expanding rapidly. Millions of Americans proudly drove the automobiles that were pouring off assembly lines in Detroit.

Optimism abounded—at least outside of agriculture and "sick" industries such as textile and coal. In December 1928, in his final State of the Union address, President Calvin Coolidge had observed that "no Congress of the United States ever assembled . . . has met with a more pleasing prospect than that which appears at the present time." Memories of past recessions—even the sharp downturn of 1920–21—had faded, and most experts detected few clouds on the horizon. Andrew Mellon, the powerful secretary of the treasury and pre-eminent spokesman for the business community, had assured the nation that "the high tide of prosperity will continue." Safeguarding the future was the immensely capable Herbert Hoover, who was inaugurated as president in March 1929.

Nowhere was this optimism more palpable than in the stock market. Stock prices had risen significantly after 1921, with many stocks doubling in value by 1927. The climb had been interrupted periodically, but it had always recovered quickly, and with each recovery more Americans had turned their savings over to Wall Street. And why not? With corporations thriving and stock prices surging, it seemed only sensible for those with a bit of cash on hand to share in the profits of boundless prosperity. Only 3 percent of Americans actually owned stock, but a far larger number followed the market attentively, viewing it as a barometer of the nation's well-being.

Stock prices rose into the stratosphere in 1928 and continued soaring through the summer of 1929. At some unspecifiable moment in this giddy climb, the alchemy of boom times transformed optimism into outright speculation. Investors were no longer buying stocks because of the merits and profits of individual corporations but because they were convinced that stock prices, however high, would continue to climb higher. A share of General Electric stock that cost $128 in March 1928 was worth nearly $400 by September 1929; Anaconda Copper leapt from $54 to $131 in the same period.

This speculative impulse was encouraged by Wall Street itself, which permitted investors to buy stocks "on margin," putting up only 50 or 30 or even 10 percent of the purchase price. Using the shares themselves as collateral, investors then borrowed the rest of the needed amount from their brokers, who in turn borrowed from banks and large corporations. These loans could be "called" in by brokers if stock prices dropped substantially, but that possibility seemed remote in the great bull market of 1928–29. As long as prices kept soaring, it seemed that a man with $30 could buy a $100 stock and sell it a year later for $130 or $150, pocketing a profit of 100 percent or more, minus a small interest charge for the loan. To many, the lure was irresistible.

But the bubble burst—as speculative bubbles always do. In early September, stock prices slid sharply, partially recovered, and then remained jittery for the next month. On October 23, the market plunged again, and the next day, "Black Thursday," pandemonium broke out on the floor of the New York Stock Exchange as prices plummeted in trading so heavy that the ticker lagged hours behind sales. The drop triggered margin calls that forced investors to sell their stocks to repay loans to brokers—which drove prices down even further. After a one-day respite, during which major broker-age houses and banks ostentatiously tried to display their confidence in the market, the rout resumed the following Monday, with what the *New York Times* called a "nation-wide stampede to unload." "Black Tuesday," October 29, was even worse than Black Thursday had been: panicked selling cut the prices of most leading stocks by 10–20 percent, while the trading volume exceeded the previous record by 30 percent. The *Times* called it the "most disastrous" day in Wall Street's history. "Hysteria swept the country and stocks went overboard for just what they would bring at forced sale."

The financial carnage did not end on Black Tuesday. By mid-November, the value of leading stocks was roughly half what it had been in early September. General Electric was down to $168; Anaconda Copper had sunk from $131 to $70. In a matter of weeks, great wealth had disappeared from the ledgers of American compa-nies and individuals; with it vanished what journalist Frederick Lewis Allen described as "the psychological cli-mate" or "the state of mind" induced by the "Big Bull Market." Throughout the nation, Allen observed, there were men and women who experienced the stock market's fall as "the sudden and brutal shattering of hope."

The stock market crash was a dra-matic and spectacular event that left many of the rich feeling less rich and that wiped out the savings of hundreds of thousands of middle-class house-holds. In so doing, it made Americans wary about investing in stocks in sub-sequent decades. But the debacle on Wall Street did not cause the economic catastrophe that came to be known as the Great Depression. The economy had begun a serious slowdown months before the stock market plummeted, and a downturn in the business cycle was more than due. The crash accelerated that downturn in late 1929 and the first months of 1930, but it had little impact on the subsequent depth and length of the Depression. The bursting of the speculative bubble did not make inevitable the suffering and devastation that were to come.

The Great Depression

THE ECONOMY IN FREE-FALL

Indeed, even as the country settled into an economic slow-down in 1930, there were few expressions of alarm: the nation had experienced panics or depressions every decade since the 1870s, and there was no reason to think this one would be much different. In the spring of 1930, experts voiced the belief that the economy was starting to recover, and the stock mar-ket regained some of the ground it had lost. The *Baltimore Sun,* voicing a widely held view, described the crash as "a

A worried crowd gathers on Wall Street at the news of the stock market crash, October 1929.

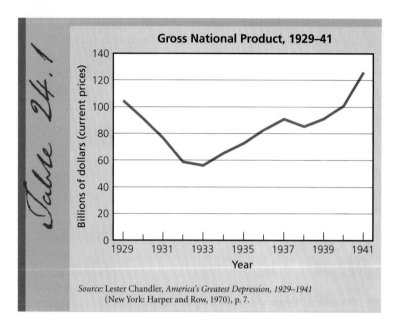

Table 24.1

Gross National Product, 1929–41

Billions of dollars (current prices)

Source: Lester Chandler, *America's Greatest Depression, 1929–1941* (New York: Harper and Row, 1970), p. 7.

to pay for more than 700,000 schools or 36 million homes or 3.6 million miles of highway. For nearly twelve years, the human and technological capacities of the economy were underutilized, and the Depression finally came to an end only when the nation was gearing up for war.

THE SOURCES OF DISASTER

There was no single or simple cause of the Great Depression. Multiple factors, domestic and international, converged to transform a cyclical downturn into a prolonged economic catastrophe. One was the structural weakness of a banking system that had many independent units and few mechanisms for propping up banks that were in difficulty: in the early 1930s, the inability of borrowers to repay loans led to a contagious epidemic of bank failures that erased savings accounts, reduced the credit supply, and accelerated the downward plunge of the economy. A second factor was the highly unequal distribution of wealth and income, which had been accentuated by the boom of the 1920s. Between 1923 and 1929, the disposable income of the wealthiest 1 percent of Americans increased dramatically while remaining stagnant for much of the population. This inequality reinforced the

hangover" that followed "a spree" without affecting the "robust constitution" of the economy itself. Americans in 1930 and even 1931 believed that they were living through a routine undulation of the business cycle, that the stumbling economy would soon right itself.

But they were wrong. The downturn that began in 1929 proved to be of unprecedented depth, and it lasted for ten years. The economy plunged downward for the first four years of the Depression, and then recovered slowly and haltingly. The statistics are as dramatic as numerical evidence can be. The physical output of the economy dropped more than 30 percent between 1929 and 1933, rebounded slowly until 1937, and then plummeted once again (see Table 24.1). Prices also fell between 20 and 35 percent, which meant that the money value of the gross national product (combining the decline in output and the decline in prices) sank by nearly 50 percent between 1929 and 1933. The unemployment rate soared to almost 25 percent in 1933 and remained in double digits until 1941 (and even then the rate was 9.9 percent). Between 1931 and 1940, there were always between 8 million and 13 million persons unemployed, while millions more were working only part time (Table 24.2).

The magnitude of these losses is difficult to grasp. One scholar has estimated that if the economy had grown at an average rate rather than sinking into a sustained depression, the difference in economic activity would have been enough

"Sold Out": Cartoonist Rollin Kirby's portrayal of a response to "Black Thursday," October 24, 1929, when the stock market plunged.

downturn because it concentrated resources in the hands of the wealthy, who did not need to spend (or invest) the money they had available, rather than in the hands of average consumers, who typically spent almost all of their incomes. As a result, a brake was placed on the consumer spending that could have stimulated the economy. In difficult times, both investment and luxury sales always plummeted much faster than sales of necessities, such as food.

A third contributor, particularly to the length of the Depression, stemmed from a coincidence of timing. The cyclical downturn hit at a moment when the economy was shifting from a reliance on traditional industries, such as steel and textiles, to being propelled by newer industries, such as autos, processed foods, and tobacco. These newer industries were heavily dependent on equity (stock) financing and thus were particularly hard hit after the collapse of the stock market. Although they rebounded quickly, they were not large enough to pull the rest of the economy with them, and they did not employ enough workers (or workers with the right skills) to make much of a dent in unemployment. Meanwhile, the older, more labor-intensive industries, embattled even in the 1920s, lacked the dynamism to recover at all before World War II.

As important as any of these structural factors was what economist John Kenneth Galbraith has called "the poor state of economic intelligence." The thinking of most government officials, bankers, and economists was shaped by inherited orthodoxies of economic thought and by past experiences that were no longer relevant to the conditions of the 1930s. These leaders brought to the crisis a mind-set, grounded as much in moral conviction as in evidence, that prevented them from adopting policies that might have significantly aided recovery; even worse, they frequently took steps that compounded the problem.

Throughout the nation, for example, public officials at all levels reacted to the downturn by trying to balance their budgets: the conventional wisdom was that such action would help restore the health of the economy. To achieve that goal, city and state governments (as well as the federal government, when it could) cut expenditures or raised taxes or did both. The effect of these measures, however, was counterproductive: they slowed the economy further by reducing the amount of money available to consumers to spend.

Even more important were failures of international economic policy: the Depression was international in scope and was caused in part by misguided policies adopted by both Eu-

ropean governments and the United States. In response to falling production and rising unemployment, numerous governments, including that of the United States, instituted protectionist measures, such as high tariffs. Designed to protect domestic industries, these actions served instead to slow international trade. Since the United States was the leading creditor nation in the post–World War I financial order, European nations had to export goods to the United States in order to pay their debts. High tariffs made that difficult if not impossible.

In addition, Britain, the United States, and most other countries in Europe and Latin America insisted on clinging to the gold standard, which, after an interruption occasioned by World War I, again provided the framework for international financial relations. Each country's currency had a fixed value in relation to gold, and the precious metal itself flowed between nations in payment of debts. Every nation, moreover, was required to maintain a gold reserve to back its currency, which was convertible into gold on demand. Although ill understood at the time, the gold standard of the 1920s and 1930s operated in such a way as to pressure governments and central banks to slow down their economies. National leaders and central bankers firmly believed that the gold standard would restore economic health, but in fact it did the opposite,

UNEMPLOYMENT, 1929–41		
	Number of Persons Unemployed (in thousands)	Percentage of Labor Force Unemployed
1929	1,550	3.2
1930	4,340	8.7
1931	8,020	15.9
1932	12,060	23.6
1933	12,830	24.9
1934	11,340	21.7
1935	10,610	20.1
1936	9,030	16.9
1937	7,700	14.3
1938	10,390	19
1939	9,480	17.2
1940	8,120	14.6
1941	5,560	9.9

Source: Chandler, *America's Great Depression*, p. 5.

Table 24.2

dragging one country after another deeper into depression. Most nations began to recover only after they belatedly and reluctantly abandoned the gold standard, but by then much of the damage had been done.

PORTRAITS IN GRAY

The Depression blanketed the entire nation, but its impact on different cities and sectors of the economy was highly uneven. Manufacturing, construction, and mining were hit much harder than the public or service sectors; and industries that produced capital goods, such as steel and automobiles, suffered far more than did industries processing food or other consumer products (see Table 24.3). By 1931, General Motors had laid off 100,000 of its 260,000 employees in Detroit; a year later, no one was working full time at U.S. Steel.

More than half of all households experienced direct economic consequences of the Depression. Those who were relatively lucky continued working but at lower wages or for fewer hours, significantly reducing their families' incomes. They used up their savings, cut back on spending for recreation and clothing, bought less meat, gave up their life insurance policies, and sometimes moved to cheaper apartments or houses. Married women commonly attempted to make up for the decline in income with extra domestic labor, such as repairing worn-out clothing, washing their children's few respectable clothes each night, and cooking meals that could be stretched to offer more portions.

Such modest adjustments were only the beginning for the millions of men and women who lost their jobs altogether, many of whom remained out of work for a year or two or more—periods that were without precedent in their lives or in American history. **The unemployed** coped by eating little and poorly (milk for children became a luxury), shutting off their electricity, eliminating all expenditures for nonnecessities, forgoing visits to doctors, and barely heating their houses in winter. They exhausted what little savings they had, sent women and children into the labor force, borrowed from grocers and saloon keepers, and moved in with relatives.

They also searched relentlessly for work or for odd jobs—until, as often happened, they became so pessimistic that they stopped looking for employment altogether. When word spread that an employer might have a few jobs available, hundreds or even thousands of men and women showed up, desperately jockeying to become one of the chosen. Young men took to the roads (and rails), wandering the country in search of work. Every town and city had a street corner or spot where idled men simply stood, talked, and waited for nothing in particular, day after day. The emotional toll was severe. Helpless and cut off from their normal routines, the unemployed frequently sank into depression while traditional patterns of family life disintegrated.

Extreme deprivation was almost commonplace. Coal miners' families, evicted from company housing, lived in tents during the harsh West Virginia winters. In Oklahoma City,

DECLINE IN INDUSTRIAL PRODUCTION, 1929–33	
Industry	1929–33 Percentage Decline
Shoes	3.4
Textiles	6.4
Cigarettes	6.6
Leather goods	7.4
Gasoline	7.4
Woolen and worsted cloth	7.7
Cotton	11.4
Tobacco products	16.7
Manufactured food	17.8
Cigars	34.4
Tires and tubes	34.8
Polished plate glass	42.7
Ships	53.1
Furniture	55.6
Nonferrous metals	55.9
Lumber	57.9
Iron and steel	59.3
Machinery	61.6
Cement	63.1
Nonferrous metals	63.5
Transportation equipment	64.2
Automobiles	65.0
Railroad cars	73.6
Copper	78.9
Common and face bricks	83.3
Locomotives	86.4

Table 24.3

Source: Chandler, *America's Greatest Depression*, p. 23.

people searched through garbage pails for food, while one couple and their seven children inhabited a hole dug in the ground that they outfitted with chairs and beds. Homeless men found shelter in boxes, abandoned automobiles, and shantytowns on the outskirts of cities, under bridges, in railroad yards, or in municipal dumps. Diseases such as typhoid, diphtheria, and pellagra were rampant among the most impoverished. In New York, thousands of children suffered from malnutrition, and seven-year-olds were sent to soup lines in search of nourishment; in Utah and other states, hundreds stopped going to school because they had no clothes. "It's fairly common to see children entirely naked," reported one investigator.

Things weren't much better, although they were different, on the nation's farms. For farmers, the crisis of the 1930s came in the form of drastically reduced prices for their products. Those who owned or rented land could continue to grow crops, and they produced as much as ever. But they were selling their goods for 30, 40, or even 60 percent less than they had in the 1920s. Between 1929 and 1932, net farm income (figuring in the expenses of growing crops) dropped a staggering 70 percent. Although most farm families had shelter and enough to eat (attractions sufficient to draw many urban dwellers back to the countryside, reversing the migratory trends of decades), they had little disposable cash and were

A mother and her children at a migrant camp on Highway 101 at Nipomo, California, 1936; photograph by Dorothea Lange.

unable to buy new equipment or make needed repairs. With alarming frequency, farmers also began to default on their mortgages and lose their land. Their difficulties were deepened by the high rate of failure among rural banks: three-quarters of the banks that collapsed between 1930 and 1932 were in communities with populations of less than 2,500.

Most farmers, moreover, lacked the amenities that had become standard in urban America: even in the mid-1930s, only 20 percent of all farms had electricity, and only 10 percent had indoor toilets. And those who were poor became even poorer. In the rural South, tenant farmers and sharecroppers found their circumstances deteriorating, with food scarce, school systems barely functioning, health care inaccessible, and living conditions primitive. In Florida, California, and parts of the Midwest, migrant farm workers picked crops for pitifully low wages while living in shacks with no sanitation facilities or running water.

THE DUST BOWL

In the plains states of Oklahoma, Texas, Kansas, and Colorado, nature made life even more difficult—and in some places, impossible. From 1930 to 1936, rainfall levels were abnormally low in much of the United States, and the drought

Unemployed men waiting in line for bread and soup in Los Angeles, 1930.

that afflicted the plains turned farmlands into baked, cracked expanses of dry soil in which little could grow. Farming on the plains had grown rapidly during the first thirty years of the century, thanks in part to new technology: the tractor, harvester-thresher combine, and disk plow helped farmers to conquer the difficult terrain of the plains and to greatly increase the planting of wheat and cotton as cash crops. In doing so, however, farmers had undermined the fragile ecology of the plains, plowing excessively, allowing animals to overgraze, loosening the top layers of sod, and destroying the region's natural, if sparse, vegetation.

The result was disaster, when the rains stopped. Beginning in 1932, dust storms began to afflict the region, and by 1934 they were reaching cataclysmic proportions. In May of that year, swirling winds blew the dry, loosened dust of the plains into gigantic dark clouds that turned day into night in one county after another; carried by the upper airstream, the storms deposited twelve tons of dirt on Chicago and sprinkled layers of dust on Boston, New York, and Atlanta. On the plains themselves, the dust blinded and suffocated animals,

sanded the paint off houses, spawned epidemics of respiratory diseases, and filled houses with tiny particles of dirt. "The doors and windows were all shut tightly," reported one Kansas woman in 1935, but the dust "got into cupboards and clothes closets; our faces were as dirty as if we had rolled in the dirt; our hair was gray and stiff and we ground dirt between our teeth." In March 1935, one storm took more dirt from the plains than had been excavated during construction of the Panama Canal.

This "Dust Bowl" disaster sparked an exodus from the plains, with hundreds of thousands of families abandoning farms and rural towns. As songwriter Woody Guthrie put it, "We loaded our jalopies and piled our families in, / We rattled down the highway to never come back again." Labeled "Okies" or "exodusters," many of these desperate migrants headed to California, forming a unique migratory caravan of old cars and trucks, stuffed with people and household goods, chugging down Route 66 through New Mexico and Arizona. In California, they often remained unemployed or found work as seasonal farm laborers. The migration of the Okies captured the nation's attention, particularly after its sympathetic portrayal in John Steinbeck's 1938 novel *The Grapes of Wrath,* as well as the 1939 movie based on the book, directed by John Ford.

THE MIDDLE AND UPPER CLASSES

Not everyone who felt the sting of hard times was poor. One of the distinctive characteristics of the Great Depression, in fact, was that it had a broad impact on the middle class as well as on workers and struggling farmers. For the first and only time in the twentieth century, large numbers of middle-class, white-collar employees suffered from prolonged unemployment. Laid off from their jobs and unable to find new ones, they experienced significant declines in their standard of living: their savings disappeared, their homes deteriorated, they gave up their cars as well as electrical and phone service, and they cut back on the educational plans for their children. Some, unable to meet mortgage payments, lost their houses. Similar fates befell middle-class owners of small businesses that failed and educated men and women who could find only part-time work.

For many Americans, however, the ordeal of the Great Depression was something that happened around them but not to them. Millions never lost a day's work, and the rhythms of their lives were little different than they had been

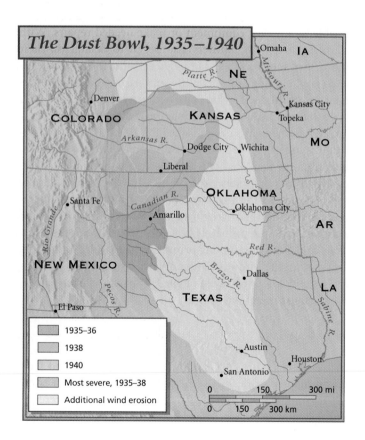

The Dust Bowl, 1935–1940

Legend:
- 1935–36
- 1938
- 1940
- Most severe, 1935–38
- Additional wind erosion

A farmer and his children running through the winds of a dust storm in Cimarron County, Oklahoma, 1936.

in the 1920s. Numerous entrepreneurs and investors took advantage of the economic decline to buy stocks at bargain prices or even to buy entire companies that were faltering. "We didn't know the depression was going on," reported one advertising executive whose business boomed as clients tried to combat the downturn by promoting their products more widely, especially on radio. He went on to make additional millions by buying and expanding the "busted, rundown" Muzak company, which tapped into the nation's growing taste for having the silence of office buildings replaced by omnipresent "music not to be listened to." Particularly for those solvent enough to weather the first storm of the stock market crash, there were fortunes to be made from the wreckage of the nation's economy.

Herbert Hoover: The Engineer as President

President Hoover, like everyone else, viewed the downturn through the prism of recent experience, which suggested that the economy would rebound after a year or two. Yet he was far from passive after the jolt of the stock market crash. Bucking the advice of ardent conservatives such as his trea-

sury secretary, Andrew Mellon, he actively intervened to prevent the stock market decline from leading to a general downturn. He quickly called to the White House bankers and other business leaders from whom he elicited promises not to cut wages or jobs, so that workers' living standards and purchasing power could be maintained. He also persuaded the Federal Reserve to ease credit and convinced railways and utility companies to accelerate planned construction projects. And he encouraged both Congress and state governments (whose collective budgets were larger than that of the federal government) to undertake public works projects.

Hoover thus took a more aggressive role in combating economic decline than any president ever had, but despite a slight (and temporary) improvement in production and employment early in 1930, his actions had little or no impact. Faced with declining revenues, business leaders soon found it impossible to honor their promises to maintain wage and employment levels; and as tax returns drooped, state and local governments had difficulty continuing planned construction projects, much less initiating new ones. Deficit financing—funding activities with loans—was not an acceptable countercyclical tool for administrators who believed in balanced budgets.

Then, as the crisis worsened in 1930–31, Hoover's political standing began to falter, and he took a series of steps that proved to be counterproductive. In 1930, despite the warnings of many economists, he signed the Hawley-Smoot Tariff, a Republican measure that raised tariffs to their highest levels in history—and, in so doing, dampened international trade and fanned nationalist flames in Europe. Hoover also insisted on keeping the United States on the gold standard and in 1932 sponsored a tax increase to balance the federal budget. That same year, he responded to the collapse of many banks—and the demands of bankers—with a series of measures designed to shore up the banking system, facilitate lending, and reduce foreclosures on home mortgages. In the eyes of some critics, these measures amounted to "bank relief," an unprecedented federal intervention in business in order to rescue millionaires.

759

Such criticism was particularly powerful because of Hoover's steadfast refusal to involve the federal government in relief of the unemployed. Hoover believed deeply that aid to the poor and the jobless should come from voluntary organizations and local governments, and he frequently reiterated the traditional conservative view that a federal "dole" would demoralize and corrupt the unemployed. As a result, he took no steps to directly relieve the suffering of the jobless, and he opposed a Senate bill, introduced by liberal Democrats, calling for unemployment insurance. Meanwhile, business leaders like Henry Ford declined to take any responsibility for helping the jobless in their communities, while others, such as the president of the National Association of Manufacturers, derided the jobless for not practicing "the habits of thrift and conservation."

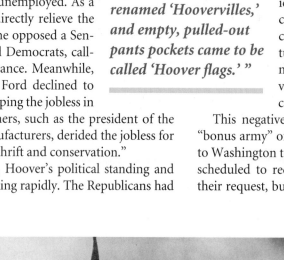

"Collections of makeshift shelters were renamed 'Hoovervilles,' and empty, pulled-out pants pockets came to be called 'Hoover flags.' "

By the beginning of 1932, Hoover's political standing and personal popularity were sinking rapidly. The Republicans had lost seats in both houses of Congress in the 1930 elections, and, rightly or wrongly, the "Great Engineer" was increasingly blamed for the Depression. Hoover's expertise and managerial skill were no match for the forces driving the economy downward; his opposition to relief made him appear insensitive to the misery of millions; and he lacked the political and oratorical talents needed to sustain the role of a compassionate leader struggling with difficult circumstances. Critics and cartoonists caricatured him as an aloof ideologue. Collections of makeshift shelters were renamed "Hoovervilles," and empty, pulled-out pants pockets came to be called "Hoover flags."

This negative image was reinforced in July 1932 when a "bonus army" of unemployed World War I veterans marched to Washington to demand early payment of a bonus they were scheduled to receive in 1945. The Senate refused to act on their request, but several thousand bonus marchers remained in Washington, squatting in buildings on Pennsylvania Avenue. Police efforts to remove the veterans led to violence and then to Hoover calling in federal troops. A cavalry unit, six tanks, and a column of infantry with fixed bayonets evicted the bonus army and burned down the shacks in Anacostia Flats, where the marchers had established a campsite. The federal government had responded to the pleas of jobless veterans by calling in the army to run them out of town.

Hoover had no chance of being reelected in 1932, and he knew it. His opponent, the popular Democratic governor of New York, Franklin D. Roosevelt, had little that was either concrete or innovative to say about the Depression, but the election was a referendum on Hoover and the Republicans, and its outcome was a foregone conclusion. Exhausted by nonstop work, wounded by barrages of criticism, the dispirited and pessimistic president campaigned listlessly and was defeated in a landslide. For Hoover

Members of the "bonus army" encamped within sight of the Capitol in July 1932.

personally, it was a bitter end to a stellar career: in four years he had gone from being the most admired man in America to being the most reviled. For the Republicans, the election of 1932 marked the end of a long period of national political dominance, as well as a repudiation of its celebratory identification of the interests of the nation with the interests of Wall Street and big business. Wall Street itself shared in the discredit, particularly as congressional hearings revealed that leading investment bankers and stock brokers had repeatedly violated the law and even profited from the distress of their clients.

In rejecting Hoover, the electorate was also registering a loss of confidence in the model of reform based on science and engineering that had become popular during the Progressive Era and preeminent in the 1920s. This model was grounded in the presumption that the interests of all Americans were the same and that the problems generated by industrial capitalism could be solved through rationality, knowledge, and good will. It was an approach to reform that relied heavily on top-down decision making and voluntary action rather than state policies. By the fall of 1932, it appeared to most Americans that some other strategy was needed.

Franklin D. Roosevelt: The First Term

Franklin Roosevelt was not an engineer but a politician. Born to an aristocratic family in Hyde Park, New York, educated at Groton and Harvard, Roosevelt, like his distant cousin Theodore, had a zeal for public service and the hurly-burly of political life. He served in the New York state legislature, was under-secretary of the navy under Woodrow Wilson, and became the Democratic vice-presidential candidate in 1920. The following year, at the age of thirty-nine, he was stricken with polio, which left him crippled for the remainder of his life, largely confined to a wheelchair, able to walk a few steps only with the aid of heavy steel leg braces. He spent much of the 1920s rebuilding his spirits and his body (acquiring a powerful torso and arms), while mapping a strategy for the pursuit of higher office. At Al Smith's urging, he ran for governor of New York in 1928 and was elected despite the defeat of the national Democratic ticket; having put together a powerful coalition of urban, ethnic voters, liberals, and upstate, more conservative Democrats, he was overwhelmingly reelected in 1930.

Roosevelt's skill at coalition building was critical to his successful pursuit of the presidency in 1932. As had been true since the late nineteenth century, the Democratic Party was split between a conservative, southern, prohibitionist wing and northern state parties that were commonly more liberal in economic matters, opposed to prohibition, and heavily populated by Catholic working-class voters. With both John Nance Garner of Texas and Al Smith also vying for the party's nomination, Roosevelt presented himself as a bridge candidate, capable of unifying the two regional branches. With the nomination in hand (and Garner as his running mate), Roosevelt also reached out to progressive Republicans who had grown disillusioned with President Hoover and the Grand Old Party's domination by big business; although his victory in the general election was not in doubt, Roosevelt's broader political goal was breaking the political dominance of the Republican Party by assembling a new coalition of progressive reformers, industrial workers, and the inevitably Democratic South.

Roosevelt did not possess a very distinctive or clearly articulated political ideology although he did believe, more deeply than most, that the role of government was to serve the people and to foster collaboration and mutuality rather than individualized competition. Alert to the changes that had transformed American society in his own lifetime, he sometimes displayed a sympathy for the disadvantaged that unnerved his more conservative backers. It was in this spirit that he declared, in accepting his party's nomination, "I pledge you, I pledge myself, to a new deal for the American people." Still, the shape of that "new deal" remained vague during the campaign, and his opinions on key issues were mainstream. Like most Democrats, he favored lower tariffs, and he signaled the orthodoxy of his economic views by criticizing Hoover for incurring deficits in the federal budget. His most innovative stance was his support for government-sponsored unemployment insurance and old-age insurance, ideas that progressive reformers had begun to place on the agenda a decade and a half earlier.

Indeed, many political figures and analysts regarded Roosevelt as something of a lightweight: "He is a pleasant man," observed Walter Lippmann, "who, without any important qualifications for the office, would very much like to be president." Although well educated, Roosevelt was not a reader and could rarely display the mastery of technical details so characteristic of his predecessor. Yet even skeptics were impressed by the extraordinary force of his personality, by his

The new president, Franklin Delano Roosevelt, speaking from the White House in the first of his "Fireside Chats," March 1933.

warmth, his restless energy, his cheery attentiveness, unshakable poise, and self-confidence, traits all the more remarkable in a man physically disabled. He has a "first-rate temperament" accompanying a "second-rate intellect," observed Justice Oliver Wendell Holmes.

That temperament, more than his past record or any systematic convictions, suggested an openness to innovation. "The country demands bold, persistent experimentation," Roosevelt had declared during the campaign. In the months between his election in November 1932 and his inauguration in March 1933, the need for such experimentation mounted. The misery of millions of jobless workers was deepening, rebellious farmers were mounting protest movements aimed at withholding food from the market, and bank failures began to accelerate, leading one state after another to close its banks to prevent panicked citizens from withdrawing their remaining deposits. Roosevelt responded by bringing to Hyde Park a steady stream of political and business leaders, academics, and intellectuals to discuss the economic crisis in all its complexity. Peppering these men and women with questions, often seeming to agree with those holding contradictory views, displaying the full range of his charm and mental agility, the president-elect soaked in ideas and proposals like a sponge and assured his visitors that they had been heard. Yet even his closest advisers were not sure what Roosevelt would actually do when he took office.

THE FIRST HUNDRED DAYS

The president's **inaugural speech,** on March 4, 1933, took clear aim at the country's mood of despair and anxiety. With the stock exchange and many banks closed, Roosevelt declared that the crisis was not due to any "failure of substance" but was rather the result of the "stubbornness" and "incompetence" of the "rulers of the exchange of mankind's goods." He promised to put people back to work, restore the health of agriculture, and regulate banking and investment. Insisting that "the only thing we have to fear is fear itself—nameless, unreasoning, unjustified terror," he announced that he was calling a special session of Congress to address all of these issues. If Congress did not act, he would ask for emergency executive powers to "wage a war" against the Depression.

The speech was followed by an extraordinary wave of activity as Roosevelt and his aides delivered one piece of legislation after another to a receptive, even pliant, Congress. The first item on the agenda was the banking crisis. After closing all banks for four days to avoid further turmoil, the administration, greatly aided by private bankers and holdovers from

This cartoon shows FDR leading his party, Congress, and the nation on a breakneck course toward emergency legislation, 1933.

the Hoover administration, drew up a multipronged reform bill designed to enhance confidence in the banking system. A thoroughly conservative measure written to satisfy leading bankers, the Emergency Banking Act was approved by Congress within hours. The night before the banks were to reopen, Roosevelt displayed his remarkable talent for mass communication as well as his mastery of the relatively new technology of radio. Holding the first of what were to be many nationally broadcast "Fireside Chats," the president explained what the banking reforms meant and assured his 60 million listeners that it was now safer to keep their money "in a reopened bank than under the mattress." The next day, deposits began to flow into, rather than out of, the nation's banks. Thanks to the radio, Roosevelt could speak directly to the people in his own voice, establishing what to many appeared to be an almost personal relationship: the number of letters written to the president from citizens throughout the nation was unprecedented.

The administration sounded another conservative note with the Economy Act, which cut payments to veterans and the wages of federal employees to balance the budget. Although many liberals opposed the bill, it passed easily. At the same time, Roosevelt proposed to increase revenues by immediately legalizing and taxing the sale of low-alcohol beer and wine. Even before Roosevelt had taken office, Congress had acted to repeal the Eighteenth Amendment, and the states, in less than a year, brought a complete end to the nation's embargo on the sale of alcohol. Roosevelt's euphemistically named "Revenue" Act meant that beer was sold legally on April 7 for the first time in more than a decade. Steam whistles and sirens sounded in the brewery city of St. Louis, while crowds filled the streets of Milwaukee to celebrate.

The Agricultural Adjustment Act. The president also acted quickly to bring some relief to farmers, both because of the protest movements spreading through the countryside and because he and his advisers believed that restoring the purchasing power of farmers would help boost the demand for manufactured goods. Led by Secretary of Agriculture Henry A. Wallace, a progressive Republican from Iowa and a highly respected authority on farming (his father had been agriculture secretary under Harding), the administration drew up the Agricultural Adjustment Act (AAA), an omnibus bill that incorporated many reform ideas that had been circulating since the 1920s. The core of the measure was the provision of incentives to farmers to restrict their acreage so that output

would be reduced and prices would rise; if they agreed to raise crops only on their "allotment" of land, farmers would be guaranteed a "parity" price for the goods by the government (parity representing a desirable ratio of farm prices to the prices of manufactured goods). The program was to be funded by a tax on the processing of farm products, paid for by processors—for example, those who milled the grain that farmers grew. The bill was a striking new departure in agricultural and economic policy, since its fundamental goal was to decrease the output of the nation's farms while having other sectors of the economy subsidize farmers who left some of their fields fallow.

The Tennessee Valley Authority. At the same time, Roosevelt launched an even more innovative program that was destined to help large numbers of farmers (among others) in the rural South. This was the Tennessee Valley Authority (TVA), a public corporation whose central goal was to generate electric power along the Tennessee River and to make and distribute nitrogen-based fertilizer from an already existing plant. The brainchild originally of Nebraska senator George Norris, the

This 1934 cartoon by Clifford Berryman depicts FDR as a doctor prescribing remedies for the ailing Uncle Sam, with Congress acquiescing.

763

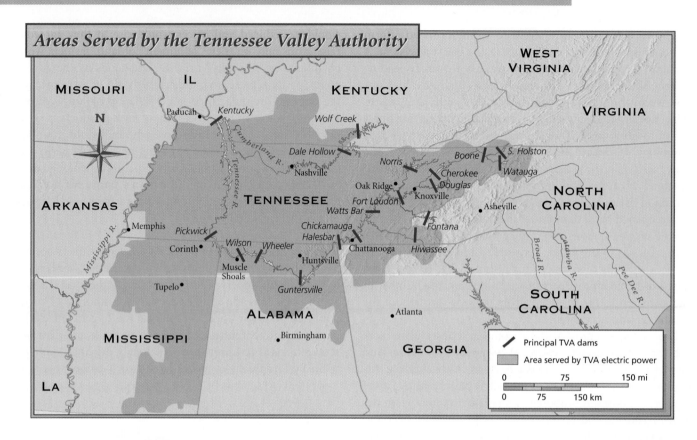

Areas Served by the Tennessee Valley Authority

Principal TVA dams

Area served by TVA electric power

TVA was designed to bring electric power, new commerce, more productive farms, and modern industry to a large segment of the long impoverished rural South, where most people were still living without the basic amenities that had become commonplace in the North. A stunning new use of federal power, the TVA was to have significant long-term effects on the development of seven states in the nation's most backward region.

The Federal Deposit Insurance Corporation. Nor was that all. The rush of activity that came to be called "the first hundred days" included bills that insulated home owners and farmers against foreclosures on their mortgages, a significant enhancement of personal security for millions. In addition, personal savings accounts were protected through the Federal Deposit Insurance Corporation (FDIC), which insured bank deposits: the FDIC was created as part of the Glass-Steagall Act, which separated investment banking from commercial banking in order to minimize the manipulation of financial institutions by bankers themselves.

Aid for the Jobless: Initial Efforts. Roosevelt also made efforts to help the unemployed. One modest program, which satisfied the president's long-standing interest in conservation, was the Civilian Conservation Corps (CCC), which put jobless young men to work in forestry and flood-control projects. The program was funded to enroll only 250,000 individuals, but it endured until the early 1940s, offering aid and new experiences to nearly 3 million men. A much larger and more controversial program, the Federal Emergency Relief Administration (FERA), involved the national government for the first time in the direct relief of the unemployed. Roosevelt, unlike his predecessor, recognized that such involvement, however ideologically uncomfortable, had become a necessity: millions were suffering, and neither private charities nor local or state governments possessed the resources to provide relief. Something had to be done, and the federal government alone was capable of acting. To administer the program, Roosevelt appointed one of his closest advisers from New York, Harry Hopkins, a crusty former social worker deeply influenced by the traditions of progressive reform.

The National Recovery Administration. Near the end of the hundred days, the administration unveiled the centerpiece of its efforts to revive the economy, the National Industrial Recovery Act (NIRA). Designed to stimulate production and inflate prices, the legislation authorized producers in each of the nation's industries to meet together to devise codes of fair competition, permitting them to set prices and divide markets much as cartels had sought to do before the antitrust laws were enacted. These codes, however, had to be approved by the government-appointed National Recovery Administration (NRA), which gave the government enormous potential power over the conduct of economic affairs. In a significant gesture to labor, the act also provided for minimum wages and maximum hours, while affirming the right of workers to form unions and engage in collective bargaining. To help jump-start the economy, the legislation provided $3 billion for public works projects, to be developed by the Public Works Administration (PWA).

The NRA was a peculiar hybrid that sought to satisfy competing interests and accommodate different analyses of the causes of the Depression itself. To many businessmen who believed that the economy was suffering from excessive capacity and competition, it promised release from the strictures of antitrust and an end to the unfettered competition that had reduced profits. To some of the economists and reformers in Roosevelt's administration, heirs to Theodore Roosevelt's New Nationalism, the NRA offered a way for the government to step up the regulation of business, to replace the chaos of the market with rational economic planning. To labor and its liberal backers, it offered Washington's support for long-standing goals. John L. Lewis, head of the miners' union, likened the NRA to the Emancipation Proclamation. The NRA was thus a political compromise, grounded largely in the debate over monopolization and the trusts that had been so prominent between 1890 and 1915. Recovery would come from a restructuring of industry and an alteration of the relationship between the state and the economy.

By the middle of June 1933—the end of the first hundred days—Roosevelt and Congress had taken action on an extraordinary array of issues. They had brought an end to the banking crisis, created several programs to aid the unemployed, created a new legal and institutional framework for the conduct of business and agriculture, lessened the odds of Americans losing their homes, farms, and savings accounts, and initiated a major experiment in regional planning in the Tennessee River valley. More a smorgasbord than a coherent reform package, the legislation was conservative in some respects, liberal in others, difficult to characterize in more than a few instances. Whatever its ideological coloration, the sheer pace of activity had broken the anxious gloom of the previous winter.

Leaving the Gold Standard. Yet there were few signs that the Depression was abating, and the president knew it. It was for this reason that Roosevelt, in early July, took one of the most controversial actions of his first term, issuing a message to a World Economic Conference in London that the United States would remain off the gold standard for the foreseeable future and would not participate in the conference's stated goal of fixing exchange rates among countries. The message was a bombshell both in Europe and domestically: although

Civilian Conservation Corps workers in the Petrified Forest of Arizona, 1938.

The National Recovery Administration's inability to stimulate the economy or satisfy the competing interests of business and labor is represented in this *Vanity Fair* cover, from September 1934, by the "Blue Eagle" (the NRA's symbol) holding an uneasy Uncle Sam aloft.

the president had effectively taken the nation off the gold standard in the spring (by placing an embargo on the export of gold), it was widely believed that this was a temporary action that would be reversed at the London conference. But Roosevelt and many of his advisers had come to realize that their strategy of inflating prices, in both agriculture and industry, was incompatible with a commitment to gold and fixed exchange rates. If the AAA and the NRA did succeed in raising the prices of goods, for example, imports would increase, gold would have to flow out of the country to pay for the imports, and price deflation would return, dampening economic activity. Faced with that scenario, Roosevelt freed American policy from the fetters of the gold standard. His doing so led to the collapse of the London conference and to widespread denunciation of his administration. It also undermined international efforts to find a collective solution to the global economic slowdown and thereby stoked the already burning fires of nationalism in Europe and the Pacific.

THE FIRST TWO YEARS

Despite the frenetic activity in Washington, the economy was slow to rebound. A few small spurts of growth spawned moments of optimism in 1933 and 1934, but each proved to be a false start on the road to recovery.

Some tangible signs of progress did appear in agriculture, thanks in part to the AAA. Although the first attempts to restrict output, in the summer and fall of 1933, produced disturbing images of cotton fields plowed under and 6 million piglets slaughtered (while millions of humans remained hungry in the cities), the incentives offered by the AAA, coupled with the fortuitous arrival of drought in 1934, did contain farm production and spark an increase in prices. Most farmers continued to demand compulsory output restriction, and militant members of the Midwestern Farmers Holiday Association went on "strike," dumping milk on highways and even blowing up dairies and creameries. But in some areas, farm incomes rose enough in the mid-1930s to stem the tide of protest.

Yet the allotment program that was at the heart of the AAA had serous negative consequences for tenant farmers everywhere, most dramatically in the South. The payments to farmers for holding some of their acreage out of cultivation were paid to the owners of farmland. In theory, owners were to share those payments with their tenants, but often they did not. In the South, typically, white landowners pocketed their subsidies, evicting tenants or sharecroppers or simply preventing them from growing cash crops. Southern tenant farmers resisted such efforts, often militantly, but in the end many were driven off the land, and some of the nation's poorest citizens became poorer still.

The NRA was even less successful. It was launched with great ballyhoo by its colorful head, Hugh Johnson: supporters throughout the nation displayed the symbol of the NRA, a "Blue Eagle," on their storefronts and workplaces, and a quarter of a million people marched through the streets of New York celebrating the new program. Buoyed by popular support, Johnson convinced most industrial producers to agree to codes of fair practice and competition by the fall of 1933. But the codes did not seem to provide any stimulus to the economy. As important, different constituencies began to complain loudly that their interests were ill served. Small businesses, as well as progressive critics, claimed that the codes were buttressing monopolies; consumers cried that prices were increasing without any increase in production and employment; big business resented the interference of the government; and labor leaders, lamenting that the prolabor clauses of the legislation were too weak, began to refer to the NRA as the National Run Around.

These conflicts within the NRA mirrored a broader problem that Roosevelt faced after his first few months in office. In the absence of any significant economic recovery, he found it increasingly difficult to hold together the broad coalition of business, labor, and farm interests that had supported him at the outset. The legislation of the first hundred days had included gestures toward many different constituencies, but nearly all found things wanting, and their dissatisfactions deepened over time. Leaders of the business and financial community, even those who were Democrats, became suspicious of Roosevelt, even accusing him of being a dangerous radical: in addition to their disenchantment with the NRA, they were appalled by his departure from the gold standard and opposed his initiatives to regulate the stock exchange and the airwaves through the creation of the Securities and Exchange Commission and the Federal Communications Commission. As a vehicle for mobilizing their anti–New Deal sentiments, many of these big businessmen, led by the chairman of General Motors and including former Democratic Party chair John J. Raskob, founded the American Liberty League.

Progressives, too, were less than ecstatic with the early New Deal: they found the pace of reform slow and Roosevelt overly inclined to compromise with big business. Both within and outside the Democratic Party, self-identified progressives ran to Roosevelt's left in the midterm congressional elections of 1934. They did exceedingly well, contributing significantly to unexpected Democratic gains and Republican losses. Reversing the long-standing pattern that parties in power lost ground during midterm elections, the Democrats emerged from the 1934 elections with sixty-nine Senate seats and a huge majority in the House. Nearly a dozen independents were also elected to Congress, and many more gained state and local offices.

One candidate who failed to win election in 1934 nonetheless gave a scare to mainstream politicians of both parties: Upton Sinclair, the aging novelist, socialist, and author of the famous muckraking novel of the Progressive Era, *The Jungle.* Sinclair lived in California, where the desperate conditions of the Depression led him to found an organization called End Poverty in California (EPIC). EPIC's program called for the state to buy or rent uncultivated land and idle factories so that workers could grow their own food and manufacture ne-

cessities such as clothing and furniture. Sinclair also announced that he would seek the Democratic nomination for governor in 1934; his program struck a strong enough chord among the state's voters that he won the Democratic primary. Squaring off in the general election against an arch-conservative Republican, he seemed to stand a good chance of being elected until conservative Democrats deserted the party in droves while Republicans launched a smear campaign against Sinclair, based on selective quotations from his early writings. With President Roosevelt standing on the sidelines, declining to endorse his own party's nominee, Sinclair went down to a decisive defeat in the general election.

STIRRINGS ON THE LEFT

Sinclair's campaign in California was only one tip of an iceberg of politicized discontent. Throughout the nation, the Depression gave birth or strength to political movements that challenged key features of traditional American political and economic life. Some questioned the viability of capitalism itself; others pressed for a wholesale redistribution of power and wealth within a free enterprise economy; still others fo-

A 1932 Socialist Party campaign poster supporting Norman Thomas for president under the slogan "Repeal Unemployment!"

cused on single issues. Despite the severity of the Depression, the nation never came near the brink of revolution, but for the first time since the late nineteenth century, radical and quasi-radical movements played a significant role in the nation's politics.

The Socialist Party, led by Norman Thomas after the death in the 1920s of Eugene Debs, experienced a resurgence of popularity, once again electing members to local offices in working-class cities such as Milwaukee and Bridgeport, Connecticut. Thomas himself polled nearly a million votes in the 1932 presidential election and was a widely respected voice for the view that the Depression was a clear demonstration of the failure of capitalism. The Socialists were challenged on the left by the Communist Party of the United States, formed after World War I and committed to the overthrow—probably not through elections—of American capitalism and the political institutions that supported it. The Communist Party never had more than 100,000 members at any one time, but the number of persons who belonged to or sympathized with the party in the course of the 1930s was far greater. Its membership consisted largely of workers and intellectuals and was concentrated in a few key cities, including New York, Chicago, and Detroit. Members of the Communist Party—as well as several dissident communist groups, including followers of Leon Trotsky—were almost alone in organizing the unemployed in the early 1930s, staging demonstrations to demand adequate relief and resisting the eviction of jobless workers from their homes; they were also almost unique in promoting full equality for African Americans. Their militance and dedication gave them a prestige among workers that went beyond their numbers.

Both Socialists and Communists were active in a wave of labor unrest that swept parts of the country in 1934. Labor had been relatively quiet during the early years of the Depression, as union membership fell off and workers feared taking any action that could risk the loss of their jobs. But stimulated in part by the hopes and disappointments generated by the NRA, workers in many cities engaged in strikes in 1934, some of them extremely militant and disruptive. Thousands of workers, for example, struck against the Electric Auto-Lite plant in Toledo, Ohio, precipitating a citywide conflict that one journalist characterized as a "civil war." Teamsters shut down Minneapolis, a longshoreman's job action led to a brief "general strike" of all workers in San Francisco, and textile workers walked off their jobs from Massachusetts to South Carolina in the largest strike in the nation's history. Blood flowed in many of these cities, as the police and private guards cracked down on workers and demonstrators: "a few hundred funerals," noted one textile industrial publication, "will have a quieting influence." Job security and wages were at issue in most of these conflicts, as was the right of workers to organize and engage in collective bargaining; fueling the militance almost everywhere was something deeper, a profound sense of injustice, anger, and exploitation.

Father Coughlin and Dr. Townsend. A sense of injustice and grievance also infused other movements, several of which were spearheaded by individuals who became prominent political figures. One was Father Charles Coughlin, a parish priest in Royal Oak, Michigan. Coughlin, beginning in the late 1920s, began delivering sermons over the radio, at first locally and then, thanks to technological changes that strengthened the power of transmitters, to audiences in Chicago and Cincinnati. He was such a popular speaker that by 1930 CBS was broadcasting his talks over a new national network, allowing him to become the first exemplar of what would become an oddly familiar type: the man of the cloth who was also a media personality and political commentator. Coughlin's political views offered a blend of progressive Catholic doctrine, support for unions, hostility to bankers, and the conviction that inflating the currency through the coinage of silver was "the key to world prosperity." He at first supported Roosevelt, but then

Police breaking up a labor gathering in San Francisco on the eve of the general strike in 1934.

LEFT: Father Charles Coughlin. **RIGHT:** Francis Townsend.

became an increasingly erratic critic of the New Deal, mixing tinges of anti-Semitism into his denunciations of a global conspiracy of bankers. Late in 1934, he founded the National Union for Social Justice, an organization that called for inflation and monetary reforms, the nationalization of important industries, and the protection of labor's rights, all rolled into a system that in some respects resembled the Italian corporatism of Mussolini. Coughlin's support was particularly strong among lower-middle-class Catholic immigrants, but his appeal was broader than that: his radio audience, the largest steady audience in the world, numbered upward of 30 million.

A much less controversial figure who rose to sudden prominence in the mid-1930s was Francis Townsend, an elderly physician from Long Beach, California. In 1934, Townsend developed a scheme for "old age revolving pensions" that he believed would solve the problem of security for the elderly in the United States while simultaneously giving a major boost to the economy. Every person aged sixty or older who retired from work would receive a check from the government for $200 each month, which they had to spend within a month of its issue: the retirements would make way for younger, unemployed workers, the elderly would have guaranteed incomes, and the spending would stimulate economic growth, enough to compensate for the 2 percent business tax required to fund the program. The Townsend plan was embraced by millions of citizens across the country, particularly older rural Protestants; its supporters constituted the first organized appearance of "senior citizens" in the nation's political debates. Although critics ridiculed the plan's arithmetic, the Townsend program was endorsed by sixteen of California's twenty congressmen, among others. In some locales, belief that the plan would soon become law was so strong that elderly citizens tried to purchase goods with the promise to pay when their first Townsend checks arrived.

Sharing the Wealth. The most important political leader to emerge during this period was Louisiana senator Huey P. Long. Brilliant, colorful, and shrewd, Long tapped a current of populist sentiment that had been underground since the 1890s. He rose to power in Louisiana in the 1920s by leading a revolt against the corrupt oligarchy of politicians and big businesses (including utility companies and Standard Oil) that had dominated the impoverished state for decades. As governor, he taxed the rich and business interests, built roads, schools, and hospitals, and constructed a political machine that became unchallengeable. With his election to the Senate in 1930 (for nearly two years he was both governor and senator), he entered the national political arena and was a key supporter of Roosevelt's nomination in 1932.

Long quickly became Roosevelt's most feared rival. Both publicly and privately, he criticized Roosevelt as being too tepid a reformer, and he positioned himself as the champion

Huey P. Long, governor of Louisiana and then U.S. senator, launched the "Share Our Wealth" movement in 1934.

of the common man doing battle against an elite that included not only big business but also educated northeasterners such as Roosevelt and many of his advisers. In 1934, Long launched a national political organization whose slogan was "Share Our Wealth" and whose goal was to confiscate and redistribute the wealth of the richest Americans so that each family would own a home, a car, and a radio. He also favored a national minimum wage, a shorter work week, support for education, and huge spending on public works to provide jobs for the unemployed. By the spring of 1935, there were thousands of Share Our Wealth Clubs in the country, as well as a mailing list of millions of adherents. Long was transformed from a regional icon to a national figure, capable of drawing enormous crowds in locales as diverse as Iowa and Philadelphia. His meteoric rise and evident presidential ambitions were deeply worrisome to Roosevelt and his fellow New Dealers. Roosevelt's primary concern was that Long would run in 1936 as an independent and drain enough votes away from him to elect a Republican; others, looking farther down the road, feared that the youthful Long would be a formidable candidate to succeed Roosevelt in 1940. Both possibilities were foreclosed in September 1935, when Long was assassinated in Baton Rouge by the son-in-law of a judge whom Long was trying to remove from office.

The energy that poured into these diverse movements revealed both an impatience with the New Deal and the critical fact that the spectrum of political opinion had lurched sharply leftward between 1929 and the mid-1930s. The moderate liberalism of Roosevelt and his allies stood in contrast not only to the conservatism of Republicans and business Democrats but also to political beliefs that were more severely critical of capitalism itself. "I am not a liberal. I am a radical," declared Minnesota governor Floyd Olson, who advocated a "cooperative commonwealth" that would include government ownership of key industries. Intellectuals like John Dewey, the nation's leading philosopher, agreed. Dewey favored a moderate form of socialism that would place the state in control of the economy while also respecting and protecting individual liberties. Other intellectuals went further, embracing the more militant program of the Communist Party; among its well-known sympathizers were novelists

John Dos Passos and Sherwood Anderson, literary critics Malcolm Cowley and Edmund Wilson, and African American poet Langston Hughes. To some, the Soviet Union (which was not experiencing a depression) stood as a model for Americans trying to build a more egalitarian society: scores of skilled American workers even went to the Soviet Union to work in its plants and catch a glimpse of the future. Such ideas were not beyond the pale in the midst of the Great Depression. "The country," observed Roosevelt's secretary of the interior Harold Ickes in his diary, "is much more radical than the Administration."

THE SECOND HUNDRED DAYS

These stirrings throughout the country were not lost on the president. Roosevelt was nothing if not a masterful politician, with extraordinary antennae for shifting political winds. The nation's mood in the spring of 1935 seemed to demand renewed action and to create the opportunity for the president to promote legislation in which he deeply believed, particularly social insurance for the elderly and the unemployed. Consequently, Roosevelt and his advisers prepared a new set of measures to present to the more liberal Congress that had been elected the previous November.

"To some, the Soviet Union (which was not experiencing a depression) stood as a model for Americans trying to build a more egalitarian society: scores of skilled American workers even went to the Soviet Union to work in its plants and catch a glimpse of the future."

Roosevelt's determination was reinforced by a striking defeat that the New Deal suffered at the hands of the Supreme Court. In May of 1935, the Court unanimously ruled in *Schechter Poultry v. the U.S.* that the NRA was unconstitutional. The case arose when Schechter Poultry, a small Brooklyn firm, was found to be in violation of the NRA's Live Poultry Code. The Court found fault with the NRA because the agency's broad authority represented an excessive delegation of the legislative powers of Congress; more ominously, the Court also concluded that the federal government had no right to be imposing the poultry code in the first place because the Schechter firm was involved exclusively in intrastate commerce, while the Constitution gave Washington the right to regulate only interstate commerce. The decision was foreshadowed by Court rulings in several earlier cases, but it nonetheless jolted New Dealers. How could the federal government possibly contend with the economic crisis without having an impact on firms whose dealings remained within the boundaries of an individual state? The Court, according to the president, had embraced a "horse-and-buggy definition of interstate commerce." The demise of the increasingly unpopular NRA was not widely mourned (although Roosevelt himself remained attached to it), but the Court's objection could potentially be applied to nearly all major pieces of legislation.

Nonetheless, Roosevelt moved forward, with one eye on the Court and another on the movements building across the nation. The result was a series of measures, all passed in 1935, that are often described as the "Second Hundred Days" or the "Second New Deal."

Aid for the Jobless. Relief for the unemployed remained a pressing issue: 8 million Americans were still jobless, for increasingly long stretches, and the initiatives launched in 1933 had come to seem flawed or inadequate. The PWA, administered by the cautious Harold Ickes, was slow in developing worthwhile construction projects, and since it was created as part of the NRA, its legal status was dubious after the *Schechter* decision. Roosevelt had shut down the Civil Works Administration (CWA) in 1934 because he was concerned about its cost and with the resemblance of many of its jobs to "make work." Giving out money for "a few hours of weekly work cutting grass, raking leaves, or picking up papers in the public parks" seemed to him not much more than a "dole" that was "fundamentally destructive to the national fibre." The FERA continued to provide funds for direct relief to the jobless poor, but it paid only a pittance and required applicants to make a demeaning declaration that they lacked the resources to support themselves.

What Roosevelt wanted—and what jobless Americans wanted—was a federal program that would relieve the urgent needs of the unemployed by paying them to perform meaningful work. In the eyes of the president and nearly all his contemporaries, work relief of some sort was preferable to paying people who remained idle. Yet the type of work that the jobless should perform was not obvious, since their abilities were diverse and it made little sense for them to engage in activities that would compete with private enterprise. Nor was it clear how pay scales could be set so that the unemployed could support themselves without earning more on work relief than they would earn in agriculture or industry.

> *"What Roosevelt wanted—and what jobless Americans wanted—was a federal program that would relieve the urgent needs of the unemployed by paying them to perform meaningful work."*

The Emergency Relief Appropriations Act, which Congress approved in the spring of 1935, tried to address many of these issues: it was grounded in the presumption that unemployment was not going to quickly disappear and that the federal government ought to step in and give work to those the private sector could not absorb. The act increased support for the previously created CCC; it also re-funded the PWA to undertake large-scale public works projects that required advance planning. Although the PWA did not really begin pumping much money into the economy until 1938, the agency did leave an enduring legacy: it built schools, courthouses, city halls, and sewage plants all across the country, as well as such landmarks as New York's Triboro Bridge and Lincoln Tunnel and the bridge linking Florida's Key West to the mainland.

At the center of the initiative was a new and more innovative agency, the Works Progress Administration (later, Works Projects Administration), or WPA. The WPA, based on the largest appropriation in the nation's history, was designed to quickly create 3.5 million jobs without compet-

"Work Pays America!" a Works Progress Administration poster.

ing with private business. Its jobs would pay more than relief but less than prevailing local wages. The WPA was also structured to take advantage of the diverse talents of the unemployed: it did construct hospitals, schools, and other public buildings, yet it also hired artists, writers, historians, and actors (among others) to paint murals on public buildings, create and perform plays, interview ex-slaves, index historical records, and write guides to individual states and regions. The WPA was a magnet for criticism from conservatives, who were appalled by its cost and feared that it was supporting the "undeserving" poor or (not without reason) serving as a massive Democratic political machine. It was also attacked by labor unions, who believed that the "security" wages paid would serve to depress wage rates, and by civil rights advocates, who were infuriated that southern blacks and Hispanic women in the West received lower wages than nearby whites. Nonetheless, the WPA had many enthusiastic supporters and by 1936 was employing a full 7 percent of American workers.

"Roosevelt was not a great fan of labor unions, but he understood that without them, workers were no match for large corporate employers."

The Wagner Act. Workers with jobs also needed attention. Although section 7 (a) of the NIRA promised workers the right to form unions and engage in collective bargaining, it lacked enforcement provisions and was generally ineffective. The *Schechter* decision gave prolabor legislators the opportunity to write a new law that would have more teeth. The driving force for such a bill was Senator Robert F. Wagner of New York, an educated, new-style Tammany Hall politician who had risen from humble, immigrant beginnings and become a powerful force for social welfare legislation. In 1935, with the somewhat less-than-enthusiastic backing of Roosevelt, Wagner successfully pressed the Democrat-dominated Congress to pass the National Labor Relations Act, often called the Wagner Act. The act gave federal protection to the right of workers to form unions and engage in collective bargaining. It also created the National Labor Relations Board (NLRB) to oversee the exercise of that right; the board was empowered to hold elections in which employees could democratically decide whether or not they wanted a union—and which union they wanted. The Wagner Act also itemized actions that would constitute illegal "unfair labor practices" on the part of employers, including firing workers because of their union membership or pro-union activity, creating company-controlled organizations in lieu of independent unions, and refusing to engage in collective bargaining with a duly certified union. In so doing, the act took away from employers some of the key weapons they had used to resist unionization.

Roosevelt was not a great fan of labor unions, but he understood that without them, workers were no match for large corporate employers. He also understood that industrial workers were a politically restive force as well as a critical constituency for the Democratic Party. The passage of the Wagner Act went a long way toward cementing the attachment of labor to the Democrats and, in so doing, helped to solidify the opposition to Roosevelt of many anti-union employers and employers' associations, such as the National Association of Manufacturers. Beyond partisan politics, the Wagner Act was significant both in serving as a charter for the unionization of American labor and in providing the basic framework of federal labor law for the remainder of the twentieth century.

Social Security. Roosevelt's heart was in the Social Security Act of 1935, a measure every bit as radical as the Wagner Act. In 1934, Roosevelt had entrusted the drafting of the legislation to a committee headed by Secretary of Labor Frances Perkins, the first woman ever to hold a cabinet position. Perkins, a Mt. Holyoke graduate schooled in social work at Jane Addams's Hull House, was a dedicated prolabor reformer who had led an official investigation of the horrific Triangle Shirtwaist Company fire (1911), which killed scores of young female workers, and served for years as an industrial commissioner in New York. She and Roosevelt agreed that the time had come for the United States to erect a system of social insurance that would help prevent the widespread destitution they were witnessing in the mid-1930s; most industrialized countries had already adopted such systems.

The Social Security Act had three key provisions, each of which tempered Roosevelt's vision of a comprehensive insurance program with political, legal, and fiscal concerns. The first was a system of unemployment insurance that would provide automatic support to men and women who had lost their jobs: in 1935, such insurance existed only in the progressive state of Wisconsin. Because of fears that the courts might find a purely federal system to be unconstitutional, it was designed as a joint state-federal program, funded largely through state taxes that would be offset by federal monies. To the dismay of many longtime advocates of such a system, some of the nation's poorest workers were not covered, and benefits in some states were utterly inadequate; but the legislation nonetheless established that workers had a right to public support when they were jobless.

The Social Security Act also created pensions for the elderly. Bowing to what Perkins called American "prejudices," the pensions were financed by payroll taxes on employers and employees, establishing a contributory system that was a curious hybrid of insurance and compulsory savings. The fact that the pensions were not funded by general tax revenues softened the principle that the elderly had a right to public support after their working years had come to an end. But Roosevelt shrewdly sensed that a contributory program would protect the pension system in the long run: since individuals were

A 1935 Social Security Board poster urging Americans to take advantage of the just-passed Social Security Act.

placing their own funds into social security accounts, "no damn politician can ever scrap my social security program." The act had other shortcomings as well: it did not cover farm workers, domestic servants (many of whom were female and/or African American), or employees in small businesses, and it did not begin payments to anyone until 1940. Nonetheless, the legislation was a pathbreaking step in the public assumption of responsibility for the welfare of its citizens and in restructuring the very idea of retirement for most workers.

The third, more modest prong of the legislation provided for immediate grants to the states to provide relief to the elderly poor and to mothers of dependent children, many of whom had been abandoned by jobless fathers who hit the road in search of work. Although the funds allocated for such programs were small, the programs were an exception to the bias against a "dole" for the nonworking poor: over time, Aid to Dependent Children (later renamed Aid to Families with Dependent Children) became a critical element of the welfare state.

Finally, it should be noted that Roosevelt wanted to begin a system of national health care as part of a "cradle to grave" insurance net. The political obstacles, however, were so formidable that this goal was relinquished except for a few minor allocations for handicapped people and some rural communities. In deciding not to press for a health care system in 1935, both the president and his advisers presumed that once the other ingredients of a social insurance system were in place, it would be soon be possible to add national health care to the mix.

Rural Electrification. For millions of farm-dwelling Americans, the creation of the Rural Electrification Administration (REA) in 1935 was a more significant event than the passage of the Wagner or Social Security Act. It reflected Roosevelt's personal belief that electricity was "no longer a luxury" but a "necessity." The goal of the REA, like that of the TVA, was to bring electricity to rural areas, something private enterprise had failed to do; unlike the TVA, the REA was national in its reach. After trying unsuccessfully to work with private utilities, the REA helped create local cooperatives to which it would lend money for the construction of electric lines; it also offered engineering and legal assistance. The program was immediately successful, leading to the construction of electric transmission lines at 40 percent below the costs estimated by private utilities. Although a shortage of funds limited the breadth of the REA, its efforts brought electricity to more than 900,000 households by 1941.

A 1937 poster for the Rural Electrification Administration, which aimed to bring electricity to rural areas around the country.

For farmers across the nation, this meant that a half century of electrical technology arrived in their homes all at once. Suddenly they had electric lights and radios; more than half of all new electric subscribers bought washing machines within a year, while more than a fourth bought refrigerators. On many farms, moreover, electricity not only improved household conditions and lightened the burden of household labor, it also altered farm production itself. Keeping electric lights burning in chicken coops increased winter egg production; refrigeration preserved milk; and electric pumps helped to irrigate semiarid lands, particularly in the West. The REA, to be sure, did not reach most of the nation's poorest farmers, but it significantly advanced the spread of electrically based technology to rural America. In so doing, it helped to increase the efficiency of the nation's farms, contributing after 1940, ironically, to the renewed exodus of farmers from the land.

The REA and the TVA were two expressions of a larger New Deal vision of state-promoted economic development and technological diffusion. In addition to the many multipurpose dams built along the Tennessee River, the government launched other major dam projects, the most notable of which were the Grand Coulee Dam in central Washington and the Hoover Dam on the Colorado River at the border of northwestern Arizona and southeastern Nevada. Planned and designed by engineers from the Department of Interior and the U.S. Army Corps of Engineers, these massive projects involved thousands of private contractors and tens of thousands of construction workers. The resulting structures were widely regarded as technological marvels. The massive turbine rooms and spillways of the Grand Coulee and Hoover Dams attracted thousands of tourists and became symbols of the New Deal's faith in public power and public action. The western dams not only generated electricity but also irrigated semiarid farmlands and provided water to rapidly growing cities like Los Angeles.

Yet these great symbols of power and progress were not without their critics, who claimed that the chief beneficiaries were large landowners and corporations. Indeed, despite the government's stated desire to provide "electricity for all," nearly half the power generated by the TVA and the Grand Coulee Dam ended up being harnessed to large industrial users. Moreover, the many dams built along the Tennessee, Colorado, and Columbia Rivers backed up water for miles, forming huge man-made lakes and forcing people to surrender their land and move. Native Americans saw their ancestral lands flooded and valued salmon runs destroyed. Advocates of the projects, however, remained convinced that their benefits far outweighed their costs. "When I think of the work which has been done" by the TVA, Senator George Norris mused in 1941, "it is too good to be true. It seems almost like a dream."

THE ELECTION OF 1936

By 1936, Roosevelt had abandoned his effort to build a broad, multiclass coalition, and he shaped his political campaign, as he had shaped the Second New Deal, to fend off the challenge from the left in a country that was becoming increasingly radicalized. The decision was not his alone: the business community had begun turning against Roosevelt as early as 1934, and its hostility mounted with the Wagner Act, the Social Security Act, and a "soak the rich" tax proposal put forward in 1936. Business and financial leaders rallied behind the Republican nominee, Governor Alf Landon of Kansas, who criticized Roosevelt for excessive spending and for violating the Constitution; yet even Landon tacitly acknowledged Roosevelt's popularity by vowing to continue some New Deal programs.

Roosevelt happily ran against the Republicans and the "economic royalists" of the business community, sometimes savagely denouncing the "greed" and "autocracy" of "organized money." At the same time, he succeeded in keeping most dissident voters on the left from bolting to third parties. With Huey Long dead, the remnants of his Share Our Wealth movement joined with followers of Dr. Townsend and Father Coughlin to form the Union Party, which nominated William Lemke, a North Dakota congressman, for president. But the Social Security Act and the tax on the wealthy had taken the steam out of these movements. Similarly, Roosevelt's prolabor stances led some socialist union leaders to urge their members to forsake third-party movements and support the Democrats instead. In November, the president won a spectacular victory. Roosevelt received almost 28 million popular votes—61 percent of the total—to Landon's 16 million; the electoral college vote was 523–8, more lopsided than any split since Monroe's election in 1820. The Union Party polled less than 900,000 votes. The Democrats also increased their hold on Congress, winning 331 members of the House of Representatives compared with the Republicans' 89.

Building on trends that had first emerged in 1928, Roosevelt had reshaped the nation's politics and transformed the Democrats into the dominant national party. He carried massive majorities in the country's industrial cities as well as among farmers in the South and West. Cracking the long-running hold of the Republican Party on African Americans, he even won majorities among the increasingly numerous blacks who had become enfranchised by migrating to the North. Most important, he had enlarged the Democratic Party: his victory owed less to the conversion of voters from the Republican to the Democratic column than to the mass mobilization of new voters. Many were immigrants who had belatedly become American citizens (the years between 1928 and 1936 witnessed an extraordinarily high incidence of naturalization) and the children of immigrants who had reached voting age in the 1930s. Italian, Irish, Slovak, and Jewish industrial workers in Detroit, Pittsburgh, Cleveland, and New York: these men and women came out to the polls in unprecedented numbers and voiced boisterous approval of the New Deal.

LABOR RISING

While Roosevelt's campaign for reelection was underway, so, too, was another campaign that promised to reshape the economic and political landscape. This was the effort, led by rebellious union leaders from the American Federation of Labor (AFL), to organize workers in mass-production industries, such as auto, steel, and rubber. Those workers, mostly semiskilled and unskilled, had remained outside of the house of organized labor when unions of skilled workers were formed in the late nineteenth and early twentieth centuries; as the Great Depression began, few belonged to unions, nearly all worked long hours for low wages, and most were either immigrants themselves or the children of immigrants. Their prospects of becoming union members seemed poor, since depressions had invariably witnessed a decline rather than an expansion of union membership.

The leader of the effort to organize these men and women was the president of the United Mine Workers, John L. Lewis. Lewis, who grew up in the coal fields of Iowa, the son of Welsh immigrants, was a charismatic figure who became one of the most prominent—and, by some, feared—men in the United States from the 1930s to the 1950s. A large man with intense eyes and huge, bushy eyebrows, he was an eloquent speaker and a shrewd strategist. Lewis had concluded as early as the 1920s that the long-run protection of his own union depended on the organization of the steel industry (since steelmakers owned many mines and were key consumers of coal) and that the union movement itself could gain strength only if all men and women who labored in the same industry belonged to the same union.

John L. Lewis, shown here addressing textile workers in Lawrence, Massachusetts, May 1937.

Lewis spent much of 1933 and 1934 building up the membership of his own union and attempting to convince the leadership of the AFL (of which he was a vice-president) to begin an organizing drive in the mass-production industries. Despite the unfavorable economic conditions, Lewis believed that rank-and-file anger as well as the prolabor provisions of the NRA had created an opening for action. The cautious, largely native-born leadership of the AFL appeared to agree but did little to support Lewis's efforts. At the AFL convention of 1935, Lewis reraised the issue, pointedly provoking a heated debate and a formal vote rejecting his proposal: after a theatrical moment in which he delivered a punch to the head of the carpenters' union, Lewis led a walk-out from the convention. With Sidney Hillman, the head of the Amalgamated Clothing Workers, and David Dubinsky, president of the International Ladies' Garment Workers' Union, Lewis then formed the Committee for Industrial Organization; it was renamed the Congress of Industrial Organizations (CIO) in 1938, two years after its leaders and their unions had been expelled from the AFL.

The CIO's first targets were the steel and auto industries. Encouraged by an improving economy (which turned out to be only temporary), as well as the new legal protections contained in the Wagner Act, the CIO hired squads of organizers to fan out into the workplaces, recreation halls, bars, and fraternal associations of industrial America. The drive was funded largely by a war chest that Lewis and the mine workers had built up over several years. Although Lewis himself was not an ideological radical, many of the organizers the CIO deployed were communists and socialists who saw unionization as both a step toward social justice and a blow against capitalism. The communists, in particular, were dedicated and skilled organizers, willing to suffer hardships and take risks for the cause.

The CIO vs. General Motors. The first major confrontation, and triumph, came in the auto industry, where a CIO-backed organizing committee squared off against General Motors, the world's largest corporation. GM was a vast, integrated network of parts manufacturing and assembly plants, centered in Detroit and the nearby city of Flint, Michigan; it employed more than 240,000 workers, only a skilled handful of whom belonged to unions. GM's workers, like those at Ford and Chrysler, suffered from annual layoffs, arbitrary hiring and firing practices, and sometimes brutally arduous working conditions. Organizers, including Socialist militant Walter Reuther, who had worked in a plant in the Soviet Union and would eventually become the president of the United Auto Workers, spent much of 1936 gathering supporters and developing a strategy to compel GM to recognize their union as the bargaining agent for all employees. Since GM was a staunchly anti-union firm that, like most other major corporations, spent a great deal of money trying to ward off unions and infiltrate organizing campaigns, a fierce strike was anticipated. The leadership of GM was also convinced that it had nothing to fear from the Wagner Act because it would soon be declared unconstitutional.

The conflict began dramatically in Flint in late December 1936, less than two months after Roosevelt's landslide reelection. In a bold strategic move, thousands of striking autoworkers, rather than leaving their jobs and forming picket lines outside, simply stopped the machinery and "sat down" inside

A picket line of supporters around the General Motors Fisher Body Plant, occupied by sit-down strikers, in Flint, Michigan, 1937.

several of GM's key plants. In doing so, they guaranteed that the company could not hire scabs (replacement workers) or take forceful action without risking damage to its machinery and facilities; by carefully selecting the sit-down targets, they hoped to prevent GM from producing cars at all, despite its large network of plants.

The action stunned GM and the public, not least because the sit-down loomed as a symbolic repudiation of private property rights. Within days, workers had seized other plants, and Flint became the center of national attention, with police guarding the plants, thousands of supporters forming picket lines outside, a "women's brigade" carrying food to the sit-down strikers, and reporters and camera crews circulating everywhere. GM denounced the strike as a Communist-inspired insurrection and demanded that the Democratic governor of Michigan, Frank Murphy, call out the national guard to evict the strikers. Murphy declined to do so, and public opinion, reflecting the era's broad political sympathy for the working class, remained on the side of the strikers. For more than six weeks, the strikers remained in the plants, carefully cleaning up and avoiding harming the machinery, doing calisthenics to remain in shape, and talking politics nonstop.

"For more than six weeks, the Flint strikers remained in the plants, carefully cleaning up and avoiding harming the machinery, doing calisthenics to remain in shape, and talking politics nonstop."

In mid-February 1937, GM surrendered and recognized the United Auto Workers as the bargaining agent for the company's employees. The company did not immediately grant the pay raises or changes in working conditions that had been demanded, but it agreed to negotiate those issues with the union. The workers' victory gave an enormous shot of adrenaline to organizing efforts throughout the nation. So, too, did the announcement a few weeks later that U.S. Steel, the nation's largest steel producer and a notoriously anti-union firm, had given up without a fight: after secret discussions with Lewis, the corporation's president, Myron Taylor, declared that it would recognize the United Steel Workers as its workers' union. Many battles remained to be fought, and some of them, including those at Chrysler, Ford, and Republic Steel, produced violent encounters and bloodshed; in Chicago, on Memorial Day 1937, police opened fire at a demonstration near Republic Steel's plant, killing ten workers, most of them shot in the back.

But the corporate bulwarks surrounding the mass-production industries had been definitively breached. By the end of 1937, more than 200,000 autoworkers and 300,000 steelworkers had joined CIO-affiliated unions; the United Rubber Workers won an eight-week strike against Firestone; and General Electric, as well as RCA, had recognized the United Electrical and Radio Workers. Total CIO membership numbered close to 4 million, as men and women in one industry after another rushed to join unions. The AFL also benefited from this surge in labor's strength and popularity, adding hundreds of thousands of new members. Some of these gains, for both the CIO and the AFL, proved short-lived, as employers counterattacked and the economy began to sink again in 1937 and 1938. Nonetheless, the union movement had acquired an institutional strength that it never had before, and it was well positioned to add millions more new members in 1941 and beyond, when wartime conditions created the tightest labor markets that had been seen in decades.

The success of the CIO in the teeth of the worst depression in the nation's history would not have been easy to predict. That the organization achieved its goal of bringing the basic protections of unionization to millions of semiskilled and unskilled workers was, in part, the result of determined leadership, both nationally and in the hundreds of locals that sprang up in cities across the nation. The CIO's success also owed a great deal to the political climate established by the New Deal, a climate that led both the federal government and state officials like Frank Murphy to encourage unionization rather than (as had often happened before) weigh in on the side of anti-union corporations.

In addition to these political factors, another process was at work as well: the development of a shared culture and sense of community among the millions of immigrant families, most of them eastern and southern European or Irish, who had come to the United States several decades earlier and who worked in its steel mills, rubber factories, and auto plants. No longer temporary sojourners in the land, these men and women had reasons to build new institutions in America; most of them, and all of their children, spoke English, and thanks to the radio and other forms of mass communication and entertainment, they possessed common frames of reference, whether their forebears hailed from Italy or Poland or County Cork. For such men and women in Flint, Pittsburgh, Chicago, Buffalo, and New York, the CIO was not simply an organization but a movement for dignity and self-improvement, in and through which they could act together.

Roosevelt's Second Term

Franklin Roosevelt's second inauguration, in January 1937—the anxious interregnum of 1933 had led Congress to permanently change inauguration day from March 4 to January 20—was a triumphant occasion for the president. Reelected by a record margin, Roosevelt enjoyed unprecedented popularity, and the economy, which had improved throughout 1936, continued to show signs of growth. Roosevelt could also point to an extraordinary string of achievements during his first term. Yet his inaugural address suggested that he would not simply rest on his record. "I see one-third of a nation ill-housed, ill-clad, ill-nourished," he declared. The president, and his administration, seemed prepared, politically and intellectually, to push the New Deal further forward.

A 1937 cartoon showing Roosevelt attempting the impossible task of pulling his Supreme Court reform plan through the Senate.

TAKING AIM AT THE SUPREME COURT

The largest cloud on the New Deal's horizon was the Supreme Court. The Court's ruling against the NRA in 1935 was followed by a series of similarly conservative decisions: it destroyed the AAA by declaring its processing tax to be unconstitutional; threw out legislation designed to shore up the coal industry after the demise of the NRA; and even overturned a New York minimum wage statute on the grounds that it interfered with the freedom of individuals to make economic contracts. The implication of these decisions seemed to be that neither the federal government nor the states could do much at all to regulate economic affairs.

The Court's posture created uncertainty in the administration about how to promote economic recovery and design further social legislation, such as a federal wage and hours bill. As important, the Court's decisions suggested that it would uphold already-pending legal challenges to other landmark measures, including the Social Security Act and the Wagner Act, effectively nullifying the heart of the New Deal. Four of the nine justices appeared to be unshakably committed to an interpretation of the Constitution that would not permit the federal government to actively intervene in the economy or erect any system of social insurance; and the conservative four were generally able to corral at least one more vote (usually from Justice Owen Roberts) to gain a majority. The conservatives were also judicial activists who had overturned legislation in the 1920s and 1930s at an unprecedented rate. Seven of the sitting justices had been appointed by Republican presidents, as had been 80 percent of all federal judges in the lower courts. The average age of the Supreme Court's justices was seventy-one; Roosevelt himself had not yet appointed a single member.

Strategies for circumventing the Supreme Court had been discussed among New Dealers for several years, but Roosevelt finally acted in early February 1937, when he sent Congress a proposal that would permit him to appoint additional justices to the Court. Couched as a measure to speed up the process of judicial review and lighten the workload of aging judges, the "Court-packing" scheme would have allowed the president to appoint one additional justice (up to a total of six) for each member of the Court who had served for ten years and did not retire within six months after reaching his seventieth birthday. It also authorized the president to appoint several dozen new judges to lower federal courts. In a characteristically mischievous twist, Roosevelt made his plan public two days after hosting a White House dinner honoring the Supreme Court—and less than a week before the Court began hearing oral arguments on the Wagner Act.

The proposal provoked an uproar, in and out of Washington. The pretext that Roosevelt was concerned about the Court's efficiency was flimsy, and he was quickly denounced for trying to alter the balance of power among different branches of government. He was also attacked for disparaging the "capacities" of the elderly—by, among others, powerful politicians who had themselves reached the age of seventy. Since Roosevelt had not alerted congressional leaders or most members of his own cabinet that the proposal was forthcoming (it had been drawn up in secrecy by his attorney general), he had few defenders, while Republicans, conservative Democrats uneasy about the administration's leftward drift, and editorial writers around the country heaped criticism upon him. Even his closest associates thought the scheme displayed "too much cleverness," and few thought it had much chance of getting through Congress.

The Court-packing scheme was widely regarded by contemporaries and historians as the most glaring mistake of Roosevelt's presidency, a rare moment when his political antennae failed him. Perhaps so: frustrated by the Court and riding a crest of personal popularity, Roosevelt may well have underestimated the opposition his proposal would provoke. Nonetheless, Roosevelt won the war, even if he eventually lost the battle for court reform. In March 1937, seven weeks after the Court-packing plan had been unveiled, the Supreme Court, by a 5–4 vote, upheld a Washington state minimum wage law not unlike the New York law that had recently been nullified. Justice Roberts had changed his mind.

In early April, the Court convened to announce its decisions in a series of legal challenges to the Wagner Act, the most important of which was *National Labor Relations Board v. Jones and Laughlin Steel*. Chief Justice Charles Evans Hughes, a white-bearded, moderate Republican, often a swing vote himself, carefully read the decision aloud to a packed courtroom in what one contemporary described as tones "of infallibility which made the whole business sound like a rehearsal for the last judgment." To the delight of New Dealers and the astonishment of legal observers, the Court, by a 5–4 vote, upheld the Wagner Act. Deploying a cir-

> *"The Roosevelt Court ushered in a new era in American jurisprudence, helping to build a powerful modern state while simultaneously protecting the civil liberties of minorities."*

cuitous logic, the majority held that unions served to maintain labor peace and prevent the disruption of interstate commerce; it was thus constitutional for the federal government to promote unionization through the mechanisms created in the Wagner Act. Justice Roberts, who had voted with the conservatives in overturning the NRA and the AAA, supported the majority decision, a change in position that came to be called "the switch in time that saved nine." Subsequent Court rulings continued in the same vein, upholding the Social Security Act and giving the federal government broad new latitude to intervene in and regulate economic affairs. Whether Roberts's shift was influenced by the pending threat of the Court-packing scheme is unclear, but there is no doubt that the Court had tacked in a new direction. Hugh Johnson, the former head of the NRA, wrote to Roosevelt that "I was taken for a ride on a chicken truck in Brooklyn two years ago and dumped out on a deserted highway and left for dead. It seems this was all a mistake."

The Supreme Court's shift took the wind out of the sails of the Court-packing scheme and prevented a confrontation between the executive and judicial branches. With the substantive war already won, Congress had little appetite for the controversial proposal, and by midsummer the president was forced to withdraw it. A month after the Court's decision on the NLRA, moreover, one of the conservative stalwarts, Justice Willis Van Devanter, announced his retirement, giving Roosevelt the opportunity to appoint liberal Alabama senator Hugo Black to the Court. By 1940, he had appointed four additional justices, including Frank Murphy, the former governor of Michigan, and Felix Frankfurter, the highly respected protégé of retiring justice Louis Brandeis. The new justices were far more open to innovation and an expansion of federal power than their predecessors had been; discarding the adherence to laissez-faire that had been the Court's hallmark for half a century, the Roosevelt Court ushered in a new era in American jurisprudence, helping to build a powerful modern state while simultaneously protecting the civil liberties of minorities.

THE EBBING OF REFORM

Roosevelt may have won the war over the Supreme Court, but the battles surrounding the Court-packing scheme left him tired and politically weakened. Sensing the president's new vulnerability—something almost unthinkable immediately after the 1936 election—a powerful conservative opposition, including many Democrats, emerged in Congress. Its members issued a "Manifesto" in late 1937 that condemned the sit-down strikes, expressed fear that the Roosevelt administration was creating a class of people permanently dependent on government welfare, demanded lower taxes and a balanced budget, and affirmed support for states' rights and private enterprise, both of which seemed imperiled by the expansion of the federal government.

Southern Democrats played a critical role in this resistance to the New Deal, because they feared that a powerful federal government committed to improving the lot of all Americans would inevitably interfere with the South's system of racial segregation and oppression. Although early New Deal programs had carefully tiptoed around matters of racial discrimination, those fears were not without cause. The president's wife, Eleanor—a niece of Theodore Roosevelt, who in the 1920s left behind the shallow social preoccupations of her upbringing to become an advocate of women's rights and an opponent of racial segregation—constantly pushed him toward more socially radical steps. Partly for this reason, the New Deal not only provided poor blacks with jobs in programs such as the PWA and the WPA, but gave educated African Americans a record-breaking number of government appointments. Roosevelt appointed the first black federal judge, William Hastie, and made the black educator and activist Mary McLeod Bethune director of Negro Affairs in the National Youth Administration. Bethune hosted meetings of African Americans who served in the Roosevelt administration (sometimes called the "black cabinet"), and used her friendship with Eleanor Roosevelt to promote African American causes. Eleanor Roosevelt, in short, formed ties with blacks that gave them unprecedented—if modest—access to the White House and helped win African American voters to the Democratic fold.

The president felt obliged to be more politically wary, as a conflict over a federal antilynching measure made grimly clear. The first years of the 1930s witnessed roughly 100 lynchings in which mobs, mostly in the South, not only killed but often tortured and mutilated blacks. In 1934, liberals in Congress introduced a bill, drawn up by the NAACP, that

"Eleanor Roosevelt, in short, formed ties with blacks that gave them unprecedented—if modest—access to the White House and helped win African American voters to the Democratic fold."

would have initiated federal prosecution for lynching and prescribed penalties for local officials who refused to prosecute lynchers. The president, prodded by his wife, favored the bill but refused to put his full political weight behind it. By virtue of their secure electoral base in a one-party region, southern Democrats had considerable seniority in Congress and consequently headed critical committees. It he alienated them, Roosevelt explained, "they will block every bill I ask Congress to pass to keep America from collapsing." The antilynching bill was stalled by a filibuster in the Senate until it was finally withdrawn in February 1938.

Despite their victory, southern Democrats looked suspiciously on any new initiatives from the Roosevelt administration. They were also aware that the climate of northern intellectual opinion about race was changing. Faith in eugenics, for example, was being supplanted by mounting evidence of the importance of cultural and social environments: Columbia University psychologist Otto Klineberg found that blacks living in the urban North scored higher on I.Q. tests than did some white rural southerners. And southerners knew that some ardent New Dealers stood poised to meddle with the South's caste system; labor unions, among others, were already active in efforts to abolish the poll tax in southern elections.

The result was a legislative stalemate. The president called a special session of Congress in November 1937 to consider a series of measures, none of which were enacted. In 1938, the administration managed to get Congress's consent to only two important measures. One, a farm bill, reenacted (with some minor changes) provisions of the old Agricultural Adjustment Act, which the Supreme Court had struck down but which it now seemed likely to endorse. It authorized the federal government to compensate farmers for limiting the amount of acreage planted and take other steps to keep market prices for agricultural goods from dropping below a fixed "parity" price. The second measure, the Fair Labor Standards Act of 1938, prohibited child labor and required industrial employers, after defined phase-in periods, to pay a minimum wage of 40 cents an hour and to honor a forty-hour work week. The act did not affect agricultural workers or domestic servants, and so had a minimal impact on low-wage black workers.

But could Roosevelt bring recovery and security to all Americans without addressing the situation in the South, which he characterized in a speech on July 4, 1938, as "the Nation's number one economic problem"? *The Report on Economic Conditions in the South,* commissioned by the president and released in August, highlighted the low living standards prevalent in the states of the old Confederacy and called for a national program to reduce the region's subordination to northern capital and integrate it into the national economy. Such a program—and perhaps all new programs—had no chance while southern conservatives remained in control of key congressional committees. As a result, Roosevelt actively intervened in the midterm elections of 1938, with disastrous consequences. The southern conservatives he opposed were triumphantly reelected; the liberals he supported lost. This personal defeat, combined with Republican gains in Congress (eight Senate seats and more than eighty seats in the House), stripped Roosevelt of the mandate he had earned in 1936. The Fair Labor Standards Act turned out to be the last New Deal measure to get through Congress.

The economy added to the president's problems. After the halting expansion of 1933–37, the country suddenly suffered a

Eleanor Roosevelt (speaking) alongside the black educator and activist Mary McLeod Bethune at a meeting on African American youth, 1939.

contraction with ominous resemblances to that of the Hoover administration. The stock market crashed in the fall of 1937; then industrial production nosedived, while unemployment surged. Some blamed Roosevelt's antibusiness campaign for undermining investors' confidence, while the president himself suggested that there was a conspiracy among his enemies to undermine the economy by cutting back capital investment—essentially a sit-down strike of the rich.

A group of committed young New Dealers such as Marriner Eccles, a former Utah banker now at the Federal Reserve, had another view. Impressed by the theories of British economist John Maynard Keynes, whose book *The General Theory of Employment, Interest, and Money* appeared in 1936, they ascribed the contraction to the mistaken policies of the Roosevelt administration itself. Keynes taught that two long-standing pillars of economic thought were, in fact, inaccurate. The first was that savings were identical to investment, a notion that underlay the impulse to balance budgets and to economize in hard times. The second was that employment levels were closely tied to wages, an idea that justified wage cuts when unemployment was rising—because cheaper labor costs would stimulate production. Keynes maintained instead that employment levels were determined primarily by the size of aggregate demand in the economy, and that savings did not necessarily promote investment. One key implication of these ideas was that governments could effectively respond to downturns in the business cycle not by tightening their belts but by spending money (to increase "aggregate demand"), even if that meant temporarily running deficits. This idea was not altogether novel—even Hoover had considered some form of deficit spending—but Keynes's work gave it a powerful intellectual rationale that began to have a great impact on the thinking of economists in the late 1930s.

If Keynes was right, then the Roosevelt administration had made serious errors in late 1936 and 1937. After incurring significant deficits in 1936 to fund the PWA and WPA and to pay veterans' bonuses, the administration cut back its expenditures sharply, as Roosevelt hoped that he might finally balance the federal budget; meanwhile, Social Security taxes kicked in for the first time. Consequently, the federal budget developed a surplus rather than a deficit, which served to reduce private expenditures and precipitate the contraction that began in the fall of 1937. According to this Keynesian reading, the solution was clear: more federal spending on a grand scale.

Roosevelt seemed to agree. But his administration was internally divided, with Secretary of the Treasury Henry Morgenthau publicly pledging to balance the federal budget and congressional conservatives firmly opposed to any more New Deal experiments. In the end, the spending initiatives the president took were far too small to make much difference, and the engine of New Deal reforms ground to a halt. The economy hobbled along for another two years until finally wartime expenditures (funded by enormous government deficits) pulled it out of its depressed state.

The Social Fabric

Not everything that happened in the 1930s was colored in depression gray. Despite the severity of the economic crisis and the often momentous conflicts going on in Washington, life went on. Social patterns that had been taking shape for decades continued unaffected or with only small detours. Scientists remained in their laboratories and novelists at their desks; New York Yankees "iron man" **Lou Gehrig** stayed on the field until he was felled by the disease that came to bear his name.

The birthrate of the nation's population, for example, continued to decline, as it had been doing since the middle of the nineteenth century. So, too, did the death rate, thanks in part to advances in medicine, such as the use of sulfa drugs, the development of a cure for pellagra (which afflicted many in the South), and the discovery of the importance of vitamins. The average life expectancy at birth rose from fifty-nine in 1930 to sixty-three in 1940.

The slowdown in immigration, begun in the teens, also continued; indeed, immigration fell off sufficiently that many of the quotas established in 1924 were not filled, and between 1931 and 1936 there was more return migration to Europe than immigration to the United States. In addition, many Mexican migrants returned to their homeland, some forced to do so by American officials who sought to lower the burden of relief-giving. (The latter half of the decade did, however, witness a significant movement of refugees from fascism to the United States, many of them well educated.) The slower flows of immigration helped those immigrants who were already in the country to become assimilated, while easing social tensions among immigrant groups and between immigrants and natives. Perhaps the foremost symbol of this shift was the election of the half-Jewish, half-Italian Fiorello La Guardia as mayor of New York in 1934.

Yankees first baseman Lou Gehrig, shown here on his baseball card, 1933.

Americans also became more educated, a perhaps ironic consequence of the Depression. Although some school systems were badly hurt in the early 1930s and many teachers did not receive their full back pay until World War II, high school enrollments rose, partly because young people decided to remain in school since they couldn't get jobs anyway. Something similar happened in colleges and universities where enrollments began to rise after a sharp dip early in the decade. By 1940, there were almost 1.5 million students on college campuses, most of them in less expensive, publicly supported schools. Not surprisingly, perhaps, a growing number were studying the social sciences and history.

Cultural trends were shaped by the Depression, although not always in straightforward ways. National mass culture became increasingly significant, as families listened to their radios for 4.5 hours per day, went to movies as often as they could, and read tabloid newspapers, which tripled their circulation between 1930 and 1940. Many filmmakers, playwrights, and writers devoted their energies to searing, thoughtful, and sometimes funny depictions of social conditions: Charlie Chaplin's classic *Modern Times* (1935) was a stunning portrait of the plight of the factory worker ricocheting between spells of unemployment and the machine-driven dehumanization of work; Par Lorenz's documentary *The Plow That Broke the Plains* captured the role of farm technology and the profit motive in setting the stage for the Dust Bowl. Yet much of popular culture was escapist, focusing on themes far removed from the realities of daily life. One of the most widely viewed films of the era was *Snow White and the Seven Dwarfs*. The tabloids were filled with stories about the love lives of entertainers and crimes of violence. The publishing sensation of the decade was the bland, cheery *Reader's Digest*, which increased its circulation from 250,000 to nearly 7 million; the best-selling novel of the decade was *Gone with the Wind*.

Advances in science and technology also marked the era. None was more important than the research of physicist Ernest O. Lawrence at the University of California at Berkeley. Funded by the federal government, the state of California, and private sources, Lawrence constructed a series of cyclotrons, or particle accelerators, that allowed him to investigate the nucleus of the atom; the cyclotron was also able to generate radioactive isotopes and neutrons that could be used for medical research and in cancer therapies. Although Lawrence's efforts were designed primarily for biomedical research, the knowledge of nuclear physics that resulted helped to set the stage for the atomic bomb project in World War II. It was also a harbinger of the big science enterprises that would become commonplace after the war. Lawrence was awarded the Nobel Prize in physics in 1939.

The 1930s were the decade when commercial aviation came of age. Building on a series of engineering advances of the 1920s, the two major manufacturers of aircraft, Boeing and Douglas, introduced passenger planes that were faster, quieter, and more efficient than any previous aircraft. The Douglas DC-3, which carried twenty-one passengers, became particularly popular, accounting for 80 percent of domestic air travel by 1938. At the same time, the Martin M-130 and later the Boeing Clipper began regular flights to convey mail and passengers across the oceans. Passenger service from San Francisco to the Philippines began in 1936, and by 1939 Pan Am was offering biweekly flights from the United States to England and France. To enhance the attractiveness of air travel, the airlines, led by United in 1930, introduced "air hostesses" to bring "home-making instincts" into the cabins. The hostesses had to meet carefully drawn qualifications of age, height, weight, and appearance.

The increasingly crowded skies—passenger traffic increased tenfold between 1932 and 1941—led to more regulations and concerted efforts to improve the safety of air travel. The first air-traffic control center went into operation in Newark, New Jersey, in 1935 and was soon followed by others. In 1938, Congress created the Civil Aeronautics Authority (CAA), which supervised all of civil aviation and had special authority to investigate accidents and recommend preventive measures. The CAA certified the training of airport and airline personnel who made decisions about weather conditions in which aircraft could safely fly.

A Martin M-130 in flight over San Francisco Bay, with the Golden Gate Bridge under construction below, mid-1930s.

Engineering advances also improved travel on the ground. Cars and trucks became cheaper, more reliable, and faster, and thanks to local, state, and federal construction projects, roads were dramatically improved. In 1940, the Pennsylvania Turnpike was completed, the first lengthy four-lane "superhighway" with no intersections. At the same time, urban public transportation systems began what would become a long-term decline in the quality and frequency of service.

Nowhere were technological changes more significant than on the nation's farms. Despite the Depression, the number of rubber-tired, gasoline-powered tractors in use doubled during the 1930s; they were particularly common in the corn belt and on large farms. Hybrid corn, developed through careful genetic selection in state agricultural experiment stations, became increasingly popular among midwestern farmers, in part because it facilitated the use of new corn-picking machines that worked best if the crop ripened all at once, stalks were strong and straight, and ears were at the same height off the ground. Hybrid corn was also more resistant to disease and insects. The spread of hybrid corn, however, increased the capital costs of farming, because it had to be purchased from seed companies (it had to be produced annually through artificial pollination). These technological advances in the corn belt, while contributing to increased productivity, drove small farmers from the land.

A harbinger of the same pattern appeared in the South, where the first successful cotton picker was patented in 1928 by two brothers named Rust. Field trials of the mechanical cotton picker in the mid-1930s demonstrated that—despite the skepticism of numerous authorities, including the secretary of agriculture—a machine actually could pick cotton. In the later 1930s, large farmers in Texas and Oklahoma began to purchase these machines, setting the stage for the widespread mechanization of cotton picking in the postwar South.

Muddling Through

Few American presidents have been as loved or as hated as Franklin Roosevelt; and few periods have been as closely identified with a political leader, or with national politics, as

> *"Few American presidents have been as loved or hated as Franklin Roosevelt; and few periods have been as closely identified with a political leader, or with national politics, as were the years between 1933 and 1940."*

were the years between 1933 and 1940. Roosevelt took office when the nation was crying out, almost desperately, for leadership, and he navigated the ship of state through some of the most troubled waters in the nation's history. The only man ever elected president four times, the charismatic and enigmatic Roosevelt—even his closest advisers often found him inscrutable—was the most important American politician of the twentieth century. Democratic successors from Harry Truman to John Kennedy to Lyndon Johnson claimed to be his heir; even the far more conservative Ronald Reagan kept a photograph of Roosevelt in his office.

Although Roosevelt did not succeed in ending the Great Depression—only World War II did that—the achievements of the New Deal were unquestionably substantial. To combat the Depression, Roosevelt presided over, indeed demanded, an immense increase in the size, authority, and influence of the federal government. With the nation watching (and listening on the radio), Washington assumed responsibility for the well-being of the economy and the welfare of the populace. The federal government became the employer of last resort to millions; it regulated financial institutions to steady the performance of banks and the stock market; it protected the owners of homes and farms; it stimulated economic and technological development in rural areas; it instituted a national minimum wage and a mandatory forty-hour work week. Inviting new constituencies into the halls of power, the government became less the representative of the business community (which it had been under long years of Republican rule) and more a "broker state" balancing the claims of diverse organized interest groups.

The New Deal also created institutions grounded in principles that reshaped the social compact linking the state to its citizenry. The Social Security Act, for example, certified the right of Americans to public support when they were jobless, when they were past their productive years, and if they were single mothers with dependent children. Through the Wagner Act, Americans were also guaranteed the right to form independent unions and not be punished for seeking to do so. Farmers meanwhile received federal aid to cope with a problem that had been building for decades: the overcapacity of agriculture. New Deal agricultural policy, although not exactly what the Populists of the 1890s had in mind, constituted a durable public commitment to intervene in the market to preserve the livelihoods and way of life of many farmers.

There were, to be sure, limits to the changes wrought by the New Deal, as both contemporaries and historians have pointed out. Overwhelmingly focused on economic issues, the Roosevelt administration paid little attention to race and tolerated legal discrimination against blacks in the South, as well as Hispanics and Asians. Although its concern for the disadvantaged produced enough gains for African Americans to draw them into the Democratic Party, the New Deal never challenged the racial boundaries drawn so starkly across the South, and its programs, responsive to the demands of southern white Democrats, often reinforced those boundaries. The outcry against the Supreme Court because of the 1935 *Schechter* decision had no parallel when the same Supreme Court, in the same year, upheld the constitutionality of the white primary in Texas.

Nor did the New Deal significantly diminish the power of large corporations. For all of Roosevelt's rhetoric against the greed of capitalists, the economic "royalists" clung to their ermine. Major banks continued to dominate the financial sector, and the extent of corporate concentration actually increased in the 1930s. The twenty largest oil companies, for example, increased their share of both crude oil production and refining capacity. By 1940, 48 percent of all employees in the nation worked for 1 percent of all employers. Similarly, in agriculture, the average size of farm units increased, as did the percentage of farms that relied on hired workers. A "broker state" may well have been formed, but labor and agriculture remained junior partners in the joint venture. As important, the poorest and most vulnerable workers, in industry and on farms, were excluded from many of the protections the New Deal had to offer, including the Wagner Act and the Fair Labor Standards Act. For all of the hostility of conservatives, the New Deal did not much alter the sway of free enterprise or the distribution of economic power.

The New Deal was thus not nearly as revolutionary as many of its most ardent supporters and ferocious detractors claimed it to be. But in critical respects, that was precisely its point—and its goal. As the bleak years of the Depression wore on, analysts of American and European societies came to doubt the viability of either capitalism or democracy and especially capitalist democracies. Fascist movements flourished in parts of Europe, socialist parties gained strength in many parts of the world, and the Soviet Union stood for some as a model of the future. Centrists and liberals alike ex-

Chronology	
October 29, 1929	"Black Tuesday" on Wall Street.
1932–36	Dust Bowl plagues the plains states.
1933	Agricultural Adjustment Act.
	Tennessee Valley Authority.
	Federal Deposit Insurance Corporation.
	National Recovery Administration.
1935	Works Projects Administration.
	Wagner Act.
	Social Security Act.
February 1937	President Roosevelt proposes Court-packing scheme.
1938	Fair Labor Standards Act.
1939	Pan Am flies biweekly from the United States to Europe.

perienced a loss of faith. In 1935, the liberal magazine *The New Republic,* founded during the Progressive Era by Walter Lippmann and Herbert Croly, observed that the choice facing the nation was between the "miseries of an essentially unregulated capitalist" or "socialism": "there is no longer a middle course." The historic achievement of the New Deal was to demonstrate that there was indeed a middle course, that an active, innovative state, at least partially responsive to the demands of different social groups and centers of power, could preserve the basic institutions of capitalism and political democracy that Americans had erected over the course of a century and a half.

Suggested Reading

Malcolm Cowley, *The Dream of the Golden Mountain: Remembering the 1930's* (1980)

Melvyn Dubofsky and Warren R. Van Tine, *An Oral History of the Great Depression* (1970)

Barry Eichengreen, *Golden Fetters: The Gold Standard and the Great Depression* (1922)

Steve Fraser and Gary Gerstle, *The Rise and Fall of the New Deal Order* (1989)

David Kennedy, *Freedom from Fear: The American People in Depression and War, 1929–1945* (1999)

Donald Worster, *Dust Bowl: The Southern Plains in the 1930's* (1979)

Chapter 25

WHIRLPOOL OF WAR:

1932-1941

Pearl Harbor, Hawaii, December 7, 1941.

QUESTIONS

■ What was the direction of foreign policy early in the Roosevelt administration?

■ What were the initial American reactions to aggressions by Germany and Japan?

■ How was America drawn into the developing war in Europe and Asia?

Shortly after noon on January 30, 1933, a little more than a month before Franklin Roosevelt's first inauguration, the president of the Weimar Republic appointed Adolf Hitler chancellor of the German government. A onetime derelict and World War I army corporal, Hitler headed the Nazi Party (German shorthand for National Socialist German Workers' Party). He was a charismatic figure, a demagogic orator, ruthless politician, and self-styled revolutionary who hated Jews, Weimar democracy, and the Versailles Treaty (1919), which had demilitarized Germany and reconstructed the political map of the Continent. That night, tens of thousands of storm troopers celebrated in a torchlight parade, strutting in tight, jackbooted columns before cheering onlookers. Hitler

Hitler in Nuremberg, September 1935.

danced joyfully while watching the spectacle from an open window of the Chancellory, raising his arm in the Nazi salute to the passing troops. The French ambassador remembered watching the procession: "The river of fire flowed past the French Embassy whence, with heavy heart and filled with foreboding, I watched its luminous wake."

Germany, its economy collapsing, was rife with fears and resentments. Hitler, whom people called *Der Führer*—the leader—attributed Germany's suffering to the Allies, Communists, and Jews. He had won popular support by promising to restore Germany to its former glory and prosperity and by relying on the Nazi Party's storm troopers, a private army of bullies in brown shirts, to intimidate dissenters of all stripes. The Nazis held only a plurality of seats in the Reichstag (the German national legislature) when Hitler was appointed chancellor. They quickly conspired to take complete control of the government, burning the Reichstag building, blaming the conflagration on Communists, and, through arrests, removing enough of them from the Reichstag to give the Nazi Party a majority. In March 1933, the Reichstag, now Hitler's Reichstag, granted him dictatorial powers. With the aid of a secret political police known as the Gestapo, **Hitler's regime** terrorized Jews, destroyed civil liberties and civil rights, and crushed all opposition with a fearsome combination of law, intimidation, force, and torture.

Hitler called his Germany the "Third Reich"—meaning the third German empire, following the Holy Roman Empire and the empire established by Bismarck—and said that it would last a thousand years. He made no secret of his aim to regain the territory Germany had lost in Central Europe as a result of the post–World War I settlement. The Nazi government repudiated the Versailles Treaty, withdrew from the League of Nations, and initiated a program of accelerated rearmament. In 1936, Hitler sent the Wehrmacht, his nation's army, into the Rhineland, the German industrial region that bordered France and Belgium, nullifying its demilitarization under the Versailles Treaty.

The threat to peace posed by Hitler was enlarged by Benito Mussolini, the fascist dictator of Italy, and by militant nationalists in Japan. A onetime socialist who had come to power in 1922, Mussolini was a dynamic though pompous figure of grandiose pretensions. In political and economic practice, his fascism constituted an authoritarian regime in which the state managed private property, suppressed Communists, Socialists, and even organized labor, and celebrated nationalism and imperialism. In 1935, Mussolini's troops struck from Italian Somalia into Ethiopia, an action of revenge that Mussolini had promised for the humiliating defeat they had suffered forty years before and that pitted bombers and fighters against villages and horsemen.

In Japan all the while, the militant nationalists, including powerful members of the military, advanced imperial ambitions in China. They had increasingly challenged the legitimacy of the settlements following World War I, especially the terms of the treaties produced by the Washington Conference in 1922 and signed by, among other nations, the United States, Britain, and Japan. Taken together, the treaties established a Washington Conference system that kept British and American naval power superior to Japan's, and sought to integrate China into the framework of international democratic capitalism and uphold that country's independence. Japanese nationalists held that the system merely maintained Western imperial interests in Asia and prevented Japan from pursuing legitimate territorial and economic aims.

In China, the government of Jiang Jieshi (Chiang Kai-shek) progressively consolidated its power while tolerating the continuation of the special privileges to which the Western powers were long accustomed. Japan enjoyed similar arrangements, but the depression intensified its hunger for the resources it might obtain in Manchuria, which already supplied major fractions of its pig iron and coal. In 1931, Japanese forces stationed in Manchuria had attacked the local Chinese troops and occupied the region, earning worldwide censure while establishing a puppet state called Manchukuo. In March 1933, Japan withdrew from the League of Nations, which had refused to recognize the new political entity. The next year, denouncing the limitations imposed by the Wash-

"In foreign as in domestic affairs, Roosevelt was a pragmatist, an innovator who refused to be bound by any single idea."

ington Naval Treaty of 1922 and its extension in the London Naval Treaty of 1930, Japan announced that it intended to abrogate the agreement.

The American people initially responded to the trends in Europe and Asia by intensifying their post-Versailles withdrawal from foreign affairs. As many of them saw it, the sacrifices of World War I had not made the world safe for democracy. If Europeans now wanted to start killing each other again, the United States had no obligation to stop them. The depth of their commitment to isolationism was made clear when in early 1935 the Senate defeated Roosevelt's proposal that the United States join the World Court, located at The Hague, in the Netherlands. In the heated debate on the measure, Senator Thomas D. Schall of Minnesota proclaimed, "To hell with Europe and the rest of those nations!"

During the 1930s, the power of isolationist sentiment handicapped Roosevelt's conduct of foreign policy. He was an internationalist, but he was compelled to walk a fine line between, on the one hand, protecting the interests of the United States and, on the other, doing so without defying domestic preferences. His capacity for leadership was increasingly taxed as events abroad bitterly divided Americans over the course for their country in a world marching toward war.

Encouraging Peace

ROOSEVELT'S BRAND OF IDEALISM

Roosevelt was at heart a Wilsonian idealist, an enthusiast of the League of Nations who wished to use power in the service of achieving and maintaining a just international order. In 1932, however, conceding to popular sentiment in the interest of winning the presidency, he publicly turned against American involvement in the League. He nevertheless appointed a fellow Wilsonian, Cordell Hull, as his secretary of state. And like his distant cousin Theodore Roosevelt, he appreciated the force of the big stick. His service as assistant secretary of the navy under President Wilson had sharpened his understanding of the realities of power. In foreign as in domestic affairs, Roosevelt was a pragmatist, an innovator who refused to be bound by any single idea. He once wrote to Hull, "In pure theory, you and I think alike but every once in a while we have to modify principle to meet a hard and disagreeable fact!"

Roosevelt realized that the hard facts of the airplane and the submarine were undermining the ability of the United States to rely for its security on the protective moats of the Atlantic and Pacific Oceans. He believed that the United States continued to have a stake in a stable world order, that its security remained linked to the international configurations established by the Versailles Treaty and the Washington Conference system. He recognized that by contesting the postwar international arrangements, Germany, Italy, and Japan all threatened American interests and security.

TRUSTING IN TRADE

Roosevelt's foreign policy early in his presidency melded concerns for national security with the principles of internationalism and the cause of economic recovery at home. Although he had torpedoed the London Economic Conference by refusing to participate in the stabilization of currencies, he recognized that the world's nations were interdependent; that the United States was intimately connected to many of them by ties of commerce, culture, and kinship; and that his country's economic well-being would ultimately be affected by the revival of their economies.

In the presidential campaign, he spoke of the need for tariff reduction. In March 1934, he made good on the implied promise, seeing to the passage of a trade bill that gave the president authority to negotiate reciprocal trade agreements, including tariff reductions that could be extended to any country that granted the United States most-favored-nation treatment or did not discriminate against it.

Shortly after entering the White House, Roosevelt began taking steps to grant recognition to the Soviet Union, which had been withheld following the Bolshevik Revolution with the aim of morally condemning and strategically isolating the Communist state. Roosevelt hoped that a rapprochement might help discourage Japanese aggressiveness and that the normalization of relations would facilitate renewed trade with the Soviets, which had plummeted since 1930. Opposition to recognition was strong among conservatives, Catholics, and labor leaders, many of whom were staunch anti-Communists. To defuse the opposition, the president obtained Soviet promises to forgo subversive activities in the United States and to guarantee religious freedom to Americans in the USSR. However, the formal recognition extended

to Soviet Russia in 1933 proved to be what one historian has called "an event of monumental unimportance" because it did little to revive trade, halt Soviet efforts at internal subversion, or discourage Japanese militancy.

THE GOOD NEIGHBOR POLICY

By 1933, trade with Latin America had fallen to roughly a quarter of the level of 1929. Roosevelt wanted to revive it and also to overcome long-standing suspicions in the region that the United States was a bad neighbor. In one of the few references to foreign affairs in his inaugural address, he declared that he would "dedicate this Nation to the policy of the good neighbor"—an initiative that was apparently intended to apply to the world in general but that soon came to connote the administration's approach specifically to Latin America.

A major source of suspicion in Latin America was the United States' past interventions in the internal affairs of countries in the region—as, for example, in Haiti in 1925. Cubans greatly resented the Platt amendment, which at the high-handed insistence of the United States had been incorporated into the new Cuban constitution in 1901 and which authorized the United States to intervene in Cuban affairs. The Hoover administration, repudiating Theodore Roosevelt's corollary to the Monroe Doctrine, had adopted a policy of nonintervention. It had also agreed to withdraw the marines in Haiti. On Pan American Day, in April 1933, Franklin Roosevelt declared that he respected the independence of the American republics and intended to deal with them on a basis of equality and cooperation.

Roosevelt's commitment to nonintervention was quickly tested in Cuba, where fighting was breaking out against the oppressive dictatorship of Gerardo Machado. Early in August 1933, pressured by Sumner Welles, the ambassador to Cuba, Machado resigned. His successor was quickly overthrown by an army coup. Welles urged armed intervention, but Roosevelt refused to send troops, although he agreed to a show of warships. Roosevelt emphasized to envoys from Mexico, Brazil, Chile, and Argentina that he had no desire to intervene in Cuba—marking the first time a president discussed U.S. policy for the hemisphere with Latin American diplomats. However, when in mid-September Cuban revolutionists formed another government, the United States declined to recognize it and adopted a wait-and-see attitude for its Cuban policy, including whether it would renegotiate the Platt amendment.

Anti-Yankee animosity was evident when, in December 1933, the Seventh International Conference of American States met at Montevideo, Uruguay. Defusing the atmosphere, the Roosevelt administration accepted, with only minor caveats, a declaration holding that no state had the right to intervene in another's "internal or external affairs." At Secretary of State Hull's urging, Roosevelt also endorsed a statement favoring the long-term liberalization of trade policy in the Americas. Hull told the president afterward that the conference had achieved a better state of good feeling toward the United States than any he had seen in a generation.

The United States soon showed that it took its Montevideo pledges seriously. When a more conservative government came to power in Cuba, the Roosevelt administration recognized it, initiated negotiations to reduce the Cuban sugar tariff, and approved a loan of $4 million to help Cuban economic recovery. In May 1934, the United States concluded a treaty with Cuba that abrogated the Platt amendment, including its right to intervene in Cuba, but that allowed it to keep the American naval base at Guantánamo Bay. That summer, Roosevelt visited the Caribbean—a Good Neighbor trip, he called it—announcing, in Haiti, an advance in the scheduled withdrawal date of the marines and, in Panama, that he would resolve all outstanding U.S.–Panamanian problems.

He was the first sitting president to cross Panama or set foot in South America. During the next two years, the United States entered reciprocal trade agreements with five Latin states, opened trade negotiations with nine others, and concluded a new treaty with Panama that, modifying the agreement of 1903, rescinded American rights to intervene unilaterally and take control of Panamanian territory.

In 1936, Roosevelt initiated a meeting of the Latin American states in Buenos Aires to devise ways to safeguard peace among themselves. At home, he explained that his aim was to "isolate" America from war, noting that he had seen the blood and agony of armed conflict, and asserting, "I hate war." The president attended the conference himself, arriving to a tumultuously enthusiastic reception. Although the conference did not give Roosevelt all he wanted, it agreed to inter-American consultation in case the hemisphere was threatened.

Avoiding the Disagreeable

JAPANESE BELLIGERENCE

Roosevelt tried to invoke the authority of law and agreements against Japan's aggressive behavior in the Far East. When the Japanese had occupied Manchuria in 1931, Hoover's secretary of state, Henry L. Stimson, declared that the United States would not recognize Japanese control of the region because it violated international law. Roosevelt endorsed the so-called Stimson Doctrine, explaining that "American foreign policy must uphold the sanctity of international treaties." Yet he had reason to think that such moral condemnation alone was inadequate to halt aggression. In May 1933, Joseph Grew, the American ambassador in Tokyo, wrote him that "Japan probably has the most complete, well-balanced, coordinated and therefore powerful fighting machine in the world today," adding that the Japanese armed forces considered the United States a "potential enemy" because it stood in the path of Japanese expansion.

To offset the increasing Japanese naval strength, in June 1933 Roosevelt directed that $238 million of funds appropriated for public works be used to construct cruisers and aircraft carriers. Added to a naval building program that Congress had already authorized, the order made for the largest peacetime naval construction program since before World War I. At the beginning of 1934, Roosevelt threw his

This cartoonist points out that Japan's seizure of Manchuria violated multiple international treaties and agreements.

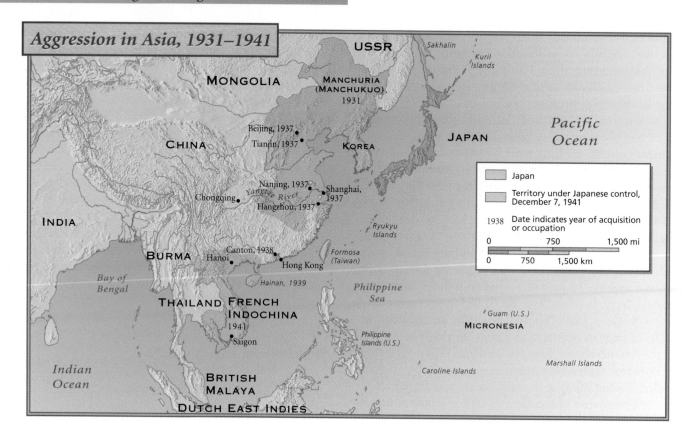

Aggression in Asia, 1931–1941

support to a congressional bill that would authorize building the United States fleet up to the Washington Conference limits. While seeking peace, the president intended to bolster his country's ability to defend itself against aggression.

Still, Roosevelt did not want his naval construction program to alienate either Japan or the sizable pacifist movement in the United States. He insisted that in the end he hoped to achieve ongoing limitation of and possibly reductions in naval armaments in the renewed negotiations of the Washington and London Naval Treaties. He feared that a departure from the treaty ratios would foster a naval arms race. In October 1934, aware that the Japanese would demand equality for their fleet, Roosevelt publicly declared, "Governments impelled by common sense and the good of humanity ought to seek Treaties reducing armaments; they have no right to seek Treaties increasing armaments."

Nevertheless, in January 1936, Japan ended its adherence to the naval treaties, walking out of the London Naval Conference after having been refused equivalence for its fleet with the major Western powers. That year, Japan also joined Hitler's Germany and Mussolini's Italy in a pact pledging the

three countries to resist the efforts of the Communist International to incite revolutions.

War in China. Japan soon dashed Roosevelt's dimming hopes for peace in Asia. In July 1937, Japan opened undeclared war on China, contending that given the Western imperial presence there, it deserved more land and resources as a matter of international justice. Striking southward, Japanese soldiers captured the key cities of Beijing, Tianjin, Shanghai, and Hangzhou as well as the national capital, Nanjing, on the Yangtze River, where they raped untold numbers of women and massacred some 200,000 civilians. In December, Japanese planes attacked British and American ships lying in the river, sinking the American gunboat *Panay*, which was evacuating American officials from the city. The Japanese government quickly apologized, explaining that the assault was unauthorized, the responsible commander was being recalled, and indemnities would be forthcoming. But it also demanded that henceforth China subordinate itself politically and economically to Tokyo. In November 1938, Japan rejected the long-standing American-backed policy of the Open

Door in China, announcing that it would create a "new order" in East Asia that would knit Manchukuo, China, and Japan into a cooperative economic and cultural bloc.

The Chinese government of Jiang Jieshi (Chiang Kai-shek) refused to submit. After the Japanese occupied the eastern region of China in 1937, Jiang had moved his capital to Chongqing (Chungking), in the interior, and continued to fight in collaboration with the Communist forces led by Mao Zedong (Mao Tse-tung). Formerly antagonists of Jiang, the Chinese Communists allied themselves with him against the Japanese—partly because of the doctrine of the Popular Front, which called for Communists to join with other enemies of fascism, and partly because they bitterly resented the Japanese invasion of their territory.

NAZI AGGRESSIONS

In the meantime, the course of events in Europe turned increasingly alarming. In July 1935, civil war broke out in Spain, pitting fascist rebel forces under General Francisco Franco against forces loyal to the country's democratic government. While the Soviet Union assisted the Loyalists with supplies and international brigades, Italy and Germany provided guns, tanks, planes, and some 60,000 troops to Franco, making the Spanish Civil War into a kind of testing ground for the newest weapons and techniques of warfare and for a contest of arms against fascist dictatorship.

In Germany, Hitler pressed to an extreme the kind of wrongheaded and racist biology that had undergirded the eugenics movement in the United States (see Chapters 19, 22, 23). By 1937, the Nazi government had sterilized more than 225,000 people found to suffer from alleged hereditary diseases and disorders, including feeblemindedness, schizophrenia, epilepsy, blindness, drug or alcohol addiction, and physical deformities that interfered with locomotion or were grossly offensive. Nazi Germany celebrated the so-called Aryan race, whose members, it claimed, constituted the genuine German *Volk*, and castigated all others, especially Jews, who, it held, were inferior to Aryans and were responsible, along with Communists, for Germany's economic breakdown.

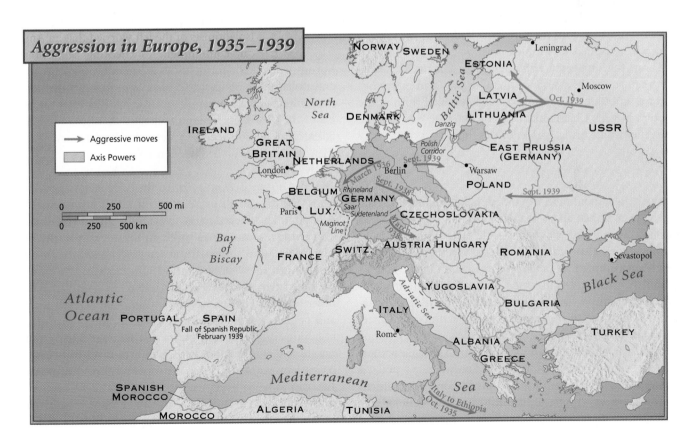

Aggression in Europe, 1935–1939

Aggressive moves
Axis Powers

In a set of laws enacted at Nuremberg in September 1935, the Nazis abolished citizenship for German Jews, and, to the end of preventing "racial pollution," prohibited their intermarriage with non-Jews while making sexual relations between Aryans and Jews punishable by death. In November 1938, the Nazis barred Jews from theaters, concerts, high schools, and universities. In retaliation for a teenage Jew's murdering a German foreign officer in Paris on November 7, Hitler fined the Jews of Germany a billion marks. In the darkness between November 9 and 10—a night people afterward called *Kristallnacht*, the "night of broken glass"—Nazi sympathizers throughout Germany and Austria burned synagogues, vandalized Jewish residences, and smashed Jewish shops and businesses.

Earlier that year, in March, Hitler had extended his racist dictatorship to the south, annexing Austria, and in September he plunged Europe into crisis by demanding the absorption into the Third Reich of the German-speaking portion of Czechoslovakia, the Sudetenland. As tensions mounted, the leaders of Europe convened in Munich. Anxious to avoid war, they appeased Hitler, allowing him the Sudetenland in return for his assurance that Germany had no further territorial ambitions. Returning to England, the British prime minister, Neville Chamberlain, predicted that the Munich Conference would bring "peace for our time."

"In the darkness between November 9 and 10—a night people afterward called Kristallnacht, *the 'night of broken glass'— Nazi sympathizers throughout Germany and Austria burned synagogues, vandalized Jewish residences, and smashed Jewish shops and businesses."*

THE INGREDIENTS OF ISOLATIONISM

Even as Hitler's dominion expanded, Japan assaulted China, and civil war ripped apart Spain, most Americans remained unwilling to confront the disagreeable facts so distant from their shores. In a speech in Chicago in October 1937, Roosevelt was prompted by Japan's recent march into China to warn that war was a dangerous "contagion" and that the world community would be warranted in imposing a "quarantine" against nations that spread the infection of violence. Isolationists denounced the quarantine idea, reminding Roosevelt of their power and compelling him to shelve mention of interventionism for the time being. According to a poll, 73 percent of Americans supported a constitutional amendment that would, except in case of invasion, require a national referendum for a declaration of war.

The isolationists of the period comprised a coalition of disparate, often overlapping groups. They were strong in the Midwest, where many people tended to be suspicious of internationalists on the Eastern Seaboard. However, isolationist attitudes were prevalent in every region of the country and were well represented across the political spectrum. They drew support from ethnic minority groups such as Irish Americans and German Americans, resistant to policies that might favor Britain or disfavor Germany; from antagonists of the Soviet Union like Joseph Kennedy, the father of the future president, who considered Germany a bulwark against the spread of Communism; from fascist sympathizers and anti-Semites, the kind of people who called Roosevelt's reforms the "Jew Deal"; but also from many of the New Deal's warmest supporters, liberals in both parties who abhorred violence.

Nationalists and pacifists found common ground in opposition to involvement in European militarism. Antiwar sentiment was widespread among women, clerics, and students. Isolationists of the left worried that an American commitment to checking aggression in Europe would kill reform, just as it had done in World War I, and isolationists of all stripes were apprehensive that an activist internationalism would enlarge the discretionary powers of the president, raising the danger that he could tilt the country away from genuine neutrality and toward war, as they believed Wilson had done in 1917.

Fear of Military Technologies. To the large majority of Americans, the bloodbath of World War I had been more than enough. Many flocked to see the antiwar film *All Quiet on the Western Front,* which was based on the German writer Erich Maria Remarque's popular antiwar novel and won an Academy Award in 1930. Since the 1920s, dozens of works had predicted that the advance of technology would make another war into an even worse conflagration. Military analysts and popular writers raised the specter of long-range aircraft bombing cities, including New York, Chicago, Detroit, Pittsburgh, and Washington, with high explosives or poison gas or, perhaps worse—if H. G. Wells's 1914 novel *The World Set Free* was to be believed—atomic weapons. To be sure, in the mid-1930s no one knew how to obtain the explosive release of atomic energy; and in 1925, the United States and forty other countries had signed the Geneva Protocol, condemning gas warfare and prohibiting its use. But Japan had refused to ratify the protocol, and so had the U.S. Senate, which found itself inundated with telegrams against the agreement from veterans, surgeons, and chemists.

The world glimpsed the realities of air attack when Italy, which had subscribed to the protocol, dropped 500-pound bombs on Ethiopian towns; the bombs sprayed mustard gas ubiquitously from 200 feet above the ground, killing numerous women and children as well as an estimated 15,000 soldiers. The British prime minister remarked apprehensively that "if a great European nation, in spite of having given its signature to the Geneva Protocol against the use of such gases, employs them in Africa, what guarantee have we that they may not be used in Europe?" During the Spanish Civil War, Italian and German planes bombed Spanish cities with high explosives, and the Japanese waged war from the air against Chinese cities. The air assaults in both countries were condemned in the United States, where a New York Times reporter declared that bombers "could destroy centuries of civilization in a few minutes." In an article in the widely read magazine Life in 1939, the humorist James Thurber deployed his signature irony in writing of a future war: "This time destruction was so complete, that nothing at all was left in the world, except one man, and one woman, and one flower."

Claims of Past Mistakes. Like Woodrow Wilson, many Americans in 1917 judged that the United States had a genuine stake in maintaining what the kaiser's government threatened: freedom of the seas and a stable balance of power in Europe. But while later generations tended to ratify their judgment, during the 1930s it was sharply challenged. Books and articles like the liberal journalist Walter Millis's The Road to War, a best-seller in 1935, argued that the country had been misled into World War I. According to this view, French and British propaganda had disposed the American public to favor the Allies by falsely portraying the Germans as monstrous, ready to burn libraries and kill innocent civilians, including those traveling on passenger liners like the Lusitania. American munitions makers and bankers were characterized as "merchants of death," who beginning in 1914 had in effect made the United States a silent partner of the Allied war effort. They were charged with having supplied the French and British with guns and credit, and then having secretly enlisted the American government to protect their investments. Such views were fueled by the public hearings that

Senator Gerald P. Nye of North Dakota held from 1934 to 1936 to investigate the munitions industry. The Nye hearings produced months of headline stories, exposed hard evidence of American arms sales to whatever nation in the world would buy them, and revealed details of financial dealings between international bankers, notably the House of Morgan, and the American and Allied governments.

Expanding on the kind of economic thinking manifest in the Nye hearings, liberal analysts like the historian Charles Beard argued that the commitment to maintaining open markets for American goods in Europe and Asia inevitably threatened to draw the country into war. To be sure, the country did have a stake in open markets, and the Roosevelt administration regarded the expansion of exports as an important instrument of economic recovery. For example, the United States held first place in China's foreign trade. Still, its investments in Japan were twice those in China and its commerce with Japan three times greater; it had an interest in remaining friendly with Japan. That interest was increasingly overridden by, among other things, widespread outrage at Japanese aggression. But if economics was not the whole story of American foreign policy, during the depression of the 1930s, when many of the country's troubles were attributed to greedy businessmen, arguments like Beard's commanded a powerful following.

LEGISLATING NEUTRALITY

In 1935, with the aim of avoiding the entanglements believed to have led the United States into war in 1917, Congress passed the first in a **series of Neutrality Acts.** As expanded in 1936, the legislation prohibited the sale to belligerents of implements of war as well as their transportation by American ships. It also forbade American loans and credits to belligerent nations and outlawed shipments of war materials to either side in the Spanish Civil War.

Critics pointed out that the neutrality laws were not, in their effects, genuinely neutral. They favored parties at war that were militarily strong and thus did not need to purchase war supplies abroad, and they disfavored parties that were militarily weak—for example, the Loyalists in Spain—and did need to purchase them. Renewing the Neutrality Act in 1937, Congress added to the previous measures a mandate forbidding travel by Americans on the vessels of nations at war, but it also enacted so-called "cash-and-carry" provisions, which permitted the export to belligerents of certain nonmilitary goods so long as they were sold for cash and carried away in ships that did not sail under the American flag. Like the rigid neutrality measures, cash-and-carry was not strictly neutral in its consequences. It gave a boost to Britain, with its powerful navy and substantial cash reserves, but it also favored Japan, which enjoyed similar advantages, in its war against China—and thus heightened the threat to U.S. interests in Asia.

In the spring of 1938, a number of Americans were growing distressed by the declining fortunes of the Loyalists in Spain. Young volunteers went to Spain as members of the Abraham Lincoln Brigade to fight for the republican cause, and influential senators, including Gerald P. Nye, suggested that the Neutrality Act ought to be revised to lift the embargo on arms sales there. Roosevelt declined to support the move, mindful that the Loyalists had no money to buy arms and that it would cost the Democrats many Catholic votes in the upcoming congressional elections, since Franco enjoyed significant support among the American Catholic hierarchy.

THE REFUGEE QUESTION

The plight of refugees from Hitler's Europe did little to diminish the insular nationalism at work in the United States. The Nazis had been encouraging the emigration of Jews, and Hitler began expelling them from Austria after annexing the country in March 1938, swelling the flood of refugees still further. Hitler's strongmen forced numerous Jewish scholars and scientists out of German universities and cultural institutions. Nazi officials justified the dismissals as a kind of purification. They maintained with Philipp Lenard, a German physicist, Nobel laureate, and supporter of the Nazis, that science "is racial and conditioned by blood"; that Einstein's physics was "Jewish physics" and as such "merely an illusion—a perversion of basic Aryan physics." Between 1933 and 1938, about 60,000 people fled Germany, Austria, and Italy for the United States. The immigrants included distinguished writers, artists, architects, musicians, scholars, and scientists, many of them aided in their flight by emergency assistance committees in Britain and the United States. Among them were the social psychologist Theodor W. Adorno, the political theorist Hannah Arendt, the psychoanalyst Karen Horney, the novelist Thomas Mann, the architect Walter Gropius, the musician Wanda Landowska, the biologist Salvador Luria, the economist Oskar Morgenstern, the composer Igor Stravinsky, and the physicist Enrico Fermi, whose wife was Jewish.

Together the refugee scholars and scientists greatly enriched American life—those in physics with the power of their mathematical techniques, experimental imagination, and frequently philosophical approach to the analysis of natural phenomena. For example, soon after arriving at Cornell University, Hans Bethe, a virtuoso in mathematical physics, decided that his colleagues needed an up-to-date summary of nuclear phenomena, especially on the theoretical side. Week after week, Bethe sat beneath a dim light, a pile of blank paper on one side and a pile of his completed text on the other, and plowed steadily through the entire corpus of nuclear studies, clarifying what was known, spotlighting what was not. In the course of two years, he produced a formidably comprehensive survey that people called "Bethe's bible" and that was soon to be found on the desk of virtually every nuclear physicist in the United States.

Many other Europeans whose only distinction was a desire to live in freedom hoped to emigrate from Nazi-controlled areas, but the welcome extended to refugees was limited everywhere, including the United States. American consular officials in Europe applied the rules of entry so strictly that even fewer refugees were being admitted than the restrictive immigration law of 1924 allowed. Congressman Emanuel Celler of Brooklyn snapped that the State Department had a "heartbeat muffled in protocol." However, the department only mirrored public sentiment: opinion polls showed strong resistance to any increase in immigration. The opposition arose partly from widespread anti-Semitism in the United States, partly from worries on the part of some American Jews that more immigrants would provoke more anti-Semitism, and partly from the fear that newcomers would take jobs that Americans wanted for themselves.

Roosevelt was appalled by the Nazi persecutions, telling the press after *Kristallnacht,* "I myself could scarcely believe that such things could occur in a twentieth-century civilization." But judging it politically futile to attempt a change in the immigration laws, he sought instead to liberalize their administration. In 1936, he ordered American consulates to afford the refugees crowding their offices "the most humane treatment under the law." Trying to ensure that the German and Austrian quotas were fully used, he arranged for 15,000 German and Austrian refugees on visitors' permits to remain in the United States.

But Roosevelt's efforts on behalf of refugees were limited. In 1938, at his invitation, a conference convened at Evian-les-Bains, in France, to seek an international solution to their

Among the refugees who fled fascist Europe in the 1930s (from left): harpsichordist Wanda Landowska, physicist Enrico Fermi, architect Walter Gropius, and physicist Hans Bethe.

plight, but it produced nothing of consequence. Roosevelt himself, his eye evidently on public opinion at home, specified that "no country would be expected or asked to receive a greater number of emigrants than is permitted by existing legislation." In 1939, although some 27,000 German and Austrian refugees arrived in America, Congress blocked a change in the immigration quotas that would have allowed the entry of 20,000 German refugee children from Europe, many of whom were Jews. Local consulates and immigration offices were often unaccommodating. In June 1939, the *St. Louis* carried 900 Jewish refugees to Havana, where it was denied a permit to land, then proceeded to Ft. Lauderdale, Florida, where immigration officials refused its passengers permission to disembark. The ship was finally forced to transport the refugees back to an uncertain fate in Europe. Between 1938 and 1941, 150,000 refugees entered the United States, roughly 62,000 fewer than the law formally allowed.

DEFENSE FOR THE AMERICAS

During the Munich crisis in September 1938, Roosevelt had privately urged Hitler to make peace, but within weeks of the settlement Hitler renewed his declarations of belligerency, and in response Roosevelt's foreign policy began to toughen. Early in 1939, he pointed out to the American people that "the world has grown so small and weapons of attack so swift" that war could no longer be contained, and "events of thunderous import have moved with lightning speed." The advance of technology had cut the time for re-

sponse. "Survival cannot be guaranteed by arming after the attack begins."

Following that logic, Roosevelt held that in a world of well-armed aggressors the military preparedness of the United States had to be strengthened. In 1935, Congress had authorized an increase in the size of the enlisted army, whose active strength when Roosevelt took office was ranked seventeenth in the world, and in January 1938 it voted to expand the navy. But in the wake of Munich, Roosevelt was convinced that far more was needed, especially for the air forces.

The Growth of Air Power. A mixture of public and private initiatives had brought military aircraft a long way from the wood-and-cloth planes of World War I, with their limited range and speed. Perhaps the most aggressive military advocate of air power had been Brigadier General William ("Billy") Mitchell, the son of a U.S. senator, who had led one of the largest army air service wings in wartime France. In exercises carried out early in the 1920s, army bombers sank several German ships captured in World War I, including a German dreadnought. Mitchell took the feat to mean that navies were obsolete and the future lay entirely with land and air forces. He put that case to Congress and the public so vigorously that he was eventually convicted in a court martial of insubordination, whereupon he resigned from the army.

The navy sensibly interpreted the sinkings to mean that it needed better security for its battleships, which could be obtained with fighter aircraft launched from aircraft carriers. The navy constructed its first carrier—the USS *Langley*—in

1922 by converting a supply ship, superposing a flight deck onto its topside and transforming its large coal-carrying holds into a hangar deck. By 1927, two more carriers had been commissioned, the *Saratoga* and the *Lexington*, each capable of carrying more than seventy aircraft; and early in Roosevelt's administration, the keels of two more—the *Yorktown* and the *Enterprise*—were laid, their construction funded by the shipbuilding program carried out under the National Industrial Recovery Act. By then, naval doctrine recognized that aircraft launched from carriers could be used not just to protect battleships but also to strike offensively against an enemy fleet.

In the meantime, progress in long-range land-based planes had hurried along, spurred by key advances in aeronautical technologies and the creation of a market for safe, commercial air services. In 1926, the philanthropist Daniel Guggenheim, convinced that the development of civil aviation required study and experimentation, established an independent fund to promote research in aeronautics; it spent more than $3 million by 1930, when the fund was dissolved, on fundamental investigations at major universities that profoundly influenced the development of aeronautics in the United States. At the California Institute of Technology, for example, the brilliant young engineer and physicist Theodor von Kármán, a recruit from Europe, forged the Guggenheim Aero-

The USS *Saratoga*, one of the first American aircraft carriers, in San Francisco Bay, August 1930.

nautical Laboratory into a world-class facility that fostered work in basic aerodynamics and shaped the burgeoning aircraft industry in southern California. In the federal government, the National Advisory Committee for Aeronautics, the agency created in 1915 to help advance aeronautical research, sponsored fruitful investigations into the design of lifting surfaces such as wings and came up with a housing for engines that reduced drag and dramatically improved engine cooling.

In commercial aviation, fledgling airlines were provided with a promise of revenue by the Airmail Act of 1925, which authorized the U.S. Post Office to contract with private companies for the delivery of airmail. Trips made to Latin America by Charles Lindbergh in the *Spirit of St. Louis* inspired millions to think about air travel. Responding to the incentives, a businessman named Juan Trippe turned his recently formed Pan American Airways into an international carrier that in a single month during 1929 flew 1 million passenger miles and transported 250,000 pounds of mail. Public demands for greater safety escalated after a plane lost a wing and crashed in 1931, killing all the passengers and crew, including the famed Notre Dame football coach Knute Rockne. The Army Air Corps' venture into the transportation of mail, begun by presidential order in 1934, was plagued by numerous crashes and a dozen deaths. An investigation attributed the disasters to inadequate training and equipment, a conclusion that the next year produced increased funding for the corps and greater autonomy for it within the army.

Major aircraft companies responded to the safety problem by designing planes that used improved flap arrangements and swept-back wings that were larger, faster, and more stable. The dominant civilian product of this effort was the DC-3 from Douglas Aircraft, which was developed with the help of the Guggenheim Laboratory at Caltech and which by the late 1930s was carrying an estimated 80 percent of U.S. airline passengers. The same technological advances that worked to the benefit of civil aviation also contributed mightily to military aviation, making possible new long-range bombers such as the B-17, a four-engine "Flying Fortress" that flew for the first time in 1935 and that could deliver 4,000 pounds of bombs from 25,000 feet.

Despite the potency of American air power, Hitler's Luftwaffe was reported to be formidably superior—notably by Charles Lindbergh, who visited Nazi Germany several times and was warmly greeted by Nazi officials. Exaggerated estimates had it that Hitler commanded hundreds of long-range bombers capable of reaching the Americas from the west

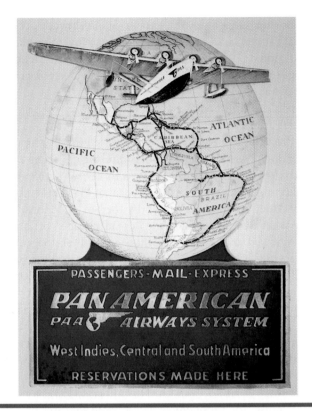

Pan American Airways advertises in 1934 its routes through the Caribbean and Central and South America.

coast of Africa. In October 1938, Roosevelt called for vastly larger military expenditures—the sum was eventually set at $500 million—and at a White House conference the next month, he said he wanted an American air force of 10,000 planes and a capacity for producing 20,000 more a year.

Only for the Neighborhood. Roosevelt justified enhanced American air power as a deterrent to war and a measure of self-defense that would prevent the spread of a European war to the Americas. Charles Lindbergh himself held that America could be well guarded by just 10,000 aircraft. Roosevelt's air-power initiative won support from both liberals and conservatives, both finding it attractive to vote for new planes—for example, the B-17 bombers for the Army Air Corps—that were not for assaulting European cities but for attacking enemy troopships if they tried to sail west across the Atlantic or east across the Pacific. The armed services argued in addition that coastal protection required long-range bombers that could fly between the East and West Coasts without refueling.

To the end of defending the Eastern Seaboard, in January 1939 the navy formed an Atlantic Squadron.

The requirements of hemispheric defense reinforced the administration's commitment to the Good Neighbor policy. That policy had been severely strained when, in March 1938, Mexico announced the nationalization of its $400 million oil industry. The U.S. ambassador to Mexico, Josephus Daniels, advised Roosevelt that upholding the policy should be "of the highest consideration in a mad world where Pan American solidarity may save democracy," adding, "Oil ought not to smear it." Roosevelt resisted pressure to intervene and steered clear of an open break with the Mexican government. He encouraged a shift in military planning—from maintaining just U.S. national security to bolstering the security of the hemisphere. In December 1938, at the eighth Pan American Conference in Lima, Peru, Secretary of State Hull won a declaration that committed the Latin American states to joint defense against foreign threats.

But while Congress was willing to bolster the means of hemispheric defense, it was reluctant to modify the Europe- and Asia-oriented neutrality laws. Roosevelt had come to regard the extension of the arms embargo to the parties in the Spanish Civil War as a grave mistake because it had seriously hampered the Loyalists. In February 1939, the war in Spain ended with the victory of Franco's fascists. In March, Hitler's armies swallowed the rest of Czechoslovakia, and in April Italy invaded Albania. Roosevelt urged repeal of at least parts of the Neutrality Act, pointing out that their cash-and-carry provisions favored the Japanese equally with the British. Isolationists in Congress, however, confidently held that no war would break out in 1939 and insisted on deferring consideration of the law until the next session.

A World at War

In Moscow on August 23, 1939, Germany and the Soviet Union signed a nonaggression pact, which included a secret protocol permitting Stalin to annex eastern Poland and the Baltic states in the event of a German-Polish war. The agreement stunned the world, since the two nations were sharp ideological antagonists, ambitious for territory in eastern Europe, and seemed on the verge of war with each other. Both Hitler and Stalin, in fact, privately saw the pact as temporary, with advantages to each for the moment. Hitler, who was

799

"Next!" Cartoonist D. R. Fitzpatrick expresses the fear in August 1939 that Poland is in jeopardy of the mechanized might of Nazi aggression.

planning to move against Poland imminently, intended to protect his troops against Soviet intervention and discourage Britain and France from coming to Poland's aid. Stalin, pleased to have the territory in eastern Europe, aimed to buy time to prepare for the German assault on his country that he was convinced was sure to come.

THE OUTBREAK OF WORLD WAR II

Hitler invaded Poland on September 1, waging a blitzkrieg, or "lightning war," spearheaded by "Panzer" divisions—phalanxes of mechanized armor, especially tanks—protected on their flanks by German Stuka dive-bombers. Roosevelt got the news in a telephone call at 3 A.M. from his ambassador to France, William Bullitt. "Well, Bill," he said, "it has come at last. God help us all."

Two days later, Britain, which had signed a pact of mutual assistance with Poland, declared war on Germany, and so did France. On September 17, the Soviet Union, following the secret protocol in its pact with Hitler, marched into eastern Poland. Less than a week later, Poland capitulated, the victim

of overwhelming power. In October, Stalin's troops occupied Latvia, Estonia, and Lithuania, and in late November they invaded Finland. After little more than a generation, a second European conflict, soon to become a world conflagration, had begun.

President Roosevelt issued a proclamation of neutrality and declared that he would expend every effort to keep war away from the United States, but he added that "even a neutral cannot be asked to close his mind or conscience." He called a special session of Congress to revise the Neutrality Act, hoping to achieve a blanket repeal of the arms embargo. Many Americans were outraged by the Soviet actions, especially what Roosevelt called the "dreadful rape" of Finland. Polls showed that while less than a third of the country thought the United States should go to war to save Britain and France from defeat, a hefty majority supported every aid to the Allies short of war. But isolationists, including Charles Lindbergh, Herbert Hoover, and now, in the wake of the Nazi-Soviet Pact, the American Communist Party, remained unbending, opposing even the administration's program of cautious aid to the Finns. To their minds, a blanket repeal of the prohibition against arms sales to belligerents would put the country at risk of war. On November 4, 1939, forced to compromise, the president signed a Neutrality Act that permitted arms trade with belligerents but required that sales be made on a cash-and-carry basis.

During the winter of 1940, the European front appeared quiet, and in the United States people jeered at what an isolationist senator derided as "the phony war." Hitler, however, was merely waiting for the drying roads and clearing skies of spring. At dawn on April 9, 1940, in a renewal of the blitzkrieg, German troops struck to the north, occupying Denmark and rapidly vanquishing Norway. On May 10, turning westward, Hitler's armies invaded the Netherlands, Belgium, and Luxembourg, then advanced into France, sidestepping the main French army, which was arrayed along the Maginot Line—a string of heavy fortifications thought to be impregnable, named after the French minister who had directed its construction—by slashing around its northern end through the Ardennes Forest and toward the channel ports. The British Expeditionary Force, troops sent to France in the months following the invasion of Poland, retreated to the northern French coast, arriving at Dunkirk at the end of May with the Germans in close pursuit. A quarter-million British troops plus 110,000 French ones were evacuated to England over several days by heroic flotillas of British destroyers and small boats, many of them seagoing civilian vessels drafted from ports on the south British coast.

On June 10, Italy, declaring war on the Allies, attacked France in the south, provoking President Roosevelt to comment, "The hand that held the dagger has struck it into the back of its neighbor." On June 22, just eleven weeks after the blitzkrieg began, France capitulated to Hitler, surrendering in the same railway car near Compiègne in which Germany had signed the armistice in November 1918. By the terms of the armistice, Germany occupied northern France, including Paris; in the south, with its capital at Vichy, the French government under Marshal Pétain collaborated with the Nazis while remaining formally sovereign and maintaining control of French imperial possessions in Africa and Indochina.

Now, through the summer and fall of 1940, Hitler mounted a relentless air assault against Britain, targeting south coast towns, air fields and factories, shipping installations, and, ultimately, London. Eventually some 1,000 German planes crossed

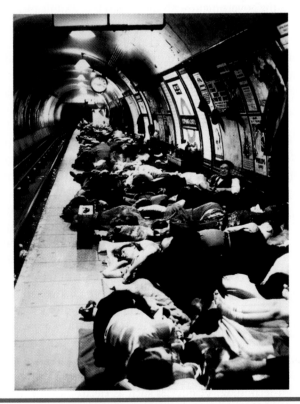

Londoners taking shelter from German air raids in the stations of the Underground, 1940.

the channel each day, aiming to destroy Britain's lifelines of trade, shatter its productive capacity, and terrorize its people in preparation for a cross-channel invasion. In the course of the Battle of Britain, German bomber forces reduced the city of Coventry, including its famed cathedral, to rubble, blasted large parts of London, and killed or wounded tens of thousands of civilians. The assaults only stiffened British resistance. In early May, Chamberlain had resigned and had been succeeded as prime minister by **Winston** **Churchill,** who had long recognized Hitler's threat to Britain but whose warnings had gone unheeded. Indefatigable, eloquent, and unswerving in his resistance to the Nazis, he now rallied his people, calling for the "blood, toil, tears, and sweat" essential to the uncompromising pursuit of victory.

The German bombers were met by hundreds of Royal Air Force (RAF) fighter craft, "Spitfires" and "Hurricanes" manned by young pilots who were guided to their targets by the new technology of radar (a term standing for "radio detection and ranging"), which had been developed independently in the United States, Britain, and Germany. Radar worked by sending out electromagnetic pulses, then detecting those reflected back by an object such as a ship or a plane. Beginning in 1937, the Air Ministry had established a line of fifty radar installations that ran along Britain's Europe-facing coast from the Orkney Islands in the north to Land's End in the southwest. Called "Chain Home," the network detected incoming enemy bombers, determined their location, altitude, and flight paths, and gave Fighter Command fifteen to twenty minutes warning of their arrival, enough time to send its forces to intercept them. Some 2,500 pilots, about 20 percent of them volunteers from conquered European nations, sortied against the German bombers and their swarms of protective fighters. More than 800 of England's fighter aircraft were destroyed, and for several weeks at a rate that exceeded production; but they downed some 600 German bombers and a comparable number of fighters, established control of the air over their country and the channel, and shattered Hitler's dream of an invasion. In August 1940, Churchill memorably told the House of Commons, "Never in the field of human conflict was so much owed by so many to so few."

THE AMERICAN RESPONSE

The swift success of Hitler's blitzkrieg stunned many Americans, but they were stirred by Churchill's resolve, the brave evacuation at Dunkirk, and the courage of both the RAF pilots and the British people. The CBS radio reporter Edward R. Murrow slowly intoning, "This is London" over the airwaves across the Atlantic, made graphic the human story of the blitz, telling of the long lines of people carrying blankets into the city's deep underground stations, where they would be safe from the night bombing. The American poet Archibald MacLeish later wrote of Murrow's broadcasts, "You burned the city of London in our homes and we felt the flames that burned it." Thousands of young men volunteered for the armed services, and some went abroad to battle Hitler by joining the RAF. Sympathy for the British was especially strong on both coasts and in the South, in academic and intellectual circles, and among businessmen with an internationalist outlook. It also flourished among Jews, old-stock Anglophiles, and groups—Polish Americans, for example—with roots in countries Hitler had conquered. Pro-British sentiment was centered among Democrats, but it reached into the ranks of the GOP, too, with strong representation in the moderate, eastern wing of the party.

The Mobilization of Science. A strong desire to assist the British marked key sectors of American science. Like their countrymen, a number of scientists had been isolationists, but most, especially those connected to physics, had moved to a strong internationalism even before the fall of France. The nation's physics leadership, which included a number of Jews, knew from firsthand visits, correspondents abroad, or the refugees the virulence of Hitler's Germany. They also knew that the Third Reich still had scientists capable of developing new military technologies. They were especially concerned with what the Nazis might do with uranium fission. Discovered experimentally in Berlin in December 1938, this released nuclear energy that conceivably might be concentrated into a bomb powerful enough to blow up a city like New York.

Albert Einstein, a pacifist before Hitler took power, had turned afterward into a staunch supporter of American rearmament and scientific involvement with the military. In August 1939, Einstein wrote a letter about nuclear fission to President Roosevelt that was to be delivered by an economist named Alexander Sachs. In October, delayed in obtaining an appointment by the press of business at the White House, Sachs

"They were especially concerned with what the Nazis might do with uranium fission, which released nuclear energy that might be concentrated into a bomb powerful enough to blow up a city like New York."

Vannevar Bush, chair of the National Defense Research Committee and a driving figure in the mobilization of civilian science for war.

brought the letter to a meeting with the president and, while they both sipped some of Roosevelt's finest brandy, succinctly explained the implications of fission, stressing that it might be used to produce explosives of unprecedented power. Roosevelt authorized action on the matter, with the result that a three-man Advisory Committee on Uranium was established to link the government with the research of atomic physicists. However, it was given a budget of only $6,000 and had made little progress by the time of the blitzkrieg.

In May 1940, a small group of prominent scientists and engineers came together, all of them moderate Republicans and internationalists who felt that civilian scientific expertise had to be brought broadly to bear on national defense. They were led by Vannevar Bush, a reedy, flint-faced electrical engineer and longtime member of the MIT faculty who had recently become head of the Carnegie Institution of Washington and chairman of the National Advisory Committee for Aeronautics. Bush could be arrogant and quick-tempered, but he possessed immense executive talents and strong devotion to public duty. During World War I, he had done research on submarine detectors at the New London, Connecticut, naval base. Between the wars, he had consulted in private industry and assisted a friend in founding a company that made vacuum tubes, the Raytheon Corporation. Like his pro-preparedness scientific colleagues, Bush knew the practical side of science, the growing respect it commanded in high-technology businesses such as electronics and aircraft, and the difficulties its practitioners faced in getting the federal government, especially the military, to take it seriously.

Through the 1930s, many army and navy officers had acknowledged what the Nobel laureate physicist Robert A. Millikan told a military gathering in 1934: defense research ought to be "a peace-time . . . and not a war-time thing. . . . [It] moves too slowly to be done after you get into trouble." In both the army and the navy, the technical bureaus now had well-equipped experimental facilities, and their chiefs considered ongoing programs of research and development a necessary part of their missions. Both services managed to bring the devices and machinery of World War I—for example, sonar and aircraft—to a state of far greater sophistication and effectiveness. They also developed radar equipment comparable to what the British deployed so effectively in the Battle of Britain. However, in keeping with the prevailing isolationist sentiment, military research and development was given little money—in 1935, only slightly more than half a percent of the combined army and navy budgets; as in aircraft, the armed services tended to draw heavily on innovation fostered in the private sector. The army and navy also maintained feeble connections with civilian science, partly because of the lack of funds, partly because the military thought civilian technical experts impractical.

In early June 1940, Bush, sure that civilian science could have a far-reaching and decidedly practical impact on military technology, obtained President Roosevelt's approval for the creation of a National Defense Research Committee (NDRC). Chaired by Bush, the NDRC included the heads of Harvard, MIT, and the National Academy of Sciences. All agreed to use the nation's existing research establishment to the limit. To that end, the NDRC resolved to assign research contracts to academic and industrial laboratories rather than build new facilities from scratch. It took over control of nuclear research from the uranium advisory committee. It also compiled a list of critical technical needs from the military.

High army and navy officers were not altogether comfortable with the intrusion of civilian scientists onto the military's technological turf, but Bush, a tough infighter, was unstoppable. The NDRC had its own budget and, behind it, the authority of the president. It also had a number of cutting-edge military devices to pursue, some from the British, especially in areas related to radar. The NDRC soon began awarding research contracts—126 of them by December, to 32 academic institutions and 19 industrial laboratories.

All the while, Roosevelt stressed to the public that it was in the national interest to help the Allies with material resources. Taking steps to make national defense a bipartisan issue, he encouraged the famed Kansas journalist William Allen White in May 1940 to form the broad-based Committee to Defend America by Aiding the Allies. In June, the president named two Republicans to his cabinet—Frank Knox, as secretary of the navy, and Henry L. Stimson, as secretary of war. In May, Roosevelt called on Congress to create an air force of 50,000 planes and an industrial capacity to produce at least 50,000 aircraft a year. Some of them he hoped could be sold to the Allies, a policy that opinion polls showed the public supported with an enthusiasm that mounted as the Nazis rolled across France. By the end of June, Congress had appropriated more than $3 billion for defense; by the end of October, $17 billion, including sufficient funds for a two-ocean navy.

THE ELECTION OF 1940

The Republican Party remained isolationist at heart, but internationalist party members successfully won the presidential nomination for a dark-horse favorite, Wendell L. Willkie of Indiana. Willkie was likable, intelligent, and articulate, a

A 1940 campaign poster for FDR.

utilities executive and foe of public power who was nevertheless sympathetic to many liberal goals. He believed that it was in the American interest to support Britain. In July, at the Democratic convention in Chicago, conservatives tried to persuade the convention against choosing Roosevelt, arguing that a third term was unprecedented and dangerous. However, anxiety about the war joined with Roosevelt's popularity to overwhelm fears and gain him the renomination. For vice-president, he chose Secretary of Agriculture Henry A. Wallace, a devoted liberal and staunch internationalist with strong credentials in the Midwest.

Willkie tried to make an issue of the third term and went so far as to promise that his secretary of labor, unlike Roosevelt's Frances Perkins, would be a man—a ploy that prompted a flood of protests, many of them from Republican women. Desperate for votes and given contradictory counsel by his advisers, he began hammering at Roosevelt's foreign policy, charging that the president was both soft on national defense and leading the country into war. Polls in mid-October showed Willkie rapidly gaining on the president. Roosevelt had been staying close to the White House, leaving the partisan campaigning to Wallace. But in late October, he went on the offensive, declaring in Philadelphia, "I'm an old campaigner and I love a good fight." When he packed Madison Square Garden in New York, 40,000 people around the city watched the event on the fuzzy screens of the early television sets, the audience for the first televised political speech. In the heat of the campaign's closing days, he told voters in Boston that "your boys are not going to be sent into any foreign wars."

On election day, Roosevelt won 27 million votes to Willkie's 22 million and trounced him in the electoral college by 449 to 82. But his popular majority had fallen 6 percentage points from 1936. The war and the New Deal had told against him among German Americans, Irish Americans, Italian Americans, and in the farms and country towns of the Midwest, while both had worked powerfully for him in the big cities, among lower-income and blue-collar groups, African Americans, Jews, and people with ties to Poland and Norway. The election revealed that much of the country remained happy with Roosevelt but divided and uncertain over its foreign course.

> *"The election revealed that much of the country remained happy with Roosevelt but divided and uncertain over its foreign course."*

BATTLE IN THE ATLANTIC

After the fall of France, in June 1940, the sea war in Europe had reached north and west from the coasts of the British Isles, France, and Spain into the North Atlantic, with German U-boats slashing at Britain's lifeline in the convoy lanes out to Iceland. The German submarine fleet, which now enjoyed the use of French ports, soon began hunting in wolf packs, coordinated groups that stalked convoys for several days at a time. Churchill had been begging for destroyers, which were crucial to protecting British shipping against Nazi submarines. Roosevelt, apprehensive about isolationist sentiment in Congress, responded to Churchill by executive action, announcing on September 3 that the United States would give fifty aging destroyers to Britain in exchange for ninety-nine-year leases of bases in the Caribbean and Newfoundland. Willkie, setting aside partisanship, endorsed the destroyers-for-bases deal. He also backed a proposal from the administration for conscription, the first such peacetime measure in the country's history. The Selective Service Act passed in September even though it aroused opposition across the political spectrum, including the charge that sending a raw, draft army against Hitler's troops would be tantamount to sending a high school football squad against a pro-football team.

In the fall of 1940, Britain was running out of cash for arms purchases, but the U.S. Neutrality Act forbade providing her any credit. In an eloquent Fireside Chat on December 29, 1940, Roosevelt declared that the United States had to serve as "the great arsenal of democracy," a resource for Britain's defense needs as well as its own. To that end, he said, the country had best forget the "silly, foolish old dollar sign." It could simply lend or lease war equipment to countries like Britain whose defense was vital to the United States on the understanding that the equipment would be returned, or returned in kind, after the war. Roosevelt likened the move to lending a garden hose to a neighbor whose house was on fire with the expectation of getting the hose back after the fire was put out. "Give us the tools and we will finish the job," Churchill pledged.

Passions on the issue ran high. When in January 1941 the president sent a lend-lease bill to Capitol Hill, congressional isolationists attacked it, with Senator Burton K. Wheeler of

Montana likening lend-lease to the New Deal's farm policy, predicting that "it will plow under every fourth American boy." Roosevelt told reporters that Wheeler's statement was "the rottenest thing that has been said in public life in my generation." No matter: the president's Fireside Chat had won huge public approval, Wendell Willkie testified in favor of lend-lease legislation, and it became law on March 11, 1941.

By then, the Germans had increased the difficulty of getting goods to Britain by intensifying their U-boat attacks and stretching the Atlantic war zone farther west to Greenland and south to the lower end of Africa. During the spring, German submarines were sending merchant ships to the bottom at twice the rate they were being replaced. In April, with the agreement of the Danish government-in-exile, Roosevelt sent American troops to Greenland, a Danish possession, to help keep it out of Nazi hands. He also authorized American air and naval patrols to cover the Atlantic out to the rugged island. On May 27, 1941, five days after the sinking of an American merchant ship by a German submarine, he warned that the war in the Atlantic was "coming very close to home" and

An English cartoonist welcomes America's lend-lease program, 1941.

proclaimed the existence of a "national emergency" in the interest of strengthening American defense to the maximum.

An Incipient Anglo-American Alliance. If all-out aid to Britain was imperative for American national security, then the United States had to ensure that it produced enough war goods for both its own defense and Britain's. After the fall of France, Roosevelt had established a commission on defense production. In January 1941, seeing that he needed more than advice on the matter, he replaced the commission with the Office of Production Management, but the new agency lacked adequate authority to accomplish its task. Defense production was being slowed by business-as-usual attitudes and strikes, some of them provoked by Communists.

Meanwhile, German-Soviet animosity had revived, partly as the result of friction between the two nations in the Balkans. Although American diplomats had advised the Kremlin that Hitler might turn against Russia, Soviet officials doubted that Hitler would be so foolish as to try to fight a two-front war. Hitler, however, realizing that he could not invade Britain, wanted to eliminate the Soviet threat on Germany's eastern flank. He may have thought he could do so with relative ease, partly because he had subdued western Europe so quickly, partly because the Red Army had fought ineptly against the determined and resourceful Finns before overwhelming them with sheer numbers. On June 22, 1941, Hitler sent 3 million troops to war against the Soviet Union (see map in Chapter 26). American Communists instantly flip-flopped, becoming passionate advocates of aid to the Allies. Britain and the United States resolved to help Stalin battle the Nazis. Echoing Churchill's reasoning, Roosevelt said that to defeat Hitler, "I would hold hands with the Devil." In October, he made the Soviet Union eligible for lend-lease and soon some American war matériel, though less than had been pledged, began making its way across the North Sea bound for Murmansk.

In August 1941, Roosevelt and Churchill rendezvoused on a warship off the coast of Newfoundland. The two men, having developed a personal relationship by letter and cable, had looked forward with pleasure to meeting each other in the flesh. A Roosevelt aide who had traveled to the meeting with the British prime minister remembered, "You'd have thought he was being carried up into the heavens to meet God." Roosevelt and Churchill each found the other greatly to his liking—self-confident, articulate, good-humored, and united in their

Roosevelt (left) and Churchill in August 1941 aboard HMS *Prince of Wales,* where they issued the Atlantic Charter.

After his meeting with Churchill, he authorized navy destroyers to escort British merchant shipping between the United States and Iceland, and he ordered the escorts to shoot any German submarine sighted anywhere in the defense zone.

On September 4, a German U-boat attacked the American destroyer *Greer,* firing its torpedoes after having been pursued by the *Greer* and depth-charged by a British plane. Roosevelt nevertheless told a national radio audience that the German submarine had "fired first" and without warning, initiating an act of "piracy." The president took advantage of the incident to announce his escort-to-Iceland policy and the order to shoot on sight, explaining, "When you see a rattlesnake poised to strike, you do not wait until he has struck before you crush him." He contended, in a slap at isolationists, that "it is time for all Americans . . . to stop being deluded by the romantic notion that the Americas can go on living happily and peacefully in a Nazi-dominated world."

In mid-October, Nazi torpedoes severely damaged one American destroyer and two weeks later sank another, the *Reuben James,* with the loss of 115 men. Following the *Greer* incident, the president had asked Congress to repeal the last key provisions of the Neutrality Act. In November 1941, act-

eagerness for Hitler's defeat. At the conference, they cemented a working union that would persist until Roosevelt's death and overcome differences in policy that inevitably cropped up between them.

Roosevelt wanted to make clear to the public that even though he might hold hands with the Soviet devil and help imperial Britain, he was not compromising fundamental American beliefs. After several days, the two governments issued a declaration of principles that became known as the Atlantic Charter. The document opposed forced or undemocratic territorial changes; endorsed equal access to resources and trade ("with due respect for . . . existing obligations"); affirmed sovereignty and self-government as universal rights; and called in the postwar period for freedom from want and fear, the disarmament of aggressor nations, and, ultimately, a system of collective security.

Roosevelt also pledged to go beyond principle to further aid the British. According to what Churchill told his cabinet soon after the meeting, Roosevelt said "that he would wage war, but not declare it," that he would do "everything" to "force an incident . . . which would justify him in opening hostilities." In July, Roosevelt had extended the American defense zone to Iceland and sent troops to help protect it.

D. R. Fitzpatrick depicts the savagery of the Nazis when a U-boat sank the *Reuben James* on November 1, 1941.

ing on Roosevelt's request, both houses voted solidly to allow the arming of merchant ships and the transport of goods through the ocean war zones all the way to Britain and the Soviet Union. Now, as American escort crews braved the gale-force winds, bitter cold, and seas rising to skyscraper heights, Roosevelt waited for a hostile encounter in the North Atlantic that would force a declaration of war against Germany. Hitler, however, having run into stiff Soviet resistance in the East, ordered his U-boats to avoid confrontations with American vessels that might bring the United States into the war.

Waging Undeclared War. According to the polls, the nation overwhelmingly supported all aid to Britain, but on August 18 the Selective Service Act had been renewed in the House by a majority of just one vote. A large number of Americans were torn, hoping that the Nazis would be defeated but unwilling to wage war against them if they were not, especially war that sent American soldiers into battle. Roosevelt himself hoped that the United States could help defeat the Nazis by using only air and naval forces, expressing a proclivity for relying more on technology than on troops that his countrymen shared. Isolationist sentiment had been strengthened by the reduction of pressure on Britain that came with the German invasion of the Soviet Union. The America First Committee, formed by isolationists in September 1940 to contest what they saw as a trend toward war that was wholly wrong and unnecessary, insisted that American security would not be jeopardized by a Nazi victory. Charles Lindbergh, a passionate America Firster, held that the real enemy was to the east (meaning Russia and the Orient), which threatened to infiltrate the West with "inferior blood." The white race was in danger from a "pressing sea of Yellow, Black, and Brown," and Germany might save it.

Some isolationists responded to Roosevelt's North Atlantic policy with nasty bitterness. In September, a special congressional committee established by Senator Burton Wheeler held hearings into whether Hollywood films sought to move public opinion in a pro-interventionist direction; several isolationists noted that a lot of Jews were Hollywood producers. That month, in a speech in Des Moines, Iowa, Lindbergh insisted that "the three most important groups who have been pressing this country toward war are the British, the Jewish, and the Roosevelt administration." Most isolationists disavowed Lindbergh's views, but many worried

> *"Roosevelt did stretch his authority to protect what he took to be the vital interests of the nation."*

about the broad discretionary powers that the president was acquiring by waging undeclared war.

Roosevelt did stretch his authority to protect what he took to be the vital interests of the nation. In addition to misrepresenting the circumstances of the *Greer* incident, he authorized the FBI to investigate "subversive activities," which extended the agency's scope to include snooping into political groups. The bureau investigated organizations such as the Veterans of the Abraham Lincoln Brigade and people who expressed support for Lindbergh; it illegally intercepted and opened private correspondence with selected foreign countries and wiretapped without warrants. In July 1941, the president appointed William J. Donovan, a wealthy, energetic, and aggressive lawyer, to the new post of coordinator of information. On the face of it, Donovan's office was to obtain information relevant to national security, but he was secretly also given responsibility for "special operations," which meant covertly waging undeclared war against the Nazis in Europe. In defending the United States, Roosevelt thus misused some of its democratic institutions and set dangerous precedents, opening the door to later abuse of presidential power in the name of national security, but at the time the heinousness of the Nazi threat made such measures seem justifiable.

THE SEARING JAPANESE SUN

As Japan pursued its war against the Chinese, its aggressive presence in China became a touchstone of U.S. policy in Asia. China held a special, if somewhat self-contradictory, place in the hearts of many Americans. On the one hand, national law had long discriminated against the immigration and naturalization of people from China (see Chapter 19), and Chinese Americans continued to suffer from a variety of injustices. On the other, Protestant missionaries often devoted much of their lives to Christianizing the Chinese, and secular evangelists of Americanism took them to be a special target for conversion to democracy and capitalism. Now that the Chinese appeared to be fighting naked Japanese aggression, they earned mounting sympathy in America and Britain.

President Roosevelt admired the aspirations of the Chinese, but his support for China was also grounded in concern for the strategic interests of the United States. He wished to maintain the Open Door so that China could further develop in a democratic, capitalist direction and help block Japan's imperial ambitions. He was worried that Japan might threaten the Philippines and the supply of strategic materials that the Allies and the United States obtained from Southeast Asia—for example, the natural rubber that came from Indonesia. Roosevelt had declined to declare that a state of war existed between China and Japan; such a declaration would have activated the Neutrality Act. The imposition of an arms embargo and of the law's cash-and-carry provisions would have hurt China, which depended heavily on imports of war goods, far more than Japan. Nevertheless, in the absence of an embargo, the sale of goods to Japan continued, legally undergirded by the Japanese-American commercial treaty of 1911. In 1938, for example, American business supplied Japan with two-thirds of its oil and nine-tenths of its metal scrap.

"In 1938, American business supplied Japan with two-thirds of its oil and nine-tenths of its metal scrap."

In late 1938, polls showed that Americans were willing to take a stand on the war in China—far more so than they were on the war in Europe—particularly by prohibiting the sale of war supplies to Japan. The isolationist senators Gerald P. Nye and George W. Norris, departing from their commitment to strict neutrality, urged that the United States embargo scrap-metal shipments to Japan. However, President Roosevelt feared that such an action would weaken Japanese moderates and risk war. In July 1939, bowing to congressional pressure, his administration told Tokyo that it intended to end the 1911 commercial treaty; but when it did, in January 1940, it declined to impose an embargo.

With the war in Europe now the primary concern, Roosevelt did not want a confrontation with Japan. Japanese expansionists, however, pressed for taking advantage of the war in Europe to break American and British economic power in Asia. In July 1940, a pro-expansionist government took office in Japan that was committed to incorporating British, French, and Dutch colonial possessions in Southeast Asia into the new Japanese order, which Japan later termed the Greater East Asia Co-Prosperity Sphere. With the aim of discouraging these ambitions, on July 31, 1940, the United States embargoed the shipment of aviation-grade gasoline to Japan, and on September 26 it extended the restriction to include shipments of iron and steel scrap. The next day, Japan joined Germany and Italy in a Tripartite Pact, pledging mutual assistance if any of the signatories was attacked by a nation with which it was currently at peace. At the end of November, the United States announced a $100 million loan and a gift of fifty fighter planes to China. The planes would be formed into a volunteer air force (later dubbed the Flying Tigers), and American citizens would be permitted to pilot them.

Japan, watchful of the Soviets in Siberia, did not immediately move into Southeast Asia, but once Hitler invaded Russia in June 1941, the Japanese government felt free to pursue its aims more aggressively. In July 1941, the Vichy government acquiesced in Japanese demands for occupational rights in French Indochina; Japanese troops marched into the country, occupying several cities in the south, including Saigon. At the end of the month, the Roo-

The battleship *Arizona* explodes at Pearl Harbor after being struck by Japanese bombs, December 7, 1941.

sevelt administration, failing in an attempt to obtain a withdrawal, froze all Japanese assets in the United States and severely reduced oil shipments to Japan. Roosevelt hoped his actions would make Japan willing to bargain. At their Atlantic conference the following month, the United States and Britain agreed that, together with the Dutch, they would warn Japan that it would suffer dire consequences if it moved south against British or Dutch possessions. It was made publicly clear to the Japanese that the warning was to be read in conjunction with the Atlantic Charter, whose endorsement of equal access to resources and markets essentially renewed the signatories' long-standing insistence on the Open Door.

Civilians in the Japanese government wanted to try to resolve the conflict with the United States, but the military, anxious about Japan's declining oil reserves, insisted that time was running out. At an Imperial Conference on September 6, Japan's leaders agreed that if by mid-October rapprochement with America appeared hopeless, the country would prepare for war against the United States, England, and Holland. Japan's conditions for peace included noninterference with its activities in China, the resumption of commercial relations, and a willingness to see its Co-Prosperity Sphere extended to Thailand and the Dutch East Indies. Roosevelt, with emphatic support from Churchill, who was anxious to keep open England's lifelines to India, refused to accept these demands, especially the abandonment of China.

In mid-October, the civilian prime minister of Japan resigned and was succeeded by General Hideki Tojo. Adamantly against compromise on China, Tojo opposed returning to any system in the western Pacific that was dominated by the United States. "Asia is the territory of the Asiatics," the Tokyo newspaper *Yomiuri* declared. Under the guise of attacking Western colonialism, however, Japan was manifestly pursuing an imperialism of its own that threatened Western security interests in the Pacific and that the United States would not accept.

Pearl Harbor. In November, while the Japanese ambassador in Washington continued to negotiate, Japanese preparations for war proceeded. On November 25, a Japanese carrier force set out from the Kuril Islands, at the northeastern tip of Japan, its objective a **surprise attack on Pearl Harbor** in Honolulu, where the American fleet was stationed. The United States had broken the codes that the Japanese used in transmitting their military and diplomatic messages. Critics of Roosevelt

The *San Francisco Chronicle* reports that the attack at Pearl Harbor means war.

later argued that the president deliberately maneuvered the United States into war, that he knew where and roughly when the attack would occur but did nothing to prepare against it because he intended to use the Japanese deceit to break the isolationist deadlock at home. The charge is flatly contradicted by the evidence. The coded Japanese traffic did not specifically identify the target, and while American military intelligence expected action and alerted the armed services in the Pacific, including those in Hawaii, the consensus was that the Japanese would strike southward, perhaps in the Philippines.

At 7 A.M. on Sunday, December 7, 1941, two army operators at the radar station on the northern tip of Oahu, at Kahuku Point, detected what seemed to be fifty planes some 132 miles to the northeast and headed for Hawaii. They telephoned their discovery to the Information Center, but the army command on Oahu had developed nothing like the British

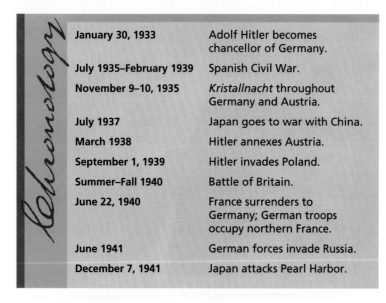

January 30, 1933	Adolf Hitler becomes chancellor of Germany.
July 1935–February 1939	Spanish Civil War.
November 9–10, 1935	*Kristallnacht* throughout Germany and Austria.
July 1937	Japan goes to war with China.
March 1938	Hitler annexes Austria.
September 1, 1939	Hitler invades Poland.
Summer–Fall 1940	Battle of Britain.
June 22, 1940	France surrenders to Germany; German troops occupy northern France.
June 1941	German forces invade Russia.
December 7, 1941	Japan attacks Pearl Harbor.

people and wounding another 1,178, destroying 188 planes, and knocking out the bulk of the American battle fleet except for its aircraft carriers, which happened to be at sea. Almost 1,000 of the dead perished when a single bomb struck the battleship *Arizona*, detonating its forward magazine and sinking the ship.

The next day, in an address before a joint session of Congress that was broadcast to millions across the country, President Roosevelt denounced the surprise attack, calling December 7, 1941, "a day which will live in infamy." At Roosevelt's urging, Congress, with only one dissenting vote, enacted a declaration of war against Japan. The president, uncertain that he could obtain a similar declaration against Germany and Italy, waited to see what action they would take. On December 11, Hitler and Mussolini declared war on the United States, triggering the nation's formal entry into the battle that Roosevelt and, by now, millions of other Americans were convinced they had to fight.

Chain Home system to act on radar intelligence. The officer on duty, thinking that the planes were a flight of B-17s arriving from the mainland, notified no one. Approaching the Pearl Harbor naval base some minutes before 8 A.M., a lead Japanese pilot radioed the carrier force, "Tora! Tora! Tora!"—a code signal that the U.S. fleet in the Pacific had been caught completely off guard.

Two waves of Japanese torpedo planes, dive-bombers, and fighters struck the American ships, planes, and military installations at Pearl Harbor for almost two hours, killing 2,403

Suggested Reading

Robert Dallek, *Franklin D. Roosevelt and American Foreign Policy, 1932–1945*, rev. ed. (1995)

Akira Iriye, *The Origins of WWII in Asia and the Pacific* (1987)

Manfred Jonas, *Isolationism in America, 1935–1941* (1966)

Daniel J. Kevles, *The Physicists: The History of a Scientific Community in Modern America* (1995)

David Wyman, *Paper Walls: America and the Refugee Crisis, 1938–1941* (1968)

Chapter 26

FIGHTING FOR FREEDOM:
1942–1945

Inspecting bomber turrets at Douglas Aircraft in Long Beach, California, 1944.

813

- ■ **What were the critical first steps America took after entering the war?**

- ■ **How did the United States mobilize its economy and scientific expertise for war?**

- ■ **What advances did Allied forces make in Europe?**

- ■ **What advances did Allied forces make in the Pacific?**

- ■ **What were the major effects of the war on American society?**

- ■ **How did the Allies finally prevail in Europe?**

After Pearl Harbor, Adolf Hitler indulged in a verbal jig, telling his cronies, "I don't see much future for the Americans. It's a decayed country. And they have their racial problems, and the problem of social inequalities. . . . American society [is] half Judaized, and the other half Negrified. How can anyone expect a State like that to hold together—a country where everything is built on the dollar." Hitler's foreign minister knew better. He warned the Führer that if the Soviet Union's huge manpower was mobilized together with the United States' immense capacity for industrial production, the prospects for a victory by the Axis powers (Germany, Italy, and Japan) would be slim.

The foreign minister was right, but he might have added that the United States had the capacity to draw strength precisely from its diversity, from its growing willingness to mobilize against racism and inequality, and from the ideas that gave that mobilization voice. Unlike Woodrow Wilson, Roosevelt declined to call the country to battle to make the world safe for democracy. The disillusion attending the collapse of Wilson's program and now the renewal of war less than a generation after his "war to end all wars" had been fought—both made appeals to his vision untenable. The ideals promulgated by the Roosevelt administration emphasized preservation of the "American way of life" by protecting the country's security. Its enemies trampled on people's rights. The United States, in contrast, was fighting to safeguard the principles of freedom, especially the Four Freedoms that Roosevelt had articulated in a message to Congress in January 1941—freedom from fear, freedom from want, freedom of worship, and freedom of speech.

> *"After Pearl Harbor, Roosevelt moved quickly to pursue the victory of ideas with the force of manpower and steel."*

After Pearl Harbor, Roosevelt moved quickly to pursue the victory of ideas with the force of manpower and steel. At the opening of 1942, the United States and Great Britain joined with the Soviet Union and twenty-three other nations to form a "Grand Alliance," pledging to commit their full resources to victory over the Axis powers. To be sure, its three principal members were divided by important differences of outlook and national interest. Winston Churchill, a staunch imperialist, headed the world's leading colonial power. Joseph Stalin, dictator of the world's only Communist state, stood for the export of Soviet ideology around the world. Roosevelt, leader of a great capitalist nation and a capitalist himself, was a critic of colonialism and Communism. They were united, however, by their ferocious opposition to Hitler, and they overrode their divisions in the interest of defeating Nazi Germany. Churchill no doubt spoke for all of them when he remarked, "There is only one thing worse than fighting with allies, and that is fighting without them."

The United States and Britain could not by themselves raise armies large enough to ensure victory by sheer numerical advantage. Their calculus of victory depended in part on the Soviet Union, with its armed forces of 8 million men and women, continuing to engage part of Hitler's Wehrmacht. It also hinged on their own achievement of overwhelming superiority in military technologies and the production of the goods of war. In the United States, the mobilization mounted in pursuit of that end greatly enlarged the federal government's powers and spending. It stimulated the economy to a blistering level of activity. It changed the lives of millions, including women and minority groups. And it transformed the relationship of the United States to the rest of the world.

Opening Gambits

Roosevelt quickly took steps to facilitate both overt and covert war. He had formed a Joint Chiefs of Staff that comprised representatives of the navy, army, and army air force, and at a meeting in Washington at the turn of 1942, he and Churchill formed a union of the American and the British military leadership. In June, Roosevelt established the Office of Strategic Services (OSS) for the centralized gathering and analysis of intelligence, and for the performance of such "special services"—they might include espionage, sabotage, and other secret operations—as the joint chiefs might direct.

STRATEGY IN EUROPE

In the months after Pearl Harbor, a debate quickly emerged between Roosevelt and Churchill over the strategy to pursue against Germany. Churchill, who linked military strategy to his country's geopolitical interests, preferred to focus first on the Mediterranean, where in central North Africa German armies were driving British forces eastward and by June were threatening Egypt. He wanted to ensure Britain's control of the Suez Canal, including its supply lines to India and the Far East, and he was fearful of repeating the slaughter of World War I by mounting a frontal assault against the German armies in France before the Allies could accumulate an overpowering invasion force. In his view, for the time being the Allies should limit their attack on the Continent to bombing Germany and encouraging native resistance in the occupied countries. He contended that the Allies should take direct action against the Nazis by invading North Africa—the plan was code-named "Operation Torch"—thus assisting the British in the battle they were waging to repel the Germans in Egypt.

General George C. Marshall, the U.S. Army chief of staff and a resolute public ser-

vant whose opinions Roosevelt respected highly, vigorously objected to Churchill's plan. The Germans were inflicting huge casualties on the Russians and had penetrated deep into Soviet territory, recently reaching the outskirts of Moscow and putting Leningrad under siege. Stalin was pressing Roosevelt and Churchill to open a second front against Hitler's forces in northern Europe at the earliest opportunity. Soviet resistance was stiffening—the Germans had been beaten back from Moscow—but Marshall worried about Stalin's ability to hold out indefinitely against Hitler. Churchill's peripheral strategy might in the end prolong the war. Marshall argued that the United States and Britain should build up a powerful military force in England, then invade the Continent in 1942, thus relieving the pressure on the Soviets as early as possible. Roosevelt himself had promised the Soviets that in 1942 a second front would be opened in the West.

Churchill countered that Operation Torch would constitute such a front and that it would serve as a preliminary to an attack across the channel in 1943. Although Roosevelt tended to defer to Marshall's military judgment, he recognized the merits of Churchill's arguments against an early cross-channel invasion. With an eye on the public's morale

U.S. troops preparing to land at Fedala, Morocco, November 1942.

815

World War II: Europe and Africa, 1940–1945

FINLAND

NORWAY

SWEDEN

ESTONIA

LATVIA

LITHUANIA

North Sea

DENMARK

Baltic Sea

Danzig

EAST PRUSSIA

Invasion of Soviet Union, June 22, 1941

SOVIET UNION

IRELAND

GREAT BRITAIN

Hamburg

Berlin

Warsaw

POLAND

Kiev

Battle of Britain (Aug.–Oct., 1940)

Amsterdam

London

NETHERLANDS

Dover

Calais

BELGIUM

Malmédy

Ardennes Forest

Bastogne

Battle of the Bulge (Dec. 1944)

GERMANY

Elbe River

Dresden

to Stalingrad (Aug. 1942–Jan. 1943)

Atlantic Ocean

Cherbourg

D day (June 6, 1944)

NORMANDY

Paris

LUX.

Reims

Prague

BOHEMIA MORAVIA

SLOVAKIA

FRANCE

Munich

Vienna

AUSTRIA

HUNGARY

SWITZ.

ROMANIA

PORTUGAL

SPAIN

Madrid

ITALY

Pisa

Rimini

Florence

Corsica

Rome

Sardinia

Salerno

Belgrade

YUGOSLAVIA

Bucharest

BULGARIA

Black Sea

Istanbul

ALBANIA

GREECE

TURKEY

Athens

Mediterranean

SPANISH MOROCCO

Oran

Sicily

Casablanca

ALGERIA

MOROCCO

TUNISIA

Sea

Tripoli

LIBYA

EGYPT

Legend:

⊛ Major battles

→ Allied forces

⇢ Heaviest Allied aerial bombing

→ Axis forces

--- Inside limit of German U-boat operations

Axis nations

Occupied by Axis

Allied nations

Neutral nations

0   200   400 mi

0   200   400 km

and the 1942 elections, he also wanted to have American ground troops engage the Germans as soon as possible, in North Africa if necessary, even at the cost of disappointing Stalin. In July, to Marshall's distress, Roosevelt agreed to Churchill's plan for an invasion of North Africa in the autumn.

On November 8, 1942, an Anglo-American force of 100,000 men landed in Morocco and Algeria in an area nominally under the control of France's Vichy government. They gained the shore in flat-bottomed, diesel-powered craft known as "Higgins Boats," after their designer Andrew Higgins of New Orleans, that would prove indispensable in carrying fighting men from troop transports to the invasion beaches throughout the European and Pacific theaters. The commander was the American brigadier general Dwight D. Eisenhower, fifty-two years old and leanly handsome, who had impressed the British with his professional competence, unpretentious directness, sunny disposition, and ability to get the forces of his nation and theirs to cooperate. Local resistance to the invasion was weak and short-lived. On November 11, Eisenhower, with Roosevelt's approval, arranged an armistice with Admiral Jean Darlan, the commander of the Vichy armed forces, who happened to be in Algiers. In the agreement, Darlan surrendered the French forces in return for being appointed governor general of French North Africa. Darlan was a prominent Nazi collaborator and exponent of the Vichy decrees against Jews, a living contradiction of the principles for which the Allies were fighting. The Darlan deal provoked a storm of protests in both Britain and the United States that ended only when a young French royalist assassinated Darlan on Christmas Eve 1942.

After the surrender of the Vichy French in North Africa, the Nazis had occupied the rest of France and Hitler had rushed troops and supplies to Tunisia, insisting, in what one of his generals later called an order of "unsurpassed madness," that his army fight to the death. Now Eisenhower's forces battled eastward across the sandy, featureless North African desert, driving into Tunisia while the British pressed westward from Tripoli. Caught between the British and American armies, the German forces faced crushing opposition. The war in North Africa ended on May 12, 1943, with the surrender of some 250,000 Axis troops.

DEMANDS IN THE PACIFIC

Roosevelt and Churchill had agreed that their nations should give priority to the defeat of Hitler, then see to Japan, but the

Cartoonist D. R. Fitzpatrick celebrates the defeat of Nazi forces in North Africa, May 1943.

war in the Pacific compelled early attention. During the first week of January 1942, the Japanese occupied Manila, the Philippine capital. In March, on Roosevelt's orders, General Douglas MacArthur, the commander in the Philippines, left his forces for Australia to prepare a counteroffensive, grandiloquently announcing, "I shall return." In April and May, American and Philippine defense forces on the Bataan Peninsula and Corregidor, at the entrance to Manila Bay, surrendered, unable to hold out any longer. The Japanese ordered the Bataan garrison of some 76,000 men, many of them exhausted and starving, to walk under a brutal sun sixty-five miles to a rail junction, where a train would take them to a prisoner's camp. Close to 1,000 Americans and several thousand Filipinos died or were murdered on what became known as the Bataan Death March. Another 6,000 men perished in the camp.

By mid-spring, the Japanese had also taken Wake Island, Guam, Sumatra, Java, Borneo, and the northern half of New Guinea. They had conquered Malaya, Thailand, and Burma, and had closed the Burma Road, the crucial overland route for transporting supplies to the forces of Jiang Jieshi (Chiang

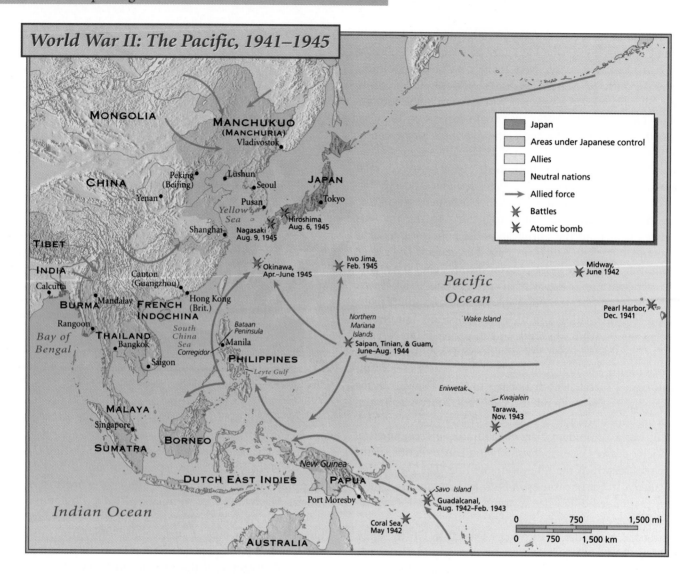

World War II: The Pacific, 1941–1945

Kai-shek) in China. All told, they had overrun roughly 1 million square miles, much of it ocean, and 150 million people. Now they moved to take the rest of New Guinea and threaten Australia, which lay to the south across the Coral Sea.

The U.S. Navy, having broken Japan's naval code, was constantly monitoring its radio traffic in the Pacific. It knew where and approximately when the Japanese forces would strike. On May 7 and 8, 1942, an American naval task force that included two carriers beat back a Japanese force headed toward New Guinea in the Battle of the Coral Sea, thus blocking Japan's drive to the southeast. A few weeks earlier, sixteen B-25 bombers under the command of Lieutenant Colonel

James H. Doolittle had flown from the carrier *Hornet*, which had brought them within 700 miles of the Japanese mainland, to bomb Tokyo. While the action produced little damage and few casualties, it stirred the American public and showed the Japanese that the war would be brought home to them.

The Doolittle raid prompted Japanese naval forces to attempt a decisive blow against the Americans in the Pacific. They set their sights on Midway, the penultimate outpost of the Hawaiian Islands chain, less than 1,200 miles to the northwest of Oahu, hoping in the course of the action to draw out and destroy what remained of the U.S. Pacific Fleet. But the fleet commanders, with their ability to decipher

Japanese radio traffic, knew once again where the attack was coming. At the Battle of Midway during the first week of June, a U.S. naval task force, although greatly outnumbered in ships and planes, destroyed almost half the Japanese aircraft and sent four carriers to the bottom.

The Battles of the Coral Sea and Midway ended Japan's naval offensive in the Pacific. Its naval forces would thereafter be placed on the defensive, retreating in the face of Allied assaults to the north and west. The outcomes of both battles depended on many ingredients, including the brilliance of the American commanders, the brave resolve of the carrier pilots, the acuity of the code breakers, and the technical advantage of radar. While the Japanese had no radar, several of the American ships and Midway itself were equipped with sets that the navy had developed and that gave early warning of oncoming Japanese aircraft. The two battles also signaled the arrival of a new era in naval warfare. The Japanese and the American surface ships never caught sight of each other. Apart from submarine attacks, all their offensive operations were carried out over long distances by carrier-based aircraft.

The Japanese nevertheless continued to threaten shipping to Australia and New Zealand from Guadalcanal, a volcanic island of tropical jungle in the Solomon Islands just 1,250 miles to the northeast of Queensland, Australia, and on which, according to intelligence reports, they were building an airfield. Early in August 1942, launching the first American ground offensive in the Pacific, marines landed on the island. They faced Japanese soldiers emerging from the jungle at night in wild, screaming suicide charges but fought to victory by early the following February.

These victories in the Pacific did not come cheaply. During the first half of 1942, the United States sent roughly quadruple the number of men and double the number of ships to the Pacific as it did to Europe. At Guadalcanal, the fighting on the ground was accompanied by several major battles at sea, as each side attempted to destroy the ability of the other to supply and support its troops. In a battle off Savo Island, near the landing beaches, the Japanese sank several ships and damaged another without suffering any losses themselves. Savo Island was a humiliating defeat for the U.S. Navy, perhaps the worst in its history, and it demonstrated that despite the reversal at Midway, the Japanese still possessed formidable naval strength.

A Japanese soldier searches U.S. prisoners of war after the fall of Bataan and Corregidor, 1942.

Mobilizing for War

PRODUCTION FOR WAR

Among the Roosevelt administration's crucial tasks after Pearl Harbor was **the conversion of American industry to a war footing**, with the aim of accelerating the mass production of war goods. In January 1942, the president established the War Production Board (WPB) and gave it broad powers, including the authority to allocate supplies of raw materials to industry and curtail civilian production. The board was headed by Donald Nelson, a former executive at Sears, Roebuck who was more familiar than most with the intricacies of American industrial capacities. Nelson was easygoing, energetic, and eager to meet military needs while fending off military pressure to take control of the economy. By 1943, war production totaled some $40 billion, accounting for 40 percent of the gross national product, some two and a half times as much as the proportion in 1941.

A critical part of the conversion involved obtaining enough raw materials to fuel the manufacture of war goods. When, in January 1942, Nelson shut down the civilian automobile industry, he not only turned its formidable manufacturing capabilities to the production of war items such as tanks and aircraft, he also freed up for war purposes the resources it used in making cars—for example, 51 percent of the nation's malleable iron, 75 percent of its plate glass, 80 percent of its rubber, and more than 18 percent of its steel output. The government adopted measures of conservation and substitution. People had to turn in their used metal toothpaste tubes in order to buy new ones, and new pennies in 1943 were minted of gray, zinc-coated steel, replacements for the familiar copper, which was in short supply.

> *"Responding to a request from Roosevelt, Americans turned in 450,000 tons of used rubber goods, including overcoats, tires, shoes, gloves, and bathing caps."*

Conservation, however, was inadequate to meet the need for rubber, which figured significantly in the construction of, for example, battleships, bomber fuel tanks, and medical adhesive tape. Japan's control of Southeast Asia had cut off 98 percent of the United States' crude rubber supply; its remaining stock would suffice for only six months. Responding to a request from Roosevelt, Americans turned in 450,000 tons of used rubber goods, including overcoats, tires, shoes, gloves, and bathing caps. But a growing chorus of voices insisted that meeting wartime rubber needs would require drastic measures. In the late summer, a blue-ribbon committee consisting of the financier Bernard Baruch and two high-ranking participants in the mobilization of science—James B. Conant, president of Harvard, and Karl Compton, president of MIT—spelled out the requirements: gasoline rationing and a national speed limit of thirty-five miles per hour to conserve the rubber on existing tires; and a major program to produce synthetic rubber. In September, on Roosevelt's orders, Nelson appointed a rubber czar who put the committee's recommendations into effect by shouldering through the construc-

tion of federally financed synthetic rubber factories and then leasing them to private corporations. In 1944, the new synthetic rubber industry turned out 750,000 tons of the material, enough to meet 90 percent of the nation's needs.

Under the guidance of the WPB, American industry achieved production miracles, turning out crucial war goods such as tanks, planes, and ships in far greater quantity than Britain, Germany, Japan, and the Soviet Union. In 1941, the Kaiser shipyards on the Pacific coast, which built about a third of the 2,700 cargo-carrying vessels called Liberty ships that came off the ways (inclined structures that support ships during launch), produced a ship in 355 days; in 1944, in fewer than 62 days. A German soldier recalled that, having broken through the American lines during an offensive in late 1944, he found himself driving through an alley of artillery shells—"stacks of shells that stretched for, I would guess, two kilometers both

Mass production of the B-17 "Flying Fortress" aircraft at the Boeing plant in Seattle.

left and right . . . I had never seen the like of it. I told my squad, 'My God, their supplies are unlimited!' "

CONTROLLING PRICES

Federal spending, pushed rapidly upward by the costs of war, amounted to more than $320 billion between 1940 and 1945, almost six times the total during Franklin Roosevelt's first two terms. The level of outlays made the federal government an unprecedentedly gigantic consumer, not only for weapons but also for items such as uniforms and shoes for the armed forces. The government's enormous demand for goods and services put high pressure on prices, and so did wartime paychecks, since the diversion of material and productive capacity to war purposes created scarcities in civilian goods. For example, new cars and kitchen appliances were unavailable, and some foodstuffs like sugar were in acutely short supply. If the civilian economy had been allowed to operate under the rules of a purely free market, too much money would have been chasing too few products, with the result that prices would have skyrocketed, injuring many people, especially those in lower-income groups.

> *"Federal taxes paid for only about 41 percent of war spending. The rest came from loans."*

Roosevelt tried to deal with the problem by paying for as much of the war as possible through taxes. The wartime revenue acts raised rates in the highest brackets to 94 percent of net income. They also reduced the level of income exempt from taxes, compelling many more people to pay them. In 1941, only 7 million Americans filed income tax returns; in 1944, some 42 million did. In 1943, to facilitate its cash flow and ensure compliance, Congress enacted the system of withholding taxes from paychecks. Still, federal taxes paid for only about 41 percent of war spending. The rest came from loans, including $100 billion in war bonds that the government sold to its citizens. Increased taxes took some money out of the civilian economy, and so did war bond sales, but even both measures together were inadequate to deal with inflation.

In August 1941, to handle the matter, Roosevelt created the Office of Price Administration (OPA). The following April, the OPA announced a freeze on prices, enforcing it through thousands of local boards, which enlisted local volunteers, most of them women, to check whether merchants complied. The OPA, which administered the rationing of gasoline and tires, extended rationing to other necessities such as meat, sugar, shoes, coffee, and canned goods, and it issued books of coupons needed to purchase them. The manufacturers of Wrigley's gum and Coca-Cola, both heavy consumers of sugar, might have been devastated by the rationing, but both got around its restrictions by convincing the army and navy that American sailors and soldiers around the world craved their products.

Similarly, farmers successfully insisted on special treatment for agricultural prices, which drove up the cost of food, and labor in turn demanded compensatory increases in wages. When in July 1942 workers in several of the comparatively smaller firms in the steel industry demanded a wage increase of a dollar a day, the National War Labor Board, which had been created in January to manage labor practices and prevent strikes, devised the "Little Steel" formula. It capped wages for the duration of the war at their level of January 1, 1941, plus the 15 percent that the cost of living had risen since that date. Prices began leveling off in mid-1943. Despite high-priced and illegal sales of some rationed goods

A poster urging the public to buy war bonds, 1942.

Choosing canned goods for sale under the Office of Price Administration's rationing system, 1942.

ECONOMIC BOOM

In the months after Pearl Harbor, as war contracts continued to energize the economy, unemployment virtually disappeared. Between 1940 and 1945, the gross national product more than doubled, reaching $211.9 billion, and so, almost, did GNP per capita. After-tax corporate profits climbed 70 percent; farm income doubled; and industrial wages shot up 50 percent even after adjustment for inflation. Partly because of higher taxes, the war economy somewhat reduced the gap between high- and low-income groups and generated a great surge in the size of the middle class. A woman who worked with her mother and sister in a shell-loading plant in Paducah, Kentucky, remembered, "We made the fabulous sum of thirty-two dollars a week. To us it was just an absolute miracle. Before that, we made nothing."

The war mobilization also greatly affected the fortunes of labor and agriculture. Labor benefited from a combination of federal policy and the wartime manpower shortage. Although the anti-inflation policy exemplified in the Little Steel formula limited wage increases, overtime pay helped drive up weekly earnings 70 percent on average. Under the circumstances, workers had little incentive to join unions, but by the end of the war organized labor had gained almost 6 million new members, largely because, in return for a no-strike

in "black markets," the OPA managed to maintain overall price stability for the rest of the war. Between 1942 and 1945, after almost four years of war, consumer prices had risen only about 10 percent, compared with the increase of 62 percent during the year and a half of war that ended in November 1918.

Wartime Washington was acutely short on housing and proliferating with federal agencies. The bureaucratic expansion occurred partly because Roosevelt had no master plan for meeting the challenges of production and price controls, partly because he was reluctant to vest too much power in any single agency director. The resulting network of jurisdictions was often beset by overlapping authority and confusion, showing as little order as the sprawl of drab gray temporary office buildings that had sprung up to accommodate the government's wartime activities. To impose sanity on the situation, in May 1943 Roosevelt established the Office of War Mobilization, under James F. Byrnes, a former Supreme Court justice, who used his considerable judicial and political skills to draw together the multiple elements of the war effort at home.

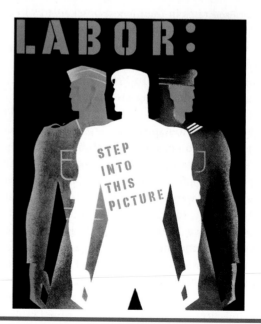

Labor is asked to do its part in the war effort.

Americans are encouraged to keep food on the table by canning the harvest of their "victory gardens."

pledge, the National War Labor Board insisted that unionized employers include a pro-union clause in their labor contracts. Getting around the cap on wages, a number of unions exercised the leverage they enjoyed amid the labor shortage to win their members unprecedented fringe benefits such as health and pension plans and paid vacations.

Although the no-strike pledge was widely observed at first, in 1943 some wildcat labor groups, discontented with the Little Steel formula, mounted short-lived work stoppages in shipyards and in factories making aircraft, leather, and steel. During the spring, John L. Lewis led the United Mine Workers out on three strikes, and for a time the government took over the mines. Although polls showed that Lewis was the most hated man in America, some administration members believed that the mine workers had legitimate grievances. In November, after further confrontations, the government approved a settlement with the mines

"The South, which accounted for about a quarter of the country measured by land and population, housed more than two-thirds of domestic army and navy bases."

whereby they got an increase in wages, among other improvements.

The war blew away hard times for farmers. Demand for agricultural goods skyrocketed, not least because the millions of men and women serving in the military had to be fed. To reduce civilian demand, in 1942 Americans planted 6 million small plots for raising their own vegetables—they were called "victory gardens"—and in 1943, 20 million, harvesting 8 million tons of produce. Farmers bought new agricultural machinery, used better fertilizers, and increased production by 50 percent. At the end of the war, agricultural output of crops such as cotton, corn, wheat, and rice far exceeded that at the beginning. The government extended price-support policies to more commodities and raised the parity rate, which tied a farmer's income for certain commodities to the prices they had fetched between 1909 and 1914, from 72 percent in 1939 to 110 percent in 1943. Agricultural income climbed steeply enough to put $11 billion into farmers' savings.

REGIONAL CHANGES

The war mobilization accelerated regional development, especially in the South and West, but the dramatic change in economic activity was felt by cities and towns across the country. One woman remembered the transformation in Seneca, Illinois, a small town turned into a shipbuilding center: "The trucks began rolling in with great loads of material. . . . Then came the new people, cars and cars and cars. . . . You'd hear the *rat-a-tat-tat* of hammering all night long. . . . Even the dogs knew enough to hide. . . . At the time we were only about a thousand people. One restaurant, an old hotel, that was all. All of a sudden Seneca and the surrounding area had about 27,000. . . . It was so crowded we had to stand in line the longest time with our ration books and food stamps."

The South, which accounted for about a quarter of the country measured by land and population, housed more than two-thirds of domestic army and navy bases, including all but one of the army training camps, which poured money into local retail and service industries. Defense manufacturing contracts came to the region in abundance, stimulating the creation of high-wage enterprises for the production of aircraft and ships in communities such as Mobile (Alabama), Marietta (Georgia), and Pasca-

823

A worker burnishing the nose of a shell at a steel plant in Birmingham, Alabama, 1942.

goula (Mississippi); of synthetic rubber in the oil-rich states of Texas and Louisiana; and of enriched uranium at an enormous plant that the atomic bomb project built for the purpose at Oak Ridge, Tennessee. The region's industrial plant doubled over what it had been in 1939, and industrial employment rose in comparable proportion. During the war, about a quarter of the southern population—some 4 million whites and blacks—left the farm, some for the North and West, most for the defense-boom areas in the South itself. It was said that for the first time since the Civil War, anyone who wanted a job in the South could get one.

Millions of people elsewhere were also on the move, migrating from farms to war production centers, from towns to cities, swelling the populations of Connecticut, Delaware, Florida, and Michigan, and especially of the far western states. California's population grew by more than 14 percent, fueled by the state's flourishing war economy. Roughly one out of eight defense contracts, amounting to a total by 1945 of $70 billion, went to

"California's population grew by more than 14 percent, fueled by the state's flourishing war economy."

California. War orders turned northern California into a huge center of shipbuilding and accelerated the growth of the aircraft industry in southern California, ensconcing the company names of Douglas, Lockheed, North American, and Hughes in the industrial firmament.

THE ENLISTMENT OF SCIENCE

The emphasis given to war production was complemented by the high priority awarded to expertise. To a degree unprecedented in the country's wars, the government relied on myriad specialists, including mathematicians to decipher codes, psychologists and linguists to devise propaganda, and economists to help manage the supply and demand of goods. But no category of experts played a more decisive role in the war than scientists and engineers, especially physicists. American analysts knew that Hitler had technical talent at his disposal; they were supplying his forces with fast planes, formidable guns, and serviceable radar. Policymakers in the United States understood that the defeat of the Axis Powers required technological innovation fast-paced enough to keep the Allies ahead.

In June 1941, to facilitate the work of war research, President Roosevelt melded the initial agency of scientific mobilization into a new Office of Scientific Research and Development (OSRD) under the leadership of Vannevar Bush, the engineer who after the fall of France had called his attention to the importance of mobilizing science. The OSRD was given direct access to congressional appropriations, responsibility for research in military medicine, and the authority to develop promising new devices into prototypes ready for production. The office fulfilled its mission handsomely, generating military technologies and medical advances that contributed mightily to victory.

Radar. One of the most important of the OSRD's projects was at the Radiation Laboratory at MIT—the "Rad Lab," as it was called, which had a staff of almost 4,000, close to 500 of whom were physicists. The laboratory developed new radars based on a powerful vacuum tube called a "magnetron," which was a British invention. The magnetron generated "microwaves"— radio waves of ten to twenty times higher frequencies than the "long" waves employed in the existing army and navy radars; and it produced them with a thousand times greater energy than the most advanced American tube. Compared with long-wave radar, microwave radar detected ships and aircraft far more accurately and at longer distances.

Microwave radar from the Radiation Laboratory first contributed significantly to the war when in the spring of 1942 it was deployed against German U-boats that threatened cargo ships coming up the East Coast from Central and South America. Army B-18 bombers equipped with new air-to-surface-vessel (ASV) radar easily detected German submarines that surfaced to take in air. Together with navy destroyers and other aircraft equipped with long-wave search radar, the B-18s drove the enemy submarines 300 miles away from the coast by the end of 1942. The victory in the eastern sea lanes demonstrated that radar-equipped aircraft were much more effective at finding submarines in the vast expanse of the sea than were destroyers.

During the spring of 1943, losses to enemy submarines on the North Atlantic shipping routes suddenly reached critical proportions. Churchill later wrote that the U-boat threat was the only one "that really frightened me during the war." Scientists and engineers called for a radical shift from the prevailing antisubmarine strategy—defensive reliance on the convoy—to a new offensive strategy: searching for the German wolf packs in mid-ocean, using hunter-killer groups of long-range and carrier-based bombers fitted out with ASV radar. The navy, although initially resistant to the idea that scientists might have something useful to say about military strategy, soon organized its antisubmarine forces into a unit that included a scientific advisory group and permitted the use of hunter-killer groups against German submarines. Shipping losses dropped from 245,000 tons in April to 18,000 tons in June. By early summer, Allied convoys were passing safely through lanes that had been perilous only a short time before. In Berlin, the chief German naval commander wrote in his diary that U-boat losses had reached "impossible heights"—because of the "increased use of land-based aircraft and aircraft carriers, combined with the possibility of surprise through the enemy radar location by day and night."

During the course of the war, the Radiation Laboratory developed a broad range of devices, including radar aids to bombing, fighter combat at night, and the navigation and ground control of aircraft. Microwave radar was also effectively coupled with new electronic systems that processed the information it provided about incoming aircraft and automatically aimed antiaircraft guns against them. Radiation Laboratory staff members would later say that the atom bomb only ended the war, that it was won by radar.

A Physicists' War. In August 1940, Vannevar Bush created an OSRD unit to provide the navy with a fuse for shells that would increase the chances of bringing down aircraft dive-bombing its ships. The likelihood of actually hitting an aircraft maneuvering evasively through the sky at some 300 miles an hour was low, and that of setting a time fuse—what the navy tended to rely on—so that a shell would detonate when it reached a plane was comparably small. The OSRD unit devised a fuse in the form of a rugged miniature radar that would trigger its carrier shell to explode when it reached a cer-

Microwave Early Warning (MEW) radar, one of the MIT Radiation Laboratory's most powerful and accurate inventions, played a crucial role during the D-day landings, detecting German aircraft and controlling Allied fighting cover.

tain proximity to the attacking aircraft. On January 5, 1943, a Japanese plane zoomed toward the relatively unprotected fantail of the cruiser *Helena*. The ship's five-inch guns fired its shells armed with proximity fuses and destroyed their target on the second salvo. Naval officers promptly began demanding huge quantities of the fuses. At the peak of wartime output, five major plants spewed forth some 70,000 of them a day, and fuse production occupied a full 25 percent of the nation's entire electronic industry.

Early in the war, physicists and engineers at the California Institute of Technology began developing rockets. Since rockets could be launched without recoil, they could arm small boats, airplanes, or even foot soldiers with firepower comparable to the five-inch guns on a battleship. Caltech rockets whooshed in ahead of the troops churning toward the beaches of North Africa in the autumn of 1942 and were used as standard naval ordnance in every subsequent landing in the Atlantic and Pacific theaters. By the end of the war, the Caltech project had produced more than 1 million rockets of different types and purposes.

"In the way World War I had been a chemists' war, World War II was a war of physicists."

By 1943, most of the nation's leading physicists had been mobilized for war research in radar, proximity fuses, rockets, the atom bomb, and numerous other OSRD projects. One professor remarked, "Almost over-night, physicists have been promoted from semi-obscurity to membership in that select group of rarities which include rubber, sugar, and coffee." Military officers now saw them as indispensable to national defense, both as progenitors of new weapons technologies and advisers on their use and implications for national security. Long before the mushroom clouds rose over Hiroshima and Nagasaki, knowledgeable observers knew that in the way World War I had been a chemists' war, World War II was a war of physicists.

THE MEDICAL WAR

OSRD medical scientists scored triumphs in saving lives on the battlefield and preventing the spread of infectious disease among the troops. During World War I, one of every seven or eight wounded soldiers treated in front-line hospitals died of infection; a powerful antibiotic would have saved many lives. In July 1941, a British biomedical scientist came to the United States in the hope of manufacturing such a pharmaceutical—a blue-green mold called "penicillium" that could

combat bacterial infections in mice and humans. At the time, the only broadly usable agents against bacteria only inhibited their growth. Penicillin—to use the name for the antibiotic that the British scientist and his colleagues hoped to make from the mold—would kill them. The mold was common, showing up on the surface of stale foods such as bread or cheese. An industrial penicillin program was started that produced the mold in quantity through a fermentation process.

Clinical tests conducted on wounded soldiers with the first yields were highly effective, and in June 1943 the army called for a major program of penicillin production. Scientists searched the world for the most promising strains of the mold. One of them said later that "the best producer of all was cultured from a moldy cantaloupe picked up in a Peoria [Illinois] fruit market." In 1945, penicillin production totaled enough to provide 21 million daily doses to soldiers suffering from wounds or infections such as venereal disease, an affliction they commonly picked up from local sexual encounters.

Fighting Malaria. Malaria at times posed a greater threat to American troops than did enemy forces. In the Pacific and Middle Eastern theaters, the disease ranked second only to gonorrhea in producing casualties from infection. Malaria is caused by a parasite that is carried by the *Anopheles* mosquito, one of whose prime developmental environments is still, fresh water, the kind that occurs naturally in ponds or that accumulates in battlefield ruts and shell holes. When in 1942 American soldiers took the offensive at Guadalcanal, malaria caused five times as many casualties as combat, bringing down 100,000 personnel from all the armed services.

The long-standing drug for both prevention and treatment of malaria was quinine, which comes from the bark of a tree grown mainly in Indonesia. The Japanese now controlled some 90 percent of the world quinine supply. In late 1942, the military and the OSRD medical unit found a synthetic substitute for quinine—a drug called Atabrine, which the Germans had first developed. Despite several drawbacks such as turning skin and nails yellow, it proved to be the best synthetic antimalarial agent available during the war. By the summer of 1943, several companies were together turning out Atabrine at the rate of 1.2 billion tablets per year, and it was available to American troops in areas at high risk for malaria the world over.

American soldiers dust their clothing with DDT powder, the new protective against typhus, 1944.

Early in the war, the army opened a second front against malaria, aiming to suppress or kill the *Anopheles* mosquito. It filled shell holes and other earthen pockets where still water might collect and spread oil over water surfaces to prevent larval maturation. But the army also wanted an insecticide that could be used to treat large, mosquito-infested areas. High hopes centered on DDT, an organic chemical that had been synthesized in the late nineteenth century and had been shown by a Swiss chemist in 1939 to kill insects. DDT, which could be spread over large areas as a spray or dust, was effective not only against mosquitoes but against lice, which carry typhus, and fleas, which carry plague. In 1944, given high priority for their task, several American companies produced 10 million pounds of the insecticide, a sixfold increase over the 1943 output. By 1945, aerial spraying with DDT was overtaking other antimosquito measures and becoming a powerful weapon in the fight against malaria and other insect-borne diseases.

Replacing Blood. Perhaps nothing was as indispensable to saving the lives of wounded soldiers, sailors, and fliers as blood—whole blood, or at least blood plasma. (Plasma comprises the fluid portion of blood other than red and white cells; it contains a variety of proteins and has a dilute, yellowish color.) The speedy replacement of blood fluids is critically important for people suffering from hemorrhage, burns, and shock. The military found practical replacements in freeze-dried plasma, a prewar development, and albumin, a postwar innovation from OSRD. (Albumin, one of the plasma proteins, increases blood volume by drawing fluids from tissue into the blood vessels.) The military established the industrial production of freeze-dried plasma and albumin that took its raw material from blood drives the Red Cross conducted in thirty-five cities throughout the war, generating more than 13 million voluntary donations. (The donations were segregated into blood that came from whites and from blacks, a practice that honored racial prejudice but that was scientifically pointless.)

Patients stabilized in hospitals often needed transfusions of whole blood. Both the British and the Americans devised methods to preserve fresh blood for twenty-one days, a five-fold increase over the prewar standard that made it practical for field-hospital use. By the end of the war, some 500,000 units of whole blood had reached armed service members in the European and Pacific theaters.

All told, the OSRD medical unit spent some $24 million—the cost of four hours of the war. Its principal projects more than repaid the investment. Blood substitutes administered on the battlefield saved thousands of soldiers who in World

Medics administer blood plasma to a wounded soldier during battlefield surgery, 1944.

War I would simply have died from shock and hemorrhage. Thanks to penicillin, only about one out of thirty front-line soldiers died in field hospitals from infection, roughly a four-fold reduction from the rate in the first war. In Naples, Italy, in 1944, a typhus epidemic was halted completely after 1.3 million people were dusted with DDT. Although DDT would later earn censure as an environmental toxin, at the end of the war it was ranked with penicillin in the pantheon of bio-medical miracles.

The War in Europe

In January 1943, as war goods and technologies were pouring out of factories and laboratories in cascading volume, Churchill and Roosevelt met in Casablanca, on the coast of Morocco, to debate the Allies' move into northern Europe. Stalin did not attend, explaining that he was needed at home because the Soviet army was locked in a savage and prolonged battle against the Wehrmacht at Stalingrad, deep in Russian territory on the Volga River. Despite his absence, Stalin's desire for a second front commanded Roosevelt's and Churchill's attention. But Churchill, eager to further secure the Mediterranean region, argued for using the troops already assembled in North Africa for an assault against Sicily that summer. Roosevelt and his military chiefs assented, not least because the United States had deployed such sizable forces in the Pacific—even more than were in North Africa and Britain—that an invasion of northern Europe in 1943 no longer seemed practical. At a press conference, Roosevelt announced that the war would end only with the unconditional surrender of the Axis Powers—a doctrine partly intended to convince Stalin of Western resolve, thus preventing another separate peace in the East.

By the spring of 1943, the Red Armies had broken out of Stalingrad; by the fall, they were on the offensive westward across a thousand-mile line. Stalin renewed his demand for the quick opening of a second front. However, in May, at a stormy meeting in Washington, Churchill insisted that the Anglo-American forces should follow up their expected capture of Sicily with an invasion of Italy. Although the proposal seemed unwise to General Marshall, since it could delay the cross-channel attack, Churchill held that it would draw German troops down from northern Europe. Roosevelt extracted an agreement from Churchill that after November the British and Americans would concentrate their troops in England for a cross-channel attack in May 1944, but that summer the Allies took Sicily and Roosevelt agreed that they should next invade the Italian mainland.

INTO ITALY

During the battle for Sicily, members of the Italian regime forced Mussolini's resignation, arrest, and imprisonment, with the formation of a new government under Marshal Pietro Badoglio. Although Badoglio was an enthusiastic fascist, official Rome recognized the deteriorating military situation for what it was and sued for peace with conditions. With Roosevelt's and Churchill's approval, Eisenhower negotiated a surrender that permitted Badoglio and his fascist associates to remain in power and eventually join the Allies as co-belligerents. But Italy remained under the control of German forces.

Early in September 1943, the Allied forces landed in Italy, with the Americans striking at the coastal city of Salerno, on the western side of the Italian boot. The Germans promptly rescued Mussolini, reinforced their armies, and put up stiff resistance. During the succeeding months, British and American troops clawed up the Italian peninsula, spilling blood for every mile they gained against the German troops, who were dug into the craggy hills and rocky spurs that descended to the coast on both sides of Italy's mountainous central spine. It took them until June 1944 to get to Rome, just 170 miles from Salerno. When they arrived, exuberant crowds, ecstatic at being rid of the Germans, bedecked their guns with flowers. But the German forces, although driven back to the north of Florence by August, dug in along a line from Pisa across Italy to Rimini and remained there, unmovable, until the last weeks of the war.

BOMBING EUROPE

In the fall of 1942, in a major preparatory step for the cross-channel invasion, Britain and the United States initiated a combined round-the-clock bomber offensive against Germany. The British had adopted a policy of carrying out raids at night so as to minimize losses, and of aiming its bombs at urban areas of war production, including sectors with workers' housing. Their purpose was to break the morale of the German civilian population. During four nights in July 1943, a British force bombed Hamburg, going after oil refineries, U-boat pens, docks, and dwellings with such relentlessness that the bombing precipitated a firestorm, burning 80 percent of the city's buildings and killing at least 30,000 civilians, including thousands of children.

The U.S. Eighth Air Force, based in Britain, made its mission precision bombing during daylight of specific industrial and transportation targets. American bomber forces had been designed to deliver large bomb loads onto small targets, but as a result of the characteristically poor weather conditions in Europe, Allied bombers could find their targets visually no more than about one day out of every five during the year, even less frequently during the fall and winter months. The MIT Radiation Laboratory developed a radar

The firestormed ruins of Hamburg after the Allied bombing in July 1943.

device, code-named "H2X," that could peer through clouds and display a map of the terrain below on the round screen of an oscilloscope. In October 1943, a squadron of B-17 bombers equipped with H2X arrived in England and began leading bombing raids over continental Europe. Soon a small contingent of civilian radar experts, most of them physicists, was established in the headquarters of the Eighth Air Force and became deeply involved in the planning and management of the air war.

U.S. Air Force leaders hoped that the B-17, a Flying Fortress bristling with .50-caliber machine guns front and back as well as top and bottom and a crew of six to ten men, could defend itself against enemy fighters. The air force also tried to protect its bombers with supersecret radar countermeasures, which a laboratory at Harvard helped develop to fool, jam, and confuse the enemy ground radars that guided German night fighters and antiaircraft guns to the attacking bombers. However, the Eighth's B-17s flying into Germany suffered grievous losses, up to 10 percent on each mission. One flight surgeon saw to it that the crews got liquor rations after each mission—to help "relax them slightly from the horrors," he said.

In June 1944, Hitler opened a new era in the bombing of civilians by sending his new V-1 rockets—the V stood for

"vengeance"—against London. Launched from Peenemünde, an offshore German island village in the Baltic, where they were designed and developed, the rockets were pilotless, radio-controlled missiles propelled by small engines that sped across the channel at 400 miles an hour; some 2,400 would strike London over several months, killing 6,000 people and wounding 40,000 more. They were a prelude to the V-2s—the first intermediate-range ballistic missiles—more than 1,000 of which were lofted from Peenemünde toward the British beginning September 8. On launch, the V-2s were powered by rockets along a 60-mile-high arc, then fell toward England, accelerating as they descended to a speed of some 3,000 miles an hour. Many V-1s sent by the Nazis did not reach London because they were shot down by radar-guided fighters and antiaircraft guns firing proximity-fused shells, but the only defense the Allies had against the V-2s was to bomb and, ultimately, capture the launch sites.

Officially, it was U.S. Army Air Force policy in Europe not to engage in terror bombing. However, bombing by radar and even visually was highly inaccurate—B-17 crews dropped almost 90 percent of their bombs more than half a mile from the target—with the result that in practice American planes bombed civilian as well as military areas. Early in 1945, the British urged the American air forces to turn practice into overt policy by joining in the air campaign to break German morale. In February 1945, heeding British arguments, the U.S. air forces began to carpet-bomb cities, setting off a firestorm in Dresden that killed 35,000 people. In the end, the combined bomber offensive killed some 600,000 German civilians, injured 800,000 more, and devastated the manufacture of German fighter aircraft and aviation fuel. However, while it depressed German morale, it neither kept people from doing their jobs nor seriously dented most other war production. And it led influential members of the U.S. military to accept terror bombing as an instrument of warfare, and to consider the German V-1 and V-2 rockets as harbingers of the strategic future.

THE INVASION OF FRANCE

To Stalin, the bombing offensive was no substitute for the second front in northern Europe. At Tehran, Iran, in November 1943, the fighting having turned in the Soviet Union, he met for the first time with Roosevelt and Churchill and pressed his case. Churchill reluctantly agreed to go ahead with the cross-channel invasion as scheduled. Roosevelt chose Dwight Eisenhower to command the effort.

Through the winter and spring of 1944, the Allied preparations for the invasion accelerated, producing a huge buildup of forces in England—thousands of guns, tanks, ships, and aircraft, and 3 million soldiers, sailors, and airmen. Just before embarking for the journey across the channel, each American soldier was given a can of DDT antilouse powder to forestall typhus. The Allies encouraged the Germans to believe the attack was coming in the Calais region, directly across the channel from Dover, but the objective was actually 150 miles to the southwest, along the channel beaches in Normandy.

The invasion began early in the gray dawn of June 6, **D day,** when thousands of ships appeared off the Normandy coast while thousands of planes thundered overhead. Technical countermeasures jammed and deceived German coastal radars, while the Eighth Air Force and its British counterpart, finding their targets with H2X, bombed the beach defenses ahead of the assault forces. The troops, disgorged from landing craft close to the shore, picked their way under heavy fire through obstacles planted by the Germans, dodging as they ran across the open sand for the shelter of the cliffs and pebbled banks. The number of casualties varied from sector to sector but was especially high at Omaha Beach, where American infantry went in. The first wave of Allied troops held on across the entire sixty-mile front, consolidated their positions on the invasion beaches, and then, followed by more waves of soldiers and guns and tanks and trucks, began the advance inland.

In the weeks after the Normandy landing, the Allied forces took northwestern France, then turned eastward in pursuit of the rapidly retreating German army. The German commander in Paris, Dietrich von Choltitz, gave up the city in defiance of Hitler's order to burn it, and on August 25 troops of the free French marched triumphantly down the Champs-Elysées, followed by the U.S. Fourth Infantry Division. On August 15, an Allied force had landed in the south of France between Toulon and Cannes; it quickly proceeded up the valley of the Rhône and joined with part of the inva-

D day: American forces landing on a Normandy beach, June 6, 1944.

sion forces in the north, thus establishing a continuous Allied line from Switzerland to the North Sea. In September, the Allies swept across France, but in the late fall the drive east slowed, beset by supply bottlenecks, stiffening German resistance, and the arrival of snowy weather.

The drive across Europe was costly. Soldiers relied for life on each other and on the medics, one of whom was attached to every platoon. Medics usually reached a soldier within ten to thirty minutes after he was hit. (One recalled "the unspeakable light of hope in the eyes of the wounded as we popped over a hedgerow.") They applied bandages and tourniquets, often under fire, then arranged for the wounded soldier's quick transport back to a battalion aid station. At one field hospital during the first week of the invasion, patients arrived at the average, unrelenting rate of one a minute. More than 85 percent of those who underwent emergency operations survived.

Combat conditions took a heavy toll on the troops, even those who remained physically whole. Trench foot—damage caused by cold and wet to the nerves and blood vessels—turned a soldier's feet white, then purple, then black, indicating the presence of gangrene; treatment could require the amputation of toes or the feet themselves. During the winter of 1945, trench foot forced some 45,000 men—the equivalent of three infantry divisions—out of the front lines. The con-

General Eisenhower talks with a G.I. at an American position in France late in 1944.

stant risk of death, the experience of it in the shattering of friends, the reminders of it in the roads and fields carpeted with bodies, all generated psychological and emotional strain. Combat efficiency fell after some ninety days at the front; after four to six months, almost everyone broke. The G.I.s nevertheless kept at their job, not out of any abstract commitment to war aims, later studies showed, but out of a desire to help each other, get the ordeal over with, and go home.

Eisenhower wanted to get it over with, too, and as quickly as possible with the V-2s descending on London, the Soviet armies storming into Central Europe, and with who knew what progress the Germans were making toward the development of an atomic bomb. Despite the adversities of the late fall of 1944, he kept the Allied troops moving across a broad front toward Germany.

The War in the Pacific

Even though the United States had halted the Japanese advance in the Battles of Midway and the Coral Sea, in 1942 the Pacific west of the Hawaiian Islands remained what the leading historian of the naval war once called "a Japanese lake." After Pearl Harbor, the Japanese had established an extensive

American troops with German prisoners of war at Omaha Beach in Normandy, France, June 6, 1944.

defense perimeter, turning the islands and atolls of the Pacific into fortified barriers extending through much of the 2,000 miles that lay between the Japanese home islands and Hawaii as well as between Japan and Australia. To get at Japan itself, American military planners resolved on a two-pronged offensive, so that the Japanese could not concentrate their forces against either line of action. One, under General MacArthur, would proceed via the large islands of the southwestern Pacific, starting with New Guinea and ultimately regaining the Philippines. The other, under Admiral Chester Nimitz, would approach Japan by taking the small islands and atolls of the central Pacific, many of them palm-treed tongues of sand and coral surrounding a lagoon.

THE NAVY'S ADVANCE

The naval offensive began in November 1943 with the invasion of Tarawa and Makin, small atolls in the Gilbert Islands at the far end of the Japanese defense perimeter. Makin fell easily, but Tarawa was heavily defended by 5,000 Japanese troops, many of them dug into pillboxes and bunkers, some of which were twenty feet deep, built of coral and concrete, coconut logs and steel. These troops had to be forced out by flamethrowers, grenades, and mortars; and when it appeared they were losing, they fought ferociously, mounting a suicidal death charge. Tarawa indicated that the brutal fighting the marines had first encountered at Guadalcanal would prove to be the rule in the Pacific. (The full, grim reality of the battle was revealed to the American public in the Oscar-winning Marine Corps documentary *With the Marines at Tarawa*, which unblinkingly—and for the first time in a war film—showed real American dead.)

Nimitz resolved simply to bypass the islands that were more strongly held, leaving them to atrophy by cutting off their lines of reinforcement and supply. His forces thus leapfrogged to the Marshall Islands, taking Eniwetok and Kwajalein, and by early 1944 they had gained control of both the Gilberts and the Marshalls. Wherever the marines landed, they were accompanied by construction battalions—commonly called "Seabees," after the first letter in each of the two words—who built roads, hospitals, harbor facilities, and airfields and thus developed a string of American military bases extending toward Japan.

Nimitz headed next for the islands of Saipan, Tinian, and Guam in the Marianas, the capture of which would bring Japan within reach of the new B-29 "Superfortresses." By now, 1944, American sea and air power in the Pacific, equipped with rockets and proximity fuses, was reaching formidable levels. During the battle for Saipan, in what was commonly called the "Great Marianas Turkey Shoot," American pilots and gunners knocked two-thirds of the Japanese aircraft out of the sky, sank three Japanese carriers, and damaged several other ships. The U.S. forces lost only twenty-nine planes, and their ships suffered negligible damage. On Saipan, the Japanese put up fierce resistance. Hundreds of Japanese civilians, propagandized to fear American atrocities, committed suicide, as did the island's defenders when they ran out of ammunition. Saipan was secured within a month of the invasion. By mid-August, so were Tinian and Guam.

MacARTHUR'S DRIVE

By January 1943, MacArthur's troops had gained control of New Guinea in the area of Papua, at the southeastern end of the 1,500-mile-long island. Now MacArthur proceeded along the northern New Guinea coast, executing a brilliant series of amphibious landings that bypassed areas heavily defended by the Japanese, leaving them, as Nimitz was doing to the north, to wither on the vine. On October 20, 1944, MacArthur waded ashore at Leyte and, while standing in a monsoon rain, announced over a truck-mounted microphone, "This is the voice of freedom, General MacArthur speaking. People of the Philippines, 'I have returned.' "

The Japanese, who had more than a quarter million troops in the Philippines, were unprepared for the landing, but they put up stiff resistance on the ground and initiated the largest naval battle in history in Leyte Gulf. For the first time, some of the Japanese planes were devoted to kamikaze attacks. A tactic of desperation, kamikazes were suicide aircraft, each armed with one 550-pound bomb, their mission to crash and explode on carrier decks. (By the end of the war, they would sink or damage more than 300 U.S. ships and cause 15,000 casualties.) The ground fighting on Leyte, though heavy, ended in victory at the end of the year. MacArthur's forces moved on to the main Philippine island of Luzon and Manila, while Nimitz's proceeded through the Pacific, toward Japan.

FRUSTRATION IN CHINA

After Pearl Harbor, Washington was all the more eager to help China wage war against Japan, especially by supplying

General Douglas MacArthur returns to the Philippines, 1944.

military equipment to the armies of Jiang Jieshi, whose government remained at Chongqing (Chungking), in south central China. Since the Japanese controlled most of Burma, including access to the Burma Road, the main overland route into southwest China, the United States mounted an air supply operation, sending cargo-laden C47 transports into China over the "hump" of the Himalayas.

The Roosevelt administration hoped that Jiang would send ground forces to help in reopening the Burma Road, but he kept wiggling away from a commitment to Burma. General Joseph Stillwell, the crusty American commander in China, found his recalcitrance exasperating and Jiang himself worthy only of contempt. (Stillwell privately called him the "Peanut.") The Nationalist regime, including its army, was weak, corrupt, and inefficient, and Jiang was far more interested in using his troops to check the advance of the Communist forces under Mao Zedong (Mao Tse-tung) to the north, at Yenan (Yan'an), than to battle the Japanese.

Churchill had no illusions about Jiang's regime (he later wrote that he "found the extraordinary significance of China in American minds, even at the top, strangely out of proportion"). Roosevelt wanted to maintain friendly relations with Jiang, partly for military reasons, partly out of fear that putting too much pressure on him might provoke his political collapse, which would virtually ensure eventual Communist control of China and cause unpredictable political trouble at home. But in mid-June 1944, with Nimitz and MacArthur making great strides in the Pacific, the most Roosevelt expected from China was that Jiang's troops might keep a large number of Japanese troops diverted from the rest of the Pacific war. Although he remained eager to avoid the collapse of the Nationalist regime, he expected that it would eventually fall and that Jiang was to blame.

The War and American Society

The more American blood spilled on far-flung battlefields, the more the administration sought to keep the nation's war aims—notably Roosevelt's Four Freedoms—before the American people, the overwhelming majority of whom told pollsters in 1942 that they did not have a clear idea what the war was about. The effort was advanced by the Office of Facts and Figures, which was replaced in the spring of 1942 with the Office of War Information (OWI). The information experts used all available media to get their message across. Advertisers, with Roosevelt's encouragement, tied the benefits of liberty to the prospect of the good postwar life, predicting consumer marvels to come from wartime technical developments. A radio program featured a boy telling a girl that the war was "about *all* young people like us. About love and gettin' hitched, and havin' a home and some kids, and breathin' fresh air out in the suburbs . . . about livin' an' workin' *decent*, like free people."

The OWI, which for a time had a Bureau of Motion Pictures, enlisted the director Frank Capra to produce the *Why We Fight* series. Capra was famous for films of social comedy as well as for productions such as *Meet John Doe* and *Mr. Smith Goes to Washington*, which celebrated the ability of the individual to make a difference in politics and the community. The *Why We Fight* films tended to heavy-handed propagandizing, using enemy footage to contrast the pliant, oppressed citizens of Hitler's Germany or militaristic Japan with the resilient independence of Americans. The OWI assured filmmakers that the motion picture industry had to remain free to do as it pleased, without censorship. By and large, Hollywood followed its normal preferences, providing films that either treated the war with sanitized sentimentality or offered entertainments to escape from it. However, some filmmakers, left to their own devices, produced arresting documentary and fictional accounts of the war. Notable among them was the uncompromising documentary of the Battle of Midway made by John Ford, which won an Academy Award, and the classic *Casablanca*, in which the cynical owner of Rick's Café, played by Humphrey Bogart, gives the impression that he believes in nothing but assists his former lover in escaping so that her husband can carry on the fight for freedom.

"During the war, more than 6 million women went to work, increasing the number who were already employed by almost 50 percent."

The very dynamics of the war helped enlarge the meaning of freedom and equality. As Americans from diverse backgrounds were thrown together in factories, ships, planes, and ground-troop units, the war helped blur ethnic and religious divisions, breaking down barriers between Protestants, Catholics, and Jews. Hollywood helped acculturate moviegoers to the trend, producing a plethora of sentimental "platoon" films in which boys of Italian, Irish, Polish, Czech, and Anglo-Saxon backgrounds became friends, fought together, and wept when their buddies fell. At the same time, the high demand for labor encouraged women and members of racial minority groups to migrate not only to different regions but also into new occupations, with results that both challenged and weakened gender and color lines. Margarita Salazar found herself mixing with Anglos—the term Hispanics tended to use for non-Hispanic whites—for the first time in her life in the war plants of Los Angeles. "We all blended in," she recalled, "men, women, Mexican, Italian." And the rhetoric of war aims prompted these Americans to insist that words like "freedom," "tolerance," and "equality" should be taken seriously.

WOMEN

During the war, more than 6 million women went to work, increasing the number who were already employed by almost 50 percent. By 1945, women accounted for a third of the workforce, even more in some defense industries. Married women came to outnumber single women in the workforce for the first time in the nation's history. Women took jobs traditionally identified with men, including work as lumberjacks, welders, miners, lathe and crane operators, machinists, taxi drivers, and even professional players in a women's baseball league. Suzie Secretary and Wendy Waitress turned into the popular wartime symbol of "Rosie the Riveter," depicted in cap and overalls, tools in hand.

The exigencies of war also opened opportunities for women in the new Women's Army Corps, commonly known as the WACs, the Navy Waves, and the Marine Corps Women's Reserve. Although initially opposed to the recruitment of women, military officers changed their minds once they realized that women could effectively fill a variety of noncombat positions ranging from clerks to chemists, mapmakers, and ferry pilots. Some 300,000 women eventually served in the armed services and affiliated organizations. Attempts to recruit several hundred thousand more for the WACs failed miserably, partly because an early recruiting campaign's theme—"Release a Man for Combat"—implied that women who enlisted could be condemning someone's loved one to death.

"Rosie the Riveter" symbolized the capability of the nation's wartime women workers.

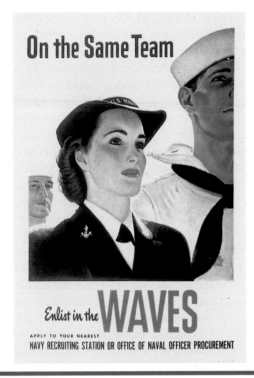

A poster recruiting women for the U.S. Navy Waves (Women Accepted for Volunteer Emergency Service).

At home, women earned far more as factory hands than they did in their previous jobs. Four states enacted laws ensuring women equal pay for equal work, and some states prohibited job discrimination against women. Still, working women encountered reminders that they were not working men and could not expect male privileges; those at the Frigidaire plant in Dayton, Ohio, for example, angrily complained that they were paid less than men for comparable work and were denied equal seniority rights. Women in the workplace were expected to fill conventional stereotypes, to "bring glamour to the job," as a female federal official put it approvingly. One personnel manager remarked, "We like the girls to be neat and trim and well put together. It helps their morale." Labor unions often stipulated that women would have to give up their jobs to men on their return from military service. "A woman is a substitute, like plastic instead of metal," a War Department brochure explained.

The forces pulling women back into the home remained powerful, especially for mothers with young children. "A mother's primary duty is to her home and children," the Children's Bureau in the Labor Department declared. Women with children under fourteen made up only 32 percent of women in the workforce. Young mothers tended to stay home, partly because while child care facilities increased in number during the war, they served too few children. In wartime Seattle, women workers were more than twice as likely to be absent from work as men. Critics who feared for the family pointed to the phenomenon of "latch-key children," sharp increases in the juvenile delinquency rate, and the jump in the divorce rate from 16 per 100 marriages in 1940 to 27 per 100 in 1944. Responding in a 1943 poll to the question of whether they would accept an offer of a war plant job, 28 percent of a national cross section of women said yes, but 51 percent said no. Still, wartime experience taught millions of women the satisfactions of paid work and independence, and set many of them to thinking that rights to both, for all the practical problems of exercising them, were worth establishing in peacetime.

AFRICAN AMERICANS

African Americans also made notable gains during the war. In the South, where the majority of blacks still lived and where they made up about a third of the population, planters and draft boards tried to keep as many as possible working on the land. Many African Americans nevertheless migrated from rural areas during the war, lured by the prospect of jobs in the thriving industrial plants. A number went to southern cities, but the majority—about 1,400,000, close to 16 percent of the blacks in the South—headed out of the region, roughly half to the north and half to the west, accelerating the Great Migration that had begun during World War I. In and out of the South, even those with high-demand skills, like welding, ran up against bald-faced discrimination. Craft unions in aircraft and shipping refused to accept African Americans, and white workers in some plants walked off their jobs to protest the hiring of blacks.

Blacks arrived in war-boom cities that were plagued by shortages in housing, social services, and police protection, and by increases in congestion, crime, and interracial tension. In 1943, several race-related riots erupted—the worst of them, a naked racial confrontation, in Detroit, where half a million people, including at least 60,000 blacks, had moved to work in war plants and formed a caldron of ethnic and racial resentments. The violence broke out on a hot Sunday evening in June, sparked by a rumor that a group of whites in the crowds leaving a recreation park had thrown a black woman and her baby off a bridge. Over the next twenty-four hours, blacks and whites fought pitched battles in and around Paradise Valley, the black ghetto near the park, while police shot looters and fired at rooftop snipers. Late the next day, at the governor's request, several thousand federal troops arrived to restore order. An elderly black woman lamented the racial animosity that the riot had exposed: "There ain't no North no more. Everything now is South."

At the outset of the war, blacks fared in the military much as they did in American society. The prewar military had denied blacks eligibility for training as army officers or air corps pilots, confined them to jobs as mess stewards in the navy, and maintained strictly segregated forces. Although the Selective Service Act of 1940 banned discrimination in recruitment and training, African Americans were assigned to all-black army units. The new WACs, following tradition, also segregated whites and blacks. African American men in military training encountered segregated theaters, post exchanges, and canteens on the bases as well as racial prejudice—and, in the South, Jim Crow laws—beyond the camp gates. While traveling in Texas to a new assignment, a group of black soldiers were denied entry to a railroad station lunchroom where two dozen German prisoners of war were being served with their guards. One of them asked in a letter to the army weekly magazine *Yank*, "If we are to die for our country, then why does the Government allow such things to go on?"

African Americans grew more and more unwilling to put up with the indignities and barriers to advancement they encountered in defense industries, the armed services, and American life. During the war, about 1 million African Americans served in the armed forces, and more than half of them went overseas. There, they tasted a freedom they did not enjoy at home. "The Europeans in our line of march had no racial hang-ups," a black master sergeant recalled, summarizing an experience that the return home would not erase. Black observers pointed out the patent contradiction between battling fascism and racism abroad while permitting racial discrimination and oppression to continue at home. Besides, they added, the United States' ongoing failures in race relations jeopardized its ability to court the good will of the rest of the world, the large majority of which was colored.

> *"Although the Selective Service Act of 1940 banned discrimination in recruitment and training, African Americans were assigned to all-black army units."*

In the spring of 1941, A. Philip Randolph, head of the Brotherhood of Sleeping Car Porters, called for 100,000 demonstrators to march in Washington to protest discrimination against blacks in the defense industries. In June, Roosevelt, eager to forestall the march, issued an executive order that banned racial discrimination in federal agencies and in companies with federal contracts and that established a Fair Employment Practices Commission (FEPC) to investigate the state of black defense employment. The FEPC exposed the ubiquity of discriminatory practices, which in turn led to efforts to increase black employment in aircraft companies, shipyards, and other defense installations.

Many African Americans insisted on pursuing a "Double V" campaign—victory over both fascism abroad and racism at home. Some 15,000 black soldiers joined the NAACP, and in the decade ending in 1945 the number of black union members rose more than eightfold. In South Carolina, blacks formed the Progressive Democratic Party, whose goals included challenging the whites-only state Democratic Party and registering more blacks to vote.

The rising aspirations of African Americans were supported by a growing number of white sympathizers. Eleanor Roosevelt lent the prestige of her position and the authority of her convictions to the African American cause, not least by participating in integrated social functions. Many white northerners who came south to the army training camps were taken aback by southern race practices. The race riots drew the attention of white liberals to the gap between the rhetoric of freedom and the realities of the home front. Nazism, with its celebration of the master race, in effect made racism a dirty idea. During the war, whites joined with blacks to form new organizations to achieve the goals declared by the name of one of them—the Congress of Racial Equality. And white politicos recognized the impact of the accelerating Great Migration northward. In 1940, the northern black vote had been larger than the majorities by which Roosevelt carried the four largest states, with 135 electoral votes—and northern politicians now felt the need to court it.

The military took steps to reform its racial practices, responding not only to protests from blacks and whites but also to the practical pressures of war. Manpower shortages demanded using as many able-bodied Americans as possible, and maintaining a segregated military was costly. Colonel

Benjamin O. Davis, a soldier since the Spanish-American War, was promoted to general, becoming the first African American to hold that rank. The army ordered on-base facilities and certain schools, hospitals, and off-base services to operate without racial restrictions. It abandoned rigid literacy standards and established Special Training Units to give draftees a basic education, ultimately providing literacy training to some 136,000 black soldiers. In 1941, the army air corps established a training base for blacks at Tuskegee Institute, in Alabama, and it created the first black air-combat unit. The navy opened its ranks to general black enlistments.

Overseas, commanders initially held that it would hurt morale and efficiency to put blacks into combat, so the army found itself assigning black units trained to fight to service positions. Eventually, however, if only because whites did not see why blacks should be protected from the risks of war that they faced, black soldiers, sailors, and airmen were sent into fire—always under white command—in both Europe and the Pacific. When in October 1944 an African American tank battalion arrived for duty with General George Patton's Third Army, Patton welcomed them heartily, saying they were "the first Negro tankers ever to fight in the American army. . . . I don't care what color you are, so long as you go up there and kill those Kraut sonsabitches." Eventually, black infantry were integrated into the combat army in Europe as platoons, and in 1944 the new secretary of the navy, James Forrestal, approved a program for integrating the crews of twenty-five combat vessels and later the whole auxiliary fleet.

Although early in the war both northern and southern soldiers favored segregation, most who served with blacks changed their minds. The captain of a black-crewed naval vessel noted in a letter to his parents that "there has been lot of bunk said about Negro crews," adding, "We can't see that they are different from others if treated the same. . . . They are anxious to make a name for themselves. They actually work harder." Blacks earned distinction wherever they served. In 1944, the Swedish sociologist Gunnar Myrdal published *An American Dilemma,* one of the most searching, thoughtful, and influential treatises on race in the United States. Myrdal emphasized that the dilemma over race was not only an economic issue but, amid the fight against Nazism, a moral one, too. He observed that "there is bound to be a redefinition of the Negro's status in America as a result of this war."

NATIVE AMERICANS AND MEXICAN AMERICANS

The war brought tensions and a taste of new possibilities to both the Native American and Hispanic communities, too. In Florida, the Seminoles declined to cooperate with the military draft, explaining that they were still technically at war with the United States, and in the Southwest the Hopis failed to appear for induction. Other Native Americans, however, saw opportunity and even duty in the war. About 75,000 Native Americans left the Indian reservations for work in defense industries and a number served in the armed forces. Some 400 Navajo comprised the Native American Code Talkers, a unit whose members did critically important duty with the Marine Corps in the Pacific by exploiting their language for secret communications—for example, *gini,* the word for

The Forty-first Corps of Engineers, an African American army battalion, at Fort Bragg, North Carolina, 1942.

Navajo code talkers near the front in the Bougainville jungle, December 1943.

"chicken hawk," was appropriated to mean "dive-bomber"—and using it at the frontlines. The Navajo code baffled the Japanese, who were unable to crack it.

Hispanics in the United States were familiar with the kind of discrimination that African Americans endured. In 1940, 90 percent of Mexican Americans lived in Texas, California, Arizona, New Mexico, and Colorado. During the war, by agreement with the American and Mexican governments, tens of thousands more entered the country in response to the labor shortage, the majority as contract agricultural labor under the *bracero* (from the Spanish word for "arm") program, which had originated in World War I. Set apart by language and skin color, Mexican Americans were subjected to segregation (a sign outside a Texas church read "For Colored and Mexicans"), forced to live in filthy shanties, barred from good jobs, and paid less than whites even when they did essentially the same work. Jose Chavez, an Arizona native employed at the Phelps Dodge Company since 1936, noted that he trained Anglo workers who got $6.22 a day, $1.32 more than he did.

Many Mexican Americans left agricultural labor for the defense and garment industries in and around Los Angeles, which was as crowded and beset by shortages as most wartime cities. Tensions with Anglos ran high. In 1942, twenty-three Mexican American gang members were tried

and seventeen found guilty by a biased court and a biased press of charges ranging from murder to assault; the charges arose from the death of a rival Hispanic gang member near a swimming hole called Sleepy Lagoon. The verdicts were later overturned on appeal for lack of evidence, but the newspapers nevertheless talked of a Mexican American "crime wave," and the police cracked down on Hispanic youth clubs, making arrests for what seemed purely racial reasons.

Young Mexican American men, seeking security and status, often joined "Pachuco" gangs and took to wearing "zoot suits," originally a Harlem ensemble of broad-brimmed hat, long draped jacket, and high-waisted baggy trousers tight at the ankles, accompanied by a lengthy key chain and duck-tailed hair. To many Anglos, zoot-suiters threatened law and order. Early in June 1943, sailors from the Chavez Ravine Naval Base, hearing that servicemen had been attacked by zoot-suiters, invaded the barrios of Los Angeles and for four days, together with soldiers on leave, beat teenagers and stripped off their zoot suits. The shore patrol, city police, and county sheriff's officers often ignored the sailors and arrested the victims. The Los Angeles City Council attempted to make it a punishable offense to wear a zoot suit. The street brawls spread to Pasadena, Long Beach, and even San Diego, soon

Japanese American children on their way to a relocation camp in Turlock, California, May 1942.

turning into what, in the judgment of some historians, was a full-fledged **race riot.** Order was not restored until mid-June, after Los Angeles was declared off-limits to naval personnel.

Draft boards in the Southwest made extensive use of their lengthy lists of eligible Mexican Americans. Yet even though Hispanics suffered discrimination in the armed services, they volunteered for military service in numbers that were disproportionately high compared with their representation in the population. More than a third of a million of them served in the wartime military. Most Mexican American draftees were assigned to the army, where, unlike African Americans, they were integrated as individuals into the infantry and saw considerable combat, some earning citations for distinguished service.

Anglos often had their eyes opened about their Spanish-speaking buddies. One trainee from the Midwest later reflected, "I always heard that [Mexican Americans] were not to be trusted. . . . But these fellows I have known here in [Camp] Roberts are just like other Americans." All the while, Mexican American activists in Texas exploited the liberal rhetoric of the war and of the Good Neighbor policy to gain some ground against segregation in schools and other public facilities, improve the chance of getting higher-paying jobs, and win acknowledgment as full-fledged citizens.

POLITICS AND THE LIMITS OF FREEDOM

Japanese American Relocation. The outbreak of the war threw a prejudiced spotlight on the 127,000 people of Japanese ancestry living in the United States in 1941, mainly on the West Coast, about two-thirds of whom were *nisei*—citizens born in the United States to the first generation of Japanese American immigrants. In the weeks after Pearl Harbor, the government rounded up some 2,300 Japanese aliens and Japanese Americans suspected of being subversives, a move that the FBI and the Justice Department both believed ended any threat to national security from the Japanese community. There was no evidence of espionage or sabotage by Americans of Japanese ancestry after Pearl Harbor, but many Americans on the West Coast were on edge enough to be acutely suspicious. Rumors abounded that the Japanese might attack—they were given a touch of credibility when in February 1942 a submarine

"In the spring of 1942, the U.S. government shipped the Japanese American populations of Washington, Oregon, and California—a total of 112,000 people—to relocation camps."

shelled a petroleum installation in Santa Barbara, California—and that Japanese Americans were preparing to assist them. Civic leaders and politicians raised a cry against the alleged internal threat. A California congressman declaimed in the House, "The only good Jap is a dead Jap."

Civic and military leaders on the West Coast clamored for the evacuation of all Japanese Americans and their internment in inland concentration camps. Proponents of the idea included liberals and moderates, notably Earl Warren, the attorney general of California, and the writer Walter Lippmann. The primary stated reason was to forestall internal subversion. Army general John DeWitt, who originally opposed evacuation but who would command it, came to hold that it was impossible to distinguish between a loyal and a disloyal Japanese American. Following an inexplicable logic, DeWitt declared, "The very fact that no sabotage has taken place to date is a disturbing and confirming indication that such action will be taken." However, the demand for internment was partly energized by ambitions to obtain land, jobs, and businesses held by Japanese Americans.

In the spring of 1942, under the authority of an executive order from President Roosevelt, the U.S. government shipped the Japanese American populations of Washington, Oregon, and California—a total of 112,000 people—to relocation camps, most of them in bleak desert areas, where they were housed in barracks, one family to a room, and forced to lead regimented lives. (No such internment occurred in Hawaii, not least because the large size of the Japanese American community there—more than a third of the population—made it impractical.) Many of the internees lost their crops, farms, and bank accounts as well as insurance coverage and licenses to practice medicine or law. Roughly two-thirds of those interned were American citizens. Nevertheless, by and large the Japanese American community went along with the evacuation program without resistance, with some of its members seemingly considering their exile, as the Japanese-American Citizens League observed, a form of "our duty to our country."

Some Japanese Americans, however, angrily renounced their citizenship. At least a dozen openly resisted the evacuation order, including Fred Korematsu, who was arrested and whose case challenging the constitutionality of the evacuation policy made its way, along with several others, to the Supreme

839

Court. In December 1944, in *Korematsu v. the United States*, the Court upheld the relocation policy by a majority of six to three, ruling that the action taken against Japanese Americans stemmed not from racial prejudice but from the requirements of military security. One of the dissenting justices castigated the removals program, declaring that it was based on an "erroneous assumption of racial guilt." (The government eventually came to agree with that view and in 1988 resolved to provide all Japanese Americans interned during the war with $20,000 in compensation.)

Despite the evacuations, some 33,000 Japanese Americans served in the armed forces, most of them as volunteers (Japanese Americans were ineligible for the draft from Pearl Harbor until January 1944). More than 6,000 served as linguists in the Pacific theater, accompanying troops into battle to interrogate Japanese prisoners and analyze letters, maps, and orders found on them and on the enemy dead. Several Japanese American units, including volunteers from the internment camps, served with distinction in North Africa and Italy, where the bravery and high casualty rate of one of them won the attention of the press and the sobriquet "the Purple Heart Battalion."

Chinese Americans, Korean Americans, and Filipinos also went into the armed forces. They were eager to fight the Axis Powers, especially Japan, because it had warred against their ancestral nations. Many considered service in the U.S. military an opportunity and a privilege—a way, as one young Filipino immigrant put it, of "serving as an equal with American boys." Fair-employment regulations helped open new job opportunities for Asian Americans. In 1943, Congress repealed the Chinese Exclusion Act, responding to demands from Chinese Americans, whose cause was aided by Madame Jiang Jieshi during a sojourn in the country.

The United States and the Holocaust. In 1942, American newspapers reported that Nazi death squads were shooting thousands of Jews in occupied territories such as Poland and the Ukraine, and the German refugee novelist Thomas Mann told of the mass atrocities in broadcasts over the British airwaves. Early that year, at a conference in Wannsee, a suburb of Berlin, senior Nazi officials established coordinated plans for a "final solution" of what they called "the Jewish problem" in Europe. In the coming months, the German government established camps at places such as Auschwitz and Bergen-Belsen, where they systematically concentrated Jews by the thousands and murdered them in gas chambers. In

1942, word of German plans to kill Jews wholesale reached the State Department, and national magazine articles reported that the Nazis had embarked on a program to exterminate the Jews of Europe.

In response to the turn of events, a number of Americans began to think less about how to deal with Jews who had escaped from Europe and more about how to rescue from almost certain death those who remained under Hitler's control. As in the 1930s, the rescue movement ran into the obstacle of anti-Semitism. Jews, who comprised about 3 percent of the American population, were still barred from moving into certain neighborhoods, faced quotas at certain colleges and universities, and were unwelcome in many jobs. It also was hampered by skepticism that the Nazis were really engaged in a program of mass extermination. When a Pole named Joseph Karski, who had posed as a guard at one of the concentration camps, told Supreme Court justice Felix Frankfurter about what he had seen, Frankfurter, a Jew, simply found it impossible to believe him. To many critics, the enormity of the alleged Nazi crimes seemed akin to the reports of German atrocities that had been a feature of Allied propaganda during World War I.

The evidence and pressure for action nevertheless grew so overwhelming that in January 1944 President Roosevelt created the War Refugee Board, charging it to rescue victims of enemy oppression in imminent danger of death and especially to forestall "Nazi plans to exterminate all the Jews." The board smuggled refugees out of threatened areas such as Hungary, sponsored Red Cross relief packages to the concentration camps, and encouraged the creation of free ports to which refugees might be temporarily admitted. In the end, the board helped save approximately 200,000 Jews and at least 20,000 non-Jews.

The American rescue record was better than that of the other Allied nations, but to many people then and since, it was by no means good enough, especially weighed against the 6 million Jews killed in the Holocaust. Rescue advocates argued for additional measures: bombing the railroads that brought Jews to the camps and their killing machinery; warning that German cities would be bombed in retribution for the slaughter; exchanging goods such as trucks for Jews. But the military did not want to divert air-force resources to nonmilitary objectives. Even some rescue advocates doubted that bombing the railroad tracks or the gas chambers would be effective, given the speed with which the Germans were able to rebuild their factories and transportation systems. Bartering trucks for blood might assist the German war effort, and retributive bombing might provoke the Germans to retaliate vindictively against prisoners of war or civilians in occupied countries. Still, the U.S. government might have done more, and sooner. The War Refugee Board's budget was limited, most of its funding consisting of contributions from Jewish organizations, and it enjoyed limited administrative support within the government. President Roosevelt dealt with the issue of mass exterminations in fits and starts, throwing neither the prestige nor power of his office behind the board's work.

A Shifting Political Agenda. Like Lincoln and Wilson before him, Roosevelt was willing to curtail civil rights and overlook atrocities in the interest of achieving military victory. Similar logic produced a rightward shift in the administration's economic policy. In 1943, Roosevelt himself remarked that "Dr. New Deal" had been succeeded by "Dr. Win the War." In order to supercharge industrial production, the government suspended antitrust prosecutions, permitted corporations tax write-offs, and guaranteed them profits by paying fixed fees above the costs they incurred in fulfilling war contracts. The system tended to benefit the largest corporations: 30 percent of defense-contract dollars went to the 10 biggest businesses. More than nine out of ten military and OSRD contracts for research and development granted the patents deriving from this publicly funded work to the contractor, a grant sure to give the contractors a competitive edge in the postwar period. As it was, in 1940 the top 100 companies accounted for 30 percent of all manufacturing in the United States; in 1943, for 70 percent.

Wartime production and prosperity revived popular admiration for business while it diminished enthusiasm for liberal reform measures. Although working time lost to strikes during the war amounted to less than a tenth of a percent of the total, many people disliked labor unions because some, like John L. Lewis's miners, went out on strike. They also resented the intrusiveness of wartime government regulations, notably the reach of the Office of Price Administration seemingly into every crevice of the consumer economy. In response to managing the demands of the war, the number of federal employees more than tripled, to 3.8 million. In 1942, the military moved into the new Pentagon, then the largest

> " *The 'G.I. Bill of Rights' provided both male and female veterans with numerous special benefits, among them low-interest loans to assist in the purchase of homes, businesses, and farms, and economic help in obtaining an education.*"

building in the world, which housed some 35,000 personnel. The trends in bureaucratic growth irritated conservatives and even gave some liberals pause. The country's totalitarian enemies had squashed the freedom of their own peoples and those they conquered. Even once they were defeated, freedom, some warned, might be jeopardized in the United States by excessive state power that was homegrown, a specter that made an increasing number of Americans wary of further federal initiatives.

In the congressional elections of 1942, the Democrats lost eight seats in the Senate and fifty in the House, dramatically moving the balance of power on Capitol Hill in a conservative direction. Republicans and southern Democrats joined to block liberal attempts to extend the New Deal and abolished some of its creations, including the Civilian Conservation Corps, the Works Progress Administration, and the National Youth Administration, all of which seemed superfluous in the full-employment economy. Congress also abolished the Rural Electrification Administration and passed the Smith-Connally Act, which was designed to curb the political and economic activities of trade unions partly by making it more difficult to strike and outlawing union contributions to political campaigns. In 1944, Congress rejected just about everything Roosevelt requested, including measures to deal with unemployment during reconversion from war to peace.

However, what Congress was unwilling to do for Americans in general, it showed itself more than willing to do for veterans when it unanimously enacted the Serviceman's Readjustment Act. Dubbed the "G.I. Bill of Rights" by the American Legion, one of its principal sponsors, the act provided both male and female veterans with numerous special benefits, among them low-interest loans to assist in the purchase of homes, businesses, and farms, and economic help in obtaining an education. The G.I. Bill would help defuse the threat of postwar recession and democratize access to home ownership, education, and business opportunity.

The 1944 Election. The Republican presidential nominee was Governor Thomas E. Dewey of New York, a forty-two-year-old moderate with internationalist inclinations who had vigorously prosecuted racketeers in New York City and had a reputation for administrative energy and efficiency. Dewey's running mate was Governor John W. Bricker of Ohio, a conservative isolationist. The Democrats, sensitive to Roosevelt's popularity and the need for stability in the middle of the war, refrained from disputing his candidacy for an unprecedented fourth term. But they fought heatedly over the choice of a vice-presidential nominee, eventually dumping Henry Wallace, the candidate of the liberal-labor wing of the party, in favor of Senator Harry S. Truman of Missouri, who had a down-the-line New Deal voting record and who, as a border-state politico, was acceptable to southerners.

> " *'I pray you to believe what I have said about Buchenwald,' said Edward R. Murrow. 'For most of it I have no words.' "*

Roosevelt struck observers who saw him as physically frail and lacking the spirit of his earlier White House days, but Dewey's harsh campaign attacks, including the charge that the Democratic Party was being captured by "the forces of Communism," provoked the president to come out swinging. In a memorable nationwide radio address, he ridiculed his opponents for attacking "my little dog Fala," declaring that he would not abide "libelous statements about my dog." Otherwise, the war and the postwar future dominated the election. Roosevelt, seeming once again to don the coat of Dr. New Deal, called for a future based on an economic bill of rights that he had proposed early in the year—a guarantee to Americans of an adequately paying job, decent farm income, sufficient medical care, decent housing, a good education, and "protection from the economic fears of old age, sickness, accident, and unemployment." He also stressed that the United States must not return to isolationism in the postwar period, that it had to remain involved in the world.

Roosevelt's campaign received an energetic boost from organized labor, angry at the passage of the Smith-Connally Act. The CIO circumvented the act's prohibitions against union political involvements by creating a separate political action committee—the first PAC—which canvassed voters on behalf of the Democratic ticket and provided almost a third of the Democratic campaign war chest. On November 7, Roosevelt defeated Dewey handily in the popular vote, 25.6 million to 22 million, and by a decisive margin of 432 to 99 in the electoral college. Democrats lost only one seat in the Senate while gaining twenty in the House. Northern black votes tipped eight states to Roosevelt. Despite the shift rightward, the large majority of Americans were unwilling to give up on the president who had carried them through the Depression and was now leading them in war.

Victory in Europe

BATTLE OF THE BULGE

The month after the election, on the morning of December 16, 1944, a quarter of a million Germans attacked Eisenhower's troops across a seventy-mile front in the thick forest of the Ardennes in Belgium and Luxembourg. By Christmas Day, the Germans had penetrated the Allied line in a bulge eighty miles long and fifty miles deep. However, despite the deep snow and subfreezing temperatures, small groups of G.I.s and even single soldiers fought back, courageously disrupting the German advance with an effectiveness far out of proportion to their numbers. Their tenacity may have been intensified by the report that on December 17, at Malmédy, Belgium, the Germans had murdered some eighty-six American prisoners of war. When the Germans invited an American force surrounded in Bastogne to surrender, their commander replied simply, "Nuts." Eisenhower, seeing that

American troops on the march during the Battle of the Bulge, winter 1944–45.

American G.I.s and inmates of the Nazi concentration camp at Dachau, Germany, celebrate its liberation, 1945.

the German venture out of their defenses made them vulnerable, took the offensive as an opportunity rather than a disaster. The American forces were aided in the Battle of the Bulge by the proximity fuse, which, in its first deployment over land, was used to air-burst shells over German troops unsuspectingly massed under cover of fog and vulnerable to the hail of shrapnel from on high. In the battle, the goriest in American history, some 20,000 Americans were killed and 40,000 wounded. But by the end of January, it was over, and the Allies were once again pressing eastward, buoyed by the taste of impending victory.

THE DEFEAT OF GERMANY

In March 1945, the Anglo-American armies in northern Europe crossed the Rhine and headed into Germany while the Russians moved into the Third Reich from the east. At the end of April, American and Russian troops met and celebrated at the Elbe River. In Italy, the Allied forces broke through the German line and headed into the northernmost regions of the country, driving toward the Alpine border with Austria and Switzerland.

As the American armies moved deeper into Germany, they encountered the concentration camps, with their gruesome

evidence of the Nazis' barbarity. When in early April the Third Armored Division entered Nordhausen, the site of a slave labor camp for the construction of V-2 rockets, its soldiers saw gaunt, skeletal creatures scarcely recognizable as human beings limping toward them. They came to what at first appeared to be piles of garbage and realized, when they saw part of a pile moving, that it contained people writhing in degradation. Eisenhower had been suspicious of the reports of such Nazi atrocities, but now he saw that they were not just propaganda. He promptly called on the Allied governments to send newsmen, photographers, and legislators to visit the camps and record firsthand what the Nazis had done. Following a visit to the concentration camp at Buchenwald, Edward R. Murrow broadcast what he had observed: "I pray you to believe what I have said about Buchenwald. . . . For most of it I have no words."

Hitler retreated into his bunker in Berlin and on April 30 killed himself. Two days later, the city was in Soviet hands. Shortly before 3 A.M. on May 7, 1945, the head of the German navy surrendered the Third Reich to Eisenhower at his headquarters in Reims, France. By now, the United States had been involved in the war more than twice as long—forty-two

June 1941	Office of Scientific Research and Development established.
1942	Twenty-six-nation "Grand Alliance" formed.
	112,000 Japanese Americans interned in desert camps.
June 1942	Battle of Midway.
November 8, 1942	English and American troops invade North Africa.
1943	Penicillin found to be an effective antibiotic.
September 1943	Allied forces land in Italy.
1944	The G.I. Bill of Rights.
June 6, 1944	Allied troops land at Normandy (D day).
June/September 1944	Germans launch V-1/V-2 rockets toward England.
December 1944	Battle of the Bulge.
May 7, 1945	Germany surrenders.

Chronology

months—as it had in World War I. Fighting on a global scale, it had successfully raised an armed force of unprecedented size, around 15 million men and women, some seven times as many Americans as had served under Woodrow Wilson. The country had equipped them handsomely, mobilizing the economy and science, and had expanded the meaning of freedom and equality at home. It had joined in creating and sustaining a Grand Alliance that had achieved victory in Europe. Now the job of defeating the Axis Powers remained to be finished in the Pacific.

Suggested Reading

Nat Brandt, *Harlem at War: The Black Experience in WWII* (1996)

Alan Brinkley, *The End of Reform: New Deal Liberalism in Recession and War* (1995)

Robert Buderi, *The Invention That Changed the World: How a Small Group of Radar Pioneers Won the Second World War and Launched a Technological Revolution* (1996)

David M. Kennedy, *Freedom from Fear: The American People in Depression and War, 1929–1945* (1999)

Harold Vatter, *The U.S. Economy in World War II* (1985)

Consumer spending on automobiles and other goods increased in the postwar 1940s.

QUESTIONS

■ **What were the purposes and effects of the atomic bombs dropped on Japan?**

■ **What were the major domestic challenges the Truman administration faced after the war?**

■ **How did the Cold War affect the priorities of the federal government?**

■ **What were the social and economic trends at the end of the war?**

■ **What were the major elements of the Fair Deal?**

■ **How did fears of domestic subversion develop during the Cold War?**

On April 12, 1945, less than a month before the defeat of Germany, the news flashed across the world from Warm Springs, Georgia: that afternoon, Franklin Roosevelt, thin and exhausted, had died of a cerebral hemorrhage. The next day, as his body was borne in a casket to the presidential train waiting to carry it north for burial at Hyde Park, New York, a black army musician stepped out from behind a portico and, tears streaming down his face, played the familiar Dvořák tune "Going Home." Millions of Americans shared his grief, producing a display of mourning not seen since the death of Lincoln. Roosevelt had filled their lives through depression and war for more than a dozen years, allaying their fears and giving them hope. Now he was gone, and the cheering that several weeks later greeted the victory in Europe was tempered by sorrow and uncertainty.

The new occupant of the Oval Office, Harry S. Truman, had to learn quickly how to deal with the Allies, manage the terrible atomic weapon that physicists were developing, and bring the war with Japan to a close. All these matters were fraught with implications for the United States' relations with the Soviet Union. Already chilling, these relations compounded the challenges looming in postwar foreign affairs, which included the country's commitment to internationalism, the prevention of another conflagration, and the establishment of a stable world order in which democracy and capitalism could flourish. Domestic needs posed problems of their own. They centered on the reconversion of the economy to a peacetime footing, the maintenance of the prosperity the war had brought, and the expansion of opportunities for all

Americans that the fight for freedom implied. No wonder that the day after Roosevelt's death Truman remarked to reporters that he felt as though "the moon, the stars, and all the planets had fallen on me."

Clouded Victory

ROOSEVELT'S ARRANGEMENTS

Truman had not been part of Roosevelt's inner circle and knew little about his wartime negotiations, agreements, projects, and plans. From 1943 onward, postwar arrangements had increasingly concerned the Big Three—the United States, Britain, and the Soviet Union—among the Allies, both in their home governments and in their joint meetings. Roosevelt brought to these encounters an eagerness to establish in the peace a structure of international relations capable of preventing war, facilitating trade and economic stability, and maintaining national self-determination. While Churchill shared some of these goals, he also wanted to safeguard the British empire, including the routes to it through the eastern Mediterranean. Stalin, bent on protecting the Soviet Union from future Western attack, was determined to establish buffer zones of influence in Eastern Europe and to enfeeble Germany so that it could never wage war again. Some of these aims conflicted with Roosevelt's, but the president was, as he said after one of the wartime conferences, "a realist." To the end of sustaining the alliance and pursuing his postwar goals, he accommodated to what he could not alter, seeking to finesse the more difficult contradictions for the time being and work out differences through personal relationships with his Allied counterparts.

At the Tehran Conference in November 1943, the Big Three considered what to do with Germany after its defeat. Stalin wanted to break it up permanently, but Churchill, suspicious of the Soviet Union, wanted Germany to be capable of maintaining a balance of power on the Continent. In the end, the Big Three agreed that Germany would be partitioned in a way to be determined. Roosevelt, who appreciated Soviet eagerness for a buffer against Germany, told Stalin that he would not oppose pro-Soviet governments in the Baltic countries, though he asked for a public commitment to elections, pointing out that American voters descended from Eastern European nationals wanted self-determination for their ancestral homelands. He and Churchill approved Stalin's intention to redraw Poland's borders by transferring eastern Poland to the Soviet Union and compensating Poland with land to the west, taken from Germany. Stalin, on his part, promised that soon after the defeat of Germany he would join the war against Japan. On his return to the United States, Roosevelt declared, "We are going to get along with him [Stalin] and the Russian people—very well indeed."

At a meeting in Moscow two months earlier, the Allied foreign ministers had committed their nations on paper to continued cooperation in the interest of postwar peace and security. In 1944, at a conference in Bretton Woods, New Hampshire, the Western powers established an International Monetary Fund, which was intended to stabilize the international value of national currencies. They also created the International Bank for Reconstruction and Development (later called the World Bank), which would lend money to countries devastated by the war and foster the revival of world trade.

The Big Three leaders convened for the last time in February 1945, at Yalta, in the Crimea, two months before Roosevelt's death. By then, the Red Armies occupied most of Eastern Europe and were establishing Communist regimes in the region. The month before, Stalin had recognized the Lublin Poles, a Soviet puppet, as the sole government of Poland, repudiating the Polish government-in-exile, which was based in London. Roosevelt and Churchill vigorously protested Stalin's action, insisting that the Polish government be broadly based and the product of free elections. Stalin countered that Poland, twice in the last thirty years a corridor

for the invasion of Russia, was a question of life and death for the Soviet Union. He nevertheless agreed to reconfigure the Polish government to include some members of the London Poles and, possibly because he thought the Communists might win, to hold general elections as soon as possible.

Stalin remained eager for the permanent partition of Germany, but he consented to its temporary division into four zones of occupation, including one for France. To gain Soviet help in the Pacific war, Roosevelt and Churchill were willing to promise Stalin concessions in Manchuria and the restoration to Russia of the territories it had lost in its war with Japan in 1904. In return, Stalin reiterated his pledge to declare war on Japan within two to three months of Germany's surrender—a crucial commitment in the minds of Roosevelt and Churchill, since, by invading Japanese-occupied Manchuria, Stalin's forces would pin down 1 million Japanese troops.

Conservative critics have long charged that Roosevelt and Churchill caved in to Stalin at Yalta, betraying Eastern Europe in a fruitless effort to appease the Soviet dictator. More

Churchill (left), Roosevelt (center), and Stalin at Yalta, February 1945.

849

recently, revisionist scholars have reversed this scenario, arguing that Stalin made most of the concessions and that the Anglo-Americans were mainly interested in keeping Eastern Europe and Asia safe for Western capitalism. However, the Red Army's presence in Eastern Europe left Roosevelt and Churchill little room for maneuver. They could only hope that Stalin would live up to his promise, made at Yalta, to consult on ways to help the peoples of Europe freely elect democratic governments. Consultation was, of course, far short of commitment. Still, contrary to the revisionists, while the Roosevelt administration strongly objected to left-wing totalitarian regimes in Eastern Europe, it was willing to accept social reformist governments friendly to the Soviet Union.

In all, Roosevelt had thought, overconfidently, that he could handle Stalin with a combination of charm, personal cajolery, and economic measures. He doubted that Stalin would be territorially aggressive and considered him more concerned with Soviet national interests than with the spread of Communism. However, soon after Yalta, Stalin violated his pledges to support political freedom in Romania and Poland. His behavior prompted Roosevelt to remark three weeks before his death, "We can't do business with Stalin. He has broken every one of the promises he made at Yalta." Still, Roosevelt declined to break with Stalin or even to push him hard, not least because he believed that the Allies needed the Soviets to conclude the war with Japan.

THE WAR IN THE PACIFIC

By the winter of 1945, the war against Japan had turned relentlessly savage. Propaganda on both sides encouraged Americans and Japanese to think of each other as subhuman, akin to insects, reptiles, rats, or apes. A U.S. Army Air Force group under the command of thirty-eight-year-old General Curtis LeMay was bombing Japan from Saipan, Tinian, and Guam, in the Marianas, going after ports, aircraft factories, and other urban industrial targets with B-29 Superfortresses, which had a range of 4,200 miles and could carry ten tons of bombs. Extending the break from long-standing American policy represented by the bombing of Dresden, LeMay introduced blanket bombing of large urban areas in Japan with incendiaries and jellied gasoline, called "napalm," for the purpose of destroying dispersed industrial targets by igniting the wood-and-paper structures around them. On the night of March 9–10, 334 B-29s fire-bombed Tokyo, killing at least 84,000 people and destroying some 16 square miles—roughly a quarter—of the city. By July, LeMay's crews had burned out 60 percent of Japan's sixty larger cities and towns.

In February, to gain better home bases for bombing runs and a staging platform for the ultimate invasion of Japan, American forces invaded the small island of Iwo Jima, just 775 miles from one of the Japanese main islands, and in April they assaulted the much larger one of Okinawa, almost 80 miles long and just 350 miles from Tokyo. The Japanese fiercely defended both islands, fighting from networks of tunnels and caves, using their bayonets and, at times, their teeth when they ran

The fire-bombing of Tokyo on March 9–10, 1945, devastated one-quarter of the city.

out of ammunition. By the time victory came on Okinawa in mid-June, the battles for the two islands had cost the American forces their heaviest losses of the war in the Pacific—77,000 casualties, including almost 19,000 dead.

In the late spring of 1945, the Joint Chiefs of Staff completed plans for the invasion of the Japanese home islands, to begin the following autumn. They were convinced by the tenacity of Japanese resistance that the costs of an assault on Kyushu, the southernmost home island, which was to be invaded first, would be huge—at least 268,000 casualties if the planned invasion force suffered losses at the same rate as did the troops on Okinawa. Sizable additional losses would be incurred during the follow-up invasion of the main island of Honshu. Truman said he "hoped there was a possibility of preventing an Okinawa from one end of Japan to the other."

THE ATOMIC BOMB

The key possibility was the **atomic bomb,** which Truman now knew about and which by the spring of 1945 seemed likely soon to become available.

The bomb was the result of the effort, which had grown gigantic, that had originated with the discovery in December 1938 of nuclear fission—the splitting of the uranium atom, with the release of nuclear energy, upon its bombardment with neutrons. If many fissions occurred rapidly, the accumulated energy would create a powerful explosion. But scientists were at first unsure whether what was feasible in principle could be achieved in practice. Natural uranium occurs in two forms—U-235 and U-238—that are mixed together. Ways had to be found to separate the U-235, which fissions, from the far more abundant U-238, which does not.

In 1941, a young physical chemist at the University of California at Berkeley named Glenn T. Seaborg discovered that after bombardment with neutrons, U-238 eventually transforms itself into a new element. Seaborg christened it "plutonium." Plutonium was found to fission, just like U-235. Thus, if the abundant but nonfissioning U-238 could be fashioned into a controlled, chain-reacting pile, it could be transformed into enough fissionable plutonium to make an atomic explosive.

In December 1941, encouraged by the progress to date, Vannevar Bush obtained a green light from President Roosevelt for a full-scale effort to build a bomb. The next month, physicists and chemists came to a new Metallurgical Laboratory at the University of Chicago that was established to build

J. Robert Oppenheimer (right) speaking to a reporter on the site of the Trinity atomic test in the desert near Almogordo, New Mexico, July 1945.

an atomic pile of uranium and determine whether it would achieve a chain reaction yielding plutonium. The physicist Enrico Fermi masterminded the construction of the pile in a doubles squash court under the stands of Stagg Field, the university's unused football stadium. On the afternoon of December 2, 1942, forty-two scientists, most of them on the spectators' balcony, watched in the near-freezing air as Fermi ordered the withdrawal of the pile's control rods until a chain reaction occurred, thus achieving human civilization's first self-sustaining release of nuclear energy. One physicist brought out a bottle of Chianti, and the group toasted the event in paper cups.

Recognizing that building an atomic bomb would require a huge industrial effort, Vannevar Bush, the head of the wartime scientific mobilization, helped arrange for the work to be assigned to a new Manhattan District of the Army Engineers. Although now a military enterprise, the project's commanding general allowed civilian scientists to retain direction of the necessary research. The scientists and engineers developed a cluster of methods for separating U-235 from U-238 and installed them in tandem at a giant facility for producing

851

uranium enriched in U-235 at Oak Ridge, Tennessee. They also designed a nuclear reactor and processing works for the production of plutonium on the Columbia River at Hanford, Washington (see pp. 860–61).

The apex of the Manhattan Project—a special laboratory for the design and development of nuclear weapons—was established on a mesa at Los Alamos, New Mexico, in March 1943 under the leadership of J. Robert Oppenheimer, a thirty-nine-year-old theoretical physicist. Soon hundreds of physicists, including some who had fled Hitler's Europe, were living and working at the isolated mesa, figuring out how to make workable atomic bombs from uranium and plutonium. To obtain a powerful explosion, sufficient fissionable material to form a critical mass had to be brought together quickly, then kept together long enough to release a lot of energy. The most direct assembly method consisted of using a gun to fire one subcritical mass of fissionable material into another with the speed and force of an artillery shell: the combination would form a critical mass that would hang together long enough to produce a powerful explosion. The gun method would work for U-235 but not for plutonium. The arrangement devised for the plutonium bomb, called "implosion," was to surround a subcritical mass of the metal with high explosives that when fired would produce a spherically symmetrical shock wave traveling inward toward the center of the bomb. The shock wave would compress the plutonium into a critical mass and, keeping it compressed while a rapid chain reaction developed, would maximize the energy released.

The Los Alamos scientists had high confidence in the gun method. In early July 1945, the laboratory assembled the uranium bomb, code-named "Little Boy," for shipment to the 509th Composite Air Group, a specially trained B-29 unit in the South Pacific. Less sure of the implosion weapon, they tested it—the exercise was code-named "Trinity"—just before dawn on July 16, in the desert near Alamogordo, New Mexico. A spot of light burst through the darkness, then boiled upward, exploding into a rainbow of fire that colored the desert wastes and dazzled the mountain ranges in the distance. Moments later, the shock wave blasted through with the roar of 20,000 tons of TNT. After the first exhilarating cheers of success, there was an awesome silence. A line from the Hindu poem the *Bhagavad Gita* flashed through

> *"Moments later, the shock wave blasted through with the roar of 20,000 tons of TNT. After the first exhilarating cheers of success, there was an awesome silence."*

Oppenheimer's mind: "I am become Death, The shatterer of worlds."

THE END OF THE WAR

The news of the successful Trinity test reached Truman at Potsdam, a suburb of Berlin, where he was attending a meeting of the Big Three. In the preceding weeks, the Japanese had sent peace feelers to the Soviets, asking for mediation but with the caveat that unconditional surrender was unacceptable. The American government was aware of the Japanese approach from intercepted cables. James F. Byrnes, now Truman's close adviser and his designated secretary of state, warned that agreeing to this concession might be taken as a sign of weakness and lead to demands for others. The United States concluded that it should seek to end the war by warning the Japanese of the grave consequences of continuing it. On July 25, an order from Secretary of War Henry Stimson and General Marshall authorized the atomic bombing of Japan as soon after August 3 as weather conditions permitted a visual attack. The next day, Truman and Clement Attlee, whom elections in Britain had just made prime minister in Churchill's place, issued a joint declaration warning Japan to surrender or suffer "prompt and utter destruction." Two days later, Japan rejected the Potsdam Declaration as "unworthy of reply." Truman, convinced by the rejection that delaying the use of the atomic bomb would be pointless, allowed the planned attack against Japan to proceed.

At 2:45 A.M. on August 6, 1945, three B-29s belonging to the 509th Composite Air Group rose from Tinian in the Marianas and headed for Japan, 1,500 miles to the north. In the belly of the lead plane, the *Enola Gay*, was Little Boy, the uranium bomb. The bombardier released Little Boy over Hiroshima, a large industrial city that was mostly untouched by bombs and included major military installations, and at 8:15 A.M., Japanese time, a great fireball incinerated the city, turning it into a wasteland of rubble covered with a huge column of smoke that rapidly swirled to 30,000 feet. Close to 80,000 people were killed in the attack, and tens of thousands more would die from burns and radiation poisoning.

The Japanese government, under the thumb of the military, nevertheless refused to surrender. Two days later, three

The rising mushroom cloud from the atomic bombing of Nagasaki, August 9, 1945.

months after the German capitulation, the Soviets declared war on Japan and invaded Manchuria. The next day, August 9, another B-29 dropped an implosive plutonium bomb, code-named "Fat Man," on Nagasaki, a major seaport, killing some 40,000 people. Still, it took the personal intervention of the emperor to counter the military's resistance to ending the war. On August 14, Japan agreed to surrender if the emperor was allowed to remain on his throne, a condition the Allies accepted on the understanding that he would be subordinated to the American commander of the occupation forces. On September 2, 1945, on the deck of the battleship *Missouri* in Tokyo Bay, Japanese officials and General Douglas MacArthur concluded the instruments of surrender.

> *"At 8:15 A.M. Japanese time, a great fireball incinerated the city, turning it into a wasteland of rubble. Close to 80,000 people were killed."*

THE DECISION TO USE THE BOMB

At the time, editorial opinion and the polled public overwhelmingly backed the atomic bombings of Japan because they brought the war to a speedy conclusion, but considerable debate has occurred since then over whether the horrendous actions were truly necessary to end the conflict without an invasion. Critics point to the Japanese peace feelers and argue that they might have been productively exploited if, as some officials advised, the United States had told the Japanese before Hiroshima that they could keep their emperor, the condition the American government eventually accepted. They cite judgments by American military and civilian officials that Japan, virtually defenseless before air attack and under effective blockade, was in fact already defeated and would have been forced to surrender by mid-autumn.

Almost all these judgments, however, were rendered later, not at the time. Moreover, conventional bombing would have continued while the Allies waited for the Japanese to surrender—it was restored to high intensity following a slowdown after Nagasaki—and would have resulted in the loss of thousands more lives. In the meantime, the Soviet army would have been marching ever farther into Manchuria. The United States might indeed have agreed earlier that the Japanese could retain their emperor, but they might have asked for further concessions. It must be remembered that Tokyo dismissed the Potsdam Declaration as late as July 28 and did not respond to its terms until after Hiroshima.

Some critics hold that the bombings were impelled by anti-Japanese racism, but abundant evidence from the war in Europe, including the firebombing of Hamburg and the comparably devastating raid on Dresden in February 1945, indicates that the United States would have dropped the atomic bomb on Germany had the weapon been ready soon enough. Others point to the recommendation by a group of Manhattan Project scientists to warn the Japanese of what they faced by demonstrating the bomb in an uninhabited area. However, a high-level scientific panel concluded that no technical demonstration would likely end the war and that it was too risky to try, not least because the demonstration bomb might be a dud. After the test at Alamogordo, the United States had only two atomic bombs available, with a third unlikely to be ready before November. Some of Stimson's scientific advisers believed that the bomb would accomplish what the firebombings had not, shock the Japanese into surrendering, and do what scientists could not—frighten both the Soviets and Americans into recognizing the need for international control of nuclear energy after the war.

According to some analysts, postwar relations with the Soviet Union figured as much in the administration's thinking

Days after atomic bombs were dropped on Hiroshima and Nagasaki, the world struggled to assess the promise and the threat of atomic power.

man's spine. At Potsdam after the Trinity test, he appeared to Churchill as "a changed man," telling "the Russians just where they got on and off." Truman merely went through the motions of informing Stalin about the bomb, casually mentioning to him at the end of a conference session that the United States had a new weapon. Stalin, who knew about the Manhattan Project from Soviet intelligence, replied merely that he hoped it would be used to good effect against the Japanese. (Back in his headquarters afterward, he re-marked that the Soviet A-bomb effort would have to be speeded up.)

Truman's expectation that the atomic bomb would make the Soviets more manageable may well have distracted him from pursuing alternative ways to end the conflict. Still, the alternative that loomed largest in his mind was an invasion, and no president able to order an atomic attack could have justified that action, with its cost of at least tens of thousands and possibly hundreds of thousands of American casualties. All things considered, the Hiroshima bomb was most likely dropped primarily to end the war promptly. So, probably, was the Nagasaki bomb, though with much less justification. But now that the destructiveness of the atomic bomb had been demonstrated, many American policymakers expected even more that it could be used to manage Stalin as the vic-tors turned to the uncertainties of the postwar world.

about the bomb as did ending the war against Japan. Indeed, the prodemonstration scientists argued that use of the bomb without warning would undercut the United States' moral position in the world, precipitate a nuclear arms race with the Soviets, and reduce the chances of obtaining international control of nuclear energy. Although the high-level scientific panel rejected a demonstration, it did urge that the United States inform the Soviet Union about the huge dangers posed by atomic weapons and call on it to join in a postwar effort to control them. Oppenheimer later recalled that Stimson went to Potsdam intent on thus reaching out to the Soviets but that once there, perceiving the Russians as viscerally resistant to Western values, he lost his nerve.

Indeed, the critics argue that Truman, Stimson, and Byrnes saw the bomb primarily as a means of keeping the Soviets in line in Eastern Europe and, if the bomb was used soon enough, keeping them out of the war—and away from the peace table—in the Pacific. The news that the United States had a workable bomb certainly added steel to Tru-

Servicemen at Pearl Harbor cheer the news of the Japanese surrender, August 1945.

854

Entering the Peace

At the opening of the peace, American power was unmatched anywhere else in the world. Although some 300,000 Americans had died in the conflict, leaving shards of pain in every home displaying a gold star in the window, losses in Europe had run much higher, reaching 20 million in the Soviet Union alone. The continental United States, unlike much of Europe and Britain, was physically undamaged, its industry and agriculture robust, its economy accounting for about half the world's gross annual product. The factories rapidly retooled for civilian production. With people now liberated from gas rationing and the thirty-five-mile-per-hour speed limit, General Motors boasted that it would convert "from tanks to Cadillacs in two months." Improvements in health, safety, and convenience were in the offing, many of them spinoffs of war research, including antibiotics like penicillin; radar guidance, navigation, and storm monitoring for air traffic and shipping; television and communication networks grounded in microwave technologies; and nuclear power reactors that would generate electricity. But the bright dawn of peace was suffused with trepidations, including anxiety about the economic and nuclear futures.

"Some 300,000 Americans had died in the conflict, leaving shards of pain in every home displaying a gold star in the window."

WORRIES, FOREIGN AND DOMESTIC

Many Americans feared that the aftermath of World War II at home might resemble that of World War I, when the country slid into recession. By V-J (victory over Japan) Day in August 1945, the armed services comprised 12 million Americans, including roughly two-thirds of all American men between eighteen and thirty-four. By mid-1947, more than 10 million of them had been mustered out, posing reentry problems of unprecedented magnitude for the veterans and their society. *The Best Years of Our Lives*, a film written by the playwright and former Roosevelt speechwriter Robert Sherwood, won multiple Academy Awards for its sensitive portrayal of the economic and emotional difficulties that many servicemen faced on their return home: finding a job; dissolving hasty wartime marriages (the divorce rate in 1945 zoomed to twice the prewar level); restoring family relationships after several years of separation; and for those who did not come back physically intact, coping with their handicaps and rebuilding a sense of self-worth.

Analysts questioned whether the economy could absorb the rapid return to civilian life of so many people, and their apprehensions were compounded by sharp cutbacks in defense spending—from slightly more than $80 billion in 1945 to about $43 billion in 1946—that resulted within days of the Japanese surrender in the cancellation of $35 billion in war contracts and the elimination of 1 million defense jobs. After V-J Day, the number of people unemployed doubled, jumping from half a million to a million. Americans wanted to revive the good times that had come with the mobilization for war, but they were divided over the role government should play in accomplishing that goal and, even more deeply, over whether the New Deal ought to be continued or curtailed.

They were less divided over what their country's role should be in the postwar world. A broad constituency for internationalism had emerged in the United States, a development indicated by the huge success in 1943

A serviceman returns home to his welcoming family after the war, 1945.

of Wendell Willkie's book *One World*—it sold a million copies in just two months—which called for an end to military alliances and the creation of a postwar international organization that would ensure the peace while spreading democracy and democratic capitalism across the planet. Senator Arthur H. Vandenberg of Michigan, a powerful Republican isolationist before the war, remembered standing in London in 1944 while German V-1s buzzed overhead and wondering to a friend, "How can there be immunity or isolation when man can devise weapons like that?" In April 1945, in a sharp break with its historic isolationism, the United States joined forty-nine other countries in formally creating the United Nations. Its structure negotiated during the war, the U.N. included a General Assembly representing each member nation and a Security Council with five permanent members—the United States, Britain, the Soviet Union, France, and China (each of which could protect its vital interest by vetoing any action the council might recommend).

Along with Vandenberg, most American policymakers believed that the United States could never again permit itself to fall into military weakness. They read the reasons for the coming of World War II—for example, the appeasement of Hitler at Munich—to mean that aggression had to be met with resistance, force with force. They held that the first line of America's defense lay far from its shores, that it was in the interest of national security to be involved in the world and shape it. Still, it was one thing to envision a strong national defense undergirding a postwar peace, quite another to bring about and maintain a stable international order in a world of political passions, conflicting national interests, and high-technology weapons.

THE NEW PRESIDENT

Under these combustible circumstances, Americans who knew something about Harry Truman (and not many did) doubted that he was up to the job of the presidency, let alone capable of filling Franklin Roosevelt's chair in the Oval Office. Truman had grown up in western Missouri helping to work his grandfather's farm and had seen combat as an artillery officer during World War I. After the war, he had failed at selling men's clothing but succeeded at politics as a protégé of the unsavory Kansas City machine, to which he owed his election to the Senate in 1934 and his squeak-through reelection in 1940. Truman loyally voted down the line with Roosevelt and the New Deal.

Harry Truman, the new president, rallies the nation after FDR's death, April 1945.

On becoming president, he disheartened observers by bringing political cronies into the White House and sometimes acting without regard for consequences. But Truman was doggedly honest, had read a lot of history, and had a straight-arrow concern for the public interest. He was scrappy, outspoken, and often courageous. He had contested the Ku Klux Klan in Missouri and declared during his reelection campaign that he believed in "not merely the brotherhood of white men, but the brotherhood of all men before the law." Remembering the profiteering during World War I, he volunteered to help prevent it this time, calling for the creation of a Senate investigative committee and chairing its probes with tenacity and evenhandedness.

Truman abhorred totalitarianism and was suspicious of the Soviets for their repression of freedom and dissent. When he entered the White House, he had limited experience in foreign affairs and knew little about Roosevelt's negotiations with the Allies on the shape of the postwar world. Still, Truman was unafraid of responsibility—a sign on his presidential desk read, "The buck stops here"—and though he vacillated at times, he had the capacity for decisiveness. His tendency to cronyism was tempered by a regard for high-minded public servants like George Marshall and for politically minded ones like James F. Byrnes, both of whom he turned to as he worked to master Roosevelt's legacy and deal with the tempestuous issues of the peace.

CONSERVATISM, PRICES, AND STRIKES

Eager to build on Roosevelt's achievements, in September 1945 Truman sent Congress a twenty-one-point package of New Deal–like legislation, calling for measures to extend Social Security, slum clearance, and public housing, to create a permanent Fair Employment Practices Commission and provide for national health insurance, and to establish a flood-control and public-power authority, like the Tennessee Valley Authority (TVA), for the Columbia River valley in the Northwest. Most of these initiatives languished in Congress, where the trend to conservatism continued. In lieu of national health insurance, which the American Medical Association (AMA) vigorously opposed, Congress passed the Hill-Burton Act, which provided federal funds for the construction of public and voluntary hospitals. The Full Employment Act of 1946, gutted by conservatives, gave the government the responsibility of achieving only "maximum" rather than "full" employment. To that end, it authorized tax cuts to stimulate investment, the promotion of government-business cooperation, and the creation of a Council of Economic Advisers.

A high postwar demand for goods brought about shortages and pressure for price increases in essentials such as cars, food, and housing. Congress ended price controls in mid-1946. The cost of consumer goods skyrocketed some 25 percent within two weeks, with the price of coffee jumping more than 50 percent and the price of meat climbing out of sight. Congress responded by reviving an attenuated version of price controls; but faced with the ire of farmers and meat producers, Truman lifted even those limp restraints shortly before the 1946 congressional elections. The rampant inflation made people angry, especially blue-collar workers, who were already reeling from the loss of wartime bonuses and overtime pay. Reports of high corporate profits and lavish executive salaries also provoked resentment.

Organized labor, which now accounted for more than a third of nonagricultural employment, flexed its considerable muscles in protest. The United Auto Workers struck General Motors in Detroit, which was earning record profits. The UAW's leader was Walter Reuther, a hard-nosed idealist who believed that unions should use their power to advance more than their bread-and-butter interests. One UAW official declared that the strike opened an "era in which labor might break away from the bonds of business unionism, to wage an economic struggle planned to advance the welfare of the community as a whole." Besides demanding a 30 percent wage increase, the UAW insisted that G.M. open its books to public scrutiny and bring labor into its decisions so as to maximize production. The strike lasted 113 days and cost the company $90 million. G.M. boosted wages, but it refused to open its books or yield any of its managerial prerogatives. The settlement added up to a defeat for Reuther's larger vision—and signaled that social vision had a diminished place in union-management negotiations.

By mid-1946, more than 2 million workers—more than one out of every fourteen members of the labor force—had struck in a number of major industries, including steel, oil refining, and meatpacking. On April 1, John L. Lewis, relentless in his advocacy of coal miners' interests, threatened the vitals of American society by calling 400,000 mine workers off their jobs. After forty days, President Truman ordered the army to seize the mines, but he also gave in to most of Lewis's demands, which he had earlier attacked as inflationary. A week later, the miners went back to work. In the spring of 1946, a railway workers strike completely shut down the nation's train system, which, in this era before superhighway travel and trucking, drastically reduced the movement of people and goods. Addressing Congress, Truman asked for government power to seize essential industries shut down by strikes, to draft strikers, and to put recalcitrant union leaders in jail. In the course of his speech, he was able to tell Congress that the unions had just settled on terms he had proposed. The applause was thunderous, but it was deeply disturbing to many across the political spectrum that the president had resorted to such means to halt the strike.

Striking United Auto workers picket a General Motors plant, 1945.

857

POLITICAL EARTHQUAKE: 1946

By the fall of 1946, Truman had alienated labor, irritated millions by his waffling on prices, and made himself vulnerable to the worst form of attack an American politician can suffer—ridicule. "To err is Truman," people gibed. Republicans saw rich political opportunity, asking people in the phrase devised by a Boston advertising executive, "Had enough?" In the 1946 elections, the Republican Party won sweeping control of both houses of Congress for the first time since the election of Herbert Hoover in 1928.

The new, Eightieth Congress, controlled by a conservative-dominated Republican majority allied with southern Democrats, aimed not only to block extension of the New Deal but to roll back as many of its advances as possible. The principal leader on Capitol Hill was Senator Robert Taft of Ohio, the son of a former president, a strongly partisan, highly intelligent, and outspoken advocate of the view that in its economic activities and relations to government the country ought to return to the "traditional American heart of things, liberty." During its first session, in 1947, Congress buried virtually every liberal initiative that came before it, enacted an income tax formula that reduced taxes on high incomes, and sought to curb the power of organized labor with the Taft-Hartley Act. The act's key provisions authorized the president to call for an eighty-day cooling-off period in nationally disruptive strikes, banned shops closed to nonunion members, and empowered the states to prohibit union shops by passing so-called right-to-work laws. The law provoked union outrage and a presidential veto that Congress promptly overrode. The actions of the Eightieth Congress seemed to place the future of the Roosevelt revolution in doubt.

The Emergence of the Cold War

In foreign affairs, the immediate postwar years were marked by the beginnings of the Cold War. That face-off eventually cost the United States trillions of dollars, half a century of the fear of nuclear annihilation, the loss of thousands of lives in local wars, and the undermining of democratic institutions in the name of the need to maintain national security. Deciding who was responsible for its origins—in many treatments Stalin, in others Truman—has thus generated energetic historical debate.

When Truman entered the White House, relations between the Western Allies and Stalin were already turning frosty. Truman's defenders point out that although, like Roosevelt, he was initially reluctant to antagonize the Soviet Union, he was rightly angered by the extension of Soviet totalitarianism to Eastern Europe. He was also concerned that Stalin's control of Eastern Europe would deny American industry access to the region, a closeout that would injure the economies of both Central Europe and the United States.

Truman's critics indict him for his determination to maintain the American atomic monopoly, pointing to his expectation as early as Potsdam that nuclear weapons would help the United States keep the Russians in line. They fault him for failing to understand that the Soviet Union had legitimate national interests in Eastern Europe. Indeed, Truman's tough stand surprised Stalin. Stalin interpreted an agreement he had reached with Churchill in 1944 and probably the Yalta agreements, too, as having acknowledged the establishment of a Soviet sphere of influence in Eastern Europe. He regarded the states in the region, especially Poland, as a first line of defense against another invasion from the West.

Truman's critics also argue that in his first days of dealing with the Soviets he tended to shoot from the hip. He postponed a response to urgent Soviet requests for $6 billion in credits. After the German surrender, he abruptly ended lend-lease shipments to them, signing the order without reading it, then modifying the action after it was pointed out to him that Stalin took the sudden termination as an undisguised provocation. The administration also hardened on the question of reparations to the Soviets, telling them the amount they could expect would have to be scaled down from $10 billion, the figure tentatively agreed to at Yalta.

Undoubtedly, misunderstandings on both sides contributed to the origins of the Cold War, and so did Truman's inexperience in foreign affairs on entering the White House. But the United States and the Soviet Union were also divided by a genuine clash of political, economic, and ideological interests that Truman could hardly ignore. Stalin, seeking to quell the impulse to independence in Poland, suppressed freedom of speech, the press, and religion there. Truman was mindful that conservatives were attacking the Yalta agreements as a "sellout" of Eastern Europe and that the imposition of pro-Soviet regimes in the region outraged millions of Catholics and Americans of Eastern European origin, many of them Democratic voters.

Early in 1946, Truman privately declared himself "tired of babying the Soviets," and in March he sat on the platform at Westminster College in Fulton, Missouri, while Winston Churchill delivered **an address** expressing apprehension about the "expansive tendencies" of the Soviet Union. "From Stettin in the Baltic to Trieste in the Adriatic, an iron curtain has descended across the Continent," Churchill declared. He added that from what he had seen of the Russians during the war, "I am convinced that there is nothing they admire so much as strength, and there is nothing for which they have less respect than weakness, especially military weakness."

Truman showed strength. Stalin, his eye on Iranian oil concessions, kept Soviet troops in Iran after they were supposed to pull out in keeping with wartime agreements. They withdrew in May 1946 after the United States protested to the United Nations and made ready to confront the Soviets directly. In August, Stalin insisted to the Turkish government that the Soviet Union share equally in control of the Dardanelles, the straits providing an opening to the Mediterranean for ships from the Black Sea. The Soviets backed down after the United States, urging the Turks to refuse, showed support by sending an aircraft carrier through the straits. In September, Henry Wallace, still in the Truman cabinet, publicly attacked American policy toward the Soviets as too tough. His speech provoked a hurricane of criticism. Before the speech, Truman himself had told reporters that it represented the policy of his administration. Once the storm broke, he hurriedly backtracked and fired Wallace from the cabinet.

DIVISION OVER THE ATOM

Whatever their ambivalence toward the Soviets, Americans took comfort in the knowledge that the United States alone possessed the atomic bomb. With demobilization rapidly proceeding—in 1947, the United States would have only 1.5 million people under arms, half the Soviet number—American policymakers like Secretary of State Byrnes saw the bomb as a means of countering Soviet superiority in conventional military forces in Eastern Europe. In 1946, the army air force established the Strategic Air Command, whose mission was to deliver nuclear bombs against the Soviet Union.

With the aim of further developing the American atomic arsenal, the administration had submitted to Congress a proposal to create an Atomic Energy Commission (AEC). The agency would be empowered to foster research and development in nuclear energy, but in tone, and to a degree in substance, the measure seemed to make the chief object of the nuclear energy program not the peaceful but the military atom. Many scientists protested the likely subjection of the AEC to so much military influence. They feared that unreasonable security restrictions would be placed on nuclear research, interfering with the free flow of information essential to scientific progress, and that military domination of the commission would jeopardize the chances for international control of nuclear energy. In July 1946, responding to the dissents, Congress established the AEC under civilian control while giving the military a voice in shaping its program.

All the while, a number of atomic scientists had kept hoping that their Soviet brethren, aware that there could be no adequate defense against nuclear weapons, might help bring about an accord for international control of nuclear energy and make it work. To many Americans, some sort of agreement seemed imperative after the appearance, in 1946, of

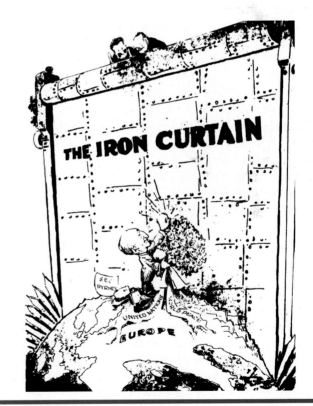

Cartoonist "Ding" Darling depicts the "iron curtain" that Winston Churchill, in his speech at Westminster College on March 5, 1946, accused the Soviets of drawing across Eastern Europe.

859

Digital History

HANFORD: THE COLD WAR ON THE COLUMBIA RIVER

One of the most significant developments of World War II and the Cold War period was the production and deployment of nuclear weapons. The nuclear production facilities at Hanford, on the Columbia River in Washington state, were critical to this effort in the United States. Opened in 1943 and employing 50,000 people at its wartime peak, the Hanford site produced the plutonium used in the atomic bomb that was dropped by the United States on Nagasaki on August 9, 1945. During the Cold War, Hanford expanded its production of plutonium for America's growing nuclear arsenal.

In the early 1970s, the Hanford facilities began converting from weapons production to electric-power production. But serious environmental problems at the site, including a leak of radioactive waste into the surrounding soil, air, and groundwater, led to a complete shutdown by 1987. The Nez Percé and other Native American peoples of the region, having lost their ancestral lands to the federal development of the facility, now suffered the further loss of fishing grounds and a contaminated food supply. The Hanford cleanup will cost the federal government an estimated $29 billion.

Above: *The nuclear power plant (completed in 1984) at the Hanford Nuclear Reservation.* ***Center:*** *Members of the Klickitat and Cascade Indian tribes marching in protest to the gates of Hanford, August 1, 1991.* ***Right:*** *Aerial view of the nuclear reactor at Hanford.*

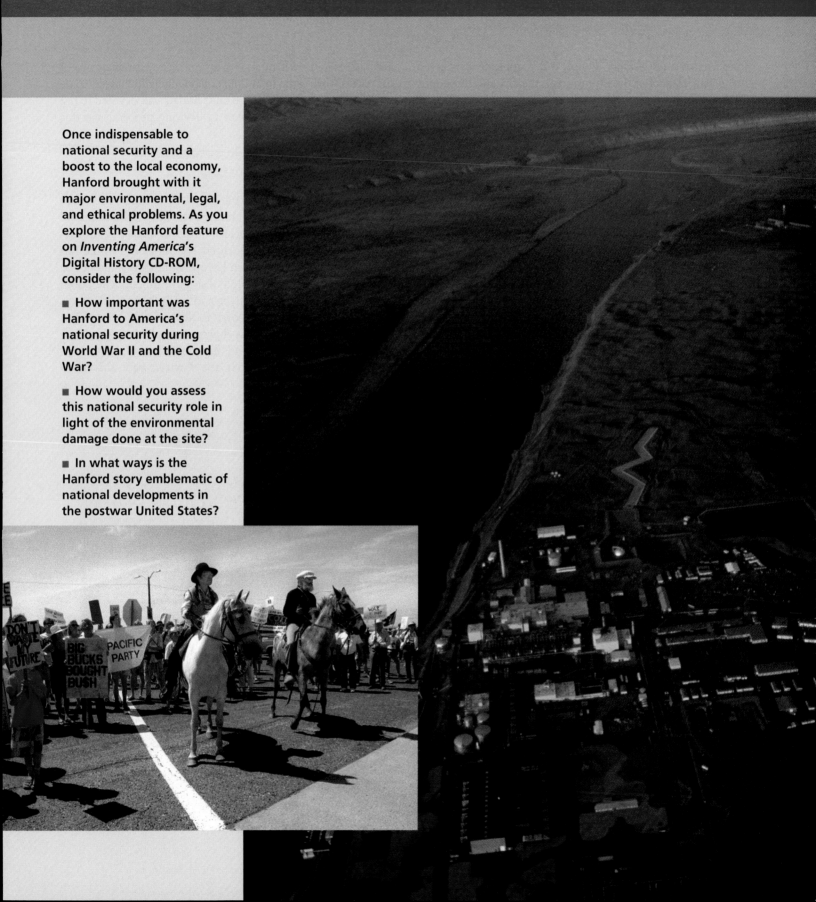

Once indispensable to national security and a boost to the local economy, Hanford brought with it major environmental, legal, and ethical problems. As you explore the Hanford feature on *Inventing America*'s Digital History CD-ROM, consider the following:

■ How important was Hanford to America's national security during World War II and the Cold War?

■ How would you assess this national security role in light of the environmental damage done at the site?

■ In what ways is the Hanford story emblematic of national developments in the postwar United States?

John Hersey's *Hiroshima*, a book that graphically portrayed the ghastly impact of the explosion on the city and its people. ("Their faces were wholly burned," Hersey wrote of some twenty soldiers in a park, "their eyesockets were hollow, the fluid from their melted eyes had run down their cheeks.") Macabre imaginings of what the United States might resemble after an atomic attack had begun to appear, exemplified by a drawing in *Life* magazine that showed the stone lions of the New York Public Library gazing over a sea of rubble as technicians crunched along testing radioactivity levels.

However, proposals for an international accord on atomic energy foundered on the United States' desire to maintain its nuclear monopoly and the Soviet determination to break it. (After Hiroshima and Nagasaki, Stalin had authorized a crash program to build a Soviet nuclear weapon.) By 1947, general discussion of nuclear weapons declined and public support rose for strengthening—and, if necessary, using—the American nuclear arsenal. The U.S. government sought to suppress or defuse information concerning the serious radiation haz-

ards associated with nuclear weapons. The vast majority of the AEC's work came to be concerned with national security—so that, for example, far more of its budget was devoted to the development of weapons than to devising peaceful uses for nuclear energy.

THE DOCTRINE OF CONTAINMENT

By 1946, some officials in the Truman administration had begun arguing for a coherent policy in Soviet relations that did not depend so heavily on nuclear weapons. It was already evident to them that the mere existence of the bomb would not affect Soviet actions in Eastern Europe and that it could not be used to force a change in the Polish government. The bomb only seemed to help heighten tensions with the Soviet Union.

Among the critics was George F. Kennan, the U.S. chief of mission in Moscow, a scholar-diplomat deeply steeped in Russian history. In February 1946, in an 8,000-word telegram to Washington, he argued that the Soviets were driven to

Cold War Europe

Members of the North Atlantic Treaty Organization (NATO)

Members of the Warsaw Pact (Soviet counterpart to NATO)

Nonaligned states

Other Communist states

aggressiveness by a "traditional and instinctive Russian sense of insecurity" arising from Russia's long-standing vulnerability to invasion from the West and its sense of the archaic inferiority of its institutions. Soviet ambitions thus ought to be contained geographically and politically, with the expectation that over time the Soviet state would mellow or break up. In an article published two months later under the pseudonym "X," Kennan provided a summary of his arguments, calling the policy "containment." His analysis increasingly influenced the Truman administration's views about how to respond to the Soviets.

Truman first articulated the doctrine of containment early in 1947, in a policy initiative prompted by the situation in Greece. Since the end of the war, Britain had been helping the Greek government fight a civil war against pro-Communist insurgents, who, it was assumed, had Soviet backing (they actually were getting assistance from Yugoslavia, not from Stalin). In February 1947, Britain informed the United States that it could no longer afford such assistance and would pull its troops out of the country. Under Secretary of State Dean Acheson, a hard-nosed, self-assured realist and a strong advocate of containment, advised Truman that a Communist takeover in Greece would make Turkey vulnerable to the Soviets and might open the Near East and Africa as well as Italy and France to Soviet penetration.

In mid-March, in a speech before a joint session of both houses of Congress, Truman went far beyond the immediate issues in the two countries, calling the battle in Greece part of a global struggle "between alternative ways of life" and warning that the "fall" of Greece would lead to losses to freedom elsewhere. "I believe that it must be the policy of the United States to support free peoples who are resisting attempted subjugation by armed minorities or by outside pressure," Truman declared, enunciating the commitment that came to be known as the Truman Doctrine. In mid-May, by substantial majorities in both houses, Congress appropriated $400 million, mainly for military aid, for Greece and Turkey over the succeeding fifteen months—thus authorizing U.S. intervention in a foreign civil conflict for the first time in the postwar era.

President Truman (left) confers with foreign-policy advisers, including George F. Kennan (second from right), the architect of containment, 1947.

Conservatives such as Senator Robert Taft questioned whether the policy of containment was practical or wise for the United States. Henry Wallace spoke for critics on the left, who contested the policy as unnecessarily aggressive. Still others worried that containment, coming on the heels of the Truman Doctrine, would encourage Americans to see disputes with the Communist world primarily in military terms that would require military responses and ally the United States with undemocratic regimes only because they were anti-Communist. Indeed, the Truman Doctrine opened the way for future interventions abroad no matter whether essential U.S. interests were involved or whether Communist agitation was the primary reason for internal unrest. Kennan himself later said that what he meant by containment was primarily political and economic resistance to the Soviets. But amid the mounting international tensions, containment was increasingly equated with the sweep and military character of the Truman Doctrine's anti-Communist commitment.

THE MARSHALL PLAN

In the spring of 1947, George C. Marshall, who had succeeded James Byrnes as secretary of state, was acutely worried about Europe, much of it impoverished and still rubble. The Communist Parties in Italy and France were gaining signifi-

863

Soviet leader Joseph Stalin attempting to block the Marshall Plan's goal of a thriving free-market economy in Europe.

cant support. Moreover, America's burgeoning prosperity depended in part on a huge export trade, largely with Europe, but Europe was running out of dollars to pay for its purchases. In a commencement address at Harvard in June, Marshall warned that if the United States did not help restore Europe's economy, "economic, social and political deterioration of a very grave character" would result. He called for extensive aid, a "cure rather than a palliative." Under the Marshall Plan, European governments would get grants of American goods that they could sell, using the proceeds to invest in their economies. Intended to stave off Communism by shoring up European democratic capitalism, the Marshall Plan amounted to the economic counterpart of the Truman Doctrine. Truman himself thought of the two programs as complementary, "two halves of the same walnut."

On Capitol Hill, conservatives in the Republican-dominated Congress derided the plan as a kind of international New Dealism. However, Senator Arthur Vandenberg championed it, calling it a "calculated risk" to "help stop World War III before it starts." Early in February 1948, Communists seized control of the government in Czechoslovakia, bringing that country into the orbit of Soviet control and sending shock waves through the West. Congress enacted the Marshall Plan before the end of the month, initially authorizing $4 billion and adding another $8.5 billion over the next three years. By 1951, the European recipients of the funds had increased their industrial output by 40 percent over that of the last prewar year.

IN DEFENSE OF EUROPE

In 1947, the Soviet Union, moving to strengthen its hold on Eastern and Central Europe, announced an economic revitalization scheme of its own—the "Molotov Plan," which it inaugurated with bilateral trade agreements with countries in the Eastern bloc. Stalin also set out to destroy political dissent in Eastern Europe, resorting to show trials, coerced confessions, and executions. In August, the Soviets forced out all left-wing anti-Communists from the Hungarian leadership and then rigged the elections to yield a pro-Soviet regime, initiatives that foreshadowed the Czech coup the following February.

The United States, Britain, and, with some reluctance, France increasingly saw the revival of the German economy as a key to fostering stability and resistance to the Soviets in Western Europe. In the spring of 1948, they pressed ahead with plans to unite the three Western zones of occupation into a West German state that would include the Western zone of Berlin and be integrated into the European economy. Defeating the Soviet determination to keep Germany weak, the effort would place the industrially rich Ruhr Valley permanently off-limits to the Soviets and foster a dynamic Western sector of Berlin deep in Soviet-held territory. In June, the Soviets cut off the flow of supplies by rail and truck from the Western zones of Germany into Berlin. Stalin's aim was to force the Western powers either to forgo the creation of a West German state or abandon West Berlin.

Truman, determined to maintain West Berlin without violent confrontation, ordered an ongoing airlift of food and medical supplies into the city. American C-54 cargo planes began flying from the Western zones to Templehof Airport in West Berlin, landing about every three minutes around the clock and delivering 13,000 tons of goods a day. In July, Truman sent two groups of nuclear-capable B-29s to England, a veiled warning to the Soviets that they should not interfere with the Berlin-bound planes. The Soviets called off the Berlin blockade on May 12, 1949, 321 days after the airlift began. That month, the United States, Britain, and France ended their occupation of the Western zones and approved their union into the Federal Republic of Germany. The Soviets turned their zone into the German Democratic Republic, thus sealing the division of postwar Germany into East and West.

The blockade, which virtually transformed the image of Berlin in American eyes from that of Hitler's capital to a heroic outpost of freedom, generated substantially increased support for a policy of toughness toward Russia. The month it began, Congress revived the peacetime military draft. In April 1949, the United States joined in creating the North Atlantic Treaty Organization (NATO), an alliance of the North Atlantic nations, each of which pledged, in the language of the treaty's Article 5, to consider "an armed attack against one or more of them in Europe or North America . . . an attack against them all." For the United States, the formal commitment to the defense of Europe marked a historic break from its tradition of avoiding peacetime alliances.

THE FAR EAST

The Truman administration also enlisted Japan in the cause of containment. At the end of the war, General Douglas MacArthur had been appointed head of the occupation forces in Japan, with sole authority to reconstitute the Japanese system of government. In keeping with U.S. policy, he imposed on Japan a new democratic constitution that included a permanent renunciation of war. MacArthur called Japan "the western outpost of our defenses." The country loomed increasingly as a stable, anti-Communist power in the Pacific, one that could counter Soviet ambitions in the region (much as the United States hoped Germany would do in Europe). In 1947–48, as U.S.-Soviet relations worsened, the United States decided to rebuild Japanese industry, reversing its earlier postwar policy, and to expand its military bases in Japan.

THE SINEWS OF NATIONAL SECURITY

Amid the emerging Cold War, national security commanded unprecedented peacetime attention. Even though defense appropriations kept falling, the defense budget in 1949 was roughly $14 billion, far higher even after adjustment for inflation than it had been in 1939. Pointing to the lessons of the war, policymakers held that the apparatus of national security needed to be better organized, more efficient, and well informed about developments elsewhere in the world. In 1947, Congress passed the National Security Act, which established an independent air force as a coequal branch of the military and unified all three armed services in a single military establishment soon named the Department of Defense (DOD). The act also created a National Security Council for better coordination between the military services and the State Department, and it established a Central Intelligence Agency (CIA) to coordinate foreign intelligence gathering. The first secretary of defense was James Forrestal, an intense and ambitious man who had been secretary of the navy and was an anti-Soviet hard-liner.

The CIA. The CIA had its roots in the wartime Office of Strategic Services, which had not only gathered intelligence

Berliners watch an American C-54 cargo plane arrive with supplies during the Soviet blockade of their city, July 1948.

but also sponsored covert activities. Although the CIA was initially limited to gathering and analyzing intelligence, after the Czech coup Truman allowed it to engage in covert operations. Among the first, the CIA influenced an Italian election by funneling several million dollars to the Christian Democrats, helping them defeat the Communists. The Central Intelligence Act of 1949 authorized the CIA to pursue covert operations without accountability to Congress. That year, secret agency funds were used to establish the ostensibly private Radio Free Europe, which broadcast propaganda to Eastern Europe. Radio Liberation, aimed at Russia, was created soon thereafter. The CIA also attempted to overthrow the Communist regime in Albania, inaugurating an era of peacetime political action hidden from public scrutiny.

> *"The Office of Naval Research provided important support for the development of a new technological innovation—electronic computers."*

Defense Research and Development. The advent of the Cold War strengthened the belief that federal support of scientific research and development (R&D) constituted a key element in the nation's defense. The armed services, eager to improve on the innovations in wartime military technology, pushed

J. W. Mauchly at work on the first electronic computer, ENIAC, February 1946.

for technological programs in areas such as nuclear weapons and nuclear-powered ships, long-range bombers and rockets, and systems of microwave detection, control, and communication. It was well understood that achieving these ends would require a steady stream of new knowledge and more trained technical personnel, especially physicists—scientists who had been in acutely short supply during the war and now, as *Life* magazine noted in the wake of Hiroshima and Nagasaki, seemed to wear the "tunic of Superman."

After the war, the military strengthened its existing technical bureaus and in 1946 established an important new one—the Office of Naval Research, whose aims included laying the technical foundation for radical new weapons. The armed services also devised an extensive system of liaisons with the civilian scientific community, while the Atomic Energy Commission called on a distinguished advisory group whose membership list read like a Who's Who of American physics and was chaired by J. Robert Oppenheimer. The AEC took over the great atomic research installations constructed during the war, but both the AEC and the military bureaus also awarded grants and contracts for R&D to industrial and academic laboratories. Some universities operated weapons laboratories for the government, notably the University of California, which managed the nuclear weapons facility at Los Alamos for the AEC.

The large majority of the military's support of research went for investigations in subjects closely related to the technologies of national security—for example, jet-powered aircraft, the newest innovation in flight. The Strategic Air Command (SAC) helped develop a jet bomber that could carry nuclear weapons from remote bases—Spain, North Africa, Iceland, and the Azores—to targets in the Soviet Union. The successful design was the Boeing Corporation's B-47, a bomber that carried its jet engines in pods under its swept-back wings and that flew twice as fast as the B-29 and with greater maneuverability over 20,000 feet than virtually any current fighter. Ordered into production by the air force in 1948, the B-47 rapidly became a mainstay of the SAC.

The Office of Naval Research provided important support for the development of a new technological innovation—electronic computers—that held great promise for a number of fields. Another product of the war, such computers had originated in the desire of some scientists and engineers to find a means to calculate artillery-firing tables better than using hundreds of people to do the necessary arithmetic with hand-operated adding machines. The first electronic computer, called ENIAC (for electronic numerical integrator and computer) and completed near the end of 1945, was devised under a military contract at the University of Pennsylvania by J. Presper Eckert, a twenty-four-year-old electronics engineer, and John W. Mauchly, a young physicist. The computer used 18,000 vacuum tubes and could perform 5,000 operations per second. Immediately exploited to do a complicated nuclear-weapons calculation that would have taken one person 100 years at a desk calculator, it finished the job in six weeks.

ENIAC excited an interest in computers on the part of John von Neumann, a brilliant mathematical physicist and prewar refugee from Hungary. In June 1945, von Neumann had published a report laying out what came to be the basic constituents of an electronic computer (units for processing, program, input, and output). ENIAC lacked crucial elements in this design—for example, a capacious physical memory and an operating program—but during the next few years, several projects aimed to develop electronic computers containing all the von Neumann elements, thus laying the foundations of the American computer industry. All were spurred ahead by the engine of national security, through direct military support or military assistance to civilian sponsoring agencies, or by the market created for computers by military contractors eager to employ them in R&D for aeronautics and rockets. The development of digital computers was part of the larger trend to what some analysts came to call "Pentagon Capitalism," the fueling of industrial growth, employment, and technological development through military expenditures.

Despite the emphasis on research in areas relevant to military technology, both civilian and defense policymakers recognized that maintaining military superiority in peacetime required vitality in every sector of the scientific enterprise, including basic research—that is, investigations of the fundamental laws and phenomena of nature without regard to their practical value. Thus, while emphasizing the development of nuclear weapons, the AEC sponsored research across a broad range of subjects, including high-energy particle physics, nuclear physics, nuclear medicine, and genetics. The Office of Naval Research became the major patron of the country's nonnuclear basic research. The United States increasingly led the world in science, partly because so many of the great centers of European research were devastated, partly because of its own richly developing capacities in the public and private sectors.

At mid-century, the AEC and the military between them accounted for some 90 percent of all federal dollars going into scientific research and training. *Time* magazine wondered whether the military was "about to take over U.S. science lock, stock, and barrel, calling the tune for U.S. universities and signing up the best scientists for work fundamentally aimed at military results." In 1950, a civilian National Science Foundation (NSF) was established to take responsibility for much of basic science, but it was a puny partner in the federal scientific complex. By then, federal R&D expenditures totaled some $1 billion, almost 50 percent more than they had been in 1946. About half came from the Defense Department, another 40 percent from the AEC.

Prosperity and Tolerance

A FLOURISHING ECONOMY

The high level of defense spending helped considerably to swell overall federal outlays and buoy the postwar economy. The federal budget, although falling after the war, turned around to reach $39 billion in 1950, more than four times what it had been in 1939. Worries about a postwar economic downturn were stilled. A clear signal of optimism came from the birthrate. During the Depression, the number of live births per 1,000 Americans had averaged around 19. By 1947, it had risen 40 percent, to 26.6, the highest since 1921. (Marking the beginning of a baby boom, it would remain 24 or higher until the end of the fifties.) Responding to demands for more schools and services, especially in the expanding suburbs, state and local spending shot up, more than doubling between 1945 and 1948 alone.

The United States led all other nations combined in the production of steel, oil, and automobiles, yielding its citizens far higher incomes on average than their counterparts elsewhere. People had money in the bank, the accumulated savings of the war years, and they proceeded to spend it on a cornucopia of products, among them electric clothes dryers, Polaroid cameras, and cars with

> *"During the Depression, the number of live births per 1,000 Americans had averaged around 19. By 1947, it had risen 40 percent, to 26.6."*

Electric washers, dryers, and refrigerators in abundance, staples of the buoyant postwar consumer economy.

automatic transmissions. The gross national product, $200 billion in 1946, climbed steadily, reaching $318 billion by 1950. Fewer veterans than expected immediately entered the labor market, since thousands of them—eventually almost half—availed themselves of the G.I. Bill to start businesses or get an education. Unemployment stayed down, hovering at slightly more than 4 percent.

FACES AGAINST THE WINDOW

Americans by no means shared equally in the prosperity of the late 1940s. In 1947, only a minority of them owned their homes, while 30 percent of the nation's dwellings had no running water and 40 percent lacked flush toilets. By the standards of the era, some 30 percent of the population fell below the poverty level. A good many of the poor were African Americans in the South, where two out of three blacks still lived. In "Operation Dixie," the AFL and the CIO attempted in rival campaigns to organize southern textile and agricultural workers, but the drives failed. They were scuttled by the Taft-Hartley law's discouragement of left-wing union

organizing, by the relatively greater strength and power that white landowners enjoyed as a result of the New Deal's assistance to agriculture, and by warnings in the region that unionization would lead to desegregation.

At the end of the war, a CIO official, noting that "people have become accustomed to new conditions, new wage scales, new ways of being treated," had added, "Rosie the Riveter isn't going back to emptying slop jars." Indeed, a majority of working women had told pollsters they wanted to keep their jobs. But many people, including some in Congress, held that women ought to go home to open up space in the labor force for men returning from the war. By early 1946, more than 3 million women had left their jobs, many of them involuntarily. Some 200 women picketed the employment office at an auto plant holding signs that read, "Stop Discrimination Because of Sex" and "The Hand That Rocks the Cradle Can Build Tractors, Too."

For women who remained in the workforce, career opportunities were limited. They tended to hold lower-level jobs, far more so than during the war. Few received the same pay as men for the same work. The fraction of women in the professions kept declining. Women trying to become doctors faced medical-school admission quotas of 5 percent and refusals by most hospitals to accept them as interns. Still, by 1950 the paid labor force included more than 18 million women, and the fraction of women working was 5 percentage points higher than in 1940. For the first time in the nation's history, more than half of working women were married, indicating that they were in the workforce for the long pull and not just biding time until the wedding day.

A TURN AGAINST INTOLERANCE

Since the war, a number of middle-class women had been calling for an Equal Rights Amendment to the Constitution, but they ran into opposition from advocates of lower-income women who feared it would lead to the abolition of protective workplace regulations. President Truman called women's rights "a lot of hooey." In 1946, the amendment won a slim majority in the House, but it got nowhere in the Senate. The *New York Times* editorialized: "Motherhood cannot be amended, and we are glad the Senate didn't try it." The drive for the amendment nevertheless signified that the American agenda was being enlarged beyond bread-and-butter issues to embrace broader issues of rights. Although at the time women's rights receded into the background as a public issue, other groups, especially racial, religious, and ethnic minorities, were insisting on an end to the discriminations they suffered in American society. In the late 1940s, such minority groups knew brightening possibilities in achieving equal rights, but they also experienced disheartening, often bitter disappointments.

The war had done a good deal to discredit intolerance. Many draftees, sent from the North to army training camps in the South, had been appalled by the region's racial customs and practices. The battlefield had diminished prejudice by throwing together men of different religions, ethnic backgrounds, and, to a limited extent, even races. Polls of G.I.s at the end of the war revealed that a majority placed above all other needs at home the necessity of eliminating racial and religious discrimination. A chaplain's remarks at a memorial service for the fallen of Iwo Jima expressed the increasingly common view that the living were obligated to ensure that all groups in America "enjoy the democracy for which all of them have paid the price."

The horrors of the Holocaust, publicized in graphic detail after the war, exposed the barbaric cruelties to which racism could lead. In November 1945, an Allied tribunal began trials of Nazi leaders at Nuremberg, Germany, charging them not only with responsibility for the war but with systematic murder and torture, especially at the concentration camps. Testimony revealed that Nazi doctors had used the inmates, the large majority of whom were Jews, as living subjects in a wide range of painful experiments. By the end of the war, biologists and social scientists had arrived at a consensus on race that rebutted the vicious theories of the Nazis and of racists in the United States. Summarized in a "Statement on Race" issued in 1950 by a branch of the United Nations, it held that there was no proof of innate differences in either mental characteristics or temperament between the groups of mankind.

The Cold War provided its own reasons for the repudiation of bigotry. "Americanism" came to be defined in contrast to Communism, as a commitment to freedom rather than in the nativist terms that had earlier disparaged immigrant ethnic minorities. The United States appeared hypocritical in preaching freedom abroad while it practiced discrimination at home, a contradiction that the Soviets did not fail to exploit. Thanks to immigration-restriction laws, only 8 percent of the population was now foreign-born, which diminished the social difficulty of assimilating foreigners. First-generation Catholics whose families had come from Eastern or southern Europe reported that they now found fewer barriers to buying homes in upper-middle-class neighborhoods. The country's ability to absorb immigrants was celebrated as a sign of its commitment to "freedom," and its "Judeo-Christian" character was touted as distinguishing it from atheistic Communism.

In the postwar climate, popular magazines attacked prejudice in editorials, articles, and cartoons. Labor, educational, and women's groups joined Jewish and civil rights organizations in preaching tolerance through such devices as "Brotherhood Weeks." The trend reached into musical theater, expressing itself in a song from Richard Rodgers and Oscar Hammerstein's popular musical drama *South Pacific* that attacks prejudice ironically: "You've got to be taught to be afraid / Of people whose eyes are oddly made / and people whose skin is a different shade / You've got to be carefully taught."

Surveys showed that anti-Semitism in the United States was steadily declining in both private speech and political debate. To be sure, job advertisements continued to specify "gentiles only"; hardly any Jews were to be found in the executive suites of banking, heavy industry, communications, transportation, or public utilities companies; and Jews were barred from membership in two-thirds of men's business and social clubs. Still, in 1945, Bess Myerson was crowned "Miss America," the first Jew to win the title, and a growing num-

NAACP staff with a poster recruiting people to join their battle against racial discrimination, 1940s.

ber of resorts dropped their restrictions against Jews. In 1947, the Oscar-winning film *Gentleman's Agreement* dramatically attacked the anti-Semitic bigotry that permeated the restricted suburbs. Legislation and voluntary action began to end quotas limiting the admission of Jews to colleges, universities, and professional schools, while barriers to Jews in employment were also coming down.

AFRICAN AMERICAN ASPIRATIONS

In 1947, the general manager of the Brooklyn Dodgers broke the major-league color barrier by signing Jackie Robinson. The product of a slum in Pasadena, California, Jack Roosevelt Robinson had gone to UCLA on an athletic scholarship, starred in multiple sports, and commanded attention as a young standout in the Negro baseball leagues. In his first weeks with the Dodgers, he faced upturned spikes from opposition runners and cold shoulders even from some of his own teammates. But he prevailed with a combination of tight-lipped dignity and play dazzling enough to make him Rookie of the Year. Robinson's triumph, widely admired and publicized, helped enlarge tolerance toward African Americans in many walks of American life. Black musicians brought their recent innovation of bebop—jazz improvisations on the harmonic structures of familiar tunes—to integrated clubs in downtown New York City; in 1947, Dizzy Gillespie—the hallmark bebopper, affecting a beret, horn-rimmed glasses, and ostrich-

> *"In 1947, the general manager of the Brooklyn Dodgers broke the major-league color barrier by signing Jackie Robinson."*

leather shoes—played Carnegie Hall, as the black jazz great Duke Ellington had done during the war. Black women were being hired as salesgirls in the swank department stores in the North; black blue-collar workers were taking on outspoken roles in labor grievance committees; and by 1946, more than two dozen blacks were serving in legislatures in every region outside the South.

Despite the tide toward tolerance, **racial discrimination** remained ubiquitous. In the South, tufts of white cotton pinched onto screen doors, an indication of restriction to whites only, were emblematic of the racial segregation that remained the norm in schools, restaurants, hotels, restrooms, and even drinking fountains. Outside the South, federal policies kept black-eligible public housing confined to black neighborhoods. The Federal Housing Administration encouraged the granting of mortgages so that "properties shall continue to be occupied by the same social and racial classes"—a policy that discouraged access to the burgeoning suburbs by blacks and other minorities. In the armed services, black soldiers traveled in Jim Crow railroad cars, lived in segregated barracks, bought only at the Negro PX, and saw films in segregated post theaters.

In the postwar years, a growing number of African Americans refused to accept the status quo. Duke Ellington crafted musical critiques of segregation and injustice, notably his *Deep South Suite*. Many returning black veterans, having tasted freedom abroad, resolved that they would no longer put up with the lack of it at home. The logic of the Cold War provided opportunities. In 1947, the NAACP, in a petition to the United Nations that gained worldwide attention, declared, "It is not Russia that threatens the United States so much as Mississippi." Increasing assistance also came from the law, including the establishment between 1945 and 1951 of Fair Employment Practices Commissions in eleven states and twenty-eight cities.

More important, suits brought by blacks and whites persuaded the Supreme Court to begin weighing in on the side of equal treatment. In the late 1930s, the Court had begun to scrutinize laws that infringed on the protections provided by the Bill of Rights. Combined with the extension of the Bill of Rights to the states that had begun with the *Gitlow* case in the 1920s, the new standard established a doctrinal foundation for revolutionary change in civil rights law. Thus, in 1944, in

Jackie Robinson, the Brooklyn Dodgers' star second baseman.

Duke Ellington (left) with fellow jazzmen Ben Webster (center) and Jimmy Hamilton, rehearsing at Carnegie Hall in New York, 1948.

Smith v. Allwright, the Supreme Court struck down the all-white primary election. In 1946, in *Morgan v. Virginia*, it held that segregation in public interstate travel was unconstitutional; and in 1950, in *Shelley v. Kraemer*, it found that restrictive covenants in housing—which prevented the sale of property to members of certain groups, in this case blacks—violated the Constitution.

In 1943, *Fortune* magazine had reported that in the South the "unity of whites against Negroes is not what it once was." In the 1930s, reported lynchings of blacks happened on average a dozen times a year; between 1945 and 1950, the annual average fell to between two and three. In the larger southern cities, an increasing number of African Americans registered to vote so that the portion of blacks on the voting rolls jumped from 2 percent in 1940 to 12 percent by 1947, the year in which, for the first time, a black alderman was elected to the city council in Winston-Salem, North Carolina.

Still, the resistance to racial tolerance was pervasive, especially in the deep South, where advocates of racial change were often smeared as Communists. After the High Court's ruling on interstate travel, the Congress of Racial Equality (CORE) initiated "Journeys of Reconciliation," in which groups of blacks and whites would sit in the whites-only section of buses bound for the South. On a CORE journey to North Carolina, the riders were intimidated by the bus drivers, arrested by southern police, and sentenced to thirty-day jail terms. In September 1948, a black army veteran who boldly cast his ballot in Wrightsville, Georgia, was dead before sundown, and an all-white jury promptly acquitted the men accused of murdering him. Black suffrage was also blocked by a maze of harassments and economic intimidations, including loss of jobs, insurance policies, and lines of credit. In Alabama, the president of the state bar association spoke for numerous whites across the South when he declared, "No Negro is good enough and no Negro will ever be good enough to participate in making the law under which the white people in Alabama have to live."

Truman Restored

POLITICS AND MINORITY RIGHTS

The rising aspirations of minority groups inspired political strategists in the White House. In the view of most observers, Truman's chances to regain the presidency in 1948 were slim. In the judgment of the strategists, however, he might well keep the presidency by counting on the South, appealing to

African Americans voting in the Democratic primary for the first time since 1890 in Jackson, Mississippi, 1946.

871

the West, and seeking the support of the coalition of groups that had returned Franklin Roosevelt to office, particularly labor, Jews, blacks, and other ethnic minorities. Truman's veto of the Taft-Hartley Act had renewed his backing among organized labor. His strategists recognized that an appeal to blacks would also be politically advantageous. In the presidential election of 1944, northern black votes had tipped the election to Roosevelt in eight states, including Michigan and Maryland, and in 1948 they could be decisive in key northern states.

Truman, already sympathetic in principle with civil rights for blacks, responded favorably to a sweeping report to the president in October 1947 entitled *To Secure These Rights*. The product of a committee of distinguished black and white citizens, it called for an end to racial discrimination and segregation in areas ranging from housing and health care to suffrage and employment. In February 1948, Truman endorsed the recommendations in a special message to the Eightieth Congress, which did nothing. He also announced that he would issue orders outlawing segregation in the armed services and the federal civil service. All along, the Truman administration filed friend-of-the-Court briefs in the civil rights cases that were coming to the Supreme Court, stressing among other things the adverse impact of segregation on foreign relations. In June 1948, Truman became the first president to address a rally of the NAACP, telling a crowd of 10,000 from the steps of the Lincoln Memorial that the "serious gap between our ideals and some of our practices . . . must be closed."

"In June 1948, Truman became the first president to address a rally of the NAACP, telling a crowd of 10,000 that the 'serious gap between our ideals and some of our practices . . . must be closed.' "

In the spring of 1948, events in the Middle East presented an opportunity to strengthen his support among Jews. The Jews of Palestine intended to create a Jewish state—Israel—finding justification for the move in the Balfour Declaration of 1917, in which the British government declared that it favored the creation of a home for the Jewish people. The move enjoyed broad public support in the United States, though most foreign policy officials opposed it, fearing that it would lead the Israelis into a losing war with Arabs, who greatly outnumbered them, and jeopardize the flow of oil to Europe and the United States. Truman believed the case for a Jewish homeland was compelling on the merits and warranted on political grounds. "I have to answer to hundreds of thousands who are anxious for the success of Zionism. I do not have hun-

dreds of thousands of Arabs among my constituents," he told the State Department. When on May 14, 1948, Israel declared statehood—prompting the predicted war with the Arabs, which Israel, to the surprise of many, won—the United States granted it recognition immediately.

THE ELECTION OF 1948

An attempt by northern Democrats to dump Truman as their presidential nominee went nowhere, but southern Democrats, angry at the president's embrace of civil rights, were threatening to boycott the party's ticket. In response, Truman waffled on civil rights, sending no specific legislation on the subject to Capitol Hill and neglecting to issue the promised executive order on the armed services. When the Democratic convention met in July, he was willing to accept a weak civil rights plank in the party platform. However, Mayor Hubert H. Humphrey of Minneapolis insisted on amending the platform from the convention floor so that it called for abolition of the poll tax, a federal antilynching law, a permanent Fair Employment Practices Commission, and desegregation of the armed forces. The convention adopted the modified platform, whereupon thirty-five delegates from the deep South walked out waving the flags of the old Confederacy.

A. Philip Randolph (head of the Brotherhood of Sleeping Car Porters), chafing at Truman's failure to move against segregation in the armed services, warned that if the president did not act, he would mount a campaign of civil disobedience. In July, shortly after the convention, the president issued executive orders banning discrimination in federal employment and establishing a committee to seek "equality of treatment and opportunity for all persons in the armed services without regard to race, color, religion or national origin." The services were slow to comply, but under pressure from the president all eventually accepted the policy of desegregation as a policy and began to inch toward making it a military reality.

The civil rights battle at the Democratic convention made Truman's reelection chances seem all the more bleak. The defectors joined with other southern segregationists to form the States' Rights Democratic Party, popularly known as the "Dixiecrats," which nominated Senator Strom Thurmond of South Carolina for the presidency. Dissidents on the Demo-

A. Philip Randolph (left) leads demonstrators demanding a strong civil rights plank at the Democratic National Convention, July 1948.

cratic left allied with Communists in a new Progressive Party that made Henry Wallace its standard-bearer and threatened to draw liberal votes from Truman in northern big-city states. The Republicans once again nominated Governor Thomas E. Dewey of New York, rejecting Robert Taft in favor of a moderate candidate who, together with his running mate, Earl Warren, the popular governor of California, might appeal to Democrats and independents. Dewey, confident that Truman had no chance, mounted a dull, listless campaign, the effort of someone who appeared to believe that he was already president.

Truman, by contrast, ran a **spirited race,** whistle-stopping across the country with his wife and daughter, telling people from the rear of his train that a vote for Republicans was a vote to turn back the New Deal. Together with his running mate, Senator Alben Barkley of Kentucky, he repeatedly attacked the "no-good, do-nothing" Eightieth Congress. He directed special attention to the groups his strategists had identified, attacking private electrical power interests in the Northwest, savaging the Republicans' indifference to farm-price supports in the Midwest, and speaking out for civil rights in Harlem in the East. Toward the end of the race, pollsters quit polling, predicting that a Dewey victory was a sure thing. But Truman was speaking to increas-ingly large and enthusiastic crowds yelling, "Give 'em hell, Harry." On election day, the voters gave him a stunning upset victory, with a margin over Dewey of 2.1 million popular votes and 114 votes in the electoral college.

Winning slightly less than 50 percent of the popular vote, Truman had run behind the Democratic ticket, which regained control of both houses of Congress. He had lost four deep South states to the Dixiecrats but only some strength in the normally Democratic Northeast to Wallace. With Truman earning kudos for the Berlin airlift, in progress during the campaign, the election tacitly endorsed the doctrine of containment. It also indicated that Americans did not want to turn back the social welfare clock. For the most part, the strategy of trying to hold together the Roosevelt coalition had succeeded triumphantly. Truman lost only Oregon out of the eleven states west of the plains. He carried Catholics, Jews, Americans of Eastern European background, and the overlapping constituency of organized labor. His majorities among blacks were enormous, with black votes proving decisive to his victory in the key states of Ohio, Illinois, and California. In January 1949, the black musicians Lionel Hampton and Lena Horne performed along with white stars at Truman's inauguration.

THE FAIR DEAL

In early 1949, Truman proposed a long list of liberal measures to the new Congress, a package designed to provide a "fair deal" for the American people. But despite the Democratic victory in November, working control on Capitol Hill remained in the hands of southern Democrats and conservative Republicans. Congress hiked the minimum wage, provided for more public housing, and broadened Social Security. But it refused to act on civil rights and federal aid to education while declining to reform the tax structure, repeal Taft-Hartley, or restructure the system of agricultural supports in ways that would benefit both small farmers and urban consumers. A renewed proposal to create a TVA-like administration for flood control and power generation in the Columbia Valley went down to defeat in the face of charges that it would put "the entire United States under socialistic government-corporation rule." Another attempt at obtaining national health insurance failed utterly. It lost partly because of a well-financed advertising campaign by the AMA warning that such a system would bring about "socialized medicine" with governmental control of the health-care system, but it also lacked public support.

Amid the strongly conservative congressional climate, organized labor tended to seek broad gains for its workers less in governmental action than in innovative contractual agreements with employers. In the spring of 1948, Walter Reuther and General Motors negotiated a pioneering cost-of-living agreement that automatically adjusted the wage level of auto workers to rises in the consumer price index (a measure of the change in cost from the previous year of the goods and services purchased by a typical wage earner). During the late 1940s, industrial corporations increasingly provided their workers with benefits such as sick pay, paid vacations, and health coverage, a trend indicating the willingness of the private sector to provide social welfare, partly in decent recognition of workers' needs, partly to forestall an enlargement of governmental programs. By 1950, roughly half the civilian population had private insurance coverage for hospital costs, about a third for surgical costs.

MEDICAL RESEARCH

Truman's first message to Congress on health care, in 1945, called for federal aid to medical research and education, a point in his package that conservatives as well as liberals were willing to support. The dramatic success of the wartime penicillin program pointed to the value of concerted attacks against disease. In 1948, Congress established the National Institutes of Health (NIH) as an umbrella for the National Cancer Institute and the new National Heart Institute, and in 1950 it authorized the establishment of whatever additional medical research institutes in the NIH the surgeon general of the United States might deem appropriate. The surgeon general promptly brought the number of such institutes to eight, covering as many different diseases and disorders. In 1950, Congress appropriated $46 million for the NIH, a small sum by the standards of defense science but enough to set the institutes on their way to forming a powerful complex for biomedical research and training.

In the meantime, private philanthropy enlarged its support of biomedical research, giving special attention to the scourges of cancer and polio. The Sloan-Kettering Institute, established in 1945 at Memorial Hospital in New York City, became one of the leading cancer research centers in the world, employing more than 100 scientists and, in 1950, spending more than twice the money on research into the disease than the entire country had devoted to it in 1937. Wartime research into defenses against gas warfare had indicated that certain chemical compounds might be employed as chemotherapeutic agents against cancer. Investigations in chemotherapy occupied a good deal of the research program at Sloan-Kettering as well as at other research centers, and effective agents were soon developed against childhood leukemias, while promising ones were found against Hodgkin's lymphoma.

THE "FALL" OF CHINA

In foreign affairs all the while, the Truman administration kept on with the policy of containment, but its aid to Jiang Jieshi (Chiang Kai-shek) in China seemed increasingly wasted. By 1949, the administration had supplied $3 billion worth of loans and war surplus goods to Jiang's Nationalist government, but Mao Zedong's (Mao Tse-tung's) Communists had kept gaining ground. Mao's forces offered the peasantry reforms that Jiang's regime refused to entertain: an end to foreign dominance, agrarian overhaul, and emancipation from the Nationalist regime's corrupt and dictatorial character. American officials concluded that to keep Jiang in power would require extensive and ongoing U.S. economic and military intervention, an option the Truman administration rejected. By mid-1949, the Nationalists had been forced to abandon Beijing, Tianjin, and Shanghai, and by the end of the year they had yielded mainland China to the Communists and left for the nearby island of Formosa (Taiwan).

Many Western nations granted recognition to the Communist regime. The American government expected to recognize it, too, hoping to encourage its independence from the Soviets. However, many American conservatives, bitter that the Truman administration had "lost" China, lobbied against recognition, and the Chinese declined to accept certain American conditions for obtaining it. The United States continued to recognize the Nationalist regime on Formosa as the legitimate government of China. Agitation from the "China lobby"—a loose alliance of individuals and groups, including many with missionary or business ties to Asia, the publisher of *Time*, and conservative Republicans from the Midwest and West—helped make recognition of the Communist regime almost unthinkable in mainstream public affairs.

DECISION FOR A HYDROGEN BOMB

The Communist takeover in China shocked Americans, and so did Truman's announcement in late September 1949 that the Soviet Union had exploded an atomic bomb. While the

What if You Get Sick?

Infectious childhood diseases such as measles, mumps, chicken pox, diphtheria, and infantile paralysis were highly contagious before vaccines against them began to be developed in the 1950s. And before broadly effective antibiotics such as penicillin became available after World War II, children who came down with these diseases were often in for a rough time. In 1946, Dr. Benjamin Spock published The Common Sense Book of Baby and Child Care, *a book that millions of parents would make their Bible and that in this first edition recommended the standard procedure for a family with a child ill with an infectious disease.*

"Quarantine.... This is first of all to prevent others—either adults or children—who have not had the disease from catching it unnecessarily. Another reason is that they will not be carrying the germs to others outside the home....

"How do you maintain a good quarantine? You keep the child in one room and keep everyone else out except the one grownup who is taking care of him. She slips on a smock which is kept hanging in the room just for this purpose. This keeps her regular clothes from collecting germs. She takes it off every time she leaves the room. All the drinking and eating utensils that leave the room should be carried to the kitchen in a dishpan and boiled in it before being handled or washed or mixed with the utensils for the rest of the family.

"In the case of scarlet fever, diphtheria, and some other serious diseases, further precautions are required by some health departments. Sheets, pillow cases, night clothes may have to be soaked in antiseptic solution before being washed. The room may have to be stripped of rugs, curtains, bureau covers, etc., at the beginning of the disease. The health department may forbid anybody outside the family from entering the home...."

Benjamin Spock, *The Common Sense Book of Baby and Child Care*

American Journal

news did not surprise most knowledgeable scientists—they had estimated that it would take the Soviets only five years or so to build their own bomb—it distressed millions of lay Americans, who, thinking the Soviets backward, had assumed it would take them much longer. Although the United States by now possessed a formidable and steadily expanding nuclear arsenal, a number of scientists and policymakers demanded that it embark on a crash program to build a thermonuclear weapon they called "the Super." Different from a fission bomb, it would work by fusing together nuclei of hydrogen, mimicking the reaction that fuels the sun. A hydrogen bomb would explode with the power of millions of tons of TNT in a blast a thousand times greater than the one that had destroyed Hiroshima. The H-bomb's most zealous advocate was Edward Teller, a theoretical physicist, refugee from Hungary, and hard-line anti-Communist, for whom the Super had become an obsession. He warned that if the Soviets beat the United States to a thermonuclear weapon, "our situation would be hopeless."

Opposed to a crash program to build an H-bomb was a distinguished complement of scientists and policymakers, J. Robert Oppenheimer among them. They hoped that American restraint would lead the Soviet Union to forgo its development, too. Their reasons were partly moral—an H-bomb would be a weapon of "genocide" and, as such, "necessarily an evil thing," in the judgment of two distinguished physicists advising the AEC—and partly prudential: the national interest of the United States lay in avoiding a thermonuclear arms race. It was also an open question whether the requirements of the H-bomb design that Teller was promoting were consistent with the known laws of physics. Subjected to analysis done in part with the new ENIAC computer, Teller's ideas repeatedly failed.

However, Teller's advocacy of an H-bomb enjoyed powerful support from physicists and top officials, including Atomic Energy Commissioner Lewis Strauss, the congressional Joint Committee on Atomic Energy, the Joint Chiefs of Staff, and Secretary of State Dean Acheson. Some could see no moral difference between slaughtering a city with several atomic bombs or a single H-bomb. The chiefs considered it "foolhardy altruism" for the United States voluntarily to renounce such a super weapon, and Acheson was unconvinced that a paranoid adversary could be persuaded to disarm by example. At the end of January 1950, President Truman authorized the crash program, telling the world, an insider physicist remembered, "that we were going to make a hydrogen bomb at a time when we didn't even know how to make one."

Subversion and Security

The advent of the Soviet atomic bomb and the so-called fall of China to Communism prompted a number of Americans to attribute Communist victories abroad to subversion at home. Shortly after the war, Canadian authorities had uncovered a Soviet atomic spy ring operating out of their country with connections to the United States, and early in February 1950, just a few days after the administration's decision to proceed with the H-bomb, the British announced that Klaus Fuchs, a Communist and a key physicist at Los Alamos during the war, had been turning over atomic secrets to the Soviet Union since 1943. Knowledgeable authorities said that Fuchs's espionage had accelerated the Soviet nuclear weapons program by a year or two (estimates that Soviet scientists later confirmed).

Communists and Communist sympathizers were to be found in various walks of American life, including universities, science, government, entertainment, and the media. Many had embraced Communism during the thirties, thinking it the answer to the Great Depression. Whatever their motives, they were automatically held to be subverting American democracy because the Communist Party, unlike ordinary political parties, usually followed the Soviet line. Communist affiliations did not in fact necessarily make someone disloyal to the United States or willing to pass secrets to Soviet agents. However, the revelations of espionage were enough to make not only Communists but non-Communists and even anti-Communists on the political left vulnerable to accusations of disloyalty. A number of Republicans red-baited their opponents in the 1946 congressional campaign, charging the Democrats, as Taft said of Truman, with "appeasing the Russians abroad and . . . fostering Communism at home."

THE TRUMAN LOYALTY PROGRAM

In March 1947, to counter Republican charges that he was soft on Communism, the president issued an executive order establishing a program to check the loyalty of the 2.5 million people who worked for the federal government. Among the criteria for suspicion of disloyalty would be past or present membership in allegedly totalitarian, fascist, or subversive organizations on a list to be drawn up by the attorney general. During the program's first year, the FBI checked out more than 2 million federal employees and conducted full investigations of over 6,000 of them. Some 1,200 workers were dismissed; another 6,000 quit. No one was ever proved to have engaged in spying or sabotage.

The loyalty program made advocates of civil liberties shudder. J. Edgar Hoover, the director of the FBI, used his agency's powers to wage investigative war against alleged Communists, smearing them with rumor and innuendo. Many people were called before loyalty boards because they were thought to be alcoholics, homosexuals, or debtors; and many were asked about the art on their walls or the recordings they owned. Truman privately wrote: "We want no

Screenwriter Dalton Trumbo, leaving the House Un-American Activities Committee's witness stand in 1947, angrily denounces its investigation of Hollywood as the start of an "American concentration camp."

Gestapo or Secret Police. FBI is tending in that direction. They are dabbling in sex life scandals and plain blackmail." In drawing up a list of subversive groups, the attorney general had no formal standard of "subversiveness"; and groups put on the list were not given the opportunity to challenge the designation. Some organizations on the list were coalitions of Communists and non-Communists who had joined together in the 1930s to oppose fascism. Despite guarantees of due process in the proceedings, the departmental loyalty boards denied federal employees even the right to know the identity of their accusers, let alone the right to confront them.

THE HOUSE UN-AMERICAN ACTIVITIES COMMITTEE

Truman established the loyalty program partly because he wanted to forestall Republican attacks during the upcoming 1948 campaign that his administration was soft on Communism, but he also said that he hoped the program would protect innocent federal workers from the extremes of the House Un-American Activities Committee (HUAC), which had been established in 1938. During the war, its chair, Congressman Martin Dies of Texas, claimed to find Communist influence in labor unions, government bureaus, and among the African Americans who rioted in Detroit; and now his successors made clear that they intended to continue the search for subversives in American life. In the late 1940s, the HUAC's members included John Rankin of Mississippi, who later decried civil rights activists as "a part of the communist program, laid down by Stalin himself," adding, "Remember, communism is Yiddish." It also included a new congressman from southern California named Richard M. Nixon. An aggressive investigator, Nixon had smeared his Democratic opponent in the 1946 elections as a "lip-service American" who consistently voted the Moscow line and who "fronted for un-American elements."

The HUAC was undeterred from its inquisitions by the Truman administration's loyalty review program. In 1948, for example, it released a report calling the physicist Edward U. Condon, the director of the National Bureau of Standards, "one of the weakest links in our atomic security." Condon was an outspoken liberal, not a Communist, and an inquiry by the Atomic Energy Commission cleared him fully. In

"After the Hollywood Ten got out of prison, they found themselves blacklisted, unable to obtain work. The message was clear: cooperate with HUAC, or the film industry would be closed to you."

1947, the HUAC, probing allegations of Communist influence in the film industry, called ten of its most successful figures, most of them screenwriters, to testify about their politics and associations. Eight of them, including Dalton Trumbo, Hollywood's highest-paid screenwriter and a veteran of the Spanish Civil War, had Communist affiliations. All refused to answer the HUAC's queries, asserting that the committee had no right to inquire into their political beliefs and associations. They enjoyed the support of many prominent entertainers. The singer Frank Sinatra, who had been denounced before the HUAC as a "front" for Communists, protested, "If you make a pitch on a nationwide radio network for a square deal for the underdog, will they call you a Commie?"

At the hearings, the Hollywood Ten, as they came to be known, were cited for contempt. All were convicted and sent to prison. Some of the outspoken stars, notably Humphrey Bogart, backed away from their criticism of the HUAC. In a meeting at the Waldorf Astoria Hotel in New York City, in November 1947, the major film producers announced that they were firing every one of the Hollywood Ten who was currently employed and vowed that they would not knowingly hire anyone who was a Communist. After the ten got out of prison, they found themselves blacklisted, unable to obtain work. The message was clear: cooperate with HUAC, or the film industry would be closed to you. A number of Hollywood witnesses subsequently called before the committee identified people whom they claimed had once belonged to left-wing groups, tarring them if the groups, which were usually perfectly lawful, happened to have included Communists. Blacklisting quickly spread to the radio and television industries, too, which relied on private consulting firms to determine who was and who was not a subversive.

THE CASE OF ALGER HISS

Many Americans were shocked by the testimony before the HUAC in August 1948 of Whittaker Chambers. A senior editor at *Time* magazine, Chambers had spied for Soviet military intelligence, breaking off his activity in 1938. He testified that during the 1930s he had received secret government documents from a State Department official named Alger Hiss.

Hiss flatly denied the allegation, and many people, especially liberals, believed him. He had impeccable credentials, including a distinguished record at Harvard Law School, a clerkship at the Supreme Court with Justice Oliver Wendell Holmes Jr., and public service as a federal attorney, member of the American delegation at Yalta, and official at the inaugural meeting of the United Nations. Since 1947, he had headed the Carnegie Foundation for International Peace. He was suave, polished, in all an unlikely spy.

Chambers, however, showed reporters a hollowed-out pumpkin on his Maryland farm containing microfilms of documents that he claimed had been given him by Hiss. At the HUAC, Congressman Richard Nixon relentlessly pursued the case. Eventually, HUAC investigators found that a typewriter once owned by Hiss had likely produced the typing on Chambers's documents. Since the statute of limitations had long since expired for Hiss's alleged treason, Hiss was indicted on charges of having perjured himself before the HUAC. After a trial in mid-1949 resulted in a hung jury, he was tried again and convicted in January 1950, serving forty-four months in prison. Although Hiss protested to his death in 1996 that he was innocent, evidence from Soviet and Eastern European sources after the end of the Cold War suggested that he had been guilty of espionage. At the time, while many people remained convinced of his innocence, many others did not, and his exposure provoked widespread doubts that national security could be entrusted to the kind of New Deal/Fair Deal liberals, even those with credentials like Hiss's, who had populated the government for twenty years.

THE EFFECTS OF FEAR

The fear of internal subversion severely damaged civil liberties in the United States. The powerful tendency to castigate and punish people not for what they did but for their political beliefs, associations, and declarations reached far beyond the hearing rooms of the administration's loyalty review program and the HUAC. In 1940, Congress had passed the Smith Act, which made it illegal merely to advocate the violent overthrow of the government. Thomas Jefferson, who had argued that the American democracy needed a revolution every generation, would have been prosecutable under the terms of the law. The act led to the trial and conviction of the leaders of the American Communist Party, who appealed their case to the Supreme Court. In 1951, in *Dennis v. the United States*, the court upheld the constitutionality of the Smith Act, with

Alger Hiss defends himself against charges of espionage before the House Un-American Activities Committee, August 1948.

the majority finding reason in the "gravity" of the Communist threat to depart from the doctrine that the right of free speech could be limited only if the exercise of it posed a "clear and present danger." Justices Hugo Black and William O. Douglas forcefully dissented, arguing that the majority opinion diluted the First Amendment to the point of protecting only "those 'safe' or orthodox views which rarely need its protection."

In 1949, the National Education Association, a body representing public-school teachers, voted almost unanimously that Communists were "unfit" to teach in the schools; and a blue-ribbon panel headed by James B. Conant of Harvard and Dwight Eisenhower, now the president of Columbia University, announced that the same criterion should apply to university professors. Loyalty oaths were enacted by fifteen states—by 1953, the total would reach thirty-four, in addition to many local governments—requiring that public employees swear that they were not Communists and did not believe in the violent overthrow of the government. Drawing national attention, the University of California fired some 10 percent of its faculty because they refused to sign a loyalty oath, and a similar fate befell professors at other universities who refused to cooperate with state and federal investigations into their political affiliations. In 1950, the Joint Committee on Atomic Energy required that all applicants for AEC fellowships obtain security clearances, whether they would be engaged in classified research or not. Albert Einstein complained to no avail that young scientists should not have to pay such a cost in "human dignity" to pursue research.

The climate of fear had a chilling effect on American culture and reform movements. It gave weight to the urging of Eric Johnston, the head of the Motion Picture Producers' Association, who wanted the film industry to make "no more *Grapes of Wrath* . . . no more *Tobacco Road*s . . . no more films that show the seamy side of American life . . . that deal with labor strikes . . . with the banker as villain." Labor unions purged Communists from their leadership, and civil rights groups similarly refused to cooperate with left-wing activists. Conservatives nevertheless charged that advocates of civil rights were Communists, a claim that Jackie Robinson denied when he testified before the HUAC, stressing, "Negroes were stirred up long before there was a Communist Party, and they'll stay stirred up long after the party has disappeared—unless Jim Crow has disappeared by then as well."

At mid-century, the United States was on tenterhooks, with the Cold War intensifying flight from the reformism of the New Deal/Fair Deal, casting doubt on the patriotism of dissenters and visionaries, and raising increasing apprehensions about the future of the nation's security. The president had asked a high-level committee for a review of defense policy in light of the Soviet acquisition of atomic weapons. In the spring of 1950, the committee produced National Security Council Memorandum Number 68 (NSC-68), which stated that the Soviet Union was a threat "not only to this Republic but to civilization itself" and that in a few years it would be capable of mounting a surprise atomic attack of potentially devastating proportions. NSC-68 urged that to deter such aggression the United States had to intensify intelligence operations, covertly encourage unrest in the satellite countries, and beef up research and development. It also had to proceed to full-scale rearmament, including the establishment of a substantial standing army and a quadrupling of the defense budget, if necessary at the sacrifice of domestic needs. But Truman was unwilling to go so far as to put the country on the virtual war footing recommended in NSC-68. In the spring of 1950, the administration sent Capitol Hill the lowest defense budget since V-J Day, and it sailed through Congress.

Since that day of victory, the Truman administration had, despite its twists and turns, carved out the essential elements of the nation's foreign and domestic policies in the postwar era. It had successfully managed reconversion to a peacetime

March 1943	Manhattan Project begins at Los Alamos, New Mexico.
1944	Western powers establish International Monetary Fund and World Bank at Bretton Woods, New Hampshire.
February 1945	Roosevelt, Churchill, and Stalin meet at Yalta.
April 1945	United Nations founded.
August 6/9, 1945	Atomic bombs dropped on Hiroshima/Nagasaki, Japan.
September 2, 1945	Japan surrenders.
July 1946	Atomic Energy Commission created.
1947	The Taft-Hartley Act.
February 1948	The Marshall Plan initiated.
April 1949	NATO created.

economy, and, despite the shift to the political right, advanced the Fair Deal version of the welfare state, explicitly placing minority rights, especially for African Americans, on the national agenda. Prompted by the technological shrinkage of the world and the emergence of the Cold War, Truman and the Congress had committed the United States to continuing international engagement, including collective security, and to a variety of programs, research and development among them, to bolster national defense. But arming the country for Cold War had unavoidably made the military a worrisomely powerful force in peacetime life. And the government's loyalty and security programs threatened to undermine the vitality of the democracy that its policies were intended to protect.

Suggested Reading

John Lewis Gaddis, *The United States and the Origins of the Cold War, 1941–1947* (1972)

Alonzo L. Hamby, *Man of the People: A Life of Harry S. Truman* (1995)

Susan M. Hartmann, *The Home Front and Beyond: American Women in the 1940s* (1982)

Arnold Rampersad, *Jackie Robinson: A Biography* (1997)

Richard Rhodes, *The Making of the Atomic Bomb* (1986)

Samuel J. Walker, *Prompt and Utter Destruction: Truman and the Use of Atomic Bombs Against Japan* (1997)

Chapter 28

KOREA, EISENHOWER, AND AFFLUENCE:

1950-1956

Levittown, one of the first suburban tract housing developments, near Philadelphia.

QUESTIONS

- How did the Korean War and McCarthyism affect the United States?

- What were Eisenhower's Cold War policies?

- What were the major technological and social developments of the 1950s?

- How did minority groups fare in the 1950s?

- How did the civil rights movement gain force in the 1950s?

Saturday, June 24, 1950: the news reached the State Department by cable at 9:26 P.M. Early that morning, military forces from Communist North Korea had crossed the 38th parallel into anti-Communist, pro-Western South Korea, initiating what appeared to be an all-out offensive. The head of North Korea had predicted to Stalin that the United States would not intervene to protect the South, perhaps because a speech that Secretary of State Dean Acheson had given in 1950 could be interpreted to mean that it was not within the American defense perimeter. Stalin promised North Korea supplies but little more. American officials were nevertheless sure that the invasion had been prompted by the Soviets. Truman told an aide, "There's no telling what they'll do, if we don't put up a fight right now." On Tuesday, June 27, the president committed air and naval forces to cover the South Korean troops. On Friday, General Douglas MacArthur, in Japan, warned that the South Korean army would be overrun without help on the ground. Truman then authorized MacArthur to send American infantry under his command to Korea.

Truman had not consulted Congress, and some members grumbled that nothing in the Constitution authorized the president to commit troops to combat on his own. The United Nations, which at the moment the Soviets happened to be boycotting, had branded the North Koreans aggressors and adopted a resolution supporting armed assistance to South Korea. The willingness to put teeth into collective security heartened delegates from Western countries, giving them hope that the fledgling U.N. would not suffer the fate of the League of Nations. Most Republicans and Democrats in Congress cheered Truman's action, and even the grumblers supported it. Relief seemed to sweep through the Capitol that at long last the country was standing up to Communism.

At a press conference, Truman insisted that the United States was not at war, but was, in a reporter's phrase, in a "police action under the United Nations." (In fact, the U.S. forces in Korea, while formally an arm of the U.N., operated under the control of Washington.) The United States had entered a war that would continue for three years and in which it would provide 50 percent of the troops, with much of the rest supplied by South Korea. In July, Congress roared through a military increase of $10 billion, inaugurating a huge enlargement in defense expenditures. In 1953, they would reach $52.8 billion, accounting for some $69 out of every $100 spent by the federal government.

As the conflict dragged on, many Americans grew angry and frustrated, intensifying suspicions of subversion and disloyalty at home. Seen as the work of the Russians, the war deepened fears of Soviet aggression, accelerated the development of atomic and conventional defense technologies, and stimulated the United States to globalize containment while reconfiguring its policies for European security. In all, the **Korean War** convinced many Americans that their country faced an era of acute danger. It fostered Cold War attitudes that would significantly affect the nation long after the war itself ended.

Korea and Its Consequences

A SEESAW WAR

In the first weeks of the war, the North Koreans overwhelmed the U.N. forces—largely American and South Korean troops under MacArthur's command. The Americans were soft from occupation duty in Japan and, like the South Korean forces, inadequately equipped. Battling Soviet-made tanks with World War II bazookas, the U.N. armies frantically retreated until they managed to establish a defense perimeter some sixty-five miles north of Pusan, at the southeastern end of the Korean peninsula. But then, on September 15, 1950, in a brilliant gamble reminiscent of his tactics in World War II, MacArthur mounted a successful amphibious assault at Inchon, on the coast just west of Seoul, the South Korean capital. The U.N. troops, their casualties extremely light, soon took Seoul while other U.N. troops, breaking out of Pusan, moved northward. By the beginning of October, the area up to the 38th parallel was under U.N. control.

MacArthur insisted that the U.N. forces continue northward to North Korea's border with China, thus reuniting Korea under Western protection. American public opinion seemed to endorse the move, and so did the United Nations, which approved it in early October. However, the Chinese had warned that it would not tolerate American troops in the neighborhood of its border. (Unknown to American strategists, Stalin had encouraged Mao Zedong [Mao Tse-tung] to resist any American march northward, sending him huge shipments of guns and planes.) In mid-October, Truman, worried about the Chinese, flew to meet with MacArthur at Wake Island in the Pacific. MacArthur—arrogant and condescending, in Truman's recollection—assured his commander in chief that the Chinese were unlikely to intervene and that if they did, they would be slaughtered. The president authorized American forces to cross the 38th parallel but not to antagonize China.

MacArthur directed his troops northward toward the Yalu River (the Chinese-Korean border), but in late November, marking a major turning point in the war, huge waves of Chinese troops began pouring into North Korea. By January 1951, the U.N. troops had been driven back through bitter cold and hazardous passages deep into South Korea. Under General Matthew Ridgway, who had taken charge of the U.S. Eighth Army in December, the U.S. forces dug in, then doggedly counterattacked to the north. By late March, they had recaptured Seoul and most of the territory south of the 38th parallel. Now the war seesawed across the 38th parallel, stalemating both sides.

THE SACKING OF MacARTHUR

The Truman administration said that the United States was fighting a "limited war" and that it wanted a diplomatic settlement, but MacArthur repeatedly and publicly insisted on taking the war to China—by, for example, bombing Chinese bases beyond the Yalu, in Manchuria. Thumbing his nose at Truman's authority as commander in chief, he disparaged the administration's Korean policies as tantamount to the "appeasement of Communism" and declared, "There is no substitute for victory." On April 11, 1951, Truman, backed by a unanimous recommendation from the Joint Chiefs of Staff, removed MacArthur from command, emphasizing that he could not tolerate such a challenge to presidential authority. Truman's action provoked widespread outrage, but by May the pro-MacArthur storm subsided. In congressional hearings, General Omar Bradley, speaking for the Joint Chiefs of Staff, persuasively argued that MacArthur's policies would have involved the United States in "the wrong war, at the wrong place, at the wrong time, and with the wrong enemy."

In June 1951, shortly before the hearings ended, the Russians intimated that they wanted a cease-fire in Korea. Peace

Marines attacking over the top during the assault on Inchon, September 1950.

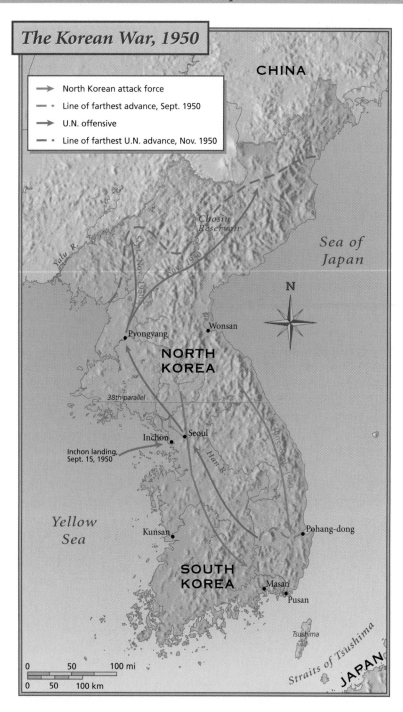

The Korean War, 1950

→ North Korean attack force
– · Line of farthest advance, Sept. 1950
→ U.N. offensive
– · Line of farthest U.N. advance, Nov. 1950

CHINA

Chosin Reservoir

Yalu R.

Sea of Japan

Sept.–Nov. 1950

Nov. 1950

N

Pyongyang

Wonsan

NORTH KOREA

38th parallel

Inchon

Seoul

Inchon landing, Sept. 15, 1950

Han R.

Chinese, June 1950

Yellow Sea

Kunsan

Pohang-dong

SOUTH KOREA

Masan

Pusan

Tsushima

Straits of Tsushima

JAPAN

0   50   100 mi
0   50   100 km

tion had to be voluntary—a condition that the North Koreans and Chinese were still refusing to accept when Truman left office in January 1953, with the result that the fighting continued.

EXTENDING CONTAINMENT

The Korean War encouraged policymakers to see the Soviet Union and Communist China as a monolithic bloc and to view the threat they posed as fundamentally military and global. The shift led the United States, even though the brutalities of World War II were still fresh in memory, to turn its recent enemies, Japan and Germany, into allies. In 1950, America persuaded its NATO allies to agree to the rearmament of Germany. The next year, in 1951, it entered pacts with Japan that restored Japanese sovereignty over the home islands and gave the United States the right to station American troops and planes on Japanese soil.

The administration stationed the Seventh Fleet between China and Formosa and strengthened American commitments to counterrevolutionary forces in Southeast Asia, a major source of rice and oil for Asia and of natural rubber for the world. Drawing a line against the Soviets in the Middle East, it obtained military bases in Saudi Arabia and Morocco. By the early 1950s, in the name of preventing the spread of Communism, the United States had extended its military presence across the globe.

A SEA CHANGE IN DEFENSE SCIENCE

The Korean War intensified the belief of policymakers that the United States had to rely on technology to offset the superior numbers of enemy troops that could be deployed against its less numerous forces. During the war, the budget for defense research and development more than doubled, reaching about $1.6 billion in 1952. In April 1951, Truman established the first science advisory committee to exist within the government, its duties to include counseling the president on scientific matters, particularly in connection with national defense. Combined with the Soviet Union's becoming a nuclear power, the Korean War generated a commitment to an expansive readiness. A high-ranking defense science ad-

negotiations began the next month, but they soon bogged down over the issue of repatriation of North Korean and Chinese prisoners of war, some 45,000 of whom did not want to go home. The Truman administration insisted that repatria-

viser observed that at times the military "seem to be fanatics in their belief of what the scientists and the technologists can do." The psychological sea change also made civilian scientists more enthusiastic about strengthening the nation's nuclear arsenal, including the integration of nuclear weapons into conventional battle plans, and it helped defuse opposition to the hydrogen bomb.

When the war broke out, no one yet knew how to make such a bomb, a weapon that, by fusing the nuclei of hydrogen, would imitate on earth the reaction that powers the sun. The main problem was to find a way to initiate the fusion of the hydrogen fuel, a process that requires enormous energy. But at Los Alamos in January 1951, the mathematical physicist Stanislaw Ulam proposed that the hydrogen might be made to fuse by compressing it with the energetic neutrons produced by an exploding fission device. Edward Teller, the principal proponent of the Super bomb, brilliantly improved on Ulam's idea, proposing the superior trick of igniting the hydrogen by compressing it with a shock wave of radiation produced by the fission trigger.

At a meeting of physicists in Princeton, New Jersey, in mid-June 1951, the new, unexpected approach was greeted as virtually miraculous. The assembled physicists did not speak of evil and genocide, as they had in 1949, when they had recommended against pressing ahead to build a hydrogen bomb. The Korean War had changed their ethical perception by raising fears for the security of Europe and heightening distrust of Soviet intentions. Besides, they expected that if American physicists could think of a radiation shock wave to fire a hydrogen bomb, so could their Soviet counterparts, especially since Klaus Fuchs, the atomic physicist at Los Alamos whose espionage had been exposed in 1950, knew all about the early ideas for the Super. In any case, as Robert Oppenheimer, who now enlisted in the H-bomb army, later explained, the Ulam-Teller breakthrough was too "technically sweet" to pass up.

On November 1, 1952, the principle of the hydrogen bomb was demonstrated to work in a spectacularly successful test in the Pacific, code-named "Mike," that yielded a ten-megaton blast, 500 times the power unleashed at Hiroshima. The explosion produced a searing white fireball more than three miles across that swiftly darkened into a boiling cloud twenty-seven miles high atop a stem eight miles wide. A sailor wrote home, "You would swear the whole world was on fire."

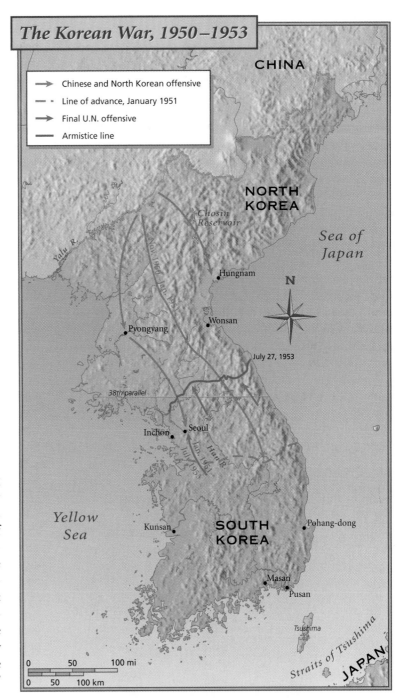

The Korean War, 1950–1953

→ Chinese and North Korean offensive
– – Line of advance, January 1951
→ Final U.N. offensive
── Armistice line

McCARTHYISM

The specter of nuclear annihilation bothered Senator Joseph McCarthy far less than the threat of internal subversion. During a speech in Wheeling, West Virginia, on February 9, 1950, McCarthy, then a little-known, first-term Republican from Wisconsin, had waved a sheet of paper, declaring, "I have here in my hand a list of 205 [employees] known to the Secretary of State as being members of the Communist Party and who nevertheless are still working and shaping the policy of the State Department." A lawyer and circuit judge before his election to the Senate in 1946, McCarthy had a history of shading the truth. Now he refused to release his "list" (which he eventually cut to 1), but amid the growing fear of internal subversion, his charges were earning headlines. In the spring, the liberal editorial cartoonist Herbert Block published a cartoon depicting a Republican elephant being dragged and pushed toward a pile of tar buckets topped by a large one labeled "McCARTHYISM"—a term that quickly entered the American language and connoted smearing attacks on character and loyalty.

Encouraged by the attention—he faced a reelection campaign in 1952—McCarthy went on a spree of raising reckless charges against alleged Communists in government. During the congressional elections of 1950, he was credited with helping to defeat four Democratic senators against whom he campaigned, including one who had called his accusations "a fraud and a hoax." (The Democratic advantage over Republicans in the Senate fell by a total of ten seats; in the House, by fifty-seven.) McCarthy blamed the Communist takeover in China on George Marshall, identifying him as part of a "conspiracy so immense and an infamy so black as to dwarf any such previous venture in the history of man" and accused the Democrats of perpetrating "twenty years of treason."

McCarthy gained a major following in the United States, especially among conservative Republicans, midwesterners, ethnic minorities of Eastern European background, and anti-Communist Catholics. What bound his supporters together was bitterness over the losses to Communism, especially in Eastern Europe and China, and a belief that privileged people like Alger Hiss, convicted of lying to Congress about his espionage, and even the resolute Cold Warrior Dean Acheson, whom McCarthy vilified as the "Red Dean," were responsible for it. A number of McCarthyites were also united by their ongoing anger at the New Deal. A conservative Republican from Nebraska sniped about Acheson, "I watch his smart aleck manner and his British clothes and that New Dealism, everlasting New Dealism in everything he says and does, and I want to shout, 'Get Out! Get Out! You stand for everything that has been wrong in the United States for years.'"

The seeming endlessness of the conflict in Korea intensified the McCarthyite atmosphere, widening suspicions that pro-Communist subversion was at work in the United States. The Christian evangelist Billy Graham warned huge crowds against "over 1,100 social-sounding organizations that are communist or communist-operated in this country," declaring that "they control the minds of a great segment of our people." Community activists forced libraries and schools to remove social reformist books such as John Steinbeck's *The Grapes of Wrath* from their shelves. Blacklisting spread in the television and film industries. The House Un-American Activities Committee continued its crusade to ferret out Communists, insisting that witnesses called before it identify other people who might have been involved years earlier in left-wing organizations. Some witnesses took the Fifth Amendment, holding that complying with the committee's demand for names would hurt innocent people. But a number cooperated.

In the federal government, where Truman had toughened the loyalty and security requirements for employees, vague innuendoes by informants about past political associations

Joseph McCarthy (second from right) used the press to level reckless charges of Communist infiltration.

often sufficed to force workers out of their jobs. The State Department denied passports to left-leaning Americans, including celebrated singers, artists, and scientists. In 1950, Congress passed an Internal Security Act that compelled Communist organizations and their members to register with a new Subversive Activities Control Board and made members of such organizations ineligible for jobs in government or defense. Truman vetoed the bill, denouncing it as the "greatest danger to freedom of press, speech, and assembly since the Sedition Act of 1798," but Congress overrode the veto by sweeping majorities. The McCarran-Walter Immigration Act (1952), which it also passed over Truman's veto, facilitated FBI surveillance of suspect groups and the deportation of aliens suspected of subversiveness.

THEY LIKED IKE

The Election of 1952. In 1952, the McCarthyite tide and frustration with the Korean conflict seemed to bode well for Republicans in the coming presidential election. So did revelations of corruption in the Truman administration, notably that payments had been made to several officials or their wives seemingly in exchange for favors such as federal loans. GOP conservatives, who were centered in the Midwest, pressed for the nomination of Robert Taft, their champion, still a resolute foe of New Dealism and suspicious of American involvements abroad. But the party's eastern wing of moderate internationalists found a powerful candidate in Dwight D. Eisenhower, the war hero and commander of the NATO forces. Although in 1948 Eisenhower had steered clear of presidential politics, he agreed to run now because he disliked Truman's tolerance for deficits and Taft's neo-isolationist leanings. Without campaigning, Eisenhower crushed Taft in the New Hampshire primary and went on to win the nomination. His running mate was thirty-nine-year-old Richard Nixon, a ferociously ambitious politico who had become a national figure by his pursuit of Alger Hiss and by his election to the Senate from California two years earlier in a red-baiting campaign that earned him the nickname "Tricky Dick."

Truman, his standing in the polls abysmal, declined to run again. The Democrats awarded their nomination to Adlai Stevenson, a wealthy lawyer, the governor of Illinois, and a critic of McCarthyism. In the hope of keeping the South in the Democratic camp, they chose Senator John Sparkman of Alabama as his running mate, a choice consistent with Stevenson's willingness to tolerate racial segregation by leav-

Dwight D. Eisenhower runs for the presidency, Lawrence, Massachusetts, 1952.

ing civil rights up to the states. During the campaign, Stevenson otherwise made eloquently good on a promise that he would "talk sense to the American people." But the crisp good sense he tried to speak, which added up to a moderate middle-of-the-roadism in foreign and domestic affairs that was close to Eisenhower's, was drowned out by the Republican din over what their party strategists called K_1C_2—Korea, Communism, and Corruption. Nixon spoke of "Adlai the appeaser . . . who got a Ph.D. from Dean Acheson's College of Cowardly Containment."

In mid-campaign, it was revealed that Nixon had a private political fund donated by rich supporters in California. He responded with a sentimental, nationally televised speech that sidestepped the issue of the propriety of the fund, emphasizing instead his watch-the-pennies upbringing and his young family's modest circumstances. He told the audience that his wife, Pat, wore a "respectable Republican cloth coat" and that among the gifts he had received was a cocker spaniel that his two young daughters loved and had named Checkers, and that "regardless of what they say about it, we're going to keep it." The speech not only saved his place on the ticket but also made the Republican Party, long identified as the party of the rich, look more like a haven for struggling, workaday Americans.

Eisenhower stayed on the high road, buoyed by his war-hero popularity and aided by the shrewd use of television in its presidential campaign debut. Staged TV advertisements brought Eisenhower's radiant smile and unpretentious forthrightness into millions of living rooms (roughly one-third of American households now had TVs). Late in the campaign, Eisenhower announced, "If elected, I shall go to Korea," a promise that stirred people even though he did not say what he would do there.

Eisenhower won in a landslide, gaining more than 55 percent of the popular vote and the overwhelming margin of 442 electoral votes against Stevenson's 89. The first Republican candidate since Herbert Hoover to break the Democratic hold on the South, he won in Florida, Texas, Virginia, and Tennessee. But the results added up more to a victory of the man rather than of the party. Although the Republicans won control of Congress, they enjoyed only a one-seat majority in the Senate and an eight-vote majority in the House.

Eisenhower the Centrist. To many Americans, Dwight Eisenhower, age sixty-two at his inaugural, was a reassuring president, publicly calm, affable, and seemingly above partisan politics, a man of sunny optimism, tested strength, and unquestionable devotion to public service. Having grown up in Abilene, Kansas, he had graduated from the U.S. Military Academy and spent his entire career in the army except for a brief stint as president of Columbia University during the late 1940s. He conducted his presidency in the manner of a general—relying on a hierarchy of aides, staff analysis, and the delegation of authority. He avoided taking the public lead on controversial issues, preferring to operate by the admonition in the Latin phrase on his desk plaque that meant "Gently in manner, strong in deed." Critics faulted him for the muddled syntax of his press conferences, but he used obfuscation as a political instrument. Advised once by his press secretary to say nothing about a controversial foreign policy issue, he replied, "Don't worry, Jim. If that question comes up, I'll just confuse them."

Eisenhower quietly but assiduously involved himself in policymaking for high-stakes matters, with special confidence

> *"Advised once by his press secretary to say nothing about a controversial foreign policy issue, Eisenhower replied, 'Don't worry, Jim. If that question comes up, I'll just confuse them.'"*

in his abilities in foreign and military affairs. Staunchly anti-Communist, he held that the United States had to shoulder its responsibilities for collective security and should continue Truman's policy of extended global containment. His views were shared by his secretary of state, John Foster Dulles, a lawyer from New York City, the son of a Presbyterian minister, and a Wilsonian with extensive experience in diplomacy. Eisenhower worked closely with Dulles and permitted him to put a righteous face on the administration's approach to the world. Dulles's evangelical moralizing may have helped hold the right wing of the Republican Party in check, but it inflamed Soviet-American relations and raised expectations that the United States was ready to crusade against Communism everywhere. In practice, Eisenhower tempered Dulles's rhetoric by restraint in action.

Ending the Korean War. Making good on his campaign pledge, Eisenhower went to Korea after the election, spending three days at the front. At the end of March, the Chinese indicated they might be willing to deal on the issue of repatriation. Although armistice talks resumed, Dulles, sensing resistance on the part of the Chinese, hinted through Indian diplomats that if the war continued, the United States might use atomic weapons. The Chinese and North Koreans, seeing that Eisenhower would offer no better terms than Truman, agreed to a cease-fire on July 27, 1953. The agreement reestablished the 38th parallel as the line of demarcation between North and South Korea and allowed Chinese and North Korean prisoners of war to decide for themselves whether they would return home; ultimately, 50,000 of them declined repatriation. The war had cost more than 33,000 Americans killed and 103,000 wounded and caused some 4 million total casualties, more than half of them civilians. It left Korea divided, with North Korea remaining a tyrannical member of the Communist bloc and South Korea developing into a prosperous, if often internally repressive, ally of the West.

Dealing with McCarthyism. Eisenhower considered Senator Joseph McCarthy's anti-Communism pathologically reckless, but he was willing to reckon politically with the climate of McCarthyism. Shortly after taking office, he issued an executive order that tightened loyalty requirements for federal employees at the cost of curtailing their civil liberties. Within a year under the new rules, some 2,200 personnel were ejected from the federal government, none of them a proved Communist. In 1954, in an attempt to curtail use of the Fifth Amendment to avoid responding to congressional queries about Communism and subversion, Congress passed the Immunity Act, which authorized federal prosecutors and congressional investigators to compel witnesses to testify by conferring on them immunity from prosecution. During the spring of 1953, Eisenhower was urged to commute the sentences of Julius and Ethel Rosenberg, who had been convicted in 1951 of obtaining technical information about the atomic bomb during the war and passing it to the Soviets. (Soviet documents released after the Cold War indicated that he was probably guilty, she probably not.) Eisenhower refused to heed the pleas on the Rosenbergs' behalf, and they were executed in June 1953.

> *" 'Until this moment, Senator, I think I had never gauged your cruelty or your recklessness,' declared Joseph Welch. 'Have you no sense of decency, sir, at long last? Have you left no sense of decency?' "*

That year, McCarthyites leveled charges that J. Robert Oppenheimer, aside from Albert Einstein the most famous physicist in America, was a security risk. They indicted him partly because he had past connections with Communists, partly because he had shown inadequate early enthusiasm for rushing ahead with the development of a hydrogen bomb. Eisenhower ordered the erection of a "blank wall" between Oppenheimer and all classified information, and in 1954, following a hearing against him, a panel of the Atomic Energy Commission ruled that he was unfit to be trusted with the nation's atomic secrets. Many Americans were shocked that not even Oppenheimer, with all he had done to develop the American nuclear arsenal, was immune from McCarthyism; they felt a chill descend on the free and open debate of controversial issues.

McCarthy himself, who headed his own investigative committee now that the Republicans controlled the Senate, hounded alleged subversives, trampling on the civil liberties of Americans in and out of government, even suggesting that Eisenhower's first year in office marked a twenty-first year of treason. Early in the spring of 1954, he took on the army, charging that it was infiltrated with Communists because it had promoted a left-wing dentist. But by now, he was running into courageous and influential criticism in the media. Once he went after the army, Eisenhower, who had been working against him privately, discreetly encouraged the formation of a special Senate committee to investigate the attempt by McCarthy to obtain special privileges for an aide who had been drafted. The committee's hearings into the dispute between McCarthy and the army ran on TV for some five weeks. They revealed McCarthy's bullying tactics to an audience of millions, especially when he suggested that the law firm representing the army included a young lawyer who had once belonged to a Communist organization. Joseph Welch, a senior member of the firm and chief counsel for the army, rebuked McCarthy for the injury he had done the lawyer, declaring, "Until this moment, Senator, I think I had never gauged your cruelty or your recklessness. . . . Have you no sense of decency, sir, at long last? Have you left no sense of decency?" When Welch finished, the room burst into applause. In December, as a result of the hearings, the Republican-controlled Senate censured McCarthy by a vote of 67 to 22 for conduct "unbecoming" a member of the Senate. McCarthyism waned, and McCarthy himself died in 1957, a broken man.

Senator Joseph McCarthy (standing) maps the location of Communists in the United States at the Army-McCarthy hearings in 1954. The army's chief counsel, Joseph Welch (seated to McCarthy's right), denounced him as a "cruelly reckless character assassin."

Accommodating to the Welfare State. In domestic affairs, Eisenhower was a middle-of-the-roader, though he leaned to the right center of the highway. His appointments made clear that he sympathized with large private corporations. His first cabinet comprised "eight millionaires and a plumber," a journalist quipped, referring to members such as Secretary of Defense Charles Wilson, the president of General Motors, and Secretary of Labor Martin Durkin, the president of the major plumbers' union. Eisenhower wanted to limit federal power, return authority to the states, and balance the budget, even if that meant cutting agricultural price supports and reducing defense expenditures. He considered himself much less liberal than Robert Taft, who in his last years (he died in 1953) had supported federal subsidies of public housing and education.

The new administration opened all the national wildlife refuges to gas and oil leasing, and in its first budget doubled funds for the construction of access roads in national forests. While many Americans believed that oil drilled from tidelands belonged to the national government, Eisenhower signed legislation making it available to the states and private interests. The administration replaced career scientific conservationists in natural resource agencies with political appointees who seemed to critics likely to relax wildlife conservation measures.

Nevertheless, Eisenhower's middle-of-the-roadism meant refusing the demands of the right for dismantling the New Deal/Fair Deal. Eisenhower was a political pragmatist, remarking that he would like to sell the Tennessee Valley Authority but figuring that "we can't go that far." And he understood that the welfare state met legitimate human needs. Although he declined to use deficit spending to stave off economic downturns, he proposed modest extensions of Social Security and the minimum wage. While acting on behalf of business and industry, he accepted and somewhat extended the accomplishments of the New Deal/Fair Deal with the result that little changed in the size and scope of the federal government during his presidency. In keeping with his propensity for fiscal restraint and limited federal power, he fashioned an approach to domestic policy that his enthusiasts cheered as Modern Republicanism.

The Election of 1956. While many Americans were happy to say, "I like Ike," they liked him personally more than they cared for the Republican Party. In 1954, the Democrats re-captured both the House and the Senate, but in 1956 Eisenhower easily won reelection, trouncing Adlai Stevenson with more than 57 percent of the popular vote and 457 of the 530 votes in the electoral college. The Democrats kept control of Congress, even gaining a seat in each house—the first time since 1848 that a victorious presidential candidate had not carried at least one house or the other on his coattails.

Eisenhower and the World

In keeping with the president's fiscal conservatism and eagerness to achieve a balanced budget, the administration's defense policies continued to rely on high technology, especially nuclear weapons, to deter aggression. Republican policymakers counted nuclear arms cheaper than conventionally equipped manpower and maintained, as had their Democratic predecessors, that they posed a formidable counter to the Communists' overwhelming land forces, which the Free World preferred not to match in any case. In January 1954, Dulles announced the administration's strategy for global security, which quickly came to be called the "New Look." The United States would rely on "massive retaliatory power" that could be deployed "instantly, by means and at places of our choosing." It would thus get "more basic security at less cost." To this end, during the 1950s the administration multiplied the country's nuclear arsenal fourfold, to about 6,000 weapons, and created a force of missiles to deliver them.

"During the 1950s, the administration multiplied the country's nuclear arsenal fourfold, to about 6,000 weapons, and created a force of missiles to deliver them."

ROCKETS AND MISSILES

At the end of World War II, eager to build on the success of Germany's wartime rocket program, the American military mounted an operation code-named "Paperclip" to search out and bring home German rocket scientists as well as captured parts and documents. Among the scientists was Wernher von Braun, head of the Nazi V-2 program, who had regarded the V-2s as a useful step toward his ultimate goal, building powerful rockets for space exploration. Early in 1950, prompted by the Soviet acquisition of nuclear weapons, the Truman administration gave the American missile program high priority, establishing a "missile czar" and bringing scientists and engineers into the chain of command. In 1951, the air force began developing an intercontinental ballistic missile (ICBM)—the Atlas. At the same time, the air force kept building its aircraft attack force so that within a few years it would have some 1,700 planes, including 400 jet-powered B-47s, capable of delivering nuclear bombs to the Soviet Union.

Dissident policymakers, including some scientists, worried that the reliance on long-range missiles and bombers—so-called "strategic" weapons—would leave the United States with no response to a Soviet attack in Europe other than a nuclear assault on Soviet territory, which could rapidly escalate into an all-out nuclear war. They proposed the development of short-range nuclear weapons, including artillery and rockets, suitable for "tactical" use against enemy troops and installations in the European theater. In the early 1950s, research and development began on such rockets, including one with a range of eighty-four miles that could deliver a nuclear warhead with an explosive power of sixty kilotons of TNT, three times the power of the Hiroshima bomb. A French official noted that if the United States again liberated Western Europe, it would "probably would be liberating a corpse." Nevertheless, tactical nuclear weapons were deployed there beginning in 1953 and later in South Korea.

STAYING AHEAD OF THE SOVIETS

By the mid-1950s, the Soviets were known to possess hydrogen bombs and to be progressing toward the development of intercontinental ballistic missiles, raising the possibility that they might become capable of launching a surprise attack against the United States. In 1955, responding to the urgent recommendations of a special panel of science advisers, the Eisenhower administration inaugurated secret photographic surveillance flights over the Soviet Union using the U-2, a plane specially built to fly at very high altitudes, beyond the reach of Soviet defenses. It was equipped with cameras designed by Edwin H. Land, the inventor of the Polaroid camera, powerful enough to discern the lines for spaces in a parking lot from 70,000 feet. While work accelerated on the Atlas ICBM, the air force began developing a new generation of intercontinental missiles, including the solid-fueled Minuteman, which was cheaper and could carry hydrogen-bomb warheads. The Minuteman would also help deter a surprise attack because it could be launched in retaliation within sixty seconds of an alert—the feature that gave the missile its

The launch of an Atlas intercontinental ballistic missile.

name—quickly enough to be off before the first wave of Soviet missiles arrived. By 1962, 150 Minuteman missiles were installed in silos west of the Mississippi River, most of them in the central Midwest and higher plains and Rocky Mountain states; by 1964, 700 were in place.

Each of the armed services embarked on the development of intermediate-range ballistic missiles (IRBMs), all of which were operational by the end of the 1950s. Among them was the navy's Polaris missile, which in its later models had a range of up to almost 3,000 miles. In 1960, the navy launched the first in a new class of submarines, built to carry sixteen of them. The ensemble of missile and ship, which was nuclear-powered and thus able to sail submerged and unseen for weeks at a time, would prove to be an essential element in the program of deterrence against surprise nuclear attack.

ARMS CONTROL INITIATIVES

Eisenhower seemed at times to regard nuclear weapons casually, publicly declaring that he saw "no reason why they shouldn't be used just exactly as you would use a bullet or anything else." Yet shortly after taking office, he had worried to an aide, "We are in an armaments race. Where will it lead us? At worst to atomic warfare. At best, to robbing every people and nation on earth of the fruits of their own toil."

The death of Stalin shortly after Eisenhower took office raised hopes that East-West differences might be resolved through "peaceful negotiation," as the Soviets put it. At the end of 1953, Eisenhower proposed "Atoms for Peace"—a plan to divert fissionable materials for purposes such as electrical power generation—but the Soviets brushed it aside. In 1955, at a summit meeting in Geneva attended by the Soviet Union, Britain, France, and the United States, he called for a commitment to "Open Skies," a system of mutual aerial surveillance to diminish the likelihood of surprise nuclear attack. Nikita Khrushchev, an earthy, outspoken party boss who was emerging as the new Soviet leader, rejected the initiative, calling it a patent means of espionage. Still, Khrushchev kept the door open to negotiating areas of mutual interest, declaring in 1956, at the Twentieth Congress of the Communist Party, that war was not inevitable, and the United States and the Soviet Union could peacefully coexist.

DEMAND FOR A TEST BAN

On March 1, 1954, the United States conducted a hydrogen bomb test, code-named "Bravo"—in the Pacific at the tip of Namu Island, in the Bikini Atoll. Within hours, a whitish ash—fallout from the blast—began speckling the *Lucky Dragon*, a Japanese fishing boat that had been some ninety miles from the site of the blast. The boat's crew arrived home suffering from radiation sickness, and by mid-March the world knew of their unlucky fate.

When the *Lucky Dragon* incident occurred, the issue of radioactive fallout was already simmering in the United States. In 1951, the Truman administration had begun testing atomic weapons in Nevada, using a tract of land larger than the state of Rhode Island that was uninhabited and owned by the government. The Atomic Energy Commission repeatedly assured the public that it had nothing to fear from the radiation released by the tests, and the military sent thousands of troops into the area of the explosions to see how they would fare physically and psychologically. But complaints that the radiation released by the tests posed hazards to health came from people downwind from the tests in Nevada and Utah and from the residents of Troy, New York, where one evening in 1953 it rained nuclear debris from an atmospheric test in

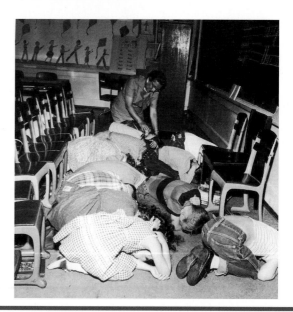
Schoolchildren practice "duck and cover" in a bomb drill, 1957.

Nevada held just a couple of days earlier. The ill fate of the *Lucky Dragon* transformed their outcries into a national concern and stimulated an increasingly vociferous demand for a ban against the testing of nuclear weapons.

Pro-test-ban scientists emphasized that thermonuclear fallout spread radioactive particles around the planet. Biologists reported that radioactive substances were being detected in the soil and in foods (notably milk), putting people, especially children, at higher risk for birth defects, leukemia, and monstrous mutations. Other scientists held that a test ban would halt further development of atomic weapons and might even encourage agreements to reduce nuclear arms. American sensitivity to the threat of radioactive fallout was no doubt heightened by a vogue of fear-provoking films that presented science-fictionalized consequences of atomic-induced genetic mutations, including giant ants (*Them!*) and a reptilian monster from the sea (*Godzilla*, an import from Japan). Schools taught children nuclear fear by teaching them to "duck and cover"—that is, to crawl under their desks and cover their heads in the event of a nuclear attack. By 1957, polls revealed that Americans had come to support a test ban by almost two to one.

In 1958, Eisenhower initiated test-ban talks with the Soviets at Geneva. Anti-test-ban scientists worked against them, insisting that testing was indispensable for national security, especially for the development of compact warheads suitable for intercontinental missiles. They predicted that the Soviets would find a way to cheat, by testing weapons in huge underground caverns that would muffle the seismic shock waves and make them undetectable by instruments located in the West. Analysts concluded that not all underground tests might in fact be detectable, but that a limited test ban—one that prohibited tests in the atmosphere while allowing underground testing—might be workable. Underground testing would permit further development of nuclear weapons while the abolition of atmospheric tests would get rid of radioactive fallout, thus defusing public fears of damage to health. By the end of the Eisenhower administration, the goal of a limited nuclear test ban was high on the national agenda.

SUPERPOWER SHIFT

In 1956, when Khrushchev affirmed the posture of peaceful coexistence at the Twentieth Party Congress, he also attacked Stalin as a tyrant and called for de-Stalinization of the Soviet Union and Eastern Europe. In the long perspective, Khrushchev's declarations opened a new era in Soviet history, but at the time his deeds contradicted his words. Later that year, taking him at face value, rioters in Poland successfully demanded the appointment of an anti-Stalinist as head of state, and insurgents in Hungary mounted an outright rebellion against Soviet rule. Although the Hungarians called for American assistance, the administration refrained from providing any while Khrushchev crushed the Hungarian rebellion (in November) with tanks and troops. Policymakers recognized that intervention against Soviet power would risk a war that might escalate into a nuclear exchange. Despite wishing the contrary, modern Republicans, like their Democratic counterparts, were compelled to face the reality that the United States could not roll back the Soviets in Eastern Europe.

Partly for that reason, by the mid-1950s, the focus of American attention in foreign affairs was beginning to shift away from Europe to what people then called the "developing world," now identified as the Third World (denoting the fact that it was at a stage of development below that of the capitalist First World and the Communist Second World). That world was emerging in the wake of nationalist revolts against colonial power and conservative monarchies in Africa, the Middle East, Latin America, and Southeast Asia. (The trend prompted the former king of Egypt, a playboy who had been ejected from power by nationalist army officers, to predict that soon only five kings would be left—"Hearts, Clubs, Diamonds, Spades, and England.") Americans expected that the nations liberated from monarchy or empire would want to follow the model of their own democratic and capitalist development. But many of these governments were weak or oppressive, vulnerable to internal challenge that could threaten Western economic and political interests. They could veer toward socialism or capitalism, submit to authoritarianism or choose democracy, ally more closely with the Soviet bloc than with the West. And since almost all comprised nonwhite peoples, the racism still prevalent in the United States might discourage their friendliness to democratic capitalism. The Soviet Union was alive to these possibilities, and in the mid-1950s initiatives to gain the loyalties of Third World countries became part of Cold War competition.

Securing the Third World. To protect its interests in these volatile regions, the United States gave economic aid to facili-

Hungarians burn the Soviet flag during their rebellion for freedom, 1956.

tate development along free-market lines and to create opportunities for American business. Several programs provided military aid to help local regimes in combating Communist threats from within as well as from without. The United States also relied on covert action mounted by the Central Intelligence Agency, often against nationalist regimes that were considered pro-Communist simply because they tried to break the power of landed oligarchies and industrial elites. By 1957, the CIA had multiplied fivefold in the ten years since its founding, stationing 15,000 people throughout the world, and it devoted more than 80 percent of its budget to covert activities. It secretly subsidized pro-American groups and newspapers, dispensed bribes to officeholders, undermined governments, and, when the administration deemed it necessary, overthrew them by force.

In the Philippines in 1953, the CIA helped a pro-American anti-Communist defeat a movement of Communist-leaning guerrillas and gain the presidency. In Iran that year, it supplied Muhammad Reza Shah Pahlevi with planning and arms for the successful coup his forces staged against the country's constitutional government, which had threatened the flow of oil to the West by nationalizing British petroleum interests. The shah promptly gave the United States and Britain favorable oil concessions and provided the West a loyal ally at the southern edge of the Soviet Union. In 1954, the CIA set its sights on the elected government in Guatemala of Colonel Jacobo Arbenz Guzmán. A reformer with some Communist backing, Arbenz had taken more than 200,000 acres belonging to the American-owned United Fruit Company without paying as much for them as the company claimed they were worth. The CIA drove him from power by arming and training a force of exiles and by providing air support for the invasion.

According to one American ambassador in Latin America, Dulles told diplomats to "do nothing to offend the dictators; they are the only people we can depend on." Eisenhower officials may have felt they had no choice but to support dictators as bulwarks against Communism, but the administration's posture fomented increasing anti-Yankee sentiment throughout the region.

The Suez Crisis and the Middle East. In 1954, power in Egypt was assumed by Gamal Abdel Nasser, an Arab nationalist eager to promote the industrialization of his country, partly by constructing the Aswan High Dam on the Upper Nile. Dulles, hoping to enlist Egypt as a counter to Russia in the Middle East, agreed that the United States would lend Egypt $56 million for the project; but he canceled the loan in mid-1956 after Nasser bought arms from Czechoslovakia while declaring neutrality in the Cold War. Nasser promptly nationalized the Suez Canal, which was owned by foreigners, claiming that its revenues would finance the dam. At the end of October, in a joint action, Israeli, British, and French forces attacked Egyptian military installations with the aim of taking back the canal.

Eisenhower was furious with his allies. None had consulted the United States before the invasion, and now Moscow was threatening to intervene, raising the grim prospect of war between the world's nuclear powers. While condemning the invasion, the president put the Strategic Air Command on alert. Eisenhower told an aide, "If those fellows start something, we may have to hit 'em—and if necessary, with *everything* in the bucket." At the joint request of

Egyptian crowds, shouting "Nasser forever," greet U.N. forces as they march through the streets of Port Said during the Suez Crisis, November 1956.

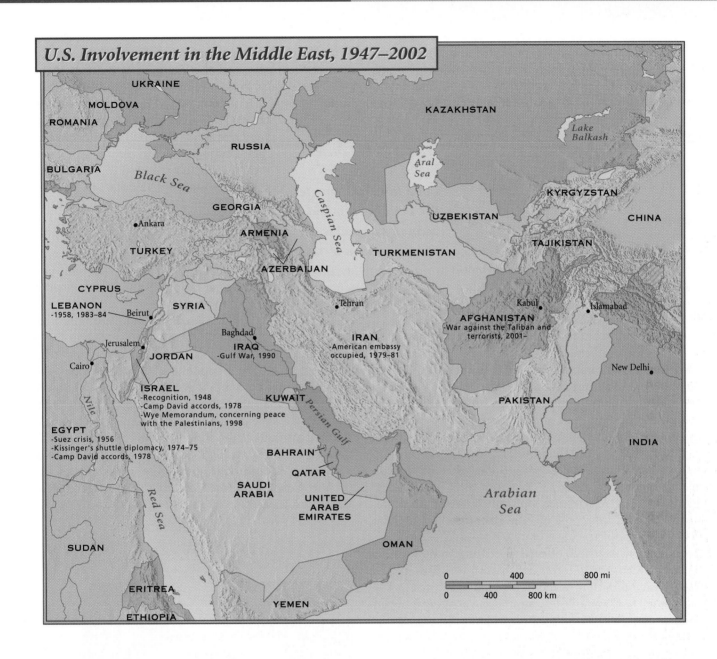

U.S. Involvement in the Middle East, 1947–2002

the United States and the Soviet Union, the United Nations urged the three invading nations to withdraw. In early November, they pledged to depart and were gone within four months. Egypt regained control of the Suez Canal and eventually built the Aswan Dam.

Eisenhower won high praise at home and abroad for his temperate handling of the Suez crisis, but the episode provoked anti-Western sentiment among the Arab nations, adding to the resentments they held against the United States for its tendency to support Israel. The crisis also greatly weakened the influence of Britain and France in the Middle East, thus leaving the United States as the principal bulwark against Russia and the guarantor of Western oil interests in the region. Eisenhower obtained approval from Congress for what became known as the Eisenhower Doctrine—a commitment to send military aid and, if required, troops to any nation in the Middle East that felt itself threatened by "international Communism."

In July 1958, Eisenhower was prompted to act on this doctrine after nationalists in Iraq overthrew the monarchy and installed an anti-Western regime, the first of many. The pro-Western government in Lebanon, fearing an overthrow there, requested American aid. Eisenhower, eager to show that the United States was ready to defend against further coups, dispatched 14,000 marines. The troops stayed in Lebanon only three months, withdrawing when it became evident that the government was not in jeopardy.

Worries over Indochina. In 1954, the Eisenhower administration faced a crisis in Indochina. After World War II, the French had sought to reestablish the authority in the region they had gained as imperialists in the late nineteenth century but had lost to the Japanese at the beginning of the war. In Vietnam, their neocolonial effort was contested by the Vietminh, a broad-based coalition led by Ho Chi Minh, a Communist nationalist. After Mao Zedong's victory in China and the outbreak of the Korean War, the Truman administration had grown fearful of a potential Communist domination of Vietnam, which was part of Southeast Asia, with its abundant rice, natural rubber, tin, and oil. The United States began providing the French with military assistance, paying 75 percent of their war costs by 1954. But that year the French found themselves trapped and facing a major defeat in the valley at Dien Bien Phu, deep in rebel territory.

A number of American officials urged Eisenhower to assist the French with ground forces and massive air strikes, possibly with tactical nuclear weapons. Eisenhower worried that if Vietnam fell to Communists, countries surrounding it might become vulnerable. He put the issue in terms that came to be called the "domino theory": "You have a row of dominoes set up. You knock over the first one, and what will happen to the last one is a certainty that it will go over quickly." However, key army and congressional leaders opposed intervention, and Eisenhower himself was reluctant to help the French with conventional air strikes, let alone nuclear ones. "You boys must be crazy," he said angrily when shown a plan for nuclear weapons in Vietnam. "We can't use those awful things against Asians for the second time in less than ten years. My God!" In May 1954, the French garrison at Dien Bien Phu capitulated.

> *"Eisenhower worried that if Vietnam fell to Communists, countries surrounding it might become vulnerable. He put the issue in terms that came to be called the 'domino theory.'"*

At the Geneva peace conference that year, the anti-Communist Vietnamese and the Vietminh agreed that Vietnam would be divided temporarily at the 17th parallel, with each sector under a separate government. The country was to be reunified in 1956 under a single government that would be freely elected. The Eisenhower administration disapproved of the Geneva settlement, fearing that the elections would produce a Vietnam unified under Ho Chi Minh, now the leader of North Vietnam. It chose to counter Ho with Ngo Dinh Diem, the new premier of South Vietnam, a staunch anti-Communist, passionate nationalist, and devout Catholic, who had strong ties in the United States with the Catholic hierarchy and the Dulles brothers.

With the Eisenhower administration's backing, Diem blocked South Vietnam's participation in the 1956 elections, deposed its French puppet emperor, and became president of the new Republic of South Vietnam. Diem sought to revive the South Vietnam economy, but he blocked land reform and suppressed political opponents. He increasingly alienated the predominantly Buddhist population, who resented his Catholicism as well as the corruption and arbitrariness of his regime. By 1958, with the assistance of North Vietnam, a National Liberation Front commonly known as the Viet Cong had formed and had begun waging guerrilla war against Diem.

Ho Chi Minh, president of the Democratic Republic of Vietnam, also known as North Vietnam, January 1955.

Security in Southeast Asia. In 1954, the French defeat at Dien Bien Phu prompted Secretary of State Dulles to create the Southeast Asia Treaty Organization (SEATO) for the purposes of mutual defense. Unlike NATO, SEATO had no standing armed forces, but it seemed to some critics to involve the United States in too open-ended a commitment to resist Communist subversion in Southeast Asia. China continued to preoccupy policymakers, partly because of the Republican right wing's absorption with Asia, partly because the Eisenhower administration assumed, wrongly, that Mao Zedong's Communists must be responsible for the turmoil in Indochina. In January 1955, at Eisenhower's urging, Congress passed the Formosa Resolution, which gave the president blanket authority to use military force to protect Formosa (Taiwan) and the nearby Pescadores Islands, which Mao's forces had been shelling. Mao's saber-rattling coupled with the French defeat in Vietnam encouraged the United States to see the Communist world even more as an expansionist monolith and to extend still further its global commitments in defense of anti-Communist regimes.

"In effect, the United States embarked on a course of what has been called 'military Keynesianism'—in this case, stimulation of the economy by military spending."

The Cold War, Technology, and the Economy

The New Look defense policy, although intended to save costs, marked a significant enlargement of the role of national security in peacetime American life. Between the end of the Korean War and 1960, defense expenditures ranged between $40 billion and $47 billion annually, accounting for about half the federal budget, compared with a third in 1949. Defense agencies were huge consumers of goods and services (in 1953, the Atomic Energy Commission alone used 12 percent of all the electrical power generated in the United States). In effect, the United States embarked on a course of what has been called "military Keynesianism," after the general theories of the British economist John Maynard Keynes—in this case, stimulation of the economy by military spending—that joined with federal investments in housing and education to fuel innovation, employment, and overall economic growth.

High defense spending enjoyed powerful support from senators representing states in the South and the far West. Both regions had long displayed a strong commitment to national defense, but their historic devotion was now reinforced by the defense contracts flowing to states such as Washington, California, Georgia, and Texas. During the 1950s, the South's share of defense contracts more than doubled, rising to 15 percent of the total; California's also doubled, reaching a whopping 24 percent of the total by the beginning of the 1960s. The money sustained numerous defense-oriented enterprises that had been revived initially by the Korean War, including shipyards and aircraft factories. Most military recruits continued to be trained in the South, with each one generating an estimated three jobs in communities surrounding military bases. Later studies concluded that during the 1950s defense spending was responsible for 10 percent of growth in the middle South and 21 percent in the Pacific region.

Apart from direct military spending, the rationale of national security helped justify federal expenditures that might otherwise have been more difficult to obtain. The most dramatic consequence of this tendency was the Interstate Highway Act of 1956, which provided $32 billion for 41,000 miles of high-speed roads throughout the country. While of potentially enormous benefit to the automobile, trucking, concrete, petroleum, and construction industries, among others, the act was justified on the grounds that it would facilitate the transportation of military supplies and personnel in a national emergency. The measure further encouraged the American devotion to the automobile, enabling people even more than in the past to pile into cars and speed over long distances. It stimulated booms in motels, fast-food restaurants, and shopping centers. By 1960, Holiday Inn and McDonald's, both born in the fifties, had turned into nationwide chains. The interstate highway system also stimulated growth by linking the rapidly developing regions such as the South and the West more efficiently to the rest of the national economy.

DEFENSE AND TECHNICAL COMPETITIVENESS

Policymakers and congressmen were determined that the United States remain ahead of the Soviet Union in all branches of science. **Cold War** competitiveness deepened the belief, born in World War II, that scientific research and training merited sustained federal action. For example, eager to maintain the United States' lead over the Soviets in physics, between 1954 and 1960 Congress quadrupled the high-energy accelerator budget, raising it to $33.2 million. Both the AEC and partisans of atomic energy in Congress also spoke of an "atomic power race" with the Soviets, considering it imperative that the United States beat the Soviet Union in bringing nuclear power to the Third World. In 1954, the Republican Congress revised the Atomic Energy Act to permit private ownership of nuclear reactors and the leasing of nuclear materials to industry. The chairman of the AEC told the public that nuclear power would bring "energy too cheap to meter." Under AEC sponsorship, industrial contractors built an AEC-owned reactor at Shippingport, Pennsylvania—the first civilian nuclear power facility in the United States. In 1957, making the environment for private nuclear power still more favorable, Congress limited liability for nuclear accidents and provided the insurance at public expense.

CIVILIAN SPINOFFS

Defense agencies and defense-related ones like the AEC continued to provide between 80 and 90 percent of federal monies for research and development in physics, electronics, aeronautics, computers, and other branches of the physical sciences and engineering. They made the development of high technology increasingly a ward of the military, with defense projects supplying an ever-larger fraction—the portion crossed the 50 percent mark in 1956—of total expenditures for industrial research. By 1960, federal dollars paid for 70 percent of the R&D carried out in the electronics business, which now ranked fifth among American industries.

During the 1950s, almost all the growth in electronics came from sales to the military services rather than from consumer products; nevertheless, the huge investments in military R&D spun off benefits to the civilian economy, including trained scientists and engineers, electronics technicians, and new knowledge as well as new technologies. All the while, industry enlarged its own spending on R&D. The steel and automobile industries invested heavily in labor-saving technology, so that, for example, between 1945 and 1960 the number of hours required to produce a car dropped by half. During the 1950s, the research-intensive plastics and chemical industries burgeoned, as did the high-technology aircraft industry. In 1958, Pan American World Airways started flying passengers to Europe with jet-powered Boeing 707 planes, which derived

from the air force's B-47, and the next year marked the debut of Air Force One, the first presidential jet.

In 1948, a trio of scientists at the Bell Telephone Laboratories had devised the transistor, a technology that would revolutionize electronics (and earn the inventors a Nobel Prize). Picking up on radar-related work during World War II, they discovered that an arrangement of small wires and a semiconducting material such as germanium could be made to control the flow of energy in electrical circuits. It would thus do the work of vacuum tubes, which were essential to every electronic device from radios to radar, but it was much smaller, consumed much less power, and promised to be more reliable. Although the invention of the transistor was accomplished with the Bell Laboratories' own funds, during the Korean War the military stepped in to speed up its development. By the end of the war, defense contracts had come to support fully half the work, and the military bought almost all the transistors first produced. However, transistors then began entering the commercial market, finding uses in hearing aids, portable radios, and, before long, computers.

The Regency, a portable transistor radio, 1955. Only five inches high, it was among the first products of the consumer electronics revolution.

COMPUTERS

The Korean War had prompted a speedup in the development of high-speed digital computers like Eckert and Mauchly's ENIAC by both IBM and the Atomic Energy Commission, which needed such computers to perform complicated calculations related to nuclear and thermonuclear weapons. IBM soon brought out a reliable workhorse that defense contractors could use for scientific computing. Other firms further developed computers, responding to demand for them in the government as well as in defense-related areas of the commercial market. In 1951, the Remington Rand Corporation delivered a machine to the Census Bureau called UNIVAC (an acronym for universal automatic computer), which fed its processors information via magnetic tape instead of punch cards. Early on election night in 1952, setting a precedent for election evenings, a UNIVAC computer at CBS forecast the Eisenhower landslide.

The air force, however, felt the need for a high-speed computer that would respond to inputs of information as they were being generated—that would operate, as computer experts liked to say, in "real time." As a result of the Soviet acquisition of the atomic bomb, the air force wanted to construct a national air warning and defense system across North America, with real-time computers that would detect a Soviet airborne nuclear attack against the United States over the North Pole. An effort to develop such a computer—it was called "Whirlwind"—was under way at MIT, and the air force stepped in with handsome support for it.

The project's prime mover was Jay Forrester, an electrical engineer in his early thirties who had gotten caught up with computers during the Korean War while helping to design feedback mechanisms for fire control. Whirlwind needed a memory that was far more capacious and readily accessible than any yet devised. Forrester conceived the idea of forging the necessary memory from small magnetizable cores, each capable of rapidly storing and returning coded information. By 1953, the Whirlwind computer was operating successfully with a magnetic core memory, which eventually became an industry standard.

During the 1950s, defense contractors devised additional computer technologies for the early airborne warning system, including printed circuits (the forerunner of the microchip)

An IBM office computer, c. 1955.

"IBM flourished partly because of its farsightedness and know-how, but as the head of the firm later remarked, 'It was the Cold War that helped IBM make itself the king of the computer business.'"

and sophisticated software—notably Fortran and Cobol, used for business analyses. Several companies exploited these technologies for the business market, but none so effectively as IBM, which in 1953 brought out its first business-oriented mainframe computer. This computer used a magnetic drum memory instead of the superior magnetic core version—an IBM executive called it computing's Model T—but to the astonishment of the company's executives, sales of the model skyrocketed. IBM also appropriated the Whirlwind technology to produce the first commercial machine with magnetic core memory in 1955, a behemoth weighing 250 tons, firing 49,000 vacuum tubes, and, like all powerful computers of the day, occupying a large room. By 1960, some 5,000 computers had been delivered in the United States and another 2,000 elsewhere in the world, with IBM's products capturing an increasing share of the market. The company flourished partly because of its farsightedness and know-how, but as the head of the firm later remarked, "It was the Cold War that helped IBM make itself the king of the computer business."

AGRICULTURE

The long-running flight from the farm continued, aided and abetted by science and technology. In 1960, only some 8 percent of the employed workforce earned their living directly in agriculture, down sharply from about 12 percent in 1950 (and still more sharply from 20 percent in 1940). Yet that diminishing fraction produced enough to feed the United States and export a surplus to the rest of the world; such a rise in productivity came from chemical fertilizers and insecticides (notably DDT), together with increasing mechanization. The larger, more richly capitalized farms were better able than small ones to exploit the tools of science and technology, with the result that the decline in agricultural population was accompanied by the consolidation of smaller, family-type farms into larger ones. The trend toward agribusiness was further accelerated by federal policies that tied farm-subsidy payments proportionally to farm size and output and thus gave the advantage to more efficient, large-scale farms.

Dramatic shifts were taking place in southern agriculture. Machines for harvesting cotton, peanuts, and tobacco had started becoming available in the late 1940s. In an hour, a human being could pick up to 20 pounds of cotton; a mechanical picker from International Harvester could pick 1,000 pounds. Federal policies that sought to protect low-wage farm workers had the effect of encouraging large producers to replace their workers with machines. So did the increasing demands of blacks, including sharecroppers, for decent jobs, housing, education, and voting rights. The more whites perceived blacks as a troublesome presence, the more they welcomed mechanization as a means to drive them off the land and out of the region.

In 1950, only 5 percent of the southern cotton crop was harvested by machine; in 1960, 50 percent (and by the end of the 1960s, more than 90 percent). Such mechanization drastically reduced the population of tenants and farm labor and, indeed, helped spur the black migration out of the South. During World War II, nonfarm had exceeded farm employment for the first time in southern history. Now the defense dollars and the mechanization of agriculture joined with probusiness boosterism to accelerate the South's shift to a more industrial economy.

The mechanization of cotton farming also led to crop diversification. Small farmers had to cope with both competition from mechanized farms and reductions in federal cotton allotments (the number of acres a planter could use to raise cotton and still qualify for federal agricultural subsidies). They thus turned to raising soybeans, grains, peanuts, and livestock. Further diversification was stimulated by a rising national demand for frozen orange juice concentrate, a recent invention, and for poultry. After World War II, chickens, historically a small side business, turned into the most rapidly expanding element of southern agriculture. An Arkansas farmer marveled, "Who'd a thought that a dadburned chicken could scratch cotton off the land."

"THE GOLDEN AGE IS NOW"

Corporal William Jensen, wounded in Korea, came home to Hastings, Nebraska, saw the stores on Second Street, and remarked with amazement, "Man, I never saw anything like it. This town is just one big boom." During the war, employment had exceeded 52 million jobs, the highest ever in the nation's history. Social Security coverage had been enlarged to include some 10 million more Americans, most of them domestic help, farm workers, and small businessmen. The stock market, long identified with the rich, was attracting middle-class investors.

After the war, the boom roared on, fueled in part by the military Keynesianism of high defense

A mechanical cotton picker enabled one man to do what had been the work of many.

spending and the economic spinoffs of basic and applied research—but also by federal socioeconomic programs, easy credit, and population growth. By 1960, monthly Social Security checks were being sent to 5.7 million families, almost five times more than the number receiving them in 1950. Federally subsidized loans permitted millions to buy homes, while private credit plans allowed them to buy goods such as cars, washing machines, and television sets. In 1960, some 33 million Americans owned homes, compared with about 23 million in 1950, and at least one television set was to be found in about 90 percent of American households, more than had running water or indoor plumbing. Buy-now, pay-later consumer habits were further stimulated by the arrival of the credit card, which Diner's Club introduced in 1950, and by commercial advertising, whose revenues more than doubled during the decade.

Between 1950 and 1960, the gross national product adjusted for inflation shot up some 37 percent, while median family income rose 30 percent. Measured by their incomes, three out of five Americans came to enjoy middle-class standing, twice the fraction in the twenties. In the dozen years before 1960, average income in constant dollars for American workers increased as much as in the previous fifty years. In 1960, at least three-quarters of American families owned an automobile, while almost one in six owned two.

Expressing the exuberant material prosperity of the era, advertising put a premium on cars that were big and flashy, heavy with chrome and tail fins. The inflation rate was low enough to keep the cost of a first-class letter at three cents until 1958, and between 1955 and 1957 the unemployment rate hovered at just above 4 percent.

Americans took advantage of their prosperity in myriad ways. They had more children, continuing the baby boom and increasing the national population some 19 percent, to 181 million, the highest growth rate since the early century. The mushrooming number of young Americans stimulated the children's clothing and toy industries as well as home and school construction (10 million more children went to school in the fifties than in the forties). Public school expenditures per pupil steadily mounted, as did the percentage of teenagers graduating from high school. Americans devoted one-seventh of the gross national prod-

A baby boomer aboard a mechanical spaceship battles aliens at a toy makers' convention, 1953.

"In 1960, some 33 million Americans owned homes, compared with about 23 million in 1950, and at least one television set was to be found in about 90 percent of American households, more than had running water or indoor plumbing."

uct to entertainment. They bought boxloads of paperback books, and they attended college and professional basketball, baseball, and football games by the millions, creating a market for the new *Sports Illustrated*, which announced that "the golden age is now."

Health. The rising economic expectations were accompanied by expanding hopes for the improvement of health. The powerful antibiotic penicillin, developed during World War II, had opened a triumphal era in the battle against disease. In 1944, the American biologist Selman Waksman discovered streptomycin, an effective agent against tuberculosis as well as other diseases of microbial origin. It became widely available in the postwar years and earned Waksman a Nobel Prize. These two discoveries inspired American pharmaceutical manufacturers to increase their annual spending on research for new drugs more than sevenfold between 1949 and 1963, to $257 million. More than 300 prescription drugs were available in 1961 that had not been twenty years earlier, including antibiotics, antihistamines, cortisone, tranquilizers, and chemi-

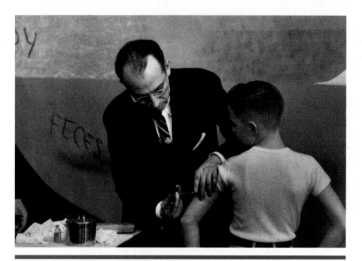

Dr. Jonas Salk administers his polio vaccine, 1955.

cal therapies against cancer. Surgeons devised means to operate on the living human heart, replacing defective valves and installing pacemakers to regulate the beat. By 1960, the average life span had risen from 63 in 1940 to almost 70.

The arsenal of vaccines expanded to protect against whooping cough and diphtheria, but the most thrilling triumph was scored against polio. Parents dreaded the disease, since it tended to attack young children, especially in the warm weather of summer, killing some, paralyzing many others. It was known from costly studies with monkeys that poliomyelitis was caused by an animal virus that attacked the cells of the nervous system. To prepare a vaccine against it, a way had to be found to cultivate the virus cheaply in large quantities. In Boston in 1949, a trio of scientists succeeded in growing poliovirus in laboratory cultures of human tissue. The feat, which earned them a Nobel Prize, transformed poliovirus production, emancipating it from the expensive use of live monkeys and pointing the way to large-scale production of the coveted vaccine. Jonas Salk, at the University of Pittsburgh Medical School, used the new methods to develop a vaccine of dead poliovirus. Church bells rang out across the country when on April 12, 1955, the tenth anniversary of the death of Franklin Roosevelt, Salk announced that a nationwide test program of inoculations had proved effective. Polio vaccinations quickly became a standard feature of preventive medicine, and by 1962 only 910 cases of the disease occurred in the United States, compared with 58,000 in 1952.

Labor. The miracles of medicine were increasingly available to unionized labor, which continued to obtain medical benefits, cost-of-living adjustments, decent working conditions, and pensions. In 1953, the United Auto Workers and the Ford Motor Company pioneered a contract that called for a guaranteed annual wage and payment to laid-off workers of two-thirds of their regular earnings. Save for a major battle in the steel industry in 1959, the number of strikes and lost worker-hours dropped significantly over the decade. Unions displayed little militancy, preferring the middle-of-the-road politics of the day. In 1955, the AFL and the CIO merged under the leadership of George Meany, an anti-Communist conservative who was disinclined to try to organize unskilled and semi-skilled workers and gave up attempting to organize labor in the South.

Unions remained influential actors in American life and politics, but their power was diminishing. Distrust of them was generated by the revelation of corruption in the Teamsters Union under Dave Beck and Jimmy Hoffa. Many Americans gained their impression of unions from *On the Waterfront*, the Academy Award–winning film of 1954 (starring Marlon Brando and Eva Marie Saint) that exposed how mobsters and goons might dominate a longshoreman's union and how ordinary members had to battle to recapture the organization.

Teamsters president Jimmy Hoffa and supporters, 1958.

Congressional hearings on union corruption led to passage of the Landrum-Griffin Act in 1959, which allowed the federal government to oversee union affairs. The spread of automation in the coal, auto, and steel industries also cost unions some members. Moreover, a mounting fraction of the workforce—roughly half by the mid-1950s—were public employees, who were prohibited from striking, and white-collar workers (for example, people in sales, banking, advertising, management, research, and clerical occupations), who traditionally resisted joining unions. In 1953, labor unions represented 36 percent of the workforce; in 1960, 31 percent.

Women and Work. Women were pressured from an array of cultural sources not to undertake careers in the paid workforce. Books, magazines, newspapers, and popular psychiatry all celebrated home, babies, and kitchen. Dr. Benjamin Spock's *Common Sense Book of Baby and Child Care* (1946), far and away the dominant book in the field, emphasized that infants and children needed the devotion of full-time mothers, at least until they were three. Films replaced the forceful, self-reliant, professionally capable women of the 1940s with saccharine and submissive types. In *The Tender Trap*, Debbie Reynolds's character tells Frank Sinatra's that she is willing to forgo her chances at an acting career: "A career is just fine, but it's no substitute for marriage. . . . A woman isn't a woman until she's been married and had children." Television might show women as shrewd within their conventional roles—like Alice Kramden, Ralph's wife on Jackie Gleason's *The Honeymooners*, or Lucille Ball in *I Love Lucy*, effective for all her wackiness in seeking her ends; but popular programs such as *Father Knows Best, Ozzie and Harriet,* and *Leave It to Beaver* projected the stereotypical suburban wife: she cheerfully cleaned the house, chauffered the children, volunteered for school or church groups, deferred to her husband's judgment even if he was wrong, and worked for success in his job.

More women went to college, but in 1960 still far fewer than men. Seniors were said to be anxious if they were not yet engaged. Compared with men, relatively few women entered graduate or professional school, many of which had quotas for women or would not admit them at all. In 1950, almost 60 percent of women between eighteen and twenty-four were married, compared with 42 percent in 1940. The preference for the stay-at-home woman was reinforced at the top of the government. Eisenhower placed twenty-eight women in high government posts, including one to his cabinet and one as ambassador to Italy, but the appointments signified a contin-

Jackie Gleason and Audrey Meadows as the bus driver Ralph and his shrewd wife, Alice, in a scene from *The Honeymooners.*

uing tokenism rather than a turn in policy or outlook. Asked at a press conference about a revival of the Equal Rights Amendment, Eisenhower laughed, saying, to the chagrin of women activists, that it was the first time in a year or so that it had been brought to his attention and that he hadn't been very active on its behalf.

Yet while many women professed to find the life of the stereotypical 1950s housewife fulfilling, others admitted to discontent. College-educated women often felt straitjacketed by the obligations of domesticity. One alumna noted her "shock" at "the plunge from the strictly intellectual college life to the 24-hour-a-day domestic one." Amid the conservative social standards of the day, women did not tend to take such discontent as warrant for divorce. Indeed, in the 1950s divorce rates fell to a stable 10 per 1,000 married women from their peak—18 per 1,000—of the immediate postwar years. But out of either dissatisfaction with homebound life or family need, or both, many women defied prevailing standards and went to work.

While women in the workforce had traditionally come from lower-income families, by 1960 a quarter of those whose husbands earned solidly middle-class incomes were employed outside the home, more than a threefold increase since 1950. Women with college degrees were 50 percent more likely to have jobs than those without them. Women from higher-income families worked to pay for children's education, the second car, or part of the bigger mortgage, or otherwise raise the family's standard of living.

"By 1960, two out of every five women over sixteen had jobs, double the fraction in 1940."

Whatever their family's social level, working women were concentrated in white-collar and clerical positions. They were paid less and promoted less frequently than their white male counterparts, although some—for example, those in the United Auto Workers and United Electrical Workers—managed to win better deals for themselves. Although the combination of home duties and outside work often proved stressful, it was turning into a virtually inexorable trend. By 1960, two out of every five women over sixteen had jobs, double the fraction in 1940. Still more striking, the proportion of married women in the workforce had also doubled, reaching 30 percent by 1960; and almost 40 percent of these women had children of school age. The trend, while contrbuting to the American family's prosperity, also sensitized an increasing number of women to the discriminations and difficulties their working sisters had long endured, including inequalities in opportunity and pay and the tensions associated with combining job and family. That sensitivity helped lay the foundation for the revival of the women's movement that would come in the 1960s.

Migrations and the Melting Pot

Opportunities were abundant, and people moved to grab them. Roughly one out of five Americans changed domiciles each year. A number migrated across regions, many of them turning south and west to the Sunbelt, the warm states that reached from the old Confederacy to southern California. They were drawn by its abundant land, warm climate, and economies stimulated by federal contracts and by the favorable business climate of tax incentives, cheap labor, and weakness or absence of unions. As one industrial promoter in the South explained, "Hell, what we've been selling is peace and order, tellin' 'em that what we've got down here is stability—friendly politicians who are not going to gut a business with taxes, and workers who are grateful for a job and are not going to be stirring up trouble." The vast uprooting added to the popularity of country music, with its nostalgic radio programs and sad songs like those of Hank Williams, whose "Ramblin' Man" and "Lonesome Whistle" told of restless wandering and lost relationships.

The most powerful magnet for migration was California, which in 1958 attracted the Brooklyn Dodgers to Los Angeles and the New York Giants to San Francisco. The California economy grew in giant leaps, energized by the construction of waterways and roads, homes and schools, a multicampus university and college system, and the dollars generated by agricultural enterprise (the state's largest income producer) and by such modern industries as aerospace, electronics, film, and television. During the 1950s, California's population exploded by almost 49 percent, reaching almost

Los Angeles welcomes the Dodgers, 1958. The team's move to the West was a blow to Brooklyn and a boon to the surging California metropolis.

16 million; and by the early 1960s, it would rank as the most populous state.

THE FLIGHT FROM DOWNTOWN

Within or across regions, people moved from farms to cities and, in pursuit of the long-standing American dream, from cities to suburbs. The suburbs away from downtown were a powerful lure, with their greenery, good public schools, and chance to own a much nicer home. Cheap suburban housing was pioneered by the brothers William and Alfred Levitt, who erected family bungalows with lawns and yards and modern appliances at the rate of one every fifteen minutes, setting them down in planned Levittowns, the first of which opened on Long Island, New York, in October 1947. New suburban houses accounted for eleven out of every thirteen homes built during the fifties.

The Federal Housing Administration helped the suburban expansion along, guaranteeing mortgages that required only a 5 percent down payment, and so did the Veterans Administration, which provided mortgages to veterans on even more favorable terms under the G.I. loan program. Federal policy further encouraged the purchase of homes by allowing property taxes and home-mortgage interest to be deducted from taxable income. The same advantages applied to urban homes, but federal mortgage agencies tended to refuse loans on dwellings in lower-income city neighborhoods as too risky. Suburban living was made easier by the federal, state, and local tax dollars that laid down freeways between suburban towns and urban workplaces. In the 1950s, more than 18 million people moved to the suburbs, generating a growth rate in those areas six times greater than that in cities, and in 1960 suburbs were home to 72 million people, almost one-quarter of the American population.

The trend cost cities dearly. Their business tax bases such as downtown retail stores began to decline as more people spent their earnings in suburban shopping centers. The automobile drove out city public transit, whose share of passenger miles, 35 percent in 1945, would plummet to 5 percent by 1965. In 1949, the federal government began providing funds to cities for urban renewal. Neighborhoods designated as "slums" were razed to make way for office buildings and expressways so that suburbanites could more easily commute to and from the cities by car. The techno-cultural critic Lewis Mumford complained that cities were turning into a "tangled mass of highways, interchanges, and parking lots." Down-

The Seagram Building, a modernist tower of glass, soaring above midtown Manhattan in 1958.

towns turned increasingly into impersonal centers of business dominated by sleek, unornamented skyscrapers, modernist towers of flat glass facades exposing interior structural steel. They were inspired by the architect Mies van der Rohe, whose principal triumph, the Seagram Building (1958), soared above Park Avenue in New York, but many of them amounted to drab glass boxes, giving city centers an aura of facelessness, aloof from ordinary human concerns.

SUBURBIA AND ASSIMILATION

During the 1950s, immigration subsided as an issue. The number of immigrants was small, averaging 250,000 a year. The percentage of foreign-born in the population, now one out of twenty, was at a low for the century, and so was the proportion of Americans born to at least one immigrant parent. To be sure, in both the suburbs and the cities ethnic loyalties remained powerful. Intermarriage between white minority group members—for example, between Poles and

Irish, or Jews and non-Jews—occurred infrequently. However, the contacts—in schools, sports, PTAs, and community groups—of different European minority groups in the suburbs was beginning to break down ethnic differences, especially among the young. Similarly, the mass media provided experiences in common—televised baseball, for example—that spanned social divides.

Frictions between ethnic minority groups and the white, Anglo-Saxon, Protestant majority were also declining. The Cold War encouraged people to think of themselves as united in their Americanism and reinforced the eagerness of numerous immigrant descendants to assimilate to the American mainstream. Films both reflected and advanced the trend, showing Catholic priests, once identified as secretive and conspiratorial, as benign figures, towers of strength to their flocks. The Catholic community's passionate anti-Communism, including the support of many Catholics for McCarthy, also commended its members to the Protestant majority. By now, few people thought of groups such as Irish Americans or Italian Americans as racially different. Genetics, anthropology, and psychology had destroyed the scientific underpinnings of that social belief. Ethnic minority group members perceived of themselves as "white," and most other Americans saw them that way, too.

ASIAN AMERICANS

Asian Americans, however, remained a group largely apart. The McCarran-Walter Act of 1952 had removed the long-standing considerations of "race" in eligibility for naturalization, thus permitting Asian immigrants to become citizens. A Japanese American remarked that "the bill established our parents as the legal equal of other Americans; it gave the Japanese equality with all other immigrants . . . a principle we had been struggling for." The act imposed low quotas on the number of people allowed to enter the United States annually from each Asian country, granting the largest quota—185—to Japan. However, laws authorizing the immigration of Asian war brides and political refugees allowed thousands of Chinese, Koreans, Japanese, and Filipinos to enter the United States outside the quotas. Between 1946 and 1965, the Chinese American population almost tripled, reaching 360,000. As a result of both natural increase and the arrival of women dependents, the historically huge imbalance between Chinese American men and women—a ratio of 7 to 1 in 1920 and 2 to 1 even in 1950—dropped to 1.3 to 1 in 1960.

Still, Asian Americans continued to face discrimination in American society. Japanese Americans in California were often unable to get back the property they had lost when they were sent to concentration camps during World War II. Because of the Communist victory in China, many Chinese Americans were subjected to surveillance by the FBI and to deportation attempts by federal authorities on grounds that they were subversive. Among those driven out was Tsien Hsue-shen, a brilliant engineer at the California Institute of Technology, who was subjected to house arrest, then returned to mainland China, where he pioneered its missile program.

As with immigrant groups before them, the children embraced America's freewheeling culture. Breaking from the values of their parents, they risked generational conflict, much as does the young Chinese American son in Rodgers and Hammerstein's musical *Flower Drum Song*, set in San Francisco's Chinatown. The son wants to marry a very Americanized Chinese American girl; but in the end, he weds the choice of his tradition-bound father, a stereotypically meek

Bishop Fulton J. Sheen delivers one of his regular television sermons, 1955.

woman recently arrived from China. Rather than melding into the suburbs, Asian Americans tended to remain concentrated in their own neighborhoods, especially on the West Coast, earning their living by running restaurants and other small businesses and dreaming of better lives for their children, especially through education.

THE REVIVAL OF RELIGION

The growth of suburbs helped stimulate a renewal of religious activity. Churches provided places for belonging and identity in the rootlessness of the suburban environment. They were as much social centers as houses of worship. One church advertised, "Lots of acquaintances, not many friends? ... Meet future friends in church next Sunday." Fortifying the suburban appeal, evangelists combined the old-time religion with new-time packaging, relying on mass mailings and television to spread the gospel. The evangelist Billy Graham called Americans to Christ through regular sermons on radio and television, a nationally syndicated newspaper column, and his Evangelistic Association, a huge operation that late in the fifties received some 10,000 letters a week and contributions of $2 million a year. Graham's Roman Catholic counterpart was Bishop Fulton J. Sheen, who attracted enormous audiences for his prime-time television program, *Life Is Worth Living.*

In 1950, about one out of two Americans belonged to a church or synagogue; in 1959, about three out of five. Toward the end of the decade, all but 3 percent of Americans declared that they believed in God. Some observers questioned the depth of the spreading religious commitment. Popular music reflected the trend, with song titles like "I Believe" and "The Man Upstairs." Hollywood produced blockbusters such as *Quo Vadis* (1951), *The Robe* (1953), and *Ben-Hur* (1959), films that pitted Christian commitment against secular temptation or oppression. "Dial-a-Prayer" offered a minute of spiritual listening on the telephone, and the film star Jane Russell told the readers of *Modern Screen* magazine that when you get to know God, "you find He's a Livin' Doll." In the *Power of Positive Thinking*, a book that ran on the best-seller list for three years, the Reverend Norman Vincent Peale extolled the marvelous effectiveness of faith for individual self-improvement.

In 1954, Congress added the phrase "one nation under God" to the Pledge of Allegiance, and the next year it agreed to imprint "In God We Trust" on the nation's currency.

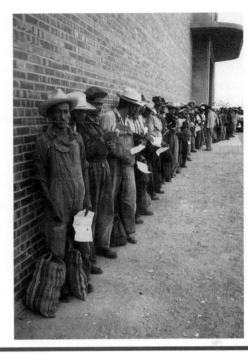

Mexican migrant workers lined up for work in the United States, 1951.

Amid the climate of the Cold War, churchgoing helped unite Americans in their anti-Communism. Anti-Communism rippled through the preachings of Billy Graham and homilies of Bishop Sheen, and religion was celebrated as evidence of the superiority of the American way of life over that of atheistic Communism.

OUTCASTS OF AFFLUENCE

The hosannas to the American way of life ignored several plain facts. The prosperity of the day bypassed millions, and for some groups the blessings of liberty remained to be fully realized. Many senior citizens barely survived on low incomes without medical or hospital insurance. While the portion of Americans who were impoverished declined by a third, more than a fifth—some 35 million people—still lived below the poverty line. Regionally, the poverty rate was highest in the South, and socially, it struck hardest at women heading households and at people of color.

Hispanic Americans. During the 1950s, the Hispanic population of the United States grew considerably. Puerto Ricans

907

Native Americans meet in the Southwest to consider a U.S. government relocation offer, 1950.

flocked to the mainland from their native island, drawn by the availability of jobs and cheap airfares to New York City. By 1960, about a million were living in the East Harlem section of New York, a fourfold increase since 1950. As people of color, they faced discrimination and indignities in housing, employment, schools, and police relations.

At the same time, Mexican Americans were entering the United States legally under the *bracero* program, expanded in the 1950s so that in 1960 these temporary workers comprised about a quarter of migrant laborers. Many stayed on after their labor permits expired, joining the thousands of Hispanics who migrated across the southwestern border illegally. The Eisenhower administration, intensifying a program begun in 1950, deported the allegedly illegal immigrants, sending some 5 million back across the Rio Grande by the end of the decade. The roundups were often conducted without due-process protections, and Mexican Americans in the country legally were often detained.

Although Hispanic organizations were powerless to stop the harassment, some did succeed in getting antidiscrimination laws passed in several southwestern cities. Many also opposed the flood of illegal migrants from the south, fearing that their arrival would undermine their own acceptance and depress wages. Ernesto Galarza, of the National Agricultural Workers' Union, tried to put an end to the *bracero* program and called on Congress to enact legislation guaranteeing farm workers decent wages, working conditions, housing, and health care, but the union's strikes were ineffective. By 1960, more than two-thirds of Mexican Americans lived in urban areas such as greater Los Angeles, leaving the jobs of agricultural labor to the recent arrivals. Hispanics began moving up the socioeconomic ladder and gaining political influence, but still a third lived below the poverty line.

Native Americans. Most Native Americans, a total of a half million people by 1960, lived on reservations and in poverty, but service in World War II had schooled some of them in the ways of the outside world and had encouraged them to claim the human rights for which they fought. Returning veterans found it outrageous that even though Native Americans were citizens of the United States, the state constitutions of Arizona and New Mexico still prohibited Indian suffrage in their state elections. One angry Navajo complained, "We went to Hell and back for what. For the people back home in America to tell us we can't vote!" In 1948, Arizona granted them the suffrage, and fourteen years later New Mexico followed suit. In 1953, Congress enacted legislation permitting Native Americans to purchase guns and alcohol on and off the reservations, rights previously denied them by federal law.

That year, too, Congress endorsed a two-pronged program for Native Americans that had begun during the Truman years. One prong—"termination"—was aimed at ending their tribal status, the federal aid that went with it, and their standing as wards of the United States. Congress, which had made them citizens in 1924, would also grant them full citizens' rights. The other prong—"relocation"—was aimed at abolishing the reservations and helping Indians to move to cities. Defenders of the program maintained that it would force Native Americans to care for themselves and to assimilate to the mainstream of society. Pressure for termination also came, however, from mining, agricultural, and lumber interests eager to obtain the remaining tribal lands. Between 1953 and 1960, armed by additional congressional legislation, the Eisenhower administration terminated more than 100 separate tribes or bands and relocated more than 60,000 Indians to urban areas.

Most Native Americans objected to termination. A Seminole petition to President Eisenhower declared, "We are not White Men but Indians, do not wish to become White Men but wish to remain Indians." Some Indians relocated to cities and succeeded; others endured low-paying jobs, inadequate schooling, and racial discrimination; about a third fled back to their tribes. For example, in Wisconsin the Menominees, having agreed to termination, suddenly found themselves subject to state and local taxes they could not pay. They often lost homes as well as tribal lands, and they were unable to afford the hospitals and medical care the federal government had previously provided. The government found itself spending three times as much on welfare for the Menominees as it had provided in subsidies before termination. By 1958, recognizing that termination was a disaster, the Eisenhower administration announced that no more tribes would be terminated without their consent. However, relocation continued, and almost half of Native Americans were placed in urban areas by 1967.

> *"A Seminole petition to President Eisenhower declared, 'We are not White Men but Indians, do not wish to become White Men but wish to remain Indians.' "*

African Americans. The Korean War had enormously speeded up racial integration of the armed services. After President Truman's 1948 order that they desegregate, the air force had quickly complied; the navy had said it would but dragged its feet; and the army, which included the largest percentage of blacks, had resisted. However, in response to the pressure for accelerating the process of military training, the color line soon disappeared from army bases across the country. In Korea itself, integration of troops was forced by battlefield emergencies. Whites took the situation in stride, and by 1953 nine out of every ten blacks were serving in integrated units.

Outside the military, however, blacks continued to suffer the debilitations of racial segregation and discrimination. The mechanization and consolidation that was transforming southern agriculture pushed African Americans out of farming, consigning them in rural areas to lives of poverty in housing with neither running water nor indoor toilets, and in urban areas to crowded, segregated neighborhoods, poorly paid jobs, or unemployment. Most blacks in the South continued to be barred from voting, and segregation continued to prevail in schools, restaurants, hotels, and most workplaces. Combined with the mechanization of agriculture, such conditions led about 2 million blacks to migrate north and west. By the end of the 1950s, some 40 percent of blacks lived outside the South, compared with 23 percent in 1940.

While northern blacks could vote, their housing and job opportunities were decidedly limited. They crowded into the central cities, which, as whites moved to the suburbs, turned increasingly into black ghettos. Federal lending agencies discriminated against blacks, making it difficult for them to buy homes or open businesses. Urban renewal was supposed to produce new, low-cost housing, but in practice it turned into what critics termed "Negro removal," accompanied by racial segregation, including heavily black housing projects. Real-estate practices closed most of the newly expanding suburbs to blacks. And many suburban whites, including ethnic minority groups who identified themselves as "white," were unwilling to accept blacks in their neighborhoods. William Levitt, who refused to sell homes to African Americans in his Levittowns, explained, "I have come to know that if we sell one house to a Negro family, then 90 or 95 per-

Florida segregation law compelled African Americans to sit in the back of public vehicles like this Tampa bus, 1956.

cent of our white customers will not buy into the community." When in 1957 a black family tried to move into Levittown, Pennsylvania, they were greeted with a barrage of rocks.

Most blacks could not afford to move into the suburbs anyway. Skilled trade unions—electrical, construction, sheet metal, plumbing—refused to admit them. Although they fared better in the United Auto Workers, an industrial union, they suffered humiliations on the shop floor and were denied a role in the union's leadership. North and South, racism continued to deny African Americans a decent material life as well as dignity and psychic comfort.

Stirrings for Civil Rights

During the heyday of McCarthyism, the chilling of dissent in so many areas of American life likely discouraged African Americans from openly protesting their condition more than they did. Many, like the protagonist in *The Invisible Man*, Ralph Ellison's searing novel of 1952, appeared to cope with their circumstances by privately distinguishing between their authentic selves and the accommodating, often humiliating behavior that white society compelled of them in order to survive. But by the mid-1950s, a tendency to challenge the status quo was emerging in the black South. Returning black veterans brought back with them the experience of the integrated armed services. Television vividly displayed images of the better life. A growing black urban middle class had formed, some of its members educated at the region's black colleges. These African Americans earned their livings as doctors, lawyers, teachers, ministers, and businesspeople serving myriad needs. Accumulating economic power, they felt a mounting impatience with segregation, with the limitations it imposed on opportunity, dignity, and equality. In 1954, their conviction that it was grossly unjust was affirmed by the Supreme Court in its historic ruling against racially segregated education. And the next year, blacks in Montgomery, Alabama, moved to abolish segregation in their city's public transportation.

BROWN V. BOARD OF EDUCATION

Since the late 1940s, civil rights lawyers had been setting their sights on the system of legally segregated public education. Virtually every student in the South attended a racially segre-

gated school, and so did some students in ten states outside the region. Segregation continued to enjoy the sanction of the Supreme Court's decision in *Plessy v. Ferguson* (1896)—that the provision of racially separate but equal facilities for blacks and whites was constitutional. But primary and secondary schools for blacks and whites were often unequal. White schools in Mississippi, for example, received four and a half times as much money per pupil as did black schools.

The civil rights lawyers had successfully chipped away at *Plessy*, winning several rulings from the Supreme Court that where schools were unequal in facilities and staff, blacks had to be allowed access to the superior white ones. Now, in the early 1950s, they resolved to attack the doctrine of separate but equal head-on. The vanguard lawyer in the drive was Thurgood Marshall, chief counsel for the NAACP, who had been taught at Howard University Law School in the 1930s that the legal system could and should be used to advance the civil rights of African Americans. Marshall had traveled the South organizing blacks to fight for their rights, often finding himself in danger of harassment or arrest for his efforts. A friend recalled that when Marshall visited the courthouses of

Thurgood Marshall (center) and his fellow attorneys celebrate their Supreme Court victory in *Brown v. Board of Education*, 1954.

the South, "folks would come from miles, some of them on muleback or horseback, to see 'the nigger lawyer' who stood up in white men's courtrooms."

In 1951, the NAACP sued the Board of Education of Topeka, Kansas, challenging the city's segregated public schools on behalf of several black families, including that of thirty-two-year-old Oliver Brown, a veteran, welder, and assistant pastor at his church. By 1952, *Brown v. Board of Education* had reached the Supreme Court. Marshall used the findings of the black social psychologist Kenneth B. Clark that segregation saddled blacks with "a permanent sense of inferiority" to contend that racially separate facilities were by their nature unequal.

The Court was now under the leadership of Chief Justice Earl Warren, a moderate Republican and three-term governor of California whom Eisenhower had appointed to the bench. While attorney general of the state during World War II, Warren had been involved in the removal of Japanese Americans to concentration camps, a chapter in his history he regretted deeply. On May 17, 1954, Warren delivered the unanimous decision of the Court: "We conclude that in the field of public education, the doctrine of 'separate but equal' has no place. Separate educational facilities are inherently unequal." On May 31, 1955, the Court gave practical force to its ruling, instructing the states to create public school systems free of racial discrimination with "all deliberate speed."

THE MONTGOMERY BUS BOYCOTT

Six months later, on December 1, 1955, Rosa Parks, a forty-five-year-old seamstress in Montgomery, Alabama, was seated toward the front of a bus on her way home. When more whites boarded, the driver yelled, "Niggers move back." Although Montgomery's black riders accounted for more than three-quarters of bus passengers, they were supposed to surrender their seats to whites. Parks was mild-mannered, reasonable, a faithful member of her church; but she was also a member of the NAACP, and the previous summer she had attended a workshop on race relations where, as she later recalled, she gained the "strength to persevere in my work for freedom." Resentful of the bus company's policies, Parks stayed put in her seat. She was arrested, convicted, and, having refused to pay a $10 fine, was given a suspended jail sentence. Some of Montgomery's black leadership, long angry at the bus system, already had plans for a **citywide bus boycott.** Now

Martin Luther King Jr., after the Montgomery bus boycott, sits with a white man on one of the city's newly desegregated buses, December 1956.

that the respectable Parks had been arrested, they put it into effect.

The black churches, the fulcrum of spiritual and social life in the black community, supported the boycott and gave it an inspiring leader: the Reverend Martin Luther King Jr., an eloquent, twenty-six-year-old Baptist minister who had come to Montgomery the year before. Raised in comfort in Atlanta, King learned from his father, himself a prominent minister who had led black voter-registration drives, that racism was to be resisted. At Morehouse College and then at Boston University, King broke away from his father's fire-and-brimstone fundamentalism, embracing a modernist Protestantism committed to combating social inequality and injustice. He found a means to that end in the doctrine of nonviolent resistance to oppression, taking inspiration from the civil disobedience of Henry David Thoreau in the 1840s against the Mexican War and Mohandas Gandhi in the 1940s against British colonial rule in India.

While a button-downed conservative in dress, King brought to the Montgomery bus boycott a socially transforming courage and vision. He shrewdly recognized that nonviolent tactics against injustice could arouse public opinion and stimulate sympathy for the black cause. He told a crowd of 5,000 blacks in a church one night, "We are here this evening to say to those who have mistreated us so long that we are tired— tired of being segregated and humiliated, tired of being kicked about by the brutal feet of oppression. . . . If you will protest courageously and yet with dignity and Christian love, when the

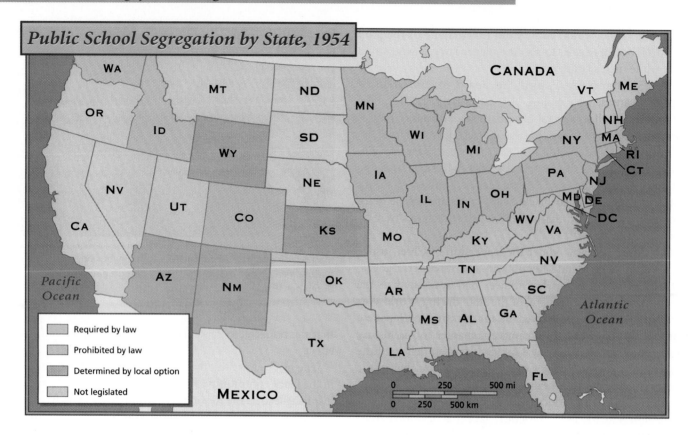

Public School Segregation by State, 1954

Required by law
Prohibited by law
Determined by local option
Not legislated

history books are written in future generations, historians will have to pause and say, 'There lived a great people—a black people—who injected a new meaning and dignity into the veins of civilization.'"

For more than ten months, black Montgomerians organized car pools, rode black-owned taxis whose drivers had agreed to carry passengers at lower fares, or simply walked. A journalist asked an old woman trudging along a road, "Aren't your feet tired?" She replied, "Yes, my feets is tired but my soul is rested." Membership in the white Citizens Council shot up; the Ku Klux Klan marched in the streets; King's house was bombed, and King, along with other leaders of the protest, was arrested, tried, and convicted of leading an illegal boycott. Still, Montgomery's blacks continued the boycott peacefully, persuaded by King that reacting with violence would undermine the righteousness of their cause.

In the meantime, the leaders of the boycott filed suit challenging the constitutionality of bus segregation. In mid-November 1956, the Supreme Court held that the city ordinances governing bus seating violated the Fourteenth Amendment. The boycott had hurt Montgomery's businesses, and their leaders were eager to see the dispute settled. Shortly before Christmas 1956, thirteen months after the boycott began, Martin Luther King Jr. sat with a white man at the front of a bus.

WHITE RESISTANCE

The victory in Montgomery was not matched by comparable success in school integration. Blacks and many whites had been cautiously heartened by the Supreme Court's ruling in *Brown*, and some southern moderates, especially in the border states, declared that they would comply with the decision, holding with Governor Jim Folsom of Alabama that "when the Supreme Court speaks, that's the law." But elsewhere, especially in the deep South, segregationists denounced the ruling, pledging with Governor Herman Talmadge of Georgia to prevent the mixing of Negroes and whites with each other "socially or in our school systems." Waves of antiblack violence broke over the South, including the murder in 1955 of

912

Emmett Till, fourteen, in Tallahatchie County, Mississippi, because he had whistled at a white woman in a grocery store. His accused killers were arrested, tried, and freed by an all-white jury. The Klan went on the march again, and respectable people organized against the Supreme Court and desegregation by joining white Citizens Councils.

But black Americans were not of a mind to retreat. The Montgomery bus boycott had dramatically demonstrated that they could press the issue of freedom by direct, nonviolent action. It also produced in Martin Luther King Jr. a new leader of protest. The boycott had been supported by black churches throughout the South. In January 1957, aware that their churches constituted an immeasurable resource in the battle for freedom, black ministers from eleven states gathered in Atlanta and founded the Southern Christian Leadership Conference (SCLC), with King as its president.

In the mid-1950s, the stirrings for civil rights were beginning to challenge the complacency and conservatism that had descended over the nation, raising questions about the merits of a golden age that excluded so many from its benefits. Amid the Cold War, a growing number were coming to agree with the response of *The Cleveland Plain Dealer* to a nationally publicized incident of racial bigotry during the Korean War: "It is high time we stopped this business. We can't do it as decent human beings and we can't do it as a nation trying to sell democracy to a world full of non-white peoples." Beyond that, the nascent movement for black civil rights aroused the conscience of white Americans. Billy Graham, who took his religious principles seriously, had been pleading for racial tolerance and an end to segregation, and now he applauded King's nonviolent campaign for "setting an example of Christian love."

But civil rights for African Americans did not seem to arouse President Eisenhower's conscience. Eisenhower, who privately disapproved of the *Brown* ruling, told reporters that while he accepted it, he would not endorse it, explaining, "I don't believe you can change the hearts of men with laws or decisions." Eisenhower now considered his appointment of Warren his "biggest damn fool mistake." He dutifully desegregated federal installations and sought to integrate public schools and accommodations in Washington, D.C., a federal jurisdiction, but he refrained from using federal power to aid school integration in the southern states. When the University of Alabama expelled its first black pupil in direct violation of a federal court order, Eisenhower refused to intervene,

1948	Scientists at Bell Laboratories invent the transistor.
June 1950–July 1953	Korean War.
1952	The McCarran-Walter Immigration Act.
November 1, 1952	United States explodes hydrogen bomb in the Pacific.
1954	Army-McCarthy Senate hearings.
May 17, 1954	*Brown v. Board of Education.*
1955	Polio vaccine proves effective.
December 1, 1955	Rosa Parks arrested, leading to Montgomery (Alabama) bus boycott.
October–November 1956	Suez Canal crisis.
November 1956	Khrushchev crushes Hungarian rebellion.
1958	President Eisenhower initiates nuclear test-ban talks with Soviets in Geneva.

Chronology

and he did not speak out against the breakdown of law and order in Mississippi exemplified by the murder of Emmett Till. Some observers took Eisenhower's reluctance to deal with the moral stain of racial segregation as a failure of leadership, an impression that a rush of subsequent events at home and abroad would soon intensify.

Suggested Reading

Stephen Ambrose, *Eisenhower*, 2 vols. (1984)

Taylor Branch, *Parting the Waters: America in the King Years, 1954–1963* (1988)

Jon Halliday and Bruce Cumings, *Korea: The Unknown War* (1988)

Kenneth Jackson, *Crabgrass Frontier: The Suburbanization of the United States* (1985)

William McDougall, *The Heavens and the Earth: A Political History of the Space Age* (1985)

Elaine Tyler May, *Homeward Bound: American Families in the Cold War Era* (1988)

Ellen Schrecker, *The Age of McCarthyism: A Brief History with Documents* (1994)

Chapter 29

RENEWAL OF REFORM:

1956-1968

Jasper Johns's *Three Flags*, 1958.

915

■ **What were the foreign and domestic conflicts Americans faced in the 1950s?**

■ **What was the significance of the Bay of Pigs invasion and the Cuban missile crisis?**

■ **How did the civil rights movement and environmentalism develop in the Kennedy years?**

■ **What were the major initiatives of LBJ's Great Society program?**

On October 5, 1957, Americans learned that the Soviet Union had launched the world's first artificial earth satellite, *Sputnik*. Twenty-nine days later, *Sputnik II* went up, weighing 1,120.9 pounds, packed with a maze of scientific instruments, and signaling back the condition of a live dog named Laika. On December 6, the United States' attempt to launch its own satellite from Cape Canaveral fizzled in a cloud of brownish black smoke. The *Sputnik*s were taken to demonstrate that the Soviets possessed the rocket and guidance capability for intercontinental ballistic missiles, and were well on the way toward putting a man into space.

The Soviet triumph stimulated a spate of national soul-searching. Sermons, editorials, and articles pronounced America chrome-plated and complacent, lax in educational standards, absorbed in materialism, and neglecting public services in favor of private indulgence. The Soviets, in contrast, were reported to be more disciplined and purposeful—educating their children more intensively, training twice as many scientists and engineers, and achieving a higher rate of economic growth. Many commentators contended with George Kennan, the architect of containment, that the country needed a greater "sense of national purpose" if it was to compete successfully with the Soviet Union for world leadership.

The Soviet satellites also stimulated calls for huge increases in defense spending. Eisenhower, avoiding panic, resisted them. He knew from secret intelligence, particularly the information gathered by overflight surveillance, that the United States was well ahead of the Soviets in intercontinental rocketry. Early in 1958, the nation did successfully launch its own satellite. Yet the Soviet satellites raised troubling questions about the soundness of American policies for defense and space. Both the questions about national security and the critique of complacency joined with the increasing energy of the civil rights movement to spur a renewal of reform that surged through the country during the presidencies of John F. Kennedy and Lyndon Johnson.

A Transitional Period

QUESTIONS OF NATIONAL SECURITY

Several weeks after *Sputnik*, Eisenhower announced in a television address that he had brought scientific expertise directly into the White House by appointing a presidential science adviser—the first in the nation's history—to assist him in national defense policymaking, with the aid of a President's Science Advisory Committee. In 1958, he signed into law the National Defense Education Act, which aimed to help needy and capable students in important fields of the humanities as well as the sciences, and which made available $250 million for the improvement of public school facilities, including laboratories.

That year, too, the government established the National Aeronautics and Space Administration (NASA) to oversee and coordinate all nonmilitary activities in space research and development. Eisenhower thought of the new agency more as a consolidation of existing ones than as a bold departure, remarking to his cabinet that he did not want to pay to learn "what's on the other side of the moon." However, Congress, resolute in its sense of Cold War competition and eager for federal contracts, pushed the president hard. "How much money would you need to . . . make us even with Russia . . .

and probably leap-frog them?" a congressman asked the head of the space agency. Between 1957 and 1961, federal expenditures for research and development more than doubled to $9 billion annually, including a tripling in outlays for basic research to $827 million a year. Eisenhower also accelerated the ICBM program and authorized the deployment of a short-range missile—the army's Jupiter, which Wernher von Braun's team had developed—in Italy and Turkey.

The renewed emphasis on missiles came at a time of intensifying criticism of the doctrine of massive retaliation. Worries about nuclear war remained powerful and were reinforced by stories such as Nevil Shute's *On the Beach* (1957), a bleak novel, made into a popular film two years later, that depicts the world after a nuclear war—everyone in the Northern Hemisphere dies from radiation, and the Southern Hemisphere awaits a similar fate. Strategic analysts argued that the threat of massive retaliation was not a realistic answer to Soviet challenges in the Third World. Yet between 1953 and 1959, the emphasis on high-technology defense was accompanied by a cost-cutting reduction of the army by more than 40 percent. To the critics, the nation lacked the capacity to wage the kind of "limited wars" that might prove necessary to protect its interests in the Third World. In an influential book titled *The Uncertain Trumpet*, General Maxwell Taylor, a former army chief of staff, argued for the doctrine of "flexible response," the ability to fight "brushfire wars" using conventional weapons in remote regions of the world.

Cuba. The most disturbing Third World upheaval occurred on the American doorstep, in Cuba, which since 1952 had been ruled by the pro-American dictator Fulgencio Batista. Although Vice-President Nixon had celebrated Batista as "Cuba's Abraham Lincoln," he was in fact a corrupt and repressive strongman. During the 1950s, an anti-Batista guerrilla movement under the leadership of Fidel Castro had steadily gathered strength, especially in the countryside, and in January 1959 Castro's forces succeeded in taking power. A reformist young lawyer, Castro intended to reconstruct Cuba's oligarchic economy and society. When he visited the United States in April, many Americans welcomed him as a hero.

But Castro soon imposed his own dictatorship, jailing and executing opponents while confiscating foreign property, in-

> *"In 1961, the United States severed diplomatic relations with Cuba, establishing a break that would last into the twenty-first century."*

cluding $1 billion worth of American investments. Announcing that he was a Communist, he allied Cuba with the Soviet Union and pledged support for leftist revolution in Latin America. In 1960, the United States cut off economic aid to Cuba and imposed a boycott on the island, prohibiting imports of Cuban sugar. The CIA began training exiles in Guatemala to invade the island and topple Castro. In a review of its Latin American policies, the Eisenhower administration concluded that more emphasis should be given to democracy, human rights, and economic development in the region, but the shift was too late to repair matters with Castro. In 1961, the United States severed diplomatic relations with Cuba, establishing a break that would last into the twenty-first century.

U.S.-Soviet Relations. In the summer of 1959, Nixon went to Moscow and fell into a spirited "kitchen debate" with Khrushchev—so called because it occurred at the kitchen display at the American National Exhibition—over the merits of the American and Soviet systems. While Khrushchev spoke with pride of the Soviet Union's productive female workers,

Sputnik I, the first earth-orbiting man-made satellite, launched by the Soviets on October 4, 1957.

Fidel Castro (waving) leads his victorious rebel forces into Havana, Cuba, January 1959.

Nixon extolled the merits and affordability of American consumer goods, emphasizing that the washing machines at the display were "designed to make things easier for our women." The next month, Khrushchev traveled to the United States, visiting Iowa cornfields and Camp David, the presidential retreat in Maryland, where he spent three days with Eisenhower. The two men agreed that they would meet together with the leaders of France and Great Britain at a summit in Paris in May 1960. Commentators celebrated the "spirit of Camp David," taking Khrushchev's earthy agreeableness as a sign of a possible thaw in the Cold War.

Hopes were dashed when two weeks before the summit, a Soviet missile brought down a U-2, the plane that had been conducting overflight surveillance of the Soviet Union. The aircraft had been specially designed to fly at very high altitudes beyond the reach of Soviet defenses. The administration quickly said that the plane had been on a meteorological mission and had lost course. But then Khrushchev announced that the Soviets had the pilot, who, having parachuted to safety, had admitted that he was on a spy flight. Eisenhower now accepted full responsibility for the flight while administration

spokesmen insisted that such flights were necessary to the security of the free world and would continue. At the summit, Khrushchev demanded an apology for the flights and the punishment of those responsible. Eisenhower refused, and Khrushchev walked out. The episode, dashing the spirit of Camp David, sent the temperature of the Cold War back down to freezing.

BREAKING WITH CONFORMITY

The post-*Sputnik* expressions of dissatisfaction with Eisenhower's United States were not new, only more intense. Through the decade, observers had been charging that much of affluent white America appeared beset by powerful pressures to conform. They dubbed its younger, college-educated members a "silent generation" in recognition of their lack of outspokenness on public issues and aversion to risk-taking. Yet in attacking conformity, these critics helped generate a culture of dissent from it, an embrace of individualism that permeated the arts and that was complemented by rebelliousness in social attitudes among younger Americans.

Even after the waning of McCarthyism, the climate of the Cold War had continued to chill iconoclasm, but the culture of conformity was also fostered by the commercial and industrial

Vice-President Richard Nixon scores a point in the "kitchen debate" with Soviet premier Nikita Khrushchev, 1959.

ethos of the era. TV had expanded into a mass commercial medium, with annual advertising revenues close to $2 billion by 1961, more than a tenfold increase over the decade. In these pre-cable days, national broadcasting was dominated by three networks, which limited diversity in programming. Fear of alienating viewers and advertisers discouraged the airing of controversial matter. Critics found commercial television willing to settle for lowest-common-denominator programming. It was less concerned with enlightenment than with mere entertainment, providing a potpourri of comedies and game shows, some of them unscrupulous. In 1958, it was revealed that two popular quiz shows, *Twenty-One* and *The $64,000 Question,* secretly provided their contestants with the answers to high-stakes questions.

Analysts contended that corporate life squashed individuality. The middle manager of a large corporation had become an "organization man," to use the title phrase of the sociologist William H. Whyte Jr.'s influential book of 1956—an employee compelled, in order to rise in the company, to get along with the group rather than assert his own convictions. A Monsanto Corporation training film showing men in white coats in a laboratory remarked, "No geniuses here; just a bunch of average Americans working together." In *The Lonely Crowd* (1950), influential in shaping social ideas through the fifties, the sociologist David Riesman and his coauthors argued that the "old middle class" had been "inner directed," using an internal "psychological gyroscope" to make moral and personal decisions. By contrast, the "new middle class" was "other directed," seeking "approval and direction from others"—a habit deadly to individuality and independence.

Personal Rebellion and Public License. Conformity and its consequences were probed critically by novelists and playwrights. In *The Man in the Gray Flannel Suit,* Sloan Wilson suggested that corporate life forced men to give the demands of their jobs priority over their families. Men wept in their seats when they saw Arthur Miller's powerful *Death of a Salesman,* a play (first produced in 1949) that showed how the traveling salesman Willy Loman's hunger to be liked and successful made his life a hollow sham. For the most part, writers were apolitical: rather than argue for social change, their fiction explored individual character, spotlighting the tensions between personal authenticity and the conformist

> *"American painters made New York City the world center of the graphic arts, forming what has been called an 'academy of authenticity.' "*

pressures of mass society. Jewish writers—notably Saul Bellow, Philip Roth, and Bernard Malamud—numbered among the most important new novelists of the period. Unlike Laura Hobson, whose *Gentleman's Agreement* focused on anti-Semitism, they probed the conflicts imposed on individuals by upward mobility and materialism, treating them by turns intellectually, comically, or ironically.

American painters made New York City the world center of the graphic arts, forming what has been called an "academy of authenticity." Many of them pursued abstract expressionism, producing compositions of colors and forms that bore no obvious relationship to reality. Such works, using the unconscious and the primordial as rich sources of imagery, indicated a recoil from the socially engaged, politically oriented art characteristic of the thirties. To be sure, several of these artists insisted on connecting with real objects. Jasper Johns, for example, painted oversize versions of the American flag, an ironic, ambiguous comment on what Americans of the fifties made into a quasi-religious icon of anti-Communist patriotism. But most practitioners of what one observer called "action painting" seemed concerned with creating their identities in the very act of painting. One of the most famous was Jackson Pollock, whose sensuous canvases of splatters and drips mirrored the violent, rebellious intensity of his life, which ended in a car crash at the age of forty-four.

A small group of writers known as the "Beats" turned themselves into a living dissent from conformism. Famous among them was the novelist Jack Kerouac, author of *On the Road.* Written in three weeks on a continuous roll of printer's papers, the book fictionalized the drug-and-sex-laden adventures of Kerouac and several friends as they traveled around the country in a state of spontaneous irresponsibility. Equally prominent was a friend of Kerouac's, the poet Allen Ginsberg, an open homosexual and political radical who wrote in his transfixing *Howl,* "I saw the best minds of my generation destroyed by madness / starving hysterical naked / dragging themselves through the negro streets at dawn looking for an angry fix." The Beats dressed in simple clothes and sneakers and grew beards; their celebrations of sexuality, alcohol, and drugs repudiated conformity and materialism while asserting the authenticity of individualism.

While Americans of the fifties did not flaunt sexuality, many tolerated an increasing frankness about it. Popular novels such as the steamy *Peyton Place* graphically recounted sexual behavior in a New England town; the new magazine *Playboy* included centerfolds of voluptuous nude women and graphically erotic fiction; and among high-art works, Vladimir Nabokov's *Lolita* narrated the obsession of an older man for the nymphet of the title. The best-selling books by the scientist Alfred Kinsey—*Sexual Behavior in the Human Male* (1948) and *Sexual Behavior in the Human Female* (1953)—reported that both men and women were increasingly engaging in sex earlier, outside of marriage, and in a variety of forms. According to Kinsey, some 10 percent of American males had engaged in homosexuality at some point in their lives. Almost half the females in the country had indulged in premarital sex, and a quarter of them had committed adultery before the age of forty.

Young America. One of the most popular writers of the fifties was J. D. Salinger, whose adolescent protagonist in *Catcher in the Rye* considers the adult world phony and opts out of it by fantasizing a heroic life for himself. Moviegoers watched James Dean in *Rebel Without a Cause* and Marlon Brando in *The Wild One* portray alienated middle-class youth journeying to the edge with motorcycles and fast cars. A car culture of risk—later memorialized in the film *American Graffiti* (1973)—was a staple of teenage suburban life, with its hot-rodding and drag racing, stag-like displays of horsepower arranged at drive-in malt shops. *Blackboard Jungle* unsparingly portrayed insolent, rebellious high school students in and out of the classroom. News reports made juvenile delinquency seem rampant, and some schools and streets appear to be combat zones.

Teenagers found a rebellious culture of their own in music. Ballads remained popular, as did jazz, but what most captured the passionate attention of young Americans was the undisguisedly sexual rock and roll. Like jazz between the wars, rock originated in the rhythm and blues of blacks, who faced barriers in performing it for white media and audiences. It was brought to the national mainstream by white musicians—notably Bill Haley and the Comets, an all-white band that in 1955 introduced "Shake Rattle and Roll," then "Rock Around the Clock," a huge hit with its pounding drums and electric guitars. Sam Phillips, a white promoter who loved black music, reportedly said, "If I could find a white man with a Negro sound, I could make a billion dollars." He discovered precisely the man in **Elvis Presley,** a twenty-year-old native of Tupelo, Mississippi, who sang blues and country in a sultry voice and with provocative motions. Presley worshiped Brando and Dean, affected their passive, alienated demeanor, and gyrated as his female fans screamed. One critic called his performances "strip-teases with clothes on." In 1956, Presley's "Heartbreak Hotel" and "Hound Dog" sold millions of records. He drew an audience of some 54 million when he appeared on a national television variety show (with the cameras catching him from the waist up).

Like jazz before it, rock was soon being performed for white audiences by black stars, too, including Chuck Berry, Fats Domino, Little Richard, and Chubby Checker. Sung by blacks or whites, rock spread rapidly through American culture. In the late 1940s, inexpensive vinyl records that played at 45 rotations per minute (r.p.m.) had begun to appear, and with them inexpensive record players. Teenagers, their spending money from odd jobs and parental allowances giving them independent purchasing power, bought 10 million portable record players a year by the late 1950s and helped double the retail sales of records between 1954 and

LEFT: The Beat poet Allen Ginsberg, 1960.

RIGHT: Marlon Brando exemplified rebellious youth in *The Wild One*, 1954.

Elvis Presley rocking his teenage audience, 1956.

1960. They also snapped up the new transistor radios, introduced in 1955, which gave them the freedom to listen to what they wanted, without relying on family radio sets. Electric guitars, becoming widely available during the fifties, were appropriated by the first high school rock bands.

Censorship and the Law. Social conservatives deplored the uninhibited sensuality of rock, and they tried to suppress the circulation of sexually explicit writings by appealing to the law. A bookstore owner in San Francisco was prosecuted for selling Ginsberg's *Howl* on the grounds that it was obscene. Federal postal and customs regulations—some went back to the Comstock Act of 1873, which blocked the distribution of obscene materials through the mails—prevented the importation and circulation of controversial materials. So did state and local officials, with the result that Americans often had difficulty getting hold of books with sexual content, including even literary classics such as Henry Miller's *Tropic of Cancer* and D. H. Lawrence's

> *"When on the first day of school black children attempted to enroll at Central, a shrieking crowd surrounded them chanting, 'Two, four, six, eight, we ain't gonna integrate.'"*

Lady Chatterley's Lover. The Hollywood Production Code continued to discourage the making of films that dealt with sex, drugs, and crime or that treated religion irreverently.

However, far greater license in expression developed during the 1950s, partly because of the expanding publication of sexually explicit materials, partly because the Supreme Court progressively tore down the legal sanction of censorship. Beginning in 1952, the Court ruled in a series of cases that movies were a form of expression protected by the First Amendment. Although in 1957, the Court held in *Roth v. United States* that obscenity was not constitutionally protected speech, it found in 1959 that a film of *Lady Chatterley's Lover* did not merit suppression for its content. And later that year, after lower federal courts held that a newly released, unexpurgated version of Lawrence's book was not obscene, the U.S. Post Office stopped trying to enforce the Comstock Act.

CIVIL RIGHTS: BECOMING A MOVEMENT

In the United States of the later 1950s, it was much easier to obtain rebellious books than to learn to read in a racially nondiscriminatory public school. By 1957, three years after the Supreme Court's ruling in *Brown v. Board of Education*, some 700 school districts had desegregated their schools, but most were in border states. School districts in the deep South fell far short of proceeding toward that goal with the deliberate speed the Court had required. In Little Rock, Arkansas, in September 1957, school officials were ready as the result of a federal court order to desegregate Central High School, but Governor Orval Faubus tried to prevent them, using the excuse that integration would threaten public safety. When on the first day of school black children attempted to enroll at Central, a shrieking crowd surrounded them chanting, "Two, four, six, eight, we ain't gonna integrate." Television broadcast the proceedings to the nation, arousing dismay and anger at the vicious display of hate. Eisenhower reluctantly federalized the Arkansas National Guard and sent 1,100 U.S. Army paratroops to protect the black students in the exercise of their legal right to attend the school.

The next academic year, Faubus, having handily won reelection, closed all the schools in Little Rock, attempting to lease them on a segregated basis to a private school corpora-

Students from North Carolina Agricultural and Technical State University start the sit-in movement at Woolworth's in Greensboro, February 1960.

tion. More than 80 percent of the city's white students went to private schools or schools outside the city, while most black high school students did not attend school at all. Faubus's action helped inspire southerners elsewhere to resist school integration by devising strategies such as diverting public funds to private segregated schools. The Supreme Court soon ruled Faubus's evasive maneuver—and by implication others like it—unconstitutional, and in August 1959 the Little Rock public schools were reopened and integrated. Still, between 1958 and 1961, the number of southern school districts that embraced integration fell to only forty-nine, a decrease of some 93 percent from the previous three years.

Voting Rights. In 1957, responding to the mounting agitation for black freedom, Congress enacted the first civil rights bill since Reconstruction. Although the bill initially included strong means of enforcement, its supporters in the Senate weakened its provisions for the protection of voting rights to avoid a southern filibuster. As passed, the bill created a Civil Rights Commission and a Civil Rights Division in the Justice Department and empowered the attorney general to intervene on behalf of citizens prevented from voting. A second act in 1960 authorized the appointment of federal referees to protect voting rights. However, the Eisenhower administration did little to exploit the powers of the legislation. By 1961, the act had not added a single southern black to the voting rolls.

Sit-Ins. In Greensboro, North Carolina, late in the afternoon of February 1, 1960, 4 black freshmen from North Carolina Agricultural and Technical State University sat down at the whites-only lunch counter in the Woolworth department store. The freshmen, aware of the Montgomery boycott, intended to desegregate Woolworth's lunch counter using nonviolent tactics of resistance. No one served them, and the store closed early. The next day, they returned with 23 classmates, and by the end of the week 1,000 students, including some whites, had come to Greensboro.

Within two months, similar protests had erupted in fifty-four cities in nine states. The protesters were often attacked by local whites, including police, who blasted them with high-pressure fire hoses and put them in jail. They nevertheless stuck to their nonviolent strategy and succeeded in desegregating several hundred lunch counters. A meeting of some 300 students over Easter weekend in 1960 led to the formation of the Student Non-Violent Coordinating Committee (SNCC), a protest organization independent of Martin Luther King's Southern Christian Leadership Conference that made sit-ins a major weapon in the battle for civil rights. By now, the agitation for civil rights had become a full-scale movement demanding responses from the nation's conscience and government.

THE ELECTION OF 1960

The Eisenhower administration's grudging response to the civil rights movement struck many observers as an abdication of moral and executive responsibility. Moreover, toward the end of the 1950s, the national debt was approaching $300 billion, and a recession in 1957–58 produced an unemployment rate of almost 8 percent, the highest since the 1930s. The setbacks of the U-2 incident and Castro's steady move leftward in Cuba cast a cloud of ineptitude over the administration's conduct of foreign policy. In the congressional elections of 1958, Democrats gained their largest majority in the House since 1936 and scored a sizable margin in the Senate.

Since the Twenty-second Amendment to the Constitution barred Eisenhower from seeking a third term, Republicans pinned their hopes for retaining the White House on Vice-President Richard M. Nixon, who won his party's presidential nomination virtually uncontested and chose as his running mate Henry Cabot Lodge, a moderate Massachusetts Republican.

The leading contender for the Democratic nomination was John Fitzgerald Kennedy of Massachusetts, at forty-three a young presidential candidate and the first Roman Catholic to make a serious run for the White House since Al Smith's failed attempt in 1928. The grandson of a Boston Irish politico, he was the son of Joseph P. Kennedy, a wealthy businessman who had been Franklin Roosevelt's ambassador to England and was ferociously ambitious to make Jack, the eldest surviving son among his nine children, president of the United States. Jack, often bedridden with a weak back, was a reader, somewhat detached and reflective. After graduating from Harvard, he enlisted in the navy and returned home a war hero for having saved the crew of his PT boat after it was sunk by a Japanese destroyer. Promptly elected to Congress and, in 1952, to the Senate, he initially embraced a hard-line anti-Communism, declined to speak out against Joseph McCarthy, and compiled a mixed record on civil rights measures. When he published *Profiles in Courage*, a book about brave leaders in the American past—it was ghostwritten for him but nevertheless won a Pulitzer Prize—critics observed tartly that he had displayed little courage on key issues in his own time.

Kennedy's youth, meager accomplishments, and Roman Catholicism raised doubts among many Americans about his suitability for the White House. But his candidacy was greatly helped by his family's rich resources and an effective political organization. He met the issue of his Catholicism head-on in the primaries, notably in predominantly Protestant West Virginia, crushed his opponents, and won the nomination on the first convention ballot. Aiming for support in the South, he chose as his running mate one of his principal rivals for the nomination—Lyndon B. Johnson of Texas, the Senate majority leader.

Campaigning on the theme of the "New Frontier," Kennedy pledged to "get the country moving again," promising to close the alleged "missile gap" between the United States and the Soviets, accelerate the country's space efforts, boost economic growth rates, and support civil rights. Nixon differed little from Kennedy in age or on the main election issues, but

he was somewhat disadvantaged by his red-baiting past. He was also unable to distance himself from the Eisenhower administration's weaknesses, notably its misstep in the U-2 affair, or answer the charges of a missile gap—which actually did not exist—because proof that it did not was classified. Moreover, Kennedy was the bolder of the two campaigners and better exploited the power of television, by now an essential instrument of politics. In a televised speech to a group of Protestant ministers, he declared that he believed "in an America where the separation of church and state is absolute." In four precedent-setting televised debates that reached an audience of more than 70 million, Kennedy was tanned, confident, and dynamic, while Nixon, recently ill, appeared drawn, haggard, and hesitant. Although radio listeners judged the contest a draw, the TV audience gave the edge to Kennedy, who shot up irreversibly in the polls.

Still, the election was remarkably close, with Kennedy beating Nixon by only 119,000 votes, winning several key states by hair-thin margins and running behind his party, which maintained its solid congressional majorities even while losing twenty seats in the House. His Catholicism apparently hurt him among southern Protestants, although

Republican Richard M. Nixon (left) and Democrat John F. Kennedy in the first televised presidential debates, 1960.

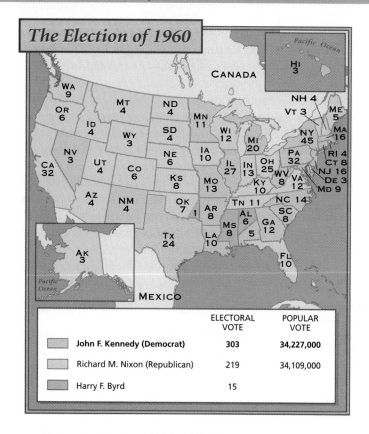

The Election of 1960

		ELECTORAL VOTE	POPULAR VOTE
	John F. Kennedy (Democrat)	303	34,227,000
	Richard M. Nixon (Republican)	219	34,109,000
	Harry F. Byrd	15	

his understanding of it in the realm of national security continued to be insightful. In his farewell address, he memorably urged Americans to guard against allowing the "military-industrial complex"—the interconnected system of the armed services and defense contractors—to gain unwarranted influence in government. And referring to the essential importance of maintaining popular control of government even in an era of nuclear weapons and intercontinental missiles, he warned that public policy must not "become the captive of a scientific-technological elite."

Yet to many of his contemporaries, Eisenhower's record was by no means unblemished. In the world at large, he tolerated an increasingly unbridled CIA and favored right-wing dictatorships over left-leaning governments, dealing heavy-handedly in particular with Vietnam and Cuba. Though he was deeply disturbed by the nuclear arms race, he had presided over its acceleration and permitted New Look cost-cutting to distort the nation's means of defense. Now, at the end of the Eisenhower years, some observers saw the country in a state of drift, vexed by urban blight, and obligated to make right at long last the condition of African Americans. The old issues left unresolved and the new ones forming out of the fifties—all were difficult, some were volatile. Together they comprised an emerging, insistent agenda for the United States and its new president.

Johnson's presence on the ticket helped him carry much of the South, including the electoral prize of Texas. He also ran strongly among blacks, and his religion also aided him among Catholic voters in the Northeast and Midwest.

THE EISENHOWER LEGACY

Eisenhower left the White House with a record of considerable accomplishment, at least during his first term. He had ended the war in Korea, kept the United States out of any other shooting conflicts, and sought cooperation with the Soviets. He had legitimized the New Deal/Fair Deal within the mainstream of the Republican Party, run his administration with quiet but effective force, and pursued policies that helped foster remarkable economic growth and technological innovation. Despite the foreign policy failures late in his administration, Eisenhower remained immensely popular. Although several scandals marred his second term, they left him personally untouched. His paramount concern for the public interest remained unquestioned, and

Kennedy: Idealism Without Illusions

Inauguration day 1961 was bright with promise, cold, crisp, the sky a clear blue, and the sun shimmering on newly fallen snow. John Kennedy declared in his **address** that the "torch has been passed to a new generation of Americans," and in a rejection of the indulgence of the fifties, he summoned his country to new beginnings, memorably proclaiming: "Ask not what your country can do for you. Ask what you can do for your country. Ask not what America will do for you, but what together we can do for the freedom of man."

Kennedy was handsome and charming, gifted with a throwaway wit and effortless eloquence, the embodiment of action and intellect. Although in chronic pain and regularly medicated because of Addison's disease, he presented himself to the public as energetic and athletic. His presidency was further assisted by his wife, Jacqueline Bouvier Kennedy, a stylish and beautiful socialite who gave the administration a patina of cultivation and chic, and by news reports about their two small children, Caroline and John Jr. Years later, Americans would learn that Kennedy indulged in extramarital affairs, even while in the White House. But at the time, the press refrained from probing the intimate private lives of presidents. Kennedy was simply "exciting," a student at the University of Nebraska remembered. "You had a guy who had little kids and who liked to play football on his front lawn . . . [who talked] about pumping new life into the nation and steering it in new directions."

Unlike Eisenhower, with his penchant for orderly, decentralized, cabinet-oriented governance, Kennedy gathered power into the Oval Office and followed a freewheeling mode of decision-making intended to facilitate action. His administration included growth-oriented investment bankers, efficiency-minded management experts, and reformist professors and intellectuals. The president also found places for longtime aides from Boston concerned primarily with his political welfare. At his father's insistence, he appointed as attorney general his brother, thirty-six-year-old Robert F. Kennedy, who had entered public life as a staff member for Joseph McCarthy's Senate investigations. Robert had never tried a case in court, but he zealously pursued the

> *"Unlike John Foster Dulles at the opening of the Eisenhower administration, Kennedy did not expect to roll back Communism, but he was determined to contest its further advance."*

administration's interests. The president gave his special assistant for national security, McGeorge Bundy, quick, tough-minded, and recently of Harvard, more authority in foreign affairs than his secretary of state, Dean Rusk, whom he found too cautious. He also permitted live television broadcasts of his press conferences, a first in American history and a practice that allowed him to shape opinion by speaking to the public directly.

As a member of the new generation, Kennedy's attitudes had been formed by the icy, restraining realities of the Cold War. He was, as his wife said of him, "an idealist without illusions." He was primarily concerned with foreign affairs, the subject to which he devoted most of his inaugural. Unlike John Foster Dulles at the opening of the Eisenhower administration, Kennedy did not expect to roll back Communism, but he was determined to contest its further advance. "We shall pay any price, bear any burden, meet any hardship, support any friend, oppose any foe to assure the survival and success of liberty," he pledged.

Despite his absorption in dangers abroad, Kennedy's arrival in the White House opened an era of profound social transformation. Rooted in the dissatisfactions that had surfaced in the late 1950s, the changes were accelerated by Kennedy's clarion call for sacrifice. Thousands of young Americans worked for civil rights at home or signed up for the new Peace Corps, which offered the opportunity at low pay and poor living conditions to assist people in the Third World. Yet the movement for change was also accompanied by resistance, turmoil, and often deadly violence.

KENNEDY AND THE THIRD WORLD

In a speech released two days before Kennedy's inauguration, Khrushchev contended that Communism would inevitably triumph, and to help it along, he promised unreserved Soviet support for "wars of national liberation." Kennedy was eager to foster prodemocratic sympathies in Third World countries by helping with their economic development, and he established warm relations with leaders in postcolonial Africa, including some who leaned toward socialism. But the administration was also determined to resist pro-Soviet uprisings while democracy took root. It extended the idea of "flexible response" to include fighting brushfire wars in undeveloped

Kennedy commands one of his televised press conferences, 1962.

regions, organizing counterinsurgency forces such as the Green Berets, and increasing research in chemical and biological warfare.

Latin America. In the opening weeks of his administration, Cuba commanded Kennedy's attention. He regarded the presence of a Communist enclave just ninety miles from the Florida coast as both an embarrassment and a threat, a potential exporter of revolution to the rest of Latin America. With Eisenhower's approval, the CIA had begun developing a scheme to train exiles from Cuba to invade their country and assassinate Fidel Castro. Despite moral and practical dissents among his advisers, Kennedy allowed the plan to proceed so long as it did not require any direct American intervention. On April 17, 1961, 1,400 Cuban exiles landed at the Bahia de Cochinos (Bay of Pigs) expecting covert air support supplied by the United States, with planes that would take off from Nicaragua with Cuban pilots. But Kennedy, now fearing that

U.S. Involvement in Latin America, 1954–2002

CUBA
-Batista is overthrown and Castro assumes power, 1959
-U.S.-sponsored Bay of Pigs invasion, April 1961
-U.S. quarantine of Cuba during missile crisis, October 1962

HAITI
-Duvalier exiled, 1986
-Jean-Bertrand Aristide elected president, 1990

GUATEMALA
-U.S.-supported overthrow of Arbenz's government, 1954

DOMINICAN REPUBLIC
-Rebellion restores power to Bosch, 1965
-Occupation by U.S. military forces, 1965–66

EL SALVADOR
-U.S. military advisers support government during 12-year civil war, 1981
-Formal peace agreement, 1992

GRENADA
-Extremist coup topples government, Reagan orders invasion, and pro-Western government installed, 1983

HONDURAS
-U.S. supports Contra rebels from bases in Honduras, 1981

NICARAGUA
-Sandinistas overthrow dictator, 1979
-U.S. (secretly) aids Contra efforts to overthrow Sandinista government, 1981
-Congress forbids military aid to Contras, 1982
-Peace accord, 1989

PANAMA
-Start of talks on Canal Zone Treaty, 1964
-Canal Zone Treaty negotiated, 1978
-U.S. invades Panama; arrests Noriega for drug trafficking, 1989
-Control of canal returned to Panama, 1999

CHILE
-U.S. tries and fails to prevent election of socialist president Allende, 1970

Gulf of Mexico

Caribbean Sea

VENEZUELA
SURINAME
GUYANA
FRENCH GUIANA
COLOMBIA
ECUADOR
Amazon R.
PERU
BRAZIL
BOLIVIA
PARAGUAY
URUGUAY
ARGENTINA

Atlantic Ocean

Pacific Ocean

0   250   500 mi
0   250   500 km

the strike would openly implicate the United States, refused to provide the support. Within two days, the island's defenders had routed the invaders. Kennedy took full responsibility for the disaster, recognizing that the action had been poorly planned, incompetently executed, and shaped by a decision-making process that needed repair. But still absorbed with Cuba, the administration established a secret CIA effort code-named "Operation Mongoose"; according to Robert Kennedy, who was in charge, the venture was meant to "stir things up on the island with espionage, sabotage, general disorder." The CIA continued to devise plans to assassinate Castro.

Meanwhile, President Kennedy had resolved to blunt the appeal of Communism in Latin America by pressing for social reform in the region. In March 1961, he announced the inauguration of the Alliance for Progress, a $20 billion program of loans for economic development to which the hemispheric nations pledged adherence. Although the Alliance for Progress encouraged land reform and other democratic measures, during the 1960s some of the assistance went to counterinsurgency programs, including training and matériel for Latin American armed forces intent on maintaining internal security.

Southeast Asia. The disaster in Cuba made Kennedy cautious in dealing with the instabilities that kept cropping up in the former French Indochina. He refused to intervene militarily in Laos, where pro-Communist rebels were warring against the pro-Western government, believing that Laos was strategically unimportant to the United States. But Kennedy did consider it vital to American interests to defend the anti-Communist government of Ngo Dinh Diem in South Vietnam.

Assuming, like most Americans at the time, that the Soviets and Chinese were backing Ho Chi Minh's drive to "liberate" the South, Kennedy wanted to demonstrate the United States' readiness to resist the spread of Communism in the Third World. He dispatched a small advisory force of Green Berets to Vietnam and initiated limited clandestine actions against the North. Still, he was wary of American overcommitment in the war. When Diem's regime was threatened in the fall of 1961, Kennedy declined to send additional forces, remarking to an aide that he would eventually have to send more, adding, "It's like taking a drink. The effect wears off, and you have to take another." Yet after becoming convinced that the credibility of American resolve was at stake, he did deploy additional troops—making a total of almost 17,000 by November 1963—for noncombat support of the South Vietnamese war effort.

A monk sacrifices himself to protest the Diem regime's discrimination against Buddhists, Saigon, 1963.

Kennedy tried to persuade Diem to widen his popularity through economic and political reform, but Diem was authoritarian by nature and bolstered in his resistance to change by his brother Ngo Dinh Nhu, a repressive politico, and Nhu's acid-tongued, arrogant wife, Madame Nhu. In mid-June 1963, a Buddhist set himself on fire, the first of several such outcries against the Diem regime. On the face of it, the Buddhists were protesting religious discrimination by the dominantly Catholic authorities, but their uprising drew support from young anti-Western nationalists hostile to the French-speaking hierarchy in charge of the country. That summer, Diem and Nhu cracked down on the dissidents, jailing hundreds of them. A group of South Vietnamese military officers resolved to remove Diem from office, and the Kennedy administration assured them that the United States would accept a coup. The plotters took over on November 1, capturing and killing Diem and his brother. Although Kennedy was upset by the murders, which he had not expected, the United States quickly recognized the new government in Saigon.

KENNEDY AND THE SOVIETS

In April 1961, the Russians launched Yury Gagarin into near-space orbit and brought him home. Although the United States sent a man into space three weeks later, the flight was only a fifteen-minute ride of less than one orbit from the

The Berlin Wall, erected in June 1961, grimly symbolized the Cold War's separation of East and West.

launch site at Cape Canaveral, Florida. The Russian feat dealt a blow to the prestige of the United States and, by extension, to the image of the capitalist system in its competition with Soviet Communism among nations in the Third World. Kennedy, sensitive to the setbacks from the Bay of Pigs and the Russian manned flight, searched for an initiative that would put the United States ahead of the Russians and soon found it.

In late May 1961, in a special message to Congress, Kennedy called for the United States to "commit itself to achieving the goal, before this decade is out, of landing a man on the moon and returning him safely to earth." Pointing to "the battle" for the Third World, he emphasized "the impact of this adventure on the minds of men everywhere, who are attempting to make a determination on which road they should take." Many scientists opposed the moon program, called Project Apollo, believing that the moon could be probed more cheaply and effectively with unmanned space vehicles; but their views were overridden by policymakers and other scientists who understood that international prestige—not to mention benefits to the aero-

> *"Kennedy, shaken by Khrushchev's bullying, declared the defense of West Berlin 'the greatest testing place of Western courage and will.'"*

space industry—was at stake. During the 1960s, the United States would spend some $30 billion on Project Apollo—fifteen times more than it had invested in the Manhattan Project—a major feat of engineering that drew on the resources of engineers and scientists, universities, aerospace firms, and hundreds of subcontractors.

Crisis over Berlin. Kennedy, fearing that the Bay of Pigs had chilled U.S.-Soviet relations, was encouraged in May 1961 to learn that Khrushchev would welcome face-to-face discussions. In a meeting in Vienna the next month, Khrushchev, taking the measure of Kennedy—"the young millionaire," he later put it—appeared to judge him easy to intimidate. Uppermost in Khrushchev's mind was the question of Germany, particularly Berlin, an island of Western capitalism deep in East Germany and a magnet for East Germans fleeing to the West. He wanted the West out of Berlin likening the presence of American troops there to "a bone stuck in the throat"; and he was determined to stop the torrent of refugees, by then totaling 3.5 million and amounting to about 30,000 a month. He told Kennedy that he intended to sign his own peace agreement with East Germany, which would likely end the West's access to Berlin and its occupation rights in the city. Kennedy replied that the United States would not tolerate such action, that to do so would shred the credibility of its commitments to collective security and lead to an unacceptable shift in the world balance of power. Khrushchev said bluntly that if the United States insisted on provoking war over Berlin, so be it.

Back in the United States, Kennedy, shaken by Khrushchev's bullying, declared the defense of West Berlin "the greatest testing place of Western courage and will." He tripled draft calls, mobilized 150,000 reservists, and requested an additional $3.2 billion in defense spending. Khrushchev likewise ordered major hikes in Russian defense spending. In mid-August, the East Germans cut off the refugee flow by building a wall of concrete and barbed wire along the line dividing East and West in Berlin. Amid the ensuing uproar, Kennedy avoided escalating the crisis but did send 1,500 troops down the autobahn to West Berlin, a signal that the United States would stand by the city. Through the fall, the Berlin crisis eased, with Khrushchev backing down from his threat to sign a peace treaty with East Germany.

In September, however, the Soviet Union resumed nuclear testing in the atmosphere, breaking a *de facto* testing moratorium in place among the world's nuclear powers since 1958. Resolved to defend the United States' strategic interests, Kennedy ordered a building up of the nation's strategic arsenal, and in April 1962 a resumption of nuclear testing. Between 1961 and 1964, defense spending jumped 13 percent, reaching $53.6 billion.

The Cuban Missile Crisis. In March 1962, Khrushchev, privately calling American nuclear behavior "particularly arrogant," declared, "It's high time their long arms were cut shorter." Two months later, he sent to Cuba at least three dozen nuclear warheads, missiles capable of carrying them to most of the continental United States, and a contingent of Soviet commanders with independent authority to launch the weapons. Policymakers at the time, including Kennedy, wondered why Khrushchev chose to pursue such a risky course, and historians since then have similarly puzzled over his reasons, especially with the increasing availability of documents and memoirs from the former Soviet Union. Khrushchev, who had inklings of Operation Mongoose, apparently wanted to bolster Cuba's defenses against a second invasion, which he feared Kennedy might mount, this time with American troops. The Soviets supplied Castro with antiaircraft missiles and some 42,000 soldiers.

Khrushchev considered Kennedy young and inexperienced, perhaps likely to let him get away with an initiative that could also redress the Soviet disadvantage in strategic nuclear forces and offset the Jupiter missiles that the United States had begun installing in Turkey after *Sputnik*. Khrushchev may also have considered the missiles in Cuba a powerful bargaining chip to force the West out of Berlin, having admonished an American visitor, "Do you need Berlin? Like hell you need it . . . we can swat your ass."

Even as the Soviets installed their offensive missiles, Khrushchev assured Kennedy that they were not doing so, but on October 16, 1962,

surveillance data obtained from a U-2 overflight showed that he had lied. Kennedy and the highest-ranking members of his administration began deliberating immediately on how to respond, with the president secretly recording much of the debate on audio tape, transcripts of which became available in the 1990s. The president observed that it "doesn't make any difference if you get blown up by an ICBM flying from the Soviet Union or one that was ninety miles away." But he could not permit this unprecedented intrusion into the American sphere of interest. If left unanswered, it would encourage Khrushchev to further action, damage American credibility, and surely provoke a savage domestic political reaction. Kennedy was resolved to get the missiles out of Cuba, one way or another.

In tense meetings during the next six days, the president and his advisers debated how to do this. One faction, including the Joint Chiefs of Staff and, at the outset, Robert F. Kennedy, argued for an invasion or a surprise air strike against the missile bases. Another faction, including Secretary of Defense Robert S. McNamara and State Department officials, argued strongly against that course, one of its members contending that an air strike would be tantamount to inflicting a Pearl Harbor on a small country. The administration eventually resolved on a naval blockade that would prevent So-

Aerial surveillance reveals a missile base at San Cristobal, Cuba, October 1962.

viet ships from bringing additional military shipments to Cuba, a policy that would demonstrate the United States' refusal to tolerate the missiles and simultaneously give Khrushchev time to withdraw. On October 22, disclosing the crisis in a major television address, Kennedy announced that he was establishing a blockade and demanding the removal of the missiles and the destruction of their bases. He also warned Khrushchev that the United States would not tolerate any retaliation in Berlin or elsewhere and that a nuclear attack originating in Cuba would require "a full retaliatory response upon the Soviet Union."

Millions of Americans spent the succeeding days fearful that nuclear war might be imminent. American forces mobilized in Florida for an invasion. While the Soviets in Cuba rushed to complete the missile bases, their ships, some presumably carrying additional missiles, neared the island. Kennedy established the blockade line close to Cuba so as to maximize Khrushchev's time for reconsideration. On Octo-

ber 24, the Soviets signaled their ships to halt at sea. The next morning, the Soviet freighters turned around, while vessels without munitions agreed to be stopped and searched on the high seas. Dean Rusk remarked, with a relief that was widely shared, "We're eyeball to eyeball, and I think the other fellow just blinked."

Still, the missiles already in Cuba remained. On October 26, a long letter from Khrushchev arrived at the White House offering to remove them if the United States would pledge not to invade Cuba. But the next day, Kennedy received a second, more demanding letter proposing a trade of the Soviet missiles in Cuba for the American missiles in Turkey. On the advice of Robert Kennedy, who by now had been persuaded by the moral arguments against an air strike, the president ignored the second letter and accepted the basic terms of the first. At the same time, in a back-channel meeting with the Soviet ambassador, Robert Kennedy dealt with the question of the Jupiters. For several years, American policymakers had considered them obsolete—"a pile of junk," McNamara put it—and had been planning to remove them anyway. The attorney general assured the ambassador that the Jupiters would be gone from Turkey soon after the crisis ended. The next day, October 28, Khrushchev agreed to withdraw the missiles from Cuba.

Khrushchev soon brought the missiles home and tore down their bases, although most of the 42,000 Soviet military personnel remained in Cuba. By the spring of 1963, the United States had removed the last of its Jupiters from Turkey, replacing them with the far more effective missiles carried on a Polaris submarine cruising the area. Although Khrushchev was widely regarded as the loser in the crisis, he later noted, "Our aim was to preserve [a Communist] Cuba. Today Cuba exists." Kennedy declined to gloat publicly, contenting himself with the praise that was showered upon him for his handling of the crisis.

The Test-Ban Treaty. Sobered by the face-off, Kennedy was all the more eager for a general nuclear test-ban treaty. He had learned about its advantages from his science adviser, Jerome Wiesner, an electrical engineer from MIT who presided over a newly created White House Office of Science and Technology, populated by scientists working on policy-related technical issues, mainly in national security. Wiesner emphasized the threat of nuclear proliferation and the danger of radioactive fallout from nuclear testing in the atmosphere. "You mean that stuff is in the rain out there?" Kennedy asked

Cartoonist Herblock's plea, May 1963, for Kennedy and Johnson (left) and Khrushchev (right) to put the nuclear genie back in the bottle by agreeing to a nuclear test-ban treaty.

him one day. In a notable speech at American University in June 1963, the president urged that both the United States and the Soviet Union rethink the Cold War, observing that both sides were "caught up in a vicious and dangerous cycle in which suspicion on one side breeds suspicion on the other, and new weapons beget counterweapons." Each side had to stop demonizing the other and join in pursuing their common interests.

That month, Kennedy and Khrushchev agreed to establish a hot line between their two countries to reduce the chance that a nuclear war might be ignited by miscalculation or misunderstanding. But achieving a test-ban treaty was made more difficult by the Joint Chiefs of Staff. Backed by conservative scientists, they insisted that a ban on underground tests was unpoliceable without more annual on-site inspections than the Soviets would accept. Kennedy compromised, obtaining an agreement with the Soviets and Britain for a test-ban treaty outlawing tests in the atmosphere, outer space, and under water. The Senate ratified the treaty by a vote of 80 to 19, subject to the proviso from the Joint Chiefs that underground testing would continue.

France, which had the bomb, and China, which wanted it, refused to sign the treaty. Moreover, the United States conducted many more tests, although underground, in the 1960s than it had in the 1950s. The Kennedy administration, having already decided to add ten Polaris submarines to the fleet and to double the Minuteman missile force to 800, continued the buildup and pressed ahead with developing MIRVs—multiple independently targetable reentry vehicles (that is, warheads) for installation on a single missile, each of them guidable to an independent target. Arms-control efforts in the future would have to concern themselves with the systems that delivered nuclear explosives even more than with the explosives themselves. Yet if the treaty did not even slow the nuclear arms race, it did greatly reduce the hazards of radioactive fallout and signaled a heartening thaw in the Cold War.

"Arms-control efforts in the future would have to concern themselves with the systems that delivered nuclear explosives even more than with the explosives themselves."

Kennedy at Home

Kennedy placed economic growth—a major factor in getting the country moving again and reducing the 7 percent unemployment rate—at the center of his domestic agenda. He won passage of several economic stimulus measures, notably an increase in the minimum wage (from $1.00 to $1.25 an hour), tax incentives for business, aid to depressed areas, and an expansion of Social Security. In 1963, he proposed a broad-based tax cut that would stimulate the economy by leaving more money in the hands of consumers and business.

Liberal critics faulted Kennedy, pointing out that a broad tax cut would favor business and the well-to-do. Kennedy argued that growth would improve conditions for everyone, including the poor.

However, he had come to recognize that the benefits of aggregate increases in national income tended to bypass many Americans. He learned from Michael Harrington's passionate *The Other America* (1962) that 40 to 50 million Americans, the large majority of them white, lived "at levels beneath those necessary for human decency." Experts found that the poor were marked by one or more of certain characteristics—over sixty-five, nonwhite, or living in a household headed by a woman or in a little-educated family—and that a "culture of poverty" was transmitted from generation to generation. Now as at the end of World War II, blacks earned about half what whites did, and the unemployment rate among breadwinning black males was three times higher than among comparable whites. In the hope of helping both the white and black poor, Kennedy called on his advisers to draw up a plan emphasizing job training, education, nutrition, and direct aid to the poor.

The combination of the Apollo program and the defense buildup helped produce unbalanced budgets and with them the threat of inflation. To help keep the imbalance under control, Secretary of Defense McNamara introduced new methods for analyzing budgetary and management issues at the Pentagon. To prevent inflation, Kennedy urged wage and price restraints on labor and business. In 1962, he persuaded the steelworkers' union to agree to a new contract with more moderate wage increases than it had obtained previously. He was infuriated when U.S. Steel and five other companies promptly announced price hikes. "My father always told me that all businessmen were sons-of-bitches, but I never believed it till now," he said angrily, in a widely reported remark. Declaring war on the industry, Kennedy forced the steel companies to back down.

Kennedy insisted that, having won the presidency by a mere 119,000 votes out of 68 million cast, he had no mandate for a program of sweeping change. Despite the hefty Democratic majorities on Capitol Hill, both houses were dominated by coalitions of Republicans and conservative Democrats, an obstacle to liberal legislation. He did submit several reform measures to Congress, including a federal health care program and federal aid to education, but they failed. Kennedy, never a Senate insider and caring less about domestic issues than about foreign affairs, was disinclined to pressure Congress. He made no headway on Capitol Hill with the broad tax cut, the main economic stimulus of his administration. Still, his spending on defense, a kind of military Keynesianism, helped boost economic growth, and so did the money poured into the Apollo program, which by 1964 virtually quintupled the NASA budget to more than $4 billion a year. On the whole, Kennedy's policies helped initiate a new era of prosperity, marked by a leap in the yearly economic growth rate—between 1961 and 1963, the economy expanded by a robust 13 percent—a decline in unemployment, and an annual inflation rate of less than 2 percent.

> *"Americans ranked nuclear physicists third in occupational status—ahead of everyone except Supreme Court justices and physicians."*

SCIENCE, TECHNOLOGY, AND THE ECONOMY

The economy also benefited from the new knowledge, technologies, and trained scientific manpower generated by public investment in scientific research. Defense and space took the lion's share of the federal R&D dollar, but people identified scientists and engineers as makers not only of bombs and rockets but also of the day's technological miracles—jet planes, computers, and direct dial telephoning, transistor radios, stereophonic phonographs, and color television, the videotaping that was transforming the coverage of news and sports, and the Xerox machines that were revolutionizing photocopying. Private firms were manufacturing nuclear reactors, spinoffs from the navy's reactors for submarines. Electric utilities, believing them reliable and competitive with fossil-fuel generators, were buying them—between 1963 and 1971, they would order 100 nuclear plants—and using them to power more than a million homes in the United States.

High-technology companies followed close on the heels of local Ph.D. programs—as on Route 128 outside of Boston, where the vitality of the area's remarkable electronic and computer firms was attributed to the scientific might of Cambridge's universities; or along the San Francisco Bay peninsula, where scientists and engineers trained at Stanford University and the University of California at Berkeley spawned a microelectronics industry and staked out the beginnings of Silicon Valley. Americans ranked nuclear physicists third in occupational status—they had been fifteenth in 1947—ahead of everyone except Supreme Court justices and physicians.

Federal funds for research and development continued to climb, reaching almost $15 billion by 1965, accounting for almost one-sixth of the federal budget. The fraction of the money that went to basic research increased about a third over what it had been in 1960. The federal money drew many European scientists to the United States, enough to raise cries abroad of an alarming "brain drain." Between 1956 and 1965, Americans won or shared in eight of the ten Nobel Prizes awarded in physics and three of the prizes in both chemistry and biology. In this era—the "age of the knowledge industry," a leading university president called it—support for R&D generated commanding prestige and was expected to stimulate endless economic expansion.

HORIZONS OF HEALTH

Affluence, the march of scientific medicine, and the rise in the number of older Americans all combined to raise the demands Americans placed on the health care system. Liberals, having been beaten on national health insurance in the late forties, now addressed the issue by spotlighting the needs of the elderly. One in six people over sixty-five required hospital care, the price of which had doubled in the 1950s. By 1963, with Kennedy's endorsement, medical care for the aged had won a place on the nation's legislative agenda. That year, Congress passed the first of several measures to expand education in the health professions. By 1967, it had also raised the health research budget to $1.4 billion, almost quadrupling the level in 1960.

By the early 1960s, Americans were recognizing that mental illness was a malady to be dealt with openly rather than hidden away in snake-pit asylums. In 1963, President Kennedy, who had a mentally ill sister, endorsed the establishment of new "community-based" mental health services, with the result that Congress passed the Mental Retardation Facilities and Community Mental Health Centers Act, which provided out-patient services for such problems as alcoholism, unwed motherhood, and delinquency. The law was part of a broader movement to deinstitutionalize the mentally disabled and return them to the community. The effort would reduce the number of patients in mental hospitals, including some who were severely ill, from about 500,000 in 1965 to 100,000 in 1985, consigning many of them to homelessness and drug addiction because many communities had neither the resources nor the will to care for them. But at the time, advocates of deinstitutionalization expected that, as Kennedy put it, "reliance on the cold mercy of custodial isolation will be supplanted by the open warmth of community concern and capability."

KENNEDY AND CIVIL RIGHTS

 John Kennedy did not embrace the **civil rights movement** when he was in the Senate, and he kept his distance during the first two years of his presidency, finding it a distraction from foreign affairs. He feared that endorsing the movement would alienate southern Democrats, jeopardize his legislative program, and risk the loss of the 1964 election. Kennedy nominated several hard-core segregationists to federal judgeships in the South and stalled for two years before fulfilling a campaign pledge to end segregation in federally assisted housing with a "stroke of the [presidential] pen." He displayed little empathy for black anger and resentments, seeming to regard them as irritants to be managed rather than addressed.

However, black activism and white violence compelled the administration to act. In May 1961, the Congress of Racial Equality (CORE) launched Freedom Rides on buses into the deep South to spotlight the widespread violation of a recent Supreme Court order outlawing segregation in interstate bus stations. At a stop in Alabama, the Freedom Riders, more than half of them black, many of them students, were beaten with pipes, bicycle chains, and baseball bats; at another, they were mobbed, and the tires of one of their buses were slashed. On the eve of his meeting with Khrushchev, President Kennedy fearing that racial confrontations diminished the United States' world stature,

"John Kennedy did not embrace the civil rights movement when he was in the Senate, and he kept his distance during the first two years of his presidency, finding it a distraction from foreign affairs."

Federal marshals escort James Meredith at the University of Mississippi, 1962.

called for a cooling off. James Farmer, the head of CORE, retorted that blacks "have been cooling off for 150 years. If we cool off any more, we'll be in a deep freeze."

Attorney General Robert Kennedy, deciding that the Supreme Court's order had to be enforced, dispatched several hundred federal marshals to quell the violence. At his request, the Interstate Commerce Commission prohibited the use of segregated facilities by interstate carriers. He brought Justice Department suits to protect voting rights in 145 counties and authorized department attorneys to appear as "friends of the court" in a broad spectrum of civil rights suits. He quintupled the number of black staff in the department and nominated five blacks to the federal bench. Still, much to the disappointment of blacks, the attorney general tried to discourage direct action, urging reliance on the ballot and the courts, and refrained from intervening with federal force unless local law enforcement broke down.

But southern blacks knew from experience that local government, including law enforcement, often tolerated or even encouraged antiblack violence. In October 1962, a federal court ordered the University of Mississippi to admit a black

933

Martin Luther King declares, "I have a dream" before a quarter million marchers at the Lincoln Memorial, August 28, 1963.

air force veteran, James Meredith, who wished to complete his education there. Governor Ross Barnett adamantly opposed the action, and at the university, in Oxford, a riotous mob tried to prevent Meredith's enrollment, attacking his escort of federal marshals. Robert Kennedy dispatched 5,000 federal troops to restore order. Meredith went to school under the protection of federal guards, graduating in 1963.

Birmingham and Beyond. The pressure kept mounting on the Kennedy administration to act on civil rights, as black activists, supported by increasing numbers of students and fed-up adults, challenged white racism in cities and towns across the South. The Reverend Fred Shuttlesworth of Birmingham, Alabama, the courageous head of the Alabama Christian Movement for Human Rights, urged Martin Luther King Jr. to confront the rabid segregationists who dominated his city, the state's largest and a striving business center, two out of five of whose citizens were black. "I assure you," he told King, "if you come to Birmingham, this movement . . . can really shake the country."

Eager to force Kennedy's hand, King came, initiating demonstrations on Good Friday 1963. In early May, more than a thousand children joined him in a protest march only to be slammed by torrential streams from high-pressure water hoses that the police chief, Bull Connor, had ordered his force

to turn on them. Americans were revolted to see television images of children blasted by water, shocked by electric cattle prods, and attacked by snarling dogs. Kennedy remarked that Bull Connor had "helped [the civil rights movement] as much as Abraham Lincoln." The Kennedy administration quietly negotiated a settlement with Birmingham's anxious business establishment that halted the demonstrations in exchange for the desegregation of stores and lunch counters and the opening of clerical and sales jobs to blacks.

Civil rights protests swept through the South, and the Kennedy administration, worried that the movement might turn more militant, urged national business and civic organizations to pressure their local members to desegregate. The resistance of many white southerners was exemplified by Governor George Wallace of Alabama, who at his inauguration had pledged, "Segregation now . . . tomorrow . . . [and] forever!" and who, in June 1963, defied a federal court order compelling the University of Alabama to admit two black students. President Kennedy won their admission by sending federal troops to Tuscaloosa and enlisting the aid of Alabama's business leaders.

By now, the black revolution had engaged Kennedy's sense of right and wrong. In mid-June, in a passionate television address, he told the nation that civil rights was "a moral issue," at the heart of which was "the question . . . whether all Americans are to be afforded equal rights and equal opportunities." The president pointedly asked, if an American, simply "because his skin is dark . . . cannot enjoy the full and free life which all of us want, then who among us would be content to have the color of his skin changed and stand in his place?" Within a week, Kennedy sent Congress a civil rights bill that aimed primarily at desegregating public accommodations and protecting voting rights.

Thousands of white Americans, many of them college students, had become civil rights activists or sympathizers, drawn to the movement by its moral purpose, the camaraderie of its marches, and its folk-rock music. The young Bob Dylan rapidly emerged in the early 1960s as a leading musical voice, a raspy, sardonic bard of protest who put Americans on notice that "The Times They Are a-Changin'." Dylan's "Blowin' in the Wind," recorded in spirited harmony by Peter, Paul, and Mary, was the first protest song to make the Hit Parade. In late August 1963, some 250,000 people, including 50,000 whites, gathered before the Lincoln Memorial, where, along with a rapt national television audience, they heard Dylan twang out his warnings, the folksinger Joan Baez soar silver-toned through the movement's anthem, "We Shall Overcome," and Martin Luther King Jr. memorably sermonize, "I have a dream that my four little children will one day live in a nation where they will not be judged by the color of their skin but by the content of their character."

But much of the South was deaf to the impassioned calls for justice. In Jackson, Mississippi, late the same night of the president's speech in June, a sniper gunned down Medgar Evers, an activist in the local NAACP who had been organizing sit-ins in the downtown Woolworth's. In Birmingham, Alabama, less than three weeks after the March on Washington, a black church was bombed, killing four girls attending a Bible school class.

THE QUALITY OF LIFE

By what he said and often by what he did, Kennedy celebrated admirable human endeavor for its own sake, beyond considerations of Cold War competition and economic pump priming (stimulation). His natural inclinations in this direction were strengthened by his wife, Jackie, who redecorated the White House to showcase American art and history and guided the nation on a television tour of the results. The Kennedys hosted elegant evenings for artists, writers, and musicians such as the great cellist Pablo Casals, who concertized in the East Room. The president celebrated scientific and technological achievement for its own sake, embossing it with a kind of cultural pride. One evening, he brought several dozen Nobel laureates in science to the White House for dinner, calling the group "the most extraordinary collection of talent, of human knowledge, that has ever been gathered together at the White House ... with the possible exception of when Thomas Jefferson dined alone."

The Kennedy rhetoric and images resonated with the new generation of Americans, better educated and more affluent than their predecessors, eager for material rewards but hungry for satisfactions beyond materialism for themselves and their children. In the 1960s, Americans grew increasingly concerned about their quality of life, including the vitality of the arts, the face of the urban landscape, and the health of the natural environment.

> *"In Birmingham, Alabama, less than three weeks after the March on Washington, a black church was bombed, killing four girls attending a Bible school class."*

Cultural Stirrings. The early 1960s marked the beginning of an explosion of high-cultural consumption. When in 1962 Leonardo da Vinci's serene and enigmatic painting *Mona Lisa* came to the United States, more than half a million people visited the National Gallery in Washington, D.C., to catch a glimpse, and another million swept past it in New York City. Many Americans tuned in to the growing number of FM radio stations, about a quarter of which were nonprofits devoted to broadcasting educational material and classical music. The growth of public television was encouraged by Newton Minow, the new chairman of the Federal Communications Commission, who in his first speech to broadcasters called TV a "vast wasteland." Minow failed to budge commercial broadcasting, but the number of public television stations burgeoned, reaching about 100 by mid-decade and providing a menu of serious music, debate, and drama.

During the 1950s, the promotion of high culture had been urged as a weapon in the Cold War—a way to compete against the Soviet export of stunning ballet dancers and to convince suspicious foreigners that American capitalism was capable of more than shallow materialism. Now people contended that the arts should also be embraced as a community responsibility. Philanthropic foundations—notably the Ford Foundation, which became the largest patron of the arts in the country—helped vitalize operas, symphony orchestras, repertory theaters, and ballet companies in cities across the country. Such enterprises were assisted locally by coalitions of wealthy individuals and public-spirited corporations—notably in Los Angeles, where Dorothy Chandler, the doyenne of the city's leading newspaper family, led its business and financial elite to establish the Los Angeles Music Center; and in New York City, where even several foreign governments joined in the spectacularly successful effort to create the Lincoln Center for the Performing Arts, at a cost of $185 million. The Kennedys added cachet to these cultural stirrings. They also brought a cultural consultant into the White House who in 1963 produced a report that, going far beyond the New Deal's relief assistance to artists, called for a full-scale federal program in support of the arts.

Just as art was becoming a part of chic consumer culture, a new school of artists broke from abstract expressionism and began producing what was dubbed "pop art"—paintings,

Campbell's Soup Can, by the pop artist Andy Warhol, 1962.

collage, and sculpture in the accessible idiom of the commonplace. One pioneer of the trend was Roy Lichtenstein, who painted canvases resembling comic-strip panels. Another was Andy Warhol, originally a commercial illustrator, who made art out of repetitive images of Campbell's Soup cans, traffic accidents, and faces of the movie stars Marlon Brando and Marilyn Monroe. The Swedish-born artist Claes Oldenburg found his materials in such everyday objects as food, chairs, neon lights, and smoke. "I am for an art that embroils itself with everyday crap and still comes out on top," he said. Critics interpreted pop art as, variously, deadpan satire or celebrations of commercial culture, at once an acceptance of corporate dominance and an ironic commentary upon it. Whatever its intentions, pop art quickly won national attention and commanded skyrocketing prices. Its products, exhibited by museums and snapped up by private collectors, fed the hunger in the United States for the consumption of culture.

Architectural Preservation. Even as the flow to the suburbs continued, the architectural fate of the nation's cities began

to capture the public's attention. Many objected to urban renewal because it was destroying neighborhoods and communities, often replacing them with modernist structures, tall, faceless piles of steel and glass that lacked human connection to the city life around them. Roughly a quarter of the country's historical pieces of architecture, most of them built before 1830, had been destroyed, largely as a result of urban renewal. In *The Death and Life of Great American Cities* (1961), the magazine writer Jane Jacobs insisted on the "need for aged buildings," not only for their architectural value but for what they contributed to the multiply textured, vibrant qualities of urban life.

The preservation of buildings, practiced in the United States since the nineteenth century, had long been energized by a desire to preserve structures associated with important historical figures—for example, George Washington's home in Mount Vernon, Virginia. Now, urban Americans agitated to preserve older buildings, including the ornamental products of Victorian and Romanesque sensibilities that the modernists despised because of their scale and detail and their integral connection to their architectural surroundings. In 1963, hundreds of New Yorkers protested the destruction of Pennsylvania Station, McKim, Mead and White's soaring combination of Roman bath and modern train shed, by its utilitarian-oriented railroad owners.

Two years later, New York City established a City Landmarks Preservation Commission empowered to designate any building over thirty years old as a historical landmark and penalize owners who disregarded the law. Other cities soon followed suit, and in 1966, Congress passed the National Historic Preservation Act, which stipulated that major historic works of architecture were to be preserved. Across the country, community groups raised money for preservation efforts. Buildings that had outlived their initial purpose were saved by giving them new functions: in San Antonio, Texas, for example, the Lone Star Brewery building became an art museum, and in San Francisco an old chocolate factory was converted to the centerpiece of a retail complex called Ghirardelli Square.

Environmental Preservation. The concern for quality in life included a renewed emphasis on the value of uncorrupted preserves of nature—forests, streams, deserts, and mountains. The constituency for preservation of nature had been growing since the late 1940s, becoming more democratized than before World War I, when John Muir had fought to preserve the Hetch Hetchy Valley in Yosemite from inundation caused by damming. The country's spreading affluence gave people the time and means to visit the national parks, and many Americans hoped to find the unspoiled beauty of sights such as the Grand Teton Mountains relief from the sameness of suburbs, television, and fast-food restaurants.

In the developing West, the imperatives of the Cold War, particularly the dependence of national security on dynamic economic growth, added force to the conservation-for-use doctrine that had dominated environmental policies since the 1930s. As the geologist John Wesley Powell had recognized in the late nineteenth century, much of the West was arid, with not enough rain falling to sustain conventional agriculture. It required enormous supplies of water and electricity that were provided largely by federal water and power projects—irrigation canals, hydroelectric dams, and reservoirs. But irrigation tended to favor agribusiness over small farms and ranches. Dams inundated canyons and valleys, many of them belonging to Native Americans, and they angered people who cared about protecting western lands from human damage.

The revival of preservationism burst into full view during the early 1950s in the battle over Dinosaur National Monument in northwestern Colorado, near the Utah border. The monument covered hundreds of miles of wild, gorgeously colored canyons carved by the Green and Yampu Rivers, part of the Upper Basin of the Colorado River. Since the Truman years, the federal government's plans for the basin included the construction of two dams in Dinosaur, one of them at Echo Park. Western advocates of the dams argued that they were badly needed for the electric power and irrigation that would bolster economic development and national security. Preservationists fought the dams partly to protect the national park system, but mainly to prevent the loss forever of the river canyons of Echo Park itself. In 1956, with the Dinosaur dams becoming the most controversial environmental issue since Hetch Hetchy, Congress passed an omnibus bill authorizing the Upper Colorado Basin project without the two dams, substituting for them a dam at Glen Canyon in Arizona.

The Dinosaur battle united preservationists into a powerful coalition, including enthusiasts of white water, wildlife, and wilderness, and armed them with political, legal, and technical expertise. The victory encouraged them to go on the

> *"The revival of preservationism burst into full view during the early 1950s in the battle over Dinosaur National Monument in northwestern Colorado."*

offensive, lobbying for a law of broad-gauged wilderness preservation to prevent any future Echo Park initiatives. Unlike Eisenhower, Kennedy supported the proposed act, which would pass in 1964, defining wilderness as "an area where the earth and its community of life are untrammelled by man, where man himself is a visitor who does not remain." During the 1960s, membership in traditional environmental organizations skyrocketed, the Audubon Society's doubling, the Sierra Club's quintupling.

Poisons and Pollutions. The environmental agenda was significantly enlarged when in 1962 Rachel Carson, a biologist and gifted writer, published *Silent Spring*, a powerful dissection of the myriad ways that herbicides and pesticides, particularly DDT, were poisoning man and nature. Carson called the chemicals of weed and insect control "elixirs of death," explaining that they killed wildlife, especially birds, as they accumulated in the wild food chain, and that they threatened human health. "For the first time in the history of the world, every human being is now subjected to contact with dangerous chemicals, from the moment of conception until death," she wrote. Despite Carson's credentials, the book was greeted with a barrage of ridicule and denunciation from the chemical industry,

Rachel Carson, author of the eloquent environmental warning *Silent Spring*.

Smog blankets downtown Los Angeles.

parts of the food industry, academic scientists allied with both, and powerful sectors of the media. However, in a report published in May 1963, a special panel of Kennedy's Science Advisory Committee endorsed Carson's main conclusions, especially her view that pesticides, rather than being used until they were proved to be dangerous, should be demonstrated as safe before they were deployed. In 1972, the federal government banned the use of DDT, largely as a result of the outcry that Carson's book had raised.

In the meantime, *Silent Spring* captured enormous attention, prompting the environmental movement to embrace the goals of protecting nature and health against poisonous pollutions. Evidence of such pollution seemed to be everywhere. Smog beclouded the cities, and in the countryside green algae and dead fish marked the pollution of streams, the seepage of chemicals and sewage into the soil and lakes. Television showed millions the consequences of an oil spill off the coast of Santa Barbara, California, in 1969, broadcasting images of black slicks covering the sea surface, the beaches, and untold numbers of hapless birds. Expectations of good health and longer life spans were rising as conventional sanitation combined with antibiotics appeared to be wiping out infectious disease. There was a corresponding increase in the attribution of noninfectious diseases—notably cancer—to environmental causes, and a comparable growth in eagerness to wipe the causes out.

The new issues of poisons and pollution drew a new generation of activists into environmentalism. They responded to Paul Ehrlich's *Population Bomb* (1968) and Barry Commoner's *The Closing Circle* (1970), which together warned against the threat to the viability of an endlessly exploited and overpopulated planet. In 1970, they spearheaded Earth Day, a nationwide manifestation of antipollution protests and environmental cleanups. The new activists, eager to distance themselves from what they called "the birds and squirrels people," stood for a new agenda of environmental reform, especially the restoration of the land, air, and water to their unpolluted states.

THE THOUSANDTH DAY

On November 22, 1963, John Kennedy and his wife were motorcading in an open car through cheering crowds in Dallas, Texas. Suddenly he crumpled, his head shattered by an assassin's rifle fire. The news of the president's death flashed across the country and around the globe. An outpouring of disbelieving sorrow flooded through the United States and washed over the planet. Television, aided since 1962 by communications satellites, carried the succeeding events to the world: the capture of a prime suspect, Lee Harvey Oswald, an unstable Soviet sympathizer and champion of Castro; the murder of Oswald in a Dallas police station by Jack Ruby, the owner of a strip joint who said he had been overcome with grief for the slain president; the funeral cortege with its riderless black horse and the brave salute given it by the president's small son; and, finally the burial at Arlington National Cemetery, where his grieving family lit an eternal flame.

Jackie Kennedy, in an interview that soon appeared in *Life* magazine, likened the Kennedy administration to King Arthur's Camelot, stating that it comprised "a magic moment in American history, when gallant men danced with beautiful women, when great deeds were done, when artists, writers, and poets met at the White House and the barbarians beyond the walls were held back." Perhaps John Kennedy, resistant to illusions, would have been the first to raise a skeptical brow to his widow's mythmaking. He had achieved the test-ban treaty, committed federal powers on behalf of the civil rights movement, got the economy moving again; but he had also presided over an escalation of the nuclear arms race, temporized on civil rights, and stimulated the economy with heavy expenditures on missiles and space. At the time of his death, key elements of his legislative program—the tax cut, the civil rights bill, and Medicare—were stalled in Congress.

How Kennedy would have dealt with Vietnam had he not been assassinated is beyond knowing. It is also highly disputed. The government of South Vietnam remained unstable and in danger of losing the war to Ho Chi Minh. Kennedy's defenders argue that in the fall of 1963 he had begun to talk privately of withdrawing American troops from Vietnam after the 1964 election and that he said in a CBS television interview, "In the final analysis, it is their war. They are the ones who will have to win it or lose it." But he added in the interview that he did not believe the United States should withdraw. Invoking the domino theory, he equated the support of South Vietnam with the defense of Asia declaring, "This is a very important struggle." Most of his close advisers agreed, and they would bring that view to his successor's administration.

Still, Kennedy's achievements were not inconsiderable for the limited time—the thousand-plus days—he had occupied the White House and for the conservative majorities he faced on Capitol Hill. His bright wit, ironic humor, and zestful open-mindedness greatly advanced the breakaway from the solemn conformities of the Eisenhower years. He electrified the young, inspiring many of them to political engagement, made irreverence fashionable once again, and put the quality of life, including culture and health, on the national agenda. During the months before his death, Kennedy himself appeared to be thinking anew about the fraught issues of war and peace, race and poverty. He was cut down before his contemporaries or, for that matter, history could know where he might have tried to lead his country.

Lyndon Johnson: Taking Charge

Moments after Kennedy was shot, the Secret Service rushed Vice-President Lyndon Johnson to Air Force One, where he was sworn in as the thirty-sixth president of the United States as his wife and Jackie Kennedy, her clothing spattered with blood, looked on. In the harrowing days that followed, Johnson reassured the American people and foreign leaders that the government of the United States was intact and shouldered his presidential duties with surefooted strength. To deal with the storm of questions swirling around the assassi-

nation, he promptly appointed an investigative commission under Chief Justice Earl Warren. It concluded in 1964 that the murder had in fact been committed by Lee Harvey Oswald and that he had acted alone. Critics then and later challenged these conclusions, claiming that Kennedy was the victim of one kind of conspiracy or another. But most scholars have found no credible evidence for any of these theories and have upheld the judgment of the commission.

Few politicos were as well prepared to take charge of the presidency as Lyndon Baines Johnson. Fifty-five years old, he had spent twenty-four years in Congress, half of them in the Senate, including his last six as majority leader. He began as an acolyte of Franklin Roosevelt and the New Deal—he liked to be called LBJ, just as Roosevelt was known as FDR—but he turned conservative after World War II, defending big corporations, especially those in Texas oil and gas, against big government. At the same time, he steered federal projects like the Manned Spacecraft Center into his state, growing rich himself with the help of his political connections and the shrewd business acumen of his wife, Claudia Taylor ("Ladybird") Johnson. As majority leader, he adopted flexible, middle-of-the-road positions, pursuing a politics of consensus to mobilize the Senate behind Eisenhower's internationalist foreign policy and moderate domestic programs.

Lyndon Johnson, with his wife on his right and Jackie Kennedy at his left, takes the presidential oath of office aboard *Air Force One*, November 22, 1963.

Tall and physically imposing, Johnson built consensus with a formidable combination of persuasiveness, intelligence, and instinct for the jugular—what insiders called the Johnson treatment. His detractors considered him a wheeler-dealer, often devious, cruel, and vindictive. Still, he was capable of generosity and compassion. Before turning to politics, he had taught briefly in a public school with many Hispanic children, and the experience had helped make him a passionate enemy of poverty and the illiteracy and disease that accompanied it. He knew that, as a southerner especially, he had to confront the issue of race, and he felt deeply that blacks suffered from historic wrongs that should be made right. Now he came to the presidency emancipated from the constraints of his southern base, saddened by how he had arrived in office but relishing the opportunity to use his considerable talents, experience, and knowledge of government in service of an expansive view of American possibilities.

> *"Johnson built consensus with a formidable combination of persuasiveness, intelligence, and instinct for the jugular—what insiders called the Johnson treatment."*

ENACTING THE KENNEDY PROGRAM

Johnson kept Kennedy's cabinet and urged Congress to memorialize the martyred president by moving quickly on his bills for a tax cut and for civil rights. Within four months of taking office, he won passage of a $10 billion tax reduction, with the result that by 1966 the economy grew by almost another 25 percent, driving unemployment down to 4.5 percent and producing a budget surplus. The civil rights bill, passing the House with equal rapidity, ran into a southern filibuster in the Senate. LBJ intervened, applying the Johnson treatment to key Republicans who then led party centrists to join with northern Democrats to shut off the filibuster and pass the bill.

The most sweeping such legislation since Reconstruction, the Civil Rights Act of 1964 outlawed racial discrimination in public accommodations engaged in interstate commerce such as restaurants and hotels, empowered the attorney general to bring suits against school segregation, and strengthened federal protection of voting rights. The bill also prohibited discrimination in employment on the basis of race, color, religion, or national origin, and it established the Equal Employment Opportunity Commission to enforce the prohibition. In 1965, to open wider the doors of opportunity,

President Johnson issued an executive order requiring federal institutions and contractors to take affirmative action toward employing more nonwhites.

The day after Johnson took office, his chief economic adviser, drawing on the work that Kennedy had initiated, presented a series of antipoverty proposals to the president. "That's my kind of program," Johnson responded. Soon announcing to Congress that it was time to declare "unconditional war on poverty in America," he proposed an attack of unprecedented magnitude and scope. The Economic Opportunity Act, which Congress passed in mid-1964, authorized almost $1 billion for a variety of efforts, including Head Start for disadvantaged youngsters and the Community Action Program, whose purpose was to obtain "maximum feasible participation" of the poor in devising and running the antipoverty effort.

LIBERTY, EQUALITY, AND THE SUPREME COURT

During the 1960s, a cascade of landmark decisions issued from the Warren Court that strengthened political equality and enlarged the scope of civil liberties. In *Baker v. Carr* (1962), it held unconstitutional the creation of state legislative districts that made one district grossly unequal in population to another, a malapportionment that gave rural districts in many states greater power than the more populous urban and suburban districts. In several follow-up cases in 1964, the Court laid down the standard of one person, one vote—which meant that every citizen was entitled to equal representation in the legislature. The Court ruled against officially sponsored Bible reading and prayer in the public schools. It also strengthened freedom of the press, holding in *Times v. Sullivan* (1964) that newspapers that published criticisms of public officials could not be held libelous unless they could be shown to have done so with "actual malice."

The justices ruled unanimously in *Gideon v. Wainwright* (1963) that an indigent defendant charged with a felony must be provided with an attorney at public expense. In a later case, they decided that suspects also had a right to a lawyer when under police interrogation. Dramatically extending these rulings in the case of *Miranda v. Arizona* (1966), the Warren Court found that police had to protect suspects against inadvertent self-incrimination by advising them when taken into custody that they had a right to an attorney and a right to remain silent. In *Griswold v. Connecticut* (1965), the Court struck down state bans on the use of contraceptives by married couples—it would do the same for single people in 1972—finding for the first time that the Constitution established a "zone of privacy" into which it would be "repulsive," as one justice observed, for the state to reach. In the late 1960s, the Court seemed likely to continue its bolstering of political equality and civil liberties, since it now included several Kennedy and Johnson appointees, including Thurgood Marshall, the first black justice.

TOWARD THE GREAT SOCIETY

The New Right and the Election of 1964. Lyndon Johnson, nominated in his own right for president at the Democratic convention, chose as his running mate Hubert Humphrey, a liberal senator from Minnesota and a spirited campaigner. Johnson ran on the theme of the Great Society, a vision for his domestic agenda that he had begun advancing in the spring. In conception, the Great Society melded the themes that ran through the president's initiatives against poverty and racism, the Supreme Court's enlargements of the meanings of liberty and equality, and the desire in the land for satisfactions beyond material abundance. The Great Society "is a place where the city of man serves not only the needs of the body and the demands of commerce but the desire for beauty and the hunger for community," Johnson said. "It is a place where man can renew contact with nature. It is a place which honors creation for its own sake . . . [and] where men are more concerned with the quality of their goals than with the quantity of their goods."

The Great Society flew against the tenets of a reenergized conservative movement that was seeking control of the Republican Party. Originating in the 1950s, the movement owed its revival in part to ideologues such as the journalist William F. Buckley, the son of a wealthy right-wing Catholic businessman and himself a fervent anti-Communist, defender of Joseph McCarthy, enemy of government regulation, and founder of the *National Review*, a journal devoted to the creation of a New Right. The movement spawned new activist groups such as the Young Americans for Freedom, which espoused views similar to Buckley's. It found adherents among Americans, many of them Catholics and evangelical Christians, who were angry at the failure of the United States to roll back Communism, and

among antagonists of big government, especially in the Southwest and West, who resented federal intrusions, taxation, and programs for lower-income and minority groups.

Many white southerners, furious at black gains and the federal role in fostering them, embraced the New Right. So did a growing number of white blue-collar workers in the North, worried that the drive for racial equality would lead to the integration of their workplaces and neighborhoods. During the spring of 1964, these workers voted heavily for George Wallace in the Democratic primaries in Wisconsin, Indiana, and Maryland, helping him win between 30 and 45 percent of the vote in these states and revealing that a white backlash against the civil rights movement was taking hold. North and South, the renewed conservatism was also stimulated by wrath against the Supreme Court's rulings on integration, censorship, and religion in the schools. Since the late 1950s, parts of the country had been dotted with billboards that read, "Impeach Earl Warren." A congressman from Alabama snapped that the Court had "put the Negroes in the schools and now they've driven God out."

At the Republican convention in July, a conservative coalition, wresting control of the proceedings from moderates, nominated Barry Goldwater, a likable but rigidly right-wing senator from Arizona, then designated William Miller, an

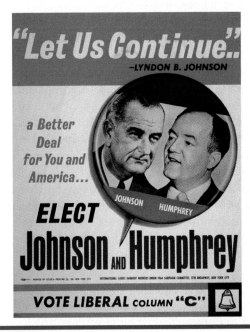

The Johnson-Humphrey ticket won a landslide victory in 1964.

undistinguished congressman from upstate New York, as his running mate. A champion of severely limited government, Goldwater wanted to abolish the progressive income tax, sell TVA's steam-generating plants, and make Social Security voluntary. Although decidedly not a bigot, he had voted against the Civil Rights Act and opposed the War on Poverty. He criticized the Supreme Court for showing a lack of judicial restraint in its decisions on school integration, school prayer, and the rights of criminal defendants. Goldwater's candor and élan, his declaration that "extremism in the defense of liberty is no vice," stimulated his followers to passionate enthusiasm.

But many Americans were made apprehensive by his evident desire to turn back the clock to the kind of limited-government Republicanism that Herbert Hoover had exemplified. They were also frightened by his shoot-from-the-hip approach to national security, particularly his seeming willingness to threaten the country's adversaries, notably North Vietnam, with the use of nuclear weapons, an impression that the Democratic campaign encouraged. Goldwater faulted Johnson for temporizing in Vietnam rather than pushing for total victory. Johnson reassured the American people, "We are not going to send American boys nine or ten thousand miles from home to do what Asian boys ought to be doing for themselves."

President Johnson, perceived as a stable centrist compared with the extremists of the right, crushed Goldwater, winning 61 percent of the popular vote—breaking the previous twentieth-century record of Roosevelt's majority over Alf Landon in 1936 and losing only six states—Arizona and five in the deep South. Yet if Goldwater had been defeated, his inroads in the South and the white backlash in the North sounded the early rumblings of a seismic political shift arising from the collision of black aspirations and white resistance. For the moment, however, what counted was the gain of thirty-seven northern Democratic seats in the House, which gave liberals a sufficient working majority to legislate Johnson's Great Society.

Enacting the Great Society. During Johnson's presidency, Congress produced a torrent of **Great Society** legislation, much of it in 1965, inviting comparison to the record legislative pace set during Franklin Roosevelt's first hundred days. The huge Democratic majorities made the legislative juggernaut possible, but

> *"If Goldwater had been defeated, his inroads in the South and the white backlash in the North sounded the early rumblings of a seismic political shift arising from the collision of black aspirations and white resistance."*

so did the tireless interventions of Lyndon Johnson, the consummate practitioner of consensus politics, who maneuvered the bills through roadblocks with a mixture of cajolery, threats, deal-making, and appeals to the national interest.

A number of measures addressed material issues: Congress established Medicare, a high priority for Johnson, which covered most medical and hospital costs for senior Americans, financing it through additional payments to Social Security; and Medicaid, which offered health care independent of age to the indigent, blind, and disabled. The minimum wage was increased from $1.25 to $1.60 and extended to more retail and service workers. Funds were allocated for the redevelopment of Appalachia, one of the country's most impoverished regions. The Higher Education Act provided the first federal scholarship program for undergraduates. The Elementary and Secondary Education Act authorized federal funds for distribution to schools, including parochial and private ones, on the basis of their numbers of needy children. The Model Cities Act aimed to rehabilitate slums, while additional measures financed the construction of low-income housing and rent supplements to low-income families.

Responding to the Great Society's attentiveness to the quality of life, Congress created National Endowments for the Arts and for the Humanities that would subsidize scholarships, museums, and the creative and performing arts and a program of federal support for public radio and television. It empowered the federal government to protect consumers against untruthful labeling and lending practices and to promote health and safety in the workplace. It set automobile safety standards, responding to the outcry stimulated by Ralph Nader's *Unsafe at Any Speed* (1965), a relentless indictment of the auto industry for putting looks and luxury ahead of survivability in a crash. Profoundly reforming immigration law, Congress abolished the preference given to people from northern Europe, opening the gates to all nationals on an equal basis. It established a Department of Transportation, a step toward dealing with metropolitan congestion, and a Department of Housing and Urban Development. The latter department was headed by Robert Weaver, the first African American to serve in the cabinet.

To protect the environment, Congress passed laws to clean up the nation's waters and to beef up the Clean Air Act of

1963, giving the federal government power to set emissions standards for automobiles (scientists had learned that cars were responsible for a sizable fraction of smog). It passed measures to preserve wild and scenic rivers, establish a national system of trails, and maintain endangered species. It set aside 58,000 acres for Redwood National Park and another 1.2 million acres for North Cascades National Park. In response to a campaign by Ladybird Johnson, it also passed a law intended to reduce the number of highway billboards and get rid of highway junkyards.

Voting Rights. Black activists, their expectations heightened after the Civil Rights Act of 1964, wanted equal access to the voting booth in the South perhaps more than to restaurants. But blacks who tried to vote faced loss of jobs and credit, threats of violence, poll taxes they could not afford, and literacy tests administered to make them fail.

In 1964, the Student Non-Violent Coordinating Committee (SNCC) and CORE organized the Freedom Summer Project in Mississippi, bringing volunteers, many of them white college students, into the state to set up "freedom schools" for black children, register black voters, and create the Mississippi Freedom Democratic Party (MFDP) to challenge the state's white-only regular party structure. The summer workers were arrested and beaten, drawing national attention to the battle for freedom in the state. The disappearance of three of them—Michael Schwerner and Andrew Goodman, both from New York, and James Chaney, a local African American—in June compelled a presidential dispatch of more than 200 federal personnel to search for them; in early August, the officials discovered that they had been murdered, then buried in an earthen dam. At the Democratic convention, the MFDP insisted that its delegates be seated in place of the regulars from Mississippi. Hubert Humphrey pushed through a compromise that gave the MFDP two at-large seats and barred from future conventions delegations from states that denied blacks the ballot. Although the compromise left the MFDP dissatisfied, it signaled a recog-

nition by the national Democratic Party that voting rights loomed next on the agenda of civil rights.

The outcome accelerated a break that had been developing between the SNCC and Martin Luther King Jr.'s Southern Christian Leadership Conference (SCLC). The SNCC, encountering violence in the field and inadequate protection by federal law enforcement agencies, considered the SCLC, which was dominated by ministers, too conservative and ready to work with whites. The SNCC's leadership felt themselves, one observer put it, "the vanguard of a revolution which seeks to transform the system while King seems to be in the middle of an effort to reform it." The SNCC's increasing militancy, however, helped make King more active in pursuit of political and economic power for blacks.

In January 1965, King and the SCLC came to Selma, Alabama, a town of about 30,000 people, to join the SNCC in organizing mass protests that would dramatize the need of federal action on behalf of voting rights. Although blacks made up about 50 percent of the voting-age population, only 1 percent of them had managed to register to vote. The protesters were arrested when they marched to the Selma courthouse. When 600 of them, having resolved to petition Governor Wallace, strode across a bridge on the way to

Whites and blacks march for voting rights from Selma to Montgomery, Alabama, March 1965.

943

Montgomery, state troopers teargassed them, then clattered through the scattering crowd on horseback, whacking them with whips and clubs. The assault, televised nationally, outraged the nation. Within days, President Johnson, in an address to Congress, called for passage of a voting rights bill, declaring that the cause of the protesters "must be our cause, too" and bringing lumps to the throats of millions watching on television when he concluded, "We *shall* overcome."

The Voting Rights Act of 1965—signed by President Johnson in August 1965, in the same room in the Capitol where President Lincoln had signed the Emancipation Proclamation—abolished discriminatory literacy tests, provided federal officers to assist black voters to register, and authorized the Justice Department to suspend any test and to use federal examiners to register qualified black voters in counties where less than half the eligible black population was unregistered. The measure was complemented by the Twenty-fourth Amendment, ratified the year before, which abolished poll-tax requirements in federal elections, and by a Supreme Court decision in 1966 that outlawed poll taxes in all elections. By 1969, the percentage of black adults registered to vote in the South had jumped dramatically, reaching more than 60 percent in Alabama, Georgia, Louisiana, and Mississippi. The number of black voters across the South tripled, totaling 3.1 million. The black exercise of the ballot helped defeat segregationist officials and compelled white candidates to court black voters. Over time, it would have a transforming effect on southern politics and the realization of black aspirations.

The Revival of Feminism. During the 1960s, the women's movement jolted back to life, winning gains under the Great Society and bringing about irreversible changes in what women expected of themselves and of their treatment. One source of the revival was the 1963 report of a Presidential Commission on the Status of Women. Addressing the issue from the orientation of labor, the report documented that women were paid less than men for the same work and were poorly represented in managerial or professional careers. Women, though roughly half the population, accounted for 7 percent of the nation's doctors, fewer than 4 percent of its lawyers, and only a minuscule percentage of its scientists. The commission's findings reflected the fact that 36 percent of

> *"Women, though roughly half the population, accounted for 7 percent of the nation's doctors, fewer than 4 percent of its lawyers, and only a minuscule percentage of its scientists."*

American women were working, and that an increasing fraction of those working had children—in 1960, 20 percent with youngsters under six, 40 percent with children between six and seventeen. Its recommendations included paid maternity leaves, tax deductions for child care, and child-care services for all income groups.

The feminist revival was also stimulated by the civil rights movement. Many young women involved in the movement were inspired by the strength, independence, and bravery of the black women of all ages who helped energize it. They took to heart its claims to equality, acquired the self-confidence to pursue them, and learned the strategy and tactics of protest. Yet women in the movement found that they were expected to make the coffee but not to participate in decision making. "The only position for women in SNCC is prone," Stokely Carmichael declared. Sexually exploited and relegated to second-class status, many women graduated from the civil rights effort convinced that the drive for equality had to be extended to gender.

The constituency for feminism was greatly increased by Betty Friedan's best-selling 1963 book *The Feminine Mystique.* Friedan, a suburbanite and mother with a background in labor journalism, described the mystique as a cluster of cultural assumptions—that women were by nature passive, subordinate, and nurturing, ideally suited to the domestic roles of making a home and raising children but unsuited for careers in business or the professions. Although millions of women led materially comfortable lives in the suburbs, Friedan argued, their conformity to the mystique left them with feelings of emptiness, suffering from "the problem that has no name." Friedan contended that women had to be free to pursue careers outside the home, embrace "goals that will permit them to find their own identity."

The feminine mystique was actually not so pervasive as Friedan believed, especially among lower-income and minority women, but her book electrified many middle-class, educated women. Beginning in the sixties, thousands of women joined "consciousness-raising" groups, gathering to recount their experiences and explore their dissatisfactions. The groups cropped up in cities and on college campuses across the country and often led to efforts to create day-care centers or women's health collectives. The group sessions taught

Betty Friedan (right), author of *The Feminine Mystique*, at a meeting of the National Organization for Women (NOW), 1967.

women that "the personal is political," that many of their personal difficulties were, as the feminist Jo Freeman explained, "common problems with social causes and political solutions." Friedan's thesis, intensified in the consciousness-raising movement, generated a shock of recognition among women and transformed them into supporters of a feminism that would break the bonds of their cultural imprisonment.

John Kennedy had initiated action on women's issues, ending separate federal job lists for men and women. In 1963, Congress passed the Equal Pay Act, which forbade employers to pay women less than men for the same work; and in 1964, at the behest of women labor activists, it incorporated into the civil rights bill of that year a provision—Title VII—that barred discrimination for reasons of sex. However, the new Equal Employment Opportunity Commission (EEOC) refused to enforce Title VII, its director calling the provision a "fluke conceived out of wedlock." In 1966, at a national meeting of state women's commissions, Betty Friedan moved to pressure the EEOC to enforce the law by helping to establish the National Organization for Women (NOW), its mission "to take the actions needed to bring women into the mainstream of American society, now, full equality for women, in fully equal partnership with men, NOW." In response to agitation by NOW, the EEOC began to enforce Title VII, beginning with the abolition of separate male and female help-wanted ads in

"In the mid-1960s, half of Americans over sixty-five had no medical insurance; twenty years later, every senior citizen was covered."

the newspapers. And in 1967, by executive order, President Johnson required federal contractors to include "sex" in their nondiscrimination and affirmative-action policies. By then, the new feminist movement was beginning to change the minds of many men, compelling them to recognize the barriers to women's ambitions and the merits of tearing them down.

DOMESTIC RECKONING

Lyndon Johnson, whose list of legislative achievements exceeded that of most presidents, broadly affected American life. During the 1960s, in dollars adjusted for inflation, per capita income shot up by 41 percent. By 1968, average family income had reached $8,000, double the amount of a decade earlier; the unemployment rate had fallen to 3.5 percent; and the poverty rate had been cut almost in half, dropping to 12 percent of the population. Although the economic boom that came from the tax cut and defense expenditures helped fuel the decline in both unemployment and poverty, a good deal of it was attributable to Great Society programs—notably the War on Poverty, expanded Social Security coverage, Medicare and Medicaid, housing subsidies, and aid to dependent children—that put cash and services in the hands of lower-income groups.

Blacks received a proportionately smaller share of the mushrooming prosperity than did whites, but some poverty programs—the Job Corps and Head Start, for example—assisted minority groups. The civil rights acts of the Johnson years revolutionized blacks' access to both public amenities and the ballot box. Johnson's orders to federal contractors to practice nondiscrimination and affirmative action in hiring and promotion eventually yielded important benefits for women as well as minority groups, since federal contracts affected about a third of the labor force. In the mid-1960s, half of Americans over sixty-five had no medical insurance; twenty years later, every senior citizen was covered.

Still, then and since, critics attacked Johnson for overreaching and charged that the War on Poverty and related programs accomplished little or nothing. Not all the critics were conservatives; some came from the core Democratic constituencies in the northern cities. Community action programs, giving voice and power to the poor in housing, education, and welfare

945

Chronology		
1957	Soviets launch the first earth satellite, *Sputnik*.	
1958	National Aeronautics and Space Administration (NASA) established.	
1960	Soviet missile brings down American U-2 plane.	
1961	United States severs diplomatic relations with Cuba.	
April 17, 1961	Bay of Pigs invasion in Cuba.	
May 1961	Freedom Rides begin into deep South.	
August 1961	Berlin Wall built.	
October 1962	Cuban missile crisis.	
	James Meredith, a black student, enters the University of Mississippi.	
November 22, 1963	President Kennedy assassinated.	
1964	The Civil Rights Act.	
1965	The Voting Rights Act.	

lenge that feminists were raising to the existing hierarchy of gender.

Together, the dissatisfactions imposed a severe strain on the consensus politics that Johnson had pursued to the end of the Great Society. In the fall of 1966, Republicans regained enough seats in Congress to reestablish the conservative coalition that had blocked reform during Kennedy's administration and to slow the Johnson legislative drive considerably. Johnson himself was thrown increasingly on the defensive for his domestic program, but the resentments provoked by his initiatives for the Great Society were enormously intensified by the fury unleashed by his policies in Vietnam.

Suggested Reading

William Chafe, *The Unfinished Journey: America Since World War II*, 4th ed. (1999)

Robert Dallek, *Flawed Giant: Lyndon Johnson and His Times, 1961–1973* (1998)

Robert Gottlieb, *Forcing the Spring: The Transformation of the American Environmental Movement* (1993)

Manning Marable, *Race, Reform, and Rebellion: The Second Reconstruction in Black America, 1945–1982*, 2nd ed. (1991)

Ernest May and Philip D. Zelikow, eds. *The Kennedy Tapes: Inside the White House During the Cuban Missile Crisis* (1997)

Richard Reeves, *President Kennedy: Profile of Power* (1993)

agencies, offended big-city mayors, northern governors, and many northern whites, especially blue-collar ethnic minorities, while many southern whites resented black advances. Many men, and a number of women, too, were irritated by the chal-

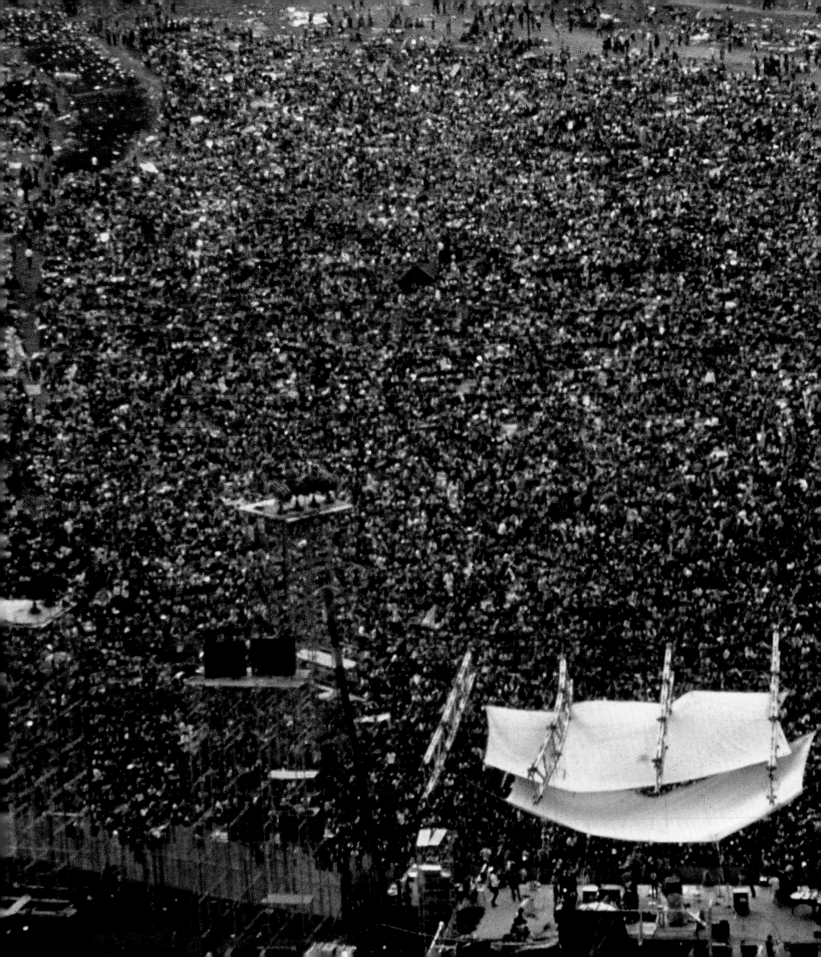

Chapter 30

YEARS OF RAGE:
1964-1974

A landmark celebration of peace and music: the Woodstock Festival in Bethel, New York, August 15–17, 1969.

QUESTIONS

■ **What problems did LBJ face in fighting Communist aggression in Vietnam?**

■ **How did the antiwar and countercultural movements make themselves felt throughout American society?**

■ **How successful was Nixon's policy of détente?**

■ **How did the Nixon administration deal with the major health and environmental issues in this period?**

■ **What was the series of events that led to Nixon's resignation?**

On August 1, 1964, a North Vietnamese torpedo boat fired at the American destroyer *Maddox* in the Gulf of Tonkin. The *Maddox,* on patrol under a secret policy that President Johnson had initiated earlier in the year, was protecting South Vietnamese PT boats that were bombarding coastal bases in North Vietnam. Three days later, the *Maddox* and another American destroyer reported that they were both under attack. Although the reliability of the report was uncertain, Johnson promptly ordered air strikes against North Vietnam. He told the nation about the action that evening in a televised speech and asked Congress for support in resisting aggression against U.S. armed forces in the region. By the end of the evening, Congress had overwhelmingly passed the so-called Gulf of Tonkin Resolution, authorizing the president "to take all necessary measures to repel any armed attacks against the forces of the United States and to prevent further aggression in the area." Several senators had cautioned that such a resolution would grant the president a blank check to wage war against North Vietnam, but pro-Johnson senators assured their colleagues that the president had no such intention.

Whatever Johnson's intention may have been at the time, it is beyond dispute that he was convinced that the United States had to prevent the fall of South Vietnam to Communism. Johnson embraced the bipartisan consensus that had dominated American foreign policy since the end of World War II: that the United States had to play a major role in resisting aggression, preferably through collective security but if necessary alone. Johnson tended to see leftist or pro-Communist movements in the Third World as instruments of a Soviet and Chinese drive for greater territorial domination—an outlook that

was reinforced by his principal advisers in national security, Dean Rusk, Robert McNamara, and McGeorge Bundy, all of whom he had asked to remain at their posts after John Kennedy's death and on whom he relied heavily.

In the end, Johnson vastly enlarged the United States' military role in Vietnam, later interpreting the Gulf of Tonkin Resolution as a warrant for his actions and thus—deviously, it seemed—committing the country to its **longest and most divisive war.** The conflict provoked bitter dissent and helped destroy the prospects for achieving the Great Society. Together, the furies unleashed by the war and the social changes of the sixties rendered Johnson's presidency untenable. They put Richard Nixon into the White House and initiated a seismic shift in American politics and government.

Johnson, a Reluctant Globalist

Unlike Kennedy, Lyndon Johnson preferred to devote his energies to reform at home. But the unruly world kept pressing in on him, compelling his attention not only in Vietnam but elsewhere in Asia, in the Middle East, and in Latin America. Johnson avoided unnecessary provocations of the Soviet Union and China while seeking cooperation in matters of global mutual interest, notably in slowing the arms race and quelling armed hostilities in the Middle East. But he was disposed to intervene where he judged that Communist advances jeopardized the United States' capacity to maintain world security and might also draw domestic criticism to his

President Johnson meets with the National Security Council, including Secretary of State Dean Rusk (on his right) and Secretary of Defense Robert McNamara (on his left), to discuss the attack on the *Maddox* by a North Vietnamese torpedo boat, August 4, 1964.

administration. He thus acted high-handedly toward Latin American countries, especially those he feared had been targeted by Fidel Castro for export of the Cuban revolution.

MISSILE DEFENSE

In the view of Johnson's national security policymakers, nothing was mutually more advantageous to the superpowers than avoiding a nuclear Armageddon. During the sixties, the expanding Soviet arsenal of intercontinental ballistic missiles had begun to equal that of the United States. And in 1964, the Chinese exploded their first nuclear weapon, enlarging the potential nuclear threat. In response, the American military and congressional Republicans began agitating for the deployment of antiballistic missiles (ABMs) that would knock out incoming Soviet nuclear warheads. The Russians themselves were known to be deploying a primitive ABM around Moscow. Along with a number of leading scientists, McNamara opposed the ABM, partly because it could be fooled by decoy warheads but also because it would cost the United States far more to build a missile defense than it would the Russians to counter the system. McNamara, with Johnson's support, tried unsuccessfully to persuade the Soviets that both sides should refrain from establishing an ABM when, in June 1967, Johnson, in the only summit with the Soviets of his presidency, met with Premier Aleksey Kosygin at Glassboro, New Jersey.

Partly to overwhelm the Soviet ABM, the United States began installing MIRVs—multiple, independently targetable warheads—on single missiles. The United States also deployed a "thin" ABM system designed to protect cities against a Chinese attack. One highly placed science adviser remarked that the system was not an "anti-Chinese ABM" but "an anti-Republican one." Nevertheless, despite the renewed nuclear bristling, the United States remained engaged with the Soviets on arms control, seeking agreements on both offensive and defensive missiles that would bear fruit during the Nixon administration.

THE MIDDLE EAST

The United States remained committed to Israel because of that country's pro-American posture, the strong support it enjoyed among American Jews, and the counter it provided to Soviet influence in the Middle East. In the spring of 1967, Israel felt itself threatened on two fronts because of a series of hostile acts by neighboring Syria and Jordan to the east and Egypt to the west. On June 5, declaring that it was acting in self-defense, Israel launched a preemptive attack, destroying

Israeli troops occupying Syrian territory during the Six-Day War, June 1967.

951

the Jordanian and Syrian air forces, slashing through the Egyptian army, and heavily bloodying Jordan's. The Soviets, sensitive to the rapidly increasing Arab losses, threatened to come to their assistance militarily. Johnson told the Israelis on June 10 that an immediate cease-fire was imperative and sent the Sixth Fleet to the eastern Mediterranean, a show of force against Russian intervention. The next day the Six-Day War ended, with the Israelis having gained control of the Old City of Jerusalem, the West Bank of the Jordan River, the hills on its border with Syria called the Golan Heights, and the Sinai Peninsula, the expanse of desert on its border with Egypt.

In November, the United Nations Security Council passed Resolution 242, calling for Israel to withdraw from the territories it had recently occupied and, by implication, for the Arab states to acknowledge Israel's sovereignty and independence. But the Arab states were still unwilling to recognize Israel, and Israeli forces remained in the captured territories.

LATIN AMERICA

Johnson considered John Kennedy's Alliance for Progress a "thoroughgoing mess," judging that as a means of fostering economic growth and democratic development in the country's neighbors to the south, it was too antibusiness and unrealistic. He made his point man for Latin America Assistant Secretary of State Thomas Mann, a tough fellow-Texan and a hard-line anti-Communist eager to promote private investment in the area. Mann signaled a rightward shift in administration policy, telling American ambassadors to the region that the United States would no longer seek to punish military overthrows of elected governments and explaining that blocking Communism was more important than supporting constitutional norms.

The shift shaped the administration's response to civil unrest in Panama in 1964 against U.S. control of the Canal Zone. In January, the Panamanian president broke off diplomatic relations with the United States and, outraging many Americans, demanded a renegotiation of the 1903 treaty that had granted the United States rights in the zone. Johnson, along with Mann and his chief national security advisers, attributed the disturbances to pro-Castro sympathizers who threatened to establish another Cuba in Central America. Eager to keep the canal open, Johnson achieved a restoration of relations in April without ceding any control of it to Panama, agreeing instead to "review" rather than "negotiate" the differences dividing the two countries.

In the Dominican Republic a year later, a rebellion against the reigning military junta restored power to Juan Bosch, a left-leaning non-Communist. At the end of April 1965, Johnson sent 14,000 troops there—the number was soon increased to 22,000—explaining that the force was intended to protect American lives and to forestall a Communist takeover. Many observers believed that Johnson had grossly exaggerated the threats, and journalists began writing about the "credibility gap," a sign of emerging distrust of the administration's foreign policy.

VIETNAM

At the time of Johnson's smashing election victory in 1964, the situation in Vietnam was rapidly deteriorating. North Vietnam and the Viet Cong, the military arm of the National Liberation Front (NLF) in the South, had recently initiated an energetic political and military offensive. They now controlled roughly 40 percent of the land and 50 percent of the people in South Vietnam. Since the murder of Diem in 1963, the South Vietnamese government had become unstable, frequently changing hands, and lacked any real authority. During the year following the incident in the Gulf of Tonkin, Johnson and his key advisers debated their course of action. Johnson was anxious that he would lose the Great Society if he "got involved with that bitch of a war." He was at first reluctant to send more American troops—about 23,000 were in Vietnam at the end of 1964—into what might prove to be an endless ground conflict like Korea. Wariness of the Soviet Union and China made him all the more skittish about enlarging the military role of the United States in the conflict.

Yet the president felt himself on the horns of a dilemma, confiding to McGeorge Bundy, "I don't think it's worth fightin' for," but adding, "I don't think we can get out." McNamara called Vietnam "a test case for the new Communist strategy": conquest by wars of national liberation. Johnson felt that the United States had to honor its commitment to South Vietnam, fearing if it did not follow through, its pledges to defend freedom against Communist aggression might lose credibility. Convinced by Eisenhower's domino theory—if one country were permitted to fall to Communism, others in the region would follow—he told reporters, "We learned from Hitler at Munich that success only feeds the appetite of aggression." Abandon Vietnam, and "the battle would be renewed in one country and then in another country." Johnson held vivid in memory the bitter woes that

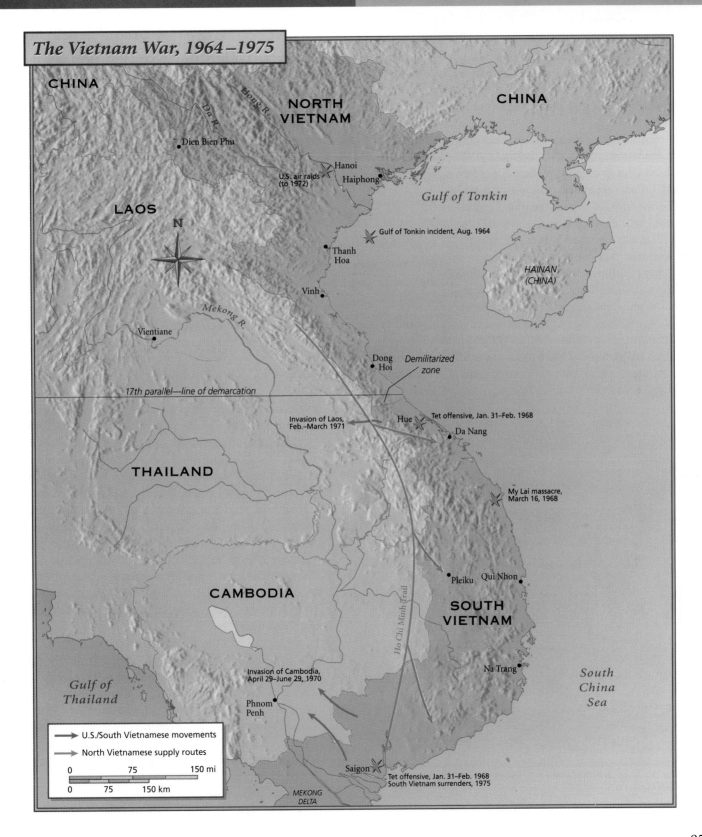

The Vietnam War, 1964–1975

CHINA

NORTH VIETNAM

CHINA

Dien Bien Phu

U.S. air raids (to 1972)

Hanoi
Haiphong

LAOS

N

Gulf of Tonkin

Gulf of Tonkin incident, Aug. 1964

Thanh Hoa

HAINAN (CHINA)

Vinh

Mekong R.

Vientiane

Dong Hoi

Demilitarized zone

17th parallel—line of demarcation

Invasion of Laos, Feb.–March 1971

Hue
Tet offensive, Jan. 31–Feb. 1968
Da Nang

THAILAND

My Lai massacre, March 16, 1968

CAMBODIA

Pleiku
Qui Nhon

SOUTH VIETNAM

Ho Chi Minh Trail

Na Trang

South China Sea

Invasion of Cambodia, April 29–June 29, 1970

Gulf of Thailand

Phnom Penh

→ U.S./South Vietnamese movements

→ North Vietnamese supply routes

| 0 | 75 | 150 mi |
| 0 | 75 | 150 km |

Saigon
Tet offensive, Jan. 31–Feb. 1968
South Vietnam surrenders, 1975

MEKONG DELTA

had befallen Truman, among them McCarthyism, following the loss of China. He was determined not "to be the president who saw Southeast Asia go the way China went," apprehensive that such a defeat would boomerang against his own presidency.

Such considerations formed the background for Johnson's decision to escalate the war in February 1965, when South Vietnam was on the verge of defeat. In response to a Vietcong attack against an American military base at Pleiku, in the Central Highlands, the Pentagon launched Operation Rolling Thunder, an air campaign against North Vietnam that Johnson authorized because "doing nothing was more dangerous than doing something." The bombing, launched from naval air carriers and bases in South Vietnam, was immediately intended to hamper the flow of troops and supplies southward from North Vietnam and bolster the morale of the Saigon government. The next month, Johnson sent two battalions of marines to the air base at Da Nang, contending that American pilots had to be pro-

> *"Johnson was determined not 'to be the president who saw Southeast Asia go the way China went.' "*

tected by American soldiers. He expected that, faced with the escalation of armed force, Ho Chi Minh would sooner or later "sober up and unload his pistol."

In the summer, as the situation of the South Vietnamese continued to deteriorate, Johnson ordered a review of U.S. policy. The chief opponent of escalation was Under Secretary of State George Ball, who had argued against the bombing campaign, predicting that it would not restore political stability in the South and would only heighten North Vietnam's resolve. Now Ball recommended abandoning South Vietnam altogether, expressing doubts that "an army of westerners can fight orientals in [an] Asian jungle and succeed." But he was a loner among White House policymakers. The debate ended in favor of the hawks, with Johnson authorizing a major increase in the American military commitment in Vietnam. By the end of 1965, 125,000 American soldiers were fighting there.

"Where does it all end?" The bombing and troop deployments failed to accomplish their immediate purpose—or their ultimate one, which was to force the North Vietnamese into peace negotiations. The military pressed Johnson to escalate further by sending ground forces against enemy sanctuaries in Laos and Cambodia, mining the harbor of Haiphong, a vital gateway for the North's supplies, and, as General Curtis LeMay, the air force chief of staff, urged, bombing North Vietnam "back to the Stone Age." Johnson, fearful of angering America's allies and provoking China and the Soviet Union, refused. Instead, he chose a middle way, steadily increasing the number of troops but confining them to South Vietnam and intensifying the bombing without striking North Vietnam's vital centers.

By early 1968, the number of American troops in Vietnam exceeded 500,000, and American planes had dropped more tons of bombs on the country than the total let loose in all theaters during World War II. To the end of removing the enemy's ground cover, the United States released chemical defoliants such as Agent Orange over millions of acres, destroying half the timberlands in the South. Ground troops, authorized in 1965 to conduct "search and destroy" missions, demolished villages, killed civilians, and

Marines in the Ninth Expeditionary Brigade landing on the beach at Da Nang, March 1965.

alienated the peasantry. In 1968, following the destruction of the village Ben Tre, an American major inadvertently expressed the growing illogic of the war, declaring, "We had to destroy the village in order to save it."

From time to time, Johnson halted the bombing in the hope of enticing Ho Chi Minh to the peace table, but the attempts repeatedly foundered on the administration's unwillingness to permit the negotiations to include the Viet Cong, the coalition in the South that had been waging war against the government with the North's support. Relative stability had returned to the South Vietnamese government when in mid-1965 General Nguyen Van Thieu won control of it together with his swashbuckling and bizarre prime minister, Nguyen Cao Ky (who considered Adolf Hitler a hero "because he pulled his country together"). The regime commanded diminishing support among the Vietnamese, especially in the countryside. Progress in the war was measured by "body counts"—estimates of the number of enemy troops killed. The number was in fact high—perhaps 220,000 by late 1967—but the estimates padded the toll by as much as 30 percent, stimulating misleading claims that the United States and the South Vietnamese were winning the war.

The North Vietnamese nevertheless fought on tenaciously despite the bombing of their cities, digging thousands of miles of tunnels to protect their citizens. They steadily replenished their troops and their Viet Cong allies in the South, sending men and supplies along the camouflaged routes through Laos of the Ho Chi Minh Trail. They infuriated American troops by their elusiveness, their ability to melt into the jungle and disappear into the local population. One American soldier wrote: "During the day they'll smile and take your money. At night they'll creep in and slit your throat." Some soldiers vented their anger, as at the My Lai massacre in 1968, by raping and murdering Vietnamese villagers. "We don't take any land. We don't give it back. We just mutilate bodies. What the fuck are we doing here?" one G.I. wrote.

Many of the American troops were confused by the war. On average, they were nineteen years old, seven years younger than their counterparts in World War II, less experienced in life and less clear about their country's war aims. They were supposedly risking their lives to defend democracy in South Vietnam, but antiwar protesters at home considered them

American troops probe a tunnel in search of North Vietnamese troops, 1968

"In 1968, following the destruction of the village Ben Tre, an American major inadvertently expressed the growing illogic of the war, declaring, 'We had to destroy the village in order to save it.'"

criminals and the South Vietnamese often treated them with contempt. As the war dragged on, their watchword became survival rather than victory. Between 1966 and 1971, desertion rates quadrupled, to almost 74 per 1,000, triple the worst rates of the Korean War. They took to assassinating officers—the process was called "fragging"—who ordered them into seemingly pointless battle. Many turned to the comfort of drugs, every variety of which was available cheaply and in abundance. In 1969, almost two out of three G.I.s were using marijuana, and one out of four had tried heroin.

A growing number of Johnson's advisers, notably Robert McNamara, knew that the war was not being won, that it was producing only killing and devastation, including, by late 1967, some 13,500 American dead. But Johnson was intolerant of the doubters, many of whom left the administration. Increasingly frustrated, like his troops in the field, Johnson was depressed by the lack of progress in the war and infuriated that "a little piss-ant country" should be so embarrassing the United States. When in the spring of 1967 General William Westmoreland, the American commander in Vietnam, requested 200,000 more troops, Johnson gave him only a fraction of that number. "Where does it all end?" he asked despairingly.

Upheaval at Home

THE ANTIWAR MOVEMENT

When the bombing campaign began, outspoken questioning of the war emerged almost immediately among the press and on the campuses. At the University of Michigan in March 1965, students and faculty introduced the teach-in—a gathering to question the merits of the intervention—and such gatherings quickly spread to other campuses. Many critics of the war held that Ho Chi Minh was a nationalist rather than an agent of either Soviet or Chinese hegemony, and that he had no interest in knocking over any dominoes in Southeast Asia. Some argued that the war was unwinnable, costly, and threatening to the Great Society. It was a civil war, the dissenters insisted. The United States had no vital interest at stake and thus had no business being in Vietnam.

For the first time, television brought a war into the nation's living rooms, the screens flickering with taped footage

> *"For the first time, television brought a war into the nation's living rooms, the screens flickering with taped footage of battle and death."*

of battle and death. As troop commitments, casualties, and draft calls mounted, the questioning of the war turned into a full-scale movement against it. Newspaper columnists like Walter Lippmann attacked the country's involvement in Vietnam, and so did foreign policy experts such as George F. Kennan, civil rights leaders like Martin Luther King Jr., and the nation's leading baby doctor, Benjamin Spock. Although Congress regularly appropriated funds for the war, virtually without debate because its members felt obligated to support the troops in the field, opposition grew steadily on Capitol Hill. By 1967, in cities and towns across the land, people were marching in protest against the war, including 35,000 who in October demonstrated at the entrance to the Pentagon.

The antiwar movement was especially strong on the campuses of the leading universities, where students—and some faculty—occupied university buildings, disrupted the work of draft boards and army recruiters, and demonstrated with angry chants ("Hey, hey, LBJ, how many kids did you kill today?"). They made common cause with songs of protest that addressed the war in the sardonic vein of Country Joe and the Fish's *I Feel Like I'm Fixin' to Die Rag* ("What are we fightin' for / Don't ask me, I don't give a damn / Next stop is Vietnam. . . . So put down your books and pick up a gun / We're gonna have a whole lot of fun"). Seeing the war as an indictment of American society, students felt linked to protesters in European capitals such as Paris and Berlin who in 1968 battled police in the streets. A growing number were attracted to the New Left, a program of social radicalism expressed on campuses by the Students for a Democratic Society (SDS). The society's Port Huron Statement of 1962, drafted by Tom Hayden, acknowledged the material benefits of prosperity but deplored the alienation, racism, and bureaucratization that accompanied it. The SDS called for a new emphasis on community and the

Students gather at a teach-in on Vietnam at the University of California, Berkeley, May 21, 1965.

achievement of social change through "participatory democracy." Hayden, a veteran of the Student Nonviolent Coordinating Committee (SNCC) who on a visit to North Vietnam gullibly accepted Ho Chi Minh's view of the war, denounced the United States' actions there as immoral, equating them with the racism rampant in the American South.

The war threw a powerful spotlight on the enormous influence of the Defense Department in academic science through its supply of funds for research to at least 100 universities. In protest, students occupied physics laboratories, demanded that universities divorce themselves from defense programs, and bombed several research facilities, including one at the University of Wisconsin, killing a postdoctoral scientist. Antiwar activists denounced their country's bombing with napalm, a jellied gasoline invented during World War II that was used to burn away the jungle, thus denying the Vietcong cover, but that often led to the incineration of civilians. The activists demanded that the principal manufacturer of napalm, the Dow Chemical Company, be prohibited from recruiting on campuses.

Critics of the war also pointed out that the burdens of armed service were marked by glaring inequities. Student deferments kept many young middle-class men out of Vietnam, while the enlisted men and draftees sent there came disproportionately from low-income, working-class, and minority-group backgrounds. Draftees, who comprised only a quarter of those who served in Vietnam, made up most of the infantry and accounted for between 50 and 70 percent of combat deaths. Black enlistees died in action at about twice the rate of enlisted men on the whole. Many draft-eligible young men ducked armed service by getting married, going to school, or joining the National Guard. Some fled to Canada or went underground.

Black activists attacked the selective service system, charging that most local draft boards were all white. The charismatic heavyweight boxing champion Muhammad Ali refused induction on grounds of his Muslim religion and conscientious objection to the war, declaring, "I ain't got nothing against them Vietcong." (He was promptly relieved of his heavyweight title and prosecuted for draft evasion.) Protesters burned their draft cards, and the Reverend Philip Berrigan, a Catholic priest, broke into a Baltimore draft board to spill duck's blood over its records. Bombings linked to radical groups targeted draft boards, induction centers, and buildings housing the Reserve Officers Training Corps (ROTC).

Muhammad Ali, having refused induction into the army on religious grounds, was stripped of his heavyweight title and prosecuted for draft evasion in 1967.

The seeming illogic of the Vietnam War machine was attacked obliquely in several popular novels about World War II. Joseph Heller's *Catch-22*, first published in 1961, brilliantly satirized the military for holding pompously to rules that made common sense into craziness and insanity into reason; and Kurt Vonnegut Jr.'s best-selling *Slaughterhouse-Five, or The Children's Crusade* (1969), a science-fiction version of his World War II experiences in the firebombing of Dresden, indicted the war machine for producing madness and disintegration. The film industry, its memories of McCarthyism and the blacklist still fresh, declined to produce movies critical of the government's policy during Vietnam; but in 1970, *M*A*S*H*, a subversive comedy about an army field hospital in the Korean conflict, indirectly spotlighted the war as an absurd waste of life.

THE COUNTERCULTURAL REBELLION

Campus dissidents had early been inspired by Mario Savio, a mathematics graduate student at the University of California at Berkeley, who amid the free-speech movement there in 1964 likened the university to a machine and cried to a

The Grateful Dead (Jerry Garcia, left) at ease in San Francisco's Haight-Ashbury district, a center of the counterculture, in the late 1960s.

throng occupying the administration building: "It becomes odious, so we must put our bodies against the gears, against the wheels . . . and make the machine stop until we're free." On many campuses by the late 1960s, young Americans, products of the baby boom, were defying social norms of hard work, getting ahead, self-denial, and sexual restraint. Their numbers gave them strength. During the 1960s, the co-hort between ages fifteen and twenty-four increased by almost 50 percent, accounting by 1970 for almost 18 percent of the population, a postwar high; a sizable fraction of them— half the eighteen-year-olds—were in college. They were active and vociferous enough to compel national attention as a youth-dominated **"counterculture"** who had opened a "generation gap" between themselves and their elders.

The counterculture, a kind of chemically aided neoromanticism, expressed skepticism of science and reason while embracing psychedelic drugs, psychedelic art, acid rock, and sexual liberation. The historian Theodore Roszak, who coined the term "counterculture," indicted science for providing "the image of nature that invited the rape [of the environment] and . . . the sensibility that has licensed it." He called reason noth-

ing more than "a handmaiden to the aggressive . . . urban industrialization of the world . . . to the scientist's universe as the only sane reality . . . [to] an unavoidable technocratic elitism."

Many young Americans fled from reason, at least temporarily, by getting high on marijuana. Some tried LSD or mescaline for pleasure as well as (so they saw it) for opening their minds to the intuitive truths of life. In January 1967, 20,000 people gathered in San Francisco's Golden Gate Park for a Human Be-In, where they listened to the acid-rocking Grateful Dead and heard Timothy Leary, formerly a Harvard psychologist, urge everyone to "drop out, turn on, tune in." Withdrawing from order, competition, and materialism, some counterculturalists adopted "hippie" life-styles—living in a commune, sharing housing and property and often each other's bodies and beds. Wherever they lived, many displayed their contempt for consumerism by dressing in military fatigues, torn jeans, and tie-dyed T-shirts. The men often grew beards and long hair; some of the women went without bras.

The youth of the era had been "trained by music and linked by music," a critic in San Francisco remarked. Popular rock groups reached huge audiences—and often got rich—through radio and LP (long-playing) record albums, which had first been introduced in the late 1940s, and which permitted the popular music industry to sell multiple songs on a single record. Rock groups sang increasingly about sex, drugs, and personal freedom. The Sopwith Camel band urged, "Stamp out reality . . . / Before reality stamps out you." The Beatles, the enormously popular group from Britain, exuded sexual energy in their mop-headed persons and mocking irreverence for everything adult in their music. Their songs, like "Lucy in the Sky with Diamonds," extolled the ecstasies of LSD and imported the mystical tonalities of the East. Anti-war convictions were combined with celebrations of love, drugs, and sex in the exuberant musical *Hair,* which mixed attacks on the draft with frontal nudity and simulated orgies.

In August 1969, an estimated 400,000 young people traveled to a 600-acre, rain-soaked farm in upstate New York for the Woodstock Festival. Some of them wandered in the nude and engaged in public sex, many indulged in marijuana and other drugs, and most listened through the din to the music of the day's rock and pop stars. That year, the popular film *Easy Rider* depicted the pleasures of drug highs and motorcycling on the open road.

By 1970, the counterculture was losing force, its image of love and gentleness shattered where its devotees tended to concentrate—notably the Haight-Ashbury district in San

Francisco and the East Village in New York City—by muggers, rapists, and drug dealers. When in 1969 a melee erupted at a Rolling Stones concert at the Altamont Speedway in California, a teenager was stabbed to death. A member of the motorcycle gang Hell's Angels, who had been hired for security, was indicted for the killing but was eventually acquitted. In Los Angeles in 1969, the hippie Charles Manson and his communal "family" brutally murdered five people, including a pregnant actress.

But features of the counterculture had spread beyond the campuses and Haight-Ashbury to upper-middle-class suburbia. They left a legacy of changed fashions—in dress, hairstyles, and drug use—and modified attitudes toward sex roles and sexual behavior, especially for women. In 1968, demonstrating against the Miss America beauty pageant in Atlantic City, New Jersey, women marchers threw girdles and bras into a trash can, calling them "instruments of torture" and intending to burn them. (Although thwarted in that attempt by the city, the organizers nevertheless earned militant feminists the nickname "bra burners.") The cause of women's sexual liberty was advanced in the pages of middlebrow *Cosmopolitan* magazine by its editor, Helen Gurley Brown, and in books like Germaine Greer's *Female Eunuch,* which urged women to take an assertive role in claiming their sexuality and sexual pleasure, and Erica Jong's best-selling *Fear of Flying,* which celebrated the "zipless fuck," sex free of all guilt and ulterior aims.

The spread of sexual permissiveness was aided by the new technologies of contraception. For several decades, advocates of planned parenthood and population control had been sponsoring research to develop chemical means of birth control. In 1960, in no small part as a result of this effort, contraceptive pills became commercially available. By 1970, some 12 million women were using them, drawn by their reliability even though they posed a small risk of adverse side effects. More relied on the new IUD (intrauterine device), which was later prohibited as unsafe, or the long-standing mainstay, the diaphragm. Obtaining these devices required a doctor's pre-

The College Scene

Before the 1960s, colleges acting in the place of parents (that is, in loco parentis) imposed a variety of rules on women undergraduates that were intended to inhibit sexual activity. In 1921, for example, Stanford University prohibited women both from "motoring" and from walking in the nearby hills "unchaperoned, after dark." Although by the 1950s many such restrictions had disappeared, most colleges required women students to be back in their dormitories by a certain hour—the times varied with class level—and men who brought their dates back late were expected to send them candy or flowers. By and large, women were not permitted to entertain men in their rooms, and where they were, the rules required that the door must remain open and at least three feet had to be kept on the floor. The sexual revolution that began in the 1960s virtually ended college governance of when, how, and where men and women students could get together.

Indeed, by the 1980s, men and women students at many colleges were living in coed dorms and sharing bathrooms. A popular guide later addressed a feature of life under the new circumstances.

"Many young men worry about having an erection in . . . a coed bathroom. Surprising as it may seem, most of the women around you won't be staring at your crotch so you needn't be overly concerned. And the one good thing about a coed bathroom is if you do get an erection, you'll be in close proximity to a cold shower.

"College women can be certain that the men around them will be looking, but how much the men get to see is up to them. While it can be annoying to be under constant scrutiny, it also presents certain opportunities to attract the attention of Mr. Right."

Ruth K. Westheimer and Pierre Lehu, *Dr. Ruth's Guide to College Life: The Savvy Student's Handbook*

American Journal

scription or insertion or fitting. Some states limited their distribution to married women, but many doctors were willing to defy the law by providing them to single women.

The countercultural skepticism of science and technology also spread into mainstream culture. If people welcomed products of science such as the pill and stereos, they worried about technological threats, such as microelectronic bugging, and reminders of the fragility of technological civilization—notably the 1965 power failure in New York that blacked out 80,000 square miles of the northeastern United States. Stanley Kubrick's widely admired film *2001: A Space Odyssey* (1968) was pervaded by a love-fear relationship with the computer Hal. Pollsters found public confidence in scientists rapidly falling, down by 1971 to a "very favorable" rating of only 37 percent.

"James Baldwin noted, 'To be a Negro in this country and to be relatively conscious is to be in a rage all the time.'"

Bolstered by Supreme Court rulings that found unconstitutional most laws restricting sexually explicit materials, nudity and sex became commonplaces in magazines, films, and theatrical productions. Pornographic theaters proliferated along downtown streets and highway strips, as did "adult" bookstores and topless bars. By the early 1970s, the sexual revolution was ensconced in American life.

MILITANCY AND BACKLASH

While the antiwar and countercultural movements gathered force, minority groups of color expressed their dissatisfactions with American society with greater militancy. Many were angered by the disproportionately large burden of the war that their young men were compelled to shoulder. Still more were made increasingly furious by the continuing inequalities they were forced to endure.

The fury was especially strong among blacks in the North. Although they could vote and, in principle, go where they pleased, the large majority remained segregated in slum housing, inadequate schools, and impoverished lives, and felt themselves constantly in peril of both crime and police brutality. The unemployment rate of sixteen- and seventeen-year-old black males in 1966 was almost 23 percent and rising (it would reach 39 percent in 1974). In 1960, some 3 mil-

lion blacks, many of them high school dropouts, were on welfare (the total would reach 11 million in 1972). During the eight years after 1966, a period of soaring increase in the overall crime rate, the arrest rate for black males between ages thirteen and thirty-nine shot up almost 50 percent.

James Baldwin, a powerful writer and a black, noted, "To be a Negro in this country and to be relatively conscious is to be in a rage all the time." In 1963, Baldwin published *The Fire Next Time*, an eloquent warning of the explosive resentments simmering in the black community that took its pointed title from a line in a Negro spiritual, "God gave Noah the rainbow sign, No more water, The fire next time." The next year, Congressman Adam Clayton Powell Jr. of Harlem remarked that the southern phase of the "black revolution"—a middle-class movement with middle-class aims like equal rights before the law—was ending. Now the northern, "proletarian," "rough" phase was imminent, raising the "gut issue of who gets the money." Powell added, "Watch out."

The Fire Ignited. One hot afternoon in July 1964, a white policeman shot and killed one of three black teenagers in an encounter in New York City. Angry blacks lashed out, rioting for

In 1967, racial tensions burst into riots here in Detroit and in more than 160 other cities.

five days in Harlem and Brooklyn. The next summer, in the Watts section of Los Angeles, a confrontation between white police and young blacks set off six days of looting, fire-bombings, and sniping at firefighters, police, and National Guard troops. The violence killed 34 people. In Detroit, a riot injured 1,000, left 43 dead, and destroyed $50 million worth of property. Almost forty such upheavals occurred in cities in 1966, more than 160 in 1967. All told, the riots between 1964 and 1968 killed some 200 people, injured 7,000, and destroyed almost $200 million worth of property.

In a report released in 1968, a National Advisory Commission on Civil Disorders, headed by Governor Otto Kerner of Illinois, laid responsibility for the riots at the door of "white racism," which had produced an "explosive mixture" of conditions in the northern black ghettos, and warned that "our nation is moving toward two societies, one black, one white—separate and unequal." Johnson declined to act on the commission's recommendations for additional governmental programs of jobs, housing, and income subsidies, counting the estimated price tag of some $24 billion too expensive. He did, however, win passage of a federal open-housing law that would eventually eliminate discrimination in the sale and rental of 80 percent of the nation's housing, and of a safe-streets act that was intended to reduce urban crime but that authorized federal, state, and local law-enforcement agencies to engage in wiretapping and bugging in particular situations.

Black Power. The urban rioting was accompanied by the growing embrace among northern blacks of the militant Nation of Islam, the Black Muslim religion led by Elijah Muhammad and articulated by Malcolm X. Eloquent and charismatic, Malcolm X repudiated integration and nonviolence, preaching instead black separatism from the "white devil," armed self-defense, and freedom by "any means necessary." A reformed petty criminal, he also emphasized self-reliance and black pride, telling African Americans to see themselves through their "own eyes, not the white man's." After falling out with the Muslims in 1964, Malcolm X began to speak of cooperation with integrationist civil rights leaders and with whites. The next year he was assassinated, allegedly by adherents of Elijah

LEFT: Black Muslim leader Malcolm X.

RIGHT: Stokely Carmichael, leader of the Student Nonviolent Coordinating Committee (SNCC).

Muhammad resentful of his growing power. However, his compelling *Autobiography* (1965) became a Bible for young blacks intent on asserting their identity and gaining independence from the power of whites.

In 1966, Stokely Carmichael, then leader of the SNCC and an exemplar of its increasing militancy, exhorted, "The only way we gonna stop them white men from whippin' us is to take over. . . . What we gonna start saying now is Black Power!" In part, Black Power stood for the kind of racial self-respect that Malcolm X had called for and that the soul singer James Brown extolled in his line "Say it loud, I'm black and I'm proud." Yet for militants, it rippled with racial separatism, derision of whites as "honkies," and a slogan for the riots, "Burn, baby, burn." In Oakland, California, the Black Panther Party for Self-Defense preached black nationalism and socialism and set up educational and breakfast programs, but its members also illegally armed themselves and patrolled the streets to monitor the police. They liked to quote Chairman Mao's observation that "Power grows out of the barrel of a gun."

Martin Luther King Jr. condemned the violence and separatism, declaring that "there is no salvation for the Negro through isolation." Surveys showed that most blacks continued to favor nonviolence, equality of opportunity, and integration. Black Power left its mark in expressions of cultural pride such as Afro hairstyles, soul food, and black studies programs in universities. It also added energy to the drive of

African Americans for political power. They demanded local control of their schools, ran with increasing success for election to school boards and antipoverty boards—and in 1967, for the first time in American history, black candidates won big-city mayoralties, in Gary, Indiana, and Cleveland, Ohio.

Red Power, Chicano Power. Amid the booming economy and reformist climate of the 1960s, Native Americans and Hispanics expressed rising expectations. Officials in the Kennedy administration recognized that even though the Eisenhower administration had ended the policy of termination for Native American tribes, it had failed to ensure the vitality of the tribes and their well-being on the reservations. Kennedy emphasized tribal economic development, a policy dubbed the "New Trail." By 1963, with the authorization of the Area Redevelopment and Manpower-Training Acts, the policy had created public-works and job-training programs on reservations in twenty-one states. The next year, Native Americans demanded and received recognition in LBJ's War on Poverty, pointing out that they were more greatly disadvantaged than any other group. A special Indian "desk" was established in the Office of Economic Opportunity, and the government provided Indians with new housing, food assistance, rural electrification, health counseling, and jobs.

> *"In 1967, for the first time in American history, black candidates won big-city mayoralties, in Gary, Indiana, and Cleveland, Ohio."*

In the meantime, young Indian activists had been deriding "Uncle Tomahawks" the way black militants assailed "Uncle Toms." Demanding "Red Power," they insisted on the designation "Native Americans" and on greater control over federal programs for Indians. Under the War on Poverty's Community Action Programs, tribal councils came to administer federal grants for Native Americans. In 1968, in a remarkably strong speech, Johnson promised "a standard of living for the Indian equal to that of the country as a whole" and freedom to choose whether to live in their homelands or in towns and cities. Within a few weeks, Congress passed the Indian Civil Rights Act, which sought both to strengthen constitutional protections for individual Native Americans and also, somewhat contradictorily, to exempt the tribes from having to respect those protections. For example, the act strengthened the role of tribal courts while repealing the 1953 law that, with the aim of facilitating termination, had granted states criminal and civil jurisdiction over tribes without their consent.

The activists also called for compensation for the lands that had been taken from them in violation of federal laws and treaties. In 1964, the National Indian Youth Council held "fish-ins" to protest the state of Washington's depriving local tribes of treaty rights by arresting their members for fishing without licenses and out of season in the Columbia River and Puget Sound. Other fish-ins were staged across the Northwest with the participation of celebrities such as Marlon Brando and the comedian Dick Gregory. Federal court decisions upheld the tribal treaty rights in Washington, and the tribes developed long-term fish-conservation measures in cooperation with state agencies.

Mexican American activism was boosted by César Chavez, whose family had suffered exploitation as migrant agricultural workers in California. In 1962, he and Dolores Huerta, a community activist, organized the National Farm Workers' Association. The NFWA fought for union recognition, higher wages, and better working conditions with a strike

César Chavez (left), head of the National Farm Workers' Association and leader of the grape workers' strike (right) in Delano, California, 1966.

that began in 1965 against the grape growers in Delano, in California's San Joaquin Valley. A devout Roman Catholic, Chavez spotlighted the merits of the cause of the agricultural workers and its commitment to nonviolence through personal fasts and by calling for a national boycott of California grapes (and later, lettuce) picked by nonunion labor. In 1970, the major grape growers in Delano signed a three-year contract with the NFWA.

By the 1960s, however, Mexican Americans had reason to be more concerned with urban than with rural issues. Of the 3.8 million Mexican Americans then living in the United States, close to 80 percent resided in metropolitan regions—2 million lived in the barrios of Los Angeles alone—where they endured racism, discrimination, and poverty. Asserting "brown pride," young Mexican American activists, many of them educated, rejected assimilation, insisted on the designations "Chicano" and "Chicana," and raised the banner of "Chicano Power." They demanded bilingual education and college Chicano studies programs. The Brown Berets, created in Los Angeles to defend Chicanos against both street crime and the police, spread through the Southwest. In Colorado, Rodolpho "Corky" Gonzales formed the Crusade for Justice, which organized community services in Denver, and in New Mexico, Reies Lopez Tijerina created the Alianza Federal de Mercedes (Federal Land Grant Alliance), which agitated for the repossession of lands that Chicanos considered historically theirs. In Texas, Jose Angel Gutierrez built the alternative political party La Raza Unida, which by the 1970s began to elect Mexican Americans to school boards and city councils. Some of the new Chicano action organizations would be short-lived, but the claims to rights and respect that they expressed would take root and continue to be heard.

Backlash. The upheavals of the day provoked angry disgust among a growing number of people, especially among groups comprising what was often termed "Middle America"—middle- to lower-middle-class whites, many of them from recent immigrant backgrounds, in blue-collar occupations, and worshiping at Catholic or Protestant (including evangelical) churches. A number had been Goldwaterites in 1964. They adhered to traditional social values and cultural commitments, and they liked the resolute parents and obedient, fresh-faced children in the film *The Sound of Music,* which enjoyed far more popularity than *Easy Rider.* They celebrated the astronauts who went to the moon, heroes of a day that had few heroes. The moon voyagers were described by *Time*

magazine as men "redolent of charcoal cookouts, their vocabularies an engaging mix of space jargon and 'gee whiz'"; their spectacular voyages, a NASA engineer observed, constituted a "triumph of the squares." Middle American "squares" were sufficiently antagonized not only by the sexual revolution but by the counterculture, the antiwar movement, feminist assertiveness, minority-group militancy, and urban riots to form a backlash against the trends of the sixties.

Even though the women of Middle America were offended by sex discrimination, they challenged the disparagement by some feminists of raising children and the emphasis given by the women's movement to working outside the home. The discontents disliked the permissiveness and secularism of contemporary society, including the Supreme Court's rulings against prayer in the schools. Worried about the rising incidence of crime, they assailed the Court for rulings on the rights of suspects that seemed to risk returning rapists and murderers to the streets. Their disapproval of ghetto riots and campus demonstrations catapulted the former screen actor Ronald Reagan into the governor's mansion of California in 1966 and helped elect other conservatives to office elsewhere in the nation. Reagan denounced radicals at the state university and quipped that a hippie was someone who "dresses like Tarzan, has hair like Jane, and smells like Cheetah."

White Middle Americans felt threatened by the civil rights revolution's turn to the North. Many were infuriated by court orders to open their neighborhoods, often segregated,

Carroll O'Connor (left) and Jean Stapleton as Archie and Edith Bunker in the popular TV series *All in the Family.*

tight-knit ethnic enclaves, and their occupations, often controlled by white craft unions, to blacks. They were enraged by court rulings compelling young children to be bused to integrated schools. Lower-income whites, unable to flee to the safe suburbs, were made apprehensive by the high crime rates in the nearby ghettos. Wherever they lived, many Middle American whites blamed rising rates of out-of-wedlock births among blacks for the high incidence of black delinquency, crime, and school dropouts and for the skyrocketing costs of welfare programs—they almost tripled in the sixties, rising to $10 billion annually—for single women with children. Many working-class whites said they identified with Archie Bunker, the bluntly bigoted protagonist of the popular television series *All in the Family.* One city worker exclaimed, "These welfare people get as much as I do, and I work my ass off and come home dead tired. They get up late and can shack up all day long and watch the tube. . . . I see them with their forty dollars of food stamps in the supermarket, living and eating better than me."

Although Lyndon Johnson's personal popularity had plummeted by late 1967, polls revealed that the war enjoyed wide bipartisan support, especially among Middle Americans. Many felt toward antiwar protesters like the construction worker who exploded, "Here were those kids, rich kids who could go to college, didn't have to fight. They are telling you your son died in vain. It makes you feel your whole life is shit, just nothing." The AFL-CIO convention rejected an antiwar resolution by a vote of 2,000 to 6, the head of the organization attesting, "I would rather fight the Communists in South Vietnam than fight them down here in the Chesapeake Bay."

The war commanded support among the overwhelming majority of college students, many of them working to get ahead in public and private schools (some of them religiously affiliated) and junior colleges operating outside the orbit of the elite universities. Middle Americans continued to hold the military in high regard. Robin Moore's *Green Berets,* a book about the Special Forces in Vietnam, sold more than 1 million copies and was made into a movie starring John Wayne, the popular and politically conservative actor. The film *Patton,* a sympathetic portrait of General George Patton, who was famed for his uncompromising pursuit of victory in World War II, extolled the American commitment to

"The scope and daring of the Tet offensive jolted American public opinion, prompting many to conclude that, despite the administration's optimistic reports of progress in the war, the enemy remained resiliently capable."

winning. That credo was echoed in the famous remark of Vincent Lombardi, the coach of the powerhouse Green Bay Packers in the popular National Football League—whose games ABC began televising in 1970 on Monday nights—that "winning isn't everything; it's the only thing." Unlike most members of the antiwar movement, Middle Americans craved military victory in Vietnam.

1968: THE POLITICS OF PROTEST

Early in the morning of January 31, 1968—the first day of Tet, the Vietnamese New Year—a small corps of Vietcong burst into the guarded compound of the U.S. embassy in Saigon, inaugurating a wave of attacks by the North Vietnamese and the National Liberation Front that struck virtually every city, district capital, provincial capital, and significant hamlet in South Vietnam. The battles, which raged for three weeks, inflicted devastating losses on the NLF and North Vietnamese troops. For them, it was a major military defeat—but a political victory. The scope and daring of the Tet offensive jolted American public opinion, prompting many to conclude that, despite the administration's optimistic reports of progress in the war, the enemy remained resiliently capable.

In the aftermath of the Tet offensive, polls showed that half the public believed that it had been a mistake for the United States to get involved in Vietnam. The fraction of Americans opposed to the war shot up—those from the antiwar left joined the ranks because Tet had intensified their moral objections, those from the prowar right because Tet had confirmed their conviction that the United States should withdraw if it was unwilling to take the hard steps to win the war. President Johnson's approval ratings plummeted to 35 percent, not much higher than Truman's rating at the time of the Korean stalemate. The CBS reporter Walter Cronkite, the country's most trusted television anchor, observed, "It seems now more certain than ever that the bloody experience in Vietnam is to end in stalemate . . . [and] that the only rational way out . . . will be to negotiate."

In late 1967, Senator Eugene McCarthy, a Democrat from Minnesota, had announced that he would challenge Johnson for the presidential nomination as an antiwar candidate. A devout Catholic with a bent for poetry and ideas, McCarthy

LEFT: In 1968, Minnesota senator Eugene McCarthy challenged President Johnson's war policies as a candidate for the Democratic nomination.

RIGHT: In March, New York senator Robert F. Kennedy also entered the race.

self, an unimpeachable Cold Warrior, told Johnson that the Joint Chiefs of Staff "don't know what they're talking about." By now, Johnson was embittered, convinced that he had accomplished a great deal for his country, yet, as he told an aide, feeling "chased on all sides by a giant stampede coming at me from all directions."

On March 31, in a televised speech to the nation, Johnson announced a partial halt in the bombing of North Vietnam as well as a reduction in hostilities and invited the North Vietnamese to respond for peace. Then he declared that he wished to devote all his efforts to the quest for peace and, shocking even his closest advisers, concluded: "Accordingly, I shall not seek, and I will not accept, the nomination of my party for another term as your president." Two days later, in a telling sign of the coming close of Lyndon Johnson's presidency, McCarthy smashed the president in the Wisconsin primary.

had long been raising moral objections to the war. Given little chance at the time, his candidacy brightened in the wake of the Tet offensive; in the New Hampshire Democratic primary in February, he gained 42 percent of the vote to Johnson's 49 percent, a stunning showing against an incumbent president. In mid-March 1968, Robert Kennedy, who had turned against the war and who was now a senator from New York, also entered the presidential race. Although attacked as a political opportunist who was cynically attempting to steal McCarthy's thunder, he ran a rousing campaign, electrifying the poor, racial minorities, and white ethnic blue-collar groups, stirring the antiwar movement with calls for peace negotiations that would include the NLF, and inspiring devotees of Camelot to hope for a Kennedy restoration.

Within the administration, Tet, and a request by General Westmoreland for 200,000 more troops, prompted a wide-ranging review of war policy that was conducted by Clark Clifford, who had succeeded McNamara as secretary of defense. Doves warned that trying to press the war to victory would tear American society apart and alienate America's allies. Dean Acheson him-

Death and Confrontation. At the time of the Wisconsin primary, Martin Luther King Jr. was in Memphis, assisting sanitation workers who were striking for union recognition and

Mourners attend the funeral procession of Martin Luther King Jr. in Atlanta, April 9, 1968.

965

better working conditions. On April 4, 1968, while standing on the balcony outside his motel room, he was shot and killed by James Earl Ray, a white convict escaped from prison. The crime devastated many whites, and angry blacks took to the streets in 125 cities, some of which erupted in violence and flame. The rioting put almost 27,000 people in jail, injured more than 3,000, and left 46 dead.

By then, Hubert Humphrey, Johnson's vice-president, had joined McCarthy and Kennedy in the contest for the Democratic nomination. Although a longtime fighter for liberal causes who enjoyed strong support among party regulars, Humphrey was weakened by his close association with Johnson and the war. Kennedy beat both him and McCarthy in the California primary on June 5. But that night, as he left his victory celebration in a Los Angeles hotel, he was assassinated by Sirhan Sirhan, a Palestinian immigrant who detested Kennedy's support of Israel. Kennedy's death, coming so soon after King's, was like a hammer blow to millions, black and white. Grieving throngs lined the railroad track awaiting the train that carried Kennedy's body from New York to Washington, where he was to be buried alongside his brother.

The killings of King and Kennedy led many Democrats to despair for the future of peace and racial justice. McCarthy continued to campaign, but he was cold, aloof, uncomfortable with blacks—he said nothing when King was murdered; his candidacy failed to catch on beyond the issue of the war. When in August 1968 the Democratic convention convened in Chicago under the taut control of Mayor Richard J. Daley, the boss of the city's Democratic machine and a staunch Johnson loyalist, Humphrey's nomination was a foregone conclusion.

Taking matters into their own hands, around 5,000 demonstrators had come to the city—many to protest the administration's war policies, some, like Tom Hayden, to discredit the Democrats by provoking confrontations. Some marched outside the convention hall yelling obscenities ("Fuck you, LBJ"). A few, calling themselves the Youth International Party ("Yippies"), intended to mock the system through, among other stunts, nominating a pig ("Pigasus") for the presidency. The police, on tenterhooks after the violence that had shaken the city following Martin Luther King's assassination, erupted in their own riot, clubbing demonstrators, hurling some of them through plate-glass windows, and assaulting the press. From the convention podium, Senator Abraham Ribicoff of Connecticut denounced "Gestapo tactics on the streets of Chicago."

Humphrey defended Mayor Daley and his police in the face of the extreme provocations of filth they had faced, and polls revealed that a majority of Americans agreed with him. But the brutal uproar in Chicago damaged the ticket of Humphrey and his running mate, Senator Edmund Muskie of Maine, further tearing apart the Democratic Party. It propelled many of its adherents into the arms of Richard Nixon, whom the Republicans had nominated several weeks earlier, and George Wallace, who was running as the nominee of the new American Independent Party and whose hold on voters, only 11 percent in January, shot up to 21 percent in the month after the Chicago convention.

Police tangle with demonstrators in the streets outside the Democratic convention in Chicago, August 28, 1968.

Campaigning for Conservatism. Wallace was a spoiler. With no chance to win the election, he hoped to capture enough votes in the South and the border states to throw it into the House of Representatives. Exploiting the backlash North and South, he attacked feminists, welfare mothers, hippies, radicals, school integrationists, antiwar demonstrators, and liberal intellectuals. "If

Richard Nixon (left) and Spiro Agnew, the Republican nominees, greet the party's national convention in Miami, 1968.

any demonstrator ever lays [*sic*] down in front of my car, it'll be the *last* car he'll ever lay down in front of," he pledged. But he chose as his running mate General Curtis LeMay, who frightened people with statements about nuclear weapons reminiscent of the mad general in the film *Dr. Strangelove.* Wallace steadily lost support to both Nixon and Humphrey.

Richard Nixon presented himself as a high-minded centrist, but with the aid of his running mate, Governor Spiro Agnew of Maryland, a onetime moderate who had turned rightward with the backlash, he also courted potential Wallace voters, appealing to blue-collar Catholics and white southerners. He also solicited sunbelt suburbanites, whom he considered natural Republicans—comfortable beneficiaries of the new high-technology industries of plastics, electronics, aerospace, and chemicals that stretched from the Old South into Texas and California. Nixon stressed the need for a restoration of "law and order" and assailed the Supreme Court for expanding the rights of criminals and upholding the "forced busing" of schoolchildren to achieve integration. He proclaimed himself a spokesman for the "silent Americans," mute in the face of cacophonous protesters. Of Vietnam, he said only that he had a "secret plan" to end the war.

Humphrey, far behind Nixon at the beginning of the campaign, gained on him at the end of it, partly as a result of Johnson's announcement on October 31 of a complete bombing halt. Nixon nevertheless held on to score a narrow victory, winning 43.4 percent of the popular vote to Humphrey's 42.7 percent, distributed to translate into a margin of 301–191 in the electoral college. Wallace took 13.5 percent of the popular vote while gaining the 46 electoral votes of five deep South states. The Democrats retained control of the House, whose new members included Shirley Chisolm, from the Bedford-Stuyvesant section of Brooklyn, the first black woman ever elected to that body; and they kept control of the Senate, even though they lost seven seats. Humphrey won almost the entire black vote and a majority of blue-collar Catholics in the North.

Still, Nixon and Wallace together scored 57 percent of the vote, commanding not only the deep South but the upper South and the border region. Nixon also did exceptionally well in the West, where resentments of the distant federal bureaucracy ran high among natural-resource users like ranchers and oil companies; and where the backlash helped shape the white vote. Nationwide, Humphrey received fewer than 35 percent of white ballots. It was evident that the Roosevelt coalition was badly damaged, riven by race, cultural conflict, and war, and that the United States was verging toward a new conservative majority.

Nixon: World Strategist

Campaign commentators had spoken of a "new Nixon." The old Nixon, a product in part of the California of rampant developers, resentment of the East, and savage red-baiting, had a reputation for valuing no principle higher than the pursuit of political advantage. He was often distrustful, self-pitying, and suspicious, especially of the media. "You won't have Nixon to kick around anymore," he snapped at a press conference after losing the California gubernatorial race in 1962. During the next several years, Nixon resurrected himself politically, tirelessly helping Republican candidates for office and forging the new Nixon in the foreign and domestic fires of the mid-sixties.

The new Nixon, drawing on broad historical reading and reflection on contemporary geopolitical trends, envisioned himself a statesman. More judicious in his anti-Communism, he was a realist rather than a moralizer in world affairs. He was prepared to exploit the plain fact that the Communist world was no longer monolithic, if it ever had been, seen especially in a rift that was developing in Chinese-Soviet relations. While keeping the Soviet Union in check, he intended to pursue a strategy of détente—reducing tensions with the Communist world, slowing the nuclear arms race, and refraining from armed intervention where the United States' vital interests were not at risk. But his strategy depended first on ending the war in Vietnam, removing what one of his speechwriters called "a bone in the nation's throat."

In pursuit of these ends, Nixon concentrated control of foreign policy in the White House, relying heavily on his national security adviser, Henry Kissinger, who in 1973 became secretary of state. A refugee from Nazi Germany, a onetime Harvard professor, and a brilliant analyst of world nuclear politics, Kissinger was ambitious to be a foreign-policy maker in his own right. He admired the balance-of-power strategies of Prince Metternich, the Austrian statesman who brought stability to Europe after the Napoleonic Wars; indeed, he seemed to rank stability ahead of democracy. His views of how to deal with the world dovetailed with Nixon's, and so did his penchant for intrigue and secretiveness in the conduct of foreign affairs.

> *"Nixon was determined not 'to end up like LBJ, holed up in the White House afraid to show my face on the street. I'm going to stop that war. Fast.' "*

Whatever Nixon's "secret plan" to end the war, in Vietnam the Nixon Doctrine translated into a huge increase in American aid that enabled the South Vietnamese forces to expand and, in a process called Vietnamization, take over responsibility for most of the ground war. As they did, the number of American troops in Vietnam fell steadily, dropping from more than 500,000 in 1969 to some 30,000 by 1972. At Nixon's initiative, the draft was ended in 1973, twenty-five years after it was reestablished, with the United States henceforth to rely on an all-volunteer army. Nixon also sidestepped the obstacles to peace persistently raised by the South Vietnamese by sending Kissinger to negotiate secretly in Paris with the North Vietnamese foreign minister, Le Duc Tho. Meanwhile, in March 1969, he intensified the American bombing campaign against North Vietnam and secretly extended it to North Vietnamese bases and supply routes in neighboring Laos and Cambodia. Nixon told an aide, "I want the North Vietnamese to

EXITING VIETNAM

Nixon was determined not "to end up like LBJ, holed up in the White House afraid to show my face on the street. I'm going to stop that war. Fast." But while resolved to bring the American troops home, he felt compelled to accomplish the withdrawal in an "honorable" way, which meant preserving an independent, pro-U.S. government in Saigon. In mid-1969, he announced what became known as the Nixon Doctrine: the United States would no longer act as a military protagonist in combating Communist subversion in the Third World. Asian nations could count on America's moral and financial assistance, but "Asian hands must shape the Asian future." If faced with armed challenges, they would have to defend themselves.

A horrified student at Kent State University kneels beside the body of one of the four demonstrators killed by National Guardsmen during antiwar protests on the campus, May 4, 1970.

believe I've reached the point where I might do *anything* to stop the war."

A Prolonged War. Nixon's strategy failed to disrupt the North Vietnamese operations in Laos or Cambodia, where a civil war broke out between pro-Communist and pro-American forces. Nor did it persuade the North to plead for peace. In April 1970, Nixon ordered American and South Vietnamese troops to invade Cambodia, explaining to the country: "If when the chips are down the U.S. acts like a pitiful helpless giant, the forces of totalitarianism will threaten free nations and free institutions throughout the world." The venture proved indecisive militarily and stimulated the North Vietnamese to increase their support to the Cambodian Communist cadres (the Khmer Rouge), thus widening the war in Indochina. (After the Khmer Rouge triumphed, in 1976, it embarked on a savage policy of genocide that lasted until 1979, killing 2 million people.)

The invasion of Cambodia prompted widespread denunciations at home as well as abroad—some of Nixon's own staff resigned in protest—and provoked a wave of student demonstrations reminiscent of 1968. At Kent State University in Ohio, the governor called out the National Guard after rioting broke out downtown and the ROTC building was firebombed. On May 4, as students—some throwing stones but all unarmed—protested the governor's action, guardsmen on campus opened fire, killing four students and wounding eleven others. Ten days later, two students were killed at Jackson State University in Mississippi when police fired into a women's dormitory.

In February 1971, the South Vietnamese, prompted by Nixon, invaded Laos; the president believed that a major campaign against North Vietnam's bases there would aid Vietnamization. But the North Vietnamese trapped the invading troops in the dense Laotian forests and forced them to withdraw precipitously in six weeks. The next year, at Easter, North Vietnam launched a major offensive, the largest since 1968. The number of American troops in Vietnam now substantially reduced, Nixon responded with what the *New York Times* called "diplomacy through terror"—mining Haiphong Harbor and sending B-52s over North Vietnam's major cities. "The bastards have never been bombed like they are going to be bombed this time," he promised.

Henry Kissinger (right) and Foreign Minister Le Duc Tho of North Vietnam, after agreeing to the settlement that ended the United States' military involvement in Vietnam, Paris, 1973.

End of the American War. All the while, Kissinger had continued his secret negotiations in Paris with Le Duc Tho, North Vietnam's negotiator. By the fall of 1972, the two men had arrived at a cease-fire agreement that required the withdrawal of all remaining American troops, arranged for the return of U.S. prisoners of war, and permitted North Vietnam to maintain troops in the South and the Vietcong to participate in a government of reconciliation. Kissinger returned home shortly before the upcoming presidential election announcing that "peace is at hand." However, South Vietnam's President Thieu balked at the terms pertaining to the North Vietnamese troops and the Vietcong. Nixon tolerated Thieu's recalcitrance, but Le Duc Tho, angry at his obstinacy, pressed for still greater concessions. Nixon responded by ordering the most extensive bombing of North Vietnam yet during Christmas week 1972, with B-52s destroying factories, hospitals, houses, and transportation facilities in Hanoi and Haiphong.

In Paris at the opening of 1973, the United States and North Vietnam agreed to a settlement much like the one Kissinger had negotiated in October, thus ending America's longest involvement in a war.

DÉTENTE

The withdrawal from Vietnam enabled Nixon to pursue his grand strategy of détente, particularly to seek a transformation of the United States' relations with China. Following Mao Zedong's victory in 1949, the United States had refused to recognize the Communist regime, had vetoed the admission of the People's Republic to the United Nations, and had cut off America's trade with China while pressuring other Western nations to restrict theirs. But since the mid-1960s, China and the Soviet Union had been growing apart. The Soviets were made apprehensive by Mao's Great Proletarian Cultural Revolution, begun in 1966, which proposed to install a purer form of Communism in China, thus by implication challenging Soviet leadership in the Communist world. Chinese leaders, on their part, were shocked by the Soviet announcement of the Brezhnev Doctrine, which claimed a Soviet right to intervene in the affairs of any other socialist country for the sake of "proletarian internationalism." The doctrine, made real in 1968 when Soviet troops suppressed a reformist government in Czechoslovakia, now seemed all the more threatening to Beijing because the Soviets had been beefing up their forces along China's northern and western frontiers.

"Nixon's visit to China marked a historic turning point in the Cold War, opening the way to the restoration of full diplomatic relations with China, achieved in 1979."

After Soviet tanks entered Prague, the Chinese signaled to the United States that they wanted to talk. Nixon and Kissinger welcomed the offer, seeing in China a counter to Soviet expansionism. In 1969, the United States eased its trade and travel restrictions on China. Publicly indicating its new flexibility, China hosted a U.S. Ping-Pong team in Beijing in April 1971. Two months later, his way prepared in secret negotiations conducted by Kissinger, Nixon announced that he would visit the People's Republic "to seek normalization of relations."

On February 21, 1972, Nixon's plane touched down in China, making him the first sitting U.S. president to visit that country and initiating a media spectacle. Television cameras and newsmen sent daily reports to American homes of Nixon's triumphal tour, including the president beaming at the Great Wall and exchanging rice-liquor toasts with Mao Zedong and the Chinese premier, Jou En-lai (Chou En-lai), at the Great Hall of the People. Nixon agreed to the eventual withdrawal of American troops from Taiwan, the island off the Chinese mainland that remained under the control of the anti-Communist Chinese Nationalist government, and accepted Beijing's claim that Taiwan was part of China. He was disappointed that those concessions failed to persuade the Chinese, in return, to withdraw support from the North Vietnamese. Otherwise, his visit marked a historic turning point in the Cold War, opening the way to the restoration of full diplomatic relations with China, achieved in 1979. It also made the future of relations with the principal Communist powers what Kissinger called a "three-dimensional game," allowing the United States to play the Soviet Union and China off against each other.

Missiles and the Soviets. In May, scoring another presidential first, Nixon went to Moscow, returning with several agreements indicating that the United States' opening to China had made the Soviets eager to improve their relations with the West. The accords covered the sale of American grain to the Soviet Union, cooperation in the exploration of space, and a limitation on offensive and defensive missiles.

Building on the Johnson administration's attempt to engage Moscow in some sort of freeze on strategic weapons, the Nixon administration had begun serious strategic arms limitation talks (SALT) with the Soviets in 1969. Nixon proposed to deploy an antiballistic missile system (ABM) to defend the country's offensive missile installations. The move prompted protest rallies and teach-ins on college campuses and renewed opposition by distinguished scientists, who warned that the system would not work. In August 1969, Nixon's ABM program cleared the Senate by just one vote.

Nixon was aware not only that the ABM system was technically vulnerable but that it would stimulate further Soviet missile development to overwhelm it. He authorized the United States' SALT negotiators to use it as a bargaining chip, but, thinking that offensive multiple warheads gave the United States an advantage, he insisted that under no circumstances might they even discuss MIRV. The SALT Treaty that he signed in Moscow allowed each country two ABM systems—

President Nixon (second from right) meets with Mao Zedong (center), the leader of the People's Republic of China, in Beijing, February 21, 1972.

one to protect its capital city, the other to defend a field of offensive missiles. A complementary agreement capped the number of offensive missiles allowed either side for five years to those already under construction or deployed. But the MIRV race continued, since the cap on the number of each side's missiles only encouraged each to pack their vehicles with as many warheads as possible. Still, the SALT Treaty, which the Senate ratified by an overwhelming majority, did dampen the ABM branch of the arms race, at least for the time being.

THE THIRD WORLD

Neither the United States nor the Soviet Union saw any contradiction between the pursuit of détente in their direct relations and otherwise continuing to compete against the other. Outside of Europe, where relations between the two superpowers had stabilized, many regions were marked by instabilities that were seen to jeopardize American interests or make them ripe for the continued Soviet support of national liberation movements. Nixon and Kissinger were eager to thwart Communist advances in the Third World without resorting to armed intervention. They lent support to authoritarian right-wing governments and covertly sought to replace left-leaning regimes by staunchly anti-Communist ones.

Anti-Communism by Other Means. After the election of the Marxist Salvador Allende to the presidency of Chile in 1970,

Kissinger declared, "I don't see why we need to stand by and watch a country go Communist due to the irresponsibility of its own people." At Kissinger's direction, the CIA, in cooperation with several multinational corporations, had energized the right wing against Allende's candidacy. Now Kissinger instructed the agency to "destabilize" his new government. The United States also terminated economic aid to Chile and successfully pressured public and private international lenders to limit Chile's credit. Allende's government, which had been elected with only 36 percent of the vote and whose economic policies were questioned by many Chileans, might have lost power anyway. But in 1973, he was ousted and killed in a military coup in which the CIA was complicit. The new regime, a dictatorial military junta led by General Augusto Pinochet, aroused condemnation around the world for its practices of torture and oppression. Nixon nevertheless not only immediately recognized it but supplied it with generous economic aid.

Concerned with increasing Soviet influence among the Arab states, Nixon turned to the shah of Iran, who had come to power through a CIA-backed coup in the 1950s, to protect American interests in the area of the Persian Gulf. In exchange, the shah was able to purchase advanced American weapons—almost $20 billion worth between 1972 and 1979, nearly sixteen times the total during the preceding twenty-two years. Although the shah partially Westernized his country, he suppressed political dissent through murder and torture, practices the United States overlooked because of his regime's pro-Americanism and seeming stability.

971

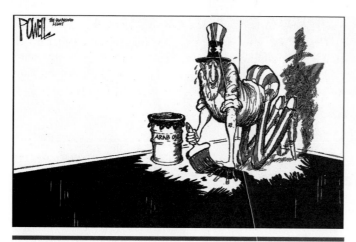

This 1973 cartoon illustrates how the United States' foreign policy in the Middle East has been constrained by the country's reliance on Arab oil supplies.

In Africa, Nixon backed the Portuguese colonial authorities in Angola and supplied aid and comfort to the white regimes in Rhodesia and South Africa, both brutal in their treatment of their black inhabitants. When Portugal quit Angola in 1975, the newly independent state was savaged by guerrilla warfare, one side supported by the Soviets, the other by the United States together with South Africa and China. With Kissinger's authorization, the CIA undertook covert armed intervention on behalf of the pro-American guerrillas, a move that the Soviets countered by importing 10,000 Cuban troops.

Kissinger ultimately endorsed black majority rule in Africa, convinced on grounds of realpolitik (realistic politics) that it was essential to gain the support of the vast majority of people living there. But throughout the Third World, the Nixon-Kissinger policies had intensified the impression that the United States was less an inspiration to freedom than a bulwark of counterrevolution and right-wing authoritarianism.

Israel, Arabs, and Oil. Since the Six-Day War in 1967, Arab-Israeli tensions had mounted, exacerbated by the bitterness of the Palestinians who had been expelled from Israel. The Palestinians had formed the Palestine Liberation Organization, a political pressure group based in Jordan that sometimes resorted to terrorism. In Egypt, Anwar el-Sadat, a modernizing nationalist like his predecessor, Gamal Abdel Nasser, had come to power following Nasser's death in 1970. Faced with a steadily weakening economy, he decided to go to war against Israel in the hope of regaining control of the Suez Canal.

On October 6, 1973—Yom Kippur, the holiest day of the Jewish year—Egypt and Syria launched a full-scale attack against Israel. The United States pressed for a quick cease-fire and offered to mediate the conflict. However, the Israelis, caught off guard, facing advanced Soviet weapons, and suffering high losses, sent Nixon a desperate plea for aid. The president announced that the United States would immediately send an airlift of arms to counter the Soviet's supply to Egypt. Pulling themselves together after ten days, the Israelis counterattacked, cutting off the Egyptian Third Army in the Sinai Peninsula. Although Israel, Egypt, and Syria accepted a U.N. call for a cease-fire, sporadic fighting continued. The Soviets, unwilling to let the Third Army be annihilated, threatened to intervene militarily. Then on the night of October 24, Nixon took the unusual step of ordering American nuclear forces around the world onto an alert. At the same time, according to later claims by Israeli officials, the United States warned that it would abandon Israel unless Israel spared the Egyptian force and quit fighting. The next day, the cease-fire went fully into effect, and six days later the United States pulled back from the alert.

The American shipment of arms to Israel nevertheless angered the oil-producing Arab states. Acting through the Organization of Petroleum-Exporting Countries (OPEC), which they dominated, they embargoed all shipments of crude oil to the United States and Western Europe. The embargo, which lasted until March 1974, sent shock waves through the industrial world, quadrupling the price of a barrel of crude oil, precipitating acute fuel shortages, and driving a wedge in the Western alliance, whose European members and Japan depended heavily on oil imported from the Middle East. In the United States, domestic oil was in short supply, and oil imports, much of it from the Middle East, jumped by almost a factor of two from 1970 to 1974. The price of gasoline at the pump shot up 40 percent, motorists waited in long lines to fill up, and many service stations simply ran out of gas. Since oil was essential for the transportation of both goods and people, the jump in oil prices threatened to affect the entire economy. To conserve oil, Nixon called for stepped-up licensing of nuclear power plants and a national speed limit of fifty miles per hour.

Nixon at Home, Bright and Dark

Domestic affairs did not engage Richard Nixon as much as foreign policy. He had long thought the country "could run itself domestically without a President," relying only on "a competent cabinet." But Nixon was faced with governing a bitterly divided nation and dealing with a troublesome economy. The day after his election in 1968, he issued a victory statement inspired, he said, by a sign he saw a teenager carrying during the campaign: "We want to bridge the generation gap. We want to bridge the gap between the races. We want to bring America together."

Reconciliation was good politics, at least so Nixon thought during the early years of his administration. It dovetailed with his long-standing Eisenhower-like centrism in much of domestic affairs, which was reinforced by the urging of Daniel Patrick Moynihan, a Harvard sociologist and domestic adviser to Nixon, to maintain Johnson's antipoverty programs and pursue a moderate reformism. He was further pushed in a reformist direction by the blunt political fact that both houses of Congress remained under Democratic control throughout his presidency.

To Nixon, moderate reformism meant dealing with social problems by relying less on direct action from the federal government and more on federal encouragement of reformist efforts by the states, private enterprise, and individuals. He launched several such initiatives, but most failed. The boldest was a proposal for scrapping the welfare system, whose clients, half of them children, had doubled between 1961 and 1972, and replacing it with a Family Assistance Plan that would guarantee direct annual incomes to the poor—for a family of four, $1,600 in cash and $800 in food stamps. The initiative passed the House, but it died in the Senate, caught in a political crossfire between liberals who considered the benefits too small and conservatives dead set against the concept of a guaranteed income. Nixon also recommended that the federal government share its revenues with the states in the form of earmarked block grants to spend as they wished, a plan that Congress did enact in 1972 and that the president hailed as the arrival of a "New Federalism."

Despite his moderate inclinations, Nixon remained suspicious, combative, prone to anger, equating opposition to his policies with drives to bring him down personally. He fre-

"In 1971, Americans imported $3 billion more goods than they exported, the first deficit in the balance of trade since 1893."

quently felt himself embattled, especially by the "eastern liberal establishment." Dissents from his policies brought out the darker angels of his nature. Drawing away from reconciliation, he turned toward confrontation, vengefulness, abuse of power, and, ultimately, the destruction of his presidency.

STRUGGLING WITH THE ECONOMY

Nixon's presidency was vexed by increasingly acute economic problems. In fighting the Vietnam War, Lyndon Johnson had refused to scale back the programs of the Great Society or raise taxes, insisting that the United States could have both "guns and butter." The resulting federal deficits combined with high consumer spending to drive prices upward at an increasing rate, producing a rise in the consumer price index between 1967 and 1970 of 16 percent, a major jump over the inflation rate that had prevailed since the mid-1950s. Nixon responded by encouraging the Federal Reserve Board to tighten the money supply and raise interest rates. Between January 1969 and mid-1971, these initiatives resulted in a recession accompanied by still higher inflation, with unemployment rising to 6 percent and the cost of living shooting up a stunning 14.5 percent. Sensitive to the needs and political power of senior citizens, Nixon approved legislation that increased Social Security benefits while tying them to changes in the cost of living.

The rise in prices, weakening the dollar abroad, adversely affected American exports. The recovered industries of Western Europe and Japan, many of their factories new and of superior efficiency, had already been increasing their share of the American market, notably in automobiles and consumer electronics. In 1971, Americans imported $3 billion more goods than they exported, the first deficit in the balance of trade since 1893. To stanch the wound, Nixon raised the price of gold in the middle of the year. At the end of it, dissolving the international monetary system established at Bretton Woods (see Chapter 27), he formally devalued the dollar, ending its convertibility into gold and allowing its price to rise and fall in response to the demand for it in foreign currencies.

Desperate to curb "stagflation"—the debilitating mixture of stagnation and inflation that was besetting the economy—

973

Nixon declared himself a Keynesian. In 1970, he had announced that he would never impose wage and price controls in the interest of political expediency. Now, in August 1971, partly with an eye to the next year's election, he announced a ninety-day wage-price freeze—for the first time since Truman took a similar action during the Korean War, in 1951—and in early November he imposed wage and price controls. The inflation rate fell, but after his reelection Nixon substituted voluntary guidelines for controls. Prices then swiftly moved higher, inflating at a 10 percent annual rate by the end of 1973.

SCIENCE, CANCER, AND THE ENVIRONMENT

In the new arena of the quality of life that had opened in the 1960s, Nixon reacted to political initiatives from the Democratic Congress and to the climate of opinion as it shifted in response to the beleaguered state of the economy and the inequities in society. The president approved the creation of the Occupational Safety and Health Administration, which would oversee conditions in the workplace, and he endorsed enlarged funding for the National Endowments for the Arts and the Humanities. When *Apollo 11* landed on the moon in July 1969, Nixon joined millions of thrilled people around the world in listening to Neil Armstrong say, as his foot touched the lunar surface, "That's one small step for man; one giant leap for mankind."

But Americans could also understand the reaction of a university student who, though "very proud," had to confess that he also "thought of all the people who live in the ghettos," adding, "The flag may be flying on the moon, but it is also flying in their neighborhoods, where there are poverty, disease, and rats." Pollsters discovered that Americans ranked the space race far lower in importance as a national problem than water and air pollution or job training and poverty. The United States sent five more successful manned missions to the moon, the last of which occurred in 1972, by which time public interest in the Apollo Program had fallen sharply. By then it was evident that the Soviets had given up the goal of sending their own crews to the moon and were more interested in cooperation rather than competition in space. In 1975, in the last manned mission of the decade, an American crew linked up with the orbiting Soviet *Soyuz 19* and jointly conducted experiments with its two cosmonauts.

Nixon followed public opinion as it translated into hard times for basic science. In 1967, the overall federal budget for

Astronaut Edwin "Buzz" Aldrin on the moon, July 20, 1969. Neil Armstrong, commander of the *Apollo 11*, took the picture.

research and development had turned downward for the first time since the Depression, falling 18 percent by 1973. In 1969, Senator Mike Mansfield, a liberal Democrat from Montana, pushed through an amendment to the military authorization bill that was intended to reduce the presence of the military on the campuses. Amid the social turmoil churning through the country, policymakers wanted science to help solve social problems.

The cutbacks hit the physical sciences and engineering, the sciences most closely related to defense, particularly hard. High-energy physicists ran into a blitz of opposition when they asked for $280 million to build a giant new particle accelerator. The *New York Times* pointed out the expensive "irrelevance" of the machine to problems such as poverty, riots, and inadequate medical care. In the end, the accelerator was authorized at the cost of phasing out a number of other machines and reducing money for still others. Built south of Chicago and designated as the Fermi National Laboratory, after the Nobel physicist Enrico Fermi, one of the refugees from Hitler's Europe who had played a decisive role in the atom bomb project, the accelerator proved to be a jewel in the crown of American science, an instrument that enabled world-class work in high-energy physics to be carried out during the rest of the century.

War on Cancer. In contrast, both Congress and the president, eager for R&D programs that would pay social dividends, responded readily to a proposal for action against cancer. Since the 1950s, confirming an observation made early in the century with chickens, biologists had found that viruses would produce tumors in a variety of animals. How they did so was now being illuminated by the rapidly developing science of molecular genetics.

Molecular genetics had begun in 1953, when the young American biologist James D. Watson and two British co-workers, Francis Crick and Maurice Wilkins, identified the structure of DNA, the molecule present in the nucleus of every cell that carries the inheritable essence of an organism—its genes—from one generation to the next. They showed that DNA (deoxyribonucleic acid) comprises a double helix joined at regular intervals across the distance between them by one or another of two pairs of chemicals. During the next decade, scientists in the United States and Europe found that the sequence in which these chemical pairs occur along the helix forms a genetic code that determines the physical characteristics of an organism. The genetic material of tumor viruses consists of either DNA or a molecule similar to it called RNA. A discovery in 1970 revealed that these viruses cause tumors by integrating their genetic information with the DNA of an animal's cells, perverting the machinery that governs their growth so that the cells multiply with abandon.

These accumulating discoveries implied to some biologists that viruses might be a major cause of tumors in human beings. Pressed by health activists and congressmen, Nixon endorsed a national commitment to the goal of wiping out cancer, declaring in 1971 that "the time has come in America when the same kind of concentrated effort that split the atom and took man to the moon should be turned toward conquering this dread disease." At the end of the year, Congress and the president inaugurated the so-called War on Cancer, which by mid-decade more than tripled the funds available for cancer research.

> *"By now, the data were overwhelming that the most significant environmental carcinogen was self-inflicted—the smoking of tobacco."*

By the late 1970s, research thus supported led to a historic breakthrough in understanding of the disease: most human cancers are not caused by viruses. They arise when normal genes involved in critical cellular functions go wrong. Their transformation into cancer-causing genes can arise spontaneously from mutations; it can also be provoked by interactions between genes and what people ingest, inhale, or encounter in the environment.

At the time, scientific studies began to link specific chemicals to human cancer. The studies were reinforced by tests of chemical carcinogenicity carried out on animals and by increasing knowledge of the genetic damage caused by chemicals. By now, the data were overwhelming that the most significant environmental carcinogen was self-inflicted—the smoking of tobacco. In 1970, the federal government toughened the law requiring warning labels on cigarette packages and banned advertisements for smoking from radio and television. The Nixon administration also prohibited the use of DDT and cyclamates, a sweetener said to cause cancer.

James D. Watson (right) and Francis Crick, shortly after they discovered the structure of DNA in 1953.

Environmental Pollution. Before his presidency, Nixon had been indifferent to environmental matters. He favored job growth, especially in the auto industry, over strict environmental restrictions. But he was sensitive enough to the environmental movement's swelling political power to want to be kept "out of trouble" in dealing with it, as he told his aide John Ehrlichman, a land-use lawyer sympathetic to environmental protection. During the Nixon years, a torrent of environmental measures cascaded through Congress and the White House. In January 1970, Nixon signed the National Environmental Policy Act, which opened the way to his establishment later that year of the Environmental Protection Agency (EPA), a body with sweeping regulatory powers. The act also directed all federal agencies to take into account the environmental impact of their activities, a requirement that gave ordinary citizens the opportunity to take them to court if they did not. Congress cast a cold eye on new irrigation and dam projects in the West. It also enacted laws to clean up oil spills, improve air and water quality, and protect endangered species.

A number of environmentalists were taking aim at the rapidly developing nuclear power industry. By 1967, more than a dozen nuclear plants were operating in the United States, and many more were under construction. The critics raised questions about the disposal of radioactive wastes; about the safety of reactors themselves, particularly their emergency core-cooling systems, which were designed to prevent overheating and meltdown; and about the impact of the heated water that reactors disgorged into rivers, lakes, and streams, endangering aquatic life.

Beginning in 1970, environmental groups brought suit under the National Environmental Policy Act against the Atomic Energy Commission (AEC) for licensing the Baltimore Gas and Electric Company to build a nuclear reactor at Calvert Cliffs, Maryland, some thirty miles from Washington, D.C. Analysts predicted that the reactor's discharged cooling water would likely thermally pollute the Chesapeake Bay. The AEC, on its part, refused to deal with any issues that did not concern radiation. After a series of legal maneuvers, the judge in the case ruled for the environmental protectionists in a strongly worded opinion that compelled the AEC to take into account all potential environmental hazards in the licensing of nuclear plants, on pain of incurring suits if it did not.

Many observers came to question the structure of atomic energy policymaking itself. The AEC combined in one institution mutually compromising aims—both the promotion and the regulation of nuclear power. In 1973, Congress broke up the agency, awarding its promotional research and development to the newly created Energy Research and Development Administration, which in 1977 became the Department of Energy, and its regulatory functions to the brand-new Nuclear Regulatory Commission.

APPEAL TO THE SILENT MAJORITY

Despite his stated eagerness to unite the country, Nixon turned confrontational as he devised a strategy for reelection. He resolved to mobilize what in 1969 he would call the "great silent majority," another term for Middle America, appealing in particular to whites in the South along with ethnic Catholics and blue-collar workers in the North. Convinced that people were "fed up with liberals," he aimed to solidify the conservative majority that appeared to be forming in the United States by exploiting the mounting resentment of inflation, taxes, and government bureaucrats, crime, riots, and welfare cheats, pornography, drugs, and sexual permissiveness, demanding blacks and domestic radicals.

> *"The domestic upheavals after Cambodia brought out Nixon's tendency, as an aide later wrote, to be 'absolutely paranoid about criticism,' and his attitudes shaped the outlook of his staff."*

Covert War. Nixon himself had come to feel some of these resentments with venomous force. The domestic upheavals after Cambodia brought out his tendency, as an aide later wrote, to be "absolutely paranoid about criticism," and his attitudes shaped the outlook of his staff. A lawyer recalled that when he joined the White House in July 1970, he encountered "a climate of excessive concern over the political impact of demonstrators, excessive concern over leaks, an insatiable appetite for political intelligence, all coupled with a do-it-yourself White House staff, regardless of the law."

Nixon mounted a largely secret war against liberal, dissident, and radical groups and individuals, using federal agencies to harass them with tax audits, spy on them with wiretapping, disrupt them by infiltration, and break them by prosecution. Previous presidents had indulged in one such tactic or another—most recently, John Kennedy and Lyndon Johnson in waging war against, respectively, organized crime and radical antiwar protesters. But Nixon's willingness to use such means was far more sweeping. He ordered the FBI and the CIA into the battle, even though the CIA was legally prohibited from engaging in domestic activities. In 1970, he approved the plan drawn up by a young aide, Tom C. Huston, whereby both agencies would protect national security through a program of legal surveillance and illegal activities such as break-ins. J. Edgar Hoover, fearful that his FBI might lose power to the CIA, persuaded Nixon to kill the plan.

But in 1971, the *New York Times* published the Pentagon Papers, a classified documentary history of American involvement in the Vietnam War that the Defense Department had compiled during the Johnson administration and that Daniel Ellsberg, a former department analyst, had given to the newspaper. Nixon, furious, exploded to an aide, "Those sons of bitches are killing me. . . . We're up against an enemy, a conspiracy. They're using any means. We are going to use any means. Is that clear?" Nixon established a secret White House unit to stop such leaks—its members were known as the "plumbers"—using the Huston plan's methods. In September 1971, in the first of a series of covert forays, the plumbers broke into the office of Ellsberg's psychiatrist in search of materials that might discredit him.

Nixon also constructed an "enemies list" made up of influential opponents of his policies whom he targeted for harassment. Among them was John Kennedy's science adviser, Jerome Wiesner, now the president of MIT and an outspoken opponent of the ABM. Nixon similarly applied ABM litmus tests to appointees to high scientific posts. In 1973, he abolished the President's Science Advisory Committee, many of whose members doubted the wisdom of a missile defense.

During the midterm election season of 1969–70, which coincided with the heated demonstrations against U.S. actions in Cambodia, Nixon unleashed Vice-President Agnew to attack the administration's enemies openly. Agnew, speaking to the resentments of the silent majority, disparaged antiwar protesters as "an effete corps of impudent snobs" and denounced the news media as "nattering nabobs of negativism." Nixon, hoping to exploit the widespread discontent with protests and violence, stressed that the nation needed law and order. But many Democrats also embraced that theme. The Republicans gained two seats in the Senate but lost nine in the House as well as eleven governorships.

The Southern Strategy. Nixon's moderate reformism extended to bread-and-butter issues for minorities. He created the Office of Minority Enterprises to promote black capitalism, and he approved subsidized housing for lower-income groups. In actions that affected corporations employing more than a third of the national labor force, he required that a fixed percentage of federal contracts be set aside for minority businesses and compelled federal contractors to create goals and timetables for the hiring and promotion of minorities. His Labor Department ordered unions across the country to enroll a specific number of blacks. However, Nixon was increasingly eager to woo whites—in the North, but especially the South—who felt threatened by the black drive for equality. He tried to block the protection of voting rights, impair the enforcement of fair housing, and halt the desegregation of public schools, especially through court-ordered busing.

Further in pursuit of his southern strategy, Nixon sought to reshape the Supreme Court by filling vacancies with appointees whose views were more congenial to his own. In 1969, he successfully nominated Warren Burger, a conservative federal judge, to succeed the retiring Earl Warren as chief justice. His nominees for the next open seat, both from the deep South, were rejected by the Senate—because of conflict of interest in the first case, intellectual mediocrity in the second. His next three appointees, all with strict-constructionist legal reputations, were approved. Contrary to expectations, however, the Burger Court hewed to a moderate course, retaining the essence of the *Miranda* rule and holding, in *Furman v. Georgia* (1972), against mandatory capital punishment. When the Nixon administration attempted to block publication of the Pentagon Papers, the Court decided, in *New York Times v. the United States* (1971), that the federal government did not have the power to prevent such material from being published. In 1971, in *Swann v. Charlotte-Mecklenburg Board of Education,* the Court upheld the constitutionality of busing to achieve school integration. Nixon, angry, went on national television to denounce the decision and call for Congress to enact a busing moratorium.

The Election of 1972. The Republicans renominated Nixon and Agnew. George Wallace, this time bringing his denunciations of integrationists and war protesters to the race for the Democratic nomination, piled up victories and strong showings in the South and Midwest, and on May 16 he won the primaries in Maryland and Michigan. But his candidacy was ended the day before, when he was shot and paralyzed from the waist down. The Democrats chose George McGovern, a former history professor, now a liberal senator from South

Dakota and a passionate opponent of the Vietnam War. McGovern's first-ballot victory was aided by new party rules—McGovern himself had headed the commission that established them—requiring that every state delegation include young, minority, and female members in rough proportion to their presence in the population. An old-guard labor leader complained that the convention displayed "too much hair and not enough cigars," a crack that caught the convention's nationally televised image.

The image likely impaired McGovern's chances, but so did his withdrawal of support from his vice-presidential running mate, Senator Thomas Eagleton of Missouri, after it was revealed that Eagleton had undergone electric-shock therapy for depression. His replacement by Sargent Shriver of Maryland, a high official in both the Kennedy and Johnson administrations, failed to revive the McGovern campaign's prospects. McGovern sounded like a radical, calling for immediate withdrawal from Vietnam, the easing of penalties for marijuana use, and a program of income redistribution. Republicans, exploiting the resentments pervading Middle America, attacked him as a defender of "abortion, acid, and amnesty."

Nixon swept to an overwhelming victory, gaining nearly 61 percent of the popular vote, losing only Massachusetts and the District of Columbia, and dominating the electoral college 520 to 17. He appeared to have solidified the new conservative majority, winning solidly among blue-collar workers and Catholics in the North while carrying the entire South. However, the Democrats retained control of the House and increased their majority in the Senate by two seats, a sign that the New Deal coalition was not entirely shattered. While many Americans might have turned conservative on some issues, notably race, they remained moderate to liberal on others, especially the management of the economy.

Watergate

Early in the election campaign, Nixon appointed Attorney General John Mitchell head of a new Committee to Reelect the President, later known as CREEP. Collecting millions in contributions, CREEP used some of the money to support a campaign of "dirty tricks" and espionage against Democrats. Possibly with Mitchell's approval, two of the White House plumbers planned a spying expedition to the Democratic Na-

tional Committee Headquarters in the Watergate building in Washington. Early in the morning of June 17, 1972, a security guard caught five men breaking in to the headquarters with cameras and electronic surveillance devices in hand. Evidence found in their hotel rooms linked them to the White House, and one, James McCord, was quickly determined to work for CREEP.

Whether Nixon knew of the break-in beforehand or not, he was well aware of it within just a few days. Tapes produced by a voice-activated recording system that he had installed in the White House later revealed his response: cover up the crime. "Play it tough," he ordered H. R. Haldeman, one of his top aides. On June 23, Nixon ordered the CIA to tell the FBI that national security required a halt to the inquiry it had begun into the incident. The order, caught on tape, amounted to an obstruction of justice. The CIA refused to comply. Pursuing the cover-up, Nixon tried to buy silence from the burglars with some $400,000. He insisted publicly and privately that they had acted purely on their own, telling a press conference in July "categorically" that "no one in the White House staff, no one in this administration presently employed, was involved in this bizarre incident."

In January 1973, the five burglars together with the two plumbers came to trial before Judge John J. Sirica, in the U.S. District Court in Washington. In early February, not satisfied that his court had heard the full story, Sirica promised them stiff sentences unless they told the full truth. On March 23, McCord confessed that the defendants had perjured themselves and been pressured by the White House "to plead guilty and remain silent." In the meantime, two young reporters on the *Washington Post* began publishing revealing articles about CREEP's activities and the cover-up, drawing heavily on a knowledgeable administration source whom they called Deep Throat, a pseudonym borrowed from the title of a pornographic film of the day.

John Dean, the White House counsel, warned Nixon that "we have a cancer . . . close to the presidency, that's growing." In April, Nixon fired Dean, who, fearing that he would be saddled with the rap, decided to tell investigators what he knew. Later that month, Nixon announced that Haldeman and Ehrlichman had resigned and that he would clear up the spreading scandal. He appointed Secretary of Defense Elliot Richardson, a man of impeccable character, as his new attorney general. Under pressure from the Senate, Richardson appointed an independent special prosecutor for the spreading scandal of Watergate—Archibald Cox of the Harvard Law School, formerly Kennedy's solicitor general.

In May, a select Senate committee under Senator Sam Ervin of North Carolina began televised hearings into charges of corruption during the 1972 election. The proceedings held millions in thrall as Ervin, disarmingly casting himself as "a plain country lawyer," and his committee revealed the existence of Nixon's enemies list, his subjection of opponents to IRS audits, and his administration's responsiveness to illegal campaign contributions. Late in May, Nixon declared that his close aides, including Dean, had fashioned a cover-up without his knowledge. In June, Dean testified before the Ervin committee that the president had been fully involved in the cover-up. The question of Nixon's culpability pivoted on resolving the conflict between his word and Dean's, a seemingly impossible task.

But in July, the Ervin committee learned about the White House's voice-activated taping system. Cox and Ervin both sought access to the tapes. Nixon stonewalled, defending his action on grounds of executive privilege and national security. In October, as the result of a suit by Cox, a federal appeals court ordered Nixon to turn over nine of the tapes to Judge Sirica. Nixon refused—and ordered Richardson to fire Cox. Richardson resigned rather than do so, and so did his deputy attorney general. The next ranking official in the Justice Department, Solicitor General Robert Bork, then did Nixon's bidding, carrying out what became known as the "Saturday night massacre." An avalanche of outrage swept across the nation and descended on the White House. In its face, Nixon relinquished the nine tapes to Sirica and appointed a new special prosecutor, Leon Jaworski, a conservative attorney from Houston.

DOWNFALL

Nixon's troubles compounded when the U.S. district attorney in Maryland found that Vice-President Agnew had taken bribes while he was governor of Maryland and as vice-president. On October 10, 1973, Agnew resigned his office,

The Senate Watergate committee, chaired by Sam Ervin of North Carolina (second from left), listens to testimony from one of the burglars, May 1973.

pleading no contest to both the bribery counts and charges of income-tax evasion. He was fined $10,000 and given three years probation. Following the procedures specified in the Twenty-fifth Amendment, which had been ratified in 1967, Nixon appointed the amiable Gerald R. Ford, the House minority leader, as his new vice-president.

Meanwhile, evidence surfaced that Nixon, in order to obtain a substantial tax deduction, had illegally backdated the gift of his vice-presidential papers and that the federal government had paid for improvements to his homes in San Clemente, California, and Key Biscayne, Florida. Nixon himself remained defiant, declaring at a nationally televised press session in November, "I am not a crook." The next month, the House Judiciary Committee began an impeachment inquiry. In March 1974, responding to evidence supplied by Jaworski, a grand jury recommended the indictment of seven Nixon aides including Haldeman, Ehrlichman, and Mitchell on grounds of perjury, obstruction of justice, and impeding the investigation of Watergate. Nixon was named as an unindicted "co-conspirator" because Jaworski believed he could not indict a sitting president.

That month, Jaworski and the House Judiciary Committee subpoenaed more tapes, particularly those of Nixon's conversations after the Watergate break-in. Nixon contested the subpoenas in court but, trying to wriggle out of the closing vise, did provide edited transcripts of the tapes. Dotted throughout with the bracketed phrase "expletive deleted," they revealed him as vindictive, bigoted, amoral, and foul-mouthed. Although they did not contain decisive evidence that he had obstructed justice—a smoking gun—they appalled even hard-line Republicans and intensified demands for his resignation.

> *"The unedited transcripts of the tapes finally provided the smoking gun, incontrovertible evidence that Nixon had personally managed the cover-up."*

In late July, the House Judiciary Committee adopted three articles of impeachment, accusing the president of obstructing justice in the Watergate investigation, abusing his power by exploiting agencies such as the CIA and the IRS for partisan purposes, and unconstitutionally resisting the committee's subpoenas. Of the twenty-one Republicans on the committee, six voted with the Democratic majority on the first charge, seven on the second, and two on the third.

At the same time, the Supreme Court, rejecting Nixon's claims of executive privilege, ruled that he had to give up the subpoenaed tapes. The unedited transcripts of the tapes finally provided the smoking gun, incontrovertible evidence that he had personally managed the cover-up, starting with his conversation with Haldeman six days after the break-in. Four anti-impeachment Republicans on the Judiciary Committee switched in favor of impeachment. A delegation of Republicans led by Barry Goldwater told Nixon that he could count on no more than fifteen votes in the Senate against conviction. On August 9, 1974, Richard Nixon made history again, becoming the **first president to resign.** Gerald Ford, promptly sworn in as president, declared, "Our long national nightmare is over."

COLD, GRAY MORNING

The nightmare may have ended, but it left consequences, and so did the explosive developments in foreign and domestic affairs that had transpired since Johnson's escalation of the war in Vietnam. The consequences were for both the better and the worse. With détente and the opening to China, Nixon had moved American foreign policy away from the post–World War II framework of a bipolar conflict between capitalism and Communism and adapted it to the reality—which the Vietnam War had demonstrated—that the Communist world comprised multiple centers only loosely joined. The hard-line Cold Warrior had made the search for accommodations with Communism a legitimate goal for the United States. By ending the Vietnam War, he implicitly recognized that American power had limits. His enunciation of the Nixon Doctrine—marking a shift in foreign commitments that most Americans welcomed—declared, in effect, that the United States would no longer act as the world's military policeman, that in a world seething with postcolonial nationalist aspirations, there would be no more Vietnams.

Richard Nixon flashes his signature salute on his departure from Washington after resigning the presidency, August 9, 1974.

Still, Nixon had wound down the Vietnam War in ways that threatened American democratic institutions. His high-handedness had been made possible by the steady accretion of presidential power, and the corresponding loss of congressional control, over national security since the beginning of the Cold War. In the War Powers Act of 1973, Congress attempted to restrict a president's power to make war indefinitely on his own while allowing him enough short-term autonomy to counter immediate threats to national security. Congressional investigations of the CIA and the FBI in 1975–76 revealed that both agencies grossly abused their power and provoked demands that they be reined in.

Since the 1930s, through World War II and much of the Cold War, Americans had tended to trust their government, especially the man in the White House. Now, both the Vietnam War and Watergate, with their lies and corruptions, encouraged distrust of the presidency, government in general, and indeed most authority in the United States. More than forty members of the Nixon administration were prosecuted for crimes. In 1974, aiming to reduce the incentive for politicos to sell favors, Congress provided for partial public financing of presidential campaigns and limitations on the role of private campaign contributions. Voter turnout had fallen from almost 64 percent in 1960 to just under 56 percent in 1972, an indication that Americans' expectations from government were steadily diminishing.

	Chronology
June 5–11, 1967	Six-Day War in the Middle East.
January 31, 1968	Tet offensive in Vietnam.
April 4, 1968	Martin Luther King Jr. assassinated in Memphis.
June 5, 1968	Robert Kennedy assassinated in Los Angeles.
July 1969	*Apollo 11* lands on the moon.
April 1970	U. S. troops invade Cambodia.
June 17, 1972	Watergate break-in.
1973–74	OPEC oil embargo.
August 9, 1974	President Nixon resigns.

Suggested Reading

Todd Gitlin, *The Sixties: Years of Hope, Days of Rage* (1987)

George Herring, *America's Longest War: The United States and Vietnam, 1950–1975*, 3rd ed. (1996)

Allen Matusow, *The Unravelling of America* (1984)

Kim McQuaid, *The Anxious Years: America in the Vietnam-Watergate Era* (1989)

Herbert Parmet, *Richard Nixon and His America* (1990)

Chapter 31

CONSERVATIVE REVIVAL:
1974–1980

The National Women's Conference, 1977. Among those onstage are Shirley Chisholm, Bella Abzug, Rosalynn Carter, Betty Ford, and Lady Bird Johnson.

QUESTIONS

■ **What were Ford's main achievements in foreign affairs?**

■ **What were the major environmental issues and technological achievements of the 1970s?**

■ **How did Carter show conservatism at home and idealism abroad?**

■ **How did social divisions emerge in this period?**

■ **What caused the New Right to emerge?**

Although the nation's first centennial, in 1876, had occurred during one of its worst depressions, the celebrations had optimistically extolled the economic and technological future, powerfully symbolized in the exhibition at Machinery Hall by George Corliss's giant steam engine. The festivals in 1976 were marked less by high expectations of marvelous tomorrows than by wistful nostalgia for a mythic past. Communities staged pie-eating contests and hog-calling competitions, while El Paso, Texas, enacted a Pony Express ride. A national television audience watched fireworks light up the sky over an armada of more than 200 tall sailing ships come from around the world to lie at anchor in New York Harbor.

The nostalgia bespoke discontent with the present and apprehension about the future. Americans were accustomed to expecting a better future for themselves and their children, but in the 1970s their confidence was eroding in the face of bedeviling difficulties. Abroad, the Soviet Union blew hot and cold in its commitment to peace, OPEC remained willful, and anti-Americanism flared in the Middle East. At home, major industries faced mounting international competition; stagflation continued to weaken the economy; and the specter of energy shortages raised nagging doubts about the nation's economic future. Environmental protection appeared to threaten economic growth. The country remained divided over the claims of minority groups and, increasingly, of women and homosexuals. Resentments lingered over the war in Vietnam.

In 1978, *Time* magazine declared the 1970s "elusive, unfocused, a patchwork of dramatics awaiting a drama"—in all, a historical pause not "worth remembering." Ford had dealt ineffectually with most of the problems vexing the country. While Jimmy Carter took them on, his efforts fell short of the task. In the post-Nixon seventies, the United States was suffused with a rare pessimism—a fear that it was now vulnerable, that it had lost the blessings of nature. But behind the gloom, key changes were taking place, enough to make the seventies a transforming decade in the nation's history. Public and private initiatives were mounted to restructure the economy, revive investment in research and development, and establish new industries by exploiting science and technology, notably in personal computers and biotechnology. The divisions over minority aspirations, women's reproductive autonomy, and gay rights increasingly expressed themselves in politics and the courts. Overall, these changes shifted the political center of gravity steadily to the right. They laid the foundation for the national agenda that would shape the United States for the rest of the century.

Ford's Stewardship

"I am a Ford, not a Lincoln," the new president self-deprecatingly once said of himself. In 1974, Gerald R. Ford, sixty-one, was a veteran Michigan congressman and right-of-center Republican, a dutiful party workhorse who had been rewarded with the House minority leadership before his elevation to the vice-presidency. The first chief executive unelected to either the presidency or the vice-presidency, Ford struck many Americans as less able than they liked their leaders to be. Lyndon Johnson was wont to say of him that he was "so dumb that he can't walk and chew gum at the same time." Still, he was unpretentious, affable, open, and honest, a refreshing change from Nixon. People were willing to allow him the benefit of the doubt, given the extraordinary circumstances of his ascent to the nation's highest office. Shortly after he entered the White House, Ford appointed Nelson Rockefeller, the former governor of New York, as his vice-president, widely considered a sound choice.

But within a month of taking office, Ford stunned the country by fully and absolutely pardoning Nixon for "any and all crimes" he had committed against the United States during his presidency. While the aides who had done Nixon's bidding were punished, the pardon meant that his own offenses would never even be fully aired. Although Ford declared that his aim was "to heal the wounds throughout the United States," millions of Americans were outraged. Suspicions abounded that Ford had secretly agreed to the pardon in return for Nixon's appointing him vice-president. Whatever the truth of the matter, the deed greatly undermined Ford's credibility, heightening the nation's widespread distrust of its government.

THE ECONOMY AND ENERGY

The continuing ripple effects of the OPEC price hikes drove up other prices, generating an inflation rate in 1974 of more than 12 percent. Ford responded with a program called Whip Inflation Now (WIN), which called for voluntary restraint in energy consumption (like Ford, people pinned on WIN buttons) and policy initiatives to slow the economy, notably higher interest rates and reductions in federal spending. The inflation rate fell to slightly more than 9 percent the next year, but the price-cutting measures produced a severe recession. Between 1973 and 1975, the gross national product plunged 6 percent. In 1974, unemployment doubled to almost 9 percent, and the next year it climbed to 11 percent.

The economic troubles joined with resentments over Watergate in the 1974 congressional elections to produce a Democratic gain of forty-three seats in the House and three seats in the Senate. To stimulate the economy, Congress passed tax reductions in March and December 1975 that totaled $31 billion, but at Ford's insistence the first was indirectly and the second directly coupled to caps on spending. By 1976, the inflation rate had dropped to just under 5 percent, but at considerable cost in jobs. Ford responded to most of the Democratic Congress's initiatives in the vein of the Republican he was, vetoing thirty-nine bills, including measures for federal aid to education and health care.

Ford also differed with Congress over energy policy. The administration wanted to decontrol oil prices, thinking that higher prices would discourage consumption while encouraging the development of new sources. Many Democrats, sure that the rise in prices had already provided oil companies with excessive profits, resisted measures that would further increase their earnings at the expense of consumers. However, Congress and the president agreed on the need for energy conservation. The Energy Policy and Conservation Act of 1975 established a 1-billion-barrel strategic petroleum reserve and required that domestic and imported automobiles meet average fuel efficiency standards—roughly doubling in ten years from 13 miles per gallon to 27.5 miles per gallon. The new standard promised to have a big impact on the oil supply, since at the time American cars and trucks burned one out of every seven barrels of oil used daily in the world.

FOREIGN AFFAIRS

Ford kept Henry Kissinger on as secretary of state, reestablished a presidential science advisory apparatus, and continued Nixon's pursuit of détente with the Soviets, but he was handicapped by growing congressional concerns over Soviet violations of human rights. Congress responded to strong ev-

President Ford encourages Americans to enlist in WIN, his war against inflation, October 1974.

985

idence of anti-Semitism in the Soviet Union by tying a grant of most-favored-nation trade status to an increase of 60,000 in the rate of allowed Jewish emigration. In the SALT II arms-control agreement, arrived at in Vladivostok, Siberia, in 1974, Ford and Brezhnev agreed to limit the number of strategic nuclear missiles on each side, about half of which could be MIRVed. In Helsinki the next year, Ford, Brezhnev, and the leaders of thirty-three other nations adopted a set of accords that formalized the post–World War II territorial boundaries and declared respect for human rights and greater freedom of travel. However, the Senate surrounded the fate of SALT II with uncertainty by delaying its ratification, and the Helsinki Accords were attacked by some Democrats as well as by the Republican right on grounds that they accepted the denial of freedom to the peoples of Eastern Europe.

The Middle East. The demonstrated vulnerability of Israel to concerted attack and of the United States to the oil embargo sent Kissinger to the Middle East to forge a political settlement. During much of 1974–75, he flew from one capital to another in what became known as "shuttle diplomacy." Kissinger kept the Soviets out of the peacemaking process so

as to reduce their influence in the region. He achieved a pull-back of forces along the Suez Canal, helped bring about an end to the oil embargo, and produced an Israeli-Syrian disengagement across the Golan Heights. Pressing Egypt and Israel to resolve their differences, he brought about a historic accord in the Sinai in September 1975 that provided for the withdrawal of Israeli troops from strategic parts of the peninsula and Egypt's opening of the Suez Canal to nonmilitary Israeli cargoes. Its way was greased by a U.S. commitment to supply advanced arms to Israel and a pledge not to deal with the Palestine Liberation Organization while it refused to recognize Israel's right to exist.

Egypt drew closer to the United States, gaining economic assistance but arousing enmity among other Arab states. Syria turned away from Egyptian president Sadat and adopted even a harder line against Israel. Nevertheless, Kissinger's tenacious shuttle diplomacy had added to Israel's security by neutralizing Egypt on its western flank. It had also improved the United States' own position in the Middle East.

Asia. Ford maintained the United States' distance from Vietnam, even after North Vietnam revived the war in 1974 and South Vietnam was threatened with defeat. In April 1975, Ford declared, "Today, America can regain the sense of pride that existed before Vietnam. But it cannot be achieved by refighting a war that is finished as far as America is concerned." The next month, Saigon fell to North Vietnamese troops and was immediately renamed Ho Chi Minh City. Television networks carried pictures of the desperate last exit of Americans joined by South Vietnamese terrified of reprisals from the helipad atop the U.S. embassy.

A few weeks later, the Khmer Rouge in Cambodia captured the American merchant ship *Mayaguez* in the Gulf of Siam. Ford got the crew back by ordering air strikes against Cambodia and sending the marines to the rescue, but more American lives were lost in the operation than

South Vietnamese, desperate to reach the evacuation helicopters, crowd the walls of the U.S. embassy in Saigon as North Vietnamese forces take the city, April 29, 1975.

the number of crew returned. The Vietnam War had cost the United States more than $150 billion and more than 360,000 casualties, including 58,000 dead, about 40 percent of whom were killed after Nixon took office. Some analysts consider the U.S. intervention in Vietnam as a necessary battle in the Cold War, but most historians consider it at best a tragic, costly error in policy, a misguided sacrifice of American blood and treasure.

THE ELECTION OF 1976

Ford won the Republican nomination after fending off a strong challenge from Ronald Reagan, the onetime film actor, former governor of California, and champion of right-wing Republicans. He appeased conservatives by dumping Vice-President Nelson Rockefeller and designating Senator Robert Dole of Kansas as his running mate. James Earl Carter, a former governor of Georgia with virtually no standing in national affairs, emerged from among a crowded field of Democratic hopefuls to sweep the primaries and win his party's presidential nomination. A wealthy peanut grower and born-again Christian, he appealed to Americans disillusioned with Washington by styling himself an unpretentious outsider, encouraging people to call him Jimmy, and promising that he would never lie. The Democratic vice-presidential nominee was Senator Walter Mondale, a liberal from Minnesota.

In the aftermath of Watergate, it seemed to many Democrats that, as one of them put it, "We could run an aardvark and win." Ford ran a lackluster campaign—and he astonished listeners in a debate with Carter by asserting, "There is no Soviet domination of Eastern Europe"—but Carter's campaign was also unimpressive. He promised little beyond honesty, decency, and goodness in government, appearing to believe that the high morality of his purpose would substitute for the murkiness of his proposals. By election day, Carter's sizable early lead in the polls had eroded. He squeaked to victory with only 51 percent of the popular vote but enough to gain him a margin of 297 to 240 in the electoral college. Apathy marked the election—only 53.3 percent of eligible voters cast ballots, down from 55.4 percent in 1972—an indication that Americans, disillusioned with government in the wake of Watergate, expected Washington to do little about the problems vexing the country at the opening of its third century since independence.

The Economy and Technology

A FALTERING ECONOMY

When Jimmy Carter entered the White House, it was evident that the economy was suffering from deep and dispiriting structural problems. Between 1945 and 1965, industrial productivity, measured as output per man-hour, had climbed at an annual rate of 3 percent; now it was rising at a mere 1 percent per year, only a quarter of the rate in Germany and a fifth of that in Japan. The standard of living in the United States dropped to fifth in the world, below that of four European nations. Stagflation severely threatened the country's economic pillars, forcing federal bailouts of the Chrysler Corporation and of New York City just a year before the tall ships sailed into the harbor.

By the end of the decade, people had to pay twice as much as they did at the beginning for basic necessities and for an average single-family home. Real spending power for the average worker fell to its lowest point since 1961. Credit cards became consumer commonplaces as people bought goods on credit one day that would be payable in cheaper dollars the next. Private debt rose sharply. In California, many homeowners reeled under the skyrocketing property taxes generated by the sharp increase in property values. In 1978, angrily resorting to the initiative process, Californians passed Proposition 13, which slashed property taxes in half, capped the annual rate of possible increases, and inspired similar tax revolts in other states.

The economic malaise was especially acute in the nation's industrial heartland. During the 1960s, foreign-car imports had quadrupled their share of the American market, to 17 percent; by 1980, their share had almost doubled again, to about 33 percent. Electronic goods from abroad captured a comparable fraction of the market. At the end of World War

"I'm glad I majored in economics. I now have a clearer understanding of why there's no job waiting for me out there."

This 1978 cartoon expresses the economic malaise of the time.

II, the United States had produced almost two out of every three tons of the world's steel; by the opening of the 1970s, it accounted for only 15 percent. Japanese steel was better and cheaper than most of the American, and the Japanese were selling more than 4 million tons of it a year in the United States. Foreign products gained a competitive advantage in part because of cheaper labor costs abroad, but domestic products suffered from short-sightedness among American industrial managers. Detroit's auto executives, for example, considered a preference for the smaller, more fuel-efficient cars coming from Europe and Asia "unpatriotic" and "un-American," as one of them put it. The captains of steel neglected to modernize their plants and invested only a paltry fraction of profits in research and development.

Since the end of World War II, job-growth rates had been far higher in the clerical than in the blue-collar sector. Now the decline in the major manufacturing industries sent many workers downward on the economic and social ladder, especially in the region from Pennsylvania through upper Illinois and into Michigan, Wisconsin, and Minnesota, the centers of steel, auto, coal, and iron production. Once brawny and prosperous, the region was now a "rust belt," its smokestacks cold and factories closed. Like Aurora, in the iron range of Minnesota, many of its towns were dying, with their Main Street stores boarded up and "For Sale" signs on houses, cars, motorcycles, and campers.

Union membership continued to decline, accounting for only a quarter of the nonagricultural workforce, and unions faced intensifying efforts by management to weaken them. Some major corporations tried to meet the mounting foreign competition by demanding higher output from their workers. At the General Motors plant in Lordstown, Ohio, management sought to double its assembly-line output of cars by giving workers only thirty-six seconds to perform their tasks. The head of the United Auto Workers charged that business leaders had broken the fragile compact of cooperativeness that had prevailed during the good years in favor of conducting a "one-sided class war." In industries that continued to thrive, complicated manufacturing tasks were increasingly being taken over by robots and computers, a process that steadily eliminated skilled jobs. Unskilled jobs were being created in their place, many of them in the service sector, ex-

> *"To many environmentalists in the seventies, technology seemed less a savior than a hazard. Their eagerness to curb its use threatened economic growth and thus pitted them against labor and lower-income groups."*

emplified by the growth of fast-food restaurants like McDonald's and discount stores like Wal-Mart.

Signs of worker alienation appeared in rising absenteeism and drug addiction. The young rock star Bruce Springsteen caught the mood, rasping—in songs like "The River" and "Thunder Road"—of bleak, blue-collar towns short on work and long on losers, where "things that seemed so important" had "vanished right into the air." Many young Americans flocked to discotheques, dancing amid flashing lights and high-decibel sound to the recordings of groups like the Bee Gees, who celebrated "staying alive." The film *Saturday Night Fever* showcased John Travolta escaping into the glittering world of the disco dance hall from the desperation of his otherwise no-exit blue-collar milieu.

In the mid-1970s, fewer than three out of five non-college-educated people thought that hard work would pay off, down from four out of five at the close of the sixties. By 1979, most Americans came to think that inflation would be with them always, and were convinced that the next year would be worse than the current one. They had it on the authority of the chairman of the Federal Reserve Board that "under [current economic] conditions the standard of living for the average American has got to decline." Pollsters found almost three out of four people agreeing that "we are fast coming to a turning point in our history. The land of plenty is becoming the land of want."

THE ENVIRONMENT AND PUBLIC HEALTH

American optimism had historically been grounded in no small part in the natural abundance of the continent and faith that technological change brought social progress. But now experts were predicting that the industrialized world, including the United States, was depleting the planet's natural resources at an accelerating rate, that the resources were finite, and that they were bound to run out. One such prognostication—based on computerized analyses at MIT and published as *Limits to Growth*, in 1972—sold 4 million copies in thirty languages.

Many environmentalists welcomed that dark prediction, seeing in it a solid reason for the United States to reject the exuberant consumerism that ravaged the land, air, and water.

They made a cult classic of the 1973 book *Small Is Beautiful* by the German-born economist E. F. Schumacher, an attack against unbridled material growth. In California, Governor Jerry Brown, an evangelist of the new age, proclaimed that the country had entered an era of limits and celebrated Schumacher's notion that "less is more." Many people embraced an ecological life-style that emphasized personal responsibility for the impact of daily living on the natural world. A number grew organic gardens, gave up gas-guzzling cars, and embraced recycling, composting, and natural fibers.

To many environmentalists in the seventies, technology seemed less a savior than a hazard. Their eagerness to curb its use threatened economic growth and thus pitted them against labor and lower-income groups. Whitney Young, the head of the Urban League, an organization of black moderates, had declared after the first Earth Day that "the war on pollution . . . should be waged after the war on poverty is won." Still, Americans of all classes and colors found worrisome the revelation that the soil under a housing development at Love Canal, near Buffalo, New York, was contaminated by chemical wastes that were believed to cause cancer and genetic defects among the residents. They were also worried about the danger to public health and safety that appeared to be posed by nuclear power and genetic manipulations.

Nuclear Power. The shortage of energy, the natural resource most crucial to American prosperity, divided the country, often bitterly. Many policymakers as well as environmentalists emphasized conservation, but some analysts continued to hold that the nation's energy supplies also needed to be increased—by finding new caches of oil and natural gas and by further developing nuclear power. In 1975, about 225 nuclear plants were ordered, under construction, or in operation. They would generate enough electrical power for some 100 million people, providing as much energy as six major oil fields. Utility companies reported that nuclear plants had already saved Americans more than $750 million on their 1974 electric bills. In 1976, addressing a widespread concern, a federal report concluded that, with 1,000 reactors operating continuously, only one serious accident would occur in 10,000 years.

Such estimates were challenged by scientific experts who intervened in the process to license nuclear plants. The interventions helped double the time required to construct a nuclear plant to about ten years and, amid the climate of high interest rates, substantially increased the cost of building

them. At the opening of a congressional hearing on nuclear safety, one senator complained about being given "a lot of gobbledegook" and expostulated that he wished "somebody would . . . tell the committee categorically a nuclear reactor is safe or it isn't safe." For the public, such a verdict issued in March 1979, when design flaws and errors committed by operators of the nuclear power plant at **Three Mile Island,** near Harrisburg, Pennsylvania, combined to cause a failure in the cooling system, a partial meltdown of the nuclear fuel, and the expulsion of some 800,000 gallons of radioactive steam into the air above the surrounding Susquehanna Valley. Coincidentally, the film *The China Syndrome*, a dramatic tale of an accident at a nuclear power plant, had just opened in the nation's theaters. The one-two punch of the real accident and the fictional one dealt the nuclear industry a setback that environmental activists by themselves might not have achieved. Utilities canceled orders for more than thirty nuclear plants, and no new orders were placed.

Fearful children protest the hazardous wastes dumped at the nearby Love Canal site in Niagara Falls, New York, August 1978.

989

The Hazards of Genetics. Americans had earlier been reminded from the agricultural quarter of the hazards of attempting to subordinate nature to human will. Beginning in 1968, a disease known as southern corn leaf blight swept from the southeastern United States westward to Texas and northward to Wisconsin, destroying 15 percent of the 1970 corn crop at a cost to farmers of about $1 billion. The disease was caused by a fungus dubbed "Race T" that thrived on a type of cytoplasm contained in 80 percent of the hybrid corn grown in the United States. The blight was eliminated within a year by breeding genes from other varieties of corn into the dominant hybrid strains, but it called national attention to the susceptibility to disease of genetically homogeneous crops. Just six varieties accounted for nearly 40 percent of the country's wheat; four varieties for 65 percent of its rice; three for 76 percent of its snap beans; and only two for 96 percent of its peas. In 1972, the National Academy of Sciences declared in a widely quoted report, "Most major crops are impressively uniform genetically and impressively vulnerable."

Apprehensions about the manipulation of genetic material widened and intensified in the mid-1970s, when genetic engineering, a term coined a decade earlier, suddenly appeared on the verge of becoming an achievable reality. The breakthrough arose from a technique, invented by two biologists in the Bay Area in northern California, that permitted scientists to snip out a gene from the DNA of one organism and insert it into the DNA of another. This method of recombinant DNA opened the door to the transformation of organisms—plants, animals, and possibly even human beings—by changing their hereditary essence. Some biologists worried that recombinant microorganisms carrying, for example, tumor genes might threaten life or health or whole ecosystems. Others warned that the ability to modify human genes might lead to a revival of eugenics (see Chapters 19, 22, 23). Some questioned the reconfiguring of life itself as an act of hubris that would lead to unpredictable and dangerous consequences.

> *"The method of recombinant DNA opened the door to the transformation of organisms—plants, animals, and possibly even human beings—by changing their hereditary essence."*

In an unprecedented action, biologists voluntarily imposed a moratorium on most research with recombinant DNA, then reviewed its potential hazards at a 1975 meeting at Asilomar, near Pacific Grove, California; as a result, government guidelines were imposed for federally sponsored work using the new techniques. In the later 1970s, however, the dangers explored at Asilomar provoked widespread public apprehension, especially in areas where universities engaged in recombinant research. Local and state governments and Congress geared up to legislate tough, mandatory restrictions on such research. The biologist James D. Watson, a signer of the call for a moratorium, argued that the hazards of recombinant research were no greater than those of traditional work with virulent organisms and that, left alone, recombinant methods would lead to revolutionary practical and commercial benefits in medicine and agriculture. Molecular biologists beat back the state and federal legislative threats to their research and gradually achieved an easing of the restrictions on investigations using recombinant DNA. But the skeptics remained suspicious that genetic engineering jeopardized public health and safety as well as the environment.

The cooling towers of the Metropolitan Edison Nuclear Power Plant at Three Mile Island, shut down after the accident in March 1979.

INNOVATION AND RENEWAL

In the circles of high technology, anxiety was mounting about the impact of the downturn in spending for research and development on the nation's military and economic vitality. Some analysts contended that the reductions in overall defense spending, including research and development (R&D), were making the United States militarily vulnerable. Others pointed to the increasingly vigorous foreign competition that the United States faced, especially from Japan. The relative power of American innovation seemed to be falling. The number of patents issued by the United States in 1978 was about the same—some 66,000—as it had been in 1966; the proportion issued to foreigners had almost doubled, from 20 percent to almost 40 percent.

Corporate and academic leaders faulted the country for allowing investment in nondefense R&D to remain flat in the 1970s, at about 1.68 percent of GNP, while the proportional Japanese investment had been steadily rising, reaching 1.92 percent in 1977. The critics argued that American military and economic security required a greater investment in R&D, including more money from nonfederal sources, particularly industry. They stressed that innovation was emerging as the new currency of foreign affairs. Throughout the decade, the United States' annual trade deficit in conventional manufactured goods doubled. The loss was offset by a trade surplus in high-technology goods, which almost quadrupled. Among the leading high-tech products of the seventies were mainframe computers, semiconductors, chemicals, and pharmaceuticals. Now it was evident that the leading prospects for the 1980s included biotechnology and personal computers.

The Birth of Biotechnology. Even while molecular biologists were fighting off excessive restrictions on recombinant DNA research, some were beginning to commercialize it. Herbert Boyer, one of the co-inventors of the technique of recombinant DNA, led the way, joining in 1976 with a venture capitalist to form the biotechnology firm Genentech—short for "genetic engineering technology." The company set out to produce human insulin, a protein in which diabetics are deficient and which was unavailable in large quantities. (Diabetics then relied on injections of insulin obtained from pigs.) In 1978, Genentech announced in a press conference that its scientists had succeeded in producing the human protein by isolating the gene for it, then inserting it into bacteria, turning them into human insulin factories. Along with other

newspapers and magazines, *Newsweek* heralded the achievement, proclaiming that "recombinant DNA technology can undoubtedly be used to make scores of other vital proteins, such as growth and thyroid hormones, as well as antibodies against specific diseases."

That expectation was stimulating the creation of a biotechnology industry in the United States. New companies were being founded at a high pace, while major pharmaceutical firms as well as oil and chemical giants were plunging into molecular biological research. The fledgling industry was given a triple boost in 1980, when the government ended most restrictions on recombinant research; Congress passed the Bayh-Dole Act, which encouraged universities to patent and privatize the results of federally sponsored high-technology research; and, in June, the Supreme Court held in *Diamond v. Chakrabarty* that a patent could be issued on genetically modified bacteria. During arguments in the Supreme Court case, critics of genetic engineering objected that allowing patents on living creatures was unwarranted and would lead to patents on higher organisms, perhaps even human beings. The Court argued that whether an invention was living or dead was irrelevant to its qualification for a patent. Following that logic, in 1985 the Patent and Trademark Office allowed patents on any kind of plant. In 1987, it declared that patents were allowable on animals though not on human beings, and the next year it issued the world's first patent on an animal—a laboratory mouse that had been genetically engineered to be supersusceptible to cancer.

Computers for the People. One of the most significant technical developments of the 1970s was the personal computer. Personal computers (PCs) sprang from several sources, notably the military's patronage of microelectronics and the interests of hobbyists in democratizing the use of computers. An essential component of the PC was the integrated circuit, which formed all its electrical parts out of a flat piece of silicon, photoetching the connections between them. It was devised independently at Texas Instruments and at Fairchild Semiconductor Laboratories, in Palo Alto, California, which was an incubator for many of the engineers who would develop the computing industry in what came to be known as Silicon Valley, the region heavy with computer firms on the peninsula south of San Francisco. Although integrated circuits were not developed with military patronage, the Defense Department and NASA provided a sizable fraction of the early market for them. One Minuteman II missile used

The Microsoft Albuquerque Group, December 1978. Top row: Steve Wood, Bob Wallace, Jim Lane. Middle row: Bob O'Rear, Bob Greenberg, Marc McDonald, Gordon Letwin. Front row: Bill Gates, Andrea Lewis, Marla Wood, Paul Allen.

2,000; the Apollo guidance system, 5,000. By the late 1960s, engineers in Silicon Valley were creating an integrated circuit on a small chip containing the calculating circuits equivalent to all those in a mainframe computer of the 1950s. In 1973, the Intel Corporation, founded by several veterans of Fairchild, announced that it had produced such a chip: the 8080.

The development of the personal computer was encouraged by the abundant technical resources of Silicon Valley—notably the electronics graduates from nearby Stanford University and the University of California at Berkeley and the engineering innovations from local firms such as Hewlett-Packard—and by the inspiration that hobbyists drew from time-sharing computers. Built around a central computer that automatically allocated processing time to different individuals, time-sharing gave users in their offices access to their personal files and encouraged them to think they could have interactive access to their own computers at any time for any purpose. Computer hobbyists, some of them in tune with the countercultural ambience of the San Francisco Bay Peninsula, called for bringing computing power to the people by, for example, providing the public with free access to time-shared terminals. One enthusiast recalled the "strong feeling that we were subversives. We were subverting the way the giant corporations had run things."

In 1974, a small firm that three hobbyists had founded in Albuquerque, New Mexico, to sell radio transmitters for model airplanes went beyond the dream of universal terminal access to put computers themselves into everyone's hands. They started marketing a personal computer kit called the Altair. Selling for $397, the Altair ran on the Intel 8080 chip and was an instant hit with hobbyists, even though it had no keyboard or monitor. It spurred Bill Gates, a twenty-year-old Harvard student, and his high school friend Paul Allen, twenty-two, to write a software program for it that they licensed to the Albuquerque firm. Gates dropped out of Harvard to develop the Microsoft Corporation, a software firm he and Allen founded in 1975 for the Altair venture. In 1976, Steve Wozniak, twenty-five, and Steve Jobs, twenty, began marketing a comparable personal computer, the Apple. Both were T-shirts-and-jeans devotees of the hobbyist electronics culture in Silicon Valley, where they grew up; Jobs, with long hair and sandals, was an acolyte of vegetarianism, the Beatles, and transcendental meditation. They built the first Apples in the home garage of Jobs's parents.

Eager to expand the business, Jobs and Wozniak relinquished their T-shirts for suits, obtained venture capital, and in 1977 brought out the Apple II, which included a keyboard,

Steve Jobs introduces the Apple II computer in Cupertino, California, 1977.

992

a monitor, and a floppy-disk drive for storage. A later version, introduced in 1983, operated with a mouse and pull-down menus, both of which had been originally developed under contracts from the Defense Department and NASA. By this time, several other companies were selling personal computers. The software for them was initially confined to educational programs and games such as the wildly popular "Pac-man," but in 1979 VisiCalc, a spreadsheet program, came on the market and demonstrated the value of the PC for business.

Bill Gates had already warned the hobbyists that he would consider free sharing of the software that Microsoft had produced for the Altair a form of piracy. By the late 1970s, personal computing was rapidly turning away from its countercultural origins into a lucrative for-profit enterprise. In 1981, IBM entered the PC market, enlisting Microsoft to provide the operating software for its machines. In response, Microsoft bought a software package that had been devised at Seattle Computer Products by Tim Paterson, a recent college graduate, and provided it to IBM as MS-DOS (short for "Microsoft Disk Operating System"). Gates sold IBM the right to use the system but maintained Microsoft's ownership, an arrangement that permitted the company eventually to earn billions of dollars by selling the right to use the system, which soon became an industry standard, to other makers of personal computers. The PC caught on so fast that two years later *Time* magazine designated the personal computer its "Man of the Year."

President Jimmy Carter walks with his wife, Rosalynn, from the Capitol to the White House following his inauguration, January 20, 1977.

Carter: A Presidency of Limits

On inauguration day in January 1977, Jimmy Carter forswore the traditional motorcade and formal dress to walk down Pennsylvania Avenue hand in hand with his wife, Rosalynn, wearing a standard business suit and overcoat. People appreciated the gesture of unpretentiousness, but they soon discovered that modest simplicity did not by itself make for an effective presidency. Carter's governmental experience had been confined to a stint in the Georgia legislature and one term as governor. He surrounded himself with a staff that was young, mainly from Georgia, and even less practiced than he was in national affairs. He dealt at a distance with Capitol Hill, declining to cultivate its leadership. As a result, "Carter couldn't get the Pledge of Allegiance through Congress," one politico noted.

Carter had campaigned as a kind of populist, yet, like the inauguration walk, his populism was more symbolic than substantive. He was an Annapolis graduate, a nuclear engineer, a successful businessman. Like Herbert Hoover, another engineer and businessman, he believed that complex issues would yield to careful rational analysis and that government would be more effective if it were made more efficient. Carter was highly intelligent and well intentioned; and though he lacked Woodrow Wilson's righteousness, his born-again Christianity added a touch of moral energy to his public purposes. In line with his gubernatorial record, he endorsed social progressivism, including civil rights for women and minorities. But Carter was not a liberal in the bread-and-butter manner of Lyndon Johnson. His commitment to progressive action was constrained by a reluctance to incur high federal costs. As his first budget director remarked, "He campaigns liberal, but he governs conservative."

A TOUCH OF LIBERALISM

Making good on a campaign pledge to heal the wounds of Vietnam, Carter granted full pardon to draft evaders the day after his inauguration. His action was applauded by liberals such as Senator Edward Kennedy, but it was denounced by conservatives, including the American Legion and the Republican national chairman, who declared it "a slap in the face to all those Americans and their families who did their duty." Sentiment on this issue reflected the ongoing division over the war itself. There had been neither celebratory parades for soldiers returning from Vietnam nor even national events of mourning for those who did not come back. But a few films debuted in the late seventies—*The Deer Hunter* (1978), *Coming Home* (1978), and *Apocalypse Now* (1979)—that aroused sympathy for the men who fought in the war.

> *"There were neither celebratory parades for soldiers returning from Vietnam nor even national events of mourning for those who did not come back."*

The Vietnam Veterans Memorial, designed by Maya Lin (with a reflection of the Washington Monument), on the Mall in Washington, D.C.

In 1980, Congress authorized the Vietnam Veterans Memorial on the National Mall in Washington. Maya Ying Lin, a twenty-one-year-old student of architecture at Yale University, produced the winning design, a simple wall of polished black granite inscribed with the names of the 57,661 American servicemen and -women who had died in the war. Some veterans and conservatives attacked Lin's design as inappropriate or insulting, partly because, unlike conventional war memorials, it did not portray flags or soldiers, partly because she was of Asian extraction ("How can you let a gook design this memorial?" one dissenter asked). Completed in 1982, the wall attracted millions of visitors, many of whom deposited flowers, flags, and tears at the site. Carter's pardon initiated a process whereby both supporters and opponents of the war began to find common, reconciling ground in concern for the Vietnam vets.

Carter instituted a wide-ranging reform of the civil service and otherwise advanced the liberal agenda through appointments and enforcement of civil rights laws. In addition to naming three women to his cabinet and a black as ambassador to the United Nations, he put more women, blacks, and Hispanic Americans into federal jobs, judgeships, and regulatory posts than had any previous president. He approved the congressional expansion of programs allocating federal work to minority contractors. He beefed up the Equal Employment Opportunity Commission, making it the lead agency in its area, and consolidating a confusing hodgepodge of activities into the renamed Office of Federal Contract Compliance and Programs. His administration fought racial and sexual discrimination by bringing class-action lawsuits against employers and called business to account for hiring methods such as employee tests that unfairly disadvantaged minority groups.

Carter's regulatory appointments reenergized the protection of consumers, the workplace, highway safety, and the environment. In December 1980, the president signed an environmental protection bill that preserved one-third of Alaska from development, thus doubling the entire area of the country's national parks and wildlife refuges. He also established an environmental superfund to clean up areas polluted with toxic wastes. Although he was deferential to the tobacco industry, his secretary of health, education, and welfare (HEW), Joseph Califano, was not. A reformed three-pack-a-day smoker, Califano labeled cigarettes "Public Health Enemy No. 1," called for smoking bans on all commercial flights, and urged Congress to increase federal cigarette taxes. In 1979, fulfilling a long-standing desire of teachers and their allies, Carter persuaded Congress to split HEW into two new agencies, the Department of Health and Human Services and the Department of Education.

A SHIFT TO ECONOMIC CONSERVATISM

Carter maintained that the country's renewal would come less from government than from voluntarism, private enterprise, and the free market. In the 1970s, conservative economic doctrines were enjoying a revival, and the president responded to them. Experts, analyzing how the nation's economic woes might be fixed, turned to reconfiguring the relationship of government to business, particularly through deregulation. Federal regulatory agencies controlled the allocation of airline routes and the price of tickets, determined interstate trucking charges, decided banking interest rates and services, and regulated the rates of the nation's private telephone monopoly, AT&T. Economists increasingly agreed that such regulation was costly to businesses and to the public. The regulators too often collaborated with the regulated, maintaining artificially high prices and protecting inefficient corporations from market risks. The critics argued that the regulatory system stifled competition and slowed economic growth. By the mid-1970s, a bipartisan movement had emerged in Congress in favor of deregulating major industries.

> "In 1977, Carter said that one of his 'major goals is to free the American people from the burden of over-regulation.' In collaboration with Congress, he deregulated the airlines, the trucking industry, the railroads, and household movers; and he initiated the deregulation of the banking industry."

In 1977, Carter said that one of his "major goals is to free the American people from the burden of over-regulation." In collaboration with Congress, he deregulated the airlines, the trucking industry, the railroads, and household movers; and he initiated the deregulation of the banking industry. Partly in the long-term interest of strengthening international competitiveness, he increased the overall budget for research and development by 5 percent in inflation-adjusted dollars, accelerating the reversal from the trend of the early 1970s. To stimulate the economy in the short term, he settled for modest public works programs and tax cuts, which hardly helped people earning too little to pay much in taxes. Federal spending on social programs peaked in 1976, then steadily declined.

ENERGY AND INFLATION

Two weeks after his inauguration, Carter donned a cardigan sweater, sat down in an armchair in the White House library, and told a national television audience that "the energy shortage is permanent" but that the country could adjust to this new reality with individual and corporate conservation and "sacrifice." Carter did not mention foreign oil, but concern for U.S. dependence on it formed part of the background of his talk. In 1973, imported oil accounted for 35 percent of consumption; in 1977, 46 percent. Although domestic oil prices had almost doubled since 1970, domestic production was falling.

In April, the president sent Congress an overarching energy plan intended to encourage both the conservation of energy and the development of new sources. He called his program the "moral equivalent of war"; its detractors preferred the acronym MEOW. Congress balked at the complexity of the proposals and the president did little to press for their passage. Finally, in November 1978, a much-diminished version of the original plan cleared Capitol Hill, gutted of its most effective conservation features, notably a tax on gas-guzzling vehicles.

However, shortly after Carter signed the energy bill, the Iranian revolution (see p. 997) sent a second oil shock through the United States, causing fuel shortages, lengthy lines at gas stations, and a spike in prices from 30 cents to almost $1 a gallon. By now, nuclear power plants were generating 13 percent of the nation's electricity, but the accident at Three Mile Island in March 1979 diminished expectations that nuclear power would eventually offset oil as a prime energy generator. Greater hope rested with more fuel-efficient automobiles, which Detroit was developing under the goad of federal fuel standards. A doubling of the average miles per gallon—only fourteen in 1978—would by itself almost halve oil imports. Addressing the short term, in 1979–80, Carter decontrolled oil prices, to encourage both conservation and the search for new oil fields. He obtained passage of a windfall profits tax on the resulting increase in oil-company income that would help pay for, among other things, mass transit. He encouraged the exploitation of solar energy through devices that convert sunlight to electricity or heat. And at his urging, Congress created a Synthetic Fuels Corporation to extract oil from tar sands, oil shale, and coal with the aim of producing more than 160 million barrels of oil a year by the early 1990s.

Between 1978 and 1980, U.S. oil consumption declined by 10 percent, but the inflation rate, which had begun creeping up after the 1974–75 recession, jumped from 7.6 percent in 1977 to more than 11 percent in 1979. Carter had been exhorting business and labor to hold the line voluntarily on prices and wages. Now faced with such a staggering rise in prices, he appointed Paul Volcker, a devotee of monetary policy, to head the Federal Reserve Board (Fed). To tighten the money supply, the Fed hiked the discount rate, helping to produce by 1980 exorbitantly high bank-interest rates of 20 percent and a recession accompanied by 7.8 percent unemployment. The inflation rate nevertheless moved higher, to more than 13 percent, which made for the worst year of stagflation yet.

CARTER AND THE WORLD

Carter came to the presidency with hardly any experience in foreign affairs. Breaking with the realpolitik of Nixon and Kissinger, he revived idealism in the stated aims of American foreign policy. But at times he jettisoned idealism, renewing covert action by the CIA and endorsing authoritarian regimes. He often appeared to waver in his approach to the Soviets, seeking accommodation on some matters, pursuing confrontation on others. One of his chief aides remarked privately, "Who the hell knows whether the President will not veer in some direction tomorrow or the day after tomorrow." His vacillation reflected the sharp differences between the two architects of foreign policy on whom he relied— Secretary of State Cyrus Vance, a principled lawyer of conciliating temperament, and Carter's assistant for national security affairs, Zbigniew Brzezinski, a Pole by birth and a scholar of international relations who saw most foreign issues through the lens of a hard-line anti-Sovietism.

Carter declared in his inaugural address, "We can never be indifferent to the fate of freedom elsewhere. . . . Our commitment to human rights must be absolute." Formal international commitment to human rights had been proclaimed several times, most recently in the Helsinki Agreement (1975). In the early 1970s, Congress, in a slap at Kissinger's realpolitik, had required the president to refuse aid to countries "engaged in a consistent pattern of gross violations of internationally recognized human rights." Carter attempted to enforce that mandate against countries with poor human rights records, including, though with only gentle pressure, friends and allies. Critics attacked Carter's human rights efforts for jeopardizing détente and undercutting some of the nation's staunchest allies, such as South Korea. But Vance strongly supported the effort, contesting egregious human rights abuses in Chile, Argentina, and South Africa, among other countries. Carter successfully put human rights on the world agenda, and by establishing a Human Rights Office in the State Department, he endowed it with an ongoing role in the making of American foreign policy.

Carter's signal achievement in Latin America was to bring to final fruition the efforts of presidents going back to Lyndon Johnson to resolve differences with the Panamanians over the Panama Canal. Carter submitted to the Senate two treaties transferring control of the Canal Zone to Panama by 1999. Conservatives, smarting over the loss in Vietnam and the OPEC oil crisis, opposed the treaties as another national humiliation. "We stole [Panama] fair and square," one senator said, expressing chauvinist indignation. But by lobbying hard for the agreement, Carter eked out one of his few congressional victories, obtaining ratification of the canal treaties in 1978 by only one vote. The outcome ended one of Latin America's long-standing grievances against the *Yanqui* colossus.

The Middle East. Carter may be remembered most for the peace accords that he facilitated between the president of

Egyptian president Anwar el-Sadat (left), President Carter, and Israeli prime minister Menachem Begin (right) sign the Camp David agreement, September 17, 1978.

Egypt, Anwar el-Sadat, and the prime minister of Israel, Menachem Begin. In November 1977, Sadat, his country's economy burdened by defense expenditures, announced that he was ready to go "to the ends of the earth" for peace. Invited to Jerusalem by Begin, he flew to Israel despite opposition from Arab recalcitrants, hoping to negotiate an end to the formal state of war that still existed between the two countries. In September 1978, building on Sadat's initiative, Carter brought the two leaders to Camp David, the presidential retreat in rural Maryland, for two weeks of difficult talks that produced a "framework" for peace. Carter pressed them to resolve their remaining differences, and at the White House the following March, Sadat and Begin signed a formal peace treaty that ended thirty years of war in exchange for Israel's returning the Sinai Peninsula to Egypt.

The Camp David accords provided that Israel would retain control of the West Bank and the Gaza Strip but that during a five-year transitional period the Palestinians there would be granted self-rule and "autonomy." At that point, the final status of the areas would be worked out by Israel, Egypt, Jordan, and—in a vague reference to the PLO—"representatives of the Palestinian people." The other Arab states, however, rejected the accords and ostracized Egypt, partly because the agreement left control of the territories in Israeli hands. Begin, bent on strengthening Israel's position in the territories, continued to expand Israeli settlements in the West Bank. In 1981, Sadat was assassinated by Islamic fundamentalists, punishment for having negotiated with Israel. Although his successor, Hosni Mubarak, continued his conciliatory policies, explosive tensions persisted between Israel on the one side and, on the other, the Palestinians and Arab irreconcilables led by Syria. The peace treaty nevertheless seemed a significant step toward a settlement in the region and a triumph for Carter.

The Middle East also provided Carter's most anguishing reverse. Like Nixon, Carter valued Shah Mohammad Reza Pahlavi of Iran, whom the United States had been supporting since 1953, when the CIA helped pave his way to power, as an instrument of American interests in the Persian Gulf region. On a visit to Tehran in 1977, Carter complimented the shah on "the admiration and love which your people give to you." In fact, the shah had long been violating his subjects' human rights—his secret police, which had close ties to the CIA, had tortured and imprisoned some 50,000 people—and had been spending unprecedented amounts of Iranian wealth on arms from the United States instead of investing it in economic development. Opposition to his regime was bitter and widen-

November 8, 1979: Crowds chant before a billboard taunting President Carter outside the U.S. embassy in Tehran, where militants held the American staff hostage for 444 days.

ing, especially among the country's religious leaders, who strongly disliked the Westernizing trends the shah supported. In January 1979, a revolution led by Shiite fundamentalists forced the shah to flee to Europe. The new head of Iran was Ayatollah Ruhollah Khomeini, seventy-nine years old and a religious zealot, who rapidly turned the government into a theocracy that condemned modernization and preached hatred of the West.

In early November, Carter admitted the shah to the United States for cancer treatment, despite warnings that the action would jeopardize American diplomats in Iran. On November 4, 1979, armed students broke into the American embassy compound in Tehran and held fifty Americans hostage, opening a prolonged captivity and a chasm in U.S.-Iranian relations. **The crisis** increasingly frustrated and angered Americans as television carried nightly clips from Tehran of anti-American mobs demonstrating at the embassy and shouting "Death to America." Carter immediately froze Iranian assets in the United States and prohibited the importation of Iranian oil. A mission to rescue the hostages in 1980 fell apart when two American aircraft crashed into each other in the desert. The rescue attempt, which was pushed by Brzezinski over the misgivings of the military, including the secretary of defense, Harold Brown, provoked Vance to resign in protest of the action and the overall course of American policy.

The Soviets. Carter was initially conciliatory toward the Soviets, hoping to diminish the chances of nuclear war by completing the SALT II arms-control treaty. But his emphasis on human rights for Soviet dissidents alienated them, as did his decision in December 1978 to restore full diplomatic relations with the People's Republic of China and his announcement that the United States would not oppose arms sales to Beijing. Still, at a meeting in Vienna in June 1979, the Soviets, recognizing a mutual interest in arms control, signed the SALT II agreement. The treaty called for equal limits on Soviet and American strategic forces. It nevertheless ran into trouble in the Senate, where critics insisted that it favored the Russians.

The trouble greatly intensified when, in December 1979, the Soviets invaded Afghanistan, where a pro-Moscow coup had brought a Marxist regime to power almost two years before. The Soviets were prompted to send the troops by their inability to suppress the mujahideen—Muslims whose insurgency was supported by the CIA. Carter, declaring that the invasion had forced a "drastic change" in his opinion of Soviet goals, pronounced the action "a stepping stone to their possible control over much of the world's oil supplies." He tabled the SALT II Treaty, embargoed exports of high technology and grain to Russia, reinstituted registration for the draft, and banned American participation in the 1980 Summer Olympics in Moscow. Reflecting the influence of Brzezinski, he also promulgated the Carter Doctrine, declaring that the United States would repel any attempt to gain control of the Persian Gulf region "by any means necessary, including military force." Critics held that the president had misjudged Soviet intentions in the region and that the Carter Doctrine was unrealistic.

But Carter had turned into a hard-liner. After his first two years in office, he had reversed the trend of reduced defense budgets and initiated the largest new-weapons program since before the Korean War. Part of the change was justified by the Soviet introduction of highly accurate intermediate-range missiles with three warheads into Eastern Europe; Carter responded by pledging to update the NATO missile force with the new Pershing IIs.

However, part of the change was stimulated by the contention of strategic theorists that the United States now had a nuclear "window of vulnerability." Although like the "missile gap" of the late 1950s, no such window existed, Carter included in his new hardware the MX, an accurate, MIRV-carrying missile that, because of its vulnerability to Soviet attack, could only be used as a first-strike weapon. After the Soviet invasion of Afghanistan, Carter requested 5 percent annual increases in military spending adjusted for inflation, with the aim of achieving military superiority over the Soviet Union. In July 1980,

Mujahideen resistance fighters at rest in the mountains of Afghanistan during their war against the Soviets, May 1980.

he signed Presidential Directive No. 59, which called for suffi-cient arms to fight a prolonged nuclear war and to win it at every level of escalation. To critics, the directive, coupled with the move to a first-strike capability, threatened a dangerous escalation of the arms race.

A Divided Society

During the 1970s, the programs and protections deriving from the sixties—the civil rights laws, affirmative action, and court decisions—helped change the condition of a growing number of ethnic and racial minority group members. So did their new pride, their unleashed ambition, and a greater tol-erance on the part of the white majority. In 1963, half of whites who were asked if they would object to a family member's bringing a black person home to dinner said yes; in 1982, fewer than a quarter did. About the same time, 80 percent of whites said they would support a well-qualified black candidate for president, a sharp reversal from the late 1950s, when two-thirds said they would not. In these changing circumstances, a rising number of minority-group members made their way in American society, attending college, obtaining better jobs, moving to better neighborhoods. But many were left behind, partly because of discrimination, partly because of the era's economic difficulties. In greater or lesser degree, Americans of color grew increasingly divided among themselves between a burgeoning middle class and a deprived, impoverished lower one. The divide between peo-ple of color and the white majority also continued, exacer-bated not only by the weakness of the economy but also by a rising tide of immigration.

"In 1976, only 32 percent of blacks said that their position in American society had been marked by 'real change,' a sharp drop from the 60 percent who had agreed with that view in 1964."

AFRICAN AMERICANS

Between 1959 and 1969, the fraction of blacks living in poverty had fallen from a little more than half to a little less than one-third. In 1970, one out of four blacks was in a middle-class oc-cupation, almost double the number a decade earlier, and at the end of the seventies the number of blacks attending college reached 27 percent, up from 5 percent in 1965. In 1975, eigh-teen blacks were serving in Congress, including several from

the South, more than triple the number in 1965, all of whom had been from the North. During roughly the same period, the number of black elected officials in the South shot up tenfold, with the trend producing a black mayor of Atlanta, one of the South's principal cities.

Still, faced with white ambivalence and resistance, African Americans were growing more pessimistic about their prospects. The percentage of blacks who perceived discrimi-nation in the workplace increased steadily. In 1976, only 32 percent said that their position in American society had been marked by "real change," a sharp drop from the 60 percent who had agreed with that view in 1964. Racism and discrimi-nation remained realities; so did poverty along the dusty back roads of the South and, especially, in the ghettos of the North, where the decline of the smokestack industries had a disproportionately high impact on unskilled labor.

Poverty was now mainly metropolitan and nonwhite. Although the national poverty rate hovered between 7 and 8 percent during the seventies (down sharply from more than 12 percent in 1965), in the inner cities it in-creased by 30 percent. The number of people in the impoverished underclass more than doubled in Philadelphia and Chicago; in New York, it almost tripled. Part of it was ac-counted for by single mothers whose children were not supported by their fathers. The frac-tion of unemployed nonwhite males who were neither in school nor in the military shot up from 10 percent in 1964 to more than 25 percent in 1980. The inner cities were pervaded by violent crime and the use of drugs like cocaine. Depending on their age, the murder rate for black males between fifteen and forty-four was between eight and fourteen times higher than the national murder rate, itself the highest in the indus-trial world.

HISPANICS

As the result of a federal district court decision in 1971, Mexican Americans were deemed to constitute an identifi-able minority group with rights to special federal assistance. The grant of official recognition encouraged Mexican Amer-ican activists to greater organization and political effort as an ethnic group. At the beginning of the decade, Congress in-cluded five Hispanics; at the beginning of the eighties, there

999

American Journal

What's for Dinner?

In the mid-twentieth century, popular cookbooks featured traditional dishes—meat, fowl, potatoes, corn, green vegetables, and breads—that required time and labor to prepare. But in the 1950s, Americans, increasingly on the go, hungered for fast and cheap cooked food, and the new McDonald's restaurants, offering the menu at right, provided them with it. In the 1970s, the microwave oven began bringing the quick cooking of food into the home, with its mushrooming number of working wives. By the early 1990s, four out of five American homes had microwaves. By then, too, The Fannie Farmer Cookbook, an American standard, had added recipes that captured "the new ethnic flavors that have become a part of American cooking—such as some lively risottos, polentas, and pastas, and stir-frys." Many of these dishes could be bought ready for the microwave or ready to eat in chains like El Pollo Loco in southern California—an indication that most minority groups, busy like everyone else, had joined the fast-food revolution.

McDonald's Speedee Service

MENU

HAMBURGERS	15¢
CHEESEBURGERS	19¢
MALT SHAKES	20¢
FRENCH FRIES	10¢
ORANGE	10¢
ROOT BEER	10¢
COFFEE	10¢
COKE	10¢
MILK	10¢

were eleven, all beneficiaries of the federal voting rights laws and increased turnout by Hispanic voters. In 1975, César Chavez's United Farm Workers union was helped by the passage of a state labor-relations act that guaranteed such rights as elections by secret ballot and voting for migrant seasonal workers. That year, the UFW won a special victory, the outlawing of the short-handled hoe, which had forced field laborers to stoop or work on their knees.

Hispanic cultural nationalism also made gains, particularly in Hispanics' demands for bilingual education. Organizations such as La Raza Unida maintained that bilingualism in the schools would facilitate the education of children who spoke Spanish at home and strengthen respect for Hispanic American culture. In 1974, the Supreme Court held that the San Francisco School Board was obligated to provide special accommodations in the public schools for children who did not speak English. The children in question were Chinese speakers; the issue was their right to be taught English, not fostering of respect for their culture; and bilingual education

was only one of the remedies suggested by the Court. Nevertheless, the ruling was broadly taken as a warrant for bilingual instruction, and it had its broadest impact among Hispanics.

Minority-language students in the United States comprised 17 percent of the school-age population; most were in California, New York, and Texas; and in 1980, more than half of them spoke Spanish. In 1974, New York City, responding to Puerto Rican activists, established bilingual classes for some 200,000 students. By 1980, twenty-four states either mandated or permitted bilingual education. Federal spending on it jumped from $7.5 million in 1968 to $150 million in 1979. Such instruction also created a high demand for certified bilingual teachers. In 1975, the federal government, paralleling the educational trend, required that bilingual ballots be provided to all voters if more than 5 percent of them constituted a language minority.

But like black America, the Hispanic American population also included a growing urban underclass, comprising mainly new immigrants. During the 1970s, more than 2.5 million Hispanics legally entered the United States, while an estimated 10 million did so illegally. About three-quarters of them lived in the band of southwestern states from Texas to California. These new immigrants, most of them unskilled, tended to care for the gardens, houses, and children of the better-off or to fill menial jobs in the garment and service industries as well as the agricultural fields. One out of five Hispanic families fell below the poverty line, compared with the national average of one out of eleven.

ASIAN AMERICANS

During the 1970s, immigration began to transform the Asian American community. The Immigration Act of 1965 allowed the admission of 170,000 immigrants annually from the Eastern Hemisphere and gave preference to specific categories of people, including family members of American citizens and permanent residents, professional and technical workers, and refugees. Hundreds of thousands of Asians took advantage of the act to flee the persecution that targeted former American allies in Vietnam, Laos, and Cambodia; the authoritarianism in the Philippines and the People's Republic of China; and the instability in Korea, Taiwan, and Hong Kong. An additional stimulus to emigration was simply the economic hardship that characterized life in some of these countries, including, in Korea, India, and the Philippines, the underemployment or unemployment of many well-educated and professionally trained men and women.

"A Chinese immigrant trained in physics complained, 'We are college graduates but are working in sewing or electronic factories. We all have taken a big step backwards in our profession or work.'"

Unlike the Asian migration of the nineteenth and early twentieth centuries, the new wave initially comprised a large fraction of urban, college-educated people, many of them doctors, scientists, engineers, and nurses. The influx of professional and technical workers diminished after the Immigration Act was amended in 1976 to tighten their eligibility for entry, and the national quotas were taken up increasingly by relatives of those already in the United States. A growing number of Asian immigrants tended to be poor, uneducated, rural in background, and commanding little English. In the five years after the Communist takeovers in Southeast Asia, more than 400,000 Vietnamese, Laotians, and Cambodians came to America, many of them risking treacherous journeys by boat to escape. In 1980, Congress capped the annual quota for refugees at 50,000 and provided a more orderly system for their resettlement as well as a fixed period of economic and medical assistance. In the 1970s, all told, about 1,600,000 Asians entered the country, almost four times as many as in the 1960s, including 124,000 from China and 355,000 from the Philippines, making the Asian American community far more diverse than other ethnic communities.

The Asian immigrants tended to concentrate geographically—some in Texas, Louisiana, and Hawaii, but most in California and New York, especially in the greater metropolitan regions centered on Los Angeles, San Francisco, and New York City. Many of those with professional skills prospered rapidly, like the nurse from the Philippines who noted, "My one day's earning here in America is more than my one month's salary in Manila." But others, unable to find work that matched their qualifications, endured occupational downgrading that often left them frustrated and depressed. They earned their livings in blue-collar and service work or in family-operated small businesses such as dry cleaners, restaurants, and greengrocers. A Chinese immigrant trained in physics complained, "We are college graduates but are working in sewing or electronic factories. We all have taken a big step backwards in our profession or work." Racial discrimination and lack of skills compounded the difficulties of Asian immigrants who were impoverished when they arrived. In 1980, more than a third of the refugees from Southeast Asia lived below the poverty line. Like other minorities of color, Asian Americans were divided within themselves between those who were advancing in society and those who were not.

NATIVE AMERICANS

Native Americans were gaining increasing popular sympathy, aided by the success of entertainers such as the singer Buffy Sainte-Marie, a Cree. The film *Little Big Man*, a sharp departure from the stereotypical arrows-and-rifles treatment, dealt with a survivor of the Indian wars of the late nineteenth century. Its director was inspired by the Vietnam War, and one of its supporting actors, Chief Dan George, a Squamish, won an Academy Award. The Native American cause was also advanced by Red Power advocates, many of them young, urban

1001

based, and college educated, who had turned more militant, organizing activist groups such as the American Indian Movement (AIM) and, beginning in 1969, occupying federal sites to call attention to Native American issues. In 1973, 200 armed men led by Russell Means and Dennis Banks of the AIM took control of Wounded Knee, a village on the Pine Ridge reservation, hoping to establish a type of tribal traditional governance free of federal control. Federal troops placed the occupiers under siege; gunfire killed two activists and paralyzed a federal marshal. The White House, however, declined to use sustained force against the occupiers, and the siege ended peacefully in May 1973, seventy-three days after it began.

During the Nixon administration, Native Americans witnessed the creation of a cabinet-level Committee on Indian Affairs and more than a doubling of the budget of the Bureau of Indian Affairs. Tribal economic development was encouraged through federal loans, greater tribal control of natural resources, and the return to the tribes of thousands of acres of former Indian lands. The largest such cession, authorized by the Alaskan Native Claims Settlement Act in 1971, transferred 40 million acres, including mineral rights, to the Alaska Federation of Natives. With support from Nixon, who condemned the termination policies enacted in 1953 as "morally and legally unacceptable," Congress soon passed the Menominee Restoration Act, which overturned the termina-

tion of that tribe. In 1974, it approved the landmark Indian Self-Determination and Education Assistance Act, which decisively ended termination and made the achievement of Indian self-determination an explicit federal goal.

In the late seventies and early eighties, the Supreme Court significantly enlarged the rights and powers of Indian tribes, holding that they could be governed by their traditional laws even if the laws conflicted with most constitutional rights. The Court also invigorated tribal rights guaranteed by past treaties, including the right of Native Americans to half the annual salmon harvest in the Pacific Northwest; the right to share water resources with the states; and the right to certain lands in the state of New York. In 1978, Congress added to the anti-assimilationist predilections of most tribes by passing the Indian Child Welfare Act, which discouraged the adoption of Indian children by non-Indians. But the enhancement of Indian civic pride and power did little by itself to ease the poverty, unemployment, alcoholism, and disease that continued to plague the reservations.

MAJORITY RESISTANCE

The minority drive for equality was constantly contested. Court orders to desegregate the public schools by busing prompted whites who could afford it to send their children to private schools or to move to the predominantly white suburbs. The flight to the suburbs was further encouraged in 1974 by the case of *Milliken v. Bradley,* when a bare majority of the Supreme Court held that students could not be bused for the purpose of achieving racial integration between predominantly black cities and the largely white suburbs. To many whites remaining in the cities, such suburban insulation from the strains of school integration seemed arbitrary and unfair. Desegregation orders provoked angry confrontations in some cities, notably Louisville (Kentucky) and Boston, where people in white enclaves put up signs declaring, "We don't want any niggers in our school." A mother from a section of Boston vulnerable to busing complained to the judge who had ordered it: "How can it be the law of the land, as we are told, when you can move less than one mile away and be out from

Leaders of the American Indian Movement march at Wounded Knee, South Dakota, during their confrontation with federal troops, March 1973.

Workers and students in New York demonstrate for affirmative action and against the Supreme Court's Bakke decision, June 1978.

under this law?" In the late 1970s, pollsters found that 70 percent of whites strongly opposed "forced" busing, and that only 53 percent of blacks favored it.

White English-speakers, resentful at having to send their children to polyglot schools, began taking aim at bilingualism. Many considered affirmative action—particularly in hiring practices and college admissions—an indefensible replacement of equality of opportunity with equality of outcomes, and thus a violation of their constitutional right to equal protection under the law.

Allan Bakke, a student, brought that view to court when he sued the Medical School of the University of California at Davis for refusing him admission. Bakke argued that the university had denied him equal protection of the laws because it regularly set aside 16 percent of its slots for minority students, many of whom were academically less qualified than he was. In 1978, in *Regents of University of California v. Bakke,* a sharply divided Supreme Court granted him victory, holding that a university could consider racial criteria as part of a competitive admissions process but that it could not rely on "fixed quotas" in determining its student body. The next year, however, in *Weber v. United Steelworkers,* the Court upheld the union's agreement to a black hiring quota for all the 350,000 steel-making jobs in the country. And in 1980, it ruled in favor of a congressionally mandated set-aside of 10 percent of public-works-program funds for minority contractors. The disparate nature of these rulings revealed that

the Court was divided on the issue of affirmative action, but perhaps no more so than the country at large.

FAULT LINES: SEXUAL AND CULTURAL

The **women's movement** continued to score victories across a broad economic, cultural, and sexual front. Gay men and lesbian women sought to gain acceptance and establish rights for themselves. Features of the counterculture spread to parts of the middle and working classes. These trends left many Americans uncertain, groping for ways to deal with each other, their children, and even themselves. And echoing the response to the advance of colored minorities, they also provoked anger and resistance among social conservatives.

Women. In 1969, NOW invaded the Oak Room of the Plaza Hotel in New York City to protest the restaurant's men-only lunch service. The action reflected feminism's expanding scope, its eagerness to break down the barriers to equality of opportunity in education and the workplace. In 1971, Betty Friedan and the congresswomen Shirley Chisholm and Bella Abzug established the National Women's Political Caucus (NWPC), a bipartisan effort to increase women's presence in politics. At their nominating conventions the next year, both

New York Democratic congresswomen Bella Abzug (left) and Shirley Chisholm confer in a House corridor, 1971.

Members of the Women's Political Caucus march for equality in New York City, August 1971.

Democrats and Republicans increased the number of women delegates and adopted much of the NWPC's platform, including ratification of the Equal Rights Amendment (ERA, which prohibited the federal and state governments from abridging a person's rights on account of sex) and greater equity for women in education.

Although Nixon vetoed legislation for national day care, he called for making child care expenses tax-deductible when both parents worked. In 1972, Congress passed the ERA, which was quickly ratified by thirty states, leaving endorsement by only eight more to complete the process. Title IX in the Educational Amendments Act of 1972 barred discrimination for reasons of sex in any educational program receiving federal assistance. The measure produced a dramatic impact in women's sports—for example, a threefold increase, to 25 percent, in the participation of girls in high school athletics. Doubts about the athletic capabilities of women were significantly dispelled when in 1973 the tennis champion Billie Jean King, an outspoken enemy of sexism in sports and a founder of the Virginia Slims tennis tour, trounced the 1939 Wimbledon champion, Bobby Riggs, who had challenged her to prove that she could beat "a tired old man."

Stereotyping was in retreat. Universities launched women's studies programs, while television aired the popular *Mary Tyler Moore Show*, featuring a single career woman who was strongly interested in men but not desperate to get married. In 1978, the Weather Service decided that henceforth it would give hurricanes male as well as female names. It was national news when in February 1977 fifty secretaries used their lunch hour to protest the firing of a legal secretary because she refused to make the office coffee, a task not included in her job description. The protest appeared to generate minor office revolutions across the country.

Early in the seventies, after a state judge in Pennsylvania ruled that newspapers in Pittsburgh could no longer list jobs for men and women separately, the practice vanished from the nationwide press. Toward the end of the decade, responding to court orders, New York City permitted women to apply for jobs as firefighters, the navy allowed women to serve on most of its regular vessels, and professional baseball—soon followed by basketball and football—opened its locker rooms to women journalists. In 1976, Barbara Walters became the first woman to anchor a regular television newscast.

In 1979, women accounted for roughly one in four graduates from medical and law schools, compared with, respectively, one in twelve and one in twenty in 1970. In 1981, they earned triple the share of the nation's doctorates that they had a decade earlier. At the end of the seventies, slightly more than half of all adult women held jobs outside the home, including almost half of women with children under six. Among the ripple effects of so many women working during the day was a growing demand that stores remain open in the evening. Partly because more women could work for their livelihood instead of having to find it in marriage, the fraction of the population who were single increased by a third between 1965 and 1979, to 20 percent. In the same period, the divorce rate more than doubled, to half of all marriages, facilitated by the passage of no-fault divorce laws in many states.

> "It was national news when in February 1977 fifty secretaries used their lunch hour to protest the firing of a legal secretary because she refused to make the office coffee, a task not included in her job description."

The cause of sexual freedom for women had become deeply embedded in American culture. In 1969, about three-quarters of American women believed premarital sex to be wrong; in 1973, only about a half did. Sexual liberty was reinforced by feminists' insistence that women ought to have the right to control their own bodies, in defiance of male or middle-class standards of propriety. The demand for women's autonomy made a commercial success of *Our Bodies, Ourselves,* a book intended to provide women with greater control over their health. It also led to mounting agitation from both women and physicians for the legalization of abortion.

Between 1967 and 1970, a dozen states eased their anti-abortion laws, making women eligible for the procedure who were the victims of rape or incest or whose lives were threatened by their pregnancies. In Texas, where abortion restrictions were not eased, Norma McGorvey, using the name Jane Roe, sued for the right to abort her unwanted fetus. Deciding the case of *Roe v. Wade* on appeal in 1973, the Supreme Court drew on the right of privacy it had established to hold that the state could not interfere with a woman's right to abortion during the first three months of pregnancy; that during the next three months it could regulate that right in the interest of preserving maternal health; and that in the last three months it could bar abortions.

Sexual Backlash. Despite their gains, women continued to feel aggrieved and threatened. Probably because so many more were employed and also had higher expectations, a growing fraction of women—two-thirds by 1974—felt discriminated against in the workplace. Some feminists called attention to physical crimes against women, and sought to deal with them by staffing rape-crisis centers and shelters for battered women. Many redoubled their efforts on behalf of the Equal Rights Amendment. But even though they won an extension of the deadline for ratification to June 30, 1982, the amendment failed to pass.

One reason for the defeat was that the women's movement was weakened by internal disputes between moderates and radicals. While radical women favored uncompromised legal and constitutional equality, moderates, especially those in the unionized workforce, worried that such equality might cost them the special dispensations—such as limits on the weight they could be asked to lift or a monthly sick day—they had fought so hard to achieve. But another reason for its defeat was the backlash against the women's movement that formed in the seventies not only among men but among women themselves. Energized by socially conservative women, it targeted both the ERA and abortion rights.

The chief enemy of the ERA was Phyllis Schlafly, a devout Catholic who proudly kept her own interests subordinate to those of her husband and six children. She disparaged feminists as "a bunch of bitter women" and denounced the advocates of the ERA as "unkempt, lesbians, radicals, and socialists . . .

women who had rejected womanhood—the God-given roles of wife and motherhood." Anti-ERA activists preyed on the fears of middle-class women that the amendment might lead to the end of alimony and maternal custody of children in divorces, the drafting of women, and the decriminalization of rape. Schlafly warned that absolute equality would seriously risk the security of middle-aged women who had been housewives all their adult lives.

The Supreme Court's decision in *Roe v. Wade* provoked an antiabortion movement. Convinced that life was sacred from the moment of conception, its adherents claimed that abortion was murder. The movement drew leadership and support disproportionately from Catholics, fundamentalist Protestants, and women who had devoted themselves to being wives and mothers. Its advocates challenged the decision in court and protested at abortion clinics. A few resorted to violence, torching a Planned Parenthood facility in St. Paul, Minnesota, in 1973. The movement sought to pass state laws that would require parental or spousal consent before an

Antiabortion demonstrators, carrying a sign with a symbolic fetus on top, protest outside the Capitol on the third anniversary of *Roe v. Wade,* January 22, 1976.

1005

Phyllis Schlafly speaks against the Equal Rights Amendment, 1977.

abortion. In *Planned Parenthood of Central Missouri v. Danforth* (1976), the Supreme Court rejected such requirements, but in *H. L. v. Matheson* (1981), it upheld a parental notification rule for minors because parental consent is required before a minor can receive medical treatment. Antiabortionists won a victory in Congress in 1976 with the so-called Hyde Amendment, which prohibited the use of Medicaid funds for abortions except in cases of rape, incest, and endangerment of the woman's life, a restriction that the Court upheld.

Gay Liberation. For decades, gay men and lesbian women had hidden their sexual preferences, fearing that to reveal them would cost them jobs or housing and make them vulnerable to blackmail or persecution, including physical assault. But now, adding to the broad-based insistence on sexual liberty, a growing number of gays and lesbians openly acknowledged their sexual orientation—that is, "came out of the closet," to use the popular phrase. A number of prominent feminists publicly declared that they were lesbians—for example, Kate Millet, the author of *Sexual Politics*, who earned national headlines when she told a Columbia University audience that she was bisexual. When in mid-1969 New York police descended on the Stonewall Inn, a gay men's bar in Greenwich Village, the patrons fought back, initiating five

days of confrontation and arousing an assertive group consciousness among male homosexuals. By the early 1970s, hundreds of openly gay groups were battling the homophobia that pervaded American society. In 1973, the American Psychiatric Association removed homosexuality from its catalogue of mental disorders, emphasizing that gays and lesbians were by and large satisfied with their sexual orientation and exhibited no signs of psychopathology directly arising from it.

Many homosexuals migrated to New York and the even more tolerant environment of San Francisco, making it a gay mecca: the writer Armistead Maupin chronicled life there in a newspaper series, *Tales of the City*, that was later turned into a popular book and TV movie. Some gays turned New York and San Francisco into centers of an outlaw sexual culture that was defiant of the heterosexual majority's, marked by the practice of unprotected anal and oral sex with dozens to hundreds of partners, mainly in bathhouses, discos, and sex clubs. But apart from their sexual orientation, large numbers of homosexuals, male and female alike, were conventional in their overall attitudes and demanded only the right to pursue their lives free of harassment and discrimination. Together with various allies, homosexuals mounted initiatives for gay-rights ordinances in cities across the country.

Social conservatives, however, defeated the initiatives in St. Paul, Minnesota; Wichita, Kansas; Eugene, Oregon; and Dade County, Florida. Taking the offensive against gay liberation, state legislators in Oklahoma and Arkansas enacted

Activists demand gay liberation, New York City, April 1978.

measures that banned homosexuals from teaching in public schools and, in Arkansas, also denied them credentials as pediatricians and social workers. In California in 1978, liberals managed to defeat a statewide initiative mandating the firing of any schoolteacher who advocated homosexuality. But just a few weeks after the victory, the leader in the gay opposition to the initiative, San Francisco supervisor Harvey Milk, was gunned down in his office by Dan White, a former city official. When a predominantly blue-collar Catholic jury found White guilty only of voluntary manslaughter, riots broke out in the gay district of San Francisco.

Searching for Self-Fulfillment. Amid the social and cultural stresses of the seventies, many Americans responded to nostalgic television shows such as *The Waltons,* the sentimental story of a rural, intact family coping with life during the Depression and World War II. But in the wake of Watergate, many turned away from tradition and traditional authority. They made hits of the irreverent TV show *Saturday Night Live,* which mocked presidents and preachers, the new values as well as the old; network productions, such as *Charlie's Angels,* that reflected the breakaway from traditional gender roles; and, in 1976, the bizarre *Mary Hartman, Mary Hartman,* whose characters, including a philandering alcoholic minister and an unfaithful wife, represented a world in moral chaos.

Ingredients of the chaos were addressed on daytime TV talk shows, notably those hosted by Phil Donahue and later (1986) Oprah Winfrey. Featuring audience participation in discussions of hitherto taboo subjects such as premarital sex, adultery, and divorce, they helped give rise to a confessional culture. Betty Ford, while still First Lady, reinforced the trend by declaring in a CBS television interview that she approved of abortion, would not "be a bit surprised" to learn that her unmarried daughter had had an affair, assumed that her children had tried pot, and, if she were young, might do the same herself.

Many Americans turned inward for insight, abandoning politics in favor of personal fulfillment. They looked to pop music for entertainment and escape, providing enthusiastic audiences for a dizzying array of pop-music groups virtually none of which urged social change in the vein of Bob Dylan a decade earlier. Bruce Springsteen's songs, while they lamented rusting factories and blue-collar despair, often suggested that the modes of survival lay in flight or the magic of love.

By the late seventies, more than a third of young adults were using marijuana. Even truck drivers now let their hair grow long and smoked pot. Thousands of veterans brought

Bruce Springsteen—"The Boss," to his fans—connects with his audience at a New Jersey concert, 1981.

drug habits home from Vietnam, while it became fashionable among well-to-do whites, including pop celebrities and young business executives, to indulge in **cocaine.** Drug dealing and drug use became a growing industry in the inner cities, where children apprenticing in the trade earned as much as $100 a day. Law enforcement officials estimated that perhaps one half of all robberies, muggings, and burglaries were committed by drug addicts in need of money to pay for their habit.

Untold numbers of Americans sought to take control of their lives through faddish methods of self-realization. They participated, for example, in encounter groups, which aimed to reveal the authentic self by stripping away the armor of self-protection. They practiced transcendental meditation, taught at more than 200 centers. They spent some $10 million a year on EST (Erhard Seminar Training) self-discovery programs devised and marketed by the pop psychologist Werner Erhard, which denied participants use of the bathroom for long periods in order to force self-revelations. They went to the Esselen Institute on a cliff overlooking the Pacific at Big Sur, California, in the hope of learning about themselves through techniques such as confessional encounter sessions, bathing nude with strangers, and group touching.

For millions, the quest for the sound spirit led through the healthy body. Middle-class Americans began taking themselves to tennis courts, racquet-ball clubs, swimming pools, jogging paths, and hiking and biking trails. *Newsweek,* covering the national exercise craze, noted with a Whitmanesque turn, "I hear America puffing." People coupled their absorption with physical fitness to a concern for healthy diet, limiting their intake of fat, sugar, and salt, eating less beef and more fish or chicken, preferring "natural" and organic foods to processed types.

As in other periods of stress, millions of Americans sought solace in religion. Unlike the religious revival of the 1950s, with its focus on suburban community and respectability, that of the 1970s was fueled in part by the drive for spiritual self-renewal, in part by the rise of Christian radio and TV programs. Surveys late in the decade revealed that 70 million Americans—more than one of every three adults—identified themselves as born-again Christians. The revival was intensified by charismatic leaders such as the Reverend Sun Myung Moon, a native of South Korea who touted himself as the new Messiah and whose Unification Church evangelized thousands of young Americans to a blend of Christian faith and anti-Communism. Eastern religions such as Zen Buddhism also gained adherents, while some college-age Americans devoted themselves to chanting "Hare Krishna."

The revival made its way into popular music, including Led Zeppelin's *Stairway to Heaven,* and into the hit musicals *Jesus Christ Superstar* and *Godspell.* Robert Pirsig's *Zen and the Art of Motorcycle Maintenance,* a novel of a journey to the American West in search of spiritual fulfillment, sold widely, while Hal Lindsey's perennial best-seller *The Late Great Planet Earth* foretold a nuclear apocalypse precipitated by an anti-Christ and then redeemed by Jesus' return to earth. In George Lucas's blockbuster film *Star Wars,* an intergalactic tale of battle between good and evil, the heroic Luke Skywalker destroys the Evil Empire's superweapon after a guru-like figure named Obi-Wan Kenobi helps him achieve his "human potential" by putting him in touch with a quasi-religious, mystical Force.

The commitment to achieving individual potential—whether through pop psychology, physical fitness, or religious renewal—prompted the writer Tom Wolfe to dub the seventies the "me decade." In a book indicting *The Culture of Narcissism* (1979), the historian Christopher Lasch wrote, "To live for the moment is the prevailing passion—to live for yourself, not for your predecessors or posterity." Another best-seller of the era was a book titled *Looking Out for No. 1.* In all, the cultural trends of the seventies, coupled with the flight from public issues, helped lay the groundwork for a politics less concerned with an overarching public interest than with a self-absorbed individualism.

Bid for Power

THE CHRISTIAN RIGHT

The cultural trends of the day angered the Reverend Jerry Falwell, a fundamentalist Baptist based in Lynchburg, Virginia, who reached an estimated 15 million people weekly through his televised *Old Time Gospel Hour.* Falwell objected strongly to the rising rates of divorce and drug use, the women's movement, the ERA, and abortion on demand; the spread of pornography and homosexuality; and liberalism's invasion of the schools in the form of sex education, the prohibition against prayer, and the teaching of biological evolution instead of biblical creationism. In the mid-sixties, he had claimed that the purpose of religion was to regenerate the inner being, not to rid society of its evils. At that time, fundamentalist Protestants were one of the most apolitical groups in the country; few of them even registered to vote. But now Falwell, finding social evil pervasive in American society, resolved to contest it politically.

Other fundamentalist Protestants had come to see the cultural trends of the seventies the way Falwell did, as threats to their way of life and the moral future of their children. In many parts of the country, concerned parents tried to rid their schools of morally subversive books, protested sex education, and urged that biology courses include "scientific creationism"—natural evidence for the truth of the biblical Genesis. In Kanawha County, West Virginia, in 1974, fundamentalist ministers and parents closed down the public

> *"In all, the cultural trends of the seventies, coupled with the flight from public issues, helped lay the groundwork for a politics less concerned with an overarching public interest than with a self-absorbed individualism."*

The Reverend Jerry Falwell, 1979.

schools to protest the use of texts they claimed were un-Christian, unpatriotic, and destructive of the family. Fundamentalist dissidents increasingly sent their children to "Christian" private schools, some 16,000 of which were operating by 1980, mostly in the South, more than a tenfold increase since the early 1960s. In 1978, a ruling by the Internal Revenue Service that appeared to threaten the tax-deductible status of these schools reinforced the political engagement of Falwell and his followers.

In 1979, Falwell founded the Moral Majority, a religious-oriented group that operated as a conservative political lobby and was eagerly welcomed by Washington-based political organizers intent on building a conservative coalition. Called the New Right, the movement was an updated though somewhat different version of the New Right that had emerged in the early 1960s. It effectively exploited television, computerized databases, and direct mail to raise money from millions of small contributors; it used the same means to mobilize them in support of right-wing candidates and legislative initiatives. At the movement's emotional core was a ferocious social conservatism that sought to rescue the United States from the libertine legacy of the sixties.

A CONSERVATIVE COALITION

The emergence of the New Right on social issues was accompanied by a shift rightward on economic issues that went far beyond calls for deregulation. The tax rebellion that began with the passage of Proposition 13 in California fueled attacks on government for taking money from people's pockets. In the mountain West, resentment of the environmental movement prompted the so-called Sagebrush Rebellion, whose participants demanded that restrictions on the exploitation of natural resources be lifted. Everywhere opponents of affirmative action demanded a reduction or elimination of the special dispensations granted to women and minorities of color.

The shift gained intellectual force from former liberals who had turned right in appalled response to the radicalism of the sixties. Labeled "neoconservatives," they contributed articles to magazines such as *Commentary* and *Public Interest* warning against the dangers of excessive governmental controls at home and Soviet expansionism abroad. Conservatives sought to counter the liberal dominance of policy analysis by establishing their own think tanks such as the Heritage Foundation, funded by gifts and subscriptions from individuals and corporations. By and large, the economic conservatives were unsympathetic to the social conservatism of the Falwells and proposed instead to reduce the role of government. The Falwells, generally indifferent to issues such as regulation and taxes, aimed to use government to restrict social behavior. Nevertheless, in the later 1970s they formed an alliance, albeit an uneasy one, of mounting influence against the liberal welfare state and the enlargement of personal liberties that had paralleled its growth.

THE ELECTION OF 1980

In July 1979, in a nationally televised address that was quickly dubbed the "national malaise" speech, Carter attributed the difficulties in dealing with energy and inflation to "a crisis of the American spirit," declaring that the people had lost "confidence in the future." Critics countered that what the country had lost confidence in was its president. In the hope of revitalizing his administration, Carter forced out five members of his cabinet, including his energy secretary.

Jimmy Carter brought honesty and integrity to the task of government. But while he had a good grasp of specific issues, he failed to articulate a larger vision in foreign or domestic af-

Chronology		
1973	*Roe v. Wade.*
1975	Microsoft Corporation founded.
April 1975	Vietnam War ends.
1976	Apple Computer founded.
1978	Treaties transferring control of Canal Zone to Panama ratified.
March 1979	Egyptian president Sadat and Israeli prime minister Begin sign peace treaty.
	Accident at Three Mile Island nuclear plant.
November 4, 1979	Fifty Americans taken hostage in Iran.
1981	Sadat assassinated.

bolster national defense and reassert American power in the world. He bested Carter in their single television debate, countering attacks with affable rejoinders and calling the sum of the unemployment rate and the inflation rate Carter's "misery index." "Are you better off than you were four years ago?" Reagan asked viewers. With the misery index, 14 in 1977, now at 20, the answer did not need to be spelled out. He told campaign audiences, "A recession is when your neighbor loses his job. A depression is when you lose yours. And recovery is when Jimmy Carter loses his."

On election day, Reagan won 50.8 percent (44 million) of the popular vote to Carter's 41 percent (35 million), with most of the remainder (7 percent) going to John Anderson, a liberal Republican congressman from Illinois who ran on an independent ticket. Turnout fell once again; almost 47 percent of eligible voters stayed home, which meant that Reagan was elected by only about a quarter of eligible voters. Still,

fairs that moved either legislators or his fellow citizens. His approval rating remained at 25 percent in the polls, comparable to Nixon's just before his resignation.

Challenged for the nomination by the liberal senator Edward M. Kennedy, Carter ran a White House Rose Garden campaign during the primaries, refusing to leave Washington so that he could deal full time with the Iran hostage crisis. Kennedy's candidacy failed, partly because of doubts about his character arising from a 1969 accident at Chappaquiddick, Massachusetts, in which a young woman riding in his car was killed. Carter, as a sitting president, gained support amid the crises in Afghanistan and Iran, and he and Mondale were renominated handily. On the Republican side, Ronald Reagan, the former movie actor, television host, two-term governor of California, and hero of the party's right wing, triumphed over a broad field in the primaries and won the nomination on the first ballot. His vice-presidential choice was his principal primary opponent, George Bush of Texas, a moderate with a long career in public service, including a stint as a congressman and, most recently, as director of the CIA.

Reagan ran on a platform that favored tax cuts, a balanced budget, prayer in the schools, and a ban on abortions. He appealed to both economic and social conservatives, attracting support from the new religious right, tax-sensitive suburban Republicans, anxious blue-collar Democrats, and people simply out of patience with Carter's ineffectuality. He spoke to the frustrations felt by many in foreign affairs, promising to

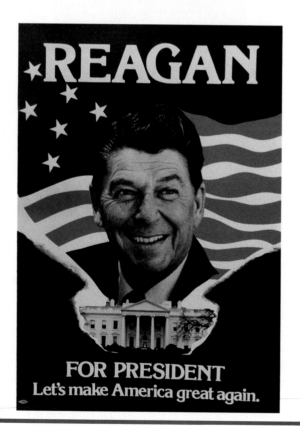

Ronald Reagan's 1980 campaign for the presidency spoke to the foreign and domestic frustrations pervading the country.

he carried forty-four states, gaining 489 electoral votes to Carter's 49. Almost a quarter of previously Democratic voters voted for Reagan, the largest portion among them saying they switched because they resented government assistance to minority groups. The Republicans recaptured the Senate for the first time since 1952. Some liberal Democrats were defeated with the help of conservative televangelists and of the Moral Majority, which had registered more than 2 million new voters in 1979. Iran's humiliation of Carter also contributed to his loss. But after being invaded by Iraq in September, the Ayatollah Khomeini's government decided it did not want to deal with two enemies at once. It released the hostages on Carter's last day in office, having held them for 444 days.

Suggested Reading

Paul E. Ceruzzi, *A History of Modern Computing* (1998)

Gary M. Fink and Hugh Davis Graham, eds., *The Carter Presidency: Policy Choices in the Post–New Deal Era* (1998)

Ronald Formisano, *Boston Against Busing: Race, Class, and Ethnicity in the 1960s and 1970s* (1991)

John Robert Greene, *The Presidency of Gerald Ford* (1995)

Sheldon Krimsky, *Biotechnics and Society: The Rise of Industrial Genetics* (1991)

Bruce J. Schulman, *The Seventies: The Great Shift in American Culture, Society, and Politics* (2001)

Gaddis Smith, *Morality, Reason, and Power: American Diplomacy in the Carter Years* (1986)

THE REAGAN REVOLUTION:

1980-1988

The AIDS quilt, begun in 1987 and displayed on the Mall in Washington, D.C., in 1992, commemorated the deaths from the disease of more than 20,000 people.

Focus QUESTIONS

■ What were the main elements of Reaganomics?

■ How did Reagan's view of the Soviet Union affect his dealings with the Soviets and Third World countries?

■ What troubles arose in the greed-is-good culture?

■ What were Reagan's major achievements in office, and what prices did the country pay for them?

At the Reagan inaugural events, the guests poured out of limousines, the men in tuxedos, the women in designer dresses, their diamonds glittering in an unabashed display of opulence. The new president avidly expressed their credo, a conviction that the scope of government ought to be reduced and private enterprise unleashed. "Government is not the solution to our problem," he declared in his inaugural address. "Government *is* the problem."

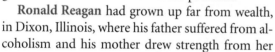

Ronald Reagan had grown up far from wealth, in Dixon, Illinois, where his father suffered from alcoholism and his mother drew strength from her participation in the evangelical Disciples of Christ Church. In his political youth, he was a devotee of Franklin Roosevelt and after World War II a leader of the screen actor's union, but the Cold War brought out in him a staunch anti-Communism, including a McCarthyite eagerness to root out reds in Hollywood. In the fifties, leaving his waning acting career to become a corporate spokesman for General Electric, he increasingly identified with big business and turned sharply to the right.

Reagan entered politics as a supporter of Barry Goldwater's 1964 presidential campaign, and in 1966, with the help of a group of wealthy California Republicans, he was elected governor of the state. Yet his ideology was tempered by a political expediency that made him effective in the office. While denouncing campus antiwar protests and "welfare cheats," he compromised with the Democratic legislature to enact moderate programs, including strong budgets for the state university, welfare reform, and a liberalized abortion law. He embodied an easygoing, "aw, shucks" likability that reinforced his praise of rugged individualism. People admired his courage and humor when in March 1981 he was seriously wounded in an assassination attempt by a lone gunman. "Honey, I forgot to duck," he told his wife, Nancy.

No one seemed to know Reagan well besides Nancy Reagan, a onetime actress whose father had helped initiate her husband's move to the right. A strong-minded, somewhat insensitive woman, she provoked criticism early in the administration, when the country was suffering double-digit inflation and high unemployment, for wearing a costly inauguration wardrobe and ordering (with private funds) expensive new china for the White House. She relied on an astrologer to determine the dates of her husband's important public engagements, but she eventually nudged him to improve relations with the Soviets and took the lead in the administration's battle against drugs, urging young people tempted by them to "Just say no."

Ronald and Nancy Reagan greet the crowds at the president's first inauguration, January 20, 1981.

Unlike Carter, Reagan was unconcerned with the details of policy, leaving them mainly to subordinates. His laissez-faire approach to administration made him seem detached from affairs of state. He sometimes told stories about purportedly real incidents that actually came from films. Critics considered him an ill-informed lightweight, a puppet whom others manipulated for their own ends. His seeming disengagement tended to insulate him from his administration's setbacks; a congresswoman tartly called him a "Teflon president," meaning that virtually nothing said against him stuck.

But Reagan knew a lot about the issues that interested him, and he took charge when he cared to. If indifferent to accuracy or details, he articulated major themes for his administration in simple, understandable terms—observers called him "The Great Communicator"—and he insisted that his subordinates operate within the broad framework of his conservative principles. Reagan sought to reconfigure the nation's agenda, deploying Rooseveltian activism and flexibility in pursuit of policies reminiscent of Calvin Coolidge, whose portrait he hung in the Cabinet Room. And although he was a hard-line Cold Warrior when he entered office, events both in the Soviet Union and at home led him to help bring an end to the Cold War.

> *"Reagan knew a lot about the issues that interested him, and he took charge when he cared to. If indifferent to accuracy or details, he articulated major themes for his administration in simple, understandable terms."*

Reaganomics

Reagan proposed to halt inflation with high interest rates, stimulate the economy with tax reductions, and balance the budget by spending cuts while simultaneously beefing up defense appropriations—a contradictory agenda that George Bush had disparaged during the primaries as "voodoo economics." Conservative theorists argued that the necessary magic would be achieved by "supply-side economics": tax reductions, this theory had it, would generate enough new taxable economic activity to pay for both the reductions and necessary federal spending. In 1981, Congress slashed income taxes by 25 percent—5 percent in the first year and 10 percent in 1982 and 1983. The top rate was cut from 70 percent to 50 percent, a shift that made public policy out of the old trickle-down theory of conservatives—that investment en-

couraged at the top of society would eventually trickle down to benefit the bottom. Reagan's budget director conceded to a reporter that the administration's supply-side proposals were mainly intended as "a Trojan horse" to reduce the top tax rates.

Before the reductions had time to work their stimulating magic, the high interest rates the Federal Reserve Board was maintaining (and which Reagan privately supported) threw the economy into a severe recession. In 1982, unemployment shot up to almost 10 percent, almost 16 percent among industrial workers—the highest level of ongoing unemployment since the Depression of the 1930s. On a visit to Minneapolis early that year, Reagan was greeted with a banner proclaiming, "Welcome President Hoover." But by 1984, the steep interest rates had brought inflation down to 3.2 percent. Moreover, the economy had revived, partly because oil prices declined in response to the worldwide economic slump of the early 1980s, the development of new sources of non-OPEC oil in places such as Alaska and the North Sea, and

GEORGE FISHER
Courtesy Arkansas Gazette

This 1984 cartoon pointedly illustrates the mushrooming budget deficit arising from the Reagan administration's combination of deep tax cuts and huge defense spending.

reductions in oil use arising from conservation measures and technological innovations such as higher mileage-per-gallon cars. The revival was also a product of the large federal deficits, which in a Keynesian manner had increased the money available for the purchase of goods and services. Unemployment was down to 7.5 percent, and the GNP rose 6.8 percent, the largest annual increase since the Korean War.

Meanwhile, to balance the budget, Reagan took aim at federal spending. Social Security and Medicare, entitlements that accounted for almost half the federal budget, were politically untouchable. Interest on the national debt, another 10 percent of it, was legally so. Reagan's determination to increase defense spending left targetable for cuts only the 15 percent of federal outlays that included programs such as housing subsidies and Aid to Families with Dependent Children. The president pledged to maintain a "safety net" under the "truly needy." But 60 cents in every dollar of his 1981 spending cuts was hacked from the budget for social assistance—a total of $41 billion, including $2 billion from food stamps and $1 billion from school lunches.

Reagan sought to shrink the federal government further through the New Federalism, a policy of returning responsibility for welfare and regulatory programs to the states. It was an echo, but a hollow one, of Nixon's initiative to restore power to the states through revenue sharing. While state responsibilities were enlarged, however, the Reagan administration failed to provide enough funds to carry them out. During the 1980s, federal allocations to the states fell in constant dollars almost 13 percent. Among the consequences of Reaganomics was a striking shortfall of investment in the nation's infrastructure such as roads, bridges, and air-traffic control systems. In this decade, capital outlays for basic public works fell to barely 1 percent of GNP, less than half the level in the 1960s.

Critics warned that education, an investment in human capital, was of such low quality as to threaten the national welfare. A blue-ribbon commission convened by Reagan's first secretary of education concluded in its 1983 report, "If an unfriendly foreign power had attempted to impose on America the mediocre educational performance that exists today, we might well have viewed it as an act of war." The commission's report prompted local efforts by primary and secondary schools to improve their quality, but it did not move Reagan to help them with federal aid. During the Reagan years, fed-

"In 1985, the United States became a debtor nation for the first time since 1914, while Japan became the world's biggest creditor."

eral outlays for primary and secondary education fell in constant dollars. Reagan's second secretary of education contended that more important than enlarging funds for schools was focusing on values in the curriculum, including religion.

DEFICITS

Reagan's budgetary slashes were substantially offset by his huge increases in military spending—$1.6 trillion was authorized over five years—and the tax-cut losses. The budgetary calculus was further distorted by high interest payments on the national debt and the additional revenue declines that accompanied the recession. Reaganomics, rather than achieving progress toward a balanced budget, led to deficits of unprecedented magnitude. The administration borrowed to meet the shortfall, nearly tripling the national debt by the time Reagan left office to $2.7 trillion. Interest payments on the debt moved up to the third rank in the national budget, behind only Social Security and national defense. "I'm not worried about the deficit," Reagan joked. "It's big enough to take care of itself."

Reagan's willingness to tolerate huge deficits was a sharp departure from the Republican Party's traditional dislike of deficit spending. A mirror shift occurred among Democrats, who now emerged as the deficit's principal critics. The reasons for this exchange of positions were the reasons for the mounting deficit: high defense spending, reduced social spending, and tax cuts that favored upper-income groups—a package that Republicans welcomed and Democrats did not. In another reversal, funding the escalating debt involved heavy borrowing from abroad, with the result that in 1985 the United States became a debtor nation for the first time since 1914, while Japan became the world's biggest creditor.

DEREGULATION

Reagan greatly extended the deregulation process that Carter had initiated, expanding it in banking, the savings-and-loan industry, communications, and transportation. He also weakened federal controls by cutting regulatory budgets, staffing regulatory agencies with people hostile to their purposes, restraining enforcement, and scrapping regulations. His appointee to the chairmanship of the Federal Communications Commission, for example, was a former lawyer for broadcast-

PAUL DUGINSKI
Courtesy Sacramento Union

A cartoonist ridicules Reagan's secretary of the interior, James Watt, for advocating the drilling for oil and gas in environmentally sensitive areas.

ers who called television "just another appliance . . . a toaster with pictures." The chairman abolished long-standing FCC rules requiring broadcasters to devote a minimum portion of airtime to news, public affairs, and public service programs aimed at groups such as children.

Deregulation did foster competition, bringing advantages as well as disadvantages to consumers. It permitted banks and brokerages to offer attractive interest rates and an array of consumer services from cash-management accounts to automatic teller machines. It also allowed savings and loans to extend credit for purposes other than home mortgages. Many S&Ls headed for failure by making available to chancy ventures billions in credit from federally insured deposits—a practice that, a federal official said, made the government a "full partner in a nationwide casino" and that ultimately cost taxpayers hundreds of billions of dollars in bailouts. Airline competition produced lower fares for travelers, saving the public an estimated $6 billion a year, according to one study; but it allowed the airlines to shut down service or charge much higher fares to out-of-the-way locations. By 1989, some 140 small towns no longer had air service.

Coincidentally, competition also entered the telephone industry when in 1982, climaxing a long-developing antitrust action, a federal judge ordered AT&T, the regulated telephone monopoly, broken up into one long-distance company and twenty-two separate local telephone companies. The breakup inconvenienced many customers, who found themselves paying multiple monthly telephone bills. But new long-distance companies such as MCI and Sprint sprang into existence, driving down interstate calling rates; and new suppliers began providing innovative services and hardware, including answering machines, cordless phones, and cell phones.

Reaganite deregulation tended to favor private advantage over the public interest in the areas of health, safety, and the environment. Regulations that compelled car and truck manufacturers to improve safety and reduce air pollution, that forced employers to maintain safe and healthy working conditions, and that protected people from hazardous food and drugs were all eased. As president, Reagan displayed the casual indifference to environmental preservation that he had expressed during his first gubernatorial campaign, when he remarked, "You know, a tree is a tree—how many more do you need to look at?" Secretary of the Interior James Watt, a leader in the Sagebrush Rebellion, gave private developers a green light to cut timber in the national forests, drill for offshore oil and gas, and strip-mine for coal on public lands. Watt invited increasing attacks for his uncompromising commitment to privatization and his likening of environmentalists to "Nazis." He was finally forced to resign in 1983 for sarcastically commenting that one of his commissions contained "a black . . . a woman, two Jews and a cripple."

Sandra Day O'Connor, the first woman appointed to the Supreme Court, with Chief Justice Warren Burger, September 25, 1981.

Deregulation ran counter to the agenda of social conservatives like Jerry Falwell. But Reagan, eager to remove government from the private economy, was disinclined to install it in the bedroom. He gave the Falwell conservatives rhetorical support, sending Justice Department lawyers into court to argue for school prayer and against abortion, and calling for a constitutional amendment that would prohibit abortions except to save the mother's life. But he did not invest much political energy in the issue. Indeed, in 1981, despite Falwell's opposition, he appointed Sandra Day O'Connor to the Supreme Court. An able jurist from Arizona, she was the first woman to serve on the high bench. Falwell, among other right-to-life activists, opposed her nomination on grounds that she appeared sympathetic to abortion rights, and declared that all "good Christians" should be concerned about O'Connor. Senator Barry Goldwater of Arizona—like Reagan more an economic than a social conservative—retorted, "Every good Christian ought to kick Falwell right in the ass."

Reagan and the World

Reagan's approach to foreign affairs was dominated for much of his presidency by his conviction that the Soviet Union was an "evil empire," the United States' chief opponent in a world contest "between right and wrong and good and evil." His view of the Soviets was shared by his first secretary of state, General Alexander Haig, a protégé of Henry Kissinger and a flamboyant, self-assured Cold Warrior. The Soviets appeared to confirm the administration's outlook when in September 1983 one of their fighters shot down a Korean airliner that had misnavigated into Soviet airspace—the Soviets claimed it was on a spy mission—killing all 239 passengers and outraging most Americans.

Reagan found the Soviets especially menacing in the realm of "strategic" weapons, the arsenal of nuclear arms that directly threatened the vital interests of the United States. Since the Soviets had superiority in the number of land-based ICBMs (intercontinental ballistic missiles), he was convinced that the U.S.'s "window of vulnerability" remained to be

> *"Reagan's approach to foreign affairs was dominated for much of his presidency by his conviction that the Soviet Union was an 'evil empire,' the United States' chief opponent in a world contest 'between right and wrong and good and evil.'"*

closed. Critics countered that the Soviet Union did not enjoy an overall strategic superiority because it had no effective defense against the nuclear missiles borne by U.S. submarines and the cruise missiles carried by American bombers. What truly threatened American security, the physicist Hans Bethe pointed out, was "the grotesque size and continuing growth of both nuclear arsenals."

But Reagan, persisting in his belief about American vulnerability, pursued the buildup of American arms, strategic and otherwise, carrying forward weapons programs begun under Carter and initiating a number of his own. Annual defense outlays mushroomed from $157 billion in 1981 to $227 billion in 1984. Further increases were projected that would bring the total to nearly $3 trillion for the decade, representing a renewal of military Keynesianism that helped fuel the prosperity of the Reagan years as it had during the Kennedy era. Secretary Haig considered aloud the possibility of firing "nuclear warning shots" in a conventional war. Pursuing Carter's commitments to deploy an accurate, MIRV-carrying land-based missile, the administration resolved to install the MX, now renamed the Peacekeeper, in vulnerable silos, implying that they were intended as first-strike weapons; and it began deploying almost 600 cruise and Pershing II missiles in Western Europe. The United States established contingency plans to "prevail" in a "protracted nuclear war," even reviving serious discussion of shelters to protect civilians from nuclear attacks. An assistant secretary in charge of civil defense, contending that backyard shelters would spare millions, expressed confidence in the protectiveness of dirt: "If there are enough shovels to go around, everybody's going to make it."

STAR WARS

The administration's promotion of nuclear weapons together with its militant anti-Sovietism generated mounting public apprehension. Antinuclear activists began calling for a verifiable mutual freeze on the testing, production, and deployment of nuclear weapons. By the summer of 1982, the nuclear freeze movement had gained strength enough to rally 800,000 demonstrators against nuclear weapons in New York's Central Park, an antinuclear demonstration of unprecedented size. That year, the dangers posed by the escalating nuclear arms race were eloquently articulated in the journalist Jonathan Schell's widely read *The Fate of the Earth*. In the fall, freeze resolutions were passed in nine states, including California and Wisconsin, and in 1983 the TV film *The Day After*, a horrific account of a nuclear attack against the United States, drew an audience estimated at 100 million. In the fall of that year, several scientists announced that clouds of black, sooty smoke generated by urban fires ignited in a nuclear war would envelope the earth, drastically reduce its surface temperature, and bring about a nuclear winter of long duration. George F. Kennan, among others, urged that the United States pledge "no first use" of nuclear weapons and enter into a comprehensive test-ban treaty with the Soviet Union.

In June 1982, seeking to defuse the emerging antinuclear movement, the administration proposed removing all medium-range nuclear weapons from Europe, and it revived

Thousands of Americans march against nuclear weapons in New York City, June 12, 1982.

strategic arms reduction talks with the Soviets. Then in March 1983, Reagan announced plans for a Strategic Defense Initiative (SDI), a technological system that would forever protect the United States from assault by nuclear missiles. SDI, which was quickly dubbed "Star Wars," after the popular film, would deploy sophisticated devices, including high-powered lasers and particle beams, some of them already being developed in the national laboratories, to detect and disable or destroy incoming enemy warheads. A number of policy analysts attacked SDI because it would violate the Anti-Ballistic Missile Treaty that the United States had ratified during the Nixon administration. And many scientists and engineers derided it as a technical fantasy—a prohibitively expensive system that could be tricked by decoys and overwhelmed by multiple warheads. In the end, they said, it would not work and would only further escalate the arms race.

SDI nevertheless appealed to Reagan and to millions of other Americans. It promised to restore the United States to the condition of security that the Atlantic and Pacific Oceans had once provided. It would substitute an invulnerable technological shield for the distasteful and polluting task of dealing with the evil empire. It would render nuclear weapons, Reagan declared, "impotent and obsolete." In 1985, Congress endorsed SDI, authorizing $3 billion as the first installment on the necessary research and development.

Boosted by Star Wars appropriations, federal expenditures for R&D continued climbing; in 1986, they would reach some $57 billion—27 percent higher, in constant dollars, than the predownturn peak, reached in 1967. The largest share of the increase went to defense, which in the late 1980s commanded about 70 percent of the federal R&D budget, a share approaching that of the 1950s. A major feature of the trend was a renewed emphasis by the Defense Department on academic research, amounting to a threefold increase over what it had been in 1975.

AFFIRMATION: THE ELECTION OF 1984

In the 1982 elections, the Republicans retained control of the Senate but lost twenty-five seats in the House, a signal of dissatisfaction with the high unemployment and tight money at that point of Reaganomics. But as the presidential election approached amid the renewal of prosperity, the Republicans cheered through the renomination of Reagan and Bush. The Reverend Jesse Jackson, a black advocate of the poor, won more than 20 percent of the vote in the Democratic primaries, but that party's nominations went to Walter Mondale, the former vice-president, and Congresswoman Geraldine Ferraro from New York City, the first woman ever nominated by a major party for the second-highest office. Mondale emphasized Reagan's seeming lack of substance, attacked the administration for increasing the gap between rich and poor, and warned that its rapidly accumulating deficit was dangerously mortgaging the country's future.

Republicans, for their part, derided Mondale as a "tax-and-spend liberal," an exemplar of the failures of the Carter years. Ferraro, who might have added electricity to the campaign, ran into trouble because of violations of campaign-spending laws and controversy surrounding her husband's business interests. On election day, Reagan won every state but Minnesota, smashing Mondale in the popular vote 59 percent to 41 percent and burying him in the electoral college with a majority of 525 to 13, a margin second only to Roosevelt's in 1936. He won or scored well in almost every major group except blacks and Jews, and continued to attract sizable numbers of blue-collar defectors from the Democrats. The Democrats retained control of the House, Republicans of the Senate.

During the campaign, Reagan had declared, "America is back: it's morning again," a sentiment that his television advertisements modified into a phrase that caught on: "It's morning in America." Reagan might not have commanded the nitty-gritty of government; he was nonetheless able to beat down inflation, restore prosperity, and get tough with the Russians. It was not, of course, morning for many Americans, particularly those living in the inner cities or worried by the escalation of the arms race. But a solid majority found reasons enough to let the Reagan revolution continue.

THE THIRD WORLD

In his second inaugural address, Reagan called for supporting anti-Communist "freedom fighters" throughout the Third World. Soon dubbed the Reagan Doctrine, his declaration expressed an evangelical outlook that pervaded his foreign policy: it was the special mission of the United States not only to stand as a beacon of democracy and freedom but to help spread those blessings to the rest of the planet. The Reagan Doctrine complemented the claim of the ambassador to the United Nations, Jeane Kirkpatrick, that it made good sense for the United States to support "positively friendly" autocrats and "right-wing autocracies" on grounds that, unlike left-wing totalitarian regimes, they "do sometimes evolve into democracies."

Reagan, in sympathy with Kirkpatrick's view, was ignorant of and indifferent to the indigenous forces in the Third World that challenged pro-Western governments for their own reasons rather than Moscow's—for example, anger at economic exploitation or the suppression of political dissidents or both. He preferred to attribute such challenges to the Soviet Union, which, he insisted, "underlies all the unrest" in the world. His anti-Sovietism strongly shaped his approach to the Middle East and, especially, Central America.

Stalemate and Terror: The Middle East. Sure that Soviet machinations were responsible for the instability in the Middle East, Reagan hoped to bring moderate Arab states and Israel together into an anti-Soviet combination. But the prospective parties considered the future of the Palestinians far more important than any Soviet threat. Although, honoring the Camp David accords, Prime Minister Begin had returned the Sinai to Egypt, he refrained from granting the Palestinians any autonomy in the West Bank and the Gaza Strip. Indeed, he expanded Israeli settlements with an evident eye toward future annexation of the territories. Reagan called for a freeze on settlements and independence for the West Bank "in association with Jordan," but Begin refused the proposal.

U.S. Marines carry a corpse from the rubble of the barracks destroyed by a truck bomb that killed 241 fellow marines, Beirut, October 1983.

Palestinian guerrillas, on their part, mounted continual armed attacks against Israel from sanctuaries in southern Lebanon. In June 1982, Israel invaded Lebanon to drive out the guerrillas, but succeeded mainly in intensifying the civil war under way between Muslims, Palestinians, and Christians and in heightening Arab-Israeli tensions. Secretary of State George Shultz recognized that the problems in the Middle East were specific to the region, not the result of Soviet ambitions. At his urging, Reagan proposed a comprehensive peace plan as a basis for negotiations between Israel and the moderate Arab states, but neither side accepted it. In 1983, in the hope of quelling the violence in Lebanon, the administration sent 2,000 marines there as part of a multinational peacekeeping force. Seen as favoring the Israelis and the Christians, they were attacked by guerrillas and terrorists. In October, a suicide truck bomber killed 241 marines in a poorly guarded barracks in Beirut. The murders provoked grief and outrage at home, including a growing demand to pull the remaining marines out of Lebanon. In early 1984, Reagan reluctantly brought the troops home, his efforts toward a settlement in the Middle East scuttled by the intractability of the region's political rivalries and hatreds.

In December 1987, Palestinians living in occupied Gaza and the West Bank began an *intifada,* a civilian uprising against the Israeli authorities. Secretary Shultz attempted to work out an agreement for Palestinian autonomy between Israel, Jordan, and the Palestinians; but his proposals dissatisfied the Palestinians, and the Israeli government refused to negotiate until the *intifada* ended. Unwilling to tolerate the uprising, Israeli forces repeatedly clashed with the Palestinian rebels, killing some 800 of them during the next three years. Despite opposition from the United States, Israel also continued to establish Jewish settlements on the West Bank.

In the meantime, terrorists brought the turbulence in the Middle East to the West, hijacking a TWA flight and an Italian cruise ship, killing an American aboard each. The attacks were attributed to Palestinians and their supporters, including Colonel Muammar al-Gadhafi, the head of Libya. In mid-1981, with Reagan's authorization, American jets had downed two Libyan planes that had fired on them; Reagan said that he wanted it known that "there was new management in the White House." In April 1986, Libyans were implicated in the bombing of a Berlin nightclub that American soldiers frequented. Reagan retaliated by bombing Tripoli, including Gadhafi's compound, killing one of Gadhafi's daughters but not, to use Reagan's term, "the mad dog of the Middle East" himself.

Rock-throwing Palestinians confront Israeli troops on the West Bank in the *intifada*, 1988.

Although Gadhafi acted with restraint for a time, Libya appeared to retaliate when in December 1988 a concealed bomb downed a Pan American jet flying over Lockerbie, Scotland, killing all 259 passengers and crew. Three years later, after an exhaustive investigation, the United States and Scotland charged two operatives of the Libyan Intelligence System with responsibility for the crime. Gadhafi denied any Libyan involvement and refused to extradite the two men until 1999, when they were sent to the Netherlands for trial before a three-judge Scottish court. In January 2001, one of them was found not guilty, the other was convicted and sentenced to life in prison.

Central America. In Nicaragua in 1979, a popular insurrection threw out a right-wing dictatorship and installed a leftist government, the Sandinistas, which received support from Castro and the Soviet bloc. In El Salvador, where a right-wing government held sway, leftist guerrillas, encouraged by the Sandinista victory, fought to overturn the regime, drawing military assistance from Cuba and Nicaragua. Both Reagan and Haig held that Central America was threatened by "Communist aggression," ignoring the roots of political instability and resentment in poverty and repression.

In 1981, to deal with Nicaragua, Reagan directed the CIA to begin arming and organizing a guerrilla army—the Contras, many of them with ties to the deposed dictatorship—to wage war against the Sandinistas from bases in neighboring Honduras and Costa Rica. The next year, Congress responded with legislation forbidding the CIA or the Defense Department to provide any aid "for the purpose of overthrowing" the Nicaraguan regime. Despite the prohibition, the Reagan administration secretly continued to fund the Contras, obtaining support from private sources and foreign governments. (George Shultz, who in 1982 had succeeded Haig as secretary of state, warned Reagan that thus circumventing the Congress might constitute "an impeachable offense.") Reagan publicly celebrated the Contras as "the moral equivalent of our Founding Fathers." All the while, the administration tenaciously sought to bolster the regime in El Salvador, even though right-wing "death squads" were operating freely against members of the opposition.

The administration found an opportunity to strike more decisively against Communism in Grenada, a small Caribbean island where in October 1983 a Marxist government was overthrown by a more radical regime. On Reagan's orders, 2,000 marines invaded the island, partly to protect American students in medical school there. They drove out the new government and established a pro-American replacement. Most Americans hailed the invasion, as did the Grenadans and nearby Caribbean states. The action impelled the Nicaraguan Sandinistas to improve their behavior, at least for a time, and even to talk about negotiations.

Reagan justified his policies in Latin America by warning of the implications of Marxist success. "Our credibility would collapse, our alliances would crumble, and the safety of our homeland would be in jeopardy. . . . If we cannot act decisively so close to home, who will believe us anywhere?"

Scandal: Iran-Contra. On November 3, 1986, a Beirut newspaper reported that the year before, the United States had sold antitank missiles to Iran in exchange for American hostages. (There were seven hostages, all but one private citizens, who had been captured in Lebanon and held by Hezbollah, an Iranian-backed terrorist group.) Hezbollah released one of the hostages the same day. The story was promptly confirmed by the Iranian prime minister, who said

that in May Robert McFarlane, the president's national security adviser, had brought a small shipment of missile parts to Iran together with gifts, including a Bible inscribed by Reagan for the Ayatollah Khomeini and a cake decorated with a brass key for the mother of the principal Iranian go-between.

In the United States, outrage greeted the revelations that the administration had violated its own stated policy, and the government's long-standing one, against bargaining with terrorists. In fact, Reagan had privately deviated from that rule on several occasions. Now, in November 1986, he went on television to say that the United States had indeed shipped small caches of arms to Iran in an attempt to encourage a restoration of relations and assist Iran in its war with Iraq. He insisted that the charge that the arms had been sent in exchange for hostages was "utterly false." Later that month, the attorney general discovered and released to the public evidence of still worse activities: Lieutenant Colonel Oliver North, a staff member of the National Security Council (NSC) and a much-decorated Vietnam veteran, had diverted millions of dollars from the arms sales to provide the Contras in Nicaragua with military assistance. North's action, carried out with the knowledge of the head of the NSC, Admiral John Poindexter, was illegal, a defiance of the congressional mandate against military aid to the Contras. During the attorney general's investigation, North and his staff at the NSC purged computer files, shredded incriminating documents, and, together with the head of the CIA, William Casey, concocted cover-up stories about the affair.

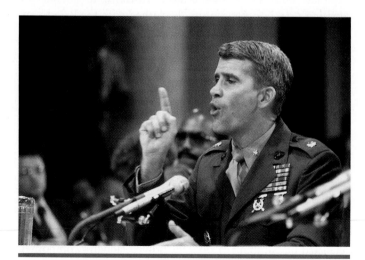

Lieutenant Colonel Oliver North testifies at the congressional hearings on Iran-Contra, July 7, 1987.

By early December, Reagan's public approval rating had plummeted 21 points, to 46 percent, the sharpest one-month drop ever recorded for a president. At the end of February 1987, a bipartisan commission rapped Reagan for his lax "management style" and for trading arms for hostages; but it concluded that the president had not known "anything whatsoever" about the illegal payments to the Contras. In a **televised address** a few days later, Reagan conceded that while he had not thought he was trading arms for hostages, he had in fact mistakenly done so. In congressional hearings that summer, North, bemedaled in his uniform, defended all he had done as an act of selfless duty. While North suggested that Reagan had known everything, Poindexter testified that he had kept the diversion of funds to the Contras secret from the president. Casey might have brought to light key facts in the matter, but he was beyond testifying to Congress, having died of a stroke in May.

In 1988, a special prosecutor brought criminal indictments against Poindexter, North, and others. All were eventually found guilty of charges such as perjury and misuse of government funds. The convictions of North and Poindexter were later overturned on grounds that some of the evidence against them had been given under a congressional grant of immunity from prosecution. At his trial, Poindexter repudiated his testimony in the hearings, declaring instead that Reagan had been fully aware of the diversion of funds to the Contras and had ordered the destruction of documents. In videotaped testimony, Reagan denied the allegation while seeming confused and claiming to be unable to recall most of the details of the scandal.

All the while, Reagan urged Congress to authorize military aid to the Contras, but Congress refused, insisting on a negotiated settlement in Nicaragua. A peace plan devised by President Oscar Arias of Costa Rica gained the support of the Central American governments and, by early 1988, of the Sandinistas. The Sandinistas entered into talks with the Contras, and a cease-fire was declared.

For a time, Reagan's complicity in Iran-Contra, whatever it was, gave rise to talk of impeachment. But the talk quickly subsided, not least because it seemed unsupportable to impeach a president for not knowing what his subordinates were doing.

> *"For Reagan, as for the American people in the aftermath of Vietnam, any armed intervention would have to be a short-term venture costing little in dollars or American lives."*

Flexibility: Africa, the Philippines, and Haiti. While Reagan revived John Foster Dulles's moralism in foreign affairs, he would go only so far in pursuit of higher purposes. He was guided by an overarching inclination to avoid committing American forces, especially on the ground, to sustained conflict. For Reagan, as for the American people in the aftermath of Vietnam, any armed intervention would have to be a short-term venture costing little in dollars or American lives: thus the compactness of the intervention in Grenada, the speediness of the withdrawal from Lebanon, and the mode of warring largely by proxy against the left in Nicaragua and El Salvador. Reagan was also capable of ignoring ideology to satisfy domestic political interests, defuse the objections of allies, and pursue practical geopolitics. The Reagan Doctrine was thus flexible, responsive to events, notably in South Africa, the Philippines, and Haiti.

Throughout his first term, Reagan had adopted a policy of what a State Department official called "constructive engagement" in dealing with South Africa. The president called its harsh system of apartheid (racial segregation) "morally wrong and politically unacceptable," but while he urged the government to release its political prisoners and legalize black political movements such as the African National Congress (ANC), he was reluctant to back his rhetoric with coercive measures. Nevertheless, in September 1985, responding to nationwide demands for action, especially on the campuses, Reagan issued an executive order that prohibited computer sales, bank loans, and the export of nuclear technology to South Africa. The next year, Congress, overriding Reagan's veto, imposed still tougher economic sanctions on the regime, including a ban on all imports from South Africa, that could be lifted only after the country had made significant progress toward democratization.

In the Philippines, Reagan clung to the hope of saving the repressive regime of Ferdinand Marcos against the intensifying democratic protest movement led by Corazon Aquino, the widow of a murdered opposition leader. Reagan, who considered Aquino weak, feared Marcos's fall would lead to a Communist takeover. Shultz, however, pressed Reagan to withdraw U.S. support from Marcos and provide him safe haven. In 1986, Shultz overcame Reagan's resistance. Marcos fled the country with his extensive entourage, and Corazon Aquino together with her followers joyfully established democratic government in the Philippines.

In Haiti, in mid-1985, the corrupt and dictatorial Jean-Claude ("Baby Doc") Duvalier got himself elected president for life with 99.9 percent of the vote. Dissent from the apparently rigged result soon turned into a tidal wave of protest that brought the country to the edge of chaos. The Reagan administration, seeing that Duvalier's government would topple, arranged for him to flee into exile. It then pressed policies of liberalization on the Haitian military, which took control. The subsequent democratization led to the election in 1990 of a new president, Jean-Bertrand Aristide.

DOING BUSINESS WITH THE SOVIETS

Although the Iran-Contra scandal impaired Reagan's authority, he recovered from the shadow it cast by a dramatic transformation in U.S.-Soviet relations that occurred during his second term. Brezhnev had died in 1982, and death had cut short the terms of the two men who succeeded him. (Asked why he was seemingly unwilling to meet with his Soviet counterparts, Reagan had quipped, "They keep dying on me.") But in November 1985, Reagan journeyed to Geneva for his first summit with a Soviet leader—Mikhail Gorbachev, who had become the new head of the Soviet Union in March. At fifty-four, Gorbachev was vigorous, articulate, knowledgeable about the West, where he had traveled, and brimming with ideas for change. With his country beset by mounting economic difficulties, he intended to pursue a program of domestic reform. To this end, he wanted to ease Cold War tensions, cut expenditures on armaments, and, like Russian reformers before him, reach out to the West. After meeting him in London, Prime Minister Margaret Thatcher of Britain, Reagan's friend and fellow conservative, had remarked, "I like Mr. Gorbachev. We can do business together."

The Geneva summit made for a fresh start in U.S.-Soviet relations. Reagan and Gorbachev spent hours in candid conversation, often alone save for their interpreters. In public, Gorbachev conducted himself with flair, assiduously cultivating the media, as did his wife, Raisa. She was a sophisticated university graduate and something of a fashion plate, the first wife of a Soviet premier to capture the West's attention. The Gorbachevs were movie buffs, enthralled by Reagan's tales of Hollywood and happy to dine with someone who had known Jimmy Stewart, Humphrey Bogart, and John Wayne. Little substantive business was accomplished at Geneva, but at the end of the meeting Reagan and Gorbachev announced that they had agreed to hold two more summits. The striking news of the conference was the rapport that had developed between the two men. "[We] got very friendly," Reagan said.

During the next several years, Gorbachev sought arms agreements with the United States and boldly pursued an expanding program of domestic political and economic reform. An increasing number of analysts in the United States dared to hope that, with Reagan's help, the Cold War might actually be ending. But the Reagan administration initially responded to Gorbachev's efforts with suspicion, some of its hard-liners counting them as mere window dressing for continued Soviet oppression at home and imperialism abroad.

Setback over Star Wars. In October 1986, when Reagan and Gorbachev held their second summit, in Reykjavik, Iceland, the then-budding miracle had seemed to wilt. Gorbachev, who had proclaimed that it was imperative for the superpowers to reduce the threat of nuclear annihilation, arrived at the meeting with a sheaf of detailed proposals for arms control, including the elimination of all intermediate-range nuclear weapons in Europe. Reagan countered by proposing an agreement to destroy all nuclear weapons. To the surprise of many, Gorbachev agreed, on the condition that the United States continue to honor the ABM Treaty of 1972 by keeping its Star Wars research confined to the laboratory for ten years.

Hard-liners in the administration had been urging Reagan to embrace a "broad" interpretation of the treaty that would

Soviet leader Mikhail Gorbachev (left) and Ronald Reagan at their first summit, Geneva, Switzerland, November 19, 1985.

allow not only for laboratory research on Star Wars but also for testing in the field. Arms-control advocates had denounced the idea as an unwarranted reading of the treaty that would lead to its renunciation and encourage an acceleration of the arms race. Reagan, his own enthusiasm for Star Wars undiminished, rejected Gorbachev's condition, explaining later that it would "have killed our defensive shield." On the evening of October 12, he and Gorbachev emerged grim-faced from their final negotiating session, with neither an arms-control agreement nor much good to say about each other. Secretary of State Shultz, one of the few in the administration who thought the Soviets were genuinely changing, had trouble concealing his distress. Gorbachev told reporters, "We have missed a historical chance. Never have our positions been so close."

The administration mounted a public relations blitz to turn the disaster at Reykjavik into a triumph, earning cheers from the public for Reagan for seeking to abolish nuclear weaponry and for SDI as a means of gaining such an agreement. However, in the succeeding months, the seeming success of Reykjavik was overshadowed by the revelations of Iran-Contra, the lack of concrete progress on arms control, and growing doubts about SDI. The Joint Chiefs of Staff, along with defense experts, expressed shock that Reagan would have bargained away the nuclear deterrent, pointing out that maintaining the nation's security without ballistic missiles would require a huge increase in military spending, enough to bring the defense budget to $1 trillion by the mid-1990s. Reports surfaced from SDI scientists that no great technical progress had occurred and from analysts that a blanket national missile defense would not work and would be enormously expensive. And in mid-March 1987, in a lengthy presentation to his fellow senators, Sam Nunn of Georgia, one of the chamber's leading authorities on defense, demonstrated that the "broad" interpretation of the ABM Treaty had no legal support whatsoever.

The Making of a Miracle. In the meantime, Gorbachev had been reconsidering his view that arms control had to be accompanied by restraint on SDI. The Soviet physicist Andrei Sakharov, isolated in internal exile, had urged that the two issues be decoupled, predicting that SDI would be costly to the United States, easily overwhelmed by the Soviets, and in the end amount to nothing more than a "Maginot line in space." At the end of 1986, by Gorbachev's personal order, Sakharov returned to Moscow and now pressed his case for arms con-

A cartoonist blames Reagan's Star Wars program for dashing arms-control hopes at the Reykjavik summit, October 1986.

trol at the center of Soviet policymaking. In late February 1987, Gorbachev told the Reagan administration that he was willing to proceed with arms-control negotiations without regard to SDI and wanted to conclude a treaty on intermediate-range nuclear weapons (INF) in Europe.

Gorbachev was simultaneously initiating profound changes inside the Soviet Union. In 1986, in order to bring pressure to bear on the Soviet bureaucracy, he had proclaimed *glasnost*, an opening of the Soviet system via greater freedom of expression and freedom of the press and the release of political prisoners. Now he was pushing ahead with *perestroika*, a restructuring of the Soviet economy to encourage private entrepreneurship as well as foreign trade and investment. In 1987, the Soviets announced that their troops would begin leaving Afghanistan within the next year.

Reagan, in deepening political trouble at home, speedily took up Gorbachev's offer for a meeting on the INF Treaty, expecting it to lead to a prestige-restoring summit before the end of the year. Anti-Soviet hard-liners were departing, leaving Shultz the key figure in a national security team disposed to think that the changes underway in the Soviet Union boded well for the United States and the world. In mid-June 1987, while in Berlin near the wall dividing the eastern and western zones of the city, Reagan called on Gorbachev to show unequivocally that the opening of Soviet society was more than a token gesture, declaring, "Mr. Gorbachev, tear down this wall."

At the summit, held in Washington in December, little of substance was accomplished beyond coming to a final agreement on the INF Treaty. When Reagan told Gorbachev that the United States would proceed with its research and development on SDI, Gorbachev responded flatly, "Mr. President, you do what you think you have to do. . . . And if in the end you think you have a system you want to deploy, go ahead and deploy it. . . . I think you're wasting your money. I don't think it will work. But if that's what you want to do, go ahead." The INF Treaty—signed precisely at 1:45 P.M. on December 8 because Nancy Reagan's astrologer had advised her that this was the most propitious moment—eliminated about 1,280 Soviet warheads and about 429 American ones. Although the reduction comprised only about 4 percent of the combined Soviet and American nuclear arsenals, the agreement represented a significant step because it was the first to abolish an entire class of nuclear weapons and the first to provide for on-site verification that the Soviet missiles were being destroyed.

> *"In a first in Gallup polling, the general secretary of the Communist Party of the Soviet Union made the list of the ten most admired men in the United States."*

The achievement of the treaty was reinforced by the good cheer that marked the summit, where the two leaders called each other "Ron" and "Mikhail," and Gorbachev kept popping out of his car to shake hands in the crowds. Expressing the "Gorbymania" that swept through the country, *Time* magazine designated Gorbachev its "Man of the Year," and—a first in Gallup polling—the general secretary of the Communist Party of the Soviet Union made the list of the ten most admired men in the United States. The following spring, Gorbachev initiated a restructuring of Soviet relations with its satellites and a transformation of the Soviet system into a political democracy, including an elected legislature and executive, an independent judiciary, and freedom of speech and assembly.

A follow-up summit in Moscow that May was still shorter on substance but even longer on happy symbolism, notably the image of Reagan and Gorbachev chatting on a morning stroll through Red Square, with Reagan putting his arm around Gorbachev's shoulder near Lenin's tomb. Asked by a reporter about his attack in 1983 on the evil empire, Reagan replied, "I was talking about another time, another era." In London on the way home, Reagan took stock of the momentous changes under way in the Soviet Union, remarking, to "all those familiar with the postwar era, this is a cause for shaking the head in wonder."

Reagan's America

Reagan's triumphal summitry abroad was accompanied by an exuberant prosperity at home. The rising economic tide lifted many boats, restoring the satisfactions of abundance to much of white America and further propelling the growth of the middle class among African Americans, Hispanics, and Asians. Many women prospered, too. Yet the tranquillity of Reagan's administration was disturbed by evidence emerging during his second term that tax reductions and deregulation did not always serve the public interest, notably in the arenas of the federal debt, the stock market, and the savings-and-loan industry. It became increasingly clear that in the prosperity of the eighties, some benefited hugely more than others.

The conservative **economic policies** and social attitudes that Reagan both reflected and encouraged left many Americans, but especially many of color, impoverished, degraded, and virtually hopeless. They dampened women's drive for equality. Their consequences were further compounded by ongoing increases in the immigration that had begun in the seventies, in part a product of political and economic upheaval elsewhere in the world, and by the ever-stiffening competitive pressures that American industry faced in a globalizing economy.

GREED IS GOOD

The Reagan years reminded some observers of the 1920s, not only in the ebullience of the prosperity but in the unevenness of it, and in the naked materialism of the culture associated with it. Between 1982 and 1988, the gross domestic product grew at an average annual rate of about 4 percent, generating more than 630,000 new businesses, 11 million jobs, and a drop in the unemployment rate from 7.4 percent to 5.5 percent. By 1988, mortgage rates had plummeted roughly 40 percent, and by 1989 median family income corrected for inflation had shot up 12.5 percent.

Corporate profits broke records, and so did the stock market—at least until October 19, 1987, when the Dow Jones industrial average (an indicator of stock-market value) plummeted 508 points, losing almost a quarter of its worth, wiping out $750 billion in paper wealth, and generating fears that the country might be headed for another Depression. But the jitters were short-lived. By 1989, the Dow Jones had more than doubled its level in 1982.

The decade produced a new group called "yuppies," a derisive acronym for "young urban professionals," upwardly mobile men and women with degrees in law or business, dressed for success and exuding the ambitions of an unrestrained materialism. Americans of all sorts became absorbed with celebrities—professional athletes, television newscasters, entertainers, clothing designers, even chefs, most of whom were admired for their professional skills but also for their opulent incomes. Among the heroes of Wall Street were manipulators of junk bonds, loans issued to finance the purchase of corporations for prices far higher than the corporations were worth. Some of the heroes, who received several hundred million dollars a year in commissions, were later exposed as crooked and went to jail.

Tom Wolfe's best-selling novel *Bonfire of the Vanities* relentlessly explored the culture of avarice, but reality outdid fiction. Amid the weakened oversight of Reaganite deregulation, a number of savings-and-loan institutions were looted by white-collar thieves, some of whom bought yachts and threw lavish entertainments. Ivan Boesky, one of the financial buccaneers of the decade—he later went to jail for fraudulent manipulations—proclaimed, "Greed is all right . . . everybody should be a little greedy," a sentiment that pervaded the popular film *Wall Street.*

Some religious ministries combined evangelism with profiteering in ways reminiscent of *Elmer Gantry*, Sinclair Lewis's famed novel of the 1920s. Taking advantage of the rapid proliferation of cable TV, some 336 of them were broadcasting by 1989. One such televangelist and his wife were found to enjoy an annual income of at least $1.6 million and to own six homes, including an extravaganza with gold-plated fixtures and an air-conditioned doghouse. He was also revealed to have had a sexual relationship with a young volunteer, who provided enough information about his business affairs to have him convicted on twenty-four counts of fraud and conspiracy. Nevertheless, the popularity of the televangelists remained undiminished. Some 33 million people subscribed to the Christian Broadcast Network's "700 Club," run by Marion

> *"Between 1979 and 1988, the disparity in earnings between the chairman of the board and the average factory worker more than tripled, reaching a ratio of 93 to 1."*

Actor Michael Douglas as a greed-driven business executive, in the award-winning film *Wall Street*, 1987.

G. "Pat" Robertson, and in 1987 the network, including its multiple enterprises, brought in $230 million.

Critics understandably disparaged Reaganomics as "welfare for the rich." Reagan's initial tax changes had channeled one dollar out of every twelve to Americans earning less than $15,000 a year, one in three to those with annual incomes greater than $50,000. His Tax Reform Act of 1986, a major overhaul of the tax system, closed numerous loopholes and removed nearly 6 million people from the tax rolls; but it also further slashed the top rate for individuals, from 50 percent to 28 percent. Then, too, throughout most of the country the reductions in federal income taxes were offset by increases in state taxes and in Social Security taxes, which were imposed to keep the system solvent. Together, these tax increases in effect nullified the Reagan tax cut for most working Americans, keeping their overall tax burden relatively unchanged. By the end of the decade, families earning under $10,000 wound up with a $95 net loss, while those making more than $200,000 gained more than $17,000. Between 1979 and 1988, the disparity in earnings between the chairman of the board and the average factory worker more than tripled, reaching a ratio of 93 to 1. In 1988, the richest 1 percent of Americans owned almost 15 percent of national wealth, almost twice the fraction of 1980.

STRESSES IN THE WORKFORCE

Reagan threw down a gauntlet to organized labor when in August 1981 about two-thirds of the air-traffic controllers' union (PATCO) walked off their jobs in a demand for higher wages. The action defied the law and a no-strike pledge that all 17,000 members of the union had signed. Two days later, Reagan fired the controllers, ordering military controllers to take their places until civilian substitutes could be trained. Air travel continued uninterrupted, and within two years the strikers had been replaced. Reagan's victory had a chilling effect on American labor, and so did his National Labor Relations Board, which after 1983 was headed by an antiunion lawyer. Although public-sector-employee unions were growing, those in the private sector were shrinking. Total union membership fell to 16.9 million in 1987, down almost 25 percent from the level in 1975. Major manufacturing unions ran scared, settling for smaller wage increases in favor of job security and retraining programs.

Labor was made more apprehensive by the wave of mergers, takeovers, and restructurings—the most extensive in the na-

Hundreds demonstrated for jobs when President Reagan stopped in Philadelphia in 1982.

tion's history—that were sweeping through corporate America. Encouraged by the administration's laissez-faire policies, corporate raiders engineered hostile takeovers, often financing their conquests partly by selling some of the assets of the companies they acquired. Corporate directors resorted to restructuring to defend against takeover threats or respond to increased competition or both. Aimed at increasing a company's efficiency and reducing its vulnerability, restructuring tended to involve selling parts of the company unrelated to its main business and cutting the workforce. Many workers, including middle managers, thus found themselves laid off from jobs they had assumed would be theirs for life.

Labor's difficulties were intensified by the ongoing decline of the smokestack industries, which were reeling still more from foreign competition in major industries such as steel, automobiles, and electronics. The challenges from abroad were compounded by the foreign capital that flooded into the United States in the early 1980s, drawn by the high interest rates at that time. The influx drove up the value of the dollar against other currencies, raising the relative price on the world market of American products and reducing that of foreign ones. Exports plummeted and imports soared, eliminating manufacturing jobs and more than tripling the trade deficit between 1981 and 1984, from $31 billion to $111 billion.

Farmers also suffered setbacks. Many had expanded their operations during the 1970s in response to a rising global demand for farm products. But now that the strong dollar had driven down exports, they were overproducing for the available domestic market. Between 1980 and 1986, crop prices dropped; in Iowa, the average value of farmland fell 55 percent. Farm foreclosures and bankruptcies climbed, reaching a post-Depression high. The downturn struck hard at related industries such as food processing and farm equipment and at small towns throughout the Midwest.

In 1985, jolted by the trade imbalance, the dollar began to slide, losing by 1989 almost a third of its value against the West German mark and almost half its value against the Japanese yen. The shift, reversing the strong-dollar trend of the early 1980s, resulted in more exports and fewer imports. A modicum of prosperity returned to the farms, as a result of a rebound in agricultural exports, increased domestic demand, and a drought in 1988 that reduced supply. But foreign manufacturers remained strongly competitive against domestic producers, notably in steel and automobiles.

By the mid-1980s, high-school-educated blue-collar workers earned $18,000 a year, a quarter less than they had fifteen years earlier. Faced with the rigors of competition, both old companies and new ones hired skilled workers at lower wages and benefits than those paid to senior, union-protected employees. The average compensation of truck drivers fell by a quarter, of pilots and flight attendants by as much as two-thirds. Many firms relied increasingly on part-time or temporary workers. Between 1982 and 1987, real hourly wages declined a half percent per year, making the period unique among those of economic boom since World War II. In his smash hit song "Born in the USA," Bruce Springsteen sang in the bitter, ironic voice of a Vietnam veteran who could gain neither work nor help: "Down in the shadow of the penitentiary / Out by the gas fires of the refinery / I'm ten years burning down the road / Nowhere to run, ain't got nowhere to go."

Many middle-class Americans stayed even only by working additional hours, taking more than one job, or becoming two-earner couples. Employers, taking advantage of the high demand for work, expanded temporary jobs and cut back on full-time jobs with benefits. In 1984, the cash income of more than one in seven Americans fell below the poverty line, a sharp increase from one in nine in 1979, and the highest proportion since the beginning of Johnson's War on Poverty in 1965. For the first time since the Depression, the streets and parks of the United States were speckled with homeless people, an estimated three-quarters of a million in 1988, some of them mentally disabled but many of them working poor, including more than a third who were families with children.

"For the first time since the Depression, the streets and parks of the United States were speckled with homeless people, an estimated three-quarters of a million in 1988."

WOMEN

During the 1980s, women continued to gain in the workforce. On average, they still earned less than men in the same occupations. But while the median salaries of men fell 8 percent, those of women rose almost 11 percent. A number of women benefited from the drive for "comparable worth"—the claim by feminist labor advocates that women performing jobs comparable in difficulty and skills with those held by men should be paid the same for their work. By 1987, 40 states and 1,700 localities had enacted comparable-worth laws. Under these laws, women gained sizable wage increases—in some cases up to 15 percent—over their previous rate of compensation. Further protecting women at work, in

1986 the Supreme Court ruled unanimously in *Meritor Savings Bank v. Vinson* that sexual harassment in the workplace, even if it does not result in job or promotion loss, violates Title VII of the Civil Rights Act.

A growing number of women were also achieving positions of status and authority, both in reality and in popular culture. Between 1975 and 1988, the number of women elected to Congress rose from nineteen to twenty-seven. And women began appearing on television as coequals with men—tough, competent, yet still feminine—as in the popular series *Cagney and Lacey,* about the adventures of two female police detectives in New York City, and *Star Trek: The Next Generation,* where women officers carried out their duties with cool authority in the face of mechanical breakdown and enemy attack. By the late 1980s, women comprised one-quarter of the graduates of law, medicine, and business schools, a dramatic increase from 5 percent in 1970. Women also occupied more managerial and professional positions (47 percent of them by 1992, compared with 40 percent in 1983).

Yet women's issues remained a flash point in American society, in part because of the independence so many women were achieving. Many men resented women's advancement in the workforce, claiming that affirmative action was denying them jobs on grounds of their sex. In 1989, in *Webster v. Reproductive Health Services,* the Supreme Court mirrored the ongoing divisions over abortion by upholding *Roe v. Wade* but also seeming to open the door to broad state regulation by permitting states to require medical tests to determine whether the fetus was yet viable or not. Social conservatives continued to consider feminism threatening to religion, traditional sexual standards, the dignity of homemakers, and the raising of children. Highly visible in the New Right, they enjoyed the sympathetic attention of the White House. If Reagan did not press their agenda, neither did he embrace the cause of women's rights. He awarded fewer women influential appointments than had his three immediate predecessors.

In this conservative decade, many younger women distanced themselves from feminism. They had benefited from the women's movement—most endorsed the right of sexual freedom and reproductive choice—but did not identify with it. The young pop stars Cyndi Lauper and Madonna posed a contrasting liberation to the buttoned-up young women in business

Martha Stewart, here conducting a cooking seminar, built a successful national business in the 1980s by marketing stylish housekeeping, dining, and entertaining.

and law with songs such as "Girls Just Wanna Have Fun" and "Material Girl"; and they flaunted an unbuttoned sexuality in their self-presentation, wearing their underwear on the outside of their scanty clothes. A number of better-off young women left the workplace at least temporarily for home and children, many of them seeking to perfect their domestic lives with the help of Martha Stewart, who published guides to elegant entertaining and home decoration.

Some feminists held that the women's movement was vulnerable to the social conservatives' family-oriented attacks against it. In 1981, Betty Friedan, a bellwether among them, argued in her widely read *Second Stage* that feminists had to recognize that women wanted both careers *and* families and that "the real battle for equality" turned on the arrangements that would allow them to have both. Equal rights had to be undergirded by measures that would let women take advantage of them, including decent child care, child support, alimony, and maternity leave. Instead of taking men as the "enemy," Friedan contended, the women's movement had to challenge the structures and customs of corporate society with calls for flexible hours and family-friendly policies.

Some feminists, though, argued that Friedan's emphasis on family straitjacketed many women into unwanted roles and accepted the traditional view that women rightly shouldered the greater share of domestic and child-rearing responsibilities. NOW attacked a federal amendment to the Civil Rights Act in 1978 that compelled employers not to penalize women who took maternity leave; members feared that such

leaves would discourage employers from hiring women at all. But in 1987, in *California Federal Savings and Loan v. Guerra*, the Supreme Court upheld the right of a state to mandate maternity leaves and, by implication, parental leaves for fathers. In the wake of the decision, feminists united behind the cause of the sex-neutral parental leave and placed the practicalities of family responsibilities high on the agenda of the women's movement.

PEOPLES OF COLOR

During the 1980s, the socioeconomic divisions among African Americans, Hispanic Americans, and Asian Americans that had emerged during the 1970s widened. In each group, a burgeoning middle class shared in the prosperity of the decade, creating a market for cable TV programs targeted to blacks or to Spanish or Asian-language speakers. *Star Trek*, the hugely popular mainstream TV show (and its successor, *Star Trek: The Next Generation*), depicted multi-alien relationships that both reflected and encouraged, at least among the young, tolerance for the multiracial character of American society.

Yet each group also included a beleaguered underclass. The persistence of poverty in minority enclaves resulted in part from discrimination, in part from the growing demand for skilled workers, in part from the restructuring of American industry, especially its smokestack sector, with its widespread job cutbacks. The inflow of immigrants, which increased in the 1980s, added to the economic burdens of the Hispanic and Asian communities. And the problems of all peoples of color were exacerbated by the policies and climate of Reaganism.

Native Minorities. By the late 1980s, almost half of black workers occupied white-collar jobs, and three out of five black families were in the middle or blue-collar class, twice the fraction in 1947. More than 1 million black families were affluent, double the fraction twenty years before. More African Americans were completing high school, and in 1990 those who did were going to college at more than twice the rate they had in 1965 and at almost the same rate as their fellow white graduates. About the same fraction of black high school graduates were going on to higher education as white high school graduates. The trend was reflected in the highly popular TV comedy, *The Cosby Show*, which featured the adventures of a black middle-class family, the father a doctor and the mother a lawyer. The black actor Eddie Murphy exploited black-white differences with a street-smart yet comic, unabrasive edge in *Trading Places* (1983) and *Beverly Hills Cop* (1984) and its sequels. The young African American singer Michael Jackson won megastar status, admired not only for his dazzling performances but also for his wealth and cross-racial self-presentation.

Black advances were paralleled among Native Americans, some of whom were becoming hardheaded businesspeople. Exercising a right the federal government had provided in 1961 to use their lands for commercial or industrial purposes, they developed tourist attractions such as the White Mountain Apache ski resort, leased land for the construction of factories, and, like the Passamaquoddies and Penobscots, who bought the third-largest blueberry farm in Maine, invested in commercial enterprises. In 1979, the Seminoles, in Florida, exploiting their tribal autonomy, opened a high-stakes bingo hall on their land. Although the state of Florida challenged the venture, a federal court upheld their right to pursue it. Netting $10 million a year from the games, the Seminoles provided a compelling moneymaking model for other Indian tribes to follow. The Bureau of Indian Affairs provided $64 million to finance casino construction. In 1986, the Mashantucket Pequot opened a bingo operation on their reservation in Connecticut that evolved by 1991 into the Foxwoods Gambling Casino, the most profitable casino outside of Las Vegas.

Yet in the eighties, Reagan's policies made the climb up the socioeconomic ladder difficult for many blacks and Native Americans. In its first year, the administration slashed

Members of the Crips gang in Los Angeles, one of many urban gangs that fought for turf in cities around the country.

the budget of the Bureau of Indian Affairs by $76 million, funds for Indian education by 40 percent, and funds for health services intended for urban Indians by 50 percent. One tribal leader observed, "Trickle-down economics feels a lot like being pissed on." Similarly, the administration sliced the welfare rolls by 10 percent and reduced the benefits of an additional 300,000 families receiving assistance.

Reagan and the leaders of his Justice Department had long opposed school busing and affirmative action. Extending deregulation to civil rights, the administration cut back on civil rights enforcement and sought to restore tax benefits to segregated private schools and colleges. Although the Supreme Court rebuffed that attempt, the Court diluted prior rulings on affirmative action programs that set aside a certain fraction of awards for women and minority contractors. One prominent civil rights leader noted ruefully, "The Reagan counter-revolution is based on re-segregating society." Over the decade, even though a growing number of blacks prospered, the fraction of blacks living in poverty held steady at 30 percent. The inner cities, still caldrons of crime and drugs, turned into battlegrounds for black gangs such as the Bloods and the Crips in Los Angeles, whose warfare took at least 400 lives.

Immigrant Minorities. During the 1980s, legal immigration reached 733,000 people per year on average, almost twice as many annually as in the late 1970s. Like the wave of immigrants at the turn of the century, most spoke foreign languages and came with few job skills. But unlike the earlier immigrants, the overwhelming majority originated outside Europe, in the Caribbean, Central and South America, and Asia. During the 1980s, largely as a result of the influx, the number of Hispanics in the United States increased more than 50 percent, and the number of Asians more than 100 percent, including a rise of 135 percent in immigrants from Southeast Asia. In 1990, the Asian American population comprised more than thirty distinct ethnic groups, with Chinese, Filipinos, and Japanese accounting for slightly more than half, and Vietnamese, Koreans, and Asian Indians a third.

The legal immigration was accompanied by a huge, continuing wave of illegal newcomers, mainly from Mexico and Haiti, estimated to total some 12 million by the early 1990s. In one year during the mid-1980s, the federal government apprehended more than 1.25 million illegal aliens, 95 percent of whom were Mexican. In 1986, with the administration's

U.S. Border Patrol agents arrest Mexicans attempting to enter the United States illegally near San Diego, 1980.

country illegally. But they increasingly organized themselves into activist groups, and a revision of the Voting Rights Act in 1982 required the redrawing of congressional district lines to give designated minority populations a fair shot at winning elections if the configuration of an existing district in which they lived appeared to disadvantage them. Soon put into effect, the requirement helped increase the number of Hispanic congressional representatives to ten by 1990, twice the number at the end of the 1970s.

The expanding immigrant communities established a presence on cable TV through stations broadcasting in Spanish and Asian languages. Hispanic subjects were taken up in films, including *Zoot Suit* (1981), a musical that dealt with the convictions of Chicano gang members in 1942; *El Norte,* which dealt sensitively with the aspirations and pain of migrants from Central America desperately trying to overcome the obstacles to entering the United States; and *Stand and Deliver,* which was based on the story of a mathematics teacher in the barrio of East Los Angeles who inspired his students to score high on an advanced calculus test and overcome the unjust accusation of the testers that they must have cheated. Many Asian Americans attracted notice for their academic achievements, winning prizes in national science competitions and entering elite universities in disproportionately high numbers.

support, Congress passed the Immigration Reform and Control Act. Aiming to stem the flow of illegals while dealing practically with those already in the country, the act offered undocumented workers the right to become resident aliens— foreigners permitted to reside and work in the United States—or citizens and extended amnesty to all aliens who had entered the country illegally since January 1, 1982. It also imposed fines on employers who hired undocumented workers in the future. By May 4, 1988, the deadline for amnesty, 1.4 million people had sought it, 71 percent of them from Mexico.

Like their predecessors at the turn of the century, the new immigrants made their way into unskilled jobs in manufacturing but even more so in the burgeoning service sector, finding employment as, for example, gardeners, domestics, janitors, and fast-food clerks. A growing number opened small businesses that served their rapidly expanding communities, including groceries and restaurants that whites also patronized. There was no path to political power for them through the big-city machines that had served earlier immigrants but were now long gone. Besides, many of them could not vote because they were not yet citizens or were in the

Immigration during the eighties amounted to 83 percent of the newcomer total during the first decade of the twentieth century, but the new wave did not provoke comparable fears and resentments. The earlier wave represented roughly 12 percent of the population in 1900; the later one, slightly more than 3 percent of the population in 1980. The new arrivals were thus far less disruptive to the arrangements of the country as a whole and, as a result, were far more tolerated nationally. However, the immigrant population jumped dramatically in some states, notably California, where it reached almost 22 percent, largely as a result of the continuing concentration of Hispanics and Asians. In those regions, the newcomers encountered considerable resentment and discrimination. In Los Angeles, a white man complained, "No one speaks English, and it bothers me. I feel it's not my country anymore."

The backlash against bilingualism—which had come to include ballots and services as well as education—was intensifying. Senator S. I. Hayakawa of California, a feisty professor of linguistics before entering politics, called for a constitutional amendment to declare English the nation's official language. Voters in Arizona, Colorado, and Florida passed English-only referenda. By the late 1980s, however, responses to bilingualism had become less ideological and more pragmatic. Areas inhabited by multiple ethnic minorities expressed a preference for English over the multilingual cacophony that might otherwise prevail in schools and government offices. For example, Monterey Park, California, where Asians made up more than a third of the population and Hispanics another third, passed a resolution that English be made the official language. Increasing numbers of immigrant parents, well aware of the economic advantages of fluency in English, wanted their children to have enriched instruction in the language. In 1988, responding to the demand, Congress amended the Bilingual Education Act and authorized funds for alternative programs.

As of 1989, only 61 percent of Hispanics in their late twenties had completed high school, compared with 82 percent of blacks and 86 percent of whites, and poverty held in its grip almost 20 percent of Mexican Americans and 30 percent of Puerto Ricans. While Asian Americans were regarded as "model minorities" because of their high-profile educational achievements, many were handicapped by poor neighborhood schools, inadequate proficiency in English, and, for those from rural backgrounds, the difficulty of adjusting to American life. A recent arrival from Southeast Asia remarked, "We have been living in a jungle for a long time in Laos. This is another kind of jungle—a technological and bureaucratic jungle." Southeast Asians suffered white resentment, vandalism, and violence. "There's too many of them," one white fisherman on the Gulf Coast of Texas said of his Vietnamese counterparts. The attorney general of Massachusetts reported that often Southeast Asians "cannot even walk along the public streets without being physically attacked and threatened."

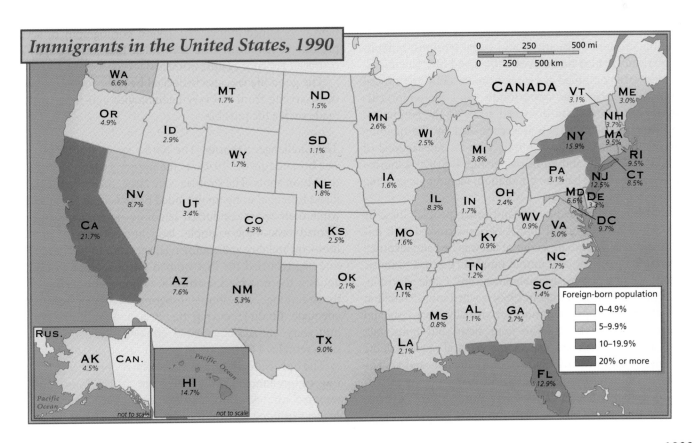

Immigrants in the United States, 1990

Foreign-born population
- 0–4.9%
- 5–9.9%
- 10–19.9%
- 20% or more

WA 6.6%
OR 4.9%
MT 1.7%
ND 1.5%
MN 2.6%
VT 3.1%
ME 3.0%
NH 3.7%
ID 2.9%
SD 1.1%
WI 2.5%
MI 3.8%
NY 15.9%
MA 9.5%
RI 9.5%
CT 8.5%
WY 1.7%
IA 1.6%
PA 3.1%
NJ 12.5%
NV 8.7%
UT 3.4%
NE 1.8%
IL 8.3%
IN 1.7%
OH 2.4%
MD 6.6%
DE 3.3%
CA 21.7%
CO 4.3%
KS 2.5%
MO 1.6%
KY 0.9%
WV 0.9%
VA 5.0%
DC 9.7%
NC 1.7%
AZ 7.6%
NM 5.3%
OK 2.1%
AR 1.1%
TN 1.2%
SC 1.4%
MS 0.8%
AL 1.1%
GA 2.7%
TX 9.0%
LA 2.1%
AK 4.5%
HI 14.7%
FL 12.9%

A Vietnamese businessman in front of his store in the Little Vietnam district of Garden Grove, California, 1980s.

In the mid-1980s, half of all Southeast Asians in the United States lived below the poverty line.

TROUBLES IN THE GOOD LIFE

Amid the economic disparities and social tensions, millions of Americans availed themselves of the good life. The migration westward continued as people from virtually every social group sought economic opportunity—and for senior citizens, repose—in the sun-drenched states of the Southwest. The geographical migration was paralleled by the ongoing movement from cities to suburbs, with its satisfactions of space, greenery, air, and home ownership. By 1990, suburbia was home to almost half the population, including a growing number of people of color.

Technology continued to ease and enrich people's lives. By the late 1980s, three out of four Americans cooked with microwave ovens; more than six out of ten watched and recorded video tapes on a VCR, and untold numbers listened to music on compact disc players, available since 1982. Cable television, available in 20 million homes in 1980, reached some 53 million in 1990, providing programming for virtually every taste and interest, including twenty-four-hour news, old films, talk shows and sex shows, soap opera and classical opera, wildlife and nature, and professional as well as amateur sports. The personal computer was revolutionizing the workplace, including the scientific laboratory, helping workers keep records, generate documents, and do accounting and data analysis. By

the end of the decade, 109 million computers had been sold. An increasing fraction were bought for the home, though many Americans were not sure what to use them for other than game-playing machines for their children.

But the good life in the eighties was by no means free of troubles, some of them ongoing. The flight to suburbia reflected in part the long-standing desire for escape from urban problems such as crime, rundown neighborhoods, and declining urban schools. A number of Americans, eager for more protection than open living might provide, settled in gated communities, some 80,000 of which now dotted the suburban landscape, an eightyfold increase in just two decades. Similarly, senior citizens segregated themselves in communities restricted to older people, a number of them predominantly white, such as Leisure World in California and New Jersey. Despite the scandals in some televangelical ministries, religious conservatism grew in the eighties, gaining support from adherents of Orthodox Judaism and Orthodox Islam. A rabbi in St. Louis explained, "Fear motivates some of the drift to this old-time religion"—fear of moral dissolution and its impact on children, including drugs and violence in the schools and pornography everywhere. (In this decade, conservative Christians were joined in their war against pornography by several prominent feminists, who contended that pornography encouraged violence against women.)

The good life was also bedeviled by new troubles, some of them arising from the very technologies and freedoms that made such a life possible.

The* Challenger *Disaster. The NASA space shuttle program was initiated in the 1970s as the agency's main successor to the Moon shots. The shuttles were large, rocket-launched vehicles intended to fly for extended periods in near-earth orbit while their crews conducted scientific experiments and performed tasks—for example, launching or retrieving satellites—for military and commercial agencies. In the early 1980s, one flight carried the first woman astronaut, Sally Ride, and another the first black astronaut, Guion S. Bluford Jr. Since its beginnings, the shuttle program had been granted inadequate funding; during the Reagan administration, the budgetary cutbacks increased while performance expectations remained high.

The pressure to perform helped produce tragedy on January 28, 1986, when, as millions watched on television, **the space shuttle *Challenger* exploded** seventy-four seconds after lift-off, killing all seven astronauts aboard. The victims included Christa McAuliffe, a New Hampshire schoolteacher, who was to instruct the nation's children about science during the flight. In an investigation of the disaster, a presidential commission sharply criticized NASA and some of its contractors for subordinating safety to public relations. In order to keep to its announced shuttle-launch schedule, the agency had overworked its employees and allowed its contractors to take too many risks. The rockets bearing the *Challenger* had exploded because a small seal had cracked in the prelaunch cold air. Several engineers employed by the rocket manufacturer, aware of this possibility, had urged postponement of the launch, but, goaded by NASA managers, the company's executives had overridden their recommendation.

The crew of the doomed space shuttle *Challenger* on the way to the launch pad, January 28, 1986. At front, Commander Francis R. Scobee (right) and Mission Specialist Judith A. Resnick.

MEDICINE AND PUBLIC HEALTH

During the 1980s, Americans were offered still more marvels in medical care. For example, new and powerful technologies were coming into use that could generate three-dimensional images of the interior of the body. When the would-be assassin who shot President Reagan also wounded his press secretary, James Brady, in the head, doctors located a blood clot produced by a fragment of an exploding bullet that had entered Brady's brain using the CT-scan, which had recently been developed largely by the British and which used X-rays and computers to reveal objects and abnormalities in flesh and bone. They then removed both the clot and the fragment with precision surgery, thus saving his life. (Brady and his wife became outspoken crusaders for gun control.) Later in the decade, physicians were also beginning to make use of magnetic resonance imaging (MRI), a new, powerful technology that Americans helped devise, which exploited computers and the magnetic fields of water-rich molecules in the body to provide a detailed picture of soft tissue troubled by injury or disease. Together, CT-scans and MRI, by revealing the interior condition of the body, amounted to a revolution in medical assessment, not least because they greatly diminished the need for exploratory surgery.

The future appeared to promise still more miracles as a result of federal policy for biomedical research. Between 1981 and 1990, the annual budget of the National Institutes of Health jumped by 50 percent after adjustment for inflation, reaching almost $8 billion. In 1986, to promote the commercialization of the practical results arising in federal research laboratories, Congress authorized governmental agencies or their employees to license patents on them to private industry. Between 1977 and 1986, industrial patronage of academic research grew more than fourfold. In the early 1980s, for the first time since 1939, the business sector spent more on research and development than the federal government, with biomedical research receiving a sizable fraction of the money.

Still, the exhilarating expectations for the biomedical future were tempered by worrisome health issues. The miracle technologies, for example, intervened between doctors and patients, rendering the delivery of medical care more impersonal. The expense of technologies such as MRI were helping to drive up the cost of medical care, as were the prices of hospitalization and drugs. Americans with medical insurance were better protected against the trend than those without it. In 1990, almost 14 percent of the population were uninsured, many because they could not afford to be. Moreover, the miracles of medical technology could do little against the propensity of people to put themselves at risk from the damages of smoking or drugs or the deadly AIDS (acquired immune deficiency syndrome).

Smoking and Drugs. In the eighties, state and local governments passed antismoking laws, government agencies restricted smoking in the workplace, and many businesses banned it. Surgeon General C. Everett Koop, an avowed public enemy of smoking, called it as addictive as heroin or opium. The portion of adults who smoked continued to decline—it would fall to 26 percent by 1993, down from 42 percent in the late 1960s and 50 percent in 1950—but the number of Americans under eighteen who took up tobacco, almost one out of five, remained unchanged over the decade.

The war against drugs won fewer victories. The use of drugs was glamorized in the fiction of the young, hard-edged writers Bret Easton Ellis, Tama Janowitz, and Jay McInerney—the "Brat Pack," critics called them. In novels such as *Bright Lights, Big City* (McInerney), *Less than Zero* (Ellis), and *Slaves of New York* (Janowitz), they chronicled their gilded contemporaries, devotees of cocaine, damaged or destroyed by too much affluence and too few responsibilities. Experts reported that drug use actually declined in the 1980s among middle-class whites but that the popularity of cocaine and the more potent crack cocaine grew among the urban poor and people of color. The inner cities were fraught with fierce competition for control of the drug trade that erupted in gang-related violence. At the end of the decade, more than half of Americans considered drugs a grave threat to the nation's well-being and security. The combined state, federal, and local bill for the war on drugs was $15 billion a year, three-quarters of which went to law enforcement and imprisonment. Drug offenders comprised the fastest-growing fraction of people sent to jail.

AIDS. Americans on all sides of the political spectrum grew increasingly worried about the mounting incidence of AIDS,

What if You Get Sick?

American Journal

The physician Lewis Thomas recalled that in the 1920s his father, also a doctor, paid house calls, often in the middle of the night, and lingered to comfort his patients. But he could provide them with little more medically than the contents of his doctor's bag, a small black suitcase that held a handful of items, notably a stethoscope for diagnosis and morphine to kill pain. A half century later, Thomas, having fallen ill, found himself in a hospital undergoing diagnostic tests drawn from a powerful arsenal of tools that had not existed in his father's day. After one diagnosis was ruled out by an illuminated examination of his colon with a quartz-fiber optical tube, a second diagnosis was checked by an X-ray examination of his arteries. Thomas described the procedure:

"A catheter was inserted in the femoral artery, high up in the right leg, and pushed up into the aorta until its tip reached the level of the main arteries branching off to supply the large intestine. At this point, an opaque dye was injected, to fill all those arteries. . . . Meanwhile, movies were being taken of the entire vascular bed reached by the dye, and the diagnosis was solidly confirmed. . . . [Seeing the pictures,] I was enchanted. There, in just one spot on the right side of my colon, was a spilled blur of dye, and the issue was settled. It struck me as a masterpiece of technological precision. . . . While it was going on I felt less like a human in trouble and more like a scientific problem to be solved as quickly as possible. What made it work, and kept such notions as 'depersonalization' and 'dehumanization' from even popping into my mind, was the absolute confidence I felt in the skill and intelligence of the people who had hold of me."

Lewis Thomas, *The Youngest Science: Notes of a Medicine Watcher*

which was recognized in 1981 as the root cause of several different diseases, notably pneumonia and certain cancers, that were breaking out among special groups, most commonly homosexual men. In 1984, scientists in the United States and France determined that AIDS is caused by an infectious virus (HIV) that attacks the immune system, making people vulnerable to one or more of these wasting assaults. The virus enters the body mainly by transfusion with infected blood, intravenous drug injection with infected needles, or sexual intercourse with an infected person.

Blood-screening tests greatly diminished the risk of infection to people who depended on blood transfusions, notably hemophiliacs. Analysts called for public distribution of clean needles to drug addicts, but the initiative failed in most places, since it ran into fierce opposition from conservatives and others fearful that it would encourage more drug use. In San Francisco, with its heavy concentration of homosexuals, public health authorities closed down the city's bathhouses and sex clubs in 1984 on grounds that the promiscuous gay sex they encouraged fostered disease and death. Other cities as well as gay activists waged public-information campaigns urging "safe sex" through condom use.

Demonstrators march in support of gays and lesbians, Market Street, San Francisco, 1983.

Although AIDS was initially concentrated among homosexuals and Haitian immigrants, who were heavy drug users, in the mid-1980s *Time* reported that "anxiety over AIDS is verging on hysteria in some parts of the country." Churchgoers feared infection from taking communion with a common cup; children shunned infected schoolmates; a number of employers and health providers turned away AIDS victims. According to a Gallup poll, more than two out of five Americans thought AIDS a punishment for moral decline. Television networks refused to carry announcements advocating the use of condoms, and the Reagan White House balked on moral grounds at endorsing condom messages.

But a growing number of Americans realized that moral condemnation would do little to retard the mounting incidence of the disease. Between 1981 and 1990, more than 157,000 people in the country were reported to have AIDS, and more than 98,000 of them died of it. The casualties included the Hollywood star Rock Hudson, whose death raised public awareness of the issue and also appeared to arouse Reagan's empathy for AIDS victims. In 1986, the president called AIDS research a top priority, and in a report prepared at his request, Surgeon General Koop urged Americans to halt the spread of AIDS with sexual abstinence, monogamy, and condoms. In the last Reagan years, federal funds for AIDS research almost doubled, reaching $655 million in 1988, and a presidential commission called for an end to discrimination against AIDS victims.

THE ENVIRONMENT, LOCAL AND GLOBAL

Grass-roots activism for wilderness preservation, clean air and water, control of toxics, and shutting down nuclear power remained energetic. The leadership included a disproportionately large number of women, many of whom were drawn to such activism by being sensitive to risks that appeared to threaten themselves and their families.

The cold-blooded efforts of James Watt, Reagan's first secretary of the interior, to turn over as much of nature as possible to private developers angered many Americans, driving up membership in the Sierra Club as much as 25 percent. Between the grass-roots activists and the established groups, the environmental movement remained powerful enough to counter a number of Watts's initiatives. Congress blocked his attempt to turn strip-mining controls back to the states, and it expanded the National Park System over his opposition. But by the late 1980s, scientific experts were confronting the administration with a new class of environmental hazards that were global in reach and threatening enough to warrant a place on the public agenda.

The most immediately pressing new environmental issue was depletion of the ozone layer in the upper atmosphere. Since the ozone layer blocks the passage of cancer-causing ultraviolet light from the sun, the depletion threatened human, plant, and animal life. The thinning of the layer had been predicted in the early 1970s by two American chemists, Sherwood Rowland and Mario Molina, who later won a Nobel Prize for their achievement. The depletion arose from the growing commercial and industrial uses of chlorofluorocarbons (CFCs) in, for example, spray cans and air-conditioners. The prediction, though disputed for years, was gradually confirmed by scientists conducting computer simulations of the atmosphere and, most dramatically, by a British team who in 1985 detected an enormous depletion of the ozone layer over a huge region of Antarctica.

In 1987, the United States took the lead in negotiating the Montreal Protocol on Substances That Deplete the Ozone Layer. Designed to impose international controls on the release of CFCs into the atmosphere, the protocol called for cutting them to 50 percent of their 1986 levels by the end of the century. The agreement was ratified by twenty-nine nations and the Commission of the European Community, which together accounted for 83 percent of global consumption of CFCs and a related class of chemicals called halons. In 1990, in response to evidence that the ozone layer was being depleted over heavily populated areas of the world, the Montreal Protocol was toughened by expanding the types of ozone-depleting chemicals it covered and speeding up the rate at which they were to be reduced and phased out. Special assistance was also granted to Third World countries so that they would not be hampered in raising their living standards.

Political Reckoning

Through the eighties, an undercurrent of disquiet with the era's greed-is-good culture pervaded the country, as did dissatisfaction with the Reagan administration's approach to poverty, civil rights, and the environment, and with its high-handed subversion of the law in Iran-Contra. Signs of the uneasiness appeared in popular culture—not only in the songs of Bruce Springsteen but in benefit concerts mounted for farmers in the Midwest and the impoverished people of Africa. One of the most popular Broadway shows of the decade was *Les Misérables,* a musical adaptation of Victor Hugo's searing portrait of the Parisian poor, surrogates for the homeless whom playgoers encountered on the streets outside the theaters.

The dissatisfaction expressed itself politically as well. In the 1986 elections, following the first revelations of Iran-Contra, the Democrats recaptured the Senate, winning a majority of ten seats. Now in control of both houses of Congress, they pressed for a more liberal legislative agenda, passing an $80 billion extension of the Clean Water Act over Reagan's veto, crushing a Republican attempt to cut back Medicare, and enacting a civil rights bill and a measure strengthening the bargaining power of labor. They also expanded the food stamp program, provided aid to the homeless and protection against catastrophic illness, and beefed up elementary and secondary education.

Since appointing Sandra Day O'Connor to the Supreme Court, Reagan had shifted it further in a conservative direction by adding Antonin Scalia to the high bench and by promoting William Rehnquist to chief justice. But in the fall of 1987, the Democratic Senate decisively defeated Reagan's nomination to the Court of Robert Bork, a strict constructionist who contended that the Constitution did not support *Roe v. Wade,* the controversial decision upholding a woman's right to abortion. After another nominee was forced to withdraw because he admitted to having smoked marijuana, the Senate confirmed Reagan's nomination of Anthony Kennedy, a conservative jurist from California.

THE ELECTION OF 1988

Expecting a victory over Reagan Republicanism, a number of Democrats sought their party's presidential nomination, but the field rapidly narrowed to Jesse Jackson, who emphasized the needs of the poor, and Michael Dukakis, the moderate governor of Massachusetts. After winning the primaries in major states, Dukakis took the nomination and chose for his vice-president Lloyd Bentsen, a right-of-center senator from Texas. Vice-President George Bush handily won the Republican nomination against Senator Robert Dole of Kansas. Bush then surprised his supporters by choosing as his running mate J. Danforth "Dan" Quayle, a

The Republican candidates in 1988: Vice-President George Bush (left) and Dan Quayle.

young, hardworking, but undistinguished senator from Indiana whose gaffes during the campaign earned him widespread ridicule in the press.

Bush dissociated himself from the Iran-Contra scandal and moved toward the center by calling for "a kinder, gentler America." Otherwise, he embraced the Reagan record, stressing the restoration of prosperity, the reduction in inflation, and the dramatic turn for the better in Soviet-American relations. He campaigned on the pledge, "Read my lips: no new taxes," the first phrase of which was borrowed from a toughguy film. Bush's supporters, playing on the fears of crime and race, broadcast a television advertisement featuring a black man, a convicted killer, who under a Massachusetts program had been furloughed from state prison only to commit rape and murder. Bush also attacked Dukakis for vetoing a bill that required students to recite the Pledge of Allegiance, a law that was likely unconstitutional, and, in a suggestive echo of McCarthyism, called Dukakis a "card-carrying member of the American Civil Liberties Union."

Dukakis, for his part, pointed to the failures of Reaganomics, stressed his gubernatorial accomplishments, but otherwise seemed wooden. Asked on television whether he would favor the death penalty for a man who had raped and murdered his wife, he answered without a hint of outrage at the thought. Attempting to demonstrate that he was tough on defense, he was filmed in a helmet too large for his head in an M-1 tank that seemed to swallow him up. In the November election, which produced the lowest turnout since 1924, Bush won 54 percent of the vote and carried forty states. The Democrats, however, kept control of both houses of Congress.

THE REAGAN LEGACY

Ronald Reagan tamed inflation, revived the economy, and presided over a historic thawing of the Cold War. Conservatives came to assert that Reagan had prompted the stunning change in the Soviet Union with his military buildup and SDI. According to them, Gorbachev tried to compete with the United States in defense, realized that the Soviet economy was not up to the task, and concluded that change was imperative because the Soviet system was so inherently flawed. However, the claim is contradicted by the evidence. The Soviets neither responded to the Reagan administration's military buildup nor spent anything to create or counter SDI, especially since by 1987 Gorbachev was convinced that it would not work. What moved Gorbachev to his reforms was not any pressure from Reagan but his own recognition of the indigenous weaknesses in the Soviet economy. What changed the Soviet Union was his desire to reconstruct it, and what Reagan contributed to the transformation of U.S.-Soviet relations was his willingness, person to person, to endorse Gorbachev's efforts.

A number of Reagan's accomplishments were won at a high price. He left the country with escalating trade deficits and a staggering debt. His laissez-faire policies helped American corporations restructure themselves to deal with mounting competition, especially from abroad; but his administration did little to assist the people whose jobs were lost or downgraded in the process. His tax reductions, government cutbacks, and resistance to civil rights exacerbated the inequalities in American society, a condition symbolized by the homeless wandering the big-city streets. Still, Reagan refurbished the image of American prowess and revived confidence in the nation's world purpose. He left office with his popularity buoyed by

1039

Chronology

1981	Sandra Day O'Connor appointed to the Supreme Court.
August 1981	President Reagan fires two-thirds of air-traffic controllers' union.
March 1983	Plans for Strategic Defense Initiative (Star Wars) announced.
October 1983	241 U.S. marines killed by suicide bomber in Beirut.
1984	French and American scientists identify the HIV virus.
January 28, 1986	Space shuttle *Challenger* explodes.
1986	Mikhail Gorbachev proclaims *glasnost* in Soviet Union.
Summer 1987	Iran-Contra Senate hearings.
December 1987	Reagan and Gorbachev sign INF Treaty.
December 1988	Pan Am jet explodes over Lockerbie, Scotland, killing 259.

courts had also permitted him to bolster the shift by appointing almost 400 federal judges, a majority of all those sitting in 1989. When Reagan left office, the middle of the political road ran through less regulation, lower taxes, more limited government. It remained to be seen whether such a restrained role for government would suffice to deal with the economic, environmental, and security issues already evident in a globalizing, post–Cold War era.

Suggested Reading

Elliott Robert Barkan, *And Still They Came: Immigrants and American Society, 1920 to the 1990s* (1996)

Susan Faludi, *Backlash: The Undeclared War Against American Women* (1991)

Frances Fitzgerald, *Way Out There in the Blue: Reagan, Star Wars, and the End of the Cold War* (2000)

Haynes Johnson, *Sleepwalking Through History: America in the Reagan Years* (1991)

Kevin Phillips, *The Politics of Rich and Poor: Wealth and the American Electorate in the Reagan Aftermath* (1990)

Michael Schaller, *Reckoning with Reagan: America and Its President in the 1980s* (1991)

William Julius Wilson, *The Truly Disadvantaged: The Inner City, the Underclass, and Public Policy* (1987)

the increasingly likely end of the Cold War. He had succeeded in shifting the center of American political culture away from the liberalism of the postwar decades. A combination of attrition and the creation of new seats in the federal

Chapter 33

TRIUMPHANT AND TROUBLED NATION:

1989-2000

"Multitasking" and "24/7" have become features of our everyday lives as microchip technology transforms our society and economy.

QUESTIONS

- How did the end of the Cold War bring both freedom and war?

- How would you describe President Bush's approach to the slumping economy and other domestic affairs?

- How did Clinton's move to the political center help advance his domestic agenda?

- What strategies did the Clinton administration use to promote democracy in the post–Cold War world?

- What were the major social issues and technological innovations of the booming nineties?

- How was Clinton's impeachment viewed by most Americans in light of his domestic record?

"The Cold War is over," Ronald Reagan remarked to a friend on leaving Washington at the end of his presidency. It was not quite over, but it soon would be, leaving Reagan's immediate successors in the White House with the enviable if difficult task of devising a new global order. Their principal challenge abroad was to protect American security while responding to the rising aspirations of peoples freed from Soviet control and to the growing problems of globalization, such as environmental degradation. At home, in the near term, the challenge was to deal with the legacy of Reaganomics and an economic downturn that emerged in the wake of the Cold War. Prosperity returned in the early 1990s, inaugurating a record-setting economic expansion that was driven to a significant extent by technological innovations such as the Internet. But the United States remained divided over social and cultural issues such as race, immigration, abortion, and sexual behavior. And the nation encountered violence stoked by resentments of its power among extremists both at home and abroad.

Foreign Affairs

George Herbert Walker Bush's inaugural celebration was twice as expensive as Reagan's, but the next day, in a gesture unseen since William Howard Taft had taken office, the new president and his wife threw open the doors of the White House, greeting some 4,000 people who had been waiting in line all night. The son of a U.S. senator from Connecticut, Bush was at once a product of privilege and a devotee of accomplishment. As a navy pilot during World War II—the youngest then in the service—he won a Distinguished Flying Cross. After graduating with a Phi Beta Kappa key from Yale in 1949, he moved to Texas, became a successful oilman, and in 1966 won election to the U.S. House of Representatives. Defeated for the Senate four years later, he served during the 1970s in a series of federal posts, including ambassador to the United Nations, head of the U.S. Liaison Office in China, and director of the CIA, before his election as Ronald Reagan's vice-president.

In all, Bush was a kind of regional and social hybrid, a Republican of the old internationalist Northeast and the new entrepreneurial Southwest, an embodiment of patrician obligation and business ambition. Closer to the domestic center than Reagan, he brought to the task of his presidency broad experience in government, in foreign affairs the attitudes of a hard-line but pragmatic Cold Warrior, and in domestic ones the convictions of a moderate conservative.

THE END OF THE COLD WAR

When he entered the White House in 1989, George Bush was suspicious of the genuineness of Mikhail Gorbachev's commitment to *perestroika* and *glasnost*. But Bush's caution was overwhelmed by volcanic demands for freedom that redrew the political map of Central Europe with stunning speed. During the first year of his presidency, Hungary cast off most of its Communist leadership, and so did Poland, where, with the help of the administration, free elections were arranged, and Solidarity, the union movement that had initiated the drive for liberalization, won control of the National Assembly. In May, Estonia and Lithuania declared themselves independent of the Soviet Union, and in August Latvia broke free. Upheaval followed in East Germany, where in early November, with Gorbachev having declared a hands-off policy, thousands forced the regime to open the gates to the West and started tearing down the hated wall dividing Berlin. That winter, the Communist governments in Yugoslavia, Bulgaria, and Romania were overthrown, and a pro-democracy playwright became president of Czechoslovakia.

> *"In January 1993, Bush and Yeltsin signed the START II Treaty, which called for a two-thirds reduction in long-range nuclear weapons within ten years and complete elimination of land-based missiles. The Cold War was now indisputably over."*

Bush navigated this tidal wave of change by trying to maintain a stable balance of power while fostering democratic capitalism in post–Cold War Europe. He was ably assisted by Secretary of State James Baker, a veteran of the Reagan administration and a long-standing ally. In East and West Germany, sentiment for reunification was mounting rapidly. Gorbachev, anxious about Russian security in the face of a united Germany and under pressure from hard-liners at home, resisted the union. But Bush opted for it, fearing otherwise an unpredictable instability in East Germany. In May 1990, during a summit in Washington, he granted Gorbachev a trade package to help shore him up against the hard-liners, and Gorbachev, in exchange, agreed to German reunification by 1994. In July 1991, at a summit in Moscow, Bush and Gorbachev signed the Strategic Arms Reduction Treaty (START I), an agreement to cut strategic nuclear weaponry ultimately by 30–40 percent.

The following month, however, Russian hard-liners attempted a coup against Gorbachev and his reforms. In defiance, hundreds of thousands of people protectively cordoned off the parliament, and Boris Yeltsin, the president of the Russian republic, rallied the crowd, courageously mounting a tank to denounce the plotters. Although the coup failed and Gorbachev retained power, he was increasingly overshadowed by Yeltsin and, in the end, overwhelmed by the liberalizing forces he had unleashed. In December 1991, the Soviet Union came to an end, replaced by a Commonwealth of Independent States comprising the eleven former Soviet republics. Gorbachev resigned, and Yeltsin reigned over Russia. In January 1993, Bush and Yeltsin signed START II, which called for a two-thirds reduction in long-range nuclear weapons within ten years and complete elimination of land-based missiles. The Cold War was now indisputably over.

RIPPLES OF FREEDOM

The end of the Cold War produced ripple effects in world affairs far beyond the borders of what people for a time called "the former Soviet Union." The decline in Russian power permitted the United States to maneuver more freely in foreign affairs and to deal with regional issues more evenhandedly, taking demands for freedom on their merits rather than refracting them through fears of Soviet imperialism. The new conditions helped the United States resolve long-standing conflicts and tensions in South Africa and the Third World,

A man chisels a piece of the Berlin Wall for a souvenir, December 1989, a month after the East German regime was forced to open the gates to the West.

Nelson Mandela, shortly after his release from prison in South Africa in 1990.

though China dishearteningly demonstrated that American leverage for freedom was far from limitless.

South Africa. Together with the winding down of the Cold War, the economic sanctions imposed on South Africa during the Reagan years yielded dramatic changes in the region. In 1988, a State Department official negotiated a de-escalation of the civil war in Angola, persuading Cuba and South Africa to withdraw their troops from the country and South Africa to withdraw its forces from neighboring Namibia, thereby granting it independence. In South Africa itself in 1990, a more moderate regime, come to power the year before, legalized the African National Congress and released its leader, Nelson Mandela, who had been in prison for twenty-seven years. President Bush ended the economic sanctions when in 1991 South Africa got rid of most of its apartheid laws. In 1992, white South Africans voted decisively to end apartheid, and negotiations were initiated to establish full democracy in the country.

The Third World. Secretary of State Baker acknowledged that Reagan's pro-Contra policy against the left-wing Sandinista government in Nicaragua had "basically failed." Changing course, Bush and the Congress devised an accord in 1989 that won the support of both the Sandinistas and the Contras. It provided for an end to the war, the release of political prisoners, enlarged freedom of the press, and national elections the next year—which in the event produced the victory of an anti-Sandinista coalition. In El Salvador, where the United States had backed the right-wing government against leftist guerrillas, both sides concluded a peace agreement in 1992 that ended their twelve-year civil war and provided for a variety of reforms.

General Manuel Noriega, the dictator in Panama, had assisted the Reagan administration by helping to get arms to the Contras in Nicaragua, but he had imprisoned political opponents and grown personally wealthy by trafficking in drugs. In December 1989, with Noriega threatening American citizens in Panama, Bush launched Operation Just Cause, a military action that within twenty-four hours—and at the cost of 23 Americans dead and 394 wounded—freed the political opposition from prison and drove Noriega from power. Taken to the United States to stand trial, Noriega was convicted in April 1992 on multiple charges, including cocaine trafficking, money laundering, and racketeering, and sentenced to a U.S. prison.

China. The changes in the former Soviet Union emboldened advocates of liberalization in the People's Republic of China. During the spring of 1989, numerous young Chinese dissidents demonstrated for freedom. But while the Chinese government craved friendly relations and expanded trade, it was unwilling to tolerate the growing outspokenness of protesters. When several thousand of them occupied Tiananmen Square in Beijing, Deng Xiaoping, China's leader, labeled them "counterrevolutionaries," prompting the protesters to go on a hunger strike. On June 4, the army drove them out of the square, generating images on world television of unarmed youth defying tanks and machine guns. The crackdown killed 3,000 people, wounded 10,000 more, and thoroughly angered millions around the world.

Bush, eager to avoid a break with China, responded with sanctions such as delaying World Bank loans to Beijing; but, resisting pressure from Congress to impose harsher measures, he refrained from strongly condemning its actions. Instead, he sought to find common ground for further cooperation, urging, for example, that China release the dissidents arrested after the episode at Tiananmen Square. By the fall, the Beijing government had released some. In late May 1990, Bush renewed China's most-favored-nation trade status, and in the succeeding months he continued to press for improvement in Sino-American relations.

THE GULF WAR

In the Middle East, the end of the Cold War provided militarily capable rogue states with greater latitude for aggression. The Soviet Union had at times exercised a stabilizing influence in the region, but it was now so weakened that the burden of maintaining order there fell more heavily on the United States.

In August 1990, Iraq invaded oil-rich Kuwait, its 140,000 troops rapidly overwhelming Kuwait's 16,000-man army. The action caught the United States as well as Egypt and Jordan by surprise, even though Iraqi troops had been observed moving toward the Kuwaiti border. The Iraqi dictator, Saddam Hussein, now had control of enough oil to make Iraq a major oil power. The United States had supported Iraq in its war with Iran during the 1980s, but along with other governments it had worried about Iraq's growing programs for the production of chemical and nuclear weapons. The Bush administration considered the invasion an unacceptable violation of international law, a threat to regional stability, and a danger to American energy security.

In an address to the nation on August 8, the president declared "a line drawn in the sand" and insisted on the immediate withdrawal of all Iraqi forces from Kuwait. By then, eager to avoid Lyndon Johnson's errors during the Vietnam War, Bush, with the help of Secretary of Defense Dick Cheney, was building support for his policy both abroad and at home. He mobilized a thirty-nation coalition against Iraq, including the leading Arab states but not Israel, which he excluded so as not to antagonize the Arab allies. He also obtained a virtually unanimous resolution from the U.N. Security Council, including Russia, calling for a complete shutdown of trade with Iraq and authorizing nonmilitary measures to enforce the sanctions. Stepping up the pressure, the Bush administration sent 100,000 American troops to Saudi Arabia to protect that country and its oil against possible invasion and won pledges from Middle Eastern, European, and Asian nations for financial support of whatever actions might be necessary to force Saddam Hussein's troops out of Kuwait.

In early November, with Saddam's troops still in Kuwait, Bush announced an increase in the American forces in Saudi Arabia to 500,000, and at the end of the month the United Nations set a deadline of January 15, 1991, for Iraq to withdraw. Congress, with many Democrats in both houses dissenting, approved military action against Iraq. On January 16, one day after the U.N. deadline, the United States began attacking Iraq relentlessly from the air.

Americans had round-the-clock access to the war via the satellite television broadcasts of the Cable News Network (CNN), some of whose reporters spoke live and regularly from Baghdad even as it was under bombardment from coalition forces. The broadcasts provided a sanitized, distorted version of the war, however. The Pentagon, mindful of how the relatively freewheeling press in Vietnam had affected public opinion of that conflict, heavily managed coverage of this one, refusing to allow filming of the gore of combat while exaggerating the effectiveness of the U.S. military's high-technology weapons. Saddam launched Soviet-made Scud missiles at Israeli cities, attempting, unsuccessfully, to provoke Israel to enter the war and thus break up the coalition against him.

On February 23, 200,000 coalition troops, most of them American, moved against the Iraqi forces in Kuwait. In command was General Norman Schwarzkopf, a theatrical, self-confident, and much-decorated veteran of Vietnam. Just over four days after the invasion, Saddam agreed to a cease-fire that left him in power in Iraq. American casualties came to 148 dead and 458 wounded, compared with some tens of thousands of Iraqi dead. Bush, who won widespread approval for his handling of the conflict, proclaimed, "We went

General Norman Schwarzkopf (right) chats with marines in Saudi Arabia before the start of the ground war against Iraq, February 1991.

halfway around the world to do what is moral and just and right. . . . We're coming home now proud, confident, heads held high." Alluding to the recriminations and a self-doubt that had pervaded the country after its defeat in Southeast Asia, he added, "By God, we've kicked the Vietnam syndrome once and for all."

Still, although the armistice conditions subjected Iraq to trade embargoes and on-site inspections to prevent Saddam from rearming, the Bush administration was criticized for preventing General Schwarzkopf from advancing to Baghdad and ridding Iraq of its dictator. Bush responded that Kuwait had been freed and that he wanted to avoid further American losses. His advisers, concerned with the balance of power in the region, were also worried that deposing Saddam might so weaken Iraq as to enlarge the influence of Iran or Syria in the Middle East, an eventuality that would be adverse to American interests. However, Saddam's continuation in power forced the United States to be constantly on guard against him. Near the end of his presidency, Bush sent air strikes against Iraq when Saddam moved missiles into areas where the armistice prohibited them.

> *"Alluding to the recriminations and self-doubt that had pervaded the country after its defeat in Southeast Asia, Bush added, 'By God, we've kicked the Vietnam syndrome once and for all.' "*

Some Reasons for Hope. Despite the persistence of the Iraqi threat, the United States' handling of the war had gained it good will among the principal Arab states. Bush, exploiting the advantage, revived efforts at achieving peace in the Middle East, an initiative that was supported by Syria, which was unable any longer to rely on the Soviets. In November 1991, talks began between Israel, the Palestinians, and several Arab countries. Progress was slowed by Palestinian violence against Jews and by the Israeli government's continued installation of Jewish settlements on the West Bank of the Jordan River. But the peace process nevertheless struggled forward, raising cautious hopes that eventually a settlement might be achieved.

A Domestic Guardian

At home, Bush was frequently criticized for lacking "vision." Far less adept and engaged in domestic than in foreign affairs,

he had no overarching legislative agenda. He conducted what some historians have termed a "guardianship presidency." Bush aimed to consolidate the changes of the Reagan years, moderating some of their harsh impacts but on the whole hewing to policies of low taxes and limited government. He emphasized voluntarism in dealing with social problems, likening charitable efforts brightening the land to "a thousand points of light." This idea only prompted skeptics to claim that he wanted the pleasure of promoting a good society without incurring the pain of finding a way to pay for it. The *Los Angeles Times* cartoonist Paul Conrad caught the overall rationale of Bush's domestic policies in a drawing of the United States dotted with small, dark circles that was captioned, "Bush's thousand points of light (batteries not included)."

But adverse economic trends compelled the president to find ways beyond guardianship and voluntarism. He had to deal with the ongoing failures in the savings and loan industry and the mounting annual federal deficit—$155 billion in 1988, $221 billion in 1990—both legacies of Reaganism. And he was forced to confront a severely slumping economy, a consequence largely of the end of the Cold War, along with the social strains accompanying the downturn.

THE TROUBLED ECONOMY

When Bush took office, the failures of savings and loan institutions (S&Ls) were reaching crisis proportions. By 1989, 350 S&Ls had gone bankrupt, the majority of them in New England and the Southwest; hundreds more bank failures were predicted. Deposits in these institutions were insured by the federal government, and bailout costs were estimated at up to $200 billion. In August 1989, responding to the crisis, Bush won passage of a measure that overhauled the federal regulatory structure for the S&Ls with the aim of making it more effective.

Polls showed that the federal deficit concerned Americans more than any other issue. Moreover, if the White House and Congress did not produce budgets that met the deficit-reduction targets in a 1987 law known as Gramm-Rudman-Hollings, federal spending would be automatically reduced, forcing a shutdown of certain government services. Faced with that possibility, Bush reneged on a campaign promise—"Read my lips; no new taxes"—and angered many of his supporters by agreeing to the passage in 1990 of a combination of spending slashes and higher taxes intended to reduce the deficit over five years. Nevertheless, the annual deficit kept climbing, reaching $290 billion in 1992 and pushing the accumulated federal debt to more than $4 trillion.

Recession. With the end of the Cold War, defense spending fell between 1989 and 1992 by 12.6 percent in inflation-adjusted dollars. Industrial corporations, focusing more on their ability to compete in the international marketplace, intensified the restructuring that had begun in the 1970s. Many companies laid off workers and shifted operations to countries where wages were lower than in the United States. A recession began in 1990. Followed by a weak recovery the next year, it set off a decline in consumer confidence, reductions in retail sales and housing starts, an increase in poverty, and a growth in unemployment to almost 7.8 percent in 1992.

Bush, seeing signs that the downturn might well affect his reelection chances, declared economic recovery his "No. 1 priority." In January 1992, he proposed to combat the recession with reduced taxes on gains from investments (capital gains) as well as tax incentives for business investment and for first-time home buyers. But although he had reached a compromise with Congress in 1991 that raised the minimum wage to $4.25, the president refrained from advancing any measures that would directly increase the spending power of lower-income groups. Democrats derided his proposals as too little and nothing more than political.

Bush held that the long-term strategy for the post–Cold War economy was economic growth, achieved in part by an expansion of international trade. Reagan had concluded a free-trade agreement with Canada in 1987, and Bush proposed to enlarge the free-trade zone to include Mexico. In 1991, he obtained authority from Congress to negotiate the North American Free Trade Agreement (NAFTA) on a fast track, despite opposition from some Democrats who feared that under NAFTA, jobs would be lost to Mexico. He concluded the treaty in December 1992, but it awaited ratification at the end of his term. Earlier that year, he had led a trade mission to Japan, but he was unable to open the Japanese market more widely to American goods, a failure symbolized by his collapse from the flu at a state dinner in Tokyo.

CIVIL RIGHTS

Bush put the face of social diversity on his administration, choosing General Colin Powell as head of the Joint Chiefs of Staff, the first African American to hold that post, and for the first time appointing a Hispanic American to the cabinet. He also tapped a record-setting number of women for high federal posts, including secretary of labor, surgeon general, and, later in his administration, secretary of commerce.

Unlike Reagan, Bush was a friend of civil rights laws that protected minority groups against discrimination. In July 1990, he signed the Americans with Disabilities Act—a congressional study had shown that the vast majority of the 43 million Americans with disabilities suffered from segregation and discrimination—which prohibited employers from discriminating against people with disabilities who were otherwise qualified, required them to provide physical access for disabled people, and expanded transportation services for them. To strengthen public education, Bush proposed to distribute federal vouchers to parents that could be used for tuition in private schools if they withdrew their children from public ones. Widely attacked as a threat to the public school system, the voucher scheme along with the constraints on the budget and the president's own fiscal conservatism prevented any major educational policy initiatives.

In Los Angeles in April 1992, a riot erupted in a poor black area when a jury acquitted four policemen of assaulting an unarmed black man named Rodney King, even though a videotape that was repeatedly shown on national television plainly showed the officers beating him. The uprising was marked by widespread looting, an indication that it was energized by anger at the recession as well as by rage at the police. More than 50 people died and 22,500 were injured, and damage to the downtown area ran to hundreds of millions of dollars. Bush flew to Los Angeles to see the destruction and meet with local leaders. His Justice Department charged the officers with violations of federal civil rights laws; two were ultimately convicted, the other two acquitted.

Like Reagan, Bush opposed affirmative action, and so, despite their social diversity, did key members of his administration. Moderate conservatives like himself, they represented the small but growing number of women and people of color in the United States who drew the line against racial and sexual preferences. In December 1989, the Department of Education, headed by a Hispanic American, ruled that scholarships set aside for minorities were illegal. The action provoked widespread outcries that prompted the resignation of the education secretary, but the administration continued to resist college aid linked to race.

THE SUPREME COURT

In 1990, Bush nominated David H. Souter, a respected centrist jurist from New Hampshire, to a vacancy on the Supreme Court, and he was confirmed without controversy. Then, in 1991, when Thurgood Marshall, the longtime champion of civil rights, retired from the high bench, Bush nominated Clarence Thomas, a conservative African American, to succeed him. Recently appointed to the U.S. Court of Appeals, Thomas was a graduate of Yale Law School, but he had only a brief and undistinguished record as a jurist, and though he had headed the Equal Employment Opportunity Commission (EEOC) in the Reagan years, he staunchly opposed affirmative action. Liberals charged that Bush was exploiting Thomas's race to place a conservative of mediocre talents on the Court.

Thomas nevertheless seemed headed for confirmation when in October 1991 Anita Hill, a black lawyer who had worked for Thomas at the EEOC, raised serious charges against him, first to the FBI and then in a dramatic hearing before the Senate Judiciary Committee. Hill claimed that Thomas had sexually harassed her, repeatedly asking her out

and discussing pornographic films. Thomas flatly denied Hill's charges, calling the Senate hearing a "high-tech lynching." Members of the Senate committee, all of them male, tended to treat Hill's claims skeptically, while car bumper stickers declared, "We Believe You Anita." In the end, the Senate confirmed Thomas by the slim margin of 52 to 48.

The Hill-Thomas controversy raised the profile of sexual harassment as an issue in the United States, but Thomas's appointment added an unswervingly conservative vote to the Supreme Court, which had already been moving steadily to the right. Since 1989, it had upheld laws limiting remedies available to women and minorities against employment discrimination and prohibiting the dissemination of information about abortion in federally funded clinics. In 1992, in *Planned Parenthood of Southeastern Pennsylvania v. Casey*, the Court by the narrow margin of 5 to 4 upheld a woman's right to choose an abortion, declaring that *Roe v. Wade* had "established a rule of law and a component of liberty that the Court would not renounce," but also ruling that the state could impose certain restrictions on the exercise of reproductive choice.

Through the rest of the nineties, the Court was neither consistently nor predictably conservative on any given case. It continued to resist school-sponsored prayer and restrictions on speech. But in several cases, it also bolstered the power of the states against federal authority, ruling, for example, that state employees could not sue in state courts for violations of federal labor laws. In all, as in the eighties, the Court reflected

Clarence Thomas (left) and Anita Hill testify before the Senate Judiciary Committee on Thomas's nomination to the Supreme Court, October 1991.

the social and ideological divisions in the country at large.

HEALTH AND THE ENVIRONMENT

Bush's political antennae were not tuned to the problem of rising health care costs, but they were fully resonant with the threats to public health and safety posed by illegal drugs and environmental pollution.

A War on Drugs. Early in the Bush presidency, more than half of Americans considered drug use a grave threat to national security. Bush declared a "War on Drugs" at both the domestic and international levels, an initiative that helped justify his ousting of Noriega in Panama. He appointed a drug czar—former Secretary of Education William Bennett, a loquacious idol of the conservative right. Bennett moved to replace Nancy Reagan's pleas to "just say no" with more effective measures, including federal funds to enlarge the capacity of the criminal justice system to handle drug offenders, alternative sentencing programs for nonviolent drug offenders, and a strengthening of the interdiction of drug trafficking at the borders.

The Environment: Pollution and Warming. In March 1989, the oil tanker *Exxon Valdez* ran aground in Prince William Sound, Alaska, staining the surrounding beauty and jeopardizing its wildlife with a spill of more than 10 million gallons of crude oil. That summer, the Environmental Protection Agency reported that air pollution in more than 100 cities exceeded federal standards. Both events renewed attention to the dangers of environmental degradation.

When Bush took office, virtually no major industry or community had yet met the standards in the existing Clean Air Act. In 1990, at the president's initiative, Congress passed amendments to the act that would impose on all cities tightened controls on emissions from automobiles, utilities, and industrial plants and that would use market incentives to encourage compliance. The Bush administration also began the huge task of ridding the areas around nuclear weapons facili-

Cleaning up the huge oil spill from the *Exxon Valdez* tanker in Prince William Sound, Alaska, March 1989.

ties and nuclear power plants of the radioactive wastes that had been deposited during the Cold War. But Bush often gave development-oriented industrial corporations the edge in determinations of environmental policy; for example, he called for opening wilderness preserves in Alaska to oil exploration. He was also reluctant to respond vigorously to what appeared to be a new environmental threat—global warming.

Scientific theory held that global warming was occurring as a result of concentrations in the atmosphere of certain gases, especially carbon dioxide (CO_2), which is a product of the burning of fossil fuels (coal, oil, or natural gas). The gases trap radiation reflected from the earth, creating a greenhouse effect that raises temperatures in the region close to the planet's surface. Analysts predicted dire consequences, including a tripling of the annual number of 90-degree days in cities of the mid-Atlantic region; a drying out of the great wheat baskets of the world; and inundations of coastal areas arising from wholesale melting of polar ice. Yet save for nuclear power, a politically and economically unacceptable alternative in the late eighties, there were no obvious substitutes for the fossil fuels that powered the engines of industrial civilization. The Bush administration stressed that the relationship of CO_2 emissions to global warming was too uncertain

1051

to warrant the economic dislocations that major restrictions on fossil-fuel burning would entail. Nevertheless, in 1992, at an Earth Summit of 200 nations in Rio de Janeiro, the American delegates did pledge to reduce the amount of greenhouse gases emitted.

THE ELECTION OF 1992

Well into the second half of his term, the triumph of the Gulf War made Bush seem so strong a bet for reelection that few leading Democrats were willing to enter the presidential race. But William Jefferson (Bill) Clinton, the forty-six-year-old governor of Arkansas, resolved to defy the odds. After prevailing in an arduous round of primaries, Clinton won the party's nomination and chose as his running mate Albert Gore Jr., a liberal senator from Tennessee who had a serious interest in environmental protection. By then, George Bush's reelection appeared decidedly more problematic, largely because of the toll taken by the slumping economy.

Clinton brought to the campaign dashes of both the cool and the confessional, appearing on one TV show wearing dark glasses and playing the saxophone, revealing on another the type of underwear he wore ("Boxers or briefs?" the interviewer had asked). Rumors had long abounded that he indulged in sexual dalliances, but Clinton was capable of reinventing himself in the face of adversity. When the press reported an extramarital affair with a former nightclub

The newly nominated Democratic candidates Bill Clinton (right) and Al Gore stop at a town meeting during their cross-country bus tour, July 1992.

singer, he appeared with his wife, Hillary Rodham Clinton, on the widely watched TV program *Sixty Minutes* and admitted that their marriage had encountered problems but insisted that it had emerged the stronger because of them. The Clinton campaign instructed its workers to remember, "It's the economy, stupid," the main issue on the minds of the American people. Clinton promised to bring about economic recovery, welfare reform, national health coverage, and the development of new technologies.

Bush dealt with the downturn by cutting withholding tax rates, increasing federal spending, and freezing federal regulation of business. In truth, statistics showed that the recession was ending—the economy had grown at a modest rate during the first two quarters of 1992—but many Americans felt bruised by the recession, the ongoing rise in health costs, and the impact of restructuring and reductions in corporate size. Bush was also undermined by attacks from the Republican right led by Patrick Buchanan, an economic isolationist and social conservative. Given the podium at the Republican convention, Buchanan and the evangelist Pat Robertson shocked moderates in and out of the party by savaging feminists, homosexuals, and advocates of reproductive choice. Bush, renominated with Dan Quayle, kept the party together, but his embrace of the right disturbed many voters. His campaign disparaged Clinton's devious (and successful) efforts to avoid the draft during the Vietnam War as well as his disingenuous admission that he had smoked marijuana but "had never inhaled." Late in the campaign, as polls showed Clinton pulling ahead, Bush derided Clinton and Gore as "crazies" and "bozos."

A challenge to both Bush and Clinton came from H. Ross Perot, a Texan who financed his own third-party campaign using some of the fortune he had made in the data-processing business. Outspoken and iconoclastic, Perot pilloried both Democrats and Republicans for absorbing themselves too much in party politics and too little in dealing with the recession and the deficit. For a time, he enjoyed strong support in the polls, an indication that many Americans were dissatisfied with the political status quo. But Perot's remedies—for example, direct popular voting on issues by electronic means—struck some analysts as unworkable and possibly unconstitutional. Perot himself was hypersensitive, willful, and volatile. He dropped out of the race in July, then at the beginning of October jumped back in, advancing his candidacy with millions of dollars' worth of television spots and in the presidential debates.

Clinton's political skills—commentators dubbed him "The Comeback Kid"—and the hangover of the recession combined to win him 43 percent of the vote to Bush's 38 percent. Perot gained 19 percent, the largest fraction ever won by a third-party candidate, taking probably far more of his share from Bush than from Clinton and helping to stimulate interest in the election. Voter turnout totaled 55 percent, up from 50 percent in 1988. Clinton won thirty-two states, carrying the Northeast and the Pacific Northwest, running strongly in the Midwest and the South, and accumulating 370 electoral votes compared with Bush's 168. Clinton attracted middle-income, blue-collar Democrats who had defected to Reagan. He also ran strongly among blacks, Hispanics, labor, and women, many of whom simmered with resentment against the treatment of Anita Hill and who helped elect six women (five of them fresh faces) to the Senate and forty-seven to the House. Colorado sent a Native American to the Senate. The number of African Americans in Congress almost doubled, reaching twenty-five; and the number of Hispanic Americans more than doubled, to seventeen. Democrats retained control in both houses.

> *"Fascinated by the process of globalization, Clinton followed Bush in making a major goal of his foreign policy the strengthening of American economic competitiveness in the post–Cold War world."*

Bush had managed the end of the Cold War shrewdly and energetically, encouraging democratic capitalism in former Communist countries and establishing a precedent for limited, multilateral military intervention against local aggression. But he dealt only fitfully with domestic concerns, courageously seeking to enlarge the North American free-trade zone yet responding to the nation's economic troubles with a peculiar lack of either empathy or effectiveness. Now, with the Cold War over, the focus of national attention turned inward, and people waited expectantly to see what Bill Clinton would do.

The Clinton Presidency

Clinton, a Rhodes Scholar at Oxford University and a graduate of Yale Law School, was prodigiously intelligent, ambitious, and resilient, a politico of disarming charm and resourcefulness. He had been elected governor of Arkansas at age thirty-two and had spent most of his adult life in state public office. Believing that the national political center had moved to the right, he presented himself as a "New Democrat," a devotee of opportunity, equality, and economic growth achieved with fiscal restraint and encouragement of the private sector.

As a New Democrat, Clinton courted the powerful, but perhaps because he had grown up in a small-town broken family, he also possessed considerable empathy for the disadvantaged and dispossessed. "I feel your pain," he would often tell people suffering from adversity. Such empathy made for good politics amid the continuing demands for equality in the United States, especially by women and members of racial and immigrant minorities. Hillary Clinton, a fellow graduate of Yale Law School, was an ambitious, politically involved lawyer—she told a reporter that she had not "stayed home baking cookies"—and her husband promised that she would play an active role in his presidency, noting that voters would get two for the price of one.

Tolerant of diversity in life-styles and attitudes, Bill Clinton was a staunch friend of affirmative action, abortion rights, and gay rights. He established a rainbow administration, appointing a woman as attorney general for the first time in the nation's history, and an African American, a Hispanic, and several other women to cabinet and subcabinet posts. He also successfully nominated Ruth Bader Ginsberg to the Supreme Court. He placed the issues of economic revival, the national debt, and health care high on his New Democrat agenda. Fascinated by the process of globalization, he followed Bush in making a major goal of his foreign policy the strengthening of American economic competitiveness in the post–Cold War world. In all, Clinton brought to the presidency a propensity for social liberalism combined with economic centrism, and an unembarrassed capacity to use personal revelation, hardball maneuver, tireless effort, or whatever else might be required to achieve his ends.

THE ECONOMY AND FREE TRADE

A month after taking office, Clinton sent a tax-and-spending package to Capitol Hill that was intended to stimulate the economy and lower the debt. Congress rejected the proposal for stimulus spending, but in August 1993, despite outcries from Republicans, it raised taxes on high incomes, reduced them on low ones, and cut spending by $225 billion.

The Clinton administration regarded free trade as essential to a thriving economy but found itself in a battle royal when it sought congressional ratification of the expanded version of NAFTA that had been negotiated by the Bush administration and that would create the world's largest free-trade zone. The measure drew support and provoked dissent from both Democrats and Republicans, advocates contending that it would create thousands of jobs, critics holding that it would result in the loss of thousands of jobs to Mexico, where goods would be produced free of the environmental and safety standards for manufacturing in the United States. In November 1993, with Clinton lobbying for the measure assiduously, NAFTA passed Congress by a comfortable margin.

Within a year, NAFTA was estimated to have cost some 12,000 people their jobs but to have created an additional 130,000 jobs by increasing exports to Mexico some 23 percent. By October 1994, 3.5 million more Americans were employed than had been at the end of 1993; and by the close of the year, the unemployment rate had fallen to 5.4 percent, its lowest level since 1990. The deficit, down to $220 billion in 1994, was predicted to be lower still the next year. Consumer confidence was up, and retail sales were rising.

In December 1994, Clinton, with congressional support, signed an international trade agreement that abolished trade quotas, lowered tariffs worldwide by $744 billion—the largest such cut in history—and created a new international trade regime called the World Trade Organization.

SETBACKS: HEALTH CARE AND GAY RIGHTS

Shortly after taking office, Clinton appointed a task force headed by his wife to recommend a comprehensive system of health coverage. By then, Americans were spending more per capita on medical care than people in any other nation, and some 39 million lacked health insurance. After five months, the task force, which became huge and worked in secret, recommended an enormously complex hybrid of federal and private arrangements that would provide universal health coverage while employing market competition to keep costs down.

The plan drew a hailstorm of criticism. It was disparaged as a bureaucratic nightmare, an infringement on the freedom of both doctors and patients, and unacceptably expensive to employers, especially small businesses, and the government itself. By early 1994, despite Hillary Clinton's vigorous campaign on its behalf, the plan was dead. The effort, however, prompted

Hillary Rodham Clinton and congressional leaders speak to the press on the administration's proposals for health care reform, April 1993.

the health care industry on its own to reorganize, expand its insurance coverage, and seek to control costs by using some of the mechanisms proposed by the Clinton commission. The Clinton administration, chastened by the defeat, henceforth took a small-step approach to health care—for example, obtaining legislation in 1996 that helped workers and their families keep their medical insurance if they changed or lost jobs.

In January 1993, Clinton announced that he intended to integrate homosexual men and women into all branches of the armed services—a departure from existing policy, which prohibited them from the military. Gays and lesbians were already serving in the military, but they had to keep their sexual orientation secret. Clinton's proposal outraged many conservatives, who felt that it implicitly legitimated homosexuality. It also generated considerable dissent from within the armed services on the grounds that the presence in the ranks of overtly homosexual men and women would create tension among straights. In July, a compromise dubbed "Don't ask, don't tell" was adopted: the armed services would not inquire into the sexual orientation of recruits and would not discharge men or women suspected of being homosexuals. But gays and lesbians could not openly acknowledge their sexual preferences or engage in homosexual acts on or off the base. The compromise dissatisfied Americans on both sides of the dispute, and later assessments revealed that it did little to make the military more tolerant of homosexuals.

The Clinton administration also stepped up the sexual integration of the armed services, with the result that women soon served aboard ships at sea, underwent basic training with men, and lived in sexually integrated barracks. By 1998, women comprised one out of seven members of the armed services on active duty.

ELECTIONS, 1994: A REPUBLICAN EARTHQUAKE

In 1994, responding to what polls revealed about voter concerns, the Clinton administration pressed for measures against crime and for welfare reform. Its anticrime bill banned assault weapons and provided $30 billion for drug treatment, prevention efforts, more prisons, and more police on the streets. Congress wrangled over the bill, then passed one similar to it. Clinton also introduced a bill intended to make good on his campaign pledge to "end welfare as we know it." The measure aimed especially to rein in the skyrocketing cost of Aid to Families with Dependent Children—it had jumped 31 percent since 1989—and to address the growing apprehension that the welfare system was encouraging many Americans into a condition of permanent dependency. In Congress, however, welfare reform took a back seat to the pending midterm elections.

Republicans sensed that both Clintons had made the Democrats vulnerable by fueling suspicion about their characters. Questions centered on the Clintons' involvement during his gubernatorial years in the Whitewater Development Corporation, a speculative real-estate venture in Arkansas that was suffused with indications of fraud and conspiracy. The questions compounded when in July 1993 Vincent Foster, then White House deputy counsel and a close friend of the Clintons who had been part of the Whitewater project, committed suicide; and when in March 1994 the press revealed that Hillary Clinton had earlier profited one-hundred-fold from an investment of $1,000 in cattle futures, a quick return that struck some as a bribe from Arkansas business interests. Then in May, Paula Jones, a young woman from Arkansas, sued Clinton for sexual harassment, charging that three years before, she had been brought to his hotel room by a state trooper, whereupon he had dropped his trousers and asked her to give him oral sex.

The Clintons denied all the charges, but the accusations received ongoing attention in the media. The couple's puta-

"The Clinton administration also stepped up the sexual integration of the armed services. By 1998, women comprised one out of seven members of the armed services on active duty."

tive peccadillos helped intensify continuing resentments over immigration, abortion, women's rights, pornography, sexual freedom, the breakaway from "family values." Right-wing talk-show hosts such as the popular Rush Limbaugh held up the Clintons as exemplars of all that his listeners considered wrong with the country. In 1992, concern for the economy may have papered over the social and cultural resentments evident since the 1970s, but now, despite the surge in the economy and Clinton's victory with NAFTA, many Americans, especially those vulnerable to automation, corporate downsizing, and foreign competition, felt no better off economically. Moreover, many appeared alienated by the administration's stand on homosexuals in the military and by the big-government flavor of its health care plan.

The "Contract with America." Newt Gingrich, a Republican congressman from Georgia, sensed the resentments and in the summer of 1994 shrewdly capitalized on them by drawing up an election-year "Contract with America," a ten-point conservative plan that included middle-class tax cuts, welfare reform, congressional term limits, a tough anticrime measure, and a balanced-budget amendment. In a November landslide, the Republicans gained fifty-two seats in the House and eight in the Senate, recapturing Congress for the first time since 1954. They won eleven governorships, bringing their total to thirty and giving them command of a majority of statehouses for the first time since 1970; and they took control of seventeen more state legislative bodies. Republican leaders celebrated the landslide as a repudiation of big, activist government and the moral decline they claimed had come to plague the United States.

In January 1995, the 104th Congress arrived in Washington righteously ready, like the 80th Congress in 1947, to turn back the clock on the recent accomplishments of the New Deal / Fair Deal state. The House elected Gingrich its Speaker by acclamation—*Time* magazine declared him "King of the Hill"—and appointed Rush Limbaugh an "honorary member." The new members of Congress aimed to overhaul the welfare system, limit federal regulatory power, roll back gun control, beef up the defense budget, cut taxes, and reduce foreign aid. The House, afire with cultural as well as economic conservatism, sought to slash the budgets for several federal science agencies, the National Endowments for the Arts and Humanities, and the Public Broadcasting Corporation. Its efforts were tempered in the Senate, which also narrowly defeated a constitutional amendment for a balanced budget that the House had passed. The Republicans then attempted to enact a legislative program that would balance the budget in seven years. But without reducing a number of social programs, it was impossible to balance the budget while simultaneously increasing defense spending and cutting taxes.

Face-Off. Clinton asserted that he would not tolerate hacking into the bone of social programs, notably Medicare, Medicaid, and education. When the Republican Congress sent him spending bills that slashed appropriations for such programs, Clinton vetoed them, with the result that the federal government was partially shut down twice in the fall of 1995. The president also vetoed a bill to ban so-called partial-birth abortions, a late-term abortion usually done to safeguard the health of the mother that many conservatives nevertheless vehemently opposed.

> *"Clinton embraced the Republican emphasis on budget balancing and debt reduction, basically vowing, as an aide recalled, 'that he was never going to get caught in that big-government, big-this, big-that trap again.'"*

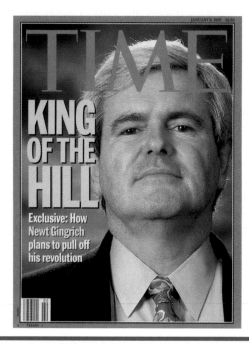

Newt Gingrich's "Contract with America" helped produce a Republican landslide in the 1994 congressional elections.

Clinton had the better of the face-off, managing to blame Gingrich and his right-wing allies for the shutdown. The Republicans surrendered on the budget and voted an increase in the minimum wage to $5.15 an hour. They had been weakened by the consequences of the shutdown, including the laying off of thousands of federal workers near Christmastime. However, Clinton on his part recognized that the forces behind the Republican earthquake had to be reckoned with. His eye on the 1996 election, he moved closer to the political center of the day, which Reagan and now the Gingrich Republicans had drawn a good deal farther to the right from where it had been in, say, the Eisenhower years. He embraced the Republican emphasis on budget balancing and debt reduction, basically vowing, as an aide recalled, "that he was never going to get caught in that big-government, big-this, big-that trap again."

The rightward shift helped prompt Clinton in August 1996 to sign a welfare reform act that reversed policies that had prevailed since the New Deal. The law reduced spending on food stamps, but most important, it abolished the largest federal welfare program, Aid to Families with Dependent Children, thus scrapping a sixty-year federal commitment to children in poverty. Welfare was turned over to the states, which would be given federal block grants accompanied by stringent rules. Coverage for most welfare recipients was limited to two years at a stretch, with a lifetime total of five years, and the recipients were required to move from welfare to work.

Critics, including many Democrats, angrily attacked the law, warning that it would adversely affect mothers and children in the inner cities. But in September, the welfare rolls were down by some 2 million people from 1993, a result of both the reform measure and the booming economy. Now with the presidential election just weeks away, Clinton focused like a laser beam on voters in the new political center.

THE 1996 ELECTION

The Republican nominee was Senator Bob Dole, a seventy-three-old warhorse from Kansas, a pragmatic conservative with a dry wit. His running mate was Congressman Jack Kemp, a former quarterback for upstate New York's Buffalo Bills. Dole and Kemp faulted Clinton for lack of leadership, character, and trustworthiness. But they ran a dull campaign, were dogged by memories of the federal shutdown the previous fall, and were swamped by the wave of prosperity that was sweeping the country.

Economic abundance was proclaimed by every indicator. In the preceding five years, the principal stock market average had more than doubled, and in the preceding six, corporate profits had risen 70 percent, to $437 billion. The federal deficit was down by 60 percent, more than Clinton had promised. Even before the passage of the welfare reform act, the growth of the economy had shrunk welfare roles 37 percent since the last presidential election year. Clinton celebrated the creation of more than 10 million new jobs during his administration, an increase in family income of $1,600 after inflation, and the lowest unemployment rate (5.1 percent) in seven years as well as the biggest drop in poverty in twenty-seven years (from more than 15 percent to less than 14 percent of the population).

On election day, Clinton beat Dole handily in the electoral college, 379 to 159. He gained 49 percent of the popular vote to Dole's 41 percent, with most of the rest going to Ross Perot, who had mounted another independent candidacy. The Republicans lost ten seats in the House but maintained control of Congress. Voter turnout fell to 54.2 percent, an indicator that interest in the political system remained desultory.

The Post–Cold War World

"Foreign policy is not what I came here to do," Clinton remarked several months after entering the White House. His heart in domestic affairs, he lacked an overarching vision for the post–Cold War world, and so did his secretary of state, Warren Christopher, a conscientious lawyer and effective negotiator. Nevertheless, Clinton did bring a set of guiding principles to foreign policy. Foreshadowed by Bush and dubbed "democratic enlargement" by the Clinton White House, these principles aimed, as his staff laid them out, to "strengthen the community of market democracies, foster and consolidate new democracies and market economies where possible, and counter the aggression and support the liberalization of states hostile to democracy." A replacement of the Cold War policy of containment, democratic enlarge-

" 'The old rules have been turned upside down,' observed one analyst. 'Instead of containing the Russians, we now subsidize them.' "

ment echoed Franklin Roosevelt's goal of promoting democratic capitalism in the world, but it gave far more attention to the demands of globalization than FDR could have dreamed of. Clinton told Congress in 1994, "We have put our economic competitiveness at the heart of our foreign policy."

Disparate problems abroad, some of them new, most ongoing, intruded on Clinton's presidency from the beginning. Some arose from the Soviet Union's collapse, others from the indirect consequences of its disappearance as a major player on the world stage, still others from indigenous antagonisms and conflicts. While the strategy of democratic enlargement helped resolve some of these disputes, several required military action.

RUSSIA

American policymakers continued to fear instability in Russia, specifically the fragility of its new capitalist economy, the threat of political upheaval, and the uncertain control of its formidable nuclear arsenal. Between 1993 and 1996, Clinton produced $4.5 billion in bilateral assistance for Yeltsin's government, helping to curb inflation and stabilize the ruble. "The old rules have been turned upside down," observed one analyst. "Instead of containing the Russians, we now subsidize them." As a result, by 1996 more than 60 percent of Russia's gross domestic product was generated by its private sector, and foreign trade was up 65 percent compared with 1993. Clinton brought to fruition efforts begun by the Bush administration to arrange for the removal of nuclear stockpiles from the former Soviet satellites, now independent nations. Clinton also agreed with Yeltsin to detarget U.S. and Russian strategic missiles, so that for the first time since the early 1950s, neither side would have missiles pointed at the other. Acting in accord with START I and START II, Clinton and Yeltsin reduced their countries' strategically deployed warheads from 20,000 to 7,000 by 1996, aiming eventually to bring the number down to 3,000.

VIOLENCE IN THE FORMER YUGOSLAVIA

The lifting of Communist rule in Yugoslavia led to the breakup of that country into five independent states, all of them divided against each other, and some within themselves, by ethnic and religious animosities. In 1991, one of them, Serbia, its people predominantly Orthodox Christian, attacked another, Croatia, whose population was largely Roman Catholic. In the spring of 1992, Serbs living in still another, Bosnia (Bosnia and Herzegovina), mounted a war that combined conventional military means with rape, murder, and terror to "cleanse" the new country of its almost 2 million Muslims, about half the population. During the winter of 1993, the Bosnian Serbs laid siege to Srebrenica, a predominantly Muslim city and one of the richest in the Balkans (countries occupying the Balkan Peninsula), its people now starving and freezing. By 1993, the post–Cold War hostilities in the former Yugoslavia had left more than 100,000 dead and produced 3.5 million refugees.

> *"By 1993, the post-Cold War hostilities in the former Yugoslavia had left more than 100,000 dead and produced 3.5 million refugees."*

Print and television reports of the Serbian atrocities angered many Americans, but they were reluctant to commit troops to stop the fighting. While the Bush administration recognized Bosnia, it endorsed a U.N. embargo on arms shipments to all of the former Yugoslavia, a policy that in effect favored the Serbs, since they were much better equipped militarily than the Bosnian or Croatian forces. During the presidential campaign, Clinton had attacked Bush for "failing to stop the horror in Bosnia." Once in the White House, however, he was reluctant to send troops, fearing a lack of public support and jeopardy to his domestic program. He went no further than endorsing multinational peacekeeping efforts by the U.N., which were largely ineffective.

However, after sixty-five Bosnian civilians died in a mortar attack on Sarajevo in early February 1994, Clinton pledged to shelter the Bosnian Muslims in "safe havens." In July, the Serbs overwhelmed the safe havens of Srebrenica and Zepa, killing thousands of Muslim civilians and undercutting the credibility of NATO. The next month, Clinton, pressured by Congress, authorized NATO air strikes against Bosnian Serb air defenses.

Post–Cold War Europe

In October, the administration obtained a cease-fire in Bosnia and in November brought the leaders of Croatia, Serbia, and Bosnia to Dayton, Ohio, for peace talks that resulted in mid-December in an agreement dubbed the "Dayton Accords." Bosnia would be a single nation divided into a Serb republic and a Muslim-Croat federation, both nominally loyal to a central national government. The peace would be ensured by a multinational Bosnian Implementation Force (IFOR). NATO would send 60,000 troops, 20,000 of them American. By now, NATO had been expanded to include Poland, Hungary, and the Czech Republic, an enlargement that the Russians found threatening. To ease their fears, in a watershed move Clinton included Russian troops in the NATO peacekeeping forces.

The signing of the peace accords in Dayton, Ohio, November 1994, ended the bloodshed and destruction in Bosnia.

Pollsters found that more than half of Americans opposed sending troops to Bosnia, but the Dayton Accords together with the IFOR halted the bloodshed in Bosnia and led to democratic elections in September 1998, arrangements for the return of refugees, and the prosecution for war crimes of certain Serbian leaders.

Secretary of State Madeleine Albright, flanked by Defense Secretary William Cohen (left) and President Clinton at a briefing on the crisis in Kosovo, April 1999.

Kosovo. Violence in the former Yugoslavia was not over, however. In Kosovo, a province of Serbia on the Albanian border, ethnic Albanians were agitating for independence. In 1998, Slobodan Milosevic, the head of Serbia, set out to suppress what he called an internal rebellion, sending in troops that resorted to impaling and decapitating residents and killing pregnant women. Madeleine Albright, who had replaced Christopher as secretary of state in January 1997—the first woman to hold the office—warned, "We are not going to stand by and watch the Serbian authorities do in Kosovo what they can no longer get away with doing in Bosnia."

The Clinton administration, once again reluctant to intervene militarily, tried to bring about a negotiated settlement but failed. In March 1999, after more than a year of continued "ethnic cleansing" in Kosovo, NATO forces supported by some 31,000 American personnel began bombing military and communications targets in Serbia. The bombing ended in June, and, as in Bosnia, the United States, NATO, and the United Nations sent troops to maintain peace in Kosovo.

CHINA AND THE PACIFIC RIM

In keeping with the economic emphasis of its foreign policy, the Clinton administration sought to create a huge free-trade zone in Asia, obtaining a pledge from the multinational Asia-Pacific Economic Cooperative forum in 1994 to develop a free-trading Pacific Rim by 2010. It also pressured Japan to open its domestic markets to American goods; renegotiating various market-access agreements, it achieved an increase in exports of 85 percent in areas the agreements covered. In February 1994, the Clinton administration lifted the U.S. trade embargo on Vietnam; the next year, it opened liaison offices there and normalized diplomatic relations.

China was rapidly emerging as a colossal market opportunity, but the Clinton administration's economic enthusiasm for China was offset by the Chinese government's capacity for high-handed behavior. China defied U.S. demands to halt sales of missile and nuclear technology to nations such as Pakistan and Libya. It continued to jail dissidents and cracked down on a movement for independence in Tibet. It also pirated American intellectual property, including films and compact discs, a rapidly growing fraction of U.S. exports.

Clinton tried to persuade the Chinese to behave differently by threatening trade sanctions and withholding shipments of high-tech goods such as communication satellites. During a visit to China in 1998, he engaged in an unprecedented television debate reminiscent of Nixon's kitchen confrontation with Khrushchev, challenging Premier Jiang Zemin on China's human rights record (Jiang stubbornly defended the crackdown at Tiananmen Square). But Clinton was willing to push the threats and punishments only so far. By the end of the 1990s, China was the United States' fifth-largest trading partner, a market for exports that accounted for approximately 170,000 American jobs and a beneficiary of tariff advantages that saved American consumers about $500 million a year on products such as shoes and clothing.

North Korea. North Korea, now the biggest supplier of missiles to Iran, Syria, and Pakistan, posed a nuclear hazard that spread far beyond its borders. In 1993, it withdrew from the nuclear nonproliferation treaty (an agreement banning the spread of nuclear weapons that was signed by more than sixty nations in 1969) and the following year refused to permit the International Atomic Energy Agency to inspect installations where it was suspected of producing plutonium. Clinton tried to establish closer ties to North Korea to dissuade it from pursuing its nuclear program, but in 1998 the country was found to be hollowing out an underground cavern—a possible nuclear test or production site—and that year it also test-fired a medium-range ballistic missile over Japan.

Tensions eased somewhat when in June 2000, just short of the fiftieth anniversary of the outbreak of the Korean War, the leaders of North and South Korea met in Pyongyang and signed an agreement allowing members of long-separated families from each country to visit each other. The Clinton administration announced that it would end economic sanctions against North Korea. But in negotiations with the United States, the North Koreans insisted on compensation for curtailing their export of missile technologies, a demand that Clinton rejected. At the end of Clinton's presidency, American policymakers remained suspicious of North Korea's intentions and worried that it might be developing nuclear-tipped missiles that could reach U.S. shores.

PEACEMAKING IN HAITI AND NORTHERN IRELAND

In 1991, a year after Jean-Bertrand Aristide was elected to head the Haitian government, he was ousted by a military junta. The junta imposed a reign of terror, driving thousands into exile, many of them fleeing in small boats across the sea for Florida. (Between 1991 and 1994, the Coast Guard rescued more than 68,000 such "boat people.") The Bush administration, fearing that admitting them would only encourage more to come and overload Florida's tolerance, began turning them back. Clinton, too, turned the boat people away. But in May 1994, responding to protests at home, he initiated economic sanctions against Haiti and obtained a U.N. Security Council resolution allowing a multinational force to oust the Haitian junta. Threatened with military intervention, the junta gave way. A multinational peacekeeping force, to which the United States contributed 21,000 troops, restored Aristide to power and enforced order in the country. The outflow of boat people dropped sharply. In elections at the end of 1995, Aristide was defeated by René Préval, marking the first democratic transition of power in Haiti's history.

During his first year in office, Clinton made good on a campaign promise to try to bring about a settlement in Northern Ireland, long plagued by a declining economy and sectarian violence that pitted predominantly Catholic nationalists against predominantly Protestant loyalists to Britain. The president was convinced that renewed economic development would diminish the conflicts. In 1994, at a White House–sponsored economic summit in Ireland, Clinton won the British government's assent to an American role in its disarmament talks with the Irish Republican Army (IRA), which had long conducted a terrorist campaign against British rule in Northern Ireland. Chaired by former Senate majority leader George Mitchell, the talks developed so well that both Britain and Ireland invited Mitchell to preside over negotiations, which produced a comprehensive agreement in April 1998. The terms called for the IRA to lay down its arms and for the creation of a popularly elected assembly in Northern Ireland that would replace the British government as the local governing authority. In May, the agreement was ratified by voters in Northern Ireland and the Republic of Ireland. Initially a triumph for Clinton, it was jeopardized during the rest of his administration by the IRA's foot-dragging reluctance to honor the disarmament terms, but in October 2001 its leaders declared that they would begin turning in their weapons.

FAILURE IN SOMALIA AND RWANDA

In December 1992, Bush had sent 25,000 troops to Somalia, in northeastern Africa, with the humanitarian aim of ending months of famine and anarchy. Soon the threat of starvation was over, and the view of Bush policymakers was that the incoming Clinton administration should accordingly end the mission. Clinton, however, decided to continue the intervention in the interest of nation building, expanding the famine-relief effort and assigning the troops the job of tracking down and arresting local warlords thought to be preying on the population. But on October 3, 1993, eighteen U.S. Army Rangers were ambushed and killed in a raid on a warlord's headquarters. Another twelve American soldiers died in other skirmishes, and by December 1993, responding to strong domestic pressure, Clinton had withdrawn all the American forces.

The failure in Somalia discouraged the United States and other Western nations from intervening in the central African nation of Rwanda in 1994, when the Hutu majority slaughtered an estimated half a million Tutsi. The Tutsi rebels retaliated, stimulating the flight of a tidal wave of Hutu refugees into neighboring Zaire. In 1998, on a visit to Rwanda, Clinton apologized for the United States' role in slavery, for its role in "crushing the aspirations" of Africa during the Cold War, and for the West's failure to halt the killing of so many Tutsis by Rwandan Hutu extremists.

THE MIDDLE EAST AND THE SPREAD OF TERROR

As in Ireland, Clinton worked hard to bring the Israelis and Palestinians further along the road to peace. But his efforts were thwarted by outbreaks of violence on both sides, including terrorist attacks. Moreover, Iraq, where Saddam Hussein remained in power, continued to court conflict, and some of the hatreds that suffused the Middle East produced an increasing incidence of terrorism against the United States itself.

The Palestinian-Israeli Conflict. For a while during the Clinton administration, the Middle East seemed headed for peace. The Norwegians brokered an agreement—the Oslo Accords—between the Israelis and the Palestinian Liberation Organization (PLO) in which the Israelis gave the Palestinians self-government in the Gaza Strip and parts of the West Bank, while Yasir Arafat, the PLO chief, renounced terrorism

Prompted by Clinton, Israeli prime minister Yitzhak Rabin (left) shakes hands with PLO leader Yasir Arafat after signing the Oslo Accords at the White House, September 1993.

1061

and pledged to extend diplomatic recognition to Israel. At the request of the two parties, the agreement was formally signed in Washington, D.C., in September 1993 at a ceremony presided over by President Clinton, who prevailed on Arafat and the Israeli prime minister, Yitzhak Rabin, to shake hands.

In 1994, Clinton assisted Jordan and Israel in resolving their long-standing differences and concluding a formal peace treaty. The United States also persuaded Israel and Syria to agree in writing that they would provide security to civilians on both sides of the Israeli-Lebanese border and that Syria would stop attacks against Israelis by Hezbollah, a terrorist group that was Syria's client in the area. Otherwise, however, the Clinton administration made little headway toward a general peace between Syria and Israel. Moreover, in November 1995, a right-wing Israeli fanatic assassinated Rabin in retaliation for his peacemaking, and Benjamin Netanyahu, a hard-line conservative, soon wrested the Israeli leadership from Rabin's party and put the peace process in cold storage.

In 1998, Clinton, determined, brought Netanyahu and Arafat to talks on the Wye River in Maryland and nudged them into an agreement called the "Wye Memorandum." The PLO pledged to rid its charter of language calling for the destruction of Israel and to exert tighter control over gun running. Israel committed itself to relinquish 14 percent of the West Bank to the Palestinians and release 750 of them from jail. But extremists on both sides remained adamantly opposed to compromise. In the summer of 2000, sustained violence erupted on the West Bank and the Gaza Strip, pitting Palestinians, often armed only with rocks, against Israeli troops, who often responded with gunfire. Anger on both sides increased as the casualties mounted. Clinton kept trying to mediate, but by the time he left office, the killing was still going on and the peace process seemed moribund.

Iraq. Despite the allied victory in the Gulf War, Iraq remained a persistent source of tension in the Middle East. In the mid-1990s, the country occasionally fired missiles against U.S. planes patrolling the no-fly zones that had been established over parts of the country. In retaliation, the allies used missiles to attack intelligence headquarters in Baghdad as well as Iraq's own missile and radar sites, and sent air, ground, and naval forces to the Persian Gulf region.

The allies maintained most of the economic sanctions they had imposed after the Gulf War, a policy that severely damaged the Iraqi economy. They also insisted that Iraq open its

Osama bin Laden, financier and mastermind of the Al Qaeda terrorist network.

facilities for potentially producing chemical, biological, or nuclear weapons to their inspection. In November 1997, Saddam Hussein, impatient with the sanctions, accused the American inspectors of spying and ordered them to leave, opening a new round of disputes between Iraq on the one side and, on the other, the allies and the United Nations. In the following months, Saddam grew more defiant, trying to use the inspection issue to obtain a lifting of the sanctions. The allies, their suspicions of Saddam's intentions undiminished, refused. In mid-December, the United States and Britain launched sustained air strikes against Iraq's weapons-making program. In 2000, the sanctions remained in place, and Iraq seemed to be rebuilding its damaged military and industrial sites.

Terrorism. The sanctions against Iraq and the civilian suffering they generated, the presence of American troops on Saudi Arabian soil during and after the Gulf War, and the United States' support of Israel all angered a number of Muslims in the Middle East. They infuriated Osama bin Laden, a rich Saudi exile living in Afghanistan. Bin Laden hated the United States enough to finance a network of terror called Al Qaeda, directed against the country. In February 1993, four Muslim terrorists connected to bin Laden exploded a car bomb in the garage under one of the World Trade Center towers in New

York City; although they failed in their ambition to topple the tower into its twin, they succeeding in killing 6 and injuring more than 1,000. In 1996, terrorists drove a truck bomb into an American army barracks in Saudi Arabia itself, killing 19 U.S. military service people. And in 1998, several other suicide truck bombers blew up an American embassy in Tanzania, killing 11, and another in Kenya, killing 213 Kenyan citizens and injuring thousands of civilians.

A few hours after the attacks in 1998, Clinton declared, "We will use all the means at our disposal to bring those responsible to justice, no matter what or how long it takes." In an operation code-named "Infinite Reach," U.S. planes attacked two targets believed to be associated with bin Laden—the Al Shifa pharmaceuticals plant in Sudan, alleged to be a source of biochemical weapons, and a temporary base camp in Afghanistan, labeled by Clinton "one of the most active terrorist bases in the world." (The owner of the plant denied that he had anything to do with bin Laden, and reporters visiting the site saw no evidence that he did.) During the trial of the organizers of the Africa bombings, testimony indicated that bin Laden and Al Qaeda had attempted to acquire weapons of mass destruction about five years earlier.

In 1996, the Taliban, a group of extreme Islamic fundamentalists, gained control of Afghanistan and extended their protection to bin Laden as a "guest." In October 1999, the U.N. Security Council, alarmed, resolved to impose limited sanctions against the Taliban in an effort to force them to turn over bin Laden immediately to a country where he could be brought to justice. The Taliban refused, and bin Laden and Al Qaeda grew bolder. A year later, terrorists linked to bin Laden attacked the USS *Cole* while it was anchored in the Yemeni port of Aden, killing seventeen of its crew and injuring forty-two.

Between 1993 and 1999, the FBI's counterterrorism budget more than tripled, to some $300 million a year. Still, in the wake of so many successful assaults, a number of analysts believed that the United States was inadequately on guard against the war of terrorism that was increasingly being waged against it. Some contended that it was only a matter of time before the terrorists would strike on American shores with far greater destructive effect than they had achieved in the 1993 bombing at the World Trade Center.

> *"While a record number of people, including a record number of minorities, held jobs, many of the new jobs were in the low end of the service sector—for example, in tele-marketing and sales, fast foods, and custodial and domestic work."*

The Prosperous Nineties

During Clinton's second term, the economic boom that had begun early in the nineties grew more exuberant. Unemployment fell steadily, reaching 4 percent in 2000, a thirty-year low. Between 1994 and 1998, the gross domestic product jumped by more than 14 percent, and during the first three months of 1999 it grew at an even faster annual pace. In 1997, three out of four homes had air-conditioning, four out of five had washing machines, one out of two had automatic dishwashers and personal computers, and almost all had television sets. In 1998, wages and benefits rose at twice the rate of inflation, which was only 1.7 percent. The poverty rate was down to 13.3 percent, and even a majority of the poor possessed amenities such as cars, TVs, and microwave ovens that most people in the world could only dream about.

Like the prosperity of the 1980s, that of the 1990s was spread unevenly. While a record number of people, including a record number of minorities, held jobs, many of the new jobs were in the low end of the service sector—for example, in telemarketing and sales, fast foods, and custodial and domestic work. In mid-decade, more than one out of five Americans worked part time, with few or no benefits and no

Sales of notebook computers, cell phones, and other high-tech consumer goods helped fuel the economic boom of the 1990s.

security or prospects of advancement. The unemployment rate among teenage job seekers ran to 16 percent in 1997, symptomatic of the growing requirement for skills and the deficiency of skills among many young people. Just one out of seven workers belonged to a labor union, only 40 percent of the fraction in 1945, which meant that standards for wages, hours, and working conditions for all of labor were weakened.

Between 1989 and 1998, inflation-adjusted wages rose just 1 percent for the bottom fifth of workers but 16 percent for the top fifth. Adding to the disparity, the average chief executive earned 400 times more than his employees, a tenfold increase in that ratio since the 1960s. Many of the low-skilled people working in Silicon Valley could not afford the area's stratospheric housing prices and lived long commuting distances from their places of employment.

Unlike the eighties, the nineties lacked naked celebrations of greed, but disquiet with the profit-maximizing practices of the marketplace were evident in the popularity of Scott Adams's cartoon strip *Dilbert,* which satirized corporate culture from the point of view of the hapless victims of restructuring and downsizing. Millions of Americans watched *The Sopranos,* a TV series about an extended Mafia family in New Jersey whose members were absorbed with ordinary personal relationships at home while routinely conducting murder and mayhem in their business—in all, a metaphor for how the conflicts and decencies of private life coexisted with the cold-blooded indecencies that the marketplace often fostered.

Democrats and Republicans disputed which party's policies were responsible for the robustness of the economy, but analysts at all points on the political spectrum agreed that a good deal of the economic miracle was attributable to technological innovation. The market for personal computers alone was projected to reach $240 billion in 1998, almost a threefold increase over 1992. Technology was steadily boosting worker productivity, producing low unemployment without significant inflation. And according to a chorus of commentators, revolutions in biotechnology and communications were creating a "new economy" whose capacities were as unbounded as human ingenuity.

BIOTECHNOLOGY: THE HUMAN GENOME PROJECT

In the late 1980s, a number of geneticists urged the federal government to create a project in which they could learn all the details of the DNA (deoxyribonucleic acid) in the human

A biologist informs the press that the public and private projects to sequence all the DNA in the human genome have been completed, Washington, D.C., February 12, 2001.

genome. (DNA forms the essence of genes, which control the development of organisms; the term "human genome" refers to all the genes contained in human cells.) Federal policymakers responded favorably, seeing in the project rich benefits for understanding and treating disease and for adding to the strength of the United States in the post–Cold War international economy. Begun in 1989, **the project** was soon producing a torrent of genetic information. In the late 1990s, a private company named Celera initiated its own effort to obtain the complete structure of human DNA. Both the federal project and Celera reached the goal simultaneously in June 2000, announcing their results at a White House press conference in the company of President Clinton.

All the while, new biotechnology companies sprang up to exploit the accumulating genetic knowledge—for example, genes that predisposed women to breast cancer and were responsible for 5–10 percent of breast cancer cases. The companies devised new drugs and new methods of medical diagnosis. Many Americans watched these developments apprehensively, fearing that a new eugenics (state interference in human reproduction for the sake of biological "improvement") might occur, with all the social bias that characterized the old eugenics, and that medical insurers or employers might use genetic information to deny applicants policies or jobs. Others worried that genetic manipulation of the natural world might run out of control, a theme that was chillingly explored in Steven Spielberg's widely popular film *Jurassic Park* (1993) and in the best-selling novel by Michael Crichton on which it was based. However, people set aside their fears in favor of the hopes for treating disease that the genome project raised.

COMMUNICATIONS: THE INTERNET

Electronics continued to revolutionize communications, as they had done since World War II. By the mid-1990s, two-thirds of the country was wired for cable television. By 1995, 33 million Americans subscribed to cell phone services, which had arrived on the consumer scene in 1988, and thousands more were signing up every month. Satellites provided individual radio and TV stations with an increasingly diverse menu of programs, and the Telecommunications Act of 1996, the first major overhaul of policy in this area since the New Deal, sought to promote competition in the telecommunica-tions sector. But the innovation with the most dramatic impact was the democratization and commercialization of the Internet into an electronics network that linked individual computers across the globe.

Like so many innovations that changed the way people lived, the Internet originated in the national defense program's patronage of science and technology. It was principally conceived in the late 1960s by a computer scientist at MIT named J. C. R. Licklider as a network that would preserve communications in the event of nuclear attack. In the seventies, scientists and engineers at different institutions developed the essential hardware and software that would permit different types of computers and networks to communicate with each other through an intermediate service provider. With the sponsorship of the Defense Department, a nationwide network rapidly developed among industrial and university scientists. It was used mainly for e-mail, which was pioneered in 1971 and which

---

American Journal

What Do You Do for Fun?

In 1975, video games burst into the Christmas market as a sell-out item, fetching prices of $100 and up. Products of the high-technology electronics industry, they worked by converting television sets into controllable fields of play. The consumer marketing director of the National Semiconductor Corporation noted happily, "The toy and game market is limited only by our imagination." Designers in the new personal computer industry were already dreaming up circuits to generate TV images that players could manipulate with the turn of a knob. Since then, computer games have become a huge industry. But to many parents and policymakers, their contents, like those of films and television, have seemed to encourage antisocial behavior, and the games thus helped fuel opposition to the libertine quality of American culture. The 1998 edition of Dr. Spock's Baby and Child Care, *the most popular book in its field for half a century, advised parents that computers served many constructive educational purposes but that they had "a darker side."*

"I'm speaking about the majority of computer games. Most of these are variations on the theme of kill (shoot, laser, karate, kick, maim, beat up) the bad guys. These games are unimaginative carryovers of violent Saturday morning cartoons. The best that can be said of them is that they may help promote eye-hand coordination in children. The worst that can be said is that they sanction, and even promote, aggression and violent responses to conflict. But what can be said with much greater certainty is this: most computer games are a colossal waste of time. . . .

"Your job with regard to video games is much the same as it is with television viewing: to help pick the right video games and to set limits on how much time is to be spent playing them. Which video games are acceptable? Generally these are ones intended to teach, that convey information in an interactive and fun fashion. Others, while not primarily educational in intent, rely on intellectual skills (like deciphering clues) to achieve the goal."

Benjamin Spock and Steven J. Parker, *Dr. Spock's Baby and Child Care,* 7th ed.

an authoritative 1978 report dubbed a "smashing success" that would "sweep the country."

Between the mid-1980s and early 1990s, partly at the initiative of then-Senator Al Gore, the Internet was transferred to civilian control and then opened up to commercial use. In the meantime, scientists in Europe developed a program to retrieve information from any computer connected to the Internet by latching on to its standard address (called a "URL," for universal resource locator). They also devised a language ("html," for hypertext markup language) for presenting text and images, and protocols ("http," for hypertext transfer protocol) for transferring them from one computer to another. Programmers at a government computing facility in Illinois, having devised a browser, left in 1994 to develop a new, commercial version that they called Netscape. Together, these innovations led to the birth of the World Wide Web. After the mid-1990s, the Web spread with the freely accessible Internet across the globe. Its diffusion was accompanied by an avalanche of companies founded to exploit it commercially, most of them with URLs that ended in the designation ".com" and were known accordingly as "dot com" companies. By early 1999, about 74 million people, including two out of five adults, were accessing the Internet.

THE BULL MARKET

The rapid growth, or expectations of such growth, of the new high-tech companies helped inflame the stock market. Between December 1990 and September 2000, the Dow Jones Industrial Average, a measure of the market's value, climbed more than 400 percent to over 11,000; and the index of the NASDAQ, a market heavy with stocks of high-tech companies, skyrocketed more than 1,000 percent, to over 4,000. America Online (AOL), the biggest Internet service provider, was valued at $26 billion, equaling the combined capital worth of the three major broadcasting networks. The inflation in stock values made billionaires of some of the men and women who pioneered the new-economy companies. The wealth of William H. Gates, one of the two founders of the Microsoft Corporation, mushroomed to more than $100 billion in 2000, which exceeded the combined assets of one-third of the American population.

Americans were tantalized by the prospect of quick stock market riches, an absorption that was reflected in the popularity during 1999 of the TV game show *Who Wants to Be a Millionaire?* An unprecedented number of people began putting their money into stocks, aided by discount brokerage houses such as Charles Schwab and the wide availability of stock information on the Internet. By the end of the decade, stocks accounted for more than a quarter of the assets of American householders, a fifty-year peak. But the willingness to buy stocks at prices that were historically very high compared with earnings reminded some observers of the 1920s. The chairman of the Federal Reserve Board remarked that the performance of the stock market expressed an "irrational exuberance" on the part of investors.

AFRICAN AMERICANS

The social and economic trends among people of color recapitulated those of the eighties, producing greater material comfort and standing for many while consigning others to poverty and despair. More African Americans (four out of ten) counted themselves members of the middle class, more lived in suburbs (one out of three, double the fraction of the seventies), and more had attended college (about 37 percent, compared with 10 percent in 1970).

African Americans were gaining prominent roles in public life. More were in professional occupations such as law, journalism, and engineering; more had been elected big-city mayors; and the House of Representatives included more than forty blacks. Several blacks, notably talk-show host Oprah

Television talk-show host Oprah Winfrey (left) and golf champion Tiger Woods.

Winfrey and comedian Whoopi Goldberg, commanded enormous power in the entertainment world. Many were a notable presence in professional sports, accounting for 80 percent of the players in the National Basketball Association, 66 percent of those in the National Football League, and 17 percent of those in major-league baseball. Several black sportsmen—golfer Tiger Woods, basketball players Michael Jordan and Grant Hill—earned fortunes.

The poverty rate among African Americans declined in the nineties, as did the inner-city murder rate and the birthrate among unmarried teenagers. Still, at the end of the nineties, over a quarter of African Americans lived in poverty; many continued to contend with slum housing, inadequate medical care, dilapidated public schools, and gang violence that often took innocent lives. The black unemployment rate was 10 percent, more than twice the national one. Black males were seven times more likely than white males to spend time in prison.

The "Million Man March," a gathering of African American men from around the nation in Washington, D.C., October 1995.

Relatively few films and TV shows starred blacks, and by most measures African Americans lagged behind whites in college attendance, occupational opportunity, status, and health. The income of the median black family in 1997 amounted to $28,000 a year, $16,000 less than that for white families. African Americans continued to encounter discrimination in ordinary commerce—for example, at food chains such as the International House of Pancakes or Denny's—and in corporate boardrooms such as the oil company Texaco's, where executives spoke of African American employees as "black jelly beans." Despite black protests, several southern states insisted on continuing to fly the Confederate flag over their capitols. And in June 1998 near Jasper, Texas, three white men chained a black man to a pickup truck and dragged him over the roads to his death.

Although the three were ultimately convicted of murder (and two sentenced to death), African Americans had little confidence in law enforcement. They were often subjected to racial profiling—stopped on the highways, for example, simply because of the color of their skin, an offense that African Americans sarcastically dubbed "driving while black." Black males were especially vulnerable to discrimination and suspicion. What they suffered at the hands of whites they often took out on the women in their lives. The troubles that black women endured from black men and white racism were sensitively explored in the novels of writers such as Toni Morrison, whose works—notably *Beloved*—became popular in the nineties and who in 1993 won the Nobel Prize for literature.

Anger and Accommodation. Folk expressions of black anger appeared in rap music, a kind of rhythmic rhyming spoken against an instrumental background known as hip-hop. Early in the nineties, rap lyrics tended to attack white racism, with performers like Ice-T seeming to celebrate a cop killer and Public Enemy urging his audiences to "fight the power." Its more militant forms, notably "gangsta rap," proclaimed hatred of women and advocated violence. Some whites, including candidate Bill Clinton in 1992, attacked its seeming admonitions for blacks to kill whites. But rap's rebelliousness increasingly appealed to young whites, who by the late nineties bought 70 percent of its albums. Rap entered mainstream culture, even outselling country music, and became associated with a commercially lucrative style of teenage dress (oversize shirts, loose jeans bunching down the buttocks, and baseball caps often worn backward). Its stars formed alliances with chic clothing manufacturers such as Calvin Klein. An executive at a black radio station in New York City remarked that rap was "not revolutionary," adding, "It's just 'Give me a piece of the action.'"

Black activists continued trying to mobilize against white racism and for social justice. In October 1995, minister Louis Farrakhan of the Nation of Islam, a kind of latter-day Malcolm X, led 400,000 black men on what was advertised as a "Million Man March" in Washington, D.C., where he called on them to accept greater responsibility for their families. But while Farrakhan preached self-help and racial pride, he also advocated black separatism and made anti-Semitic remarks, leaving an impression that alienated whites and many blacks. The Reverend Jesse Jackson persistently called for social justice, but his appeals made no headway against the prevailing devotion to the free market and limited government.

> *"Demographers predicted that Hispanics would soon likely outnumber African Americans and by 2050 account for a quarter of the population."*

IMMIGRANTS AND NATIVE AMERICANS

During the nineties, people migrated legally to the United States in numbers comparable to those of the 1980s. Almost 7 million arrived on the nation's shores, including 1 million from Europe, 2.1 million from Asia, and 3.3 million from Latin America. Hispanics, their numbers continuing to swell from illegal as well as legal immigration, comprised almost 30 million people, or about 11 percent of the population. Demographers predicted that they would soon likely outnumber African Americans and by 2050 account for a quarter of the population.

Asian and Hispanic newcomers continued to concentrate in the Southwest, especially California, where in 2000 Hispanics comprised about one-third of the population and held more than 4,000 public offices. Both groups tended to be marked by strong families, low crime rates, and rising wages. By 1998, the number of Latino and Asian-owned businesses in the Los Angeles metropolitan region had grown to 220,000, a threefold increase from the early 1980s. The growing concentrations of Hispanics provided enthusiastic audiences for new musical forms, including salsa, merengue, and Tejano, an energetic hybrid of rock, rhythm and blues, and rancheras melodies with a mixture of Spanish and English

lyrics. The rapidly expanding market for Spanish cultural products prompted *People* magazine to create a national Spanish-language edition, *People en Español,* which compiled record-breaking sales for a memorial issue devoted to the young Tejano singer Selena, who had been murdered by an obsessed fan.

The immigrant success stories masked the persistence of low incomes and poverty in the newcomer communities. While about one in eight immigrants were college graduates and moved into skilled work, most were young, much less educated, and candidates for unskilled jobs such as domestic helpers, gardeners, and agricultural labor. In the late nineties, for example, more than a quarter of Hispanics lived in poverty, and about 8 percent had no jobs. Some 6 percent of immigrants wound up on welfare, twice the fraction of people born in the United States.

All the while, anti-immigrant resentments were evident. In 1994, California voters approved an initiative that denied nonemergency welfare benefits and public-school access to the children of illegal immigrants; four years later, they passed another initiative that largely eliminated bilingual education in the state's public schools. In September 1996,

Many legal and illegal immigrant women found work caring for the children of working parents.

Pawnee Indian attorney Walter Echo-Hawk, a leader in the fight for Indian rights on tribal lands.

President Clinton signed immigration legislation that restricted the eligibility of legal immigrants for public assistance, placed higher income requirements on sponsors, and doubled the strength of the border patrol. A poll found that more than two-thirds of respondents believed that Chinese Americans were "taking away too many jobs from Americans," "don't care what happens to anyone but their own kind," and "have too much power in the business world." In Dearborn, Michigan, when the schools superintendent proposed an Arabic-English program in a school where 90 percent of the students spoke Arabic, a number of residents attacked bilingual education, with one insisting, "This is America. Public money for public education should be used for English only."

Safeguarding Indian Rights. Following in Nixon's policy footsteps, President George Bush encouraged self-determination for Native Americans. During his presidency, the federal government relied more on Native Americans to run the programs of the Bureau of Indian Affairs and, giving them preference in hirings and promotions, increased their representation among the bureau's employees to 87 percent. In 1994, President Clinton, who had said he was one-eighth Native American, brought leaders from all the nation's tribes to the White House—a first in the nation's

history—and signed a directive to safeguard Indian rights on tribal lands and to protect the use of eagle feathers for ceremonial purposes. In 2000, the Clinton administration returned 84,000 acres to the Ute tribe in northern Utah, the largest restoration of land in a century, and apologized for the federal government's treatment of Native Americans, including its "futile and destructive efforts to annihilate Indian cultures."

Indian reservations looked increasingly to gambling for revenues; by 1995, more than 100 had opened casinos, often against state opposition arising from fear of losing revenue from lotteries. The tribes used some of their revenues to address the long-standing social problems on their reservations, funding tribal colleges, community centers, and programs for treating alcoholism.

WOMEN

By the mid-1990s, six in ten women were employed outside the home, including two-thirds of married women and more than half of women with children under age one. While on average women still earned less than men, the gap had narrowed since the mid-1980s. They owned more than a third of the nation's small businesses and accounted for about a quarter of all physicians, lawyers, and judges and a third of all professional athletes. In the mid-1990s, forty-eight women were serving in the House and eight in the Senate. Women represented about one in five state legislators and almost the same portion of mayors in all but the smallest cities.

Entertainment media still provided traditional portraits of women, in, for example, films such as *Pretty Woman* (1990), in which a prostitute is rescued from degradation and loneliness by a rich man. But more offerings celebrated traits of independence in body, mind, and spirit. In the popular television comedies *Sex and the City, Seinfeld,* and *Roseanne,* the women were saucy, strong-minded, and sexually liberated. The film *Courage under Fire,* released in 1996, starred Meg Ryan as a servicewoman fighting and dying in the Gulf War valiantly enough to earn consideration for a Congressional Medal of Honor. The same year, in *United States v. Virginia,* the Supreme Court, deciding that the Virginia Military Institute could not refuse to admit women, implied that men-only admissions policies at state-supported colleges were unconstitutional.

> *"In 2000, the Clinton administration returned 84,000 acres to the Ute tribe in northern Utah, the largest restoration of land in a century."*

1069

HEALTH AND SAFETY

By many measures, Americans on the whole were healthier than they had ever been. Infant mortality was down to an all-time low of 7.2 per 1,000 live births. Life expectancy for children born in 1996 was 76.1 years, with the expectancy for blacks at 70.2 years, a narrowing to just over six years of the historic gap with whites. About one in two Americans exercised regularly, while many consumed low-fat and low-calorie foods to avoid clogging their arteries and thus to reduce the risk of heart disease and stroke.

An arsenal of biomedical knowledge and technologies was available to prevent people from falling ill and to cure them if they got sick. Heart, lung, and kidney transplants lengthened and improved lives. Lasers rendered surgery, dentistry, and ophthalmology more effective. Recent imaging technologies—magnetic resonance imaging (MRI), ultrasound, positron scans, and CT-scans—were continuing to revolutionize diagnostic medicine. Increasingly for young couples, the first picture entered in the baby album was an ultrasound of the fetus in the womb. Pharmaceutical companies produced not only antibiotics against infectious disease but also drugs for functional disorders, including high blood pressure, emotional distress, menopausal symptoms, and male sexual dysfunction.

Tolerance of AIDS victims was encouraged by the film *Philadelphia* (1993), in which Tom Hanks portrayed a lawyer who contracted the disease, was fired by his firm, and sued in response. In 1998, the Supreme Court ruled that the Americans with Disabilities Act applied to people with AIDS even if they showed no symptoms. By 1996, 320,000 Americans had died of AIDS and another 650,000 to 900,000 were infected with HIV, the virus responsible for the disease. But the incidence of new infections had fallen sharply since the 1980s, partly as a result of safer sex practices among homosexual males; and between 1993 and 1997, the incidence of AIDS itself in the United States declined by almost half, to 22 per 100,000 people. It continued to decline thereafter even among people infected with HIV because of the development of a cocktail of drugs devised from molecular biological studies that suppressed the virus's multiplication in the body. Still, new strains resistant to drugs evolved constantly. Moreover, by the end of the decade, confidence in the cocktail was leading young gay men to revive the practice of promiscuous, unprotected sex, and public health officials were worried that the incidence of HIV infection might rise once again.

At the end of the century, health was one of the nation's largest industries. In 1998, drug company revenues totaled $102 billion, 85 percent higher than just five years earlier. Almost nine in ten Americans were covered by some form of health insurance.

Crime and the Schools. The crime rate steadily declined between 1991 and 1998, with especially sharp drops in murder and robbery. Analysts found the reasons partly in the job-rich prosperity, which diminished desperation, partly in the get-tough policies of state and local law enforcement. In mid-1998, the United States led the world in the size of its prison system, holding 1.8 million men and women behind bars—1 in every 150 Americans, a rate double that of the mid-80s. In New York City, Mayor Rudolph Giuliani, elected in 1993 after pledging to crack down on criminals, strongly backed the police; crime in the city fell 44 percent in five years, while the murder rate dropped 48 percent.

But while the streets grew safer, the schools appeared to grow dangerous. A series of deadly school shootings that began in 1997 took the lives of a number of teenagers. The worst such episode occurred at Columbine High School in the Denver suburb of Littleton, Colorado, where on April 20, 1999, two heavily armed students stalked through the school at lunchtime, spraying gunfire on their classmates and eventually turning their guns on themselves. Thirteen students and faculty died, while twenty-three were wounded. The two

The father of a child killed at Columbine High School at a protest for gun control outside the National Rifle Association convention in Denver, April 1999.

murderers, like most of their classmates the product of white, middle-class families, were said to be angry about being teased.

Stunned by the school violence, Americans wondered whether safety could be found anywhere. In fact, the number of students killed in violent incidents across the country had not increased, but the shootings stimulated debate about dysfunctional families, gun control, the impact on teenage behavior of violence on television and in popular music such as gangsta rap, and the effect of deaths of rock stars like Kurt Cobain, the lead singer of Nirvana, who took his life in 1994.

RESENTMENTS

The resentments that produced the Republican earthquake in 1994 remained in force. As in the 1980s, membership in conservative and fundamentalist Christian denominations grew steadily. Attacks on abortion rights, feminism, affirmative action, immigrants, and the Clintons pervaded talk radio, Christian radio as well as TV stations, and, increasingly, the Internet. The Web, whose content was unregulated, provided a medium for some conservatives to billboard venomous, usually unfounded disparagements of public figures and social trends. Radical anti-abortionists defaced or bombed abortion clinics. Outside an abortion clinic in Florida in 1995, one of them shot and killed a physician and his bodyguard, and at a clinic near Boston another killed two and wounded five others.

Secularism, freewheeling behavior, and now violence in the public schools troubled many Americans, social conservatives especially. Many supported a voucher system that would permit them to send their children to private (including parochial) schools at public expense. The conservatives, unhappy with the breakdown of "family values," were also disquieted by the ongoing decline of the traditional nuclear family, in which a married couple lived with their minor children under the same roof, and its replacement by a dizzying diversity of spousal, partnering, and parenting relationships.

Conservatives were also angered by the support the National Endowment for the Humanities provided to artists whom they considered sacrilegious or morally offensive—for example, Andreas Serrano, whose photographs included a depiction of a crucifix in a container of urine. They contended that traditional views of American history and culture were being excluded from the classroom in favor of a "politically correct" but intellectually distorted emphasis on "multiculturalism," women, and minority groups.

Conservatives of all stripes, including women and the growing number of people of color who counted themselves in the fold, found common ground in warring against affirmative action. In 1996, Californians passed Proposition 209, an initiative that ended racial preferences in college admissions. That year, too, a federal appeals court in Texas barred the use within its jurisdiction of race in university admissions. Universities devised ways to get around the prohibition—for example, by taking social and economic disadvantage into account in evaluating applicants—but like Proposition 209, the court's ruling set back efforts at achieving racial and cultural diversity in higher education. In 1995, in *Adarand Construction v. Pena,* the Supreme Court bolstered the turn away from broad programs of affirmative action. Deciding against the federal programs that gave preference to minority contractors, the Court indicated that affirmative action programs had to assist individual victims of past discrimination rather than simply benefit minorities.

Violence on the Right. One theme that ran through the discontent among conservatives (but was not confined to them) was suspicion of government. Such misgivings were reflected in the popularity later in the decade of the TV show *The X-Files,* a fictional series about investigations into paranormal events that seemed attributable to space aliens but that shadowy powers always covered up. Wariness of government could be found across the political spectrum, but it was made especially acute on the far right by the government's own tragic actions.

At Ruby Ridge, Idaho, in 1992, dozens of FBI agents, federal marshals, and local as well as state police laid siege for months against an armed white separatist named Randy Weaver, who was convinced that the United States had come under the control of Jews, communists, atheists, homosexuals, perhaps even Satan himself. Weaver had committed a minor crime and was holed up in a cabin with his family. The confrontation resulted in the deaths of his wife and thirteen-year-old son before Weaver was persuaded to give himself up. Then in Waco, Texas, during February the next year, federal agents tried to search for illegal firearms at a fortified religious community occupied by the Branch Davidians and their apocalyptic leader, David Koresh. The Davidians opened fire, and in the ensuing gun battle people on both sides were killed and wounded. In April, federal agents acting under orders from Attorney General Janet Reno assaulted the compound. A fire broke out—whether Koresh or the agents ignited it is disputed—wiping out all seventy-six of the occupants, including women and children.

The episodes at Ruby Ridge and Waco galvanized the far right, stimulating the formation of more than 1,000 patriot groups and armed militias in thirty-six states. On the Internet, theories that the government was intent on wiping out white Christians were posted, along with information about how to construct bombs and other weapons. While such theories ranged ideologically from traditional conservatism to blatant racism, most viewed the federal government as an instrument of a conspiracy to impose a totalitarian regime on the United States. Such angry convictions led Timothy McVeigh, a decorated veteran of the Gulf War, and his ally, Terry Nichols, in April 1995 to truck-bomb the federal building in Oklahoma City, killing 168 people, including children in a day-care nursery on the second floor, and injuring scores more. Tried and convicted of the crime, McVeigh was executed in 2001, and Nichols was sentenced to life in prison.

Renewing the Domestic Agenda

In domestic affairs during his second term, Clinton continued the cautious and fiscally conservative strategy he had adopted after the Republican victory in 1994. Mindful that Republicans still controlled Congress, he generally refrained from major legislative initiatives, preferring modest, at times tepid proposals. But he placed high on his agenda issues that he knew his Democratic constituency and centrist Republicans cared about, notably the environment, gun control, and tobacco.

Clinton paid no more than lip service to the cause of reforming campaign financing, an issue that had been stimulated by the increasingly large amounts of money that candidates and the major parties raised to pay for electioneering. Vice-President Al Gore was accused of having raised funds illegally during a gathering at a Buddhist temple in Los Angeles and of using his office telephone to contact donors. Gore pleaded that he was ignorant of the nature of the temple event and that there was no "controlling legal authority" over how he used his telephone. In 1998, Senators John McCain, a Republican, and Russell Feingold, a Democrat,

"Clinton issued executive orders to protect from development more than 72 million acres of wildlife habitats, wetlands, and roadless forests, a total that placed him third behind only Jimmy Carter and Theodore Roosevelt in land protection."

introduced a bill to curb reliance on large campaign contributions, but Republican senators blocked the measure, alleging that it was unconstitutional and did nothing to stop the advertisements by labor unions and other groups that tended to favor Democrats.

In 1997, Clinton signed a bill that provided some tax cuts and committed the federal government to achieving a balanced budget by 2002. By the opening of 1998, the combination of the government's fiscal restraint and the economic boom, which raised tax revenues, seemed likely to produce a balanced budget three years ahead of schedule. In his State of the Union address in January, Clinton predicted a small budgetary surplus for the next fiscal year, and the following January the Congressional Budget Office predicted that federal surpluses would total $2.6 trillion during the next decade. Although some Republicans wanted to bite into the surplus with tax cuts, Clinton successfully refused, insisting that most of it should go first to protecting Social Security, a position that enjoyed widespread support.

GUN CONTROL, THE ENVIRONMENT, AND TOBACCO

Clinton responded to the mounting demand for gun control—including a "Million Mom March" on Washington, D.C., in May 2000—that followed the Columbine shootings. Together with congressional Democrats, he pushed for background checks on people who bought guns at gun shows, the one remaining major gun-sale venue that was completely unregulated. But gun-show promoters blocked the necessary legislation, arguing that such checks would put them out of business.

The president provided funds to deal with more than 1,000 hazardous waste sites, including those at nuclear-weapons facilities. He established or expanded several national monuments, one of which added 1 million acres to the Grand Canyon National Park. He also issued executive orders to protect from development more than 72 million acres of wildlife habitats, wetlands, and roadless forests, a total that placed him third behind only Jimmy Carter and Theodore Roosevelt in land protection. In 1996–97, at Clinton's urging, Congress enacted a bill to bolster the regulation of pesticides, and the administration put new air-quality standards in place to reduce the levels of soot and ozone on the ground. And at an international conference in Kyoto, Japan, in 1997, the Clinton administration, building on the Bush administration's agreements at Rio de Janeiro in 1992, pushed for a treaty that would reduce the emission of gases that contribute to global warming.

Early in the decade, the federal government banned smoking on interstate buses and airline flights of six hours or less; in 1994, Amtrak followed suit for train trips of short and medium duration. The war against smoking scored enormous victories in suits against the tobacco companies by numerous states, all of them seeking compensation for the millions of dollars they spent through Medicaid for smokers' illnesses. In June 1997, the tobacco companies reached a preliminary joint settlement with forty states that called for their industry to spend $368 billion over twenty-five years mainly on antismoking campaigns. In return, the tobacco companies would gain immunity from further lawsuits. Clinton fought for the congressional assent that the joint settlement required, but approval was defeated in the Senate as the result of a multimillion-dollar lobbying campaign by the tobacco industry and the opposition of key tobacco-state senators. Still, by November 1998, acting independently of Congress, all fifty states had reached a $206 billion settlement with the industry for the costs of caring for sick smokers.

In 1997, responding to a sustained campaign by David Kessler, the head of the Food and Drug Administration, the Clinton administration declared tobacco an addictive drug subject to regulation by the FDA. In March 2000, the Supreme Court, in a 5-to-4 decision, ruled that the FDA lacked jurisdiction over tobacco, but the year before, Clinton's Justice Department, following the precedent set by the states, sued the tobacco industry to recover billions of federal dollars spent on smoking-related health care, accusing cigarette makers of a "coordinated campaign of fraud and deceit."

SEX, LIES, AND IMPEACHMENT

From early 1998, Clinton's ability to advance even a modest domestic agenda was greatly undermined by the scandals that

> *"Clinton's Justice Department, following the precedent set by the states, sued the tobacco industry to recover billions of federal dollars spent on smoking-related health care, accusing cigarette makers of a 'coordinated campaign of fraud and deceit.'"*

began washing over him and led to his impeachment the following year. The scandals came to light as a result of the work conducted by Kenneth Starr, who in August 1994 had been appointed a special prosecutor to look into the Whitewater affair. During the next several years, Starr was authorized to investigate several other allegations of impropriety in the Clinton administration. Then in January 1998, Starr received evidence from a government employee named Linda Tripp that Monica Lewinsky, a young government intern, had been having an affair with the president that included her performing oral sex on him during visits to the Oval Office.

Meanwhile, in late 1997, the attorneys for Paula Jones, who was still pursuing her sexual harassment suit against the president, had heard rumors of an affair between Lewinsky and Clinton. Hoping to demonstrate that Clinton showed a pattern of predatory sexual behavior, they obtained a ruling from the Supreme Court requiring Clinton to answer their questions, establishing the precedent that a sitting president could be compelled to testify in a civil suit concerning actions that took place before his presidency. On January 17, responding under oath to questions by Jones's lawyers, Clinton denied having a romantic relationship with Lewinsky.

At Starr's request, Attorney General Janet Reno authorized him to enlarge his multiple investigations of Clinton into whether the president had lied in his testimony to Jones's lawyers and had sought to obstruct justice by encouraging Lewinsky to cover up their affair.

Tightening the Noose. By now, January 1998, word of the information Tripp had given Starr was making headlines. In a statement on national television at the end of January, Clinton, shaking his finger, emphatically declared, "I did not have sexual relations with that woman." He refused to discuss the matter further publicly, but he told his family, cabinet, and advisers that the stories about his relationship with Lewinsky were absolutely untrue. Hillary Clinton blamed the array of investigations into the couple's activities on a "vast right-wing conspiracy." Frenzied discussions of the case filled newspapers, television, radio, and the Internet for months. In 2000, Philip Roth remarked in his novel *The Human Stain* that in the summer of 1998 "a president's penis was on everyone's mind," and his alleged Oval Office peccadilloes "revived America's oldest communal passion . . . the ecstasy of sanctimony."

In August, Lewinsky, whom Starr had threatened to prosecute, agreed to testify in return for a grant of immunity. Besides telling a federal grand jury in graphic detail about her affair with Clinton, she turned over a blue dress that, according to her, was stained with the president's semen. Clinton realized that DNA testing of the stain would demonstrate that the semen was his. In mid-August, in videotaped testimony to Starr and the federal grand jury, he conceded that his conduct with Lewinsky had been "wrong," but insisted that he been legally accurate in denying to Jones's lawyers that he had engaged in a "sexual relationship" with Lewinsky because he took such a relationship to mean intercourse. He told the American people in a four-minute nationally televised address that he had "misled" them and done injury to his family. Still, he defiantly insisted that he had not lied under oath nor asked anyone to lie for him.

On September 9, Starr gave Congress a videotape of Clinton's grand jury testimony and a 445-page report. The report detailed Clinton's sexual contacts with Lewinsky and listed eleven possible grounds for impeachment, some of which focused on charges that he had lied under oath. Congress quickly released both the full report and the videotape to the public. On October 8, the House voted to launch an impeachment inquiry by a solid majority of 258 to 176, with 31 Democrats joining most of the Republicans in support.

Slipping Through. The public had long thought Clinton was lying about his relationship with Lewinsky, but it had persistently registered high approval of his performance in office. Now Clinton's conduct was brushed off by leading Democrats and his supporters among feminists, blacks, gays, and union officials as sex between two consenting adults, covered up as anyone might conceal an illicit affair, but by no means worthy of impeachment. "It's hard to get really excited," a waitress remarked. "What does the Clintons' sex life have to do with me?" Meanwhile, the public standing of Starr, Linda Tripp, and the Republican Congress plummeted. In the congressional elections in November, the Democrats gained five seats in the House while maintaining their number in the Senate and in state contests. Newt Gingrich, under fire himself for questionable financial dealings, announced that he would leave Congress.

His expected successor in the speakership, Robert Livingston of Louisiana, also left as news stories began to circulate that he had engaged in adultery.

All the same, on December 19, 1998, the House in a strongly partisan vote **resolved to impeach Clinton** on two articles—perjury and obstruction of justice—making him the second president (after Andrew Johnson) to be so treated. On January 27, 1999, the impeachment trial began in the Senate, with the House leadership presenting the case against the president. After more than a month of partisan debate, the prosecutors failed to come near the two-thirds majority (67 votes) necessary for conviction. The Senate voted 55 to 45 against the perjury charge and 50 to 50 on the charge of obstructing justice. Neither charge gained a single Democratic vote; 10 Republicans opposed the charge of perjury, 5 the charge of obstructing justice.

THE CLINTON RECORD

Pollsters found that Americans overwhelmingly believed Clinton guilty of the charges, but that the vast majority did not want him removed from office. People, wiseacres were saying, were far more interested in the Dow Jones (the stock

President Clinton, in the White House Rose Garden, apologizes for the behavior that led the House to impeach him, December 1998. Behind him is Vice-President Al Gore, and to the right Hillary Rodham Clinton.

market indicator) than in Paula Jones. Indeed, they cared much more about the booming economy, not to mention how to deal with the looming surplus, the solvency of Social Security, the increasing costs of medical care, and the emerging need to revitalize the military in the wake of post–Cold War budget reductions. Many had nodded vigorous assent when shortly before the impeachment trial began, Clinton delivered a confident State of the Union address exhorting the assembled Congress to deal with the people's business in "a spirit of civility and bipartisanship." Now that the ordeal of impeachment was over, they wanted their government to get on with their business.

So far as a large majority of Americans were concerned, Clinton had attended to their business very well. He had successfully pursued the post–Cold War work of resolving or controlling bitter antagonisms abroad and extending the global reach of democratic capitalism. Wrestling with a Congress that was often hostile, he had managed the economy through a record-breaking prosperity, reformed the welfare system, safeguarded Social Security, protected the environment, advanced the interests of minority groups and women, and made millions of people feel that he cared about them.

Democrats, savoring Clinton's victory and confident in his accomplishments, felt optimistic about keeping the presidency in the upcoming 2000 election. But a deep-seated ambivalence had emerged about the United States' role in the post–Cold War world, doubts among many—revealed, for example, by the lack of support for sending troops to Kosovo—that its military commitments ought to match its global economic engagements. And the glow of good times had been persistently blotched through the nineties by the dark spots of social and cultural division. The United States remained in a sense two nations, the one secular, multiracial, and supportive of widening civil liberties, the other religious, predominantly white, and discontented with the consequences of broad social freedom. The differences had expressed themselves in the partisan divisions that had prevailed through most of Clinton's two terms. Clinton had managed to straddle them to a remarkable degree, but the revelations of shortcomings that led

	Chronology
March 1989	*Exxon Valdez* oil spill in Prince William Sound, Alaska.
January–February 1991	The Gulf War.
December 1991	Soviet Union falls, replaced by the Commonwealth of Independent States.
1992	Apartheid ends in South Africa.
November 1993	The North American Free Trade Agreement (NAFTA).
April 1995	Truck bomb kills 168 in federal building at Oklahoma City.
December 19, 1998	House votes to impeach President Clinton.
April 20, 1999	Shooting at Columbine High School in Littleton, Colorado.
2000	The complete structure of human DNA is deciphered.

to his impeachment had given character and morality unusually high places on the election agenda. In 2000, despite their defeat on impeachment, Republicans hopefully geared up to battle for control of the White House.

Suggested Reading

Janet Abbate, *Inventing the Internet* (1999)

James McGregor Burns and Georgia Sorenson, *Dead Center: Clinton-Gore Leadership and the Perils of Moderation* (1999)

George Bush and Brent Scowcroft, *A World Transformed* (1998)

Haynes Johnson, *The Best of Times: America in the Clinton Years* (2001)

Herbert Parmet, *George Bush: The Life of a Lone Star Yankee* (1997)

Richard Posner, *An Affair of State: The Investigation, Impeachment, and Trial of President Clinton* (1999)

Roberto Suro, *Strangers Among Us: How Latino Immigration Is Transforming America* (1998)

Stephen and Abigail Thernstrom, *America in Black and White: One Nation, Indivisible, Race in Modern America* (1997)

A STATE OF SHOCK: 2000–2001

The election of 2000 proved to be one of the closest in American history. It was hardly over before the economy suddenly began slowing and throwing its dot-com sector into a tailspin. Then, some nine months later, terrorists struck New York City and Washington, D.C., shocking the nation and the world.

Election 2000

The Democratic nominee was Vice-President Al Gore, a native of Tennessee and a Harvard graduate, the son of a U.S. senator and himself the holder of national elective office since he won a House seat at age twenty-eight. Gore lacked Clinton's personal magnetism—people thought him wooden—but he was respected for his staunch environmentalism, enthusiasm for technological innovation, and detailed knowledge of public policy. In an apparent appeal to religious and social conservatives, he chose as his running mate Connecticut senator Joseph Lieberman, a middle-of-the-roader and an openly observant orthodox Jew who had publicly denounced Clinton for his sexual conduct. He was the first member of his faith to be nominated for the vice-presidency by a major party.

The Republican nomination went to George W. Bush of Texas, a son of the former president. A graduate of Yale and the Harvard Business School, Bush had compiled a reputation as a heavy drinker, mediocre businessman, and intellectual lightweight. But then, at age forty, he had become a teetotaler and born-again Christian. Affable and self-confident, he won election and then reelection to the Texas governorship, establishing a reputation for bipartisanship in the service of socially and economically conservative policies. He used his family name and contacts to accumulate a formidable presidential war chest. Bush's choice for vice-president, an attempt to offset his relative youth and inexperience in government, especially in foreign affairs, was Richard (Dick) Cheney, a Republican stalwart who had been President Bush's secretary of defense during the Gulf War.

Gore distanced himself from Clinton the man, whose character the voters so disapproved of, while associating himself in a gingerly fashion with the Clinton record, which they so much admired—22 million new jobs, the lowest unemployment in thirty years, the highest home ownership ever, the longest economic expansion in history. Gore promised to defend ordinary Americans against high medical drug prices, inadequate education, and the Republican insistence on using the surplus to finance tax reductions that would mainly benefit the wealthy.

Bush, on his part, campaigned for "compassionate conservatism"—by which he seemed to mean a government that was lean and limited but willing to care for those in need, especially by enlisting the private sector, including religious groups. He argued for overhauling Social Security by giving people the right to divert some of their payroll taxes into private investments; advocated educational improvement through a federal program of school vouchers that parents could use for tuition at private schools; and defended the Republican tax-cut proposals on grounds that the money in the surplus belonged to the American people and ought rightfully to be returned to them. He also insisted that the country deserved trustworthy leaders of character, a clear allusion to the scandals of the Clinton White House. Contrary to expectations, Bush fared well in several televised presidential debates, holding his own with Gore on the issues and besting him, many thought, in the realm of personal demeanor and likability.

The field included two third-party candidates: Patrick Buchanan on the right and Ralph Nader on the left, both attacking the influence of big money on politics and the North American Free Trade Agreement. While Buchanan seemed no problem to Bush, it appeared that Nader might siphon off enough votes from Gore to cost him more than one state. Pollsters predicted that the election would be close.

DISPUTED OUTCOME

On election evening, November 7, the television networks followed their long-standing practice of calling the election state by state, using polls that asked people how they had voted. According to their projections, Bush had won most of the states from the Appalachian Mountains to the Rockies and from the Canadian border to the Gulf of Mexico. Gore had taken most of the West Coast and the Northeast as well as the industrial states in the upper Midwest. By late evening, it was evident that the next president would be the candidate who won Florida. The networks had earlier given the state to Gore, then decided it was too close to call, and finally, at 2:15 A.M., announced that it had gone for Bush.

In accord with Florida law, the closeness of the vote triggered an automatic recount of the entire state, which gave the victory to Bush by 930 votes. However, Democrats charged that the balloting had been distorted by irregularities, the most important involving the counting of punch-card ballots. In the punch-card method of voting, people registered their choices by poking out and removing a small indented rectangle (called a "chad"). A machine counted the votes by detecting the holes, but if the chads were not completely removed, the machine would likely not record the vote.

The election was contested for a month in a storm of press conferences, demonstrations, and, most important, lawsuits. In the crucial round of litigation, the Gore campaign, believing their candidate had really won the election, sought manual recounts of the punch cards in selected counties, while the Bush campaign, seeing victory in the status quo, fought to block any recounts. The Florida state supreme court, ruling in favor of the Gore campaign, authorized the manual recounts and instructed the secretary of state to accept them after the date by which, according to state law, the counties had to submit their voting results. The recounts proceeded, and Bush's margin of victory steadily diminished.

Republicans cried foul, angrily contending that the Gore forces were attempting to steal the election. They said that the Democrats' insistence on manual recounts invited partisan vote counting, since deciding whether, for example, a partially removed chad was evidence of an intent to vote for Bush or Gore would be subjective. The Bush campaign appealed the Florida court decision to the Supreme Court, claiming that it denied their candidate equal protection of the laws.

The Court's decision in *Bush v. Gore*, handed down on December 12, consisted of two rulings. By 7 to 2, the Court halted the recounts ordered by the Florida court because, as Bush's lawyers had argued, they violated equal protection of the laws. But going further, a majority of only 5 to 4 held that no constitutionally acceptable recount procedure could be completed before the electoral college was to meet to cast

Democratic and Republican Party observers oversee the manual recount of presidential ballots, West Palm Beach, Florida, November 11, 2000.

its votes. The latter ruling effectively gave Florida to Bush, and Gore conceded in a gracious statement on nationwide television.

Many Americans considered the Court's decision blatantly partisan. Commentators quickly pointed out that the majority of 5 had all been appointed by Republicans and were the Court's most conservative members. They also noted that while the majority usually preferred to leave the states to govern their own affairs, in this case they had usurped Florida's right to manage its election procedures. In a blistering dissent, Justice John Paul Stevens observed: "Although we may never know with complete certainty the identity of the winner of this year's presidential election, the identity of the loser is perfectly clear. It is the nation's confidence in the judge as an impartial guardian of the rule of law."

The outrage was intensified by the fact that Gore had won the popular vote, beating Bush by a margin of 540,000. The election was the first since 1892, when Benjamin Harrison had gained the presidency, in which the loser in the popular vote won in the electoral vote. The outcome spotlighted the undemocratic nature of the electoral college, which awards voters in states with a small population far greater weight in presidential contests than it does voters in states with a large population. It also called attention to the variations in quality of vote-counting machines in different areas within states—and to the fact that the more error-prone machines tended to be used in counties with relatively large numbers of low-income and minority voters.

No matter the dispute: analysis of the nationwide vote revealed that Bush won because the prosperity of the nineties had not helped Gore as much as good times historically tended to benefit the candidate of the incumbent party. Despite Gore's attempts to distance himself from Clinton, he suffered from his association with the scandals of the administration. He also lost significant support to Ralph Nader, who called for ridding politics of the corruptions of big money and who won 2.7 million votes, including almost 100,000 in Florida. Democrats won enough Senate races—including a victory for Hillary Rodham Clinton in New York—to produce a 50–50 tie in that chamber, and they narrowed the Republican margin of control in the House from 19 to 10.

> *"The election was the first since 1892, when Benjamin Harrison had gained the presidency, in which the loser in the popular vote won in the electoral vote."*

The Bush Presidency: Beginnings

The night the Supreme Court ended the election, Bush promised the nation, "Whether you voted for me or not, I will do my best to serve your interests, and I will work to earn your respect." In his inaugural address, an eloquent reminder of the nation's principles, he adopted a conciliatory tone reminiscent of Jefferson's two centuries earlier, declaring, "America has never been united by blood or birth or soil. We are bound by ideals that move us beyond our backgrounds, lift us above our interests and teach us what it means to be citizens."

Bush appointed to his cabinet several women and African Americans, including Colin Powell as secretary of state, a Hispanic American, and two Asian Americans. But while some of his domestic appointees were moderates—for example, the head of the Environmental Protection Agency—his choices for the most powerful domestic posts were decidedly to the right of center. His secretary of the interior, a protégé of James Watt in Colorado, opposed strong federal control of land use and favored allowing corporations to assess their own performance in meeting environmental regulations. His head of Health and Human Services was a staunch opponent of abortion and, as governor of Wisconsin, had cut the state's welfare rolls by 90 percent by pushing through the nation's toughest welfare-to-work program. Bush's most controversial appointment was his nominee for attorney general, John Ashcroft, who had just been defeated for reelection to a Senate seat from Missouri. A devout fundamentalist Christian, Ashcroft had sought to criminalize abortion, fought desegregation of the St. Louis schools, and blocked the appointment of a black state jurist to a federal judgeship by grossly misrepresenting his record on the death penalty. Critics wondered how anyone with such right-wing convictions could fairly enforce the nation's laws, including those guaranteeing civil rights and a woman's right to choose. Ashcroft was nevertheless confirmed by his former Senate colleagues, some of whom said he was in fact highly ethical and fair-minded.

GOVERNING FROM THE RIGHT

Bush's cabinet appointments revealed that, for all his attention to conciliation, he saw no reason in the closeness of the election to back away from his fundamentally conservative domestic agenda. Political circumstances augured well for getting what he wanted. For the first time since 1954, Republicans controlled the presidency, the House, and the Senate (the latter because Vice-President Cheney could vote when it split evenly on a measure). Bush asked Congress to enact a $1.6 trillion tax cut, an education bill that authorized school vouchers, and a measure (called a "faith-based initiative") authorizing religious organizations to give federal welfare assistance. He appointed a commission to look into the safeguarding of Social Security, choosing members who, observers predicted, were likely to recommend at least partial privatization of the system.

The tax cut loomed as Bush's highest priority, especially now that the economy might be heading toward recession. The downturn had begun suddenly at the end of 2000, revealing itself in the collapse of new-economy companies, the dot-coms that had seemed to defy the economic laws of gravity by operating at a loss while their stock prices soared. By early 2001, the NASDAQ stock index had plummeted some 60 percent from its high in March 2000, and the Dow Jones index had fallen about 10 percent. Corporations were cutting back on capital spending and production, consumer confidence was declining, and the unemployment rate was going up.

Bush now contended that the tax cut was needed to stimulate the economy. Democrats and some moderate Republicans objected that it largely favored the wealthy, would put little into the pockets of people who needed money, and would impact the economy too far in the future to avoid recession in the near term. Although the administration met critics of the bill partway, the bulk of the tax relief remained slated for upper-income taxpayers. The bill reduced income-tax rates across all brackets, abolished the so-called marriage penalty, and provided for the eventual elimination of the estate tax. On May 26, a heavily Republican but bipartisan majority sent Bush for signature a $1.35 trillion tax cut, the largest in a generation, to be spread over ten years. Analysts estimated that the reduction in tax revenues promised to starve new spending programs far into the future, which made the Bush tax cut a means to the Republican end of reducing the size and influence of the federal government.

RESISTANCE AND SENATOR JEFFORDS

In the areas of energy and environment, Bush quickly reversed a regulatory rule that Clinton had issued to reduce the amount of the poison arsenic allowed in drinking water and proposed to roll back Clinton's orders removing millions of national-forest acres from development. Sidestepping energy conservation, he emphasized policies to increase supplies. Bush issued an energy plan that called for a revived commitment to nuclear power, noting that nuclear plants already supplied about one-fifth of the nation's electricity "safely and without pollution," and he asked Congress for authority to open up the Arctic National Wildlife Preserve to drilling for gas and oil.

Bush's aggressive conservatism, however, aroused resistance, both among the public at large and within Congress, especially in the closely divided Senate. His action on arsenic provoked especially widespread criticism. Polls showed that two out of three people thought he cared more about protecting large corporate interests than about protecting ordinary working people. His faith-based initiative was stalled, and his call for opening the wildlife preserve to drilling faced vigorous opposition in the Senate. Congress refused to endorse school vouchers. In December, though, after Bush agreed to leave that provision out, Congress passed—and the president

signed—a bill that made schools accountable for higher standards of student achievement and provided federal funds to assist them in reaching that goal.

The prospects for Bush's conservative initiatives suddenly dimmed further on May 24, 2001, when James M. Jeffords, a veteran Republican senator from Vermont, stunned the nation by announcing that he was quitting the Republican Party to become an independent and that he would vote to give control of the Senate to the Democrats. A moderate Republican, Jeffords was an environmentalist and an advocate of abortion rights and gay rights. In disagreement with Bush over the size of the tax cut, he was willing to support it if Bush had agreed to fully finance programs for special education, a commitment the president and the Senate leadership were willing to make. Announcing his defection, Jeffords declared that the Republican Party had grown too conservative, adding, "Given the changing nature of the national party, it has become a struggle for our leaders to deal with me and for me to deal with them."

Democrats, jubilant, predicted that measures such as drilling in the wildlife preserve and the privatization of Social Security stood much less chance of passage. But while they now controlled the Senate, that body remained one of the most closely divided in American history; and conservative Republicans continued to dominate the House. If moderates could block Bush's conservative programs, conservatives could foil moderate or liberal initiatives. Indicative of the possibilities for standoff, a bill to reform campaign financing passed the Senate in the spring but languished in the House. (It cleared Congress and was signed into law by President Bush at the end of March 2002. By then, the bill had gained support from Republicans eager after the scandalous collapse of the Enron Corporation, an energy conglomerate whose books had been cooked, to sanitize their campaign connections to large corporations.)

AMERICA FIRST

Bush's domestic conservatism was complemented by what many observers saw as a tendency to reduce the United States' engagement in the world, to adopt a go-it-alone posture toward the nation's friends and an antagonizing one toward others. On taking office, Bush treated the Russians coldly, delaying a meeting with their president, Vladimir V. Putin, expelling their diplomats for spying, and charging them with selling dangerous military technology to the Middle East. The administration scrapped an eight-year effort to achieve stronger international controls over chemical and biological weapons on grounds that the proposed agreement jeopardized the privacy of pharmaceutical laboratories and the secrecy of government programs. Bush also froze negotiations with North Korea that Clinton, partly to discourage that nation's development of a nuclear arsenal, had initiated.

Most important, Bush insisted that the United States would pursue the development of a National Missile Defense (NMD) even if it jeopardized relations with Russia. And he seemed to repudiate American participation in the international effort to combat global warming.

National Missile Defense. After the end of the Cold War and the scrapping of Reagan's Strategic Defense Initiative, enthusiasts of missile defense called for protecting the country against the relatively small number of warheads that might be launched either by accident or by design from rogue states like North Korea or Iraq. Skeptics continued to question whether any such system could ever be effective, but by the end of Clinton's administration, antimissile technologies had advanced far enough—or so their advocates said—to warrant taking steps toward the installation of test facilities. The steps, however, would violate the Anti-Ballistic Missile (ABM) Treaty, which the United States and the Soviet Union had concluded in 1972. Clinton left the decision on the matter to the next president.

On May 1, 2001, Bush announced that the United States intended to develop and deploy a National Missile Defense. He implied that the ABM Treaty was out of date and should be abandoned if necessary. To allay Russian fears, he proposed that the NMD would be accompanied by substantial unilateral cuts in the U.S. nuclear arsenal. Reaction at home was mixed, with some observers assailing the president for withdrawing the nation's support from an agreement that had helped keep the world from nuclear war for thirty years. The dissenters pointed out, echoing the opponents of Star Wars, that the NMD would cost more than $100 billion, would be technically dubious, and would provoke a renewal of the nuclear arms race with Russia.

At first, Putin's reaction to the plan was unfavorable, but at a meeting with Bush in Genoa, Italy, in July he said that coupling NMD with cuts in nuclear arms might allow modification of the ABM Treaty without precipitating a renewal of the arms race. The Europeans remained unpersuaded that the NMD either was needed or would be dependable, but they were willing to go along with Bush's plans if they did not upset relations with Russia. In mid-December, Bush, rejecting compromise, formally notified Russia that the United States would withdraw from the ABM Treaty completely so that it could proceed with the development of the NMD. Putin called the withdrawal a "mistake" but said little else, an indication that, like Gorbachev before him, he expected that the Russian nuclear arsenal could likely overwhelm an NMD for at least the next quarter century.

Global Warming. In March 2001, Bush announced that the United States would not abide by the 1997 Kyoto Protocol to reduce the emission of greenhouse gases that cause global warming. An extension of the accord on climate that the first President Bush had signed at Rio de Janeiro in 1992, the Kyoto agreement committed its signatories, including the United States, to reduce their greenhouse gas output to 5.2 percent below the level of 1990 within fifteen years. Bush withdrew from the protocol partly because it did not require reductions by China and India, developing nations that were major emitters of greenhouse gases. But his most important objection rested on his unwillingness to limit carbon dioxide emission when the economy was slowing. Bush explained to the chancellor of Germany, who was visiting the White House, "We will not do anything that harms our economy, because first things first are the people who live in America."

Bush's decision infuriated European leaders. The United States was in effect asserting that it had the right to pervert the atmosphere covering every other nation: since the United States emitted fully one-quarter of the world's greenhouse gases, its withdrawal from the Kyoto agreement jeopardized the prospects of significantly reducing their presence in the atmosphere.

Before departing on a trip to Europe in June, Bush tried to soften the impression of his seeming indifference to the rest of the world by publicly acknowledging that temperatures were in fact rising because of human activities. But while he insisted that the United States remained committed to join with other nations under the 1992 accord to reduce the threat of global warming, he did little more than appoint a committee to review the issue. In late July, 178 nations arrived at a final agreement for putting the Kyoto accords into effect. One European official, alluding to the nonparticipation of the United States, remarked, "I prefer an imperfect agreement that is living than a perfect agreement that doesn't exist."

Struck by Terror

On Tuesday, September 11, 2001, America's world was suddenly and dramatically transformed. Within the space of an hour and a half that morning, two passenger airlines took off from Logan Airport in Boston, and two others took off from Newark Airport in New Jersey and Dulles Airport in Washington, D.C. All four, bound for California, were loaded with fuel. At some point not long after the planes were airborne, each was commandeered by four or five hijackers armed with box cutters and knives.

At 8:45 A.M., one of the planes from Boston crashed into the north tower of the 110-story World Trade Center in lower Manhattan, tearing a huge hole in the building and setting it ablaze. Eighteen minutes later, the second plane out of Boston struck the south tower and exploded. At 9:43, the plane from Dulles crashed into the Pentagon. Shortly after 10, the south tower of the World Trade Center, its reinforced concrete supports severely weakened by the intense heat of the jet-fuel fire, collapsed, showering a torrent of debris into the streets below. Just before 10:30, the north tower followed its twin into the dust, releasing a tremendous cloud of debris and smoke and severely damaging a nearby 47-story building—later in the day it, too, fell—and setting others in the area on fire. In Washington, in the meantime, the portion of the Pentagon that had been hit also collapsed.

> "Within less than an hour of the first crash at the World Trade Center, the Federal Aviation Administration halted all flights at American airports for the first time in the nation's history."

Passengers on the fourth flight, in touch with relatives via cell phones, learned about the attacks on the Trade Center and the Pentagon; they concluded that their plane was being flown to a target as well. Some decided to storm the cockpit, with the result that the plane crashed in a field southeast of Pittsburgh rather than into a building. (It was, in fact, headed toward the nation's capital.) All forty-four people aboard were killed.

Within less than an hour of the first crash at the World Trade Center, the Federal Aviation Administration halted all flights at American airports for the first time in the nation's history and diverted to Canada all transatlantic aircraft bound for the United States. President Bush was in Florida, but the White House was evacuated and so were all other federal office buildings in the capital. Secret Service agents armed with automatic rifles were deployed opposite the White House in Lafayette Park. In New York, the stock exchanges and all state government offices were closed.

At a news conference in the mid-afternoon, New York's Mayor Rudolph Giuliani, asked about the number killed, said, "I don't think we want to speculate about that—more than any of us can bear." That evening, the city reported that hundreds of its police officers and firefighters on the scene were dead or missing. In the weeks that followed, estimates of the deaths at the World Trade Center ran as high as 6,000 (they were later reduced to 3,000). Some 200 people died in the crash at the Pentagon.

BUSH TAKES CHARGE

Less than an hour after the attacks, President Bush said that the country had suffered an "apparent terrorist attack." Later in the day, having been flown to an air force base in Louisiana for his protection, he assured the country that appropriate steps were being taken to protect American security, including the placement of the U.S. military on high alert. By the late afternoon, investigations had identified nineteen Middle Eastern men as the hijackers, and as the likely sponsor of the attack Osama bin Laden, who was still living in Afghanistan under the protection of the Taliban, the radical Islamic group that controlled the country. That evening, Bush addressed the nation from the White House, declaring that "thousands of lives were suddenly ended by evil" and promising to hunt down the responsible parties.

On Friday, September 14, the president visited "Ground Zero," the site where the World Trade Center's twin towers had stood and where rescue crews were frantically digging through the rubble in the hope of finding survivors. As the workers chanted "USA, USA," some people in the crowd shouted to Bush that they could not hear him. "I can hear you," he responded. "The rest of the world hears you. And the people who knocked these buildings down will hear all of us soon." The workers roared approval. That same Friday, the Senate unanimously and the House by a margin of 420 to 1 voted to authorize the use of force against those responsible for the terrorist attacks, and both bodies enacted a $40 billion emergency spending bill to combat terrorism and assist the recovery efforts in New York and Washington. Bush ordered the De-

President Bush speaks to New York City firefighters at the site of the World Trade Center, three days after September 11, 2001.

fense Department to mobilize up to 50,000 reservists for "homeland defense."

On the evening of September 20, in a somber address to a joint session of Congress, Bush announced the start of a "War on Terror." Reasonably confident that Osama bin Laden was responsible for the crimes of September 11, he demanded that the Taliban turn bin Laden and all the leaders of the Al Qaeda terrorist group over to the appropriate authorities and shut down all the terrorist training camps in the country. "These demands are not open to negotiation or discussion," he went on, warning that if the Taliban did not hand over the terrorists, they would "share in their fate." Bush added that the United States' humanitarian aid to the people of Afghanistan, a severely impoverished country, would increase. He stressed that America's war was with the terrorists, not with Muslims or Islam, whose texts and teachings did not sanction terror. But he pledged that the war would extend to terrorists everywhere and to the nations that harbored them; indeed, that it would "not end until every terrorist group of global reach has been found, stopped, and defeated."

Bush announced to Congress that he was naming Pennsylvania governor Tom Ridge to a newly established post of homeland security director. During the following two weeks, he issued an executive order authorizing the government to freeze whatever funds terrorists might have access to in the United States. He also visited mosques, met with Muslim leaders, and strongly condemned violence and discrimination against Muslims. Islam was a religion of love, not hate, he said.

Like his father in the period before the Gulf War, Bush built a coalition of support for military action against the Taliban that included predominantly Muslim Pakistan and the nations of the former Soviet Union, whose populations also included many Muslims. The United Nations Security Council unanimously resolved to mount wide-ranging measures against terrorism, focusing especially on the financial support terrorists needed to carry out their acts. A key element in the work of persuasion was the increasingly convincing evidence that the United States compiled demonstrating Osama bin Laden's complicity in the September 11 attacks. The evidence was presented to the nation's European allies, and on October 4 Prime Minister Tony Blair of Britain detailed its contents in an address to Parliament that was broadcast to the world.

At home, some observers worried that the War on Terror would be endless, and they wondered just how the president would deal with the many nations that provided terrorists safe harbor. They were also apprehensive that war against terrorists abroad would lead to the deaths of many innocent people and that the search for them at home would threaten civil liberties. But Bush won high praise for the caution and deliberativeness with which he was handling the crisis, including his strong admonitions against intolerance toward Muslims. Polls showed that the overwhelming majority of Americans supported military action if the Taliban refused to comply with Bush's demands. The Pakistanis tried to get them to comply but failed.

On October 7, the United States began air strikes against Al Qaeda terrorist camps and Taliban military installations in Afghanistan, using improved versions of the precision bombing employed in the Gulf War. The ultimate aim was to force the Taliban out of power, replace them with a broadly representative government, capture or kill bin Laden, and destroy the Al Qaeda terrorist network and its facilities. Most of the ground forces were supplied by the Northern Alliance, a collection of anti-Taliban factions, tribesmen, and warlords. They were soon joined by small contingents of American special forces trained to operate in Afghanistan's forbidding deserts and mountains, which in the south and east included warrens of caves where bin Laden and his forces were believed to be based.

The war progressed rapidly, with the Taliban abandoning Kabul, the capital city, in late November, leaving their southern stronghold of Kandahar several weeks later, then fleeing into the mountains. The progress was aided by the support of many Afghans, joyful at being released from the oppressive Taliban rule—from, for example, their prohibitions against music, games, television, and radios, their insistence that men not shave, and their consignment of women to virtual imprisonment in their homes. In late December, an anti-Taliban coalition government was preparing to take power, and the Taliban and the Al Qaeda network were virtually defeated in Afghanistan. But bin Laden remained at large, and Washington was alive with talk that the United States might soon extend the war to other countries suspected of harboring terrorists, particularly Iraq and Somalia.

STATE OF THE NATION

The attacks of September 11 prompted an outpouring of patriotism rarely seen since Pearl Harbor. American flags appeared in shop windows and on homes, buildings, cars and trucks, overpasses, and bridges. Millions of Americans pinned red, white, and blue streamers on their jackets. Across the country, people attended services for the victims, sent money to assist their families, and gave blood for the survivors. Commentators everywhere extolled the heroism of the firefighters and police who died in the line of duty at the

Displays of memorials and pleas for information about loved ones missing in the attacks sprang up all over the streets of New York. This one was in Union Square.

World Trade Center. Thousands flocked to Ground Zero, now hallowed ground, solemnly peering at the smoldering ruins and the workmen removing the debris. Many posted prayers, notices of the missing, and poems on the protective chain-link fences at the site and on any available wall space (including phone booths) around the city.

September 11 heightened awareness of the fact that the United States, as the world's sole superpower, was an integral part of what was becoming a global civilization. The day after the attacks, the French newspaper *Le Monde* ran the headline "Nous sommes toutes les Américaines" (We are all Americans). The victims at the World Trade Center included the nationals of more than eighty nations. The multinational and multicultural nature of American society was revealed by the names of lost spouses, parents, and children, hundreds of them on posterboards pleading for information about them—people named Schwartzstein, Henrique and Calderon, Kikuchihara and Tsoy, Cassino, Staub, and Egan, Williams, Caulfield, and Wiswall.

On a sheet of paper tacked up in New York's Grand Central Station in late October, an anonymous poet cried out:

> Six thousand fallen heroes . . .
> The six thousand angels, their trumpets blaring
> Are calling us to arms,
> Waking us up from our selfish slumber
> To the truth of our lives, the evil in the world . . .
> We must stop, turn, stand up together as one,
> Arm in arm, pillars of strength.

A Sense of Vulnerability. To many Americans, national strength and unity seemed all the more necessary because September 11 had exposed a degree of anti-Americanism in parts of the Muslim world that spilled over into hatred. Some of it was rooted in the United States' support of Israel (Palestinian demonstrators celebrated the destruction of the World Trade Center towers). Perhaps more of it derived from America's vanguard role in globalization. After the Cold War, Americans had trumpeted the spread through the world of global corporations and free markets, but the widening power of international capitalism prompted protests even in the West, the most recent occurring at a meeting of the Group

"These events ended the nation's long-standing sense of domestic security and dramatically demonstrated that the marvelous technologies of contemporary civilization, from jet aircraft to the Internet, could be used to breach its defenses."

of Eight, the major powers in international trade, in Genoa, Italy, in July 2001. Similar economic resentments festered in the Third World, and they were compounded there by the intrusion of the social and cultural accompaniments of globalization, notably secularism and personal freedom, especially for women. The resentments helped fuel the growth of Islamic fundamentalism, including the militant-minority version invoked by Osama bin Laden.

Foreigners had not attacked the mainland United States since the War of 1812. Americans watched the television broadcasts of September 11—the planes veering into the Trade Center towers, the towers collapsing—with disbelief. "This is impossible," an observer remarked, capturing the widespread reaction. Nothing in the nation's experience had prepared it for these events. They ended its longstanding sense of domestic security and dramatically demonstrated that the marvelous technologies of contemporary civilization, from jet aircraft to the Internet, could be used to breach its defenses. Now the government warned its citizens that terrorist attacks might occur again, even predicting specific time spans of heightened risk. Officials noted that some of the attacks might draw on the technologies of biology.

The warnings seemed to come true early in October, when it was reported that an employee at a tabloid newspaper in Florida had died of anthrax and that one of his co-workers had been infected with the deadly microbe. During the next several weeks, anthrax cropped up elsewhere, notably in the form of a subcutaneous infection suffered by an assistant to the NBC newscaster Tom Brokaw and in a white powder that arrived in an envelope mailed to the office of Tom Daschle of North Dakota, the Senate majority leader. An anthrax scare swept the country, prompting people to buy out local stocks of Cipro, the principal antibiotic against it. No one knew who was responsible for sending the anthrax, but President Bush said he would not be surprised if it was Osama bin Laden.

America Is an Idea. A commentator suggested that between the end of the Cold War and September 11, the United States had been on "a holiday from history"—a decade-long romp free of cares about the economy at home and threats from abroad. But now the holiday was over. Indeed, the post–September 11 jitters worsened the economic slowdown.

1085

Letter to Tom Brokaw

Letter to Senator Daschle

Letters sent to Senator Tom Daschle, NBC news anchor Tom Brokaw, and others were found to be laden with deadly anthrax spores that spread through postal centers and the mail.

Many people refused to fly, stopped going to restaurants, theaters, or malls, and huddled close to home. War expenditures did not make up for the loss of commercial income. In December, taking further steps to stimulate the economy, the Federal Reserve Board reduced interest rates to their lowest levels since 1962. President Bush urged Americans to return to their normal pastimes, especially shopping, and pushed for a second round of tax reductions.

To thwart terrorism at home, Congress passed the Patriot Act, an administration measure that expanded the power of law-enforcement agencies to detain alien suspects and conduct secret searches—for example, of private records of telephone calls. Without asking Congress, Attorney General John Ashcroft authorized eavesdropping on communications between detained suspects and their lawyers. And he announced that the government would try suspected terrorists who were not citizens in secret military tribunals, where the legal safeguards for fair proceedings and the standards for conviction were much weaker than in open civilian courts. The secrecy meant that a defendant could be charged, tried, and put to death without public knowledge.

Many observers declared that September 11 had ushered the United States into a new era. Perhaps it had. Officials in the Bush administration had been saying since September 11 that the war against terrorism would be a long one, without a decisive end. Critics passionately protested the curtailment of civil rights and civil liberties inherent in the administration's antiterrorist legal weapons, especially the military tribunals. Many Americans across the political spectrum were outraged when Attorney General Ashcroft, called to the Senate to explain the curtailments, admonished the critics: "Your tactics only aid terrorists, for they erode our national unity and diminish our resolve. They give ammunition to America's enemies and pause to America's friends." But even though observers detected widening unease about the prospect of endless war and the erosion of rights, polls showed strong support for the administration's measures against terrorism.

The open debate under way about the restrictions on rights and liberties indicated to *Time* magazine that "America's enemies, who hate us because we are free, have undeniably lost." Another poem posted at Grand Central Station told the perpetrators of September 11 why the nation remained strong and resilient:

> Well, you hit the World Trade Center, but you missed America. . . .
> America isn't about a place, America isn't even about a bunch of
>   buildings,
> America is about an IDEA.

The idea, forged and enlarged through almost four centuries of struggle, had come to include many elements. The overarching ones—the Fourth of July standards of freedom, equality, democracy, and opportunity—continued to transcend the nation's diversity, bind it together, and at once invigorate and temper its response to the shadowy threats it was now compelled to confront.

Suggested Reading

Strobe Talbott and Nayan Chand, eds., *The Age of Terror: America and the World After September 11* (2001)

Washington Post political staff, *Deadlock: The Inside Story of America's Closest Election* (2001)

THE DECLARATION OF INDEPENDENCE

When in the course of human events, it becomes necessary for one people to dissolve the political bands which have connected them with another, and to assume among the Powers of the earth, the separate and equal station to which the Laws of Nature and of Nature's God entitle them, a decent respect to the opinions of mankind requires that they should declare the causes which impel them to the separation.

We hold these truths to be self-evident, that all men are created equal, that they are endowed by their Creator with certain unalienable rights, that among these are Life, Liberty, and the pursuit of Happiness. That to secure these rights, Governments are instituted among Men, deriving their just powers from the consent of the governed. That whenever any Form of Government becomes destructive of these ends, it is the Right of the People to alter or to abolish it, and to institute new Government, laying its foundation on such principles and organizing its powers in such form, as to them shall seem most likely to effect their Safety and Happiness. Prudence, indeed, will dictate that Governments long established should not be changed for light and transient causes; and accordingly all experience hath shown, that mankind are more disposed to suffer, while evils are sufferable, than to right themselves by abolishing the forms to which they are accustomed. But when a long train of abuses and usurpations, pursuing invariably the same Object evinces a design to reduce them under absolute Despotism, it is their right, it is their duty, to throw off such Government, and to provide new Guards for their future security.—Such has been the patient sufferance of these Colonies; and such is now the necessity which constrains them to alter their former Systems of Government. The history of the present King of Great Britain is a history of repeated injuries and usurpations, all having in direct object the establishment of an absolute Tyranny over these States. To prove this, let Facts be submitted to a candid world.

He has refused his Assent to Laws, the most wholesome and necessary for the public good.

He has forbidden his Governors to pass Laws of immediate and pressing importance, unless suspended in their operation till his Assent should be obtained; and when so suspended, he has utterly neglected to attend to them.

He has refused to pass other Laws for the accommodation of large districts of people, unless those people would relinquish the right of Representation in the Legislature, a right inestimable to them and formidable to tyrants only.

He has called together legislative bodies at places unusual, uncomfortable, and distant from the depository of their public Records, for the sole purpose of fatiguing them into compliance with his measures.

He has dissolved Representative Houses repeatedly, for opposing with manly firmness his invasions on the rights of the people.

He has refused for a long time, after such dissolutions, to cause others to be elected; whereby the Legislative powers, incapable of Annihilation, have returned to the People at large for their exercise; the State remaining in the mean time exposed to all dangers of invasion from without, and convulsions within.

He has endeavoured to prevent the population of these States; for that purpose obstructing the Laws of Naturalization of Foreigners; refusing to pass others to encourage their migrations hither, and raising the conditions of new Appropriations of Lands.

He has obstructed the Administration of Justice, by refusing his Assent to Laws for establishing Judiciary powers.

He has made Judges dependent on his Will alone, for the tenure of their offices, and the amount and payment of their salaries.

He has erected a multitude of New Offices, and sent hither swarms of Officers to harass our People, and eat out their substance.

He has kept among us, in times of peace, Standing Armies without the Consent of our legislatures.

He has affected to render the Military independent of and superior to the Civil Power.

He has combined with others to subject us to a jurisdiction foreign to our constitution, and unacknowledged by our laws; giving his Assent to their Acts of pretended Legislation:

For quartering large bodies of armed troops among us:

For protecting them, by a mock Trial, from Punishment for any Murders which they should commit on the Inhabitants of these States:

For cutting off our Trade with all parts of the world:

For imposing taxes on us without our Consent:

For depriving us of many cases, of the benefits of Trial by jury:

For transporting us beyond Seas to be tried for pretended offences:

For abolishing the free System of English Laws in a neighbouring Province, establishing therein an Arbitrary government, and enlarging its Boundaries so as to render it at once an example and fit instrument for introducing the same absolute rule into these Colonies:

For taking away our Charters, abolishing our most valuable Laws, and altering fundamentally the Forms of our Governments:

For suspending our own Legislatures, and declaring themselves invested with Power to legislate for us in all cases whatsoever.

He has abdicated Government here, by declaring us out of his Protection and waging War against us.

He has plundered our seas, ravaged our Coasts, burnt our towns, and destroyed the lives of our people.

He is at this time transporting large armies of foreign mercenaries to compleat the works of death, desolation, and tyranny, already begun with circumstances of Cruelty & perfidy scarcely paralleled in the most barbarous ages, and totally unworthy the Head of a civilized nation.

He has constrained our fellow Citizens taken Captive on the high Seas to bear Arms against their Country, to become the executioners of their friends and Brethren, or to fall themselves by their Hands.

He has excited domestic insurrections amongst us, and has endeavoured to bring on the inhabitants of our frontiers, the merciless Indian Savages, whose known rule of warfare, is an undistinguished destruction of all ages, sexes, and conditions.

In every stage of these Oppressions We have Petitioned for Redress in the most humble terms: Our repeated Petitions have been answered only by repeated injury. A Prince, whose character is thus marked by every act which may define a Tyrant, is unfit to be the ruler of a free people.

Nor have We been wanting in attention to our British brethren. We have warned them from time to time of attempts by their legislature to extend an unwarrantable jurisdiction over us. We have reminded them of the circumstances of our emigration and settlement here. We have appealed to their native justice and magnanimity, and we have conjured them by the ties of our common kindred to disavow these usurpations, which, would inevitably interrupt our connections and correspondence. They too must have been deaf to the voice of justice and of consanguinity. We must, therefore, acquiesce in the necessity, which denounces our Separation, and hold them, as we hold the rest of mankind, Enemies in War, in Peace Friends.

WE, THEREFORE, the Representatives of the UNITED STATES OF AMERICA, in General Congress, Assembled, appealing to the Supreme Judge of the world for the rectitude of our intentions, do, in the Name, and by Authority of the good People of these Colonies, solemnly publish and declare, That these United Colonies are, and of Right ought to be FREE AND INDEPENDENT STATES; that they are Absolved from all Allegiance to the British Crown, and that all political connection between them and the State of Great Britain, is and ought to be totally dissolved; and that as Free and Independent States, they have full Power to levy War, conclude Peace, contract Alliances, establish Commerce, and to do all other Acts and Things which Independent States may of right do. And for the support of this Declaration, with a firm reliance on the Protection of Divine Providence, we mutually pledge to each other our Lives, our Fortunes, and our sacred Honor.

The foregoing Declaration was, by order of Congress, engrossed, and signed by the following members:

John Hancock

NEW HAMPSHIRE
Josiah Bartlett
William Whipple
Matthew Thornton

MASSACHUSETTS BAY
Samuel Adams
John Adams
Robert Treat Paine
Elbridge Gerry

RHODE ISLAND
Stephen Hopkins
William Ellery

CONNECTICUT
Roger Sherman
Samuel Huntington
William Williams
Oliver Wolcott

NEW YORK
William Floyd
Philip Livingston
Francis Lewis
Lewis Morris

NEW JERSEY
Richard Stockton
John Witherspoon
Francis Hopkinson
John Hart
Abraham Clark

PENNSYLVANIA
Robert Morris
Benjamin Rush
Benjamin Franklin
John Morton
George Clymer
James Smith
George Taylor
James Wilson
George Ross

DELAWARE
Caesar Rodney
George Read
Thomas M'Kean

MARYLAND
Samuel Chase
William Paca
Thomas Stone
Charles Carroll,
  of Carrollton

VIRGINIA
George Wythe
Richard Henry Lee
Thomas Jefferson
Benjamin Harrison
Thomas Nelson, Jr.
Francis Lightfoot Lee
Carter Braxton

NORTH CAROLINA
William Hooper
Joseph Hewes
John Penn

SOUTH CAROLINA
Edward Rutledge
Thomas Heyward, Jr.
Thomas Lynch, Jr.
Arthur Middleton

GEORGIA
Button Gwinnett
Lyman Hall
George Walton

Resolved, That copies of the Declaration be sent to the several assemblies, conventions, and committees, or councils of safety, and to the several commanding officers of the continental troops; that it be proclaimed in each of the United States, at the head of the army.

ARTICLES OF CONFEDERATION

To all to whom these Presents shall come, we the undersigned Delegates of the States affixed to our Names send greeting.

Whereas the Delegates of the United States of America in Congress assembled did on the fifteenth day of November in the Year of our Lord One Thousand Seven Hundred and Seventy-seven, and in the Second Year of the Independence of America agree to certain articles of Confederation and perpetual Union between the States of Newhampshire, Massachusetts-bay, Rhodeisland and Providence Plantations, Connecticut, New York, New Jersey, Pennsylvania, Delaware, Maryland, Virginia, North-Carolina, South-Carolina and Georgia in the Words following, viz.

Articles of Confederation and perpetual Union between the States of Newhampshire, Massachusetts-bay, Rhodeisland and Providence Plantations, Connecticut, New-York, New-Jersey, Pennsylvania, Delaware, Maryland, Virginia, North-Carolina, South-Carolina and Georgia.

ARTICLE I. The stile of this confederacy shall be "The United States of America."

ARTICLE II. Each State retains its sovereignty, freedom and independence, and every power, jurisdiction and right, which is not by this confederation expressly delegated to the United States, in Congress assembled.

ARTICLE III. The said States hereby severally enter into a firm league of friendship with each other, for their common defence, the security of their liberties, and their mutual and general welfare, binding themselves to assist each other, against all force offered to, or attacks made upon them, or any of them, on account of religion, sovereignty, trade or any other pretence whatever.

ARTICLE IV. The better to secure and perpetuate mutual friendship and intercourse among the people of the different States in this Union, the free inhabitants of each of these States, paupers, vagabonds and fugitives from justice excepted, shall be entitled to all privileges and immunities of free citizens in the several States; and the people of each State shall have free ingress and regress to and from any other State, and shall enjoy therein all the privileges of trade and commerce, subject to the same duties, impositions and restrictions as the inhabitants thereof respectively, provided that such restrictions shall not extend so far as to prevent the removal of property imported into any State, to any other State of which the owner is an inhabitant; provided also that no imposition, duties or restriction shall be laid by any State, on the property of the United States, or either of them.

If any person guilty of, or charged with treason, felony, or other high misdemeanor in any State, shall flee from justice, and be found in any of the United States, he shall upon demand of the Governor or Executive power, of the State from which he fled, be delivered up and removed to the State having jurisdiction of his offence.

Full faith and credit shall be given in each of these States to the records, acts and judicial proceedings of the courts and magistrates of every other State.

ARTICLE V. For the more convenient management of the general interests of the United States, delegates shall be annually appointed in such manner as the legislature of each State shall direct, to meet in Congress on the first Monday in November, in every year, with a power reserved to each State, to recall its delegates, or any of them, at any time within the year, and to send others in their stead, for the remainder of the year.

No State shall be represented in Congress by less than two, nor by more than seven members; and no person shall be capable of being a delegate for more than three years in any term of six years; nor shall any person, being a delegate, be capable of holding any office under the United States, for which he, or another for his benefit receives any salary, fees or emolument of any kind.

Each State shall maintain its own delegates in a meeting of the States, and while they act as members of the committee of the States.

In determining questions in the United States, in Congress assembled, each State shall have one vote.

Freedom of speech and debate in Congress shall not be impeached or questioned in any court, or place out of Congress, and the members of Congress shall be protected in their persons from arrests and imprisonments, during the time of their going to and from, and attendance on Congress, except for treason, felony, or breach of the peace.

ARTICLE VI. No State without the consent of the United States in Congress assembled, shall send any embassy to, or receive any embassy from, or enter into any conference, agreement, alliance or treaty with any king, prince or state; nor shall any person holding any office of profit or trust under the United States, or any of them, accept of any present, emolument, office or title of any kind whatever from any king, prince or foreign state; nor shall the United States in Congress assembled, or any of them, grant any title of nobility.

No two or more States shall enter into any treaty, confederation or alliance whatever between them, without the consent of the

United States in Congress assembled, specifying accurately the purposes for which the same is to be entered into, and how long it shall continue.

No State shall lay any imposts or duties, which may interfere with any stipulations in treaties, entered into by the United States in Congress assembled, with any king, prince or state, in pursuance of any treaties already proposed by Congress, to the courts of France and Spain.

No vessels of war shall be kept up in time of peace by any State, except such number only, as shall be deemed necessary by the United States in Congress assembled, for the defence of such State, or its trade; nor shall any body of forces be kept up by any State, in time of peace, except such number only, as in the judgment of the United States, in Congress assembled, shall be deemed requisite to garrison the forts necessary for the defence of such State; but every State shall always keep up a well regulated and disciplined militia, sufficiently armed and accoutred, and shall provide and constantly have ready for use, in public stores, a due number of field pieces and tents, and a proper quantity of arms, ammunition and camp equipage.

No State shall engage in any war without the consent of the United States in Congress assembled, unless such State be actually invaded by enemies, or shall have received certain advice of a resolution being formed by some nation of Indians to invade such State, and the danger is so imminent as not to admit of a delay, till the United States in Congress assembled can be consulted: nor shall any State grant commissions to any ships or vessels of war, nor letters of marque or reprisal, except it be after a declaration of war by the United States in Congress assembled, and then only against the kingdom or state and the subjects thereof, against which war has been so declared, and under such regulations as shall be established by the United States in Congress assembled, unless such State be infested by pirates, in which case vessels of war may be fitted out for that occasion, and kept so long as the danger shall continue, or until the United States in Congress assembled shall determine otherwise.

ARTICLE VII. When land-forces are raised by any State of the common defence, all officers of or under the rank of colonel, shall be appointed by the Legislature of each State respectively by whom such forces shall be raised, or in such manner as such State shall direct, and all vacancies shall be filled up by the State which first made the appointment.

ARTICLE VIII. All charges of war, and all other expenses that shall be incurred for the common defence or general welfare, and allowed by the United States in Congress assembled, shall be defrayed out of a common treasury, which shall be supplied by the several States, in proportion to the value of all land within each State, granted to or surveyed for any person, as such land and the buildings and improvements thereon shall be estimated according to such mode as the United States in Congress assembled, shall from time to time direct and appoint.

The taxes for paying that proportion shall be laid and levied by the authority and direction of the Legislatures of the several States within the time agreed upon by the United States in Congress assembled.

ARTICLE IX. The United States in Congress assembled, shall have the sole and exclusive right and power of determining on peace and war, except in the cases mentioned in the sixth article—of sending and receiving ambassadors—entering into treaties and alliances, provided that no treaty of commerce shall be made whereby the legislative power of the respective States shall be restrained from imposing such imposts and duties on foreigners, as their own people are subjected to, or from prohibiting the exportation or importation of and species of goods or commodities whatsoever—of establishing rules for deciding in all cases, what captures on land or water shall be legal, and in what manner prizes taken by land or naval forces in the service of the United States shall be divided or appropriated—of granting letters of marque and reprisal in times of peace—appointing courts for the trial of piracies and felonies committed on the high seas and establishing courts for receiving and determining finally appeals in all cases of captures, provided that no member of Congress shall be appointed a judge of any of the said courts.

The United States in Congress assembled shall also be the last resort on appeal in all disputes and differences now subsisting or that hereafter may arise between two or more States concerning boundary, jurisdiction or any other cause whatever; which authority shall always be exercised in the manner following. Whenever the legislative or executive authority or lawful agent of any State in controversy with another shall present a petition to Congress, stating the matter in question and praying for a hearing, notice thereof shall be given by order of Congress to the legislative or executive authority of the other State in controversy, and a day assigned for the appearance of the parties by their lawful agents, who shall then be directed to appoint by joint consent, commissioners or judges to constitute a court for hearing and determining the matter in question: but if they cannot agree, Congress shall name three persons out of each of the United States, and from the list of such persons each party shall alternately strike out one, the petitioners beginning, until the number shall be reduced to thirteen; and from that number not less than seven, nor more than nine names as Congress shall direct, shall in the presence of Congress be drawn out by lot, and the persons whose names shall be so drawn or any five of them, shall be commissioners or judges, to hear and finally determine the controversy, so always as a major part of the judges who shall hear the cause shall agree in the determination: and if either party shall neglect to attend at the day appointed, without reasons, which Congress shall judge sufficient, or being present shall refuse to strike, the Congress shall proceed to nominate three persons out of each State, and the Secretary of Congress shall strike in behalf of such party absent or refusing; and the judgment and sentence of the court to be appointed, in the manner before prescribed, shall be final and conclusive; and if any of the parties shall refuse to submit to the authority of such court, or to appear or defend their claim or cause, the court shall nevertheless proceed to pronounce sentence, or judgment, which shall in like manner be final and decisive, the judgment or sentence and other proceedings being in either case transmitted to Congress, and lodged among the acts of Congress for the security of the parties concerned: provided that every commissioner, before he sits in judgment, shall take an oath to be administered by one of the judges of the supreme or superior court of the State where the case shall be tried, "well and truly to hear and determine the matter in question, according to the best of his judgment, without favour, affection or hope of reward:" provided also that no State shall be deprived of territory for the benefit of the United States.

All controversies concerning the private right of soil claimed under different grants of two or more States, whose jurisdiction as they may respect such lands, and the states which passed such grants are adjusted, the said grants or either of them being at the same time claimed to have originated antecedent to such settlement of jurisdiction, shall on the petition of either party to the Congress of the United States, be finally determined as near as may be in the same manner as is before prescribed for deciding disputes respecting territorial jurisdiction between different States.

The United States in Congress assembled shall also have the sole and exclusive right and power of regulating the alloy and value of coin struck by their own authority, or by that of the respective States—fixing the standard of weights and measures throughout the United States—regulating the trade and managing all affairs with the Indians, not members of any of the States, provided that the legislative right of any State within its own limits be not infringed or violated—establishing and regulating post-offices from one State to another, throughout all of the United States, and exacting such postage on the papers passing thro' the same as may be requisite to defray the expenses of the said office—appointing all officers of the land forces, in the service of the United States, excepting regimental officers—appointing all the officers of the naval forces, and commissioning all officers whatever in the service of the United States—making rules for the government and regulation of the said land and naval forces, and directing their operations.

The United States in Congress assembled shall have authority to appoint a committee, to sit in the recess of Congress, to be denominated "a Committee of the States," and to consist of one delegate from each State; and to appoint such other committees and civil officers as may be necessary for managing the general affairs of the United States under their direction—to appoint one of their number to preside, provided that no person be allowed to serve in the office of president more than one year in any term of three years; to

ascertain the necessary sums of money to be raised for the service of the United States, and to appropriate and apply the same for defraying the public expenses—to borrow money, or emit bills on the credit of the United States, transmitting every half year to the respective States an account of the sums of money so borrowed or emitted,—to build and equip a navy—to agree upon the number of land forces, and to make requisitions from each State for its quota, in proportion to the number of white inhabitants in such State; which requisition shall be binding, and thereupon the Legislature of each State shall appoint the regimental officers, raise the men and cloath, arm and equip them in a soldier like manner, at the expense of the United States; and the officers and men so cloathed, armed and equipped shall march to the place appointed, and within the time agreed on by the United States in Congress assembled: but if the United States in Congress assembled shall, on consideration of circumstances judge proper that any State should not raise men, or should raise a smaller number of men than the quota thereof, such extra number shall be raised, officered, cloathed, armed and equipped in the same manner as the quota of such State, unless the legislature of such State shall judge that such extra number cannot be safely spared out of the same, in which case they shall raise officer, cloath, arm and equip as many of such extra number as they judge can be safely spared. And the officers and men so cloathed, armed and equipped, shall march to the place appointed, and within the time agreed on by the United States in Congress assembled.

The United States in Congress assembled shall never engage in a war, nor grant letters of marque and reprisal in time of peace, nor enter into any treaties or alliances, nor coin money, nor regulate the value thereof, nor ascertain the sums and expenses necessary for the defence and welfare of the United States, or any of them, nor emit bills, nor borrow money on the credit of the United States, nor appropriate money, nor agree upon the number of vessels to be built or purchased, or the number of land or sea forces to be raised, nor appoint a commander in chief of the army or navy, unless nine States assent to the same: nor shall a question on any other point, except for adjourning from day to day be determined, unless by the votes of a majority of the United States in Congress assembled.

The Congress of the United States shall have power to adjourn to any time within the year, and to any place within the United States, so that no period of adjournment be for a longer duration than the space of six months, and shall publish the journal of their proceedings monthly, except such parts thereof relating to treaties, alliances or military operations, as in their judgment require secrecy; and the yeas and nays of the delegates of each State on any question shall be entered on the Journal, when it is desired by any delegate; and the delegates of a State, or any of them, at his or their request shall be furnished with a transcript of the said journal, except such parts as are above excepted, to lay before the Legislatures of the several States.

ARTICLE X. The committee of the States, or any nine of them, shall be authorized to execute, in the recess of Congress, such of the powers of Congress as the United States in Congress assembled, by the consent of nine States, shall from time to time think expedient to vest them with; provided that no power be delegated to the said committee, for the exercise of which, by the articles of confederation, the voice of nine States in the Congress of the United States assembled is requisite.

ARTICLE XI. Canada acceding to this confederation, and joining in the measures of the United States, shall be admitted into, and entitled to all the advantages of this Union: but no other colony shall be admitted into the same, unless such admission be agreed to by nine States.

ARTICLE XII. All bills of credit emitted, monies borrowed and debts contracted by, or under the authority of Congress, before the assembling of the United States, in pursuance of the present confederation, shall be deemed and considered as a charge against the United States, for payment and satisfaction whereof the said United States, and the public faith are hereby solemnly pledged.

ARTICLE XIII. Every State shall abide by the determinations of the United States in Congress assembled, on all questions which by this confederation are submitted to them. And the articles of this confederation shall be inviolably observed by every State, and the Union shall be perpetual; nor shall any alteration at any time hereafter be made in any of them; unless such alteration be agreed to in a Congress of the United States, and be afterwards confirmed by the Legislatures of every State.

And whereas it has pleased the Great Governor of the world to incline the hearts of the Legislatures we respectively represent in Congress, to approve of, and to authorize us to ratify the said articles of confederation and perpetual union. Know ye that we the undersigned delegates, by virtue of the power and authority to us given for that purpose, do by these presents, in the name and in behalf of our respective constituents, fully and entirely ratify and confirm each and every of the said articles of confederation and perpetual union, and all and singular the matters and things therein contained: and we do further solemnly plight and engage the faith of our respective constituents, that they shall abide by the determinations of the United States in Congress assembled, on all questions, which by the said confederation are submitted to them. And that the articles thereof shall be inviolably observed by the States we respectively represent, and that the Union shall be perpetual.

In witness thereof we have hereunto set our hands in Congress. Done at Philadelphia in the State of Pennsylvania the ninth day of July in the year of our Lord one thousand seven hundred and seventy-eight, and in the third year of the independence of America.

THE CONSTITUTION OF THE UNITED STATES

We the People of the United States, in order to form a more perfect Union, establish Justice, insure domestic Tranquility, provide for the common defence, promote the general Welfare, and secure the Blessings of Liberty to ourselves and our Posterity, do ordain and establish this Constitution for the United States of America.

ARTICLE. I.

Section. 1. All legislative Powers herein granted shall be vested in a Congress of the United States, which shall consist of a Senate and House of Representatives.

Section. 2. The House of Representatives shall be composed of Members chosen every second Year by the People of the several States, and the Electors in each State shall have the Qualifications requisite for Electors of the most numerous Branch of the State Legislature.

No Person shall be a Representative who shall not have attained to the Age of twenty five Years, and been seven Years a Citizen of the United States, and who shall not, when elected, be an Inhabitant of that State in which he shall be chosen.

Representatives and direct Taxes shall be apportioned among the several States which may be included within this Union, according to their respective Numbers, which shall be determined by adding to the whole Number of free Persons, including those bound to Service for a Term of Years, and excluding Indians not taxed, three fifths of all other Persons. The actual Enumeration shall be made within three Years after the first Meeting of the Congress of the United States, and within every subsequent Term of ten Years, in such Manner as they shall by Law direct. The Number of Representatives shall not exceed one for every thirty Thousand, but each State shall have at Least one Representative; and until such enumeration shall be made, the State of New Hampshire shall be entitled to chuse three, Massachusetts eight, Rhode-Island and Providence Plantations one, Connecticut five, New York six, New Jersey four, Pennsylvania eight, Delaware one, Maryland six, Virginia ten, North Carolina five, South Carolina five, and Georgia three.

When vacancies happen in the Representation from any state, the Executive Authority thereof shall issue Writs of Election to fill such Vacancies.

The House of Representatives shall chuse their Speaker and other Officers; and shall have the sole Power of Impeachment.

Section. 3. The Senate of the United States shall be composed of two Senators from each State, chosen by the legislature thereof, for six Years; and each Senator shall have one Vote.

Immediately after they shall be assembled in Consequence of the first Election, they shall be divided as equally as may be into three Classes. The Seats of the Senators of the first Class shall be vacated at the Expiration of the second Year, of the second Class at the Expiration of the fourth Year, and of the third Class at the Expiration of the sixth Year, so that one third maybe chosen every second Year; and if Vacancies happen by Resignation, or otherwise, during the Recess of the Legislature of any State, the Executive thereof may make temporary Appointments until the next Meeting of the Legislature, which shall then fill such Vacancies.

No Person shall be a Senator who shall not have attained to the Age of thirty Years, and been nine Years a Citizen of the United States, and who shall not, when elected, be an Inhabitant of that State for which he shall be chosen.

The Vice President of the United States shall be President of the Senate, but shall have no Vote, unless they be equally divided.

The Senate shall chuse their other Officers, and also a President pro tempore, in the Absence of the Vice President, or when he shall exercise the Office of President of the United States.

The Senate shall have the sole Power to try all Impeachments. When sitting for that Purpose, they shall be on Oath or Affirmation. When the President of the United States is tried, the Chief Justice shall preside: And no Person shall be convicted without the Concurrence of two thirds of the Members present.

Judgment in Cases of Impeachment shall not extend further than to removal from Office, and disqualification to hold and enjoy any Office of honor, Trust or Profit under the United States: but the Party convicted shall nevertheless be liable and subject to Indictment, Trial, Judgment and Punishment, according to Law.

Section. 4. The Times, Places and Manner of holding Elections for Senators and Representatives, shall be prescribed in each State by the Legislature thereof; but the Congress may at any time by Law make or alter such Regulations, except as to the Places of chusing Senators.

The Congress shall assemble at least once in every Year, and such Meeting shall be on the first Monday in December, unless they shall by Law appoint a different Day.

Section. 5. Each House shall be the Judge of the Elections, Returns and Qualifications of its own Members, and a Majority of each shall constitute a Quorum to do Business; but a smaller Number may adjourn from day to day, and may be authorized to compel the Attendance of absent Members, in such Manner, and under such Penalties as each House may provide.

Each House may determine the Rules of its Proceedings, punish its Members for disorderly Behaviour, and, with the Concurrence of two thirds, expel a Member.

Each House shall keep a Journal of its Proceedings, and from time to time publish the same, excepting such Parts as may in their

Judgment require Secrecy; and the Yeas and Nays of the Members of either House on any question shall, at the Desire of one fifth of those Present, be entered on the Journal.

Neither House, during the Session of Congress, shall, without the Consent of the other, adjourn for more than three days, not to any other Place than that in which the two Houses shall be sitting.

Section. 6. The Senators and Representatives shall receive a Compensation for their Services, to be ascertained by Law, and paid out of the Treasury of the United States. They shall in all Cases, except Treason, Felony and Breach of the Peace, be privileged from Arrest during their Attendance at the Session of their respective Houses, and in going to and returning from the same; and for any Speech or Debate in either House, they shall not be questioned in any other Place.

No Senator or Representative shall, during the Time for which he was elected, be appointed to any civil Office under the Authority of the United States, which shall have been created, or the Emoluments whereof shall have been encreased during such time; and no Person holding any Office under the United States, shall be a Member of either House during his Continuance in Office.

Section. 7. All Bills for raising Revenue shall originate in the House of Representatives; but the Senate may propose or concur with Amendments as on other Bills.

Every Bill which shall have passed the House of Representatives and the Senate shall, before it become a Law, be presented to the President of the United States; If he approve he shall sign it, but if not he shall return it, with his Objections to that House in which it shall have originated, who shall enter the Objections at large on their Journal, and proceed to reconsider it. If after such Reconsideration two thirds of that House shall agree to pass the Bill, it shall be sent, together with the Objections, to the other House, by which it shall likewise be reconsidered, and if approved by two thirds of that House, it shall become a Law. But in all such Cases the Votes of both Houses shall be determined by Yeas and Nays, and the Names of the Persons voting for and against the Bill shall be entered on the Journal of each House respectively. If any Bill shall not be returned by the President within ten Days (Sundays excepted) after it shall have been presented to him, the Same shall be a Law, in like Manner as if he had signed it, unless the Congress by their Adjournment prevent its Return, in which Case it shall not be a Law.

Every Order, Resolution, or Vote to which the Concurrence of the Senate and House of Representatives may be necessary (except on a question of Adjournment) shall be presented to the President of the United States; and before the Same shall take Effect, shall be approved by him, or being disapproved by him, shall be repassed by two thirds of the Senate and House of Representatives, according to the Rules and Limitations prescribed in the Case of a Bill.

Section. 8. The Congress shall have Power To lay and collect Taxes, Duties, Imposts and Excises, to pay the Debts and provide for the common Defence and general Welfare of the United States; but all Duties, Imposts and Excises shall be uniform throughout the United States;

To borrow Money on the credit of the United States;

To regulate Commerce with foreign Nations, and among the several States, and with the Indian Tribes;

To establish an uniform Rule of Naturalization, and uniform Laws on the subject of Bankruptcies throughout the United States;

To coin Money, regulate the Value thereof, and of foreign Coin, and fix the Standard of Weights and Measures;

To provide for the Punishment of counterfeiting the Securities and current Coin of the United States;

To establish Post Offices and Post Roads;

To promote the Progress of Science and useful Arts, by securing for limited Times to Authors and Inventors the exclusive Right to their respective Writings and Discoveries;

To constitute Tribunals inferior to the supreme Court;

To define and punish Piracies and Felonies committed on the high Seas, and Offences against the Law of Nations;

To declare War, grant Letters of Marque and Reprisal, and make Rules concerning Captures on Land and Water;

To raise and support Armies, but no Appropriation of Money to that Use shall be for a longer Term than two Years;

To provide and maintain a Navy;

To make Rules for the Government and Regulation of the land and naval Forces;

To provide for calling forth the Militia to execute the Laws of the Union, suppress Insurrections and repel Invasions;

To provide for organizing, arming, and disciplining, the Militia, and for governing such Part of them as may be employed in the Service of the United States, reserving to the States respectively, the Appointment of the Officers, and the Authority of training the Militia according to the discipline prescribed by Congress;

To exercise exclusive Legislation in all Cases whatsoever, over such District (not exceeding ten Miles square) as may, by Cession of Particular States, and the Acceptance of Congress, become the Seat of the Government of the United States, and to exercise like Authority over all Places purchased by the Consent of the Legislature of the State in which the Same shall be, for the Erection of Forts, Magazines, Arsenals, dock-Yards, and other needful Buildings;—And

To make all Laws which shall be necessary and proper for carrying into Execution the foregoing Powers, and all other Powers vested by this Constitution in the Government of the United States, or in any Department or Officer thereof.

Section. 9. The Migration or Importation of such Persons as any of the States now existing shall think proper to admit, shall not be prohibited by the Congress prior to the Year one thousand eight hundred and eight, but a Tax or duty may be imposed on such Importation, not exceeding ten dollars for each Person.

The Privilege of the Writ of Habeas Corpus shall not be suspended, unless when in Cases of Rebellion or Invasion the public Safety may require it.

No Bill of Attainder or ex post facto Law shall be passed.

No Capitation, or other direct, Tax shall be laid, unless in Proportion to the Census or Enumeration herein before directed to be taken.

No Tax or Duty shall be laid on Articles exported from any State.

No Preference shall be given by any Regulation of Commerce or Revenue to the Ports of one State over those of another: nor shall Vessels bound to, or from, one State, be obliged to enter, clear, or pay Duties in another.

No Money shall be drawn from the Treasury, but in Consequence of Appropriations made by Law; and a regular Statement and Account of the Receipts and Expenditures of all public Money shall be published from time to time.

No Title of Nobility shall be granted by the United States: And no Person holding any Office of Profit or Trust under them, shall, without the Consent of the Congress, accept of any present, Emolument, Office, or Title, of any kind whatever, from any King, Prince, or foreign State.

Section. 10. No State shall enter into any Treaty, Alliance, or Confederation; grant Letters of Marque and Reprisal; coin Money; emit Bills of Credit; make any Thing but gold and silver Coin a Tender in Payment of Debts; pass any Bill of Attainder, ex post facto Law, or Law impairing the Obligation of Contracts, or grant any Title of Nobility.

No State shall, without the Consent of the Congress, lay any Imposts or Duties on Imports or Exports, except what may be absolutely necessary for executing its inspection Laws: and the net Produce of all Duties and Imposts, laid by any State on Imports or Exports, shall be for the Use of the Treasury of the United States; and all such Laws shall be subject to the Revision and Controul of the Congress.

No State shall, without the Consent of Congress, lay any Duty of Tonnage, keep Troops, or Ships of War in time of Peace, enter into any Agreement or Compact with another State, or with a foreign Power, or engage in War, unless actually invaded, or in such imminent Danger as will not admit of delay.

ARTICLE. II.

Section. 1. The executive Power shall be vested in a President of the United States of America. He shall hold his Office during the term of four Years, and, together with the Vice President, chosen for the same Term, be elected, as follows:

Each State shall appoint, in such Manner as the Legislature thereof may direct, a Number of Electors, equal to the whole Number of Senators and Representatives to which the State may be entitled in the Congress: but no Senator or Representative, or Person holding an Office of Trust or Profit under the United States, shall be appointed an Elector.

The Electors shall meet in their respective States, and vote by Ballot for two Persons, of whom one at least shall not be an Inhabitant of the same State with themselves. And they shall make a List of all the Persons voted for, and of the Number of Votes for each; which List they shall sign and certify, and transmit sealed to the Seat of the Government of the United States, directed to the President of the Senate. The President of the Senate shall, in the Presence of the Senate and House of Representatives, open all the Certificates, and the Votes shall then be counted. The Person having the greatest Number of Votes shall be the President, if such Number be a Majority of the whole Number of Electors appointed; and if there be more than one who have such Majority, and have an equal Number of Votes, then the House of Representatives shall immediately chuse by Ballot one of them for President; and if no Person have a Majority, then from the five highest on the List the said House shall in like Manner chuse the President. But in chusing the President, the Votes shall be taken by States, the Representation from each State having one Vote; A quorum for this Purpose shall consist of a Member or Members from two thirds of the States, and a Majority of all the States shall be necessary to a Choice. In every Case, after the Choice of the President, the Person having the greatest Number of Votes of the Electors shall be the Vice President. But if there should remain two or more who have equal Votes, the Senate shall chuse from them by Ballot the Vice President.

The Congress may determine the Time of chusing the Electors, and the Day on which they shall give their Votes; which Day shall be the same throughout the United States.

No Person except a natural born Citizen, or a Citizen of the United States, at the time of the Adoption of this Constitution, shall be eligible to the Office of President; neither shall any Person be eligible to that Office who shall not have attained to the Age of thirty five Years, and been fourteen Years a Resident within the United States.

In Case of the Removal of the President from Office, or of his Death, Resignation, or Inability to discharge the Powers and Duties of the said Office, the Same shall devolve on the Vice President, and the Congress may by Law provide for the Case of Removal, Death, Resignation or Inability, both of the President and Vice President, declaring what Officer shall then act as President, and such Officer shall act accordingly, until the Disability be removed, or a President shall be elected.

The President shall, at stated Times, receive for his Services, a Compensation, which shall neither be encreased or diminished during the Period for which he shall have been elected, and he shall not receive within that Period any other Emolument from the United States, or any of them.

Before he enters on the Execution of his Office, he shall take the following Oath or Affirmation:—"I do solemnly swear (or affirm) that I will faithfully execute the Office of President of the United States, and will to the best of my Ability, preserve, protect and defend the Constitution of the United States."

Section. 2. The President shall be Commander in Chief of the Army and Navy of the United States, and of the Militia of the several States, when called into the actual Service of the United States; he may require the Opinion, in writing, of the principal Officer in each of the executive Departments, upon any Subject relating to the Duties of their respective Offices, and he shall have Power to grant Reprieves and Pardons for Offences against the United States, except in Cases of Impeachment.

He shall have Power, by and with the Advice and Consent of the Senate, to make Treaties, provided two thirds of the Senators present concur; and he shall nominate, and by and with the Advice and Consent of the Senate, shall appoint Ambassadors, other public Ministers and Consuls, Judges of the supreme Court, and all other Officers of the United States, whose Appointments are not herein otherwise provided for, and which shall be established by Law; but the Congress may by Law vest the Appointment of such inferior Officers, as they think proper, in the President alone, in the Courts of Law, or in the Heads of Departments.

The President shall have Power to fill up all Vacancies that may happen during the Recess of the Senate, by granting Commissions which shall expire at the End of their next Session.

Section. 3. He shall from time to time give to the Congress Information of the State of the Union, and recommend to their Consideration such Measures as he shall judge necessary and expedient; he may, on extraordinary Occasions, convene both Houses, or either of them, and in Case of Disagreement between them, with Respect to the Time of Adjournment, he may adjourn them to such Time as he shall think proper; he shall receive Ambassadors and other public Ministers; he shall take Care that the Laws be faithfully executed, and shall Commission all the Officers of the United States.

Section. 4. The President, Vice President and all civil Officers of the United States, shall be removed from Office on Impeachment for, and Conviction of, Treason, Bribery, or other high Crimes and Misdemeanors.

ARTICLE. III.

Section. 1. The judicial Power of the United States, shall be vested in one supreme Court, and in such inferior Courts as the Congress may from time to time ordain and establish. The Judges, both of the supreme and inferior Courts, shall hold their Offices during good Behavior, and shall, at stated Times, receive for their Services, a Compensation, which shall not be diminished during their Continuance in Office.

Section. 2. The judicial Power shall extend to all Cases, in Law and Equity, arising under this Constitution, the Laws of the United States, and Treaties made, or which shall be made, under their Authority;—to all Cases affecting Ambassadors, other public Ministers and Consuls;—to all Cases of admiralty and maritime Jurisdiction;—the Controversies to which the United States shall be a Party;—to Controversies between two or more States;—between a State and Citizens of another State;—between Citizens of different States;—between Citizens of the same State claiming Lands under Grants of different States, and between a State, or the Citizens thereof, and foreign States, Citizens or Subjects.

In all cases affecting Ambassadors, other public Ministers and Consuls, and those in which a State shall be Party, the supreme Court shall have original Jurisdiction. In all the other Cases before mentioned, the supreme Court shall have appellate Jurisdiction, both as to Law and Fact, with such Exceptions, and under such Regulations as the Congress shall make.

The Trial of all Crimes, except in Cases of Impeachment, shall be by Jury; and such Trial shall be held in the State where the said Crimes shall have been committed; but when not committed within any State, the Trial shall be at such Place or Places as the Congress may by Law have directed.

Section. 3. Treason against the United States, shall consist only in levying War against them, or in adhering to their Enemies, giving them Aid and Comfort. No Person shall be convicted of Treason unless on the Testimony of two Witnesses to the same overt Act, or on Confession in open Court.

The Congress shall have Power to declare the Punishment of Treason, but no Attainder of Treason shall work Corruption of Blood, or Forfeiture except during the Life of the Person attainted.

ARTICLE. IV.

Section. 1. Full Faith and Credit shall be given in each State to the public Acts, Records, and judicial Proceedings of every other State. And the Congress may by general Laws prescribe the Manner in which such Acts, Records and Proceedings shall be proved, and the Effect thereof.

Section. 2. The Citizens of each State shall be entitled to all Privileges and Immunities of Citizens in the several States.

A Person charged in any State with Treason, Felony, or other Crime, who shall flee from Justice, and be found in another State, shall on Demand of the executive Authority of the State from which he fled, be delivered up, to be removed to the State having Jurisdiction of the Crime.

No Person held to Service or Labour in one State, under the Laws thereof, escaping into another, shall, in Consequence of any Law or Regulation therein, be discharged from such Service or Labour, but shall be delivered up on Claim of the Party to whom such Service or Labour may be due.

Section. 3. New States may be admitted by the Congress into this Union; but no new State shall be formed or erected within the Jurisdiction of any other State; nor any State be formed by the Junction of two or more States, or Parts of States, without the consent of the Legislatures of the States concerned as well as of the Congress.

The Congress shall have Power to dispose of and make all needful Rules and Regulations respecting the Territory or other Property belonging to the United States; and nothing in this Constitution shall be so construed as to Prejudice any Claims of the United States, or of any particular States.

Section. 4. The United States shall guarantee to every State in this Union a Republican Form of Government, and shall protect each of them against Invasion; and on Application of the Legislature, or of the Executive (when the Legislature cannot be convened) against domestic Violence.

ARTICLE. V.

The Congress, whenever two thirds of both Houses shall deem it necessary, shall propose Amendments to this Constitution, or, on the Application of the Legislatures of two thirds of the several States, shall call a Convention for proposing Amendments, which, in either Case, shall be valid to all Intents and Purposes, as Part of this Constitution, when ratified by the Legislatures of three fourths of the several States, or by Conventions in three fourths thereof, as the one or the other Mode of Ratification may be proposed by the Congress; Provided that no Amendment which may be made prior to the Year One thousand eight hundred and eight shall in any Manner affect the first and fourth Clauses in the Ninth Section of the first Article; and that no State, without its Consent, shall be deprived of its equal Suffrage in the Senate.

ARTICLE. VI.

All Debts contracted and Engagements entered into, before the Adoption of this Constitution, shall be as valid against the United States under this Constitution, as under the Confederation.

This Constitution, and the Laws of the United States which shall be made in Pursuance thereof; and all Treaties made, or which shall be made, under the Authority of the United States, shall be the supreme Law of the Land; and the Judges in every State shall be bound thereby, any Thing in the Constitution or Laws of any State to the Contrary notwithstanding.

The Senators and Representatives before mentioned, and the Members of the several State Legislatures, and all executive and judicial Officers, both of the United States and of the several States, shall be bound by Oath or Affirmation, to support this Constitution; but no religious Test shall ever be required as a Qualification to any Office or public Trust under the United States.

ARTICLE. VII.

The Ratification of the Conventions of nine States, shall be sufficient for the Establishment of this Constitution between the States so ratifying the Same.

Done in Convention by the Unanimous Consent of the States present the Seventeenth Day of September in the Year of our Lord one thousand seven hundred and Eighty seven and of the Independence of the United States of America the Twelfth. In witness thereof We have hereunto subscribed our Names,

G°. WASHINGTON—Presd^t.
and deputy from Virginia.

NEW HAMPSHIRE
John Langdon
Nicholas Gilman

MASSACHUSETTS
Nathaniel Gorham
Rufus King

CONNECTICUT
Wm Saml Johnson
Roger Sherman

NEW YORK
Alexander Hamilton

NEW JERSEY
Wil: Livingston
David A. Brearley
Wm Paterson
Jona: Dayton

PENNSYLVANIA
B Franklin
Thomas Mifflin
Robt Morris
Geo. Clymer
Thos FitzSimons
Jared Ingersoll
James Wilson
Gouv Morris

DELAWARE
Geo: Read
Gunning Bedford jun
John Dickinson
Richard Bassett
Jaco: Broom

MARYLAND
James McHenry
Dan of St Thos Jenifer
Danl Carroll

VIRGINIA
John Blair—
James Madison Jr.

NORTH CAROLINA
Wm Blount
Richd Dobbs Spaight
Hu Williamson

SOUTH CAROLINA
J. Rutledge
Charles Cotesworth
Pinckney
Charles Pinckney
Pierce Butler

GEORGIA
William Few
Abr Baldwin

Amendments to the Constitution

Articles in addition to, and Amendment of the Constitution of the United States of America, proposed by Congress, and ratified by the Legislatures of the several States, pursuant to the fifth Article of the original Constitution.

AMENDMENT I.

Congress shall make no law respecting an establishment of religion, or prohibiting the free exercise thereof; or abridging the freedom of speech, or of the press; or the right of the people peaceably to assemble, and to petition the Government for a redress of grievances.

AMENDMENT II.

A well regulated Militia, being necessary to the security of a free State, the right of the people to keep and bear Arms, shall not be infringed.

AMENDMENT III.

No Soldier shall, in time of peace be quartered in any house, without the consent of the Owner, nor in time of war, but in a manner to be prescribed by law.

AMENDMENT IV.

The right of the people to be secure in their persons, houses, papers, and effects, against unreasonable searches and seizures, shall not be violated, and no Warrants shall issue, but upon probable cause, supported by Oath or affirmation, and particularly describing the place to be searched, and the persons or things to be seized.

AMENDMENT V.

No person shall be held to answer for a capital, or otherwise infamous crime, unless on a presentment or indictment of a Grand Jury, except in cases arising in the land or naval forces, or in the Militia, when in actual service in time of War or public danger; nor shall any person be subject for the same offence to be twice put in jeopardy of life or limb; nor shall be compelled in any criminal case to be a witness against himself, nor be deprived of life, liberty, or property, without due process of law; nor shall private property be taken for public use, without just compensation.

AMENDMENT VI.

In all criminal prosecutions, the accused shall enjoy the right to a speedy and public trial, by an impartial jury of the State and district wherein the crime shall have been committed, which district shall have been previously ascertained by law, and to be informed of the nature and cause of the accusation; to be confronted with the witnesses against him; to have compulsory process for obtaining witnesses in his favor, and to have the Assistance of Counsel for his defence.

AMENDMENT VII.

In Suits at common law, where the value in controversy shall exceed twenty dollars, the right of trial by jury shall be preserved, and no fact tried by a jury, shall be otherwise re-examined in any Court of the United States, than according to the rules of the common law.

AMENDMENT VIII.

Excessive bail shall not be required, nor excessive fines imposed, nor cruel and unusual punishments inflicted.

AMENDMENT IX.

The enumeration in the Constitution, of certain rights, shall not be construed to deny or disparage others retained by the people.

AMENDMENT X.

The powers not delegated to the United States by the Constitution, nor prohibited by it to the States, are reserved to the States respectively, or to the people. [The first ten amendments went into effect December 15, 1791.]

AMENDMENT XI.

The Judicial power of the United States shall not be construed to extend to any suit in law or equity, commenced or prosecuted against one of the United States by Citizens of another State, or by Citizens or Subjects of any Foreign State. [January 8, 1798]

AMENDMENT XII.

The Electors shall meet in their respective states, and vote by ballot for President and Vice-President, one of whom, at least, shall not be an inhabitant of the same state with themselves; they shall name in their ballots the person voted for as President, and in distinct ballots the person voted for as Vice-President, and they shall make distinct lists of all persons voted for as President, and of all persons voted for as Vice President, and of the number of votes for each, which lists they shall sign and certify, and transmit sealed to the seat of the government of the United States, directed to the President of the Senate;—The President of the Senate shall, in the presence of the Senate and House of Representatives, open all the certificates and the votes shall then be counted;—The person having the greatest number of votes for President, shall be the President, if such number be a majority of the whole number of Electors appointed; and if no person have such majority, then from the persons having the highest numbers not exceeding three on the list of those voted for as President, the House of Representatives shall choose immediately, by ballot, the President. But in choosing the President, the votes shall be taken by states, the representation from each state having one vote; a quorum for this purpose shall consist of a member or members from two-thirds of the states, and a majority of all the states shall be necessary to a choice. And if the House of Representatives shall not choose a President whenever the right of choice shall devolve upon them, before the fourth day of March next following, then the Vice-President shall act as President, as in the case of the death or other constitutional disability of the President.—The person having the greatest number of votes as Vice-President, shall be the Vice-President, if such number be a majority of the whole number of Electors appointed, and if no person have a majority, then from the two highest numbers on the list, the Senate shall choose the Vice-President; a quorum for the purpose shall consist of two-thirds of the whole number of Senators, and a majority of the whole number shall be necessary to a choice. But no person constitutionally ineligible to the office of President shall be eligible to that of Vice-President of the United States. [September 25, 1804]

AMENDMENT XIII.

Section 1. Neither slavery nor involuntary servitude, except as a punishment for crime whereof the party shall have been duly convicted, shall exist within the United States, or any place subject to their jurisdiction.

Section 2. Congress shall have power to enforce this article by appropriate legislation. [December 18, 1865]

AMENDMENT XIV.

Section 1. All persons born or naturalized in the United States, and subject to the jurisdiction thereof, are citizens of the United States and of the State wherein they reside. No State shall make or enforce any law which shall abridge the privileges or immunities of citizens of the United States; nor shall any State deprive any person of life, liberty, or property, without due process of law; nor deny to any person within its jurisdiction the equal protection of the laws.

Section 2. Representatives shall be apportioned among the several States according to their respective numbers, counting the whole number of persons in each State, excluding Indians not taxed. But when the right to vote at any election for the choice of electors for President and Vice President of the United States, Representatives in Congress, the Executive and Judicial officers of a State, or the members of the Legislature thereof, is denied to any of the male inhabitants of such State, being twenty-one years of age, and citizens of the United States, or in any way abridged, except for participation in rebellion, or other crime, the basis of representation therein shall be reduced in the proportion which the number of such male citizens shall bear to the whole number of male citizens twenty-one years of age in such State.

Section 3. No person shall be a Senator or Representative in Congress, or elector of President and Vice President, or hold any office, civil or military, under the United States, or under any State, who, having previously taken an oath, as a member of Congress, or as an officer of the United States, or as a member of any State legislature, or as an executive or judicial officer of any State, to support the Constitution of the United States, shall have engaged in insurrection or rebellion against the same, or given aid or comfort to the enemies thereof. But Congress may by a vote of two-thirds of each House, remove such disability.

Section 4. The validity of the public debt of the United States, authorized by law, including debts incurred for payment of pensions and bounties for services in suppressing insurrection or rebellion, shall not be questioned. But neither the United States nor any State shall assume or pay any debt or obligation incurred in aid of insurrection or rebellion against the United States, or any claim for the loss or emancipation of any slave; but all such debts, obligations and claims shall be held illegal and void.

Section 5. The Congress shall have power to enforce, by appropriate legislation, the provisions of this article. [July 28, 1868]

AMENDMENT XV.

Section 1. The right of citizens of the United States to vote shall not be denied or abridged by the United States or by any State on account of race, color, or previous condition of servitude—

Section 2. The Congress shall have power to enforce this article by appropriate legislation. [March 30, 1870]

AMENDMENT XVI.

The Congress shall have power to lay and collect taxes on incomes, from whatever source derived, without apportionment among the several States, and without regard to any census or enumeration. [February 25, 1913]

AMENDMENT XVII.

The Senate of the United States shall be composed of two senators from each State, elected by the people thereof, for six years; and each Senator shall have one vote. The electors in each State shall have the qualifications requisite for electors of the most numerous branch of the State legislatures.

When vacancies happen in the representation of any State in the Senate, the executive authority of such State shall issue writs of election to fill such vacancies: *Provided,* That the legislature of any State may empower the executive thereof to make temporary appointments until the people fill the vacancies by election as the legislature may direct.

This amendment shall not be so construed as to affect the election or term of any senator chosen before it becomes valid as part of the Constitution. [May 31, 1913]

AMENDMENT XVIII.

After one year from the ratification of this article, the manufacture, sale, or transportation of intoxicating liquors within, the importation thereof into, or the exportation thereof from the United States and all territory subject to the jurisdiction thereof for beverage purposes is hereby prohibited.

The Congress and the several States shall have concurrent power to enforce this article by appropriate legislation.

This article shall be inoperative unless it shall have been ratified as an amendment to the Constitution by the legislatures of the several States, as provided in the Constitution, within seven years from the date of the submission thereof to the States by Congress. [January 29, 1919]

AMENDMENT XIX.

The right of citizens of the United States to vote shall not be denied or abridged by the United States or by any State on account of sex.

The Congress shall have power by appropriate legislation to enforce the provisions of this article. [August 26, 1920]

AMENDMENT XX.

Section 1. The terms of the President and Vice-President shall end at noon on the twentieth day of January, and the terms of Senators and Representatives at noon on the third day of January, of the years in which such terms would have ended if this article had not been ratified; and the terms of their successors shall then begin.

Section 2. The Congress shall assemble at least once in every year, and such meeting shall begin at noon on the third day of January, unless they shall by law appoint a different day.

Section 3. If, at the time fixed for the beginning of the term of the President, the President-elect shall have died, the Vice-President-elect shall become President. If a President shall not have been chosen before the time fixed for the beginning of his term, or if the President-elect shall have failed to qualify, then the Vice-President-elect shall act as President until a President shall have qualified; and the Congress may by law provide for the case wherein neither a President-elect nor a Vice-President-elect shall have qualified, declaring who shall then act as President, or the manner in which one who is to act shall be selected, and such person shall act accordingly until a President or Vice-President shall have qualified.

Section 4. The Congress may by law provide for the case of the death of any of the persons from whom the House of Representatives may choose a President whenever the right of choice shall have devolved upon them, and for the case of the death of any of the persons from whom the Senate may choose a Vice-President whenever the right of choice shall have devolved upon them.

Section 5. Sections 1 and 2 shall take effect on the 15th day of October following the ratification of this article.

Section 6. This article shall be inoperative unless it shall have been ratified as an amendment to the Constitution by the legislatures of three-fourths of the several States within seven years from the date of its submission. [February 6, 1933]

AMENDMENT XXI.

Section 1. The eighteenth article of amendment to the Constitution of the United States is hereby repealed.

Section 2. The transportation or importation into any State, Territory or possession of the United States for delivery or use therein of intoxicating liquors, in violation of the laws thereof, is hereby prohibited.

Section 3. This article shall be inoperative unless it shall have been ratified as an amendment to the Constitution by convention in the several States, as provided in the Constitution, within seven years from the date of the submission thereof to the States by the Congress. [December 5, 1933]

AMENDMENT XXII.

Section 1. No person shall be elected to the office of the President more than twice, and no person who has held the office of President, or acted as President, for more than two years of a term to which some other person was elected President shall be elected to the office of the President more than once. But this Article shall not apply to any person holding the office of President when this Article was proposed by the Congress, and shall not prevent any person who may be holding the office of President, or acting as President, during the term within which this Article becomes operative from holding the office of President or acting as President during the remainder of such term.

Section 2. This article shall be inoperative unless it shall have been ratified as an amendment to the Constitution by the legislatures of three-fourths of the several states within seven years from the date of its submission to the States by the Congress. [February 27, 1951]

AMENDMENT XXIII.

Section 1. The District constituting the seat of government of the United States shall appoint in such manner as the Congress may direct:

A number of electors of President and Vice-President equal to the whole number of Senators and Representatives in Congress to which the District would be entitled if it were a State, but in no event more than the least populous State; they shall be in addition to those appointed by the States, but they shall be considered, for the purposes of the election of President and Vice-President, to be electors appointed by a State; and they shall meet in the District and perform such duties as provided by the twelfth article of amendment.

Section 2. The Congress shall have the power to enforce this article by appropriate legislation. [March 29, 1961]

AMENDMENT XXIV.

Section 1. The right of citizens of the United States to vote in any primary or other election for President or Vice President, for electors for President or Vice President, or for Senator or Representative in Congress, shall not be denied or abridged by the United States or any State by reason of failure to pay any poll tax or other tax.

Section 2. The Congress shall have power to enforce this article by appropriate legislation. [January 23, 1964]

AMENDMENT XXV.

Section 1. In case of the removal of the President from office or of his death or resignation, the Vice President shall become President.

Section 2. Whenever there is a vacancy in the office of Vice President, the President shall nominate a Vice President who shall take office upon confirmation by a majority vote of both Houses of Congress.

Section 3. Whenever the President transmits to the President pro tempore of the Senate and the Speaker of the House of Representatives his written declaration that he is unable to discharge the powers and duties of his office, and until he transmits to them a written declaration to the contrary, such powers and duties shall be discharged by the Vice President as Acting President.

Section 4. Whenever the Vice President and a majority of either the principal officers of the executive departments or of such other body as Congress may by law provide, transmit to the President pro tempore of the Senate and the Speaker of the House of Representatives their written declaration that the President is unable to discharge the powers and duties of his office, the Vice President shall immediately assume the powers and duties of the office as Acting President.

Thereafter, when the President transmits to the President pro tempore of the Senate and the Speaker of the House of Representatives his written declaration that no inability exists, he shall resume the powers and duties of his office unless the Vice President and a majority of either the principal officers of the executive departments or of such other body as Congress may by law provide, transmit within four days to the President pro tempore of the Senate and the Speaker of the House of Representatives their written declaration that the President is unable to discharge the powers and duties of his office. Thereupon Congress shall decide the issue, assembling within forty-eight hours for that purpose if not in session. If the Congress, within twenty-one days after receipt of the latter written declaration, or, if Congress is not in session, within twenty-one days after Congress is required to assemble, determines by two-thirds vote of both Houses that the President is unable to discharge the powers and duties of his office, the Vice President shall continue to discharge the same as Acting President; otherwise, the President shall resume the powers and duties of his office. [February 10, 1967]

AMENDMENT XXVI.

Section 1. The right of citizens of the United States, who are eighteen years of age or older, to vote shall not be denied or abridged by the United States or by any State on account of age.

Section 2. The Congress shall have power to enforce this article by appropriate legislation. [June 30, 1971]

AMENDMENT XXVII.

No law, varying the compensation for the services of the Senators and Representatives shall take effect, until an election of Representatives shall have intervened. [May 8, 1992]

PRESIDENTIAL ELECTIONS

Year	Number of States	Candidates	Parties	Popular Vote	% of Popular Vote	Electoral Vote	% Voter Participation
1789	11	**GEORGE WASHINGTON**	NO PARTY DESIGNATIONS			69	
		John Adams				34	
		Other candidates				35	
1792	15	**GEORGE WASHINGTON**	NO PARTY DESIGNATIONS			132	
		John Adams				77	
		George Clinton				50	
		Other candidates				5	
1796	16	**JOHN ADAMS**	FEDERALIST			71	
		Thomas Jefferson	Democratic-Republican			68	
		Thomas Pinckney	Federalist			59	
		Aaron Burr	Democratic-Republican			30	
		Other candidates				48	
1800	16	**THOMAS JEFFERSON**	DEMOCRATIC-REPUBLICAN			73	
		Aaron Burr	Democratic-Republican			73	
		John Adams	Federalist			65	
		Charles C. Pinckney	Federalist			64	
		John Jay	Federalist			1	
1804	17	**THOMAS JEFFERSON**	DEMOCRATIC-REPUBLICAN			162	
		Charles C. Pinckney	Federalist			14	
1808	17	**JAMES MADISON**	DEMOCRATIC-REPUBLICAN			122	
		Charles C. Pinckney	Federalist			47	
		George Clinton	Democratic-Republican			6	
1812	18	**JAMES MADISON**	DEMOCRATIC-REPUBLICAN			128	
		DeWitt Clinton	Federalist			89	
1816	19	**JAMES MONROE**	DEMOCRATIC-REPUBLICAN			183	
		Rufus King	Federalist			34	
1820	24	**JAMES MONROE**	DEMOCRATIC-REPUBLICAN			231	
		John Quincy Adams	Independent			1	
1824	24	**JOHN QUINCY ADAMS**	DEMOCRATIC-REPUBLICAN	108,740	30.5	84	26.9
		Andrew Jackson	Democratic-Republican	153,544	43.1	99	
		Henry Clay	Democratic-Republican	47,136	13.2	37	
		William H. Crawford	Democratic-Republican	46,618	13.1	41	
1828	24	**ANDREW JACKSON**	DEMOCRATIC	647,286	56.0	178	57.6
		John Quincy Adams	National Republican	508,064	44.0	83	
1832	24	**ANDREW JACKSON**	DEMOCRATIC	688,242	54.5	219	55.4
		Henry Clay	National Republican	473,462	37.5	49	
		William Wirt	Anti-Masonic	101,051	8.0	7	
		John Floyd	Democratic			11	

Year	Number of States	Candidates	Parties	Popular Vote	% of Popular Vote	Electoral Vote	% Voter Participation
1836	26	**MARTIN VAN BUREN**	DEMOCRATIC	765,483	50.9	170	57.8
		William H. Harrison	Whig			73	
		Hugh L. White	Whig	739,795	49.1	26	
		Daniel Webster	Whig			14	
		W. P. Mangum	Whig			11	
1840	26	**WILLIAM H. HARRISON**	WHIG	1,274,624	53.1	234	80.2
		Martin Van Buren	Democratic	1,127,781	46.9	60	
1844	26	**JAMES K. POLK**	DEMOCRATIC	1,338,464	49.6	170	78.9
		Henry Clay	Whig	1,300,097	48.1	105	
		James G. Birney	Liberty	62,300	2.3		
1848	30	**ZACHARY TAYLOR**	WHIG	1,360,967	47.4	163	72.7
		Lewis Cass	Democratic	1,222,342	42.5	127	
		Martin Van Buren	Free Soil	291,263	10.1		
1852	31	**FRANKLIN PIERCE**	DEMOCRATIC	1,601,117	50.9	254	69.6
		Winfield Scott	Whig	1,385,453	44.1	42	
		John P. Hale	Free Soil	155,825	5.0		
1856	31	**JAMES BUCHANAN**	DEMOCRATIC	1,832,955	45.3	174	78.9
		John C. Frémont	Republican	1,339,932	33.1	114	
		Millard Fillmore	American	871,731	21.6	8	
1860	33	**ABRAHAM LINCOLN**	REPUBLICAN	1,865,593	39.8	180	81.2
		Stephen A. Douglas	Democratic	1,382,713	29.5	12	
		John C. Breckinridge	Democratic	848,356	18.1	72	
		John Bell	Constitutional Union	592,906	12.6	39	
1864	36	**ABRAHAM LINCOLN**	REPUBLICAN	2,206,938	55.0	212	73.8
		George B. McClellan	Democratic	1,803,787	45.0	21	
1868	37	**ULYSSES S. GRANT**	REPUBLICAN	3,013,421	52.7	214	78.1
		Horatio Seymour	Democratic	2,706,829	47.3	80	
1872	37	**ULYSSES S. GRANT**	REPUBLICAN	3,596,745	55.6	286	71.3
		Horace Greeley	Democratic	2,843,446	43.9	66	
1876	38	**RUTHERFORD B. HAYES**	REPUBLICAN	4,036,572	48.0	185	81.8
		Samuel J. Tilden	Democratic	4,284,020	51.0	184	
1880	38	**JAMES A. GARFIELD**	REPUBLICAN	4,453,295	48.5	214	79.4
		Winfield S. Hancock	Democratic	4,414,082	48.1	155	
		James B. Weaver	Greenback-Labor	308,578	3.4		
1884	38	**GROVER CLEVELAND**	DEMOCRATIC	4,879,507	48.5	219	77.5
		James G. Blaine	Republican	4,850,293	48.2	182	
		Benjamin F. Butler	Greenback-Labor	175,370	1.8		
		John P. St. John	Prohibition	150,369	1.5		
1888	38	**BENJAMIN HARRISON**	REPUBLICAN	5,477,129	47.9	233	79.3
		Grover Cleveland	Democratic	5,537,857	48.6	168	
		Clinton B. Fisk	Prohibition	249,506	2.2		
		Anson J. Streeter	Union Labor	146,935	1.3		

Year	Number of States	Candidates	Parties	Popular Vote	% of Popular Vote	Electoral Vote	% Voter Participation
1892	44	**GROVER CLEVELAND**	DEMOCRATIC	5,555,426	46.1	277	74.7
		Benjamin Harrison	Republican	5,182,690	43.0	145	
		James B. Weaver	People's	1,029,846	8.5	22	
		John Bidwell	Prohibition	264,133	2.2		
1896	45	**WILLIAM McKINLEY**	REPUBLICAN	7,102,246	51.1	271	79.3
		William J. Bryan	Democratic	6,492,559	47.7	176	
1900	45	**WILLIAM McKINLEY**	REPUBLICAN	7,218,491	51.7	292	73.2
		William J. Bryan	Democratic; Populist	6,356,734	45.5	155	
		John C. Wooley	Prohibition	208,914	1.5		
1904	45	**THEODORE ROOSEVELT**	REPUBLICAN	7,628,461	57.4	336	65.2
		Alton B. Parker	Democratic	5,084,223	37.6	140	
		Eugene V. Debs	Socialist	402,283	3.0		
		Silas C. Swallow	Prohibition	258,536	1.9		
1908	46	**WILLIAM H. TAFT**	REPUBLICAN	7,675,320	51.6	321	65.4
		William J. Bryan	Democratic	6,412,294	43.1	162	
		Eugene V. Debs	Socialist	420,793	2.8		
		Eugene W. Chafin	Prohibition	253,840	1.7		
1912	48	**WOODROW WILSON**	DEMOCRATIC	6,296,547	41.9	435	58.8
		Theodore Roosevelt	Progressive	4,118,571	27.4	88	
		William H. Taft	Republican	3,486,720	23.2	8	
		Eugene V. Debs	Socialist	900,672	6.0		
		Eugene W. Chafin	Prohibition	206,275	1.4		
1916	48	**WOODROW WILSON**	DEMOCRATIC	9,127,695	49.4	277	61.6
		Charles E. Hughes	Republican	8,533,507	46.2	254	
		A. L. Benson	Socialist	585,113	3.2		
		J. Frank Hanly	Prohibition	220,506	1.2		
1920	48	**WARREN G. HARDING**	REPUBLICAN	16,143,407	60.4	404	49.2
		James M. Cox	Democratic	9,130,328	34.2	127	
		Eugene V. Debs	Socialist	919,799	3.4		
		P. P. Christensen	Farmer-Labor	265,411	1.0		
1924	48	**CALVIN COOLIDGE**	REPUBLICAN	15,718,211	54.0	382	48.9
		John W. Davis	Democratic	8,385,283	28.8	136	
		Robert M. La Follette	Progressive	4,831,289	16.6	13	
1928	48	**HERBERT C. HOOVER**	REPUBLICAN	21,391,993	58.2	444	56.9
		Alfred E. Smith	Democratic	15,016,169	40.9	87	
1932	48	**FRANKLIN D. ROOSEVELT**	DEMOCRATIC	22,809,638	57.4	472	56.9
		Herbert C. Hoover	Republican	15,758,901	39.7	59	
		Norman Thomas	Socialist	881,951	2.2		
1936	48	**FRANKLIN D. ROOSEVELT**	DEMOCRATIC	27,752,869	60.8	523	61.0
		Alfred M. Landon	Republican	16,674,665	36.5	8	
		William Lemke	Union	882,479	1.9		
1940	48	**FRANKLIN D. ROOSEVELT**	DEMOCRATIC	27,307,819	54.8	449	62.5
		Wendell L. Willkie	Republican	22,321,018	44.8	82	

Year	Number of States	Candidates	Parties	Popular Vote	% of Popular Vote	Electoral Vote	% Voter Participation
1944	48	**FRANKLIN D. ROOSEVELT**	DEMOCRATIC	25,606,585	53.5	432	55.9
		Thomas E. Dewey	Republican	22,014,745	46.0	99	
1948	48	**HARRY S. TRUMAN**	DEMOCRATIC	24,179,345	49.6	303	53.0
		Thomas E. Dewey	Republican	21,991,291	45.1	189	
		J. Strom Thurmond	States' Rights	1,176,125	2.4	39	
		Henry A. Wallace	Progressive	1,157,326	2.4		
1952	48	**DWIGHT D. EISENHOWER**	REPUBLICAN	33,936,234	55.1	442	63.3
		Adlai E. Stevenson	Democratic	27,314,992	44.4	89	
1956	48	**DWIGHT D. EISENHOWER**	REPUBLICAN	35,590,472	57.6	457	60.6
		Adlai E. Stevenson	Democratic	26,022,752	42.1	73	
1960	50	**JOHN F. KENNEDY**	DEMOCRATIC	34,226,731	49.7	303	62.8
		Richard M. Nixon	Republican	34,108,157	49.5	219	
1964	50	**LYNDON B. JOHNSON**	DEMOCRATIC	43,129,566	61.1	486	61.9
		Barry M. Goldwater	Republican	27,178,188	38.5	52	
1968	50	**RICHARD M. NIXON**	REPUBLICAN	31,785,480	43.4	301	60.9
		Hubert H. Humphrey	Democratic	31,275,166	42.7	191	
		George C. Wallace	American Independent	9,906,473	13.5	46	
1972	50	**RICHARD M. NIXON**	REPUBLICAN	47,169,911	60.7	520	55.2
		George S. McGovern	Democratic	29,170,383	37.5	17	
		John G. Schmitz	American	1,099,482	1.4		
1976	50	**JIMMY CARTER**	DEMOCRATIC	40,830,763	50.1	297	53.5
		Gerald R. Ford	Republican	39,147,793	48.0	240	
1980	50	**RONALD REAGAN**	REPUBLICAN	43,901,812	50.7	489	52.6
		Jimmy Carter	Democratic	35,483,820	41.0	49	
		John B. Anderson	Independent	5,719,437	6.6		
		Ed Clark	Libertarian	921,188	1.1		
1984	50	**RONALD REAGAN**	REPUBLICAN	54,451,521	58.8	525	53.1
		Walter F. Mondale	Democratic	37,565,334	40.6	13	
1988	50	**GEORGE H. BUSH**	REPUBLICAN	47,917,341	53.4	426	50.1
		Michael Dukakis	Democratic	41,013,030	45.6	111	
1992	50	**BILL CLINTON**	DEMOCRATIC	44,908,254	43.0	370	55.0
		George H. Bush	Republican	39,102,343	37.4	168	
		H. Ross Perot	Independent	19,741,065	18.9	0	
1996	50	**BILL CLINTON**	DEMOCRATIC	47,401,185	49.0	379	49.0
		Bob Dole	Republican	39,197,469	41.0	159	
		H. Ross Perot	Independent	8,085,295	8.0	0	
2000	50	**GEORGE W. BUSH**	REPUBLICAN	50,455,156	47.9	271	50.4
		Albert Gore	Democratic	50,997,335	48.4	266	
		Ralph Nader	Green Party	2,882,897	2.7	0	

Candidates receiving less than 1 percent of the popular vote have been omitted. Thus, the percentage of popular vote given for any election year may not total 100 percent. Before the passage of the Twelfth Amendment in 1804, the electoral college voted for two presidential candidates; the runner-up became vice-president.

ADMISSION OF STATES

Order of Admission	State	Date of Admission	Order of Admission	State	Date of Admission
1	Delaware	December 7, 1787	26	Michigan	January 26, 1837
2	Pennsylvania	December 12, 1787	27	Florida	March 3, 1845
3	New Jersey	December 18, 1787	28	Texas	December 29, 1845
4	Georgia	January 2, 1788	29	Iowa	December 28, 1846
5	Connecticut	January 9, 1788	30	Wisconsin	May 29, 1848
6	Massachusetts	February 7, 1788	31	California	September 9, 1850
7	Maryland	April 28, 1788	32	Minnesota	May 11, 1858
8	South Carolina	May 23, 1788	33	Oregon	February 14, 1859
9	New Hampshire	June 21, 1788	34	Kansas	January 29, 1861
10	Virginia	June 25, 1788	35	West Virginia	June 30, 1863
11	New York	July 26, 1788	36	Nevada	October 31, 1864
12	North Carolina	November 21, 1789	37	Nebraska	March 1, 1867
13	Rhode Island	May 29, 1790	38	Colorado	August 1, 1876
14	Vermont	March 4, 1791	39	North Dakota	November 2, 1889
15	Kentucky	June 1, 1792	40	South Dakota	November 2, 1889
16	Tennessee	June 1, 1796	41	Montana	November 8, 1889
17	Ohio	March 1, 1803	42	Washington	November 11, 1889
18	Louisiana	April 30, 1812	43	Idaho	July 3, 1890
19	Indiana	December 11, 1816	44	Wyoming	July 10, 1890
20	Mississippi	December 10, 1817	45	Utah	January 4, 1896
21	Illinois	December 3, 1818	46	Oklahoma	November 16, 1907
22	Alabama	December 14, 1819	47	New Mexico	January 6, 1912
23	Maine	March 15, 1820	48	Arizona	February 14, 1912
24	Missouri	August 10, 1821	49	Alaska	January 3, 1959
25	Arkansas	June 15, 1836	50	Hawaii	August 21, 1959

POPULATION OF THE UNITED STATES

Year	Number of States	Population	% Increase	Population per Square Mile
1790	13	3,929,214		4.5
1800	16	5,308,483	35.1	6.1
1810	17	7,239,881	36.4	4.3
1820	23	9,638,453	33.1	5.5
1830	24	12,866,020	33.5	7.4
1840	26	17,069,453	32.7	9.8
1850	31	23,191,876	35.9	7.9
1860	33	31,443,321	35.6	10.6
1870	37	39,818,449	26.6	13.4
1880	38	50,155,783	26.0	16.9
1890	44	62,947,714	25.5	21.1
1900	45	75,994,575	20.7	25.6
1910	46	91,972,266	21.0	31.0
1920	48	105,710,620	14.9	35.6
1930	48	122,775,046	16.1	41.2
1940	48	131,669,275	7.2	44.2
1950	48	150,697,361	14.5	50.7
1960	50	179,323,175	19.0	50.6
1970	50	203,235,298	13.3	57.5
1980	50	226,504,825	11.4	64.0
1985	50	237,839,000	5.0	67.2
1990	50	250,122,000	5.2	70.6
1995	50	263,411,707	5.3	74.4
2000	50	281,421,906	6.8	77.0

IMMIGRATION TO THE UNITED STATES (1820–1998)

Year	Number	Year	Number	Year	Number	Year	Number
1820–1998	**64,599,082**						
1820	8,385						
1821–30	**143,439**	**1871–80**	**2,812,191**	**1921–30**	**4,107,209**	**1971–80**	**4,493,314**
1821	9,127	1871	321,350	1921	805,228	1971	370,478
1822	6,911	1872	404,806	1922	309,556	1972	384,685
1823	6,354	1873	459,803	1923	522,919	1973	400,063
1824	7,912	1874	313,339	1924	706,896	1974	394,861
1825	10,199	1875	227,498	1925	294,314	1975	386,194
1826	10,837	1876	169,986	1926	304,488	1976	398,613
1827	18,875	1877	141,857	1927	335,175	1976, TQ[1]	103,676
1828	27,382	1878	138,469	1928	307,255	1977	462,315
1829	22,520	1879	177,826	1929	279,678	1978	601,442
1830	23,322	1880	457,257	1930	241,700	1979	460,348
						1980	530,639
1831–40	**599,125**	**1881–90**	**5,246,613**	**1931–40**	**528,431**		
1831	22,633	1881	669,431	1931	97,139	**1981–90**	**7,338,062**
1832	60,482	1822	788,992	1932	35,576	1981	596,600
1833	58,640	1883	603,322	1933	23,068	1982	594,131
1834	65,365	1884	518,592	1934	29,470	1983	559,763
1835	45,374	1885	395,346	1935	34,956	1984	543,903
1836	76,242	1886	334,203	1936	36,329	1985	570,009
1837	79,340	1887	490,109	1937	50,244	1986	601,708
1838	38,914	1888	546,889	1938	67,895	1987	601,516
1839	68,069	1889	444,427	1939	82,998	1988	643,025
1840	84,066	1890	455,302	1940	70,756	1989	1,090,924
						1990	1,536,483
1841–50	**1,713,251**	**1891–1900**	**3,687,564**	**1941–50**	**1,035,039**		
1841	80,289	1891	560,319	1941	51,776	**1991–98**	**7,605,068**
1842	104,565	1892	579,663	1942	28,781	1991	1,827,167
1843	52,496	1893	439,730	1943	23,725	1992	973,977
1844	78,615	1894	285,631	1944	28,551	1993	904,292
1845	114,371	1895	258,536	1945	38,119	1994	804,416
1846	154,416	1896	343,267	1946	108,721	1995	720,461
1847	234,968	1897	230,832	1947	147,292	1996	915,900
1848	226,527	1898	229,299	1948	170,570	1997	798,378
1849	297,024	1899	311,715	1949	188,317	1998	660,477
1850	369,980	1900	448,572	1950	249,187		
1851–60	**2,598,214**	**1901–10**	**8,795,386**	**1951–60**	**2,515,479**		
1851	379,466	1901	487,918	1951	205,717		
1852	371,603	1902	648,743	1952	265,520		
1853	368,645	1903	857,046	1953	170,434		
1854	427,833	1904	812,870	1954	208,177		
1855	200,877	1905	1,026,499	1955	237,790		
1856	200,436	1906	1,100,735	1956	321,625		
1857	251,306	1907	1,285,349	1957	326,867		
1858	123,126	1908	782,870	1958	253,265		
1859	121,282	1909	751,786	1959	260,686		
1860	153,640	1910	1,041,570	1960	265,398		
1861–70	**2,314,824**	**1911–20**	**5,735,811**	**1961–70**	**3,321,677**		
1861	91,918	1911	878,587	1961	271,344		
1862	91,985	1912	838,172	1962	283,763		
1863	176,282	1913	1,197,892	1963	306,260		
1864	193,418	1914	1,218,480	1964	292,248		
1865	248,120	1915	326,700	1965	296,697		
1866	318,568	1916	298,826	1966	323,040		
1867	315,722	1917	295,403	1967	361,972		
1868	138,840	1918	110,618	1968	454,448		
1869	352,768	1919	141,132	1969	358,579		
1870	387,203	1920	430,001	1970	373,326		

[1] Transition quarter, July 1 through September 30, 1976.

NOTE: The numbers shown are as follows: from 1820 to 1867, figures represent alien passengers arrived at seaports; from 1868 to 1892 and 1895 to 1897, immigrant aliens arrived; from 1892 to 1894 and 1898 to 1998, immigrant aliens admitted for permanent residence. From 1892 to 1903, aliens entering by cabin class were not counted as immigrants. Land arrivals were not completely enumerated until 1908.

PRESIDENTS, VICE-PRESIDENTS, AND SECRETARIES OF STATE

President	Vice-President	Secretary of State
1. George Washington, Federalist 1789	John Adams, Federalist 1789	Thomas Jefferson 1789 Edmund Randolph 1794 Timothy Pickering 1795
2. John Adams, Federalist 1797	Thomas Jefferson, Democratic-Republican 1797	Timothy Pickering 1797 John Marshall 1800
3. Thomas Jefferson, Democratic-Republican 1801	Aaron Burr, Democratic-Republican 1801 George Clinton, Democratic-Republican 1805	James Madison 1801
4. James Madison, Democratic-Republican 1809	George Clinton, Democratic-Republican 1809 Elbridge Gerry, Democratic-Republican 1813	Robert Smith 1809 James Monroe 1811
5. James Monroe, Democratic-Republican 1817	Daniel D. Tompkins, Democratic-Republican 1817	John Q. Adams 1817
6. John Quincy Adams, Democratic-Republican 1825	John C. Calhoun, Democratic-Republican 1825	Henry Clay 1825
7. Andrew Jackson, Democratic 1829	John C. Calhoun, Democratic 1829 Martin Van Buren, Democratic 1833	Martin Van Buren 1829 Edward Livingston 1831 Louis McLane 1833 John Forsyth 1834
8. Martin Van Buren, Democratic 1837	Richard M. Johnson, Democratic 1837	John Forsyth 1837
9. William H. Harrison, Whig 1841	John Tyler, Whig 1841	Daniel Webster 1841
10. John Tyler, Whig and Democratic 1841	None	Daniel Webster 1841 Hugh S. Legaré 1843 Abel P. Upshur 1843 John C. Calhoun 1844
11. James K. Polk, Democratic 1845	George M. Dallas, Democratic 1845	James Buchanan 1845
12. Zachary Taylor, Whig 1849	Millard Fillmore, Whig 1849	John M. Clayton 1849
13. Millard Fillmore, Whig 1850	None	Daniel Webster 1850 Edward Everett 1852
14. Franklin Pierce, Democratic 1853	William R. King, Democratic 1853	William L. Marcy 1853
15. James Buchanan, Democratic 1857	John C. Breckinridge, Democratic 1857	Lewis Cass 1857 Jeremiah S. Black 1860
16. Abraham Lincoln, Republican 1861	Hannibal Hamlin, Republican 1861 Andrew Johnson, Unionist 1865	William H. Seward 1861
17. Andrew Johnson, Unionist 1865	None	William H. Seward 1865

President	Vice-President	Secretary of State
18. Ulysses S. Grant, Republican 1869	Schuyler Colfax, Republican 1869 Henry Wilson, Republican 1873	Elihu B. Washburne 1869 Hamilton Fish 1869
19. Rutherford B. Hayes, Republican 1877	William A. Wheeler, Republican 1877	William M. Evarts 1877
20. James A. Garfield, Republican 1881	Chester A. Arthur, Republican 1881	James G. Blaine 1881
21. Chester A. Arthur, Republican 1881	None	Frederick T. Frelinghuysen 1881
22. Grover Cleveland, Democratic 1885	Thomas A. Hendricks, Democratic 1885	Thomas F. Bayard 1885
23. Benjamin Harrison, Republican 1889	Levi P. Morton, Republican 1889	James G. Blaine 1889 John W. Foster 1892
24. Grover Cleveland, Democratic 1893	Adlai E. Stevenson, Democratic 1893	Walter Q. Gresham 1893 Richard Olney 1895
25. William McKinley, Republican 1897	Garret A. Hobart, Republican 1897 Theodore Roosevelt, Republican 1901	John Sherman 1897 William R. Day 1898 John Hay, 1898
26. Theodore Roosevelt, Republican 1901	Charles Fairbanks, Republican 1905	John Hay 1901 Elihu Root 1905 Robert Bacon 1909
27. William H. Taft, Republican 1909	James S. Sherman, Republican 1909	Philander C. Knox 1909
28. Woodrow Wilson, Democratic 1913	Thomas R. Marshall, Democratic 1913	William J. Bryan 1913 Robert Lansing 1915 Bainbridge Colby 1920
29. Warren G. Harding, Republican 1921	Calvin Coolidge, Republican 1921	Charles E. Hughes 1921
30. Calvin Coolidge, Republican 1923	Charles G. Dawes, Republican 1925	Charles E. Hughes 1923 Frank B. Kellogg 1925
31. Herbert Hoover, Republican 1929	Charles Curtis, Republican 1929	Henry L. Stimson 1929
32. Franklin D. Roosevelt, Democratic 1933	John Nance Garner, Democratic 1933 Henry A. Wallace, Democratic 1941 Harry S. Truman, Democratic 1945	Cordell Hull 1933 Edward R. Stettinius Jr. 1944
33. Harry S. Truman, Democratic 1945	Alben W. Barkley, Democratic 1949	Edward R. Stettinius Jr. 1945 James F. Byrnes 1945 George C. Marshall 1947 Dean G. Acheson 1949
34. Dwight D. Eisenhower, Republican 1953	Richard M. Nixon, Republican 1953	John F. Dulles 1953 Christian A. Herter 1959

President	Vice-President	Secretary of State
35. John F. Kennedy, Democratic 1961	Lyndon B. Johnson, Democratic 1961	Dean Rusk 1961
36. Lyndon B. Johnson, Democratic 1963	Hubert H. Humphrey, Democratic 1965	Dean Rusk 1963
37. Richard M. Nixon, Republican 1969	Spiro T. Agnew, Republican 1969 Gerald R. Ford, Republican 1973	William P. Rogers 1969 Henry Kissinger 1973
38. Gerald R. Ford, Republican 1974	Nelson Rockefeller, Republican 1974	Henry Kissinger 1974
39. Jimmy Carter, Democratic 1977	Walter Mondale, Democratic 1977	Cyrus Vance 1977 Edmund Muskie 1980
40. Ronald Reagan, Republican 1981	George Bush, Republican 1981	Alexander Haig 1981 George Shultz 1982
41. George Bush, Republican 1989	J. Danforth Quayle, Republican 1989	James A. Baker 1989 Lawrence Eagleburger 1992
42. William J. Clinton, Democratic 1993	Albert Gore Jr., Democratic 1993	Warren Christopher 1993 Madeleine Albright 1997
43. George W. Bush, Republican 2001	Richard B. Cheney, Republican 2001	Colin L. Powell 2001

728: Mary Evans Picture Library; 729: Mary Evans Picture Library; 730: (*left*) The Granger Collection, New York; (*right*) Library of Congress; 731: The Granger Collection, New York; 732: Hulton|Archive by Getty Images; 734: The New York Public Library: Astor, Lenox, and Tilden Foundations; 735: (*left and right*) 2002 General Motors Corporation. Used with permission of GM Media Archives; 736: The New York Public Library: Astor, Lenox, and Tilden Foundations; 737: From the Collections of Henry Ford Museum and Greenfield Village; 739: Courtesy of Bill and Ruth Dick, Newton, Kansas, Collection of Ronald Kline; 740: (*left*) Hulton|Archive by Getty Images; (*right*) The Kobal Collection; 742: Minnesota Historical Society/Corbis; 743: Hulton|Archive by Getty Images; 744: The Granger Collection, New York; 747: The Granger Collection, New York; 748: (*left*) Bettmann/Corbis; (*right*) The Granger Collection, New York; 750: Smithsonian American Art Museum, Washington, D.C./Art Resource, N.Y.; 753: Mary Evans Picture Library; 754: (*left*) Hulton|Archive by Getty Images; (*right*) The Granger Collection, New York; 757: (*left*) Hulton|Archive by Getty Images; (*right*) The Granger Collection, New York; 759: The Granger Collection, New York; 760: Hulton|Archive by Getty Images; 762: (*left*) Corbis; (*right*) The Granger Collection, New York; 763: The Granger Collection, New York; 765: The Granger Collection, New York; 766: The Granger Collection, New York; 767: The Granger Collection, New York; 768: Hulton|Archive by Getty Images; 769: (*far left*) Underwood & Underwood/Corbis; (*left*) Bettmann/Corbis; (*right*) Hulton|Archive by Getty Images; 771: The Granger Collection, New York; 773: The Granger Collection, New York; 774: The Granger Collection, New York; 775: Bettmann/Corbis; 776: Bettmann/Corbis; 778: The Granger Collection, New York; 781: Bettmann/Corbis; 782: The Granger Collection, New York; 783: TRH Pictures; 786: The Granger Collection, New York; 788: Mary Evans Picture Library; 791: The Granger Collection, New York; 797: Mary Evans Picture Library; 798: TRH Pictures; 799: The Granger Collection, New York; 800: The Granger Collection, New York; 801: Mary Evans Picture Library; 802: Hulton-Deutsch Collection/Corbis; 803: The Granger Collection, New York; 805: The Granger Collection, New York; 806: (*left and right*) The Granger Collection, New York; 808: TRH Pictures; 809: Hulton|Archive by Getty Images; 812: The Granger Collection, New York; 815: The Granger Collection, New York; 817: The Granger Collection, New York; 819: Hulton|Archive by Getty Images; 820: TRH Pictures; 821: The Granger Collection, New York; 822: (*left*) Thomas McAvoy/TimePix; (*right*) The Granger Collection, New York; 823: The Granger Collection, New York; 824: Dmitri Kessel/TimePix; 825: Photos12.com—Collection Bernard Crochet; 827: (*left*) Bettmann/Corbis; (*right*) The Granger Collec-

tion, New York; 829: Hulton|Archive by Getty Images; 830: TRH/US Army; 831: (*left*) Mary Evans Picture Library; (*right*) The Granger Collection, New York; 833: Photos12.com—Keystone Pressedienst; 834: The Granger Collection, New York; 835: The Granger Collection, New York; 837: Hulton|Archive by Getty Images; 838: (*left*) TRH/USMC; (*right*) Corbis; 842: The Granger Collection, New York; 843: Mary Evans Picture Library; 846: 2002 General Motors Corporation. Used with permission of GM Media Archives; 849: The Granger Collection, New York; 850: TRH/US Air Force; 851: Fritz Goro/TimePix; 852: Hulton|Archive by Getty Images; 853: The New York Public Library: Astor, Lenox, and Tilden Foundations; 854: SuperStock; 855: Lambert/Hulton|Archive by Getty Images; 856: Hulton|Archive by Getty Images; 857: William Shrout/TimePix; 859: The New York Public Library: Astor, Lenox, and Tilden Foundations; 863: Bettmann/Corbis; 864: Corbis; 865: Walter Sanders/TimePix; 866: Bettmann/Corbis; 868: SuperStock; 869: Anthony Potter Collection/Hulton|Archive by Getty Images; 870: Hulton|Archive by Getty Images; 871: (*left*) Frank Driggs Collection/Hulton|Archive by Getty Images; (*right*) Bettmann/Corbis; 873: Bettmann/Corbis; 876: Bettmann/Corbis; 878: Hulton|Archive by Getty Images; 880: Van Bucher/Photo Researchers, Inc.; 883: TRH/US National Archives; 886: Hulton|Archive by Getty Images; 887: Mark Kauffman/TimePix; 889: Bettmann/Corbis; 891: SuperStock; 892: American Stock/Hulton|Archive by Getty Images; 893: Hulton-Deutsch Collection/Corbis; 894: Hulton|Archive by Getty Images; 896: Sovfoto/Eastfoto; 898: Courtesy Ede Rothaus; 899: Edwin Levick/Hulton|Archive by Getty Images; 900: SuperStock; 901: Hulton|Archive by Getty Images; 902: (*left*) Al Fenn/TimePix; (*right*) Robert W. Kelley/TimePix; 903: Leonard McCombe/TimePix; 904: John Bryson/TimePix; 905: Rafael Macia/Photo Researchers, Inc.; 906: Walter Sanders/TimePix; 907: Bernard Hoffman/TimePix; 908: Carl Iwasaki/TimePix; 909: Stan Wayman/TimePix; 910: Bettmann/Corbis; 911: Bettmann/Corbis; 914: SuperStock; 917: Sovfoto/Eastfoto; 918: (*left and right*) Sovfoto; 920: (*left*) Mario Jorrin/ Pix Inc./TimePix; (*right*) SuperStock; 921: Bettmann/Corbis; 922: Bettmann/Corbis; 923: Hulton|Archive by Getty Images; 925: Hulton|Archive by Getty Images; 927: Hulton|Archive by Getty Images; 928: TRH Pictures; 929: Photos12.com—Oasis; 930: Library of Congress; 933: Hulton|Archive by Getty Images; 934: Bettmann/Corbis; 936: Saatchi Collection, London/SuperStock; 937: Underwood & Underwood/Corbis; 938: Will & Deni McIntyre/Photo Researchers, Inc.; 939: Hulton|Archive by Getty Images; 941: David J. & Janice L. Frent Collection/Corbis; 943: Hulton|Archive by Getty Images; 945: Bettmann/Corbis; 948: Image Works/Dan McCoy; 951: (*left*) Bettmann/Corbis; (*right*) Hulton|Archive by Getty Images; 954: TRH Pictures; 955: TRH